MEMBERS OF THE UNITED STATES SUPREME COURT
1789-1976

★DENOTES CHIEF JUSTICE

JAMES IREDELL
1790-1799

ALFRED MOORE
1799-1804

WILLIAM JOHNSON
1804-1834

THOMAS TODD
1807-1826

ROBERT TRIMBLE
1826-1828

JOHN McLEAN
1829-1861

JOHN McKINLEY
1837-1852

JAMES M. WAYNE
1835-1867

JOHN CATRON
1837-1865

JOHN A. CAMPBELL
1853-1861

CHART CONTINUED

ON BACK ENDPAPER

DAVID DAVIS
1862-1877

STEPHEN J. FIELD
1863-1897

NOAH H. SWAYNE
1862-1881

JOSEPH P. BRADLEY
1870-1892

JOHN MARSHALL
HARLAN
1877-1911

STANLEY MATTHEWS
1881-1889

The American Constitution

FIFTH EDITION

THE American Constitution

Its Origins and Development

By

Alfred H. Kelly & Winfred A. Harbison

FIFTH EDITION

W · W · NORTON & COMPANY · *New York · London*

Fifth Edition.

Library of Congress Cataloging in Publication Data
Kelly, Alfred Hinsey, 1907-
  The American Constitution.
  Bibliography: p.
  Includes index.
  1. United States--Constitutional history.
I. Harbison, Winfred Audif, 1904- joint
author. II. Title.
JK31.K4   1976   342'.73'029   76-23106
ISBN 0-393-09176-7

Printed in the United States of America.

5 6 7 8 9 0

T O
OCIE and EMILY MAY

Contents

Preface

IN THIS BOOK we have attempted to present a general picture of the growth and development of the American constitutional system. It is an introductory work, in the sense that it presupposes no extensive technical knowledge of constitutional law or political theory on the part of the reader. The intellectual problems encountered in constitutional history are often complex, and the book makes no attempt at false oversimplification. At the same time there has been every effort at proper emphasis and clarity of presentation, so that the average undergraduate student or general reader should be able to follow the narrative successfully.

The work emphasizes strongly those aspects of constitutional growth that relate closely to the fundamental structure of the American government and social order. For example, it deals at length with the emergence of limited government, or "constitutionalism," with the growth of federalism and its concomitant problems of sovereignty and state-federal relations, with the rise of judicial review, and with the constitutional aspects of civil liberties. It devotes about equal attention to the "classical" period of American constitutional history (1760–1877), and to the equally important constitutional developments since that time—the growth of substantive due process of law, the emergence of a modern federalism based upon the commerce and taxing power, the constitutional crisis of the New Deal, the impact of World War II and of America's new role in world affairs upon the constitutional system, and the extraordinary constitutional developments associated with the Warren Court including its treatment of the

"Black Revolution" and of radical and dissident political activity, its intervention in the field of legislative apportionment, and its evolution of a new and highly egalitarian constitutional law of civil liberties. In addition, the present edition reviews the Burger Court experience, which has seen a Court divided between libertarian activist Warren Court veterans and more conservative Nixon appointees grapple with procedural guarantees of the Bill of Rights, civil rights issues, and executive privilege. The crisis of the Presidency which culminated in the initiation of impeachment proceedings against Richard Nixon and his subsequent resignation is scrutinized within the broad historical context of the expansion of executive prerogative power in foreign and domestic affairs.

The present edition also takes into account certain important recent contributions to the scholarship of American constitutional history. The main corpus of American constitutional history obviously changes slowly, but the fact remains that recent studies have substantially altered the historical profession's view of such variegated matters as impeachment, the Progressive Movement, and the Smith Act prosecutions. Accordingly, we have attempted to incorporate in the text numerous new insights gained from current research.

It seems appropriate here to give some recognition to the numerous colleagues and friends who have assisted us greatly over the years with criticism, advice, and suggestions. These persons include Professors Benjamin F. Wright of the University of Texas, Robert K. Carr, Leonard Levy of the Claremont Graduate School, Winton U. Solberg of the University of Illinois, Paul Murphy of the University of Minnesota, and Charles Burton Marshall. In addition, Professors Stanley N. Katz of the University of Chicago Law School, Richard E. Ellis of the State University of New York at Buffalo, Herman Belz of the University of Maryland, Loren Beth of the University of Massachusetts, and Michal R. Belknap of the University of Texas provided detailed critiques of the fourth edition which have proved extremely useful in the preparation of the present revision. Finally, we remain indebted to the late Addison Burnham, whose encouragement and assistance in the first instance helped make this book possible. We are grateful to all the foregoing, whose generous aid, we believe, has made this a substantially stronger work than it would have been otherwise.

Introduction

WILLIAM GLADSTONE, the great British statesman and prime minister, once described the American Constitution as "the most wonderful work ever struck off at a given time by the brain and purpose of man." Americans cannot but be pleased by this tribute, and a historian may well accept it as having a large measure of truth. The Philadelphia Convention of 1787 was one of the great creative assemblages of the modern world. It did not, of course, depend upon pure inspiration, for it had several centuries of English and colonial constitutional growth to draw upon, and many of the main principles of American government were already fairly well established. Yet the creative role of the convention is undeniable. It fashioned a frame of government embodying the most adequate mechanism for a federal state ever achieved by man, and it produced at the same time a brilliant compromise between the requirements of adequate governmental authority and effective controls upon the exercise of political power.

Certainly the American Constitution has withstood the most decisive of all tests—that of time. The Charter drafted at Philadelphia in 1787 is now the oldest written constitution in the world. It has survived the trials of practical politics, the holocaust of civil war, and the immense and relentless tide of social and economic change induced by the industrial revolution. Drafted for an eighteenth-century agrarian republic of less than four million people, the Constitution now functions adequately as the fundamental law of a great urban industrial democracy of some one hundred and sixty million souls.

The American Constitution would not have survived 160 years had it not been an extraordinarily flexible instrument of government. Flexibility is commonly achieved most readily in those governments which function without the limitations of a supreme written charter. But it has been the peculiar genius of the American Constitution that while its provisions are sufficiently specific and detailed to provide a necessary element of stability to government, it has nonetheless proved to be broad and general enough in its institutional arrangements and grants of power to allow for steady growth of the "living constitution" to meet the altered requirements of a changing social order.

This implies that the American Constitution is something more than a mere written document. And indeed, in all but the narrowest sense this is true. A constitution might well be defined as the fundamental supreme law by which the state is organized and governed. But a written document, however important, can never contain more than a very small proportion of the whole body of custom, tradition, governmental practice, and statutory and judicial interpretation that functions at any one time as the fundamental law. Indeed, in the past most states managed to get along well enough without a formal written charter, although since 1787 nation after nation has adopted the American idea of committing at least the bare outlines of its constitutional system to paper. Written charters still occupy a position of peculiar sanctity and supremacy in our constitutional system, but the United States is no exception to the general rule that most of a "living constitution" at any one time is to be found in contemporary governmental practice.

This fact sets the limits of inquiry and analysis for the study of American constitutional history. Constitutional history necessarily concerns itself with tracing the origin and development of all the principal institutions, practices, customs, traditions, and fundamental legal ideas that go to make up the whole body of the "living constitution" today.

What are the forces in American history upon which the student of constitutional history must turn his particular attention? In one sense, of course, constitutional history is inextricably bound up with the entire fabric of American social and economic development. It is therefore frequently necessary to examine various important phases of the nation's economic life or a political conflict which may have altered the nation's entire destiny and the constitutional system along with it.

In a more immediate sense, actual governmental practice has prob-

ably been the greatest single force in shaping the evolution of the
American constitutional system. The first settlers along the Atlantic
seaboard brought with them a certain English political heritage, but
they began at once to evolve the unique institutions and ideas of
American constitutional government. Before the close of the colonial
era, governmental practice had produced the bicameral system, a
mass of legislative practices relating to procedure and prerogative,
the theory of the separation of powers, and the idea of a supreme
written constitution.

Since 1787 day-to-day governmental practice has been of no less
importance. The first Congress, for example, created the principal
executive departments of government, and turned the barren language of Article I, Section 8, of the Constitution into the actual
assertion of national authority through the creation of a national
bank, an army and navy, and a nationalistic judicial system. President Washington found it necessary to make several important decisions about the nature of the executive office, decisions which
have had a permanent influence upon the scope and character of
presidential authority. The presidential cabinet made its appearance
in his administration, and executive ascendancy in the control of
foreign policy also began at this time. Needless to say, constitutional growth through actual governmental practice is still going
on. Several of the major federal statutes adopted by Congress in the
"New Deal" era, for example, have apparently worked a more or
less permanent alteration in the scope of national power.

In the seven decades between 1790 and the Civil War, congressional debate was a major source of constitutional doctrine. Supreme
Court dictum, although already important, was not then universally
accepted as the final word upon constitutional questions. Instead,
prevailing ideas about the constitutional system were in the main
derived from congressional politics. Henry Clay, John C. Calhoun,
Daniel Webster, Robert Y. Hayne, Thomas H. Benton, and the
other great sectional leaders of the day frequently engaged one another in great debates upon the nature of the Union and the powers
of the states and of the national government. After Webster's brilliant oration, "Reply to Hayne," delivered in January 1830, during
the course of an epoch-making Senate debate on the nature of the
Union, most Northerners regarded Webster's forensic effort as the
most authoritative statement upon the sovereign character of the
national government. Southerners, on the other hand, usually relied
upon the constitutional arguments of Calhoun, Hayne, or Robert
Barnwell Rhett. Even today, congressional debate upon constitu-

tional matters is frequently significant, although it is rarely decisive in deciding major constitutional issues, most of which are referred to the courts.

In the last eighty years the Constitution has become more and more, as Charles Evans Hughes put it in 1926, "what the Supreme Court says it is." The Court has become the final arbiter of the American constitutional system. Its opinions on the nature and scope of federal and state power, on the functions of the various departments of government, and on the meaning of the written language of the Constitution have built up a great body of living and growing constitutional law. Supreme Court opinions are almost universally accepted as the final word on constitutional questions, so that in a practical, everyday sense it is this body of constitutional law rather than the document of 1787 which comprises the "living constitution" today.

In spite of judicial supremacy, however, it is public opinion and not the Court that has the last word on constitutional matters. Although the justices hold office during good behavior and so are protected against popular political resentment of a momentary or sporadic nature, they cannot maintain a constitutional doctrine against long-range, deep-seated majority popular conviction. Judges are mortal and perforce must eventually die or resign. A constitutional philosophy dominant for any great length of time in the nation at large will eventually find expression through Congress and the President. This in turn means the nomination and confirmation of judges who accept the verdict of the election returns.

The greatest constitutional issue in all American history, however, was not settled by the Court or in the halls of Congress but on the battlefield. The whole nature and destiny of the American Union was at stake in the Civil War. Lee's surrender to Grant at Appomattox Court House settled once and for all that the United States was a sovereign nation and not a mere loose confederation of sovereign states. Until 1865 that question had been undecided; since that time no one has questioned either national sovereignty or the permanent nature of the Union.

American constitutional history falls into three fairly well-defined periods. The first, from 1607 to 1789, covers the whole colonial era, the break with Britain, and the achievement of national unity under the Articles of Confederation and the Constitution. Most of the principal institutions and ideas of the American constitutional system made their appearance in this period of almost two centuries, among them the idea of a supreme written constitution, the doctrine of limited government, the concept of a federal state, the separation of powers, bicameralism, and the main principles of American legislative practice. The era closed with the ratification of the Constitution, a document embodying the political experience of the preceding two centuries.

The second period, from 1789 to 1865, began with the establishment of the national government under the Constitution and ended with the collapse and failure of the Confederacy's attempt to break up the Union. The great constitutional issue of this entire period was that of the ultimate nature of the Union. Had the Constitution created a supreme sovereign central government or had it merely brought into being a loose confederation or league of sovereign states? Closely correlated with this issue was the question of who had the final power to interpret the Constitution. Secession finally transferred both questions from the political arena to the battle-field, where the "locus of sovereignty" was settled decisively in favor of the national government.

The third great period in American constitutional history began in 1865, and has extended to our own time. The era has been one of large-scale industrialization and urbanization of American life, and most of its constitutional problems have arisen from successive attempts to adjust the constitutional system to the requirements of modern urban industrial society. The powers delegated to the national government in 1789 contemplated but little assertion of federal authority beyond the general areas of defense, finance, foreign policy, and commerce. No one in the Convention had any knowledge of modern means of communication, railroads, holding companies, labor unions, hydroelectric power, mass production, or mechanized agriculture. Modern government has to deal with social and economic problems arising from all these developments and many more. The result is a body of modern constitutional law which the delegates to Philadelphia would no doubt have some difficulty in recognizing as their handiwork.

One grand theme runs through all three centuries of American constitutional history. It is the idea of limited government, or what Professor C. H. McIlwain has called "constitutionalism." The doctrine of limited government holds that government should proceed within the authority of established institutions and laws, that governmental authority should be limited and defined by law, and that governmental officials should be responsible to law. A government of this kind is often, somewhat loosely, described as one of laws and not of men. Without doubt the evolution of limited government constitutes one of the most significant chapters in the history of human freedom. In the twentieth century, when free political institutions are once again under powerful attack in the Western world, the central thesis of American constitutionalism is that free men can solve the problems of modern society under processes of law and without resort to tyranny.

English and Colonial Origins

THE FIRST English colonies in America were the work of private enterprise, not of the British government itself. The role of the Crown in colonial ventures was passive rather than active; it granted charters, conveyed lands, conferred monopoly rights in trade, and permitted migration, but its officials were not at all aware that they were giving encouragement to men laying the foundations of a great colonial empire. Early colonial government, in short, bore the marks of private enterprise, of the men and institutions that first participated in colonial activity.

Speaking generally, early colonial adventurers were of three types: merchant capitalists seeking new markets, raw materials, and trade; English Calvinists seeking to found religious Zions in the wilderness; and Stuart courtiers hoping to establish feudal proprieties in the New World. Merchant-capitalists, already accustomed to the joint-stock company as a method of organization, quite naturally founded governments in their colonies closely modeled upon joint-stock corporate structure. Separatists, accustomed to founding church government by compact, or mutual consent, formed political bodies in that fashion. Stuart courtiers, holding a feudal grant from the Crown, attempted to organize colonial government as a feudal barony. Thus the three early types of colony—joint-stock, compact, and proprietary—all resulted from some form of private initiative.

THE JOINT-STOCK COMPANY: VIRGINIA AND
MASSACHUSETTS BAY

The joint-stock company was an important instrument in the great English commercial expansion of the sixteenth and seventeenth centuries. The origins of the institution are to be found in the Middle Ages. The merchants and industrialists of fifteenth-century Italy developed the business technique of pooling capital resources to expand operations and distribute risk, and later English merchants no doubt borrowed somewhat from the Italian idea.

The English joint-stock companies, however, also evolved directly out of the medieval guild-merchant. Since the twelfth century it had been customary for the merchants of a community to organize guilds-merchant for the purpose of carrying on trade. The guild often became a kind of closed corporation—that is, one to which admission was necessary if a merchant wished to trade within the area over which the guild had control. Very often it sought and obtained from the Crown a charter giving legal recognition to the trade rights it claimed, a step particularly important to the guild when it had secured a monopoly over some segment of foreign trade.

Organizations of "merchant-adventurers," as this type of guild was sometimes called, were fairly common in fifteenth-century England. They were not joint-stock companies in the later sense of the term, for they seldom undertook any common group venture. The membership simply carried on individual operations under the protection of the privileges assured by membership in the guild.

In the great commercial development of the sixteenth century, the principle of the "company of merchant-adventurers," a corporate entity licensed by the crown and having certain trade privileges, was combined with the continental device of pooling the capital of investors to share both risk and profits in a common enterprise. The result was the emergence of the great English trading companies of the late sixteenth and early seventeenth centuries as the principal media of English commercial and colonial expansion.

In the case of at least one company, the Merchant-Adventurers of London, it is possible to trace the transition from a mere company of merchant-adventurers into an actual joint-stock enterprise. This organization had originally been one of the trading guilds of the kind discussed above. Later, having acquired a virtual monopoly of the Netherlands trade, it sought and obtained incorporation in 1564, as the Merchant-Adventurers of London.

About the same time that the Merchant-Adventurers of London

were incorporating, various groups of traders approached the Crown and sought and received charters affording commercial favors, prescribing their form of organization, and granting the right to raise money by selling stock. One of the earliest of such enterprises was the Muscovy Company, chartered in 1555 to carry on trade with Russia and central Asia. It enjoyed a profitable career until the early seventeenth century, when the growth of Dutch influence in Russia intervened. The Eastland Company, chartered in 1579, received a monopoly of English trade with the Baltic and for some years carried on a prosperous trade in naval stores and cloth. The Levant Company, chartered in 1592 to trade with the eastern Mediterranean, counted Queen Elizabeth herself among its investors. Most famous of all was the East India Company, chartered in 1600, on the eve of Elizabeth's death. This concern eventually became not only the medium through which English commercial interests penetrated India and wrested control of that great subcontinent from the Portuguese, the Dutch, and the French, but also a virtual state-within-a-state, through which British control of India was gradually effected.

A typical joint-stock charter of this time gave the company a name and a formally recognized legal position, and specified the terms of organization. The charter usually vested control in a council, the original members of which were customarily named in the document. Generally, the membership of this body varied from six to more than twenty, and the direction of the affairs of the company was in its hands. Sometimes the charter provided for a governor as the head of the company, in which case he was chosen by the council, usually from its own membership. Membership in the company was secured through stock ownership. The smaller stockholders had little to say about general policy; however, they met periodically in a general court to elect members to vacancies in the council and occasionally to express their opinion upon some major question of policy.

The typical charter also granted a number of privileges thought to be of some financial advantage. These might include a grant of land, the right to convey title to any portion of its domains, and the title to all precious metals discovered within the specified region. A monopoly of trade within the area was an almost invariable provision.

Finally, the charter sometimes conferred upon the company extensive governing powers. This was necessary either because the contemplated region to be exploited was unsettled wilderness, as in America, or because the company was to be the actual instrument of English conquest in an already civilized region, as in India. In either case the company needed authority to establish law and order within its domains, and therefore the charter commonly bestowed the right to set up some local governing body, to maintain defense, to coin money, to establish courts, and to enact ordinances for local government. Thus certain of the companies took on a quasi-sovereign character, becoming virtual states within the British Empire. In this respect those companies trading to America were not at all unique; the East India Company, for example, long exercised an almost unlimited authority over much of India.

Virginia, the earliest successful English colony, was founded by a joint-stock company. In 1606, two influential groups of English merchants, one at London and one at Plymouth, obtained two separate grants from the crown under a single charter. The London group was organized as The Virginia Company of London, while the Plymouth adventurers were incorporated as the Virginia Company of Plymouth. The London Company was given the right to found a colony anywhere between the thirty-fourth and forty-first parallels on the North American continent, and the Plymouth group was granted the corresponding right between the thirty-eighth and forty-fifth parallels. Neither company might colonize within one hundred miles of the other. The two companies were technically "semi-joint-stock" organizations, separate stock subscriptions being anticipated for each successive voyage.

The London Company's charter provided for a governor, who with an advisory council of thirteen was empowered to direct the general affairs of the company. The stockholders were also instructed to assemble from time to time in a general court. A novel provision was one establishing a Royal Council in London, quite apart from the company's council, with power to supervise all activities in so far as they concerned the interests of the English Crown. Under this charter, the Virginia Company of London founded the settlement at Jamestown in 1607.

There was at first little local self-government in Virginia; rather, as in any joint-stock enterprise, the governor and council directed operations from London. Local matters within the colony were in the hands of a governor and local council, all appointed from London, and ordinary settlers were given no share in the government. Political quarrels between governor and council, together with recurrent economic crises, inspired Governor John Smith in 1608 to resort to stern measures to check the colony's disintegration.

In 1609, the London Company secured a new charter designed to end mismanagement and to encourage new stock subscriptions. This charter severed the company's connection with the Virginia Company of Plymouth after the latter had already failed in its attempt to establish the Sagadahoc Colony in Maine. The London Company now became a regular joint-stock concern, with some seven hundred permanent stockholders. The separate royal council in London was abolished, control now being vested in the company's treasurer and the London council. The Crown also extended the company's lands to include all the lands from sea to sea for two hundred miles on either side of its settlement. A supplementary charter of 1612 strengthened the stockholders' control of company affairs by providing for four "great courts" or stockholders' meetings each year to dispose of matters of great importance. The 1612 charter also extended the company's boundaries three hundred leagues seaward to include Bermuda.

In 1610 the reorganized company resorted to outright despotism in Virginia. The treasurer and council revoked the authority of the local governor and council and vested absolute authority in a "lord-governor and captain-general" who was given full military, executive, and lawmaking power. By this experiment in autocracy the company hoped to end the indolence and petty wrangling which had so far crippled the colony's life.

The enterprise nonetheless did not prosper, mainly because it lacked an adequate economic base. The settlers had attempted more or less unsuccessfully to raise corn, produce wine and silk, and mine gold. Although the cultivation of tobacco, begun in 1612, brought some prosperity, the significance of the new crop was not appreciated, and the company still failed to pay dividends. Furthermore, the despotic local government gave the settlement a bad name and discouraged immigration.

In 1618 the company, in an effort to encourage immigration and to promote a better spirit among the colonists, attempted a general reorganization of local government in Virginia. The governor's instructions for 1619 contained an order for the establishment of a local representative assembly. This body, patterned after the company's general court or stockholders' meeting in London, was the beginning of the Virginia colonial legislature. The local council, which at first sat with the assembly to compose one chamber, was a counterpart of the company's council in London.

Thus, through the establishment of a local governor, a council, and a representative assembly, the Virginia Company of London had finally evolved a colonial government for Virginia modeled upon its own charter provisions. Substantially the same pattern of government eventually appeared in all the English colonies. The Virginia Company of London, beset by financial failure and internal dissension, lost its charter in 1624. The King now named a royal governor and, the following year, formally incorporated Virginia in the royal domain. Virginia thereby became the first royal colony in America. The assembly, a mere creature of the company, might well have expired at this time, and in fact no regular assemblies met in Virginia from 1623 to 1628. Thereafter the legislature met annually, although it was not until 1639 that the king recognized the right of the assembly to permanent existence. By that time the future of Virginia as a royal colony was assured, but the frame of government of the Old Dominion, both as colony and as state, continued to be that imposed by the joint-stock company.

Like Virginia, Massachusetts Bay was founded by a trading company, but in its case the company's charter became the actual constitution of the colony. The company's founders were for the most part middle-class Puritans who desired to found a Calvinist religious refuge in the wilderness. Many of the stockholders had mercantile backgrounds, however, and some were interested primarily in the venture's commercial possibilities. Hence it was not unnatural for the interested parties to organize as a joint-stock company.

The charter of the Massachusetts Bay Company, secured in 1629, provided for a governor, a deputy governor, and eighteen assistants, who together were to constitute the council. Provision was made for four "great and general courts" each year, to be attended by the freemen of the company. The power to make laws and ordinances not contrary to the laws of England was bestowed in a somewhat ambiguous fashion upon the governor, the deputy governor, the assistants, and the general court. The charter granted also the right to establish all necessary offices and to appoint appropriate magistrates. Included also was a grant of all the land lying between a point three miles south of the Charles River and three miles north of the Merrimac River, extending to the "Westerne Sea."

While the foregoing provisions were not unusual, the charter in one important respect differed vitally from others of the period in that it failed to specify where the seat of government was to be located. The omission may have been an inadvertent one, for it was only reasonable to assume that the governor and assistants would normally reside in London; or it may have been intentional, at least on the part of some of the grantees. In either case, the absence of any such stipulation opened the way for the eventual transfer, in 1630, of the seat of government of the colony from London to Massachusetts.

At this time most of the influential members of the Massachusetts Bay Company belonged to the faction interested in a religious colony rather than a commercial enterprise. Many of them preferred to migrate to Massachusetts along with other religious dissidents and direct company affairs on the scene rather than stay in England. The mercantile group still had some influence, however, and they would not concur in a move which might foreclose the possibility of future profits from the venture. The result was a compromise, arrived at in the famous Cambridge Agreement of 1629. The mercantile group assented to the removal of the company to Massachusetts Bay, and in return the merchants were given certain exclusive trading concessions with the colony. This made possible the transfer of the seat of government to Massachusetts Bay, a move which actually took place in July 1630, some months after the Cambridge Agreement was signed. The company's connection with any superior governing body in England within the corporation forthwith ceased.

The council, once it became located in Massachusetts, attempted to run the colony as a closed corporation in the hands of the select without the assistance of the General Court. However, this oligarchical conception, fitting precisely with the aristocratic Calvinism of Governor John Winthrop and his associates, was not at all to the liking of the stockholders, or, as they now became, freeholders, in the colony. In 1634, certain of the freeholders, of whom there were then about two hundred in Massachusetts, demanded to see the charter. With some reluctance, the governor and his assistants produced it, and by it, the freeholders were able to demonstrate that the lawmaking powers of the corporation were vested in the General Court. The governor and assistants were forced to consent to the calling of the General Court at regular intervals to function as a legislature, and from that time on, the supremacy of the General Court was never questioned.

The metamorphosis of a trading company charter into the constitution of an English colony thus determined the outlines of the government of Massachusetts. The governor, the deputy governor, and the eighteen assistants, who together had constituted the board of directors of the trading corporation, functioned almost from the start as the executive council which handled day-to-day affairs of the colony. The "Great and General Court," formerly the quarterly meeting of the stockholders, now became the legislature. The only important subsequent modification in the structure of the General Court was the introduction of bicameralism in 1644.[1] The rights of self-government which the charter granted the company proved sufficient to give Massachusetts almost complete internal autonomy during most of the seventeenth century. Though the original charter was annulled in 1684, subsequent grants did not seriously alter the colony's form of government. Meantime the general pattern of Massachusetts' government had spread among the other New England colonies.

GOVERNMENT BY COMPACT: PLYMOUTH, PROVIDENCE, CONNECTICUT, AND NEW HAVEN

Several of the smaller New England colonies, notably Plymouth, The Providence Plantations, the Connecticut River towns, and New Haven, owed their early governments to compacts among the settlers, an idea borrowed directly from Puritan church theory.

The Puritans were English Calvinists, who began to win a following among English Protestants about the beginning of Elizabeth's reign (1558–1603). They derived their name from a desire to purify the English church of its remaining taint of "Popery," or Catholicism. Most of them wished also to restore the Bible as the principal source of religious authority, and emphatically rejected all doctrine and ceremonial not justified by the Scriptures.

A principal subject of Puritan concern was church organization. Puritans were nearly unanimous in rejecting episcopacy, but they were far from united in their belief as to what should be substituted. Before 1600, the Presbyterians seem to have been the most numerous Puritan group. They wished to organize the church into regional synods controlled by boards of presbyters or church magistrates, each synod having full charge of the churches within its district. Prior to 1600, most of the Presbyterians were conformists —that is, they were content to seek reform from within the Church of England.

In the 1570's there appeared in England a Calvinist sect, the Separatists or Brownists, who advocated separation from the Church of England and the formation of churches by compact or covenant among the church members. Church organization by compact was even then not new to Calvinist thought. In Protestant theory, every man was ultimately his own source of authority in religious

---

[1] The development of bicameralism in the colonies is discussed in Chapter 2.

matters, and it followed logically from this that mere agreement among individuals was all that was necessary for church organization. Calvin himself had asserted in his *Institutes* that the church came into existence by "common consent," while Richard Hooker, author of a famous Elizabethan theological work, *The Laws of Ecclesiastical Polity*, had supported the same theory.

Robert Browne, an early Separatist divine, whose contentiousness in matters theological earned him the title of "Trouble-Church Browne," contended that any two believers could come together and form a church, which needed no other source of authority than the compact that brought it into existence. Following Browne's advice, the Separatists proceeded to form their churches by common compact among the members and refused to acknowledge any connection with the Church of England.

Separatist theory and practice very soon brought the adherents of the faith into direct conflict with established Anglican authorities and with the English government itself. In England, as in other Protestant and Catholic nations of the time, the church was still regarded as an arm of the state. To deny the authority of the episcopacy was hence to attack the authority of the state itself. This was particularly the case in England, where the king was himself the personal head of the church. Anglican theologians therefore condemned Separatist compact theories as both heretical and seditious. Even under the tolerant Elizabeth, the Separatists were subjected to some mild persecution, while under James I (1603–1625) the condition of the Separatists as well as that of other Puritan groups became decidedly uncomfortable.

Various Separatist groups in search of greater religious freedom therefore migrated shortly after 1600 to the Netherlands, a country already practicing almost complete religious toleration. Possessed with the desire to form a wilderness Zion, a number of Separatist families resident in Holland decided to migrate to America, and after some negotiation they secured consent from the Virginia Company of London to settle within its domain. There followed the voyage on the *Mayflower* and the founding of Plymouth colony in November 1620.

The Plymouth colonists thus found themselves presented with a unique opportunity to apply the compact doctrine, hitherto used by the Separatists only for church organization, to the organization of a new body politic. In theory, the idea was not an original one, for various medieval political writers had held that the Holy Roman Emperor's authority flowed from a compact to which the people assented; also Calvin had argued for common consent or covenant as the origin of lawful government. However, Calvin's aristocratic theory of election was in conflict with this notion, for it implied that the magistrates, presumably chosen from among the elect, held office by the superior authority of God's grace.

In the Mayflower Compact, the Plymouth settlers translated abstract theory into practice. Their grant from the Virginia Company of London was meaningless, since the portion of the New England coast upon which they were to settle lay entirely outside the company's domains, and hence they were without any recognized political authority. Before landing, therefore, the adult males of the little body of Separatists gathered in the cabin of the *Mayflower*, and there set their hands to a covenant intended to provide the basis for civil government:

We whose names are underwritten . . Do by these Presents, solemnly and mutually in the Presence of God and one another, covenant and combine ourselves together into a civil Body Politick . . .

Here for the first time the compact theory of the state found expression in America. Plymouth Colony, in fact, had no other formal basis for its political order throughout its seventy-one years of existence.

The Mayflower Compact was only the first of many such covenants by which civil authority was established within the various New England settlements. When Roger Williams and his followers fled from Massachusetts to Rhode Island in the winter of 1636 and founded the town of Providence, they also found themselves outside all organized government. They solved their problem as the settlers at Plymouth had, binding themselves by a compact very similar to that executed aboard the *Mayflower*. The other principal Rhode Island towns founded within the next few years, notably Newport and Portsmouth, established governments in the same fashion.

The most famous of all early covenants after the Mayflower Compact was the Fundamental Orders of Connecticut, executed in 1639 among the settlers in the Connecticut River towns of Hartford, Windsor, and Wethersfield. The covenant created a government patterned after the joint-stock company organization, probably in direct imitation of the Massachusetts Bay charter.

Once a year all freemen in the colony were to assemble in a "Courte of Election" to choose a governor and a board of magistrates. In addition, each of the three towns elected four deputies to meet with the governor and magistrates in a General Court or legislature. The General Court possessed all law-making authority for the colony, including the power to raise taxes, admit freemen, make grants of undisposed lands, and call the magistrates to account for misconduct. The General Court was more powerful than the governor; it could meet and adjourn without the consent of the governor and magistrates, while the governor possessed no veto but only a casting vote in case of a tie.

The Fundamental Orders of Connecticut were for all practical purposes the first of modern written constitutions. Like modern American constitutions, they were a written compact of the people by which a fundamental frame of government was erected. They differed from modern constitutions in one important respect: they could be modified or abolished by a vote of the General Court. Thus they did not make the distinction, as does modern American constitutional law, between organic supreme law and ordinary enactments of the legislature. This distinction was late in making its appearance in American political theory; indeed, it was not clearly stated in most of the early state constitutions adopted after 1776.

The Puritan followers of John Davenport and Theophilus Eaton, who founded New Haven Colony, likewise organized their body politic through compact. They first met at New Haven in 1639, and with the declaration that the Bible offered perfect guidance for establishing government, they covenanted together in a body politic to enforce the laws of God. Seven men, known as the "seven Pillars," were chosen to constitute the government; and to them was granted virtual dictatorial power to make laws, administer affairs, and admit new freemen to the colony.

Eventually a number of towns grew up around New Haven, and in 1643 they united to form the colony of New Haven. Under this compact the freemen of the colony elected a governor, deputy governor, and magistrates, while the several towns each sent two delegates to a General Court. The governor, deputy governor, and magistrates sat with the delegates to compose a one-house legislature with general lawmaking and taxing powers and supreme judicial authority.

For a long time the covenant colonies were concerned with their lack of formal recognition from the English government, a condition that might well have resulted in their dissolution through a royal grant of their lands to a joint-stock company or proprietor. Actually there was comparatively little danger of such a development during the Puritan Revolution in England, since for some years after 1642 the mother country was thoroughly preoccupied with civil war, the trial and execution of the king, and the establishment of the Puritan Protectorate. In any event, the Puritan leaders in England were friendly to the Calvinist colonies in America, although Rhode Island in 1644 took the precaution of obtaining a charter from the Long Parliament.

With the restoration in 1660 of Charles II, who certainly had no cause to love Puritans either in England or in America, the covenant colonies feared greatly that the new sovereign might refuse to recognize their existing governments. Accordingly they all hastened to make their submission to royal authority and to obtain formal recognition of their right to existence. John Winthrop, Jr., son of the renowned governor of Massachusetts, acting as agent for Connecticut, secured a charter from the Crown for that colony in 1662 This document, with some minor modifications, confirmed the constitutional system already functioning in Connecticut under the Fundamental Orders. The colony was obliged, however, to submit to royal customs control and to the limitation that its laws could not be contrary to those of England. The colony's eastern boundary was fixed at Narragansett Bay, a provision which by implication brought New Haven under Connecticut's jurisdiction. While London officialdom probably had not intended thus to destroy Davenport's colony, Connecticut nevertheless insisted upon interpreting the charter literally, and in 1664 the weak and uninfluential New Haven settlement ended its separate existence by accepting Connecticut's jurisdiction.

Like Connecticut, Rhode Island recognized Charles II, and the colony was rewarded with a royal charter granted in 1663. This document also substantially confirmed the existing governmental pattern. There is reason to believe that Plymouth also made an attempt to obtain a royal charter at this time but was unsuccessful, and the colony continued to have no other legal basis than its own covenant until it was formally merged with Massachusetts Bay in 1691.

These charters of 1662 and 1663 gave Rhode Island and Connecticut a constitutional base substantially like that of Massachusetts under the charter of 1629. In erecting government by compact, the various covenant settlements had already imitated closely the Bay Company's corporate structure, and the new charters therefore merely confirmed the joint-stock frame of government in the two colonies. In a technical sense, also, Rhode Island and Connecticut were after 1663 little less than joint-stock companies—legal entities owing their existence to the Crown's prerogative.

Rhode Island and Connecticut eventually came to occupy a unique position among the English colonies, for after granting their charters the Crown recognized no more corporate colonies, and in 1684 Massachusetts lost its corporate charter.[2] The two former covenant settlements, however, continued to enjoy an extraordinary autonomy and freedom from outside interference. Although under the terms of their charters their laws were supposed to conform to those of England, they were never required to send them to England for review. Alone of all the colonies in the eighteenth century, their assemblies elected their own governors. The two colonies had to recognize appeals from their courts to the Privy Council, and they were also subject to the Navigation Acts and customs system. Otherwise they were nearly autonomous states whose self-government was interrupted only by the short-lived attempt at a single royal government for New England between 1686 and 1689.[3]

Rhode Island and Connecticut never forgot that they had created their governments by covenant and compact. Indeed, they merely transferred the original Separatist doctrine to the later royal charters, which they came to regard as binding compacts between themselves and the English Crown. Thus the Separatist compact theory remained alive in colonial New England and contributed substantially to the later American constitutional idea: the compact theory of the state. New Englanders never ceased to regard government as an instrument created by general agreement and resting therefore upon a contract binding the sovereign as well as the people.

THE PROPRIETARY COLONIES

Several colonial ventures, notably Maryland, New York, New Jersey, Pennsylvania, Delaware, the Carolinas, and Georgia grew out of feudal grants made by Stuart sovereigns to court favorites. As such, they reflected the persistence of feudal institutions in seventeenth-century England and the attempt to transfer those institutions to America.

The first proprietary grant on the mainland, that for Maryland, came very close to erecting an autonomous feudal principality in America. In the warrant issued in 1632, Charles I as overlord granted Lord Baltimore all the rights, privileges, and immunities possessed

---

[2] Abrogation of the Massachusetts charter is discussed on pp. 56–57.
[3] See pp. 55–57.

then or in the past by the Bishop of Durham. Between the years 1300 and 1500 the Palatinate of Durham in England had been little less than an independent feudal state, and thus by implication reference to Durham's past status made Baltimore a virtually independent feudal lord, with but very slight obligation to the Crown.

The Maryland charter also gave the proprietor complete control over local administration, lawmaking, and military matters in his province. He could establish an assembly, but was not required to do so. All writs ran in his name, and no appeals could be taken to England from his courts. He possessed the right of sub-infeudation, and the charter provided further that grantees owed allegiance only to Baltimore and not directly to the king. In short, Baltimore enjoyed a status not unlike that of a king except that he had no crown.

The proprietary grant for the Carolinas was in origin and character substantially similar to that for Maryland. In 1662, Charles II granted Carolina to eight court favorites, including the Earl of Clarendon and the Duke of Albemarle, who were thus rewarded for faithful service during the king's exile or for their influence in effecting his restoration. As in the case of Lord Baltimore, the proprietors received all the rights and privileges of the Bishop of Durham, and full ordinance-making power, subject only to the restriction that local legislation must conform as far as possible to the laws of England. No restrictions of consequence were imposed upon proprietary autonomy.

The warrant of 1664 granting New York to the Duke of York was in some respects even more extreme in its recognition of proprietary sovereignty, although it also contained certain new limitations. The Duke received full control of lawmaking, appointive and judicial powers, customs duties, land grants, and military matters. The charter made no mention of the Durham Palatinate, however, and the king specifically reserved the right to hear appeals from the colony's courts.

Perhaps because the Duke of York was the king's brother, he was able to exercise extraordinary freedom in disposing of his grant. Three months after receiving his patent he handed over the Jerseys as an independent proprietary to John Berkeley and George Carteret. York's action in parting with his own sovereignty over the region was illegal, but nonetheless the grant brought New Jersey into existence as a proprietary colony.

The charter issued to William Penn in 1681 reflected the growing belief among the more responsible English statesmen that proprietary colonies were undesirable, and that England ought to assert a more positive authority over her growing colonial empire. The king's advisers were unable to block the grant to Penn, but they did succeed in imposing certain unprecedented limitations upon his powers as proprietor. Within the colony, Penn's sovereignty was limited by the requirement that all laws be promulgated with the assent of an assembly of freemen. The Lords of Trade, the new body charged with administering English commercial policy, insisted also upon seven additional charter provisions intended to secure the colony's submission to English authority: First, the colony must obey the Navigation Acts. Second, the proprietor must keep an agent resident in London to answer in court for any violations of the Navigation Acts. Third, the proprietor must admit royal customs officers to his province. Fourth, he must forward all provincial laws within five years of their passage, to the Privy Council for acceptance or disallowance, the crown thus reserving a kind of veto over all the colony's legislation. Fifth, the Crown reserved the right to hear appeals from the colony's courts. Sixth, the proprietor assented to the erection of Anglican churches in the colony, should any twenty persons ask for one. And seventh, the king reserved the right to levy taxes on the colony, subject to consent of the provincial assembly, the proprietor, or Parliament.

These provisions anticipated many of the main elements of eighteenth-century British colonial policy. Submission to the Navigation Acts and customs control, maintenance of a London agent, disallowance, and judicial appeals—all shortly became requirements imposed upon most of the American colonies. The clause reserving Britain's right to tax the colonies is of special interest in the light of the American claim advanced in the Revolutionary period that Britain had no lawful authority to tax the colonies, and that no colony had ever acknowledged such a right. In fact, however, Britain never resorted to the authority established by the provision to impose taxes upon Pennsylvania. The considered and sustained assertion by Britain of a right to tax the American colonies did not develop until after 1763.

In all of the proprietary colonies, the proprietor specified the details of local government. In Maryland, Lord Baltimore at first merely provided for a governor and advisory council and put complete control of the colony's government in their hands. In 1637, however, he instructed his governor to call an assembly of the freemen. Although for some years after this the proprietor insisted upon his unlimited lawmaking powers, by 1650 the assembly had forced recognition of its right to initiate legislation. The council and assembly were by that date sitting separately to compose a bicameral body.

Likewise in New York the Duke of York at first attempted to rule through a local governor and advisory council vested with complete sovereign authority. In 1665, for example, the first governor, Richard Nicolls, with the consent of a temporary assembly, promulgated a legal code known as the "Duke's laws." Not until 1681 did York yield to popular pressure and instruct Governor Thomas Dongan to call a popular assembly with full legislative powers.

In the Carolinas, the proprietors promulgated a comprehensive constitutional system for their colony soon after its formation. The Fundamental Constitutions of Carolina, drawn up by John Locke, the famous English political philosopher,[4] and issued in 1669, reflected the proprietors' intention of establishing a comprehensive feudal society in their grant. Carolina was to be divided into several counties, within each of which there were to be eight seigniories of twelve thousand acres each, one for each proprietor. Each county was also to contain eight baronies of equal size, to be granted to one "landgrave" and two "caciques." These highly artificial titles were borrowed from the German nobility and the Indians because the charter prohibited resort to English titles of nobility.[5] The remaining lands in each county were to be divided into twenty-four "colonies," to be apportioned among the resident freemen. The eight proprietors sitting in England were to constitute a palatinate court, which was in turn to appoint the colonial governor. There was to be an assembly, composed of the governor, a deputy for each proprietor, landgraves, caciques, and elected deputies representing the freeholders. The scheme, an attempt to reproduce in the colony the social and political structure of medieval Europe, was destined never to function as the proprietors intended. There was too much good land readily available in America to enable a feudal system based upon land scarcity to survive.

In Pennsylvania, William Penn between 1682 and 1701 made a series of constitutional grants for his colony. In 1682, he issued a "frame of government," providing for a council of seventy-two members, and an assembly of two hundred, both elected by the landholders. The Council alone could propose bills; the assembly alone could enact them. The proprietor was to appoint the gov-

---

[4] Locke's contribution to American political theory is discussed on pp. 38–39.
[5] A landgrave was a kind of German count; a cacique originally was a West Indian native chief.

ernor, who was given three votes in the council, but no veto. A so-called "second frame" which Penn issued in 1683 reduced the size of the assembly to thirty-six and the council to eighteen, and authorized the assembly to amend legislation proposed by the council. It also granted the franchise to all who owned a fifty-acre freehold or £50 worth of other property.

These provisions were liberal for the time, but Penn's colonists did not appreciate the restrictions imposed upon the assembly's powers, and they agitated to give the chamber full legislative authority. Penn's absence from the colony for some years after 1683 led to a series of brawls between Penn's deputy governors, the council, and the assembly, and greatly strengthened the assembly's sense of independence. Furthermore, Penn fell out of favor in England after the fall of James II in the Glorious Revolution, and in 1692 the Crown suspended his proprietorship, appointing a royal governor for Pennsylvania. When in 1694 Penn's proprietary rights were restored, he found his control over the assembly still further weakened. As a result, the assembly in 1696 was itself emboldened to enact a new frame of government, which it forced Governor Markham to accept. The Markham Frame reduced the size of both council and assembly by one-third, gave both houses the right to propose and consider legislation, and deprived the governor of the right to perform any public act without the council's consent.

Penn returned to his colony in 1699, and after some negotiation with the assembly he promulgated the famous "Charter of Liberties" of 1701, in which he surrendered all control over Pennsylvania's government except the right to appoint the governor. The charter also put all legislative power in the assembly's hands, that body thereby becoming a unicameral legislature, the only one in colonial America. Under the Charter of Liberties, which remained in effect until the Revolution, Pennsylvania presented a curious anomaly: a proprietary colony virtually free from proprietary control.

A by-product of the Charter of Liberties was the eventual emergence of Delaware as a distinct propriety. Penn had earlier acquired the three "lower counties" from the Duke of York, who had a dubious title to them through conquest from the Dutch. The charter of 1701 provided that Delaware in three years might organize a separate assembly, a step actually taken in 1704. Penn remained the Delaware proprietor and continued to appoint a common governor for the two colonies.

The last proprietary colony in America was that established by the Georgia grant to James Oglethorpe in 1732, made with the understanding that the proprietor's control would expire in 1752. British officials had reached the conclusion, following Penn's grant, that the establishment of additional autonomous colonies would be unwise and that existing settlements of whatever form ought to be brought under more effective royal control.

By the end of the seventeenth century, the proprietary colony was rapidly becoming an anachronism. Manorial feudalism was a dying institution in England, and the system did not thrive on American soil. It was difficult to erect a social and political system based upon land scarcity in a country where there was a surplus of unoccupied land. Moreover, most of the small landholders in the proprietary colonies were of lower middle-class rather than peasant origins, and they did not take kindly to manorial and feudal restrictions. Had the British government supported the attempt to introduce feudalism in the American colonies with the same strong hand the Spanish and French used to protect similar institutions in their settlements, it is conceivable that the proprietary colonies might have survived for a longer period. Instead the English government permitted the colonists in the proprietaries to engage their overlords in protracted conflicts eventually ending in the destruction of both the legal and the social elements of manorial feudalism.

The proprietary colonies nonetheless made a distinct contribution to colonial government in that they promoted the transfer of English parliamentary institutions to America. Since the average proprietor found himself in his relations to his colonists in a position analogous to that of the king in England, he tended to establish a local administrative and parliamentary system strongly resembling that in London. The proprietary colonists recognized the parallel, and in their dealings with the proprietor they insisted upon the rights and privileges which the English House of Commons had lately wrested from the Crown. After 1688, in particular, the proprietary colonies tended to re-enact to a degree the Glorious Revolution; as a result the whole body of English parliamentary institutions and attitudes appeared in the proprietaries somewhat earlier than in the other colonies.

By the end of the seventeenth century, the private agencies which had founded the early colonies and thus established the first colonial governments were of declining importance in America. The impulse to covenant settlements had passed with the Puritan Revolution. Joint-stock enterprise in America was not financially successful, and after the Virginia Company of London and the Massachusetts

Bay Company had in turn disappointed their investors, the experiment was not repeated. Likewise the proprietary ventures, except that in Maryland, proved for the most part unprofitable. Moreover, the Crown after 1681 discouraged applications for proprietary favors.

While the earlier forms of colonial enterprise passed from the scene, they left behind them a residue of political institutions of permanent importance in the American constitutional system. The joint-stock company contributed the basic framework of colonial and later state government. The Separatist church contributed the doctrine of government by compact. The feudal proprietaries contributed little of themselves, but they hastened the transfer of English parliamentary institutions to America. The influence of seventeenth-century colonial government is still noticeable in the twentieth-century American constitutional system.

A Century of Colonial Government

DESPITE ITS heterogeneous origins, colonial government in America progressed rapidly toward a common constitutional pattern, which became clearly discernible by the early eighteenth century. Most British settlements tended eventually to become royal colonies. A royal colony was in theory a part of the king's domains, and was administered by a governor appointed by the Crown. Virginia became a royal colony virtually by default in 1625. For a time no others appeared, since the Stuarts long deliberately favored the establishment of proprietary colonies. After 1681, however, most of the colonies were converted to the royal type, either by accident or because London officials after that time deliberately sought to establish direct royal government. Massachusetts, for example, lost its original charter in 1684, when the Crown acted to end the colony's high-handed autonomy. New York became a royal colony in 1685, when its proprietor, the Duke of York, became King of England, while the Carolinas became royal colonies in 1729 following the virtual collapse of proprietary government. By 1752, there remained but three proprietary colonies—Maryland, Pennsylvania, and Delaware—and two charter colonies, Rhode Island and Connecticut. Royal government obtained in the remaining eight.

The differences between the governments of royal, proprietary, and charter colonies were slight in actual practice. All had governments established by written charter, either proprietary or royal. All had approximately the same legislative, executive, and judicial systems; all had about the same degree of internal autonomy, and all maintained about the same relations with the English government. It is therefore possible to subject all colonial government to common analysis.

THE COLONIAL LEGISLATURE

All but one of the eighteenth-century colonial legislatures were bicameral bodies. The upper house, usually known as a council, consisted of from twelve to eighteen members who were appointed by the Crown or proprietor upon the governor's recommendation. The council ordinarily had three fairly distinct functions: it acted as a legislative chamber, as an advisory cabinet for the governor, and as a court of last resort in certain types of judicial cases. Its members were usually drawn from the ranks of the great landed gentry or merchant class and thus represented the dominant social groups in the colony.

The lower house was an elective body, usually chosen from the colony's smaller-propertied classes. It varied considerably in size; in Massachusetts, for example, the house consisted of about one hundred members; the Virginia House of Burgesses seated about seventy-five; and the Maryland House of Delegates had about fifty members. There were invariably substantial property qualifications for membership, the common requirements being possession of a forty-shilling freehold (the traditional English suffrage prerequisite of a piece of land returning an income of at least forty shillings a year), or possession of fifty acres of land or other property valued at fifty to three hundred pounds. The privilege of voting for members of the lower house was also restricted.[1] The lower house thus

---

[1] All the colonies imposed a variety of restrictions upon the franchise. A majority recognized in some fashion the forty-shilling freehold requirement, although this condition was often altered to meet American conditions. Massachusetts and Connecticut, for example, both observed the forty-shilling freehold requirement in the eighteenth century, but New York merely stipulated ownership of a piece of land worth forty pounds. The colonies south of New York fixed the requirement in acres rather than in income or value; thus New Jersey stipulated one hundred acres, while Pennsylvania, Delaware, Maryland, the Carolinas, and Georgia all required fifty acres. After 1736, Virginia fixed the franchise prerequisite at one hundred acres of unimproved land, or twenty-five acres with a house. Most of the colonies at one time or another imposed various religious qualifications for the franchise. Until 1664, Massachusetts required all freemen to be Congregational church members; after that date and until 1691 a certificate of religious orthodoxy was a franchise prerequisite. Several of the colonies disfranchised Catholics and Jews at various

represented the more prosperous middle-class farmers and smaller merchants. The squatter, tenant, artisan, indentured servant, laborer, and Negro had little or no voice in political affairs.

In several of the very early colonial legislatures, the council and the assembly sat together to compose one representative body. This practice failed to give full recognition to the superior economic and social prestige of the council members, who eventually insisted upon sitting separately in order to exercise a veto over the assembly's enactments. In Massachusetts, for example, the assistants and deputies at first sat together in the General Court. From the first, however, the assistants insisted upon a separate veto, and in 1644, after a serious crisis precipitated over the amusing matter of a lost pig, the assistants withdrew and thereafter met as a separate chamber. In Maryland, where the council represented the proprietary interest and great landlords, and the assembly represented the middle-class farmers, constant quarreling over the council's right to a negative vote led to permanent separation by 1650. In the Carolinas, Locke's Fundamental Orders nominally established a one-house legislature consisting of the governor and four estates: proprietary deputies, landgraves, caciques, and elected deputies. From the beginning, however, the various orders of nobility coalesced as a council, while the elected deputies sat separately as an assembly. In a few colonies, notably in Virginia and New York, the council antedated the assembly, and the lower house when created sat apart from the council from the beginning.

American bicameralism was thus largely an outgrowth of colonial social and economic distinctions, with the council and assembly drawing apart because they represented different economic interests. No doubt the fact that British parliamentary structure already recognized bicameralism based upon class differences made the development an altogether natural one in America.

Eighteenth-century colonial legislatures commonly thought of themselves as small-scale models of the English parliament, and they tend to assume both the practice and prerogatives of the Lords and Commons. The committee system and parliamentary rules of debate and order were adopted with little change; so also, were many parliamentary ceremonies so dear to English tradition. The governor's

---

times. Virginia excluded all non-Protestants from voting after 1699, and Maryland, New York, and Rhode Island all disfranchised Catholics in the eighteenth century, as did South Carolina after 1759. Pennsylvania, New York, Rhode Island, South Carolina, and Virginia all disfranchised Jews in the later colonial period. The Southern colonies all barred Negroes and mulattoes from voting, while nearly all the colonies at all times barred Indians and indentured servants.

address imitated the speech from the throne, and the speaker was presented to the governor in the same fashion as the House of Commons presented its speaker to the king.

More important were the privileges and prerogatives claimed by the assemblies in imitation of the rights lately won by Parliament in its struggle with the Stuarts. These included the full right of local legislation, control over taxes and expenditures, the right to fix the qualifications and judge of the eligibility of house members, the power to apportion legislative districts, freedom of debate and immunity from arrest, and the right of the assemblies to choose their own speakers. In Britain, these privileges had been fully vindicated by the Glorious Revolution, and in insisting upon them the colonial assemblies believed that they were assuming the normal prerogatives of all sovereign legislative bodies.

English officials, however, held that the colonies were technically mere subordinate corporations without inherent sovereignty, and they were unwilling to recognize colonial legislative prerogative as identical with that of Parliament. Colonial legislatures, they said, existed only upon sufferance and could exercise only such privileges as the king chose to grant them. Legally, they said, the colonial assemblies had a right of legislation analogous to that of any other private corporate body—the power to make by-laws. London officials also insisted that the benefits gained by Parliament in the Glorious Revolution did not automatically extend to the colonial assemblies, and that the royal prerogative was therefore much more extensive over the American assemblies than over Parliament.

This difference of opinion upon colonial legislative prerogative resulted in a long series of disputes between governor and assembly in most of the colonies. In some matters the assemblies were successful in asserting their rights. In all of the colonies they soon won full internal legislative power, and the early attempts in New York and Maryland to rule without an assembly ended in failure, as did Penn's attempt to give the lower house mere veto power. Also the assemblies eventually established the right to judge the eligibility of their own members and to fix the qualifications for membership in the lower house.

On the other hand, British officials consistently refused to allow the assemblies to create new legislative districts or to pass "triennial acts" providing for automatic meetings of the assembly at regular intervals. Further, they refused requests of the assemblies for the automatic acceptance of their speakers by the governor. In Massachusetts, for example, a dispute between the General Court and

Governor Samuel Shute over automatic acceptance of the speaker led to the issuance in 1725 of an "explanatory charter" confirming the governor's right to disapprove the speaker at his discretion.

In the sphere of finance, the assemblies won a great and decisive victory. From the first they were able to resist the insistent demands of royal governors acting on instructions from London that they pass permanent revenue acts making annual appropriations unnecessary. In New York, for example, the assembly by 1740 customarily limited its appropriations to one year, stipulated in great detail how the money was to be spent, and refused to accept amendments to revenue bills. When, in 1748, Governor George Clinton attempted to regain some authority over fiscal matters by use of his veto power, the assembly blocked all legislation and eventually forced him to capitulate. Similar incidents occurred in Massachusetts, Pennsylvania, and the Carolinas.

This victory over the purse strings, recapitulating as it did a like victory by the House of Commons over the Crown, was of tremendous importance in the growth of colonial internal autonomy. Governors could hardly support royal or proprietary prerogative against assemblies that could specify the expenditure of every penny and withhold money from any governmental function, however vital. This situation contributed substantially to a gradual depletion of internal British authority in America.

If colonial legislative prerogative was substantially modeled upon that of Parliament, the theory of representation which prevailed in eighteenth-century America was vitally different from that in England. In England, members of Parliament were held to represent the nation at large rather than the particular district which elected them, and never considered themselves bound to obey local interests at the expense of national policy. In America, however, the representative was regarded primarily as a deputy, sent to the assembly by the people of his district simply because they were too numerous and too preoccupied to go themselves. This concept arose very early in Virginia and Massachusetts. When instructions were prepared for summoning the Virginia assembly of 1619, Governor George Yeardley suggested that distances were too great and that there were too many freemen to permit the attendance of all. Hence the instructions called upon the freemen in each of eleven districts to choose two deputies to attend the assembly for them. In Massachusetts Bay, Governor John Winthrop made a similar suggestion in 1634, proposing that the freemen in the various towns choose deputies to meet with the assistants as the General Court. The idea of the representative as a deputy soon spread to the other colonies. This American concept of representation was to prove a potent factor in colonial unwillingness to submit to Parliamentary taxation after 1763 and was thus of some consequence in promoting the Revolution itself.

THE COLONIAL GOVERNOR

The principal executive officer in the colonies was the governor. In the royal colonies he was an appointee of the Crown, named usually upon the recommendation of the Board of Trade, although on occasion the opinion of influential colonials was consulted. In the proprietary colonies, the governor owed his office to the proprietor, while Rhode Island and Connecticut chose their own governors.

As the representative of the Crown in the colony, the governor exercised virtually all the traditional prerogatives of the executive. Thus he summoned and prorogued the assembly; he possessed an absolute veto over legislation; by his commission from the Board of Trade he exercised nominal control over appropriations and expenditures; he had full appointive power for subordinate colonial offices; he was commander in chief of the colony's military forces and was vice-admiral of the province; he was the head of the Established Church in the colony; and, with the council, he frequently constituted a court of last resort. In short, he was the principal symbol of royal or proprietary authority and as such carried high prestige. The office was certainly sufficiently important to call for the appointment of men of position and character, and in general the Crown so regarded it. The colonists' recurring charge that the English government placed inferior men in the governorships was on the whole not true.

Colonial governors were of three types: Englishmen who owed their offices to political influence with London officialdom, English military and naval officers, and provincials. The first group was the most numerous and the most distinguished. In eighteenth-century England, most offices were obtained by political favoritism, or even by bribery. Yet this was not thought to be immoral, and many distinguished men entered colonial service in this fashion. Fully a fourth of the English civil appointees were drawn from the ranks of the nobility or the lower English gentry, and others had long been influential in English public life.

Occasionally a rogue secured the office. The classic example cited by historians is that of Lord Cornbury, cousin of Queen Anne and governor of New York and New Jersey for a time at the opening of the eighteenth century. Cornbury was apparently a profligate scoundrel, devoid of any sense of public or private morality.[2] On the other hand, the list of distinguished men whom England sent to the colonies was long and impressive. The able and upright Thomas Pownall, governor of Massachusetts from 1767 to 1770, is an excellent example of this type of official. The provincial appointees were also often of high caliber. Thomas Hutchinson, who governed Massachusetts on the eve of the Revolution, has a bad name in American history because he supported the king in the break with England. Yet he was a man of integrity, a historian of estimable scholarship, and a talented official. Cadwallader Colden, who governed New York at intervals after 1760, was, with the possible exception of Benjamin Franklin, perhaps the most learned man of his time in America.

Notwithstanding the prestige of the office, however, the colonial governor's lot generally was not a happy one. As the king's representative, he was expected to defend the interests of Britain and to maintain the prestige of the Crown unimpaired. A governor who disregarded instructions from London to curry favor with provincial interests courted loss of favor in London and eventual removal. On the other hand, a governor who attempted honestly to execute instructions from London was in danger of involving himself in a long and bitter struggle with the assembly, a struggle from which he was only too likely to come off second best. The British government thought in terms of imperial interests and British authority; the colonials thought in terms of provincial interests and the prestige of their own governments. The two points of view were incompatible. The whole conflict of interests between a colony and England thus centered upon the person of the governor, who nearly always incurred colonial wrath in the defense of imperial interest.

In spite of the governor's legal powers, in the many struggles between governor and assembly in eighteenth-century America it was generally the governor who was defeated. The real authority in colonial government was in the hands of those who controlled taxes and expenditures, and the assembly knew it. Time after time, the governor's failure to control expenditures defeated his attempts to carry out his instructions from London.

Sometimes the method used to defeat the governor was a simple

---

[2] A few of Cornbury's deficiencies: he was chronically drunk in public, embezzled large sums from the New York treasury, cruelly oppressed the Quakers, and displayed tendencies toward abnormal sexual behavior.

and direct threat to withhold his salary. In certain colonies, notably in Massachusetts and New York, the governor's stipend was dependent upon annual appropriations by the assembly. If the governor was un-co-operative, it was easy to withhold this appropriation. In 1721, for example, the Massachusetts General Court informed Governor Shute that it would approve the annual salary grant only after he had signed all the bills passed by the legislature. The same thing happened occasionally in New York, New Jersey, and Pennsylvania. While the exercise of direct pressure of this sort was not common, the governor was almost invariably the victim of the control which the assembly exercised over the purse strings. The failure of the Board of Trade to obtain a permanent civil list for any colony confirmed the financial ascendancy of the legislatures.

The long conflicts between the assembly and the governor in the American colonies had at least two important consequences for American constitutional development. First, the colonists became extremely suspicious of executive power. They came to look upon executive authority as almost inherently evil and corrupt, and suspect on every occasion. In the Revolution this attitude was strengthened by the popular hatred for monarchy symbolized by the person of George III. As a result, when the new states wrote their first constitutions, they tried to reduce their governors to virtual nonentities. It took a century of practical experience in state and national government to convince Americans that a comparatively strong executive authority was imperative to sound statesmanship.

Second, the colonists became accustomed to regard the executive and legislative departments of government as being entirely separate, as fundamentally opposed in interest and policy. It is sometimes said that the American states borrowed the doctrine of the separation of powers from Montesquieu, whose great work, *The Spirit of the Laws*, was known and read in America before the Revolution. It seems more fitting, however, to regard Montesquieu's doctrines as a confirmation of something in which Americans had been conditioned for a century or more. Long before Montesquieu they had become convinced of the desirability of a legislature removed from and independent of executive controls.

COLONIAL JUDICIAL AND LEGAL INSTITUTIONS

In the course of the century and a half before the Revolution, the colonies developed a legal and judicial structure largely adapted from its English counterpart. The growth was a slow one. Some conception of the basic principles of the common law came to America with the first settlers, while the early charters, with their provisions guaranteeing the inhabitants the rights of Englishmen and requiring that local laws conform to the laws of England, also tended ultimately to promote acceptance of the common law. But there were very few lawyers professionally trained in the common law, and in some of the early colonies, notably in Massachusetts Bay, they were forbidden to practice. As a result, the law administered by seventeenth-century colonial courts was a melange of common law, English local law, continental law, church law, and rough-and-ready "homemade" law. As colonial civilization became more complex, the common law, present from the beginning in outline, gained more and more recognition. By the middle of the eighteenth century, the common law, with some adaptation to American conditions, had triumphed more or less completely, while legal practice also had passed principally into the hands of professionally trained common-law lawyers, although as late as 1818 the Chief Justice of Rhode Island was a blacksmith.

In most of the colonies of the early period, judicial authority was in the hands of the governor and council. Whenever an extension of judicial functions became necessary, local courts of original jurisdiction were established, usually by executive fiat, with the governor and council continuing to exercise appellate jurisdiction. In Massachusetts, for example, the Board of Assistants at first acted as a court of first resort; but in 1636 quarterly courts were formed at Ipswich, Salem, Newton, and Boston, and in 1639 four counties were formed, one around each of these jurisdictions.

Similar development occurred in the other colonies. In New York, the assembly of 1683 put the judiciary on a statutory base with the establishment of a court of sessions in each county. These were county courts with original jurisdiction over a variety of types of small criminal and civil cases. A like statute was enacted in Pennsylvania, where the county courts were given original jurisdiction over nearly all cases except capital crimes, which were tried by the provincial court.

With the emergence of local courts, the council in most cases ceased to serve as a court of original jurisdiction and retained merely its appellate functions. In nearly all the colonies, the governor and council constituted for a time a kind of supreme court. In Massachusetts, New York, and Virginia, the upper chamber functioned as a supreme court to the end of the colonial period. In the other colonies, however, the appellate jurisdiction of the council was either limited or taken away by the establishment of a provincial court of appeals. In South Carolina, a peculiar situation existed. There the Court of Berkeley County, erected in 1685, was given power to try all criminal and civil cases for the entire colony. For a long time, it was not merely the sole court of original jurisdiction, except for justices of the peace, but it also functioned as the supreme court of the colony.

DEVELOPMENT OF COLONIAL POLITICAL THEORY

Of great importance for the future of American constitutional theory was the body of political ideas developed in colonial times. Colonial political theory had two principal sources: seventeenth- and eighteenth-century writers on natural law, and certain ideas derived from English legalists.

The theory of a law of nature or natural law first arose in the ancient world. Its basic concept was that certain eternal principles of law were inherent in the very nature of the universe itself, man-made law being a mere affirmation of natural law. In the *Republic*, Plato advanced the conception of an absolute justice which existed whether or not it found expression in any human enactment. The Stoic philosophers, who emphasized the necessity of harmonizing man's institutions with those of nature, spread the same idea throughout the Hellenistic and Roman world. Cicero, the great Roman essayist, orator, and statesman, expressed the essential notion in his *De Legibus*, where he stated that the binding quality of civil law rose out of its harmony with the eternal principles of right and justice. He contended that man-made law was valid only when it did not transgress the principles of right and justice, and that it would be impossible to make "robbery, adultery, or the falsification of wills" true law by mere enactment.

In the medieval period the idea of natural law continued to receive recognition. The Roman law as codified by the Emperor Justinian was thought to be largely a reflection of natural law; the *Decretum*, Gratian's great canonical code of the twelfth century, also paid homage to natural law. In England, John of Salisbury, a great theologian of the twelfth century, wrote that "there are certain principles of law which have perpetual necessity, having the force of law among all nations, and which absolutely cannot be broken." Henry de Bracton, the thirteenth-century English legal theorist, made much the same observation, as did Sir John Fortescue, who wrote two centuries later.[3]

Modern natural-law theory, however, arose in the late sixteenth century. The great problem confronting political theorists of the day was the rise of the modern national state, which had freed itself of ecclesiastical controls, feudal decentralization, and theoretical allegiance to the Holy Roman Empire. The essential political quality of the new national state was its sovereign irresponsibility, that is, its refusal to acknowledge superior controls exercised by any political or religious body. Jean Bodin, a sixteenth-century French theorist, first adequately defined the new sovereignty when he said that it was "supreme power over citizens and subjects unrestrained by the laws."

The sovereign secular state created a new problem in political theory. The state and its sovereign attributes could not be explained or justified by any notion of a divinely ordained political order as had medieval government, for the new nations had renounced theocratic controls. The national state and the theory of irresponsible sovereignty upon which it operated therefore required a new theoretical justification, and political theorists set to work to supply it.

The problem was solved in the seventeenth century by combining the ancient Stoic idea of natural law with the Calvinist-Separatist doctrine of the social compact. Political theorists turned the more readily to the idea of natural law as a sanction for social theory because the new science, particularly in astronomy and physics, seemed to demonstrate that all nature operated by immutable and eternal laws inherent in the nature of the universe itself. It was an easy step to transfer this idea from science to the foundations of social theory. The idea that a society or body politic might be based on a covenant or compact among the people had been seized upon by Calvin as the theoretical foundation for all church organization. The little Separatist communities in England and America had used the covenant principle to organize their churches, and it was but a short step for them to move from the creation of a

---

[3] John of Salisbury (d. 1180) was a great English scholar, cleric, and early humanist, who did much to revive medieval interest in the ancient classics. Henry de Bracton (d. 1268) was England's greatest legal authority of the Middle Ages. His *De Legibus Consuetudinibus Angliae* combined English with Continental Roman legal practice, and had a pronounced influence on seventeenth- and eighteenth-century British writers. Sir John Fortescue (d. 1476) was a noted English jurist, justice of the King's Bench, and political theorist. His *De Natura Legis Naturae* is a leading early treatise on natural law, which he carefully distinguished from divine law. He argued that natural law was the fountainhead of the English constitutional system.

church by covenant to the founding of the social order and the state itself by the same process. This the Fundamental Orders of Connecticut and the other Puritan covenants were to demonstrate.

A Dutch writer, Johannes Althusius (d. 1638), was perhaps the first to associate a modernized conception of natural law with the Calvinist compact theory. Althusius was himself a pronounced Calvinist, and he thus supplied a definite link between Calvinist theory and the secular philosophers. Althusius also was well known to the early Separatists, a fact which may explain the well-developed ideas on natural law present in the New England of Roger Williams and Thomas Hooker. Hugo Grotius, the great Dutch authority on international law, shortly presented the natural law–compact theory of the state anew in his immortal treatise, De Jure Belli ac Pacis, published in 1625. Thereafter the same general body of ideas, with some important variations in detail, was explored by a host of brilliant seventeenth- and eighteenth-century figures, among them the Englishmen John Milton,[4] James Harrington,[5] Algernon Sidney,[6] and John Locke,[7] and the continental writers Samuel Pufendorf, Emmerich Vattel, and Jean Jacques Burlamaqui.[8]

Seventeenth-century natural-law theorists took their departure not from divine sanctions for the state or from an Aristotelian conception of society as inherently political, but from the idea of an original state of nature, the presumed condition of man prior to the creation of all government. There being no man-made law in the state of nature, man's relations were then governed by natural law and by the long familiar principles of right and justice inherent in the nature of things. All theorists agreed that for the better protection of natural law and natural right men had covenanted

---

[4] John Milton (1608–1674), the great Puritan poet, was also a political theorist of some consequence. His Areopagitica (1644) was a classic defense of the right of free speech. In later essays he used the natural-law theory to champion the doctrine of limited government and the right of revolution against a tyrannous king.

[5] James Harrington (1611–1677) was an aristocratic political philosopher whose Utopian essay, The Commonwealth of Oceana, advocated equitable distribution of land, written constitutions, free elections, and the separation of powers. Oceana had considerable influence in America.

[6] Algernon Sidney (1622–1683), Puritan political philosopher and opponent of Charles I, wrote a Discourse Concerning Government advocating limited republican government and resistance to tyranny. He had much influence upon the revolutionary era in America.

[7] John Locke (1632–1704), a Whig politician and secretary to the Earl of Shaftesbury, was both political theorist and abstract philosopher. His best-known political works are his Two Treatises of Government (1690), the second of which is discussed on p. 40.

[8] Jean Jacques Burlamaqui (1694–1748) was a Swiss jurist and political theorist. His Principes du droit naturel derived natural law from the divine order and from man's reason and moral sense. Pufendorf and Vattel are discussed below.

together to create the state and erect a sovereign who was thereby endowed with the responsibility for protecting and enforcing natural law, a function originally inherent in separate individuals. Most philosophers held that the sovereign was a party to the compact and was bound by its terms, an idea pointing directly toward the doctrine of limited government, the theory of ultimate popular sovereignty, and the right of revolution.

An important derivation of certain seventeenth-century theorists was the distinct formulation of the idea of natural rights, hitherto not given clear and decisive expression. The doctrine was first expounded emphatically by John Milton and was later reiterated by the great John Locke, who was to exercise an immeasurable influence on colonial political thought. These writers conceived of a detailed body of inalienable rights and privileges possessed by every individual in the state of nature and reserved by him even in organized society. It was the state's duty to protect these rights, which were virtually immune to infringement, even by government in the name of the general welfare.

In 1690 Locke published his *Second Treatise on Government*, written some ten years earlier, which now served to justify the Glorious Revolution. It spoke of natural rights as those of "life, liberty and estate," the last term being a general one for property. The right to property, he said, was created by the union of a man's labor with the fruits of nature, and was therefore absolutely inalienable; even governmental restrictions upon usage in the light of the general welfare must be narrowly circumscribed. Locke's attitude toward the sanctity of private property and its virtual immunity from governmental regulation was largely a rationalization of the economic interests of England's new mercantile and industrialist groups, who were disgusted with outworn governmental restrictions upon economic enterprise. The doctrine of inalienable natural rights was later to enter American constitutional law, eventually becoming identified with the due process clause of the Fifth and Fourteenth amendments.

Locke associated his doctrine of natural rights with the concept of limited legislative power, also of great significance in American constitutional development. The legislature, he contended, could not lawfully enact "arbitrary" or unjust measures violating natural right, and it must rule through promulgated standing laws, not through capricious decrees. It could take no man's property without his consent, and it could not delegate its legislative authority to any other person or body. Locke also drew a sharp distinction between executive and legislative functions, and thus contributed to the growth of the doctrine of separation of powers in later colonial and national political theory. All these ideas substantially affected later American constitutional thought, both before and after the American Revolution.

Locke went further in defense of the right of revolution than had earlier theorists. He drew a distinction between the occasional violations of natural law and right inevitable under any government, and chronic habitual violations constituting a "long train of abuses, prevarications, and artifices" marking a government's degeneration into a tyranny. The former circumstance did not justify rebellion, but in the latter instance, the sovereign broke the compact by which the people's obedience was commanded, and rebellion became a right, even a duty.

Natural-law and compact theory early made their way into the oligarchical semitheocratic societies of seventeenth-century New England. John Winthrop, governor of Massachusetts Bay and head of the oligarchical clique of ministers and aristocrats who ruled the colony, could assert that both churches and government properly originated by compact among regenerate men. He could assert also that the people ought to elect their own magistrates, and that the latter are responsible to the covenant and to God. John Cotton, the colony's leading churchman, could demand that "all power that is on earth be limited." Natural law also had a place in the pattern; it was identified with the law of God as revealed in the Bible through Christ and the prophets.

But these ideas hardly implied belief in any modern conception of popular constitutional democracy. In his *Little Speech on Liberty*, delivered in 1645, Winthrop drew a sharp distinction between "natural" liberty, which men shared with the beasts and which was corrupt and degenerate, and "civil or federal" liberty. This latter, which arose out of the covenant between God and man and also out of lawful civil covenants setting up the state, Winthrop likened to that liberty which the Church enjoyed in subjection to Christ or a good woman in submission to her husband. It obligated men "quietly and cheerfully" to "submit to the authority which is set over you," since only by this means could the people "enjoy such civil and lawful liberties as Christ allows you." In short, in the exercise of their powers the magistrates enjoyed both divine and secular sanctions; as for the common people, it was their duty to submit to lawful authority.

Yet compact social theory had in it the seeds of a modern secular

constitutional system, and occasionally there were hints of the contemporary concepts of democracy even in early New England.
Thomas Hooker, one of the founders of Connecticut, has on occasion been described as a believer in limited constitutional government based upon popular democratic controls. This point of view
is undoubtedly exaggerated; Hooker's ideas on government, church.
and society were for the most part good orthodox Calvinism, and
he never quarreled seriously with the Bay Colony oligarchy. Nonetheless his writings do contain somewhat more emphasis upon the
popular foundations and limited character of government than was
common among early Calvinist divines. He early accepted the ideas
of fundamental supreme law and the limitation of magistrates by
an organic constitution. In a notable sermon of 1638 Hooker emphasized three points: (1) The choice of public magistrates belongs
to the people by God's own allowance; (2) the privilege of election which belongs to the people must therefore be exercised according to the law of God; (3) since the people choose the magistrates, it is within their power also to set bounds and limitations
upon the magistrates' office.

His *Survey of the Summe of Church Discipline*, published in
1648, was mainly orthodox Calvinist doctrine; yet he emphasized
not so much the sovereignty of magistrates or the duty of submission, but rather the continued responsibility of officials to the people, who remained the ultimate source of sovereignty even after
the compact. It is perhaps no accident that the Fundamental Orders
of Connecticut, for which Hooker was in part responsible, placed
no limitations upon the franchise, and subjected the magistrates to
the control of the General Court. If Hooker was not a modern
liberal democrat, he at least revealed something of the implications
of Calvinist compact theory for later constitutional government.

Roger Williams, founder of Rhode Island and rebel against the
Massachusetts oligarchy, was a religious radical whose passionate
pursuit of theological truth led him to anticipate, in a certain sense
at least, some of the basic ideas of later American constitutional
thought. Williams was not at all a libertarian in any twentieth-
century sense of the term. He has been called an "irrepressible
democrat," but there is little evidence that he advocated anything
remotely resembling modern political democracy, while the notion
of economic and social equalitarianism, which in his time was already being propounded by the Levellers in England, apparently
never occurred to him.

Like any good Calvinist thinker, Williams believed that the state rested upon a formal social compact entered into by the people, and he even observed further that "governments properly ought to have no more power—nor for a longer time—than the civil power of a people consenting and agreeing shall entrust them with." This statement indisputably contains something of the modern idea of constitutionalism, and it sounds superficially as though Williams' concept of the social compact were thoroughly democratic and even anticipated something of a Jeffersonian "right of revolution." The difficulty for a modern reader, however, lies in the word "people," which for Williams and other seventeenth-century political theorists meant only the compacting freemen, not the aggregate mass of individuals in society.

Like other Calvinist theorists, also, Williams took for granted the idea of natural law and of a body of natural rights derived therefrom. Religious liberty was the most important of these, but other rights also were sacred. Government, he wrote, must guarantee liberty of persons, by which he meant freedom from arbitrary punishment or restraint, and liberty of "estates," that is, the right to property. He held these rights to be guaranteed by Magna Charta, and he was thus among the first of many colonists to assume that the great English charters incorporated certain natural rights fundamental to liberty.

Williams' major contribution to later American thought lay in his firm advocacy of separation of church and state and in his complete dedication to religious liberty. His two principal essays, *The Bloudy Tenent of Persecution* (1643) and *The Bloudy Tenent Yet More Bloudy* (1652), were both attacks upon the theocratic conception of government as maintained by John Cotton of the Bay Colony oligarchy. Even here, however, Williams' basic premises were medieval rather than modern and have but little in common with the Enlightenment rationalism and skepticism that inspired Jefferson nearly two centuries later to advocate "a wall of separation" between church and state. Williams began with the idea that the life of the soul was the only form of human existence which had any importance or ultimate reality, and he developed elaborate arguments drawn from both the Old and New Testaments to prove to his own satisfaction that the state had absolutely no responsibility for the soul or its welfare. By the same token, Williams believed that the Bible enjoined freedom of conscience as a means of saving men's souls. Forced worship, he argued, "stinks in God's nostrils," denied the second coming of Christ, and threatened civil peace.

Only the last of these points, that concerned with civil peace, has much of any resemblance to those which a modern advocate of separation of church and state and freedom of worship would invoke to support his position. One may conclude generally that Williams ought not to be labeled a modern political thinker, but that there are nonetheless certain evidences of later constitutional ideas embedded in his writings.

Williams was an extreme radical for his time, and he stood almost alone in New England, denounced by most magistrates and divines as a dangerous firebrand. At the end of the seventeenth century, however, New England society began to lose its oligarchical, theocratic character. As the eighteenth century progressed it assumed more and more a secular democratic cast. Religious and political theory reflected these changes, so that after 1700 declarations of belief in natural rights, compact theory, limited government, popular sovereignty, and the right of revolution became more and more common.

One of the earliest writers to reflect the growth of a secular democratic social order was John Wise, pastor of the church at Ipswich, Massachusetts, and lifelong champion of popular causes. In 1717 Wise published his *Vindication of the Government of New England Churches*, a defense of the Congregational system of church organization against certain Boston ministers who had agitated for a close-knit hierarchical church system. Wise was concerned in the first instance entirely with church government, but he made as well an interesting inquiry into the foundations of the secular state in order to support his argument. He openly borrowed his political ideas from Samuel Pufendorf, the noted German writer on international law whose *De Jure Naturae et Gentium* had appeared in 1672. John Locke's *Second Treatise of Government* would have served his purposes better, but apparently Wise was not acquainted with this work.

As Roger Williams had done, Wise turned natural-law theory into a powerful defense of individualism, liberty, and even democracy. Natural law, Wise said, emanated ultimately from God himself. In the state of nature men had possessed inherent rational capacity to discover natural law. They also possessed an inherent political equality and a body of natural rights of which no man could rightfully be deprived. Because some men violated natural law, men were driven into combination for their common safety. The state, Wise emphasized, was a mere instrument of human convenience, not any divinely sanctioned agent of God's will. Therefore in covenanting together the people had a right to determine their own form of government and to alter it at will. Of the three forms of government, democracy, aristocracy, and monarchy, Wise thought democracy to be the best, since it gave recognition to man's natural equality and was best calculated to protect society against tyranny and despotism.[9]

In the course of the eighteenth century natural-law and compact theory assumed a position of increasing importance in the minds of colonial statesmen, lawyers, and clergymen. Educated colonials in New England, and the other colonies as well, read and adopted as their own the ideas of Locke, Harrington, Milton, Sidney, Pufendorf, and the other notable political theorists of the day. Locke, hardly known in America before 1740, became familiar to the generation of Americans before the Revolution. The New England clergy in particular filled their sermons with references to the law of nature, government by compact, natural rights, and the right of revolution.

To this body of ideas the colonists added one of their own—the notion of a written constitution. Since the days of the Mayflower Compact and the Fundamental Orders of Connecticut they had been accustomed to form governments upon written compacts. The idea of a written instrument of government was strengthened by the later charter grants to Rhode Island, Connecticut, and Massachusetts, and by the various written proprietary charters, notably Penn's Charter of Liberties of 1701.

The colonists thus became accustomed to viewing the charter as a visible embodiment of the compact setting up government, which specified and guaranteed certain natural rights, presumably derived ultimately from natural law and reserved to the people. The frame of government and the rights specified in the written constitution could not lawfully be altered by the government. The constitution, in other words, was supreme, and government was fixed and limited by its terms.

On the eve of the Revolution Emmerich de Vattel's *Law of Nations*, published in London in 1758, became known in the colonies and attracted much interest.[10] Significantly, Vattel emphasized

---

[9] Because the *Vindication* was republished in 1772 and had some circulation at that time, Wise has sometimes been described as the father of the Revolution. It is doubtful whether his influence upon the revolutionary era was large in any direct sense, for the *Vindication* in certain passages attacks the right of revolution as contrary to natural law. The passages on rebellion and revolution appear to be confused and contradictory.

[10] Emmerich de Vattel (1714–1767) was a Swiss diplomat, jurist, and writer on international law. He emphasized the customary practice of states as well as natural law as the origin of international law.

the importance of a fixed written constitution which could not be altered by the legislature. He also drew a sharp distinction between the fundamental constitution, which he regarded as supreme, and mere legislative enactments, which must conform to the written constitution.

Colonial theories of natural law and natural rights, compact, written constitutions, and the right of revolution bore fruit in the Revolutionary era, when they formed the legal basis of the colonial argument against England. Patrick Henry's Resolves, John Dickinson's essays, and Jefferson's ideas as set forth in the Declaration of Independence all were applications of well-matured colonial ideas upon natural law and natural rights.

THE INFLUENCE OF SIR EDWARD COKE

Sir Edward Coke, the great seventeenth-century authority on the common law of England, also contributed substantially to colonial ideas on limited government. In his *Institutes*, Coke contended that the Magna Charta had embodied certain fundamental principles of right and justice, and that the common law contained a further expression of the same principles. Magna Charta and the common law, he argued, were therefore supreme law, having such force that they controlled both the king and acts of Parliament.

Coke's opinion in Dr. Bonham's Case, delivered in 1610, when Coke was Chief Justice of the King's Bench, contained a notable expression of this viewpoint. An act of Parliament had authorized the London College of Physicians to license the practice of medicine in the City and empowered the college to punish physicians practicing without the required license. When one Dr. Bonham appeared before Coke on appeal on a charge of having violated the statute, the Chief Justice held Dr. Bonham innocent upon the grounds that the law in question was void. He went on to observe: "And it appears in our books, that in many cases, the common law will control acts of Parliament, and sometimes adjudge them to be utterly void; for when an act of Parliament is against common right and reason, or repugnant, or impossible to be performed, the common law will control it and adjudge such act to be void."

This case upon casual examination appears to be a seventeenth-century application of the doctrine of judicial review. Actually, it may not be so regarded. The modern American concept of judicial review has to do with the power of a court to hold an act of a coequal legislative body invalid as repugnant to the Constitution.

In Coke's day, however, no clear-cut idea of Parliament as being strictly a legislative body had yet emerged, nor had the later notion of the separation of powers any hold upon political thought at the time. Coke was thus upholding the validity of one set of courts, those of the common law, as against another, the High Court of Parliament. Notwithstanding this, the case certainly contains the idea that the common law embodies the principles of natural law and natural right, and that it therefore can control the acts of an important agency of the government.

Coke became the principal legal authority in colonial America in the eighteenth century, in part because his *Institutes* and *Commentaries on the Common Law* were among the very few legal works accessible to colonial lawyers, in part because many colonists studied law at the Inns of Court in London, where Coke's ideas were still given wide currency, even though many of them were no longer generally recognized in English practice. Coke's notion that the common law and Magna Charta reflected natural law and could therefore control acts of Parliament thus gained wide acceptance in America, even though the doctrine was generally rejected in England after 1700.

The best evidence for this statement is the Writs of Assistance Case, which occurred in Massachusetts in 1761, on the very eve of the Revolution. A writ of assistance was simply a "John Doe" search warrant; that is, it permitted the bearer to search virtually any premises at virtually any time. The English government often issued them to customs officers to facilitate search of warehouses. ships, and private dwellings, their use having been authorized by an Act of Parliament of 1662.

Writs of assistance, like other writs, were issued in the name of the king. Hence, when George II died in 1760, the writs of colonial customs officials had to be renewed, so as to bear the name of the new sovereign, George III. At this time, the British government was already tightening the enforcement of commmercial regulations, much to the resentment of colonial merchants. When the Massachusetts customs officials applied to the Superior Court of the colony for new writs, certain Boston merchants determined to resist their issuance, and they retained James Otis, a young Boston lawyer of the day, to represent them. The case came before the Superior Court in 1761, and Thomas Hutchinson, recently appointed Chief Justice, heard the case.

Otis advanced the argument that writs of assistance were illegal, since they violated a fundamental principle of the common law —that every man should be secure in his own home. As the writs were authorized by an act of Parliament, the statute was also illegal, for it contravened the common law, which was supreme. Otis' actual words to the court as reported by John Adams were:

> Thus reason and the constitution are both against this writ. . . . No Acts of Parliament can establish such a writ; though it should be made in the very words of the petition, it would be void. An act against the Constitution is void.

As authority, Otis cited Dr. Bonham's Case and Coke's works. Thus on the eve of the Revolution an American lawyer, citing Coke, had contended that the common law constituted a kind of supreme law for England, and that acts of Parliament violating its principles were void, a clear defense of the doctrine that legislative power is limited by higher law. Otis lost his case, but the important thing is that he made the argument. Three years later, he used the same reasoning in the attack on the Sugar Act, at the opening of the Revolutionary crisis.

THE COLONIES IN THE EMPIRE

Although the colonies were in most respects internally autonomous, they were but small units in a vast and complicated imperial system, which by 1763 was the greatest the world had seen since the day of the Roman Empire. The British government, however, awoke only gradually to the fact that its subjects had created a far-flung network of colonies requiring some control and administration. The main outlines of commercial policy first appeared in the so-called Navigation Acts, enacted between 1660 and 1696, while the administrative machinery of the empire was not complete until after 1700.

The policy and attitude evolved by Britain toward her new empire was commercial rather than imperial in the modern sense. That is, London officialdom was not interested in political control of the colonies for its own sake, or for taxes or military power. Rather, Britain viewed the colonies as a great commercial reservoir, to be exploited for the benefit of English traders and the material prosperity of the mother country. Mercantilism, the body of economic theories about trade and empire which gained currency in the latter seventeenth century, emphasized the importance of a favorable balance of trade and the importance of colonies as markets and as sources of raw materials.

The Navigation Acts, anticipated by Cromwell and enacted formally between 1660 and 1696, reflected the prevailing mercantilist trend of thought. They embodied three main principles: First, all trade with the "plantations" must be in English or colonial ships manned by English crews or colonial crews. Second, certain colonial products, the so-called enumerated commodities, must be shipped to England alone; these included tobacco, sugar, indigo, rice, cotton, and naval stores. Third, the plantations must, with certain exceptions, take their imports only from Britain, this rule being intended to give English merchants the benefits of the middleman's position in continental exports to the colonies. The Molasses Act of 1733 placed an additional restriction on colonial trade; it required all sugar and molasses imported into the colonies from other than British plantations to pay a duty of sixpence per gallon. This statute, passed at the instance of absentee West Indies plantation owners, was intended to give the British sugar islands a monopoly in sugar production for the colonial rum industry.

Largely because England's interest in the colonies was commercial rather than political, the development of colonial administrative agencies proceeded in a comparatively unplanned and haphazard fashion, no single agency ever being charged with the primary function of colonial government and administration until the very eve of the Revolution. By the early eighteenth century, however, six principal agencies of the British government in London shared the responsibility for administering the colonies: the Secretary of State for the Southern Department, the Privy Council, the Board of Trade, the Treasury and Customs Office, the Admiralty, and Parliament.

The cabinet officer immediately charged with the administration of colonial affairs was the Secretary of State for the Southern Department. This official was one of two secretaries for foreign affairs whose duties were theoretically interchangeable, but by custom and convenience the Secretary of State for the Northern Department confined his activities to the north of Europe, while the Secretary of State for the Southern Department was concerned mainly with the region south of a line drawn roughly from Paris to Constantinople. After 1704, American affairs were also placed in the Southern Department.

The power of the Secretary over colonial affairs rested mainly upon his appointment of colonial governors. In practice he gave little attention to their duties, once they had taken office. The Secretary's interest in the colonies was confined to military affairs, foreign policy, and piracy, while matters relating to commerce and trade were turned over to the Board of Trade for study and recommendation. Between the Board and the Secretary there was a constant exchange of papers and information, and a fairly well recognized division of interest obtained.

Since the Secretary of State enjoyed the right of approach to the king, his office functioned as a clearing house between the king and other parts of the English government. This increased his importance in colonial administration, for all petitions, suggestions, and requests for the royal favor passed through his hands. All matters relating to colonial affairs were also relayed by him to the proper official. Thus if Parliament sought information from the Board of Trade, the request was presented through the office of the Secretary.

Although the Secretaries of State were usually competent men, it was unfortunate that they were so little informed about colonial matters. The Duke of Newcastle, for example, who occupied the office from 1724 to 1748, was interested mainly in English party politics and cared little about America. The other duties of the Secretaries were so burdensome that they had little time for administrative detail and policies. It was administration of this kind which accounted for the fact that English officials eventually fell completely out of touch with American problems.

The Board of Trade was in theory a mere advisory body; actually, however, it was more directly and exclusively concerned with American matters than any other agency. The Board's immediate predecessor was the Lords of Trade, a committee of the Privy Council erected in 1675, when Crown officials were just becoming aware of the desirability of a more positive and coherent colonial policy. The Lords were placed in direct charge of American affairs, and for some years administered their duties with efficiency. They strengthened the customs service, placed the proprietaries under more direct control, and took steps toward the unification and centralization of the entire colonial system. After the Glorious Revolution, however, the Lords ceased to function effectively, and in 1696 King William replaced it with the "Lords Commissioners of Trade and Plantation," a sixteen-man body better known as the Board of Trade.

The Board had a great variety of duties, the most important being the instruction of colonial governors, control of colonial patronage, the review and disallowance of colonial legislation, assistance to the Privy Council in appeals from the colonial courts, and advice to the Crown and Parliament upon matters of colonial policy.

Although the Board did not appoint colonial governors, it nonetheless was charged with instructing them in virtually all questions of policy except foreign affairs, military matters, and piracy. In practice, it carried on a constant correspondence with the governors, advising, admonishing, and seeking information to be forwarded to other governmental departments in need of it. While the Board's supervision over the governors was in theory purely advisory, its prestige was usually great enough for it to command respect for its policies. It had no removal power, but it sometimes could and did force the removal of governors who violated its instructions too flagrantly.

The Board also had some control over royal patronage within the colonies. By established custom, its nominations for members of the governors' councils were accepted by the Crown, and it sometimes was able to control the appointments of royal governors, although here its wishes were very often ignored by the Secretary of State.

The power to review and disallow colonial legislation was nominally lodged in the Privy Council; actually, however, the Council invariably referred colonial legislation to the Board for investigation, and then abode by the Board's recommendations as a matter of course. Colonial legislation went into effect immediately upon being signed by the governor, but the king reserved the right to "disallow" statutes within a prescribed time. In Pennsylvania the charter required that all laws be submitted within five years to the Crown, which might then nullify them within six months after they were received; in Massachusetts the time allowed was three years; and in the royal colonies a statute could be disallowed at any time after passage. Disallowance differed from the modern veto in that its effect was to repeal a law already in operation rather than to block the proposed enactment of a law.

The Board's decisions on disallowance were in general guided by well-defined principles. It was quick to disallow encroachments upon the royal prerogative, such as the colonial triennial acts providing for automatic meetings of the assembly. It also disallowed laws which were considered to be inconsistent with fundamental principles of English law and justice. In this category were the various acts which attempted to classify slaves as personal property. It usually disallowed laws regarded as detrimental to British commercial policy, and those which it felt endangered the welfare of the colonies enacting them. Thus, the Board refused its assent to the Virginia Land Act of 1707, which permitted the patenting of two hundred acres of land per taxable servant imported. It also frowned upon badly drawn, obscure, and absurd laws.

Some four hundred acts of colonial legislatures were recommended for disallowance by the Board between 1696 and the outbreak of the American Revolution. The Board was sometimes exceedingly dilatory in the performance of its duties; laws were often disallowed after they had been in effect for years and had already accomplished their intended purpose. Yet with all its weaknesses disallowance constituted one of the few genuine checks which the British government exercised upon the internal life of the colonies. In general, the Board was attentive to its review of legislation, and arrived at its judgments only after grave consideration.

The function of disallowance was in some degree anticipatory of the role which the Supreme Court of the United States was to play with respect to state legislation at a later date. An agency of the central government reviewed legislation passed by local legislatures and decided whether or not it was in accordance with the fundamental law of the central government. It is true that the Supreme Court is a judicial body, reviewing the decisions of inferior courts rather than legislative enactments as such, and that it passes upon state legislation in the light of a written constitution. Yet the essential idea of harmonizing local legislation with central supreme law obtains in both instances.

The Board also played an important role in advising the Privy Council on appeals from the colonial courts. It was usually given the task of investigating disputed facts or questions of policy behind cases on appeal, and as a rule its recommendations were accepted by the Council.

Upon occasion, the Board furnished both factual information and advice to the various ministries and to Parliament, a function of some consequence, particularly at those periods when the Board possessed sufficient prestige to make its recommendations effective. Board members often had seats in the Lords or Commons, a fact making relations with Parliament fairly intimate. The Board frequently submitted information to Parliament on request, and it sometimes even successfully recommended the passage of specific pieces of legislation for the colonies.

Since the Board possessed only advisory powers, its importance in the last analysis was dependent upon the quality of the men who served on it, their prestige, and their relations with other branches of the government. The original Board included John Locke, the famous statesman-philosopher, and William Blathwayt, a man endowed with an extraordinary knowledge of colonial affairs, as well as two members of the House of Commons and two members of the Privy Council. Its prestige was therefore very high. After 1714, however, few men of distinction served on the Board, and its importance entered upon a long decline. Appointment in 1748 of the Earl of Halifax as President of the Board gave the body renewed significance. After 1751 Halifax was a member of the Board and of the Cabinet at the same time. After 1763 the Board again became unimportant, and it was abolished in 1782.

Nominally, at least, the Privy Council had two important functions with respect to the colonies. These were the review of colonial court decisions and the disallowance of colonial laws. The Privy Council had once been an important executive body, but by 1700 the full committee had ceased to be anything more than a ceremonial body. Its theoretical functions were actually performed by a series of committees, whose acts the Council ratified as a matter of course.

The Committee on Appeals of the Privy Council was a court of last resort for the American colonies. If one party to a colonial action was dissatisfied with the decision of the court of highest resort in the colony, he could petition the governor to grant an appeal to the Council. Ordinarily, the governor's instructions limited such appeals to civil cases involving £200 or more, although appeals were occasionally granted in criminal cases. The Council as a matter of course transferred such cases to the Committee on Appeals, which in turn usually referred the facts to the Board of Trade. As a rule, the Committee embodied the Board's finding in its decision, although occasionally it exercised some independent judgment. The Committee's decisions were then promulgated as the decisions of the king-in-council.

Certain principles were observed regularly by the Committee and the Board in arriving at decisions. As far as possible, opinions were rendered in accordance with the local law of the colony in question, unless some fundamental rule of English procedure or justice were involved. The Committee sought to protect English subjects against grave miscarriages of natural justice, and it also attempted to use appeals as a method of controlling the administration of justice in the colonies. Certain common colonial legal practices were definitely frowned upon—for example, evidence by affidavit, general verdicts, improper jury procedure, and the like.

Although the Committee attempted to function efficiently as a supreme court for the empire, its jurisdiction was subject to serious weaknesses. The expense of appeals was great. Numerous documents and records and occasionally even witnesses had to be sent to England. English solicitors must be retained to argue the case before the Committee and the Board of Trade. The cost of appeal often amounted to several hundred or several thousand pounds.

Appeals sometimes took years to carry through to a final judgment. For instance, the Stanton Case, which arose in Rhode Island, required ten years from petition to verdict. Moreover, the colonial courts, like other departments of the colonial governments, often resented outside interference with their jurisdiction, and in extreme instances, sometimes actually refused to give effect to the orders of the Council. For example, in *Frost v. Leighton*, taken on appeal from the Massachusetts Courts in 1735, the Council reversed a two-hundred-pound judgment which had been assessed against Leighton for cutting timber upon the public lands in Maine, although Leighton had a license to do so. The Privy Council ordered a refund and a new trial. After three years of dallying, however, the Superior Court of Massachusetts refused either to give the necessary order for a new trial or to restore Leighton his £200. When Governor Belcher and the Council failed to give him any relief, Leighton obtained a second order from the Privy Council directing Frost to pay the disputed sum immediately and ordering the governor and council to "support the royal authority."

The treasury and customs commissioners in London controlled the colonial customs service, which was not separated from that of Great Britain until 1767. A body of customs officials confusing in variety appointed by the Crown and responsible to the treasury—collectors, surveyors, naval officers, controllers, and the like—gradually grew up in the colonies, these officials being charged with the enforcement of the Navigation Acts and the collection of the duties imposed therein. Heading the American customs was a surveyor-general, who exercised a general supervisory authority over all colonial customs houses. In 1709, the continental colonies were divided into a northern and a southern department, a separate surveyor-general being appointed for each. Each customs house was in charge of a collector, whose principal function was the enforcement of the navigation laws and the collection of the duties incidental thereto. The resident naval officer performed much of the work of clearing vessels entering or leaving the port, this official being responsible not to the customs office but to the Crown.

In 1696 the High Court of Admiralty in England, acting on instructions from the Privy Council, created eleven vice-admiralty courts in the American colonies. The colonial vice-admiralty courts, which were subject to the High Court of Admiralty and the Admiralty Board in England, were given control of the usual marine, prize, and salvage causes, as well as certain cases arising out of violation of the various acts of trade. They remained an important agency of British control in America until the Revolution and succeeded in building up a substantial body of American admiralty law, most of which was later adopted by the federal courts under the Constitution.

Finally, Parliament exercised an uncertain degree of authority over the colonies. The theoretical extent of Parliamentary authority in America hardly concerned British officials at all before 1763, although colonial writers occasionally discussed the matter. Some colonists held that the colonies were not part of the realm of England but merely part of the king's domain and were therefore not subject to acts of Parliament at all. Others contended that an act of Parliament might be recognized in a colony in the absence of any specific colonial legislation on the point. Still others believed that a colony was subject only to those parliamentary acts which were in force when the colony was founded.

Such theories had little relation to reality. In practice, many acts of Parliament had effect in the colonies. Thus, the colonies were subject to the various Navigation Acts passed by Parliament from Cromwell's time onward and to the acts erecting a colonial customs service and the Admiralty Courts. Several important statutes were directly concerned with the internal affairs of the colonies. Among these were the three statutes prohibiting certain classes of colonial manufactures: the Woolens Act (1699), the Hat Act (1733), and the Iron Act (1750); the act fixing the value of foreign coins in the colonies (1708); the act establishing an intercolonial post office (1710); the act making colonial realty and slaves chargeable with debts (1732); the colonial Naturalization Act (1740); the act extending the Bubble Act to the colonies (1741); and the act forbidding the issuance of paper money by the New England colonies (1751).

These parliamentary statutes were for the most part concerned with major considerations of imperial policy. Parliament legislated only on the major affairs of the empire at large; it was not interested in the purely domestic internal affairs of any one colony.

When the vast complex mechanism of the British Empire in the eighteenth century is examined, it appears that the empire had become something very like a modern federal state. The government at London controlled matters of general imperial importance, while local affairs were left to the care of the provincial governments. Thus, London was concerned with the commerce and trade of the empire, and with defense, Indian affairs, the post office, and money. These functions upon examination appear to be remarkably like those later delegated to Congress by the Constitution of the United States. Only one important power accorded Congress was not exercised by the British government. That was the right of taxation, the very right which caused such an uproar in the Revolutionary era.

No political theorist before 1765 recognized the empire for the federal state it had become. English legalists still thought of the colonies as subordinate political corporations and held that Parliament and the Crown were supreme over them. The theory of divided sovereignty, upon which American federalism was later to rest, had not as yet been formulated. The empire was a federal state in practice but not in theory.

EARLY ATTEMPTS AT IMPERIAL REORGANIZATION

Though on the whole the empire's governmental mechanism worked smoothly enough, it was subject to certain difficulties. A very important one was the general absence of unity and coherence in colonial administration, a situation arising mainly because no single agency in Britain was in control of American affairs. While the Board of Trade was largely concerned with colonial matters, it had only advisory authority and hence could enforce no unity in administration or policy. Other officials, the Secretary of State, for example, regarded colonial matters as of incidental importance in relation to their other duties; as a result they were usually badly informed on colonial affairs and gave them but little attention. Division of authority among many officials resulted in a general absence of any sense of responsibility for colonial policy and a disinclination to undertake the reform of colonial administration. This situation explains in part why colonial affairs were allowed to drift along for three-quarters of a century after 1689 with little attention given the development of a more logical, unified, and rational colonial system.

A second difficulty arose out of the conflict between local provincial interests and the larger interests of the empire. Each of the various colonies tended quite naturally to adopt a narrow and provincial view of its relations with the mother country, considering questions of war, trade, land, and Indian relations strictly in the light of its own interests. This attitude exasperated London officials, who looked upon these problems in the light of the larger welfare of the empire and the prosperity of the mother country. This conflict of interest focused in the interminable quarrels between governors and assemblies upon money matters, defense, Indian affairs, and the like. Since, for reasons already explained, the assemblies usually more than held their own in these differences, provincial interests more often than not triumphed over what London officials conceived to be the larger imperial welfare.

There were in general two possible remedies for this situation. One solution, some form of imperial absolutism, repeatedly suggested itself to exasperated British officialdom. Under this plan, the existing colonies might well be combined into a small number of larger royal colonies. Were the existing colonies permitted to continue, then, at the very least, proprietary and charter governments would be abolished and a uniform pattern of royal government imposed on all colonies alike. In any event, colonial autonomy would be virtually ended, local administration being placed in the hands of royal officials paid and directed from London. The assemblies would either disappear or be greatly reduced in importance.

The other solution would nowadays be termed "dominion government." It would involve the erection of an intercolonial federal government in America to handle common problems. This government would maintain an army and a navy, treat with the Indians, handle western lands, operate a post office, and possibly coin money. It would support itself either by direct taxation or by levies upon the various component governments. The administrative duties of London would be reduced to a minimum, although English officials would exercise a general supervision, retaining enough control to protect British interests.

There were great difficulties in the way of either royal absolutism or colonial dominion government. London officials were interested only sporadically in the problem of colonial administration, while the prevailing divided responsibility for the colonies made it difficult for any single agency to propose and carry through a comprehensive plan of reform. The almost total absence of any sense of cultural or political unity among the American colonies, before 1763, was a fatal stumbling block to the development of dominion government, for the colonies lacked any desire for sustained cooperation in the handling of their common problems. In spite of these difficulties, however, two attempts at voluntary colonial federalism and one attempt at royal absolutism were made before 1763.

The earliest attempt at voluntary colonial co-operation occurred in 1643, when Massachusetts Bay, Plymouth, Connecticut, and New Haven formed the Confederation of New England. While the various New England colonies were fearful and jealous of one another, they were nonetheless drawn together by the Indian menace, fear of the Dutch and French, certain boundary problems, and common religious interests. Rhode Island and the New Hampshire towns were not permitted to join the Confederation, for Massachusetts still hoped at this time to enforce her title to these settlements.

The Confederation's articles of union called the Confederation a "firm and perpetual league of friendship for offense and defense." Each colony was to send two commissioners to meet with the delegates from the other colonies once a year and in emergencies. The commissioners were to elect one of their own number as a presiding officer. They could declare war, make peace, and settle boundary disputes with the consent of any six of the eight delegates. The articles also guaranteed the mutual return of fugitive servants and the extradition of criminals, two provisions later incorporated in the Constitution of the United States.

Though the Confederation was of some importance for a time, it was sabotaged from the start by Massachusetts Bay, which felt itself stronger and more important than the other colonies. The Bay Colony negotiated independently with the French in Arcadia, handled its own Indian problems, and in 1652 refused to co-operate in a projected war against the Dutch voted by seven commissioners. The Restoration of 1660 in England, which re-established some measure of direct English control over the colonies, also dealt a severe blow to the Confederation's vitality, and Connecticut's annexation of New Haven further weakened the league. The commissioners continued to meet occasionally, however, until Massachusetts lost its charter in 1684, when the Confederation was formally dissolved.

The one important attempt to establish unified royal absolutism, extending from 1675 to 1689, culminated in the erection of the Dominion of New England in 1686. When the Lords of Trade were established in 1675 they at once began working toward closer royal control over the colonies. They discouraged the establishment of any additional proprietary colonies and sought means for converting existing proprietaries and charter colonies to the royal type. They were forced to make an exception in the proprietary grant to

William Penn in 1681, but as already observed, they hedged the grant about with several restrictions intended to bring the new colony under certain royal controls. Meantime, in 1679, New Hampshire was converted to a royal colony, and in 1682 the Lords blocked a proprietary grant for Florida. Two years later, after lengthy judicial proceedings, the lords secured the annulment of the Massachusetts charter of 1629, in order to reduce the semi-autonomous Puritan republic to some degree of royal authority.

This policy of royal centralization came to a head in 1686, when the Crown established the Dominion of New England. Apparently modeled on absolutist French Canada, the Dominion dissolved all existing governments in the New England colonies, New York, and New Jersey, and united the colonies involved under a single royal government. A governor and council, both appointed by the Crown, were the sole governing bodies; there was no provision for a legislature. The governor and council were given power to promulgate laws in the name of the king, to tax, and to provide for the administration of justice. Sir Edmund Andros was named governor of the Dominion.

The Dominion of New England failed mainly because the tradition of colonial self-government was already too well established to be destroyed in such summary fashion. New Englanders remained in a state of silent animosity to the new regime and seized the first opportunity to destroy it. That opportunity came in 1689, when news of the Glorious Revolution reached America. The former colonies of the Dominion immediately rose in rebellion, and in the name of King William imprisoned Andros and his subordinates as agents of the deposed James II. The Dominion disappeared overnight.

William III wisely allowed the colonies to reassume their old identity and autonomy. Only in Massachusetts were matters somewhat changed. The Crown refused to restore the trading company charter, and instead issued a new charter in 1691. While most features of the old government were retained, the governor was now appointed from England and the colony was obliged to send its laws to England for review. Under the new charter Plymouth and Maine were incorporated in Massachusetts.

NEED FOR IMPERIAL REORGANIZATION AFTER 1750

After the Dominion's failure, no further concerted attempt at colonial reform was projected by British officials until the close of the Seven Years' War in 1763. England in the early eighteenth century was preoccupied with her protracted struggle with France for control of North America, and could pay little attention to colonial government. Meanwhile the old habits of colonial self-government, limited only by the imperfect controls of the British federal system, were left undisturbed.

In 1754, Benjamin Franklin, aware of the need for greater colonial co-operation in certain common problems, proposed the erection of what was in effect a self-governing confederation for the colonies. The occasion was the Albany Conference, composed of delegates from the northern colonies called together by the Board of Trade to negotiate with representatives of the Iroquois Indians, in order to cement the very valuable military alliance with that tribe. Franklin, a delegate from Pennsylvania, obtained the adoption of a resolution that some union of the colonies "was absolutely necessary for their preservation." He then presented a plan of union, which the congress adopted and recommended to the various colonial assemblies.

The Albany Plan was essentially a scheme for a federal government for all the continental colonies. There was to be a "grand council," composed of delegates elected by the various provincial assemblies. Very cleverly, Franklin provided that the number of delegates from any one colony was to be dependent upon the size of the monetary contribution which that colony made. There was to be a "president-general" appointed by the Crown as executive officer. To this government the respective colonies were to delegate the powers to raise military and naval forces, to make war and peace with the Indians, to regulate trade with the tribes, to control the purchase of Indian lands, and—significantly—to levy taxes and collect customs duties.

Franklin's plan of union was foredoomed to failure. Not a single assembly accepted the plan. It appealed neither to the colonies nor to the Crown. To the colonists it seemed to involve too much a surrender of local prerogative to the central government, and they wanted none of it. On the other hand, British officials probably would have rejected the plan for the opposite reason: to them it seemed to concentrate too much power in colonial hands and strengthen colonial autonomy too far. Franklin reported that in England it was "thought to have too much of the democratic" in it.

Though the Albany Plan thus failed of adoption, Franklin's proposal was nonetheless significant, for it is the first clear evidence that the colonists were groping their way toward the conception of federalism later embodied in the American constitutional system.

The Articles of Confederation and the Constitution later delegated to a central government substantially the same group of powers as Franklin's plan had proposed be delegated in 1754.

It is also possible that the adoption of Franklin's proposal would have averted the revolutionary crisis which shortly arose out of Britain's attempt to reorganize her colonial system. The Albany Plan was essentially an anticipation of the scheme of dominion government evolved in the British Empire in the twentieth century. Successful operation of the dominion system would have solved the problem of imperial organization for an indefinite period, and would have averted the strains which became so apparent in the Seven Years' War and which led directly to the attempt at imperial reorganization.

Some attempt to reform the imperial structure was virtually inevitable, and if the colonies would not initiate the movement, sooner or later the attempt was certain to be made from London. It was the inefficient operation of the imperial system during the Seven Years' War which finally crystallized the determination of British officials to impose certain reforms on the empire. During the war, the prevailing scheme of defense, which allowed each colony almost complete discretion in raising and supplying armed forces, broke down completely, and the Navigation Acts were also flagrantly violated. Such a state of affairs was intolerable to Britain. At the same time, the Peace of 1763 paved the way for an attempt at reform, for it cleared the French from North America and allowed Britain to pay some attention to colonial policy, undistracted by the French conflict. In 1763, therefore, London, deeply dissatisfied with the existing colonial system, launched a far-reaching plan of imperial reorganization. The attempted reform led directly into the American Revolution.

Chapter

3

The American Revolution

THE FORCES producing the American Revolution were exceedingly complex, and even today historians are not in general agreement upon them. The immediate cause was the attempted British reform program inaugurated at the close of the Seven Years' War, in which Britain sought to bring the colonies under more direct control. The attempt at reform was inspired by British disgust with colonial defense measures and American evasions of the Empire's commercial restrictions.

Behind this disgust there lay a changing conception of empire. British officials were abandoning the older ideal of mercantilism for a new conception—that of imperialism. Mercantilism had sought colonies as markets and sources of raw materials, and was interested in political control only as incidental to these ends. Imperialism, the newer policy, sought colonies primarily as a means to greater political, financial, and military power, ends to be achieved through sharper and more efficient political and military control of the colonies and a program of direct taxation.

The British reform program affected adversely the economic interests of nearly all classes of colonists. Merchants, lawyers, and land speculators were particularly affected, however, and they led the attack on the earlier Parliamentary measures.

The underlying basis of the American objection to the British program was in part a conviction that the new measures would prove economically ruinous, but in accordance with Anglo-Saxon tradition the colonists couched their objections very largely in constitutional and legal terms. This led to a protracted debate between England and America as to the fundamental nature of the empire's constitutional system. The developing crisis thus had somewhat the appearance of a lawyers' quarrel, though it is scarcely conceivable that the colonists would have pursued the argument so vigorously had they not felt the immediate severity of the new tax laws and the commercial menace of tighter trade regulations.

Colonial resistance to Britain was intensified by a growing American sense of independence, and an awareness of cultural and economic divergence between America and England. The destruction of French control in Canada removed much of the old sense of military insecurity and dependence on Britain, while their growing population and economic power gave the colonists an additional sense of self-sufficiency. Many Americans were also coming to realize how profoundly Britain's culture and economic interests differed from those of the colonists; they saw that their economic, social, and political institutions were in many respects entirely unlike England's. This realization contributed substantially toward a breakdown in sympathy, respect, and understanding between the colonists and the mother country. Thus, one underlying cause of the Revolution was the growth of a distinct and independent American culture and a growing American awareness of that cultural difference.

The quarrel with Britain brought to a climax long-standing social and class conflicts within the colonies, between the wealthy planter and merchant classes on the one hand and the small farmer, laborer, and artisan groups on the other. These conflicts involved differences over land systems and quitrent, defense of the frontier, the support of established religion, the franchise, and the like. Eventually the middle and lower classes came to identify their animosities toward the ruling groups with hatred for Britain, and after 1774 they formed the core of the revolutionary Patriot Party. The great merchants and landed gentry, though at first they had led the attack on British tax and commercial measures, eventually drew back from the abyss of social revolution, and with some very important exceptions, notably in Virginia, the colonial elite became Tories and supported Britain in the Revolutionary War. The Revolution was therefore an internal social upheaval as well as a political break with Britain.

However, while the Revolution was a conflict based on economic and social as well as political grounds, the constitutional crisis was of great significance in American history. It brought colonial political ideas on natural rights, compact theory, legislative limitation, and federalism to maturity and fixed them firmly in the American mind. Immediately following the Revolution the political concepts developed and expressed during the crisis found application in the creation of state governments, the Articles of Confederation, and the federal Constitution of 1787.

GRENVILLE'S REFORMS: THE SUGAR AND STAMP ACTS

Whatever the more remote causes of the Revolution, the immediate crisis was precipitated by the attempt of the ministry of George Grenville to impose certain reforms upon the administration of the colonies. Colonial military co-operation with Britain, based upon voluntary appropriations by the colonial assemblies, had all but collapsed in the Seven Years' War. Grenville and his associates therefore concluded, with much justice, that since the colonies would not voluntarily defend either themselves or the Empire, regular British troops must be sent to the colonies. As Britain had already incurred a heavy indebtedness in defense of the Empire, and since her tax burden was considered already too heavy, the ministry determined to levy taxes on the colonies to pay for the new army. In addition, Grenville decided to tighten enforcement of the custom laws, a step which might be made to yield still further revenue.

The ministry was also concerned with the problem of the trans-Allegheny West. Extensive colonial migration into this region appeared to be imminent, and such a development might injure British speculative landholdings on the seaboard, prejudice imperial relations with the Indian tribes controlling the valuable fur trade, and ultimately build a new colonial world too remote for effective British control. Grenville therefore determined to check western settlement for the moment.

The ministry resorted to three principal measures to accomplish these ends: The Proclamation of 1763, the Sugar Act of 1764, and the Stamp Act of 1765. The Proclamation of 1763 closed the frontier west of the Alleghenies to further settlement and forbade further land purchases or patents in the region. Although the decree was of slight constitutional significance, it greatly annoyed colonial land speculators and western settlers.

The Sugar Act, however, provoked powerful constitutional objections in the colonies. The statute levied a duty of threepence per gallon on molasses imported into the colonies, and it also levied small duties on a variety of other imports, among them sugar, indigo, coffee, wines, calicoes, and linens. On the surface there was nothing revolutionary in the character of these duties, for England had long imposed small tariffs upon the colonies for the regulation of trade, and under the Molasses Act of 1733 Britain had levied a duty of six-pence per gallon on molasses imported into the colonies from other than the British West Indies.

What was revolutionary in the Sugar Act was the statement in the preamble of the statute that the proceeds were to be applied toward "defraying the expenses of defending, protecting, and se-curing the colonies." In other words, the Sugar Act was a revenue measure, not a regulation of trade, and thus it raised the whole ques-tion of the power of Britain to tax the colonies.

The ensuing uproar against the law was inspired not only by nice legal theories, but also by the conviction that the law would prove ruinous to colonial commerce and industry. Although the law low-ered the duty on molasses, this was done to facilitate enforcement by reducing the incentive to smuggling. Strict enforcement of the duty, the colonists believed, would destroy the molasses trade and the manufacture of rum, thus bringing ruin to the whole structure of colonial commerce.

The colonial constitutional argument against the Sugar Act found cogent statement in a famous pamphlet by James Otis, a young Boston lawyer who had first attracted attention with his argument in the Writs of Assistance case in 1761. His pamphlet *The Rights of the Colonists Asserted and Proved* began with an inquiry into the origins of government. He mentioned with approval Harring-ton's assertion in *Oceana* [1] that government is "evidently founded on the necessities of our nature," but warned that "the natural lib-erty of man is to be free from any supreme power on earth . . . but only to have the law of nature for his rule. . . ." It followed that power, even the power of Parliament, was not arbitrary but was merely a declaration of natural law, which Otis identified closely with the divine law of God. "Should an Act of Parliament be against any of His natural laws, which are immutably true, their declaration would be contrary to eternal truth, equity, and justice, and conse-quently void." Recapitulating his argument in the Writs of Assist-ance case, he asserted that where an act of Parliament was obviously against natural right and equity, "the judges of the executive courts have declared the Act 'of a whole Parliament void,'" an evident reference to Dr. Bonham's Case. And he concluded, "That acts of

[1] See Note 5, p. 37.

Parliament against natural equity are void. That acts against the fundamental principles of the British constitution are void." These words embodied ideas long familiar to New England minds: the supremacy of natural law, the idea of a supreme constitution, the doctrine of natural rights, and the limited power of human government.

It would be an error to insist that Otis saw clearly the whole theory of judicial review, as later exercised in the American courts. He was interested in the idea of limited government, the doctrine that the legislature was controlled by natural law and the constitution, and his reference to the courts was evidently incidental. Yet the fact of that reference illustrates clearly that the doctrine of judicial review sprang directly out of the political philosophy of the American Revolution.

Otis then asserted that since the Americans had no representation in Parliament, that body had no power to tax the colonies. Thus he assumed the deputy theory of representation and rejected the English conception that Parliament virtually represents the entire Empire. A difference in the respective theories of representation in America and Britain, traceable to the action of early seventeenth-century Virginia and Massachusetts in substituting elected deputies for the actual presence of all electors in the legislature, was at last coming into the open.[2] The American and English conceptions of representation were to be dramatically revealed as irreconcilable.

Otis also saw clearly a point not yet discerned by many Americans—that there was no essential constitutional difference between external and internal taxation. The alleged distinction Otis declared to be entirely specious. The Sugar Act was taxation—and as such was as obnoxious in principle as any internal excise.

While the colonies were resounding to the attack on the Sugar Act, Parliament in February 1765 passed the Stamp Act, the second revenue measure in Grenville's series of imperial reforms. This law provided for excise duties, to be paid by affixing revenue stamps upon a variety of legal documents, bills of sale, liquor licenses, playing cards, newspapers, and so on. The duties ranged from one half-penny to six pounds and were required to be paid in specie. Here was no abstract question of constitutional right. The duties were direct and heavy. They touched nearly every aspect of commercial and industrial life in the colonies, and the power of Parliament to

---

[2] On the early development of the deputy system of representation, see pp. 30–31.

lay them immediately became of vital concern. The indignation which swept the seaboard produced a flood of pamphlets, tracts, and resolutions, nearly all of them setting forth essentially the same arguments as Otis had advanced the previous year.

At the suggestion of Massachusetts, a colonial conference known as the Stamp Act Congress, to which nine colonies sent delegates, was held in New York in October to protest against the law. This marked the first time that so many of the colonies had resorted to voluntary concerted action for a political purpose. In a sense, the meeting was a forerunner of the Continental Congress.

The Stamp Act Congress adopted a series of resolutions, the work of John Dickinson of Philadelphia, conservative in phraseology and full of polite protestations of loyalty to the Crown. However, their polite phraseology was a mere façade for a number of sharp and ominous political observations. The British government was reminded that the king's subjects in America were "intitled to all the inherent rights and liberties of his natural born subjects within the kingdom of Great Britain," and that it was "the undoubted right of Englishmen, that no taxes be imposed on them but with their own consent, given personally or by their representatives." The people of the colonies, said the resolutions, "are not, and from their local circumstances cannot be, represented in the House of Commons," and hence "no taxes ever have been, or can be constitutionally imposed on them, but by their respective legislatures." The Stamp Act, the resolutions concluded, had "a manifest tendency to subvert the rights and liberties of the colonists."

More sweeping and more ominous were the resolves submitted in May 1765 to the Virginia House of Burgesses by a fiery young backwoods radical, Patrick Henry. It was on this occasion that Henry reputedly cried that "Caesar had his Brutus, Charles I had his Cromwell, and George III . . . ," at which point he was interrupted by cries of "Treason! treason!" from outraged conservatives. His Resolves were a powerful statement of the whole colonial argument. They claimed for Virginians all the rights, privileges, and immunities of Englishmen by virtue of the charters granted by James I, and asserted that "taxation of the people by themselves" is "the distinguishing characteristick of British freedom, without which the ancient constitution cannot exist." They stated that "the General Assembly of this Colony have the only and sole exclusive right and power to lay taxes and impositions upon the inhabitants of this Colony." In short, Henry identified resistance to British authority as loyalty to the Crown and a defense of British authority as treason to the colony—a claim destined to be heard from the lips of many a revolutionary patriot within the next ten years.

Several of the most important colonial arguments appeared in pamphlet form. Pamphlets then functioned as a public forum, much as the newspaper and radio do today, and they attracted a wide audience. The flood of pamphlets that poured from the pens of colonial writers expressed substantially the ideas of the Stamp Act Congress and the Virginia Resolves.

One of the most brilliant and influential pamphlets was that of Governor Stephen Hopkins of Rhode Island. Like other American writers, he observed that the British government was founded on compact and that the colonial charters guaranteed "all the rights and privileges of free-born Englishmen." One of those rights was immunity from taxation except by consent of lawfully elected representatives. Those "whose Property may be taken from them by taxes, or otherwise, without their own consent," he said, "are in the miserable condition of slaves."

Hopkins then presented the British Empire as a great federal state in which "each of the colonies hath a legislature within itself, to take care of its Interests . . . yet there are things of a more general nature, quite out of reach of these particular legislatures, which it is necessary should be regulated, ordered and governed." These things, among them commerce, money, and credit, were properly in the keeping of Parliament. This notion of a division of authority was a realistic appraisal of the actual state of affairs within the empire; yet few men of 1765 had the vision to see reality so clearly. Not until John Dickinson popularized the notion of a federal state two years later did the federal idea gain wide acceptance in America.

Other colonial writers rested their case upon the supposed distinction between external and internal taxation which Otis and Hopkins had already attacked as specious but which still had much currency. Daniel Dulany, distinguished Maryland lawyer, legislator, and plantation aristocrat, accepted the distinction but at the same time attacked the theory that the colonies were virtually represented in Parliament as "a mere cobweb, spread to catch the unwary, and intangle the weak." Richard Bland, a leader of the Popular faction in the Virginia House of Burgesses, who also confined his attack to internal taxation, declared: "I cannot comprehend how Men who are excluded from voting at the Election of Members of Parliament can be represented in that Assembly . . ." He conceded that the colonies were subordinate to the authority of Parliament, but "subordinate I mean in Degree, but not absolutely so." He even implied cautiously the possibility of rebellion against injustice.

The points in the argument advanced against the Stamp Act may be summed up somewhat as follows:

Most of the resolutions and pamphlets attempted to return to first principles of government. Nearly all colonial thinkers accepted the idea of a state of nature in which men were naturally free, and they accepted the compact theory of the state as the beginning of free government.

They also assumed the existence of a supreme British constitution, to be found in a variety of documents from Magna Charta to the Bill of Rights. Their own charters they regarded as contractual, embodying the principles of natural law and natural right and granting them all the rights of freeborn Englishmen.

They upheld the doctrine of limited government. While they admitted that Parliament was the supreme legislature of the empire, they insisted that Parliament had no power to violate natural law or natural right, which they identified with the great principles of English liberty, the English constitution, and the colonial charters.

In attacking the power of Parliament to tax the colonies they accepted the American doctrine of deputy representation and repudiated the idea that the colonists were "virtually represented" in Parliament.

A few colonial writers, notably Stephen Hopkins, presented a federal conception of the empire, the power of Parliament being represented as properly confined to matters of broad imperial interest, while local internal affairs were dealt with by the colonies' own governments. Most colonists, however, were as yet confused about the extent of parliamentary authority. In this they could doubtless sympathize with the position of the Massachusetts General Court, which in October 1765 stated that "it by no means appertains to us to presume to adjust the boundaries of the Power of Parliament, but boundaries there undoubtedly are. . . ."

On the whole, it will be seen that these ideas were exceedingly conservative in the literal sense. Unlike the ideas put forward in many revolutionary movements, they made no attack upon the existing body of symbols and ideas commanding loyalty to the state, nor did they attempt to formulate a new body of political philosophy. The colonists merely took the theories laid down by Hooker, Milton, Harrington, Locke, and Vattel, propagated among them by their own clergy and lawyers, and applied them to the current controversy. To Americans the statesmen in London, and not themselves, were the revolutionaries. Westminster, not Boston, New York, or Philadelphia, had launched an attack upon the precedents of a century and a half of colonial growth.

REPEAL OF THE STAMP ACT; THE DECLARATORY ACT

Not all of the colonial reaction to the Stamp Act took the form of high-flown appeals to constitutional theory. There was rioting and street fighting, intimidation of tax collectors, and the beginnings of a merchants' and consumers' boycott directed against English products. London merchants, their trade badly injured, clamored for repeal. All this had its effect upon the government in London. The ministry of the Marquis of Rockingham, which succeeded that of Grenville in 1766, was not averse to discrediting the work of men now out of power, and it therefore determined upon repeal of the law.

Before the act was repealed, however, an extensive debate in both houses of Parliament revealed how greatly the thinking of British statesmen was at odds with that of their American cousins. Almost without exception, the lords and gentlemen of Parliament were unable to understand either the American conception of direct representation or the idea that there were limits to the authority of Parliament over the colonies. Lord Mansfield, for example, held that the British legislature "represents the whole British Empire, and has authority to bind every part and every subject without the least distinction." Lord Lyttleton stated the case for the unlimited authority of Parliament very brilliantly with the remark that "in all states . . . the government must rest somewhere, and that must be fixed, or otherwise there is an end of all government. . . . The only question before your lordships is, whether the American colonies are a part of the dominions or the crown of Great Britain? If not, Parliament has no jurisdiction, if they are, as many statutes have declared them to be, they must be proper subjects of our legislation."

Lord Lyttleton's rejection of federalism as incomprehensible was a good argument in the abstract, for it rested upon the assumption that within the state there must be some one supreme authority, without which there would be chaos. If sovereignty is supreme authority, it is by definition destroyed when divided. Yet Lyttleton's argument lacked realism; for however convincing his logic, the British Empire had in fact become a federal state, and the American colonies had long exercised a considerable degree of sovereign autonomy.

In the debate in Commons, most members were unwilling to accept the American doctrine of deputy representation. George Grenville, author of the Stamp Act, declared for the complete sovereignty of Parliament and added that "taxation is a part of the sovereign power." Another member stated that "enacting laws and laying taxes so intirely go together that if we surrender the one we lose the others." With reference to the claim that taxation and representation were inseparable, a third member said: "I thought that argument had been beat out of the House. There never was a time when that Idea was true."

However, America was not without friends in Parliament. In the Commons the great William Pitt lent the weight of his immense prestige to the American cause. He upheld the supremacy of Parliament, but almost alone among Englishmen he insisted at the same time that "taxation is no part of the governing or legislating power." He followed this assertion with a direct attack upon the whole theory of virtual representation, which he called "the most contemptible idea that ever entered the head of man." In the House of Lords, Lord Camden put forth the same idea with the statement that "taxation and representation are inseparable;—this position is founded on the laws of nature." Camden alluded to the American doctrine of limited government in his categorical claim that "the legislature cannot enact anything against the divine law."

The shrewdest commentary upon the whole conflict was made by Edmund Burke, in after years to become known as the great English champion of American rights. On parliamentary taxation, he pointed out that "some of the Charters declare the Right, others suppose it, none deny it." But he saw "a real Distinction in every Country between the speculative and practical constitution of that country . . . The British empire must be governed on a plan of freedom, for it will be governed by no other." The colonies, he continued, "were mere Corporations, Fishermen and Furriers, they are now commonwealths. Give them an interest in his [the king's] Allegiance, give them some Resemblance to the British Constitution . . . ," and American loyalty would then follow as a matter of course.

Burke was issuing a warning that if dead constitutional theories were allowed to blind Parliament to the fact that the colonies were rapidly becoming great and powerful states, then the empire was headed for disaster. The colonies were not corporations, but great states, whose population, commerce, and industry were thriving and whose economic and social order was now powerful enough to stand alone, even if British politicians were unaware of it. Their requests for freedom from taxation and for internal autonomy were demands, however confused, that this situation be recognized. Should British statesmen persist in their failure to recognize it, the empire's disruption was highly probable.

At the end of a lengthy debate, Parliament repealed the Stamp Act, but it was a surrender of convenience, not of principle; for Parliament accompanied repeal with the emphatic words of the Declaratory Act affirming the absolute supremacy of Parliament over the colonies "in all cases whatsoever."

THE TOWNSHEND ACTS; COLONIAL OPPOSITION

The words of the Declaratory Act were largely ignored in the rejoicing in America upon the repeal of the stamp duties. But Parliament had not abandoned the principle of colonial taxation. In 1767, a new shift in the ministry brought Pitt, now Earl of Chatham, into office as prime minister. As he was too sick to play an active role in the government, actual power fell to young Charles Townshend, Chancellor of the Exchequer. Townshend now prepared to take advantage of a supposed distinction the colonists had raised between external and internal taxation, admitting the legality of the external but denying the legality of the internal. In fact, this notion had almost no standing in America. But Benjamin Franklin, in his famous examination before the House of Commons in 1766, had drawn the distinction, and Townshend might be excused for his assumption that the colonists would not object seriously to duties levied on colonial imports.

The Townshend Revenue Act, which was passed by Parliament in June 1767, accordingly levied a series of duties upon glass, red and white lead, painters' colors, tea, and paper imported into the colonies. While the manner of collection was not different from those older duties incident to the enforcement of the Navigation Laws, the law's preamble specifically stated that it was a revenue measure for "the support of civil government, in such provinces as it shall be found necessary." The law was an undisguised tax measure, not a commercial regulation.

The Americans were alarmed particularly by Townshend's proposal to use the proceeds of the law to create a colonial civil list, from which colonial governors and judges would receive their salaries. This struck directly at the hard-won control which the assemblies had come to exercise over the colonial governors. If the governors were given independent salaries and a civil list independent of assembly control, much of colonial autonomy would be destroyed.

Another statute sponsored by Townshend and passed at this time created a separate five-man board of customs commissioners for the American colonies. The ministry hoped to administer the customs more efficiently by this reform, and oddly, it believed this would help reconcile the Americans to the new tax program. The colonists, however, saw the board merely as another instrument of sharpened British control and unconstitutional taxation. The board, seated at Boston, immediately became a source of additional irritation to the resentful colonists. Still another Townshend statute created new admiralty courts and specifically authorized the hated Writs of Assistance in customs cases.

Colonial opposition to the Townshend measures was intense and took the form of merchant boycotts and mob action as well as pamphleteering. And true to the Anglo-Saxon legalistic tradition, the colonists did not neglect constitutional argument. There now appeared one of the most brilliant interpretations of the colonial position written during the entire Revolutionary controversy, *The Letters of a Pennsylvania Farmer*, by John Dickinson. Appearing serially in several newspapers of America for some weeks beginning in November 1767, the letters almost immediately won the attention and respect of a wide audience.

Dickinson's convincing argument began with an attack upon the supposed distinction between external and internal taxation. No such difference could be admitted; instead he held that Parliament had no authority "to lay upon these colonies any tax whatever." He admitted that Parliament had in the past levied certain charges incident to the regulation of trade. These were in no way taxes, however, for their main purpose was the regulation of commerce, and the duties were purely incidental to that end. To Dickinson, there was a profound difference between the power to regulate commerce and the power to tax. That Parliament properly could regulate the trade of the colonies no one denied; that it could tax the colonies in any guise, Dickinson utterly denied.

This statement clearly implied that two types of governmental powers were exercised within the empire, those properly exercised by Parliament, and those properly exercised by the local or colonial governments. Here was plainly a federal conception of the British Empire. Dickinson went on to describe the empire as it had in fact existed for a century—a great federal state with a practical distribution of authority between local and central governments. The description did not fit the elaborate constitutional theories of the gentlemen in London, but it did fit that "practical constitution" to which Burke had referred.

The *Farmer* played no small part in leading the colonists toward an understanding of the federal principle, shortly to become a cornerstone of the American constitutional system. The Constitution of 1787 was to embody much the same distribution of authority between local and central governments as Dickinson had set forth twenty years earlier.

Dickinson also emphasized heavily the doctrine of the supremacy of the constitution and the requirement that government operate within the limitations there imposed. In one famous passage he inquired rhetorically, "For who are a free people?" and then gave this stirring answer: "Not those over whom government is reasonably and equitably exercised, but those, who live under a government so constitutionally checked and controuled, that proper provision is made against its being otherwise exercised." In summary, Dickinson expounded the two principles which are the essence of the American constitutional system, federalism and limited government.

Very similar to the ideas in the *Farmer* were those incorporated in the *Massachusetts Circular Letter*, an address by the Massachusetts General Court to the assemblies of the other colonies informing them of Massachusetts' attitude toward the Townshend Acts. The *Circular Letter* was adopted in February 1768, after considerable political maneuvering. It was primarily the work of a radical faction in the legislature under the leadership of Sam and John Adams and James Otis. These men had already made the General Court a hotbed of opposition to the Crown in New England, and the Townshend Acts gave them further opportunity to continue their attacks on royal authority. The actual drafting of the *Circular Letter* was done by Sam Adams, whose brilliant mind and vitriolic pen were from that time on to render much service to the extremists in the colonies.

The *Circular Letter* was a classic exposition of the twin doctrines of constitutional supremacy and limited government. Adams began with the observation that "in all Free states the Constitution is fixed; and as the supreme Legislative derives its Power and Authority from the Constitution, it cannot overleap the Bounds of it, without destroying its own foundation." The British constitution was of this sort, and engrafted in it was the "fundamental Law" that what a man has honestly acquired "cannot be taken from him without his consent." The Townshend Acts violated this principle because they were imposed "with the sole and express purpose of raising a Revenue," and because, since the people "are not represented in the British Parliament, his Majestys Commons in Britain, by those Acts, grant their property without their consent."

These were stirring words, adopted as they were by a vote of the General Court, and they provoked a wrathful response from Lord Hillsborough, the Secretary of State for the Colonies. The Secretary instructed Governor Sir Francis Bernard to order the General Court to rescind its action on pain of dissolution. In July, however, the General Court refused to take this step, and Bernard thereupon dissolved it. The whole incident was a victory for the radicals, for the *Circular Letter* was a deliberate move toward concerted colonial resistance to British authority. By it, the breach between Massachusetts and the government in London was definitely widened.

Legislative remonstrance, colonial boycotts, and declining trade soon made the British ministry aware of the ominous nature of the colonial temper. In 1769 Parliament repealed all the obnoxious duties except the tax on tea, with the result that colonial boycotts for the most part collapsed. By 1770 the crisis precipitated by the Townshend Acts was at an end.

THE PERIOD OF QUIESCENCE; EMERGENCE OF THE DOMINION THEORY OF EMPIRE

There now ensued a period of quiescence in the quarrel between Britain and her colonies, lasting from 1770 to 1773. Many moderate men in the colonies had become frightened by the frequent outbursts of mob violence and by the intemperate character of radical leadership. They drew back in alarm from the specter of revolution, especially abhorrent to conservative men of position and property. Moreover, the period 1770–1773 was one of revived commercial prosperity, in which merchants, craftsmen, planters, and farmers were more interested in making money than in pursuing what now seemed to be a dead political quarrel with the mother country. Even the Boston "Massacre" in March 1770 produced little more than a temporary flurry. It was followed by long months of quiet which thoroughly discouraged Sam Adams and other radicals in their efforts to keep alive the controversy with England.

Toward the end of this period of comparative calm a great debate occurred in Massachusetts between Governor Thomas Hutchinson and the legislature on the nature of the British Empire. The controversy was precipitated by Hutchinson, who would have been better off to let sleeping dogs lie. In a message to the General Court in 1773, he tactlessly challenged the whole theory of colonial autonomy. The governor held that the colonies had always admitted the supreme authority of Parliament and it was absurd to suppose that there was any limit to the sovereignty of that body. He knew of no line that could be drawn between the supreme authority of Parliament over America and the complete independence of the colonies. In Hutchinson's thinking it was impossible to imagine two independent legislatures within the same state. The colonial legislatures, he said, were mere corporations, similar to those erected in England, with power to make by-laws for their own convenience, but completely subject to the supreme authority of the government in London.

Such a theory was anathema even to the moderates in the assembly. It gave Sam Adams a fine new opportunity to exercise his pen in behalf of the radical cause. He now had the audacity to deny that Parliament had any authority whatever over the colonies. The original domain of North America, he wrote in the message returned to the governor by the House, was not part of the realm of England but adhered to the Crown alone, as the king's personal property. The king, through his prerogative, had the power to dispose of his domains as he wished. Queen Elizabeth and James I and their successors had exercised this right by granting away portions of the royal domain in a series of charters to various of their subjects. These grants, Adams contended, established a direct relationship between the colonies and the Crown, but they were outside the authority of Parliament, not a party to the contract.

Adams then fired at Hutchinson a categorical denial of any parliamentary authority whatever over the colonies: "Your Excellency tells us, 'you know of no line that can be drawn between the supreme authority of Parliament and the total independence of the colonies.' If there be no such line, the consequence is, either that the colonies are the vassals of the Parliament, or that they are totally independent. As it cannot be supposed to have been the intention of the parties in the compact, that we should be reduced to a state of vassalage, the conclusion is, that it was their sense, that we were thus independent."

This theory was a remarkable forerunner of the idea of dominion status which long afterward was to come into being within the

British Empire. It presented the empire as a confederation of sovereign states, a commonwealth of nations, each with its own independent government united with Britain only through the person of the Crown. The theory denied all parliamentary authority whatever within the various American colonies. The dominion idea was to be realized within the British Empire during the late nineteenth and twentieth centuries, when Canada, South Africa, Australia, and New Zealand achieved almost precisely the autonomous status for which Sam Adams had argued in 1773. Obviously, however, Adams' theory did not present a realistic portrayal of the British Empire of his own time, and his ideas appeared to be little less than seditious and treasonable to conservative Englishmen and loyalist Americans. Nonetheless the dominion conception of the colonies' status became more and more prevalent in American thought on the eve of the final break with England, and it proved ultimately to be the theory of empire incorporated in the Declaration of Independence.

THE CRISIS OF 1774 AND THE RISE OF REVOLUTIONARY GOVERNMENT

In spite of the attitude adopted by the extremists, it is quite possible that the differences between the colonies and the mother country might in time have been adjusted had it not been for the colossal blunder committed by the ministry of Lord North, in May 1773. The venerable East India Company was in serious financial straits. To rescue it from bankruptcy, Parliament granted it a bounty on its tea exports to America, thereby making it possible for the company to sell its tea in the colonies at a price below that offered by any other importer, including smugglers. As the company proposed to establish its own agents in America, the act threatened to destroy the lucrative tea business of colonial merchants. The uproar which followed the passage of the act rivaled even the row over the Stamp Act.

The most famous incident was of course the affair since dignified by the title of the Boston Tea Party. The tea thrown overboard in Boston harbor that gray December afternoon in 1773 was valued by the East India Company at more than £20,000.

In London, the reaction to the Boston Tea Party was one of furious anger. Parliament under the leadership of the North ministry prepared immediately to enact a series of punitive measures to bring the colonists to their senses and break the power of the radical party in Massachusetts.

The Boston Port Act, March 31, 1774, closed the port of Boston until the town should make restitution to the East India Company. The Massachusetts Government Act, May 20, 1774, altered the charter of Massachusetts in an attempt to bring the colony more directly under the control of the English government. The assistants were no longer to be elected by the General Court but appointed by the Crown. The governor was also given the power to appoint, without consent of the council, all judges of inferior courts, and to nominate all judges of superior courts. In the future, also, no town was to call any meeting of its selectmen other than the annual meeting without the consent of the governor.

The Administration of Justice Act, May 20, 1774, provided that in case of alleged felonies committed by Crown officers, magistrates, and so on, in pursuit of their duties in Massachusetts Bay, trial was, upon order of the governor, to be moved to some other colony or to Great Britain. The act was intended to protect officials in the discharge of their duties by guaranteeing them against the wrath of colonial juries. The Quartering Act, June 2, 1774, permitted officials in any colony to quarter royal troops upon the inhabitants of a town when necessary. This law was intended to force the colonists to make adequate provision for housing soldiers wherever they might be needed; yet clearly it violated one of the traditional guarantees of the Petition of Right.

The Quebec Act, passed June 22, 1774, although not intended as a punitive measure, was so regarded in America. The law extended the boundaries of the Province of Quebec to include the area north of the Ohio and west of the Proclamation Line of 1763, and it thus appeared to violate several colonial charters by stripping the colonies of their trans-Allegheny possessions. The law also extended religious liberty to the Catholics of Quebec. While this provision was of no constitutional or social significance to the seaboard colonies, it was nonetheless represented by Sam Adams and other radicals as an attempt to impose the hated Church of Rome upon Protestant America.

Amid the indignation and determination to resist that swept America when the so-called Intolerable Acts became known, the colonists took their first steps toward extralegal or revolutionary government. Perhaps the earliest move of this kind had occurred in Massachusetts, when, in November 1772, Sam Adams brought about the formation by the town of Boston of a "Committee of Correspondence." Similar committees were soon established in most New England towns and in Virginia; and in the agitation against the Intolerable Acts, the committee system spread rapidly through all the continental American colonies.

Although the ostensible purpose of the committees of correspondence was innocent enough—they supposedly served to communicate matters of mutual interest to other towns—the committees from the start assumed duties commonly vested only in sovereign political bodies. Most important was their attempt to give colonial boycott agreements the force of law by means of publicity, intimidation, and resolutions against offenders. In reality the committees were revolutionary bodies, taking the lead in concerted resistance to British authority.

These committees soon gave rise to colony-wide revolutionary governments. Thus in Massachusetts, General Thomas Gage, now governor of the colony, dissolved the regularly constituted General Court in June,[3] and the Boston committee of correspondence thereupon demanded the election of a provincial congress to take charge of the government of Massachusetts until Parliament and the Crown should accept their constitutional functions. The provincial congress met in October 1774, and henceforth the effective government of Massachusetts Bay was no longer in the hands of the governor and the other regularly constituted Crown officers, but in the hands of the provincial congress.

Events took a similar turn in the other colonies. In Virginia, the royal governor, the Earl of Dunmore, dissolved the assembly in May because of its rebellious temper. Thereupon a portion of the House of Burgesses under the leadership of Patrick Henry, Thomas Jefferson, and others, issued a call for an election of members of a provincial congress to meet in Williamsburg on August 1. By the close of 1774, all the royal and proprietary colonies except New York, Pennsylvania, and Georgia had established provincial congresses, and these three colonies took this step the following year. In the two charter colonies of Connecticut and Rhode Island, the legal governments were so nearly autonomous that no such move was necessary. The existing governments simply accepted the patriot cause.

In most of the colonies the governor's dissolution of the regularly constituted legislature or his refusal to call it into session was the immediate occasion for the erection of the provincial congress. In

---

[3] At the last session of the old Massachusetts legislature, held in Salem on June 17, the assembly hastily chose five delegates to the forthcoming Continental Congress at Philadelphia, while the governor's secretary vainly hammered at the locked doors with the message of dissolution.

some cases, a congress was a rump of the regular assembly, composed of delegates in sympathy with the popular cause. This was true in Massachusetts, New Hampshire, Delaware, Virginia, and North Carolina. In New Jersey, Maryland, and South Carolina, delegates to the congresses were chosen through elections held at popular meetings throughout the colonies.

As noted, the provincial congresses were in fact revolutionary state governments. Although the members loudly protested their loyalty to the Crown, they engaged in steady suppression of the remnants of royal authority in the colonies. Thus the Massachusetts Congress, late in 1774, took over the tax machinery and the operation of the courts, and began raising an army for the field. Much the same seizure of power occurred in all the colonies. The American colonies were now in the process of becoming the American states, a metamorphosis completed by 1776, some time before the Declaration of Independence was signed.

THE FIRST CONTINENTAL CONGRESS

While this revolution was going on within the various colonies, the pyramid of revolutionary government was completed by the establishment of an intercolonial congress. In September 1774 the First Continental Congress, called at the suggestion of several of the provincial congresses, met in Philadelphia. All the colonies except Georgia were represented, and some of the most distinguished men in America were present, among them Sam and John Adams of Massachusetts, Stephen Hopkins of Rhode Island, Roger Sherman of Connecticut, John Jay and Philip Livingston of New York, John Dickinson and Joseph Galloway of Pennsylvania, George Washington, Richard Henry Lee, and Patrick Henry of Virginia, and John Rutledge of South Carolina.

Although the delegations varied in size and represented colonies of different territorial extent and population, it was nevertheless shortly decided that the vote would be taken by states, each state present having one vote. Thus the principle of state equality was established, a principle soon to be incorporated in the Articles of Confederation and later to gain limited recognition in the Constitution of the United States.

The temper of the Congress, despite its revolutionary status, was at first somewhat conservative. The delegates were inclined to listen to men of caution in the persons of Dickinson, Jay, Galloway, and Rutledge. These men advocated a constructive solution of the imperial problem rather than a break with England. The more radical and revolutionary views of the two Adamses, Hopkins, Lee, and Henry were thrust temporarily into the background.

For a time the delegates considered a plan of union submitted by Joseph Galloway of Pennsylvania, not unlike Franklin's proposals at the Albany Congress some twenty years before. This plan proposed the establishment of an intercolonial legislature or "grand council" composed of delegates chosen for three years by the respective colonial assemblies. A president-general appointed by the king would preside. The grand council would be "an inferior and distinct branch of the British Legislature," and would have authority over the general affairs of the colonies. Either the British Parliament or the grand council would enact legislation for intercolonial matters, but the assent of both legislatures would be necessary before any statute became valid.

In a calmer day the plan might have been adopted and might have paved the way for dominion status for America, but the trend was against conciliatory measures. After some indecision the plan was tabled by a majority of one vote, and the Congress turned toward more radical proposals.

The first evidence that the extremist faction was obtaining the upper hand came with the introduction of the Suffolk Resolves, a series of resolutions of a popular convention in Suffolk County, Massachusetts. The Resolves asserted that no obedience was due the Intolerable Acts and that no taxes should be paid into the provincial treasury until constitutional government was restored in the colony. Their introduction was in reality a successful stratagem to force the Congress toward a more radical position. Although the Congress took no positive action upon the Resolves, the reaction toward the measures nonetheless indicated the steady growth of radical opinion among the delegates.

The Declaration and Resolves of the First Continental Congress, a series of resolutions adopted by Congress on October 14, showed how far radical sentiment had progressed in the gathering. This document, though conciliatory in tone, virtually reiterated the dominion conception of colonial status which had been advanced by Sam Adams in his argument of 1773 with Governor Hutchinson and which had become extremely popular among the colonial radicals. The Declaration and Resolves held the colonists to be "entitled to a free and exclusive power of legislation in their several provincial legislatures . . . in all cases of taxation and internal polity, subject only to the negative of their sovereign. . . ." The only concession to parliamentary authority was a provision that "from the necessity of the case, and a regard to the mutual interest of both countries, we cheerfully consent to the operation of such acts of the British parliament, as are bona fide restrained to the regulation of our external commerce. . . ." Apparently this slight concession to the power of Parliament over the colonies, admitted as a matter of convenience and not of right, was a necessary gesture by the radicals in Congress to win the support of certain moderate delegates to the resolutions. The Declaration and Resolves came close to a flat assertion of a commonwealth-of-nations theory of the empire.

Other provisions of the resolutions amounted essentially to an assertion of a colonial bill of rights as against even royal authority. The colonists were declared entitled to "life, liberty, and property," and to "all the rights, liberties, and immunities of free and natural-born subjects within the realm of England." They were further declared entitled to the common law of England, to the benefits of such English statutes as had existed at the time of their colonization and which had been found applicable to American circumstances, and to all the privileges and immunities granted by the several royal charters or secured by their own legal systems. The resolutions affirmed further the colonists' right to assemble peaceably, consider their grievances, and petition the king. They denounced as "against law" the maintenance of a standing army in any colony in time of peace without the consent of the legislature of that colony. Finally, they condemned appointment of colonial councils by the Crown as "unconstitutional, dangerous, and destructive to the freedom of American legislation."

Six days after the adoption of the Declaration and Resolves came the formation of the Continental Association, the first positive measure of resistance to British authority taken by the colonies acting in their united capacity. Through this organization Congress laid down an intercolonial non-importation agreement against all British goods, effective December 1, 1774. The slave trade as well was banned as of the same date. The Congress also threatened to invoke non-exportation to Britain, to be effective September 1, 1775, unless the obnoxious acts of Parliament were repealed. The boycott was given sanctions by recommending the formation of local committees "whose business it shall be attentively to observe the conduct of all persons touching this association."

With the creation of the Continental Congress, the pyramid of local, state, and federal revolutionary governments was complete. However, neither the local committees of correspondence, the provincial assemblies, nor the Continental Congress before January 1776 laid claim to any regular sovereign political authority. Nor, at first, was it their overt intention to engage in armed rebellion against England. Actually, however, they not only steadily carried out the seizure of authority from agents of the Crown, but in April 1775 they began an armed rebellion against British troops.

THE COMING OF INDEPENDENCE

When the Second Continental Congress met in May 1775, the battle of Lexington and Concord had been fought, armed clashes had occurred in Virginia, and the major battle of Bunker Hill was in the offing. The Congress responded to the challenge by raising and appointing an army and naming Washington to command it. In July, the Congress issued a Declaration of the Causes and Necessity of Taking Up Arms, a document prepared by Dickinson and Jefferson. It disavowed any intention of seeking independence, but pledged resistance until Parliament abandoned its unconstitutional rule in America. The estrangement between England and America was now complete, though there was a general reluctance in the colonies to admit the fact. The king's Proclamation of Rebellion in August 1775, the Prohibitory Act of December 1775, by which Parliament declared the colonies outside Britain's protection and proclaimed a blockade of all colonial ports, and the steady extension of military engagements, made reconciliation impossible. Throughout 1775 most colonials denounced the idea of independence, but early in 1776 there developed a marked increase in the sentiment for formal separation from the mother country.

In January 1776, Thomas Paine's famous pamphlet *Common Sense* made its appearance and at once attained extraordinary circulation and popularity. *Common Sense* greatly accelerated the growth of colonial sentiment for independence, for it went far to undermine attachment to the English king and loyalty to Britain.

There were two principal ideas in the pamphlet: a slashing attack upon the institution of monarchy, and a plea for immediate separation from the mother country. Government, Paine thought, was but "the badge of lost innocence: the palaces of kings are built on the ruins of the bowers of paradise." Human corruption rendered government necessary, but this also offered a clue to the only proper sphere and function of government: "freedom and security." But how poorly the English monarchical system accorded with this ideal! Paine admitted that the English constitution was "noble for the dark and slavish times in which it was erected," but its component parts were nonetheless "the base remains of two ancient tyrannies, compounded with some new republican materials." The king was a remnant of monarchical tyranny; the Peers were a remnant of aristocratic tyranny. Only in the Commons were there republican elements, and upon their virtue depended the freedom of England. But Paine made it clear that there was far too little republicanism in Britain to protect freedom and security; the survival of monarchy hopelessly corrupted the English political system.

The institution of monarchy, Paine added, was a base insult to intelligent free men. "There is something exceedingly ridiculous," he observed, "in the composition of monarchy; it first excludes a man from the means of information; yet empowers him to act in cases where the highest judgment is required." Nature herself disapproved of the principle of hereditary right; "otherwise she would not so frequently turn it into ridicule by giving mankind an ass for a lion." The first kings had been nothing better than "the principal ruffian of some restless gang," and the English monarch's title was no better: "A French bastard, landing with an armed banditti and establishing himself King of England against the consent of the natives, is in plain terms a very paltry, rascally origin." Paine concluded that "of more worth is one honest man to society, and in the sight of God, than all the crowned ruffians that ever lived."

Paine then attacked sentimental loyalty to Britain as stupid. Britain had founded, nurtured, and protected the colonies from motives of pure selfishness; "she would have defended Turkey from the same motives, viz. for the sake of trade and dominion." England was no loving parent; the colonists had fled to America "not from the tender embraces of a mother, but from the cruelty of the monster; and it is so far true of England that the same tyranny which drove the first emigrants from home, pursues their descendants still."

Further dependence upon Britain, Paine contended, had become ruinous; "the injuries and disadvantages we sustain by that connection are without number. . . ." Submission to Britain "tends directly to involve this continent in European wars and quarrels; and sets us at variance with nations who would otherwise seek our friendship, and against whom we have neither anger nor complaint." Moreover the association was commercially disastrous, since in any European war "the trade of America goes to ruin because of her connection with Britain." Dependence was absurd from a political and governmental point of view: "To be always running three or four thousand miles with a tale or a petition . . . will in a few years be looked upon as folly and childishness—there was a time when it was proper, and there is a proper time for it to cease." In any event, "there is something very absurd in supposing a continent to be perpetually governed by an island." Every possible argument, Paine concluded, pointed to the wisdom of immediate separation. "The blood of the slain, the weeping voice of nature cries, 'tis time to part."

Powerful as it was, Paine's pamphlet did no more than hasten an already inevitable separation. By 1776 the rebellious colonists had carried their movement too far to turn back without abandoning the whole cause and placing their very lives in danger. They had organized *de facto* state and national governments and had shot the king's troops, ousted his officials, and destroyed his trade. Conciliation, as Paine had said, was impossible. Independence was already a fact, and it remained only to make it true in theory and law as well.

In the spring of 1776 events moved swiftly toward the establishment of formal independence. On April 6 the Congress declared all colonial ports open to foreign trade. On May 10 it adopted a resolution calling upon the several colonies to create regular state governments. A preamble to this resolution, adopted on May 15, went even further; it stated that since Great Britain had placed the colonies outside her protection and made war upon them it was now necessary that every kind of authority under the Crown should be totally suppressed and all governmental powers transferred to the people of the several colonies.

On June 7, Richard Henry Lee, acting in accordance with instructions from the state of Virginia, laid the following resolution before Congress:

> *Resolved*, that these United Colonies are, and of right ought to be, free and independent States, and that they are absolved from all allegiance to the British Crown, and that all connection between them and the State of Great Britain is, and ought to be, totally dissolved.

On June 11, Congress referred the foregoing to a committee of five men, Thomas Jefferson, John Adams, Benjamin Franklin, Roger Sherman, and Robert Livingston, who were assigned the task of drafting a "declaration to the effect of the said resolution."

It was still not certain, however, that Congress would adopt a formal declaration of independence. On the first day of July, the delegations of only nine states were positively in favor of this move.

The Maryland delegation had been instructed late in May to oppose any such declaration, while in New York, division of sentiment was so great that the delegates were uninstructed. Members from Pennsylvania were also badly divided on the question. John Dickinson, although loyal to the American cause, opposed a formal break, and not until the last moment was Franklin able to swing the delegation to independence. On July 2, a resolution of independence was finally adopted by a unanimous vote of twelve states; the New York delegation, still being uninstructed, did not vote. After some further debate, the document we know as the Declaration of Independence was unanimously adopted on July 4.

The Declaration of Independence was mainly the work of Thomas Jefferson, although Adams and Franklin suggested certain minor alterations. The document consists of five parts: an introductory paragraph setting forth the intent of the Congress in issuing the Declaration, a brief statement of contemporary American political philosophy, an indictment leveled against the misgovernment of George III, the resolution of independence adopted on July 2, and the signatures.

The opening paragraph in words of solemn magnificence reveals at once the purpose behind the Declaration:

> When in the course of human events, it becomes necessary for one people to dissolve the political bands which have connected them with another, and to assume among the powers of the earth the separate and equal station to which the Laws of Nature and of Nature's God entitle them, a decent respect to the opinions of mankind requires that they should declare the causes which impel them to the separation.

These words reveal the Declaration to have been intended as an appeal to public opinion—an attempt to draw favorable attention to the revolutionary cause—among the French, among America's friends in Britain, and even among waverers in the colonies. Treason is at best an ominous business, and the Congress was determined that Great Britain and not the revolting colonies should stand condemned before the bar of world public opinion.

Jefferson next presented a condensed statement of the natural law–compact philosophy then prevalent in America:

> We hold these truths to be self-evident, that all men are created equal, that they are endowed by their Creator with certain unalienable rights, that among these are life, liberty, and the pursuit of happiness. That to secure these rights, governments are instituted

among men, deriving their just powers from the consent of the governed. That whenever any form of government becomes destructive of these ends, it is the right of the people to alter or to abolish it, and to institute new government. . . . Prudence, indeed, will dictate that governments long established should not be changed for light and transient causes; . . . But when a long train of abuses and usurpations, pursuing invariably the same object, evinces a design to reduce them under absolute despotism, it is their right, it is their duty, to throw off such government, and to provide new guards for their future security.

There are four fundamental political ideas here: the doctrine of natural law and natural rights, the compact theory of the state, the doctrine of popular sovereignty, and the right of revolution. These conceptions were common to nearly all seventeenth- and eighteenth-century natural-law theorists, but Jefferson's phraseology was closely modeled on John Locke's *Second Treatise*. Several of Jefferson's most telling phrases were borrowed directly from Locke's essay. Jefferson had in fact succeeded admirably in condensing Locke's fundamental argument into a few hundred words.

Jefferson's declaration that "all men are created equal" is of special interest, since later these words were to take on a significance quite different from their eighteenth-century meaning. In Andrew Jackson's day, they became one of the cornerstones of equalitarian democracy. Indeed, in our own time the words seem to have a self-evident meaning. However, Jefferson did not intend to lay down any broad premise of extreme democratic equality. Natural-law theory did indeed hold that in a state of nature all men were equal in the possession of certain inalienable rights—"life, liberty, and the pursuit of happiness," as Jefferson put it. Government was instituted to protect those rights and could not impair them. It was in this sense that all men were created equal—equal, that is, before the law. This concept did not imply intellectual, moral, or spiritual equality, although a later generation imbued with the spirit of democracy might read it so.

Jefferson's "life, liberty, and the pursuit of happiness" was a variation from the expression "life, liberty, and property" sanctioned by Locke. Why did Jefferson substitute "the pursuit of happiness" for property? The idea was not entirely new. James Wilson, noted Pennsylvania lawyer and later justice of the United States Supreme Court, had asserted in a pamphlet of 1774 that government was founded "to increase the happiness of the governed" and that "the happiness of society is the first law of every government." The

Virginia Bill of Rights, drafted by George Mason a few weeks before the Congress adopted the Declaration, also anticipated Jefferson. It stated "That all men are by nature equally free and independent, and have certain inherent rights . . . namely, the enjoyment of life and liberty, with the means of acquiring and possessing property, and pursuing and obtaining happiness and safety." One can only conclude that Wilson, Mason, and Jefferson all rejected the emphasis in Locke and the common law upon the protection of property as the fundamental end of government. They believed rather that government existed to protect human rights as well as property rights. Jefferson was among the earliest statesmen of importance in Western culture to draw sharply the difference between the conservative and liberal conceptions of the role of the state in human affairs. He believed that even property rights must in the last analysis yield before the imperatives of the common social welfare.

Ironically, Jefferson made his declaration of natural rights in a society which countenanced slavery. Of the signers of the Declaration of Independence a considerable number were slaveholders. Jefferson was aware of the inconsistency involved in a slaveholders' avowal that freedom was an inalienable human right, and it was in part for this reason that he sought to transfer the responsibility for slavery to Britain. His original draft of the Declaration contained a passage condemning George III for conspiring to perpetuate the slave trade and slavery in America. Upon the insistence of the delegates from South Carolina and Georgia, the Congress struck this paragraph out of the final draft, but the implication of natural rights for the institution of slavery was not lost upon the leaders of the revolutionary cause. The antislavery movement in America dated from Revolutionary days.

The indictment of George III was presented by Jefferson to illustrate "the long train of abuses" which had spurred the colonies to revolt. Most of the alleged offenses had grown out of issues that had arisen since 1763 and which involved disputes over the validity of various acts of Parliament asserting authority over the colonies. Yet the Declaration attacked the misgovernment of George and said virtually nothing of Parliament. This seeming incongruity occurred because Jefferson and the Congress had come generally to accept the dominion theory of colonial status, first broached by Sam Adams in the Great Debate in 1773. This theory, it will be recalled, presented the colonies as united to Britain only through the person of the Crown, and it denied all parliamentary authority over the colonies. The colonists could hardly revolt against a parliamentary sovereignty whose very existence they denied. Hence, for good reason, the Declaration inveighed not against Parliament but against the tyranny of George III, although that mild-mannered monarch was responsible only in a very minor degree for American grievances.

The Declaration of Independence consummated the Revolution. From a constitutional standpoint the Revolution and the Revolutionary War must not be confused. The Revolution was the transfer of power and sovereignty from Great Britain to the states and to the United States, the shift of authority from agencies of the Crown to agencies of the states and of Congress. This process was complete by 1776. The war that followed was fought to confirm it.

Chapter

4

The First State Constitutions and the Articles of Confederation

THE FORMATION of legally constituted state and federal governments was early recognized by patriot leaders as a strategic move in the revolutionary process. The provincial congresses and the Continental Congress were mere *ad hoc* revolutionary bodies, poorly adapted to everyday matters of government. Moreover, the old colonial assemblies, some of which survived even until 1776, became the resort of Tories who worked to impede the Revolution. By establishing governments recognized as the sole legally constituted authorities, the radicals would go far toward winning ascendancy over their opponents.

In all the states and in the Congress as well, the problem was solved by drafting a written constitution erecting a government, providing for its main outlines, and stipulating certain rights reserved to the people. This resort to written constitutions was based upon tradition and colonial custom. The early colonies invariably had some kind of written fundamental law setting up government —either a trading company, proprietary, or royal charter—and this custom of establishing government under a written constitution had continued throughout the colonial period. By 1776 the habit of living under a fundamental supreme law was a century and a half old in America. Moreover, since the days of the Fundamental Orders of Connecticut the colonists had had some experience with the actual creation of written constitutions by formal covenant. It was easy to revive that practice now.

Prevailing political philosophy in 1776 also encouraged the creation of new governments by a formal compact. Locke and other recognized philosophers had held that revolution destroyed all existing political compacts, although not necessarily the social compact itself, and left the people free to enter into a new political compact setting up government once more. Locke did not advocate formal written constitutions, but Vattel, whose *Law of Nations* gained some attention in America on the eve of the Revolution, insisted that the fundamental law ought to be a fixed and written document. The revolutionists were also much concerned with natural rights. They were familiar with English charters, notably Magna Charta and the Bill of Rights, granting certain rights to the people, and upon breaking with Britain they hastened to reaffirm in writing not only the traditionally recognized rights but also certain new ones— the product of the recent quarrel with Britain.

THE FIRST STATE CONSTITUTIONS

The Congress very early encouraged the formation of regularized state governments. In June 1775 it suggested to the Massachusetts provincial congress that it would be wise to erect a new government which would restore to the commonwealth the privileges of the original charter, and in November it made a like recommendation to New Hampshire and South Carolina. Thus inspired, New Hampshire adopted a very brief, temporary constitution in January 1776, and South Carolina did the same in March. In May 1776, Congress ordered the formal suppression of all remnants of royal authority in the states, so that the way was then cleared for the erection of permanent constitutional systems. Between 1776 and 1780, therefore, all the states except two adopted new written constitutions. In Rhode Island and Connecticut the old charters were still regarded as acceptable frames of government, and they continued to serve well into the nineteenth century.

Judged by later-day standards, the process of constitution-making was in most instances an exceedingly irregular one. While revolutionary political philosophy emphasized the distinction between organic supreme law and mere statute law, the distinction between a constitutional convention and a legislature was as yet little understood or appreciated. In New Jersey, Virginia, and South Carolina the revolutionary provincial congresses drafted the permanent constitutions, without seeking any new authority from the people and while engaged in other legislative business. New Hampshire, New York, Pennsylvania, Delaware, Maryland, North Carolina, and Georgia all held special elections for new congresses to draft constitutions, but these conventions also concerned themselves with legislative matters. In none of the states acting in 1776 and 1777 did the conventions submit their work to the people for approval; rather, they merely proclaimed the new constitution in effect.

In Massachusetts, however, the distinction in theory between a legislative body and a constitutional convention called to perform the organic function of drafting the supreme law received dramatic recognition. The provincial congress first drafted a constitution in 1777. When submitted to the people, this document was rejected, in part on the grounds that it was not the product of an organic convention but had been drafted by the legislature. The congress then called for the election of delegates to a separate constitutional convention. This body met in 1779 and drafted a second constitution, which was submitted to the people and accepted by the required two-thirds constitutional majority the following year.

Considerations of theory alone were not always decisive in keeping the other states from following the example of Massachusetts. In many states it would have been dangerous to call conventions or to submit the proposed constitutions to a popular vote. Nowhere were the radicals in a heavy majority; yet the new constitutions were intended to place power in their hands. Had the Tories and moderates been permitted to vote, they might in some states have undone the work of the revolutionaries.

Compared with the constitutions of a later day, those of 1776 are notable for their brevity, most of them being but five to seven pages in length. They provided merely for the skeletal outlines of government, and save for a few simple restrictions the legislatures were left to fill in the details. The people had not yet had instilled in them the deep distrust of the legislature which was to become prevalent during the nineteenth century.

Seven of the state constitutions contained separate bills of rights, while the remainder incorporated certain provisions of this kind. They set forth, often in declamatory style, the now familiar idea of natural rights and the compact theory of the state. Many provisions reflected those in the famous English Bill of Rights of 1689; others were the product of the century-long struggle between colonial legislatures and governors over local self-government. Still others reflected the recent quarrel between the colonies and England; thus Virginia and Massachusetts banned writs of assistance, while several constitutions prohibited the levying of taxes without the consent of the people or their representatives. All the bills of rights incorporated the now traditional guarantees of Magna Charta and the common law concerning procedural rights and fair trials in criminal cases.

The Virginia Bill of Rights, drafted largely by George Mason and adopted in June 1776, has long been recognized as a masterpiece of revolutionary political philosophy. This document set forth the doctrine of natural rights, the compact theory of the state, and the right of revolution in language remarkably like that which Jefferson was shortly to employ in the Declaration of Independence. There followed guarantees of the separation of powers and free elections, and prohibitions against writs of assistance and taxation without the consent of the people or their representatives. Other provisions extended the rights of jury trial, moderate bail, and fair procedure in criminal cases. The document also guaranteed freedom of the press, espoused the principle of a free militia, declaimed against standing armies in peacetime, and ended by enunciating the principle of religious liberty.

All the constitutions except those of Pennsylvania and Georgia provided for a bicameral legislature. The lower house was invariably based upon district representation; the upper house was usually elected separately on the same basis. In South Carolina, however, the upper chamber was elected from and by the lower, while in Maryland a system of indirect election was used.

The bitter rivalry between governors and assemblies in colonial times had instilled in the people a deep distrust of the executive, and the new constitutions reflected this. The governor's term was short—from one to three years—and his authority was closely hedged. Under most of the state constitutions the governor was elected by the assembly and was intended to be its creature, but in New York and Massachusetts and under the rejected New Hampshire constitution of 1779 [1] the governor was elected by popular vote. Most of the states made the governor's veto subordinate to a mere majority of the legislature, although Massachusetts required a two-thirds majority to override. North Carolina provided merely that bills be signed by the speaker before becoming law, thus obviating the veto, while New

---

[1] New Hampshire wrote four constitutions in all during the Revolutionary era: in 1776, 1779, 1781, and 1783. The constitution of 1776 was intended to be temporary; those of 1779 and 1781 were rejected. The constitution of 1783 was adopted the following year.

York vested the veto in a separate Council of Revision composed of the governor and several judges, a body distinct from the Senate. Even the appointive power, by long tradition an executive prerogative, was often drastically impaired by provisions for appointments by the legislature or council. In New York the appointive power was given to the governor's council, in which the governor had but one vote. In New Jersey the appointive power was bestowed upon the legislature.

The ascendancy of legislature over executive was in curious contrast to another provision, concerning the separation of powers. Some of the constitutions specified the distinct existence of the three principal departments of government. Thus the Virginia constitution provided that "The legislative, executive, and judiciary department, shall be separate and distinct, so that neither exercise the powers properly belonging to the other." Provisions of this kind were in part the product of contemporary political thought as exemplified by Montesquieu;[2] in part they were the product of more than a century of colonial practice in which executive and legislature had derived their authority from separate and distinct sources, the Crown and the electorate, and in which the differences between the two branches had been accentuated by recurrent conflict.

Were the early state constitutions democratic instruments of government? By present-day standards the answer is a qualified No, but they were decidedly more democratic than were the charters of colonial times. Most constitutions retained simple property qualifications for the suffrage; all of them set up heavy property requirements for legislators and governors. In Massachusetts, for example, the governor must possess not less than £1,000 in property, and members of the General Court must possess £300 and £100 for the upper and lower houses respectively; in Maryland, deputies must have £500 in property, senators £1,000, and the governor £5,000, including a £1,000 freehold estate. Possession of a simple freehold was the most common suffrage qualification, but the Pennsylvania constitution opened the franchise to all taxpayers and sons of freeholders.

Many of the colonial religious qualifications for suffrage and for office were swept away. Also, all of the constitutions guaranteed religious liberty and equal political rights for all Protestants, while

---

[2] Baron de Montesquieu (1689–1755) was a renowned political philosopher of the French Enlightenment. His *Spirit of the Laws* (1748), in which he argued that liberty could best be secured by a balance and separation of power between different governmental functions, had much influence in America.

several extended this guarantee to all Christians, Protestants and Catholics alike. Several of the constitutions, among them those of New York, New Jersey, Pennsylvania, Virginia, and the Carolinas, expressly provided against compulsory support of any church. In Maryland, the legislature might still appropriate for the support of various churches, but only in New Hampshire, Massachusetts, Connecticut, and Virginia did state churches survive the Revolution.

By and large, these provisions were more liberal than those of the colonial period, and generally they were far more liberal than those of the same day in Europe. Certainly they were moving toward the democratic principles recognized in later state constitutions.

An important constitutional practice was the new institution of judicial review, which, although not embodied in the new constitutions, attained formal recognition in several state cases between 1778 and 1787. Judicial review was fundamentally an outgrowth of colonial and Revolutionary political philosophy. Its basic postulates were the supremacy of the constitution, the limited power of the legislature, and the independence of the judiciary, achieved through the separation of powers. If one grants that the constitution is supreme, that the legislature cannot modify it or act against its provisions, and that the judiciary is an independent branch of the government with the right to interpret the constitution, the groundwork is established for judicial review—for the right of the judiciary to refuse to recognize a legislative enactment which in its opinion violates the constitution. It will be recalled that James Otis, in the Writs of Assistance Case, had held that an act against the supreme constitution was void and that it was the duty of the courts to "pass the law into disuse." Judicial review thus arose out of the revolutionary climate of ideas.

Most state cases involving judicial review which arose before 1787 were somewhat shadowy and uncertain in character. *Holmes v. Walton*, a New Jersey case of 1780, widely cited as a fairly clear instance, involved an appeal to the Supreme Court from a trial under a state law of 1778 for forfeiture of property taken in trade with the enemy. The law in question provided for trial of "small causes" (those involving less than £10) by six-man juries in apparent violation of the guarantee of twelve-man jury trial in the Constitution of 1776. Upon review, the Supreme Court threw out the conviction. The difficulty with the precedent, however, is that the Walton case itself was not a "small cause" and the court apparently reversed the trial court because the latter had violated the law itself as much as because six-man juries violated the constitution. However, the New Jersey assembly, in a strenuous protest, indicated that it considered the court actually to have declared the law void.

In the more famous case of *Trevett v. Weeden* (1786), the Rhode Island Superior Court went to the verge of specifically declaring unconstitutional the state's recently enacted paper-money force act. Technically, however, the judges merely refused to entertain an action for damages under the law on the ground that the act was "internally repugnant," in that it contradicted itself in providing for trials without jury "according to the law of the land." It is quite clear, nonetheless, that they took this position because they thought the law violated the property guarantees of the old charter.

Bayard v. Singleton, a North Carolina case of 1787, is an even clearer instance of judicial review. Here the Supreme Court held unconstitutional a law of 1785 requiring a trial court to dismiss forthwith any action for the recovery of property under an earlier Tory confiscation law, on the ground that the statute in question violated the constitutional guarantee that "every citizen had undoubtedly a right to a decision of his property by trial by jury."

The doctrine of judicial review was by no means universally accepted in the Confederation era. It was in direct conflict with the idea of legislative ascendancy so prevalent at the time. Both in *Trevett v. Weeden* and *Bayard v. Singleton,* the decision of the court provoked strong protest in the assembly, the judges in each instance being called before the bar of the house for examination. In spite of popular opposition, however, the idea of judicial review persisted. Between 1787 and 1803, state courts held void state laws in more than twenty instances, and after 1789 the doctrine of judicial review passed into the new federal judiciary under the Constitution.[3]

THE ARTICLES OF CONFEDERATION

While the various states drafted constitutions, the Congress took steps to establish a regular government for the entire nation. Benjamin Franklin, making the first move in July 1775, introduced into the Congress a plan for a "league of friendship," which would have given the Congress much the same powers as were ultimately delegated to that body under the Articles of Confederation. The

---

[3] See Chapters 7 and 9 for the rise of judicial review under the Constitution.

idea was too advanced, however, for the state of opinion at that time, and Franklin dropped his suggestion.

When, on June 7, 1776, Richard Henry Lee's resolution looking toward the Declaration of Independence was introduced into the Congress, it was accompanied by a resolution that the Congress set up a committee to draft a constitution for the "United Colonies." The suggestion was adopted, and John Dickinson was placed in charge of the committee. After some weeks of labor the committee reported a plan of confederation on July 12.

Some months of intermittent debate followed, during which certain changes were made in the original draft. The principal points of dispute on the floor of Congress were the provision apportioning the expenses of the government among the states according to population and the provision giving Congress power to adjust disputed state boundaries. The conflict between localists and small-state men on the one hand and nationalists and large-state men on the other was already taking shape. The states' rights group won a most important victory when it secured the introduction of a clause guaranteeing to each state "sovereignty, freedom and independence."

The Articles of Confederation were submitted to the states by the Congress in November 1777, and all states except Maryland ratified within the next two years. However, Maryland insisted on a cession of all the states' trans-Allegheny land claims to Congress before she would enter the Confederation. These claims, based upon old royal charters, overlapped in a manner creating serious confusion. Thus Virginia, Pennsylvania, Massachusetts, New York, and Connecticut all had rival claims to the region north of the Ohio. Five states—New Hampshire, Rhode Island, New Jersey, Delaware, and Maryland—had no western land claims, and among these states there was a strong feeling that all western lands were properly the common possession of the nation and ought therefore to be ceded to Congress.

In 1779 Congress adopted a resolution which asked that all states transfer the titles to all trans-Allegheny lands to Congress. New York made the first important concession in February 1780, releasing its entire western land claim to Congress. Maryland, convinced that similar cessions by other states were only a matter of time, now yielded and ratified the Articles in March 1781.

The Articles of Confederation were largely a legalization of the *ad hoc* government which had developed long before 1781 with Congress as its center. The Articles placed the full authority of the

Confederation government in the hands of Congress, while the principle of state equality in that body, first recognized in September 1774, was also retained, each state delegation being allowed but one vote. The powers granted to Congress were those which it had already been exercising, and significantly they were essentially those of Parliament and the Crown under the old empire. Thus Congress was given the authority to make war and peace, to send and receive ambassadors, to enter into treaties and alliances, to coin money, to regulate Indian affairs, and to establish a post office.

Two extremely important powers, taxation and the regulation of commerce, were withheld from Congress. Both of these powers had but recently been involved in the dispute with England, and the new states were apparently reluctant to grant them to any central government. Failure to grant Congress the right to levy taxes obliged the Confederation to rely upon the system of state appropriations that had proved so inefficient in the colonial period. The result was financial chaos. Before many years had passed statesmen would realize that it was impossible to operate even a confederation government effectively unless it had the power to levy taxes and exercise some control over commercial activity.

The Articles made no direct provision for executive authority. Instead Congress was authorized to establish such "committees and civil officers as may be necessary for managing the general affairs of the united states under their direction." Congress might also appoint one of their number to preside over Congress, this "president" to serve for but one term of one year in any three years. In practice, the "president" of Congress proved to be little more than a presiding officer possessing almost no executive authority.

Executive authority rested in a series of committees erected to deal with various problems as they arose. Some of these, notably the Committee on Foreign Affairs, the Marine Committee, the Committee on Finance, and the Board of War, eventually attained the status of permanent departments. The basic weakness of this system lay in the divided character of executive responsibility. Even within a given committee there was at first no one individually responsible for policy, while the multiplicity of the committees created—at one time there were ninety-nine—and the overlapping of the functions of various committees aggravated the confusion.

In 1781, Congress remedied much of this confusion when, after extensive study, it created departments of Foreign Affairs, War, Marine, and Treasury, and placed each under a single permanent secretary. The number of lesser committees was also successively reduced. Had the Confederation government lasted, it is probable that the various departments would have drawn together under the control of a single executive committee or cabinet. Indeed, the Committee of the States, established in 1784, was a step in that direction, although Congress by that time lacked sufficient energy to inaugurate the idea successfully.

This development leads to the speculation that a parliamentary cabinet system was in evolution under the Confederation. The Articles have often been criticized for executive feebleness, yet those who voice this criticism usually accept the doctrine of separation of powers. For the moment the executive was indeed weak; potentially, however, it was at least as efficient as that later provided under the Constitution, and it was more responsive to popular will. Cabinet government, properly correlated with a two-party system in the legislature, has many advantages over the presidential system, not the least of which are freedom from paralysis in crisis and greater responsiveness to popular will.

One of the weakest features of the Articles of Confederation was the lack of a federal judiciary. The central government was given but four types of jurisdiction over causes, all narrow. Congress was given power, through an involved process, to establish *ad hoc* courts to deal with interstate disputes, should any state, a party to such dispute, appeal to Congress. The decision of such a court was to be final, the verdict, by implication at least, having the force of an act of Congress. Congress was given power to settle in a like manner certain cases arising out of private land title controversies involving land grants from two or more different states. In addition, the Articles authorized Congress to establish courts to try cases of piracy and felony committed on the high seas, and to establish courts to determine finally appeals in "cases of captures," or prize cases.

Congress settled some six interstate disputes during the Confederation period, the most important being a case between Connecticut and Pennsylvania over conflicting claims to what is now western Pennsylvania. The judicial power thus granted to settle disputes between the states may be regarded as establishing a precedent for the like power of the Supreme Court of the United States under the Constitution of 1787.

How is the government under the Articles of Confederation to be classified? In some respects, it was like a "league of friendship" or loose confederation among independent states, each with practically undepleted sovereignty. The Articles specifically provided for the "sovereignty, freedom and independence" of the separate states, evidence that the states were regarded in theory as the ultimate repositories of sovereignty. This provision was incorporated by amendment in Congress before submission to the states. It is clear that Congress was aware of its meaning.

Other portions of the Articles seemingly support the idea that they envisioned an association of states each of which would continue to act in most respects as a free and independent nation. The provision for the extradition of fugitives from one state to another is an example. Extradition is ordinarily a feature of international comity between friendly states in the family of nations; it does not exist automatically in international law, but it may be established by treaty.

The Articles also contained a clause by which "full faith and credit shall be given in each of these states to the records, acts and judicial proceedings of the courts and magistrates of every other state"—a form of recognition common among members of the family of nations. A marriage performed in New York, for example, is ordinarily recognized as valid in France, while a contract in Massachusetts for sale of land in that state may be enforced in the British courts in accordance with the provisions of the Massachusetts law.

Finally the Articles provided that the inhabitants of every state were "entitled to all the privileges and immunities of free citizens in the several states." Thus citizens of Virginia, for example, might freely enter and leave the state of New York, might own land, carry on any lawful business which the state of New York permitted its own citizens, have the same recourse to the courts, and expect the same police protection of life and property, and the same guarantees of liberty and human rights as New York extended to her own people. These are again courtesies which sovereign states commonly extend to one another, sometimes voluntarily, sometimes by treaty.

These three provisions, adapted as they were from international comity, were to pass over directly into the Constitution of 1787. As such they live and function at the present time. Obviously, however, the United States in the twentieth century is no mere league of sovereign states, nor is there anything left of the doctrine of complete state sovereignty. The presence of these provisions in the Articles of Confederation, therefore, can hardly be regarded as conclusive evidence that the Confederation was nothing more than a loose-knit league. Rather it must be said that, although the provisions were adopted from international comity, they have since proven their value to a rather close-knit federal state.

There is some evidence also that the Articles of Confederation and acts of Congress were intended to be accorded the status of law within the various states. Article XIII provided that "every state shall abide by the determinations of the united states in congress assembled, on all questions which by this confederation are submitted to them." The Articles were also to be "inviolably observed by every state." This is in a sense anticipatory of Article VI of the Constitution of 1787, which makes the Constitution, treaties, and acts of Congress the supreme law of the land. At this point, however, a difference appears, for the Articles merely charged the states with the preservation of the Articles, while Article VI specifies how the Constitution is to be observed: it is to be enforced in the courts. Therein lies the vital difference: the Articles made no provision for their enforcement as law, while the Constitution does. The very fact that the Articles could not be enforced as law constituted one of their most serious weaknesses.

Alexander Hamilton saw this clearly and must be given credit for the idea that the Articles ought to be enforced as supreme law. In a New York case in 1784, *Rutgers v. Waddington*, involving a conflict between an act of the state legislature confiscating Tory property and the Treaty of Peace, he argued that the treaty as an act of Congress must be recognized by the New York courts. He won his point, but even so the principle was not given general recognition at the time.

The weaknesses of the Articles may appropriately be recapitulated:

Most serious, perhaps, was the failure to delegate an adequate group of powers to the central government. Without the power to tax, the Confederation was forced to depend upon the old levy system, which had failed in colonial and Revolutionary times. Levies upon the states for the most part went unpaid, or were paid only in part, and the government was thus doomed to operate under the handicap of chronic bankruptcy. Failure to delegate to the Confederation the power to regulate interstate commerce led to disastrous "economic wars" among the various states, and made a national commercial policy impossible. It is conceivable that, had the power to tax and the power to regulate commerce been granted to the Confederation government, that government might have succeeded in overcoming its other weaknesses. Failure to grant these two powers doomed the Articles.

Almost as serious was the fact that the government was obliged to depend upon the states as agents for certain necessary functions of the central government. It is an overstatement to say, as has sometimes been said, that the Confederation depended entirely upon the states to perform its functions, whereas under the Constitution the federal government was able to discharge its functions without any intermediary. The Confederation government performed many of its functions without the aid of an agent; for instance, Congress through its committees sold western lands, carried on foreign affairs and relations with the Indians, maintained an army and a navy, and operated a post office.

In two very important respects, however, the states did act as agents of the Confederation government. First, they supplied the Congress with revenue. Second, in so far as the Articles and acts of Congress gave rise to rights, titles, and interests at law, it was necessary to enforce them in the state courts.

The states failed miserably as agents of the national government. They were repeatedly derelict on annual requisitions levied upon them by Congress—to such an extent that they put the Confederation government into chronic bankruptcy. The states were equally irresponsible as agents for the enforcement of Confederation law. They flouted the Treaty of Peace of 1783 with England: their legislatures violated its provisions at will, while their courts generally refused to recognize any rights other than those arising under the laws of their own respective states.

The solution lay in the elimination of the states as agencies of the national government. This would mean that the central government would be given the power to levy taxes directly and collect them through its own officials. Equally important would be the establishment of a system of national courts in which individuals could sue out rights pursuant to national law, and the central government could enforce its interests against private citizens and even against the states.

There was much confusion about this problem during the Confederation period. Most of the suggested remedies involved some plan to coerce the states into proper performance of their duties. Yet if the states were eliminated as agents, such coercion would be unnecessary.

Allied to this problem was the one inherent in all federal systems: the need of a mechanism to determine the proper respective spheres of the states and the national government. The Confederation government had certain powers, while the residue remained with the states; but there was no one to settle conflicts of authority which arose between the two bodies. If a state legislature chose to ignore the Articles and legislate upon Indian affairs, there was no federal agency to gainsay it. Since the national government lacked agencies to enforce its will, the decision of the separate states as to the extent of national authority almost invariably prevailed. This problem was also to be solved by the establishment of a national judiciary.

The lack of a clearly defined executive has already been discussed. The weakness, however, did not lie in the fact that the functions of the executive were exercised by a committee, for if given an opportunity a committee could have developed into the parliamentary-cabinet type of executive. The real difficulty was the lack of executive unity. Instead of many committees, there should have been one to formulate a common policy and control a number of co-ordinated ministries. There is evidence that this development was under way when the Constitutional Convention brought it to an abrupt end.

Finally the extreme difficulty of passing effective legislation through Congress may be mentioned. This was due primarily to the fact that a vote of nine of the thirteen states was required for enactment. Since the principle of state equality prevailed, the votes of any five of the less populous states could block a measure desired by eight of the more important states and a great popular majority of the nation.

Further amendment of the Articles could be obtained only by a unanimous vote of all states. In 1781, for example, the refusal of Rhode Island blocked an amendment to permit the Confederation to collect a five per cent import duty which would have solved, at least in part, the revenue problem.

Yet, when all the weaknesses of the Articles are surveyed, it is clear that in principle they were fundamentally sound. They might have been amended into a highly satisfactory instrument of government. Had the federal government been given the power to tax and to regulate commerce, had federal law been made supreme and enforceable by a federal judiciary, had steps been taken to hasten the unification of the executive branch, and had proportional representation been substituted for state equality in Congress and a workable amendment provision adopted, the Articles might well have served as the basis for a sound and lasting union.

FAILURE OF THE CONFEDERATION GOVERNMENT

Whatever the theoretical deficiencies of the Articles of Confederation, there was no doubt about the failures of the Confedera-

tion government in practice. Most of Congress's difficulties between 1776 and 1787 were connected in some degree with its
financial incompetence, in turn ascribable to its lack of taxing power
and the habitual failure of the states to meet their assessments
promptly. During the Revolutionary War, the army went chronically unpaid, while in 1783 the officers encamped at Newburg,
New York, threatened mutiny in attempt to recover back salaries.
In despair the Continental Congress resorted to the printing presses
to finance itself, issuing, by 1780, some $40,000,000 in paper money,
the entire issue ultimately being virtually repudiated. Also Congress borrowed several millions between 1778 and 1783 from the
French and Dutch governments; during the Confederation period
it was unable even to meet the interest on these loans, and interest
and principal accumulated until the national debt was refunded
under the Constitution. Financial weakness after 1783 also made
it difficult to protect the great trans-Allegheny wilderness region
acquired in the Peace of 1783, for Congress was utterly without the
resources to garrison the West properly in order to protect settlers,
keep out British and Spanish intruders and control the Indian tribes.
As a result, Britain, contrary to the provisions of peace, retained her
forts in the Northwest Territory, both Spain and England intrigued
to separate the West from the new republic, and Indians ravaged
the settlements in Kentucky and Tennessee.

Another important series of difficulties arose out of congressional
impotence in the field of foreign and interstate commerce. It was
almost impossible for Congress to negotiate commercial treaties
with foreign states, in part because they realized that Congress
could not guarantee compliance by the states with any commercial
policy agreed to. When John Adams, American Minister to England, sought a commercial treaty with Britain, Foreign Secretary
Charles James Fox contemptuously suggested that ambassadors
from the thirteen states ought to be present, since Congress had
no authority over the subject. Recognizing that Congress was im-
potent to impose a retaliatory commercial policy, Britain closed
the West Indies to American trade, and discriminated against
Yankee merchantmen in her own ports. Within the Confederation, the various states carried on retaliatory trade wars against one
another, Congress being powerless to interfere. New York, for example, profiting by her port of entry, laid duties upon incoming
commerce destined for New Jersey and Connecticut, while these
states in return taxed interstate commerce with New York.

Further numerous difficulties arose out of the inability of Congress to compel obedience by the states and individuals to acts of Congress and treaties. The weakness of Confederation foreign policy was in part due to this fact. Congress was unable to compel the states to execute the provisions in the treaty of peace with respect to the return of Tory property and the payment of merchant debts, and Britain used this as an excuse to retain control of the Northwest forts. France and Holland also hesitated to negotiate treaties with a nation which could not meet its commitments.

Inability on the part of Congress to prevent the states from intruding upon the sphere of congressional authority also contributed to an extremely bad financial situation within the various states. Theoretically, the monetary power was delegated to Congress; however, the states did not regard this as prohibiting their own issues. Within most of the states, a continuous struggle went on between a paper-money faction, composed of small farmers, debtors, and artisans, and a hard-money faction composed of creditors, merchants, and large planters. Very often the paper-money faction won control, and several states passed acts fixing prices in paper and making it a misdemeanor to refuse paper currency at its face value. Other states passed stay-laws suspending the collection of debts and forbidding courts to grant judgments for debt.

In Massachusetts, the quarrel over money and credit precipitated in 1786 the outbreak known as Shays' Rebellion, a conflict in which armed bands of farmers closed the courts in the interior of the state and even threatened to lay siege to Boston in order to force passage of inflationary legislation. Difficulties of this kind frightened conservatives, accelerated the movement for constitutional reform, and were directly responsible for those clauses in the Constitution of 1787 which prohibit the states from coining money, emitting bills of credit, making anything but gold and silver legal tender in payment of debt, or impairing the obligation of contracts.

However, not all the difficulties of the Confederation era were chargeable to deficiencies in the form of government. The period was one of great agricultural and commercial prostration, and the causes for this condition were only in small part political. The United States was now outside the British mercantile system. The West Indies were closed, while goods could be sold in England only over British tariff walls. The war had nearly destroyed New England's fisheries; the ravages of war and the loss of English bounties on rice and indigo had much to do with the agricultural decay of the South. These conditions were to be greatly improved by the onset of the French Revolution and by the long period of European war beginning in 1792, which created a war market for American agriculture. Recovery from depression was thus ultimately brought about primarily by developments outside the country. Yet to conservatives in the Confederation period the economic difficulties of the day appeared to rise in considerable part out of the weakness of the government, and the economic crisis thus contributed to the impetus for constitutional reform.

THE MOVEMENT FOR CONSTITUTIONAL REFORM

The move for constitutional reform began even before the Articles of Confederation had been ratified. In a letter to James Duane in September 1780, Alexander Hamilton suggested that Congress reassume its revolutionary powers and call a "convention of all the states" to draft plans for a "general confederation." In a pamphlet published about the same time, Tom Paine made the same proposal. The following year, Hamilton, writing under the pseudonym of "The Continentalist," asserted that "we ought without delay to enlarge the powers of Congress." A convention of the New England states at Boston in 1780 proposed that the American states immediately form a "more solid union," and both in 1781 and in 1782 the New York Assembly recommended "a general convention of the states specifically authorized to revise and amend the Confederation."

Such agitation made itself felt upon the floor of Congress. In February 1781, Congress submitted to the states for ratification a proposed amendment to the Articles to permit the Confederation government to levy a five per cent *ad valorem* import duty for independent revenue. A month later, a special committee headed by James Madison recommended that Congress request of the states authority to "employ the force of the United States as well by sea as by land to compel the states to fulfill their federal engagements." In August, a second committee of three, Oliver Ellsworth, James Varnum, and Edmund Randolph, reported twenty-one deficiencies in the Articles and recommended a general enlargement of the powers of Congress to include taxation, the admission of new states, the embargoing of commerce, control of suffrage, and the right to distrain the property of states delinquent in their financial obligations to the central government.

For the time being these fine words came to nothing. Twelve states responded favorably to the request for authority to levy an import duty, but Rhode Island, obsessed with the importance of her own commercial system, refused. The recommendations of

Madison's committee and those of the committee of three were too strong for Congress, which took no action on either report. Congress in 1783 again asked the states for permission to levy an import duty; again Rhode Island refused and several other states failed to take action. The idea was several times alluded to within the next few years, but nothing ever came of it.

By 1786, many, especially nationalists, thought the United States was a political failure. The Confederation treasury was empty. A weak and helpless government was unable to defend its sovereignty against Britain, Spain, or the western Indians; Congressional foreign policy seemed equally ineffective. Alarmed conservatives believed the sharp social struggles within the states presaged civil war. There was talk of forming three new confederacies, one for each section— New England, the Middle States, and the South.

In a final surge of energy, Congress again turned its attention to the reform of the Articles. Charles Pinckney of South Carolina led the way in forcing the issue of a constitutional convention upon the floor. But Congress refused to call a convention, the self-love of the chamber being apparently too great to deliver into other hands the task of reform.

Failing in this step, Pinckney finally obtained the appointment of a "grand committee" to "report such amendments to the Confederation as it may be necessary to recommend to the several states." When the committee reported, it recommended only that Congress be given power to regulate foreign and domestic commerce and collect duties on imports. The requisition system was to be retained, but Congress might specify when the appropriations were to be paid by the states. A defaulting state would be charged ten per cent interest, and if, after an interval, the levy remained unpaid, a federal tax might be collected directly from the township and county governments. Congress took no action on this scheme, which was cumbersome beyond belief and devoid of ingenuity. It was apparent that the vitality and prestige of Congress had sunk too low for positive action.

Before this impasse in Congress had been reached, however, the series of events which finally resulted in a constitutional convention in Philadelphia were under way. In 1785, Virginia and Maryland signed an agreement settling a long-standing dispute over commercial regulation of the Potomac. The idea of interstate agreement proved so attractive to the Maryland legislature that it now proposed to Virginia a general commercial convention to include Delaware and Pennsylvania. Virginia suggested that the invitation be extended to all the states and that the convention consider a common interstate commercial policy.

The convention met in Annapolis, Maryland, in September 1786. In one sense the meeting was a failure, for delegates from but five states were in attendance, those from New England, the Carolinas, and Georgia failing to appear. Yet Hamilton and Madison, the moving spirits of the gathering, used the occasion to issue a call for a new convention. At their instance, the Annapolis convention unanimously adopted an address to the states to send delegates to a constitutional convention to meet in Philadelphia the following May.

Congress was too jealous of its prerogative to give this call the formal sanction of the central government, but the Virginia assembly saved the day with a stirring resolution adopted in November 1786, calling upon the other states to send delegates to Philadelphia. Pennsylvania and New Jersey responded within a few days, North Carolina followed in January, and Delaware in February. In February, Congress perceived the inevitable and saved face with a recommendation for a convention to meet at the same time and place, although the resolution said nothing of the Annapolis convention or its recommendation. Within a short time the other states, with the exception of Rhode Island, also nominated delegates.

Thus by 1787 the country's leading statesmen had come to recognize fatal deficiencies in the Articles of Confederation, and the movement for reform had finally resulted in a constitutional convention whose efforts were to be crowned with spectacular success. Yet the failure of the Confederation government should not obscure the substantial contributions made by the Articles to the Constitution drafted in 1787. The Articles and the Constitution contained essentially the same conception of a federal state, inherited from the old British empire. Each adopted the same system of interstate comity taken over from the society of nations. The Constitutional Convention was to adopt sweeping reforms of a profoundly important character, but nevertheless it built upon the constitutional foundations erected in the Confederation era.

Chapter

5

The Constitutional Convention

THE CONSTITUTIONAL CONVENTION marked in a sense both the culmination and the close of the Revolutionary period. The crisis of 1765–1775 had been precipitated by the failures of the old British imperial system. When Britain had attempted greater centralization, the colonies had resisted, and had finally broken up the empire. The states had in turn established a central government of their own, but they had consented only to the erection of an extremely weak confederation in place of the vacated British position of control. Yet the Confederation's weakness had produced chaos and had finally convinced thoughtful men that a much more centralized federal system was essential to the nation's stability and welfare. By 1787 most statesmen were ready to accept what some twenty years before they had so bitterly resisted at the hands of Britain—a central government having the power to tax and to regulate commerce. However, in place of the unity Britain would have imposed from London, there now appeared a self-imposed unity, controlled by a central government in America.

THE CONVENTION'S PERSONNEL AND ORGANIZATION

Although the Convention had been scheduled to convene on the second Monday in May, only a few delegates were actually on hand at the appointed time. Those present simply adjourned from day to day for want of a quorum. It was not until May 25 that delegates from seven states were present and the Convention was able to proceed. Not until the end of June were eleven states represented, and individual delegates continued to straggle into the Convention during the next two months. Rhode Island sent no delegation to the Convention, and the New Hampshire deputies did not put in an appearance until late July. Meanwhile two of the New York delegates had withdrawn, and the remaining man from New York, Alexander Hamilton, was not allowed to cast the vote of his state. Hence no more than eleven states were ever represented at one time for voting purposes.

Of the seventy-four men named by the various state legislatures as delegates, only fifty-five appeared at the Convention. The real work was done by not more than a dozen men. But this small group included several of the most eminent figures in America.

George Washington, a delegate from Virginia, was present at very great personal sacrifice. He had been reluctant to attend, for his health was bad, his finances were in poor shape, and his estates were in need of immediate attention. Only when Madison and others made it plain to him that his immense prestige would go far to assure the Convention's success did he consent to come to Philadelphia. Elected the Convention's presiding officer, he proved to be an invaluable asset. Though he took little direct part in the proceedings, his presence did much to keep the Convention at its task when the heat of argument might otherwise have ruptured proceedings beyond repair.

James Madison without doubt supplied the greatest measure of intellect and leadership in the Convention. Unprepossessing in appearance and a somewhat mediocre speaker, he was nonetheless a brilliant scholar and public servant. The Virginia Plan, which the Convention took as the starting point in its labors, was probably mainly his work, and from start to finish he played a leading role in the struggle for a strong nationalist government. Also, historians are indebted to Madison for his careful notes on the Convention's proceedings. Published more than fifty years later, they constitute the most important source of what happened on the floor, and they are far more valuable than the Convention's official journal, comprising nothing more than the bare bones of motions and votes, often inaccurately recorded. Altogether, Madison deserved the title later bestowed upon him—"the father of the Constitution."

James Wilson, a member of the Pennsylvania delegation, was the outstanding legal theorist of America in the latter eighteenth century. A Scot by birth, Wilson had emigrated to America about the time of the Stamp Act. After studying law under John Dickinson, he had first won wide attention in 1774 with his *Considerations on the Nature and Extent of the Authority of the British Parliament*, in which he was among the first to conclude that Parliament had no legal authority whatever over the colonies. In the Convention, he emerged as one of the four or five firm believers in a completely national government founded upon a popular electoral base, and he also fathered the electoral college idea when he saw that election of the executive by a direct popular vote could not win the support of the Convention. In after years he was a lecturer in law at the University of Pennsylvania, and in 1789 Washington appointed him an associate justice of the Supreme Court.

Gouverneur Morris, also a Pennsylvania delegate, was another important leader in the fight for strong national government. A product of the landed aristocracy of New York, his political philosophy was characterized by an outspoken contempt for democracy. His suave air and too smooth mannerisms won him the distrust of many Convention members, but his marked ability as a statesman and public speaker nonetheless gave him great influence. The task of putting the Constitution into its final literary form was probably entrusted to him.

The outstanding member of the New York delegation was Alexander Hamilton. A West Indian by birth, Hamilton had married into the aristocratic Schuyler family of New York and had already acquired reputation as an officer on Washington's staff, a lawyer, and an ardent advocate of strong national government. Yet Hamilton was not able to exercise an influence in the Convention proportionate to his national stature. The explanation lay in part in the opposition of the other two members of the New York delegation, John Lansing and Robert Yates, who consistently outvoted Hamilton to place New York with the states supporting weak government. In part, also, Hamilton's outspoken affection for the institutions of constitutional monarchy and the British government, and his known belief that effective government required complete centralization, placed him out of line with the general sympathies of the Convention. When Lansing and Yates left the Convention, Hamilton was left without the right to vote, and since it was then apparent that he could not influence the course of affairs appreciably, he left the Convention and thereafter seldom put in an appearance.

Connecticut furnished three men of first importance to the Convention. Oliver Ellsworth already had a great reputation as a lawyer; he had also served in Congress and was now chief justice of the highest court in his state. He was brilliant in debate, a master parliamentarian, and a stubborn fighter in any cause in which his convictions were thoroughly aroused. Later he was to sit in the United States Senate, where he acquired a reputation for legislative skill so tremendous that the tradition of it lingered on in the upper chamber for more than a century. In 1796 he became Chief Justice of the United States Supreme Court. Among his later accomplishments was authorship of the Judiciary Act of 1789, a great landmark in the development of the American constitutional system.

William Samuel Johnson—Dr. Johnson, as he was known to his contemporaries because of his Oxford degree of Doctor of Laws— had one of the most respected legal minds of America. He had been a judge of the Superior Court of Connecticut and a member of the Continental Congress. His gentle manner and able intellect gave him an important position in the Convention. An advocate of moderate national government, he did his most valuable work in the compromise of disputes. He was one of the men who kept the Convention at its task when differences threatened to tear it asunder.

The third Connecticut delegate, Roger Sherman, was an example of the American ideal—a self-made man. He had risen from shoemaker to lawyer, judge, and public leader. Long a member of the Continental Congress, he holds the unique distinction of having signed the Articles of Association of 1774, the Declaration of Independence, the Articles of Confederation, and the Constitution of 1787. He favored strong central government, but his principal efforts in the Convention were directed to the end that state autonomy should not be completely destroyed.

In Rufus King, Massachusetts contributed one of the more important figures of the Convention. Most of his distinguished career lay in the future, but at Philadelphia he revealed himself as a strong nationalist, a lucid thinker, and an eloquent speaker. Later Senator from New York and minister to England under John Adams, he was the Federalist candidate for the presidency in 1816. In his old age he found himself again in the Senate, where he played an important part in the Missouri Compromise debates.

Elbridge Gerry, also of Massachusetts, played a prominent but curiously inconsistent role in the Convention. A former satellite of Sam Adams, he had become a member of the Continental Congress in 1776, and he continued to sit in that body throughout the Confederation period. In the Convention he often voiced fears of popular government; yet he more than once professed adherence to "republican principles" and refused to sign the finished Constitution on the grounds that it was "monarchical" in character. In later years, Gerry became a noted Jeffersonian politician, serving as a member of Adams' XYZ mission to France in 1797, governor of Massachusetts, and Vice-President under Madison. The term *gerrymander* remains today as testimony to the manipulative skill in Massachusetts politics attributed to him by his contemporaries.

John Rutledge, head of the South Carolina delegation, was a polished lawyer-statesman of the kind his state made famous in later years. A former leader of the revolutionary party in South Carolina, he helped draft the state's constitution of 1776 and served as governor of the beleaguered state in the late years of the war. In the Convention, he supported effective national government, but spent his principal energies in defense of Southern sectional interests by proposals that wealth be made the basis of representation and that no restrictions be placed upon the slave trade. Washington appointed him an associate justice of the Supreme Court in 1789, and named him to be Chief Justice in 1794, the latter nomination being defeated by the Senate because of his opposition to the Jay Treaty.

Charles Cotesworth Pinckney, usually designated "C. C." or "General" Pinckney to distinguish him from his younger cousin, was also a South Carolina planter and lawyer-statesman. He had won his military title as a brigadier general in the Revolutionary War; later he became a leading Federalist and was the party's candidate for the vice-presidency in 1800 and for the presidency in 1804 and 1808. In the Convention, he also championed Southern interests, insisting that slaves be counted in the basis of representation and that no limitations be placed upon imports.

The outstanding champion of state sovereignty in the Convention was Luther Martin of Maryland, who as attorney general of his state had achieved a reputation as one of the most eminent lawyers in America. In the Convention he battled with all his strength against the nationalistic tendencies of the majority. Unfortunately for his cause, he was a rambling, diffuse, and interminable speaker, who on occasion held the floor for hours to the mortification and boredom of everyone present. Though his role in the proceedings was largely negative, he deserves credit for moving that the section in the New Jersey Plan making the constitution the supreme law of the respective states be incorporated in the Convention's draft. In spite of his early opposition to any powerful central government, Martin after 1789 became a strong Federalist. Eventually, he ruined his career by drunkenness, although he was to achieve brilliant heights in the defense of Justice Chase and in the trial of Aaron Burr.

Another distinguished member of the small-state bloc [1] was William Paterson, author of the so-called New Jersey Plan. Paterson already had a distinguished legal career behind him, having served successively as a member of New Jersey's revolutionary provincial congress, the state's constitutional convention, the New Jersey legislative council and the Continental Congress. Later he was to serve with distinction as a United States Senator from New Jersey and as an associate justice of the Supreme Court. While a defender of small-state interests, he was moderate of speech and thought and readily accepted the Constitution as a satisfactory compromise.

Other delegates deserve some mention. Benjamin Franklin, renowned the world over as a statesman and scientist, was a member of the Pennsylvania delegation. Franklin's contribution to the Convention was spiritual rather than technical—as an influence for harmony and compromise he was second in importance only to Washington. Franklin was now eighty-two years of age, and while he was by no means in his dotage, he was not his old brilliant self. His speeches were rambling and somewhat off the point, and seldom contained much of immediate practical value. Robert Morris, the financier of the Revolution, was another Pennsylvania delegate. Although he never once took the floor, he probably exercised considerable influence within the eight-man Pennsylvania delegation. Edmund Randolph of Virginia was the nominal author of the Virginia plan. While he was a man of moderate learning and capacity, his fine manners and ingratiating air made him an excellent asset to the Convention's nationalists. George Mason, also of Virginia, was an outstanding liberal of late eighteenth-century America. A friend of Jefferson and author of the Virginia Declaration of Rights of 1776, he was far ahead of his time in his democratic social philosophy. He refused to sign the finished Constitution, which he regarded as too aristocratic. Charles Pinckney, twenty-nine-year-old cousin of C. C. Pinckney, was the author of the so-called Pinckney Plan, now known to have had little influence on the Convention's proceedings. He spoke often and at length, but his ideas were erratic and probably carried little weight with the other delegates.

Abraham Baldwin of Georgia, a native of Connecticut, formerly a professor of divinity at Yale and later the founder of the University of Georgia, was respected both for his good sense and for his moderate temperament. He probably had some influence in

---

[1] For a discussion of the controversy between the large and the small states see p. 117.

bringing about the great compromise on the composition of the legislature. John Langdon, a merchant who had sacrificed his personal fortune in the Revolutionary cause, threw the influence of New Hampshire on the side of moderate nationalism. John Dickinson, delegate from Delaware, hardly exercised an influence proportionate to his ability and former reputation. In the Convention he was chiefly concerned for the rights of the small states, although he accepted the necessity for a more effective central government. Nathaniel Gorham of Massachusetts, silversmith, businessman, and member of the Confederation Congress, was a quiet man who lent some weight to the cause of strong national government.

These men constituted as distinguished and brilliant a body of statesmen as America could have brought together, nearly all of America's great men of the day being present.[2] Most of the delegates had long experience in public office, and many were to rise to further eminence in the service of the government they were creating. While most were lawyers and statesmen, the mercantile and landed classes were also well represented. There were a few weaklings among them; yet it is difficult to imagine the young nation calling an abler group to serve in the great task that confronted the Convention.

It may clarify matters to explain the organization and procedure of the Convention. Much of the work was done in committee, so that most of the debate on the floor of the Convention was devoted to a discussion of committee reports. The delegates devoted the first two days after May 25 to the details of organization. They elected Washington presiding officer, chose William Jackson as secretary, and appointed a Committee on Rules. This committee recommended that voting be by states, and that a majority of the states present decide any question. Each state decided its own vote by polling its delegation; occasionally this resulted in a divided vote which eliminated the state from the count on the point at issue.

On May 27, Edmund Randolph presented the Virginia Plan to the Convention. This was referred to the Committee of the Whole in order to permit informal discussion of its provisions. The Committee of the Whole sat from May 31 to June 19, during which time it debated the Virginia Plan point by point, voting to accept, re-

---

[2] Thomas Jefferson was then serving as minister to France; John Adams as minister to Great Britain. Patrick Henry had been chosen a delegate from Virginia but had declined to serve. Sam Adams, who opposed strong national government, was not named a delegate.

ject, or modify each item in the resolutions. From June 19 to July 26, the full Convention debated the report of the Committee of the Whole. The deadlock over the composition of the legislature resulted early in July in the appointment of a Compromise Committee of one delegate from each state, which reported the details of the so-called Connecticut Compromise.

On July 26, the Convention handed some twenty-three resolutions upon which it had been able to reach an agreement to a five-man Committee on Detail. This committee on August 6 reported a draft constitution of twenty-three articles, embodying the substance of the resolutions hitherto agreed upon by the Convention. The full Convention then debated this draft for several weeks. Early in September, certain unsettled matters were referred to a committee of eleven on unfinished business. This committee recommended the method finally adopted for choosing the President. The final draft of the Constitution was the work of the Committee of Style, appointed on September 8.

THE VIRGINIA PLAN

The Virginia Plan served as the original point of departure for the subsequent work of the Convention. It provided for a legislative body of two chambers, the lower house to be elected by the people of the respective states, and the upper house to be chosen by the lower house from nominations submitted by the state legislatures. The powers of Congress were to be those enjoyed under the Articles of Confederation, with the important addition of the right "to legislate in all cases in which the separate States are incompetent." The executive was to be chosen by the legislature for an unspecified term and was to be ineligible for re-election. The executive, together with a portion of the national judiciary, was to constitute a Council of Revision, with an absolute veto over acts of the legislature. A national judiciary was to be established, consisting of one or more supreme courts, and such inferior tribunals as the legislature might determine upon. Federal judicial authority was to extend to all cases involving piracies and felonies on the high seas, captures from an enemy, foreigners or citizens of different states, collection of the national revenue, impeachment of national officers, and questions involving national peace and harmony.

The Virginia Plan contained an exceedingly nationalistic solution for the problem created under the Articles of Confederation by the absence of any mechanism for defining the respective spheres of the central government and the states. What was needed was some arrangement by which the central and state governments would each exercise effective jurisdiction unhampered within their respective spheres without intruding upon the functions entrusted to the other, and which would settle any disputes which might arise as to the extent of state or national power.

The Virginia Plan attempted to solve this problem by several devices. It gave Congress a right to disallow state legislation. Congress was empowered to "negative all laws passed by the several States, contravening in the opinion of the National Legislature the articles of Union." This was a power similar to that which had been exercised by the Board of Trade over the various colonial legislatures before the Revolution. The Virginia Plan also gave Congress a broad and indefinite grant of legislative authority in all cases where the states were "incompetent." It is not clear from the phraseology whether the plan intended to give Congress the power to alter at will the extent of its authority and that of the states; at the very least, however, *the plan proposed to solve the problem of federalism by giving Congress the power to define the extent of its own authority and that of the states.* There was to be but one check upon this power: the Council of Revision was authorized to examine "every act of a particular legislature before a negative thereon shall be final."

The disallowance provision was rendered the more impressive by the succeeding clause, which empowered Congress to coerce a state—by force if necessary. Congress was authorized "to call forth the force of the Union against any member of the Union failing to fulfill its duty under the articles thereof." This proposal may be considered from two quite different viewpoints. The fact that it followed immediately the proposal to allow Congress to define the extent of its own authority gives rise to the assumption that the plan intended that the national government be given the authority to support, with force if necessary, its own interpretation of the compact between the states and the national government. On the other hand, it will be recalled that under the Confederation the states had been derelict as agents of the central government in the execution of its will. On the assumption that the states were to continue as such agents, coercion might be regarded as a device for enabling the national government to exact a more conscientious performance from the states.

Yet in this sense, coercion would be unnecessary under the Virginia Plan. *The new government was to be truly national in character, in that it would operate directly upon individuals, rather than upon the states, and would possess its own agents—courts, attorneys, marshals, revenue officers, and the like—to carry out its functions and impose its will.* It was for this reason that the nationalists in the Convention, who had originally considered coercion essential to any effective government, eventually abandoned the idea as irrelevant and unnecessary for the truly national government they were creating.

With the Virginia Plan before it, the Convention went into a committee of the whole house. Immediately thereafter, the nationalists scored an important victory when, at the suggestion of Gouverneur Morris, Randolph moved the postponement of the first point in his plan in order to present a new resolution. This asserted that no "Union of the States merely federal" nor any "treaty or treaties among the whole or part of the States" would be sufficient. It concluded:

> That a *national* government ought to be established consisting of a *supreme* Legislative, Executive and Judiciary.

The meaning of this resolution was clear. It went beyond any proposal to establish a federal state with limited powers in the central government. In the discussion that followed, Morris contended "that in all Communities there must be one supreme power, and one only," and proposed that this supreme power be lodged unequivocally in the national government. Several delegates objected to the proposal as meaning that state sovereignty was to be obliterated and replaced by a powerful national government. The resolution was nevertheless adopted, only Connecticut voting in the negative.

This was an astounding victory for nationalism in a Convention which had been commissioned merely to modify the Articles of Confederation. It put to rout at the very beginning proponents of state sovereignty and those who wished merely to patch up the Articles. Later the localists were to rally sufficiently to secure the formation of a government based upon the principles of divided sovereignty, but for the moment it appeared that the proponents of national sovereignty were in complete control and that any suggestions for preserving state autonomy would be swept aside.

The Convention had thus committed itself to a serious breach of its authority. Called to amend the Articles, a majority of the delegates had boldly decided to disregard their instructions and instead to create an entirely new frame of government. Only the tremendous prestige of many of the delegates and the common recognition of national danger could secure acceptance of their work.

THE PROBLEM OF THE LEGISLATURE

With this crucial decision disposed of, the Committee of the Whole now took up the provisions of the Randolph plan point by point. Most of the early discussion was centered on the composition of the legislature. On this issue a major cleavage between the large and small states arose. One faction, the large-state bloc, comprised the delegations of Massachusetts, Pennsylvania, and Virginia, with support on most occasions from North Carolina, South Carolina, Georgia, and Connecticut. The small-state bloc was composed of the delegates of New Jersey, Delaware, Maryland, and New York, and, on certain issues, of Connecticut and Georgia. New Hampshire's delegates were not yet present. Although on most occasions the large states were at first able to control the vote of the Convention, the small states were able eventually to force a compromise by implying that they would withdraw from the Convention unless their views were heard.

The composition of the legislature involved two main issues: the method of electing the membership of the two chambers, and the method of apportioning representatives among the states. The nationalistic large-state party desired direct popular election for both houses, a method implying that the central government rested directly upon individuals rather than upon the states and was truly sovereign in character. The large-state faction also wanted representation in both houses apportioned according to population, a nationalistic scheme which would give them a superior position in the legislature. On the other hand, the small-state group, intent on preserving states' rights, wanted state representation and state control of the national government, and therefore it favored retaining the Confederation plan of having the state legislatures elect delegates to Congress. The small-state faction also desired the retention of state equality, which not only would bolster the influence of the small states in national affairs but would also imply state sovereignty rather than national ascendancy.

On the mode of election both sides showed a disposition to compromise. The small states offered no serious opposition to the Virginia Plan's proposal for direct popular election of the lower house, the resolution to this effect being approved on May 31, 6 to 2. However, almost no one approved of the proposal that the lower house elect members of the upper, and that resolution was voted down, 7 to 3, when it was first considered.

After some delay, Dickinson moved on June 7 that the Senate

be elected by the various state legislatures. In the debate that followed, Madison and Wilson contended that authority in a truly national government ought to flow directly from the people, while Sherman, speaking for the small-state faction, argued that representation of the states as such would maintain balance and harmony between the states and the national government. It was clear that the small states were prepared to insist upon representation of the states as such in at least one chamber, and at the end of the discussion, the Convention adopted Dickinson's resolution unanimously.

Meanwhile, the Convention attacked the more vital issue of whether representation in the two houses should be apportioned according to population or based upon state equality. Debate continued for some days, and at times became very heated. Madison and Wilson repeatedly insisted that in a proportionate system, the people as such, rather than states, would be represented, and that on this basis the people of Delaware would have the same representation in Congress as would those of Pennsylvania or Virginia. They were nonetheless unable to quiet the apprehensions of the small-state faction that proportional representation would swallow up the existence of the small states, and Paterson proclaimed that his state would "rather submit to a monarch, to a despot, than to such a fate." Wilson impatiently struck back with the warning that "if New Jersey will not part with her Sovereignty, it is in vain to talk of government."

Many moderates in the small-state faction were in reality prepared to compromise on the issue of proportionate versus equal representation, and to concede proportionate representation in the lower house, insisting only upon state equality in the Senate. Sherman suggested this solution on June 11, at the opening of an important debate on the question.

However, the nationalists were at the moment in control of affairs, and they carried the day without compromise. Sherman's proposal was silently rejected, and immediately thereafter Rufus King moved that suffrage in the lower house ought to be "according to some equitable ratio of representation." [3] After some debate, the resolution was carried, 7 to 3, only New York, New Jersey, and Delaware opposing, with Maryland divided. Sherman thereupon moved that each state have one vote in the upper house. "Everything," he said, "depended upon this," since "the smaller states would

---

[3] This formula implied possible representation of land and slaves, as well as free population.

never agree to the plan on any other principle than an equality of suffrage in this branch." In spite of this warning, the Convention rejected his motion, 6 to 5; and then adopted by the same vote a resolution of Wilson and Hamilton that representation in the upper house be apportioned "according to the same rule as in the 1st branch."

Thus as the Committee of the Whole neared completion of its work, the nationalists had scored victories on three out of four points. They had won proportionate representation in both chambers and popular election in the lower house, and had conceded only that state legislatures might still elect the Senate. Whether the nationalists could retain their gains, however, remained to be seen.

THE NEW JERSEY PLAN

On June 15, the Committee of the Whole finished its discussion of the Virginia Plan and prepared to report the revised draft out upon the floor of the Convention; but at this point the small-state party counterattacked powerfully. Their ranks had been augmented by the arrival of additional delegates from the small states, among them Luther Martin of Maryland, Gunning Bedford of Delaware, and John Lansing of New York, and they evidently felt that if the drift toward complete centralization was to be checked at all, it must be done then and there. Accordingly, Paterson of New Jersey now asked permission to introduce an alternate plan, of which the small states approved and which was "purely federal" in principle as opposed to the nationalistic Randolph Plan.

The New Jersey Plan proved to be merely a modification of the Articles of Confederation. It would have expanded the powers of Congress by adding the right to tax and the right to regulate commerce. It retained state equality in the legislature and erected an executive directly subject to state control. It would also have granted the federal government the right to coerce recalcitrant states, strong evidence that coercion was now regarded as more consistent with state sovereignty than the Congressional veto, of which the plan said nothing.

The most significant clause in the New Jersey Plan was one which would have made all treaties and all acts of Congress under the Confederation the supreme law of the respective states, enforceable in the state courts. This was in reality the key to solution of the problem of federalism, but at the time it escaped notice, for momentarily the Convention was altogether preoccupied with the legislature.

After acrimonious discussion in the Committee of the Whole, in which the deficiencies of the Articles were again treated at length, the New Jersey Plan was voted down, 7 to 3. Again the nationalists had triumphed. Yet the small states were now determined to force a compromise between nationalism and state sovereignty, and because of the certainty that no plan emerging from the Convention could succeed unless the small-state group supported it, they were aware of the strength of their position.

The modified Virginia Plan was reported from the Committee of the Whole on June 19, and the legislative fight continued on the open floor. By large majorities the Convention accepted popular election of the lower house and election of the upper chamber by state legislatures, but when, on June 27, the Convention touched upon the question of proportionate representation versus state equality in the two chambers, all the differences between the large- and small-state factions flared up again. Luther Martin harangued the Convention for two days, insisting that the central government existed merely to preserve the states and that state equality was "essential to the federal idea." Madison in reply made the astute observation that the small states in reality need not fear a combination of large states against them, for the economic interests of the large states were altogether diverse: Massachusetts, he said, depended largely on fish, Pennsylvania on flour, Virginia on tobacco. As the discussion grew embittered, some delegates openly hinted that the Convention was on the verge of failure. Benjamin Franklin, free-thinking skeptic that he was, piously appealed to the power of prayer and suggested that the Convention solve its dilemma with a daily invocation to the Deity.

On June 29, the Convention again voted, six states to four, for proportionate representation in the lower house. The moderates on both sides at once saw in this vote the possibility of compromise— the small-state faction would grant proportionate representation in the lower house in return for state equality in the upper. Arguing for this solution, Oliver Ellsworth pointed out that "we were partly federal, partly national." The compromise, he said, recognized both the national and federal elements and would mutually protect the large and small states against one another. The nationalists were not yet ready to accept this solution, however, and several days of acrimonious debate followed in which all the well-known arguments on both sides were restated. On July 2, the question of proportionate representation in the upper house was put, and the small-state faction succeeded in deadlocking the vote, 5 to 5.

The moderate nationalists now recognized that compromise was necessary. At C. C. Pinckney's suggestion, therefore, the Convention appointed a committee of eleven, one man from each state, to devise a compromise. The committee chosen was composed of Gerry, Ellsworth, Yates, Paterson, Franklin, Bedford, Martin, Mason, Davie, Rutledge, and Baldwin. Significantly, all these men were either moderates or die-hard defenders of state sovereignty. The compromise which they reported on July 5 was regarded by the nationalists as a distinct setback to their cause. The committee recommended:

That in the lower house each state be allowed one member for every 40,000 inhabitants.

That all bills for raising or appropriating money originate in the lower house, and not be amended by the upper.

That each state have an equal vote in the upper house.[4]

Further discussion by the Convention led to the acceptance of one other proposition, introduced by Elbridge Gerry: that the vote in the Senate be by individuals, and not by state delegations. With this one modification the Convention accepted the committee report substantially without change.

SIGNIFICANCE OF THE GREAT COMPROMISE

This plan was the "Great Compromise" of the Convention. Without it, the gathering probably would have broken up in failure. Historians have sometimes called the settlement the "Connecticut Compromise," because of the role which the Connecticut delegation is supposed to have played in bringing it about, but the phrase is not altogether justified. Roger Sherman of Connecticut seems to have been the first delegate to suggest that the Convention allow an equal vote in the Senate, and Oliver Ellsworth of Connecticut was not only a member of the committee of eleven, but also aided in the defense of the scheme on the floor. Also, Connecticut had paved the way for compromise by acceding in some degree to the demand of the large states for nationalism, and in supporting the demands of the small-state men for equality in the Senate. Yet Nathaniel Gorham, George Mason, John Dickinson, and Elbridge Gerry all contributed something to the compromise, and one may

---

[4] It had already been decided that the Senate was to be elected by the legislatures of the several states.

doubt that the Connecticut delegation acted together in a concerted and prearranged fashion to bring about the final settlement.

The Great Compromise did not, in fact, affect the subsequent development of the constitutional system very profoundly. The supposed conflict between small-state interests in the Senate and large-state interests in the House failed to materialize. Nor did the Senate become the champion of the states against the national government. As Madison predicted in the Convention, the great controversies of American history have been drawn along sectional rather than interstate lines. Hence, though the Senate theoretically represents the states, the chamber has on most occasions been as nationalistic as the House, if not more so, and has divided along the same sectional lines.

The one notable exception occurred during the slavery controversy, when the Senate tended to become the champion of states' rights and Southern sectional interests, while the House became the champion of Northern nationalism and Northern sectional interests. The explanation for this division lay in the relative power of the North and South in the Senate and the House. Early in the slavery controversy the more populous Northern states with their larger delegations in Congress proved able to control the House of Representatives, which thereafter reflected the growing spirit of Northern nationalism as well as Northern attitudes on the slavery question. The number of slave and free states long remained about the same, however, so that the less populous Southern states could control about half the votes in the Senate, where the states were represented on a basis of equality. Party organization on most occasions enabled the South to pick up some Northern votes in the Senate, so that the Senate usually reflected Southern attitudes on slavery and Southern states' rights doctrine. Save for Southern dominance in the Senate, the history of the slavery controversy might have been quite different, for in a national legislature based entirely upon proportionate representation by population, the South would have been forced either to submit to the national will or to withdraw from the Union long before 1860.

In many of the great sectional conflicts since 1865 the Senate has actually been more nationalistic than the House. This is largely because the less populous states, now western as well as southern, have sought from the national government various forms of assistance which could be conveyed only under a broad interpretation of national power.

As Madison predicted, the provision that all revenue bills must originate in the House of Representatives has been inconsequential. The provision nominally is still observed; however, the Senate is free to accept, amend, or reject any House measure, and by those means it exercises as much control over revenue measures as does the lower chamber. The fact that the Senate cannot initiate revenue bills has been of small importance; the essential fact is that it can amend such bills into any form which both the Senate and the House may be willing to pass.

A much more serious consideration was the import of the compromise for the problem of sovereignty. The compromise was undoubtedly a concession to the principle of state equality, and hence by implication, to the principle of state sovereignty. The nationalists—Madison, Wilson, Morris, and their supporters—perceived this fact clearly and accordingly fought the compromise bitterly. Gouverneur Morris warned in a stirring speech that "this country must be united. If persuasion does not unite it, the sword will." He predicted that the Senate would become the bulwark of the small-state interests, eventuating in a collapse of the national government.

The final contest over state sovereignty did not develop precisely as Morris had predicted, but in their fear that state sovereignty might at length endanger the nation the nationalists were overwhelmingly right. They yielded to the majority only when they saw that no other solution was possible and that the compromise was necessary if the Convention was to proceed with its work. In later days the doctrine of state sovereignty, partially recognized in the structure of the Senate, helped pave the way for the great controversies on the nature of the Union and for the recurring revival of the contention that the federal government was a mere league of sovereign states and that the ultimate repositories of sovereignty were still the states.

Other details concerning the legislature were adjusted with relative ease. Certain of the delegates, notably Rutledge and the two Pinckneys, thought that property ought to be recognized in the apportionment of representatives in the House. The committee of eleven nonetheless adopted population as the sole basis of representation, although the Convention later gave limited representation to property in slaves by accepting the so-called "three-fifths clause," suggested by C. C. Pinckney, by which three-fifths of the slave population was counted for purposes of representation. In the absence of any certain knowledge of the population of the various states, the Convention fixed temporary arbitrary quotas for representation in the House and provided for subsequent apportionment by decennial census.

THE EXECUTIVE OFFICE

Although the Convention's great crisis developed over the legislature, the delegates spent even more time thrashing out certain vexatious problems relating to the executive. At no time did these difficulties threaten to break up the Convention; yet they caused long discussion and many stalemates.

The delegates were divided into two schools of thought on the executive. One group, represented chiefly by Sherman, Dickinson, and Martin, believed in a weak executive, chosen by and responsible to the legislature, a mere instrument of legislative will. Their belief reflected the prevalent Revolutionary doctrine of legislative ascendancy. A second group, led by Wilson, Madison, Gouverneur Morris, and Hamilton, believed in a powerful independent executive, preferably chosen by direct popular election. This attitude was inspired to some extent by the doctrine of separation of powers, a notion theoretically inconsistent with legislative ascendancy. The strong-executive men were also the Convention's nationalists, and they were convinced that a powerful executive representing the nation at large was essential if the new government was to have the capacity for decisive action. As Wilson put it, they wanted the executive possessed of "energy, dispatch, and responsibility."

These two conceptions of the executive office came into conflict the moment the Committee of the Whole took up the matter. The strong-executive men attacked the Randolph Plan's provision for an executive elected by Congress, and Wilson suggested direct popular election as an alternative. This idea received little favor with most of the delegates, in part because of the antidemocratic views of many delegates, in part because the idea of a popularly elected executive was as yet largely foreign to American experience.

Wilson then suggested as a compromise that the people of the various states choose presidential electors, who should then meet and choose the executive magistrate. This proposal, with some modifications, was eventually adopted by the Convention, but when first set forth the idea attracted little favor. On a vote, Wilson's motion was defeated, eight states to two. The Convention immediately thereafter by the same margin ratified the plan for the election of the President by Congress, and there matters stood when the Committee of the Whole reported on June 15.

The strong-executive party, however, simply would not allow the election of the executive by the legislature to stand. In a series of debates throughout July, Wilson, Morris, and Madison hammered away at the idea that an executive chosen by Congress would be corrupt and incompetent, and that free government demanded that the executive, legislature, and judiciary be independently constituted. They scored a temporary success when, on July 19, the Convention voted, 6 to 3, to accept the electoral college idea, the electors to be chosen by the state legislatures. Yet a few days later, on July 26, after an able speech by George Mason defending legislative choice, the Convention voted, 7 to 2, to return to legislative election. And in spite of repeated attacks by the strong-executive party, this decision was embodied in the Report of the Committee on Detail submitted early in August.

On August 31, as the Convention neared its close, it appointed a new committee of eleven, one delegate from each state, to "Consider such parts of the Constitution as have been postponed." This committee settled a number of minor details, but its most important accomplishment was a lengthy paragraph describing a proposed compromise method of choosing the executive.

The committee recommended the choice of the President by an Electoral College, with certain modifications designed to win the favor of the adherents of legislative ascendancy and states' rights. Each state was to "choose its electors in such a manner as its legislature may direct." This plan recognized the states; yet left the door open for popular choice of electors. The electors were to vote by ballot for two persons, the man receiving the greatest number of votes to be President, provided the number of votes cast for him constituted a majority of all the electors. If no candidate received a majority, the Senate was to elect the President from among the five candidates receiving the highest number of electoral votes. This last clause was a direct concession to the doctrine of legislative ascendancy.

When the matter was debated on the floor of the Convention, several delegates expressed the opinion that in most elections no candidate would receive a majority, and that the choice would therefore usually devolve upon the upper house. Although the strong-executive adherents objected to this feature, it was precisely what was needed to win over such proponents of legislative ascendancy as Mason and Randolph. The Convention accordingly adopted the report almost in its entirety.

Only one substantial modification of the committee's recommendation was made. At Sherman's suggestion, the election of the President was referred to the House of Representatives instead of the Senate. A majority of the delegates approved of this change on the ground that election of the executive by the House rather than by the Senate was less aristocratic in character. To insure against a possible combination by which three or four of the large states might band together and elect the President, it was provided that the vote in the House should be by states, and that a majority of all the states be required to elect.

The Electoral College was thus a compromise device, adopted to meet the objections which various delegates had raised to other proposed methods of election. A distinct majority who believed in the separation of powers opposed choice of the executive by the national legislature, but another majority feared both the nationalism and the democracy of direct popular election. Election by state legislatures, the only other alternative, was equally repugnant to the nationalists. The Electoral College, though an artificial device, provided the only apparent way out of the difficulty.

What was the significance of the compromise on the executive? At the time the answer was not clear, but from the vantage point of today, two things are plain. First, the plan turned out to be a victory for both nationalism and democracy. Within a very few years after 1789, nearly all the states had by law established popular election of their presidential electors, who were rapidly reduced to figureheads.[5] Thus the proponents of a truly national foundation for the executive eventually had their way.

Second, the plan was a substantial victory for the doctrine of the separation of powers and hence for a separately constituted and independent presidency. Had the choice of the President by Congress been permitted to stand, it is probable that the executive would have become simply an arm of the legislature, and the United States would have emerged with what is known as a parliamentary-cabinet form of government, in which the executive is a committee of the legislature.

This conclusion has been disputed by certain theorists, notably Edward S. Corwin. Professor Corwin contends that the distinctive

---

[5] By 1800 the principle was fairly well established that electors were mere creatures of party will and could exercise no personal discretion in voting, but instead must vote for the designated party candidates for President and Vice-President. Thereafter electors virtually never acted as other than mere instruments of party will. In 1820, one elector, William Plumer of New Hampshire, failed to vote for Monroe, his party's candidate, apparently on the grounds that he disapproved personally of Monroe's re-election to the presidency.

feature of a parliamentary government is the power of the cabinet to coerce the legislature through the right to prorogue the legislature whenever the latter fails to do the cabinet's bidding. This is the situation in England, where the Cabinet maintains its ascendancy and control of Parliament by this method. Corwin concludes that the emergence of a parliamentary government would have been impossible under the Constitution, even had the Convention provided for election of the President by Congress, for the executive would still have had no general power to prorogue a dissident legislature.

The power to prorogue is not, however, absolutely essential to all types of parliamentary government. In the Third French Republic, the power to prorogue existed in theory, but was seldom resorted to. There a vote of non-confidence in a government immediately resulted in the cabinet's resignation and the formation of a new cabinet which was formed with the intention of winning a vote of confidence in the Chamber of Deputies. Unlike the English system, that in France assured unity between executive and legislature by providing for the dominance of the latter. It was the cabinet, and not the legislature, which re-formed in case of differences between the two. Hence there existed no need to prorogue the legislature. In short, while it may be conceded that the British cabinet system could not have developed under the Constitution, there seems to be no reason why a parliamentary system like that of France could not have emerged. It would have been necessary to develop the principle of ministerial responsibility, but this would not have been difficult once Congress controlled the election of the President and could put a man of its own viewpoint in the office. This is precisely what happened in France, where the president was elected by the legislature for a fixed term, but eventually came to perform no real functions, all of which were taken over by a ministry responsible to parliament. Indeed, congressional control of the executive would not have involved a new principle in the United States, for it already existed under the Articles of Confederation.

The committee of eleven also settled the question of the executive's eligibility for re-election. The Virginia Plan had made the executive ineligible for re-election. When the matter first arose in the Convention, the delegates expressed the fear that an executive chosen by Congress and eligible for re-election would court the favor of Congress so completely as to destroy all executive independence. Once the provision for independent election was adopted, however, this objection to re-election became irrelevant, and the

Convention therefore removed all limitations upon eligibility to re-election. A president might remain in office indefinitely, but a four-year term was specified so that he would have to ask for a vote of confidence at regular and fairly frequent intervals.

THE FEDERAL PROBLEM AND THE JUDICIARY

Intermittently the Convention returned to the two related problems that lay at the heart of the central government's difficulties under the Articles of Confederation: the use of the states as agencies of the central government, and the issue of the respective spheres of the state and federal governments.

The proposal in the Virginia Plan to solve the problem of Federalism by empowering the national government to coerce a state deficient in its obligations to the federal union appeared to be more and more irrelevant as discussion in the Convention progressed. As explained above, it became obvious that the new government would rest directly upon individuals, and would carry out its functions through its own agents without the assistance of the states. For example, the new government would impose excise and customs taxes directly upon individual citizens in the country, and it would proceed to collect them through its own revenue officers. The states would play no part in the imposition or collection of federal taxes. Coercion, in short, would be meaningless in a truly national government functioning directly upon individuals.

Viewed in this light, the very idea of coercion implied that the Union was still to be a league of sovereignties and that the central government would still be dependent upon the will of the various sovereign states. Coercion of a state would then come dangerously close to an act of war. Madison observed that the use of force "would look more like a declaration of war, than an infliction of punishment, and would probably be considered by the party attacked as a dissolution of the union." At his suggestion, therefore, the idea of coercion was dropped. The nationalists also had in mind the congressional veto of state legislation as a more effective device for controlling the states, and were therefore the more willing to abandon coercion.

Coercion reappeared in the New Jersey Plan, proof that the notion was dear to the proponents of state sovereignty, but after the failure of that plan, it was not heard of again. As Randolph remarked at the time, "we must resort to a national legislation over individuals"; and coercion had therefore become undesirable.

The more serious and difficult problem remained. Who was to

define and safeguard the respective spheres of the states and the national government? The position of the nationalists on this question was conditioned by the fear that the states would gradually usurp the functions of the central government and reduce it to impotence, while the attitude of the states' rights men reflected the fear that the new government would supersede the states altogether and reduce them to "mere corporations."

The Virginia Plan, it will be recalled, had sought to solve this problem by stating the national government's sphere of authority in indefinitely broad terms and empowering Congress to disallow state laws contravening the Constitution. Had this plan been followed, the new Constitution would have settled the question of the locus of sovereignty. While a sphere of autonomous authority would have been left to the states, the ultimate power to define and interpret both state and national spheres would have rested plainly with the national government.

At first it seemed certain that the Convention would adopt this extremely nationalistic solution of the federal problem. In spite of some resistance from the states' rights men, the Committee of the Whole incorporated in its report to the floor on June 15, congressional disallowance of state legislation. However, a growing number of moderates and states' rights delegates thereafter became convinced that the congressional negative constituted a genuine menace to the states, and they determined to eliminate it. The critical debate occurred on July 17. Roger Sherman contended that the congressional negative involved a "wrong principle" in that every state law not negatived would by implication remain operative, even though contrary to the fundamental nature of the Constitution. This idea, drawn from a well-known doctrine of the common law, was highly suggestive to the lawyers present. They saw at once that Congress would have to consider every state law passed to determine whether or not it was contrary to federal legislation or to the Constitution. Such a provision would not only place an onerous burden on Congress; it would have the further result of allowing any state law not acted upon by Congress to remain operative, no matter how seriously it violated the Constitution.

A second highly constructive criticism of the Congressional negative was advanced by Gouverneur Morris, who, though a strong nationalist, now denounced it as "terrible to the states" and then observed that the device was not really necessary, since a law contrary to the articles of union would in any event not be recognized by the courts. Although Madison argued vigorously that the negative was utterly necessary to effective national government, his words were unavailing. At the end of debate the Convention voted to abandon the device, only Massachusetts, Virginia, and North Carolina favoring its retention.

Luther Martin now brought forward a provision of the New Jersey Plan, hitherto little noticed, designed to solve the federal problem by making federal law supreme but making the state courts the agency by which the states and federal government would be kept within their respective spheres. After the debate of July 17, the delegates accepted without opposition Martin's suggestion, the nationalists apparently believing this solution to be better than none. After some modification, the provision read as follows:

> This Constitution, and the Laws of the United States which shall be made in Pursuance thereof; and all Treaties made, or which shall be made, under the Authority of the United States, shall be the supreme Law of the Land, and the Judges in every State shall be bound thereby, any Thing in the Constitution or Laws of any State to the Contrary notwithstanding.

The provision ultimately appeared in Article VI of the finished Constitution.

The states' rights men evidently regarded this provision as something of a victory. While it made the Constitution, treaties, and acts of Congress supreme over state law, it apparently lodged in an agency of the state governments—the state courts—the power to determine the extent of state and federal authority under the Constitution. This was precisely the opposite of what the nationalists had sought. Late in August the nationalists therefore made a final plea for the restoration of the Congressional negative. Wilson called the negative the "key-stone wanted to compleate the wide arch of Government we are raising." But his eloquence was wasted, the Convention rejecting the negative by the close vote of six states to five.

Yet the nationalists' apparent defeat on this issue was actually a victory. The supremacy clause of Article VI, inserted at the suggestion of Luther Martin, arch-champion of states' rights, later became the cornerstone of national sovereignty. This occurred because the Judiciary Act of 1789 provided for appeals from state courts to the federal judiciary, and finally to the Supreme Court of the United States. The ultimate effect of this statute was to give the Supreme Court, an agent of the national government, the final power to interpret the extent of state and national authority under the Constitution.

Was this the intent of the members of the Constitutional Convention? It certainly was not the intent of William Paterson, author of the New Jersey Plan, or of Luther Martin. They and the other states' rights men were interested in preserving the autonomy, even the sovereignty, of the states. Had they known that the very principle against which they had fought so bitterly in the congressional negative would later be established by legislative fiat and constitutional growth, they would have regarded their proposal in a very different light. It was certainly not their intent to establish national supremacy. Furthermore, the dissatisfaction of Madison and Wilson with the guarantees established by the provision against encroachment by the states upon national authority and their repeated attempts to win adoption of the negative make it clear that the nationalists also were unaware of the potentialities of the provision.

The Constitution does not provide specifically for appeals from state to federal courts. There is substantial evidence, however, that certain members of the Convention assumed that such a right would exist. The original Virginia Plan provided not only for one or more supreme tribunals, but for a lower federal judiciary. This provision was attacked in the Committee of the Whole by the states' rights men, who contended that lower federal courts were unnecessary. Rutledge of South Carolina argued that the state courts could decide federal cases in the first instance, and that uniformity of decisions could be secured by granting a right of appeal to the supreme national tribunal. Behind this contention apparently was a fear that a lower federal judiciary would take away certain types of cases from the state courts, which would suffer a loss of business and prestige. Although Wilson and Madison both defended the necessity for an inferior federal judiciary, the Convention rejected the provision by a 5-to-3 vote. Immediately thereafter, Madison and Wilson moved to make inferior federal tribunals optional with Congress, and this provision carried, 8 to 2.

It is clear, therefore, that the Convention contemplated the possibility of appeals from state courts to the Supreme Court in the event that Congress should choose not to erect inferior federal tribunals. Thus, ironically enough, it was the states' rights faction which insisted upon the right of appeals, later to play a vital part in confirming national sovereignty, as a substitute for a lower federal judiciary.

Perhaps the soundest conclusion is that most members of the Convention did not regard the right of appeals as establishing a general power in the federal judiciary to interpret the extent of state authority under the Constitution. Eventually, the supremacy of national law and the right of appeal from state courts to national courts helped to establish not only the supremacy of the national government but also the right of the Supreme Court to determine the extent of state and national authority. To the men of 1787, however, the compelling logic of their work and of future events was not as clear as it is to us now.[6]

Closely related to the whole matter of federal sovereignty and the right of appeals from state to federal courts is the question of whether the Convention intended to vest the federal judiciary with the power to determine the limits of state and congressional authority under the Constitution. This problem has usually been assumed to be identical with that of whether the Convention intended to bestow upon the federal judiciary the power to declare acts of Congress void. However, there are reasons for questioning this assumption.

There is substantial evidence in the debates of the Convention that many of the delegates believed that the federal judiciary would have the right to refuse to recognize an unconstitutional federal law. At one time or another this viewpoint was expressed by several members, including James Wilson, Elbridge Gerry, Nathaniel Gorham, Luther Martin, and George Mason. It is probable that a majority of the delegates would have agreed with Morris, who "could not agree that the judiciary should be bound to say that a direct violation of the constitution was law." On the other hand John Mercer of Maryland "disapproved of the doctrine that the Judges as expositors of the Constitution should have the authority to declare a law void," while John Dickinson thought that "no such power ought to exist."

If we grant for the sake of argument that most of the delegates assumed this power to be inherent in the judiciary, this question remains: Was the power to declare void an act of Congress recog-

---

[6] In No. 80 of *The Federalist* Hamilton asserted that the right of appeal from the state courts to the federal judiciary upon constitutional questions was an imperative necessity, as the only available means of enforcing constitutional limitations upon the state legislatures and securing a final interpretation on such constitutional questions. There must, he said, be some "effectual power" in the national government to "restrain or correct the infractions" of the prohibitions upon the states. "This power must either be a direct negative on the State laws, or an authority in the federal courts to overrule such as might be in manifest contravention of the articles of Union. There is no third course that I can imagine. The latter appears to have been thought by the convention preferable to the former, and, I presume, will be most agreeable to the States." It must be remembered, however, that Hamilton, a thoroughgoing nationalist, was here propagandizing the cause of strong national government.

nized as tantamount to a general power to interpret the Constitution and to define the ultimate limits of national and state authority? Direct evidence upon this point is small, but one incident which Madison records is significant. On August 27, the provisions dealing with the Supreme Court in the resolutions prepared by the Committee on Detail came up for discussion. One section read that "the jurisdiction of the supreme court shall extend to all cases arising under the laws passed by the legislature of the United States." Dr. Johnson then moved to insert the words "this Constitution and the" before the word "laws," so that the jurisdiction of the Supreme Court would extend to all cases arising under the Constitution and laws of the United States. Let Madison's notes speak:

> Mr. Madison doubted whether it was not going too far to extend the jurisdiction of the Court generally to cases arising under the Constitution & whether it ought not to be limited to cases of a Judiciary Nature. The right of expounding the Constitution in cases not of this nature ought not to be given to that Department.
>
> The motion of Dr. Johnson was agreed to nem: con: it being generally supposed that the jurisdiction given was constructively limited to cases of a Judiciary nature.

If the import of this passage is correct, the delegates were generally agreed that the federal judiciary was not to possess the general right of expounding the Constitution. In other words, the right to declare void an unconstitutional federal law was not supposed to confer any general power to interpret the compact. In the twentieth century "the Constitution is what the Supreme Court says it is," to quote Charles Evans Hughes. But this condition came about only as the result of a long process of evolution which was not freely confirmed until the latter portion of the nineteenth century. It was a development not foreseen by the members of the Convention.

Regardless of where the final power to interpret the Constitution was to be lodged, there is no doubt that the Convention intended the federal sphere of sovereignty to be a limited one. In the original Virginia Plan, the scope of federal power was defined in a very broad and general fashion to include power over all matters in which the states were incompetent as well as those matters over which power was exercised by the Confederation Congress. This proposal, had it been allowed to stand, would have given Congress vast authority of a vague and undefined character, inconsistent with the very nature of a federal state. The problem of federal spheres would have been solved by permitting Congress to define the extent of its own authority.

Although two or three delegates expressed alarm at the sweeping grant of congressional power implied in the Virginia Plan, the Convention took no positive action until the Committee on Detail produced a draft constitution early in August. In this draft the Committee had abandoned the original vague statement of congressional authority, and incorporated instead a series of specific delegated powers. Madison's notes give us no hint as to why this was done, although certain members of the Convention had expressed strong fear of an indefinite grant of legislative authority to the national government. The personnel of the Committee on Detail—Rutledge, Randolph, Gorham, Ellsworth, and Wilson—yields no specific clue as to what occurred in committee, although three of these men were moderate states' rights men and only one, Wilson, was a powerful nationalist. The likelihood is, however, that Rutledge, Gorham, and Ellsworth insisted upon a limitation of congressional authority by enumeration, and they may have pointed out that in no other way could the state courts be counted upon to give supremacy and precedence to national law. Perhaps the committee was also convinced that only if the powers of Congress were specified and enumerated would the states consent to ratify the new Constitution. At any rate, enumeration marked another moderate victory for the states' rights bloc, for it meant that those powers not specifically delegated to the national government would reside in the states. A great majority of the Convention apparently took enumeration for granted. It was in the tradition of American federalism, and occasioned little discussion.

THE LOCUS OF SOVEREIGNTY

In summary, it is clear that the Convention did not make a decisive disposition of the locus of sovereignty in the new union. A partial solution of the problem was indeed made. The federal government was given only limited and enumerated powers; the residue of sovereignty was left by implication with the states. Yet within its sphere, the federal government had most of the appurtenances of a truly sovereign national government. Unlike the government of the Articles, it functioned directly upon individuals in all instances, and had its own agencies, executive and courts, to execute its will. Moreover, the Constitution, treaties, and acts of the national government were made the supreme law of the land, and the state courts were required to enforce that law regardless of any provision in their own state constitutions or laws. The new legislature was in large part national in character, although the principle of state equality received implied recognition in the upper chamber.

No one body received specific final authority to interpret the Constitution. Article VI seemingly lodged that power with the state courts, and this would seem to be what Martin, Paterson, and other champions of states' rights intended. It is possible to demonstrate logically, however, that the Constitution by implication authorizes appeals from state courts to federal courts, and some delegates apparently took such appeals for granted. In all probability, however, neither the nationalists nor the states' rights bloc understood that this procedure would eventually lodge the general power to interpret the Constitution with the Supreme Court.

Certainly the Convention did not anticipate the future role of the Supreme Court as the final arbiter of the constitutional system. Some of the members of the Convention obviously believed that the federal courts had the power to declare acts of Congress void, but they hardly assumed that this was synonymous with the power to interpret the general nature of the Constitution or to settle all constitutional issues.

The vague and uncertain character of the Convention's solution of the problems of sovereignty opened the way to the development of two constitutional issues of great importance.

The first of these was the question of state sovereignty. Were the states still sovereign? Was the national government supreme within its limited sphere of powers, or was it a mere agency of the states? Who had the ultimate power to interpret the nature of the Constitution and to decide disputes between state and national authority? By failing to provide specifically for an indisputable negative upon state laws, by failing to make it clear beyond question that the national government had sole power to interpret the Constitution, the Convention had opened the way for the assertion that the states had the right to interpret the nature and extent of their powers under the Constitution. Madison himself was to advance that assertion before eleven years had passed.

Fifty years later, statesmen and theorists were to quarrel about whether the Constitution was a compact or an "instrument of government." The argument had little meaning as of 1787. The Constitution was indeed a compact, for it was an agreement by which the people of the United States set up government by covenant or consent. Revolutionary political philosophy assumed that all free government was created by compact. Calhoun later tried to argue that as a compact the Constitution was a mere voluntary agreement between the states and as such of no binding force. The argument, however, ignored the whole implication of eighteenth-century compact philosophy. Eighteenth-century political philosophers regarded the compact upon which the state was founded as supreme law.

Later northern nationalists were to hold that the sovereignty of the national government was above and beyond the states because the Constitution was ratified by the people of the states, rather than by the states themselves. This raises a question in sheer metaphysics. The Constitution was referred by the Convention to the states, which had the power to act or not as they chose. The Constitution required that the act of ratification itself be performed by organic conventions which in theory represented the people of the various states. Did this reduce the states themselves to mere convenient electoral districts for the purpose of ratification? To put it differently, was the Constitution ratified by the State of Virginia, or by the people of the state of Virginia? One can only say that the question lacks historical reality, for it did not even occur to the men of 1787.

Ultimately the question of sovereignty was not settled by any fine-drawn political debates about the meaning of the Constitution. The Constitution became the instrument of government in a country which at first had little sense of unity and nationalism. But the advancing years saw the growth of a powerful nationalism in America which bound the various sections firmly together into one nation, and which gave most Americans a new conviction that the federal union was no mere league but a truly national government. In the face of this belief, the question of the sovereignty of the federal government in 1787 becomes insignificant. Only in the South was there after 1820 a serious disposition to challenge the new nationalism. The attempt of the South to use the doctrine of state sovereignty to defend its economic institutions led to war, and to the permanent destruction of any claim that the federal government was not supreme, or that the United States was not a nation.

The second important issue which grew out of the vague solution of the problem of respective spheres was that of the role of the judiciary in relation to the Constitution. From 1803, when John Marshall expounded at length the dictum that the federal courts had a right to declare void an act of Congress, down to 1937, when the great battle over President Roosevelt's attempt to curb the judiciary was fought, the role of the federal judiciary in constitutional interpretation became at intervals a matter of bitter controversy.

THE CONSTITUTION COMPLETED

In early September the Convention neared the end of its work. On September 8, with all details of consequence disposed of, the Convention appointed a Committee of Style, consisting of Hamilton, Johnson, Gouverneur Morris, and King. The actual task of drafting the finished Constitution was performed mainly by Morris, and the result was the brilliant clarity of legal style which characterizes the document. Here and there ambiguities remained to puzzle future generations, but the Convention could not have ironed them all out had it sat for another decade. The Committee's draft was accepted almost as it stood, the only substantial change being a reduction of the ratio of representation for members of the lower house from 40,000 to 30,000, a change proposed by Hugh Williamson of North Carolina and supported by Washington.

A debate on the method of ratification then took place. The Convention had previously decided upon ratification by state conventions, favorable action by any nine states to be sufficient to establish the Constitution among those states so acting. This plan was in a sense illegal, for it violated the method of amendment in the Articles of Confederation, which stipulated that proposed amendments must be submitted by Congress and must be ratified by all the states before becoming effective. Several delegates, among them Hamilton, Gerry, and Randolph, were of the opinion that the Convention's plan of ratification was a bit high-handed, but their alternative suggestion that the Convention submit its work to Congress for approval in the regular manner was voted down on the ground that such action would endanger the chances of adoption.

An overwhelming majority of the delegates present in mid-September approved of the final draft. Although a few extreme states' rights men who disapproved of the Convention's work, among them Luther Martin, Lansing, and Yates, had left in disgust well before the day of adjournment, both the nationalists and the moderate champions of states' rights signed the document. To lend an appearance of harmony Franklin suggested that the Convention submit its work to the nation over the formula: "Done in Convention by the Unanimous Consent of the states present," and this somewhat disingenuous proposal was adopted. Only three of the delegates then present refused to sign: Randolph, in the belief that the Constitution would fail of adoption and in the wish to be free to support a second convention; George Mason in the conviction that the Constitution was too aristocratic; Elbridge Gerry on the grounds that the new government would have too much irresponsible authority. On September 17, 1787, the remaining thirty-nine members affixed their signatures to the document.

The Convention then adjourned. Most of the delegates prepared to return home to champion the Constitution in their respective states. The fate of their efforts now rested with the state conventions.

Chapter

6

Ratification of the Constitution

TEN DAYS after the Convention adjourned, an unenthusiastic Congress submitted the Constitution to the states. The Constitution provided for ratification by state conventions, and the various state legislatures therefore proceeded to set convention dates and issue calls for the election of delegates. In Rhode Island, where the paper-money faction that was in control objected to the financial provisions in the Constitution, the assembly refused to do this, and as a consequence that state remained completely aloof during the struggle over ratification. In all the other states, however, the attempts of opponents to block the calling of conventions were defeated. Within the next few months, delegates met in twelve states to debate and vote upon the great question of entry into the new union.

In the course of the fight for adoption, the supporters of the new instrument of government shortly became known as Federalists, a name which anticipated that of the later political party, although the Federalists of 1787 should not be confused with the partisan organization that emerged a few years later. The Federalists dubbed the enemies of ratification Antifederalists, a title that reflected no great credit upon the latter, for it seemed to imply that they were opponents of all national union.

ECONOMIC AND CLASS DIVISION

Although local issues confused the division, it is possible to perceive not only an economic and class separation but also a sectional demarcation between the Federalists and Antifederalists. Long ago O. G. Libby, a student of the Constitution, observed that if a line were drawn along the coastal plain from Maine to Georgia, parallel to the sea and fifty miles inland, it would separate "pretty accurately" the Federalist tidewater area from the Antifederalist interior. Broadly speaking, the statement is true, although there were several important exceptions. Certainly the tidewater, with the exception of North Carolina and Rhode Island, was generally heavily Federalist. But, although the interior was for the most part strongly opposed to the Constitution, the presence of sizable Federalist groups in the back country of New Hampshire, Massachusetts, Pennsylvania, Virginia, and Georgia was of great importance. Without the support of these areas the Constitution probably would have failed of adoption.

The sectional division between tidewater and back country was related closely to the economic and class differences which marked the two parties. The merchants, the larger planters, the land speculators, the men of wealth who held the bonds of the Confederation, groups dwelling in the cities or plantations on the seaboard, were generally in favor of a government which would protect commerce and remove the burdens of interstate tariffs. They were enemies of the paper money experiments then prevalent in most of the states. Some of them desired a national policy to protect the large investor in western lands. Most of all they wanted a sound national credit established.

A notable exception, however, occurred in New York, where the owners of the great estates along the Hudson were for the most part opposed to adoption. The reason was simple: New York's government was supported by the taxes the state was able to levy upon interstate commerce. The Constitution would end state tariffs and necessitate land taxes, a development which the landed aristocracy feared and objected to. Also in New York, and to some extent elsewhere, many lawyers opposed adoption in the fear that a new federal court system would deprive them of favorite state connections and practice.

The great interior upland plain, running back into the Allegheny foothills, was the home of a numerous class of small farmers and frontiersmen who constituted an important part of the population of the United States at that time. Many of these men believed they had small reason to support the Constitution. They cared little for the promotion of interstate commerce, and the Constitution appeared to offer but few benefits in the marketing of small agricultural surpluses. The small farmers' monetary interests, then as always, were inflationary. Nearly always disappointed in grain, livestock, and whisky prices, knowing that paper money would increase agricultural income, and wishing to meet obligations with cheap money, the small farmers had fought in all the state legislatures for paper issues to relieve the postwar deflation of the 1780's. To them a constitution which promised to make state paper illegal and which was dedicated to "sound"—that is, deflationary—credit policies was anything but attractive.

Small farmers and frontiersmen were also interested in a weak national land policy. They were extremely hostile to large land speculators, and they feared that the new government might fall into the hands of "the speculative blood-suckers." Also some were squatters upon the public domain, and they did not like the idea of a government which might force them to pay for lands they occupied illegally.

Certain farmer and frontier groups, however, threw in their lot with the Federalist tidewater. The farmers living along the waterway of the upper Connecticut River in New Hampshire felt themselves economically and culturally associated with the downriver communities in Massachusetts and Connecticut and therefore supported a government which would facilitate interstate commerce and break down state provincialism.

In Massachusetts there were alignments of a similar character. In the central interior over four-fifths of the people were opposed to the Constitution, for this was the area from which the followers of Daniel Shays had so recently risen in rebellion. But in western Massachusetts, in the Springfield area, sentiment was about evenly divided, for here the farmers were interested in downriver Connecticut markets.

In Virginia the tidewater coastal area was very heavily in favor of the Constitution, while the interior farming upland or piedmont was almost as heavily opposed, with only about a fourth of the people favoring ratification. But still farther west, in the Shenandoah Valley and in what is now West Virginia, sentiment was almost unanimously pro-Federalist. Here again the chief explanation lay in market connections. The Shenandoah Valley, already a booming wheat area, opened toward the north into Maryland and Pennsylvania, northeastward toward the tidewater. The natural market outlets of this region were Baltimore and Philadelphia. A government that would assure free access to markets in other states was of prime importance to farmers already beginning to produce an important cash crop. The vote of this region was in marked contrast to that of Kentucky, then a part of Virginia, for this typically frontier area was heavily against adoption.

In Georgia, still a frontier state, even outlying settlements supported the Constitution. The state was one of the first to ratify. Here the reason lay in the people's fear of the Creek Indians, with whom the Georgians were experiencing difficulties. Georgians believed that a strong national government would take a firm line with the southwestern tribes and would perhaps send troops to pacify the frontier.

THE DEBATE OVER RATIFICATION

The native American propensity for translating economic conflicts into legalistic and constitutional terms characterized the discussion carried on in press and pamphlet and in the state conventions on the Constitution's merits. The argument revolved chiefly around the Constitution's mechanical details; occasionally it was concerned with abstract principles of government; almost never did it touch directly upon the proposed government's economic aspect. Opponents of adoption posed as friends of an "adequate" or "correct" federal union, but attacked the proposed constitution as inimical to good government and as destructive of the rights of the states and the liberties of the people. Although endless trivial objections were raised, many thoughtful criticisms were presented. Some of these appear to be irrelevant or immaterial today; yet they reveal the hopes and fears of the men of 1787 in their struggle for a "more effective union."

One criticism repeatedly advanced was the absence of a bill of rights. This matter had been discussed very briefly on the floor of the Philadelphia Convention, where George Mason had introduced a resolution, supported by Elbridge Gerry, to appoint a committee to prepare a bill of rights. Roger Sherman had replied briefly that the various state constitutions already had bills of rights, which should prove sufficient under the new government, and Mason's motion had then been defeated 10 to 0. But in the ratification controversy, absence of a federal bill of rights became a focal point of attack upon the Constitution by the Antifederalists, who pointed out that since the new government had a sphere of sovereignty of its own and functioned directly upon individuals, the absence of a bill of rights prepared the way for encroachments upon the liberties of the people.

In reply, several of the recent delegates to Philadelphia offered two explanations as to why they had not included a bill of rights in the Constitution. The first, advanced by Madison and C. C. Pinckney among others, was that the new government was one of specific and enumerated powers and possessed no authority except in those spheres where it had received a grant of power. The various state legislatures possessed residual plenary powers; hence it was advisable to place limitations upon those powers in the state constitutions. But since the powers of Congress were limited by enumeration, it would be absurd to attach an additional section to the Constitution specifying what Congress could not do. The second explanation, advanced by Washington and James Wilson among others, was that an enumeration of the rights of the people as against the new government was by implication restrictive. The delegates, said Wilson, had found a bill of rights "not only unnecessary, but it was found impracticable—for who will be bold enough to enumerate all the rights of the people?—and when the attempt to enumerate them is made it must be remembered that if the enumeration is not complete, everything not expressly mentioned will be presumed to be purposely omitted." Since it was hopeless to attempt to enumerate all natural rights, the delegates had preferred to fall back again upon their insistence that all natural rights were guaranteed to the people by the very nature of constitutional government.

The absence of a bill of rights proved a bargaining point for the Federalists in some of the state conventions, for they were able to pledge the adoption of a new bill of rights by amendment once the new government was established. In several conventions, among them those in Massachusetts, New York, and Virginia, the Federalists at the last moment won over certain moderates in the opposition with this understanding. Several of the state conventions submitted proposed amendments containing bills of rights at the time that they ratified. These were made the basis of the first ten amendments to the Constitution, adopted by Congress in 1789 and by the states within two years after the establishment of the new government.

The Antifederalists also repeatedly expressed the fear that in one way or another the new government would destroy the sovereignty and even the autonomy of the states. This was the line of attack selected by Patrick Henry, who led the Antifederalist forces in

Virginia, and by Luther Martin in Maryland. The argument had several variations. One was that the "necessary and proper" clause in Article I, Section 8, was a grant of plenary legislative authority in disguise, and that the federal government would be able to use it to usurp the powers of the states. Another was directed against Article VI, which made the Constitution supreme law and established national supremacy and by implication thus seemed to challenge the sovereignty of the states. Another pointed out the vast size of the new nation, the distance of the new capital from its sources of authority, the people, and the consequent probability of abusing the grant of authority by usurpation. And still another pointed to the broad powers of taxation possessed by the new government and warned that these could be used to drain the states' sources of revenue and thus reduce them to impotence.

These arguments the Federalists met in various ways. In the Virginia convention Madison explained that the new government was not altogether national and was in some respects "federal," for the states were still given direct representation in one branch of the legislature. As for fear of the new government's taxing powers, the Federalists everywhere were able to point out the disastrous financial record of the Confederation, the failure of the requisition system, and the necessity of guaranteeing the new government an adequate revenue.

An objection commonly raised in the New England states was directed against the biennial system of election to the House of Representatives, and the long term in the Senate. New Englanders had a long tradition of annual elections to their legislative bodies which they disliked to disturb. In Massachusetts, for example, several delegates insisted that congressmen absent from home for two years would lose touch with their constituents and would conspire to seize dictatorial power and perpetuate themselves in office. The argument seems totally without meaning in the twentieth century, when a two-year term of office is regarded as brief rather than lengthy. But at the time it had to be met with observations on the great difficulties of wintertime travel over long distances and the difficulties which legislators from one state would encounter in conspiring together to seize power.

The ten months' struggle for ratification produced several worthwhile pieces of political literature, by far the most important of which was The Federalist. This work was inspired by Hamilton, who was greatly concerned by the large number of Antifederalist pamphlets that made their appearance in New York soon after the

Philadelphia Convention had adjourned. He therefore decided to publish a series of scholarly and analytical articles which would examine the Constitution point by point. Hamilton secured the support of Madison and John Jay for his project, and in October the articles began appearing in the New York press under the pseudonym of "Publius." Eighty-five articles in all appeared between October 1787 and July 1788. Of these, about fifty were the work of Hamilton, thirty of Madison, and five of Jay.

Notable for penetration of argument, *The Federalist* is one of the great treatises upon the American constitutional system. The amazing thing about the work is the accuracy with which it predicted the behavior of the constitutional system in actual operation. Even today one marvels at the ability of the authors to describe accurately the operation of a government which at the time existed only on paper.

The Federalist was not an objective treatment of the Constitution but a restrained work of partisanship. Its authors had two distinct and not altogether harmonious objectives in mind. First of all they sought to win over doubters and hesitant Antifederalists to the support of the Constitution. For this purpose, the power and authority of the national government had in certain respects to be portrayed in subdued colors. Many pages of *The Federalist* were thus devoted to explanations of the necessity for various provisions of the Constitution and to reassurances that the new government would not destroy the sovereignty of the states or become an instrument of tyranny. Madison pointed out the now familiar argument that Congress would have only enumerated powers beyond which it could not go. Unwise, tyrannical, or unconstitutional legislation would have to run the gamut of two houses of Congress, the presidential veto, and the courts before becoming effective. If past experience was any criterion, the states had little to fear from usurpations by the national government; rather the national government would have to fear usurpations by the states. If by some mischance liberty should be endangered by the tyranny of the federal government, Americans should remember that they had once before defended their rights by resort to the sword, and if necessary could do so again.

Hamilton, Madison, and Jay were also strong nationalists, and somewhat inconsistently with their purpose of reassuring Antifederalists, they made their treatise a defense of the doctrine of national ascendancy. They insisted on the necessity of appeals from state courts to federal courts as essential to a uniform interpretation of the Constitution and to national unity, and Hamilton also argued for the right of the federal judiciary to declare acts of Congress void. Madison even went so far as to interpret the "necessary and proper" clause in a guarded fashion as giving Congress the power to make all laws directed toward constitutional ends not specifically denied by the Constitution. This was a direct anticipation of the doctrine of loose construction laid down two years later in Hamilton's bank paper.

The nationalistic character of these ideas explains in part the success of *The Federalist* in predicting the course of later constitutional development. After 1789, this line of constitutional interpretation was sponsored by Hamilton and the Federalist party. Between 1800 and 1835 Chief Justice John Marshall was to write the doctrine of national supremacy into the growing body of constitutional law, and the idea ultimately triumphed completely through the verdict of the Civil War. It would be interesting to know to what extent *The Federalist* served as a guidebook for the congressmen who wrote the Judiciary Act of 1789, and for the decisions of John Marshall. There is no way of settling this question with complete certainty, but there is some evidence that the influence of *The Federalist* was considerable.

The most effective Antifederalist work to appear was *The Letters from the Federal Farmer*, published by Richard Henry Lee of Virginia in December 1787. This work, moderate and reasoned in tone, immediately won a wide audience in Virginia and the other states. Lee admitted that the Constitution contained many excellent features, but he thought it "aimed too strongly at one consolidated government of the United States." He thought that centralized government was impractical and dangerous to liberty. The Constitution, he said, was also undemocratic, for it placed the majority under minority control. The congressional scheme was bad, since the small House of Representatives could not possibly represent all the people, while state equality in the Senate constituted an injustice to the large states. He also deplored the absence of a bill of rights. While he did not absolutely oppose ratification, he deemed certain reforms essential, and he cautioned Virginians not to rush into ratification before these changes were secured.

TRIUMPH OF THE FEDERALISTS

The successful issue of the struggle for adoption was not assured until June 1788. In seven states the Constitution was ratified by two-to-one majorities or better, but in four others ratification was secured only with difficulty and by narrow majorities, while in two states it was at first rejected.

The Constitution was thought generally to be more favorable to the less populous states because of the provision for equal representation in the Senate, and it was mostly the small states that were the first to ratify. Delaware and New Jersey gave their assent in December 1787; Georgia and Connecticut followed in January, and Maryland ratified in April after an unsuccessful attempt by Luther Martin to filibuster the Convention. Of these states, four were small and without any back country, while Georgia was small in population and influenced by fear of the Indians.

The Federalists also won impressive victories in Pennsylvania and South Carolina. Pennsylvania was the second state to ratify. Here the critical struggle over ratification occurred in the state legislature, where the Antifederalists stayed away from the assembly in an attempt to defeat the quorum necessary to do business, and so block the call for a convention. But the assembly, without a quorum present, voted to call the convention, and the next afternoon the necessary quorum to validate this vote was secured when a mob dragged two Antifederalist assemblymen into the state house and held them in their seats by force. The Federalists under the leadership of James Wilson controlled without difficulty the convention that followed, and secured ratification in December, 46 to 19, after a three weeks' session. Similarly in South Carolina, the real struggle took place in the state legislature, where the Antifederalists attempted to block the motion to call a convention, on the grounds that the Philadelphia Convention had exceeded its authority. This move failed, and when the convention met, the Antifederalists were unable to offer serious opposition to ratification.

In Massachusetts, Virginia, New York, and New Hampshire, ratification was secured only by narrow margins and after hard-fought struggles. Indeed, in Massachusetts it appeared at first as though the enemies of the Constitution had the upper hand. Shays' Rebellion was but lately concluded, and the convention which met in January was filled with the bitter consciousness of social conflict. Most of the distinguished men present, among them Nathaniel Gorham, Rufus King, Caleb Strong, and James Bowdoin, favored ratification. But the Antifederalists seemed to have the weight of numbers on their side, while John Hancock, whose prestige in the state was very high and who was nominal chairman of the convention, at first avoided taking a stand on the issue by failing to put in an appearance. Sam Adams also hung back from endorsement in the belief that the Constitution provided for a too centralized government.

The Federalists overcame these handicaps very skillfully. They won over Hancock by dangling before him the promise of support in his campaign for the governorship or even the vice-presidency. Hancock then took the chair and proposed a number of amendments to the Constitution in order to win over certain moderate Antifederalists. The proposed amendments were of course not mandatory; yet there was some assurance that they would be adopted. This reconciled Sam Adams and several other delegates to ratification. Although the Antifederalists tried to filibuster the convention and later sought to adjourn the meeting without action, these tactics were unsuccessful, and on February 6, 1788, the Constitution was ratified by the narrow vote of 187 to 168.

In Virginia, the support of the Constitution by Washington, Madison, Randolph, and Marshall was offset by the opposition of Patrick Henry, George Mason, and Richard Henry Lee, all of whom had much influence. When the state convention met in June 1788, Patrick Henry at once launched an intemperate attack upon the Constitution, in which he spared no invective in his denunciation of the proposed frame of government. He demanded an investigation of the Federal Convention and even implied that the delegates at Philadelphia had engaged in a criminal conspiracy. He sneered at the Constitution as a bastard hybrid, "so new, it wants a name." He warned that the Constitution would destroy the liberties of the people; aristocracy would give way to monarchy and despotism. Mason attacked the clause guaranteeing the slave trade until 1808, while other delegates feared that the new government would destroy the states once it was set in operation.

Madison met the impassioned pleas of Henry and his followers with quiet reasoned arguments which eventually won over doubters. The Constitution, he admitted, did indeed establish a government difficult of description; it was "partly national, partly federal." The new government did not threaten liberty, however, for it had only specific derived powers, though he implied that he had no objection to a bill of rights. An effective national government was essential to the protection of liberty, and Madison made it clear that the greater danger of despotism arose out of the deficiencies of the present system.

As in Massachusetts, the technique of offering proposals for amendments to appease the moderate Antifederalists was successful, and Virginia ratified the Constitution on June 25, by the close vote of 89 to 79. Forty suggested amendments accompanied ratification. Earlier in the month New Hampshire had also ratified, so that with ratification by ten states the adoption of the Constitution was now assured.

New York was another state in which ratification was secured only after a long fight and by the narrowest of majorities. Governor George Clinton, an Antifederalist, refused to convene the legislature in special session to consider a convention, and not until the regular session in February 1788 did the assembly call for the election of delegates. This election the Antifederalists won by an impressive majority, so that when the convention met, forty-six of the delegates were supposedly hostile to the Constitution while but nineteen favored adoption.

The convention assembled in June. Since over two-thirds of the delegates were Antifederalists, it appeared that ratification of the Constitution was destined for speedy defeat. Robert Livingston, John Lansing, and Governor Clinton,[1] representatives of the local aristocracy who feared the effect of the Constitution upon the state's revenue system, led the opposition. Hamilton, an ardent champion of ratification, was known to regard the Constitution as defective and to favor adoption only because the document was the best available under the circumstances. Yet the skill of Hamilton in debate and the news that Virginia and New Hampshire had ratified eventually carried the day. A portion of the opposition was at length won over under the promise of conciliatory amendments. A proposal was made to make ratification conditional upon adoption of a large number of concomitant amendments, with the specification that the state would quit the union if the amendments were not adopted within a certain time; but this proposal was defeated. The convention then adopted the Constitution unconditionally by a vote of 30 to 27, although, as a conciliatory gesture toward the Antifederalists, a resolution proposing a second constitutional convention was adopted unanimously.

By late July, only North Carolina and Rhode Island had failed to ratify the Constitution. The North Carolina convention did not meet until July 4, when ten states had already ratified. Probably because of the predominance of the rural and frontier elements in the state, an overwhelming majority of the delegates were Antifederalists. They did not reject the Constitution outright, but in-

---

[1] Governor Clinton served as president of the convention.

stead refused, 184 to 83, to ratify until a long list of proposed amendments were adopted. No other action was taken by the state until November 1789, when, with the new federal government already functioning, a second convention met and ratified the Constitution without serious opposition, 195 to 77.

In Rhode Island the paper-money faction in control of the state legislature continued to refuse to call a convention. Instead, it submitted the Constitution to a vote of the town meetings, where it was overwhelmingly defeated, the Federalists refusing to vote. In 1790 the paper-money faction lost control of the state legislature to the conservatives. The new assembly promptly called a convention which on May 29, 1790, ratified the Constitution by the narrow margin of 34 to 32.

REASONS FOR RATIFICATION

The triumph of the Federalists was due in part to the superiority of their arguments, in part to the tactical strength of their position in the ratification conflict.

The Federalists had the advantage of a positive program. They stood in the position of offering the country a remedy for the many ills besetting the nation. They freely admitted many of the shortcomings of the Constitution; and many leading proponents of adoption, among them Washington and Hamilton, were known to regard it as far from perfect as a frame of government. Yet the Federalists could truthfully say that it was the best available remedy for the obvious evils of the Confederation and that it was the most perfect instrument of government that the best minds of the nation working over a period of several months had been able to devise. If the opponents of the Constitution brought about its rejection, responsibility would be theirs for the chaos and disunion to follow.

Everywhere the proponents of ratification drew a terrifying picture of the results of rejection: monetary chaos and national bankruptcy, division of the Confederation into three or more separate nations, civil war, reconquest of the separate states by Britain or some other foreign power. It was because the Antifederalists could not answer such arguments, because they had no remedy except the feeble demand for amendment of the Articles of Confederation or the calling of another convention, that their position was gradually weakened and undermined.

The method by which the state constitutional conventions were elected also favored the Federalists. The delegates were elected from the existing legislative districts in the same proportion and on the same basis as were delegates to the state legislatures. The back country and the frontier had for decades been notoriously underrepresented in most of the assemblies. Reforms coincident with the Revolution had worked some increase in the representation of the back country; yet in 1788 it was still true that state legislatures were controlled by the tidewater, which had many more delegates than they were entitled to on the basis of population. Hence the proponents of ratification, most of them from the tidewater, were in a much stronger position than public sentiment probably warranted. Overrepresentation of the tidewater was an important if not decisive factor in the triumph of the Constitution.

Suffrage requirements for the election of delegates to the convention were also such as to disqualify the landless and propertyless groups among whom sentiment against the Constitution was strong. Again, this was true simply because in every state except New York suffrage requirements duplicated those for ordinary state elections, in which persons of no property were for the most part disfranchised. Many of these people—artisans, squatter-farmers, and debtors, would have opposed adoption, but they were without influence in the choice of delegates simply because they could not vote.

The Constitution nonetheless was adopted by a process as democratic as any available at that time—certainly more democratic than that by which either the Declaration of Independence or the Articles of Confederation were adopted—and its ratification probably reflected popular will more accurately than did either of those two documents. It has sometimes been said that the Constitution would have been rejected had it been submitted directly to a referendum vote of the people in all the states, on a basis of free white male suffrage such as came to prevail some forty years later. The narrow margin by which the Constitution was adopted in four states plus the underrepresentation or disfranchisement of substantial elements presumably opposed to adoption lends some support to this contention. Probably not more than three per cent of the male population actually balloted upon the choice of delegates to the various state conventions. Yet this was due not only to the suffrage system, but also to the fact that only a small portion, seldom more than a fourth, of the population who were qualified to vote actually took the trouble to do so. Apparently the great question before the nation was greeted with apathy and indifference by many people. Circumstances of this kind make it extremely difficult to make any absolute statement as to whether or not the Constitution would have received a majority in a direct referendum based on universal suffrage. In 1788, indeed, the idea of a mass democratic popular majority had hardly been entertained.

THE VENERATION OF THE CONSTITUTION

Although the battle over ratification was strenuous, all serious controversy over the Constitution ceased abruptly once it had been adopted. The enemies of ratification, if not convinced, were at least silent. If a few men, like Patrick Henry, sulked in their tents, their attitude did not seriously affect the steady growth of an effective sentiment in favor of the new instrument. Before a decade had passed, the Constitution, from being an object of partisan contention, became one of veneration. The new political parties, Federalists and Jeffersonians, which rose in the early years of the Republic, vied with one another in their expressions of respect for the supreme law. Men might differ as to the true meaning of the basic document; they might even come to blows over the nature of the government it erected; but the Constitution itself in time became sacrosanct.

As a common symbol of American patriotism and nationality, the Constitution eventually came to occupy a position rivaled only by the Declaration of Independence and in after years by Lincoln's Gettysburg Address. The men who had drafted it were honored as the Founding Fathers, and their achievement was celebrated as one of the great events in the nation's history. When George Bancroft in the mid-nineteenth century wrote of the Constitution, he treated the Convention's work as a culmination of the entire development of all preceding civilizations up to that time. To him, as to other Americans, the hand of God was clearly visible in the background. Although the men who drafted the Constitution had known little and believed less of the dogma of democracy, by Jackson's time the Constitution was regarded as a principal bulwark of a democratic state. In short, veneration of the Constitution became an integral part of popular political thought.

Why did this happen? One explanation lies in the relative absence of visible common symbols of sovereignty and national unity in American life. In England the king is the great symbol of political unity, above party and class, commanding the common loyalty of all Englishmen. The majesty of his position and the ceremony and trappings with which he has been surrounded are visible symbols of the tremendous authority of the state of which he is the ceremonial head. The Constitution gave America no king. Even great political leaders do not stand above partisan hatred during their lives; only after death may they become common symbols of unity. The Constitution, it may be said, is America's uncrowned king. It is above party, a common object of veneration, a living symbol of national unity.

Doubtless it was because of the pinnacle of veneration to which historians and Americans in general had lifted the Constitution that a somewhat different interpretation of the place of the Constitution in the nation's history produced a strong popular and professional reaction. In 1913, Professor Charles A. Beard published his now famous *Economic Interpretation of the Constitution of the United States*. Briefly, his thesis was that the Constitution was the work of a particular economic elite, which he labeled the "personalty," because their wealth was represented by "paper": merchants, wealthy lawyers, western land speculators, public bondholders and moneyed creditors generally. These men, Beard argued, wrote a Constitution which reflected their peculiar interests and then drove the document through to ratification over the opposition of the "realty"—the small farmer and planter class.

Beard offered several pieces of evidence in support of his argument. Many delegates, he demonstrated, were wealthy lawyers, planters, or merchants; many were substantial Confederation bondholders; others held large blocks of land in the western domain. The Constitution, Beard argued, directly reflected the interests of these groups. He cited the clause prohibiting the states from coining money or emitting bills of credit, or impairing the obligations of contracts, obviously aimed at the paper money issues and stay-laws then prevalent in many states. The provisions giving the national government control over money and credit and guaranteeing the national debt, he pointed out, were of obvious benefit to the creditor class.

Beard's thesis has recently come under severe attack from several scholars, who have argued with some success that his evidence does not support his conclusions. Several of the most prominent nationalists in the Convention, among them Madison himself, owned no bonds, western lands, or other substantial "personalty," while many others held only insignificant amounts. By contrast, several states' rights men or delegates who later fought ratification of the Constitution, notably Luther Martin and Elbridge Gerry, held very large blocks of "personalty."

Quite naturally, however, the delegates were drawn from the dominant social groups in the various states, for the idea of mass participation in government had not yet been born. The Convention's personnel was not in the least aristocratic beyond the average political gathering of the time. The same general group of men had written the Declaration of Independence, the Articles of Confederation, and the state constitutions, documents neither more nor less aristocratic than the Constitution of 1787.

Moreover, the Constitution must be judged by the political and social standards of the late eighteenth century, rather than by those of twentieth-century democratic liberalism. It was certainly as liberal a document as the state constitutions then drafted, and in some respects more so. The popular base of representation in the House was made identical with that in the various states, while the Senate merely continued the system of state representation prevailing under the Articles of Confederation. The electoral college was a cumbersome mechanism, but it was the result of compromise, not of attempts at aristocracy, and it opened the way for potential election of the President virtually by popular election, a fact well understood by some delegates.

The Constitution forbade religious tests or qualifications for office, banned titles of nobility, and laid down a very narrow definition of treason, all exceedingly liberal provisions by eighteenth-century standards. It incorporated certain of the traditional guarantees of English civil liberty, forbidding the states and federal government alike to pass bills of attainder and ex post facto laws and guaranteeing the federal writ of habeas corpus against suspension except when rebellion or emergency made such suspension necessary. Even the property guarantees were of a moderate character and were not at all designed merely to keep a landed or mercantile aristocracy in power. Most of them, that guaranteeing the national debt, for example, would be regarded as acceptable and even necessary in a constitution drafted today. The Constitution was in fact a sufficiently progressive frame of government so that, although penned in a day when the democratic ideal was as yet little known, it was able to provide the framework for a democratic national government of the twentieth century.

THE CONSTITUTION AS A PRODUCT OF EIGHTEENTH-CENTURY POLITICAL IDEAS

Much of the discussion over whether the Constitution was a liberal or democratic document can be put aside with the observation that the Constitution was a product of the Age of Enlightenment and of colonial political philosophy and experience.

The Constitutional Convention was an expression of the Enlightenment's abiding faith in the supremacy of reason. Man was a rational being. It was therefore possible for men of various and conflicting interests to meet together and by discussion, by argument, by the application of reason, solve the problems of the state in a rational manner. This solution could then be embodied in a compact based upon the reign of law, simply because it was to the mutual interest of all rational men to accept the most intelligent solution of the problem of government which human reason could devise. The Convention inaugurated an era of formal constitution-making; the French Revolutionists and early nineteenth-century European liberals were also to engage in the same practice with the same implicit faith in the supremacy of reason.

The Constitution gave recognition to several ideas of colonial and Revolutionary political philosophy: the compact theory of the state, the notion of a written constitution, the conception of constitutional supremacy and limited legislative capacity, the doctrine of natural rights, and the separation of powers. As a formal compact setting up government, the Constitution's antecedents ran back to the Mayflower Compact, the Fundamental Orders of Connecticut, the great natural-law philosophers, and the state constitutions of the Revolutionary era. As a written document, the Constitution reflected the late colonial and Revolutionary belief that the compact ought to be a written one. The notion of constitutional supremacy was also recognized; the Constitution was made supreme law, controlling state law and by implication federal law as well. Federal legislative capacity was strictly defined and enumerated; by implication it was limited to the express terms of the grant. Although the Constitution contained no separate bill of rights, certain natural rights were specifically guaranteed against invasion in the clauses prohibiting ex post facto laws and bills of attainder and guaranteeing the writ of habeas corpus. The doctrine of the separation of powers was implied in the Constitution's organization and content, legislative, executive, and judicial powers being granted separately in three different articles.

The powers granted the new government reflected in part American experience with federalism under the British Empire and the Articles of Confederation, in part the Enlightenment belief in the negative state. The scope of federal authority was essentially the same as that of the central governments under the old British Empire and under the Articles of Confederation. Experience had taught the statesmen of the Revolutionary era that a central government could not function effectively without the right to tax and to regulate commerce, and they now added these items to the grant of federal authority. Yet the federal government was still conceived of as having few other functions than the maintenance of peace against external and internal disturbance, though for this purpose it was thought that it must also be financially sound and efficient. Even the power over interstate commerce, eventually to become so potent an arm of federal authority, was apparently granted for negative rather than positive reasons—to protect trade from the manifold abuses of state control rather than to make possible extensive regulation by the central government.

The Constitution was thus an expression of eighteenth-century political ideas. It was conceived as the instrument of government in an eighteenth-century agrarian republic of less than four million people. Yet today the document of 1787 functions as supreme law in a twentieth-century state of more than two hundred million people having an urban industrial economy. The success of the Constitution in bridging the gap between the eighteenth and twentieth centuries is due in part to the general soundness of the frame of government provided, but even more it is due to the remarkable growth in the meaning of the Constitution itself. Though nominally a fixed written document, the Constitution began to grow, evolve, and change with the first meeting of Congress, and it has been changing ever since. This process of growth made possible the adaptation of the Constitution as a frame of government for the modern world's first great experiment in democracy; it also preserved the document of 1787 in a twentieth-century society bearing little resemblance to that in which the delegates of 1787 lived and moved.

Chapter

7

Establishing the New Government

THE DOCUMENT drafted at Philadelphia in 1787 provided a sound foundation for subsequent constitutional development, but the actual task of erecting the living structure of government devolved upon successive generations of statesmen and jurists. The ultimate character of the American constitutional system depended as much upon the objectives, methods, and policies of these men as it did upon the provisions of the original Constitution itself.

The decisions made by the statesmen who launched the new government were of especial importance, for the institutions they erected and the policies they inaugurated established precedents that were certain to affect profoundly the entire subsequent development of the constitutional system. Some decisions upon institutions and policy could be made with relative ease, either because the Constitution itself was explicit and clear upon the point in question, or because there was very general agreement among all interests as to what ought to be done. Other issues, however, gave rise to extended controversy, either because the Constitution was vague or silent upon the matter at hand, or because the question seriously affected the political or economic welfare of one or more sectional or class interests in the nation. Out of these controversies, there emerged many of those institutions and policies and practices which came to make up the living organism of government.

LAUNCHING THE NEW GOVERNMENT

In September 1788, after eleven states had ratified the Constitution, the Confederation Congress designated the first Wednesday of the following January for the selection of presidential electors, the first Wednesday in February for the casting of the electoral vote, and the first Wednesday in March (March 4) for the inauguration of the new government. The Constitution had left the method of selecting presidential electors to the state legislatures. In the first election the states accordingly chose their electors in a variety of ways, some by popular election on a general ticket, some by popular district election, and some by legislative vote. This lack of uniform electoral procedure was to continue for several elections, and it was not until after 1860 that the choice of electors on a general ticket became universal.

When the electoral vote was counted, George Washington was found to have received one of the two votes cast by every elector. This unanimity was not caused by any party mechanism, for political parties had not yet developed; rather, it was ascribable to a general sentiment that Washington was the new nation's transcendent leader and the logical choice for the presidency. The electors scattered their other ballots among a half-dozen candidates. John Adams received the second highest number of electoral votes and thereby became Vice-President.

Meanwhile the various states held elections for members of the House of Representatives, and the state legislatures chose their senators. A large majority of the successful candidates for both houses had actively supported ratification of the new Constitution, although a few opponents of ratification won seats. The success of the Federalists was due in part to the prestige these men had gained through sponsorship of the Constitution and to the discomfiture of the Constitution's opponents, and in part to the fact that the Constitution's champions were vitally interested in the successful operation of the new government and hence sought office in greater numbers than did the Antifederalists.

The first Congress was thus decidedly more nationalistic than the Constitutional Convention had been; furthermore, President Washington and Alexander Hamilton, who shortly became Washington's principal adviser, were also proponents of strong central government. This situation resulted in a persistently nationalistic interpretation of the Constitution during the early years of the new government. Those conflicts between nationalism and localism which the Convention had left unresolved were usually settled in favor of the champions of nationalism. Thus the first Congress, assisted by the executive, supplemented and strengthened the handiwork of the nationalists in the late Convention.

Congress, meeting in New York by direction of the Confederation Congress, did not obtain a quorum in both houses until early in April. The two chambers then organized for business, a task involving the appointment of the few necessary officers and the delineation of rules of procedure. Legislative progress was somewhat delayed in the first Congress by the entire absence of systematic rules of procedure and by the fear of establishing undesirable precedents or of giving some agency too much power.

The Committee of the Whole, in which the entire chamber sat as a committee, very soon assumed a position of outstanding importance in procedure, particularly in the House of Representatives. The relatively small membership of the two houses, the successful experience with a like committee in the Virginia legislature and in the Philadelphia Convention, and the need for informal debate, all encouraged the use of the committee. When important legislation was under consideration, the Committee of the Whole usually worked out the general principles of the projected statute and then submitted its findings to a select committee to settle remaining details and to draft a bill. Standing committees were very seldom employed in the early sessions of Congress. For assistance in framing a measure the select committee usually relied heavily upon the head of the executive department most directly concerned, so that the bill reported actually was the result of co-operation between executive and legislature. Following the select committee's report, the House debated the measure anew, accepted or rejected proposed amendments, and put the bill to a final vote. If the proposed law passed, it went to the other house.

Because of the important place held by department heads in lawmaking, the first Congress seriously considered giving chief administrative officers the right to participate in debates on the floor. Had this step been taken it might have stimulated the development of a parliamentary system of ministerial responsibility in the relations between executive and legislature. Though certain members ardently supported the idea, it was defeated after some discussion.

In early sessions of Congress, the House of Representatives assumed a position of considerably more importance than the Senate. Most important legislation was initiated in the lower chamber, the Senate functioning mainly as a body for modification and revision. The House was regarded as representing the people directly, an attitude attributable in part to the fact that until 1794 the Senate held its legislative as well as its executive sessions behind closed doors.

ORGANIZATION OF THE EXECUTIVE DEPARTMENT

Among the first statutes enacted by Congress were laws providing for the establishment of three executive departments—the State, Treasury, and War departments. The Constitution made no direct provision for administrative departments. Congress thus had a large measure of discretion in the matter, though the system of administrative departments evolved in the later Confederation period was available as a precedent. James Madison, now a member of the House of Representatives, took a prominent part in formulating the statutes providing for the establishment of departments, as he did for much of the other legislation passed by the First Congress.

Madison's proposal of May 1789 to create a Department of Foreign Affairs precipitated a prolonged debate on the President's removal power. The bill expressly granted the President the right to remove the head of the prospective department. The Constitution was silent on the removal power, an omission which was to open the way for a century and a half of intermittent controversy on the question. Some congressmen now opposed the provision in Madison's bill on the grounds that the Senate, being associated with the President in appointments, was by implication properly associated with him in removals as well. Others contended that the removal power was an inherent part of the executive prerogative and a proper means of implementing the President's duty to take care that the laws be faithfully executed; hence, they held, the President could properly make removals without the Senate's consent. Still others argued that the Constitution permitted Congress to locate the removal power according to its judgment. The bill in question was finally phrased so as to imply that the power of removal had already been lodged in the President by the Convention. While this precedent was for a time generally followed in subsequent legislation, the question of the removal power arose again during the administrations of Jackson and Johnson and in the twentieth century.[1]

In the debate on the bill creating a Treasury Department an argument arose over whether a single individual or a board of commissioners should be placed at its head. Elbridge Gerry, who as a delegate from Massachusetts had sat in the Constitutional Convention, argued that the Treasury's duties were too arduous and important to be conferred upon a single individual. Although the House decided against him, Congress nonetheless took the precaution of surrounding the secretary with a comptroller, an auditor, a treasurer, and a register, thereby providing adequate safeguards against unauthorized payments.

Congress also took deliberate steps to make the Secretary of the Treasury responsible to Congress as well as to the President. The Secretary was required from time to time to make reports and "give information to either branch of the legislature, in person or in writing (as may be required), respecting all matters referred to him by the Senate or the House of Representatives, or which shall appertain to his office; and generally shall perform all such services relative to the finances, as he shall be directed to perform." Thus, while Congress made the heads of other departments subordinates of the President, it made the Secretary of the Treasury, primarily at least, its own agent to execute its constitutional powers in the field of finance.

Here again was an important move toward ministerial responsibility and parliamentary government. The basic proposition implied in the Treasury Act was that Congress could constitutionally make an executive department responsible to itself rather than to the President. Subsequent developments, however, were to arrest the trend toward ministerial responsibility.

The creation of other departments involved no major controversies. The War Department received supervision over both military and naval affairs, an arrangement continued until 1798, when the quasi-war with France led to the establishment of a separate Navy Department. The Judiciary Act of 1789 provided for an Attorney General, whose chief duties were to prosecute cases for the United States before the Supreme Court and to give legal advice to the President and the heads of departments. Although he did not become the official head of a department until 1870, he became

---

[1] For later controversies involving the removal power, see the discussion on pp. 319–321, 443–448, 675–677.

immediately a principal executive officer and presidential adviser. The post office was organized on an annual basis until 1794, when it was given permanent standing; not until 1829, however, did the Postmaster General become a regular cabinet member.

A proposal of August 1789 to create a Home Department failed because of the implied invasion of state authority; instead, Congress altered the name of the Department of Foreign Affairs to the Department of State, a title general enough to cover a variety of small additional duties then assigned to the department—among them the custody of public records and correspondence with the states.

THE JUDICIARY ACT OF 1789

No law enacted by the first session of Congress was of greater importance than the Judiciary Act of September 24, 1789, which incorporated the principle of national supremacy into the federal judicial system. The act was largely the work of a Senate committee dominated by staunch Federalists, with Oliver Ellsworth of Connecticut taking the leading role. It provided for a Supreme Court consisting of a Chief Justice and five associate justices, for thirteen federal district courts of one judge each—one district for each of the eleven existing states and two additional districts, in Virginia and Massachusetts, for Kentucky and Maine—and for three circuit courts, each composed of two justices of the Supreme Court sitting in conjunction with one district court judge. The jurisdiction of the various courts was stated in great detail, and to a lesser degree their organization and procedure were set forth in detail. Although this arrangement constituted a victory for those who advocated a complete system of federal courts, state courts were given concurrent jurisdiction in certain cases involving federal law. Thus the state courts became a part of the judicial system of the United States.

Section 25 of the act, a tremendous victory for the principle of national sovereignty, provided in certain instances for appeals from state courts to the federal judiciary. Under this section, appeals could be taken to the United States Supreme Court whenever the highest state court having jurisdiction of a case (1) ruled against the constitutionality of a federal treaty or law; (2) ruled in favor of the validity of a state act which had been challenged as contrary to the Constitution, treaties, or laws of the United States; or (3) ruled against a right or privilege claimed under the Constitution or fed-

eral law. In effect, this meant that appeals would be taken in all instances where the state judiciary assertedly failed to give full recognition to the supremacy of the Constitution, or to the treaties and
laws of the United States, as provided by Article VI of the Constitution.

This provision, which solved the problem of conflicts between
state and national spheres of authority, was to become the very
heart of the American federal system of government. If the Constitution and federal laws and treaties were to be "the supreme Law
of the Land," it was vital that they be upheld against state law and
that they be interpreted with reasonable uniformity. Unless the Supreme Court were given authority to review the decisions of state
courts in disputes between the states and the federal government
over their respective powers, it would be possible for state courts
practically to nullify federal authority, just as state legislatures had
virtually nullified the authority of Congress under the Confederation. Therefore the nationalists insisted that the Supreme Court
must be the final interpreter of the Constitution and as such must
have the right to receive appeals from state courts.

The Constitutional Convention had not specifically provided for
appeals from state to federal courts, but Ellsworth and the other
nationalists of Congress boldly assumed the right to be implied in
the Constitution. In 1789 and for many years afterward, the critics
of Section 25 of the Judiciary Act claimed that the Constitution
specifically placed the responsibility for upholding federal supremacy upon the state courts and that Congress had no authority
to subject their decisions to review by the Supreme Court of the
United States. This opposition was motivated by the fear that the
state judiciaries and state powers would be gradually absorbed by
federal authority, a fear that made it almost impossible for this
group to see the necessity for the uniform upholding of federal
supremacy throughout the Union.

In view of its later importance, it should be noted that the power
of the Supreme Court to determine with finality the constitutionality of acts of Congress was not specifically recognized in the Judiciary Act of 1789. It might have been considered as implied, however, since decisions of state courts involving the constitutional construction of acts of Congress might be appealed to the Supreme
Court and there presumably either affirmed or reversed. But to
go beyond this implication was apparently considered either
unnecessary or politically inexpedient at the time.

THE BILL OF RIGHTS

It will be recalled that during the contest over adoption of the Constitution, ratification had been won in several states through the technique of promising a series of constitutional amendments embodying a bill of rights. Many men in the First Congress now felt that the national government was under a moral obligation to fulfill these promises. Moreover, advocates of amendments believed that many persons still lukewarm or unfriendly to the new government might be won over should such amendments be adopted. One of the very few specific recommendations made by President Washington in his inaugural address was that Congress should give careful attention to the demand for these amendments.

In Congress, Madison took the initiative in advocating amendments, co-ordinating the suggestions of the state ratifying conventions and introducing them in the House. Although a majority of his colleagues supported this move, a few conservative nationalists, notably Fisher Ames of Massachusetts and Roger Sherman of Connecticut, opposed it as unnecessary and unwise. Since the federal government was one of enumerated powers, they said, the Constitution did not endanger the rights of the people, and it should be given a fair trial before attempts were made to amend it. On the other hand, certain champions of states' rights, among them Elbridge Gerry of Massachusetts and Thomas Tucker of South Carolina, were determined to add amendments protecting both citizens and the states against federal power. The partial victory of the nationalists is evident in the substantial curtailment of the amendments originally proposed.

Madison's proposal was not to add the amendments in a body at the end of the Constitution but to incorporate them in their proper places in the text by changes, omissions, and additions. Although this plan was later abandoned, it was at first agreed to by the House. The most numerous changes were to be additional limitations upon the power of Congress over citizens, to follow the clause in Article I, Section 9, prohibiting bills of attainder. By the proposed amendments, Congress was to be prohibited from abridging the freedom of religion, of speech, of the press, of assembly, of petition, or of bearing arms; and federal authority was closely restricted in quartering troops, in prosecuting citizens for crimes, and in inflicting punishments. Out of these proposals grew the first five and the Eighth and Ninth amendments. Extensive changes designed to guarantee to the citizen more fully a fair trial by a jury in his own district and the benefits of the common law were also proposed for Article III, Section 2, of the Constitution. These proposals eventually became the Sixth and Seventh amendments.

The proposed amendments were debated at length in both houses, several additions, alterations, and eliminations being made. The House at first agreed to add to the Constitution's preamble a statement reminiscent of the Declaration of Independence to the effect that government was intended for the benefit of the people and was derived from their authority alone, but this plan was eventually dropped on the grounds that the phrase "We the People" was sufficient evidence and proof of the popular basis of the Constitution.

Some of the ardent states' rights advocates also attempted to add to the proposed amendment guaranteeing the rights of assembly and petition a phrase guaranteeing the right of the people to instruct their congressmen on public questions. A combination of moderate and extreme Federalists, alleging that this proposal would undermine the representative and deliberative character of Congress by subjecting its members to direct popular control, succeeded in defeating the move.

The Senate, even more conservative than the House, killed several other suggestions, among them a clause exempting conscientious objectors from compulsory military service, an article specifically prohibiting any of the three departments of the federal government from exercising powers vested in the other two, and a limitation upon the states' police power proposed by the House, that "no State shall infringe the right of trial by jury in criminal cases, nor the rights of conscience, nor the freedom of speech or of the press."

One of the most significant events in the course of the debate was the failure of the states' rights advocates in their attempts to alter the proposal that was to become the Tenth Amendment so as to limit the federal government to those powers "expressly" delegated by the Constitution. This move was blocked by Madison and other moderates as well as the nationalists, all of whom believed that in any effective government "powers must necessarily be admitted by implication." In later years, however, extreme strict constructionists, adhering to a narrowly circumscribed conception of federal powers, were frequently but incorrectly to insist that the Tenth Amendment had made implied federal powers illegal.

In September 1789, Congress submitted twelve proposed amendments to the states. But before they were ratified by the existing states, the number of states in the Union increased from eleven to fourteen through the ratification of the Constitution by North Carolina and Rhode Island and the admission in 1791 of Vermont to the Union. Ratification by eleven states was therefore necessary. During the two years from 1789 to 1791 various states took favorable action on all or most of the amendments, and in November 1791 Virginia's vote made ten of the amendments part of the Constitution, although Massachusetts, Connecticut, and Georgia failed to ratify them. The first two proposals, one providing that there should be not less than one representative in the lower house for every fifty thousand persons, and another postponing the effect of any alteration in the compensation of Senators and Representatives until an election had intervened, failed to secure favorable action by the necessary number of states and thus were defeated.

The ten amendments adopted worked no real alteration in federal power. They gave formal recognition to certain traditionally accepted "natural rights," hitherto incorporated in the great English charters, colonial grants, and state bills of rights. They took no substantive powers from Congress which could reasonably have been implied before the amendments had been passed, and most of the procedural limitations, trial by jury and the like, probably would have been taken for granted in any event. Only gradually did there emerge the now almost universal conception of the first ten amendments as a great Bill of Rights.

THE HAMILTONIAN PROGRAM

In 1790, the national government having been safely organized, Alexander Hamilton, now Washington's closest adviser, launched an extensive financial program, conceived in the interests of conservative mercantilistic nationalism.

Though not an aristocrat in origin, Hamilton soon became the national spokesman for those of wealth and standing, and the resourceful leader of what he hoped would become a national aristocracy. He neither understood nor sympathized with the great mass of people of little or no property; he simply attributed their condition to their incapacity and indolence. While he recognized that it was perhaps impolitic to exclude the masses from all political activity, he had a strong conviction that control of government should be lodged securely in the hands of the manufacturing, commercial, and landed aristocracies.

Hamilton therefore favored an efficient, coercive, and highly centralized state, which would foster commerce, manufacturing, and capitalistic development. Since he considered self-interest to be the mainspring of human conduct, he was confident that such a program would give the aristocracy a definite interest in the new federal government and thereby assure its ultimate stability and success.

Hamilton's opportunity came when Congress asked him to submit a report on the public credit. In reply, Hamilton in 1790 and 1791 made a series of reports embodying a number of proposals calculated to place federal finances upon a sound basis and to enhance the public credit both at home and abroad. He believed that a properly funded national debt would add to the stability of the government and would provide the equivalent of money for major private business transactions. He recommended that the national government refund the outstanding Confederation debt at face value, assume and refund the unpaid debts contracted by the several states to carry on the Revolutionary War, charter a national bank to assist in handling the government's monetary and financial problems, and enact a protective tariff law.

There was comparatively little opposition to the refunding of the national debt, which was guaranteed by the Constitution itself. However, certain congressmen did object to paying the old obligations off at face value, a step which they argued would redound to the advantage of the speculator class. And the states' rights faction attacked the assumption of state debts by the federal government as a scheme to consolidate national authority at the expense of the states. The Virginia legislature adopted a resolution declaring assumption to be both dangerous to the states and repugnant to the Constitution. Representatives from states which had already paid off a large part of their debts also objected to assumption as inequitable. Hamilton nonetheless carried his proposal through Congress with the aid of a political bargain by which certain Southern members voted for assumption in return for some Northern support for a bill to locate the future national capital on the Potomac River.

Hamilton's proposal to charter a national bank was severely attacked in Congress on constitutional grounds. The opposition was led by Madison, who was becoming increasingly hostile to Hamilton's program. Although the two men had supported strong national government in the Convention and had worked together to secure ratification of the Constitution, neither their constitutional philosophies nor their economic interests were harmonious. Hamilton wished to push still further in the direction of a powerful central government, while Madison, now conscious of the economic implications of Hamilton's program and aware of the hostility which the drift toward nationalism had aroused in his own section of the country, favored a middle course between nationalism and states' rights.

In the Constitutional Convention Madison had proposed that Congress be empowered to "grant charters of incorporation," but the delegates had rejected his suggestion. In view of this action, he now believed that to assume that the power of incorporation could rightfully be implied either from the power to borrow money or from the "necessary and proper" clause in Article I, Section 8, would be an unwarranted and dangerous precedent.

In February 1791, the bank bill was passed by Congress, but President Washington, who still considered himself a sort of mediator between conflicting factions, wished to be certain of its constitutionality before signing it. Among others Jefferson was asked for his view, which in turn was submitted to Hamilton for rebuttal.

In a strong argument Jefferson advocated the doctrine of strict construction and maintained that the bank bill was unconstitutional. Taking as his premise the Tenth Amendment (which had not yet become a part of the Constitution), he contended that the incorporation of a bank was neither an enumerated power of Congress nor a part of any granted power, and that implied powers were inadmissible.

He further denied that authority to establish a bank could be derived either from the "general welfare" or the "necessary and proper" clause. The constitutional clause granting Congress power to impose taxes for the "general welfare" was not of all-inclusive scope, he said, but was merely a general statement to indicate the sum of the enumerated powers of Congress. In short, the "general welfare" clause did not even convey the power to appropriate for the general welfare but merely the right to appropriate pursuant to the enumerated powers of Congress.

With reference to the clause empowering Congress to make all laws necessary and proper for carrying into execution the enumerated powers, Jefferson emphasized the word "necessary," and argued that the means employed to carry out the delegated powers must be indispensable and not merely "convenient." Consequently the Constitution, he said, restrained Congress "to those means without which the grant of power would be nugatory." Later as President, however, Jefferson was to become aware that those charged with the responsibility of the federal government must have some discretionary authority in the choice of means to perform its function.

In rebuttal Hamilton presented what was to become the classic exposition of the doctrine of the broad construction of federal powers under the Constitution. He claimed for Congress two kinds of powers in addition to those expressly enumerated in the Constitution, resultant and implied powers. Resultant powers were those resulting from the powers that had been granted to the government, such as the right of the United States to possess sovereign jurisdiction over conquered territory. Implied powers, upon which Hamilton placed his chief reliance, were those derived from the "necessary and proper" clause. He rejected the doctrine that the Constitution restricted Congress to those means which are absolutely indispensable. According to his interpretation, "necessary often means no more than needful, requisite, incidental, useful, or conducive to. . . . The degree in which a measure is necessary, can never be a test of the legal right to adopt it; that must be a matter of opinion, and can only be a test of expediency."

Then followed Hamilton's famous test for determining the constitutionality of a proposed act of Congress: "This criterion is the *end*, to which the measure relates as a *mean*. If the *end* be clearly comprehended within any of the specified powers, and if the measure have an obvious relation to that *end*, and is not forbidden by any particular provision of the Constitution, it may safely be deemed to come within the compass of the national authority." This conception of implied powers was later to be adopted by John Marshall and incorporated in the Supreme Court's opinion in *McCulloch v. Maryland* on the constitutionality of the second national bank.

Hamilton had his way and the national bank was established. It served well most of the purposes he had outlined for it and in addition proved to be a decided boon to the nation's financial and commercial interests. Eventually also his broad interpretation of the scope of the authority of the central government was to be acquiesced in by practically all political and sectional groups. Before that time arrived, however, there were to be almost interminable debates and controversies over such an interpretation of the Constitution—controversies involving nullification, secession, civil war, and virtual congressional dictatorship.

In his report on manufactures, Hamilton presented a powerful argument for a protective tariff for certain industries, as a means of attaining a proper balance between agriculture, commerce, and manufacturing, and a prosperous and expanding economy. Since the protection of industry was not an enumerated power of Congress, the authority for such action had to rest again upon the doctrine of implied powers. Although Hamilton's recommendation to Congress was adopted in only a modified form, the opposition to the protective tariff was based more upon policy than upon alleged unconstitutionality. Many times in later years, however, the constitutionality of the protective tariff was to be attacked with strong argument, although never with complete success.

THE TEST OF FEDERAL COERCIVE POWER

One of the basic difficulties of the Confederation period had been the lack of any coercive power on the part of the central government against either states or individuals. It will be recalled that the Constitutional Convention had considered and later abandoned a proposal to give the new government the right to coerce the states, largely on the ground that the government would function directly upon individuals and that coercion of states would therefore be irrelevant and unnecessary. This in turn, however, implied that the national government would have the right to coerce individuals who resisted its lawful authority. In line with this assumption the Convention had in fact empowered Congress "to provide for calling forth the Militia to execute the Laws of the Union, suppress Insurrections and repel Invasions."

The first occasion for the exercise of this vital authority came in the so-called Whisky Rebellion of 1794. In 1790 Congress, as a part of its new revenue program, had levied a direct excise tax upon whisky. The tax was very much resented in the frontier regions of the middle and southern states, for whisky was the frontiersman's principal medium for marketing his surplus grain. A considerable majority of westerners had been opposed to the adoption of the Constitution, and they did not now appreciate the necessity for an effective federal revenue program. The law therefore aroused much political unrest in western regions, where farmers, spurred on by antiadministration politicians, held meetings of protest and threatened forcibly to block the execution of the excise law.

Alarmed by frontier unrest and eager to assert national authority, the Federalist-controlled Congress on May 2, 1792, enacted a law authorizing the President to call out the militia in case an insurrection occurred against federal authority or in case a state, threatened by internal disorder beyond its control, called for federal aid. Although there were sharp divisions both in Congress and among the people over the expediency of such an enforcement measure, all factions were agreed that the employment of military power should be unequivocally subordinated to the processes of civil government. The act therefore provided that the militia were to be employed only when "the laws of the United States shall be opposed, or the execution thereof obstructed, in any state, by combinations too powerful to be suppressed by the ordinary course of judicial proceedings, or by the powers vested in the marshals." Even then the President was required first to issue a proclamation warning the insurrectionists to disperse peaceably.

Meanwhile, although Congress lowered somewhat the whisky tax as a concession to western sentiment, resistance in western Pennsylvania became more and more extreme. In 1794 it took on an organized character and threatened to result in a serious breakdown of the federal revenue laws.

Spurred on by Hamilton, Washington now determined to seize this occasion to demonstrate the strength and sovereignty of the national government before the decentralizing effects of frontier provincialism should undermine the federal constitutional system. On August 7, 1794, Washington therefore issued a proclamation in accordance with the Act of 1792, commanding all insurgents to submit to federal authority by September 1. When they failed to do so in the required time, he proceeded to call out 13,000 militiamen from Pennsylvania and near-by states to suppress the insurrection. Though federal military prestige was at the moment suffering from a series of defeats administered by the Indian tribes of the northwest frontier, the necessary troops were raised with but little difficulty, and an expedition was dispatched against the insurgents. The threatened insurrection quickly disintegrated. A few of the leading rebels were arrested and tried for treason; two were convicted but were subsequently pardoned by the President. The whole episode had demonstrated conclusively that the new federal government possessed ample power to enforce its authority over individuals, even recalcitrant ones.

EXECUTIVE RELATIONS WITH CONGRESS

The Constitutional Convention had contemplated a strong executive, who would not only execute federal laws but would also take a prominent part in the formulation of legislation. The Constitution provided several possible instruments for executive leadership in Congress, among them the President's duty to advise Congress on the state of the Union and to "recommend to their Consideration such Measures as he shall judge necessary and expedient," and his veto power. Eventually, also, the appointive power was to become an important device for the control of policy, although it did not develop as such during Washington's time.

In advising Congress on the state of the Union, Washington early adopted the practice of appearing in person before Congress at the opening of each session to review the developments of the preceding year and to recommend matters for congressional consideration. During sessions also he sent special messages, chiefly to provide Congress with information as occasion arose. Although early Congresses followed an elaborate ceremonial in making formal response to the President's annual messages, they did not always accept his recommendations. The annual message was in fact not destined to become a major instrument of executive leadership in Congress.

The veto was also potentially an important instrument for the control of legislative policy, but it too did not become significant in the early national period. Federalist leaders favored the exercise of the veto power as a part of a desirable strong executive. Their opponents, on the other hand, conscious of the unpopularity of the governor's veto power in the colonial era and aware of the weak veto given most state governors, believed that the power should be used very sparingly.

Washington first used the veto in 1791, when he refused his assent to a bill apportioning representation in the House in such a manner that some states would have more than the one representative for every 30,000 inhabitants permissible under the Constitution. The President sympathized with Jefferson's argument that he ought not to refuse his assent to any bill unless he was certain that it was unauthorized by the Constitution. However, in his opinion the bill under consideration was unquestionably unconstitutional, and he finally vetoed it on that ground. While use of the veto in this case aroused little opposition, the veto power was to be used very rarely for a long time. Neither Adams nor Jefferson vetoed a single law, and not until Jackson's time was the veto used to defeat any measure which the President considered objectionable for reasons of policy.

During Washington's first administration, department heads took an active part in advising Congress upon legislative policy, even to the extent of drafting legislation. Hamilton in particular considered himself to be a kind of prime minister, a co-ordinator between Congress and the President. Washington, other department heads, and many members of Congress were at first inclined to accept him as such. The House refused to allow Hamilton to appear before it in person; but by means of written reports, the domination of party caucuses, and the control of congressional committee personnel, the Secretary of the Treasury became for a time the most important person in the government in the determination of legislative policy.

This trend toward executive leadership in Congress was sharply checked during Washington's second term and the Adams administration. The change was due not to an altered conception of the presidency by either incumbent, but to a less favorable response to such leadership from Congress. With the rapid growth and crystallization of the Republican opposition in Congress,[2] Hamilton and his colleagues were faced by 1793 with a hostile majority in the House. Not only did Hamilton's hopes for a premiership disappear but also he was subjected to various attacks in both houses charging him with intruding upon congressional authority and with certain improprieties and actual violations of law.

For several years thereafter, Congress struggled along without any definite or effective leadership. Eventually both houses were to develop standing committees as a means of providing responsible internal leadership, but the early Republicans moved in that direction with hesitation and even with trepidation.

DEVELOPMENT OF THE CABINET

The Constitutional Convention had made no specific provision for an advisory council for the President. The Virginia Plan had provided for a Council of Revision, but this had been proposed primarily as a veto agency and not as a real advisory council, and it had been abandoned without much consideration.

To some extent the finished Constitution implied that the Senate was to be a kind of advisory council to the President. It was given two specific advisory functions—treaty making and the appointment of diplomatic, judicial, and administrative officers. The Sen-

---

[2] For a discussion of the development of the Republican or Jeffersonian Party, see Chapter 8.

ate's small size—before 1796 it had not more than thirty members—and the fact that since colonial times the upper house in certain states had constituted an executive council strengthened the concept of the Senate as a presidential advisory body.

Influenced by this idea, Washington at first assumed that the Senate's advice and consent in treaty making would be obtained by personal consultation between the President and the Senate. In August 1789 he appeared in person with the Secretary of War before the Senate to discuss the terms of a treaty to be negotiated with certain Indian tribes. Washington had the important papers read to the Senators and then asked their advice upon several points in the negotiations and in the treaties. The Senators were embarrassingly hesitant about responding and finally asked that the papers be assigned to a Senate committee for study before they gave their advice and consent. Washington, obviously irritated at this unexpected delay, exclaimed, "This defeats every purpose of my coming here." Though he returned later to conclude the discussion, the inconvenience involved and the lack of responsiveness on the part of the senators discouraged him from repeating the procedure.

Thereafter, both in treaty making and in appointments, the President carried forward negotiations without formally seeking the Senate's advice. Individual senators were often consulted, and very occasionally the Senate was asked for instructions during negotiations. As a rule, however, the President merely submitted finished treaties to the Senate for their acceptance or rejection, and appointments were handled in the same fashion.

The development of a cabinet composed of department heads was both a cause and a result of the failure of the Senate to function effectively as an advisory body. While the cabinet was unknown as of 1789, Washington very early took advantage of the constitutional provision authorizing the President to request written opinions from department heads. Such formal opinions, however, did not satisfy the President's need to discuss problems fully and freely with a small body of trusted advisers.

In 1791 Washington, being personally absent from the capital, suggested that the department heads and the Vice-President should consult together upon any important problems arising during his absence. The resultant conference was in a sense the first cabinet meeting. The following year other consultations were held, and by 1793 regular meetings had become the rule and the term "cabinet" had come into fairly common usage.

The cabinet shortly came to be made up exclusively of men who were personally loyal to the President and in essential agreement with him and with one another upon administration policies. Washington's attempt to draw advice from men of conflicting political philosophy, as he was obliged to do when Jefferson and Hamilton both headed departments, soon proved unsatisfactory, and he became accustomed to accepting Hamilton's opinion in most matters. Jefferson's retirement in 1793 followed as a consequence. This trend was conclusively emphasized in 1795, when Secretary of State Edmund Randolph was forced to resign because of his failure to support Washington's foreign policy. The President's power to remove principal policy-making subordinates, first confirmed by Congress in 1789, was eventually to become an additional important factor in establishing cabinet unity.

The administration of John Adams, who entered the presidency on March 4, 1797, experienced a partial and temporary disintegration of executive unity, largely because Adams retained Washington's cabinet, several members of which were loyal to Hamilton, now a factional rival of the new President. But when Jefferson became President, he formed a cabinet of men who willingly accepted his leadership and strove to carry out his program. Only on rare occasions thereafter were cabinet officers to be much more than the President's subordinates and agents.

The cabinet thus became a reasonably coherent consultative body where the major policies of the administration were discussed and formulated. Because of the extraconstitutional nature of the cabinet the President was not under legal obligation to abide by the vote or decision of his advisers, but as a matter of policy most Presidents have been inclined to do so except in extraordinary cases.

FOREIGN POLICY AND EXECUTIVE PREROGATIVE

The idea of the President as a powerful independent executive capable of initiating policy and controlling events on his own responsibility was strongly reinforced by the exercise of executive policy in foreign affairs during Washington's administration.

At the outbreak of war between France and Britain in 1793, France sent a new minister to the United States, one Edmund Genêt, to obtain this country's co-operation with the French war effort. Genêt came as emissary from the new French Republic, the monarchy having been overturned in 1792 by revolution. His reception by the United States would under international law constitute formal recognition of the new French government, and the question therefore arose as to whether under the Constitution the President was authorized to take this step. The cabinet nonetheless agreed that Washington should receive Genêt, an action which set a precedent for the absorption by the executive of the right to extend recognition to a foreign government.

Though the United States had signed a treaty of alliance with monarchist France in 1778, Washington's cabinet was unanimously of the opinion that the nation ought to remain neutral in the current war. It was accordingly agreed that Washington should issue a proclamation of neutrality, a step shortly taken.

The administration's opponents immediately charged that Washington's proclamation of neutrality had infringed upon the province of Congress, to which the Constitution had assigned the authority to declare war. Hamilton replied by publishing in the press, under the pseudonym of "Pacificus," an elaborate statement of his theory of the strong executive. "If, on the one hand," he concluded, "the Legislature have a right to declare war, it is on the other, the duty of the executive to preserve peace till the declaration is made."

Hamilton then advanced the startling contention that the President possessed an inherent body of executive prerogative, above and beyond those rights and duties specifically mentioned in the Constitution. "The general doctrine of our Constitution, then, is," he asserted, "that the *executive power* of the nation is vested in the President; subject only to the *exceptions* and *qualifications* which are expressed in the instrument." To put it differently, the clause in the Constitution vesting executive authority in the President was itself a general grant of executive power, and the subsequent enumeration of functions was not in any sense all-inclusive. Part of the inherent executive prerogative, Hamilton added, was the general authority to conduct foreign relations and to interpret treaties in their non-judicial aspects.

This broad claim of inherent executive prerogative caused Jefferson and Madison to believe with some reason that Hamilton was contriving to attach to the President powers approximating the royal prerogatives of the British Crown. To Jefferson and his colleagues the executive authority was limited by the specific grants of the Constitution and of laws, and in domestic affairs this concept has since largely prevailed.[3] The Hamiltonian doctrine, however, strongly supported by the hard fact that the executive department is always available and has superior sources of information regard-

---

[3] In 1861 President Lincoln was to assume that the President possessed very broad executive powers to deal with the emergency of an extensive rebellion against national authority. For a discussion of this and related issues see Chapter 16.

ing foreign affairs, has succeeded in giving the President very broad powers in the conduct of foreign relations. This development was to become especially significant in the twentieth century and since 1950 has become a controversial issue among statesmen and scholars.

The phase of the foreign policy of the Washington administration that aroused the bitterest opposition was the treaty drawn up by John Jay with Great Britain in 1794. It provided for the clarification of commercial relationships as well as for an amicable settlement of outstanding differences growing out of the misunderstanding and nonfulfillment of the Treaty of Peace of 1783. Since Britain now occupied an advantageous diplomatic position, most of the terms of the Jay Treaty were more favorable to her than to the United States. The treaty was therefore unpopular in many parts of the country, but the Federalist-dominated Senate in 1795 agreed to all of it except one clause.

Certain provisions in the treaty required appropriations of money before they could be put into effect. This necessitated action by the House of Representatives, where the opponents of the treaty were especially strong. By a considerable majority the House requested the President to furnish that body with a copy of the instructions to Jay and of other documents relative to the treaty. In taking this bold step the House was following the leadership of Albert Gallatin. He insisted that the House had a constitutional right to ask for the papers because its co-operation and sanction were necessary to carry the treaty into full effect and make it an integral part of the law of the land.

Washington, with the approval of his cabinet, refused to comply with this request, on the ground that the papers demanded had no relation to the functions of the House. He also reminded the representatives that the Constitutional Convention had very deliberately assigned the power of making treaties to the President and the Senate, and he insisted that "the boundaries fixed by the Constitution between the different departments should be preserved." The House then disclaimed any part in the treaty-making power but insisted upon its rights to originate all appropriations, even those for treaties, and therefore upon its inherent right to deliberate upon the expediency of carrying the treaty into effect. Washington held to his position and finally, by a very narrow margin, the House acquiesced and voted the necessary appropriation.

The controversy illustrated well the potentialities for conflict arising out of the difference between the procedure required for enacting a statute and that for making a treaty. The House technically cannot make a treaty nor control foreign policy, yet by withholding an appropriation necessary to execute a treaty it might in effect well do so. However, on most occasions after 1795, the House has responded almost automatically to the request that it vote funds for the execution of treaties, and it has never defeated a treaty by refusing to appropriate, though it very nearly did so upon occasion of the Alaskan purchase in 1867.

FEDERALIST JUDICIAL INTERPRETATON

Nowhere was Federalist control upon the developing constitutional system more pronounced than in the realm of judicial interpretation. Then, as now, opinions and decisions depended to a large degree upon the social and political philosophy of the presiding judges. To practically all federal judicial posts Washington appointed conservatives and supporters of strong central government. Hence a majority of the federal opinions written between 1789 and 1801 reflected Federalist political ideas and a conservative nationalist point of view.

The federal judiciary was relatively slow in acquiring a position of prestige and importance. During the first three years of its existence the Supreme Court had no cases to decide. Most legal matters were handled through the state courts, and many people were jealous of the potential power of the new federal judicial system. Only gradually did the Supreme Court's work grow in volume and importance.

It was the federal circuit courts, where Supreme Court justices also presided, that first brought federal judicial authority home to the people. Through the charges to grand juries by judges of these courts, the public was informed regarding the basic principles of the new government and the provisions of important federal statutes. Under such circumstances the federal courts began the delicate and endless process of refining the details of the American constitutional system, for which the Constitution had provided the broad outline.

Federal justices almost at once adopted a policy of restricting their decisions and opinions to the adjudication of specific cases duly brought before the courts. Thus in 1792, in the so-called Hayburn's Case, certain circuit court justices unofficially challenged the constitutionality of a recent act of Congress which provided that the circuit courts should pass upon certain claims of disabled veterans of the Revolutionary War. "Neither the Legislative nor the Executive branches," said the judges, "can constitutionally assign to the judicial any duties but such as are properly judicial and to be performed in a judicial manner."

The following year President Washington, desiring legal advice on the questions of neutrality, had his Secretary of State address a letter to Chief Justice John Jay asking the justices of the Supreme Court whether the Chief Executive might seek their advice on questions of law. The judges were also presented with a list of specific questions on international law and neutrality. After due consideration the judges declined to give their opinion on the questions of law on the grounds that the constitutional separation of the three departments prevented them from deciding extra-judicial questions. This procedure became the permanent policy of the Supreme Court and tended to entrench that body as a tribunal of last resort whose decisions and opinions were beyond the authority of any other branch of the government.

The function of the federal judiciary that was of the greatest public concern during its first decade, and by and large until 1861, was its determination of the compatibility of state constitutions, statutes, and court decisions with "the supreme Law of the Land." This function was of the utmost importance in the operation of the federal system of government, for it not only tended to establish the Court as the final interpreter of the Constitution, but it also emphasized the supremacy of the national government. It will be remembered that the guardianship of the distribution of powers between the states and the central government was not explicitly assigned by the Constitution to the federal courts, but that the Judiciary Act of 1789 had taken a long step in that direction by providing for appeals from state to federal courts on constitutional questions.

In May 1791 the United States Circuit Court for Connecticut took the lead in asserting federal judicial authority over state law when it held an act of that state unconstitutional as an infringement of the treaty of peace with Great Britain. The following year the Circuit Court for Rhode Island, in *Champion v. Casey*, declared void a state law giving a debtor citizen an extension of three years in which to pay his debts. "The Legislature of a State," the court said, "have no right to make a law . . . impairing the obligation of contracts, and therefore contrary to the Constitution of the United States." It will be remembered that many laws similar to this one had been enacted by various states during the period of the Articles of Confederation, and that the creditor element had been influenced by the resulting apprehension to strive for a stronger central government to check such "radicalism." However, the return of prosperity and the popular acceptance of the new federal government obviated any widespread opposition to this decision. In subsequent years various laws of other states were invalidated by the federal circuit courts without any serious challenge by states' rights advocates to the exercise of such power.

Considerable popular dissatisfaction, however, was aroused by the Supreme Court in 1796 in the case of *Ware v. Hylton*, which declared invalid a Virginia statute of 1777 sequestering pre-Revolutionary debts of British creditors. The treaty of peace had provided that no impediment was to be placed on the recovery by British subjects of debts due to them from Americans. Under the Articles of Confederation this provision had been of little practical value to British creditors. The Court now held that the treaty nullified the earlier law of Virginia, destroyed the payment made under it, revived the debt, and gave a right of recovery against the debtor, notwithstanding the payment made under the authority of the state law. Such a sweeping and retroactive interpretation of the supremacy of treaties over state law on the sensitive issue of Revolutionary debts naturally led to Republican criticism of the judges as pro-British Federalists.

Even more serious opposition to federal judicial authority was excited by the decision in *Chisholm v. Georgia* (1793), a case involving the right of the federal judiciary to summon a state as defendant and to adjudicate its rights and liabilities. The Constitution expressly gave the federal courts jurisdiction over "controversies between a state and citizens of another state." In the campaign for the ratification of the Constitution in the various states prominent Federalists had assured their apprehensive opponents that this provision would not encompass suits against states without their consent. Almost from the establishment of the federal judiciary, however, suits were instituted against states by citizens of other states. In *Chisholm v. Georgia*, two citizens of South Carolina, executors of a British creditor, brought suit in the Supreme Court against the state of Georgia for recovery of confiscated property. The state refused to appear and presented a written protest denying the jurisdiction of the Court. Meanwhile the Georgia legislature considered a resolution declaring that the exercise of such authority by the federal judiciary "would effectually destroy the retained sovereignty of the States."

The Supreme Court rendered its decision in favor of Chisholm, and the individual justices presented elaborate opinions explaining the nature of the federal union and the extent of federal judicial authority. The majority of justices, especially John Jay and James Wilson, discussed at length the nature of sovereignty and maintained that under the Constitution sovereignty was vested in the people of the United States for "purposes of Union" and in the people of the several states for "more domestic concerns." In ordaining and establishing the Constitution the people acted "as sovereigns of the whole country." They established, said Chief Justice Jay, "a constitution by which it was their will, that the state governments should be bound, and to which the state constitutions should be made to conform." Consequently the state of Georgia, "by being a party to the national compact," in order "to establish justice," consented to be suable by individual citizens of another state. In dissenting from the decision Justice James Iredell, while admitting that sovereignty under the Constitution was divided between the United States and the individual states, denied that the English common law, under which a sovereignty could not be sued without its consent, had been superseded either by constitutional provision or by statute law in this case.

In this case, however, the Supreme Court did not have the final word. The old Antifederalist hostility to a nationalistic or consolidated government flared up, especially in those states where suits similar to Chisholm's were pending or were instituted against the state. Georgia refused to permit the Chisholm verdict to be executed. The day following the decision there was initiated congressional action, which a year later resulted in the submission of the Eleventh Amendment to the states for ratification. It provided: "The Judicial power of the United States shall not be construed to extend to any suit in law or equity, commenced or prosecuted against one of the United States by Citizens of another State, or by Citizens or Subjects of any Foreign State." Because of indifference or Federalist opposition the amendment was not ratified by the requisite number of states until January 1798. Thus for the only time in its history the federal judiciary had its jurisdiction directly curtailed by constitutional amendment.

The Federalist-minded national judiciary soon took steps toward asserting its authority to declare null and void any act of Congress found to be incompatible with the Constitution. In Hayburn's Case, previously referred to, several circuit judges successfully challenged the authority of Congress to assign them duties as pension commissioners, although the opinions handed down in this case were not of a strictly judicial character.

In *Hylton v. United States* (1796) the question of the constitutionality of an act of Congress, a measure levying a tax on carriages, came squarely before the Supreme Court. The specific issue was whether the levy in question was a direct tax or an excise. If the former, it would conflict with the constitutional provision requiring all direct taxes to be apportioned among the states according to population. The Court held that only land taxes and capitations or head taxes were direct taxes, and that the carriage tax was an indirect tax and therefore constitutional. The opinion openly assumed that the Court had the right to declare an act of Congress void, should the justices find that the law conflicted with the Constitution. By 1800, nearly all federal justices, as well as a majority of the legal profession, had accepted the principle that the Supreme Court could declare acts of Congress unconstitutional and therefore invalid.

THE DOCTRINE OF VESTED RIGHTS

Meanwhile some of the federal judges were attempting to incorporate the English common law and a doctrine of vested rights into American constitutional law. In May 1791 the Circuit Court for Connecticut, relying on principles of common law, invalidated a Connecticut statute which sought to restrict the recovery of interest that had accrued to British creditors during the period of the Revolution. In the early national period, certain Federalist-appointed justices asserted the jurisdiction of the federal courts in cases involving criminal jurisdiction based on the common law in the absence of any federal penal statute. Such a judicial policy was viewed by many men of Antifederalist leanings as a dangerous and unwarranted extension of the authority of the central government, especially since most of those prosecuted under the common law were political opponents of the Washington and Adams administrations. Eventually, however, the Supreme Court was to hold, in *United States v. Hudson* (1812), that there was no criminal common law of the United States, nor any civil common law enabling individuals to bring actions in the absence of statutory provisions.

The doctrine of vested rights was a direct outgrowth of the natural rights philosophy of the Revolutionary period, which held that certain rights were so fundamental to an individual as to be beyond governmental control. Constitutional government existed for the protection of these natural rights, which were derived from the very nature of justice. Some of these rights were specified in the bills of rights to state constitutions, but these lists were not to be considered exclusive. Among the most important of these rights was the individual's right to be secure in his possession of private property. Therefore the legislature of a state did not have an unlimited right to interfere in an arbitrary manner with private property. According to the Federalist doctrine of vested rights, it was the duty of the courts to declare invalid statutes considered violative of existing property rights, not necessarily by virtue of any specific provision in the federal or state constitution but rather on the grounds that such statutes violated the fundamental nature of all constitutional government. The Federalist espousal of this principle of abstract justice implied the vesting of final governmental authority over certain important matters in the federal judiciary rather than in the state legislatures as the representatives of the people.

In 1795, Justice William Paterson in the Circuit Court for Pennsylvania stated this doctrine of vested rights in guarded terms in the case of *Vanhorne's Lessee v. Dorrance.* The decision turned upon the invalidity of an act of the Pennsylvania legislature which attempted to vest the ownership of some disputed land in one party after the land had been originally granted to another party. Paterson asserted that "the right of acquiring and possessing property and having it protected, is one of the natural inherent and unalienable rights of man. . . . The legislature, therefore, had no authority to make an act divesting one citizen of his freehold, and vesting it in another, without a just compensation. It is inconsistent with the principles of reason, justice, and moral rectitude; it is incompatible with the comfort, peace, and happiness of mankind; it is contrary to the principles of social alliance in every free government." Paterson also declared the Pennsylvania act unconstitutional because it impaired the obligation of a contract and thus was prohibited by Article I, Section 10, of the Constitution.

This doctrine of vested rights was refined and restricted somewhat by the Supreme Court in *Calder v. Bull* (1798). The decision in this case hinged upon whether the provision in Article I, Section 10, of the federal Constitution forbidding states to enact ex post facto laws encompassed a prohibition upon state laws which interfered with the decisions of the state courts affecting property and contractual rights. The justices hesitated to interfere with a legislative practice which had been employed extensively in certain states and decided that "ex post facto laws extend to criminal, and not to civil cases." As Justice Iredell expressed it, "Some of the most necessary and important acts of legislation are . . . founded upon the principle, that private rights must yield to public exigencies."

In another opinion Justice Samuel Chase nonetheless found occasion to pay homage to the doctrine of vested rights. "There are certain vital principles in our free Republican governments," he said, "which will determine and overrule an apparent and flagrant abuse of legislative powers; as to authorize manifest injustice by positive law; or to take away that security for personal liberty, or private property, for the protection whereof the government was established. An act of the Legislature (for I cannot call it a law) contrary to the great first principles of the social compact, cannot be considered a rightful exercise of legislative authority."

To carry this doctrine of vested rights to its logical conclusion would have meant the investment in the federal judiciary of a comprehensive and indefinite veto power over state legislation without specific provision in the Constitution. Such a move was bound to arouse strenuous opposition from those who believed in popular sovereignty and states' rights. That such a development did not occur was due in large measure to the fact that the clause of the Constitution prohibiting states from impairing the obligation of contracts was soon to be substantially broadened to provide protection of private property from interference by the states. As was indicated in connection with *Vanhorne's Lessee v. Dorrance*, the foundation for the expansion of the scope of the contract clause was being laid during the Federalist period, but its important development was not to begin until John Marshall's first contract decision in 1810.[4] Then during the late nineteenth century the doctrine of vested rights was to be revived, tied to due process of law, and used to defend corporate property rights.

THE RISE OF POLITICAL PARTIES: FEDERALIST DEFEAT

A significant yet unanticipated development of the Federalist period was the rapid growth of political parties. As Richard Hofstadter has emphasized, the idea of a legitimate and responsible opposition party was one of the major constitutional contributions of Thomas Jefferson, James Madison, and their Republican allies during the 1790's.

The development of national parties, however, was somewhat irregular and sporadic. The establishment of the new government between 1789 and 1791 and in particular the enactment of Hamilton's nationalistic economic program aroused substantial opposition among agrarian and frontier elements, which early led to the formation of embryonic political parties in several of the states.

---

4 See pp. 261–262.

But the general success of the new government at home and abroad, the prestige of President Washington, and the involvement of both Jefferson and Madison in the new regime for a time inhibited the development of a national opposition party. Moreover, the restricted use of ideological concepts and labels and the limited divisiveness of domestic issues served to restrain open partisan feeling.

Beginning in 1792, however, the sharp ideological division which developed in the country over the nature and significance of the French Revolution rapidly widened the gulf between the supporters and opponents of the Federalist economic, constitutional, and diplomatic programs. Since 1776, the vast majority of Americans had been opposed to monarchy; yet few or no conservatives would admit to being "democrats," and even liberal leaders were sensitive about the use of the term. With the growth of radicalism and violence in France, however, politicians in America resorted increasingly to such terms as "monarchist," "aristocrat," "democrat," and even "mobocrat" to describe their opponents. No genuine political or social revolution was taking place in America, but certain progressive changes were indeed under way which would inevitably affect the political process. By the early 1790's, for example, old property and religious restrictions on the franchise and on office-holding were gradually being relaxed; the result was to contribute substantially to the growth of political democracy.

The French Revolution had a profound impact upon American thought and politics. Few Americans had regretted the overthrow of the despotic Bourbon monarchy. But when, in 1792, the revolutionaries proceeded to set up a democratic republic and to institute a Reign of Terror directed against nearly all conservative groups in France, public opinion in the United States divided sharply.

The war which broke out between France and Great Britain early in 1793 further sharpened this division. The Federalists strongly favored Britain, and denounced those who sympathized with the French Republic as anarchists, mobocrats, and Jacobins. To conservatives, the violence of the Reign of Terror was proof that the untutored and unpropertied masses were interested primarily in despoiling the propertied classes and were unfit for the responsibilities of governing. Most Federalists now looked to the aristocratic British government as a principal bulwark against atheistic Jacobinism. At the same time they favored strengthening the conservative controls of the American government.

The followers of Jefferson and Madison, on the other hand, were already calling themselves Republicans and heralding the establishment of a democratic republic in France as the dawn of a new era for the world at large. Many Republicans also applauded the views of Tom Paine, who in his *Rights of Man* proclaimed that sovereignty was inherent in the majority will. They boldly accepted the leveling implications of democracy and popular sovereignty; throughout America they organized democratic political clubs to disseminate their principles of government. The label "democrat" now was enthusiastically accepted by many Republicans, while a definite philosophy of democracy was now proclaimed for the first time, even in those localities where a considerable degree of political democracy had long existed. The new democratic enthusiasm tended to bind the various anti-Federalist elements together into an effective political movement designed to wrest control of the national government from the Federalists and thereby to put an end to Hamiltonian "perversion" of the Constitution.

By 1796, the Jeffersonian Republicans had a nearly nationwide party organization and were steadily growing in power. They lost the presidential election of 1796 to John Adams by only three electoral votes. Under the prevailing constitutional provision, Jefferson, with the second highest number of electoral votes, thereby became Vice-President. The Federalists succeeded in retaining control of Congress, but it was apparent that should the Republicans' position continue to improve, they might soon win control of the national government.

THE ALIEN AND SEDITION ACTS

The undeclared naval war with France which broke out in the spring of 1798 greatly exacerbated the prevailing spirit of partisan bitterness. In Congress, the Federalist majority deliberately took advantage of the intense excitement generated by the war to enact into law the so-called Alien and Sedition Acts. These measures, of which there were four, were deliberately designed to suppress the partisan activities of the Republican political opposition.

Least open to constitutional attack was a new Naturalization Act, which stipulated that an alien, to be eligible for citizenship, must prove fourteen years of residence within the United States. Although reactionary in spirit, the law posed no serious constitutional difficulties.

Far more controversial were the Alien Act, the Alien Enemies Act, and the Sedition Act. The Alien Act authorized the President to order the deportation of an alien whom he deemed dangerous to the peace and safety of the United States. The Alien Enemies Act empowered the President in case of war to deport aliens of an enemy country or to subject them to important restraints if they were permitted to remain in this country. The Sedition Act not only made it a high misdemeanor for any person to conspire to oppose any measure or to impede the operation of any law of the United States but also made it illegal for any person to write, print, or publish "any false, scandalous and malicious writing . . . against the government of the United States, or either house of the Congress . . . , or the President . . . , with intent to defame . . . , or to bring them, or either of them, into contempt or disrepute; or to excite against them, or either or any of them, the hatred of the good people of the United States. . . ."

The two Alien Acts were obviously aimed at French and pro-French foreigners in the United States, who were virtually unanimous in their support of the Republican Party. Jefferson's followers at once attacked the laws as grossly unconstitutional. They argued, first, that the acts would deprive persons of their liberty without due process of law in violation of the Fifth Amendment and, second, that they contemplated the imposition of penalties without judicial process upon persons not convicted of any offense.

These arguments were plausible enough at the time; nonetheless the Alien Acts were unquestionably constitutional by twentieth-century standards. In part because President Adams was not enthusiastic about the laws, no alien was actually deported under either statute. However, the Enemy Alien Act is still on the statute books and in 1948 was in effect held valid by the Supreme Court.[5]

The Sedition Act posed a far more difficult constitutional problem. The sponsors of the law admittedly had intended virtually to re-enact the English common law of seditious libel as a congressional statute. The First Amendment, the Federalists contended, had merely incorporated the English common-law guarantee of "no prior restraint," which prohibited censorship before publication but which permitted very broad prosecution for "seditious libel" subsequent to the publication of anything unfriendly to the government. The truth of the published matter at issue did not constitute a defense, and the judge had sole power to decide whether or not it was

---

[5] In *Ludecke v. Watkins* (1948), discussed below, p. 811.

libelous. English "freedom of the press" thus meant little more than a prior right to publish. The present law, the Federalists could point out, softened the traditional law of seditious libel, for it permitted truth as a defense and allowed the jury to decide whether an utterance was libelous, two reforms for which the champions of free speech had long contended.

Certain Federalists argued also that there was a federal criminal common law, which had carried over from the English courts and those of the states and could be enforced in the federal judiciary. Under this law, they contended, it would be constitutional to institute prosecutions in the federal courts for seditious libel without benefit of any statute against critics of the government. However, certain federal judges had already expressed some doubt about the existence of a federal criminal common law. To remove all question about the matter, therefore, the Federalist advocates of a common law of sedition had assented to the passage of a statute to the same end.

The Jeffersonians in turn attacked the Sedition Act as flagrantly unconstitutional. Madison and Gallatin argued, first, that the First Amendment had been intended to sweep the old law of seditious libel into the rubbish heap and thereby make all federal sedition laws constitutionally impossible. This argument, going well beyond anything asserted on the floor of Congress in 1789, thus stated virtually for the first time what was to become the classic "extreme liberal" position on the amendment. Jefferson's followers also applied strict-construction theory in attacking the law: there was no enumerated power to enact a sedition act and it could not properly be construed from the "necessary and proper" clause. Finally, they argued, there could be no federal criminal statute law running beyond those crimes mentioned in the Constitution itself, nor could there be any federal criminal common law, a notion offensive to limited federal sovereignty.

The Adams administration enforced the Sedition Act with vigor, securing some fifteen indictments and ten convictions. The hope at first entertained by certain Jeffersonians that the federal courts might declare the law unconstitutional proved false; the Federalist-dominated judiciary refused to allow counsel to challenge its constitutionality. Technically, most presiding judges allowed defense counsel to plead the truth of alleged libel, but in their charges to the jury refused to admit proof of libel, so this defense invariably failed.

In addition, Federalist-minded judges conducted trials under the law in a grossly partisan manner, browbeating counsel and witnesses and delivering Federalist political harangues to the jury. The behavior of Justice Samuel Chase, in particular, was so notorious as to rouse vast indignation among Jefferson's followers. In the case of James Callender, a Virginia Republican, who wrote a pamphlet criticizing the Federalist administration, Chase openly boasted before the trial that he would teach the Virginians the difference between the liberty and the licentiousness of the press. His refusal to permit Callender's counsel either to challenge the constitutionality of the law or offer proof of the statements at issue virtually brought about an automatic conviction.

In the light of modern constitutional law it has become clear, however, that Congress has the constitutional power to enact a sedition statute. The power may be reasonably inferred from the "necessary and proper" clause, since it is evident that extreme attacks on the government may well interfere with the performance of federal functions, the prosecution of a war, or the conduct of duty by its officers. Moreover, the guarantees of the First Amendment do not protect conspiracies to overthrow the government, even though such attempts may technically not be treason. Jefferson's argument that there is no federal criminal common law has since been sustained by the Court. However, there is a federal criminal statutory law, and contrary to the Jeffersonian argument it is not limited to crimes mentioned in the Constitution. Congress may punish offenses in connection with its enumerated powers—robbery of the mails, for example.

The Sedition Act of 1798 nonetheless was unquestionably unconstitutional when adjudged by modern standards, for it undertook to punish mere political criticism of government officials, something no modern law attempts to do. By contrast, the Sedition Act of 1918 punished attempts to interfere with the prosecution of the war. Even the much controverted Smith Act of 1940 does not undertake to punish mere political utterance; instead, it makes punishable conspiracy to advocate overthrow of the government by force and violence. It is now generally recognized, in short, that the First Amendment outlawed seditious libel in the United States. Political criticism not directed to interference with the conduct of a war, incitement to riot or insurrection, or the overthrow of the government by violence generally is protected by the First Amendment.[6]

---

[6] For discussion of the 1918 and 1940 acts, see pp. 631f., 906ff.

THE CLOSING ERA OF FEDERALIST POWER

In the election of 1800, the Federalists lost control of the presidency and both houses of Congress to the Jeffersonian Republicans. Thereupon the Federalist-dominated lame-duck Congress rushed through to completion a bill for the reorganization of the Federalist judiciary upon which party leaders had been at work for the past two years. On February 13, 1801, President Adams signed the measure into law.

The Judiciary Act of 1801 was an extraordinary combination of sheer partisanship, Federalist nationalism, and intelligent judicial reform. The law established six new circuit courts with their own judiciary, thereby requiring the appointment of sixteen circuit judges, and it provided also for several new district courts, all with appropriate numbers of marshals and clerks. The law also greatly enlarged the original jurisdiction of the circuit courts, while it made cases that arose in the state courts involving the Constitution, treaties, and laws of the United States removable to the federal courts without regard to the sums of money involved. In addition, it expanded substantially the jurisdiction of federal circuit courts in diversity cases (those between citizens of different states), particularly those that concerned disputes over land titles.

The partisan character of much of this was evident enough. The act promised to provide the dying Adams administration with a fat piece of judicial patronage and at the same time to entrench the Federalists in control of the national judiciary indefinitely. An additional provision, reducing the size of the Supreme Court from six justices to five effective with the next vacancy, obviously intended to deprive the incoming President of his first appointment to the Court, further emphasized the law's partisan intent.

Despite its evident partisan purpose, the Judiciary Act of 1801 embodied a number of intelligent reforms, particularly when considered from a nationalist point of view. Creation of a separate circuit court judiciary was a step for which numerous judges and congressmen had been contending ever since John Jay's time. It promised to relieve Supreme Court justices, who were often elderly men, of the onerous necessity of riding circuit, while it would also provide a new national forum for numerous classes of lawsuits hitherto handled only by the state courts, a prospect particularly attractive to the business community. Land speculators were particularly delighted with the provisions broadening the resort to the federal courts in disputes over land titles, since many of them had been faring rather badly of late in their suits in the state courts.

In the closing days of his administration, President Adams appointed good Federalists to all of the various judicial positions created under the law. He also commissioned forty-two new justices of the peace for the sparsely populated District of Columbia, as a separate law passed late in February authorized him to do. The Republicans quite naturally denounced both the act and the appointments as a grave abuse of power and an attempt to defeat the popular will. "They have retired into the judiciary as a stronghold," wrote Jefferson bitterly, ". . . and from that battery all the works of Republicanism are to be beaten down and destroyed." It was a remark that forecast the repeal of the new law the following year.

The Federalist cause, however, did receive a powerful new lease on life in the appointment of John Marshall as Chief Justice of the United States, replacing Oliver Ellsworth, who had resigned the previous December. Marshall was a staunch Federalist-nationalist, but he had demonstrated repeatedly a greater moderation of view and independence of character than had many of his fellow party members. To the disgust of Hamilton and other "High Federalists," he had publicly condemned the Alien and Sedition Acts as unsound, while he had participated also in the unfortunate "XYZ" mission and, almost alone in his party, had supported Adams' recent attempt to make peace with France. In 1798 he had declined an appointment from Adams as an associate justice of the Supreme Court to succeed James Wilson, preferring for the moment the congressional arena. But in 1800, he had consented to become Adams' Secretary of State and now, after John Jay had declined reappointment to his former position, he accepted the nomination to the Chief Justiceship. In his new role he would one day emerge as a veritable colossus of the constitutional system.

The Federalist defeat at the polls in 1800 had been by a relatively small margin, but the party was never again to secure control of either the legislative or the executive branch of the federal government, and within twenty years it was dead. The party of Hamilton, Washington, and their cohorts had represented the superior classes and had made valuable contributions to American constitutionalism by providing an effective organization for the new government and by guiding it through the early experimental stages. The first third of the nineteenth century, however, was to witness an increasingly successful demand for popular participation in government, and any party which proclaimed the incompetence of the masses was bound to go down before the rising tide of democracy. In the future, conservative groups and vested interests were to use political organization as a means to influence and control governmental policies, but they would pretend to be concerned primarily with the welfare of the people as a whole and would not openly espouse aristocratic political principles. Under these circumstances the federal judiciary under the able leadership of Marshall was to become a conservative and nationalistic bulwark against the dominant political forces of democracy and states' rights.

Chapter

8

The Rise of Jeffersonianism

JEFFERSON sometimes spoke of the popular defeat of the Federalists as the "Revolution of 1800." In reality, however, the transformation of Hamiltonian constitutional and political principles into Jeffersonian Republicanism was an evolutionary and protracted development. This reflected the generally moderate temper of most Americans and the definite division within both political parties, particularly in Congress. The events of the late 1790's, as well as basic philosophical differences, had divided the party in power into High Federalists or conservative Hamiltonians and the more moderate or Adams Federalists, with John Marshall in their midst. The Jeffersonians also were divided between the moderate, Madison-type Republicans and the more radical or militant members of the dominant party, who advocated the outright abandonment or destruction of many Federalist institutions, measures, and programs. Thus on certain issues the Republicans, once in power, consisted of different groups or factions holding conflicting views and political positions. Under such circumstances the key personality was of course President Jefferson.

Few political leaders have ever reflected the genius of their country or inspired their fellow citizens of their own and succeeding generations as effectively as did the author of the Declaration of Independence. Throughout a long and illustrious public career Jefferson's social and political philosophy remained relatively constant in basic principles but quite flexible in means and solutions. Although a visionary he certainly was no wild-eyed revolutionary but rather a philosophical statesman of moderate principles, conciliatory methods and deep dedication to the prevailing values and free institutions of his beloved country. He also fully appreciated the validity of the pragmatic test and often made the compromises and modifications necessary to the performance of public duty. He was, moreover, the leader of a great political movement and of a party which represented varied and even diverse interests, ideas, and programs. Jeffersonian Democracy encompassed a few fundamental political and constitutional principles which received shifting emphasis depending upon time, locale, and circumstances.

THE ORIGINS OF JEFFERSONIAN DEMOCRACY

Organized opposition to the Constitution had largely disappeared after its adoption. The favorable launching of the new federal government, the return of economic prosperity, and the adoption of the first ten amendments had eliminated all thought of returning to the constitutional system of the Confederation. As memories of the ratification struggles dimmed, the Constitution of the United States attained a practically universal acceptance and approval.

Almost simultaneously, however, disputes as to the meaning of certain portions of the Constitution and as to the nature of the "more perfect Union" began to arise. Economic interests and social groups tended to form political organizations and sectional blocs which in turn developed constitutional doctrines and explanations to uphold their position on important public issues. For much of the period from 1789 to 1861 there persisted a basic clash between the political leaders who upheld the Hamilton-Marshall-Federalist conception of a strong, active, nationalistic government, and those who insisted with Jefferson that the Constitution provided for a federal government of limited delegated authority with the residue of powers reserved to the states and to the people.

The student will miss much of the significance of American constitutional development, however, if he assumes that the struggle from the Philadelphia Convention to the battlefield of Appomattox was a simple and ever-present contest between capitalistic nationalists and agrarian champions of states' rights. At one time or another every major economic interest, every geographical section, and almost every state, expounded a theory of states' rights to justify its opposition to the prevailing policies of the federal government. Likewise every interest, section, and state supported some federal measures of a strongly nationalistic character, and practically every state eventually went on record in condemnation of what it considered an excessive states' rights position of a sister state. Much depended upon the particular issue involved and upon which political, economic, or sectional group was in control of the federal government.

Although the fears of a consolidated government were stirred again by the passage of the Judiciary Act of 1789, comparatively little popular opposition to the policies of Hamilton and the Federalists developed until 1790, when the issues of the federal assumption of state debts, the creation of a national bank, and the enactment of a protective tariff were raised. To many of the small farmers and southern planters such legislation seemed to be using the federal government to provide special favors for the mercantile and capitalistic interests at the expense of agrarian taxpayers. Many rural citizens opposed any governmental action that was favorable to speculators and stock-jobbers, while some of the more informed advanced a definite agrarian social and political philosophy.

One of the most intelligent and vocal agrarian philosophers was John Taylor of Caroline County, Virginia. In several pamphlets he expressed the belief that the liberty and happiness of the individual could be maintained only in a free society of tillers of the soil. He accepted the physiocratic doctrine that agriculture was the only really productive enterprise and maintained that the mercantile and financial interests actually prospered at the expense of the great mass of people who were agriculturists. Perceiving the close tie between politics and economics, Taylor denounced the Federalist laws as steps in a selfish scheme to subvert the Constitution by the creation of a consolidated nationalistic government. He held that the Declaration of Independence made each state a separate sovereignty and that each remained sovereign under the Constitution. These states he proclaimed to be the most inspiring examples of free republican government in the world. The state governments were considered the farmers' most "intimate associates and allies," while the federal government was criticized as "the associate and ally of patronage, funding, armies, and of many other interests" subsisting upon agriculture.

Although Jefferson was not as extreme in his agrarianism as his friend Taylor, he regarded a free yeomanry as the producers of real wealth, the guardians of liberty, and the backbone of the nation. Since the overwhelming majority of people were farmers and villagers, Jefferson felt that their welfare and happiness should be the primary concern of government. He distrusted the mercantilistic minority and opposed a constitutional development that would allow this or any other minority to control the policies of government.

Jefferson believed that the simple economic life of the time required little regulation, and that the welfare of the people could best be secured through the state and local units of government, which would naturally understand the needs of each community better than a more distant federal government. He realized the necessity of having a central government of sufficient strength and prestige to control commercial and diplomatic relations with foreign countries, but in the field of domestic affairs he strongly believed that federal authority should be confined strictly to those powers enumerated in the Constitution and that other matters should be left to the states and to individuals. He therefore viewed Hamilton's broad-constructionist program with increasing concern, and in December 1793 he resigned from Washington's cabinet, convinced that the President was definitely committed to the Federalist program. Jefferson would have nothing to do with the creation of the leviathan state. Increasingly after 1793 he became the leader and director of the opposition to the Federalist interpretation of the Constitution as well as to Federalist political and economic policies.

Individualistic frontiersmen, most of whom had been either hostile or indifferent to the adoption of the Constitution, were made active opponents of the Federalist interpretation of the Constitution by the excise tax on liquor and the untoward incident of its enforcement. The Jeffersonian leaders carefully cultivated frontier discontent by emphasizing that the obnoxious tax was imposed to pay the increased expenses necessitated by Federalist financial policies. The American frontier was to remain for a century or more one of the main outposts of the Jeffersonian concept of government; many a frontier orator was to offer as his toast: "Equal rights for all, special privileges for none."

THE VIRGINIA AND KENTUCKY RESOLUTIONS

As was mentioned earlier, in 1798 the crisis with France following the X Y Z affair inspired the Federalist-controlled Congress to enact the Alien and Sedition Acts in order to restrict the activities of aliens and citizens of pro-French and anti-Federalist sympathies. Republicans were greatly incensed by the laws, which they regarded as a flagrant and unconstitutional invasion of the rights of individuals and of the states. Many contended that the obnoxious statutes were another long step in the scheme of the Federalists to consolidate all authority in the central government and then to establish a monarchy. John Taylor and other extreme Republicans talked of having Virginia and some of the other states secede from the Union and establish a separate confederacy. But Jefferson and his colleagues would not countenance such a move. They believed that if the American people were made fully aware of the unconstitutionality of the Alien and Sedition Acts and of the danger inherent in the Federalist constitutional interpretation, the people would effectively voice their disapproval through existing political channels.

The strategic problem was to find a way to bring effective pressure for the repeal of the odious laws. The Federalist judges refused to permit the constitutionality of the controversial laws to be challenged in court. Although the Republican press and public meetings repeatedly denounced the measures, Jefferson and his associates felt that mere partisan unofficial opposition was insufficient, and they accordingly sought some formal legalistic mode of disapproval. Their choice fell upon the state legislatures, which at that period were bodies of considerably greater prestige and relative importance than now. This was not the first and certainly it was not to be the last time that state legislatures were to sit in judgment on the constitutionality of acts of Congress.

Jefferson, working in collaboration with his party lieutenants, had Madison draft a set of resolutions denouncing the laws, and John Taylor presently submitted Madison's work to the Virginia legislature. The Vice-President himself secretly drafted similar resolutions, which his friend John Breckinridge introduced into the Kentucky legislature. After slight but not insignificant modifications, the resolutions were adopted by the respective legislatures and sent to the legislatures of the other states, a step attracting wide public attention. The immediate objective of the Virginia and Kentucky Resolutions was to rally the various states in an effort to get rid of the obnoxious laws and to discredit the constitutional tenets upon which the whole Federalist program rested. However, the resolutions are of permanent significance because of the constitutional theories which they promulgated.

The Virginia legislature expressed "a warm attachment to the union of the states" and a firm resolve to support the government of the United States in all of its legitimate powers, but it declared that it viewed "the powers of the Federal Government as resulting from the compact to which the states are parties, as limited by the plain sense and intention of the instrument constituting that compact; as no further valid than they are authorized by the grants enumerated in that compact." The resolutions added that "in case of a deliberate, palpable, and dangerous exercise of other powers not granted by the said compact, the states, who are parties thereto, have the right and are in duty bound to interpose for arresting the progress of the evil, and for maintaining within their respective limits the authorities, rights, and liberties appertaining to them." After protesting most emphatically that the Alien and Sedition Acts were a violation of the Constitution and of the First Amendment, the legislature expressed confidence that the other states would join in declaring the acts unconstitutional and in taking "the necessary and proper measures" to maintain unimpaired "the authorities, rights, and liberties reserved to the states respectively, or to the people."

The Kentucky Resolutions also declared the Constitution of the United States to be a compact to which "each State acceded as a State, and is an integral party, its co-States forming, as to itself, the other party." Therefore, they added, "the government created by this compact was not made the exclusive or final judge of the extent of the powers delegated to itself; since that would make its discretion, and not the Constitution, the measure of its powers." Each state as a party to the compact, the Resolutions declared, "*has an equal right to judge for itself, as well of infractions as of the mode and measure of redress.*" The Alien and Sedition Laws exceeded the constitutional power of Congress and were therefore "not law," but "altogether void and of no force." The legislature warned that the states would not tamely submit to such extension of congressional authority beyond the constitutional limits, and it added ominously that "these and successive acts of the same character, unless arrested on the threshold, may tend to drive these States into revolution and blood."

Jefferson's original draft had declared that "where powers are assumed which have not been delegated, a nullification of the act is the right remedy," and had expressed hope that the "co-States . . . will concur in declaring these [Alien and Sedition] acts void and of no force, and will each take measures of its own for providing that neither of these acts . . . shall be exercised within their respective territories." For expediency or other reasons this section was replaced by an appeal to the other states and by instructions to Kentucky's congressional representatives "to use their best endeavors to procure, at the next session of Congress, a repeal of the . . .

unconstitutional and obnoxious acts." [1]

There were three fundamental constitutional ideas involved in the Virginia and Kentucky Resolutions—first, a theory of the nature of the Union; second, a theory of the extent of federal powers; and third, an argument that the final power to interpret the Constitution was lodged with the states.

The precise meaning of the argument that the Constitution was a compact to which "each State acceded as a State" is not clear even today. Conceivably this was nothing more than a somewhat self-evident statement of political philosophy derived from the Revolution—the compact theory of the state and the limited character of federal sovereignty. Jefferson's language, in particular, would seem to imply, however, that the actual ultimate locus of sovereignty still lay within the states. Calhoun was later to interpret the Resolutions as statements of extreme state sovereignty and as implicit assertions that the federal government was a mere agent of the several states. A more probable estimate of Madison's and Jefferson's opinions, however, is that both men accepted the Revolutionary conception of divided sovereignty—both state and national governments had some sovereignty. Precisely where the ultimate abstract locus of sovereignty lay did not greatly concern them—they were primarily interested in achieving a political objective, not in setting up an academic speculation on the ultimate nature of sovereignty.

Although the Resolutions' theory of union was equivocal, they were clear and specific in their defense of strict constructionism. Madison's assertion that the federal authority was limited by the "plain sense and implication" of the Constitution and by the powers enumerated therein was a flat denial of the whole Hamiltonian nationalist program.

On the question of who had the final power to pass upon constitutional questions involving the extent of state and federal authority the Resolutions were again somewhat equivocal. They denied categorically that the federal government had any exclusive right to judge of the extent of its own powers. By implication this constituted a denial of the whole system of constitutional controls erected in the Judiciary Act of 1789 and the presumed right of the Supreme Court to settle constitutional questions.

---

[1] In January 1800, the House of Representatives actually voted for the repeal of part of the Sedition Act, but the Federalist-dominated Senate refused to support the repeal. Early in 1801 the Republicans in Congress were able, after extensive debate, to block Federalist attempts to extend the Sedition Act beyond its expiration date of March 3, 1801.

Just how the Resolutions did propose to settle constitutional issues is less certain. Each state might interpret the Constitution for itself, but how could it enforce that interpretation? The Virginia Resolutions asserted that the states were in duty bound to "interpose"; the Kentucky Resolutions, even with the word "nullification" deleted, still warned that the states would not "tamely submit" to unconstitutional extensions of federal authority. These were strong words; conceivably they implied the use of force. However, a suggestion of the resort to force was not so radical in the post-Revolutionary era as it now sounds—the right of revolution had only lately been on all patriot lips. Certainly Madison and Jefferson set forth no elaborate mechanism for "interposition" such as Calhoun later offered; indeed they offered no specific suggestions at all for the peaceable settlement of constitutional questions. This fact has made it possible for subsequent constitutional theorists to read virtually any desired constitutional implication into the Resolutions —to support the interpreters' own theories. Both statesmen and constitutional historians have played this game.

The success of the Jefferson-Madison attempt to establish their concept of constitutional theory as well as of their efforts to put an end to the Alien and Sedition Acts depended upon the co-operation of the other states. In most of the other southern states political sentiment was fairly closely divided, and no official responses were made to the Resolutions. On the other hand, the legislatures of all the northern states, which were controlled by the Federalists, adopted resolutions endorsing both the constitutionality and the propriety of the Alien and Sedition Acts. In practically every case, however, the Republican minority in the legislature dissented from the Federalist position and in different degrees approved of the position taken by the legislatures of Kentucky and Virginia.

The replies of the Federalist-controlled northern state legislatures maintained that the federal courts and not the state legislatures were the "proper tribunals" to determine the constitutionality of acts of Congress. Only Vermont, however, directly challenged the assertion of the Kentucky and Virginia Resolutions that the Constitution was a compact between the separate states. "The people of the United States," declared the Vermont Federalists, "formed the federal constitution, and not the states, or their legislatures." The other legislatures apparently either accepted the compact theory (though not necessarily the immediate implications thereof), or considered the constitutionality of the Alien and Sedition Acts to be the vital question, or perhaps believed that an assertion of the authority of the federal judiciary to make the final decision was a denial of the particular compact theory involved.

The replies of the northern states and other public discussions induced Virginia and Kentucky to make rebuttals. In the former state a committee headed by Madison prepared a report reaffirming the principles of the original Resolutions. Madison also explained that the word "states" as used in 1798 meant "the people composing those political societies, in their highest sovereign capacity," a conception that Calhoun was to employ to advantage a generation later.

Kentucky was much more emphatic in its defense of the rights of the states. Irked by charges of their disloyalty to the Union, the Kentuckians in their second Resolutions (1799) unequivocally declared their attachment to the Union and to the Constitution. But they vigorously reasserted their conviction that if the general government was the exclusive judge of the extent of its delegated powers, as several states had contended, the result would be "despotism." The heart of the new Resolutions was the bold declaration: "That the several states who formed that instrument [the Constitution] being sovereign and independent, have the unquestionable right to judge of the infraction; and, *That a nullification of those sovereignties, of all unauthorized acts done under color of that instrument is the rightful remedy.*"

Whether such a doctrine approximated the Calhoun doctrine of nullification, as the South Carolinian later claimed, has been debated for over a century.[2] The phrase "nullification of those sovereignties" indicates a decided similarity to Calhoun's concept. On the other hand the Kentucky Resolutions, after declaring that the Alien and Sedition Acts were "palpable violations of the . . . Constitution," concluded not with a recommendation for extreme action but merely with a "solemn PROTEST" in order to prevent "similar future violations of the federal compact." This moderation and the fact that Kentucky took no overt steps to prevent the enforcement of the obnoxious acts lead to a conclusion that the Resolutions were a declaration primarily of constitutional theory and not of a mode of action.

Behind all this controversy lay the fact that there was as yet no general agreement as to the precise nature of the Union. Everybody agreed that the powers of government were divided between the states and the central government. It was also evident that the Con-

---

[2] The nullification controversy is discussed at length in Chapter 12.

stitution had made no explicit provision for the settlement of disputes over power between the two units of government. Article VI, which provides for the supremacy of the Constitution and federal laws, might be balanced against the Tenth Amendment, which provides for the reservation of undelegated powers to the states, without producing a conclusive answer. The government established under the Constitution was essentially a compromise between a confederation and a national state. In limited and varying degrees the political leaders realized that in the long run such a compromise might prove unworkable and that the federal system might evolve either into modified confederation or into a strongly centralized national government. The Republicans were essentially right in claiming that if a branch of the federal government had the final power to judge of the extent of federal authority, the states would ultimately and inevitably be reduced to a subordinate position. On the other hand, the Federalists were correct in asserting that the recognition of the right of each state to act as final judge in case of vital disputes would lead to utter confusion and probably to "an interruption of the peace of the states by civil discord." No decision on this all-important issue was reached in 1799, and in one form or another the question was to crop up almost continuously through the years until it was finally settled on the battlefield.

ADOPTION OF THE TWELFTH AMENDMENT

As indicated earlier, the framers of the Constitution had assumed that the administration of the federal government would naturally be entrusted to nonpartisan representatives of the upper classes, and therefore made no provision in the Constitution for political parties. In particular, the Convention's scheme for electing the President implied no recognition of political parties. Under the method finally decided upon, each elector was to cast two votes for two different men, without differentiating between the vote for President and the vote for Vice-President. The candidate having the highest number of votes then became President, and the man with the next highest number became Vice-President. It was expected that most presidential contests would be staged between rival sectional or state candidates, and that in most elections no candidate would receive a majority of votes and final choice would therefore devolve upon the House of Representatives.

The rise of political parties was to make this mode of election impracticable. Under a party system, the men chosen President and Vice-President might well be, and in the election of 1796 were, members of two different political parties, an undesirable situation both for executive unity and for continuity of administration should the President die in office. More serious, should the party mechanism function with sufficient rigidity, each elector could very conceivably cast a ballot for each of his party's two candidates, and a tie would thereupon result between the man whom the winning party had intended for the presidency and the man intended for the vice-presidency. The resultant tie, under the Constitution, would then have to be decided by the House of Representatives.

In the first election, that of 1789, no definite party division existed, and presidential electors were chosen on the basis of their personal appeal to the voters. By 1792, however, Federalist and Republican or opposition party organizations had been developed in every state. The Republicans did not oppose President Washington's re-election, but their electors supported a Republican, George Clinton of New York, against John Adams for Vice-President.

For the campaign of 1796 both the Federalists and the Republicans nominated candidates for President and Vice-President by means of the congressional caucus, and both conducted a partisan campaign. The result was the election of a Federalist President, Adams, and a Republican Vice-President, Jefferson. It was becoming increasingly evident that the constitutional provisions for choosing the President were being outmoded by the growth of political parties. Several proposals were made to amend the Constitution, but for the moment Congress took no action.

In the election of 1800, however, increased party discipline resulted in a tie for the presidency. More Republican than Federalist electors were chosen, and each Republican elector cast one vote for Jefferson and one vote for Jefferson's running mate, Aaron Burr of New York. The election was thus thrown into the House of Representatives, where prolonged balloting and political maneuvering occurred before the Federalists finally, in February 1801, permitted the Republicans to elect Jefferson to the presidency with Burr receiving the vice-presidency.

This episode led to an immediate demand for an amendment to the Constitution to require electors to cast one set of ballots for President, and a second distinct set of ballots for Vice-President. At the next session of Congress the House adopted such a proposal, but it was not until December 1803 that it received the requisite two-thirds vote of both houses. Congressmen from some of the small states opposed the proposal on the ground that it would reduce the weight of their states in choosing Presidents and that it would reduce the chances of anyone from their states being elected. Some Federalists opposed the amendment because it gave the majority party virtually complete choice in selecting the President and Vice-President. Republicans controlled most of the state legislatures, however, and they were anxious to avoid another experience like that of 1801. They rushed the ratification through the requisite thirteen states by September 1804, so that the Twelfth Amendment became effective before the presidential election of that year.

Under the new amendment it was still possible, though not so probable as before, that a President would be elected by the House of Representatives. In case no candidate received a majority of electoral votes, the House, voting by states, was required to choose the President from among the three candidates having the largest number of votes. Actually, however, this provision was to operate in only one presidential election, that of 1824, although in several subsequent closely contested elections as late as 1868 it remained a distinct possibility.

The speed with which the Twelfth Amendment was ratified created a false impression of the ease of changing the Constitution by the amending process. Jefferson in particular favored easy and frequent amendment in order to keep the Constitution abreast of the changing needs of the people. Later experience, however, was to furnish ample proof that only under extraordinary circumstances would any proposal receive the necessary two-thirds vote in Congress and subsequent favorable action by three-fourths of the states. More than sixty years were to elapse before another amendment was to be added to the Constitution. Meanwhile many constitutional changes were to be effected by less formal processes.

THE JEFFERSONIAN CONSTITUTIONAL PROGRAM

Although some of the constitutional and political concepts held by Thomas Jefferson and John Adams were decidedly opposed and although the emotions of the people were greatly aroused by the issues of the campaign of 1800, Jefferson succeeded Adams as President on March 4, 1801, in an orderly and constitutional manner. This, at a time when such a procedure was impossible in all but a few countries in the world, was in itself a notable achievement for the constitutional system of the new nation and was in a sense prophetic of the new century which was to witness the progress of constitutional government, slow and irregular though it often was, in nearly all nations of the world where the impact of Western civilization was felt.

In his inaugural address, Jefferson set forth the general principles which would guide his administration. Urging a unity of heart and mind among his fellow-citizens, he proclaimed as a "sacred principle": "that though the will of the majority is in all cases to prevail, that will to be rightful must be reasonable; that the minority possess their equal rights, which equal law must protect." He stoutly disagreed with those who contended that republican self-government contained the seeds of its own destruction; he believed that it was "the strongest Government on earth" and could successfully combat with reason alone those few dissenters who "wish to dissolve this Union or to change its republican form."

"The sum of good government," asserted the champion of agrarian democracy, is "a wise and frugal Government, which shall restrain men from injuring one another, shall leave them otherwise free to regulate their own pursuits of industry and improvement, and shall not take from the mouth of labor the bread it has earned." Jefferson then proceeded to outline the objectives of his administration in greater detail, though still in general terms:

Equal and exact justice to all men, of whatever state or persuasion, religious or political; peace, commerce, and honest friendship with all nations, entangling alliances with none; the support of the State governments in all their rights, as the most competent administrations for our domestic concerns and the surest bulwarks against antirepublican tendencies; the preservation of the General Government in its whole constitutional vigor, as the sheet anchor of our peace at home and safety abroad; a jealous care of the right of election by the people—a mild and safe corrective of abuses which are lopped by the sword of revolution where peaceable remedies are unprovided; absolute acquiescence in the decisions of the majority, the vital principle of republics, from which is no appeal but to force, the vital principle and immediate parent of despotism; a well-disciplined militia, our best reliance in peace and for the first moments of war, till regulars may relieve them; the supremacy of the civil over the military authority; economy in the public expense, that labor may be lightly burthened; the honest payment of our debts and sacred preservation of the public faith; encouragement of agriculture, and of commerce as its handmaid; the diffusion of information and arraignment of all abuses at the bar of the public reason; freedom of religion; freedom of the press, and freedom of person under the protection of the habeas corpus, and trial by juries impartially selected.

The new President recommended that the country could "safely dispense with all the internal taxes" and rely upon customs duties and revenue from the sales of public land. Congress responded with enthusiasm by repealing the excise on whisky which had been so obnoxious to the western farmers.

In keeping with their policy of governmental economy, the Jeffersonians reduced expenses substantially by eliminating certain civil offices and instituting a more effective accounting system as well as by curtailing the military and naval expansion program which the Federalists had launched during the trouble with France.

The Republican Party disagreed sharply with the Hamiltonian concept of the value of a national debt to the stability of the Government. Led by Albert Gallatin, Jefferson's able Secretary of the Treasury, Congress adopted a program of paying off the national debt as rapidly as possible. Jefferson also revealed his moderate and balanced economic principles by declaring that "agriculture, manufacture, commerce, and navigation, the four pillars of our prosperity, are most thriving when left most free to individual enterprise." In practice, if not always in theory, the Republicans were to foster the balanced development of the vast and varied natural resources of their country during the next quarter-century.

A cardinal constitutional principle of the Jeffersonian creed was belief in a system of checks and balances among the three departments of the federal government in order to prevent any one of them from assuming despotic or unconstitutional power. During the Federalist regime the Republicans had repeatedly criticized what they considered unwarranted assumptions of authority by the executive and judicial branches. As the institution most directly responsible to the people, Congress was thought by Republicans to have a priority in a system of separated powers. The organization of Congress, however, had not been developed sufficiently to provide machinery for the assumption by that body of effective direction of the federal government. The party therefore had to devise ways of constructive leadership and co-operation between the executive and Congress without violating the principle of legislative priority or supremacy.

Jefferson solved the problem through his position as party leader, a solution made possible because of his tremendous prestige and unquestioned ascendancy in Republican ranks. Nominally, he accepted the theory of congressional ascendancy in legislation. Unlike Washington and Adams, he sent his messages to Congress by a clerk rather than reading them in person, and he was uniformly deferential in his messages and in his other relationships with Congress. He did not veto a single bill.

At the same time, Jefferson used a variety of methods to assert a strong executive leadership in Congress. Although his practice varied, depending upon conditions, he often had his political lieutenants placed in key legislative and political positions and worked through them to effect his legislative program. Also, Treasury Secretary Gallatin served as an effective and valuable liaison officer between the President and Congress. Although the Republicans had earlier condemned the Federalist practice of referring legislative matters to Hamilton as Secretary of the Treasury, they now revived the practice by asking Gallatin to make reports and proposals to the House. He attended committee meetings and assisted in the preparation of reports to be presented to the House. In general he became a sort of executive manager who co-operated with the congressional leaders in steering measures through Congress.

This unofficial fusion of the executive and legislative departments would have been very difficult if not impossible without the employment of another extra-constitutional device, the party caucus. From time to time the President, cabinet officers, and party members in Congress met in caucus and discussed proposed legislation fully and came to a conclusion upon policy before specific measures reached the floor of either house. It was alleged that Jefferson himself upon occasion presided at these secret meetings. By holding doubtful members in line, the caucus increased party solidarity in Congress and facilitated enactment of important measures.

The effectiveness of this close though unofficial relationship between the executive department and Congress depended largely upon the President's prestige and recognized ascendancy in his own party, and upon his capacity for leadership. From 1801 to 1809 such leadership was provided by Jefferson, and it resulted in a comprehensive legislative achievement. His successor, James Madison, lacked Jefferson's flair for political leadership, however, and during his term of office, the executive rapidly declined to a position subordinate to that of Congress.

THE ANNEXATION OF LOUISIANA

The outstanding achievement of Jefferson's presidency was the incorporation in 1803 of the Louisiana Territory into the United States. The occasion gave rise to two important and interrelated constitutional issues. The first concerned the constitutional right of the United States to acquire foreign territory; the second involved the right ultimately to admit the territory to the status of statehood without altering unconstitutionally the nature of the Union.

Upon their succession to power, the Jeffersonians were confronted with a difficult domestic and international problem. The lower Mississippi River flowed entirely through Spanish territory and for the people west of the Appalachians the Mississippi furnished. an indispensable avenue of commerce. The American frontiersmen were an aggressive lot, not inclined to be restrained by unappreciated restrictions—even those of an international nature—and there were repeated protests when the Spanish increased the restrictions on American trade through New Orleans.

Jefferson was sympathetic with the westerners. When he learned that the Louisiana Territory had been ceded to France, then powerful and aggressive under Napoleon's leadership, the President moved to secure American control of enough land in the New Orleans region to insure unrestricted navigation and use of the lower Mississippi. The result of the negotiations with France was America's greatest windfall: the purchase by treaty in April 1803 of the entire Louisiana Territory for approximately $15,000,000.

The American response to the acquisition was generally favorable, but the administration and Congress were confronted with a basic question of constitutionality. Republicans professed adherence to the doctrine of strict construction, according to which federal authority was definitely limited to those powers specifically mentioned in the Constitution. Yet the Constitution said nothing of any right to acquire territory, the framers of 1787 having simply neglected to make any statement on the point. If so sweeping a power as the right to acquire territory were considered to be implied merely because it was now convenient to do so, it would render the whole doctrine of strict construction absurd and instead confirm the Hamiltonian theory of implied powers.

More serious, to admit a given federal power as a matter of convenience would go far to impair the validity of the Tenth Amendment. The doctrine that the federal government was one of enumerated powers would then be replaced by the theory that federal authority could encompass any matter of sufficient importance to the national welfare. The whole Jeffersonian conception of the Union would thus be subtly altered, or even destroyed.

Jefferson at first wished to solve this dilemma by amending the Constitution to grant the federal government the requisite authority to purchase territory. He actually drafted proposals for a constitutional amendment to this end and submitted them to his advisers for their consideration. They argued, however, that it would be dangerous to allow the treaty to be delayed awaiting the slow and doubtful process of constitutional amendment, for Napoleon might change his mind and the great opportunity be lost. They also contended that the power to purchase territory could reasonably be implied from the treaty-making power. Reluctantly the champion of strict construction acquiesced, trusting, as he said, "that the good sense of our country will correct the evil of loose construction when it shall produce ill effects." Thus did the Jeffersonians deliver a severe blow to their own doctrine of strict construction of the Constitution.

The President called Congress into special session in order to obtain the advice and consent of the Senate for the treaty and to secure the action of both houses for measures to carry the treaty into effect. Constitutional issues played the leading role in the congressional debate. While the Federalists raised little objection to the mere acquisition of the territory, they vehemently denounced certain provisions of the treaty and their implications. They centered their attack upon Article III, which provided: "The inhabitants of the ceded territory shall be incorporated in the Union of the United States, and admitted as soon as possible, according to the principles of the Federal Constitution, to the enjoyment of all the rights, advantages, and immunities of citizens of the United States; and in the mean time they shall be maintained and protected in the free enjoyment of their liberty, property, and the Religion which they profess." This provision was essentially a promise of eventual statehood for the people of Louisiana, although under the Constitution the admission of new states was left to the discretion of Congress.

Since the Federalist Party was centered in New England, its spokesmen objected to the creation in the South and West of new states which would almost inevitably add to the strength of the Jeffersonian cause. Probably most Federalists agreed with the declaration of Representative Roger Griswold of Connecticut: "A new territory and new subjects may undoubtedly be obtained by conquest and by purchase; but neither the conquest nor the purchase can incorporate them into the Union. They must remain in the condition of colonies and be governed accordingly." Griswold's policy, if adopted, would have made the United States at this early date an imperialistic nation.

The most extreme Federalist view was reflected by Senator Timothy Pickering of Massachusetts, who maintained that new states could not be admitted from the acquired territory even by constitutional amendment unless every state gave its consent, since the Union was a partnership to which the consent of each member was necessary to admit a new partner. Later, when the Federalists were defeated on the Louisiana issue, Pickering became the leader of the extremists who contemplated the secession of the northern states from the Union and the formation of a separate confederacy.

Fortunately for the future of the United States, the Republicans preferred realistic and progressive statesmanship to consistency. They emphasized the authority to acquire territory under the war and treaty-making clauses of the Constitution, a position later upheld unequivocally by Marshall and the Supreme Court in *American Insurance Company v. Canter* (1828). Also, Republican spokesmen insisted that the treaty did not positively guarantee statehood, inasmuch as territorial status would satisfy the requirements of Article III of the treaty. Whether states should be admitted from the Louisiana Territory would be left to the future discretion of Congress.

The Senate ratified the treaty in October 1803, 26 to 5, and both houses then appropriated the money and made temporary provisions for the government of the new territory. Since a majority of Congress did not believe that the people of the acquired territory were yet ready for a large amount of self-government, the first governing act provided that all military, civil, and judicial authority in Louisiana should be vested in appointees of the President. As the Constitution explicitly gave Congress the power to "make all needful Rules and Regulations" respecting the territory of the United States there was inherent in this measure no serious question of congressional authority. However, objection was raised to the autocratic nature of the territorial government, and soon the administration sponsored another measure providing for a gradual preparation of the French and Spanish inhabitants of Louisiana for self-government. This second law provided for government by a powerful governor and a weak council to be appointed by the President from the property-holding residents of the territory.

American immigrants were soon settling in Louisiana and demanding greater participation in the government. Consequently in 1805 a third act gave the Territory of Orleans, as the lower part of the Louisiana purchase was termed, a territorial government very similar to that outlined in the Northwest Ordinance of 1787. The vast area north of the present state of Louisiana contained few white people and was temporarily attached to Indiana Territory for purposes of administration. Thus did the territory acquired from France rapidly come to have a constitutional status practically identical with that of the original territory of the United States.

Opposition to the constitutional incorporation of Louisiana and its people into the federal union continued among the New England Federalists for several years. They saw the balance of power among the original states being undermined to the detriment of New England. To provide a partial corrective Massachusetts and her sister states repeatedly proposed a constitutional amendment to increase their relative influence by entirely eliminating slaves in the apportionment of representatives in Congress. In 1812 the admission of Louisiana as a state encountered bitter opposition from the Federalists, who reiterated most of their former arguments against the incorporation of "outsiders" into the Union.

To be compelled to accept as political equals the untold and untutored masses who would settle beyond the Mississippi seemed to believers in government by the good, the wise, and the rich to constitute a catastrophe. "This Constitution," declared the conservative Josiah Quincy of Massachusetts, "never was, and never can be, strained to lap over all the wilderness of the West," without virtually subverting the rights of the original states and endangering the Union which they created.

In sponsoring the admission of a state from the Louisiana Territory the Republicans delivered a severe blow, consciously or otherwise, to their former concept of the Union as a compact among the original states and to the related doctrine of strict construction. The Louisiana Purchase doubled the size of the country; and the Republicans, by adopting a policy of admitting new states from that territory into the Union on an equal basis with the old states, greatly extended the liberal and successful program of nation-building launched by the Ordinance of 1787. No other modern nation has had an opportunity to incorporate a virtually unoccupied region as large and potentially valuable as the Mississippi Basin, and fortunately both the constitutional structure and the statesmanship of the United States were equal to the occasion.

Chapter

9

The Triumph of Jeffersonian Republicanism

NOWHERE did the impact of Jeffersonianism upon the American constitutional system produce such a sharp reaction as in the federal judiciary. While the judiciary, still in the hands of Federalists appointed prior to Jefferson's inauguration, looked to long-established law and precedent, Jefferson and his followers looked to the present and the future and insisted upon the right of the contemporary majority to shape its own institutions. This basic conflict had been sharpened by the enforcement of the Sedition Act and by the partisan enactment of the Judiciary Act of 1801. With the accession of the Republicans to power, a clash was inevitable.

REPEAL OF THE JUDICIARY ACT OF 1801

In the original draft of his first message to Congress, Jefferson had set forth his own theory of constitutional interpretation. Each of the three equal and independent departments "must have a right in cases which arise within the line of its proper functions, where, equally with the others, it acts in the last resort and without appeal, to decide on the validity of an act according to its own judgment, and uncontrolled by the opinions of any other department." Such a public challenge to the advocates of judicial supremacy was not actually issued. Instead, in the message as delivered on December 8,

1801, Jefferson discreetly contented himself with calling the attention of Congress to the Judiciary Act of 1801 and with submitting a summary of the business of the federal courts since their establishment, designed to demonstrate that the courts created by the recent act were unnecessary.

On January 6, 1802, Senator John Breckinridge of Kentucky introduced a motion to repeal the disputed law. This precipitated a long debate on the question of Congress' constitutional authority to deprive the judges appointed under the act of their offices by abolishing the offices they held. Federalist spokesmen answered the question emphatically in the negative by maintaining that repeal would violate the provision of the Constitution which guaranteed tenure during good behavior to federal judges. Republicans replied that the creation and abolition of inferior courts were left by the Constitution to the discretion of Congress, and that the offices did not become the vested property of the judges. Senators and congressmen from Kentucky and Virginia in particular were well aware of the widespread sentiment among their constituents for the complete abolition of the inferior federal courts lest the decisions of those courts jeopardize existing land titles in those states. To the Federalist charge that the repeal bill was a partisan attempt to control what the Constitution had placed above partisanship, the Republicans retorted that the Judiciary Act of 1801 was the original sin in that respect.

Repeatedly during the debates the Federalists asserted the power of the Supreme Court to declare acts of Congress unconstitutional. The Constitution, they said, had provided for an "independent" judiciary which had "the power of checking the Legislature in case it should pass any laws in violation of the Constitution." In reply, Breckinridge reiterated Jefferson's doctrine, that the three departments are equal and co-ordinate, each having "exclusive authority on subjects committed to it." He concluded that "the construction of one department of the powers vested in it, is of higher authority than the construction of any other department; . . . that therefore the Legislature have the exclusive right to interpret the Constitution, in what regards the law making power, and the judges are bound to execute the laws they [Congress] make." In the House John Randolph of Virginia emphatically denied the need for a judicial check on Congress by the blunt rhetorical questions: "Are we not as deeply interested in the true exposition of the Constitution as the judges can be? Is not Congress as capable of self-government?"

The forces of Jeffersonian democracy had their way, and on March 31, 1802, the repeal bill became law. The immediate effect was to revive the judicial system based on the Judiciary Act of 1789. Promptly the Republicans enacted another law providing for annual instead of semiannual sessions of the Supreme Court, the effect being to postpone the Court's next session until February 1803. The law's sponsors evidently hoped thereby to discourage any of the displaced circuit judges from attacking the validity of the Repeal Act before the Court.

In April 1802, the Republican-dominated Congress passed a new Circuit Court Act by which the country was divided into six instead of three circuits, to each of which was assigned a separate justice of the Supreme Court, who, together with a district judge, should compose the circuit court. As new states were later admitted into the Union this federal judicial system was extended, with no basic change being made until after the Civil War.

MARBURY V. MADISON

Chief Justice Marshall realized the need for immediate and bold action if he were to prevent Federalist constitutionalism from being overwhelmed by the triumphant Republicans. Jefferson and his congressional supporters had carried through a comprehensive legislative program based upon their own interpretation of the constitutional division of power, and then in the congressional elections of 1802 they had received the equivalent of a vote of confidence from the people. Marshall was aware that a frontal assault upon the power of the executive or of Congress might accomplish little of lasting value and might lead to the impeachment of judges in retaliation. A skillful political tactician, he therefore decided upon a flanking movement. He found his opportunity in *Marbury v. Madison* (1803), a case giving rise to his most celebrated opinion, if not his most important one.

William Marbury was one of President Adams' "midnight" appointees as justice of the peace for the District of Columbia. His commission had been signed and sealed but not delivered when Jefferson took office. The new President, believing that the appointment had not been consummated, ordered James Madison, his Secretary of State, to withhold the commission. Thereupon Marbury, acting under Section 13 of the Judiciary Act of 1789, applied to the Supreme Court for a "rule" or preliminary writ to Madison to show cause why a mandamus should not be issued directing the Secretary of State to deliver the commission. When the preliminary writ was granted Madison ignored it as a judicial interference with the executive department.

At the Court's next session in February 1803, Marshall handed down an opinion on Marbury's application for a mandamus. Ignoring for the moment the issue of whether or not the Supreme Court could properly take jurisdiction of the cause, Marshall first considered the question: "Has the applicant a right to the commission he demands?" His answer was that when a commission has been signed and sealed the appointment is legally complete. For Jefferson's and Madison's benefit he added: "To withhold his commission, therefore, is an act deemed by the court not warranted by law, but violative of a vested legal right." In leaving the question of the Court's jurisdiction to the last Marshall reversed the usual and logical order of procedure, and by so doing he created for himself an opportunity to lecture the Secretary of State on his duty to deliver the commission and thus to obey the law.

If the applicant's rights have been violated, the Chief Justice next asked, "do the laws of his country afford him a remedy?" This question Marshall also answered in the affirmative: "Having this legal title to the office, he [the applicant] has a consequent right to the commission; a refusal to deliver which is a plain violation of that right, for which the laws of his country afford him a remedy." Marshall denied that the Court in exercising its duty to decide on the rights of individuals was attempting "to intrude into the cabinet, and to intermeddle with the prerogatives of the executive." In the exercise of "certain important political powers" the President is free to use his own discretion, but where he is directed by act of Congress to perform certain acts which involve the rights of individuals he is "amenable to the laws for his conduct."

A third, and the determining question in the case was whether the proper remedy for the applicant was "a mandamus issuing from this Court." Under the Judiciary Act of 1789, Section 13, the Supreme Court had been authorized "to issue . . . writs of *mandamus* . . . to . . . persons holding office under the authority of the United States." Since the Secretary of State definitely came within that description, "if this court is not authorized to issue a writ of mandamus to such an officer, it must be because the law is unconstitutional." Marshall then argued that the Constitution prescribed specifically the Supreme Court's original jurisdiction, that this jurisdiction did not include the power to issue writs of mandamus to federal officials, and that Congress had no power to alter this jurisdiction. Therefore the attempt of Congress in the Judiciary Act of

1789 to give the Supreme Court authority to issue writs of mandamus to public officers "appears not to be warranted by the constitution." Consequently Marbury's application for a mandamus was denied.

Having declared void a section of the Judiciary Act of 1789, Marshall then passed to his now famous argument defending the Court's power to hold acts of Congress unconstitutional. His argument rested more upon certain general principles of constitutional government than upon specific provisions in the Constitution itself. First he observed that the Constitution was the "fundamental and paramount law of the nation." Second, it was the particular duty of the Courts to interpret the law—that is, "to say what the law is." "Thus," the Chief Justice concluded, "the particular phraseology of the constitution of the United States confirms and strengthens the principle, supposed to be essential to all written constitutions, that a law repugnant to the constitution is void, and that the courts, as well as other departments, are bound by that instrument." Therefore, in conflicts between the Constitution and acts of Congress, it is the Court's duty to enforce the Constitution and to ignore the statute, that is, to refuse to enforce the unconstitutional law.

Marshall's opinion was in reality a shrewd and audacious political attack on Jefferson's administration, in which the Chief Justice went out of his way to lecture his political antagonist in the Executive Mansion. In order to do so, he carefully avoided a prior consideration of the question of jurisdiction and instead treated first and at great length the constitutional duties and obligations of the executive. Much of this material was mere *obiter dictum*, since later in the opinion Marshall held that the Court had no proper jurisdiction of the cause.

At the same time, Marshall carefully protected himself against political reprisals. He decided the immediate issue in favor of the administration and thereby avoided giving Madison and Jefferson any opportunity to defy the Court's authority. Had he issued the writ of mandamus requested, Madison would almost certainly have refused to comply, and the Court, its authority flouted, would have been made to look ridiculous. Moreover, in declaring void a portion of a statute on the grounds that it gave the Court authority in excess of constitutional limitations, he evaded any possible charge that the Court was engaged in self-aggrandizement of power.

In declaring void a section of the Judiciary Act of 1789, Marshall also violated a basic rule of statutory construction—that a law ought not to be held unconstitutional when it might be held valid by any other possible reasonable construction. A careful reading of the Judiciary Act of 1789 does not reveal any obvious and distinct attempt on the part of Congress to confer any additional category of original jurisdiction upon the Court beyond that authorized in the Constitution. The plain intent of Section 13 was to authorize the issuance of writs of mandamus in cases where the Court did have jurisdiction under the Constitution. In short, Marshall's interpretation of the section in question was a strained and unreasonable one, and was out of accord with the principles of statutory construction laid down by Marshall himself in subsequent opinions, in which he argued for a broad and liberal construction of statutes and of congressional powers under the Constitution.

Marshall's argument in favor of the Court's power to declare an act of Congress void was not of major significance at the time he made it, and the importance of *Marbury v. Madison* in the history of judicial review has in fact been somewhat exaggerated. The idea that the Court could invalidate acts of Congress was not then new. More than a score of analogous state cases, in which state courts had declared void the acts of their legislatures, had already occurred. In *The Federalist*, Hamilton had argued for the right of judicial review in the forthcoming federal judiciary, and the reader will recall that in *Hylton v. United States* (1796) [1] the Court had assumed the right, although it had decided that the statute in question was constitutional. Prior to 1803, a decided majority of the bench and bar had apparently considered judicial review a necessary part of the constitutional system, and the principle had not been seriously disputed until the recent debate on the highly controversial Repeal Act of 1802. Marshall's reaffirmation of the Court's power therefore received but little attention from either the friends or the foes of the federal judiciary.

Moreover, Marshall's opinion is of doubtful significance as a precedent for the later exercise of the Court's power to act as the final arbiter of constitutional questions involving the validity of acts of Congress. Marshall nowhere asserted that the Court's decision regarding the constitutionality of acts of Congress was final and binding upon the other two departments of government, nor did he make the express claim that the judiciary's interpretation was superior to or entitled to precedence over that of Congress or the executive. The act he invalidated in part was not a general law, but dealt exclusively with the judicial department. In asserting the

---

[1] For a discussion of this case see pp. 181–182.

Court's right to pass on the constitutionality of such a statute, Marshall did not claim much more than that each department of the government rightfully should have the final authority to pass on constitutional matters affecting that department.

That the Court was not anxious at this time to assert too boldly and comprehensively its rights of judicial review was demonstrated a few days after the delivery of the Marbury opinion, when a majority of the justices officially acquiesced in the assignment to them of circuit court duty by the Judiciary Act of 1789 and the Circuit Court Act of April 1802. Marshall and some of the associate justices strongly believed that the Constitution did not authorize the assignment of Supreme Court justices to the circuit courts. But when the issue came before the Court in *Stuart v. Laird* (1803), the pertinent provisions of these acts of Congress were held to be valid for the remarkable reason that "practice and acquiescence" in the assignment of circuit court duty to the justices "for a period of several years, commencing with the organization of the judicial system [in 1789], affords an irresistible answer, and has indeed fixed the construction."

For more than half a century after *Marbury v. Madison* Congress and the President continued to consider themselves at least the equals of the judiciary in determining the constitutionality of legislation. In several important cases before the Supreme Court the validity of certain congressional acts was challenged, but in each case the Court upheld the act in question. Furthermore, practically every session of Congress was to witness lengthy constitutional debates in which the members would rely upon their own rather than the judges' interpretation. Likewise until after 1869 many more bills were vetoed by Presidents on the ground of their unconstitutionality than were invalidated by the Supreme Court. During that time it was generally assumed that the people of the United States could make the final interpretation of the Constitution themselves through the politically responsible departments or through amendments. Not until the latter decades of the nineteenth century was this theory of constitutional interpretation replaced by the juristic concept of judicial review, according to which the decisions of the Supreme Court determined constitutional issues with finality unless changed by amendment.

The reaction of the Republicans to the Marbury decision was limited and less critical than were their responses to some of Marshall's later decisions. Few grasped the potentialities of judicial review, and as a consequence the portions of the opinion affirming the Court's right to declare acts of Congress void aroused relatively little opposition. Most Republican leaders were determined that the politically responsible departments should have their way in important conflicts with the Federalist judiciary and were not deterred by the elaborate pronouncement of the Chief Justice. This attitude was encouraged by the decision in *Stuart v. Laird*, which virtually upheld the Republican cause as represented in the Repeal Act. And since the decision on the immediate issue between Marbury and Madison was in favor of the Jeffersonians, their chief criticism was directed against Marshall's "interference" with the Executive Department. This they considered a political act, and they were determined to reply in kind.

IMPEACHMENT OF FEDERAL JUDGES

Under the Constitution impeachment is the only legal method of removing federal executive and judicial officers. The House of Representatives is authorized to impeach "all civil Officers of the United States" for "Treason, Bribery, or other high Crimes and Misdemeanors," whereupon they are to be tried before the Senate. As in many other provisions of the Constitution, the real scope and meaning of impeachment could be determined only by practical application and experiment.

Although the Constitution prescribed the impeachment of federal judges only for high crimes and misdemeanors, Jefferson's supporters were inclined to take an extremely broad view of the impeachment power. By the more partisan Republicans impeachment was considered a proper instrument for removing from office judges who had fallen too far out of step with public opinion. This conception made impeachment largely a political proceeding in which any judge could be removed from office should both the House and the Senate think it expedient to do so.

To the Federalist argument that the judiciary should be above political considerations, Jefferson's supporters replied that the federal judiciary had already entered the political arena and that it must abide by the consequences. More moderate Republicans were not willing to go this far, but they held that "high crimes and misdemeanors" might be construed broadly, so that bad judicial ethics or misconduct on the bench would become impeachable offenses. Some judges had taken advantage of their responsibility in charging grand juries to make political speeches from the bench; others had left their work to participate in political campaigns; still others had interpreted and applied the Sedition Law with gross partisanship. Many moderate Republicans thought these offenses properly impeachable.

The Republicans first tested the impeachment process against Judge John Pickering of the District Court of New Hampshire. In February 1803, while the Marbury case was pending, Jefferson sent to the House of Representatives a message accompanied by documentary evidence showing that Pickering was guilty of intoxication and profanity on the bench. The House later impeached the judge on charges of malfeasance and general unfitness for office because of his loose morals and intemperate habits. In March 1804, Pickering was tried before the Senate, where it became obvious that he was insane.

This raised the question of the extent of the impeachment power in a most embarrassing form. It could hardly be argued plausibly that an insane man's conduct constituted either high crime or misdemeanor, since such offenses implied "a vicious will" on the part of the person involved. Yet unless the impeachment power was to be construed broadly enough to remove Pickering, the precedent would be established that there was actually no method of removing an incompetent or incapacitated judge from office.

A majority even of the Republican senators were apparently persuaded that Pickering, being insane, could not properly be convicted on any of the specific counts in the House impeachment. Nonetheless they believed Pickering unfit for office and either abstained from voting or joined their colleagues in voting that the accused was "guilty as charged." He was convicted by a 19-to-7 vote and removed from office. The Pickering impeachment was so confused and contradictory, however, that it was not thereafter treated as having established the general right of impeachment for mere incompetence or incapacity in office.

Following Pickering's conviction, the Republicans moved to impeach Justice Samuel Chase of the Supreme Court. Republican leaders were generally agreed that Chase's conduct on the bench in the Sedition cases had been inexcusable; moreover, they felt that he had forfeited any claim to judicial impartiality by actively campaigning for Adams in 1800. In 1803 he provided additional grounds for impeachment, when in a long charge to a Baltimore grand jury he severely criticized Congress for abolishing the circuit judges and jeopardizing the "independence" of the judiciary. He also attacked the Jefferson administration and its doctrine "that all men, in a state of society, are entitled to enjoy equal liberty and equal rights," a doctrine which he said had "brought this mighty mischief upon us," a mischief that would "rapidly progress, until peace and order, freedom and property, shall be destroyed." Universal suffrage, he contended, would cause "our republican Constitution" to "sink into a mobocracy."

Led by John Randolph of Virginia, a radical Republican strongly committed to the twin doctrines of States' rights and agrarianism, the House of Representatives in January 1804 appointed a committee to inquire into Chase's conduct. This resulted in the House's impeachment of Chase on March 12 by a strictly partisan vote of 73 to 32. To prosecute the case against Chase the House appointed a committee of managers, headed by Randolph, who presented eight articles of impeachment. No infraction of law was alleged. The first seven articles concerned Chase's "oppressive conduct" as a presiding judge in several criminal trials of 1800 which had arisen under the Sedition Act. The final article related to the Baltimore address, which was characterized as "an intemperate and inflammatory political harangue," designed "to excite the fears and resentment . . . of the good people of Maryland against their State government . . . [and] against the Government of the United States."

In February 1805 the trial got under way before the Senate, presided over by Vice-President Aaron Burr, fresh from his duel with Hamilton. Justice Chase was defended by five eminent Federalist lawyers, headed by Luther Martin, whose hatred of the President was so great that in an age of intense partisanship his worst damnation of a man was to call him "as great a scoundrel as Tom Jefferson." It was evident to observers that although the fate of the federal judiciary might hinge on the verdict, the trial was to be an heroic partisan contest. At first the Republican leaders were confident of success, but as the trial progressed their confidence declined. The House managers were less competent lawyers than the defense counsel, while the testimony of their star witnesses proved to be contradictory and less damaging to Chase than anticipated.

It was generally recognized both in the presentation of the evidence and in the arguments of the case that the vital issue concerned the proper scope of impeachment under the Constitution. The counsel for the defense did not claim that Chase was above reproach, but they consistently maintained that an offense to be impeachable must be indictable in law.

On the other hand, certain members of the impeachment committee, notably Randolph, took the extreme view that impeachment was not necessarily a criminal proceeding at all, but rather that on occasion it could be resorted to as a constitutional means of keeping the courts in reasonable harmony with the will of the nation, as expressed through politically responsible departments. The weight of this argument was increased by the fact that President Jefferson had just been re-elected in the presidential campaign of 1804 by an overwhelming electoral vote, with increased Republican majorities in Congress.

The other House managers did not adhere to such a broad interpretation of impeachment. They merely argued logically that, since impeachment was the only constitutionally recognized method of removing federal judges, the terms "high Crimes and Misdemeanors" must necessarily include all cases of willful misconduct in office, whether indictable in law or not.

The Senate was composed of thirty-four members, twenty-five Republicans and nine Federalists. With twenty-three votes necessary for conviction, the Republicans clearly had the requisite two-thirds majority, provided balloting on the articles of impeachment followed strict party lines. But several moderate Republicans remained unconvinced of Chase's guilt, being persuaded neither by the evidence nor by the prosecution's arguments. Several Republican Senators also had been antagonized either by Randolph's extreme position or by his opposition to certain legislative measures sponsored by party moderates. Moreover, the President himself maintained a hands-off policy. The prosecution's efforts to enlist Vice-President Burr's influence with northern Republican Senators also proved futile.

As a consequence, the Republican leadership failed to obtain the necessary two-thirds majority for conviction on each article of impeachment. On three articles there was a simple majority to convict, but even on the last article, where the prosecution had its strongest case, the vote fell four short of the necessary twenty-three. Failure convinced Jefferson and many of his supporters that impeachment was "a bungling way of removing Judges," "a farce which will not be tried again." Immediately Republican leaders introduced into both houses of Congress resolutions to amend the Constitution so as to provide for the removal of federal judges "by the President on joint address of both Houses of Congress." Although this action was in part a gesture—since the Republicans could hardly have expected to secure the adoption of such an amendment at that time—they repeatedly used the threat of an amendment of this kind in their struggles with the Federalist judges.

That the abandonment of impeachment as a political device was salutary has been the general verdict of statesmen and historians. To say, however, that the conviction of Justice Chase would inevitably have led to the removal of his associates and to the destruction of the "independence" of the federal judiciary is to engage in unwarranted speculation. Elective judiciaries or other means of making judges responsible to public opinion were later adopted by most of the states without noticeable curtailment of the legal rights of the individual citizen.

Chase's impeachment had some beneficial consequences in that thereafter federal judges were more inclined to confine their official opinions and actions to judicial matters and to refrain from lecturing the public on political and moral issues. But the Chase case did not settle the basic constitutional issue of whether impeachment was limited to indictable offenses or could be employed more broadly. This unresolved issue was to reappear later, notable in the impeachment proceedings against both Presidents Andrew Johnson and Richard Nixon.

THE BURR TRIAL AND THE DEFINITION OF TREASON

Treason is the most serious crime which a citizen can commit against his country. In Britain and in many European countries, however, the offense has often been defined very loosely, to include a variety of political offenses against the state. To guard against this possibility, the Convention of 1787 wrote into the Constitution, Article III, Section 3, an extremely narrow definition of treason: "Treason against the United States, shall consist only in levying War against them, or in adhering to their Enemies, giving them Aid and Comfort. No person shall be convicted of Treason unless on the Testimony of two Witnesses to the same overt Act, or on Confession in open Court."

The first federal treason trials of constitutional significance were those arising out of the celebrated conspiracy of Aaron Burr. Burr had a brilliant though opportunistic political career which carried him to the vice-presidency, but his political break with Jefferson and his tragic duel with Hamilton in July 1804 brought his career to a premature end. To recoup his political fortunes he turned to the West, where popular discontent still prevailed. In the summer of 1806 Burr procured, although he did not actually attend, the assemblage of a small armed force at Blennerhassett's Island in the upper Ohio River and subsequently conducted it down the Mississippi toward New Orleans. What his ultimate objectives were is still a matter of controversy, but many men were then convinced that he plotted the treasonable separation of the Southwest from the remainder of the Union, and there is some evidence to substantiate this view. Jefferson was at first not much alarmed by Burr's activities, but in November 1806 he issued a proclamation calling for the seizure of Burr and his associates. The expedition ultimately reached the lower Mississippi, where it disintegrated. Burr fled into the wilderness of the Southwest Territory but was shortly captured and brought east for trial.

Burr's trial opened at Richmond early in August 1807, in the United States Circuit Court for Virginia, presided over by Chief Justice John Marshall. The prosecution was in charge of District Attorney George Hay and the immature but brilliant William Wirt; defense counsel included Burr himself, Luther Martin, and several other famous lawyers of the day. The serious nature of the alleged offense, Burr's former high office, the administration's grim determination to secure a conviction, and Marshall's known antagonism toward Jefferson, all combined to produce one of the most dramatic trials in American history.

The first important constitutional issue presented by the case arose during the proceedings before the grand jury, when Burr moved that the court issue a subpoena to President Jefferson requiring him to appear with certain papers in his possession material to the case. A heated debate between counsel developed over the power of the court to issue a subpoena to the President, with Marshall finally ruling in favor of the court's authority. Both the Constitution and federal law, he said, gave an accused person the right "to the process of the court to compel the attendance of his witnesses," and neither the Constitution nor any law exempted the President from this rule.

Jefferson refused to obey the order on the ground that the independence of the executive would be jeopardized were the President amenable to the court's writ. The President, he added, had duties which were superior to his duties as a citizen. In general, Jefferson's argument has since been sustained as correct, in particular where the court seeks to interfere with the conduct of executive affairs.

The main issue during the trial itself was whether Burr's actions constituted treason as defined in the Constitution of the United States. The defense maintained that Burr could have had no direct part in any overt act of levying war against the United States, since he had not been present during the assemblage of armed forces at Blennerhassett's Island. The defense thus attempted to draw a distinction between the real act of levying war and the mere act of advising such action, the former admittedly being treason but the latter being only "constructive treason." The prosecution, on the other hand, relied on the English common-law doctrine that "in treason all are principals," and argued accordingly that Burr as procurer of the unlawful assemblage was as guilty as any of the men who assembled on the fateful night.

In a very elaborate opinion Marshall accepted the defense contention. He drew a sharp distinction between actual presence with an armed force levying war against the United States and mere advice or procurement. The latter, he said, was conspiracy, not treason.[2] "To advise or procure a treason . . . is not treason in itself." The Chief Justice admitted, however, that procuring the armed force might be treason, but the procurement must then be charged in the indictment and proved by the testimony of two witnesses to the same overt act of procurement, as required by the Constitution. To the objection that procurement was by its very nature a secret act and that "scarcely ever" could two witnesses be produced to testify to the same overt act connecting procurement with assemblage, Marshall replied that "the difficulty of proving a fact will not justify conviction without proof."

Since the prosecution could not produce two witnesses to overt procurement, the jury found Burr not guilty. Administration supporters widely condemned this outcome as a miscarriage of justice and attacked Marshall for "screening a criminal and degrading a judge." However, Burr's guilt has never been definitely established; moreover, Marshall's narrow construction of treason has not damaged the national welfare. Not until World War II was the Supreme Court to pass on the treason clause in the Constitution, when it finally construed "overt act" more broadly than Marshall had done.

After 1807 several factors worked toward a gradual diminution of the antagonism between the judiciary and the dominant Republicans. In March 1809, with the accession of Madison to the presidency, the personal hostility between Chief Executive and Chief Justice that had prevailed during the Jefferson administrations disappeared. Also Madison realized the nationalizing value of the federal judiciary even when he disagreed with its policies. After 1811 a majority of the Supreme Court justices were Republican appointees, although on the bench they generally conformed more

---

[2] During the Civil War Congress by statute drew a distinction between conspiracy and treason. For a discussion of this and other aspects of treason during the Civil War, see pp. 394–396, and 410–420.

closely to Marshall's than to Jefferson's constitutional creed. Then the disintegration of the Federalist party after the War of 1812 removed much of the partisan motive for conflict between the judiciary and the politically responsible departments. And previous to this last development the predominance of foreign over domestic issues in the public mind tended to temper the resentment against John Marshall and his associates. Meanwhile the center of constitutional controversy shifted to the northern states, where the Federalists were still strong and decidedly opposed to Jeffersonian policies.

THE EMBARGO AND NORTHERN CHAMPIONSHIP OF STATES' RIGHTS

While the first few years of Jefferson's administration were prosperous and relatively free from the encroachments of international strife, after 1804 the bitter international struggle between Britain and Napoleon gradually projected itself more and more into American affairs. As the European war progressed, American commerce became increasingly important to both belligerents, the result being both increased profits and increased hazards for American merchantmen. Unfortunately for the United States, both Britain and France in their determination to destroy one another had little regard for the maritime rights of neutral nations. Both belligerents in their attacks on neutral commerce with their enemies followed blockade and contraband policies which the American government regarded as flagrantly illegal, while Britain insisted also upon the supposed right of impressment—the seizure of seamen from American merchant vessels on the high seas on the ground that they were deserters from the Royal Navy.

Attacks on American commerce speedily became a source of controversy between the administration and the Federalists. Jefferson's followers, generally pro-French and anti-British in sentiment, were inclined to resent the British blockade, contraband, and impressment policies as affronts to American national dignity. Republican congressmen from the middle and southern states therefore clamored for measures of reprisal to protect American honor and dignity, and the administration was inclined to listen to their demands. The great merchants and shipmasters of the Federalist-dominated Northeast, however, were making very large profits out of the neutral carrying trade, and they were inclined to accept captures and impressments as a necessary business hazard. Accordingly they were loud in their disapproval of all suggestions that the administration resort to reprisals against Britain and France, for such measures would almost surely ruin a highly prosperous business.

After the failure of less drastic measures to compel observance of American neutral rights, Jefferson in December 1807 proposed that Congress pass an embargo act banning outright all foreign trade, both imports and exports. The theory behind the proposal was that American commerce was so indispensable to all belligerents concerned that Britain and France would relax their obnoxious regulations and practices in order to gain the benefits of American commerce once more. After but four days' debate, Congress passed the Embargo Act by large majorities, and it became law on December 22, 1807. A number of subsidiary enforcement acts were adopted within the next few months. As a coercive device the law was unsuccessful, for it hurt American commerce more than it hurt Britain and France. From the start, both violations of the embargo and demands for repeal were widespread, and in March 1809, just as Jefferson was retiring from the presidency, the law was finally repealed.

The embargo produced an intense constitutional debate both in Congress and in the press. Republicans justified the law by pointing to the federal power to regulate foreign commerce. The commerce power, they said, was complete, and could be extended to include outright prohibitions upon all commercial activity. Some administration supporters drew a distinction between federal power over interstate commerce and federal power over foreign commerce. They admitted that Congress could not constitutionally lay any outright prohibitions upon commerce between the states, but they insisted that federal power over commerce with foreign nations was of a more complete character, since the commerce clause was reinforced in that field by the government's control over foreign affairs. This distinction between federal power over interstate commerce and federal power over foreign commerce was to arise on other occasions and was to have a certain limited acceptance in the early twentieth century.[3]

The Federalist opposition, on the other hand, insisted upon an extremely narrow definition of the commerce power. The right to regulate, they said, implied only the right to protect in order to extend benefits thereto. The power was not restrictive, and certainly was not prohibitive. Neither, they said, could the commerce power be used for any ulterior purpose—that is, any purpose other than the protection of commerce itself. Here was the question of the

[3] See pp. 552ff.

motive behind the exercise of federal power, another issue of substantial consequence in later constitutional law.

It is interesting to note that the Jeffersonians and Federalists had now virtually exchanged places in their constitutional philosophy. The former strict constructionists now insisted upon a broad and liberal construction of the powers of Congress, while the former nationalists of Hamilton's day now fell back upon the Tenth Amendment, states' rights, and a narrow interpretation of congressional authority. Constitutional theory in both instances was apparently little more than the creature of economic and political interest.

In general, the federal judiciary supported the embargo's constitutionality. On October 3, 1808, Judge John Davis of the federal District Court for Massachusetts, though a Federalist, upheld the embargo's constitutionality in very broad terms. "The degree or extent of the prohibition" imposed upon foreign commerce, he said, must properly be left to "the discretion of the national government, to whom the subject appears to be committed." He rejected the contention that the commerce power could be used only for the protection of commerce itself: "the power to regulate commerce is not confined to the adoption of measures exclusively beneficial to commerce itself, or tending to its advancement; but in our national system, as in all modern sovereignties, it is also to be considered as an instrument for other purposes of general policy and interest." He also sustained the embargo under the war power as a preparation for war, and under the "necessary and proper" clause as appropriate for the protection of the nation's inherent sovereignty.

The Federalists were now no longer willing to acknowledge the federal judiciary as the final arbiter of constitutional questions, and like the Republicans of 1798 they turned to the state legislatures in order to register constitutional objections to national policy. The legislatures of both Massachusetts and Connecticut, for example, adopted resolutions reminiscent of those promulgated by Virginia and Kentucky in protesting the Alien and Sedition Laws. The Massachusetts Resolutions of February 1809 declared that the embargo was "unjust, oppressive, and unconstitutional, and not legally binding upon the citizens of this state." The legislature added: "It would be derogatory to the honour of the commonwealth to presume that it is unable to protect its subjects against all violations of their rights, by peaceable and legal remedies." The Connecticut legislature, in similar vein, endorsed Governor Jonathan Trumbull's declaration that "whenever our national legislature is led to overleap the prescribed bounds of their constitutional powers," it was the right and duty of the state legislatures "to interpose their protecting shield between the rights and liberties of the people, and the assumed power of the general government."

These resolutions virtually affirmed the right of state legislatures to judge of the validity of acts of Congress and to block the enforcement of unconstitutional national policies. However, neither Massachusetts nor Connecticut proposed any actual machinery for nullification, nor did they advance any clear-cut theory of state sovereignty or secession. A few Federalist extremists, notably Senator Timothy Pickering of Massachusetts, supported the idea of secession on several occasions after 1803, but most opponents of the administration thought mainly in terms of political activity as a method for defeating what they considered to be unconstitutional legislation. The New England Federalists, in short, were closer to the position taken by Virginia and Kentucky in 1798 than they were to the well-defined theories of state sovereignty, nullification, and secession that were later to be advanced by Calhoun and his followers.

In 1809 the Pennsylvania legislature also found occasion to evoke the doctrine of states' rights and to challenge the authority of the federal judiciary. The occasion arose out of the so-called Olmstead Case, in which one Gideon Olmstead sought to recover from the state certain proceeds from the sale of a prize ship captured and sold during the Revolution. After some years, Olmstead's title was finally affirmed by Judge Richard Peters, in the United States District Court for Pennsylvania. The state legislature thereupon authorized the governor to use the state militia to prevent the federal marshal from serving a writ of execution. Olmstead then appealed to the Supreme Court of the United States, where he sought and obtained a writ of mandamus directing Judge Peters to issue the writ of execution.

Chief Justice Marshall's opinion in *United States v. Peters* (1809) was a characteristic defense of federal authority. "If the legislatures of the several states," he said, "may, at will, annul the judgments of the courts of the United States, and destroy the rights acquired under those judgments, the constitution itself becomes a solemn mockery, and the nation is deprived of the means of enforcing its laws by the instrumentality of its own tribunals." Marshall also denied that the suit was either commenced or prosecuted against the state in violation of the Eleventh Amendment.

The Pennsylvania legislature ultimately yielded, but not without issuing another challenge to the federal judiciary's right to final judgment on constitutional questions. The assembly warned that it could not permit any infringement of the state's rights by the federal judiciary and added that "no provision is made in the constitution for determining disputes between the general and state governments." The legislature therefore recommended that a constitutional amendment be adopted creating an impartial tribunal to settle constitutional questions.

This suggestion was disapproved by at least eleven of the other sixteen states, including Virginia, Kentucky, and Massachusetts, each of which had formerly issued resolutions similar to those of Pennsylvania. Apparently unconscious of any irony in its position, Virginia declared that the Constitution had already provided for a tribunal to act as final judge—"the Supreme Court," which was "more eminently qualified . . . to decide the disputes aforesaid in an enlightened and impartial manner, than any other tribunal that could be erected."

The Pennsylvania legislature was not convinced by this chorus of disapproval and soon found a new grievance in the attempt to renew the charter for the United States Bank. Accordingly the next year the legislators made their constitutional theory more definite, and perhaps more extreme, by declaring: "The act of union thus entered into being to all intents and purposes a treaty between sovereign states, the general government by this treaty was not constituted the exclusive or final judge of the powers it was to exercise." The resolutions as a whole make it reasonably clear, however, that the legislature was still appealing to the bar of public opinion, and was neither threatening to leave the Union nor setting itself unalterably against the measures of the federal government.

THE WAR OF 1812

The War of 1812, the first war fought by the United States under the Constitution, revealed how far the American people still were from being a really united nation. After years of diplomatic frustration and ill-treatment by belligerent Britain and France, President Madison in June 1812 recommended a declaration of war upon Great Britain. Congress thereupon voted for war, although only by fairly small majorities in both houses.

The war that followed was conducted with general military ineffectiveness amid sectional dissension and constitutional controversy. Principal support of the conflict came from "Warhawk" Republicans from the South and West, who expected to add both

Canada and Florida to the United States by military conquest and to redress British violations of American rights on the high seas. Meanwhile, however, the Northeast, preponderantly Federalist in political sentiment and mindful of its commercial interests, strongly opposed the conflict.

The war produced a serious constitutional controversy on the nature and extent of federal power over state militia. The Constitution gave Congress the power "To provide for calling forth the Militia to execute the Laws of the Union, suppress Insurrections, and repel Invasions." Congress was also authorized "To provide for organizing, arming, and disciplining the Militia, and for governing such Part of them as may be employed in the Service of the United States."

These provisions apparently gave the national government full authority over state militia whenever necessary, but several New England states, where Federalists were in control, refused to permit their militia to be commanded by federal officers or to become an integral part of the army of the United States. In Massachusetts, the state Supreme Court ruled that neither the President nor Congress had the authority to determine *when* the militia should be called out, since this right was not specifically mentioned in the Constitution and could not be inferred from the actual right to call out the militia as mentioned in the Constitution. This was strict construction with a vengeance. The Connecticut legislature resolved that the Constitution did not authorize the use of state militia to support an offensive war. All the New England states attempted to ban service of their militia outside the respective states and in effect built up separate state armies for their own defense against British attack.

Several years after the war had closed, the Supreme Court in *Martin v. Mott* (1827) upheld the President's right, under authority of Congress, to be the sole judge of the existence of those contingencies specified in the Constitution upon which the militia might be called out. The Court added that the President's decision was binding upon state authorities and that the state militia in federal service was subject to the authority of officers appointed by the President. This opinion and subsequent similar ones, however, did not prevent the assertion of a large amount of state autonomy in the organization and administration of armies in both the Mexican War and the Civil War.

Connecticut and Massachusetts also practically nullified the so-called "Enlistment of Minors Act," passed in 1814, which authorized the army to accept enlistment of men aged eighteen to twenty-one. Both states passed acts directing the judges to release on writs of habeas corpus all minors enlisted without the consent of their parents. At the same time, the prospective passage of a federal conscription law inspired the Connecticut legislature to denounce the pending bill as "utterly subversive of the rights and liberties of the people of this state," and as "inconsistent with the principles of the constitution of the United States." Probably the only thing that averted a serious clash between federal and state authorities over army matters was the termination of the war early in 1815.

Meanwhile the Massachusetts legislature had issued a call to the New England states for a convention to meet at Hartford, Connecticut, to discuss the possibility of amending the Constitution for the better protection of New England's sectional interests. Convening in December 1814, the convention deliberated in secret for three weeks. Whatever the real intent behind the gathering, there was much open talk of disunion among Federalists in New England and in Congress at the time, and many Republicans feared that the convention was designed to effect the secession of the New England states. Whether the convention actually considered anything of a treasonable nature, however, is very doubtful; certainly there was nothing treasonable in the measures actually taken.

The Hartford Convention adopted several resolutions of a states' rights and obstructionist character. The states were urged to protect their citizens against unconstitutional federal militia and draft legislation, and to request the federal government to permit the separate states to defend themselves and to receive federal tax credits for such action.

The convention also proposed seven amendments to the federal Constitution. These proposals were obviously designed to provide remedies for the chief grievances of New England and to increase the influence of that minority section in the federal government. In order to limit the power of the South, one proposal would eliminate the "three-fifths" compromise clause in the Constitution and base representation in the House of Representatives solely upon free population. Embargoes were to be limited to sixty days. A two-thirds vote of both houses of Congress would be required to admit a new state, to interdict commerce with foreign nations, or to declare war except in case of actual invasion. Naturalized citizens were to be disqualified from federal elective or appointive office. No President was to serve two terms, and no two successive Presidents were to come from the same state. The final resolution proposed the calling of another convention if the war continued and the federal government failed to respond favorably to the recommendations of the convention.

Commissioners were appointed to carry the resolutions to Washington, but they were met with the news of the termination of hostilities by the Treaty of Ghent and of Andrew Jackson's notable victory at New Orleans and so abandoned their mission. Only Massachusetts and Connecticut acted favorably upon the Convention's proposals, while nine states passed resolutions of disapproval or nonconcurrence. Thus the Hartford Convention and New England Federalism were repudiated by events and rejected by the American people.

How far the New England Federalists were ready to go to attain their objectives is questionable, since constitutional arguments cannot always be taken literally. It is difficult to determine from all the resolutions and protests, from all the claims of "sovereignty" and "independence," just what concept of the Union they were using as a basis of action. The non-co-operation and resistance of some of the states to war measures of the federal government amounted practically to nullification, although there was lacking the complete theoretical justification later found in Calhoun's doctrine. Some Federalist extremists were so strongly convinced of the existence of an irrepressible conflict of political and economic interests with the Republican forces of the South and the West that they were willing to have the "more perfect Union" broken up. The vast majority of Federalists, however, evidently preferred to work for the defeat or modification of their opponents' policies within the existing constitutional system.

The Hartford Convention revealed the constitutional degeneration that had occurred in Federalism. It had become increasingly provincial and devoid of that broad national outlook that distinguished the statesmanship of Washington, Hamilton, and Marshall. There was little philosophical justification even in the Federalists' states' rights doctrines; they were devised simply to protect their own sectional and class interests from the dominant forces of Jeffersonian democracy. The party had lost all capacity for constructive statesmanship, had been deserted by many of its younger statesmen, and was thoroughly out of touch with the rising spirit of democracy and political equalitarianism. The Federalist organization did not long survive the War of 1812.

Nationalism versus Sectionalism

THE CLOSE of the War of 1812 marked the beginning of a new era in the development of the youthful American nation and of its immature constitutional system. After 1815 the United States embarked upon a remarkable period of westward expansion, population growth, and agricultural, commercial, and industrial development. A new generation had grown up since the days of the Revolution and the Confederation, and the men of this generation were determined to make the United States into an effective union and a prosperous country. But the processes of American national growth involved a basic contradiction—a conflict between centralizing and nationalizing forces on the one hand and decentralizing and sectionalizing forces on the other. For a few years after 1815 nationalism was to be in the ascendancy, and after the Civil War it was again to become the dominant force in the United States. During the period from 1820 to 1865, however, nationalism generally was to be overshadowed by decentralization and sectionalism, which were to challenge some of the basic principles of the Constitution and eventually were to shake the nation to its very foundation.

INTERNAL EXPANSION AND THE CONSTITUTION

The United States was growing at an astonishing rate. Its territory was more than trebled during the half-century between the

Louisiana Purchase in 1803 and the Gadsden Purchase in 1853. Meanwhile the area of settlement increased in approximately the same proportion. The population of the country was likewise growing at an amazing pace, increasing from 7,200,000 in 1810 to 17,000,-000 in 1840, and to more than 31,000,000 in 1860. By 1850 the population of the United States had surpassed that of Great Britain, and it continued to increase with extraordinary rapidity. The American birth rate was very high and Europeans were immigrating in large numbers, especially after 1840. This population growth affected all sections and all states but was most pronounced in the new western states. In fact, westward migration within the United States was practically continual and was one of the outstanding developments of this period.

Thus the American people were spreading across the continent more rapidly than they were developing means to bind themselves into a unified nation. Under such a decentralized condition the people considered most of their problems to be of a local or state character rather than national. This situation encouraged the growth of provincialism and a widespread demand for local democracy, state autonomy, and freedom from interference by any "outside" body, such as the United States Supreme Court.

Meanwhile the economic development of the country was producing an intensified sectionalism that was to have serious constitutional consequences. By 1815 the northeastern section was undergoing an industrial revolution, at first predominantly in textiles, but later expanding to include such products as shoes, coal, iron and steel, brass, and glass. Extensive urbanization also occurred in this region. Along the north Atlantic seaboard the cities of Boston, Philadelphia, and above all New York were expanding their commercial and industrial activities and were growing rapidly in population and influence. Their prosperity was based upon their favored positions as gateways to the great continental hinterland and as centers of trade with London, Constantinople, Canton, and other remote markets of the world.

At the same time the southern states were experiencing a remarkable boom in short-staple cotton, a boom that carried the plantation system into the rich bottom lands of the Gulf coastal plain, that was instrumental in bringing a new group of slave states into the Union, and that gave a new impetus to the institution of Negro slavery. While cotton was becoming "King" in the South, a great expansion in grain and livestock production was taking place in the new West—a somewhat indefinite and expanding area which included the Ohio River valley, the upper Mississippi valley, the Great Lakes region, and for a time even the western portions of New York and Pennsylvania.

This new era of expansion produced a whole new series of national political and constitutional problems to replace the older matters that had formerly occupied the attention of Congress and the nation. The political and economic problems of the United States in the first generation of independence had grown principally out of American relations with Europe. American commercial and agricultural prosperity had been dependent upon the exigencies of European war markets; party loyalties had been to some extent guided by support or opposition to the French Revolution; and the principal matters occupying the attention of Congress were diplomatic in origin and turned upon American relations with Britain and France. In a sense, the United States, still mainly concerned with its relations with the Old World, had remained virtually a colony of Europe.

The political questions of the new era rose chiefly out of internal expansion and national growth and were concerned mainly with the conflict of sectional interests incident to that growth. A section was sometimes divided on an important issue, and local prejudices and interests often cut across sectional lines; but in general a decided majority in each section either favored or opposed specific national policies. The expanding industries of the Northeast sought a protective tariff, an objective that soon came into sharp conflict with the agrarian interests of the South and eventually with those of the West, and ultimately precipitated the tariff and nullification crisis of 1833. Northeastern merchants and manufacturers also wanted a national banking system and a conservative federal money policy, but most of the westerners and southerners were farmers and debtors and as such were suspicious of banks in general and especially of a strong national bank. The West, badly in need of roads and canals, constantly sought federal assistance for a program of internal improvements, but the Northeast had no desire to be taxed for westward expansion. West and East also quarreled over federal land policy: the West wanted the federal government to sell small farms at low prices and on liberal credit terms, while the East, viewing the national domain as a source of revenue and desiring to check a western expansion that menaced the political ascendancy of the older states, preferred that western lands be sold in large blocks at a high price. The South generally opposed federal internal improvements and was divided on public land policies, but above all it sought to protect the interests of its "peculiar institution," Negro slavery. In the Missouri controversy around 1820 and in later controversies over questions of slavery, the West divided roughly along the Ohio River into the slave West which supported the South and the free West or Northwest which aligned itself with the Northeast.

The clash of sectional interests helped make the era one of great constitutional debate in Congress. The recognized ascendancy of Congress in national affairs throughout most of the period, the tremendous forensic skill and intellectual powers of John C. Calhoun, Henry Clay, Daniel Webster, Thomas Hart Benton, Robert Y. Hayne, and other great legislators, and the fact that the Supreme Court was not yet generally recognized as the final arbiter of constitutional questions gave congressional debate an importance never possessed before or since in American politics. The Missouri Compromise debates, those between Webster and Hayne in 1830, and those preceding the Compromise of 1850 were only the most famous of many prolonged and important discussions of constitutional questions.

Constitutional debate very often turned ultimately to a discussion of the fundamental nature of the Union. The question had many facets, among them the extent of federal authority under the enumerated powers of Congress, the implications of the general welfare clause, whether or not the Constitution was a compact between the states, and the methods by which constitutional disputes between a state and the federal government were to be settled. The ultimate question, however, was whether the United States was a sovereign nation or essentially a confederacy of state sovereignties.

The constitutional doctrines advanced in Congress were generally based upon sectional interests. Whether a congressman championed nationalism and broad construction or states' rights and strict construction was largely a matter of the political and economic interests of his state or section. Daniel Webster, for example, began his career as a strict constructionist who opposed the protective tariff on constitutional grounds. At that time New England's commercial interests were opposed to a protective tariff, which they feared would interfere with foreign trade. However, as industry developed in New England, sentiment changed in favor of the protective tariff, and Webster became ultimately an exponent of protectionism and a champion of nationalism.

Calhoun, on the other hand, began his career as a nationalist advocating an expansion of federal power and broad construction of the Constitution. As the South fell behind in population and began to realize that ultimately it could not control the course of national policies, the section began to view nationalism and broad construction with concern. Calhoun shifted with his section, and from 1830 to 1850 he was the great champion of the doctrine of state sovereignty.

On most occasions between 1815 and 1860 sectionalism and provincialism proved to be stronger forces than nationalism. There was as yet but little genuine national sentiment in the country. True, following the War of 1812 there was a temporary outburst of nationalistic feeling in Congress, and the Supreme Court under John Marshall's leadership for some years after 1815 consistently adhered to a nationalistic policy in constitutional interpretation. But the various sections and states were quick to oppose their own interests to national welfare and to raise the constitutional arguments necessary to do so. In spite of judicial nationalism there was probably an actual decline in nationalist constitutional philosophy in the nation between 1815 and 1850. By the latter year, certain congressmen commonly spoke of the United States as a "confederacy," while a large majority in the Senate in 1837 acquiesced in a resolution describing the Union as a mere league of sovereignties.

POSTWAR NATIONALISM: THE NATIONAL BANK

Congressional sentiment in the postwar period beginning in 1815 was at first decidedly nationalistic. The young Republican leaders who dominated both houses had grown up under the Constitution, and they had also witnessed the difficulties of the United States since 1806 in both foreign affairs and domestic matters growing out of an inadequate sense of national unity and the limited character of federal power. They were determined to remedy these defects. They had little sympathy with the old Republican doctrine of extreme strict constructionism. As Calhoun expressed it, there was less danger of federal political and military usurpation than there was that justice and liberty would be destroyed because of the weakness of the central government. Clay, Calhoun, and other young nationalists admitted that they were more advanced than a majority of the people in their desire for a strong central government, but they believed that it was the duty of Congress to educate and lead public opinion in that direction.

The strict-constructionist bloc in Congress was still strong, however, both among the older Republican agrarians and among the dwindling Federalist minority. The strict-constructionist Republicans insisted that the new nationalistic measures were not only unconstitutional but in fact threatened to destroy the states by prostrating them "at the feet of the General Government." The able but eccentric John Randolph of Virginia was the House leader of this group, while Nathaniel Macon of North Carolina championed the same cause most effectively in the Senate. Outside Congress, John Taylor of Virginia still argued elaborately in favor of state sovereignty and strict constructionism, while Jefferson, now relieved of the responsibilities of high office, also returned in part to his earlier constitutional position.

With the coming of peace in 1815 President Madison had given the Congressional nationalists a decided advantage by advocating a comprehensive program of national legislation. In December 1815, he recommended the enlargement of the Military Academy and of the country's naval and militia organization, and Congress responded with legislation providing for some expansion. He urged Congress to pay particular attention in revising the tariff to the establishment of protective duties for those commodities considered essential to national independence and prosperity. Led by Calhoun, Congress enacted the Tariff Act of 1816, which definitely adopted the protective principle as a national tariff policy, although eventually this policy was to provide a serious constitutional controversy.[1] The President also advocated a new national bank, a system of roads and canals to be "executed under the national authority," and the establishment of a "national" university for the purpose of developing and diffusing those "national feelings" and "liberal sentiments" which "contribute cement to our Union." Congress provided for a national bank but unfortunately did not succeed in establishing either a national transportation system or a national university.

The first postwar issue to provoke extended constitutional controversy was the proposal to recharter a national bank. In 1811 a Republican-dominated Congress had refused to grant a new charter to the Bank of the United States, but since that time many strict-constructionist Republicans had changed their viewpoint on both the wisdom and the constitutionality of a national bank. The disappearance of the first bank in 1811 had caused the states to charter a

---

[1] See Chapter 12.

number of state banking institutions, many of which failed to observe the elementary rules of sound banking practice. They had issued large quantities of paper money, much of it of little or no value, which circulated as part of the nation's monetary system and often caused great confusion in commercial and industrial circles. The Constitution specifically forbade the states to coin money and emit bills of credit, but as Calhoun pointed out, the chartering of state banks had enabled the states to elude this restriction and usurp control of the monetary system. The absence of a national bank also proved a serious handicap to federal fiscal policy and financial activities during the War of 1812, for the government not only lacked any adequate agency of deposit, but it also missed the financial assistance such a bank might have been able to extend.

The Republican nationalists accordingly brought about the passage of a national bank bill in January 1815. Madison vetoed the measure as inadequate, but at the same time indicated his belief that the bank was constitutional, and in his annual message of December 1815 he again recommended passage of a national bank law. In January 1816, accordingly, Calhoun, as chairman of the special committee on uniform national currency, introduced a bill to incorporate a new bank of the United States for twenty years with a capital of $35,000,000, one-fifth of which was to be subscribed by the federal government.

Calhoun defended this measure's constitutionality by holding that it was a necessary and proper means to the establishment of a uniform national currency. The main object of the framers of the Constitution in giving Congress the power to coin money and regulate its value, he thought, must have been to give steadiness and fixed value to the currency of the United States. The various states, through their banking activities, had recently worked the defeat of this end and had actually taken over control of the nation's monetary system. Consequently, he concluded, it was the duty of Congress to recover control over the monetary system, and this could best be done through the medium of a national bank.

Clay also presented an ingenious argument to explain his change of attitude toward the proposed national bank. He had voted against the bill to recharter the old bank, in part on constitutional grounds. Now, however, he explained that in 1811 he had opposed the bank because it had not then been necessary to carry into effect any power specifically granted to Congress; at that time, therefore, the bank had been unconstitutional. Conditions had now so changed, he said, that a national bank was necessary to give effect to the enumerated powers of Congress, and Congress thus now possessed an implied power not possessed five years before.

Another popular Republican argument in Congress in favor of the bill was that the bank's constitutionality was now a settled matter simply because Congress and public opinion had for some time recognized a bank as constitutional. Madison had advanced this argument even while vetoing the bill of 1815, observing that all question as to the bank's constitutionality had now been precluded by "repeated recognition under varied circumstances of the validity of such an institution in acts of the legislative, executive, and judicial branches of the Government, accompanied by indications, in different modes, of a concurrence of the general will of the nation." Madison's argument amounted to the contention that a constitutional question could be settled by a kind of prescriptive process —by prolonged common recognition of a particular practice or constitutional doctrine. The notion was unorthodox Republicanism, but most students of constitutional history will recognize it as not far from the truth.

The strict-constructionist argument against the bank, best stated by Representative John Clopton of Virginia, rested on the old Jeffersonian narrow interpretation of the necessary and proper clause. This clause, Clopton said, "imparts not a scintilla of power to Congress which the preceding enumeration does not grant." Should it be admitted that the necessary and proper clause conveyed any substantive powers, it would "give to Congress general, unlimited, discretionary powers," an idea which would eventually sweep away "every vestige of authority reserved to the States." Clopton also denounced Madison's argument that acquiescence in federal legislation could conclusively settle any constitutional question. Were this doctrine adhered to, he argued, the Constitution would in time "be superseded and rendered altogether a dead letter" by various acts of Congress.

Clopton and his sympathizers, however, were not able to stay the tide of nationalism in Congress. Although the Federalists joined the strict-constructionist Republicans in opposition, the bill to charter a second Bank of the United States became law on April 10, 1816. Future developments were to demonstrate, however, that the constitutionality of the national bank was far from being a dead issue.

THE INTERNAL IMPROVEMENTS ISSUE

Few issues were to be as repeatedly involved in constitutional controversy during the first half of the nineteenth century as that contemporaneously termed "internal improvements." The American people were constantly pushing westward into new and unoccupied regions, conquering the wilderness and building a nation. The great extent of fertile territory open to settlement encouraged the growth of widely scattered and largely isolated communities. As settlement increased, the people clamored for improved natural waterways, canals, and roads, to enable them to transport their products to market and to have manufactured and other needed goods imported at reasonable prices.

The individual states generally provided some internal improvements, often by chartering private turnpike and canal companies. Most of the trans-Appalachian region, however, was too sparsely settled and too undeveloped to make internal improvements attractive to private capital or financially possible for the new state governments. Moreover, there was obvious need for large interstate projects, beyond the financial and constitutional competence of the separate states. Such improvements would enhance the national prosperity and help to bind the states into a more effective union. Also many westerners thought it only fair that the substantial federal revenues derived from the sale of public land should be used for internal improvements.

Constitutional theorists in Congress were sharply divided on the internal improvements issue. The strict constructionists held that the general welfare clause did not authorize Congress to spend money for any purpose not directly related to the enumerated powers of Congress. Internal improvements, they said, were not so related, and congressional appropriations for that purpose were therefore illegal. They could be made legal only by constitutional amendment.

The broad constructionists, on the other hand, argued that the general welfare clause authorized Congress to spend money for any broad national purpose, whether or not that purpose lay within the enumerated powers of Congress. Since Congress could spend the money, they contended, it could also control its expenditure, and even come into the possession of internal improvements which could be maintained as government property.

Some moderately broad constructionists in Congress drew a distinction between the power to appropriate for internal improvements and the power to own and operate. They agreed with other nationalists that the general welfare clause authorized appropriations beyond the enumerated powers of Congress but insisted that the appropriation of money must not lead to a new sphere of congressional authority. Hence, while Congress might constitutionally grant money to state or local governments or subsidize private enterprise for internal improvement purposes, it could not authorize the federal government itself to build or operate any improvement such as a canal or national highway. A few legalists, drawing a still finer distinction, insisted that while Congress might appropriate for and construct internal improvements, it could not operate them, but would have to surrender completed improvements to state or private hands.

The internal improvements issue first rose in Congress in 1806, when Jefferson recommended to Congress the application of surplus federal revenue to "public education, roads, rivers, canals, and such other objects of public improvement as it may be thought proper to add to the constitutional enumeration of Federal powers." As an orthodox strict constructionist, he added that he supposed a constitutional amendment was necessary, "because the objects now recommended are not among those enumerated in the Constitution, and to which it permits the public moneys to be applied."

Congress did not act on the President's suggestion that the Constitution be amended; it did, however, authorize the construction of the Cumberland National Road from Cumberland, Maryland, to the Mississippi River, a few miles of which were presently constructed. After 1806 internal improvements were for a time almost forgotten, as commercial restrictions and war eliminated the federal surplus.

The War of 1812 emphasized the need for internal transportation and communication facilities for purposes of effective national defense. In his annual messages of 1815 and 1816, Madison strongly recommended that Congress provide for a federal internal improvements program of roads and canals. In the latter message he took his stand with the strict constructionists, and asked that Congress submit a constitutional amendment to the states to make the program possible.

Led by Calhoun, the nationalists in Congress responded in December 1816 by sponsoring a "Bonus Bill" setting aside the $1,-500,000 bonus paid by the national bank for its charter and the United States government's bank dividends as a permanent fund for internal improvements. In supporting the measure in the House, Calhoun delivered an exceptionally able speech, rivaling the broad constructionism of Webster and Marshall at their best. "No country, enjoying freedom," he said, "ever occupied any thing like as great an extent of country as this Republic. . . . We are great, and rapidly . . . growing. . . . We are under the most imperious obligation to counteract every tendency to disunion." Arguing for a broad construction of the general welfare power, he pointed out that "if the framers had intended to limit the use of the money to the powers afterward enumerated and defined, nothing could be more easy than to have expressed it plainly." While he admitted that the Constitution was founded upon "positive and written principles" rather than upon precedents, he nonetheless insisted that continuous popular approval of congressional action in favor of internal improvements furnished "better evidence of the true interpretation of the constitution, than the most refined and subtle arguments."

Although other members of Congress raised constitutional objections to the "Bonus Bill," the opposition was predominantly sectional in scope and based upon expediency. Many members from New England and the South Atlantic states opposed a rapid development of internal improvements, not only because relatively few would be constructed in their states, but also because improved transportation facilities would tend to drain off their population to the West. Population was generally considered the mark of economic prosperity and the measure of political power. On the other hand, the Middle Atlantic region and especially the western states would benefit from the appropriation, and the members from these sections supported the measure with enthusiasm. Because of this sectional clash the "Bonus Bill" barely passed the House by a vote of 86 to 84, and the Senate by a vote of 20 to 15.

To the surprise of many, Madison vetoed the "Bonus Bill" on constitutional grounds. He adopted the narrowest possible interpretation of the general welfare clause, holding not only that it did not constitute any general grant of legislative power but also that it did not even authorize appropriations of money beyond the enumerated powers of Congress. He reasserted the benefits of internal improvements but insisted that a constitutional amendment was necessary to legalize them. Thus by a paradox of history the man who in the Constitutional Convention had championed a strong central government vetoed a nationalistic measure sponsored by the man who was soon to become the most celebrated proponent of state sovereignty.

In his first message to Congress in December 1817, President James Monroe also adopted a stand in favor of a constitutional amendment authorizing an internal improvements program. In the Senate, James Barbour of Virginia responded by introducing an amendment granting Congress the power "to pass laws appropriating money for constructing roads and canals, and improving the navigation of water-courses," provided that no action was taken without the consent of any state involved and provided that the money appropriated was distributed among the states in proportion to their representation in the lower house of Congress. In the House, a select committee headed by St. George Tucker of Virginia also took the constitutional question under advisement.

The broad constructionists in Congress killed the proposals for a constitutional amendment to legalize internal improvements. Barbour's amendment was ultimately tabled, 22 to 9, while Tucker's committee made a report rejecting Monroe's constitutional viewpoint and recommending once more that the bank bonus be set aside as a fund for roads and canals. Tucker explained why the broad constructionists opposed a constitutional amendment: If they believed they already had the power in question, they would be wrong to ask the states to grant it. "For, if an amendment be recommended, and should not be obtained, we should have surrendered a power, which we are bound to maintain if we think we possess it." Henry Clay, then emerging as the great western champion of internal improvements, took the same ground. In support of this position the House shortly resolved, 90 to 75, that Congress had the power to appropriate money for post roads, military highways, and canals, although it rejected, 84 to 82, a resolution declaring that Congress had the power to construct such improvements.

Even had Congress submitted a constitutional amendment to the states, it would have had very little chance of adoption. New England and the South Atlantic states were largely opposed to a national internal improvements program. The eastern states would have gained very few direct benefits from internal improvements, while they, as the more populous portion of the Union, would have been obliged to pay a disproportionate share of the costs.

The constitutional impasse between President and Congress arrived at in 1818 ended for a time the hope for any broad federal internal improvements program. In 1819, Calhoun, now Secretary of War, submitted to Congress plans for a comprehensive system of internal improvements that he considered necessary for national defense, but the panic of 1819 reduced federal funds and prevented Congress from taking any action for the next three years.

In 1822 Congress passed a bill providing for federal toll gates and federal maintenance of the Cumberland National Road and giving the federal government certain jurisdictional rights over the road within the various states. Monroe had approved earlier Cumberland Road grants, but he vetoed the present measure as unconstitutional. Unlike Madison, he admitted that Congress could appropriate money for the general welfare, but he denied that the federal government could construct or operate any such improvement. Again constitutional amendments were introduced empowering Congress to construct roads and canals, and again Congress refused to adopt them. The impasse therefore continued.

The result of this situation was the gradual abandonment by Congress of plans for a national system of internal improvements and the adoption of a policy of appropriations to the states for this purpose, a device which all but a small minority of strict constructionists thought constitutional. Many western states now preferred to undertake their own canal- and road-building programs, and accordingly they sought financial assistance from the federal government rather than a separate national program. Consequently representatives from different states increasingly entered into "logrolling" agreements to secure mutual support for appropriations for state-owned improvements and even for private canal corporations. Congress also adopted the policy of granting public lands to western states which the states could sell or use as security to obtain money for their programs. When President John Quincy Adams, a nationalist and broad constructionist, in 1825 submitted new plans for a national internal improvements program, Congress ignored the suggestion and instead appropriated still larger sums to the various states for their own use.

Thus the internal improvements controversy resulted in a victory for states' rights and decentralization. Calhoun, Clay, Adams, and the other broad constructionists were defeated in their attempts to create a great national system of internal improvements. Undoubtedly such a system would have supplied a powerful and very badly needed force for unification in the youthful nation. Instead, internal transportation passed almost exclusively under state control at the very time that interstate commerce, by roads, canals, and railroads, was becoming important. Even the Cumberland Road was shortly relinquished to the states through which it passed. More than a generation was to elapse before a really national transportation system was to be developed, and then it was to be controlled by private corporations rather than by the federal government. In the intervening period, localism, sectionalism, and the doctrine of state sovereignty were to score their greatest successes.

NEGRO SLAVERY AND THE MISSOURI CONTROVERSY

No political conflict of this period emphasized more powerfully the sectionalist character of the federal Union than did the great controversy over the admission of Missouri into the Union. Now for the first time a distinct political cleavage between North and South, based on the question of the westward extension of slavery, made its appearance.

In the first generation of national life, slavery had not constituted an important sectional issue, and indeed there seemed to be some grounds for belief that the institution was dying. Between 1777 and 1804 all the states north of Maryland took action to abolish slavery within their borders, usually by gradual emancipation laws, while all the Southern states abandoned the importation of Negro slaves from abroad. Both Northern and Southern delegates in the Confederation Congress supported the provision of the Ordinance of 1787 prohibiting slavery in the Northwest Territory, and representatives from both North and South also supported the Act of 1807 banning the foreign slave trade. Philosophic and humanitarian opposition to slavery was also fairly widespread in the South before 1815, particularly in the older plantation areas, where the institution was beginning to be unprofitable. There were numerous small antislavery societies south of the Mason and Dixon Line, and many prominent Southerners hoped that the institution would soon die.

The differing economic and cultural evolution of the Northern and Southern states nonetheless gradually laid the foundations for the sectional controversy over slavery. Slavery had no adequate economic foundation in the North, and by 1800 the gradual emancipation laws had assured its extinction. The Northwest Territory also remained free soil, and the states formed from it, beginning with Ohio in 1803, entered the Union as free states. In the South, however, the widespread introduction of short-staple cotton after 1795 created a new plantation boom, first in South Carolina and Georgia and then in the Gulf coastal plain. As a result, Alabama and Mississippi entered the Union as slave states, and slavery already existed in Louisiana when the territory was acquired in 1803. By 1819, the Mason and Dixon Line and the Ohio River divided the eleven free states from the eleven slave states, although this division was not as yet a matter provoking any great sectional selfconsciousness.

While the legal status of Negro slavery was primarily a local matter under the control of the individual states, certain provisions in the Constitution gave the federal government some control, either direct or indirect, over the institution and so supplied the legal groundwork for a constitutional controversy if slavery should become a subject of serious dispute.

Though the Constitution nowhere used the word "slavery," three provisions dealt directly with Negro servitude. Article I, Section 2, provided that three-fifths of the slaves should be counted in apportioning direct taxes and representatives in the House. Article I, Section 9, prohibited Congress from interfering with the importation of slaves before 1808. Article IV, Section 2, provided for the return of fugitive slaves. The three-fifths clause, a compromise provision satisfying in part the contention of Southern delegates to the Constitutional Convention that property as well as population should be included in the representative base, was never a source of serious controversy, although this provision was occasionally challenged by Northerners—in the Hartford Convention, for example. The section forbidding interference with the foreign slave trade before 1808 had been a concession to certain Southern states which felt the need of an increased labor supply, but both Northern and Southern congressmen had voted in 1807 to end the importation of slaves in 1808, and no large groups of Southern congressmen ever thereafter seriously proposed to reopen the foreign slave trade. The fugitive slave clause seemingly left enforcement to the states, but Congress nonetheless in 1793 enacted a statute to supplement state machinery. The law worked well enough for several decades.

There were other constitutional provisions which, although they did not deal directly with slavery, nonetheless ultimately became involved even more than the direct provisions in the slavery controversy. The Constitution gave Congress the power "to dispose of and make all needful Rules and Regulations respecting the Territory or other Property belonging to the United States." Congress at first apparently assumed that this provision gave it full authority over slavery in the territories, but ultimately the clause became the source of a long and embittered argument as to whether Congress could legally ban slavery in the territories.

The Constitution also gave Congress the power to regulate commerce between the states; in the later slavery controversy some Northern extremists argued that Congress thereby had power to regulate or forbid the interstate slave trade. Although such a contention would seem plausible today, it was not then taken seriously by most Northerners and never became an important cause of sectional friction.

The provision which became the center of conflict in the Missouri controversy was that part of Article IV, Section 3, which stated that "New States may be admitted by the Congress into this Union." This phraseology had resulted from a compromise in the Convention of 1787 between those who wished new states admitted upon terms of equality with the original members of the Union and those who wished to preserve the dominance of the older states. Constitutional theorists in Congress generally agreed that by the terms of this clause, Congress was permitted to admit new states but was not required to do so. But to what extent could Congress impose conditions upon new states before their admission to the Union? Could Congress, for instance, require that a prospective state ban slavery or impose other limitations upon Negro servitude? This was to be the crucial constitutional question in the prolonged controversy over the admission of Missouri.

Prior to the admission of Missouri, Congress had admitted nine new states into the Union without any important controversy over the matter of slavery. In every instance, geography and prior territorial legislation had previously largely disposed of the slavery issue and had made apparent the state's future status as slave or free soil. Thus Congress, almost by accident, had been able to balance the admission of a new free state with the admission of a corresponding slave state, so that the political equilibrium of free and slave states remained undisturbed.

Missouri's case was not disposed of so easily. The prospective state lay athwart a projection of the dividing line between free and slave states and had not been definitely committed for or against slavery either by history or by geography. During the territorial period, however, Missourians had been permitted by Congress to hold slaves, and some expected to continue the practice after attaining statehood. Furthermore, Missouri's admission into the Union would disturb the existing balance between free and slave states.

In 1818 the Missouri territorial legislature petitioned for statehood, and in January 1819 the House of Representatives took up the consideration of an enabling bill—that is, a measure that would permit Missouri to draft a constitution, organize a state government, and make formal application for admission to the Union, the usual procedure for admitting a new state.

Representative James Tallmadge of New York now offered an amendment to the bill prohibiting the further introduction of slavery in Missouri and declaring free at the age of twenty-five all slaves born after the state's admission to the Union. The House adopted the Tallmadge Amendment by an almost straight sectional vote, nearly all the proposal's supporters coming from Northern states. However, with two senators from each state the Southern position in the Senate was stronger, and the upper chamber refused to concur in the Tallmadge Amendment. Neither the House nor the Senate would recede, and Congress adjourned in March without further action on the Missouri Bill.

Throughout 1819 the public was much aroused over the Missouri issue. The predominant sentiment in the free states was strongly in favor of the Tallmadge Amendment. In the slave states, on the other hand, public protests were made against congressional restrictions on slavery expansion. The people of Missouri also protested in various ways against the attempt of Congress to restrict their freedom in drawing up a state constitution. Simultaneously with the development of this issue the alarm of many states' rightists was increased by the restriction of state authority over bankruptcy and banking brought about through the Supreme Court's decisions in the Sturges case and the McCulloch case.[2] The combination of congressional and judicial nationalism was very disturbing to the champions of states' rights and strict constructionism.

In December 1819 Missouri renewed its application for statehood, and at this time Maine, then a part of Massachusetts, also asked for admission as a separate state. The House promptly passed a bill for Maine's admission to the Union as a free state. The Senate then added two important amendments to the Maine bill. The first provided for Missouri's admission without restriction as to slavery; the second, introduced by Senator Jesse Thomas of Illinois, prohibited slavery forever in any remaining portion of the Louisiana Purchase above the parallel of 36° 30′ north latitude, an extension of the line forming the southern boundary of Missouri.

While the House at first refused to concur in the Senate's proposals, a Senate-House conference committee ultimately made the

---

[2] These decisions will be discussed in detail in the following chapter.

Thomas Amendment the basis for compromise. The committee recommended the passage of a separate act admitting Maine as a free state and the passage of the bill to admit Missouri as a slave state with the Thomas Amendment attached. Both houses concurred, although the antislavery men in the lower chamber fought to the end against the compromise and lost in a very close vote.

President Monroe at first considered vetoing the Missouri Act as unconstitutional on the ground that Congress had no authority to prohibit slavery in the territories. But when his cabinet, which included three slaveholders, unanimously assured him that the bill did not violate the Constitution, he signed the measure.

THE CONSTITUTIONAL DEBATE

The principal constitutional issue in the Missouri debates was whether or not the constitutional provision, "New states may be admitted by the Congress into this Union," empowered Congress to impose restrictions upon a new state as a condition of admission to statehood. If so, then Congress could ban slavery in Missouri as a prior condition of the state's entry into the Union.

Northern antislavery men insisted that Congress had a right to impose such conditions. They emphasized the word "may" which implied that Congress had complete discretion as to whether or not it wished to admit any state. Admission to the Union, they said, was "a privilege and not a right," and when Congress granted the favor of statehood, it could "annex just and reasonable terms." This argument they enforced with historical precedent—Congress had imposed a variety of restrictions upon the various states admitted to the Union since 1789, while the enabling acts for Ohio, Indiana, and Illinois had required those states to prohibit slavery in their constitutions.

Southerners admitted that Congress could reject a state's application for admission, but denied that Congress could impose any conditions upon its entry. The Union, they argued, was one of equal states. Were additional states admitted under limitations not required of the older states in the Union, the result would be a union of states unequal in "sovereignty" and a consequent fundamental alteration in the nature of the Union. Therefore they held that since the original states of the Union were under no limitations on the subject of slavery, Congress could not impose such limitations upon Missouri.

The antislavery men also brought the territories clause of the

Constitution to bear on their argument. Congress, they said, had complete authority to dispose of the territories as it wished, and to govern them in any fashion it saw fit. Congress could therefore impose any restrictions or requirements it wished upon the Territory of Missouri. Conditions so imposed became a contract between the Territory of Missouri and the United States and could be enforced after the territory's admission to statehood.

Most Southerners admitted that Congress could prohibit slavery in the territories, a point later to become a matter of great controversy. They were almost unanimous, however, in their insistence that such a restriction had no binding effect upon the state after its admission to the Union.

Proslavery men argued also that the Louisiana Purchase Treaty had imposed a condition upon the federal government which obligated it to admit Missouri without any restrictions as to slaves. Article III of the treaty, they pointed out, guaranteed that the inhabitants of Louisiana would be admitted to all the rights, privileges and immunities of citizens of the United States. This, they said, amounted to a guarantee of slavery in the Louisiana Territory, since slaveholding might be construed as a privilege of citizens of the United States, and the federal government could not revoke the guarantees extended in the treaty of 1803.

Northerners denied, on the other hand, that any treaty could work a diminution of the constitutional right of Congress to exercise discretion in the admission of new states. "The treaty-making power," declared Tallmadge, encompassed "neither the right nor the power to stipulate, by a treaty, the terms upon which a people shall be admitted into the Union."

Many years later, the Supreme Court ruled upon various aspects of the right of Congress to impose restrictions upon a state entering the Union. The Court's general position was that Congress may require a territory to fulfill certain conditions as a precedent to statehood, but that such conditions, with certain exceptions, are not binding upon a state after admission. Certain conditions involving private rights of a non-political character, such as land titles, constitute such exceptions. In any case, Congress may not impose restrictions which impair the state's political equality in the Union.

On the other hand, it is recognized today that a treaty cannot deprive Congress of legislative power which it would otherwise possess. Even though a treaty has placed an obligation or limitation upon the United States, Congress may subsequently set that obligation aside in the ordinary legislative process. To do so may constitute a violation of the international obligations of the United States, but congressional competence to do this is beyond question. In short, the Southern argument that the Louisiana treaty had worked a permanent limitation of federal authority in the territories encompassed in the purchase would nowadays be regarded as untenable.

NEGRO CITIZENSHIP AND THE SECOND
MISSOURI COMPROMISE

Missouri's constitution, presented for final approval to the next session of Congress (1820–21), provoked another controversy. The constitution submitted contained a clause requiring the state legislature to pass a law banning free Negroes from entering the state. Northerners at once attacked the provision, and another prolonged debate ensued, provoking considerable bitterness and sectional feeling.

Northern congressmen contended that the clause banning free Negroes from Missouri violated Article IV, Section 2, of the federal Constitution, which provided that "The Citizens of each State shall be entitled to all Privileges and Immunities of Citizens in the several States." They pointed out that in some of the Northern states— Massachusetts, New Hampshire, and Vermont—Negroes were granted citizenship rights. Were such a Negro, a citizen of one of these states, to go to Missouri, he would be denied entrance in violation of his constitutional rights. The Northern congressmen maintained that the right to enter and settle in a state was one of the most important privileges enjoyed in common by the citizens of the several states.

In reply, Southern spokesmen contended that the privileges and immunities of citizens were not extended to free Negroes and mulattoes by the Constitution. Although their definitions of citizenship varied, most Southerners held that Negroes could not be considered citizens unless they possessed all the civil and political rights of white citizens living under the same circumstances. Since the free Negroes of none of the states actually possessed equal rights with white citizens, Negroes could not be recognized as citizens under the Constitution. The privileges and immunities clause, in short, did not apply to Negroes. In support of this contention, Charles Pinckney of South Carolina, a member of the Constitutional

Convention in 1787, claimed that he was the author of the privileges and immunities clause of the Constitution and that it was designed on the positive belief that Negroes were not and never would be citizens. In essence, Southerners maintained, as Chief Justice Taney later did in the Dred Scott case, that the Constitution was a white man's document.

This argument over what constituted state citizenship was possible mainly because the federal Constitution had failed to define either state or national citizenship. Whether a state could define citizenship was uncertain; presumably in the absence of any federal definition, it could do so, but whether this meant that the other states were required to accept as citizens any group of persons so defined by a state was open to question. The whole matter of citizenship was in fact not cleared up until the Fourteenth Amendment, adopted in 1868, defined national citizenship, made it primary, and made state citizenship dependent upon it.[3]

Most Southerners insisted that in any event Missouri had already become a state by virtue of the enabling act and that Congress therefore had no further discretion whatever either in seating the state's congressmen or in imposing any further limitations upon the state's sovereignty. Northerners replied that Missouri was not a state until the formal resolution of admission had been passed by Congress. Precedent certainly supported this contention, for in the past the enabling act had been followed by a resolution of admission before the state's representatives were seated. Accordingly, the Northern-dominated House rejected the resolution of admission, 93 to 79.

Henry Clay now assumed the lead in formulating a compromise. He secured the appointment of a House committee with himself as chairman, which proposed that Missouri be admitted on condition that the state legislature should agree never to pass any law preventing the citizens of any state from entering Missouri. When the Northern majority voted down this proposal, Clay secured the appointment of a joint Senate-House committee, which reported the same formula in somewhat more exacting terms—Missouri was to be admitted upon the fundamental condition that her constitution should never be construed to authorize the passage of any law which should exclude the citizens of any state from enjoying those privileges and immunities guaranteed by the Constitution of the United States. And further, Missouri was to be required to give

---

[3] The evolution of the Fourteenth Amendment and the definition of citizenship therein are discussed on pp. 429–435 and 462–467.

her assent to this provision. Although this change in the formula was little less than pure sophistry, the House of Representatives accepted it by a close vote, and with the Senate's concurrence the resolution of admission was adopted. Missouri's forthcoming assent was hedged with some reservations, but President Monroe ended the matter by issuing a proclamation of admission on August 10, 1821.

The Missouri Compromise quieted the slavery controversy for a time. But by the close of the Missouri controversy, it had become apparent that the wave of postwar nationalism had not succeeded in submerging the fundamentally sectionalist character of the Union. It was evident not only that the various sections had highly divergent economic and political interests, but that sectional champions in Congress could not agree upon either the nature of the Union or the exact extent of federal authority. Certain statesmen of the North and West, notably Webster and Clay, continued to emphasize nationalism and broad construction of federal powers. Their position reflected the desire of certain economic interests for a protective tariff and a strong federal banking system, and a Northern awareness that the growth of Northern population assured that section ultimate control of Congress and of national policy.

At the same time Southern statesmen, led by Calhoun, gradually became aware that nationalism did not serve the political and economic interests of the South. Broad construction, they eventually realized, could be used to underwrite northeastern tariff and banking policies, which they regarded as disastrous to Southern interests. The realization also grew, although slowly at first, that national power might conceivably be used to make an attack upon the institution of slavery. Hence nationalism and broad constructionism gradually disappeared among Southern statesmen, while their adherence to the doctrines of strict construction, of states' rights, and even of state sovereignty became more and more general.

For a generation after 1821 the Northwest served as a balance between the economic interests and constitutional philosophy of the Northeast and the South. As a rapidly growing section of free states the Northwest did not share the South's fear of ultimate domination by the Northeast or of federal interference with its domestic institutions. On the other hand, as an agrarian region the Northwest generally opposed a strong federal banking system and eventually turned against the protective tariff. Also the Northwest received more support from the South than from the Northeast for its cherished policy of speedy removal of Indians and the opening of new lands to settlement. Consequently agrarian interests, moderate states' rights, and strict construction secured ascendancy in the Northwest, although the people there opposed nullification and eventually opposed the extension of slavery and secession.

Chapter

11

John Marshall and Judicial Nationalism

THE WEAKENING of the spirit of nationalism in Congress was in marked contrast to the Supreme Court's success after 1815 in building up a comprehensive body of nationalistic constitutional law. Between 1815 and 1830, the Court, dominated by the powerful and persuasive intellect of Chief Justice John Marshall, struck blow after blow in support of the doctrine that the United States was a sovereign nation and not a mere confederation of sovereign states.

For the moment the Court's influence proved unable to outweigh the realities of provincial and sectional politics, or to arrest the growing tendency in the South to embrace states' rights ideas and, after 1830, the ominous theories of state sovereignty. Yet its voice was in the long run of great importance in fostering the growth of American nationalism in the North and West and in providing the politicians in those sections with the legal arguments they needed to counter the South's attack on nationhood. In the secession crisis of 1861, it was to John Marshall's theories of national sovereignty and national supremacy that Lincoln would turn as he rallied the Republic to defend itself. In turn the Union triumph that followed meant that several of Marshall's great opinions, written between 1810 and 1830, were to emerge as the principal foundation for the modern system of American constitutional law.

Marshall was of course a former Federalist politician, and it is hardly surprising to discover that his opinions often exhibited something of the same regard for nationalism, broad construction, and property rights that had once characterized the policies and constitutional theories of Alexander Hamilton. Yet Marshall had never been a High Federalist; instead he was essentially a moderate who had consistently opposed the extremism of his party's dedicated reactionaries. Moreover he was no blind worshiper of property rights at the expense of the public welfare. Instead he seems to have regarded the protection of property not as an end in itself but rather as a means to a much more important end: the integrity and stability of society.

Marshall's moderation of spirit, powerful intellect, and great personal charm and persuasive powers all contributed to his extraordinary domination of the Court until his death in 1835. The justices appointed to the Court in the generation after 1804 all were nominally at least good Republicans, but in reality most of them proved to differ but little from Marshall in their political and social philosophy, and on most occasions they accepted his leadership without much question. This situation prevailed in part because of the strength of Marshall's personality and the quality of his intellectual leadership, in part because most of the new appointees were lawyers whose ideas and concepts contrasted markedly with those of the many men of comparatively radical tendencies who were elected to Congress and to state legislatures during those years. The very nature of the Supreme Court's position as the nation's highest judicial body also influenced the justices to view issues from a nationalistic rather than a provincial standpoint, especially when national authority tended to safeguard the established social and economic order.

Two of the new Republican justices, William Johnson (1804–1834) and Joseph Story (1811–1845), both appointed at the youthful age of 32, deserve special note. Johnson, a South Carolinian and Jefferson's first appointee to the Supreme Court, was a liberal nationalist of notable intellectual independence. He was the first great dissenter on the Supreme Court, and, like Justice Oliver Wendell Holmes a century later, his dissenting opinions served as an incisive critique and a potential check on the rulings of the majority. As a consistent champion of positive law he held that the popularly elected Congress rather than the appointed Supreme Court should be the final umpire of the federal system. Accordingly, in cases of conflict between national and state authority, he consistently upheld congressional power on the principle of broad construction. But when the action of a state clashed with questionable rights of private property without infringing positive national authority, Johnson generally opposed Marshall's broad interpretation of the constitutional restrictions upon the state's legislative competence.

Story, appointed by Madison, was without previous judicial experience, but he was exceptionally well trained, and his extensive knowledge of international and admiralty law was a distinct asset to the Court, especially during his first years on the bench. Although nominally a Republican, he showed no great attachment to Jeffersonian principles and was soon Marshall's most able and vigorous collaborator. Story's great knowledge of law and his studious habits made him a most effective complement to the Chief Justice, who was less learned in the law but who possessed a remarkable grasp of the practical needs of American government and a bold determination to make the Supreme Court a conservative nationalist safeguard against the forces of decentralization and agrarian radicalism.[1]

Marshall and his colleagues received influential support and encouragement from members of the American bar. This was a period of great forensic efforts before the Supreme Court as well as in the halls of Congress. In many of the significant cases the litigants were represented by the nation's ablest lawyers, men like Daniel Webster, William Pinckney, William Wirt, Joseph Hopkinson, and Henry Clay. In rendering the decision in several important cases, Marshall actually took the argument of counsel, stripped it of extraneous material, and welded it into the dictum of the Court, thereby making it a part of American constitutional law. In this connection the Chief Justice admitted his indebtedness, especially to Pinckney and Webster.

Beginning in 1816 the Court at almost every term decided issues touching vital spots in the American constitutional system, most of them involving the interrelationship of the states and the central government. Most of the constitutional restrictions upon the states and some of the most important powers of Congress had not previously been interpreted by the Supreme Court. By employing broad

---

[1] Joseph Story, *Commentaries on the Constitution of the United States*, 3 v. (Boston, 1833), is one of the great treatises on the American constitutional system and reveals both Story's scholarship and his nationalism.

construction in both of these fields the Court deliberately promoted legal nationalism at a time when it was greatly needed.

Social and economic conditions following the War of 1812 were similar to those that had prevailed after the Revolution. Speculation, wildcat banking, and questionable financial schemes were followed by depression and hard times. All this was accompanied by the inevitable conflicts between creditor and debtor elements. The latter turned, as had other debtors in the 1780's, to the state legislatures for relief. Widespread popular demands arose for legislation that would suspend burdensome contracts, postpone the payment of debts, and increase the volume of money in circulation. The state legislatures, being close to the people and directly responsible to the current majority, responded to the popular demand with various laws reminiscent of the Confederation period.

The conservative, propertied creditor interests turned to the courts for protection against what they considered radical and unconstitutional legislation, seeking to have such laws invalidated as invasions of national authority or as violations of the constitutional prohibitions upon the states. They secured the best legal talent in the country to represent them in court and to carry their cases to the Supreme Court of the United States if necessary to obtain a favorable decision. In most of the important cases of this character to reach the highest tribunal the verdict was against the states and in favor of the vested interests. Thus conservatism and nationalism were closely joined in American constitutional law.

Because of the disintegration of political parties after 1815, the main source of organized opposition to the nationalistic judicial interpretation was the state governments, especially those whose interests were affected adversely by the Court's decisions. Provincialism and state pride were strong in all sections, and state legislatures and state judiciaries were often exceedingly jealous of their handiwork. Consequently most of the states were greatly aroused at one time or another by what they considered outside interference with their action and restrictions upon their "sovereignty." The political leaders of the state involved usually protested strongly, and in some cases attempted to circumvent or nullify the adverse consequences of the Court's action. Marshall and his colleagues were not unaware of this popular attitude. They were willing to take their stand against it.

EXPANSION OF THE CONTRACT CLAUSE

A principal objective of the men who framed the Constitution had been to put a stop to the practices which state legislatures often adopted at that time of interfering with vested rights by enacting stay and tender laws, making paper money legal tender and setting aside court decisions. Conservatives in 1787 had been alarmed over the lack of security for property rights from what they considered arbitrary action by popularly controlled state legislatures. Consequently the Constitution, in Article I, Section 10, had forbidden the states to emit bills of credit, make anything but gold and silver legal tender in payment of debts, or enact any law impairing the obligation of contracts.

No interpretation of these prohibitions upon the states had been made by the Supreme Court during its first twenty years, although the federal judiciary early had taken some hesitant steps toward the incorporation into American constitutional law of the doctrine of vested rights.[2] This amorphous doctrine was to reappear later, but during Marshall's regime the Supreme Court with one or two exceptions relied for protection of property and contract rights primarily upon more specific restrictions imposed by the Constitution upon the states.

The first case involving the obligation of contracts clause was that of *Fletcher v. Peck* (1810), the old and notorious Yazoo Land Fraud Case. In 1795 the Georgia legislature, influenced in part by bribery of many of its members, had granted millions of acres of land along the Yazoo River to certain land companies. At the next session of the legislature the grant was rescinded, but not before some of the land had been sold to innocent third parties. The status of the Yazoo lands was debated repeatedly in Congress and dragged through the courts until it finally reached the Supreme Court in 1810. There was strong evidence that the case was a feigned or collusive one, and Justice Johnson asserted that only respect for counsel in the case had induced him to abandon his belief that it should not be adjudicated. The other justices, however, considered the case acceptable.

The Court, in unanimously invalidating the rescinding act of the Georgia legislature, for the first time in its history held a state law void because it conflicted with a provision of the Constitution of the United States. Previously state laws had been held unconstitutional because they conflicted with federal laws or treaties.

Marshall, speaking for the Court, upheld the original grant made by the Georgia legislature on the dubious grounds that the courts could not inquire into the motives of legislators no matter how corrupt those motives might be. He next challenged the valid-

---

[2] See pp. 182–184.

ity of the rescinding act on the ground that it was a fundamental interference with private rights and hence beyond the constitutional authority of any legislative body—an allusion to the old doctrine of vested rights.

Marshall was not willing to rest the decision entirely on such general principles, however, and he next held that the Georgia rescinding act came within the constitutional provision forbidding any state to impair the obligation of contracts. A contract he defined as "a compact between two or more parties," and as "either executory or executed." Either kind of contract contained obligations binding on the parties. A grant made by a state and accepted by the grantee, he added, is in substance an executed contract, the obligation of which still continues. The constitutional provision, he observed, made no distinction between public and private contracts. The rescinding act was therefore invalid.

In holding that the obligation of contracts clause applied to public grants as well as to private contracts, Marshall in all probability misconstrued the intent of the Constitution's framers. The preponderant evidence indicates that the Convention had intended merely to prohibit the states from interfering with the contractual relations of two or more private persons. By holding that contracts entered into by the state also came under the contracts clause, Marshall gave the provision a far broader meaning than the Convention had intended.

Also in this case Marshall might well have held the original grant creating the contract invalid because of the bribery involved. His failure to do so and his apparently unwarranted extension of the contract clause made the Court's decision extremely unpopular with democratic elements and states' rights leaders, who attacked Marshall as a speculator and landholder incapable of approaching the case with judicial disinterestedness.

Two years later, in *New Jersey v. Wilson* (1812), the Court extended the contract clause to protect and perpetuate a state grant of exemption from taxation. Some years before the Revolution, New Jersey had granted the Delaware Indians exemption from taxation on certain lands held by them. After the Revolution the lands in question were sold to white men, and when New Jersey attempted to tax them, the owners appealed to the courts, claiming that the original grant of tax exemption had passed to the new owners. When the case reached the Supreme Court, Marshall wrote an opinion holding that New Jersey's attempt to tax the lands involved constituted an impairment of New Jersey's obligation of contract.

The decision not only lacked adequate precedent but also had the effect of impairing New Jersey's indispensable power of taxation. Nevertheless Marshall's opinion was accepted by the entire Court and has never been repudiated by that body. As a consequence many later state constitutions either prohibited or sharply limited legislative grants of tax immunity.

Marshall's most celebrated opinion on the contract clause came in *Dartmouth College v. Woodward* (1819), in which the Court ruled that a charter of incorporation was a contract protected against legislative infringement by the Constitution. The case grew out of the efforts of the New Hampshire legislature to alter the charter granted by George III in 1769 to the trustees of Dartmouth College, conveying to them "forever" the right to govern the institution and to fill vacancies in their own body. The charter continued unchanged throughout the Revolutionary period, but in 1816 the Republican governor and legislature, believing that the old charter was based upon principles more congenial to monarchy than to "a free government," attempted to bring the college under public control. Accordingly they passed laws which virtually took the control of the institution from the hands of the Federalist-dominated trustees and placed it under a board of overseers appointed by the governor. The trustees thereupon turned for relief to the state judiciary, but the New Hampshire Superior Court upheld the legislature's acts, chiefly on the ground that the college was essentially a public corporation whose powers and franchises were exercised for public purposes and were therefore subject to public control.

The trustees of the college then appealed the case upon writ of error to the Supreme Court, before which body the college was represented by two of the most able and eloquent lawyers of the day, Daniel Webster and Joseph Hopkinson. Although the elaborate argument of the case took place in 1818, two of the justices were unable then to make up their minds, so that the Court did not render its decision until the following year. Meanwhile the two doubtful justices were persuaded of the soundness of the college's position by the arguments of such conservative legal authorities as Chancellor James Kent of New York.

Finally, by a vote of 5 to 1, the Court decided that the New Hampshire laws in question were unconstitutional as impairment of the obligation of contract. The Chief Justice, in giving the opinion of the Court, admitted an important constitutional argument of the state: that "the framers of the constitution did not intend to restrain the states in the regulation of their civil institutions, adopted for internal government." He went to great length, however, to demonstrate that Dartmouth College was not a public institution subject to state control but instead was a "private eleemosynary institution." Although he cited no authorities, Marshall declared that the charter granted by the British Crown to the trustees was a contract within the meaning of the Constitution. By virtue of the Revolution, he said, the powers and duties of government had devolved upon the people of New Hampshire. At any time prior to the adoption of the Constitution the power of the state to repeal or alter the charter was restricted only by the state constitution, but after 1789 that power was further restrained by the obligation of contract clause.

The Dartmouth case was the first in which the Court held that a charter was a contract protected by the Constitution, but its significance has nonetheless been somewhat exaggerated by lawyers and historians. The opinion made it clear that state legislatures might reserve the right to repeal or to modify the charters which they granted, and in the future most legislatures took advantage of this right. While the decision did reassure corporate interests somewhat, the rapid increase in the number and importance of private corporations in the fields of transportation, finance, and industry was due less to their legal intrenchment than to the evident economic advantages of incorporation in large-scale business enterprise. Moreover, after 1880, when the right of the states to control and regulate business corporations became a great national issue, the Supreme Court was to base its restriction of the states' regulatory powers upon the due process clause of the Fourteenth Amendment rather than upon the obligation of contracts clause.

Green v. Biddle (1823), a case involving the relationship between the contract clause and political agreements between states, was of less permanent significance than *Dartmouth College v. Woodward*, but the Court's decision aroused much greater popular opposition. At the time of Kentucky's separation from Virginia, the two states had entered into an agreement by which Kentucky recognized the validity of land titles issued under Virginia law. Land titles in Kentucky were nonetheless extremely confused because of the large number of overlapping and conflicting claims, and for many years after 1792 they gave rise to a constant procession of lawsuits in the state's courts. In order to remedy this situation, the Kentucky legislature enacted a series of laws providing that no claimant should be awarded possession of land to which he proved title without compensating the occupant for the latter's improvement; in default thereof, the disputed title was to rest in the occupant upon payment of the value of the land without improvements. By implication at least, these laws impaired the full validity of land titles secured under the Kentucky-Virginia agreement, and the acts in question were therefore attacked in the federal courts.

The Supreme Court, speaking through Justice Bushrod Washington, held that the contract clause in the Constitution applied to contracts between two states as well as those between private persons or between a state and a private individual. The Court also denied Kentucky's claim that the agreement in question was invalid because Congress had not given its assent to the agreement as required by the Constitution. The Constitution, Justice Washington observed, required no particular mode of consent by Congress, and he held that Congress had implicitly assented to the compact when it admitted Kentucky to the Union.

The opinion provoked widespread criticism, for the prevailing opinion was that the Convention of 1787 had never intended to include interstate political agreements within the contract clause. In Congress there arose a renewed demand for reform and restriction of the federal judiciary. Kentucky, embittered because the Court's decision benefited numerous absentee landowners, continued for the most part to enforce its own laws, thereby virtually ignoring the Court's ruling. Moreover, later cases involving interstate issues were usually decided under the interstate compact clause.

THE CONTRACT CLAUSE AND BANKRUPTCY LAWS

Cases involving the legality of state bankruptcy laws were closely related in social origins and constitutional import to those arising out of other impairments of contract. State legislation in the field of bankruptcy and insolvency grew both in volume and in importance after 1815, and the attitude of the Supreme Court on these matters was anxiously awaited in many circles.

Sturges v. Crowninshield (1819) involved the constitutionality of a New York law for the relief of insolvent debtors from debts contracted before the law was enacted. Two related issues were involved: first, whether the state had the right to enact any bankruptcy legislation in the light of the provision in the Constitution specifically delegating to Congress the power to make uniform laws on bankruptcy; and second, whether the New York act violated the contract clause. Marshall held that state bankruptcy legislation was permissible in the absence of any federal statute, provided the act in question did not violate other constitutional requirements. However, he also held that the New York law impaired the obligation of contracts. Any law, said Marshall, which released a man in whole or in part from his agreement to pay another man a sum of money at a certain time, impaired the obligation of contracts and could not be reconciled with the Constitution.

Sturges v. Crowninshield resulted in a general limitation of state authority over bankruptcy matters. Congress had for many years consistently refused to enact any bankruptcy law, while at the same time the Supreme Court in this case had greatly restricted the possibility of state action, though it had not entirely prohibited it. The result hardly contributed toward an effective settlement of the problem of debtor-creditor relationships.

The panic of 1819 and the subsequent economic depression led several states to seek a loophole in *Sturges v. Crowninshield* by enacting bankruptcy laws applying solely to debts contracted after the statute's passage. Presumably such a law would place a limitation on contracts subsequently entered into and hence would make bankruptcy proceedings on such contracts constitutional, notwithstanding Marshall's ruling that state power over bankruptcy was limited by the contract clause. Moreover, the membership of the Court had changed somewhat since the Sturgis decision, and a more liberal interpretation might be expected.

In *Ogden v. Saunders* (1827) the Court ruled, 4 to 3, that a state bankruptcy law discharging both the person of the debtor and his future acquisition of property did not impair the obligation of contracts entered into after the passage of the law. The decision was accompanied by six elaborate opinions, which revealed that the Court was not only badly divided on the present question but had also been divided in *Sturges v. Crowninshield*. The earlier decision, Justice Johnson now admitted, had been arrived at substantially as a compromise among the justices rather than as an act of "legal adjudication." Johnson and the other more liberal-minded justices, it appeared, had acquiesced in the invalidation of state laws regulating anterior contracts only with the proviso that the opinion be so guarded as to secure the states' power over posterior contracts. It was this latter point that the present majority now insisted upon.

The majority justices arrived at their identical position by differing logical paths. Justice Washington argued that a bankruptcy law in existence at the time the contract was made was a part of the contract itself; hence subsequent bankruptcy proceedings in accordance with the law were within the obligation of the contract in question. Both Johnson and Robert Trimble, on the other hand, argued substantially that the states had the authority to prescribe "what shall be the obligation of all contracts made within them." As Johnson expressed it, "all the contracts of men receive a relative, and not a positive interpretation: for the rights of all must be held and enjoyed in subserviency to the good of the whole. The state construes them, the state applies them, the state controls them, and the state decides how far the social exercise of the rights they give us over each other can be justly asserted." This was substantially an anticipation of the later doctrine of the state's police power.

This view sounds reasonable in the twentieth century, but it was heresy to Marshall and Story, with their conservative legal doctrines of vested rights and the inviolability of contracts. In a dissenting opinion the Chief Justice declared that the Constitution protected all contracts, past or future, from state legislation which in any manner impaired their obligation. He maintained that the position of the majority would virtually destroy the contract clause of the Constitution. Marshall admitted, however, that the constitutional prohibition of the impairment of the obligation of contracts by a state did not prohibit its legislature from changing the remedies for the enforcement of contracts. Even his sympathetic biographer, Albert J. Beveridge, labels Marshall at this time "the supreme conservative." It was symbolic of a new era of constitutional interpretation that in 1827 the Court for the first and only time voted against Marshall on an important question of constitutional law.

On another issue raised in *Ogden v. Saunders* Johnson joined Marshall and the conservatives in a majority opinion. They declared that a state's insolvency law could not discharge a contract owed to a citizen of another state, since such action would produce "a conflict of sovereign power, and a collision with the judicial powers granted to the United States."

In conclusion, then, the Supreme Court's position was, first, that state bankruptcy and insolvency laws were unconstitutional when they operated on contracts entered into before their passage but were constitutional with respect to contracts entered into after their passage; and second, that they were unconstitutional if they invalidated a contract owed to a citizen of another state. Thus the Court took the first important step in restricting the scope of the contract clause as it had been interpreted between 1810 and 1819.

The immediate effect of the decisions on the obligation of contracts clause was to make the Supreme Court a conservative stronghold against the growing power of state democracy and popular sovereignty. In most of the other important constitutional decisions of this period the Court invalidated state laws or state court decisions in order to uphold the authority of the national government. Generally such a policy proved to be beneficial to the American people, especially since the national government was responsible to them. In the contract cases, however, the Court's decisions favored vested interests at the expense of the states, without any considerable benefit accruing to the national government.

THE CONTROVERSY OVER APPELLATE JURISDICTION

While the Supreme Court was striving to determine the nature and the scope of the obligation of contracts on the part of the states, its own right to review the decisions of the highest state courts was seriously challenged by the Virginia states' rights champions. Here again were involved the persistent and basic questions of the nature of the Union and of the location of the authority to act as a final arbiter in disputes between the states and the central government.

It will be recalled that Article III, Section 1, of the Constitution was the result of a compromise in the Constitutional Convention between those who wished a completely national judicial system and those who wished to leave original jurisdiction almost entirely in the state courts, even in cases in which national issues were involved. As finally drawn, this section permitted Congress to establish inferior federal courts but did not obligate it to do so. In the Judiciary Act of 1789 the nationalists had won out by establishing a complete system of federal courts with final appellate jurisdiction vested in the Supreme Court. Although the state courts were given concurrent jurisdiction in certain types of cases, the crucial twenty-fifth section of the act provided that whenever the highest state court rendered a decision against a person who claimed rights under the federal Constitution, laws, or treaties, the judgment could be reviewed, and possibly reversed, by the Supreme Court. At the time some of the states' rights advocates approved this arrangement because it gave the state courts a share in a jurisdiction which might otherwise have been assigned exclusively to federal courts. Others saw only the danger to the sovereignty of the states if their highest courts could be overruled by the federal judiciary.

The first important controversy over the question of the Supreme Court's appellate jurisdiction from state courts grew out of an old case involving the vast lands of Lord Fairfax, a Virginia loyalist.

During the Revolution, Virginia confiscated his estate and also enacted a law denying the right of an alien to inherit real property. After the Revolution, Virginia according to this law refused to allow Fairfax's English heir to inherit the estate, despite his rights under treaties with Great Britain. The Virginia Court of Appeals eventually upheld the state laws, but the case was taken on writ of error to the United Sates Supreme Court, where the Virginia decision was reversed. Since Marshall had earlier participated in the litigation, he absented himself, and the Court's decision was rendered by Justice Story. The decision practically emasculated the state's alien-inheritance and confiscation laws, which had been enforced by the state judiciary for a generation. The Virginia judges, headed by Spencer Roane, responded by declaring unconstitutional Section 25 of the Judiciary Act and by refusing to carry into effect the Supreme Court's mandate.

This refusal caused the case to be taken again to the Supreme Court as *Martin v. Hunter's Lessee* (1816). Story again rendered the opinion and presented a powerful argument in support of the Court's right to review decisions of state courts. He maintained that, since Congress constitutionally could have vested all federal jurisdiction in the federal courts, the voluntary granting of concurrent jurisdiction in certain cases to the state courts did not divest the Supreme Court of its appellate jurisdiction. In other words, the concurrent jurisdiction clauses of the Judiciary Act had incorporated the state courts, for certain cases, into the federal judicial system. Story declared, moreover, that the Constitution, laws, and treaties of the United States could be maintained uniformly as the supreme law of the land only if the Supreme Court had the right to review and to harmonize the decisions of all inferior courts applying that supreme law.

The Court's stand was repeatedly attacked by the states' rights Virginians. Judge Spencer Roane presented their ablest argument. He maintained not only that the Constitution established a federal rather than a consolidated union, but also that it contained no provision which authorized the central government to be the final judge of the extent of its own power, legislative or judicial. Nor, he argued, was there any clause in the Constitution which expressly denied the power of state courts to pass with finality upon the validity of their own legislation. To be sure, he said, the judges in every state were bound by the Constitution to uphold "the supreme law of the land," even when it was in conflict with the constitution and laws of any state; but they were bound as state judges only, and therefore their decisions were not subject to review or correction by the courts of another jurisdiction. Hence, he contended, Section 25 of the Judiciary Act was unconstitutional. In fact, Roane concluded, the state's sovereignty could not be protected against federal encroachment if the final decision on the constitutionality of both federal and state acts rested with the Supreme Court.

The Court's opportunity to answer Roane came in *Cohens v. Virginia* (1821). The Cohens were convicted by a Virginia court of selling lottery tickets in violation of a state statute, although they claimed the protection of an act of Congress authorizing a lottery for the District of Columbia. When the Cohens appealed to the Supreme Court under Section 25 of the Judiciary Act, counsel for Virginia denied the Court's right of review and insisted that a state could never be subjected to any private individual's suit before any judicial tribunal without the state's own consent. This immunity resulted, the state claimed, in part from the sovereign nature of the states, "as properly sovereign now as they were under the confederacy," and in part from the Eleventh Amendment, which prohibited the federal judiciary from taking jurisdiction of a suit prosecuted against a state.

Marshall began his opinion by defining the extent of federal judicial power. The jurisdiction of the federal courts under the Constitution, he observed, extended to two general classes of cases. In the first class, jurisdiction depended upon the "character of the cause," and included "all cases in law and equity arising under this constitution, the laws of the United States, and treaties made, or which shall be made, under their authority." In the second class, jurisdiction depended on the character of the parties, and included controversies between two or more states, between a state and citizens of another state, and between a state and foreign states' citizens or subjects. Any case falling within either of these classes, Marshall said, came within the jurisdiction of the federal courts, even though one of the parties might be a state of the Union.

Marshall then examined Virginia's contention that because of the sovereign, independent character of the states they could not be sued without their consent. The Chief Justice replied that for some purposes the states were no longer sovereign—they had surrendered some of their sovereignty into the keeping of a national government. Maintenance of national supremacy, he continued, made it necessary for the states to submit to federal jurisdiction; the contrary situation would prostrate the government "at the feet of every state in the Union."

Nor did the Eleventh Amendment, which protected the states against suits by private individuals, exempt the state of Virginia from federal jurisdiction in the present instance. The present action, Marshall said, was not commenced or prosecuted by an individual against a state; rather the appeal was merely part of an action begun by the state against the Cohens, and thus the state could not claim immunity from that appeal by virtue of the Eleventh Amendment.

Finally Marshall turned to Virginia's argument that in any event there existed no right of appeal from the state courts to the United States Supreme Court, because the state and federal judicial systems were entirely distinct and the Constitution did not provide for such appeals. Marshall's reply again was to cite the doctrine of national supremacy and to argue that the maintenance of that supremacy made such appeals necessary. "America has chosen to be, in many respects, and to many purposes, a nation; and for all these purposes, her government is complete; to all these objects, it is competent. The people have declared, that in the exercise of all powers given for these objects it is supreme. It can, then, in effecting these objects, legitimately control all individuals or governments within the American territory." In a government so constituted, Marshall continued, the national judiciary must be able to decide whether or not the constitution and laws of any state are conformable to the federal Constitution and laws, and for this purpose the Supreme Court's right to hear appeals from the state courts was an imperative necessity.

The Court then decided the specific question at issue in favor of Virginia, holding that the congressional lottery ordinance was limited to the city of Washington and that the Cohens therefore had no legal right to sell tickets in Virginia.

Virginia's nominal victory brought the state little satisfaction. It was overshadowed by the Court's sweeping and definitive interpretation of its right of appellate jurisdiction over decisions of the highest state courts in all questions involving national powers. It was widely recognized that the Court's assertion of authority would greatly enhance its prestige and its opportunity to be the final arbiter of constitutional questions.

Although the decision was applauded by some and passively approved by many, it was vigorously attacked by the Virginia states' rightists and their numerous sympathizers. Judge Roane and his friends wrote a series of newspaper articles, bitterly attacking the Court's usurpation of authority over the states. Roane tried to persuade ex-President Madison to lead the attack, but the latter refused; in fact he agreed essentially with Marshall's position in regard to the appellate jurisdiction of the Supreme Court. Jefferson, more hostile to Marshall, denounced the decision as another step in the scheme of the Supreme Court to destroy the federal constitutional system by consolidating all authority in the central government.

John Taylor, the veteran champion of agrarian localism, elaborated the arguments against the Court in a series of pamphlets on constitutional interpretation, one graphically entitled *Construction Construed and Constitutions Vindicated*. He argued that Marshall's concept of the Court's jurisdiction would make it the supreme, irresponsible, and tyrannical arbiter of all constitutional disputes and thus would destroy the independence of both the states and the other branches of the federal government. The Court, or a bare majority of its members, he charged, was actually molding and changing the character of the Constitution, whereas this function was the rightful authority of three-fourths of the states through amendments. The great evil of the federal judiciary was the absence of any obligation on the part of the judges to act in accordance with the will of the sovereign people or of their chosen representatives. If any branch of the federal government was to be the guardian of the Constitution, it should be Congress, the politically responsible body. Constitutional change, Taylor insisted, must be effected by popular will, and not by judges who were responsible only to "God and their own conscience."

IMPLIED POWERS AND NATIONAL SUPREMACY

John Marshall's most comprehensive exposition of the American constitutional system was his opinion in *McCulloch v. Maryland* (1819). The case involved the second Bank of the United States, at that time one of the most controversial issues before the American people. The new bank had neither checked speculation nor improved financial conditions sufficiently to prevent a serious panic in 1819, followed by a depression which caused innumerable banking and business failures with resultant unemployment, hard times, and popular discontent throughout the country. Certain branches of the bank had also engaged in reckless speculation, mismanagement, and outright fraudulent financial practices, and had almost ruined the bank and its reputation for integrity.

Several of the states of the South and West, where the Bank of the United States was most unpopular, took action to prevent the operation of its branches within their borders, either by direct prohibition in the state constitution or by prohibitory taxation.

Among the latter was Maryland, where the legislature in 1818 levied a heavy tax on the bank's Baltimore branch. The validity of the Maryland law was upheld in the state courts, whereupon the bank appealed the case to the United States Supreme Court.

The case was elaborately argued by six of the greatest lawyers in the country, including Daniel Webster and William Pinckney for the bank, and Luther Martin and Joseph Hopkinson for Maryland. Three days after the close of the argument, on March 6, 1819, the Chief Justice handed down the unanimous judgment of the Court, upholding the constitutional power of Congress to charter the bank and to have exclusive control over it, denying the right of Maryland to interfere with the federal government by taxing its agencies, and declaring the state law unconstitutional.

The first important question involved in the case was: "Has Congress power to incorporate a bank?" In answering this question in the affirmative Marshall proceeded to analyze at some length the nature of the Constitution and the American Union. His argument was directed mainly to upholding the doctrines of national sovereignty and broad construction. National sovereignty he upheld by emphasizing that the federal government rested directly upon a popular base, having derived its authority from the people of the states rather than from the states as sovereign entities. Marshall admitted that sovereignty was divided between the states and national government and that the states retained a sphere of sovereign authority. But the national government, he said, "though limited in its powers, is supreme within its sphere of action." This argument that national sovereignty was derived from the direct popular base of the Constitution was later to be eloquently reasserted by Webster and Lincoln and was to become one of the main tenets of American nationalism.

Marshall then set forth what was essentially the same doctrine of broad construction and implied powers that Hamilton had advanced in his bank message of 1791.[3] He admitted that the right to establish a bank was not among the enumerated powers of Congress, but he held that the national government also possessed implied powers as well as those enumerated in the Constitution. Implied powers, he said, could be drawn from two sources. First, every legislature must by its very nature have the right to select appropriate means to carry out its powers. Second, he pointed to the necessary and proper clause, which he construed as broadly as Hamilton

---

[3] See pp. 166–170.

had previously done. "Necessary and proper," he said, did not mean "absolutely indispensable," for there were various degrees of necessity. Then followed the test for determining the constitutionality of an implied power, stated almost in the words of Hamilton's original formula: "Let the end be legitimate, let it be within the scope of the constitution, and all means which are appropriate, which are plainly adapted to that end, which are not prohibited, but consist with the letter and spirit of the constitution, are constitutional."

The second question involved in the case was whether the state of Maryland could constitutionally tax a branch of the national bank. In defending Maryland's right to tax the bank, counsel for the state had resorted to the classic states' rights argument of dual federalism. The states and the federal government, according to this view, constituted two mutually exclusive fields of power, the sphere of authority of each being an absolute barrier to the encroachment of the other. The right to charter corporations was a state power, and the state therefore had a right to regulate or exclude from its limits corporations not chartered by itself.

In refuting this argument Marshall again resorted to the principle of national supremacy. He pointed to the clause making the Constitution, treaties, and acts of Congress the supreme law of the land, and observed once more that when state law conflicted with national law, the latter must prevail. Since the bank was a lawful instrument of federal authority, the act of Congress establishing it must prevail against any state attempt to limit or control the bank's functions. The state's attempt to tax the bank was therefore illegal, for "the power to tax involves the power to destroy." If federal functions could be taxed by the states, their continuance would be dependent upon the will of the states rather than that of the national government—an inadmissible conclusion. The American people, he said, "did not design to make their government dependent on the states." The Maryland tax act was therefore unconstitutional and void.

The importance of this decision was recognized immediately, and has been ever since. It was reprinted by newspapers in all sections of the country and was widely discussed by men in public life. In conservative circles of the Northeast the decision was generally approved, partly because the national bank was favored there, and partly because nationalism and broad construction of the powers of Congress were returning to popularity in that section.

On the other hand, the decision was condemned and bitterly denounced in most of the western and southern states. There a majority of the people saw their efforts to get rid of the hated bank stopped by a tribunal beyond the control of public opinion. They seemingly forgot that the bank had been established by a majority of Congress. Newspapers, public meetings, and state legislatures protested that the effect of the decision was to obliterate the last vestige of the sovereignty and independence of the individual states. Resentment was especially strong in the South, where the concern for state sovereignty was heightened by the Missouri controversy, then in progress. In Virginia in particular, Marshall's interpretation of the Constitution was challenged by a formidable array of states' rightists, led by Judge Roane of the Court of Appeals, and supported by the leading newspaper editors and by ex-Presidents Madison and Jefferson.

Out of such strong opposition to the McCulloch decision arose a movement for a constitutional amendment designed to prevent clashes between the states and the federal government by granting power to the former to exclude branches of the national bank from their territory. Most of the state legislatures considered the question, and five states formally approved of a request to Congress for such an amendment. Nine states disapproved, however, and the movement died.

The most definite and defiant action in opposition to the Court's decision was taken by the state of Ohio. Economic and financial conditions there were particularly distressing, and much of the blame was heaped upon the national bank. In February 1819 the Ohio legislature had levied the exceedingly heavy tax of $50,000 on each branch of the bank within the state, and had granted the state auditor wide powers of search and seizure in collecting the tax. When the McCulloch decision was handed down shortly afterward, the state determined to disregard it on the ground that the case was a feigned one designed to save the bank from the effects of its "extravagant and fraudulent speculations" by exempting it from state taxation. In order to prevent the state from enforcing its act, the bank obtained an injunction from the federal Circuit Court against Ralph Osborn, the state auditor. Osborn and his aides ignored the injunction, and after demanding and being refused payment of the tax, seized the bank's specie and notes and conveyed them to the state treasury. The bank then instituted a suit for damages against the state officials involved, whereupon the legislature banned the bank from Ohio in entirety. A subsequent attempt by the state to compromise the tax question was rejected by the bank.

The controversy finally reached the Supreme Court as *Osborn v. The Bank of the United States* (1824). Although the appellant's counsel argued that the Ohio tax and outlaw acts were constitutional, the Court considered that their validity could not be maintained in face of the McCulloch decision. Chief consideration, therefore, was given to the bank's constitutional means of protection against illegal state action. The crucial question was whether the suit was an action against the state and therefore not within the jurisdiction of the federal judiciary because of the Eleventh Amendment, or whether the state's agents were personally responsible for their acts. Marshall and his colleagues held that the United States Circuit Court had jurisdiction, on the ground that the suit was not against the state, because the state was not the actual party on record. This decision was another step in the direction of limiting the states' protection from suits under the Eleventh Amendment.

Of greater importance was the Supreme Court's ruling that the agent of a state, when acting under authority of an unconstitutional statute, was personally responsible for any injury inflicted in his attempt to execute the act. This involved a transfer to constitutional law of the old English and American principle of private law that every man is responsible for the wrongs he inflicts. This principle is essential for the protection of personal liberty, for since governments or legislatures cannot be sued for torts, the injured person's only recourse is to sue their agents. Thus in this case both the state of Ohio and its agents were defeated by the United States Bank before the nation's highest judicial body.

As in the cases involving obligation of contract, the Supreme Court's decisions in the bank cases placed it in the role of defender of corporations and vested rights against popular sovereignty as embodied in the state legislatures. Again the Court's nationalism was tinged with conservatism. That fact helps to explain the defeat suffered by the bank a few years later when its request for a new charter was rejected by the veto of President Jackson, a rejection sustained by implication by the electorate.[4]

THE POWER TO REGULATE COMMERCE

Another of the chief objectives of the framers of the Constitution had been to replace the confused condition of foreign and interstate commercial relations prevailing in 1787 with an orderly and uniform system. Consequently the Constitution empowered Congress "to regulate Commerce with foreign Nations, and among the several

---

[4] Later constitutional controversies involving the national bank are discussed on pp. 314–321.

States, and with the Indian Tribes." After the adoption of the Constitution the volume of both foreign and interstate commerce increased rapidly. Congress early made legal provision for the regulation of ships and cargoes from foreign countries and passed a law providing for the licensing of vessels engaged in the important coastal trade. On the other hand, Congress took virtually no positive action for the control of interstate commerce, but such commerce flourished without much federal aid or regulation, since the states abandoned their former discriminations against vessels and products from other states.

During the first quarter of the nineteenth century the steamboat was developed into an important means of transportation in the coastal trade and especially on the rivers and lakes of the interior of the country. By the 1820's the free development of interstate trade by this new means of transportation was being threatened by attempts of various states to grant "exclusive privileges" to various interests over the steam navigation of "state waters." This policy led to retaliation of state against state. Thus monopoly and localism were joining hands in a movement of state restriction upon interstate commerce that was reminiscent of the days of the Confederation.

In 1808 Robert Fulton and Robert Livingston, pioneers in the development of a practical steamboat, secured from the New York legislature a grant of the exclusive right to operate steamboats on the state's waters. From this monopoly Aaron Ogden secured the exclusive right to certain steam navigation across the Hudson River between New York and New Jersey. Thomas Gibbons, however, proceeded to engage in competition with Ogden, claiming the right under a license granted under the federal Coasting Act. Ogden's suit to restrain Gibbons from engaging in this interstate navigation was sustained by the New York courts in 1819 and 1820, with Chancellor James Kent, perhaps the most learned jurist in America, upholding Ogden and the steamboat monopoly act.

Gibbons appealed to the United States Supreme Court, where the case of *Gibbons v. Ogden* was finally heard in 1824. Thus thirty-five years after its establishment, the Court was first called upon to give a general interpretation of the nature and scope of the power of Congress to regulate interstate commerce. Moreover, the case was decided when the Court was under serious attack in Congress and in the public press for previous nationalistic decisions.

Although the argument of the case took a wide range, Chief Justice Marshall, in handing down the unanimous decision of the

Court, devoted himself to four main points or questions. First, what does commerce comprehend? Second, to what extent may Congress exercise its commercial regulatory power within the separate states? Third, is congressional power to regulate interstate commerce exclusive, or does a state have concurrent power in this field? Fourth, should the commerce power of Congress (and inferentially other powers too) be construed broadly for the national welfare or be construed strictly in order to protect the reserved police powers of the states?

In discussing the first question, Marshall rejected the argument of Ogden's counsel that commerce should be narrowly defined as "traffic" or the mere buying or selling of goods, including only such transportation as was purely auxiliary thereto. "Commerce, undoubtedly, is traffic," he said, "but it is something more; it is intercourse." It encompasses navigation and general commercial relations. The meaning of the word, he added, is just as comprehensive when applied to "commerce among the several states" as when applied to foreign commerce, where it admittedly comprehends "every species of commercial intercourse."

Turning to the second and vital question of the power to regulate commerce, the Chief Justice admitted that "the completely internal commerce of a state" was reserved to the state. Interstate commerce, however, cannot stop at "the external boundary-line of each state," but "comprehends navigation within the limits of every state in the Union." Congress' power to regulate foreign and interstate commerce, "like all others vested in Congress, is complete in itself, may be exercised to its utmost extent, and acknowledges no limitations other than are prescribed in the constitution," which did not apply to the case under consideration.

Marshall's clear-cut and emphatic disposition of the first two points was lacking in his treatment of the question of the concurrent power of the states over interstate commerce within their own limits. Marshall did not actually hold that federal power over interstate commerce was exclusive, although he almost appeared to do so. Instead he merely held that the state law in question violated the federal Coasting Act, and he left in great uncertainty the question of whether the states had any actual concurrent power over interstate commerce in the absence of federal regulation.[5]

In failing to hold that the commerce power was exclusive and

[5] In a concurring opinion Justice Johnson held that Congress' power to regulate commerce was not only very broad but definitely exclusive.

in suggesting by implication that the states could therefore exercise some jurisdiction over interstate commerce, Marshall took a much less nationalistic position than he did in most of his other opinions. He might have foreclosed conclusively the field of interstate commerce from any state regulation; instead he left the door open to that possibility. Why he did so is uncertain. Perhaps he recognized the necessity for some state regulation of commerce which might incidentally touch upon interstate commercial activities. It is possible, also, that he hoped to enlarge the sphere of the Court's jurisdiction, since it would now be necessary in the future to define the extent of permissible state activity.

To the fourth and more general question of whether the enumerated powers of Congress should be construed narrowly or broadly, the Chief Justice gave an emphatic answer. At the outset he rejected narrow construction on the ground that it "would cripple the government and render it unequal to the objects for which it is declared [in the preamble] to be instituted, and to which the powers given, as fairly understood, render it competent."

Gibbons v. Ogden was Marshall's last great decision, and, as if it were his valedictory, he closed with a vigorous and significant protest against the swelling chorus of strict construction and state sovereignty: "Powerful and ingenious minds, taking, as postulates, that the powers expressly granted to the government of the Union are to be contracted, by construction, into the narrowest possible compass, and that the original powers of the States are retained, if any possible construction will retain them, may, by a course of well digested, but refined and metaphysical reasoning, founded on these premises, explain away the constitution of our country, and leave it a magnificent structure indeed, to look at, but totally unfit for use. . . . In such a case, it is peculiarly necessary to recur to safe and fundamental principles. . . ."

For once John Marshall had handed down a popular decision. It was a death blow to the steamboat monopoly, and at the time monopolies were very unpopular. This aspect of the decision received so much attention that few people fully appreciated its nationalistic implications. The popularity of the decision temporarily checked the agitation and movement in Congress for changes in the size and powers of the Supreme Court. The only serious opposition to the principles of *Gibbons v. Ogden* came from the extreme adherents of localism, especially in Virginia and North Carolina. In the Court's broad construction of national control over interstate commerce these men perceived a serious danger to states' rights in general and to the interstate slave trade in particular.

The broader significance of *Gibbons v. Ogden* became evident only with the passage of time. Steamboat navigation, freed from the restraint of state-created monopolies, both actual and potential, increased at an astonishing rate. Within a few years steam railroads, encouraged by the freedom of interstate commerce from state restraints, were to begin a practical revolution of internal transportation. The importance of national control of commerce in the rapid economic development of the country is almost incalculable. For many years after 1824 Congress enacted but few important regulatory measures, and commerce was thus free to develop without serious monopolistic or governmental restraint.

The constitutional result of this situation was that the Supreme Court became a virtual collaborator with Congress in the regulation of foreign and interstate commerce.[6] Pursuing its policy of selective exclusiveness of national authority, the Court was repeatedly called upon to draw a line between the commerce power and the rights of the states, especially their taxing and police powers. Within five years after 1824 Marshall himself rendered two opinions making such distinctions.

In the first of these, *Brown v. Maryland* (1827), Marshall formulated the "original package" doctrine. The question at issue was whether a Maryland statute requiring wholesalers of imported goods to take out a special license came within the state's taxing power or infringed upon the federal commerce power. The Chief Justice declared that whenever imported goods became "mixed up with the mass of property in the country" they became subject to the state's taxing power, but that as long as the goods remained the property of the importer and in the original form or package any state tax upon them constituted an unconstitutional interference with the regulation of commerce. The principle was stated so broadly that it would apply to interstate as well as foreign commerce and to any degree of state taxation.

Two years later, however, in *Willson v. Black Bird Creek Marsh Company* (1829), Marshall upheld a Delaware law authorizing the damming of a creek to exclude water from a marsh, even though the stream was navigable and had occasionally been used in the coasting trade. Willson's vessel was licensed under the same coasting act as that cited in *Gibbons v. Ogden*, and Marshall therefore might

---

[6] Later developments of the interstate commerce power are discussed in detail especially in Chapters 13, 21, and 22.

have held that the state statute infringed upon the federal commerce power. Instead, however, he held that the federal government had not yet acted, and that the state's regulation was therefore valid in the absence of any federal statute. Thus Marshall and the Court inaugurated the policy of judicial determination of whether a challenged state law was a valid exercise of its police power or was an unconstitutional infringement upon the federal power to regulate foreign and interstate commerce.

FAILURE AND SUCCESS OF MARSHALL'S LEGAL NATIONALISM

During Marshall's tenure the Supreme Court declared unconstitutional acts of more than half of the states. In practically every case the state involved naturally objected in some form to the Court's decision, and often the state received sympathetic support from other states with similar statutes or interests. Frequently, however, other states supported the Court. In nearly every instance the state was motivated primarily by concern for its immediate interests rather than by a broad political theory or constitutional concept. Paradoxically, the greatest theoretical opposition to the Court's legal nationalism came from Virginia at a time when one of its citizens, James Monroe, was the nation's President and another was the Chief Justice of the United States Supreme Court. Jefferson, Madison, Taylor, and Roane formed a very talented quartet to argue the cause for states' rights even though their argument was essentially the one formulated in 1798.

The Court's repeated invalidation of state statutes demonstrated that the states' rights adherents had largely failed in their efforts to make the states rather than the Court the final arbiter in disputes between the states and the central government. Consequently the Court's opponents attempted to curb its power by congressional action, especially between 1819 and 1827, when state statutes were being set aside at almost every session of the Court. The chief arguments in Congress against the Court were the same ones used by state agents and legislatures: the absence of any specific constitutional authority on the part of the Court to invalidate state statutes or judicial decisions, the Court's lack of responsibility to the people, its natural policy of upholding federal authority at the expense of the state, and the threat of such a powerful body to the "sovereignty" of the states and the liberties of the people.

The most drastic attempt to restrict the Court's authority was that initiated by Senator Richard Johnson of Kentucky, who proposed to constitute the Senate a court of last resort in all cases which involved the constitutionality of state laws or to which a state should be a party. More numerous were the efforts to increase the size of the Court and to require more than a bare majority decision to invalidate a state law. None of these proposals was adopted by Congress. Rejected also were the bills sponsored by friends of the Court to relieve Supreme Court justices from circuit court duties. The House did pass a bill increasing to ten the membership of the Supreme Court and rearranging the circuits, but the measure failed in the Senate.

The continued refusal of Congress to make any changes in the federal judiciary was due to a combination of several factors: political and sectional cross currents, the absence of definite party organization, the confidence of many groups in the Supreme Court, realization that the proposed remedies involved greater disadvantages than the existing system, and belief that the veteran justices would soon be replaced by jurists more sympathetic toward states' rights and popular sovereignty.

The anticipated transformation in the Court's personnel and viewpoint was already under way by appointments made during the late 1820's, although it did not become thorough until after Marshall's death in 1835. Ultimately some of the principles of constitutional law announced by Marshall and his colleagues were gradually modified, and a few were virtually abandoned.

In the new political atmosphere judicial nationalism often seemed less relevant than local democracy, popular sovereignty, and the states' police power. Eventually these popular ideas and institutions became badly confused, both politically and legally, with extreme states' rights and the defense of slavery. The practical result was secession and civil war.

Yet the impact of Marshall's nationalism upon the American constitutional system could not be effaced. For a third of a century the great Chief Justice had stood for law and justice, firmly and fairly applied to all groups and segments of American society, despite widespread opposition and some vigorous protests. For a long time after 1824 Marshall's constitutional law was to serve as a check upon the strong popular trend toward decentralization and states' rights. Although the Supreme Court under a new Chief Justice, Roger B. Taney, modified some phases of Marshall's law, it did not abandon judicial nationalism and it still insisted that the Court was the ultimate arbiter of all judicial cases involving the respective limits of federal and state constitutional powers.

Marshall's most important contribution was his insistence that the Constitution was an ordinance of the American people and not a compact of sovereign states, and therefore that the United States was a sovereign nation and not a mere federation of states. In the generation following Marshall's death this concept often seemed to be in eclipse, but it was still potent when the supreme crisis arrived. Between 1861 and 1865 more than a million men voluntarily took up arms to maintain an indissoluble Union, and tens of thousands of them gave their lives "that that nation might live."

The Nullification Controversy

CONFLICTS between national and state interests had been a fruitful source of political and constitutional controversy since the establishment of the government under the Constitution in 1789. At one time or another most of the states had resorted to states rights or state sovereignty doctrines to challenge the authority of the national government and had developed a variety of ideas, concepts, and arguments in defense of their positions.

The constitutional crises growing out of the conflict over Indian rights in Georgia and the tariff dispute between the federal government and South Carolina nonetheless differed significantly from earlier federal-state conflicts. In the first place, both Georgia and South Carolina openly flouted federal authority, while South Carolina actually took steps to block the enforcement of a major federal statute within the state. Equally important, the South Carolina nullifiers developed a far more elaborate and coherent theory of the Union as a mere league of sovereign states and of nullification as a remedy for unconstitutional federal legislation than anyone had advanced at any time between 1798 and 1828. Calhoun's theories were in fact so well developed that they were adopted as the legal basis of the South's argument in the slavery crisis, and they were ultimately used to justify secession in 1860–61.

284

GEORGIA'S DEFIANCE OF THE UNITED STATES
ON THE INDIAN QUESTION

South Carolina's defiance of federal law was anticipated by a controversy between Georgia and the United States, inspired by Georgia's attempt to remove the remaining Creek and Cherokee Indians from the western portion of the state. In the course of the controversy Georgia openly flouted the authority of federal treaties governing the Indians' status and even threatened to use force against United States troops if that proved necessary to defend state interests.

The status of the American Indians, like so many other matters, was left indefinite under the Constitution. By implication the Indians were almost outside the constitutional system. They were denied citizenship, exempted from taxation, and not counted in the apportionment of representation and direct taxes. Congress was authorized merely to regulate commerce with the Indian tribes. Under this authority and the treaty-making and war powers the federal government from the beginning had dealt with the Indians as autonomous nations and had pursued a policy of removing the Indians from the paths of the white men as the tide of settlement moved westward.

In accordance with this policy, the federal government at the time of Georgia's cession of her western domains had undertaken to secure for the state at federal expense all Indian lands lying within the state "as early as the same can possibly be obtained on reasonable terms." The Indians in Georgia were the relatively civilized Creeks and Cherokees, who were determined not to give up their homeland, and federal evacuation therefore proceeded very slowly.

During the 1820's Georgia became extremely dissatisfied with the slowness of the United States government in removing the Creeks and determined to assert its authority over the tribe's territory. Although in 1826 the Creeks had been "persuaded" by the federal government to cede all their lands except a small strip along the western border of the state, Georgia's militant Governor George M. Troup nonetheless bitterly charged the government with failure to carry out its promises, and ordered state surveys to be made of the lands in question. When President Adams threatened to use the army to restrain Georgia's surveyors, the arrogant governor informed the President that such action would precipitate civil war, and he prepared to defend Georgia's "sovereignty" by force of arms. An open clash between the state and federal governments was averted only by the capitulation of the Creeks and their removal beyond the Mississippi.

A few years later the attempt of the Cherokee Indians within Georgia to organize themselves as an "independent nation" led the state to defy the authority of the federal judiciary. In 1827 the Cherokees adopted a written constitution and proclaimed themselves an independent state, whereupon the indignant Georgia legislature extended state law over Indian territory, annulled all Indian law, and directed the seizure of all Cherokee lands. In accordance with the newly asserted jurisdiction, the state presently tried and convicted a Cherokee Indian, one Corn Tassel, for murder. The United States Supreme Court shortly granted Corn Tassel a writ of error, but the state refused to honor it, and Governor Troup with the support of the legislature declared that he would resist all interference from whatever quarter with the state's courts. Suiting action to words, the state promptly executed the Indian.

President Jackson refused to take any action in defense of Indian treaty rights such as Adams had done, but friends of the Cherokees sought an injunction in the Supreme Court to restrain Georgia from enforcing its laws over the Indians and from seizing their lands. In *Cherokee Nation v. Georgia* (1831) the Court held in a cautious opinion of Chief Justice Marshall that an Indian tribe was neither a state in the Union nor a foreign nation within the meaning of the Constitution, and therefore could not maintain an action in the federal courts. But he added that the Indians were "domestic dependent nations" under the sovereignty and dominion of the United States, and that they had an unquestionable right to the lands they occupied until title should be extinguished by voluntary cession to the United States. This equivocal decision left Georgia defiant and the Cherokees unprotected.

The following year, in *Worcester v. Georgia* (1832), a case involving Samuel Worcester's conviction by the state for residence upon Indian lands without a license from the state, Marshall went further and held that the Cherokee nation was a distinct political community, having territorial boundaries within which "the laws of Georgia can have no force, and which the citizens of Georgia have no right to enter but with the assent of the Cherokees themselves or in conformity with treaties and with the acts of Congress." Georgia openly flouted this decision, refusing either to appear at the bar of the Court or to order Worcester's release. Many people applauded Georgia's defiance.

President Jackson refused to take any steps to implement the Court's opinions in these cases, and it appeared that there was no practical way to force him to do so. In the Worcester case Marshall strongly implied that it was the President's duty to uphold the appellant's rights under federal law, to which admonition Jackson is reputed to have replied: "John Marshall has made his decision, now let him enforce it." Jackson in fact could rightfully claim some discretion in the choice of means for the execution of laws, and in this instance he chose to pressure the Cherokees to sign new treaties providing for the cession of their lands and for migration to new lands west of the Mississippi River.

The Cherokee episode had two significant aspects. In the first place, the mean and disgraceful treatment of the Cherokees by Georgia and Jackson, which undoubtedly had widespread popular support, constituted one of the great blots upon the character of white American society in the nineteenth century. Unfortunately, the treatment accorded the Cherokees was hardly unique. Most of the western states were also taking effective if more legal steps to force the Indians to move beyond the Mississippi against their wishes. Neither the national government nor any state made any serious effort to divide the country's abundant land between whites and red men or to follow a policy of live and let live. Although the fact was not fully appreciated until the twentieth century, the American Constitution had failed in a major sense to provide adequate protection for one of the nation's largest minorities, the American Indians.

Of more immediate significance for American constitutional development was the ominous precedent set by Georgia's deliberate defiance of federal authority. Within a few months of the Worcester decision, South Carolina attempted to nullify the tariff act of 1832. A constitutional crisis of major proportions resulted.

FROM NATIONALISM TO NULLIFICATION
IN SOUTH CAROLINA

For thirty years after the establishment of the Constitution, South Carolina was relatively nationalistic. The state repeatedly championed the central government against charges of usurping state authority and favored broad construction of national power. As late as 1820 the lower house of the state legislature, although opposed to the tariff, deprecated the tendency of certain states to array themselves as sovereign entities in opposition to national authority.

In harmony with this view, South Carolina's great statesman, John C. Calhoun, at first stood forth as a thoroughgoing nationalist and a strong advocate of broad construction. It will be recalled that he had sponsored the second national bank, and had argued effectively for both a protective tariff and a national system of internal improvements. He urged the adoption of these measures in order to bind together the sprawling young nation, asserting at the same time that disunion was the worst evil that could befall the American people.[1]

During the 1820's, however, the South Atlantic states entered upon a period of decline in economic prosperity and population growth. South Carolina in particular suffered a severe commercial and agricultural depression. The fundamental cause of this collapse was the spread of cotton cultivation to the up-country and ultimately to the Southwest or "lower South," especially to the fertile region stretching across Georgia, Alabama, Mississippi, and Louisiana. Increased cotton production brought lower prices, to the ruination of eastern planters, many of whom in despair picked up families and slaves and migrated westward. The resultant population loss still further accelerated the economic decline. It also had political significance, since the older seaboard states would inevitably lose power in Congress both to the thriving Southwest and to the rapidly growing North.

Most statesmen of the Southeast, however, did not engage in economic analysis of this kind; instead they tended to lay the responsibility for their section's ills upon the protective tariff, which rapidly became a kind of evil political symbol for all the economic difficulties into which the Southeast had fallen. The drift of sentiment in South Carolina became apparent in 1824, when George McDuffie, long an outstanding protariff nationalist representative of the state in Congress, joined the opponents of the tariff act of that year. The state senate also denounced the new law as unconstitutional, and while the lower house at first opposed this position, it changed its own stand within a year and passed a resolution attacking the tariff as illegal. Behind this change in attitude there lay a gradual abandonment of the original Southern expectation that the South would share in the benefits of industrial expansion, an expectation now recognized as unrealistic. It was true, also, that the

---

[1] Calhoun's nationalistic leadership is discussed in Chapter 10.

agricultural South received almost no direct benefit from the protective tariff, and the popular Southern argument that the tariff was in effect a tax upon Southern agriculture for the benefit of Northern industry contained more than a little truth in spite of the fact that the antitariff argument oversimplified the South's economic difficulties.

South Carolina's attitude toward the tariff now inspired her statesmen to formulate an extremely advanced doctrine of state sovereignty and nullification. When Congress in 1828 enacted the so-called "Tariff of Abominations," the most highly protective tariff to that date, the South Carolina legislature officially protested against it as "unconstitutional," and published, as a committee report, the South Carolina Exposition. This document was secretly drafted by Calhoun, who was Vice-President from 1825 to 1832 and who was not yet ready in 1828 to repudiate openly his former nationalistic position. The Exposition declared that a sovereign state had the right to determine through a convention whether an act of Congress was unconstitutional and whether it constituted such a dangerous violation "as to justify the interposition of the State to protect its rights." If so, the convention would then decide in what manner the act ought to be declared null and void within the limits of the state, and this declaration would be obligatory, not only on her own citizens, but also on the national government. The state's action would be definitive unless the federal Constitution were subsequently altered by constitutional amendment.

Although South Carolina's reliance in 1828 was still upon words rather than action, the people of the state were rapidly dividing into two parties over the policy of nullification. The more radical elements, who eventually became the majority, gradually coalesced into the States' Rights Party and advocated the active nullification of the tariff unless the protective principle was abandoned. They strove to combat the popular apprehension that nullification might involve disunion and civil war by insisting that their program was legal, constitutional, and peaceful. The more moderate elements within the state formed the Union Party; although they opposed the protective tariff, they condemned nullification as fallacious and revolutionary. Many of these Unionists were willing to secede from the Union if that became necessary as a last resort, but they considered secession an exercise of the right of revolution.

The doctrine of nullification was given national publicity in January 1830 by the famous Webster-Hayne debate in the United States Senate. The controversy originated over public land policy, but it culminated in a great debate between Robert Hayne of South Carolina and Daniel Webster of Massachusetts on the nature of the Union and the validity of nullification. Hayne maintained more definitely than had the South Carolina Exposition that sovereignty was indivisible and resided in each state and that therefore nullification was constitutional. Webster replied with a powerful defense of national sovereignty, insisting that the Constitution emanated not from the states as such but from the American people, that the national government was not a creature of the states, and that nullification was nothing less than revolutionary.

CALHOUN'S THEORIES ON SOVEREIGNTY AND THE UNION

The following year Calhoun added the weight of his position as Vice-President to the States' Rights Party with an open espousal of nullification and soon won recognition as the foremost theorist and advocate of nullification and state sovereignty.

Calhoun rested his theoretical position upon the general proposition that sovereignty was by its very nature absolute and indivisible. In asserting the indivisibility of sovereignty he was adopting a conception common in Europe, but one which had previously exercised very little influence upon American thought and institutions. According to this view, sovereignty was not the sum of a number of governmental powers, but rather the ultimate will of the political community, which hence could not be divided without being destroyed. In a federal state, governmental powers were distributed between local and central governments, but ultimate sovereignty must rest in one or the other. It could not be inherent in both.

From this premise Calhoun then argued that ultimate sovereignty in the American Union rested in the separate states and not in the central government. He supported this proposition with both historical and analytical arguments. The American colonies, he maintained, had always existed as distinct political communities, which by revolution became free, sovereign, and independent states. As such they were leagued together under the Articles of Confederation. The Constitution had also been drafted by delegates acting and voting as states and had been ratified by the separate states, each state acting as a sovereign entity. The various states had indeed delegated a portion of their functions to the federal government, but they had not surrendered their ultimate sovereignty, something by nature indivisible, and consequently they still retained the latter undiminished under the Constitution.

Calhoun reached the same conclusion as to the nature of the

Union by an analysis of the nature of the Constitution, which he concluded was not supreme law but a mere contract or agreement between sovereign states. Law was by definition, he said, the fiat of a superior sovereign entity imposed upon an inferior. But the Constitution was an agreement between equal sovereign states, who thereby set up the federal government to perform certain functions for the contracting parties. An agreement between equals, however, was not law, but rather a compact—something in the nature of a treaty. It followed that the central government organized under the Constitution could not pretend to sovereignty; instead it was the mere agent of the various sovereign states. There was no such thing, he said, as the American nation.

Calhoun also argued his cause from the fundamental nature and purpose of government. Free government, he observed, was instituted to insure liberty and justice to all citizens. The basic problem, then, was to restrain government by constitutional checks in order that it be kept just. In his early career, Calhoun said, he had believed that the good sense of the people and the popular checks provided for in the Constitution were adequate safeguards for liberty and justice. Ultimately, however, he had become convinced that "the people" were a political fiction, and that governmental policies in reality resulted from combinations of the strong against the weak. Those in control of the central government would strive to extend its power and prerogatives. Thus the numerical majority would become tyrannical and would disregard the Constitution in order to destroy the power of minority groups. Calhoun believed that within the various states the popular majority might somehow be kept in check, but that neither the American people nor the Constitution would prevent a majority in control of the national government from using its power to destroy minority rights. Hence he became more and more fearful of the growth of the federal government and of broad construction of national powers. The more he observed the behavior of congressional majorities on the various issues of the day, the more he became convinced that the only safeguard for minority rights lay in state sovereignty and nullification.

Calhoun's theories were in reality a thorough rationalization of the South's new political position within the Union. The great South Carolina statesman recognized before other Southerners that the North was fast outstripping the South in population, economic power, and western settlement. In the not far distant future a Northern majority would control both houses of Congress and the presidency, as it already controlled the House of Representatives. The South would then have to submit to unfriendly federal legislation on the tariff, money, land, and internal improvements, and it might ultimately see the federal government used to attack slavery itself. In the last analysis it was not state sovereignty but rather Southern sectional interests that Calhoun sought to protect, and his analysis of the South's future weak position in national policy making was fundamentally sound.

Nullification offered a method for protecting the Southern minority against the Northern majority. Since, according to Calhoun's theory, the states possessed complete and undivided sovereignty, it followed that they were possessed of the final authority to interpret the Constitution. Hence, whenever a state found a congressional act to be a dangerous violation of the Constitution, the state could declare the law void and make it inoperative within its limits. Nullification was "simply a declaration on the part of the principal, made in due form, that an act of the agent transcending his power is null and void."

Calhoun admitted that a nullifying state might be overruled by a federal constitutional convention or by constitutional amendment. This meant in effect that a nullifying state's interpretation of the Constitution would stand unless three-fourths of its sister states disagreed. The obligation to clarify or alter the Constitution rested upon the majority favoring the nullified act and not upon the nullifying state, since only thus would the minority have protection against the majority.

Should three-fourths of the states overrule the nullifying state, Calhoun added, the state might still exercise its ultimate sovereign right to withdraw from the Union. At this time the right of secession was not emphasized by Calhoun, since he advocated nullification as a method of preserving the original Constitution and the Union. He recognized, however, that if the national government persisted in enforcing a nullified law the state's final resort could only be secession. In fact, because of the practical failure of nullification, the right of secession ultimately became the most significant element in Calhoun's theories.

Calhoun's doctrines were open to very serious objections on historical, theoretical, and practical grounds. The historical foundation of his theories was exceedingly weak. At no time during the Revolutionary period had the various states ever acted as though they were completely sovereign entities. Though the Articles of Confederation declared that each state retained its "sovereignty," the Articles also conferred upon Congress, and denied to the states, certain powers and governmental functions—such as the power to make war, peace, and treaties—without which no state could be wholly sovereign. Informed public opinion of the 1770's took it for granted that sovereignty could in fact be divided, as it had been in practice under the old British Empire.

Calhoun also ignored the overwhelming evidence that the Constitutional Convention had intended to erect a government that was truly national, though functioning within a limited sphere of sovereignty. The Convention had early resolved to establish a national government, and had proceeded to create one functioning for most purposes directly upon individuals without the intervention or control of the states. A whole series of powers, all essentially sovereign in character, had been vested in the new government. Finally the Constitution and federal treaties and laws had been expressly declared to be "the supreme law of the land," a situation incompatible with undiluted state sovereignty.

Calhoun also misconstrued the eighteenth-century theory of compact government. In his insistence that the Constitution was a compact entered into by "co-states" Calhoun thought he had demonstrated that the Constitution could not be law and that the federal government could not be possessed of sovereignty. Yet the men of the Revolutionary era had regarded compact as the only possible method by which legitimate sovereign government could be created. Contrary to Calhoun's later belief, they had thought of all lawful government as flowing from agreement between equals, not as imposed by the fiat of a superior. In other words, to assert that the Constitution was a compact was in reality to offer historical evidence that it was the foundation of a sovereign government.

Nullification itself was open to criticism on several counts. At best the idea was extraconstitutional and rested upon a tenuous and overelaborate argument as to the nature of the Union and the Constitution. Most men outside South Carolina refused to believe that so important and complicated a constitutional process as nullification had been left to mere implication.

A more serious consideration was that nullification in practice would have paralyzed the entire constitutional system. The doctrine gave any one of the states the right to veto any federal act, no matter how vital its importance, even when the law in question had supposedly been authorized by the Constitution. Since it could be expected that nearly every federal statute of consequence would meet opposition in some section of the Union, the result would be a general breakdown of federal authority. The only appeal from a state's action under the doctrine would be to a general convention of all the states. Such a body would presumably have to sit almost continuously to handle a recurrent series of constitutional crises provoked by state nullification. Uncertainty regarding federal law would be widespread, a situation that might well lead to open conflict and violence should either party to a controversy press home its case with determination.

Finally the nullification theory disregarded the fact that forty years of constitutional growth had evolved a very different and quite workable method for the settlement of constitutional disputes. The Convention had specifically made federal law supreme over state law, and the Judiciary Act of 1789 had provided for appeals from state courts to the federal judiciary and so had lodged the final right to decide constitutional questions in the Supreme Court, an agent of the national government. This right had been repeatedly exercised by the Court; and although the system had occasionally been challenged, as in the writings of John Taylor and Judge Roane and by counsel for Virginia in *Cohens v. Virginia*,[2] the dissenters had not been successful in disturbing the practice. As of 1832 the Court's right to act as arbiter of the Constitution was widely though not universally accepted by American statesmen, lawyers, and common citizens.

In short, Calhoun and his fellows of the States' Rights Party wanted a constitutional system different from that created in 1787 and developed by more than forty years of orderly growth. Almost half a century after the creation of a limited national government, during which time the main trend had been toward the confirmation of federal authority, they were now attempting to substitute a confederation of sovereign states for the prevailing federal system. Such an attempt was in reality little short of revolutionary.

THE ATTEMPT AT NULLIFICATION

By 1832 the South Carolina extremists were ready to put theory into action. In July Congress passed a new tariff law continuing the protective system but moderating some of the higher duties of the previous act. Three South Carolina Unionist congressmen supported the new tariff as a move in the right direction, but the others formally denounced the measure as unconstitutional and oppressive to the Southern people. In the subsequent state election that fall, the

2 See pp. 270–271.

States' Rights and Unionist parties made the tariff and nullification the chief issues, and when the States' Rights group elected more than two-thirds of the legislature, it promptly called a state convention.

The convention met in November 1832 and by a vote of 136 to 26 adopted an ordinance of nullification. The ordinance, drawn up by Chancellor William Harper, declared the tariff acts of 1828 and 1832 "unauthorized by the Constitution" and therefore "null, void, and no law, nor binding upon this State, its officers or citizens." It instructed the legislature to adopt all measures necessary to give full effect to the ordinance and to prevent the enforcement of the tariff acts after February 1, 1833. It declared that in no case at law or equity in the courts of the state could the validity of the ordinance or the legislative acts pursuant to it be questioned, and that no appeal in such a case could be taken to the Supreme Court of the United States. State officers and jurors impaneled in any case involving the ordinance and subsidiary acts were required to take an oath to obey and enforce the ordinance. Finally, the nullifiers declared that any effort of the federal government to employ naval or military force to coerce the state, close its ports, destroy or harass its commerce, or enforce the tariff acts, would impel the people of South Carolina to secede from the Union and organize a separate independent government.

A separate address to the people of the state warned them that citizens of South Carolina owed no direct allegiance to the federal government and reminded them of their sole allegiance to the state. Still another appeal, defending South Carolina's position and suggesting a general convention of the states for further consideration of the tariff problem, was directed to the citizens of the other states.

A few days later the legislature reassembled and proceeded to enact measures giving effect to the ordinance of nullification. Unionists in and out of the legislature opposed such action as the "mad edict of a despotic majority," provocative of civil war. Nonetheless the extremist majority pushed through a test oath act for judges and jurors, and a replevin act authorizing the owner of imported goods seized for nonpayment of duties to recover them or twice their value from customs officials. Since this was the point where an actual clash was most likely to occur between state and federal authority, the law also authorized the governor to call out the militia to enforce the laws of the state.

The success of nullification would depend upon the stand taken by the federal government and by the other Southern states. Andrew Jackson as President was the key man in formulating federal policy, and in this case he was determined to uphold national authority at all hazards. During the fall of 1832 he dropped quiet hints that federal law must be obeyed, encouraged the South Carolina Unionists, and took military precautions for a possible emergency requiring force. Then on December 10, the President issued a proclamation to the people of South Carolina, refuting the doctrines of nullification, appealing to the intelligence and patriotism of the people of the states, and rebuking the nullifiers for provoking a national crisis. He asserted that the people of the United States for many purposes constituted a sovereign nation, and that the Constitution formed "a government, not a league." Using the most emphatic and sweeping language, Jackson said he considered "the power to annul a law of the United States, assumed by one State, *incompatible with the existence of the Union, contradicted expressly by the letter of the Constitution, unauthorized by its spirit, inconsistent with every principle on which it was founded, and destructive of the great object for which it was formed.*" Therefore, he said, not only was nullification illegal, but secession was revolutionary, and disunion by armed force was treason. He warned that he would enforce the tariff law in all the states, by force if necessary, and he asked the people of South Carolina not to bring dishonor upon themselves in a futile attempt to destroy the nation's unity.

On January 16, 1833, Jackson officially informed Congress of South Carolina's actions, and requested that body to take steps that would "solemnly proclaim that the Constitution and the laws are supreme and the *Union indissoluble.*" He asked for additional authority to support the tariff act, and to employ the army and navy to overcome any resistance to the enforcement of federal law.

The nationalists in Congress came to Jackson's support with the introduction of the so-called Force Bill. This measure authorized the President to employ his authority in support of federal law against any obstruction, civil or military, even if the obstruction be made by authority of a state. The President might also close ports of entry or alter collection districts, were such steps necessary to the collection of customs duties. The bill thus asserted the supreme sovereignty of the national government and its right to enforce its statutes directly upon individuals by force if necessary. It constituted an effective denial of the whole of Calhoun's constitutional theories.

While the national government prepared to use force against nullification if necessary, South Carolina's position was weakened by the failure of the other states to come to her support. The northern and western states generally condemned nullification as unconstitutional and revolutionary, as did North Carolina, Alabama, and Mississippi in the South. The attitude of Georgia and Virginia was especially significant since both of these states had recently talked of resistance to unconstitutional federal legislation. Georgia called a state convention, but this body thwarted the state's nullification sympathizers by condemning nullification as neither peaceful nor constitutional. Virginia's stand was even more disappointing to the South Carolina extremists. The Virginia legislature expressed sympathy with South Carolina's attitude toward the tariff, but deplored the resort to nullification and denied that the Virginia Resolutions of 1798 constituted an adequate precedent for the present nullification doctrine. In reality, there was as yet too little sense of Southern self-consciousness and sectional unity to impel the Southern states to stand together against national authority. South Carolina thus found herself abandoned by those from whom she had hoped for the most.

As the deadline of February 1, 1833, approached, South Carolina felt itself in too weak a position to risk a direct clash with national authority. A compromise tariff measure was before Congress at the moment, and although it seemingly had but little chance of passage, a States' Rights Party convention recommended virtual suspension of nullification until Congress could act on the prospective concession. The sovereign will of the state was thus set aside by a party conclave, an act which in itself made a virtual farce of state sovereignty, although the nullifiers themselves were apparently undisturbed by this irregularity.

Meanwhile events in Congress moved toward compromise. When it had become evident that the Force Bill would pass, Henry Clay introduced a compromise tariff bill providing for a slow and gradual abandonment of protectionism through a progressive reduction in duties to a 20 per cent maximum in 1842. This measure became law early in March, and Congress enacted the Force Bill at the same time. In both houses Northerners were practically unanimous in support of the Force Bill, while almost half of the Southern congressmen also voted for the measure. The new tariff act provided South Carolina with a face saver, but it was evident that a large majority in Congress were prepared to defend national sovereignty by force if necessary.

The South Carolina convention reassembled on March 11. Accepting the Compromise Tariff Act as a victory, it rescinded the ordinance of nullification against the tariff, but adopted another ordinance nullifying the Force Act. This latter action was of no practical meaning, however, since the Force Act would not be invoked unless the state attempted to interfere with some positive federal function, such as collection of the customs.

Although South Carolina obtained a moderately favorable readjustment of the tariff, nullification had failed decisively as a reliable and peaceable device for settling constitutional disputes between the states and the national government. Most Southerners became convinced that if a "sovereign" state's remonstrances against an objectionable federal policy proved unavailing, the only alternatives were to submit or to secede. Hence secession now tended to become the constitutional refuge of those Southerners who believed that their fundamental rights and liberties were endangered by the exercise of questionable national authority.

On the other hand, the effect of the nullification episode upon the Northern people was to emphasize the necessity of maintaining at all hazards the federal Union and the constitutional authority of the national government. In a more limited way, the same popular reaction occurred in the border slave states and in certain Unionist sections of the lower South. The challenge of Calhoun and his theories led such legalistic spokesmen for Northern economic interests as Webster and Story to assert with renewed vigor the claims of the Supreme Court as the final interpreter of the Constitution. Most Northerners, however, were impressed not so much with the Court's increased prestige as with the determination of the President and Congress to enforce the supreme law of the land in a state which had prepared to resist by force of arms. Jackson's determined stand in 1833 provided the national government with a powerful precedent in 1861.

Chapter

13

Democracy and Jacksonianism

FOR MORE than a century the American people have regarded their constitutional system as the foundation of the world's greatest political democracy. As has been observed in earlier chapters, the Constitution as drafted in 1787 was democratic only to a degree. It gave the people a direct role only in the election of members of the House of Representatives and even in that case it adopted the suffrage restrictions of the various states. But certainly the Constitution was enlightened and liberal for its day, and it was so constructed as to make possible the subsequent growth of democratic political institutions. At the time the Constitution was adopted, there were already some evidences of the growth of democratic institutions within the states, and the process was accelerated by the development of Jefferson's party organization and by the impact of the French Revolution upon American political ideas. By 1830 the transition to a democratic political and constitutional system was well advanced, and by 1850 the development was almost complete. At midcentury the United States could fairly be described as a constitutional federal democracy, even though there remained some limitations on equality, such as the exclusion of women, young adults, Negroes, and Indians from the suffrage.

THE GROWTH OF DEMOCRACY

Perhaps the most fundamental factor in the growth of democracy in the United States was the dynamic expansion of the American economic and social order. The tremendous rate of western settlement, the terrific growth of population, commerce, and industry, and the rapid urbanization of the eastern seaboard all tended to shatter older established class distinctions and to create new economic aristocracies that had but little pretension to superiority through birth or heritage.

The breaking down of class distinction was perhaps most evident on the western frontier, where a combination of circumstances favored the growth of social democracy with its resultant effect upon political institutions. The great western domain lay open to exploitation, inviting every man who had courage, initiative, and reasonably good fortune to make a place for himself regardless of his social antecedents. The federal government offered farmers eighty acres of fertile virgin land for the modest sum of one hundred dollars, while some states were even more generous with their public lands. The result was an extraordinary equality of opportunity for a man to win fortune and success through his own skill and industry. The resultant atmosphere was not necessarily productive of pure equalitarianism; in fact the West tended to recognize the superior prestige of those who were skillful, fortunate, or unscrupulous enough to win economic success. Nonetheless the West did cast aside the class restrictions of the earlier colonial society. Family and social background counted for little or nothing, and westerners generally insisted that every man must have a fair and equal chance in the great struggle with the wilderness.

The older and more populous East also reacted to the pulse of democracy. The growth of democracy in the older states was quickened by the impact of the frontier upon the East through the spread of political and social ideas. In the Northeast, the frontier between 1790 and 1830 lay in upper New England and upstate New York, and its proximity to the older, more settled community had a perceptible effect upon the institutions of that section. And throughout the East the frontier offered an alternate economic and social opportunity to the dissatisfied common man, and so forced the older established commercial and landed aristocracies to make concessions to political democracy in order to check the vast wave of westward migration, a movement which between 1810 and 1830 threatened to check eastern economic development and to leave this region behind in the growth of population and the race for national political control.

But the East was also dynamic in its own right. The rapid growth of seaboard cities and the steady expansion of industry and commerce both created new opportunities for ambitious, strong, and even ruthless men to push ahead, to seize new economic opportunities, and to win fame and fortune. In the East, just as on the frontier, established systems of privilege and class tended to disintegrate under the impact of new economic opportunity. Here again the result was not altogether democratic in the long run, for the ultimate result of eastern expansion was the creation of new inequalities based on wealth and power. Yet the process of terrific expansion created a fluid social order, a greater common economic opportunity for all men, and engendered a spirit of political democracy. In 1831 the aristocratic Frenchman Alexis de Tocqueville, who traveled widely throughout the country, was greatly impressed with the general belief then prevalent that the United States had a special world mission as the champion of democracy and equality.[1]

The new egalitarian spirit resulted in a steady growth of democratic political institutions, in both state and national government. Notable constitutional developments within the states were the general adoption of white manhood suffrage, the reduction of religious and property qualifications for office, and the establishment of more direct popular control of state and local government. The democratic ideal also affected the national political scene; it made possible the election to the presidency in 1828 of Andrew Jackson, and he made the presidential office a kind of tribune of the people. Even the Supreme Court, remote though it was from popular control, after 1835 recognized more frequently the popular will as expressed through Congress and the various state legislatures than it had during Marshall's ascendancy.

BROADENING THE BASE OF STATE GOVERNMENT

Motivated by the democratic impulse, most of the states rewrote their constitutions between 1815 and 1850 to make them more responsive to the popular will. The favorite medium of constitutional reform was the constitutional convention, an institution which in the first half of the nineteenth century came to be generally accepted as a kind of grand committee of the people chosen and

---

[1] De Tocqueville's *Democracy in America* was first published in France in 1835 and in the United States in 1838. A recent American edition was published in 1945.

authorized to submit a plan of government for acceptance or rejection. Between 1800 and 1865 every state in the Union held such a convention and adopted a new constitution or added important amendments to the old. During these years some states adopted two or even three constitutions, the new instruments often involving drastic changes in their systems of government. The general effect of the new constitutions was to develop a much wider and more popular participation in government.

Extension of the franchise and removal of the restrictions upon office holding were the most significant trends in the new constitutions. Even before 1800 certain of the eastern states had reduced voting qualifications to the payment of a public tax, and after 1800 the democratic forces strove to establish white manhood suffrage throughout the seaboard states, but with varying results. A few eastern states dropped both property and tax qualifications for voting before 1815, but most of those states retained such qualifications longer and abandoned them only after a bitter struggle between democratic and conservative forces. Generally they were even more reluctant to remove restrictions upon office holding.

Meanwhile the new western states were unanimous in opening the suffrage and office holding to all white adult males, although in other respects western state constitutions followed closely the pattern of eastern constitutions. Between 1816 and 1821, Indiana, Illinois, Mississippi, Alabama, and Missouri, in adopting their first constitutions, all provided for universal white manhood suffrage, and made the entire electorate eligible for election to political office. Western states subsequently entering the Union also adopted these democratic provisions in every case and without serious opposition.

In some eastern states conservative forces, which retained their faith in government by the few, were partially successful for a time in retaining the older restrictions upon the suffrage and office holding. In 1820 a Massachusetts constitutional convention, after a hard struggle, substituted taxpaying for property ownership as a qualification for the franchise. The new constitutions of Rhode Island (1842), Pennsylvania (1838), and Virginia (1830) also retained property or tax qualifications for the suffrage and office holding.

In other eastern states the champions of property were less successful. The New York convention of 1821 was typical of the conservative breakdown. Here Chancellor James Kent led the defenders of the old regime, mostly former Federalists, in a futile attempt to retain property qualifications for the right to vote for state senators. When a majority of delegates proposed only a taxpaying or militia-serving requirement, he condemned it as universal suffrage in disguise. "The tendency of universal suffrage," he declared, "is to jeopardize the rights of property, and the principles of liberty." Society, he said, "is an association for the protection of property as well as of life," and he argued that "the individual who contributes only one cent to the common stock, ought not to have the same power and influence in directing the property concerns of the partnership, as he who contributes his thousands." But Daniel Tompkins, president of the convention and Vice-President of the United States, spoke for the democratic majority when he appealed to the Declaration of Independence and declared that life, liberty and the pursuit of happiness, not property, were the important objects of civil society, and this sentiment carried the day.

In the southeastern states the popular demand for political equality led to a series of struggles for the reapportionment of state legislatures. The early constitution-makers had continued the colonial practice of allotting to the older tidewater areas a disproportionately large share of representatives at the expense of the new western counties. Since the tidewater was dominated by slave-holding planters while the upland was more largely populated by non-slaveholding small farmers, the contests over reapportionment took on a distinctly conservative-liberal character. In the Virginia convention of 1829–30 there occurred a notable instance of such a struggle, during which the conservative easterners succeeded in incorporating elaborate provisions in the new constitution for the continuation of their political control. About 1850, however, most of the southeastern states made constitutional changes granting greater representation to the western regions, although as long as slavery remained, entire equality of representation proved unattainable.

The removal of state constitutional restrictions upon voting, together with other factors, greatly increased the extent of popular participation in elections and government. Until the 1820's less than 5 per cent of the people customarily voted even in important elections. Thereafter the electorate increased rapidly, and by 1840, 17 per cent of the people, approximately half of the white adult males, ordinarily voted. This enlargement of the electorate meant a rapid increase in the number of inexperienced and ill-informed voters and the growth of new political organizations and techniques designed to influence and direct them.

THE GROWTH OF DIRECT POPULAR CONTROL IN
STATE GOVERNMENT

The new constitutions drafted between 1820 and 1850 reflected also the current demand for increased restrictions upon the power and discretion of the state legislatures. Earlier constitutions embodied the assumption that the legislature was the sovereign voice of the free people, and they had placed but few constitutional checks upon legislative authority. The extravagant state banking laws and internal improvement schemes of the generation after 1815 led to a growing popular distrust of the integrity and capacity of state legislators, a distrust that greatly increased after the financial collapse of many of the states following the Panic of 1837.

As a result, the constitutions drafted in the 1840's imposed substantial limitations upon legislative discretion. Generally they placed limitations upon the time, frequency, and expense of legislative sessions, abolished the legislature's right to enact special legislation benefiting individuals or corporations, required a two-thirds vote or popular approval for the creation of state banks or public works projects, and limited the amount of the state debt and the objects for which it could be contracted. Many of the constitutions contained lengthy provisions which were legislative in character rather than organic, an additional indication of unwillingness to trust legislative discretion completely.

While legislative authority declined, the power of the governor was increased. The earlier constitutions had in general given the governor no veto or had permitted the legislature to override a veto by a majority vote, while the new documents usually granted the executive a more effective veto power. The new constitutions also granted the governor much of the appointive power hitherto lodged in the legislature. These provisions reflected growing recognition of the governor as an influential political and executive leader and a valuable constitutional check upon the legislature rather than as a mere ceremonial head of the state.

Generally the new constitutions also provided for the popular election of nearly all state and county administrative officials, whereas formerly most of these offices had been filled by appointment. The prevailing insistence on popular sovereignty now led to the attitude that even minor administrative officials ought to be directly responsible to the popular will. While the practice was in line with the trend toward a more democratic government, it nonetheless had, in the long run, unfortunate effects upon state and local government. It multiplied the responsibilities of the electorate to the point where it often became impossible for the most intelligent voters to know the qualifications of most candidates, and it tended to inject political considerations into offices that should have been purely administrative in character. The election of a half dozen or more of the principal state administrative officers also reduced the governor's capacity to control his subordinates, led to divided responsibility, and weakened executive policy. However, these evils were mitigated to some extent by the unifying force that resulted from the growth of strong political parties.

Highly controversial were the provisions in several state constitutions for popular election of the judiciary. A few of the constitutions adopted in the 1820's provided for the popular election of judges of inferior courts, and the Mississippi constitution of 1832 carried a far more radical provision that called for the choice of supreme court judges by the electorate. For a time no other state followed Mississippi in this procedure, but in 1846 New York wrote a similar provision into her new constitution. Conservatives and even many moderates fought hard against such radicalism, but they were unable to stem the tide. Within a few years nearly all the western states framed constitutions incorporating the principle of an elective judiciary, and many of the eastern states did likewise. To guarantee popular control of the judiciary still further, many of the new constitutions empowered the legislature to remove any judge simply by a majority vote.

It is difficult to overestimate the importance of the local courts in the development of American democracy. Equality before the law was basic, and the people strove to guarantee that equality by providing for laws made by their own representatives and applied by judges of their own choice. Although plain people sometimes regarded the county courts as strongholds of local conservative influences, the courts were theoretically open on a basis of equality to all white citizens. Thus in an agrarian age the county courthouse became the widely recognized symbol of justice, equality, and security.

The new constitutions reflected also an increasing popular demand for a variety of new governmental services. People were slowly losing their fear of government, and the eighteenth-century attitude that all government was at best a necessary evil was gradually disappearing. At the same time the rising spirit of nineteenth-century humanitarianism, very much a part of the age of Liberalism in both Europe and America, made the public aware of a variety of social problems arising from the prevailing archaic and barbarous institutions for handling criminals, the insane, the handicapped, and the poor. The resultant demand for state social legislation led to the incorporation in the new constitutions of numerous provisions obligating state legislatures to establish public institutions for the care and treatment of the outcast and unfortunate members of society. In some of the free states antislavery leaders strove also to obtain more civil and political rights for the Negroes; but the constitutional conventions, made exceedingly cautious by the raging slavery controversy, actually did little to improve the lot of black people. In fact, some of the new constitutions definitely prohibited the migration or settlement of free Negroes in the state.

Further, most of the new constitutions provided for the establishment of public school systems. Although there was considerable variation in these provisions, the western states in particular created state educational administrative offices and provided for the use of public funds or public lands for the support of education. Although public school systems materialized slowly, public education and democracy were henceforth considered inseparable.

The new public temper was well exemplified in the treatment of property rights. Since this was a period of rapid and varied economic expansion, the average American expected to become a man of property, and very often he did. Therefore the new democratic constitutions provided protection for private property that was honestly and equitably acquired, especially through a clause prohibiting the legislature from passing any law impairing the obligation of contracts. Such a clause was widely regarded as a protection of a fundamental, natural right against the dangers of legislative encroachment, and hence it was usually included in the bills of rights of state constitutions.

On the other hand, the prevailing sentiment opposed monopoly and special privilege and favored an improved status for debtors and for women. Many of the new constitutions definitely prohibited the state from establishing monopolies, from creating corporations by special legislative acts, and from using its credit to aid any person or corporation. There was a strong tendency in the new constitutions to protect debtors from complete loss of equity and property to creditors and speculators. This was generally accomplished by exempting a specific amount of a citizen's property, usually a small homestead, from forced sale for payment of debts. In the same spirit some of the new constitutions for the first time granted married women the legal right to the independent control of their own property. These and similar provisions definitely indicated that the new democratic philosophy was modifying the economic and legal conservatism of Marshall, Story, and Kent. At long last the common man was legally as well as socially coming into his own.

DEMOCRACY AND THE FEDERAL CONSTITUTIONAL SYSTEM

The steady growth of democracy was bound to make a deep impression upon the federal constitutional system. The great mass of common people were determined that the national government should function more effectively in their interest through men of their own choice and viewpoint. Many believed that all three departments of the government were too unresponsive to popular wishes, and that federal officials were too remote from the people. Accordingly there arose a widespread popular demand for the democratization of the federal government.

This demand took in part the form of proposals to amend the Constitution. Most Americans accepted the Jeffersonian principle that each generation should amend the Constitution to make it expressive of the popular will. Several states on various occasions requested that Congress call a national constitutional convention to propose amendments, but the number of such requests never reached the two-thirds required by Article V for the calling of a convention. Between the years 1804 and 1860, however, over four hundred proposed amendments were submitted to Congress. Many of these proposals would have required the election of representatives by districts in order to prohibit the practice of some states of electing them on a general ticket. On three occasions the House refused to agree to such proposals, although they had been passed by the Senate; but the same objective was reached by the Congressional Apportionment Act of June 25, 1842, which made mandatory the election of representatives by districts. Another important proposal was that of 1826, which stipulated that the election of senators be by popular vote in each state instead of by the legislature. Although at the time this proposal also failed of adoption, almost a century later a similar proposal was to become the Seventeenth Amendment.

The most numerous and most significant of the proposed amendments were those designed to give the people a more direct and important part in the choice of the President. Many people believed that the indirect electoral college system, which left the method of choosing electors to the state legislatures, was inconsistent with the new democratic spirit. Members of Congress, therefore, repeatedly proposed amendments requiring all states to provide for the choice of electors by districts, and four times such a proposal passed the Senate but failed in the House. Following the presidential election of 1825, when Andrew Jackson was defeated in the House, his supporters concentrated on proposals to have the President chosen by a direct vote of the people. After he became President in 1829, Jackson repeatedly recommended the adoption of such an amendment, but his supporters in Congress were unable to secure its passage. The adoption of either of these proposals would seriously have changed the nature of future presidential campaigns and probably would have affected the results in close elections.

The only proposed amendment actually adopted by both houses of Congress and submitted to the states was the relatively unimportant proposition of 1810, which would have abrogated the citizenship of any American who accepted any title of nobility or honor from a foreign power. The proposal lacked the vote of only one state for adoption, and for many years the general public erroneously supposed that it had been ratified and was the thirteenth amendment to the Constitution.

The failure of all these proposals demonstrated the practical difficulty of democratizing the Constitution through amendments. Conflicting sectional, party, or class interests made it almost impossible to obtain a two-thirds vote in both houses of Congress and the approval of the three-fourths of the state legislatures. The opponents of a proposed amendment had too great a constitutional advantage to be overcome except under the most extraordinary circumstances. Consequently the champions of democracy turned to constitutional construction and extraconstitutional methods to advance their cause.

THE ROLE OF POLITICAL PARTIES IN THE DEVELOPMENT OF DEMOCRACY

Very effective as instruments for democratizing the federal constitutional system were the new political parties that emerged after 1824 from the ruins of the old Jeffersonian party organization. Without definite political organization it would have been practically impossible for the great mass of new voters to work out a common legislative program for the welfare of the nation. Parties also provided a means whereby the voters could elevate men of their choice to office, from the local justice of the peace to the Chief Executive of the nation. It is significant that the political organizations and techniques of this period built the road upon which Abraham Lincoln traveled from his humble origin to a position of enormous power and prestige. Of course political parties, like all human institutions, are susceptible to corruption and manipulation for selfish advantage, but these evils are subject to remedy by an enlightened and vigilant electorate. More than a century of experience has not produced a more effective instrument of democratic government.

The early Federalist and Jeffersonian parties had been almost entirely instruments of the party leaders. The general policies and principles of these men constituted the party platform. They subsidized and even wrote editorials for the few party newspapers. They largely chose from among themselves the party candidates for legislative and executive offices through legislative and congressional caucuses. The voters were then asked to support the party program.

Although there had been local and scattered efforts earlier to make political organizations more democratic, it was the Jackson men of the 1820's who first built a nationwide organization from the ground up. Believing that their hero had been cheated out of the presidency in 1825 through obsolete and undemocratic election machinery, they set out to inaugurate a more democratic method. While they hoped to be able ultimately to amend the Constitution, they also moved to achieve their objective through extraconstitutional means.

First they condemned presidential nominations made by congressmen and insisted that nominations must come directly from the people. They claimed that a class of professional officeholders and politicians composed of wealthy business and professional men dominated the national government through the congressional caucus and similar devices. As a more democratic method of nomination, Jackson's followers at first put their man forward through popular meetings, local newspapers, and state legislatures. This meant the death of "King Caucus," a caucus of a party's members of Congress, which had been the presidential nominating device in use during the first thirty years of our national history.

As a more democratic and enduring method of selecting candidates, the Jacksonians developed the nominating convention, which both major parties used to nominate presidential candidates for the first time in the election of 1832. Eventually a whole series of extraconstitutional party conventions, extending from the local meeting and the state convention to the national conclave, presented the party's nominees for office. Replacing the caucus system entirely, the convention prevailed as almost the sole nominating device until the coming of the direct primary in the twentieth century. As the reader is aware, the convention is used today in nominating presidential candidates as well as officers within many states.

Jackson's party also developed the principle of party uniformity on national issues, both through the party platform and through emphasis upon fairly well recognized party principles. This was vitally necessary to the party's success on a national scale; for if its followers were to work together in Congress, agree upon a candidate for the presidency, and support an administration in power, they were of necessity obliged to compromise or suppress sectional differences and present at least an appearance of national harmony. The opposition party, the Whigs, was at first composed of a variety of groups representing sectional interests, unified to some extent by their opposition to Jackson's forces; but as time went on they also developed a certain degree of national coherence. Thus by 1840 elementary party principles could be set forth by both of the two major political groups.

Party solidarity on principles and leadership had a powerful nationalistic effect on political life and went far to counteract the prevailing tendencies toward sectionalism and decentralization. Parties were living symbols of national political unity as well as effective instruments for the reconciliation of sectional differences. It is highly significant that as long as two nationwide political parties existed, the threatened disruption of the Union in the slavery crisis was averted by compromise.

Carrying Jefferson's philosophy to its logical conclusion, the Jacksonians attacked all forms of aristocracy and special privilege and demanded the right of all men to participate in government on an equal basis. Whereas Jeffersonian Democracy had been based upon large and small landholders, Jacksonian Democracy was based upon the common man whether propertied or unpropertied. While Jefferson had preferred government administered by men of talent and experience, Jackson acted on the expressed belief that frequent appointments from the rank and file produced more honest, efficient, and responsive government than did long tenure by the talented few. Whereas the Jeffersonians had emphasized legislative deliberation and the representative character of government, the Jacksonians stressed the imperative character of the direct demands and decisions of the people.

The Democratic Party officially placed its trust "in a clear reliance upon the intelligence, patriotism, and the discriminating justice of the American people." Jackson maintained that the right of the popular majority to govern was "the first principle of our system." Most Democrats insisted upon the people's right to "instruct" their legislators on important matters, and upon the right of the various state legislatures to "instruct" their senators and to "request" their congressmen on national issues.

It was only natural, therefore, that the Jacksonians received the support of the majority of men who had not previously participated in public affairs. Most Whigs also professed a belief in democracy, and so avoided the aristocratic pitfall that had swallowed up the Federalists; but the Whigs were never as universally or as consistently the champions of the mudsills of society as was "Old Hickory's" party.

POLITICAL PARTIES AND CONGRESSIONAL POWERS

For a decade or more prior to Jackson's taking office in 1829, sectional interests rather than political parties had dominated questions of constitutional interpretation. During the 1830's, however, the growth of two nationwide parties led to a general realignment of broad constructionists and strict constructionists along partisan lines. Jackson came into office over the opposition of John Quincy Adams and Henry Clay, both broad constructionists, and he therefore had the support of most strict constructionists. His previous record and his inaugural address indicated, however, that he was essentially a moderate in the matter of interpreting the powers of the federal government. He accepted national sovereignty but believed that the amending process rather than loose construction was the proper way for Congress to obtain additional needed powers.

The first important constitutional issue on which President Jackson was compelled to take a definite stand was that of federal appropriations for internal improvements. It will be recalled that during the Adams administration Congress had adopted the policy of appropriating federal funds for a large number of state and local transportation and navigation projects. In 1830 Jackson applied the brakes to this policy by vetoing four improvement bills, the most notable being the so-called Maysville Road Bill. He did not adopt the narrow Madisonian constitutional position, but he did insist that federal revenue could be constitutionally expended only for projects of a national character, not for those of purely state or local benefit.

This position strengthened Jackson with strict constructionists, but it tended to drive supporters of federal improvements or appropriations into the ranks of the opposition, led by Clay. For the presidential campaign of 1832 the latter group organized under the appropriate name of "National Republicans" and officially declared in favor of "a uniform system of internal improvements, sustained and supported by the general government." Jackson was re-elected and continued as a general policy to check congressional inclinations to grant financial support for local roads and canals. He was not, however, entirely consistent in this stand, for he approved aid for certain river and harbor improvements that were only remotely national in scope. Meanwhile many states launched more or less elaborate internal improvement systems of their own, generally with unfortunate results.

For a time following the Panic of 1837 the issue lost importance, but with the return of prosperity in the middle forties, the advocates of federal improvements again became active. In July 1846 Congress, by bipartisan "log-rolling" methods, passed a bill making appropriations for improving more than forty rivers and harbors in various parts of the country. President James Polk, a southern Democrat, vetoed the bill. He adopted the extreme Madisonian argument that Congress lacked constitutional authority either to construct or to appropriate money for internal improvements and warned that the policy embodied in the bill would lead to a dangerous and unconstitutional "consolidation of power in the Federal Government at the expense of the rightful authority of the States." This veto again put the issue to rest for a time, though before long the federal government was to inaugurate a policy of making huge grants to railroad corporations in the form of public lands.

Another constitutional controversy that arose during Jackson's administration developed when it became apparent that there would be a surplus in the federal treasury. The War of 1812 had left the United States with a national debt of above $200,000,000, but years of peace and rising federal revenues from the tariff and from land sales brought about its steady reduction. After 1830 a speculative boom in western lands developed, revenue from public land sales reached unprecedented heights, and the national debt approached actual extinction. The federal government was thus faced with the imminent prospect of a heavy treasury surplus, and accordingly the question arose as to its proper disposition.

The two parties gradually evolved conflicting solutions for the problem of the surplus. The Whigs, led by Clay, advocated the distribution of proceeds of land sales among the states in accordance with their congressional representation, the funds to be applied to education, internal improvements, or the reduction of state taxes. Clay based his arguments for distribution upon the need for a strong and active national government. He held that the public domain was a great national heritage and should be used by Congress for the benefit of all the people. Under the program he advocated, he said, "the States will feel and recognize the operation of the General Government, not merely in power and burdens but in benefactions and blessings." Clay's proposal made the reduction of the high tariff unnecessary and also enabled the government to maintain the current price of public lands, two considerations which made his stand attractive to his party's eastern supporters.

On the other hand, most Democrats favored a reduction in the price of public lands and the ultimate disposal of the problem by ceding all public lands to the states in which they lay. This program was calculated to appeal to westerners, hungry for cheap public lands, and to states' rights Democrats, who were apprehensive of the growth of federal power and prestige, which they believed was based in part upon the national government's control of the public domain. Jackson's supporters in Congress opposed Clay's distribution scheme largely for the same reason—it could give the federal government a potent weapon for forcing the citadel of states' rights through the persuasive power of the purse.

In 1833 Jackson killed a distribution bill with a pocket veto; but actual extinction of the national debt in 1835, the unwillingness of eastern congressmen to vote any reduction in the price of public lands, and the fact that tariff rates could not be further reduced without disturbing the Compromise of 1833 [2] brought the issue to the fore once more. In 1836 Calhoun, acting as an independent Democrat, suggested a method of distribution calculated to relieve the fears of the states' rights faction. He proposed that most of the federal surplus, then amounting to some thirty million dollars, be "deposited" on account with the states in quarterly installments. The Democrats strongly insisted upon a constitutional distinction between merely depositing the money and making an outright gift, but nearly everyone realized full well that the "deposits" would never be recalled. The deposit bill passed in June 1836 and three installments were paid the states before the Panic of 1837 eliminated the surplus. The "deposits" have remained with the states ever since.

---

[2] The constitutional issues involved in the tariff controversy of 1832 are discussed in Chapter 12.

THE BANK AND THE TRIUMPH OF STRICT CONSTRUCTION

The constitutional issue of the 1830's that divided Democrats and Whigs most sharply was the old question of the United States Bank. Banking methods and credit facilities affected people in all walks of life, and many people distrusted all banks. When Jackson entered the presidency the national bank's prestige and influence had again risen, and most people apparently now accepted the bank's constitutionality. But the institution was still unpopular in the West and South.

In December 1829 Jackson revived the issue of the bank's constitutionality in his first annual message, but at that time the institution's charter still had several years to run, and Congress therefore took no action. In January 1832, however, the bank's officers decided to seek a renewal of its charter, and Henry Clay introduced a bill in the Senate for this purpose. A protracted debate thereupon ensued. The bill's enemies generally accepted the bank's constitutionality, but they sought to attach amendments to the bill requiring the consent of any state within which a branch was to be established and granting the states the right to tax such branches. In reply, the Whigs pointed out that Marshall in *McCulloch v. Maryland* had held that the states could neither exclude the bank's branches nor subject them to taxation. States' rights Democrats answered that Congress conceivably could bestow these rights upon the states, while Senator George Bibb of Kentucky went so far as to declare flatly that the Supreme Court had "erred" in the McCulloch case and that Congress ought to ignore its opinion. Congress finally passed Clay's bill in early July in substantially its original form.

Jackson vetoed the bank bill as unconstitutional and as bad public policy. It invaded the powers of the states, he declared, and was not a necessary and proper exercise of the federal fiscal power. Since the Supreme Court in *McCulloch v. Maryland* had already accepted the bank's constitutionality, Jackson supported his stand with the argument that the Supreme Court was not the final arbiter of constitutional questions and that the President had the right to exercise an independent judgment on both constitutional issues and matters of policy. In Congress the Whigs made a bitter attack upon Jackson's constitutional theories, but they were unable to override his veto.

Jackson's re-election in November 1832 doomed the bank. The following year he virtually severed the government's connection with the institution by withdrawing federal funds from its vaults for various expenses until the government's accounts were exhausted and depositing all new funds in state banks. In 1837 the bank's charter expired without renewal. As a substitute agency to receive, transfer, and pay out federal funds the Democrats beginning in 1837, sponsored the creation of a subtreasury system, an idea which finally became law in 1840. President Martin Van Buren explained the underlying constitutional philosophy of the scheme when he declared that the federal government had no constitutional authority to associate itself in any way with private banking activities or business pursuits and that it was therefore obliged to provide for the deposit, transfer, and payment of government funds without the assistance of private institutions.

Another attempt to recharter a national bank—the last for many years—came in 1841, after the Whigs had gained control of Congress and had elected William Henry Harrison to the presidency in 1840. Under Clay's imperious leadership they repealed the Sub-Treasury Act and passed a bill to create "the Fiscal Bank of the United States," with headquarters in the District of Columbia. President John Tyler, who had taken office upon Harrison's death in April 1841, was a states' rights Virginian and strict constructionist, and he favored a provision requiring the assent of the states for the establishment of branches therein. But the Whig leaders disregarded Tyler's wishes and asserted that the question of congressional power to establish branch banks within the various states had already been settled affirmatively by the Supreme Court. They did, however, include a provision which "presumed" a state's assent unless its legislature promptly and "unconditionally" dissented.

Tyler vetoed the bill on the ground that Congress had no constitutional power "to create a national bank to operate *per se* over the Union." Admitting that Congresses and Presidents had often differed over the question of constitutionality, he reminded Congress of his own oft-expressed opinion that no such power existed. He insisted that the bill's provision for the protection of the rights of the states was entirely inadequate and hence that the bill was unconstitutional. The Whig majority in Congress now made a half-hearted attempt to meet Tyler's objections. In September they passed another bank bill, but they refused to meet his repeated request that the establishment of the bank's branches be made dependent upon positive state consent. Tyler vetoed this bill also, declaring that it was a disguised attempt on Congress' part to exercise an "assumed" power to establish a real national bank. "The question of power remains unchanged," he asserted, and concluded that the bill was unconstitutional.

The Whigs now broke completely with Tyler and never again had an opportunity to establish a national bank. In 1846 the Democrats, following President Polk's recommendation, re-established the independent treasury system and left banking to the control of the states. Not until the Civil War was a new national banking system to be created.

Thus by the mid-forties the predominantly strict constructionist Democrats had thwarted the nationalistic Whigs on every important constitutional issue of the day. The Democratic program was doubtless more in harmony with the prevailing social and economic conditions of the country as a whole. In general the Whig program was geared primarily to the commercial and industrial interests of the nation, while Democratic policies appealed more to individual westerners and to agrarian states' rights southerners, and those latter groups were still in the majority in the Union. Perhaps a more positively nationalistic program would have been of greater ultimate benefit to the nation, but at the time most Americans did not think so. The Democratic Party was nationalistic in the sense that most of its members still strongly opposed any development that would disrupt the Union, but they also believed that preservation of the Union depended upon strict construction of federal powers and the preservation of the rights and autonomy of the states.

ANDREW JACKSON AND THE NEW PRESIDENCY

Even more than Washington, Jackson laid the foundations for the modern presidential office. He sharply reversed the twenty-year old trend toward a weak executive, and in his two terms in office he evolved a new conception of presidential authority and new instruments of power which were ultimately incorporated permanently into the executive.

Jackson's determination to play a powerful role in the government rested mainly on his conception of himself as a national champion of the people. There were strong grounds for this attitude: he was the first President nominated and elected almost entirely by democratic processes, and he was also the leader of a political party which championed popular sovereignty. His naturally strong-willed temperament and his experience as a military commander no doubt strengthened his capacity for leadership and his willingness to assert presidential prerogative.

As a popular champion, Jackson was determined to play an independent role in the formulation of national policy. To this end he willingly defied both Congress and the Supreme Court when it became necessary for him to do so. Nor were instruments of presidential power wanting, even though they had long lain dormant. Jackson ultimately made use of three of these instruments of power —the veto power, his power over appointments and removals, and his extraconstitutional position as a party leader.

It was Jackson's bank veto which first led him to assert comprehensively his ideas on executive independence. His veto message set forth two fairly distinct constitutional concepts, both of which infuriated the Whigs—that the Supreme Court was not the final arbiter of all constitutional questions, and that the President could exercise a judgment independent of Congress upon matters of policy, presumably even where constitutional issues were not involved.

Constitutional questions, Jackson said, could not be regarded as settled merely because the Supreme Court had passed upon them. "The Congress, the Executive, and the Court," he asserted, "must each for itself be guided by its own opinion of the Constitution. Each public officer who takes an oath to support the Constitution swears that he will support it as he understands it, and not as it is understood by others. It is as much the duty of the House of Representatives, of the Senate, and of the President to decide upon the constitutionality of any bill or resolution which may be presented to them for passage or approval as it is of the supreme judges when it may be brought before them for judicial decision. The opinion of the judges has no more authority over Congress than the opinion of Congress has over the judges, and on that point the President is independent of both."

The difficulty with Jackson's position was in part historical, in part practical. For years before 1832 the idea that the Supreme Court had the power to pass upon constitutional questions and that its decisions were final and binding upon the other two departments of government had been asserted in Congress, first by the Federalists and later by a substantial number of Republicans. So widely accepted was this conception of the Supreme Court as the final arbiter of the constitutional system that Webster and Clay in Congress now attacked Jackson's stand as utterly unsound and revolutionary. Asserting that Jackson's message denied "first principles," Webster insisted that the judiciary alone possessed the power to pass on the constitutionality of legislation and that its opinions were binding upon the other departments of government. Although there is no statistical evidence, probably most leading statesmen and jurists of the day did accept the doctrine that the Supreme Court was the final arbiter of the constitutional system.

Jackson's theory also lacked practicality. Although he denied the Court's authority to decide constitutional issues with definity, he was vague about any alternate method of settling serious constitutional controversies. Apparently he believed that constitutional questions might be regarded as settled when Congress, President, and Court were in substantial agreement on the matter and were supported by a general concurrence of the popular will. As opposed to this vague formula, acceptance of the Court's final authority had the obvious advantage of greatly reducing the possibilities of unresolved conflicts over serious public questions and of assuring greater stability in constitutional interpretation.

One part of Jackson's message was open to serious theoretical criticism—he seemed to imply that the executive was not obligated to recognize the validity of judicial decisions even as between the parties to the case at hand. It is undeniably true, as Webster pointed out, that the decision of the Supreme Court in cases lying within the jurisdiction of the federal judiciary is final and binding as between the parties; in this respect the executive is as much bound to recognize the Court's decision as any other individual; otherwise the very judicial capacity of the Court itself is virtually destroyed. Prior to his veto message Jackson had already caused serious concern in this area by his refusal to uphold and enforce the Supreme Court's decision in the Worcester case[3] involving the Cherokee Indians. Webster's contention, although correct on the larger issue, had little relevance to Jackson's bank veto. In vetoing the recharter bill, Jackson was exercising his right of separate judgment upon both the wisdom and the constitutionality of a proposed law, and he was not refusing to give effect to a specific Court decision. Webster and Clay argued that in effect he was, since the bank bill would have continued the charter validated in *McCulloch v. Maryland;* but the argument seems tenuous at best.

In his message, Jackson had also defended the veto as an instrument of legislative policy and had contended that the President had a separate and independent right to review the wisdom and merits of proposed legislation even after a bill had been passed by

---

[3] See p. 286.

Congress. This stand the Whigs condemned as smacking of monarchy and despotism. Clay insisted that the veto was intended only for those occasions when Congress had obviously overstepped its constitutional authority, and that the President could not veto a bill merely because he thought it bad policy. To veto a bill as bad policy, he said, made the veto "royal prerogative," and totally irreconcilable with "the genius of representative government."

The Constitution does not support Clay's contention. Jackson's predecessors had used the veto very sparingly, but the fact remains that the Convention had purposely lodged the veto power in the President in order that he might check unwise legislation as well as legislation which he thought to be unconstitutional. Since Jackson's time, most Presidents have acted upon this assumption, and Jackson's position would not be seriously challenged today. Clay really objected more to Jackson's success in killing a pet legislative measure than he did to the theory behind the President's use of the veto.

The fight between Jackson and Congress reached its climax in 1833 in a bitter quarrel over the President's removal power. It will be recalled that Jackson in 1833 had decided to transfer federal deposits from the United States Bank. The bank's charter provided that this might be done by the Secretary of the Treasury if he thought it wise and if he submitted his reasons to Congress. In September 1833 Jackson ordered Secretary W. J. Duane to remove the deposits, but Duane refused to do so.

Accordingly, the President now read to the Cabinet a skillfully drawn essay prepared by Attorney General Roger B. Taney defending the President's right to impose his will upon his subordinates. The President had been chosen by the people, he contended, to see that the laws were faithfully executed; the full responsibility for the conduct of the executive department was his alone, and it was "his undoubted right to express to those whom the laws and his own choice have made his associates in the administration of the Government his opinion of their duties under circumstances as they arise." He assured the Cabinet that he would take full responsibility for the removal of the deposits. Notwithstanding this virtual ultimatum, Duane still refused to obey the President's order, whereupon Jackson removed him from office and appointed Taney to the vacated position. Taney promptly ordered the deposits transferred and submitted his reasons to Congress.

In December 1833 the Whig-controlled Senate by a strict party vote adopted a resolution drawn by Clay asking the President to communicate to the Senate a copy of his Cabinet paper on executive responsibility. Jackson refused to comply on the ground that compliance with the Senate's request would constitute an improper encroachment on the constitutional rights of the executive. "The executive," he declared, "is a co-ordinate and independent branch of the Government equally with the Senate, and I have yet to learn under what constitutional authority that branch of the Legislature has a right to require of me an account of any communication, either verbally or in writing, made to the heads of Departments acting as a Cabinet council." He then appealed to the American people, expressing his responsibility to them and his willingness to explain his conduct to them.

The basic issue in this controversy was whether the President, through his constitutionally implied power of dismissal, could dictate to the Secretary of the Treasury how he should exercise the discretionary power vested exclusively in him by Congress. The Whigs argued that the Constitution specifically granted Congress control over public funds, and that Congress in 1789 had purposely placed the Treasury Department under congressional rather than executive control. Therefore the President had no constitutional right either to dismiss Secretary Duane or to force removal of the public deposits under presidential authority. After reiterating arguments of this kind for three months, the Senate majority adopted Clay's famous resolution of censure: "That the President, in the late Executive proceedings in relation to the public revenue, has assumed upon himself authority and power not conferred by the Constitution and laws, but in derogation of both."

Although Democratic senators defended the President's constitutional position, Jackson presented his own case by sending to the Senate an elaborate "Protest" against the resolution of censure. He effectively summarized his position when he declared that it was "settled by the Constitution, the laws, and the whole practice of the Government, that the entire executive power is vested in the President of the United States; that as incident to that power the right of appointing and removing those officers who are to aid him in the execution of the laws, with such restrictions only as the Constitution prescribes, is vested in the President; that the Secretary of the Treasury is one of those officers; that the custody of the public property and money is an Executive function, which, in relation to the money, has always been exercised through the Secretary of the Treasury and his subordinates; that in the performance of these duties he is subject to the supervision and control of the President, and in all important measures having relation to them consults the Chief Magistrate and obtains his approval and sanction; that the law establishing the bank did not, as it could not, change the relation between the President and the Secretary—did not release the former from his obligation to see the law faithfully executed nor the latter from the President's supervision and control."

Jackson's argument was in the main a sound one. The Constitution provides for a unified executive, with ultimate responsibility vested in the President to see that the laws are faithfully executed. Jackson was following the Hamiltonian view in maintaining that the power of removal, like that of appointment, was inherent in executive power and subject only to specific constitutional limitations. The President was unquestionably correct when he insisted that he must have the right to discharge subordinates "when he is no longer willing to be responsible for their acts."

The only alternatives to Jackson's concept of executive authority are the parliamentary system and the decentralization of executive power that exists in many state governments. In the twentieth century Congress has actually succeeded in decentralizing the executive office to some extent and placing parts of it beyond the President's removal power. But the twentieth century also was to witness the increasing dominance of the President in the executive department, and a variety of Cabinet officers have been dismissed because they were unwilling or unable to carry out presidential policies.

Despite the frantic Whig protests that Jackson's policies would subvert the republican nature of the government and give rise to an elective monarchy, the President was able to defend his conception of executive authority successfully, mainly because his conviction that the awakening masses viewed him rather than Congress as their leader was based upon sound reality. Jackson's successors, though often less able and aggressive, also were for the most part successful in maintaining his conception of the President as a national leader and a powerful force in legislative policy. When the Whigs came into power in 1841, Clay and other party leaders expected to re-establish presidential subserviency to Congress, but President Tyler's vetoes of Whig legislation and his refusal to be dictated to by Congress preserved executive independence. In a quieter fashion Presidents Polk, Taylor, and Fillmore also refused to accept the doctrine of legislative supremacy and insisted that the executive was an equal and co-ordinate branch of the government. Lincoln was to call upon these precedents in the crisis of 1861 to establish executive control and direction of the Civil War, with marked significance.

THE JACKSONIAN JUDICIARY AND
CHIEF JUSTICE TANEY

As in every period of American history, the dominant political ideas of Jackson's time worked their way into the opinions of the Supreme Court, in part through the appointment of justices who were in sympathy with new concepts and in part because older judges yielded somewhat to the new atmosphere. There were, however, relatively few issues upon which the new constitutional interpretation was to be in sharp contrast with that of Marshall's heyday. Rather the new justices were to make modifications and refinements of constitutional points, especially as they touched upon new social and economic conditions. More striking perhaps was the fact that the new breed of justices more often than before divided widely among themselves and rendered numerous concurring and dissenting opinions.

A new judicial spirit was apparent after 1835. The Court was somewhat more inclined to recognize the rights of popular majorities as against private property rights. To a certain extent also the new Court recognized the limited retreat from nationalism then under way. Between 1835 and 1855 there were no more great decisions defending national supremacy as against the states, and during the same period the Court often recognized as legitimate certain state powers and functions which Marshall might well have argued intruded upon federal authority.

The dominant personality on the new Court was Chief Justice Roger B. Taney, a Maryland planter, lawyer, and Cabinet officer appointed to the bench upon Marshall's death in 1835. A man of strong character and great ability, Taney had once been a strong Federalist, but after the death of his old party he became an ardent supporter of Andrew Jackson. As Jackson's Attorney General he helped draft the bank veto and the President's Cabinet message on the veto power, and as Secretary of the Treasury he willingly removed the deposits of the United States Bank, a step which he had in fact long advocated. The Senate rejected his nomination as an associate justice in 1835 and confirmed his nomination as Chief Justice the following year only after several weeks of embittered debate.

Once on the bench, Taney proved to be a liberal in his defense of majority rights against corporate property rights, but throughout his career he remained a staunch defender of property rights in land and slaves. While many of his opinions were sympathetic toward the maintenance of state authority as against private rights or federal power, he nonetheless did not break sharply with Marshall's nationalism. He was at most a moderate dual federalist, believing that both the federal government and the states possessed exclusive spheres of authority in which each was supreme. Indeed, his opinion in *Ableman v. Booth* (1859) was a ringing defense of national supremacy and the Court's right to control state judiciaries in matters of constitutional interpretation.[4] The general intellectual quality of his opinions was very high—perhaps as high as Marshall's. After his death his reputation was long beclouded, mainly because of the resentment that Northern-minded historians felt toward his opinion in the Dred Scott and certain Civil War cases. Today, however, he is generally recognized as one of America's greatest jurists.

Most of Taney's colleagues were also agrarian Democrats in background. After 1835, only Story and Thompson remained from the great days of John Marshall. However, two of Jackson's appointees, John McLean of Ohio and James Wayne of Georgia, especially the latter, generally upheld national authority on important issues. In 1837, Congress was instrumental in further reducing the influence of the nationalistic minority by enlarging the Court from seven to nine members. The new justices, John McKinley of Alabama and Philip Barbour (and his successor in 1841, Peter V. Daniel) of Virginia, were particularly strong states' rights men, while John Catron of Tennessee adopted a moderate position.

An early indication of the Court's changing constitutional philosophy appeared in *Briscoe v. The Bank of Kentucky* (1837), a case involving the constitutional status of state bills of credit. In 1830, in *Craig v. Missouri*, the Court had invalidated a Missouri law which had provided for state interest-bearing certificates. Although these certificates would not have been actual legal tender, they would have been receivable for taxes and backed by certain state property. In the Briscoe decision, however, the Court took away much of the force of the Craig opinion by holding valid a Kentucky statute establishing a state-owned and state-controlled bank authorized to issue notes for public circulation. The decision hinged on the definition of a bill of credit. "To constitute a bill of credit within the Constitution," said Justice McLean for the Court, "it must be issued by a State, on the faith of the State, and be designed to circulate as money." The Kentucky act did not pledge the faith of

---

[4] See pp. 356–557.

the state for redemption of the notes; instead it established a corporation that could sue and be sued. Therefore, the Court held, state bank notes were not bills of credit within the meaning of the federal Constitution and were allowable.

The Briscoe decision, coupled with the simultaneous overthrow of the national bank by the Democrats, went far to destroy the effectiveness of the Constitution's limitations upon state issuance of currency. Justice Story in his dissent argued that the Court had in effect overturned the Craig opinion. Technically this was not true, since it is possible to distinguish between state issues and issues of a public corporation; yet Story's contention that Marshall's Court would have invalidated the Kentucky statute was no doubt correct. A new generation of jurists had arisen, freed from the old post-Revolutionary conservative fear of state currency issues and hence inclined to be more lenient toward state currency and banking activities. In any event, the states were now practically free to regulate banking and currency matters as they wished, and in fact they continued to do so until the Civil War brought about a new era of federal monetary regulation.

THE CONTRACT CLAUSE AND CORPORATE POWER

No opinion revealed more effectively the differences in the Supreme Court's complexion between Marshall's and Taney's time than did *Charles River Bridge v. Warren Bridge* (1837), a case that resulted in a substantial modification of Marshall's earlier contract doctrines.

In 1785 the Massachusetts legislature had incorporated the Charles River Bridge Company for a period of forty years, and had empowered it to erect a bridge over the Charles River and to collect tolls for passage over the bridge. In 1792 the life of the original charter was extended to seventy years. Before the expiration of the charter, however, the legislature authorized another corporation, the Warren Bridge Company, to erect another bridge over the Charles River at a point less than three hundred yards from the earlier bridge. By the terms of its charter, the new corporation was to turn its bridge over to the state as soon as its expenses of construction were paid; it was therefore potentially toll-free and threatened to destroy almost entirely the value of the earlier bridge. Accordingly, in 1829 the Charles River Bridge Company sought an injunction against the construction of the new bridge, on the grounds that the older charter by implication gave it sole and exclusive right to operate a bridge at the point in question during the

life of its charter and that the second charter therefore constituted an impairment of the obligation of contracts.

Chief Justice Taney, delivering his first opinion on a constitutional question, held that a charter grant must always be construed
narrowly, that no implied right could be assumed, and that ambiguities must be construed in favor of the state. The doctrine of vested
rights, upon which the plaintiff had placed considerable reliance,
he brushed aside as irrelevant. Taney rested his legal position upon
English precedent and earlier American cases, but Jacksonian social philosophy protruded all through his reasoning: "The object
and end of all government," he said, "is to promote the happiness
and prosperity of the community by which it is established, and it
can never be assumed that the government intended to diminish its
power of accomplishing the end for which it was created." The
Court could not consent, he said, to strip away "the rights reserved
to the States," and by "mere technical reasoning take away from
them any portion of that power over their own internal police and
improvement, which is so necessary to their well being and prosperity."

Taney's doctrine limited somewhat the earlier Marshall attitude toward the inviolability of contracts and was more progressive
and realistic than the earlier position. Corporations were becoming
numerous in the fields of banking and transportation, and they required close state supervision if the public interest was to be protected. A rapidly expanding country in search of improved means
of transportation would have been greatly handicapped had the
older turnpike and canal corporations been enabled to establish
monopolies by mere presumption or ambiguous clauses and thus
prevent the construction of parallel railroad lines. The Charles
River Bridge decision did not forsake Marshall's doctrine laid down
in the Dartmouth College decision, that a state-granted charter is a
contract protected under the contract clause; the new decision
merely restricted the contract to the actual provisions of the charter.
Therefore the new constitutional law proved to be a good balance
between the security of property rights and the state's power to
provide for the public welfare.

To Story, Webster, Kent, and other conservatives who shared
Marshall's philosophy, however, Taney's position seemed to spell
the destruction of "a great principle of constitutional morality."
Story's dissenting opinion now seems almost pathetic in its appeal
to old interpretations of English common law in support of the
proposition that the state could be bound by implied contracts with

individuals and corporations. What he really feared was the abandonment of the whole doctrine of judicial review, an institution which he viewed as the principal means of protecting property rights against legislative encroachment.

In reality, however, Taney's contract position was not so revolutionary as conservatives feared. It circumscribed but did not abandon Marshall's Dartmouth doctrine that a charter is a contract, protected from state impairment by the Constitution. In any event, it soon became common practice for states granting corporate charters to reserve therein the specific right to alter or terminate them in the interests of the public welfare. This policy, together with the Charles River Bridge opinion, tended to curtail appeals to the courts under the contract clause, but it did not cut off the right of corporations to secure judicial review of their grants.

In spite of their sensitivity to popular welfare, Taney and his associates proved to be little inclined to disturb Marshall's doctrines concerning the relationship between state legislation and private contractual rights between individuals. In part this was because much current legislation of this kind, especially the debtor-relief legislation arising out of the long depression following the Panic of 1837, concerned property rights in land and mortgages, toward which most of the justices were more sympathetic than they were toward corporate property. In the outstanding case of this kind, *Bronson v. Kinzie* (1843), the Court declared invalid as an impairment of the obligation of contracts two Illinois laws restricting foreclosure sales and giving debtors certain broad rights to repurchase foreclosed property. Most state bankruptcy statutes of the day were not as radical as these, however; they seldom attempted to reduce or modify the debt, but instead contented themselves with softening the methods of execution by permitting installment payments, extending redemption dates, and the like. The Court customarily upheld this type of law under the doctrine advanced by Marshall in *Sturges v. Crowninshield* that the state could rightfully modify the legal "remedy" or method of enforcing a contract as long as it did not impair the terms of the contract itself.

Closely related to a state's control over its chartered corporations was the question of its power to exclude corporations created by other states. This matter came before the Supreme Court in the so-called Comity Cases of 1839, the chief of which was *Bank of Augusta v. Earle*. An Alabama citizen refused to pay the bills of exchange of a Georgia bank on the ground that a "foreign" corporation had no legal right to make a contract within a "sovereign" state. Counsel for the bank argued that a corporation, like a citizen, could enter another state and engage in business there under the protection of the privileges and immunities clause of the federal Constitution.

The Court's decision, rendered by the Chief Justice, recognized the general right of a corporation to do business under interstate comity within other states, but it also recognized the right of the various states to exclude foreign corporations by positive action if they so desired. Taney also refused to recognize corporations as possessing all the legal rights guaranteed to natural persons under the Constitution. Accordingly, he held that a corporation could have legal existence only in the state creating it, and that it could not migrate to another state by virtue of any right bestowed in the privileges and immunities clause, though it might do business in other states if they consented. The immediate question was whether this consent must be expressed or merely implied. Taney maintained that "the silence of the state authorities" in face of extensive activities by outside corporations gave presumption of the state's acquiescence. As Alabama law did not expressly prohibit foreign corporations from selling bills of exchange, the activities of the Bank of Augusta were held to be legal.

Since this opinion definitely upheld the right of a state to exclude a foreign corporation or impose limits upon its entrance, it led many states to enact prohibitory or regulatory statutes upon foreign corporations seeking to do business within their limits. Such statutes often led to confusion, but on the whole they proved to be socially beneficial, since there was as yet practically no federal regulation of interstate commerce. Ultimately the Supreme Court, beginning in 1877, sapped the vitality of the Earle case by holding that a state could not unduly burden corporations doing business in interstate commerce, while the Court's assumption after 1880 that corporations were legal persons within the meaning of the Fourteenth Amendment still further weakened the Taney precedent.

THE COMMERCE POWER AND STATES' RIGHTS

As in Marshall's day, most of the cases touching upon interstate commerce which came before the Court over which Taney presided involved the validity of state legislation having some effect upon interstate commerce. There was as yet very little positive federal regulation of interstate commerce, and the critical issue was the scope of state power as against the commerce clause, rather than the extent of federal authority under it.

Taney's opinions did not break sharply with Marshall's ideas, but they did give a somewhat different scope and significance to the commerce power. Taney never had occasion to quarrel with the broad scope of the commerce clause as Marshall had interpreted it in *Gibbons v. Ogden;* [5] rather by implication he acquiesced in that opinion. It will be recalled that Marshall had almost, though not quite, held that the federal commerce power was exclusive, and that state legislation which touched upon interstate commerce was void. It was this implication that Taney's Court vigorously rejected in favor of the presumption that state police legislation was constitutional even though it might have an incidental effect upon interstate commerce, while the Court ultimately even recognized that the states possessed a limited concurrent authority over interstate commerce itself.

The first intimation of this position came in *New York v. Miln* (1837), a case involving the validity of a New York law requiring masters of ships arriving in New York to report certain data on all passengers brought into port. The law had been attacked as an interference with congressional authority over foreign commerce, but Justice Barbour, speaking for five of the seven justices, held the law valid as a legitimate exercise of the state's police power, since the state's internal welfare was the obvious end purpose of the statute. Unlike the act involved in *Gibbons v. Ogden,* he said, the New York law did not come into conflict with any act of Congress so as to raise any question of conflict between state police power and federal commerce power; and he even intimated that since Congress had not asserted authority over the matter involved, the law could also be held valid as a proper regulation of commerce by the state. In a concurring opinion Justice Thompson went further and stated flatly that the states had a certain authority over commerce in the absence of federal regulation—"the mere grant of the power to Congress does not necessarily imply a prohibition of the States to exercise the power until Congress assumes to exercise it." Justice Story alone dissented, on the ground that the law was a regulation of commerce and hence invaded an exclusive sphere of federal authority.

The divergent attitudes revealed in *New York v. Miln* were reinforced in the so-called License Cases (1847). The three cases, argued together, concerned the validity of three statutes of Massachusetts, Rhode Island, and New Hampshire regulating and taxing

---

[5] This decision is discussed in detail on pp. 277–281.

the sale of alcoholic liquors. The laws were attacked on the ground that in taxing liquor imported from outside the state they in effect imposed unconstitutional regulations upon interstate commerce and so were void. The New Hampshire case was of particular interest, for here the tax had been levied upon liquor still in the "original package," in apparent violation of the dictum in *Brown v. Maryland*.[6] There was considerable difference among the justices about certain legal details—the six justices wrote nine different opinions. But certain propositions stood out clearly amid the welter of legal reasoning. The justices were in general agreement that the fact that a state tax law levied for internal police purposes has an incidental effect upon interstate commerce did not thereby make it invalid.

Four justices—Taney, John Catron, Samuel Nelson, and Levi Woodbury—also thought the states had a concurrent right to regulate interstate commerce in the absence of federal action; and it was on this basis that the first three sustained the New Hampshire law. The federal commerce power, Taney maintained, was not exclusive. "It appears to me to be very clear," he said, "that the mere grant of power to the general government cannot, upon any just principles of construction, be construed to be an absolute prohibition to the exercise of any power over the same subject by the States. . . . In my judgment, the State may nevertheless, for the safety or convenience of trade, or for the protection of the health of its citizens, make regulations of commerce for its own ports and harbors, and for its own territory; and such regulations are valid unless they come in conflict with a law of Congress." Taney admitted the validity of the original package doctrine but distinguished the present case from *Brown v. Maryland* on the ground that that case involved a direct conflict between a state act and a congressional law regulating foreign commerce.

In the Passenger Cases (1849) it became clear, however, that the various justices were still far from agreement upon the precise line between the states' internal police power and the commerce power and upon the question of whether the commerce power was exclusive or concurrent. The cases involved the validity of New York and Massachusetts statutes imposing head taxes upon alien passengers arriving in the states' ports. Five justices thought the acts a direct regulation of interstate commerce and so void, McLean flatly declaring that the federal commerce power was lodged exclusively in the federal government and could not be exercised by the states

---

[6] See p. 280 for a discussion of *Brown v. Maryland*.

even in the absence of congressional action. The minority of four, headed by Taney, pointed out that the laws were specifically aimed at the prevention of disease and pauperism and accordingly contended that the laws were valid exercises of state police power. Taney also argued once more that the states had a concurrent power over interstate commerce in the absence of federal regulation.

The conflict within the Court as to the character of the commerce power was largely reconciled in *Cooley v. Board of Wardens* (1851), a case in which the Court upheld a Pennsylvania statute regulating pilotage in the port of Philadelphia. Justice Benjamin Curtis, a Boston Whig lawyer recently appointed to the Court, speaking for six justices, said that the power to regulate commerce involved a vast field, some phases of which were national in character and so demanded congressional action. Here federal power was properly exclusive. Other phases were local in character and demanded a diversity of local regulations; here the states properly had a concurrent power to legislate in the absence of federal action. There was thus a limited concurrent field of state power over interstate commerce, exercisable only where Congress had not yet acted. Pennsylvania's regulation of pilotage came within this power.

This doctrine of "selective exclusiveness," as it has been called, was a more restrained view of state authority over commerce than Taney had formerly assumed; yet the Chief Justice now silently assented to Curtis' position. Why he did so is uncertain; perhaps he thought Curtis' stand a satisfactory compromise of the differences among the justices. Justice Daniel alone protested that state power over local commerce was original and inherent in the states and not subject to federal control. McLean and Wayne dissented outright from the majority decision, contending to the last for the exclusive character of the federal commerce power.

At the same session at which the Cooley case was decided, the Court in *Pennsylvania v. Wheeling Bridge Company* (1851) showed its willingness to respect federal authority over commerce when the exercise of that power came into conflict with that of the states. The state of Pennsylvania had attacked the bridge company's right to construct a bridge over the Ohio River under the supposed authority of Virginia statutes, claiming that the prospective bridge would interrupt interstate river navigation. The case attracted great popular interest because it involved a conflict between rival transportation systems—rivers and railroads—an important economic issue at the time. The Court held, with Justice McLean delivering the opinion, that the bridge was an interference with the federal commerce power as already exercised by Congress in the coasting license acts and that its construction was therefore unlawful.

Taney and Daniel dissented; the Chief Justice's argument was remarkably farsighted in its insistence upon self-limitation of authority by the Court. He argued that, since the Court had never exercised jurisdiction over the construction of bridges over navigable streams and since Congress had "undoubted power over the whole subject," it was within the province of Congress to "adopt regulations by which courts of justice may be guided" in determining whether such a bridge was an interference with interstate commerce. Taney maintained that outright judicial determination of the validity of the bridge would come "too near the confines of legislation." This position soon received the endorsement of Congress through the enactment of a law declaring the bridge to be a lawful structure.

As is evident in these decisions, the Court's treatment of the commerce power in Taney's time hardly exemplified a radical championship of state sovereignty. The doctrine of a selective exclusiveness—of a limited concurrent state power over commerce—was realistic and met with popular approval, since most aspects of commerce were still more susceptible to state than to national regulation. Yet the Court did not challenge the broad construction of the commerce power as laid down by Marshall in *Gibbons v. Ogden*. In fact, a majority of the judges never seriously challenged the doctrine of national supremacy in relation to the commerce power—that is, the assumption that congressional legislation could supersede state controls when the two came into conflict.

The new commerce doctrines actually alarmed extremist champions of states' rights, who feared that the Court might sanction federal interference with the interstate slave trade or with the exclusion of free Negroes by the states. A minority of the justices had raised this question in *Groves v. Slaughter* (1841), a case involving a provision of the Mississippi constitution intended to prevent the purchase of slaves from other states for resale in Mississippi. While the majority of the Court upheld the Mississippi provision without discussing the question of whether the movement of slaves across state lines constituted interstate commerce, Henry Baldwin, Taney, and McLean discussed the relation of Congress' commerce power to the regulation or prohibition of the interstate slave trade. Baldwin stated unequivocally that slaves were "property" as well as "persons" and therefore subject to congressional regulation in interstate commerce like other kinds of property. Taney, on the other hand, declared flatly that the power over the subject of slavery rested "exclusively with the several states," and that the states' regulation of the introduction or control of slaves within their territories "cannot be controlled by Congress . . . by virtue of its power to regulate commerce." The Chief Justice reiterated this stand in his dissent in the Passenger Cases in 1849, at a time when Southern alarm over the Northern attitude toward the interstate slave traffic was growing steadily. Daniel had the same problem in mind when he declared in the same cases that an "unlimited" federal control over commerce threatened "the safety and independence of the States of this confederacy."

The fashion in which federal authority over interstate commerce gradually became involved in the slavery question was typical of the manner in which virtually all major political and constitutional questions ultimately became engulfed in the great maelstrom of the slavery controversy. So far Congress, the Court, and the President had succeeded moderately well in adjusting constitutional growth to the changing requirements of successive economic and social developments. But the slavery controversy was not to be solved by congressional compromise or judicial arbitrament; instead the constitutional crisis it precipitated had to be settled on the field of battle.

Chapter

14

The Slavery Controversy and Sectional Conflict

JACKSONIAN DEMOCRACY partially obscured but could not obliterate the steady current of sectional conflict in national politics. Before 1840, however, national controversies seldom produced a clear alignment of one half of the nation against the other half; even South Carolina's stand on the tariff had not united the South against the North. Political issues usually involved a variety of combinations between the Northeast, the middle states, the South, and the West upon matters relating to the tariff, land, bank, and internal improvements. No one section stood permanently arrayed as a hostile minority against the rest of the nation.

It was the renewal of the slavery question which gradually created a clear-cut deeply rooted sectional division between North and South. Conflict over slavery had first become serious at the time of the Missouri question, but the achievement of compromise in 1820 quieted controversy over the issue for a time. The intersectional party coalition which Van Buren organized after 1825, with its heavy emphasis upon states' rights, also served to dampen intersectional controversy over slavery. By it, Northern supporters of the coalition in effect assured Southern pro-slavery Jacksonians that they would not make an issue of the "peculiar" institution.

In the late 1830's, however, controversy broke out anew, inspired by the growth of an impassioned abolitionist movement in the North and by a substantial change in the South's attitude toward slavery. The new abolitionism was essentially but one phase of a great wave of humanitarianism which swept the North between 1820 and 1860, and which expressed itself in demands for prison reform, world peace, women's rights, prohibition, and economic utopianism as well as in attacks upon slavery. Ultimately the attack upon slavery absorbed more and more of the energies of reformers until the abolitionist movement dwarfed all other phases of reformism. The new antislavery leaders, William Lloyd Garrison, Elisha Lovejoy, James Birney, Theodore Parker, and their fellows, condemned slavery as utterly immoral and, unlike earlier opponents of the institution, demanded immediate and total emancipation.

The Southern attitude toward slavery had also altered. By 1830 the former apologist sentiment had disappeared and had been replaced by a growing belief that slavery was not only a positive good but was necessary to the South's very survival. Cotton was enjoying a new boom in the lands of the Gulf states and Southwest, and here as well as in South Carolina abolitionist attacks upon slavery produced violent resentment and alarm.

Thus inspired, the slavery controversy broke out anew in Congress shortly after 1835. At first it lacked the character of a major sectional conflict, but it gradually grew in bitterness and intensity until it forced all other sectional differences into the background.

THE RENEWAL OF CONGRESSIONAL CONTROVERSY

The abolitionists early adopted the device of flooding the mails with quantities of pamphlets, newspapers, and circulars addressed to Southerners and in some instances to slaves themselves. Southerners, not unnaturally, hotly resented this practice as an attempt to stir up servile insurrection, and postmasters in the South often took it upon themselves, without formal legal sanction, to destroy such material. President Jackson sympathized with the Southern attitude in this matter, and in December 1835 he recommended the passage of a federal censorship law.

Calhoun and other Southerners, however, feared the nationalistic effects of federal postal censorship, and they therefore opposed Jackson's suggestion. Instead, in February 1836, a Senate committee under Calhoun's chairmanship reported a bill providing that it should be unlawful for any deputy postmaster knowingly to receive and mail any matter "touching the subject of slavery, directed to any person or post-office in any state where by the laws thereof their circulation is prohibited."

Calhoun's bill thus proposed to lend federal assistance to the enforcement of state law, and moreover made a federal statute dependent upon state law for validity and interpretation. Several senators, notably Henry Clay of Kentucky and Daniel Webster of Massachusetts, attacked the bill on this ground, holding that the Constitution nowhere authorized federal enforcement of state law. States' rights proponents, by contrast, argued that the measure was unconstitutional on the ground that the federal postal power implied no congressional authority whatsoever over materials moving through the mails. Even the nationalistic Webster thought such control would constitute federal censorship in violation of the First Amendment. In vain Calhoun advanced his argument based upon absolute state sovereignty and federal agency: that the federal government as an agent of the sovereign states had an inherent right to enact legislation to assist the states in the enforcement of their laws and the protection of their domestic institutions.[1] At the close of debate, the Senate rejected the bill, 25 to 19.

In the same session of Congress in which Calhoun introduced his postal bill, a crisis developed over abolitionist petitions and memorials asking Congress to abolish slavery in the District of Columbia. Since the federal government presumably had full police power in the District, the petitions had a plausible constitutional foundation, but they infuriated Southern congressmen, who not without reason regarded them as attempts to drive a wedge into the institution of slavery. In any event, they said, Congress had no lawful authority to interfere with slavery in the District, for the institution was protected by a federal contract with the states of Virginia and Maryland. This contract had been incorporated in the Act of 1802, which organized government in the District and by which Congress had promised not to interfere with the domestic institutions and property rights of residents in the ceded areas. Senator Bedford Brown of North Carolina also contended that interference with slavery would destroy property rights and so constitute a violation of the Fifth Amendment, an extraordinary antici-

---

[1] Calhoun's contention that the federal government could lawfully act as an agent of the states has been put into practice in the twentieth century. The Webb-Kenyon Act of 1913 used the interstate commerce power to assist the states in the enforcement of their various prohibition laws, and the same principle was incorporated in the so-called "Hot Oil" Section of the National Industrial Recovery Act of 1933.

pation of Taney's opinion in the Dred Scott case twenty-one years later. Slavery in the District of Columbia continued to be a sore spot between North and South until the Civil War. Not even the Compromise of 1850, which later banned the slave trade but permitted slaveholding, was to be successful in checking the abolitionist memorials.

The right to petition Congress was seemingly protected by the First Amendment, but the steady flow of abolitionist petitions in Congress nevertheless inspired Southern congressmen to find some means of banning them. Southerners contended that the First Amendment guaranteed the right of petition only upon subjects within the constitutional competence of Congress, and that Congress was under no obligation to receive petitions upon matters beyond its lawful concern. Slavery, they pointed out, was a domestic institution of the states over which Congress had no authority; hence petitions on slavery could be lawfully rejected. Many Northern delegates in Congress, anxious to suppress antislavery agitation, were sympathetic with this attitude, although others thought that any house rule barring petitions would violate the Constitution.

After some months of intermittent debate, the House of Representatives in May 1836 adopted a "gag rule" intended to bar abolitionist petitions entirely. The rule, drawn by Representative Henry Pinckney of South Carolina, stated that "all petitions, memorials, resolutions, propositions, or papers relating in any way, or to any extent whatsoever, to the subject of slavery, or the abolition of slavery, shall, without being either printed or referred, be laid upon the table, and no further action whatever shall be had thereon." The resolution passed, 117 to 68, over the bitter protests of John Quincy Adams of Massachusetts, who denounced the proposal as "a direct violation of the constitution of the United States, the rules of this House, and the rights of my constituents." In spite of Adams' continued opposition, the House strengthened the rule in 1840 to ban outright any attempt to introduce petitions on slavery. This was a more extreme prohibition than that of 1836, which had merely established a uniform rule for disposing of memorials.

Adams made the repeal of the House gag rule a *cause célèbre*, which he carried on for years, much to the displeasure of his colleagues. He was finally successful in obtaining repeal in 1844, largely because the growth of Northern antislavery sentiment had convinced most Northern congressmen that it would be politically unwise to support the rule longer.

Very early many abolitionists seized upon the federal power over interstate commerce as a possible device by which Congress could strike a blow at slavery, and antislavery memorials very often asked Congress to prohibit the interstate slave trade entirely. Such demands received but little support, even from antislavery congressmen. Two Madisonian theories of the commerce power were popular at the time: first, that the federal power over commerce was a protective and conservative one, that the federal government could regulate commerce in order to advance or protect it but could not destroy any phase of commerce through outright prohibition; and second, that while federal power over foreign commerce was admittedly all-inclusive and complete, authority over domestic commerce was not as extensive and was perhaps only negative in character. Thus an embargo on foreign commerce would be constitutional, while an embargo on domestic commerce would not. Outlining this argument in a lengthy Senate speech in 1839, Henry Clay contended that the use of the commerce power to attack slavery would in reality amount to a perversion of the Constitution. Apparently most of his colleagues agreed with him.

On the whole the Court lent but little comfort to those who sought to invoke the federal commerce power to prohibit the interstate traffic in slaves. Justice Barbour's majority opinion in the 1837 Miln case carefully distinguished between the carrying of goods, which he held fell within the commerce power, and the carrying of persons, which did not. In *Groves v. Slaughter* (1841), Justice Baldwin alone argued that the commerce power properly embraced regulation of the interstate slave trade, while even he thought that a state could regulate or prohibit the introduction of slaves within its boundaries, an ideal position from an antislavery point of view. In the welter of opinions in the Passenger Cases of 1849, nearly all the justices seemingly agreed that the federal commerce power indeed extended to persons. But they carefully avoided any resultant implications that Congress thereby could regulate the interstate slave trade, apparently agreeing with Daniel Webster's argument as counsel deprecating the existence of any such power.[2]

SLAVERY AND INTERSTATE COMITY

Certain aspects of the slavery question involved matters of interstate comity as well as congressional power. Into this category fell

---

[2] See the discussion of the Milin, Groves, and Passenger cases, above, pp. 328–329, 331, 332.

the disputes over fugitive slaves, slaves who were sojourners in other states, and the status of free Negroes.

Article IV, Section 2, of the Constitution provided that persons "held to Service or Labour" in one state who escaped into another state were not thereby to be "discharged from Service" but were to be "delivered up on Claim of the Party to whom such Service or Labour shall be due." The precise meaning of this section was vague in that it did not make clear what agency, state or federal, was charged with its execution. Article IV of the Constitution dealt with various matters of interstate comity, and from this it might have been assumed that the mutual return of fugitive slaves was an obligation imposed upon the states rather than the federal government. This supposition was strengthened by the fact that power to enact a fugitive slave law was not among the enumerated powers of Congress.

In spite of this ambiguity, Congress in 1793 enacted a fugitive slave law. This statute provided that fugitives escaping from one state into another might be seized by the master or his agent, brought before any federal or state court within the state, and returned under warrant upon proof of identity. The act thus put the responsibility for the return of fugitives upon both federal and state courts, and so made state officials agents for the enforcement of a federal statute. Various states, North and South, also enacted fugitive slave laws which provided legal processes for the seizure, detention, and return of fugitives through state police officers and courts. This system of joint federal-state responsibility worked well enough for a long time, and no one thought to challenge its constitutionality.

With the rise of Northern antislavery feeling, however, the return of fugitive slaves speedily became a sore point between North and South. Beginning in 1824, several Northern states enacted so-called "personal liberty laws," the object of which was to throw certain safeguards around alleged fugitives and to protect free Negroes from kidnaping. Pennsylvania's statute, enacted in 1826, contained a prohibition practically banning all seizure of Negroes with intent to return the victim to slavery. Other provisions of the Pennsylvania law prohibited lower state magistrates from taking cognizance of fugitive slave cases under the federal statute. Connecticut also imposed this latter restriction on state officials and together with Indiana, New York, and Vermont guaranteed fugitives a jury trial in the state courts.

In *Prigg v. Pennsylvania* (1842) the constitutionality of such legislation and of the federal fugitive slave law came before the Supreme Court. Edward Prigg, a slaveholders' agent from Maryland, had seized a runaway in Pennsylvania, and upon being denied a warrant in the state courts, had forcibly carried the slave back to Maryland without benefit of further legal proceedings. Returning to Pennsylvania, he was indicted and convicted of violating the kidnaping clause in the act of 1826. This verdict was sustained by the Pennsylvania Supreme Court, and an appeal was thereupon taken to the United States Supreme Court.

Justice Story, who delivered the majority opinion of a divided Court, held, first, that the Pennsylvania provision banning forcible seizure and removal of a fugitive was unconstitutional. The true intent of the fugitive slave clause in the federal Constitution, he said, was to expedite the return of runaways in every possible fashion, and any state law interfering with that right was void. Secondly, Story held that execution of the fugitive slave clause in the federal Constitution was exclusively a federal power. Answering those who argued that the Constitution seemingly established a system of interstate comity, Story said that in the interest of uniform enforcement a federal act was imperative, that there were other federal powers than those listed in Article I, Section 8, and that in any event the principle of federal legislation had now stood too long to be challenged successfully. The act of 1793 was thus held to be constitutional in all its main provisions.

Story held incidentally, however, that Pennsylvania was within its rights in prohibiting its own magistrates from enforcing the federal fugitive slave law, since there was, he said, no state obligation to undertake the enforcement of federal law. This ruling opened the way for further Northern interference with the return of fugitives, and several Northern states now passed statutes prohibiting their courts and police officers from assisting in any way in the return of fugitives. Liberty laws of this kind were a further source of irritation between North and South.

The Court's opinion in the Prigg case did not win general acceptance among lawyers and statesmen in either North or South. Many Southern statesmen continued to insist that the return of fugitives was a mutual obligation of the several states rather than of the federal government, and that Northern acts prohibiting state officials from assisting in the return of fugitives were therefore void. On the other hand, certain Northern statesmen, Daniel Webster among them, often admitted that return of fugitives was properly a matter of interstate comity, but they threw emphasis upon the fact that the federal statute was thereby void, notwithstanding the Prigg opinion. By 1850 Northern violations of the Fugitive Slave Law constituted an important Southern grievance promoting the congressional crisis of that year.

Southerners visiting the North for business or pleasure often found occasion to bring their slaves with them as personal servants. The question early arose whether or not the sojourner-slave in a free state thereby became free. Most Northern states, either by statute or by court opinion, had long recognized the sojourner slave as a special case and provided by law that slaves in transit or temporarily in the state in the company of their masters did not thereby become free. The right does not seem to have been regarded generally as based on any constitutional obligation, although in *Groves v. Slaughter* Justice Baldwin had stated that the Constitution guaranteed all citizens a right of transit with all property including slaves, across any state, free or slave.

After 1830 the attitude of the Northern courts toward the sojourner-slave changed rapidly under the impact of antislavery agitation. In 1836 the Massachusetts Supreme Court, for example, held in *Commonwealth v. Aves* that slavery was contrary to the state constitution and to natural law, and that any attempt to bring a slave into the state automatically freed the slave. The court held the idea of sojourners' rights to be "wholly repugnant to our laws, entirely inconsistent with our policy and our fundamental principles," and "therefore inadmissable." Similar rulings were soon forthcoming in several other Northern courts, while most liberty laws enacted after 1840 formally withdrew all sojourners' rights.

The Southern states, indignant at the new policy toward sojourners, contended that the federal Constitution recognized slavery, and that Northern refusal to grant sojourners' rights to the slaveholder violated the privileges and immunities clause as well as the spirit of the Constitution. The issue was never decided by the Supreme Court. In theory, however, if slavery were purely a domestic institution as Southerners claimed, there could be little objection to the legality of the denial of sojourners' rights, since no state was obliged under the Constitution to extend to the citizens of other states privileges which it denied to its own citizens.

A somewhat related problem in comity arose out of South Carolina's treatment of free Negro sailors. In 1822, South Carolina passed a law that all free Negroes who came as sailors into the ports of the state should be arrested by the local sheriff and held in jail until the ship was ready to sail. Free Negroes were very often citizens of the various Northern states, and hence by implication at least, citizens of the United States. Others were British nationals. Several Northern states immediately protested that the South Carolina law violated the privileges and immunities of citizens of the United States, while Prime Minister George Canning protested that the act violated the existing commercial treaty with Great Britain.

Attorney General William Wirt shortly issued an opinion that the South Carolina law violated the Constitution's privileges and immunities clause, and in 1823 a federal district court in South Carolina also held the act void on the ground that it invaded the federal commerce power. South Carolina thereupon ceased to enforce the statute as against British Negroes but continued to do so against those from Northern states. Further, many Southern states continued to enforce laws against the entry of free Negroes, even though the latter were conceivably citizens of the United States and entitled to the benefits of the privileges and immunities clause. This practice furnished antislavery leaders with a countercharge to Southern complaints against the Northern personal liberty laws.

THE PROSLAVERY LEADERS ADOPT STATE SOVEREIGNTY

In all this early controversy, the underlying fear of Southern statesmen was that the North would eventually use its growing political power to make a direct attack upon the institution of slavery within the Southern states. Before 1845 there seemed little immediate danger of this. Abolitionists were not popular in the North; few Northern congressmen showed any inclination to adopt abolitionist arguments, or even to press for the abolition of slavery in the District of Columbia. Besides, until 1850 the slave states controlled half the Senate and two-fifths of the votes in the House, while a Southern President occupied the White House for all but eight years between 1801 and 1850. In these circumstances there seemed little prospect that national legislation unfavorable to slavery would be adopted.

Yet certain Southern statesmen, notably Calhoun, looking to the future, foresaw a far different situation. While comparatively few Northerners were abolitionists, antislavery sentiment in the North was indubitably growing. In time, most Northern congressmen might swing to the abolitionist position. Moreover, the free-state population was outstripping that of the South at an alarming rate. The North already controlled the House, and if new free states were admitted from the great trans-Mississippi Northwest, it would eventually control the Senate as well. A Congress dominated by antislavery sentiment might then repeal the fugitive slave law, abolish slavery in the District of Columbia, and prohibit the interstate slave trade. Ultimately, it might attack slavery within the Southern states, either illegally or through a constitutional amendment.

To some degree, Southern leaders could meet this situation, should it develop, by resort to strict-constructionist arguments upon federal power over slavery, and they did so. Yet Calhoun thought this remedy insufficient. Ultimately the North, already growing more and more nationalistic, might override strict construction and impose its own constitutional viewpoint on the South. What the South desired was, first, assurance that the North could not legally use national power to interfere with slavery; and second, assurance that if the North ever did so, the South could leave the Union.

An answer to the South's problem lay in the doctrines of state sovereignty and secession, already formulated by Calhoun and his fellow Carolinians in the nullification controversy. The South Carolina doctrine, holding as it did that the Union was a mere league of sovereign states and that the central government was not a separate sovereignty but only an agent of the several states, fitted the needs of the proslavery faction exactly. If the central government were an agent of the sovereign states, then it could never attack the institution of slavery in however remote or indirect a manner, since to do so would be an act of the agent against his principal's interest. Moreover, were the Union viewed as a compact among sovereign states mutually guaranteeing one another's institutions, the Southern states could with some plausibility call those in the North to account, should the latter permit any attack upon slavery. Finally, should the South's position in the Union become too difficult, Calhoun's theories made available the right of secession.

It was Calhoun himself who first realized how appropriate were his earlier ideas to the South's interests in the growing controversy over slavery. In December 1837, he introduced a series of six resolutions into the Senate, applying his constitutional theories directly to the slavery controversy. The resolutions held that the several states had voluntarily entered the Union as independent and sovereign states, retaining "sole and exclusive" control of their domestic institutions, and that the federal government was a common agent of the several states and therefore "bound so to exercise its powers as to give . . . increased stability and security to the domestic institutions of the states that compose the union." It was therefore "the solemn duty of the government to resist all attempts by one portion of the Union to use it as an instrument to attack the domestic institutions of the other states." The resolutions added that "domestic slavery, as it exists in the Southern and Western states of this Union composes an important part of their domestic institutions," and warned that all attacks against it on the part of other states of the Union, including even attempts to abolish slavery in the District of Columbia or the territories, were "a violation of the mutual and solemn pledge given to protect and defend each other" when the states adopted the Constitution. The resolutions ended with an implied threat of secession were Southern rights denied and the equality of the Union thereby destroyed. All but the last of these resolutions passed the Senate by large majorities, partly because they involved no specific political interest of the moment and partly because certain senators found it expedient to conciliate Calhoun. However, Calhoun's main argument on the nature of the Union went unchallenged in debate, so far had the conception of national sovereignty evidently disintegrated since 1789.

Calhoun's resolutions marked the firm union of the proslavery and state-sovereignty arguments. As Calhoun put it in debate, the resolutions were aimed directly at the proposition that the United States was "one great Republic." Such a doctrine, he said, would strengthen the abolitionists and prepare the ground for an attack on slavery in the Southern states through the medium of the national government. From this time onward, Calhoun invariably called forth the logic of his resolutions in support of Southern interests in the slavery debate, and other Southern statesmen were quick to see the advantage and do the same. The resolutions thus became the basis of the main Southern argument concerning slavery in the territories as developed in the great debate preceding the Compromise of 1850.

THE WILMOT PROVISO AND REVIVAL OF THE
SLAVERY-EXTENSION CONTROVERSY

The foregoing difficulties were of little moment compared with the bitter dispute over the westward extension of slavery which broke out once more after 1845, inspired by the annexation of Texas and the prospect of vast new territorial acquisitions from Mexico.

Many antislavery-minded Northerners watched the aggressive foreign policies of Tyler and Polk with growing resentment. They looked upon the annexation of Texas, consummated in 1845 by Tyler and Calhoun, as a bold-faced attempt to increase the "slavocracy's" influence in the Union. They denounced as grossly unconstitutional the annexation of Texas by joint resolution of Congress, a device resorted to when ratification by the required two-thirds majority of the Senate appeared to be impossible of attainment. Texas, they said, was a foreign state and could be dealt with only by treaty. They denounced as a mere sophistry the administration argument that since Texas was admitted as a state Congress possessed the requisite power to act. The constitutional objection to annexation of a foreign state by joint resolution had some theoretical merit. To have complied with every constitutional technicality, annexation should have been preceded by a treaty with Texas as a foreign nation followed by an enabling act and a subsequent joint resolution admitting the state of Texas to the Union. Yet annexation by joint resolution hardly had the character of a *coup d'état*, even though the device was in fact a technique for avoiding the two-thirds majority required for the ratification of treaties. The same procedure was to be employed in 1898 for the annexation of Hawaii.

The Mexican War aroused even more deep-seated resentment in the North than had the annexation of Texas. A large minority of Northerners regarded the war, begun in May 1846, as one of conquest waged for the sole purpose of gaining more slave territory. Many public figures in the North openly adopted attitudes that, if expressed in a twentieth-century war, might have led to arrest for sedition. Abraham Lincoln, for example, then a young Whig congressman serving a lone term in the House, early in 1848 introduced his so-called "Spot Resolutions," which plainly suggested that the United States rather than Mexico had been the aggressor in the border dispute prior to hostilities.

In Congress, the Northern attitude toward the war led David Wilmot, a comparatively unknown Pennsylvania congressman, to introduce the famous proviso bearing his name. When in August 1846 Polk asked Congress for $2,000,000 for diplomatic expenses, Wilmot offered the following as an amendment to the resultant appropriation bill:

Provided that, as an express and fundamental condition to the acquisition of any territory from the Republic of Mexico by the United States, between them, and to the use by the executive of the moneys therein appropriated, neither slavery nor involuntary servitude shall ever exist in any part of said territory, except for crime, whereof the party shall first be duly convicted.

In explaining his motion, Wilmot stated plainly that he thought Polk sought the appropriation in order to secure more slave territory without the consent of Congress, a sentiment in which John Quincy Adams and other Northern Whigs immediately concurred. The House presently adopted the proviso in a straight sectional vote revealing how much progress antislavery sentiment had made in the North. Not a single Northern Whig voted against the proviso, while not a single Southern representative in either party voted in favor of it. The Senate shortly adjourned without acting on the appropriation bill, so that the issue carried over to the next session.

The Wilmot Proviso signaled the beginning of a four-year congressional debate on the slavery-extension question, a debate carried on with ever increasing bitterness as the prospect of territorial annexation developed into a reality. Northern congressmen, led by Senators John Parker Hale of New Hampshire and Daniel Webster of Massachusetts, and Representatives David Wilmot of Pennsylvania, John A. King of New York, Joshua Giddings of Ohio, and John Quincy Adams of Massachusetts, took the stand that the North would not tolerate further extension of slavery in the territories. After the acquisition of the Southwest from Mexico in 1848, they met every attempt to organize California and New Mexico as territories by moving the Wilmot Proviso as an amendment. That public opinion in the North was strongly behind this attitude is evidenced by the fact that between 1846 and 1848 eleven Northern states adopted resolutions condemning any further extension of slavery and instructing their congressmen to support the proviso.

On the other hand, Southern congressmen rallied against the Proviso, aroused by this issue as they had not been since the days of the Missouri Compromise controversy. Led by Senators John C. Calhoun and Andrew Butler of South Carolina, John M. Berrien of Georgia, David L. Yulee of Florida, and Henry S. Foote of Mississippi, and Representatives Barnwell Rhett of South Carolina, and Alexander H. Stephens and Howell Cobb of Georgia, they held that the Proviso was a flagrantly unconstitutional attempt to deprive the South of its equal rights in the territories and an attack upon slavery itself so serious as to be resisted even by secession if necessary. In this stand they had the support of public opinion in their section. The Virginia legislature, for example, resolved that the Proviso's adoption would leave the South only the choice between "abject submission to aggression and outrage on the one hand, and determined resistance on the other." Other Southern states adopted similar resolutions.

CONSTITUTIONAL THEORIES ON SLAVERY
IN THE TERRITORIES

A great variety of constitutional arguments concerning slavery in the territories made their appearance during the four-year controversy. The most frequently adopted Northern position was that Congress had full sovereignty over the territories by virtue of the territory clause and federal treaty and war powers. It could therefore protect, limit, or abolish slavery in the territories as it wished. This conclusion, they pointed out, coincided with actual practice, for since the founding of the government in 1789, Congress had repeatedly exercised the right to establish freedom or slavery in its western domains.

Certain Northerners, at first few in number, insisted that the Constitution itself prohibited slavery in the territories, and that it was the duty of Congress to enforce this prohibition by positive legislation. Proponents of this position pointed out that the due process clause of the Fifth Amendment guaranteed that no person could legally be deprived of liberty without due process of law. Since the institution of slavery did precisely that, it followed that slavery was *ipso facto* illegal in all the territories. This argument first appeared in the Free Soil Party platform of 1848 and was subsequently incorporated in the Republican Party platforms of 1856 and 1860.

An early variation of the Northern argument for outright prohibition of slavery in the territories observed that the natural condition of all lands was freedom and that slavery could exist only by virtue of positive municipal legislation. In the absence of such legislation, slavery could have no lawful status. The territories acquired from Mexico, in particular, had been free under Mexican law; their normal condition therefore was freedom, and Congress, even by virtue of the territories clause, was legally powerless to disturb that condition.

One Northern argument, the so-called "higher law" doctrine advanced by Seward during the great debates of 1850, went beyond the Constitution in its insistence upon the illegality of slavery in the territories. Seward admitted that the Constitution itself countenanced slavery. But there was a higher law than the Constitution, he declared, that of natural law, and all positive law in conflict with natural law and natural right was void. Since slavery conflicted with natural law, it was lawfully void in all the territories. Thus Seward harkened back to the political ideas of the

Revolutionary epoch. But his argument now seemed at odds with the Constitution, and it attracted few followers.

The doctrine of popular sovereignty, sometimes less elegantly dubbed "squatter sovereignty," was essentially a compromise theory. It first became prominent in December 1847, when Senator Lewis Cass of Michigan, the prospective Democratic presidential nominee, outlined the theory in his so-called "Nicholson Letter." Construing the Constitution's clause on the territories very narrowly, Cass held that the federal government had no right to legislate upon the domestic concerns of the territories. The territories had certain inherent rights of self-government, among them the right to decide the local status of slavery without interference from Congress. The theory's seeming effect if adopted would have been to transfer the whole slavery-extension question from the halls of Congress to several remote territorial legislatures, where it would cease to menace party organization and national unity, and it was therefore eagerly embraced by conciliatory Northern Democrats who wished to forestall the current crisis.

Certain Southerners advanced their own version of the doctrine of squatter sovereignty, although their conclusions were very different from those of Cass. They agreed that the territories clause did not give Congress full sovereignty over the territories, but added also that a territorial legislature, the mere creature of Congress, could not be endowed with full sovereign rights not possessed by its creator, and hence could not exclude slavery by law any more than could Congress. The slaveholder therefore had an unqualified right to bring his slaves into any territory without legal hindrance, subject only to the admitted right of the territory to ban slavery upon admission to statehood.

The most frequently espoused Southern argument on slavery in the territories was that advanced by Calhoun. As already observed, it rested upon his theories of state sovereignty and federal agency. The federal government, common agent of the sovereign states, had no right to act against the property interests of any of the partner-sovereignties. The territories were the common property of the states, held in trust for them by their agent, the federal government. The agent could not administer the common properties against the interests of any of its principals; hence it could not ban slavery in the territories, an act construed as against slave-state rights in the common property.

Another Southern argument rested upon the Fifth Amendment. Occasionally advanced in Congress after 1835, it became important when Senator Jefferson Davis of Mississippi, now rapidly moving forward as a champion of Southern rights, made the argument his own. Slaves were property, the argument ran, and property was protected under the amendment against legislative confiscation. Since abolitionist legislation destroyed property rights without compensation, it therefore violated due process. Chief Justice Taney was to adopt this argument in the Dred Scott case. Superficially convincing, it nonetheless perverted the historical meaning of due process of law, which for centuries had been considered merely a guarantee of a fair trial for accused persons in criminal cases.

CRISIS AND COMPROMISE

The debate over slavery in the territories could terminate only when Congress had provided territorial government for the southwestern regions in dispute and had made some provision settling the status of slavery within them. For a long time, however, there seemed but little prospect of settling the controversy at all, for neither South nor North could carry its will through both houses of Congress. Northern Whigs and antislavery Democrats forced the Wilmot Proviso through the House for a second time early in 1847, but the Senate, where the South was stronger, refused to adopt it, and Polk finally obtained his diplomatic appropriation without it.

Two important attempts at compromise failed in 1848. An eight-man Senate committee headed by John Clayton of Delaware proposed the organization of California and New Mexico as separate territories with the status of slavery within them to be determined by the opinion of the territorial supreme court, from which there was to be a right of appeal to the Supreme Court of the United States. As a nominal concession to the North, Oregon was to be organized as a free territory. This ingenious attempt at a judicial settlement passed the Senate but failed when the House refused to concur. A proposal by Senator Stephen A. Douglas of Illinois to extend the Missouri Compromise line through the new territories to the Pacific also passed the Senate only to die in the House as Northern Congressmen stood almost to a man against surrendering the Wilmot Proviso.

The nation was now dangerously close to disunion. In South Carolina, the secessionist faction, led by Calhoun, Barnwell Rhett and Langdon Cheves, was clearly in the ascendancy over the state's Unionist Party. In Georgia, the state's great triumvirate of Alexander H. Stephens, Robert Toombs, and Howell Cobb advocated much the same policy. The extremists were still further strengthened in January 1849, when Calhoun persuaded the Southern delegates in Congress to meet and adopt an *Address to the People of the Southern States*. The address set forth Calhoun's theory of the Union, recited Northern attacks upon the South's "internal institutions," asserted that slavery was the foundation of the Union and that the Union would therefore collapse were this foundation disturbed.

When Congress during 1849 accomplished nothing but further embittered debate, the Southern extremists began to call for concerted Southern action to protect Southern rights. This attitude found expression in October, when the Mississippi legislature called for a convention of the Southern states to meet at Nashville in June 1850 and "adopt some mode of resistance" to Northern aggression. The resolution pledged Mississippi to stand by her "sister states" in whatever common measures were devised.

That the Union was not disrupted at this time was due largely to the last-minute success of Congress in achieving the settlement since known as the Compromise of 1850. Henry Clay first advocated the substance of the Compromise, while Daniel Webster, Stephen A. Douglas, and certain Southern Whigs were mainly responsible for its adoption.

The December 1849 session of Congress began most inauspiciously. The deadlock between North and South forced the House to spend three weeks electing a speaker, and threats of secession filled the air. Many members went armed and several brawls marked the proceedings in the two chambers. To make matters worse, the slavery question was now complicated by the highly irregular action of California's new settlers, who, without benefit of prior territorial status or any enabling act, had called a constitutional convention, drafted a constitution banning slavery, and were now asking for California's admission to the Union as a free state. It was not likely that Southerners would grant this without some concessions on the territory question; yet President Zachary Taylor made any such compromise exceedingly difficult, for although himself a Louisiana slaveholder, he favored California's immediate admission on her own terms and was known to oppose the formation of any more new slave territories, in the Southwest or elsewhere. A quarrel had also arisen between the Taylor administration and the state of Texas over the boundary line between the state and the Mexican cession, while an ever growing crisis over the Fugitive Slave Law and Northern demands for the abolition of slavery in the District of Columbia added fuel to the flames of discord.

The first important step toward compromise came on February 8, when Henry Clay submitted an elaborate eight-point plan for the Senate's consideration. By the first resolution, California was to be admitted to the Union at once without any restrictions upon her right to exclude or include slaves. In effect this meant California's admission as a free state. Second, the New Mexico Territory was to be organized without any restrictions or limitations upon the status of slavery. This proposal obviously was based upon the doctrine of popular sovereignty. Clay's third and fourth resolutions fixed the western Texan boundary so as to deprive the state of the disputed region between the Del Norte and the Rio Grande rivers but proposed to compensate Texas by the assumption by the federal government of the state's pre-annexation public debt. The fifth resolution submitted that it was "inexpedient" to abolish slavery in the District of Columbia, but the sixth proposed that the trade in imported and exported slaves be banned in the District. The seventh resolution asked for a more effective fugitive slave law, while the eighth stated merely that Congress had no authority over the interstate slave trade.

Debate on Clay's resolutions shortly became the order of the day in the Senate, where a series of brilliant speeches delivered over the next several weeks highlighted the various Northern and Southern positions. Especially noteworthy were those of Calhoun, Webster, and Seward. The dying Carolinian, whose speech Senator Mason of Virginia read for him on March 4 to a packed and silent Senate chamber, warned that the growth of Northern population and power threatened to destroy what he called the original balanced equilibrium of the constitutional system. Unless this tendency were checked, Calhoun declared, the South ultimately would be forced to secede. Somewhat vaguely, he suggested a constitutional amendment as a remedy; apparently he had in mind a dual presidency with one executive from the North and another from the South, each having an absolute veto upon all congressional enactments.

In an equally powerful speech three days later, Webster held out the olive branch to the South. He reaffirmed his opposition to the extension of slavery in the territories, but nonetheless repudiated the Wilmot Proviso, on the ground that the imperatives of climate and geography made it unnecessary. Further, he conceded the legitimacy of the South's demand for a more stringent fugitive slave law, condemned abolitionist agitation, deplored southern talk of secession, and ended by prophesying the glorious future the

American republic would have as a united nation. Seward's "higher law" speech of a few days later to some extent countermanded Webster's impact, but by going outside the bounds of orthodox constitutional law the New Yorker gravely weakened his influence.

Webster's appeal for moderation and compromise changed few or no votes in the Senate, but it did reflect a certain mood of conciliation and compromise that was becoming apparent in the nation at large. Within the next few weeks, a series of fortuitous events strengthened the hand of moderates in both houses. Calhoun, the very embodiment of southern extremism, died at the end of March, while President Taylor, who had opposed any concessions to the South either on California or the territories issue, died in early July. And the Nashville Convention, from which southern fire-eaters had expected so much, met in June, adopted a few meaningless hot-headed resolutions, and then adjourned.

Behind the scenes, a group of influential Senators, most of them northern Democrats, now were working to effect a compromise. In May, a compromise committee of thirteen headed by Clay reported out the substance of the Kentuckian's resolutions in a so-called Omnibus Bill. But when this measure failed in July, Stephen A. Douglas of Illinois took the lead in breaking the bill up and moving it through to passage in September as a series of five separate statutes. House action, spurred on by Democratic moderates, followed within a few days.

The New Mexico and Utah Acts, the first of these measures, both enacted September 9, 1850, created two new territories in the area lying between Texas and California. Neither act specifically banned or authorized slavery in either territory, and the territorial legislatures' authority was ambiguously defined as "extending to all rightful subjects of legislation consistent with the Constitution of the United States." In effect this language recognized the doctrine of popular sovereignty. States formed from any portion of the territories were to be admitted to the Union with or without slavery as their constitutions might provide at the time of admission. The two acts also incorporated provisions for an attempted judicial settlement of the status of slavery in the territories borrowed from the abortive Clayton Compromise of 1848. In all cases involving title to slaves, writs of error were to be allowed from the territorial district court direct to the Supreme Court of the United States. Like appeals might be taken from the district court upon writs of habeas corpus involving the question of personal freedom. In actuality no appeals involving the status of slavery in either territory ever reached the Supreme Court. Almost no slaves were taken to either territory.

The new Fugitive Slave Act, which became law September 18, 1850, put responsibility for runaway slaves upon United States marshals, allowed masters of slaves to "pursue and reclaim" with the marshal's assistance, permitted recovery upon affidavit before federal judges, and made any interference with enforcement of the act a felony. The fugitive slave was not allowed to testify in his own behalf. A fourth act of September 9 admitted California as a free state, and a fifth, adopted September 20, abolished the slave trade in the District of Columbia. The Texan boundary and debt settlement was incorporated in the New Mexico Act.

Thus by the narrowest of margins, Webster, Douglas, Clay, and the other moderates had averted secession and disruption of the Union. In the crisis, a majority in both North and South had revealed that they loved the Union enough to make substantial sacrifices for its preservation. Party politics also had played a critically important part in effecting a compromise. Douglas, Cass, and other northern Democrats, joined by a few Southerners of their party, among them Henry Foote of Mississippi, Sam Houston of Texas, and William R. King of Alabama, had recognized how essential a settlement was for their party's welfare. Whig moderates, led by Clay, Webster, and Berrien of Georgia on their part had blocked off much Whig opposition to a settlement.

In achieving the Compromise of 1850, Congress played its most important role as an agency for the settlement of constitutional and political controversy. The day of Congress as the arbiter of constitutional questions was in fact drawing to a close. Within the decade the center of authority on constitutional issues shifted decisively to the Supreme Court, as the interest in the Dred Scott case was to show. Congressional interpretation lacked the myth of political impartiality that was later to be accorded to the Court's opinions. The decline of congressional interpretation was no doubt due also to the death of the political giants of the years between 1815 and 1850. The words of Webster, Clay, and Calhoun on constitutional matters had long carried more weight than that of the Supreme Court. No men of comparable stature replaced them. Except for a brief period in Reconstruction days, the Court rather than Congress was henceforth regarded as the guardian and final interpreter of the Constitution.

While the Compromise of 1850 failed to prevent ultimate secession and civil war, it can still be considered a triumph for national unity. Between 1850 and 1860 the balance of economic power and population growth shifted ever more decidedly northward. Northern nationalism and solidarity also grew steadily stronger in the ten-year interval. The economic and sectional interests of the north-western states shifted away to some extent from the lower Mississippi Valley and drew closer to the Northeast. As a result, the North entered the Civil War both relatively and absolutely more powerful and united than it had been ten years previously. The ten years gained by the compromise of 1850 may well have been decisive in securing the ultimate triumph of Northern arms and the preservation of the Union.

Crisis and Secession—1851–1861

In the months following the achievement of compromise, an extraordinary calm settled upon the political scene. The entire slavery controversy receded temporarily into the background. In the North, the Free Soil Party almost disappeared, and the abolitionists became more unpopular than ever. In the South the failure of the Nashville Convention and the triumph of Union leaders in Georgia, Mississippi, and South Carolina indicated that most Southerners still cherished the Union and regarded the Compromise of 1850 as satisfactory. Party leaders were almost unanimous in their efforts to keep the slavery issue under cover, and both the Whig and Democratic platforms in 1852 treated the slavery issue as settled. The years between 1851 and 1853 saw an extraordinary burst of nationalism, a sentiment strengthened by the prevailing economic prosperity. In short, it appeared that the slavery crisis had been dissipated.

Indeed, there seemed no valid reason to quarrel further about the constitutional status of slavery in the territories, for in nearly all of them the future of the institution had been settled by congressional law. The Missouri Compromise Act was still in effect in all the lands of the Louisiana Purchase yet unorganized, and the acts organizing the territories of Utah and New Mexico in the lands recently acquired from Mexico incorporated the doctrine of popular sovereignty. Slavery in the territories was thus a closed issue, should the *status quo* be accepted as permanent.

There were ominous signs, however, that the slavery issue was not buried as deeply as it seemed to be. The instantaneous and tremendous success of Harriet Beecher Stowe's *Uncle Tom's Cabin*, a romanticized and distorted portrayal of slavery which appeared in 1852, revealed clearly that the average Northerner was still deeply concerned over the moral issue involved in slavery. Equally foreboding was the following retained by William L. Yancey, the Alabama "fire-eater," Senator Robert Toombs of Georgia, and other Southern extremists on the slavery question. The partial disintegration of the Whig Party, painfully apparent in the presidential election of 1852, when Southerners refused to vote for Winfield Scott because of his unsatisfactory record on the slavery issue, also heralded the demise of an important remaining bond of national unity.

THE FUGITIVE SLAVE LAW

The most vexing constitutional issue disturbing the post-compromise calm was the Fugitive Slave Law. Antislavery leaders in Congress, notably Senator Charles Sumner of Massachusetts, charged that the act's provisions for summary hearing, which permitted the master to reclaim a fugitive through *ex parte* evidence [1] and which banned the fugitive's testimony in his own defense, violated the procedural guarantees of the Fifth, Sixth, and Seventh Amendments associated with an impartial jury trial. In addition, they denounced the prohibition against any judicial interference with the fugitive's removal as a violation of the guarantee of habeas corpus in Article I, Section 9, of the Constitution.

To this argument the law's apologists replied that the constitutional guarantees cited were not relevant since the hearing was not properly a criminal trial. The slave was not an accused person, and the hearing involved no jeopardy, since it led to no sentence to be executed upon the slave. The true analogy to the hearing, Southerners said, was a hearing in extradition proceedings. Here, also, the fugitive could be surrendered on executive order without trial. The proper place for the fugitive to defend himself, both in criminal cases and in those involving fugitive slaves, was in the courts of the state to which he had been returned. The law's defenders also asserted that constitutional guarantees did not apply to slaves, who were mere property and therefore outside the protection of the Bill of Rights, a contention anticipating Taney's statement in the

---

[1] Evidence bearing upon only one side of the case.

Dred Scott case that the Constitution's benefits extended only to white men.

Antislavery advocates attacked also the provision in the Fugitive Slave Law authorizing United States commissioners and other deputies appointed by the courts to hold the necessary hearings, contending that this constituted an improper delegation of judicial power to a nonjudicial agency. This argument had some plausibility at the time, but in the light of the more recent practice of delegating quasi-judicial powers to executive and judicial commissioners it now appears to have had little validity.

Several Northern states came close to outright nullification in their attempts to block enforcement of the Fugitive Slave Act through new "Personal Liberty Laws." Thus Massachusetts and Wisconsin statutes, in direct defiance of the federal act, instructed state courts to issue writs of habeas corpus against any person detaining a fugitive, and also authorized a judicial hearing on the fugitive's status, in which the complete burden of proof was to be upon the claimant. In Massachusetts, however, the state supreme court voided the law.

In Wisconsin, conflict over the Fugitive Slave Law led to outright defiance of the United States Supreme Court by the state judiciary. The case, later known as *Ableman v. Booth*, arose in 1854 when one Sherman Booth, having forcibly assisted in the escape of a fugitive slave, was convicted in district federal court of violating the Fugitive Slave Law and was fined $1,000. The state supreme court then issued a writ of habeas corpus, and on hearing, freed Booth, holding his conviction illegal and the Fugitive Slave Law void. United States District Marshal Ableman then sought and obtained a writ of error in the United States Supreme Court, to review the Wisconsin court's finding. The Wisconsin Supreme Court, however, refused to receive notice of the United States Supreme Court's writ, and indeed ignored the subsequent review completely.

Chief Justice Taney's opinion in *Ableman v. Booth* (1859) was a masterly analysis of the conceptions of divided sovereignty and national supremacy. The Court denied the right of the state judiciary to interfere in federal cases, upheld the supremacy of the federal Constitution, and defended the role of the federal judiciary as the final tribunal to decide constitutional issues. At the close of the opinion Taney ruled briefly that the Fugitive Slave Law was constitutional, though he did not elaborate on this observation.

Thus Taney, whose private correspondence reveals him to have been almost passionately dedicated to the defense of slavery, successfully invoked the doctrine of national supremacy for pro-slavery purposes. Yet so powerful and closely reasoned was his argument that even the strongly antislavery Justice McLean joined in the Court's opinion, which won reluctant praise from many moderate Republicans.

The new Personal Liberty Laws enacted by the various Northern states made a tremendous impression in the South, where they were viewed as a violation of the "compact between the states." Many Southern theorists held that they justified secession, since they evidenced Northern unwillingness to live up to the obligations of the Constitution.

REPEAL OF THE MISSOURI COMPROMISE: THE KANSAS-NEBRASKA BILL

Early in 1854 the precarious political calm was abruptly shattered when an apparently innocuous bill to organize the Nebraska Territory led to the repeal of the Missouri Compromise and the reopening of the slavery-extension issue.

Senator Stephen A. Douglas of Illinois had been trying since 1845 to secure the territorial organization of "Nebraska," the remaining unorganized portion of the Louisiana Purchase lying north of the Indian Territory. A western expansionist, Douglas had for some years been interested in a projected transcontinental railroad from Illinois to the Pacific coast. Were such a road to be successful, it would have to pass through populated territory, and to this end, it was desirable that "Nebraska" be organized and opened for settlement. Such a program would provide the Democratic Party with an important national issue, enhance Douglas' stature as a national political figure, and even make him a logical Democratic choice for the presidency. It was by no means certain, however, that Douglas would be able to secure support in Congress for his plans. Many influential Southern statesmen, among them Jefferson Davis, the Secretary of War, were seeking to promote a Pacific railway with an eastern terminus in the South, and they were therefore indifferent to Douglas' attempts to organize Nebraska.

In December 1853, Senator Augustus C. Dodge of Iowa, another railroad promoter, introduced a bill to organize the Nebraska Territory. The bill was presently referred to the Senate Committee on Territories, of which Douglas was chairman. Douglas, who was little interested in the slavery question, now attempted to win a measure of Southern support for the bill, which might readily be construed as against Southern interests. Accordingly his committee incorporated a provision, borrowed directly from the acts organizing the Utah and New Mexico Territories, stipulating that Nebraska might ultimately be formed into states and admitted to the Union "with or without slavery, as their constitutions might prescribe at the time of their admission." Another clause provided that all questions involving title to slaves in the Territory should be tried in the Territory's courts, subject to the right of appeal to the United States Supreme Court. When these provisions evoked only mild Southern support, the bill was called back into committee and a further concession to Southern interest was made through the insertion of a provision specifically declaring the Missouri Compromise inoperative and void. The bill was also altered to provide for the erection of two territories, Kansas and Nebraska, instead of one. The plain implication of the bill now was that either Kansas or Nebraska might well be developed as slave territory. In this form the bill had the active support of President Franklin Pierce and the enthusiastic backing of the Southern delegation in Congress.

The revised Nebraska Bill at once provoked a tremendous storm, in which all the suppressed bitterness and passion of the slavery controversy burst into the open. Senators Salmon P. Chase of Ohio, William H. Seward of New York, Charles Sumner of Massachusetts, and other antislavery men in the upper house attacked the measure as a betrayal of the Missouri Compromise and an insidious conspiracy to extend slavery over the entire nation. They accused Douglas of selling out Northern interests to the "slave power" in order to gain Southern support in future presidential campaigns.

Douglas and his followers in reply asserted that the Missouri Compromise ought to be repealed, that it was in fact unconstitutional, since the federal government had no power to prohibit slavery in the territories. Southern senators used Calhoun's old argument to defend the proposition that the territories were the common property of all the states, and that the federal government was a mere agent administering them and could not administer them against the interests of the people of any state. Northern followers of Douglas, notably Lewis Cass of Michigan, resorted to the doctrine of popular sovereignty: that federal power over the territories was limited to mere administrative contracts—land sales, provisions for government and courts, and the like—and internal police measures within the territories were therefore void.

The bill's defenders also contended that the Compromise of 1850, embodying squatter sovereignty in the acts organizing the New Mexico and Utah Territories, had discarded the Missouri Compromise as outworn, in fact if not in theory, and had established popular sovereignty in its place.

In reply, antislavery men vehemently denied that the legislation of 1850 had abrogated the Missouri Compromise. The Missouri Compromise, they said, had applied only to the territory of the old Louisiana Purchase and to nothing more. The New Mexico and Utah Territories lay entirely outside this region, and the admission of popular sovereignty here did not affect the 1820 agreement. They also asserted that there was an essential difference between the kind of popular sovereignty provided for in the New Mexico and Utah bills and that in the proposed Nebraska Bill. The former granted the territories the right to choose either slavery or freedom at the time they entered the Union as states. There was nothing very revolutionary in this, since a state, once in the Union, could legalize or abolish slavery anyhow. But the Nebraska Bill gave the people of the territory immediate control over slavery. It established popular sovereignty in the territories, not in the states; and this, said free-soil champions, was a perversion of any true theory of popular sovereignty.

The Kansas-Nebraska Act went through both houses of Congress under terrific administration pressure, and became law in May 1854. As finally drafted, the provision repealing the Missouri Compromise was a declamatory defense of the doctrine of popular sovereignty. It proclaimed the eighth article of the Missouri Compromise Act, establishing the 36°30′ line, "inoperative and void; it being the true intent and meaning of this [Kansas-Nebraska] act not to legislate slavery into any territory or state, nor to exclude it therefrom, but to leave the people thereof perfectly free to form and regulate their domestic institutions in their own way, subject only to the Constitution of the United States."

The attempt to apply the doctrine of popular sovereignty to Kansas and Nebraska reopened the entire slavery-extension controversy once more. In both North and South, moderate men found their positions undermined and destroyed, while extremists steadily gained power. After 1854 more and more men on both sides plunged into the struggle, until the final result was secession and civil war.

In the North, the growth of extremist antislavery sentiment resulted in the birth of the Republican Party, which adopted an attitude of uncompromising hostility toward all extension of slavery in the territories. The Republicans absorbed the Northern Whigs almost completely, while many important antislavery Democrats, including such outstanding figures as Lyman Trumbull of Illinois and Salmon P. Chase of Ohio, also shifted to the Republican camp.

In their first national convention, held at Philadelphia in 1856, the Republicans adopted a platform announcing that it was the constitutional duty of Congress to exclude slavery from all federal territories. The platform cited the provision in the Fifth Amendment that no person shall "be deprived of life, liberty, or property, without due process of law." Since slavery denied persons their liberty without due process, it was therefore illegal in the territories, where the federal government had full sovereignty. Strangely enough, this argument was not unlike the Southern interpretation of due process in that it rested upon a substantive interpretation of the due process clause, but it drew precisely the opposite conclusion. Jefferson Davis and other Southerners contended that due process prevented any interference with the slaveholder's right to hold property in human beings. The Republicans now held that due process prevented any interference with the Negro's right to freedom.

In the South, the Democrats turned increasingly to the leadership of the proslavery extremists—W. L. Yancey, Robert Toombs, and Jefferson Davis. The more moderate Whigs disintegrated in the lower South, although in the upper South they retained their organization and in 1860 appeared nationally as the Constitutional Union Party.

The failure of popular sovereignty to function peacefully in Kansas also contributed to the growth of extremism. Following a mad rush of settlers from both North and South, civil war broke out in June 1856 between the proslavery territorial government at Shawnee, recognized in Washington as the legal government, and the rival antislavery government at Topeka. "Bleeding Kansas" greatly strengthened Northern antislavery sentiment and gave the Republicans a strong issue in the presidential election in November. Only with some difficulty did Pierce restore order and thus assure James Buchanan of victory over John C. Fremont, the Republican candidate.

The subsequent attempt of the Buchanan administration to force Kansas into the Union as a slave state placed Douglas at odds with the administration and the Southern Democrats, and still further encouraged extremists on both sides of the Mason-Dixon line. More Northern Democrats, dissatisfied with popular sovereignty and with the party's domination by Southern leaders, shifted to Republican ranks. Southern Democrats also abandoned the doctrine of popular sovereignty as inacceptable and turned instead to Taney's dictum in the Dred Scott case, which offered the South a complete constitutional victory on the territorial question.

THE DRED SCOTT CASE

Many statesmen had long held that the proper method of settling the constitutional dispute over the legal status of slavery in the territories was to have the Supreme Court rule on the issue. In March 1857, in the midst of the bitter excitement over Kansas, the Court announced its opinion in *Dred Scott v. Sandford,* wherein the Court discussed at length the federal power over slavery in the territories.

Dred Scott was a Negro slave, formerly the property of one Dr. Emerson, a surgeon in the United States Army. In 1834, Emerson took Scott to the free state of Illinois, and thence in 1836 to Fort Snelling, in what was then the Wisconsin Territory, free soil under the Missouri Compromise and the act of 1836 organizing Wisconsin's territorial government. Eventually Emerson returned to Missouri, taking Scott with him. The surgeon died shortly thereafter, and title to Scott eventually passed to John A. Sandford, a citizen of New York.

In 1846 Scott brought suit in the Missouri state courts for his freedom. At the time this action apparently had no political import. Though Scott won a favorable decision in the lower courts, the Missouri Supreme Court eventually rejected his plea, on the grounds that the laws of Illinois and of free territory did not have extraterritorial status in Missouri and could not affect his status as a slave after his return.

Scott's attorney then began, in 1854, a new suit against Sandford in the United States Circuit Court for Missouri. The case was now frankly political in character, and both sides pressed it through to a conclusion in order to obtain a judicial opinion upon slavery in the territories.

Scott's right to sue Sandford in a federal court rested upon his contention that he was a citizen of the state of Missouri, and that the case involved a suit between citizens of different states. Sandford replied to Scott's suit with a plea in abatement, that is, a demand that the court dismiss the case for want of jurisdiction, on the ground that since Scott was a Negro he was not a citizen of Missouri. To this plea, Scott demurred. The circuit court sustained the demurrer (thereby implying that Scott might be a citizen), but it then returned a verdict in favor of Sandford. Scott now appealed to the Supreme Court of the United States on a writ of error.

The Supreme Court first heard argument on the case in February 1856, at the height of the Kansas furor. Apparently most of the justices were at first inclined to dismiss the case for want of jurisdiction. A clear and recent precedent for such a decision was available, for in 1850, in *Strader v. Graham*, the Court without dissent had refused to consider the argument that a slave automatically became free through residence in a free state, and had held instead that the decision of the state courts was final in determining the slave status of a Negro. A majority of seven justices apparently now believed this precedent to be a decisive one, and in accordance with their wishes Justice Samuel Nelson actually prepared an opinion for the Court based on *Strader v. Graham*, a course avoiding all discussion of slavery in the territories.

However, the majority attempt to settle the case in this way, without reference to the status of slavery in the territories, broke down when John McLean and Benjamin Curtis, the two antislavery justices, announced that they were preparing dissenting opinions discussing the status of slavery in the territories. The majority judges, with the exception of Justice Nelson, then determined also to prepare an opinion that took into account this phase of the question. Nelson alone adhered to his original opinion. All the justices were under tremendous pressure to "solve" the constitutional controversy then raging, and apparently even the majority came to believe that a clear opinion might lessen the tension.

In February, Justice John Catron notified Buchanan, then preparing his inaugural address, that the Court would shortly pass upon the constitutionality of the Missouri Compromise. Buchanan was thus enabled to refer to the forthcoming opinion in his inaugural address, and to assert that the Court would presently settle the much-disputed territorial question. Buchanan's foreknowledge of the opinion later caused Lincoln and other Republican leaders to charge Buchanan and the Court with conspiracy. Historians now consider this charge unwarranted, although by present-day judicial standards the Court was guilty of highly unethical conduct in informing Buchanan in advance of its opinion so that he might use it for political purposes.

The Court finally delivered its long-awaited decision on March 6, 1857. Each of the nine justices, seven majority and two minority, wrote a separate opinion. In no two cases was the reasoning precisely alike; however, Chief Justice Taney's opinion was thereafter most discussed and debated.

In Taney's opinion, Scott could not sue because he was not a citizen of the United States. There were two reasons why Scott was not a citizen: first, because he was a Negro, and second, because he was a slave. Taney supported his claim that no Negro, not even a freeman, could be a citizen, by citing the Negro's long-established servile position, the slave codes, and other evidence proving that as of 1787 the states had excluded Negroes from citizenship. Hence, Negroes were not citizens of the United States within the meaning of the Constitution.

There was a weakness in the theory on which this argument was based: Since the establishment of independence certain Northern states had extended political rights to free Negroes. If a state could properly confer citizenship, as the Constitution implied, then a Negro might thus conceivably be a citizen of a state and entitled to sue in the federal courts.

Taney avoided this difficulty by drawing a distinction between state citizenship and national citizenship; that is, by evoking the doctrine of dual citizenship. The Constitution, he observed, gave Congress power to establish a uniform rule of naturalization; hence, federal citizenship was a matter specifically reserved to Congress by the Constitution and could not be conferred by a state. A state, he admitted, could confer political privileges upon its inhabitants as it saw fit, but this would not make the recipient "a citizen of the United States within the meaning of the Constitution," nor even entitle the person to the privileges and immunities conferred by the federal Constitution upon citizens of the several states.

The doctrine of dual citizenship in a federal state was a plausible one. But Taney's contention that the naturalization clause gave the federal government an exclusive right to define all the privileges of citizenship, even that of "citizens of different states" under the Constitution, was of questionable validity. The Fourteenth Amendment later made national citizenship primary and state citizenship dependent upon it, but it is at least doubtful whether before the amendment was passed a state could not have defined state citizenship within the meaning of the Constitution.

Taney had given as a second reason why Scott was not a citizen the fact that Scott was a slave. The Chief Justice might have made this point simply by citing the opinion of the lower Missouri courts on this point as conclusive, with a reference to *Strader v. Graham* as precedent. Instead he proceeded to consider the effect of Scott's residence on free soil, a matter enabling him to discuss the constitutional status of slavery in the territories. This fact caused many Republican opponents of the Court, notably Abraham Lincoln, to hold that the entire latter portion of Taney's opinion constituted a highly unwarranted *obiter dictum*, injected into the case for political purposes.

While many scholars have accepted this charge, it does Taney some injustice. The case was before the Court on a writ of error, and prevailing practice permitted the Court to consider all phases of an opinion taken from the lower courts on a writ of error, even though a decision on any one point might be sufficient to dispose of the case. In addition, were the Court to find that Scott was a slave, it would bulwark the conclusion that the plaintiff was not a citizen, whatever the status of a free Negro. Hence, while the Court could well have avoided the territorial question, Taney's inquiry into the effect of Scott's residence on free soil was not altogether immaterial to his first conclusion. Finally, it may be pointed out that Justices McLean and Curtis, by insisting upon introducing this question into their dissenting opinions, had put great pressure upon the majority justices to do likewise.

Taney began his argument on the effects of Scott's residence on free soil with the contention that federal authority over the territories was derived from the power to create new states and the power to acquire territory by treaty and not from the clause empowering Congress to make necessary rules and regulations for governing the territories. The latter clause, he said, was a mere emergency provision applying only to lands ceded by the original states to the Confederation. It did not validate federal authority in territories acquired after 1789.

It followed, Taney said, that the federal government had no general sovereignty over the territories at all. Congress had only those powers reasonably associated with the right to acquire territory and prepare it for statehood. This did not imply a general internal police power, and the people of a territory could not "be ruled as mere colonists." While Congress might organize local territorial government, it could not "infringe upon local rights of person or rights of property." Hence Congress could not prohibit slavery in the territories, since the right to hold slaves was a local property right.

This argument had been presented in Congress for some years by Cass, Douglas, and other champions of popular sovereignty. Calhoun had also denied congressional right to restrict slavery in the territories, though his argument had rested on a different premise—that the federal government was the agent of the states and hence could not act contrary to the interests of any of the states in the territories. Historically, however, Taney's contention was exceedingly doubtful, for Congress had long exercised a general police power in the territories comparable to that exercised by the states within their own boundaries.

Taney then passed almost imperceptibly to an altogether distinct argument—the doctrine of vested interest. Federal authority in the territories, he observed, was certainly limited by the various provisions in the federal Bill of Rights, among them that in the Fifth Amendment guaranteeing due process of law. "And an act of Congress," said the Chief Justice, "which deprives a citizen of the United States of his liberty or property, merely because he came himself or brought his property into a particular Territory of the United States, and who had committed no offence against the laws, could hardly be dignified with the name of due process of law." Taney thus evoked the doctrine of vested interests, tied it to the due process clause in the Fifth Amendment, and applied it to property in slaves.

Taney's association of vested rights with due process of law, while not entirely without precedent, constituted a new and questionable interpretation of the meaning and intent of the Fifth Amendment. Due process of law had for centuries been accepted as a mere procedural guarantee, extending to accused persons all the safeguards of a fair and impartial trial. Until a short time before it had never been assumed that it was an absolute limitation upon the right of a legislature to restrict property rights in the interest of the public welfare. The New York courts, however, had recently associated due process and vested interest. In 1856, in *Wynehamer v. New York*, a New York court had declared void a state prohibition law destroying certain property rights in liquor, on the ground that the act violated due process of law. It is highly probable that Taney knew of this association and was influenced by it in applying substantive due process to slavery in the territories.

Taney then concluded that the Missouri Compromise Act provision prohibiting slavery north of the line "therein mentioned" was "not warranted by the Constitution" and was therefore void. The federal government, in short, could not lawfully exclude slavery from any of the federal territories. Hence Dred Scott's residence on "free" soil had not made him a free man, since slavery actually had not lawfully been excluded from the Wisconsin Territory.

Justices Nelson, Daniel, Campbell, Catron, Wayne, and Grier all concurred in Taney's conclusion that Scott was a slave, although they arrived at this finding by varying routes. Nelson entered the opinion originally prepared for the seven majority justices, deciding the case on the authority of *Strader v. Graham*. Daniel merely restated Calhoun's doctrine of federal agency as prohibiting any interference with slavery. Campbell admitted the efficacy of the territories clause, but thought strict construction properly limited federal authority to mere administrative and conservatory acts, and to the enumerated powers of Congress. Catron thought the Louisiana Purchase treaty, which had guaranteed existing property rights in the territory, had made illegal any restriction on property rights in slaves within the confines of the original purchase. Wayne and Grier indicated more or less complete assent to Taney's opinion.

Curtis and McLean dissented from the majority opinions both on Scott's status and on the validity of the Missouri Compromise. Curtis, a native of Massachusetts, had never been an antislavery man; yet he now wrote an elaborate exposition of antislavery constitutional arguments. First, he rejected the contention that because Dred Scott was a Negro he was not a citizen. Free Negroes, he pointed out, actually had been accepted as citizens in several states as of 1787. Curtis further contended that a state could properly confer citizenship of the United States. Since there was no federal citizenship clause in the Constitution except that relating to naturalization of foreigners, state citizenship was therefore primary and citizens of the various states were thus automatically citizens of the United States.

Curtis then argued that Scott's residence in Illinois and the Wisconsin Territory had made him a free man. He observed first that in Britain slaves entering England automatically became free, and that the Northern states, including Illinois, had had similar laws, excepting only fugitive slaves and temporary sojourners as distinct from those who became domiciled. Dred Scott had lived in Illinois and Wisconsin Territory several years; he had certainly been domiciled and was therefore free. International comity and the Constitution also required Missouri to recognize Illinois law and the law of free territory in its effect on Scott, and the Missouri courts had therefore ruled improperly in holding that Scott was a slave.

Curtis next turned to the majority contention that federal authority in the territories was not complete and that the Missouri Compromise was unconstitutional. He cited Marshall's opinion in *Ameri-*

can Insurance Company v. Canter (1828), where the Court had held that federal power over the territories was derived from the territories clause as well as from the power to acquire territory, and then presented no less than fourteen specific instances since 1789 in which Congress had legislated upon slavery in the territories. Curtis therefore concluded that the Missouri Compromise was valid and that Scott's residence on free soil either in Illinois or in upper Louisiana had made him a free man.

The Dred Scott Case was on the whole a sorry episode in Supreme Court history. Both majority and minority opinions betrayed a clear attempt to interfere in a political controversy to extend aid and comfort to one side or the other in the slavery controversy. Taney's reasoning was questionable on several points. His argument that Congress had no general police power in the territories ignored historical realities, while his attempt to draw a substantive limitation upon congressional power from the due process clause of the Fifth Amendment and his assertion that a state could not define even state citizenship within the meaning of the Constitution were at least open to dispute.

Nor were the minority opinions free from logical difficulties. The refusal of Curtis and McLean to recognize that by established precedent the Missouri Supreme Court's ruling upon Scott's status was final and their determination to embark on a discussion of the status of slavery in the territories was largely responsible for the majority's equally unwarranted discussion of this question.

THE LINCOLN-DOUGLAS DEBATES

The Dred Scott opinion was a source of embarrassment for both major parties. The doctrine enunciated there, if accepted, almost destroyed the supposed reasons for the Republican Party's existence, since the demand that slavery be excluded by Congress from the territories was now legally untenable. Republican leaders availed themselves of several avenues of escape from this dilemma. They argued, first, that the Court's opinion on slavery in the territories was mere *obiter dictum* and therefore had no final binding character as constitutional law. Second, they appealed to the precedent of Jackson's attitude toward the Court, and contended that the other two departments of the government were not bound by the Court's opinion on constitutional questions. Third, they pointed out that the opinion could well be reversed by some future Court. This might be achieved should the Republicans win control of Congress and the Presidency, and then fill vacancies on the bench with loyal party men. The Court might even be "reformed," new justiceships being created if necessary. Lincoln hinted at this solution, while several Republican congressmen, including Ben Wade and Roscoe Conkling, bluntly demanded "Court packing."

While the Dred Scott Case embarrassed the Republicans, it ultimately proved a major catastrophe to the Democrats. The Southern wing of the party, led by Jefferson Davis, Robert Toombs, W. L. Yancey, and Howell Cobb, embraced Taney's dictum with enthusiasm, and called upon their party allies in the North to take the same position. The Northern Democrats, however, proved unwilling to adopt the opinion unreservedly, and instead attempted to reconcile popular sovereignty with the Court's position. This stand was furiously resented by Southern Democrats, already angered by the refusal of Douglas to support the administration's attempts to bring Kansas into the Union as a slave state, and ultimately it completed the division of the Democratic party into a Northern and a Southern wing.

Douglas made his impressive attempt to reconcile the Dred Scott opinion with popular sovereignty in a series of debates with Abraham Lincoln, his opponent in the Illinois senatorial campaign of 1858.

Defending the Republican attitude toward the Court, Lincoln asserted flatly that judicial opinions on constitutional questions were not binding upon the other two departments of government, and he cited the stand taken by Jefferson and Jackson as precedent for this position. While he did not openly advocate Court-packing, he hinted that the opinion lacked finality and that it might subsequently be overturned. Douglas replied by charging Lincoln with disrespect for the Court and with seeking to overturn the Dred Scott opinion by appealing to the mob.

Of far more significance for the fate of the Democratic Party was the question Lincoln propounded to Douglas in their Freeport debate: "Can the people of a United States Territory, in any lawful way, against the wish of any citizen of the United States, exclude slavery from its limits, prior to the formation of a state constitution?" Put differently, Lincoln's question was, how can you argue that the people of a territory have a lawful right to decide the slavery issue for themselves, when the Court has already held that slavery cannot be barred from any territory?

In reply, Douglas formulated his famous "unfriendly legislation" doctrine. In his opinion, he said, slavery could be lawfully excluded from a territory by a failure to introduce the local police regulations necessary to the protection of slavery. Slavery, in other words, could not exist except with the aid of a slave code favoring the institution, and if a territory wanted to ban slavery, they could do so, practically speaking, merely by refusing to enact such a code.

Douglas' Freeport doctrine was in reality an argument designed to hold Northern antislavery Democrats in the party by hedging against the Dred Scott opinion. The doctrine had a certain plausibility; yet it failed to check the steady exodus of antislavery Democrats to Republican ranks, an exodus which was to assure eventual Republican control of the Northern states and the victory of Abraham Lincoln in the election of 1860. Moreover, the Freeport Doctrine in effect denied to the South the fruits of the Dred Scott opinion, and hence infuriated Southern Democrats, increased the strength of the Southern extremists, and all but completed the growing split in the Democratic Party. To Jefferson Davis and other Southerners, Douglas was a Judas who had betrayed his party, the South, and the nation.

Thus the nation approached the fateful election of 1860 in an atmosphere of bitter excitement boding ill for any possibility of compromise. John Brown's raid on Harper's Ferry in 1859 made a profound impression upon the Southern mind. Many Southerners accepted it as specific evidence that a majority of Northerners sanctioned a direct attack upon the internal institutions of the Southern states, overlooking the fact that nearly all Northerners, Republicans included, strongly condemned Brown's action. The growing power of the Republican Party, the rising crescendo of abolitionism, and the passage of new and more stringent personal liberty laws in several additional Northern states were all ammunition for Southern fire-eaters, who argued that the South must soon make a stand in defense of its constitutional rights or be destroyed by the growing preponderance of Northern population and economic power. Long before November 1860 it was clear that a very large Southern faction would demand secession were a Republican to win the presidency and equally clear that the new party's steadily growing power made that eventuality a distinct possibility.

THE ELECTION OF 1860

The quarrel between Northern and Southern Democrats was presently transferred to the floor of the party's national convention at Charlestown. Here a Southern extremist faction in control of the Convention's Committee on Resolutions submitted resolutions declaring that it was "the duty of the federal government, in all its departments, to protect, when necessary, the rights of persons and property in the territories." This language was of course intended as a slap in the face to the Douglas faction, and the Northern majority on the floor therefore rejected it and adopted instead a somewhat equivocal statement pledging the party to popular sovereignty and promising to abide by the decisions of the Supreme Court.

Delegates from seven Southern states thereupon bolted the convention. The remaining delegates adjourned to Baltimore and attempted to repair the schism, but reconciliation proved impossible. Ultimately the Northern rump nominated Douglas for the presidency, while the Southerners held a convention of their own at Baltimore and nominated John C. Breckinridge of Kentucky as their candidate.

The Republican convention at Chicago nominated Abraham Lincoln on the third ballot. The party's platform proclaimed that "due process of law," properly interpreted, guaranteed freedom in the territories. It also denounced popular sovereignty as a fraud and condemned as a "dangerous political heresy" the "new dogma" that the Constitution of its own force carried slavery into the territories.

A fourth group, the Constitutional Union Party, in reality the old Whig organization still surviving in the upper South, also entered the field. Nominating John Bell of Tennessee, the party deplored the prevailing agitation on the slavery question and pronounced it "both the part of patriotism and duty to recognize no political principle other than the Constitution of the Country, the Union of the States, and the Enforcement of the Laws." The party's appeal was in reality to moderate men who feared the disastrous results that might follow the election of either Lincoln or Breckinridge.

In the election in November, Lincoln carried every Northern state but New Jersey, winning 180 electoral votes. Douglas won only Missouri and New Jersey, securing but 12 votes. Breckinridge carried eleven Southern states for 72 votes, while Kentucky, Tennessee, and Virginia gave Bell 39 votes. Thus the extremists in both North and South now dominated their respective sections in the electoral college. The vote thus resolved itself into a direct conflict between Northern and Southern extremists for control of the electoral college. Since the more populous North had more electoral votes than the South, the conflict resulted in Lincoln's election, although but a minority of the popular vote had been cast for him.

SECESSION

The doctrine of secession was not new. It will be recalled that dissident New England Federalists had broached the idea at the time of the Louisiana Purchase and again during the War of 1812. Calhoun had incorporated a "right" of secession in his constitutional theories as the last resort of a state failing to obtain its wishes through nullification. The failure of nullification in the crisis of 1832–33 discredited that doctrine, and Southern extremists thereafter inclined toward secession as the South's ultimate constitutional remedy. There had been a formidable secessionist faction in the South in 1850, as the Nashville convention of that year attested. In the succeeding decade, Senator Jefferson Davis of Mississippi had become the outstanding champion of secessionist constitutional theory.

Like Calhoun before them, the secessionist theorists of 1860 held that the several states retained complete sovereignty, and that the Union was a mere league, from which member states might withdraw at their pleasure. The Constitution was a compact between the states, not (as Lincoln was shortly to argue) between the people of the United States. Sovereignty was indivisible and could be neither divided nor delegated; therefore the federal government had no sovereignty. The Constitution was thus a mere treaty, and the Union a mere league. From this it followed that secession was a self-evident right, since it could hardly be denied that a sovereign state could withdraw from a league at any time it chose to do so.

Jefferson Davis, perhaps the most brilliant secessionist theorist of the times, frequently adduced two additional historical arguments in support of secession. First, he pointed to the fact that the Constitutional Convention had rejected state coercion. If a state could not be coerced, Davis contended, then it was manifestly impossible to prevent it from withdrawing from the Union at will. Davis also pointed to the resolutions adopted by the various state conventions when ratifying the Constitution. The Virginia Convention, in particular, had resolved that "rights granted by the people may be resumed by the people at their pleasure"; while New York and Massachusetts had enacted similar resolutions. Davis interpreted these resolutions as specifically reserving to the various states the right to withdraw from the compact should they desire to do so.

The conception of extreme state sovereignty was for the most part both historically and logically unsound. The contention that the founding fathers intended the Constitution to be nothing more than a treaty and the new national government a league or loose confederacy was manifestly absurd. As has already been observed, the contention that the national government could not be a sovereignty because it rested upon a compact was in reality a grave misconstruction of late eighteenth-century political theory, which regarded compact as the only possible way to create lawful sovereign government.[2]

Davis' strong emphasis on the Constitutional Convention's rejection of coercion attempted to prove much from very dubious evidence. It will be recalled that the Convention had rejected coercion largely because it would be unnecessary now that the state-agency was being abandoned and a government based directly upon individuals was to be substituted. Coercion of individuals would therefore replace coercion of states. It is true that Madison's language in the Convention on coercion was not altogether conclusive; he did indeed state that coercion would disrupt the Union and lead to war. But it is significant that it was the state sovereignty party in the Convention which clung to coercion, and not the nationalists, who apparently believed it unnecessary and irrelevant. If this interpretation of the problem of coercion in the Convention was correct, it was damning to the secessionist argument, for it supported the idea that individuals in states, citizens of the United States, might be coerced should they resist national authority. It was this theory that Lincoln shortly applied in using military force again the Southern secessionists.

Davis' contention that the Virginia and New York resolutions in the conventions of 1788 had reserved the right of secession was also misleading. Resolutions that rights once granted by the people may be taken back by the people might well be interpreted as no more than an affirmation of the right of revolution, an admitted right in eighteenth-century political philosophy but one not to be confused with a pretended constitutional right of a state legally to withdraw from the Union. It was not a right of revolution that most secessionists claimed in 1861; they claimed instead a constitutional right of withdrawal as a privilege of the federal system. Although some Southerners, notably Alexander H. Stephens, thought secession a revolutionary rather than a constitutional right, this viewpoint was exceptional.

Southern champions, on the eve of 1861, commonly cited several

---

[2] See the discussion of Calhoun's theories of sovereignty, nullification, and secession on pp. 290–294.

existing grievances as justifying immediate secession by the Southern states: (1) Northern violation of the Fugitive Slave Law; (2) the personal liberty laws, which they represented as a violation of the "compact" between the states of a sufficiently serious nature to justify withdrawal; (3) abolitionist agitation in the North, which they held to be an attack upon the internal institutions of the Southern states and hence a clear violation of the spirit of the Constitution, which left each state free to decide its internal institutions for itself; (4) John Brown's raid, which Southerners argued constituted a direct attack by citizens of the Northern states upon the South; (5) Republican attack upon the Dred Scott decision and the concomitant attempt to deny the constitutional rights of the Southern states in the territories, as laid down in the Dred Scott decision.

As early as the election of 1856, Southern leaders in and out of Congress had repeatedly warned the nation that the South would regard a "Black Republican" presidential victory as justifiable cause for secession. This was no idle political threat, for a large number of Southerners were firmly convinced that a Republican administration would not only destroy Southern interests in the territories but would inaugurate a direct attack upon "internal institutions" in the slave states themselves. With Lincoln's election in November 1860, the secessionists prepared to carry their threat into effect.

South Carolina acted first. As soon as the result of the election became known, the state legislature called a constitutional convention which met at Charleston on December 17. Three days later, the convention by unanimous vote adopted an ordinance of secession. The ordinance purported to repeal the ordinance of 1787, whereby the state had ratified the Constitution. The convention also adopted a declaration of the causes of secession, which presented the Southern theory of the Union and the various Southern grievances of the hour. Alabama, Georgia, Florida, Mississippi, Louisiana, and Texas had also called conventions, all of which met in January and voted for secession by large majorities. Thus all seven states of the lower South had seceded by the end of January.

ATTEMPTS AT COMPROMISE

Meanwhile Buchanan's administration in Washington was involved in a paralyzing dilemma: if it did nothing to check the secessionist movement, the Union would most assuredly be dissolved; on the other hand, if the government used force against the seceding states, a terrible civil war might result. There was no assurance that the North was ready to support such a drastic policy. More-over, the employment of force would probably precipitate seces-sion in several of the remaining slave states of the upper South, then on the verge of leaving the Union.

Confronted by this quandary, President Buchanan stalled for time and awaited developments. In his annual message in December, he laid the responsibility for the current crisis at the door of the Northern people's "intemperate interference" with slavery. He added, however, that Lincoln's election was not just cause for seces-sion, and he also warned the South that no constitutional right of secession existed, since the Union had been intended to be perma-nent. He then nullified whatever force these last observations had with the statement that if a state chose to secede, there existed no constitutional remedy against its action, however illegal it might be. Buchanan's constitutionalisms were thus the quintessence of fu-tility. Seward ironically commented that "the message shows con-clusively that it is the duty of the President to execute the law—unless someone opposes it; and that no state has the right to go out of the Union—unless it wants to." In justice to Buchanan, however, it must be observed that the political dilemma in which he found himself was a very real one, and that his policy of watchful waiting was precisely the course that Lincoln adopted after his inauguration.

In reality, Buchanan hoped that Congress would again effect some sort of last-minute compromise. Moderate Democrats, both North and South, were working desperately to that end. The House on December 4, 1860, appointed a committee of thirty-three, one mem-ber from each state, to consider compromise proposals, and two days later the Senate created a committee of thirteen for the same pur-pose. The Republicans dominated the House committee, but the Senate group represented all factions, and included William H. Seward of New York and Ben Wade of Ohio for the Republicans, Stephen A. Douglas of Illinois and John J. Crittenden of Kentucky for the moderate Democrats, and Robert Toombs of Georgia and Jefferson Davis of Mississippi for the secessionists.

The most significant proposals presented were the so-called Crit-tenden Resolutions, introduced to the Senate and the committees by Senator Crittenden on December 18. In substance, these would comprise an amendment of the Constitution extending the Mis-souri Compromise line to the Pacific, guaranteeing slavery in the ter-ritories south of the line and prohibiting slavery in the territories north of the line. States on either side of the line might be admitted with or without slavery as their constitutions provided. Congress was to have no power to abolish slavery in the District of Columbia, or to interfere with the interstate slave trade. The amendments incorporating these guarantees were to be unamendable, and still another clause prohibited any future constitutional amendment authorizing Congress to abolish or interfere with slavery within the several states.

Although Douglas and Crittenden fought hard for some compromise, their efforts failed, mainly because neither secessionists nor Republicans were inclined to make any important concessions. Senators and representatives from the seceding states were now steadily withdrawing from Congress. They were, in fact, no longer interested in compromise. The Republican attitude was that Lincoln's election did not menace the South and that concessions to the Southern states were therefore unnecessary. In reality Republican politicians could not possibly accept any amendment definitely settling the constitutional status of slavery in the territories, for by such action the party's whole constitutional argument, indeed its principal reason for being, would have been destroyed. The Crittenden proposals therefore were defeated both in committee and on the Senate floor.

In February Congress did belatedly adopt a constitutional amendment guaranteeing slavery within the states in perpetuity against federal interference. "No amendment shall be made to the Constitution," the proposal read, "which will authorize or give to Congress the power to abolish or interfere, within any state, with the domestic institutions thereof, including that of persons held to labor or service by the laws of said state." Eventually three states, Ohio, Maryland, and Illinois ratified the amendment, but it came too late and conceded too little to influence the course of events.

The "Unionist"-dominated Virginia legislature also sponsored an unsuccessful "Peace Conference." In response to Virginia's call, delegates from twenty-one states assembled at Washington on February 4, under the chairmanship of Ex-President Tyler. The conference got nowhere. The seven seceded states refused to send delegates, while the Northern delegations were for the most part controlled by Republicans determined to make no substantial concessions. Eventually the conference adopted the substance of the Crittenden amendments, with some modifications, as well as a proposed amendment that the United States acquire no new territory except by a four-fifths vote of the Senate, with a majority of both free- and slave-state Senators concurring. When presented in Congress, these proposals were overwhelmingly defeated. Almost all hope of compromise was now gone.

FORMATION OF THE CONFEDERACY

On February 4, 1861, the very day when the futile peace conference met in Washington, delegates from the seven seceded states gathered in Montgomery, Alabama, for the purpose of forming a central government. They shortly adopted a temporary constitution converting themselves into a provisional congress and instructing the congress to elect a provisional president and vice-president. On March 11, the congress adopted a permanent constitution and submitted it to the seceded states for ratification.

The Confederate Constitution closely resembled that of the United States, although it contained a number of interesting differences. Certain provisions underscored state sovereignty. The preamble read, "We the people of the Confederate States, each state acting in its sovereign capacity . . . do ordain and establish this Constitution . . ." This implied that the resultant government arose out of a compact between sovereign states, and not between the people thereof. The right of secession might thereby be inferred. Interestingly enough, however, the Constitution mentioned no such right, and in fact three different proposals guaranteeing the right were killed in convention without reaching the floor.

Other provisions grew directly out of the late slavery controversy. Congress was forbidden to pass any law impairing the right of property in slaves. Citizens with their slaves were granted the right of transit and sojourn in other states, and such sojourn did not thereby impair ownership in such slaves. Negro slavery was specifically recognized in any territories the Confederacy might acquire. The foreign slave trade, however, except with slave-holding states of the United States, was forbidden. The South's long-standing grievance against the protective tariff was reflected in a clause forbidding import duties for the benefit of industry, while congressional appropriations for internal improvements, except those in navigational facilities, were also prohibited.

Substantial changes were made in the executive department. The President and Vice-President were given six-year terms and made ineligible for re-election. The President was specifically granted a separate unconditional removal power over principal officers, and over minor officials for reasons of misconduct or incapacity. This provision evidently reflected the long quarrel over the removal power under the United States Constitution.

The President also had more effective control over money matters than did the President of the United States under the Constitution. He could veto separate items in appropriation bills, while Congress could appropriate money only by two-thirds vote of both houses unless the funds were requested by the executive. Another clause enabled Congress to grant cabinet officers a seat on the floor of either house to discuss matters pertaining to their departments. Such a provision might conceivably have led to the emergence of a parliamentary system of government, although no such tendency appeared during the Confederacy's brief history.

The new government also prepared to treat with the United States to effect a settlement with respect to "common property," the territories, debts, and the like. For this purpose the Confederate Congress accredited two commissioners to Washington. The new government also proceeded to take over certain forts, arsenals, and other United States property lying within the Confederacy. Apparently it expected the government at Washington to offer little resistance to the erection of a new nation.

LINCOLN'S POLICY TOWARD SECESSION

On March 4, 1861, the Buchanan administration expired, and the tremendous responsibilities of the presidential office devolved upon Abraham Lincoln. Lincoln laid down the outlines of his policy toward slavery, secession, and the maintenance of national authority in his inaugural address of March 4. It was a reasoned and powerful address, lucid in its constitutional theorizing, but the President offered no compromise whatever to the South on the territorial question, as many Southern Unionists desired him to do.

Lincoln first reminded the South that he had no constitutional authority to attack slavery within the Southern states, and added that he was willing and even anxious to extend all the constitutional protection possible to the "prosperity, peace and security" of every section of the Union. He sanctioned the constitutional amendment specifically guaranteeing slavery in the states against congressional interference, adding that in any case this was already implied constitutional law.

On the subject of slavery in the territories, however, he suggested that the issue was a matter of policy not adequately covered by the provisions of the written Constitution. In what was obviously an oblique repudiation of the Dred Scott opinion, he added that he could not accept the proposition that opinions of the Supreme Court on constitutional questions bound finally the other two departments of government, who must decide constitutional issues for themselves. Matters of constitutional law not specifically covered by the written constitution, he implied, ought to be settled by the majority will, presumably by the mechanism of presidential and congressional elections. In other words, the constitutional status of slavery in the territories might ultimately be settled by Republican victories in national elections and the translation of party policy into law. The new President obviously intended to abide by the substance of his party's platform and to refuse to sanction any further extension of slavery in the territories.

Moreover, there was in Lincoln's words the strong implication that the South could not secede in peace. The Union of 1789 was intended to be perpetual. Secession he denounced as the "essence of anarchy." It was "legally void," and acts of violence within any state or states "against the authority of the United States" were "insurrectionary or revolutionary, according to circumstances." He added that he would make no war upon the South, but that he would enforce federal law, collect taxes, and hold possession of federal property.

Lincoln thus saw clearly what Buchanan had not seen—that coercion of a seceding state was technically unnecessary and irrelevant, and that the proper answer to secession was the coercion of individuals resisting federal authority. To anyone accepting the doctrine of national sovereignty Lincoln's position was consistent, clear, and completely convincing.

Lincoln then warned the South to consider well the possible disadvantages involved in resorting to the undoubted right of revolution. Successful secession would solve none of the South's existing problems relating to the North and the Union; the same problems would exist after secession as before. He ended with an attempt to stir Southern sentiment and loyalty for the Union. "The mystic chords of memory stretching from every battlefield and patriot grave to every living heart and hearthstone all over this broad land, will yet swell the chorus of the Union when again touched, as surely they will be, by the better angels of our nature."

Lincoln never wavered in the policy toward secession announced in his inaugural address. He did, however, proceed with great caution in its application. He desired above all else to avoid the charge

of deliberately waging war upon the South. Moreover, he believed
that a policy of caution might hold the states of the upper South in
the Union, while the rash application of force would make their
secession certain. The Virginia Unionists, in particular, were pleading with him to make no move, lest it precipitate their state's secession.

The issue of federal authority in the South very shortly focused
upon Fort Sumter, in Charleston Harbor. Although the Confederates had taken over nearly all other federal properties, Buchanan
had refused to surrender Sumter, and Lincoln continued this policy.
When Lincoln notified the governor of South Carolina of his intention to replenish the fort's supplies, Confederate military officials replied, on April 12, 1861, with an attack on the fort. The
bombardment ended the agonizing interim between secession and
war. Four more states, Virginia, Tennessee, Arkansas, and North
Carolina, shortly seceded. Lincoln called for troops to suppress the
"rebellion," and the Civil War had begun.

LINCOLN'S RESPONSIBILITY FOR SECESSION AND WAR

Lincoln's policy before and after his inaugural has been severely
criticized by certain historians, who charge him with partial responsibility for the coming of secession and war. First, they assert, Lincoln's coldness toward the Crittenden compromise and his general
unwillingness to extend to the South any assurances on the territorial question inspired the remaining six states in the lower South
to follow South Carolina out of the Union. Second, Lincoln's critics
contend that the policy set forth in his inaugural address made war
and further secession inevitable.

It is highly probable that the attitude of Lincoln and other Republican leaders toward the South after November 1860 strengthened the hand of the secessionists and thereby contributed to disunion. When the Republicans confined their assurances to a promise
not to interfere with slavery in the Southern states, the secessionists were enabled to argue that the forthcoming administration
would ignore Southern constitutional rights in the territories as
enunciated in the Dred Scott case. Since the Republicans were willing to treat one set of constitutional rights in so cavalier a manner,
the secessionists said, what assurance was there that a Republican
administration might not ultimately attack slavery within the states
themselves?

It is doubtless true that Lincoln's policy as laid down in his inaugural made war inevitable. It was certain that the attempt to assert federal authority within the limits of the seceded states would lead to armed conflict, for the seceded states must of necessity resist such authority or their pretended status of independence would become absurd. Confederate defiance would in turn provoke federal military action and war would follow automatically.

Yet Lincoln's policy after March 4 not only was constitutionally correct but was the only possible course available if the Union was to be saved. After the formation of the Confederacy, the time for compromise had passed. Submission to the suppression of national authority in the Confederate states would ultimately have constituted a *de facto* recognition of Confederate independence, and would have confirmed disunion.

Lincoln's critics have replied that a conciliatory policy would have averted secession in the slave states yet in the Union, and that the states of the lower South would voluntarily have returned to the Union. This thesis appears highly implausible. Jefferson Davis and other Confederate leaders made it emphatically clear long before Lincoln's inauguration that under no circumstances would their states return to the Union no matter what compromises were offered the South. There was no valid reason, indeed, why the region stretching from South Carolina to Texas, now united by common institutions and political ideals, should not have functioned successfully as a southern nation. It appears probable that the unseceded slave states, forced to choose between the Confederacy and a Union dominated completely by the North, would have left the Union also.

Even if compromise had been extended after March 4 and war had thus been averted and the South brought back into the Union, the price of peace would have been catastrophically high. Secession would then have been established as a successful minority device for wrenching concessions from the national government. The technique, once successful, would have been resorted to on other occasions, and the reality of national sovereignty would have dissolved completely. Horrible as civil war was, it was a preferable alternative to the disintegration of American national unity. After March 4, in fact, state sovereignty and national sovereignty confronted one another in an unavoidable showdown. Force alone could have resolved the conflict unless state sovereignty were to triumph by default. And, as Lincoln was presently to recognize in his Gettysburg Address, the American experiment in nationhood and constitutional democracy was too full of promise for the future of mankind to allow it to be destroyed in the interests of a socio-political order which at bottom rested upon a form of human exploitation so crass and inhuman that enlightened societies elsewhere already had abandoned it as too barbarous to be tolerated.

Lincoln critics in return have maintained that had the Confederate states been brought back by compromise, then the South would ultimately have been converted peaceably to the Northern view of federal sovereignty and national supremacy. In support of this view, they argue that slavery, the economic base of Southern sectionalism, was in reality a dying institution, regardless of any Northern abolitionist pressure. Again the argument seems doubtful. Slavery was hardly a dying institution in 1860; the secessionists themselves assumed the contrary to be true. The number of slaves in the lower South was increasing, the price of Negroes was rising, and there had recently been a revival of the illicit African slave trade.

Finally, Southern constitutional philosophy was too deep-rooted to die out in a short length of time of its own accord. The South's determination to secede in 1861 was merely the final expression given a body of ideas about the nature of the Union which had been gaining ground since 1798. The Virginia and Kentucky Resolutions had contained a partial challenge to national sovereignty, while after 1815 John Taylor and Spencer Roane had taken an even more advanced stand. The metaphysics of state sovereignty as formulated by Calhoun was little less than Holy Writ in the South by 1860; and it seems questionable that it could have died other than a violent death.

At all events, the great constitutional issue underlying much political and sectional controversy since the government had been established in 1789 was now about to be settled in the most terrible and decisive fashion possible.

The Civil War

FROM A constitutional standpoint the Civil War resulted from vague and conflicting doctrines as to the nature and location of sovereignty in the federal Union. An overwhelming majority of Southerners had come to accept Calhoun's doctrine of the sovereignty of individual states. This position provided the legal basis of secession and of the Confederate States of America. In the North by 1860 a majority of people had probably come to accept a dual federalism in which the state and federal governments pursued virtually independent courses of action, but the nationalistic views of Marshall and Webster still retained much of their vitality. With the attack on Fort Sumter the North rose to resist secession and to maintain that the United States constituted an indissoluble union, an indivisible nation. The people of the four border slave states of Maryland, Delaware, Kentucky, and Missouri were reluctant to take sides in such a conflict and when forced to do so they divided sharply in their allegiance, although the states officially remained in the Union. To settle this greatest of all American constitutional issues, three million men went forth to battle, and more than half a million lost their lives through battle or disease.

While this key issue of the nature of the Union was being decided on the battlefield, other important constitutional questions grew out of the unprecedented efforts of the federal government to win the war. Many of these issues were rooted in the fact that the Constitution had been drafted primarily to meet peacetime situations and accordingly it contained comparatively brief and inadequate provisions for the exigencies of war. This fact had been obscured in the public mind by the country's relative geographic security from foreign attack, by the unmilitary character of the American people, and by the ease with which the country had won the recent war with Mexico.

The major constitutional issues raised by the war may conveniently be divided into five categories. First, the outbreak of hostilities raised questions about the nature of the war powers under the Constitution, and the relative authority of the Congress, the President, and the federal judiciary in the exercise of these powers. Second, at the very outset conflicts arose as to the nature of the war itself. Some of these persisted throughout the war and into the reconstruction struggle. Third, there were issues concerning the proper relations between the loyal states and the federal government in the prosecution of the war, especially in the raising and organizing of troops. Fourth, there developed important questions involving the effect of the war upon the authority of the federal government to deal with the highly controversial institution of slavery. And fifth, there was a varied series of controversies involving the right of the government to suspend or restrict the citizens' civil liberties when such a course was considered necessary for the success of the war. Underlying all these issues was the basic question of whether the immature, individualistic American democracy could survive a great civil war.

LINCOLN'S PRESIDENTIAL LEADERSHIP

As the preceding chapter indicates, the period between November 1860 and April 1861 witnessed the rapid disintegration of national authority, the spectacular spread of secession, and the founding of the Confederate States of America. Never before nor since has the United States government under the Constitution been so near total collapse. Despite this grave situation Congress adjourned on March 4 and most members went home. Under such foreboding circumstances the awesome responsibility for saving the nation fell upon the new and inexperienced President, fresh from the prairies of Illinois. Lincoln surprised his enemies and detractors, and pleased his friends, by responding to the attack on Fort Sumter with imagination and vigor. Unlike many of his contemporaries, Lincoln believed that the Constitution was adequate to the supreme test of self-preservation, and he acted accordingly.

Neither the nature nor the location of the war power was established beyond debate by the Constitution. Although unionists firmly believed that the national government possessed full powers to wage war successfully, they differed sharply among themselves over the relative authority of Congress and the President in the exercise of these powers. The Constitution specifically empowers Congress to declare war, to raise and support armies, to maintain a navy, and to provide for the government and the regulation of the land and naval forces, including militia employed in the United States service. On the other hand, the President is constituted the commander in chief of the national military forces and is vested with the full executive power of the government. Clashes between Congress and President during the War of 1812 and the Mexican War over the exercise of war powers had been neither serious nor conclusive in results. In this respect the Civil War was to be vastly different.

On April 15, immediately after the attack on Fort Sumter, Lincoln instituted his presidential quasi-dictatorship under which the powers of the executive were to be extended beyond their traditional limits. His first action was to call for 75,000 volunteers to suppress the insurrection. He also summoned Congress into extraordinary session but set the convening date far ahead to July 4. His failure to convene Congress immediately to provide additional legislation to cope with the grave national crisis defies conclusive explanation. His wish that members of Congress should acquaint themselves with the public temper before convening certainly did not justify the delay of eighty days. Undoubtedly Lincoln, like most Northerners, failed to realize how effectively the secessionists had overpowered the unionists in the lower South, and hence he seriously underestimated the task of restoring national authority. Perhaps he also thought that the current states' rights doctrines had so undermined Congress' power to cope with the emergency that the Union would have to be saved by some as yet largely untested source of national authority. This he found in the presidential oath and in the office of commander in chief.

Accordingly Lincoln proceeded rapidly to prepare the nation for war without either aid or new authority from Congress. He not only determined the existence of rebellion and called forth the militia to suppress it, but he also proclaimed a blockade of the ports of the rebel states, an act equivalent legally to a declaration of war. Realizing soon that such steps were inadequate for the emergency, on May 3 he called for 42,034 United States volunteers to serve for three years, and he actually received a much larger number. He also directed that large additions be made to the regular army and to the navy. He had two million dollars paid out of the federal treasury, and he pledged the government's credit for the unprecedented sum of a quarter of a billion dollars, all without statutory authority. He had the privilege of the writ of habeas corpus suspended in certain places and ordered the arrest and military detention of citizens who were represented to him as being engaged in or contemplating "treasonable practices."

The overwhelming majority of Northern people strongly endorsed the President's course, even when they were uncertain of his constitutional authority. In the nation's greatest crisis the people clamored for more action, not less—in order "to maintain the Union and to preserve the Constitution."

When Congress met in July 1861, Lincoln offered a twofold justification for his extraordinary course. He admitted that the calls for three-year volunteers and for additions to the regular army and navy were of doubtful legality, but he explained that those acts "were ventured upon under what appeared to be a popular demand and a public necessity, trusting then, as now, that Congress would readily ratify them." In other words, the President claimed the constitutional right in an emergency to take action which otherwise would be illegal, provided only that it was not "beyond the constitutional competency of Congress." This was indeed a new and remarkable doctrine to present to an American Congress, which could easily have been convened for previous authorization.

Lincoln's second and more significant justification was that the President possessed the war power and had been forced to use it in defense of the government. Thus he contended that his prescribed oath to "preserve, protect, and defend the Constitution" empowered and even obligated him in an emergency to resort to practically any action necessary to maintain the Union. This obligation stemming from the presidential oath was confirmed by a legal opinion of Attorney General Edward Bates, who held that it was the President's particular duty to suppress the rebellion, since the courts lacked the strength to do so. Lincoln therefore took the position that he might constitutionally disregard the guarantee of the habeas corpus privilege or any single law if he considered such a step necessary to preserve the government. Buttressing this contention was his fundamental concept of the nation as older than either the Constitution or the states, and therefore superior to both. In short, he held that the President's oath and his position as commander in chief constituted him a virtual dictator, like those of the ancient Roman Republic, to save the life of the nation.

CONGRESSIONAL AND JUDICIAL REACTIONS

The great majority of the members of Congress—those from the Confederate states having withdrawn or having been expelled —approved the President's course, but they divided sharply over the constitutional justification of his actions. Intermittently throughout the special session of 1861 the Senate debated a proposed joint resolution which enumerated, approved, and validated the President's extraordinary acts, proclamations, and orders. The resolution had the support of the vast majority of Republicans, including some who assumed that certain of the President's acts were illegal when performed. Other Republicans, while approving the President's course, questioned the proposed method of validating his suspension of the writ of habeas corpus and his proclamation of a blockade. Owing to this disagreement the resolution never came to a vote. Instead a less specific and less comprehensive validating clause was attached as a rider to an act to increase the pay of privates and on the last two days of the session was rushed through both houses, with only five Democratic senators from border slave states recorded in opposition. By this law all of the President's acts, proclamations, and orders respecting the army, navy, militia, and volunteers were approved and "in all respects legalized and made valid, to the same intent and with the same effect as if they had been issued and done under the previous express authority and direction of the Congress." This congressional ratification of part of the President's extraordinary acts left the blockade and the suspension of the privilege of habeas corpus resting entirely upon presidential authority.

By the time Congress reassembled in December 1861, members could see more clearly the critical nature of the war and consequently the need for the exercise of more comprehensive war powers. The relative authority of the President and of Congress in the exercise of the "rights of war" was debated repeatedly, especially in the Senate. Senator Orville Browning of Illinois, a close friend of Lincoln, contended that the rights of war were executive, not legislative, and that questions of military necessity, by their very nature, must be decided by military commanders acting under the authority of the President as commander in chief. On the other hand, Senator Charles Sumner of Massachusetts, among others, contended that Congress' constitutional power to declare war encompassed full belligerent rights against the enemy, and hence that Congress possessed complete powers of sovereignty in the conduct of war.

This contest over constitutional prerogative was heightened by differences between the President and the Republican congressional majority over the policy, methods, and personnel employed in the prosecution of the war. Lincoln appointed Democrats as well as Republicans to high military positions, particularly General George B. McClellan as general in chief of the army. These Democratic generals adhered rigidly to Lincoln's early cautious policy of prosecuting the war solely to save the Union and of not interfering with slavery except as military necessity required. When the war progressed more slowly than congressional leaders had anticipated, they attributed the slowness to a lack of determination on the part of these conservative generals and to their proslavery policies. Consequently the more radical Republicans, or Radicals as they came to be called, demanded that Congress assert its full constitutional power in order to secure a more vigorous and successful prosecution of the war.

Congress' most serious attempt to exercise the war power more effectively was the creation, in December 1861, of the Joint Committee on the Conduct of War. Originally proposed as an investigation into certain military failures, the committee was finally empowered to inquire into the general conduct of the war. Headed by Radical Senator Benjamin F. Wade of Ohio and dominated by Radicals, the committee traveled extensively, conducted many investigations, and published voluminous reports of its findings. Both the inquiries and the reports were excessively critical of Democratic or conservative military leaders and partial to antislavery generals. Committee members considered themselves empowered to supervise the plans of commanders in the field, to make military suggestions, and to dictate military appointments. At first the joint committee co-operated with the new Secretary of War, Edwin M. Stanton, himself a Radical, but later the committee tended to interfere with the President and with General in Chief Henry Halleck in their conduct of the war. After the tide of war turned definitely in favor of the Union in July 1863 and the main armies came under the command of such successful and distinctly nonpolitical generals as Grant and Sherman, the committee played a much less important role in military affairs.

The Supreme Court, like Congress, was divided over the constitutionality of Lincoln's assumption of broad war powers, but a majority of the justices upheld his position. In the Prize Cases (1863) Justice Robert Grier declared for the majority that, although the President did not have power to initiate war, when it was begun by insurrection he was "bound to accept the challenge without waiting for any special legislative authority." Grier concluded:

> Whether the President in fulfilling his duties, as Commander-in-Chief, in suppressing an insurrection, has met with such armed hostile resistance, and a civil war of such alarming proportions as will compel him to accord to them the character of belligerents, is a question to be decided by him, and this court must be governed by the decisions and acts of the Political Department of the government to which this power was intrusted. "He must determine what degree of force the crisis demands." The proclamation of blockade is, itself, official and conclusive evidence to the court that a state of war existed which demanded and authorized a recourse to such a measure, under the circumstances peculiar to the case.

A minority of four justices insisted that the basic war power belonged to Congress and not to the President. Justice Samuel Nelson summarized the minority position when he declared:

> . . . The President does not possess the power under the Constitution to declare war or recognize its existence within the meaning of the law of nations, which carries with it belligerent rights, and thus change the country and all its citizens from a state of peace to a state of war; that this power belongs exclusively to the Congress of the United States and, consequently, that the President had no power to set on foot a blockade under the law of nations.

PRESIDENTIAL ASCENDANCY CONTINUED

Under these circumstances President Lincoln continued to formulate as well as to execute most of the essential war policies. In 1862 the War Department commissioned Professor Francis Lieber, a German immigrant and an authority on international law, to codify for the first time in America the rules and regulations for the conduct of armies in the field. The result, General Orders No. 100, was promulgated in April 1863 as the laws of war for the Union armies. All this was done without congressional authorization, despite the fact that the Constitution specifically grants this power and responsibility to Congress. On the other hand, Congress on July 17, 1862, did make a thorough revision of the Articles for the Government of the Navy. Both sets of regulations, extensively revised, continued to be used through World War II.

In such other important fields as emancipation, reconstruction, and the impairment of civil rights, the President largely determined governmental policy, either in the absence of congressional action or in virtual disregard of it. In September 1862 he disregarded the emancipation section of the Second Confiscation Act and based his preliminary Emancipation Proclamation upon his power as commander in chief. In December 1863 he merely announced to the new Congress his own reconstruction program, and when Congress formulated a sterner plan in the Wade-Davis Bill he killed it with a pocket veto.[1]

For almost two years after the outbreak of hostilities Lincoln continued to suspend the habeas corpus privilege on his own authority. Both Republicans and Democrats repeatedly challenged his constitutional authority on the ground that the clause of the Constitution authorizing suspension was in Article I, Section 9, which deals with the powers of Congress and not those of the President. Nevertheless, in September 1862 he issued a proclamation subjecting broad categories of "disloyal" persons to martial law and suspending the privilege of habeas corpus in all cases involving such persons.

At its next session Congress, on March 3, 1863, finally passed the Habeas Corpus Act, by which the President, during the rebellion, was "authorized to suspend" the privilege of the writ in all cases in which he thought the public safety might require it. The phraseology was intentionally ambiguous, designed to win the support of those who believed that Congress was recognizing an existing presidential power as well as of those who believed that Congress was thereby conferring the power upon the President. Lincoln did not issue a fresh proclamation invoking this new authority until six months later, nor did the administration later materially alter its policy in making arbitrary arrests.

Although the Supreme Court never rendered a decision directly involving the location of the suspending powers, in the Prize Cases it did give indirect approval to the President's action in suspending the habeas corpus privilege. The suspension of the writ was not

---

[1] See p. 427.

directly involved, but the Court held that when war was forced upon the United States the President was obligated to take all appropriate steps to meet it "without waiting for any special legislative authority."

Thus precedent was established. During the Civil War the President did suspend the habeas corpus privilege without having been restrained in so doing by either Congress or the Supreme Court. It may well be argued that the uncertain location of the suspending power is in practice advantageous, since in time of war Congress will usually confer the power upon the President, while if in a great emergency time does not permit such action he may fall back upon the Lincoln precedent and assume the power.

In other respects also Lincoln continued his presidential domination to the end of his administration. The mounting success of Union arms, the favorable turn of international affairs, Lincoln's staunch adherence to his emancipation policy, all enhanced greatly the President's prestige and influence with Republican, independent, and even many Democratic citizens. Lincoln's remarkable ability to speak to and for the great mass of people through private conversations, public addresses, and open letters published in the newspapers tended to make him a grand tribune of the people.

Under such circumstances the Republicans in Congress after 1863 attempted less frequently and less successfully than before to challenge the President's assumed constitutional position. Some Peace Democrats or so-called Copperheads continued to denounce his position as tyrannical and unconstitutional, but what they really opposed was the government's basic policy of restoring the Union by military force. Most congressmen, however, were willing to support the President's effective leadership, particularly after his re-election in November 1864. This acquiescence in presidential control was well illustrated early in 1865, when a majority of Congress declined to revive the Radicals' reconstruction program, which had been blocked by Lincoln's pocket veto of the Wade-Davis Bill. It is significant that at no time during the war did Congress pass a law placing important restrictions upon the enormous powers exercised by the President.

The Civil War experience failed to provide a permanently satisfactory solution for the problem of wartime legislative-executive relationships. That Lincoln's assumption of broad powers as Chief Executive and commander in chief did not seriously and irretrievably pervert the constitutional relationship between President and Congress has been due to at least three important factors. First, in times of great stress the people want strong leadership. Presidential domination from 1861 to 1865 was generally approved because of the great emergency of a civil war that shook the nation to its very foundations. The outcome of the war fairly guaranteed the nation against a recurrence of that experience. Second, in times of peace presidential domination is possible only with an exceptionally strong president and a relatively weak, divided, or discredited Congress. For a generation after Lincoln, Congress was relatively stronger than the Chief Executive and thus dominated national policy. Both of these factors became operative almost immediately upon Andrew Johnson's accession to the Presidency in 1865. Third, in the war emergencies of 1917 and 1941 Presidents Wilson and Roosevelt had already established themselves as unquestioned leaders of their party and were promptly granted by Congress ample authority to cope with any foreseeable contingency.

THE LEGAL NATURE OF THE WAR

A second major constitutional issue persisted throughout the war and beyond: Was the conflict basically an insurrection, a rebellion, or an international war? This was an important question, since a variety of legal rights and responsibilities hinged upon the answer. An insurrection is legally construed to be an organized and armed uprising for public political purposes; it may seek to overthrow the government, or it may seek merely to suppress certain laws or to alter administrative practice. A rebellion in general is considered to have a much more highly developed political and military organization than an insurrection; in international law it conveys belligerent status. Generally such belligerent status implies that the belligerent government is attempting by war to free itself from the jurisdiction of the parent state, that it has an organized *de facto* government, that it is in control of at least some territory, and that it has sufficient proportions to render the issue of the conflict in doubt. An international war, on the other hand, is one between two or more independent states who are recognized members of the family of nations.

In international law the rights of parties to an armed conflict vary greatly with their status. Insurgents have a very limited status; they are not mere pirates or bandits, but their activities do not constitute "war" in the *de jure* sense, and they cannot claim against neutrals the privileges of the laws of war. A full rebellion, on the other hand, is a "war" so far as international law is concerned and the rebel government possesses all the belligerent rights of a fully recognized international state, toward both neutrals and the parent state. Needless to say, a parent state may attempt by force to suppress either an insurrection or a rebellion. In domestic law rebels may be criminals in the eyes of the parent state, and answerable to its courts if their movement fails. Thus under the United States Constitution insurrection and rebellion constitute treason, for which the laws provide severe penalties.

The Southern secessionists took the position that the armed conflict was an international war between the United States and the Confederate States of America. The Confederates believed that secession had been constitutional and that they had not only a *de facto* government entitled to full belligerent rights but also a *de jure* government whose independence and sovereignty should be recognized by foreign powers. In their hope of winning the war the Southerners counted heavily upon the aid and the intervention of foreign nations and they were bitterly disappointed when little aid was forthcoming. Even after the collapse of the Confederacy all true Southerners held that the struggle had been a "War between the States."

The official position of the Union government was that secession was a constitutional impossibility and nullity, and hence that the so-called Confederates were engaged in an insurrection against their lawful government. When the Confederates fired upon Fort Sumter, President Lincoln proclaimed on April 15, 1861, that the execution of federal laws was being obstructed "by combinations too powerful to be suppressed by the ordinary course of judicial proceedings." Therefore he called for militia to suppress the insurrection, in much the same way that Washington had done in the Whisky Rebellion of 1794. Both Congress and Supreme Court later supported Lincoln's theory of the war, even though the war attained enormous proportions.

In harmony with this insurrection theory the Union government throughout the war was meticulously careful to avoid any act that even suggested official recognition of the Confederacy as a *de jure* independent state. At first the United States attempted to deny that the Confederacy possessed even belligerent status. Thus in 1861 the State Department objected strongly to foreign powers granting belligerent rights to the Confederacy. Throughout the war the Lincoln administration invariably maintained that no peace terms could be considered unless they were premised upon the legal nonexistence of the Confederacy and the complete submission of the "rebels" to Union authority. In theory Union spokesmen commonly insisted that they were dealing only with the "pretended government" of the "so-called Confederate States of America."

In practice, however, the Union government was very soon impelled to concede belligerent rights to the Confederates. The impotency of Buchanan's administration had permitted Southern resistance to federal authority to become too extensive and powerful to be treated as mere insurrection. At the outbreak of hostilities Lincoln proclaimed a blockade of Southern ports, an act which according to international law virtually recognized the belligerency of the Confederacy. Soon afterward the Lincoln administration abandoned its declared purpose of treating Confederate seamen as pirates. Threats of reprisal upon captured Unionists as well as humanitarian considerations induced the government to treat all captives as prisoners of war.

After initial protests the United States acquiesced in the recognition by foreign nations of the belligerent status of the Confederate government. In short, practical considerations led the Union government to treat the Confederates as belligerents, even though it still refused to recognize their belligerency in any direct, formal manner.

Congress agreed fully with the President that the United States could claim against the Confederates both sovereign rights and those rights arising out of the international law of war. This double status greatly influenced federal laws and policies. For example, Congress enacted a new treason law providing severe punishment for all those found guilty of supporting the rebellion, while other congressional acts held such persons to be public enemies.

The Supreme Court also sustained this dual status for the Confederates. In this connection the most important decision was in the Prize Cases, decided in March 1863, involving the legality of the capture of neutral ships and cargoes. These seizures occurred soon after Lincoln had issued his proclamations of blockade of Confederate ports on April 19 and 27, 1861, and before Congress had formally recognized the existence of war. In upholding the legality of the captures, Justice Robert Grier declared for the Court that it would and must accept the President's decision that the armed insurgents had become so formidable by April 19, 1861, that they must be accorded belligerent status. "A civil war," he asserted, "is never solemnly declared; it becomes such by its accidents—the number, power, and organization of the persons who originate and carry it on. . . . It is not the less a civil war, with belligerent parties in hostile array, because it may be called an 'insurrection' by one side, and the insurgents be considered as rebels and traitors." Therefore the Court held that as far as foreign nationals were concerned the conflict was a civil war, fought according to the laws of nations, with both sides possessed of belligerent rights and responsibilities. In subsequent decisions the Court maintained the same position.

While the war from a military standpoint was between belligerents, in constitutional theory the insurrection doctrine remained of great importance during both the war and the reconstruction period. Many war acts and words of the Unionists were based upon the assumption that they were fighting to suppress a gigantic insurrection, even though Union officials often spoke of the war as a rebellion. At the conclusion of the war no peace treaty was drawn up. Instead the subjugated Confederates threw themselves upon the mercy of the Union government, which thus was free to develop a reconstruction program premised upon the insurrection theory.

PUNISHMENT OF TREASON

The Union government's inconsistent rebellion theory is clearly evident in the handling of the questions of treason and confiscation of property. The Constitution defined and limited treason to levying war against the United States or adhering to their enemies and giving them aid and comfort. Thus any participation in insurrection or rebellion against the federal government constituted treason. Congress was authorized to declare the punishment of treason, but no attainder of treason should work corruption of blood or forfeiture except during the life of the person attainted. Therefore the only constitutional method of procedure against traitors was by judicial conviction under treason statutes passed by Congress. Accordingly, in 1790 Congress had passed a law against treason, providing the death penalty for anyone convicted. Though no one had ever been executed for treason against the United States, this law was still operative in 1861.

The nature and scope of the Civil War soon demonstrated the practical impossibility of enforcing the existing treason law against Confederates. Several million Southern people were adhering to the "rebellion," while hundreds of thousands of them were actually bearing arms against the United States. As explained above, for practical and humanitarian reasons the captured soldiers and sailors had to be treated as prisoners of war. Few civilian Confederates were captured during the early phases of the war, and with sympathetic witnesses and juries the possibility of conviction for treason seemed remote even where the federal courts were open. Moreover, many persons in the border states and in the North were engaging in disloyal activities which did not amount to full treason.

As a consequence Congress enacted special legislation to adapt the punishment of treason to the emergency. The Conspiracies Act of July 31, 1861, provided heavy fine and imprisonment for anyone convicted of conspiring to overthrow the United States government, or to levy war against the United States, or to oppose by force the authority of the government, or to interfere forcibly with the execution of federal laws, or to seize property of the United States. Technically this act dealt with conspiracy and not with treason. Yet critics of the measure were partly right in contending that it nullified existing constitutional law prohibiting "constructive treason." However, they overlooked the fact that new emergencies often call for new statutes or new construction laws.

On July 17, 1862, at a time when recent military failures were causing great anxiety throughout the North, Congress enacted a more comprehensive war measure known as the Treason Act, or more commonly as the Second Confiscation Act. This measure dealt with three important subjects: (1) the punishment of treason and rebellion, (2) the confiscation of enemies' property, and (3) the emancipation of rebels' slaves. For treason the penalty was henceforth to be either death or heavy fine and imprisonment at the discretion of the court. Engaging in or aiding rebellion against the United States was declared to be distinct from the crime of treason with a separate penalty of fine and imprisonment. Reflecting the rising emancipationist sentiment, the act provided also for freeing the slaves of anyone convicted of either treason or rebellion.

The chief political purpose of the new Treason Act was to induce the Lincoln administration to prosecute more vigorously those engaged in rebellion by softening the penalty. In general this purpose was not fulfilled, for the Attorney General and his subordinates pursued a cautious and lenient policy of enforcement. Grand juries brought numerous indictments for treason, especially in the border states, but few cases were prosecuted to completion. Instead, the district attorney usually continued the indictment from one term of court to another and eventually had the case dismissed. It is significant that despite the vast extent of rebellion, the government did not execute a single person for treason or even carry out completely a sentence of fine or imprisonment.

This wide gap between the treason statutes and their enforcement persisted after the cessation of hostilities in 1865. Legally and physically it was then possible to proceed against adherents of the Confederacy, and radical Unionists demanded the punishment of at least a few leading "traitors" as examples. Many Confederates were indicted, and several leaders were placed in confinement, but none was convicted and punished. Even Jefferson Davis, former President of the Confederacy and in the North a veritable symbol of high treason, escaped official punishment, although his "treason" case dragged through the federal courts for more than three years.

From a legal standpoint the Lincoln administration's cautious enforcement policy was open to criticism. Prompt and impartial application of criminal law is fundamental to civil rights. Yet from the standpoint of practical administration the government's policy worked reasonably well under difficult circumstances. Judicial punishment of treason is necessary and proper in case of a few individuals, but it is impractical when applied to vast numbers in an organized rebellion. Nevertheless the government had to preserve a semblance of enforcement, since much of its war policy was based upon the assumption that it was proceeding against rebellious citizens.

CONFISCATION

Closely interwoven with the punishment of treason was the question of confiscation of private property. Confiscation of enemy property was an ancient war usage, and such outstanding American legal authorities as Marshall, Story, and Kent had maintained that international law sanctioned a nation's right to confiscate. Yet by 1861 Western nations had largely abandoned the practice. Moreover, the United States Constitution provided safeguards for citizens' property rights by prohibiting such devices as bills of attainder and deprivation of property without due process of law.

In practice confiscation soon became an important element in congressional war policy. Following the Confederate enactment of a sequestration law, Congress on August 6, 1861, passed a statute authorizing the confiscation of all property actually used for "insurrectionary purposes" or "in aid of the rebellion." This act, of course, touched only a very small amount of enemy property, and in its enforcement most military and civil officials were careful to respect the individual property rights of Southerners. In a reaction against this lenient policy, which many radicals blamed for early military failure, congressional leaders demanded a more rigorous and comprehensive confiscation law. Such a law they secured in the Second Confiscation Act, which, it will be recalled, provided for the confiscation of property. This act provided for immediate forfeiture to the United States of all property of officials of the Confederate government and a similar forfeiture after sixty days' warning of the property of all other persons supporting the "rebellion." By this means Congress hoped to shorten the war and to make the "rebels" pay much of its cost.

The Second Confiscation Act was a curious mixture of constitutional and international law; yet it disregarded some of the restrictions ordinarily associated with both. Although the intent of the measure was to punish rebellious citizens by confiscating their property, there was no provision for the trial and conviction of those accused of rebellion. Instead confiscation was to be a separate and distinct action *in rem*, not against the property of traitors but against the property of enemies. Supporting this position, Senator Lyman Trumbull of Illinois, one of the sponsors of the measure, summarized the majority view of the power of Congress over Confederates with the words, "We may treat them as traitors, and we may treat them as enemies."

President Lincoln believed that certain features of the measure were unconstitutional and prepared a veto message. He said that the combination of punishment of treason and confiscation of property constituted, in effect, forfeiture of property beyond the life of the guilty party. Apparently assuming that the confiscation features were supposed to be based upon constitutional law, he objected also to the forfeiture of property "without a conviction of the supposed criminal, or a personal hearing given him in any proceeding." Congress, in an explanatory joint resolution, removed the President's first objection but not the second. He thereupon reluctantly signed the bill, although he never sympathized with its methods. In practice confiscation never attained the importance that its sponsors had expected; it was limited largely to rebel-owned property located in the loyal states where the federal courts were open.

The Supreme Court did not pass upon the Second Confiscation Act until after the war, and then the justices proved to be as badly divided on the measure's constitutionality as the President and Congress had been. In *Miller v. United States* (1871) a Virginia "rebel" challenged the decree of the federal district court of Michigan, declaring his stock in Michigan railroad corporations forfeited by default. The Court, relying upon the double-status doctrine already affirmed in the Prize Cases, confirmed the right of the United

States to confiscate Miller's property as an exercise of the war power. The majority judges admitted that the treason sections of the act were based upon the United States' sovereign right or upon internal or municipal law and that under such law Congress lacked authority to disregard the judicial safeguard of the Constitution and of the Fifth and Sixth Amendments. But the opinion insisted that the confiscation sections of the act were based upon "an undoubted belligerent right," and therefore were constitutional.

The Court's position was open to objection. Three justices dissented, two of them on the ground that the forfeitures were punitive in character, being based upon Congress' municipal power and not on its war power; that accordingly condemnations must depend upon owner's personal guilt; and that therefore a judgment based on mere default amounted to a denial of due process of law. Although this exact issue was not again to come before the Court, the dissenting argument is in essential harmony with recent interpretation of related issues.

The Confiscation Act was Congress' unique manifestation of a natural determination to crush the rebellion by any means within constitutional or international law, or a combination of the two. It was one of those extreme measures which a nation adopts when its very existence hangs in the balance.

FEDERAL CENTRALIZATION OF AUTHORITY

Between 1801 and 1861 an irregular but considerable decentralization of constitutional and political authority had taken place in the United States. During these years population had increased rapidly and had spread over a vast area. The states had more than doubled in number, and their governments, rather than the federal government, had assumed most of the new governmental functions that had evolved. In general during this period all three branches of the federal government had interpreted federal powers somewhat narrowly, with the result that the people looked to the state governments rather than to Washington for the performance of many positive governmental services. Relatively little federal administrative machinery had been developed. States' rights tendencies were strong in the free as well as the slave states. Consequently in 1861 the loyal state governments naturally assumed that they would play important roles in the prosecution of the war.

In 1861 and 1862 the governors and other state officials to a large degree took the lead in mobilizing the nation for war. They not only raised the militia called for initially by the President, but they also directed the recruiting of most of the regiments of federal volunteers. In addition the states often provided the troops with equipment, subsistence, and transportation. Such state governors as John A. Andrew of Massachusetts, Oliver P. Morton of Indiana, and Richard Yates of Illinois were more energetic and more efficient than Secretary of War Simon Cameron in mobilizing troops. Before Congress met in July 1861, more than a quarter of a million men had been mobilized, largely by state initiative.

Inevitably friction and confusion arose between federal and state authority in these military matters. Federal recruiting officers sometimes clashed with governors over the raising of troops and the appointing of officers. Early in the war some states actually competed with the War Department in the purchase of arms and equipment. The President had the unpleasant task of trying to placate conflicting parties and to co-ordinate their activities. This task was made somewhat easier by the fact that at the time practically all free-state governors were Republicans, but it was also made more difficult by the fact that the governors under our federal system are not constitutional subordinates of the President, even in the raising and control of troops. It was conflicting authority of this kind as well as the decline of volunteering which caused Congress and the administration eventually to turn to a national conscription policy.

A different type of controversy arose in April 1861 between the federal government and the border slave states, especially Kentucky and Maryland. Many people, perhaps a majority, in those states accepted the Calhounian doctrine of state sovereignty, yet they wanted neither secession nor war. In Kentucky the governor emphatically refused to supply troops to the federal government and the state senate formally declared that the state would maintain an armed neutrality, neither severing connection with the Union nor taking up arms for either side. This attempt to take a middle position was not only impractical but was also contrary to both the letter and the spirit of the Constitution. The power of neutrality is an integral part of the war-making power, which is specifically and necessarily assigned to the federal government.

At about the same time the state authorities of Maryland sought to prevent the passage of federal troops through the state on the way to the national capital. This action was flagrantly unconstitutional; for, as Marshall had pointed out in *McCulloch v. Maryland*, in matters which belong to the United States federal authority must be supreme and unimpeded by state interference. Within a brief time the Lincoln administration, by employing a waiting policy in

Kentucky and a firm policy in Maryland, was able to maintain federal authority in both states and to secure a considerable degree of co-operation from state authorities.

Another case where national authority definitely won out over states' rights was in the partition of Virginia. The western portion of the state was geographically a part of the Ohio Valley, and for many years before 1861 the people there had disagreed politically and economically with the eastern Virginians. When the Virginia convention adopted an ordinance of secession, the westerners refused to be bound thereby, and in June 1861 organized a new Unionist or "restored" government for Virginia, which was recognized for most purposes by the federal government. This Unionist state government, meeting at Wheeling, authorized the western counties to frame a constitution for a new state of West Virginia; this, in turn, was ratified by the voters. Thus in an irregular and somewhat fictitious manner the "state" of Virginia complied with the constitutional requirement of giving consent to the erection of a new state within its borders.

On December 31, 1862, Congress passed an act providing for the admission of West Virginia as a state as soon as it had provided for the gradual abolition of slavery. During the congressional debate on the subject the Republican majority took the position that the admission would aid in suppressing the rebellion, while conservative opponents contended that the real state of Virginia had not given its consent to partition. Although the Cabinet also was divided over the constitutionality of the act, Lincoln reluctantly signed it, believing then, as he did throughout the war, that the determining consideration should be whether the measure aided or hampered the restoration of the Union. On June 20, 1863, West Virginia officially became a separate state.

The Supreme Court in *Virginia v. West Virginia* (1870) indirectly declared the process of separation to be constitutional by affirming the existence of "a valid agreement between the two States consented to by Congress." Thus did the federal government's policy of broad constitutional construction, in conjunction with what was virtually a revolution within a state, effect the partitioning of one of the oldest and largest states in the Union.

During 1862 Congress and the administration came to realize that greater nationalization of governmental authority was necessary for the effective prosecution of the war. Two years of unwarranted decentralization and reliance upon state performance of certain war functions had proved unsatisfactory and may have prolonged the war. Gradually and reluctantly, therefore, the federal government took to itself the performance of truly national functions by adopting nationalizing measures and policies. Thus by 1863 the government of the United States was exercising authority commensurate with that intended by the framers of the Constitution, having regained much that had been dissipated during two generations dominated by states' rights doctrines and practices.

In order to finance the war the federal government had to resume definite control of the important fields of currency and banking, which had been left largely to the states since the 1830's. Between February 1862 and March 1863 Congress authorized the issuance of $450,000,000 in fiat money or greenbacks, which were made legal tender for both public and private debts. Even more significant was the enactment of the National Banking Act of February 25, 1863, with important modifications made by new laws in 1864 and 1865. Although these measures did not create a centralized national bank like those of 1791 and 1817, they did provide for an extensive system of national banking institutions, which under federal supervision could issue banknotes based largely upon United States bonds and guaranteed by the federal government. The 1865 law, which levied a 10 per cent tax on all state banknotes, soon had the intended effect of driving these notes out of existence and leaving a uniform national currency based fundamentally upon the credit of the United States.

After a lapse of some thirty years the federal government once more assumed a prominent role in the field of internal improvements and transportation. In pursuance of an act of Congress, the President in May 1862 took official possession of all railroads and directed that all railroad companies and their employees hold themselves in readiness for the transportation of troops and munitions at the order of military authorities. Only in a very few instances did the government take more than nominal control of Northern railroads, but through this act it did obtain effective co-operation from the roads. In the South the federal government, through the military authorities, actually repaired and operated many miles of railroads.

Congress took steps also to sponsor the construction of new railroad lines. In March 1863 a select committee of the House, in order to provide more adequately for the transportation of military forces and supplies, recommended that the federal government charter a special railroad line between Washington and New York to which the government would give its patronage and over which it would enjoy priorities and have extensive powers of regulation. Constitutional and political opposition to the federal government taking such a direct part in the railroad business, plus some effective lobbying by competing railroad lines, prevented the enactment of the measure. However, the Pacific Railroad Act of 1862, supplemented by another act in 1864, enabled the federal government to charter two corporations to build a railroad from Omaha to the Pacific and to grant them large tracts of land and extensive loans. This action proved to be only the beginning of the active part that the government was to play in rail transportation after the Civil War.

In general, however, the federal government attempted little or no regulation of private enterprise such as became so important in the war emergencies of the twentieth century. Congress encouraged great industrial and agricultural expansion by the enactment of increasingly high protective tariff rates and by paying high prices for food, clothing, munitions, and other military supplies. But there were no price ceilings, no rationing, and practically no governmental controls over agriculture, commerce, industry, or labor.

COMPULSORY MILITARY SERVICE

The gigantic military task of conquering the Confederacy forced the federal government to re-examine the place of military forces under the Constitution. Practically no one seriously questioned the traditional American principle that the military authority is always subject to ultimate civilian control. The Constitution, in Article I, Section 8, gave Congress blanket power "to raise and support armies" and to provide for calling forth, organizing, arming, disciplining, and governing the militia when employed in federal service. By law and precedent three forms of military organization were available in 1861: the regular army, United States volunteers called into service during emergencies for limited periods, and the militia, which was in a degree both a state and a federal organization. In the War of 1812 and the Mexican War all troops had been raised by voluntary recruiting, although in the earlier struggle conscription had been seriously considered by Congress.

In April 1861 Lincoln called for 75,000 militia under the law of 1795, but the great bulk of the army raised in 1861, and in fact throughout the war, consisted of federal volunteers. When the supply of volunteers seemed inadequate, Congress, in July 1862, enacted a new Militia Act, which provided that the militia should include all male citizens between the ages of 18 and 45 and authorized the President to issue regulations to cover any defects in state laws for employment of the militia. With no more specific basis than this provision, the President in August 1862 assigned quotas to the states and ordered a draft through the state governors to fill any unfilled quotas. Under this curious mixture of federal and state authority the first men were conscripted in 1862. The chief constitutional significance of this entire procedure lies in the small amount of statutory law considered necessary to transform the old obligation for militia duty into compulsory federal military service.

The President and Congress soon realized that the militia could not be made into an effective national army and on March 3, 1863, enacted a comprehensive conscription law. All able-bodied male citizens between 20 and 45, and foreigners who had declared their intention to become citizens, were "to constitute the national forces" and were declared liable for military service upon call by the President. No reference was made to the militia, and a complete federal system of enrollment and administration was established. Any person failing to report after due service of notice was to be considered a deserter, and any person convicted of resisting the draft or of aiding or encouraging the same was subject to fine and imprisonment.

Such a drastic departure from previous American experience was bound to encounter serious opposition on constitutional as well as political grounds. In regions where pro-Southern sentiment was strong, resistance to the draft took place in various forms, and federal troops were sometimes needed for enforcement. The Conscription Act was repeatedly denounced as un-American and unconstitutional in Congress, in the courts, in the press, in the public forums, and on the streets. From New York, where violent antidraft riots raged for four days in July 1863, Governor Horatio Seymour wrote to the President, declaring bluntly that conscription was unconstitutional and requesting its suspension. Except for minor interruptions, however, the draft was applied when necessary to meet quotas.

The constitutionality of the Conscription Act never came before the Supreme Court, but it was challenged in some of the lower courts without decisive results. Of all the constitutional arguments in support of conscription perhaps the most forceful was made by the President himself.[2] In legal logic that was reminiscent of John Marshall at his best, Lincoln declared:

---

[2] His views, however, were expressed in a paper which was not published until years afterward.

It is the first instance, I believe, in which the power of Congress to do a thing has ever been questioned in a case when the power is given by the Constitution in express terms. . . . The case simply is, the Constitution provides that the Congress shall have power to raise and support armies; and by this act the Congress has exercised the power to raise and support armies. This is the whole of it. It is a law made in literal pursuance of this part of the United States Constitution. . . . The Constitution gives Congress the power, but it does not prescribe the mode, or expressly declare who shall prescribe it. In such case Congress must prescribe the mode, or relinquish the power. There is no alternative. . . . If the Constitution had prescribed a mode, Congress could and must follow that mode; but, as it is, the mode necessarily goes to Congress, with the power expressly given. The power is given fully, completely, unconditionally. It is not a power to raise armies if State authorities consent; nor if the men to compose the armies are entirely willing; but it is a power to raise and support armies given to Congress by the Constitution without an if.

Opponents of conscription usually resorted to states' rights and strict-constructionist arguments and emphasized the distinction between the militia and the army. Many believed with Chief Justice Taney that although both federal and state governments exercised sovereign powers over the same territory and the same people at the same time, each was altogether independent of the other within its own sphere of action. They argued that the militia was primarily a state institution, and therefore the extent to which the Conscription Act interfered with this state institution by bringing state militiamen and state civil officials within the draft constituted a violation of the Constitution.

The preponderance of logic as well as legal and public opinion supported the constitutionality of conscription. The power to raise armies as well as the power to declare war is expressly given to Congress without qualification as to means, and conscription may reasonably be considered a "necessary and proper" means to "carry into effect" these powers. To restrict federal powers within the narrow limits proposed by draft opponents would in effect have denied the United States the assured power to suppress the rebellion. In fact many who opposed conscription also denied that the federal government had the constitutional power to preserve the Union by force of arms. Ironically, the Confederate Constitution copied the federal Constitution exactly in conferring upon Congress powers for raising troops, and the Confederate Congress adopted conscription before the federal Congress did. Thus the experience of the Civil War established a strong precedent for conscription, although its constitutionality was judicially open to question until 1918, when the Supreme Court upheld it unanimously.[3]

EMANCIPATION

The most revolutionary result of the Civil War, and one of the most significant, was the emancipation of Negro slaves. Emancipation was not one of the original war issues, and it only gradually became a major issue. In 1860 very few Northern people believed that the federal government had the constitutional authority to abolish or even to interfere with slavery in the Southern states. Some abolitionists in fact denounced the Constitution because it protected the institution of slavery. Although the Republican party was organized to prevent the spread of slavery into new territory, its national platform and leaders expressly denied either the intent or the federal power to interfere with slavery in the states. Moreover, most authorities on international law held that even during time of war a belligerent did not possess the legal right to emancipate the enemy's slaves except as they were used for military purposes.

As the preceding chapter has explained, Northern congressmen in the early months of 1861 had repeatedly tried to reassure the Southerners that Congress would not and legally could not interfere with slavery where it then existed. It will be recalled that in February of that year Congress had actually adopted and submitted to the states a proposed constitutional amendment which would have prohibited Congress from ever having the power, even by future amendment, to abolish or to interfere with slavery within the states. Legally this was the ultimate in congressional self-denial on the subject, and it was proposed in a futile attempt to prevent the disruption of the Union by secession. Even as late as July 1861 Congress had adopted almost unanimously the Crittenden and Johnson Resolutions, which declared that the war was not waged for any purpose of conquest or subjugation or of overthrowing or interfering with slavery or other rights of the states.

Until well after the outbreak of war, Lincoln, despite his famous "house divided" doctrine, persistently denied that he had any intention of interfering with slavery in the South. In his inaugural address he took special pains to reassure Southern and border-state

---

[3] See p. 624.

slaveholders on this point. Even after Fort Sumter the President called the nation to arms in order to preserve the Union and maintain national authority, and not to interfere with slavery. Largely to bolster the strength of unionists in both the South and the border states Lincoln was careful to keep antislavery political and military leaders from using the war to strike directly at slavery.

The magnitude and bitterness of the war, however, soon produced drastic changes in the attitude of the Northern people toward slavery. Led by the antislavery forces, more and more people came to believe that slavery was the real cause of secession and disunion and therefore that it must be destroyed before a peaceful Union could be re-established. Thus to both the people and the government the abolition of slavery gradually became an integral part of the Northern war program to preserve the Union.

In general, the Republican majority in Congress was more anxious than the President to undermine the constitutional position of slavery. In April 1862 Congress abolished slavery in the District of Columbia, with compensation for loyal owners, and in June it abolished slavery in all the territories without compensating slaveholders. Thus did the first Republican Congress repudiate the Dred Scott doctrine and assert its authority in two previously debatable fields.

Congress' first serious effort to strike at the heart of slavery—to destroy the institution of slavery in slaveholding states—was the emancipation section of the Second Confiscation Act of July 1862. This provided that all slaves of persons engaged in rebellion or in any way giving aid thereto, who should be captured or escape to the Union lines, "shall be deemed captives of war, and shall be forever free of their servitude, and not again held as slaves." Although this emancipation feature was considered an important part of the Radical program for a more vigorous prosecution of the war, there were no provisions whatever for making it effective. To determine the facts regarding which slaves should be freed would be essentially a judicial function, for which no provision was made. The President made no serious effort to enforce this section, largely because he was then developing his own program of emancipation.

Lincoln's favorite plan for the permanent solution of the slavery problem was the gradual emancipation of slaves by voluntary action of the states, with federal compensation to slaveholders, and possibly with voluntary colonization of freedmen outside the United States. He strongly believed that this program fairly recognized the constitutional rights of states and the property rights of slaveholders, and that because it was a comparatively reasonable plan it might appeal to the South and thus provide a means of shortening the war.

Upon the President's recommendation Congress in April 1862 passed a joint resolution declaring that "the United States ought to co-operate with any State which may adopt gradual abolishment of slavery, giving to such State pecuniary aid" for compensation. Lincoln strongly urged the representatives from the border slave states to take the lead in adopting compensated emancipation, but without success. In his annual message to Congress in December 1862, after he had issued his preliminary emancipation proclamation, he again discussed compensated emancipation in all its aspects and eloquently argued for its prompt adoption. Early in 1863 each house of Congress passed a different bill providing compensation for the loyal slaveholders of Missouri upon emancipation of their slaves, but the bills were never harmonized and Congress never again seriously considered the proposition. Lincoln, however, did not abandon his hope for compensated emancipation, even after events had propelled more drastic solutions into the forefront.

In his capacity of commander in chief, Lincoln on September 22, 1862, issued a preliminary proclamation of emancipation. He proclaimed that the war would continue to be prosecuted for the restoration of the Union but that in all areas where the people were still in rebellion on January 1, 1863, slavery would be abolished immediately and completely.

Since the Confederates continued in rebellion, Lincoln on January 1 issued his definitive proclamation, "sincerely believed to be an act of justice, warranted by the Constitution upon military necessity." It designated the states and parts of states which were still in rebellion and declared that all persons held as slaves therein "are, and henceforth shall be, free; and that the Executive Government of the United States, including the military and naval authorities thereof, will recognize and maintain the freedom of said persons." The freedmen were also declared to be acceptable for certain types of military duty.

An extensive controversy raged at the time over the constitutionality and the legal effect of the proclamation, and no complete agreement has ever been reached. Opponents of emancipation, North and South, condemned the proclamation as entirely unconstitutional and as a gross usurpation of power on the part of the President. They argued that the federal government had no authority over slavery in the states under any circumstances and that the laws of war did not warrant such a blanket destruction of private property.

Lincoln and his supporters fully realized that the only constitutional justification of the proclamation was in the war powers of the President. He considered liberation of the enemy's slaves an appropriate and necessary military measure coming within the laws of war. "I felt that measures otherwise unconstitutional," he later declared, "might become lawful by becoming indispensable to the preservation of the Constitution through the preservation of the nation."

It is difficult today to reach a definitive conclusion on this issue. There is no real parallel in the more recent experiences of Western nations. The Supreme Court never rendered a decision involving the proclamation's legality, although some believed that the Court's upholding of Lincoln's proclamation of blockade in the Prize Cases gave support by implication. At least it is certain that the Emancipation Proclamation was part and parcel of the expansiveness of Lincoln's theory of the presidential war power and of his belief that his primary duty was to preserve the Union by any means at his disposal.

The Emancipation Proclamation was followed by a period of doubt and confusion regarding the legal status of the freed Negroes. The Proclamation purported to free many slaves, but it did not abolish the law of slavery throughout the Confederate States. In practice most Negroes continued as slaves until their regions were conquered by Union armies. Since slavery existed on the basis of state law, new laws were needed to define the new status of Negroes. Moreover, the proclamation did not apply to the border states or to those areas of Confederate states already conquered. The antislavery men in these states were soon working for emancipation by state action, and by early 1865 Missouri, Maryland, and Tennessee had abolished slavery.

THE THIRTEENTH AMENDMENT

To make emancipation uniform throughout the nation and to eliminate all doubts as to its constitutionality, the emancipationists advocated an amendment to the federal Constitution. The Senate adopted the proposed Thirteenth Amendment on April 8, 1864, but it was not until January 31, 1865, that the required two-thirds vote could be mustered in the House. As submitted to the states, the amendment prohibited slavery and involuntary servitude, except as a punishment for crime, within the United States or any place subject to their jurisdiction, and empowered Congress to enforce it.

The constitutionality as well as the wisdom of the amendment was elaborately discussed. It was the first example of the use of the amending process to accomplish a nationwide substantive reform, as distinguished from procedural reform or limitations upon federal power. Opponents of emancipation argued that the amending power did not extend to interference in the domestic institutions of the states. For the central government thus to invade the field unquestionably reserved by the Constitution to the states would produce a revolutionary alteration of the basic American federal system. It would be equivalent to the adoption of a new constitution, for which the unanimous consent of the states would be necessary, not merely the three-fourths required for an amendment.

Though superficially plausible, this argument is untenable. Article V, containing the amending process, is an integral part of the Constitution, agreed to by all the states at the time of ratification. Except for the restriction concerning the equal vote of the states in the Senate, all parts of the Constitution are subject to the amending power. The Constitution expressly declares that an amendment properly made becomes "valid to all Intents and Purposes, as Part of this Constitution," and has as much force as any other provision. Therefore, the amending power is equivalent to the constitution-making power and as such is above the authority of the federal government or the individual states. Through it, the American people express their ultimate sovereign power.

The validity of the ratification of the Thirteenth Amendment was open to challenge. The votes of 27 of the 36 states were required for ratification; yet there were only 25 states aside from the former Confederate states, of which Kentucky and Delaware, which still had slavery, rejected the amendment. Hence four "seceded" states were necessary for ratification, and eight were actually counted in the official proclamation of December 18, 1865, which declared the amendment in force. These Southern ratifications were made by provisional governments set up under President Johnson's plan of reconstruction, which Congress later refused to recognize as valid governments within the Union. Yet Congress was willing to consider them competent for ratification of the Constitution, one of the many anomalies of reconstruction. In any event the Thirteenth Amendment definitely ended the institution of slavery, which had affected so seriously the previous constitutional development of the United States.

IMPAIRMENT OF CIVIL RIGHTS

The fifth of the major constitutional issues raised by the war concerned the government's authority to impair civil rights in wartime. Two basic factors made this issue particularly prominent. First was the prevailing Anglo-American concept of the "rule of law"—that the officers of government are always subject to the law and prohibited from exercising arbitrary authority over citizens. The peaceful conditions which had prevailed except for a few brief periods since the adoption of the Constitution had accustomed the American people to a policy of noninterference with civil rights by the federal government. There had been very few occasions for suspension of the habeas corpus privilege, censorship of the press, or the establishment of martial law. There was in America no tradition or important precedent for military rule or summary procedure even for a war emergency.

The second factor was the extensive disloyalty that prevailed in the Union states, especially in the border states. Many disloyal citizens positively sympathized with the Southerners and were eager to aid their cause. Most of their activities were designed to bring about Union defeat. These included spying, sabotage, recruiting for the enemy, stealing military supplies for potential Confederate invasions of the North, carrying treasonable correspondence, plotting to split the remaining Union states, and otherwise aiding the enemy. A larger number of wavering citizens professed loyalty to the Union but openly opposed the government's fundamental policy of suppressing the rebellion by a complete subjugation of the Confederacy. They claimed, unrealistically, that the Union could be restored peaceably by negotiation and blamed the Republican Party for the war. Their activities were generally confined to such actions as discouraging enlistments, aiding desertion, circulating disloyal literature, and denouncing the Lincoln administration and Republicans in general.

Upon the outbreak of hostilities Lincoln decided that existing laws and judicial procedures were inadequate for controlling such extensive disloyal activities. Although the old treason law was broadened by the Conspiracies Act of July 1861 and the new Treason Act of July 1862, the administration made only slight use of treason or conspiracy prosecutions. With a pro-Southern or lukewarm jury, conviction in such a technical judicial proceeding as treason would generally be difficult to obtain. Moreover, many of the disloyal activities could not legally be construed as treason. In the North grand juries often brought indictments for treason or conspiracy, but the usual practice was to keep them on the docket from term to term and eventually to drop them. The district attorneys followed the wishes of the President and the Attorney General in not pressing cases of this kind. Naturally, convictions were very few, and these sentences were seldom if ever fully carried out.

Instead of rigidly enforcing treason statutes, the Lincoln administration developed a policy of dealing with suspected persons through military arrests and the suspension of the privilege of habeas corpus. In the early part of the war this policy was restricted to definite localities specified in presidential proclamations. Its operation was entrusted to the State Department, which directed arrests through an elaborate secret service as well as through federal marshals and military authorities. The national situation was very critical at the time and hundreds of arrests were made. Prisoners were not told why they were arrested, and often the authorities acted without sufficient investigation or evidence to provide a reasonable basis for definite charges. With the habeas corpus privilege suspended, prisoners were held without legal action until the emergency which had led to their arrest had passed. Judges often sought to secure the release of such prisoners, but provost marshals and other military officers were usually under orders to disregard judicial mandates and to resist the execution of writs. This procedure resulted in numerous conflicts between civil and military authorities, with the latter naturally controlling action.

In 1862 the administration both modified and extended its policy. In February the control of arbitrary arrests was transferred to the War Department and the policy was mitigated by establishing a commission to provide for the examination and release of political prisoners. On September 24, however, the President issued a sweeping proclamation declaring that all persons discouraging enlistments, resisting the draft, or "guilty of any disloyal practice affording aid and comfort to rebels . . . shall be subject to martial law, and liable to trial and punishment by courts-martial or military commissions." Further, the habeas corpus privilege was suspended for all persons arrested cr already imprisoned on such charges. Thereafter thousands of citizens suspected of disloyalty were summarily arrested and imprisoned in all parts of the country.

In the actual use of such extraordinary powers the Lincoln administration generally manifested considerable circumspection and leniency. The broad prerogatives assumed and announced in proclamations were not always exercised. Since arrests were often precautionary, designed to prevent violence or interference with military or other governmental activities, many prisoners were released within a short time. Those detained were usually treated without undue harshness.

Lincoln's policy of suspending the privilege of habeas corpus encountered considerable criticism from the bench, including that of Chief Justice Taney in *Ex parte Merryman* (1861). John Merryman, an officer of a Maryland secessionist military organization which had destroyed some railroad bridges, was arrested in May 1861 by order of General Wm. H. Keim, commander of the district, and imprisoned in Fort McHenry. Merryman's petition for a writ of habeas corpus was presented to Taney, who seems to have gone to Baltimore chiefly for the purpose of receiving it in his capacity of circuit judge. Taney issued a writ of habeas corpus directing General Cadwalader, then Merryman's custodian, to produce Merryman in court for judicial examination. In accordance with his military instructions, the general refused to comply but sent a respectful reply indicating the cause of Merryman's arrest and citing the President's suspension of the writ. Taney then attempted to have Cadwalader himself brought into court but without success.

Having failed to secure compliance with the writ, the aged Chief Justice read an opinion vigorously denying the President's right to suspend the writ, and had a copy of it transmitted to the latter. The President's action in the Merryman case and many similar cases, said Taney, was without legal warrant, since the privilege of the writ of habeas corpus could be suspended constitutionally only by act of Congress. Taney argued for exclusive congressional control of suspension of the writ from Marshall's opinion at the time of the Burr conspiracy as well as from the fact that the habeas corpus clause occurs in Article I, Section 9, which deals with the legislative power. The President's only power where the rights of citizens are involved is to take care that the laws "be faithfully carried into execution as they are expounded and adjudged by the co-ordinate branch of the government, to which that duty is assigned by the Constitution." Instead of performing his constitutional duty of assisting the judiciary in enforcing its judgments, the Chief Executive in this case had actually thrust aside the judicial authorities and substituted military government. If such military usurpation was to be permitted, Taney concluded, "the people of the United States are no longer living under a government of laws, but every citizen holds life, liberty and property at the will and pleasure of the army officer in whose military district he may happen to be found."

Although Taney's views were hailed by Southern sympathizers as a sound defense of American civil liberties, they were disapproved by most unionists and refuted by the Lincoln administration. The President in his message to Congress in July 1861 justified the arrest and detention of certain individuals deemed "dangerous to the public safety" because of the inability of the courts to deal adequately with organized rebellion. He answered Taney's challenge for a faithful execution of the laws by arguing that it would be better for the President to violate a single law "to a very limited extent" than to have all laws go unexecuted and "the Government itself to go to pieces" through failure to suppress the rebellion. Lincoln denied, however, that he had violated any law, arguing that since the Constitution permits suspension of the writ of habeas corpus during a rebellion and does not specify which branch of the government is to exercise the suspending power, the President in an emergency must be allowed to use his discretion in the matter. Later Lincoln emphasized the precautionary or preventive purpose of the arbitrary arrests, which were made "not so much for what has been done, as for what probably would be done."

In a more elaborate opinion Attorney General Edward Bates refuted Taney's contention that the President had violated his constitutional duty of executing the laws. The executive, he insisted, was not subordinate to the judiciary, but was one of three coordinate departments of government. Moreover, the President's oath to "preserve, protect, and defend the Constitution" makes it particularly his duty to put down a rebellion since the courts are too weak to do so. Bates cited *Martin V. Mott* [4] (1827) to support the President's discretionary power in the manner of discharging his duty. Therefore, if the President in case of rebellion or insurrection considers the suspension of the habeas corpus privilege necessary for the public safety he may order it on his own authority.

Beneath all the legal arguments lay a fundamental difference in philosophy of government between the President and the Chief Justice. Lincoln strongly believed that the preservation of the Union was of such transcending importance that the federal government should, if necessary, use extraordinary powers, even at the temporary expense of civil liberties, to attain that objective. Taney, on the other hand, apparently considered the dissolution of the Union as less disastrous than the violence and bloodshed which was necessary to preserve it by civil war.

---

[4] See p. 231.

THE HABEAS CORPUS ACT AND IMMUNITY OF
FEDERAL OFFICERS

Through the Habeas Corpus Act of March 3, 1863, Congress attempted to regularize and modify the President's control of political prisoners so that the authority of the courts would be respected without restricting too seriously the executive and military authorities. The President was "authorized to suspend" the habeas corpus privilege and military officers were relieved from the obligation to answer the writ. On the other hand, the Secretaries of State and War were required to furnish lists of political prisoners to the federal courts, and if grand juries found no indictments against them they were to be released upon taking the oath of allegiance. Thus in degree congressional authority and regulations were substituted for executive authority, and judicial procedure rather than executive discretion was made the basis for the detention of prisoners.

The Habeas Corpus Act also contained indemnity sections which granted broad immunity to federal enforcement officers and extended the jurisdiction of federal courts at the expense of state judiciaries. It provided that any order made by or under the authority of the President should be a defense in all courts to any action or prosecution for any search, seizure, arrest, or imprisonment. Provision was also made for the removal of suits of this type from state to federal courts and for imposing a two-year limitation upon the initiation of such suits.

In practice the Habeas Corpus Act seems to have made little difference in the crucial matters of arrest, confinement, and release of prisoners. Not until September 1863 did the President issue a new proclamation basing his suspension of the habeas corpus privilege upon the law of March 3. The executive authorities were negligent also in furnishing the courts with lists of prisoners. Judge Advocate General Joseph Holt ruled that the new law did not apply to prisoners triable by military commissions, a ruling which left the executive department without restraint in all cases where martial law was instituted. Release of political prisoners, therefore, continued to be largely at the discretion of the War Department rather than by federal judges.

With the restoration of peace and normal judicial procedures in the loyal states in 1865, the immunity or indemnity features of the Habeas Corpus Act became important. Many people considered these sections unconstitutional, since they afforded blanket protection to military and civil officers from such prosecution as would normally follow an unwarranted invasion of private rights or an actual injury of persons and property. Beginning in 1865 many individuals previously held on suspicion of disloyalty sued federal officers for false imprisonment. Suits, both civil and criminal, were brought in state courts and efforts were made to prevent them from being transferred to federal courts. In Kentucky, where opposition to the immunity features was most determined, former federal officers were convicted of violating state laws and subjected to fines and imprisonment for such war activities as giving passes to Negroes or impressing horses for pursuit of guerillas. Special state laws were enacted to obstruct the federal law by prohibiting the removal of alleged immunity cases from Kentucky to United States courts. In 1866 Congress attempted to meet such state defiance by supplementary legislation making state judges liable if they proceeded with cases after proper action had been taken to transfer them to the federal courts. Considerable legal confusion persisted in this field for several years, with instances of injustice on both sides.

The immunity and jurisdictional features of the federal law were characteristic of hasty and extreme war legislation and were open to serious objections. Chief among these were the excessive federal jurisdiction conferred, the extraordinary methods of acquiring such jurisdiction, the setting aside of existing judicial remedies for private wrongs, the subjection of state judges to personal damages, the application of a federal statute of limitations to state causes, and the failure to provide any means of relieving those who were injured by the acts of indemnified officers. On these grounds certain state courts declared the law unconstitutional, but the Supreme Court later upheld its constitutionality in *Mitchell v. Clark* (1884). However, later legislation dealing with this subject was to avoid most of the objections that applied to the Civil War law.

MARTIAL LAW AND THE MILLIGAN CASE

The climax in the impairment of civil rights was the institution of martial law and the limited use of military tribunals for the trial of civilians in both border and free states. Since portions of all the border states were at various times during the war occupied by Confederate troops or hostile guerillas, martial law was employed there as an essential means of military security. Moreover, disloyalty to the Union in these areas was so widespread and so violent that the President considered martial law necessary for the preservation of peace and order. Usually martial law was applied in specified limited districts where the situation seemed most serious, but in July 1864 Lincoln put the whole state of Kentucky under martial law. At the time of Lee's invasion of Pennsylvania in 1863, the President, in response to the petitions of many citizens, proceeded to put that area under martial law.

In all these instances, however, actual interference with the civil authorities was generally held to a minimum and the power over citizens entrusted to the military authorities was sparingly used. Political and judicial officers continued to function except as interruption was necessary for the military authorities to preserve order and punish military crimes. In short, the federal government made no effort to carry martial law beyond certain specified objectives considered necessary for the successful prosecution of the war.

More important to constitutional law was the actual trial and conviction of citizens before military tribunals. In regions under martial law military commissions could properly be used for the trial of civilians who had committed offenses of a military character, such as sniping or spying. The vast majority of cases brought before military commissions in the border states were of this general type, and many individuals were convicted and punished, sometimes severely, for such offenses. Little adverse criticism was made at that time, and little has been made since.

A great legal controversy arose, however, when citizens were subjected to military tribunals in regions remote from military operations and where the civil courts were unimpeded by the course of the war. This situation developed during 1863 and 1864, especially in Ohio, Indiana, and Illinois, where many Democrats were so opposed to the administration's new war policies that they were demanding a negotiated peace and obstructing the prosecution of the war. Some of these so-called "Copperheads" were arrested by zealous military commanders for "disloyal practices affording aid and comfort to rebels" and in accordance with the President's proclamation of September 24, 1862, were tried and sentenced by military commissions.

Two of these cases, which attracted nationwide attention, strikingly reveal the effect war may have upon decisions of the Supreme Court. The first case involved Clement L. Vallandigham, a former Democratic congressman of Ohio. In April 1863 General Ambrose Burnside, commanding the military department of Ohio, issued a general order stating that persons declaring sympathy for the enemy would be arrested and punished by military procedure. On May 1,

Vallandigham made one of his public speeches bitterly denouncing the Lincoln administration for needlessly prolonging the war. For this offense he was placed under military arrest and promptly tried by a military commission in Cincinnati, although he strongly denied its jurisdiction. The commission found him guilty of disloyal sentiments with the object of weakening the government and sentenced him to close confinement during the war.

Vallandigham then applied to the judge of the United States Circuit Court for a writ of habeas corpus, which the judge, after the unusual procedure of requesting and receiving a statement from General Burnside, refused to issue. Whereupon the case was carried to the Supreme Court on a motion for a writ of certiorari to review the sentence of the military commission. Vallandigham's attorney argued that the jurisdiction of a military commission did not extend to a citizen who was not a member of the military forces, that the prisoner had been tried on a charge unknown to the law, and that the Supreme Court had the power to review the proceedings of the commission.

In February 1864, in *Ex parte Vallandigham*, the Supreme Court refused to review the case, declaring that its authority, derived from the Constitution and the Judiciary Act of 1789, did not extend to the proceedings of a military commission because the latter was not a court. The Supreme Court, said Justice James Wayne in the official opinion, "cannot without disregarding its frequent decisions and interpretation of the Constitution in respect to its judicial power, originate a writ of certiorari to review or pronounce any opinion upon the proceedings of a military commission." Neither in this case nor in any other during the war did the Court deny or even question officially the President's authority to establish military commissions for the trial of civilians in nonmilitary areas.

A very similar case but one destined to result in quite a different decision was that of L. P. Milligan, who with certain associates was arrested in Indiana on October 5, 1864, by the military commander of the district. A few weeks later Milligan was tried before a military commission at Indianapolis and convicted of conspiracy to release and arm rebel prisoners and to march with these men into Kentucky and Missouri in order to co-operate with rebel forces there for an invasion of Indiana. In comparison with Vallandigham, Milligan had engaged in distinctly subversive or treasonable activities. The commission sentenced him to be hanged on May 18, 1865, but President Andrew Johnson commuted the sentence to life imprisonment. Milligan petitioned the federal circuit court for a writ of habeas corpus, and the judges, disagreeing, certified the question of law to the Supreme Court.

In December 1866, in the midst of the conflict between Congress and President Johnson over reconstruction, the Supreme Court rendered its famous decision in *Ex parte Milligan*, unanimously holding the military commission authorized by the President to have been unlawful. Contrary to the Vallandigham decision, the Court asserted its right to review the action of a military commission and to nullify it if the action was without legal foundation. Since Milligan had not been indicted by a grand jury at the next session of the federal court, the Court held that according to the Habeas Corpus Act of March 1863 the government had no legal right to hold him and that he must be released.

A majority of five justices, with David Davis as their spokesman, chose to state their further opinion that Congress as well as the President was without legal power to institute a military commission to try civilians in areas remote from the actual theater of war, where the civil courts were open. Davis maintained that such a military tribunal violated the safeguards for civil liberties established by the Constitution and the Bill of Rights. "The Constitution of the United States," he declared, "is a law for rulers and people, equally in war and peace."

Davis insisted that Milligan should have been tried by the civil courts in Indiana, which were fully competent to deal with such cases, and that "no usage of war could sanction a military trial there for any offense whatever of a citizen in civil life." Martial law, he declared, might be used in case of invasion, but it cannot arise merely from "a threatened invasion." "The necessity must be actual and present, the invasion real, such as effectually closes the courts and deposes the civil administration. . . . Martial rule can never exist where the courts are open, and in the proper and unobstructed exercise of their jurisdiction. It is also confined to the locality of actual war."

Chief Justice Chase, speaking for a minority of four, dissented from the majority's narrow delimitation of military authority and insisted that "Congress had power, though not exercised, to authorize the Military Commission which was held in Indiana." Congress' constitutional powers to declare war, to raise and support armies, and to make regulations for the military forces, Chase maintained, necessarily encompass "many subordinate and auxiliary powers" and are not abridged by "the fifth or any other amendment." Therefore it cannot be doubted, the Chief Justice concluded, that "in such a time of public danger" as that prevailing in Indiana in October 1864, "Congress had power, under the Constitution, to provide for the organization of a military commission, and for trial by that commission of persons engaged in this conspiracy."

At the time the Milligan decision became part of the continuing debate over the extent of federal powers, and later certain jurists and historians were to consider it an historic landmark in American civil liberties. It proclaimed in sweeping terms that the constitutional rights of citizens would be protected by the federal judiciary against arbitrary or military rule established by either President or Congress, in war as well as in peace. It focused national attention upon what was, potentially at least, the most vulnerable phase of Lincoln's handling of the home front—the tendency to use arbitrary means to deal with disloyalty when regular civil means were available and to act on his own authority when congressional authorization could have been obtained.

It is questionable, however, whether the majority opinion in *Ex parte Milligan* was a realistic approach either to the Civil War experience or in providing for a future contingency of a similar kind. Davis' declaration that the Civil War had demonstrated that military rule in nonmilitary areas was never necessary scarcely coincided with the facts. To be sure, the rebellion might well have been suppressed without resort to martial law in the loyal states, but actually it was not. Lincoln strongly believed that disloyalty in the North might become so violent, unless held in check by military authority, that it would materially bolster Confederate morale and thus jeopardize the Union cause, or at least prolong the war and bring about additional loss of life. Therefore his policy of arbitrary arrests and military trials for suspected citizens was essentially precautionary and in case of civil war perhaps justifiable. Although as commander in chief he felt impelled in such a great crisis to employ military authority to curtail temporarily certain civil rights, he made no attempt to establish a despotic military regime. He did not believe that his policy would subvert the Constitution or permanently impair the rights of citizens, and his belief proved to be correct.

In none of the more recent wars has disloyalty seemed to have been sufficiently prevalent to require the type of arbitrary or military control of citizens employed during the Civil War. In World War II, however, Japanese-American citizens had their civil rights suspended more completely and for less justifiable cause, and with the approval of the Supreme Court.[5]

CONSTITUTIONAL SIGNIFICANCE OF THE CIVIL WAR

The Civil War was one of the great turning points in American constitutional development. Some of the most profound issues that had agitated the American people since winning their independence were now largely settled, while new ones were created or recognized.

The most significant result was the definitive decision as to the nature of the Union under the Constitution. The North's complete military victory destroyed not only the Confederacy but also the doctrine that the Constitution was a compact of sovereign states, each with the right to secede from the Union. The Supreme Court confirmed this military decision in *Texas v. White* (1869), when it declared: "The Constitution, in all its provisions, looks to an indestructible Union, composed of indestructible States." The Constitution was now recognized everywhere as the supreme law of the land, with sovereignty residing in the people of the United States collectively. A unified American nationality gradually became a reality, replacing the intense sectionalism and excessive decentralization of the preceding era. The term "national government" became almost synonymous with "federal government." This development was in harmony with the general growth of nationalism throughout Western civilization, but it had been attained at a terrible price in loss of lives and property and in the destruction of much of the culture of the pre-war South.

The war had four other important constitutional results. First, closely related to the establishment of national supremacy was the marked centralization of authority in the federal government. This national authority was extensively used during the reconstruction period and then was largely neglected for a generation before it was reasserted on a positive and permanent basis during the twentieth century. Second, Lincoln established a precedent for strong presidential leadership in case of a great national crisis, although this also was not to become important again until the twentieth century. Third, the destruction of the institution of slavery eliminated the source of great constitutional conflict, but the postwar status of the freed Negroes was to raise many new issues. Fourth, the Civil War demonstrated that American democracy could fight a gigantic war under the Constitution without critically jeopardizing the basic rights of citizens.

---

[5] See Chapter 29 for a discussion of more recent aspects of this issue.

☆ ☆

Chapter

17

☆ ☆

Reconstruction: The Presidential Phase

THE DESTRUCTION of the Confederacy settled one great constitutional issue—the nature of the Union—but it created additional constitutional issues of critical importance. What was the legal status of the defeated states, and what steps were necessary to restore them to a normal position in the Union? The Constitution, which did not contemplate the possibility of secession, contained no direct answer to either question. The way was thus opened for the formulation of a variety of constitutional theories resting in part upon certain seemingly relevant passages in the Constitution itself, and in part upon differing theoretical observations on the effect of secession and civil war. One theory became the basis for an attempted executive program of reconstruction, while a second group of related theories furnished the foundation of a congressional reconstruction advanced by the so-called Radical Republicans.

PRESIDENTIAL RECONSTRUCTION: THE FIRST PHASE

The first ideas on reconstruction to be given practical expression were those advanced by President Lincoln while the war was still in progress. Lincoln held that secession was null and void *ab initio*, and that the so-called seceded states were therefore still in the Union. He admitted that the Southern states were out of their normal relationship to the other states and the federal government, since they had no loyal governments and were controlled by persons in rebellion against federal authority. But the states, as political entities distinguished from their governments, still were in the Union. Hence all that was necessary for reconstruction was the suppression of actual military rebellion, the creation of loyal state governments by loyal citizens, and the resumption of normal relations with the federal government.

Lincoln assumed that it was the duty of the federal government to assist the states in reconstruction. The justification for this assumption he found in Article IV, Section 4, of the Constitution, by which the United States guaranteed every state a republican form of government. All subsequent reconstruction schemes, by the way, drew upon this somewhat vague constitutional provision as justification for federal controls.

Finally, Lincoln assumed that the President had authority to carry through a competent reconstruction program with little congressional assistance. A principal step in the plan was the suppression of rebellion, already being accomplished under the President's war powers. Lincoln admitted that in practice Congress would have final authority to pass upon presidential reconstruction, since it could seat delegates from Southern states at its discretion. President Andrew Johnson was later to claim that Congress could not lawfully refuse to seat delegates from reconstructed states, but Lincoln did not advance this argument.

Lincoln's plan had two great virtues. It was consistent, for it rested upon the same premise of the nullity of secession upon which the administration had prosecuted the war. And it was simple of execution and promised a rapid restoration of a normally functioning constitutional system. Its great practical weakness was that Congress could destroy it merely by refusing to seat delegates from the reconstructed states.

Presidential reconstruction began while the Civil War was still in progress. In December 1863, more than a year before the war ended, Lincoln issued a proclamation offering a pardon to anyone engaged in rebellion, certain Confederate officials excepted, provided the individual took an oath of loyalty to the United States. The proclamation further declared that whenever the number of loyal persons qualified to vote within a state should equal 10 per cent of the total qualified voters as of 1860, the loyal persons would be empowered to form a state government, which would receive federal protection under the constitutional provision guaranteeing every state a republican form of government and protecting it from domestic violence. The President also implied that the abolition of slavery would not be unwelcome, although he said nothing of Negro suffrage, believing that the Negro was not yet prepared for it.

Under this proclamation, "loyal" state governments were erected before the end of the war in Tennessee, Arkansas, and Louisiana. The loyal voters in Union-occupied areas in these states first elected delegates to constitutional conventions. These conventions repudiated secession, abolished slavery, drafted new state constitutions, and provided for new state governments which were set up during 1864. In Virginia, it will be recalled, the Pierpont government had been created under a similar arrangement in 1862, and had given its consent to the separation of West Virginia in 1863. Thus four loyal state governments existed in the South before the war ended.

These governments were exceedingly flimsy affairs. They had almost no popular support and undoubtedly would have collapsed except for federal military protection. Congress thought so little of them that with certain exceptions it refused to seat their senators and representatives. Yet Lincoln, acknowledging their weakness, insisted that they were constitutionally correct and that they represented a very real opportunity for carrying out reconstruction with as little difficulty as possible.

Soon after Johnson entered office in April 1865, he adopted the main features of Lincoln's reconstruction theory and practice. In a proclamation of May 29, Johnson pardoned all persons lately engaged in rebellion, except for high Confederate officials and Confederate supporters who possessed more than $20,000 in property. Persons accepting amnesty were required to take an oath of loyalty to the national government, which included a promise to abide by and support all federal laws and proclamations adopted during the war concerning the emancipation of slaves.

At the same time, Johnson issued a proclamation appointing W. W. Holden provisional governor of North Carolina and outlining a plan of presidential reconstruction for that state. The governor was to call a constitutional convention of delegates chosen by and from loyal voters accepting the presidential amnesty. The convention was to "alter and amend" the state constitution and to take the necessary steps to restore the state to its normal constitutional status. Significantly, the proclamation said nothing of Negro suffrage, although in subsequent statements the President advocated extension of the franchise to Negro taxpayers and to literate Negroes. In the course of the next six weeks Johnson issued similar proclamations for the remaining Southern states where Lincoln-sponsored governments had not been erected. Meanwhile, he had extended full recognition to the four Lincoln governments.

Between August 1865 and March 1866, conventions met in all of the seven unreconstructed states. These bodies, except in South Carolina, passed resolutions declaring the various ordinances of secession to have been null and void. South Carolina, clinging pathetically to dead constitutional theory, merely repealed the ordinance. All of the conventions formally abolished slavery within their respective states. With the exception of South Carolina and Mississippi, all repudiated the state debt incurred in rebellion. The conventions also provided for elections of state legislative, executive, and judicial officers.

The newly elected legislatures met shortly and, except in Mississippi, ratified the Thirteenth Amendment. Johnson virtually insisted upon ratification, and it was by this device that the requisite three-fourths majority of the states was secured for the adoption of the amendment. This requirement of ratification was altogether inconsistent with the theoretical sovereignty of the new governments; however, this technical consideration attracted little notice. The new legislatures also chose United States senators, and provided for the election of House members.

Thus by the time Congress met in December 1865, the Johnson reconstruction program was approaching completion in every Southern state. All that remained was for Congress to seat the Southern delegates and constitutional reconstruction would be complete. Instead, Congress first rejected and then overthrew the entire Johnson program.

THE RISE OF THE RADICALS

It will be recalled that during the war there had come into being a congressional bloc which sought a more vigorous prosecution of the war. Well before the war ended, this bloc, which came to be known as Radicals or Radical Republicans, assumed a more positive role in opposing the reconstruction program and favoring more extreme measures. This group objected to Lincoln's program on several counts. First, while the program implied the abolition of slavery, it guaranteed neither Negro suffrage nor Negro civil rights. Nearly all Republicans, both Radical and moderate, believed that

Congress must remedy this situation, while certain Radicals were also convinced that the Negro ought to be elevated forcibly to a position of civil, social and political equality with the whites. Second, the program contained few punitive provisions, whereas many Radicals believed that all Southerners should be punished severely for rebellion. Third, the program virtually excluded Congress from any share in reconstruction, and thus it aroused congressional jealousy. Fourth, the program contained no guarantees of Republican political ascendancy, which might be threatened were the Democratic Southern states immediately readmitted to Congress. This objection was strengthened by the consideration that the abolition of slavery presumably made obsolete the three-fifths clause for slave representation. Negroes as free men would be counted on the same basis as whites in determining representation, so that one result of abolition would be an increase in the representation in Congress of the late slave states. Ex-Confederates with increased representation would probably vote with Northern Democrats to overthrow Republican ascendancy in Congress.

In short, the Radicals were determined to guarantee black civil rights, to impose punitive measures upon ex-Confederates, to secure control of reconstruction for Congress, and to build up a Radical party organization in the South which would help assure Republican political ascendancy nationally. Not until these requirements were guaranteed were the Radicals willing to restore the Southern states to representation in Congress and to equal status in the Union.

A number of related constitutional theories were advanced to support the Radical objectives, the most important being the "conquered provinces" and "state suicide" theories.

The conquered provinces theory was advanced by Thaddeus Stevens of Pennsylvania, who emerged in 1865 as the determined and embittered leader of the Radical bloc in the House of Representatives. Stevens, a stark realist, argued that secession, constitutional or not, had been an accomplished fact. The South had organized as a foreign state and had waged war against the United States. This action, he held, had severed all existing compacts and brought the Confederacy under the international law of war. Conquest of the South had thus reduced the former states to the status of mere conquered provinces with no internal political rights whatever.

The state suicide theory was advanced by Charles Sumner, senator from Massachusetts and idealistic champion of Negro rights.

Sumner held that the mere act of secession instantly destroyed the state as well as its government as a political entity. Unlike Stevens, he contended that secession did not remove the state from the Union but that it worked "an instant forfeiture of all those functions and powers essential to the continued existence of the state as a body politic." The effect of secession was ultimately to reduce the state's domain to the status of unorganized territory. Under the Constitution, Congress had exclusive power to govern the territories; hence the late Confederate states were now completely subject to congressional authority.

Both the conquered provinces and state suicide theories were too extreme for the majority of Republicans, and neither was ever to be acted upon fully or, indeed, to assume a prominent place in congressional theorizing after 1865—1866. However, they did provide a kind of intellectual springboard for a position which most Republicans shortly came to accept: that the Southern states, despite the creation of the Johnson governments, were still out of their normal relationship to the Union and for the moment stripped of most if not all of their constitutional functions and prerogatives, including that of representation in Congress.

Under the Constitution, most Republicans shortly would insist, Congress alone had the power to "readmit" the late rebel states to representation in the Senate and House. It could do this, conceivably, in accordance with its power to admit new states to the Union or under the "guarantee clause" in Article IV, whereby Congress guaranteed to each state "a republican form of government." Under the "guarantee clause," also, Congress presumably could "reconstruct" the political and constitutional systems of the rebel states to make certain that each had a government loyal to the Union. It might also impose conditions-precedent upon the rebel states prior to their readmission to representation; these might well include disenfranchisement of Confederate supporters, a guarantee of Negro civil rights, and Negro suffrage. All this meant that the President lacked power to carry out the reconstruction of the Southern states, and that the presidential program was at best tentative and conditional; at worst, illegal and unconstitutional.

The obvious weakness of both theories was their inconsistency with the constitutional doctrines under which the Union had prosecuted the Civil War. Union theorists had repeatedly drawn a sharp distinction between the states as entities and the people and governments thereof. Northern thinkers had contended that the states themselves as distinct from their governments remained unchanged by rebellion. The congressional Radicals, however, denied this doctrine and proceeded on the premise that the rebellion of individuals destroyed the states as entities.

The first organized Radical attack on presidential reconstruction came with the passage of the Wade-Davis bill on July 2, 1864. This measure provided that a majority of the white male population in any state must take an oath of loyalty to the Constitution before a constitutional convention could be called. This body must in turn draft a constitution disenfranchising Confederate civil and military officials, formally abolishing slavery, and repudiating the Confederate debt. The President might then obtain the formal consent of Congress to recognition of the government erected under this constitution. Lincoln pocket-vetoed the bill, but its provisions anticipated future congressional reconstruction plans.

When President Johnson entered office in April 1865, the Radicals hoped with some reason that he would support their program. The new President was a fiery Tennessee unionist, recently loud in his denunciation of the "traitors" and the "slavocracy." When Johnson, after some hesitation, adopted the Lincoln program, Stevens, Sumner, and their followers were furiously indignant. For the moment, however, they could do nothing to interfere with Johnson's course, for Congress would not convene until December, and meanwhile Johnson refused to call a special session.

When Congress assembled in December 1865, the Radicals at once attacked Johnson's program. It was as yet uncertain that they could command a two-thirds majority and assume control of reconstruction, but they scored an immediate success when they blocked the admission of Southern representatives and senators, by means of a Republican party caucus order instructing the clerks in each house to ignore the seceded states in the roll-call.

Radical leaders next secured the appointment of a Joint Committee on Reconstruction, composed of nine representatives and six senators, who were instructed to make a thorough study of the entire reconstruction problem and to report upon whether any of the Southern states ought to be represented in Congress. Another resolution was passed pledging that neither house would seat representatives from the seceded states until the Joint Committee made its report.

The new committee's most powerful figure was Thaddeus Stevens, now in undisputed ascendancy among the Radicals. The chairman, Senator William P. Fessenden of Maine, was something of a moderate, but other important members, Representatives John A.

Bingham of Ohio, Roscoe Conkling of New York, and George Boutwell of Massachusetts, were all thoroughgoing Radical Republicans. The temper of the committee's report was thus virtually predetermined.

It was soon clear that the Radical Republicans had much popular support and were rapidly gaining in strength. Four long years of terrible warfare had left their mark on the Northern mind; and the assassination of Lincoln, widely attributed to Confederate machinations, greatly increased Northern bitterness. Even generous spirits desired adequate guarantees that the fruits of the war would not be lightly thrown away in a soft and careless reconstruction program.

Several developments strengthened this attitude. The so-called "Black Codes," adopted by the reconstructed states in 1865 and 1866, bore a suspicious resemblance to the ante-bellum slave codes. They contained harsh vagrancy and apprenticeship provisions whose apparent purpose was the establishment of a system of Negro peonage in which the ex-slave, while technically no longer a chattel, would nonetheless be bound to the soil and stripped of all the practical attributes of his new-found freedom. The penal sections provided for more severe and arbitrary punishment for Negroes than for whites, while several codes also called for racial segregation in schools and other public facilities. The "Black Codes," in short, imposed an inferior non-citizen status upon the freedman, along with a potential system of partial bondage. Presumably, also, they violated the Thirteenth Amendment, as many northern congressmen believed, unless the amendment's provisions against "involuntary servitude" were to be construed in the narrowest possible sense.

The South also erred politically in electing prominent ex-Confederates to high state and national offices. Georgia, for example, sent Alexander H. Stephens, former Vice-President of the Confederacy, to the Senate. Stephens had opposed secession in 1861 as thoroughly unwise and likely to bring utter ruination upon the South, but the North nonetheless thought his election to the Senate compounded treason with honor, and expressed doubt concerning Southern sincerity in accepting the results of the war.

Johnson's unimaginative constitutional conservatism and political ineptitude further strengthened the Radicals' hand. The President was a courageous fighter, and his views on reconstruction were technically identical in most respects with those of Lincoln. But he demonstrated repeatedly an almost complete lack of imagination and sympathetic insight with respect to the problem of the freedman in the South, while at the same time he assumed an intransigent states-rights constitutional position toward successive attempts on the part of Congress to deal with various aspects of the reconstruction crisis. All this, combined with his coarse mannerisms, his bitterness of speech, and his uncompromising attacks upon all who differed with him, eventually drove most moderates into the Radical camp.

EVOLUTION OF THE FOURTEENTH AMENDMENT

By early January of 1866, the Radicals were strong enough to begin formulating their own reconstruction program. Many of them now were determined to impose upon the South a legal revolution in the Negro's status that would guarantee the freedman both full citizenship and possession of the franchise as a condition precedent to readmitting the seceded states to Congress. Even the more moderate Republicans, shocked by the Black Codes and by numerous evidences of southern white intransigence toward freedmen, now believed that certain congressional guarantees of the black American's civil rights had become an imperative necessity. The more politically minded Republicans had concluded also that a revolution in Negro status was essential to pave the way for Radical control in the South and so offset the prospective increase in southern representation in Congress resulting from the abolition of slavery and the resultant obsolescence of the three-fifths clause. A series of tentative Radical measures looking to these objectives led finally to the adoption by Congress and submission to the states of the Fourteenth Amendment.

The first step in the evolution of the Fourteenth Amendment came with the passage by Congress of the Freedmen's Bureau Bill, on February 19, 1866. The Freedmen's Bureau had been created by Congress in March 1865 as an emergency wartime relief agency for distressed Negroes lately released from bondage. The law was due to expire one year after the close of the war, and many members of Congress, appalled by the chaotic social conditions in which the black American in the South still found himself, believed continuation of the Bureau to be highly advisable. The new bill, introduced by Senator Lyman Trumbull of Illinois, extended the agency's life indefinitely. More important, it placed Negro civil rights in the seceded states under federal military protection. Any person in any of the formerly seceded states charged with depriving a freedman of his civil rights was to be tried by a military tribunal or a Freedmen's Bureau agent in accordance with martial law. No presentment or indictment was required.

These provisions precipitated a serious constitutional debate in both houses of Congress. Democrats and more conservative Republicans, led by Senators Garrett Davis of Kentucky and Reverdy Johnson of Maryland, attacked the Trumbull bill as hopelessly unconstitutional, arguing that control of civil rights was not one of the enumerated or implied powers of Congress and therefore was exclusively reserved to the states. They argued also that the provisions for the military trial of civilians violated the procedural guarantees of the Fifth Amendment, which specifically enjoined presentment and indictment in federal criminal trials except in the armed forces and in the militia in time of war and which thus clearly implied a general immunity for civilians from peacetime military trial.

In reply, Trumbull contended that the Thirteenth Amendment, which empowered Congress to enforce its provisions by appropriate legislation, had endowed Congress with a new power to legislate to protect civil rights, at least those essential to the black American's new status of freedom as opposed to slavery. The military trial provisions he defended as resting upon the presumption of a continuing disturbed situation in the South brought about by the recent rebellion, in which civil authority had as yet not been completely restored.

Trumbull's contention that Congress by virtue of the Thirteenth Amendment now had at least some power to protect civil rights carried great force, as a majority in Congress recognized, since the condition of freedom could hardly be said to exist apart from certain essential rights intimately associated with that condition. His argument for the trial of civilians by military courts, however, was a far more dubious one. It could be sustained only by accepting one of two possible premises—that the South now was reduced to the status of conquered foreign territory where American constitutional guarantees did not run, or the seceded states still were in a condition of active military rebellion, as Trumbull had implied. In fact, the more enthusiastic Radicals accepted both these premises.

Johnson vetoed the Freedmen's Bureau Bill, calling the provisions for military trials a violation of the Fifth Amendment and questioning the capacity of the present Congress to function at all. A Congress that barred eleven states outright, the President said, was not legally capable of enacting any legislation, especially for the states it excluded. Congress sustained the veto by a narrow margin, but this was to be Johnson's last reconstruction victory of any consequence. In July, Congress was to pass another Freedmen's Bureau Bill, very like the earlier measure, over Johnson's veto. By that time, the President had lost control of reconstruction completely.

The Civil Rights Bill, passed by Congress on March 13, embodied another and more detailed attempt by the Radicals to extend federal protection over Negro civil rights. This measure first declared that "all persons born in the United States and not subject to any foreign power, excluding Indians not taxed," were citizens of the United States. This provision, the substance of which was shortly to be incorporated in the Fourteenth Amendment, thus bestowed citizenship upon the Negro and directly overruled Taney's opinion in the Dred Scott Case, which had held Negroes to be incapable of federal citizenship. The bill next provided that all citizens "of every race and color" were entitled to certain civil rights, which it enumerated in detail: "to make and enforce contracts, to sue, be parties, and give evidence, to inherit, purchase, lease, sell, hold, and convey real and personal property," and to enjoy the "full and equal benefit of all laws and proceedings for the security of person and property, as is enjoyed by white citizens . . ."

The Civil Rights Bill, like the Freedmen's Bill before it, led to a protracted constitutional debate in both houses of Congress. Trumbull and his fellow Republicans had a comparatively easy time defending the citizenship from conservative attack. After all, Taney himself had insisted that control over citizenship was a matter vested exclusively in Congress through the naturalization clause in Article I, Section 8, while it could be argued, also, that the Thirteenth Amendment in abolishing slavery either had already made the Negro a full citizen and member of the body politic, as Senator Charles Sumner contended, or at the very least had opened the way for Congress to declare Negroes to be so. Only extreme states-rights conservatives such as Davis and Johnson could argue the contrary.

However, the civil rights provisions in the bill gave the Republicans somewhat more difficulty. Trumbull's original draft of the measure had carried a clause providing that "there shall be no discrimination in civil rights," a guarantee so sweeping that it seemingly transferred the protection of all such rights from their historic lodgment with the states to the federal government. Replying to the conservative argument that there was no constitutional authority whatsoever for such transfer, Trumbull once again argued that the Thirteenth Amendment had endowed Congress with the power to legislate in the civil rights field. This time, however, he went further and contended also that Congress had the power to enforce by legislation the clause in Article IV of the Constitution whereby "the Citizens of each State shall be entitled to all Privileges and Immunities of Citizens in the Several States." And in particular, he pointed to *Corfield v. Coryell* (1822), a federal circuit court decision in which Justice Bushrod Washington had in effect asserted that the "privileges and immunities" placed under interstate protection by this clause included all possible civil rights except that of the franchise. The clause, Trumbull insisted further, was enforceable by a congressional statute.

However, Trumbull's contention that Congress had full authority to protect all civil rights by legislation proved too far-reaching for many Republicans. When the Civil Rights Bill reached the House, Representative John A. Binham of Ohio, an astute constitutional lawyer who would shortly become one of the principal authors of the Fourteenth Amendment, protested that Congress had no such power without benefit of a new constitutional amendment to that end. At his insistence, the bill was returned to the House Judiciary Committee, which struck out the "no discrimination" clause and replaced it with a mere enumeration of those rights that could be plausibly defended as incidences of that freedom now enjoined by the Thirteenth Amendment. In this form, the bill finally passed.

Johnson vetoed the Civil Rights Bill, advancing the same conservative states rights objections he had offered to the Freedmen's Bureau Bill. However, on April 9 Congress passed the bill over his veto. With this defeat Johnson lost all control over congressional reconstruction policy. Although the Democratic minority and a scattering of Republicans continued to support his administration, the Radical Republican majority henceforth promptly passed all reconstruction measures of any consequence over his veto.

Meanwhile the Joint Committee on Reconstruction was engaged in an extensive study of the reconstruction problem. In January, Thad Stevens and Roscoe Conkling introduced a proposed constitutional amendment to exclude outright from the basis of congressional representation any person whose political rights were denied or abridged by the state on account of race or color. By implication this measure enjoined Negro suffrage under penalty of a reduction in the representation of any state not granting it. The amendment passed the House late in January, but the less radical Senate rejected it. After some further delay, the Joint Committee on April 30 reported out a far more comprehensive constitutional amendment, destined to emerge with some modifications as the Fourteenth Amendment.

The opening sentence of Section I of the proposed amendment provided that:

> All persons born or naturalized in the United States, and subject to the jurisdiction thereof, are citizens of the United States and of the State wherein they reside.

Thus the lack of a citizenship clause in the original Constitution was formally remedied. National citizenship now became primary and state citizenship secondary; thereby the issue of the locus of citizenship, discussed in the Missouri Compromise and later debates and left in a confused condition by the Dred Scott decision, was finally put to rest. The clause also obviously conferred outright national and state citizenship upon Negroes, as was its intent.

The three remaining clauses in Section I guaranteed private rights against state interference:

> No State shall make or enforce any law which shall abridge the privileges or immunities of citizens of the United States; nor shall any State deprive any person of life, liberty, or property, without due process of law; nor deny to any person within its jurisdiction the equal protection of the laws.

These provisions, largely the work of Representative John A. Bingham of Ohio, were intended to remove all doubt as to the constitutionality of the Civil Rights Act, as Stevens presently made clear in debate. The "privileges or immunities" clause, Bingham explained several times, was borrowed directly from the similar guarantee of interstate comity in Article IV, Section 2 of the Constitution. Bingham and Senator Jacob Howard of Michigan, who presented the amendment to the upper house, agreed that the clause incorporated the entire federal Bill of Rights as a limitation upon the states.[1] The "due process" clause was lifted from the Fifth Amendment; it now also became a guarantee against state action. The "equal protection" clause was specifically intended to reinforce the

---

[1] The Supreme Court destroyed this contention in the Slaughterhouse Cases. See pp. 507–508.

Civil Rights Act; in everyday language, it warned the states not to discriminate against Negroes.

Certain historians, however, have challenged the "Negro protection" theory of Section I, and presented instead a so-called "conspiracy theory" of the amendment. This had its inception in a statement made by Roscoe Conkling in arguing a case before the Supreme Court in 1882. He claimed that the Joint Committee had deliberately drafted the equal protection and due process clauses to protect corporate property, and had employed the word "person" instead of "citizen" in these provisions to extend protection to corporations as well as humans. Charles A. Beard, taking Conkling's assertion at face value, later concluded that the Joint Committee, under the pretense of protecting human rights, had engaged in a conspiracy to protect corporate property interests.

More recent research has demolished the "conspiracy theory." It overlooks the obvious fact that the due process clause in the amendment was lifted directly from that in the Fifth Amendment, where "person" is the word used. The Journal of the Joint Committee also indicates that Bingham selected "person" instead of "citizen" because the former term covered Negroes, while the latter might not do so. But the most obvious objection to the conspiracy theory is that it assumes that the Joint Committee could foresee the intimate association between due process and corporate property interests developed after 1890, a notion scarcely heard of earlier. There is much evidence, also, that important corporations of the day were uninterested in due process; they were, instead, seeking a federal incorporation act as protection against restrictive state legislation.

A more difficult historical question, but one which has lately assumed some importance, is whether or not the "equal protection" clause was intended to ban state laws providing for racial segregation in public schools, common carriers, and the like. No certain answer is possible. The Civil Rights Act was specifically amended in the House to exclude any application to state segregation statutes, mainly on Bingham's argument that Congress lacked such power without benefit of a constitutional amendment. On the other hand, debate on the Fourteenth Amendment, while it scarcely touched segregation as such, made it very clear that the Radicals were attempting, as Howard put it, to "destroy all caste and class in the United States." And Bingham explained also that Congress was not now enacting a mere statute with a sharp and limited meaning, but that instead the precise sweep of the amendment would be determined in the future. From this point of view, prohibition upon school segregation did no violence to the Radicals' general intent.

Sections 2 and 3 dealt with the problem of Southern representation. Section 2 as reported by the Committee was a compromise based on the rejected Stevens-Conkling amendment of January. It based state representation in the House upon the whole number of people in each state and so abrogated the three-fifths clause, but it excluded from the basis of representation those persons denied the franchise for any reason other than "participation in rebellion, or other crime." This section in effect insured that the conservative white population should not be able to take advantage of increased state representation together with Negro disfranchisement to place the Southern states and Democrats in control in Washington once more. At the same time, the section did not categorically bestow the vote upon Negroes.

As originally drafted by the Joint Committee, Section 3 unconditionally disfranchised all participants in the late rebellion until March 4, 1870. Many moderate Republicans thought this at once too severe and too temporary. It passed the House, but was then unanimously stricken out in both houses and a substitute provision by Senator Jacob Howard of Michigan put in its place. Howard's provision merely barred from state and federal offices all participants in rebellion who had formerly held political office and in that capacity taken an oath to support the Constitution. It further empowered Congress to remove this disability by a two-thirds vote.

Section 4 recited the obvious—it guaranteed the United States public debt and outlawed debts incurred in rebellion against the United States. Section 5 empowered Congress to enforce the amendment by appropriate legislation.

The amendment passed both houses in its final form on June 13, 1866. The required three-fourths of the states had ratified by June 1868, and it was proclaimed the Fourteenth Amendment to the Constitution on July 28, 1868.

REPORT OF THE JOINT COMMITTEE ON RECONSTRUCTION

The amendment was one part of a comprehensive plan of reconstruction submitted by the Joint Committee. The Committee submitted its full report late in June 1866, together with a voluminous body of testimony and evidence gathered in the previous six months.

The report adopted a so-called "forfeited rights" or "dead states" theory of the effect of secession. This conception, less extreme than the state suicide or conquered provinces theories, was advanced in an effort to win the support of moderate Republicans in Congress. The Committee dodged the question of whether the Southern states were in or out of the Union. But it declared that the seceded states, by withdrawing their representatives in Congress and levying war against the United States, had forfeited all political rights incident to the Union. They were politically dead, entitled to only such rights as the conqueror should grant them. Like Sumner's and Stevens' theories, the forfeited rights theory paved the way for congressional reconstruction, since only Congress could restore "dead" states to a full position in the Union. Accordingly, the Committee disavowed presidential reconstruction and partially disavowed the governments Johnson had created. "The powers of conqueror," said the Committee, "are not so vested in the President that he can fix and regulate the terms of settlement and confer congressional representation on conquered rebels and traitors."

The Committee did not absolutely repudiate Johnson's governments, however. Instead it recommended that before any Southern state should be readmitted to Congress, steps should be taken to guarantee the civil rights of all citizens, secure a "just equality of representation," and protect against rebel debt claims.

These terms evidently referred to the Committee's constitutional amendment and to a bill submitted by the Committee the previous April providing that any state lately in insurrection might secure representation by ratifying the amendment. The bill was not formally acted upon in Congress, but it was clearly understood to be a part of the Radical program.

In declaring the Southern states to be politically dead and yet at the same time insisting that they ratify a constitutional amendment as a prelude to readmission to Congress, the Radicals had put themselves in a hopelessly inconsistent constitutional position. The seceded states were without rights; yet they could perform the highest sovereign trust reserved to a state—the power to amend the Constitution! This inconsistency the Committee of necessity overlooked, for ratification by some of the Southern states would be necessary to secure action by a requisite three-fourths of the states. The forfeited rights theory, which theoretically recognized the continued existence of the Southern states, probably also tempered the apparent inconsistency in the plan for many Republicans.

The success of the Joint Committee's plan depended upon whether the Southern states would consent to ratify the Fourteenth Amendment. Had they done so, it is probable that Congress would have then recognized the Johnson governments and restored all the Southern states to representation. Tennessee indeed did promptly ratify and was promptly "readmitted" to representation in July.

The other ten states, however, seven of them acting before the end of the year, all rejected the Fourteenth Amendment and thereby rejected the Radical overture. The states were in effect refusing to accept enfranchisement of the Negro and the social revolution in black status implicit in the Fourteenth Amendment. Many Southerners, though dissatisfied with the *status quo*, nevertheless preferred their present position to that envisioned after ratification. Evidently they also believed that the Radicals could not force their plan through against the will of the President and the nation. A congressional election would occur in November. Should Johnson's supporters win control of Congress, the President could then secure admission of the Southern states to representation on his own terms.

Both the President and the Radicals made every effort to win the congressional elections of 1866, for it was evident that the elections would resolve the conflict between them. Both the conservative Republican-Democratic coalition and the Radicals held party conventions in Philadelphia in August and September. Johnson himself made a "great circle" tour of the northern and western states. Both sides sponsored ex-soldiers' conventions.

In November the Radicals won an overwhelming victory. In the next Congress, they would now, by direct mandate of the people in the North, command better than a two-thirds majority in both houses. The Radicals had capitalized on their seizure of the old Republican Party's name and organization, now known as the party of Lincoln and the Saviors of the Union. The North was also still suspicious of Southern good faith, and a series of unfortunate race riots in the South in 1866 seemingly confirmed this suspicion. Also, Johnson's speaking tour was a disastrous failure, his coarse mannerisms disgusting many moderates.

Thus the Lincoln-Johnson program of speedy reconstruction, with its implicit rejection of any important legal, political, or social changes in the South, in particular those associated with changes in the status of the Negro, was at length utterly repudiated by Congress. An era of congressional reconstruction under control of the Radicals was about to begin, which, while its ultimate implications for the American constitutional system were in no sense revolutionary, would nonetheless carry constitutional change well beyond the conservative presidential program.

Chapter

18

Radical Congressional Reconstruction

WHEN CONGRESS MET in December 1866, the Radical leaders, now confident of popular support, determined upon a far more sweeping program for the late seceded states than that of the previous June. Their plans now contemplated outright repudiation of the Johnson governments and the creation of temporary military regimes for the South in their place. The ten unreconstructed states were to be "readmitted" to the Union only after they had drawn up new constitutions in which a majority of the white population had been disfranchised and Negro suffrage guaranteed. The result presumably would be a long-range alteration of the position of the Negro in southern society, in which the freedman would be elevated from his former servile status to full citizenship and participation in the body politic.

Horrified conservatives in both political parties looked upon this program as essentially revolutionary both in its implications for the Union and for the southern class system. But in fact a great majority of the Radical Republicans were themselves constitutional conservatives, who looked upon their program as one designed to deal with an extraordinary emergency and who very soon moved to restore "correct" constitutional government in the South, even at the risk of imperiling their own plans for the Negro. Ultimately this was to spell the virtual abandonment of much of the Radical program.

THE MILITARY RECONSTRUCTION ACTS OF 1867

The first fruit of the Radicals' new supremacy was the Military Reconstruction Act, which passed Congress on March 2, 1867, under the leadership of Thaddeus Stevens of Pennsylvania, Roscoe Conkling of New York, and George Boutwell of Massachusetts. The act declared that "no legal state governments" existed in the ten unreconstructed states. It then divided the "said rebel states" into five military districts, and placed each district in command of a general of the army appointed by the President. If the district commander thought it necessary, he could suspend or supersede entirely the functioning of the so-called Johnson governments outright, but in any case it definitely subordinated them to military rule. The commanding general could also bring "disturbers of the public peace" and criminals to trial before military tribunals.

Section 5 of the act outlined a plan by which the seceded states could secure readmittance to Congress and escape military rule. It provided that the people of a "rebel state" might call a constitutional convention. In the voting for delegates, Negroes were specifically enfranchised, while all participants in rebellion were virtually disfranchised. The convention was to draft a constitution, which was to be ratified by the same electorate and then submitted to Congress for approval. If Congress approved, and if the state legislature elected under the new constitution ratified the Fourteenth Amendment, the state was to be "declared entitled to representation in Congress," and the military provisions of the act were to become inoperative for the reconstructed state as soon as the Fourteenth Amendment had become a part of the national Constitution. The Second Reconstruction Act, passed on March 23, 1867, outlined reconstruction procedure in more detail but did not alter the plan set forth in Section 5 of the first act.

The constitutionality of the congressional plan rested in large part upon the validity of Radical reconstruction theories. Assuming that the Southern states were politically dead, conquered provinces, or unorganized territories, Congress undoubtedly had the authority to establish military government in the South. Congress by the same theory also had the constitutional right to dictate the process by which new states were to be created. It could even be argued that Congress could require a newly organized state to ratify a constitutional amendment before formal admission to the Union, not in its constitutional capacity as a state but as a condition precedent required as a gesture of good faith, such ratification to be without effect upon the adoption of the amendment by the required three-fourths of the states. Even the provision for the military trial of civilians in peacetime, constitutionally the most dubious of the entire congressional program, could be defended if one assumed that the late seceded states were so far divorced from their former connection with the Union that their inhabitants were not entitled to the protection of the Constitution.

If, on the other hand, the Lincoln-Johnson hypothesis of Southern status be accepted as correct, then the entire military reconstruction plan was hopelessly unconstitutional. The plan set aside lawful state governments, imposed military government upon sovereign states of the Union, denied representation to states lawfully entitled to it, and imposed illegal conditions precedent upon the Southern states before re-admitting them to representation.

Certain historians have contended that the ultimate constitutional issue involved in military reconstruction was that of outright national centralization versus continuation of the traditional constitutional system. This argument is untenable. Drastic as military reconstruction was, a large majority in Congress plainly intended it as a temporary policy under which the Southern states would ultimately be fully restored to the Union. The plan did not contemplate a permanent union of unequal states nor any permanent alteration in state-federal relationships except in so far as the Fourteenth Amendment placed certain private rights under federal control.

Johnson vetoed the March reconstruction acts as unconstitutional; but when Congress promptly re-enacted them, the President put them into operation. On March 11, Johnson appointed a commanding general to each of the five military districts. These officers presently registered the enfranchised population in their districts. In all of the Southern states the proportion of Negroes registering was very large. In Alabama, for example, 104,000 out of 165,000 registered voters were Negroes; in South Carolina, 80,000 out of 127,000 were Negroes. In five states Negroes were in a majority; in the others, they nearly equaled the whites. Many white voters registered with intent to frustrate ultimate ratification of the new constitutions, for the Reconstruction Act of March 23 stipulated that a constitution must be ratified in an election in which a majority of all registered voters in the state participated. They hoped to block ratification merely by remaining away from the polls.

RADICAL RECONSTRUCTION WITHIN THE SOUTH

In all ten of the unreconstructed states actual political control now rapidly passed from the conservative white population to radical political groups dominated by Northern immigrants (carpetbaggers), a native white minority group supporting the Radical program (scalawags), and Negroes. Since 1865, Southern Radical leaders had made steady progress in building up Radical political organization in the South. Union League clubs, controlled by carpetbaggers and scalawags, instructed and catechized the new Negro voters in the Radical Republican political faith. Military reconstruction officials further strengthened the Radical position by refusing to register large groups of the white population. The so-called Third Reconstruction Act of July 19, 1867 had placed almost complete discretionary authority in registering the white population in the hands of local military officers, and it had redefined in extremely broad terms the disfranchised class listed in the Second Reconstruction Act. Thus the conservative white population, largely disfranchised and demoralized, was for the moment thrust aside.

In the fall of 1867, all ten Southern states voted by large majorities to call constitutional conventions, and the various conventions met in the winter and spring of 1868. All were dominated by Radicals, and all had many Negro members. In one state, South Carolina, Negro delegates outnumbered the whites 76 to 48.

The constitutions drafted were very like other mid-century state constitutions except that they embodied Radical suffrage provisions. They all categorically guaranteed Negro suffrage and disfranchised outright large elements of the white population. Thus Louisiana disfranchised everyone who had voted for secession or "advocated treason." Certain provisions in the constitutions, however, were surprisingly enlightened. The sections dealing with taxation and finance have generally been characterized as intelligent and progressive, while the provisions which aimed at universal free public education were undoubtedly more democratic than those in earlier Southern constitutions.

When the new constitutions were submitted to the voters, most enfranchised whites stayed away from the polls in an effort to block the majority of the registered vote required for adoption. In Alabama this device succeeded temporarily, but Congress promptly took even this weapon away from the Southern Conservatives. The so-called Fourth Reconstruction Act, enacted in March 1868, provided that the new constitutions could be ratified by a simple majority of those voting. In all the remaining states except Mississippi the constitutions were ratified by large majorities.

Accordingly Congress in June 1868 voted to "readmit" Alabama, Arkansas, North and South Carolina, Georgia, Florida, and Louisiana to the Union, and to accord them representation in Congress. Alabama's admission was an altogether irregular procedure, for the state had not ratified its constitution by the majority of the registered vote then required. Nonetheless Congress voted to disregard this technicality and admit the state anyhow.

"Readmission" of Texas, Mississippi, and Virginia was delayed until June 1870. Mississippi had rejected its constitution, while in Texas and Virginia the vote had been delayed too long for Congress to act in that session. In all three states there was much opposition to the drastic disfranchisement provisions in the new constitutions. President Grant, who entered office in March 1869, sympathized with the Southern whites in this matter, and in April 1869 he asked Congress to enact legislation permitting the three unreconstructed states to vote separately upon the disfranchisement clauses.

At this time, Radical leaders in Congress were engaged in pushing through Congress a constitutional amendment intended to guarantee the franchise to Negroes. This proposal, shortly to become the Fifteenth Amendment to the Constitution, had been inspired by Radical dissatisfaction with the Fourteenth Amendment, which did not categorically enfranchise the Negro. Republican leaders in Congress accepted Grant's proposal for a separate vote on disfranchisement in Texas, Mississippi, and Virginia, but they coupled to the necessary act a clause requiring Texas, Mississippi, and Virginia to ratify the prospective amendment as an additional condition precedent to admission. This act became law in April 1869. Virginia, Mississippi, and Texas complied with its terms and were "readmitted" to the Union in 1870.

The constitutional amendment submitted to the states as a result of the foregoing political bargain stipulated that:

> The right of citizens of the United States to vote shall not be denied or abridged by the United States or by any State on account of race, color, or previous condition of servitude.

The foregoing secured ratification by the necessary three-fourths of the states in March 1870, and thereby became the Fifteenth Amendment to the Constitution.

The legal framework of congressional reconstruction was now complete. Political and social reconstruction, however, was anything but complete. The attempt to impose upon the South a revolution in the status of the Negro resulted in a series of violent up-heavals, as the white "Conservatives," gradually recovering their morale and their political power, fought to wrest control from the Radicals and their Negro allies. This conflict provoked further congressional interference in the South, although after 1871 the interest of the Radicals in Congress in maintaining southern Radical state governments underwent a progressive decline.

THE IMPEACHMENT OF JOHNSON

After the break between Johnson and Congress in the spring of 1866, all party relations between the President and the Radical Republicans had come to an end. The President had vetoed every important reconstruction measure since the Freedmen's Bureau bill, and since the passage of the Civil Rights Act the Radicals had promptly passed all their measures over the President's veto. Their bitterness at Johnson's "obstructionism" was extreme, and they feared that the President might somehow succeed in destroying the Radical program.

Beginning in March 1867, the Radicals forced through a series of acts intended to restrict the President's authority as much as possible. The Army Appropriation Act of March 2, 1867, required that all army orders be issued through the General of the Army, and that the general in command of the army should not be removed without the Senate's consent. This act virtually deprived the President of his full constitutional authority as commander in chief and was unquestionably unconstitutional. The Third Reconstruction Act of July 19, 1867, vested the entire power to appoint and remove officials under the act in the General of the Army, a direct and undoubtedly illegal transfer of the President's constitutional appointive power to a subordinate official.

Of even greater significance was the Tenure of Office Act, also enacted on March 2, 1867. This law was intended to destroy the President's power to remove subordinate officials without the Senate's consent. It provided that all executive officials appointed with the Senate's consent should hold office until a successor was appointed and qualified in the same manner. Thus no presidential removal would be valid under the act until the Senate consented by ratifying the nomination of a successor. A partial exception was made for cabinet officers, who were to hold office only during the term of the President appointing them, and for one month thereafter.

Another section of the act provided for ad interim appointments.

When the Senate was not in session, the President could remove an official for crime, misconduct, or incapacity and fill the vacancy so created with an ad interim appointment. But the President was obliged to report the removal to the Senate within twenty days after that chamber next convened. If the Senate then refused its consent to the removal, the office reverted to the former incumbent. Accepting or holding an office in violation of the statute was made a misdemeanor punishable by fine and imprisonment.

This statute reopened the old dispute over the President's removal power. As the reader is aware, the First Congress had decided that the President possessed a separate right of removal without the Senate's consent. Also, Jackson had successfully reaffirmed that right in 1833, and it had since been commonly exercised. Johnson's veto recalled these facts and denounced the bill as an unconstitutional usurpation of executive authority; however, Congress promptly passed the measure over his veto.

Meanwhile the Radical leaders had been searching for plausible grounds upon which to impeach the President. In the spring of 1867 a House investigating committee had covered every possible charge thoroughly and had been forced to report in July that no adequate grounds for impeachment existed. The investigation continued, however, and in December the committee, now under control of Representative George S. Boutwell of Massachusetts, recommended impeachment, although no specific grounds for such a step were presented.

In the debate that followed, the Radical leaders contended for a broad construction of the Constitution's impeachment clause, holding that the phrase "high crimes and misdemeanors" was not to be construed narrowly, but that it embraced all misbehavior and incompetence in office, whether or not the offense was recognized at law. Implausible as this position was, some precedent for it existed, for Judge John Pickering had been impeached and convicted in 1804, although he had technically not been guilty of any high crime or misdemeanor, his actual "offense" being insanity.[1] For the moment, however, the conservative argument—that some offense known either to federal statute or to the common law was a prerequisite to impeachment—carried the day, and the House voted down the committee report 100 to 57.

Very shortly, however, Johnson committed what appeared to be a specific violation of the Tenure of Office Act, and so opened the

---

[1] See the account of the Pickering impeachment on p. 220.

way for his impeachment. The President had long been at odds with Secretary of War Edwin M. Stanton, who had openly aligned himself with the congressional Radicals. Stanton had refused to resign and had used his position in the cabinet as a vantage point to spy on the President and to undermine the President's administration.

In August 1867, Johnson removed Stanton from office and appointed General U. S. Grant in his place. The removal and appointment were made ad interim (that is, while the Senate was not in session), and so did not constitute a violation of the Tenure of Office Act. When the Senate convened in December it refused to confirm the removal, whereupon Grant resigned and Stanton resumed office. Grant's resignation disappointed the President, for he had hoped to force Stanton to resort to the courts in an effort to recover his office. In this manner, Johnson could conceivably have obtained a judicial opinion on the constitutionality of the Tenure of Office Act. Grant's refusal to retain the office after the adverse Senate vote defeated this plan.

In February 1868 Johnson forced the issue by summarily removing Stanton as Secretary of War and appointing Major General Lorenzo Thomas as his successor. Since the Senate was then in session, the President's act appeared to be a specific violation of the Tenure of Office Act. This was precisely what the Radical leaders had been waiting for, since the President had now presumably committed the specific statutory offense that many hesitant Republicans considered necessary for impeachment. Two days later, on February 24, the House voted, 128 to 47, to impeach the President.

On March 2 and 3 the House voted eleven articles of impeachment against Johnson. The first three articles charged the President with deliberately violating the Tenure of Office Act in removing Stanton and appointing Thomas. Articles 4 to 8 charged the President with entering into a conspiracy with Thomas to violate the same law. Conspiracy to violate a federal statute was a punishable offense by a statute of July 31, 1861. Article 9 charged Johnson with having attempted to subvert the provision in the Army Appropriation Act of 1867, which made all orders issuable through the General of the Army.

Article 10, inserted at the insistence of Ben Butler, charged the President with attempting to "bring into disgrace, ridicule, hatred, contempt, and reproach the Congress of the United States." This charge was supported by reference to a number of Johnson's political speeches attacking the congressional Radicals. In substance, this article thus sought the President's conviction merely because he was a political enemy of the congressional majority. Article 11, inserted at Stevens' suggestion, was a "catch-all" provision summing up all the previous counts.

On March 30 the impeachment trial began before the Senate, with Chief Justice Salmon P. Chase presiding. The attorneys for the prosecution, or "managers," appointed by the House of Representatives to prosecute the case before the Senate, were John A. Bingham of Ohio, Ben Butler of Massachusetts, George Boutwell of Massachusetts, John A. Logan of Illinois, Thad Stevens of Pennsylvania, Thomas Williams of Pennsylvania, and James Wilson of Iowa. Johnson was defended by former Attorney General Henry Stanbery, Benjamin R. Curtis, and William M. Evarts, all more able lawyers than any of the prosecution.

The first important matter of contention was the Senate's judicial status. Was the Senate sitting as a court or as a political body? The issue was extremely important. If the Senate was a regular court, then it was bound by legal rules of evidence. Presumably, also, it could convict the President only if it found him guilty of a specific offense either at the common law or defined in a federal statute. It could not rightfully convict the President merely as a political enemy of Congress. On the other hand, if the Senate sat as a political body, not only could it hear evidence usually inadmissible in a regular court of justice, but also it might conceivably convict the President of a political offense.

Johnson's attorneys argued powerfully that the trial was strictly a judicial proceeding. The Constitution, they pointed out, adhered strictly to a common-law terminology in describing impeachment. The Senate was empowered to "try" impeachments, make a conviction, and enter a judgment. With equal force they contended that if impeachment was a mere political proceeding, then the whole long-established constitutional relationship between executive and Congress would be threatened. Were the President removable merely because he was politically inacceptable to Congress, executive independence would be destroyed and parliamentary ascendancy would replace the American presidential system.

The prosecution, on the other hand, argued that the nature of impeachment made the Senate something more than a court. Offenses other than those known to the common law were impeachable. Impeachment, they said, could be pressed for improper motive, or even "action against the public interest." If not, what other method was there for getting rid of an incompetent officeholder? Here they cited the Pickering precedent.

The issue was technically settled in favor of the defense. Early in the trial the Senate voted, 31 to 19, to permit the Chief Justice to settle all questions of law, evidence, and the like, unless the Senate overruled him. The implication was that the Chief Justice was the presiding officer in a regular court, the senators sitting as associate justices. In reality, however, this ruling hardly destroyed the political character of the proceedings, for many senators were still prepared to vote according to their political convictions regardless of evidence.

The principal argument in the trial centered on Johnson's supposed violation of the Tenure of Office Act. The prosecution argued that Johnson had committed a deliberate violation of a constitutional statute, clearly an impeachable offense. Johnson's attorneys in reply argued that the Tenure of Office Act did not apply to Johnson's removal of Stanton at all. The act specified that cabinet officers were to hold office during the term of the President appointing them, and for one month thereafter. Stanton had been appointed by Lincoln, not Johnson, and Johnson had never reappointed him but had merely tacitly assented to Stanton's continuance in office. The prosecution replied that Johnson was merely an "acting President" serving Lincoln's unexpired second term—a weak argument, for since Tyler's time Vice-Presidents succeeding to office had been considered as Presidents-in-full.[2]

The cornerstone of Johnson's defense, however, was the contention that the Tenure of Office Act was unconstitutional. Counsel for the President cited the debates in the First Congress on the removal power, Jackson's successful removal of Duane, and the established practice of eighty years, all of which supported the contention that the removal power was an executive prerogative separate and distinct from the power of appointment. Against the weight of these precedents the House managers retorted that the Tenure of Office Act was a formal declaration of the meaning of the Constitution, and therefore finally settled a long-mooted constitutional issue. This was tantamount to the assertion that Congress possessed a final right of constitutional interpretation even with regard to issues apparently settled by long-established practice—a dubious contention, since it was now generally recognized that the ultimate power to interpret the Constitution belonged to the Supreme Court.

Finally the defense contended that Johnson's deliberate violation

---

[2] In the face of some opposition in Congress, Tyler had been successful in asserting he was President in every sense, not merely acting President. The precedent here established had been recognized under Fillmore and Johnson.

of law had not been subversive, but that the President had merely
wished to test the act's constitutionality by bringing it before the
courts. The President's action was therefore not a misdemeanor but
an attempt to institute judicial proceedings. This argument the
prosecution dealt with effectively. The President, they said, must
like everyone else bear responsibility for his acts. If he violated a
law on the grounds that it was unconstitutional, he must face the
consequences if the proper tribunal, in this case the Senate, decided
that the law was valid. If the Senate decided that the Tenure of
Office Act was constitutional, then Johnson had committed a misdemeanor and must be punished regardless of intent.

On May 16 the Senate began balloting upon the impeachment
articles. The Republican majority in the Senate, intent on securing
a conviction, instructed the Chief Justice to poll the Senate first
on Article 11, which included all possible charges and supposedly
offered the greatest chance of conviction.

The final vote on Article 11 was 35 "guilty," and 19 "not guilty,"
one vote short of the two-thirds majority required by the Constitution for impeachment. Seven Republican senators—Fessenden,
Fowler, Grimes, Henderson, Ross, Trumbull, and Van Winkle—
had risked political annihilation to vote with the Democratic minority for acquittal. After an adjournment to May 26, the Senate voted
on Articles 2 and 3. On both Articles the vote was again 35 to 19.
In disgust, the Senate majority voted to adjourn as a tribunal "without day." [3] The Radical grand design had failed. The minority
Republicans, who had saved the day for Johnson, afterward made
it clear that they believed that the Tenure of Office Act was unconstitutional and that the President had not committed the statutory offense they believed necessary to conviction.

Since 1868 many analysts have held that Johnson's acquittal saved
the American presidential system from destruction. The actual basis
for Johnson's impeachment, they asserted, was the Radicals' intense
hatred for his political principles. They have concluded that had
impeachment proved successful as a weapon to remove a politically
unacceptable President, the precedent would have been established
for the removal of any President refusing persistently to co-operate
with Congress, an eventuality implying the establishment of a parliamentary form of government with legislative ascendancy.

The argument has some weight, but it ignores the political atmosphere of the reconstruction era. The Radicals were bent upon

---

[3] That is, without setting another meeting date—in other words, permanently.

the destruction of a President whom they had come to regard as a traitor, a blackguard, a drunkard, and a madman. Successful impeachment would therefore have established about the same precedent as that in the Pickering trial—that is, a loose construction of the impeachment power. While the issue of impeachment for political dissent was certainly a major factor in the case, many other long steps would have been required before impeachment became a mere routine means of voting "no-confidence" in the parliamentary sense of the word.

RECONSTRUCTION AND THE COURT

The Supreme Court in general pursued a cautious policy of neutrality throughout the turbulent struggle between Johnson and Congress. The justices were apparently well aware that the Radical majority was in no mood to tolerate any judicial tampering with their program, and they carefully avoided those situations that might have involved them in serious conflict with the two houses. And as for the Radical leaders, while they frequently attacked the Court in hot indignation on the floor of Congress for decisions they found objectionable, they apparently recognized also the justices' desire to avoid a direct clash. On several occasions Congress concerned itself with the Court's work, but in only one instance did it make an overt move of any importance to block consideration of a congressional reconstruction measure. As a consequence, no major confrontation between Court and Congress ever occurred.

The Republican Radicals first interested themselves in the Court in the spring of 1866, when they undertook consideration of a bill to alter the number of justices and at the same time to reorganize the lower federal court system. Justice John Catron had died in May, 1865, and in April, 1866, President Johnson nominated Attorney General Stanbery to the vacancy. However, the Senate refused to act upon the nomination. Instead, it took up a bill, already passed by the House, lowering the size of the Court from ten to nine members and making corresponding adjustments in the federal circuit court system. The Senate then adopted an amendment offered by Lyman Trumbull to reduce the size of the Court to seven members effective with the next two additional vacancies, and passed the bill in this form. The House concurred, and Johnson quietly signed the bill into law in July.

This measure, which deprived the President of one actual and two potential appointments to the Court, was long considered to have been intended as a deliberate blow at the Chief Executive. However, it now seems certain that the act was not aimed principally at the President, although the Radicals were well aware of its potential in that respect. Instead, Congress had acted in part upon information that Chief Justice Chase and other incumbent justices thought the Court too large. The law also represented an attempt to reduce the influence of the South in the federal judiciary both by reorganizing the existing federal circuits and by obviating the necessity for any attempt at preserving a sectional balance between the North and South on the Supreme Court, an objective accomplished simply by eliminating the next three appointments. Johnson apparently understood quite well that the act was not in the main an instrument of warfare against him, as his signature made clear.

But with the Court's opinion in *Ex parte Milligan* in December 1866, ruling that the military trial of civilians in other than an actual seat of military operations was unconstitutional,[4] a major crisis between Court and Congress loomed suddenly on the horizon. Particularly alarming for the Radicals was the dictum set forth clearly in Justice David Davis' opinion that Congress lacked the constitutional power to authorize such trials even had it attempted to do so, a position against which Chief Justice Chase and justices Wayne, Swayne, and Miller had vigorously disagreed in a concurring opinion. The plain implication of all this apparently was that the majority justices, if given an opportunity to do so, might well hold void the military trial provisions of both the Freedmen's Bureau Act and Civil Rights Act, as well as like provisions in any further reconstruction measures Congress might see fit to adopt. In private, Justice Davis protested that the Court's opinion applied only to military trials in loyal states and that "military commissions in the disloyal states have never been pronounced to be illegal," but this did little to quiet the outcry of protest in Congress.

Other decisions adverse to Radical interests soon followed. In *Cummings v. Missouri*, decided in January 1867, the Court reviewed a clause in the Missouri constitution of 1865 requiring voters, ministers, attorneys, and candidates for public office to swear that they had never engaged in rebellion against the United States, or given aid to rebels, or even expressed any sympathy for their cause. Those who could not take the oath were disfranchised or debarred from

---

[4] See pp. 415–419 for a full discussion of the Milligan case.

the profession or office in question as the case might be. Justice Field's opinion for the five majority justices called the provision a bill of attainder and an ex post facto law and held it unconstitutional.

In *Ex parte Garland*, decided the same day, the Court held, also by a 5-to-4 majority, that the Federal Test Act of 1865 imposing a similar oath upon federal attorneys was unconstitutional on the same grounds. These two decisions threatened other aspects of the Radical program, since the Radicals contemplated disfranchisement and disbarment from office of ex-Confederates and their sympathizers.

These decisions immediately evoked in both houses of Congress a bitter Radical attack on the Court. Thad Stevens called the Milligan decision "more dangerous" than that of the Dred Scott case, while Bingham suggested that Congress at once deprive the Court of all appellate jurisdiction and thereby render it impossible for the justices to interfere with the Radical program. For the moment, however, Congress took no action.

Meanwhile the Court, in *Mississippi v. Johnson* (1867), very properly refrained from seizing upon a dubious opportunity to rule upon the constitutionality of the Congressional Reconstruction Acts of March, 1867. In April, attorneys for the Johnson government in Mississippi, then about to be replaced by a federal military administration, asked the Court to issue an injunction restraining the President from enforcing the two acts in question, on the ground that they were unconstitutional. This request was, to say the least, extraordinary, for although the Court, beginning with *Marbury v. Madison*, had several times held the executive to be amenable to judicial writ, the present petition was utterly unprecedented in that it asked the justices to interpose their authority directly against that of the President in his execution of an act of Congress. Attorney General Stanbery, appearing before the Court in response to the petition, called the request "scandalous" and in derogation of the President's properly constituted authority.

In a unanimous decision, the Court rejected Mississippi's plea. In an opinion that followed Stanbery's argument almost precisely, Chief Justice Chase drew a distinction between mere ministerial acts involving no discretion and large executive acts such as those carrying into effect a statute of Congress. The former, he said, could be enjoined; the latter involved political discretion and could not be. Such an injunction would amount to interference with the political acts of the legislative and executive branches of the government; defiance of it, Chase pointed out astutely, would create an absurd situation.

In May the Court, in *Georgia v. Stanton* (1876), dismissed a similar suit in which the states of Georgia and Mississippi asked injunctions restraining the Secretary of War and General Grant from enforcing the Reconstruction Acts. The suits, said the Court, involved proposed adjudication of political questions over which the Court had no jurisdiction. Plainly the Court had drawn back from the danger involved in so direct and unprecedented an attack on congressional policy.

In February 1868, however, the Court consented to hear arguments in *Ex parte McCardle,* a case arising in a Mississippi military tribunal, and carried on appeal under the authority of the Habeas Corpus Act of 1867. The case by implication involved the constitutionality of the Reconstruction Acts, since the appellant McCardle contended that the military tribunal which existed by virtue of the acts had no lawful authority.

When it thus became apparent that the Court might dare to declare the Reconstruction Acts invalid, the Radical majority immediately moved to end the possibility. In March, Congress passed a bill dealing with appeals in customs and revenue cases. Attached was a rider repealing the Supreme Court's jurisdiction in all cases arising under the Habeas Corpus Act of 1867. The rider was admittedly designed to kill the McCardle case. Johnson gave the bill a blistering veto, but Congress immediately overrode the veto. In April, 1869, accordingly, the Court dismissed McCardle's plea on the ground that the new act had destroyed its jurisdiction in the case. Whether or not the justices had acted in part out of a sense of caution is uncertain; however, their constitutional position was entirely sound. As Chief Justice Chase pointed out in his opinion, the Court holds its appellate jurisdiction entirely at the discretion of Congress, so that it was no longer empowered to act.

On the same day that the Court bowed to Congress in *Ex parte McCardle,* it indicated even more clearly in *Texas v. White* (1869) that it had no wish to engage in a major controversy with Congress. The latter case involved an action by the Johnson government of Texas to recover title to certain United States bonds formerly the property of the state but sold by the Confederate state government during the war. The Court here found an opportunity to pass upon the status of both the Confederate and Johnson state governments, and hence to analyze at length the theories of secession and reconstruction.

Chief Justice Chase first presented very convincingly the orthodox Lincoln theory of secession. The United States, said Chase, was an indissoluble Union of indissoluble states. Hence secession did not destroy the state of Texas, nor the obligations of Texans as citizens of the United States. The pretended Confederate state government, though for some purposes a *de facto* government, was in its relations to the United States a mere illegal combination.

This analysis might have paved the way for a direct challenge to the congressional theory of reconstruction, since it held that the seceded states still were in the Union. However, the Chief Justice then made a major concession to the Radicals by holding that the constitutional right of permanent reconstruction devolved upon Congress. He quoted with evident approval the opinion in *Luther v. Borden*, growing out of the Dorr Rebellion of 1842 in Rhode Island, in which the Court had decided that Congress had power under Article IV, Section 4, of the Constitution to guarantee republican governments in the states and to recognize the correct government in any state. Chase specifically refrained from expressing any opinion upon the constitutionality of the Reconstruction Acts, but he nevertheless cited the acts as authority for the provisional character of the Johnson governments. The decision was a major victory for the Radicals, and it clearly indicated that the Court would make no direct onslaught upon congressional reconstruction.

Because the Supreme Court was unwilling to challenge Congress directly on the issue of Southern reconstruction, it must not be assumed that the Court failed to function positively during the Reconstruction era. The modern conception of judicial review began to make its appearance at this time. Between the years 1789 and 1864 the Court had declared just two acts of Congress unconstitutional; during the nine-year tenure of Chief Justice Salmon P. Chase, from 1864 to 1873, it declared void ten acts of Congress. The Court, in short, was beginning to assert its right to review congressional legislation just as in the days of John Marshall it had asserted powerfully the right to review state legislation. The Court was beginning to assume its modern role as the final arbiter of the constitutional system, the balance wheel of federalism.

THE COURT-PACKING CHARGE

In April 1869, Congress enacted a statute increasing the number of justices on the Court to nine. The fact that President Grant and not Johnson would now have the new appointments at his disposal may have been responsible in part for this measure, but Congress appears to have acted mainly out of a new conviction that an odd number of justices, with its lessened possibility of tied decisions, was the better part of wisdom. The following December, Justice Robert Grier, now aged and mentally impaired, resigned from the bench under pressure from his colleagues, and Grant was thus enabled to nominate two new justices. The President first named Edwin M. Stanton and Attorney General Ebenezer R. Hoar. However, Stanton died in December, four days after the Senate had confirmed his appointment, and the Senate rejected Hoar. Thereupon Grant in February 1870 nominated Joseph P. Bradley, a well-known Republican railroad lawyer, and William Strong, a former Pennsylvania Supreme Court Justice, both of whom the Senate confirmed.

A few hours before Grant nominated Bradley and Strong, the Supreme Court, in *Hepburn v. Griswold*, declared the Legal Tender Act of 1862 unconstitutional. This statute had made "greenbacks," the fiat money issued by the federal government during the Civil War, legal tender in payment of debts. Chief Justice Chase, speaking for four of the seven justices, said that the law was invalid in so far as it applied to contracts made before its passage. The act, said Chase, was contrary to the due process clause of the Fifth Amendment and also violated the obligation of contracts. Although there was no contract clause limiting the federal government, Chase nevertheless held that the violation was contrary to the spirit of the Constitution. Three Republican justices—Miller, Swayne, and Davis—dissented vigorously, arguing that the federal monetary power amply included the right to make paper money legal tender.

It was at once evident that this opinion might well be reversed should the Legal Tender Act come before the enlarged Court. A year later, in the *Second Legal Tender Cases* (1871) this reversal occurred; the Court directly overruled *Hepburn v. Griswold* by a majority of five to four with Bradley and Strong joining Miller, Swayne, and Davis.

This sequence of events led Grant's enemies to charge him with having deliberately packed the Court to obtain a reversal of *Hepburn v. Griswold*. The truth of this charge depends entirely upon the meaning of the expression "packing the Court." Grant disapproved of the decision in *Hepburn v. Griswold*, and it appears certain that he was aware that both Bradley and Strong were known to consider the Legal Tender Act constitutional. Apparently Grant had obtained no prior commitment or understanding, expressed or implied, from either appointee that they would vote to reverse *Hep-*

burn v. Griswold, but it is plain that he had needed none. Grant's action differed little or not at all from that of all Presidents making appointments to the Court, since Presidents invariably consider the constitutional, political, and economic implications of their judicial appointments.

THE DISINTEGRATION OF RADICAL RECONSTRUCTION

A bitter political and social struggle ensued after 1868 in all the so-called reconstructed states. The white population, at first largely disfranchised and leaderless, was nevertheless bitterly determined to resist "Negro domination," and soon re-entered the political conflict. The conservative leaders rallied whites to the polls, sought the support of Negroes disgusted with Radical tactics, and through the Ku Klux Klan resorted to night-riding and terrorism in their struggle for supremacy. The Radicals fought back with their principal weapons: the Negro vote, white disfranchisement, corruption, and appeals to Washington.

Although the Southern states were now nominally "reconstructed," Congress did not hesitate to interfere in the resultant chaos. For example, when the conservatives secured control of the Georgia legislature, Congress responded in December 1869 by a statute imposing additional requirements on the supposedly reconstructed state. The Radical governor was empowered to determine the membership of the legislature, and the state was also required to ratify the Fifteenth Amendment. The unconstitutionality of this statute is too evident to require analysis; even the extreme Radicals were embarrassed in their attempts to defend it.

Another law, the so-called Enforcement Act of May 1870, guaranteed Negro suffrage, and imposed heavy penalties upon individuals for night-riding or for infringing the right to vote secured by the Fifteenth Amendment. This statute attempted to protect the right to vote against all infringement, whether or not disfranchisement was based upon race, color, or previous condition of servitude. The Supreme Court in *United States v. Reese* (1876) was to declare these portions of the act void on the ground that the Fifteenth Amendment did not extend any positive guarantee of the franchise.

The so-called Second Enforcement Act, passed in February 1871, placed congressional elections under direct federal supervision. This statute, the real purpose of which was again to protect Negro and Radical voters, was undoubtedly constitutional, since Congress had full authority to regulate congressional elections.

Most drastic of all, however, was the Third Enforcement Act, or the "Ku Klux Klan Act," which the Radicals pushed through Congress in April 1871, on the alleged grounds that an actual state of rebellion against federal authority existed in some areas in the South. The law levied heavy penalties against persons conspiring to rebel against the United States, interfering with duties of federal officer or enforcement of federal law, or conspiring "to go in disguise" in order to deprive any person of "the equal protection of the laws." Whenever the President found that insurrection, rebellion, or conspiracy to violate the provisions of the act existed, he was authorized by proclamation to suspend the writ of habeas corpus and to employ the armed forces of the United States to suppress the conspiracy. This law was open to the objection that it attempted to enforce the guarantees of the Fourteenth Amendment against persons rather than state action; the Supreme Court, in *United States v. Harris* (1883), later declared it void on that ground.

Under the provisions of the Ku Klux Klan Act, federal troops were dispatched to suppress literally hundreds of disturbances throughout the South in the next few years. The most notable instances of federal intervention occurred in South Carolina, Louisiana, and Arkansas. In October 1871, when Klan activity became particularly violent in South Carolina, President Grant issued a proclamation declaring nine counties in that state to be in rebellion, suspended the writ of habeas corpus, and sent in federal troops to restore order.

In Louisiana, conflict between Radicals and Conservatives in 1872 resulted in the erection of rival state governments. The Radicals, claiming victory in the state election of that year, used federal troops and irregular federal processes to place the so-called Kellogg-Pinchback government [5] in power. The Conservatives nonetheless organized a separate legislature and recognized John McEnery as rightful governor. Grant sent troops to support the Radicals, but the Conservative government continued to exist, and violence, political chaos, and semi-anarchy prevailed in the state for the next four years.

In Arkansas, the followers of Robert Brooks, unsuccessful Conservative candidate for governor in 1872, raised an armed force and in April 1874 ejected the Radical governor, Elisha Baxter, from the state house. Actual civil war ensued in Little Rock, and again federal troops were called in to keep order. Eventually Grant sustained Baxter's administration.

---

[5] So called because Governor William P. Kellogg and Lieutenant-Governor P. B. S. Pinchback headed the Radical political machine.

In spite of their many handicaps—disfranchisement, the presence of federal troops, and effective Radical organization—the Conservatives made steady progress in regaining control of the reconstructed states. Several factors assisted them. Most important, the Conservatives had the support of approximately nine-tenths of the white population. In 1871, Congress modified the Test-Oath provisions which had virtually debarred ex-Confederates from voting, and in the following year, Congress took action under Section 3 of the Fourteenth Amendment and passed a broad amnesty act restoring the right of office-holding to nearly all ex-Confederates.

The Amnesty Act of 1872, significantly, was a Radical measure designed specifically to throttle the rebellion then in progress against the regular Republican Party organization. A few days before its passage in May, a number of so-called "Liberal Republicans," who disagreed sharply with their party's policies in the South and who were dismayed also both with the growth of corruption in the Grant administration and with Republican high tariff sentiment, had met in convention in Cincinnati and nominated Horace Greeley, the eccentric editor of the *New York Tribune*, for the presidency. Among other things, the Liberals' platform had called for "the immediate and absolute removal of all disabilities on account of the rebellion," and the Radicals in alarm had rushed the Amnesty Act onto the books in reply. By its passage the Radicals signaled their recognition of the fact that northern public opinion was becoming dangerously disaffected with the continued attempt to impose Radical regimes in the southern states in opposition to white wishes.

The Liberal Republican revolt ended in failure, but it threw a scare into the Radical Republicans, who thereafter hesitated to pass legislation interfering in the internal affairs of the southern states. Southern Conservatives now had virtually a free hand. By 1875, operating mainly through the Democratic Party, they had recovered control in eight of the eleven late Confederate states. Only in South Carolina, Florida, and Louisiana did Radical Republican regimes still cling to power.

Meanwhile in the election of 1874 the Republicans lost control of the House of Representatives. Dismayed Radical leaders now recognized that they were in serious trouble. In an effort to hold control of the Negro vote in the South, the lame-duck Republican Congress, acting under Representative Ben Butler's leadership, rushed through to passage the so-called Civil Rights Act of 1875 prohibiting racial segregation in inns, public conveyances, theaters, restaurants, and the like. Significantly, this measure, for which the late Charles Sumner had agitated for years, had been carefully stripped of its school desegregation features before passage, at the instance both of white southern Republican congressmen and of President Grant. The Civil Rights Act of 1875 had little practical effect in operation and was to be declared unconstitutional in the *Civil Rights Cases* (1883) as exceeding the powers of Congress under the Fourteenth Amendment.[6]

THE DISPUTED ELECTION OF 1876

The presidential election of 1876, which resulted in a bitter political and constitutional controversy, greatly hastened the final disintegration of Radical reconstruction.

The election at first appeared to have resulted in a victory for Samuel J. Tilden, the Democratic candidate. An early tabulation gave him 184 undisputed electoral votes, with but 185 votes necessary for election. Rutherford B. Hayes, the Republican candidate, had but 165 undisputed votes. However, it soon appeared that Hayes had a chance to win. South Carolina, Florida, and Louisiana, with nineteen electoral votes, emerged as disputed states. Conflict also developed in Oregon, where one Republican elector was ineligible because he was a federal officeholder. Eventually all four states submitted dual electoral returns to Congress. If the disputed electoral votes of all four were added to the Republican column, Hayes would emerge victorious.

The double returns from the Southern states resulted from a confused struggle between the Radicals and the Conservatives. In South Carolina, where the Radical machine was still in control, the Republicans had apparently carried the state, and the Republican-controlled returning board certified the Hayes electors; nevertheless the Democratic electors submitted ballots for Tilden. In Louisiana, after an utterly chaotic election, the illegally constituted Kellogg-Pinchback Radical government conducted an incredibly partisan count and certified the Hayes electors. McEnery, the Democratic gubernatorial pretender, then issued certificates to the Democratic electors, who balloted for Tilden. In Florida the Republican board certified the Hayes electors, only to have the newly elected Democratic governor and legislature establish a new returning board which certified the Tilden electors.

In Oregon, the secretary of state was the proper returning board,

---

[6] See pp. 463–464 for a discussion of the Court's opinion.

and he first certified the victory of the Republican electors. It shortly appeared, however, that one Republican elector was a postmaster, and therefore ineligible under the Constitution to serve as an elector. The Democratic governor then put forward the plausible claim that the ineligible elector had never legally been chosen, and that the office thereupon devolved upon the elector having the next highest number of votes, who was a Democrat. The governor, acting in concert with the secretary of state, then issued certificates to the two uncontested Republicans and to one Democratic elector. The two Republicans nonetheless met with their ineligible colleague, who had meanwhile resigned both as postmaster and as elector, and reappointed him an elector. The three then cast three ballots for Hayes.

Thus, when Congress met in December, it was confronted with dual returns from Florida, Louisiana, South Carolina, and Oregon. Unfortunately, there was no constitutional provision governing such a situation, nor was there any clear precedent for solving the problem. The Constitution stipulated merely that electoral returns were to be opened by the president of the Senate in the presence of both houses, and should then be counted. Did this mean that the president of the Senate had the right to count the votes and to decide between conflicting returns? If this contention, immediately advanced by the Republicans, was correct, it would presumably place Hayes in the White House, for Thomas W. Ferry, president of the Senate pro tem, was a Republican. However, the argument had but little weight, for the president of the Senate had never in the past assumed to exercise any discretionary authority in counting the vote.

The so-called Twenty-Second Joint Rule, adopted by Congress in 1865, had provided that in case objection was offered to the vote of any state, the two houses were to separate and decide independently whether the vote was to be received. The rule further provided that no vote was to be counted unless both houses assented to it. Since the House was now Democratic, the application of this rule would have made impossible a count favoring the Republicans. Unfortunately for the Democrats, the rule was no longer in effect, for in January 1876 the Senate had refused to readopt it for the coming election.

After some initial confusion, a joint Senate-House committee on January 18 reported a bill creating an Electoral Commission of Fifteen to decide all disputed returns. The Commission was to be composed of five representatives (three Democrats and two Republicans), five senators (three Republicans and two Democrats), and four justices of the Supreme Court, who were to name a fifth justice. The four justices designated were those assigned to the first, third, eighth, and ninth circuits, which in reality meant Nathan Clifford, Stephen J. Field, William Strong, and Samuel Miller—two Democrats and two Republicans. It was generally understood that the fifth justice would probably be David Davis of Illinois, who was nominally a Republican but very moderate in his viewpoint. The bill provided that the Commission's decision on all disputed returns should be final unless an objection were sustained by the separate vote of both houses.

Nearly all Democrats and most Republicans supported this proposal, though the extreme Radical Republicans, led by Senator Oliver P. Morton of Indiana, opposed it. The Democrats believed that the Commission would settle at least one disputed return in their favor and so elect Tilden. This expectation was badly shaken when the Illinois legislature elected Davis to the Senate. As a result the fifth justice named was Joseph Bradley, who was a staunch Republican, and thus the Republicans controlled the Commission by a count of eight votes to seven.

When the electoral votes were counted in joint session, the returns from the four states were all disputed and were therefore referred to the Commission.

The Commission settled the dispute by refusing "to go behind the election returns." It held that it had power merely to decide what electors had been certified in the proper manner by the correct returning board, in accordance with the state law; and that it could not investigate the actual popular vote to determine whether the returning board had correctly counted that vote. The Commission based this conclusion on the argument that each state under the Constitution was entitled to choose its electors as it saw fit. The federal government, the Commission held, had no constitutional power to control this process, for to do so would be an intrusion upon the sovereign sphere of state authority. In accordance with this rule, the Commission decided, by a vote of eight to seven in each instance, that the Republican electors in South Carolina, Florida, and Louisiana had been properly certified and that their vote was valid.

The Oregon case was more difficult, but the Commission resolved it by deciding that under Oregon law the secretary of state alone was the properly constituted returning board and that he had originally certified the election of the three Republican electors. The ineligibility of one elector the Commission held to be immaterial, since he had resigned both his federal office and his electorship and had then been reappointed by the other two electors according to law. The Commission rejected the Democratic argument that his ineligibility had resulted in election of a Tilden elector. Acceptance of this contention would have taken the board into the considerations behind the secretary of state's certificates; moreover, American legal precedent was against a defeated candidate for office being declared the winner when his opponent was revealed as ineligible.

Thus the Commission by a partisan vote of eight to seven decided every disputed return in favor of the Republicans. The House dissented from the Commission's report in every instance, but the Senate concurred, and therefore the Commission's decisions stood. Hayes was accordingly declared elected, 185 votes to 184, the final decision being formally reached on March 3, the day before the scheduled inauguration.

Then and ever since outraged Democrats have charged that the Republicans "stole the election" of 1876 and deprived Tilden of the presidency. The contention has some merit. Hayes electors were evidently "counted in" in both Florida and Louisiana under heavy Republican pressure. The Commission also clearly made all its decisions by a straight partisan majority; plainly the eight Republican members were concerned mainly with placing Hayes in the White House. The sudden concern of Morton and other Republican Commission members for the sanctity of states' rights—this by men who had sponsored a long series of attacks upon state autonomy—was not convincing. Had political expediency demanded it, they clearly would have manipulated their constitutional theories to suit the opposite approach.

The Commission's decision nevertheless had a certain consistency in constitutional theory. The contention that federal authority over state choice was limited to fixing the identity of the electors lawfully certified by the legal state agency for this purpose had a great deal of force. Electors are technically state officials, and the Constitution does indeed give each state the right to choose its electors as it wishes. To "go behind the returns" and subject a state election to scrutiny and analysis would indeed have been an act of doubtful constitutionality.

It is sometimes charged that the Commission was inconsistent in that it actually did go behind the returns in Oregon. This charge is unjustified. The Commission did not investigate the state's popular vote; it merely held that the secretary of state's original certification of three Republican electors was legal and had not been invalidated by the governor's refusal to deliver certificates to the Hayes electors.

Hayes' election marked the practical end of Radical reconstruction and federal control of the South. The Republicans had already lost control of the House, and the new President was a moderate who did not approve of continued federal interference in state affairs. Hayes at once withdrew federal troops from the three Radical-controlled Southern states. The Democrats shortly assumed control in all of them, thereby bringing the Radical Republican era in the South to an end.

AFTERMATH OF RECONSTRUCTION

After 1876 the remnants of the legal structure imposed upon the South in the Reconstruction era steadily disintegrated. The Thirteenth Amendment was of course not challenged, but the dominant white majority nevertheless succeeded in defeating for the most part the original intent of the Fourteenth and Fifteenth Amendments with respect to the Negro.

The immediate reason for the failure of the Southern social revolution the Radicals had projected was the abandonment by Congress after 1876 of support for the attempted new Southern social order. After 1876 Congress followed a policy of non-interference in Southern internal affairs. In part, this change of policy was forced upon Congress because of increasing Northern weariness and disgust at the continued violence and chaos in the South, although in fact a substantial element in Southern disorder was the direct result of Conservative policies of subversion and resistance directed at the various Republican regimes. After 1876, the Northern Democrats had far enough revived in prestige and power to compete seriously in congressional elections with Radical Republicans so that Republican candidates who "waved the bloody shirt" too violently might be defeated at the polls. In effect, the Northern electorate refused to support interference in Southern "local affairs" any longer.

Also the general character of the Republican party was undergoing alteration. Increasingly the party came to represent the big business interests of the Northeast. Reflecting this trend, the party's politicians turned their interest toward tariff and monetary policies while the reconstruction issue steadily lost importance.

After 1876, the Republican party was the more willing to abandon Southern controls because it perceived that the task of building an effective Southern Republican machine was not only apparently hopeless but also had become unnecessary to the party's national dominance. While the Democratic party had revived somewhat, it had nonetheless become apparent that the Republican party possessed such strength in the North and West that it could control Congress most of the time and win most presidential elections without the aid of a Southern Republican party. The Republican party in the South was accordingly allowed to disintegrate and to become the property of a small hierarchy of Southern Republican officeholders dependent upon patronage from Washington.

The Supreme Court also lent support to the restoration of "white supremacy" in the South. In a long series of decisions, the Court greatly reduced the significance of the Fourteenth and Fifteenth Amendments as guarantees of Negro rights.

The first big step in this development came in 1876, when the Court first decided that the Fourteenth Amendment did not place ordinary private rights under federal protection except as against state interference. The Fourteenth Amendment, said Chief Justice Morrison R. Waite in *United States v. Cruikshank* (1876), "adds nothing to the rights of one citizen as against another. It simply furnishes a federal guaranty against any encroachment by the States upon the fundamental rights which belong to every citizen as a member of society."

In 1883, in the Civil Rights Cases, the Court applied this doctrine in declaring void the Civil Rights Act of 1875. This law, the last serious effort of the Radicals to establish civil equality for Negroes, had provided that all persons, regardless of race, were entitled to "the full and equal enjoyment of the accommodations, advantages, facilities and privileges of inns, public conveyances on land or water, theatres and other places of public amusement . . . ," and made it a misdemeanor for any person to impair or deny the foregoing rights.

Justice Bradley in his opinion pointed out that the Fourteenth Amendment was "prohibitory upon the States," but not upon private individuals. The Amendment declared that no state shall "abridge the privileges or immunities of citizens of the United States . . . nor deny to any person within its jurisdiction the equal protection of the laws." The Amendment thus clearly prohibited invasion by state action of certain private rights, but, said Bradley, "Individual invasion of individual rights is not the subject-matter of the amendment."

In effect this opinion served notice that the federal government could not lawfully protect the Negro against the discrimination which private individuals might choose to exercise against him. This was another way of saying that the system of "white supremacy" was mainly beyond federal control, since the Southern social order rested very largely upon private human relationships and not upon state-made sanctions.

Equally important in the maintenance of a caste society in the South was the Court's acceptance in *Plessy v. Ferguson* (1896) of the so-called "separate but equal" rule. The case involved the constitutionality of a Louisiana "Jim Crow" law requiring separate railway coaches for whites and Negroes. Such a statute, said Justice Brown for the Court, did not deprive Negroes of the equal protection of the laws, provided Negroes were furnished accommodations equal to those for whites. Registering a vigorous lone protest, Justice Harlan insisted that "Our Constitution is color-blind" and the statute unconstitutional. Undeterred by this rebuke, the Court in *Cumming v. County Board of Education* (1899) by implication accepted the constitutionality of state laws requiring "separate but equal" schools for whites and Negroes. And in *Berea College v. Kentucky* (1908) the Court accepted a Kentucky statute prohibiting private schools from admitting whites and blacks to the same institution.

The Court made a nominal concession to Negro rights when it held in *Strauder v. West Virginia* (1880) that laws barring Negroes from jury service were a violation of the equal protection clause and were void. However the Court at once destroyed the implication of this decision when it ruled in *Virginia v. Rives* (1880) that the mere absence of Negroes from a jury did not necessarily mean a denial of right. To prove a denial of due process an accused Negro was obliged to prove that Negroes were deliberately excluded from the jury trying him. This decision paved the way for the practical exclusion of Negroes from juries through the cautious exercise of discretionary authority by local officials.

The Southern states were also able through a variety of devices to escape the intent of the Fifteenth Amendment and effectively disfranchise the Negro. In *United States v. Reese* (1876) the Supreme Court first pointed out the obvious but important fact that the Fifteenth Amendment did not "confer the right of suffrage upon anyone." It merely prohibited the states or the United States from excluding a person from the franchise because of race, color, or previous condition of servitude. The primary control of suffrage remained with the state. The Court accordingly declared Sections 3 and 4 of the Enforcement Act of 1870 to be unconstitutional since they provided penalties for obstructing or hindering any person for any reason from voting in any election. The right of Congress to legislate for state elections, said Chief Justice Waite, was limited to legislating against discrimination because of race, color, or previous condition of servitude.

Thus it was evident that if the Southern states could discover and impose certain restrictions which nominally did not bar Negroes as such but actually had that effect, such statutes might be constitutional. Eventually the South discovered four such devices, the first two of which the Court accepted as constitutional. These were the literacy test, the poll tax, the "grandfather law," and the "white-primary" law.

In *Williams v. Mississippi* (1898), the Court held that a law giving local officials authority to require any voter to read and interpret any part of the Constitution was valid. Such a law admittedly opened the way for mass disfranchisement of Negroes, since local offices could simply administer to any "undesirable" voter a reading test which few men could meet. In the same case, the Court declared that the payment of a poll tax as a prerequisite for the franchise was also valid—though again the practical effect was to disfranchise nearly all Negroes and poor whites alike.

The Court, however, refused to validate so-called "grandfather laws," in which the state disfranchised Negroes by extending the franchise only to all those whose ancestors had had the right to vote in 1866. In *Guinn v. United States* (1915), the Court said that the only possible purpose of such a law was to disfranchise the Negro, and that the law was a deliberate evasion of the Fifteenth Amendment. At the time of the decision, however, such laws had already been in effect for a generation and had largely served their purpose. Not until the mid-twentieth century, with the destruction of white primary laws, did the practical disfranchisement of the Negro in the South show signs of breaking down.[6]

In theory, the Fourteenth Amendment provided a means whereby Congress could have coerced the several Southern states into granting the franchise to the Negro. Section 2 of the amendment declares that any state which abridges the right of suffrage for any of its male inhabitants above the age of twenty-one, except as a punishment for crime, shall have its representation in Congress reduced proportionately. Had Congress chosen to enforce this provision, it could have confronted any Southern state which denied Negroes

---

[6] See pp. 881ff.

the franchise with the unpleasant choice of restoring Negroes the right to vote or losing one-fifth to one-half of its seats in the House of Representatives. In 1890, this provision inspired a Republican faction headed by Representative Henry Cabot Lodge of Massachusetts to introduce the so-called "Force Bill" for the enforcement of the amendment. This measure would have established federal supervision over state polling places in national elections, and would have reduced the representation in Congress of any state which then persisted in denying Negroes the franchise. The Force Bill for a time revived all the bitter animosities of the Reconstruction era; however, a political bargain with Southern Democrats in Congress finally shelved the proposal. Since that time, an occasional Northern congressman, usually one seeking support from Negro constituents, has introduced legislation to effect a reduction in Southern representation in accordance with the amendment, but these measures have never been taken seriously.

The Reconstruction era closed with state-federal relations on much the same plane as they had occupied before 1860. Some of the centralization effected in the Civil War, through the creation of a new national banking system and increased federal controls over the monetary system, remained in effect; by the same token, the long-time prewar trend toward the shrinkage of federal governmental prestige and power had been decisively halted. Slavery stood abolished by constitutional amendment, with Congress empowered to enforce the prohibition. The Fourteenth Amendment had at length settled definitively the status of citizenship by making national citizenship primary and state citizenship secondary. Civil rights were now guaranteed by the Constitution and by Congress against impairment by a state, though not against impairment by private individuals. There was now a federal guarantee against any state's impairing the right to vote because of race, color, or previous condition of servitude, a guarantee which, as has been observed, meant little in actual practice. But the basic character of the American constitutional system had emerged unimpaired. A few Radical extremists had desired to destroy state autonomy permanently, but there had never been any serious prospect that they would succeed in this objective. The issues of state sovereignty and the supposed right of secession had been settled forever. The Union remained essentially the same one as that described in the Federalist papers and in the great opinions of John Marshall.

In 1876, something like a constitutional revolution was in the making, but it had comparatively little to do with the great issues of the Reconstruction period. It was to be associated, rather, with the remarkable industrial revolution under way in the North. It was to be in part based upon judicial interpretation of the Fourteenth Amendment, but it had little to do with the original intent of that Amendment or with the constitutional controversies of Southern reconstruction generally. After 1876 the principal constitutional issues in national development were no longer associated with the question of the ultimate character of the Union but rather with the question of how a document, drafted in the eighteenth century for a socially decentralized agrarian state, could be adapted to the needs of a modern urban industrial society.

Chapter

19

The Revolution in Due Process of Law

IN THE generation after the Civil War a gigantic economic revolution transformed the United States from an agrarian republic into the world's leading industrial nation. Some industrial development had occurred in the two generations before the Civil War. Early industrial development had centered mainly in the Northeast and had included chiefly production in textiles, shoes, coal, iron, brass, and small ware. The Civil War, with its heavy demands upon northern manufactures, sharply accelerated industrial activity in the North. After the war a great boom began in steel, coal, railroads, meat packing, oil, milling, lumber, and textiles. This development was interrupted by panic and depression in 1873 and 1893, while a chronic depression settled down upon American agriculture for two decades after 1873. But the underlying industrial trend, inspired by the nation's matchless natural resources and remarkable technological progress and by expanding markets at home and abroad, continued unbroken.

By 1900 the United States had become the greatest industrial nation in the world. It produced more iron and steel than Great Britain and Germany combined. The value of American manufactured products exceeded eleven billion dollars annually, compared with less than two billion dollars in 1860. Whereas in 1860 there had been not more than 30,000 miles of railroads in the United States, by 1900 there were about 200,000 miles. Population growth and urbanization had kept pace with industrial development. In 1860 there were some 31,000,000 people in the United States, of whom approximately 16 per cent lived in cities; by 1900 the nation's population exceeded 70,000,000, of whom almost 50 per cent lived in cities.

The industrial revolution opened a new chapter in American constitutional history. The Constitution of 1787 was written for an eighteenth-century agrarian republic of less than four million people. The same document now had to serve as the frame of government for a modern urban industrial society with all the new complex social and economic problems inherent in such a civilization. A continuous and rapid process of constitutional growth and adjustment was therefore necessary and inevitable if the Constitution was to be adapted successfully to the modern era. In fact, nearly all constitutional development since the close of the Reconstruction period has been concerned directly or indirectly with the impact of the new social order upon government. After 1880 constitutional questions became increasingly entangled in a series of political and social issues of basic consequence to America's destiny.

REVIVAL OF THE DOCTRINE OF VESTED RIGHTS

In the generation after 1876, the new masters of industry and capital sought little in the way of positive constitutional change. Through the Republican Party they obtained favorable tariff and banking legislation and railroad subsidies in the form of land grants. but these involved no radical alteration in the constitutional system. For the rest, their interests in government were generally negative —they wished protection against the efforts of agrarian and liberal dissident groups to impose governmental controls upon big business. In part this protection could be secured in one way or another through political action. Business leaders influenced party platforms, supported promising candidates, and lobbied against what they considered to be unreasonable and arbitrary state and national legislation. However, these procedures were not always effective. In particular, many of the western states frequently fell into the hands of agrarian radicals who passed laws subjecting railroads and business enterprise to a variety of regulatory measures. Even eastern state legislatures and Congress were not immune to the liberal reformer's zeal. Against such legislation business sought and found protection in the courts.

What business needed was a means whereby the prevailing doctrine of *laissez-faire* economic theory could be written into constitutional law as a positive protection against "unreasonable" legislation. The old doctrine of vested rights, developed by the state and national judiciary between 1790 and 1830, served this purpose to some extent, since in a vague way it guaranteed private property against arbitrary or confiscatory laws. The doctrine had been identified in part with the contract clause, but otherwise it rested upon no specific provision of federal or state constitutions but rather upon the general nature of constitutional government. A more definite identification with the written constitution was highly desirable to the business leaders.

The due process clause in the first section of the Fourteenth Amendment was to serve this purpose. In a series of epoch-making decisions between 1873 and 1898, the Supreme Court revolutionized the historic interpretation of due process of law and thus established the Fourteenth Amendment as the specific constitutional authorization for the doctrine of vested rights.

This constitutional revolution was not a conspiracy. It was a reflection of the prevailing economic philosophy of *laissez faire* and the preoccupation of the country with the rapid development of its natural resources. No group of men sat down together and plotted the changes in constitutional interpretation necessary to extend maximum protection to the property of American industry. The process was a gradual one, in which the decisions responded slowly to the arguments of many different attorneys who came before it and to changes in the point of view of the judges who were appointed to the courts. So involved in legal technicalities was the shift in the meaning of due process that most judges and lawyers seem hardly to have been aware of what was happening. Yet the revolution was no less real because it was gradual and unconscious; and when it was completed, the courts occupied a new position of power and prestige in American life as the guardians of property.

The reader will recall that the doctrine of vested rights was originally a product of eighteenth-century natural rights theory and compact philosophy. Certain rights, according to this theory, were so fundamental as to be derived from the very nature of justice, even from the very nature of God. It was the purpose and function of organized society to protect these rights; indeed constitutional government existed to assure their protection. Not the least of such rights was that of private property. Therefore the legislature of a state did not have an unlimited right of interference with private property. The bill of rights set up certain specific immunities, but it did not follow that rights mentioned in the Constitution were of an exclusive character, or that the legislature could commit a violation of natural right merely because the right in question was not written down. The whole body of natural rights inhered in the people, and the legislature was powerless to interfere with them in any fashion.

The doctrine of vested rights most often found expression in the early national era by its infusion into the obligation of contracts clause in Article I, Section 10, of the Constitution. It was in this connection that the doctrine achieved its most positive and specific limitations upon legislative authority. *Vanhorne's Lessee v. Dorrance* (1795), wherein Justice Paterson condemned a Pennsylvania statute as a violation of the "primary object of the social compact," the protection of property, arose under the contract clause. It will be recalled that the doctrine was again identified with the contract clause in *Fletcher v. Peck* (1810) and in *Dartmouth College v. Woodward* (1819). And again, in *Terrett v. Taylor* (1815), a case involving Virginia's attempt to take title to certain lands of the disestablished Episcopal Church, Justice Story discoursed at length upon the doctrine of vested rights, which he identified with the contract clause in imposing limitations upon the state's legislative authority. In brief, in the early nineteenth century the contract clause played somewhat the same role in the embodiment of the doctrine of vested rights as the due process clause was to play after 1890.[1]

With the rise of popular sovereignty after 1830, the doctrine of vested rights suffered a temporary decline, for it conflicted with the growing idea of the ascendancy of popular will as expressed through legislative fiat. The prevailing attitude expressed by most courts between 1830 and 1850 was that the legislature represented

---

[1] The courts did not invariably associate the doctrine of vested rights with the contract clause, but sometimes instead rested vested rights merely upon the general nature of all constitutional government. Thus in *Calder v. Bull* (1798) Justice Samuel Chase observed that "an act of the Legislature (for I cannot call it a law) contrary to the first great principles of the social compact, cannot be considered a rightful exercise of legislative authority." Among other examples of such legislation he included "a law that takes property from A and gives it to B." Justice Story used much the same language in *Wilkinson v. Leland* (1829) when he said that "We know of no case in which a legislative Act to transfer the property of A to B without his consent has ever been held a constitutional exercise of legislative power in any State of the Union." And Chancellor Kent in his *Commentaries*, published in 1826, emphasized that vested rights were to be protected from legislative attack whether or not the constitution specifically protected them. He regarded them as associated with the general nature of all constitutional government.

the sovereign power of the people, and that the only proper limitations upon its will were those specifically imposed in the state and federal constitutions.

About 1850, the doctrine of vested rights underwent a revival and at the same time became associated to some extent with the guarantee of due process of law in state and federal constitutions. In *Wynehamer v. New York* (1856) the New York Court of Appeals declared unconstitutional a state law regulating the manufacture of liquor and in so doing tied the doctrine of vested rights to the due process clause in the state constitution. It held that this clause constituted a general restriction on the legislature's power to interfere with private property. A year later, in the Dred Scott case, Chief Justice Taney referred incidentally to the due process clause in the Fifth Amendment to the federal Constitution, construing it as prohibiting the federal government from imposing restrictions upon property in slaves within the territories. Again, in *Hepburn v. Griswold* (1870) the Court briefly invoked the due process clause of the Fifth Amendment in holding invalid federal legal tender legislation.

The guarantee of "due process of law" and its counterpart, "the law of the land," were already centuries old in the nineteenth century. In England, the thirty-ninth article of the Great Charter granted by King John to his barons in 1215 contained the pledge that "no freeman shall be taken or imprisoned or disseised or exiled or in any way destroyed . . . except by the lawful judgment of his peers and by the law of the land." Magna Charta from time to time was reaffirmed by successive English monarchs, and in the Statute of Westminster of the Liberties of London, enacted in 1354, the phrase "due process of law" occurred for the first time in English law. According to Sir Edward Coke, "due process of law" and "law of the land" had the same meaning, although no certain definition of either phrase was ever laid down.

The phrase "law of the land" was incorporated in several colonial charters, and thus became a part of the commonly accepted body of liberties of the American colonists. The Massachusetts constitution of 1780 contained the phrase "the law of the land," virtually as it had been originally embodied in Magna Charta. Most of the other early state constitutions contained the same general guarantees. In 1791 due process passed into the federal Constitution with the adoption of the Fifth Amendment, which provided that "no person shall . . . be deprived of life, liberty, or property without due process of law." Thus after some centuries of development "due process of law" found its way into the American constitutional system.

Before 1850 due process was generally assumed to be a procedural rather than a substantive restriction upon governmental authority. That is, it guaranteed certain protective rights to an accused person before he could be deprived of his life, liberty, or property. These rights included protection against arrest without a warrant, the right to counsel, the requirement of indictment by a grand jury before trial, the right of the accused to hear the nature of the evidence against him, the right to an impartial trial by a jury of the accused person's peers, and the requirement of a verdict before any sentence was executed. In other words, due process of law historically was of significance primarily in criminal cases. It promised accused persons that they would not be punished in an arbitrary and indiscriminate fashion and without the protection of long-established criminal procedure. By the same token, due process hitherto had had no relation to the doctrine of vested rights, nor had it constituted any limitation upon the right of legislatures to regulate private property in the interests of the public welfare.

The tentative association between due process of law and the doctrine of vested rights in the Wynehamer, Dred Scott, and Hepburn cases thus represented a radical departure in the historic meaning and content of due process. The new association between due process and vested rights gave due process a substantive content and made it a guarantee against unreasonable legislative interference with private property. Before 1870, the substantive conception of due process was tentative, and had appeared in only a few cases. It remained to be seen whether the due process clause in federal and state constitutions would replace the obligation of contracts clause as the principal constitutional limitation upon legislative capacity to interfere with private property and vested rights.

THE FOURTEENTH AMENDMENT AND THE
SLAUGHTERHOUSE CASES

The Fourteenth Amendment to the federal Constitution, taking effect in 1868, contained in Section 1 the clause: "Nor shall any State deprive any person of life, liberty, or property, without due process of law." Unlike the similar clause in the Fifth Amendment, which guaranteed the individual against the federal government, the due process clause in the Fourteenth Amendment was a federal guarantee against arbitrary state action interfering with individual rights.

The reader will recall that the entire history of the Fourteenth Amendment prior to passage indicated that it was passed to protect the newly acquired political and legal rights of Negroes against arbitrary state action. There is little evidence that the statesmen who wrote the amendment were interested in bringing about the intervention of the federal government in the protection of vested rights. Certainly there was nothing to indicate in their time that the due process clause of the Fourteenth Amendment was destined to become one of the most important foundation stones of modern constitutional law.

The Supreme Court first ruled upon the meaning of the Fourteenth Amendment in 1873, in the *Slaughterhouse Cases*. The legislature of Louisiana in 1869 had conferred upon one firm what was in effect a monopoly of the slaughterhouse business in New Orleans and had banned all other slaughterhouses already established within the city. Some of the businesses affected brought suit in the Louisiana courts, asserting among other things that the law in question was a violation of the Fourteenth Amendment. The Supreme Court of Louisiana, however, held that the law constituted a legitimate exercise of the police power of the state and thus upheld the constitutionality of the act. An appeal was then taken to the Supreme Court of the United States.

The most insistent claim of the appellant was that the statute in question constituted a violation of the privileges and immunities clause of the Fourteenth Amendment—"no state . . . shall abridge the privileges or immunities of citizens of the United States."

This interpretation of the clause by implication placed all civil rights under the protection of the federal government, but the Court refused to accept this contention. Instead it resorted to the doctrine of dual citizenship. "It is quite clear," said Justice Miller, "that there is a citizenship of the United States and a citizenship of a state, which are distinct from each other."

The consequence of this doctrine of dual citizenship was that the Court was enabled to draw a sharp line between those privileges and immunities which accrued to an individual by virtue of his state citizenship and those which accrued to him by virtue of his citizenship in the national government. Only the latter, said the Court, fell under the protection of the Fourteenth Amendment.

But what were the "privileges or immunities" of citizens of the several states as distinct from national citizenship? Here the Court quoted earlier decisions to demonstrate that the whole body of commonly accepted civil liberties fell within this category. It included, said Miller, "protection by the government, with the right to acquire and possess property of every kind, and to pursue and obtain happiness and safety, subject, nevertheless, to such restraints as the [state] government may prescribe for the general good of the whole." It was not the intent of the Fourteenth Amendment, said Miller, to transfer this whole body of rights to the keeping of the federal government. The consequences of such an interpretation, if accepted, were "so serious, so far-reaching and pervading," and they altered so radically "the whole theory of the relations of the state and Federal governments to each other" that the Court simply rejected this line of thought completely.

What, then, were the "privileges or immunities" of national citizenship, which the Court admitted the amendment did protect against state action? These the Court refused to define absolutely, but it suggested what some of these might be. They included the right of a citizen "to come to the seat of the government to assert any claim he may have upon that government"; the "right of free access to its seaports"; and the right "to demand the care and protection of the Federal government over his life, liberty, and property when on the high seas, or within the jurisdiction of a foreign government."

What the opinion said in effect was that the whole body of traditional rights of the common law and of state bills of rights still remained solely under the protection of the states. The "privileges or immunities" clause of the Fourteenth Amendment had not placed the federal government under an obligation to protect these rights against state violation. So far as the federal Constitution was concerned, therefore, the "privileges" and "immunities" of the citizens of the separate states were in exactly the same status as they were before the amendment was adopted. By implication, the "privileges or immunities" clause had thus done nothing to disturb or restrict the power of the various states to regulate private property interests within their boundaries.

The plaintiffs also asserted that the Louisiana statute in question deprived them of their property without due process of law, again in violation of the Fourteenth Amendment. The Court simply dismissed this contention with the observation that "under no construction of that provision that we have ever seen, or that we deem admissible, can the restraint imposed by the state of Louisiana . . . be held to be a deprivation of property within the meaning of that provision." In other words, the Court accepted without debate the procedural interpretation of due process; it acted as though it had never heard of the substantive interpretations of due process which had been stated briefly by Taney in his Dred Scott opinion and again by the majority in *Hepburn v. Griswold*.

Justice Miller gave the equal protection clause of the Fourteenth Amendment similar summary treatment. The Court simply said that it had reference to state laws discriminating against Negroes. Justice Miller doubted "whether any action of a state not directed by way of discrimination against the Negroes as a class, or on account of their race, will ever be held to come within the purview of this provision."

This interpretation of Section 1 of the Fourteenth Amendment was about as narrow a one as the Court could possibly extract from the language of the section. It came close to nullifying the apparent intent of the amendment. It seems probable that Congress had intended to place the whole generally accepted body of civil and private rights within the protection of the federal government as against state action. Yet by emphasizing the conception of dual citizenship the Supreme Court had denied that the federal government had any interest in a state's regulation of the common private rights of its citizens under the privileges and immunities clause. The Court had gone on to dismiss briefly the argument that the due process clause in the amendment was concerned with the right of a state to regulate private property, a conclusion which accorded with nearly all past interpretations of due process. It had concluded by holding that the equal protection clause was merely a warning to the states not to discriminate against Negroes.

Why had the Court refused to place the common body of "privileges or immunities" within the protection of the federal government? The answer probably is that it did not care to recognize any profound or fundamental alteration in the relations of state and federal governments as a result of the amendment. And to recognize that all private rights were now entrusted to the specific protection of the federal government would have indeed constituted a radical change in the nature of the American constitutional system. The justices on the bench at the time were political conservatives, interested in seeing the old relationships of state and federal governments maintained with as little disturbance as possible. Hence they advanced the very plausible conception of dual citizenship, which seemed to remove nearly all common private rights from the sphere of federal control.

Furthermore, a majority of the Court were not in sympathy with the argument that the meaning of the amendment extended beyond its immediate purpose—the protection of the Negro. The Court was not impressed by the attempts of counsel to make due process of law a general limitation upon the power of the state to regulate private property. Those lawyers and statesmen who wished to extend the protecting hand of the federal government over vested property rights could draw but cold comfort from the Court's contemptuous rejection of the plea that due process of law was a guarantee of vested property rights against state interference.

Four justices—Stephen J. Field, Salmon P. Chase, Noah H. Swayne, and Joseph Bradley—dissented. Field based his spirited dissent mainly upon the doctrine of vested rights, but he also insisted that the Louisiana statute violated the privileges and immunities of citizens of the United States, arguing very plausibly that the Civil Rights Act expressed the true intent of the framers of the amendment as to the general category of rights to be protected by the section. Bradley and Swayne gave more importance to the due process clause, Bradley observing that any act which banned a citizen from a lawful occupation was a violation of due process; while Swayne defined due process as the "fair and regular course of procedure" and yet implied that to impair a property right by statute was in fact a violation of procedure and hence of due process. These minority opinions anticipated the day when a majority of the Court would accept the dictum that due process was indeed a limitation upon the regulatory powers of the state.

MUNN V. ILLINOIS: THE GRANGER CASES

Four years later, in 1877, the Court was presented with an opportunity to set forth again its attitude toward due process of law. In *Munn v. Illinois* and in the other *Granger Cases*, the Court again refused to apply a substantive conception of due process. Instead, it reaffirmed at considerable length the right of the states to regulate private property in the public interest.

These cases involved a characteristic example of the way in which the new economic power was clashing with the attempts of the states to subject that power to some degree of regulation. In the seventies a profound movement of agrarian unrest and discontent swept many of the western states. The causes behind the discontent of the farmer were fairly complex. The deflation of postwar years had lowered his cash income; he had been left with debts which had been contracted during the period of high farm prices, expansion, and war prosperity; and at the same time he was suffering the more general effects of the great business depression which hung over the entire nation between 1873 and 1880.

Economic discontent is at all times likely to seek a political outlet. All over the West in the seventies the farmers joined the Granger movement. Local Grange clubs were both social and political in purpose. Politically, they sought to capture control of state legislatures in order to enact legislation in the interests of the farm group. For a time in the seventies and eighties the Grange or men sympathetic to it held control of the legislatures in most of the northwestern states.

Farmers in the Granger movement laid the blame for their plight chiefly at the door of the railroads and other public utilities. These, they felt, were controlled by eastern financiers or by selfish businessmen who operated them at exorbitant profit without regard to the interest of the farmer they were supposed to serve. Granger-controlled legislatures as a consequence passed numerous laws subjecting railroads, warehouses, and other public utilities to sharp regulation of prices charged for hauling freight, storing grain, and the like.

Munn v. Illinois arose out of an act passed in 1873 by the Granger-controlled legislature of Illinois fixing the rates for the storage of grain in warehouses located in cities of 100,000 population or more. The only city in Illinois of that size was Chicago, and the law was in reality aimed at preventing abuse of the monopoly which the elevator operators had succeeded in establishing over the grain elevator business at the mouth of the Chicago River. Some nine different elevator firms were engaged in business in this vicinity; yet the uniformity and exorbitancy of their rates indicated clearly that the various firms constituted a near-monopoly.

The elevator operators shortly attacked the constitutionality of the statute in the Illinois courts, asserting that the act constituted an infringement upon the power of Congress to regulate interstate commerce and that it violated the due process clause of the Fourteenth Amendment. The decision of the Illinois Supreme Court was favorable to the constitutionality of the act, and an appeal was then taken to the Supreme Court of the United States.

The other *Granger Cases* had a similar origin. A number of Granger-controlled western legislatures, among them those of Wisconsin, Iowa, and Minnesota, had enacted statutes fixing rail rates within the states. The railroads had attacked the constitutionality of these statutes in the courts of the several states. The issue here was the same as that in *Munn v. Illinois*, and the Court therefore settled these cases by direct reference to the former decision.

The opinion in *Munn v. Illinois*, as presented by Chief Justice Morrison R. Waite, showed that a majority of the Court still clung to the notion of due process of law laid down in the *Slaughterhouse Cases*, though the Court's reasoning showed some evidence that the traditional conception of due process as purely procedural was weakening. Waite began with an analysis of the police power, which the courts since Taney's time had defined as the inherent sovereign capacity of the several states to legislate for the health, safety, morals, and welfare of the community. He rested his argument both upon the nature of constitutional government and upon an appeal to history. He quoted the constitution of Massachusetts, which describes the body politic as "a social compact by which the whole people covenants with each citizen, and each citizen with the whole people." From this it followed that the social compact authorized "the establishment of laws requiring each citizen to . . . so use his own property as not unnecessarily to injure another." This was an old common law doctrine which Waite now invoked to support police power. Waite admitted, however, that the state could not control rights which were "purely and exclusively private," an intimation that in certain circumstances the Court might admit due process as a limitation upon police power.

Chief Justice Waite defined the extent of the state's regulatory authority by asserting that when private property is devoted to a public use it is subject to public regulation. "When, therefore," he said, "one devotes his property to a use in which the public has an interest, he, in effect, grants to the public an interest in that use, and must submit to be controlled by the public for the common good." Waite reinforced his doctrine by an appeal to English and American legal history, and cited several precedents from English and American law in which wharfs, warehouses, and private businesses had been subjected to regulation in the public interest.

As in the *Slaughterhouse Cases*, the Court did not enter into an extensive analysis of due process of law; instead Justice Waite contented himself with demonstrating that the legislative power to regulate private property in the public welfare had passed unchallenged for centuries. No one had ever held the police power to be controlled or limited by due process of law.

Yet the very statement that property vested with a public interest was subject to public regulation gave some implied recognition to a substantive conception of due process. What constituted a public interest? Suppose the property in question were vested clearly with a mere private interest? Would the state then have the power of regulation? The Court did not try to answer this embarrassing question. Yet here was a clear anticipation of the growth of substantive due process in the next twenty years.

Field again dissented, and this time he based his dissent directly upon the due process clause. He denied specifically that the mere fact that a business was vested with a public interest gave the state any regulatory power. "If this be sound law, if there be no protection, either in the principles upon which our republican government is founded, or in the prohibitions of the Constitution against such invasion of private rights, all property and all business in the State are held at the mercy of a majority of its legislature." Here was an unequivocal demand that the judiciary constitute itself the guardian of property rights against restrictive state legislation under the authority of the federal Constitution. Though only one other justice, Strong, agreed with his dissent, Field was to see his conception of due process triumph completely before he left the Court in 1897.

THE GROWTH OF SUBSTANTIVE DUE PROCESS, 1877–1898

The Supreme Court had now apparently placed its approval upon a new era of extensive economic regulation by the states. This dictum, if allowed to stand, would have provided a broad constitutional base for the states to control the mass of powerful propertied interests springing up in the nation. New and powerful corporate interests could have been controlled by law simply because they were "vested with a public interest." State government now had been assigned the right to play an important part in molding the industrial revolution then going on in the nation.

Actually no such thing occurred. The gigantic growth of industrial life in the United States in the generation after 1875—in steel, oil, railroads, sugar, lumber, and coal, proceeded substantially unaffected by state legislation. There was regulation, much of it, but it was not of a character to constitute a major checkrein upon the men who were directing the destinies of American industry.

Several factors account for this. First, the whole spirit of the times was against extensive state regulation of the new economic life in America. American industry seemed to be doing very well indeed for itself without the necessity for any governmental interference. Most of America was profiting in one way or another by the tremendous rise in industrial wealth and productive power. True, a few industries and a few men associated with them were amassing fortunes beyond the comprehension of the average person, but the great majority of Americans saw no wrong in the acquisition of wealth; they asked only an equal opportunity to use their own imagination, skills, business sense, and good fortune to enrich themselves. Most Americans despised any suggestion of paternalism in government. The modern idea of the service state had not yet arisen.

State legislatures were nonetheless sometimes controlled by men hostile to business and industry. This was particularly likely to occur in agricultural states, as the Granger laws had shown. The constitutional doctrines of *Munn v. Illinois* might be exceedingly embarrassing in such circumstances. There were, however, two remedies against restrictive state legislation, and American business availed itself of both of them.

First, business went into politics to protect its interests. It is significant that *Munn v. Illinois* was followed by a perceptible quickening of the interest of industry in politics. Since the state had been confirmed in its power to regulate industry, industrialists now became greatly concerned about the kind of regulation that was to be imposed. Control of a state legislature by a farm group hostile to the railroads, for example, might result in the establishment of rate schedules or warehouse regulations which the railroads would consider altogether inimical to their welfare.

American industry had always been in politics to some degree. After 1880, however, industry and the railroads went into state politics to an extent hitherto unknown. They put forward their own attorneys as candidates for office; they donated funds to political parties; they backed this or that faction in the state legislature. Sometimes less scrupulous industrial leaders resorted to bribery. The eighties and nineties saw a new low in the moral level of the American state legislature. That the seats of assemblymen in Harrisburg or Albany were often for sale was a matter of common knowledge. From the point of view of business these tactics, whether or not they remained within the scope of orthodox political morality, were a matter of practical necessity. State interference with industry might be dangerous. Therefore the state government must be kept out of hostile hands.

Second, business carried the fight against restrictive state legislation into the courts, where, after a long fight, it won a substantial victory in the general acceptance of due process as a substantive limitation upon the power of government to regulate private property. The doctrine propounded in *Munn v. Illinois*, that private property vested with a public interest is subject to public regulation, technically was not subsequently overturned; but by 1898 the Court was to strike down statutes imposing "unreasonable" rail rate legislation on the ground that the rates in question were confiscatory and so took property without due process of law. In the next twenty years judicial emphasis was to pass almost completely from the dictum in *Munn v. Illinois* to reiteration of the principle that due process of law offered immunity to private property and vested interest against unreasonable social legislation. In its emphasis upon the capacity of state legislatures to control private property in the interest of the public welfare, *Munn v. Illinois* was at odds with the dominant economic interests of business and industry. And it was big business and industry which, in the generation after 1876, for the most part controlled the formation of national policy in Congress and ultimately in the courts as well.

The judiciary could hardly be expected to remain immune to the "big business" conception of the role of government in society. Judges, then as now, usually reached their positions through the legal profession. The philosophy of the legal profession, as always, was generally colored by the interests and attitudes of the men it most often represented—that is, industrialists, bankers, and railroad men. The path of corporation lawyers to the bench in the two generations after the Civil War was made easier by the fact that the Republican Party controlled the presidency for all but two administrations between 1868 and 1912. The Republican Party was for the most part a party of big business, and the men its Presidents appointed to the bench were most often corporation lawyers by training. Thus, it is not surprising that the attitude of the Supreme Court, as well as that of the federal and state judiciaries in general, began to reflect the economic and social attitudes of big business. Judges of this background might be expected to interpret the Constitution in the light of the *laissez-faire* economic philosophy and to regard the Constitution and the judiciary as bulwarks of property. They did not disappoint these expectations.

After 1877 the Court gradually gave more and more recognition to the substantive conception of due process of law and its identification with the doctrine of vested rights. Between 1877 and 1898 a flood of cases came up from the lower courts, in which appellants attacked state statutes attempting to regulate corporate property or some private vested interest. Always the claim was the same: the statute in question, by imposing some limitation upon the use of private property, constituted a violation of the due process clause of the Fourteenth Amendment. And notwithstanding the Court's outright denial of the conception of substantive due process in the *Slaughterhouse Cases* and its strong insistence in *Munn v. Illinois* upon the validity of public regulation, the Court between 1890 and 1898 finally gave full recognition to substantive due process as a limitation on state legislative power.

How very much alive the doctrine of vested rights was in legal minds, even in the Supreme Court itself, at the time of the *Slaughterhouse Cases* and *Munn v. Illinois* was demonstrated in *Loan Association v. Topeka* (1875). The decision dealt with the validity of a Kansas statute authorizing municipalities to issue bonds for the encouragement, in certain instances, of private businesses. The interest and principal on such bonds were to be paid from the public treasury. The Supreme Court found that the law in question authorized taxation for a private purpose and so was unconstitutional and void. The appropriation of public money for a private purpose was, the Court held, a violation of the basic nature of constitutional government. There were limitations upon the legislative power of the states, said Justice Miller's opinion, "which grow out of the essential nature of all free governments. Implied reservations of individual rights, without which the social compact could not exist, and which are respected by all governments entitled to the name." Then followed the already classic formula illustrating the validity of the doctrine: "No court, for instance, would hesitate to declare void a statute which . . . should enact that the homestead now owned by A should no longer be his, but should henceforth be the property of B." Clearly the justices had by no means accepted the doctrine that the legislative power of the state was limited only by specific constitutional restrictions.

As yet a majority of the Court was drawing the doctrine of vested rights from the "essential nature of all free governments," as it had done years before in *Calder v. Bull*. Should it ever decide, however, that due process of law itself constituted a limitation upon the police power of the state, then the doctrine of vested rights would be tremendously strengthened. For the immunity of vested rights from legislative interference would then be supported by the authority of a specific clause in the Constitution of the United States, rather than by some vague conception of the nature of compact government. All that was necessary, in other words, was to tie the doctrine of vested rights to the due process clause of the

Fourteenth Amendment. Were that done, the police power of the states would be seriously impaired.

Evidence of the growing tendency to identify due process of law with the doctrine of vested rights came in 1878 in *Davidson v. New Orleans*. Broadly speaking, Justice Miller here again confirmed the now seemingly established opinion that the due process clause of the Fourteenth Amendment carried only procedural implication. He noted the number of cases coming up from the state courts under the amendment and concluded rather impatiently: "There is here abundant evidence that there exists some strange misconception of the scope of this provision as found in the XIVth amendment." Yet the opinion also conceded that under extreme circumstances a regularly enacted statute imposing a property regulation might be a violation of due process. A law transferring property from A to B, thought the Court, would be a violation of the Fourteenth Amendment. For the first time a majority of the Court held that at least one extreme form of property regulation by state legislation—the most extreme imaginable to be sure—would be a violation of due process of law.

In the next dozen years death and retirement depleted the conservative majority on the Court. The men who, with Justice Miller, felt that there existed "some strange misconception" of due process were dying off. Between 1877 and 1890 no less than seven of the justices who had participated in *Munn v. Illinois*—Nathan Clifford. Ward Hunt, William Strong, Morrison R. Waite, Noah H. Swayne. David Davis, and Samuel F. Miller—resigned or died. These men were all constitutional conservatives, interested in maintaining the traditional relationships of state and national governments. Upon the death of Justice Miller in 1890, only Joseph Bradley and Stephen J. Field remained of the bench that had decided the *Slaughterhouse Cases* and *Munn v. Illinois*. And both Bradley and Field had dissented strongly in the *Slaughterhouse Cases*, contending that due process constituted a guarantee of vested rights against state action, while Field had reiterated this belief in his dissent in *Munn v. Illinois*.

Most of the new appointees were the product of Reconstruction politics and accustomed to the doctrine of strong national government. Nearly all of them had legal backgrounds calculated to inspire respect for vested interests and property rights. Justice John Marshall Harlan, appointed by President Hayes in 1877, was a Kentuckian and a former slaveholder who had sided with the Union in 1861 and had subsequently fought in the Northern army. Because of his respect for property rights he had opposed the

Thirteenth Amendment. By 1868, however, he was a Radical Republican and a thoroughgoing nationalist. Eventually Harlan emerged as a strong liberal nationalist, but he was at first not at all reluctant to use the federal judiciary to protect vested interests. Horace Gray, appointed in 1882 by President Chester A. Arthur, was a property-minded Republican lawyer from Boston. Samuel Blatchford, also an Arthur appointee of 1882, was a New York Republican and a patent lawyer.

Several of Cleveland's appointees, all Democrats, were also highly property-minded. Melville Fuller, appointed Chief Justice by Cleveland in 1888, was an old-time Illinois Democrat, and his record hitherto had been that of an extremely public-spirited man. Once on the Court, however, he quickly fell under the influence of Field's ideas and became a staunch defender of private interests against social legislation. Lucius Quintus Cincinnatus Lamar, also a Cleveland appointee of 1888, was a one-time Confederate general and ardent states' rights advocate of decidedly conservative temperament. Edward D. White, appointed in 1894 during Cleveland's second term, was a wealthy conservative Louisiana sugar planter and tariff protectionist, although at the same time generally an ardent champion of states' rights. Rufus W. Peckham, appointed in 1895, was a conservative New York attorney.

David J. Brewer, appointed by President Benjamin Harrison in 1889, was a nephew of Justice Field and much under the latter's influence. At the time of his appointment he had already acquired a solid reputation as a federal circuit judge for upholding corporate property rights: in one notable decision of 1885 he had refused to accept the authority of *Munn v. Illinois* as to the broad police powers of the states. Henry B. Brown, appointed by Harrison in 1890, was a conservative Detroit admiralty lawyer.

The new appointees were conservatives, but of a very different kind from the judges who had decided the *Slaughterhouse Cases* and *Munn v. Illinois*. The conservatives of the seventies had been concerned with the protection of the old established state-federal relations against the upheavals of the Civil War and the onslaught of Radical reconstructionism. The conservatism of the new judges, on the other hand, was concerned primarily with protecting the property rights and vested interests of big business and with the defense of the prevailing economic and social order against agrarian and dissident reformers. The new appointees, in short, were extremely receptive to the constitutional theories advanced by Justice Field and by the brilliant attorneys appearing before the Court.

In 1886, the Court in *Stone v. Farmers Loan and Trust Co.* made its first great concession to the lawyers who were trying to give a substantive meaning to due process and so to link it with the doctrine of vested rights. The case involved a Mississippi statute which had erected a state railroad commission with authority to revise rates, a power which the Mobile and Ohio Railroad Company upon appeal charged was in violation of due process of law.

The Court again said "No," citing *Munn v. Illinois.* Yet the very words of the opinion carried a concession to the argument. "General statutes regulating the use of railroads in a State, or fixing maximum rates of charge for transportation," said Chief Justice Waite, "do not necessarily deprive the corporation owning or operating a railroad within the State of its property, without due process of law within the meaning of the Fourteenth Amendment." But at the same time Waite warned that "it is not to be inferred that this power of limitation or regulation is itself without limit. . . . Under pretense of regulating fares and freights, the State cannot require a railroad corporation to carry persons or property without reward; neither can it do that which in law amounts to a taking of private property for public use without just compensation, or without due process of law."

In other words, the Court now openly admitted that there were conceivable circumstances in which a legislative regulation of private property, a pretended exercise of the police power, might constitute a violation of due process. All that remained was for the Court to find a specific instance in which legislative regulation denied due process. The emergence of substantive due process would then be virtually complete.

Four years later the Court, in *Chicago, Milwaukee, and St. Paul Ry. Co. v. Minnesota* (1890), took what was practically the final step in this development, when it declared a Minnesota rail rate statute of 1887 to be in violation of the Fourteenth Amendment. The act in question had set up a rail and warehouse commission with power to examine rail rates and to revise those which it found to be unreasonable or unequal. Justice Blatchford, who wrote the majority opinion, based his argument mainly upon the fact that the law as interpreted by the Minnesota Supreme Court gave the commission final and conclusive rate-fixing powers, with the result that the rates set by it were not subject to any review by the courts as to their equality or reasonableness. Under the statute, said Blatchford, there was "no power in the courts to stay the hands of the Commission, if it chooses to establish rates that are unequal and unreasonable." In other words, he said, the statute "deprives the Company of its right to a judicial investigation, by due process of law, under the forms and with the machinery provided by the wisdom of successive ages for the investigation judicially of the truth of a matter in controversy." The question of whether a rate was reasonable, he continued, "is eminently a question for judicial investigation, requiring due process of law for its determination. If the company is deprived of the power of charging reasonable rates for the use of its property, and such deprivation takes place in the absence of an investigation by judicial machinery, it is deprived of the lawful use of its property, and thus, in substance and effect, of the property itself, without due process of law and in violation of the Constitution of the United States."

Now on the surface the Court was here concerned merely with a procedural due process and not with a substantive limitation upon the rate-fixing powers of the legislature itself. It merely found a procedural defect in the commission's prescribed method of rate-fixing. In other words, it treated the commission as though it were a court or at least a quasi-judicial body, and it described the de-termination of the reasonableness of rates as a judicial process. Act-ing on these assumptions, it found that the commission's mode of fixing rates violated one of the essential elements in procedural due process—the right of appeal.

The commission, however, was more than a quasi-court. Its rate-setting powers had been delegated by the legislature. The Court had said that the commission could not lawfully be given the power to fix rates from which there was no judicial appeal. But what if the legislature itself should set the rate directly and allow no judicial appeal? Here the substantive implication of the decision stood clearly revealed. It would be but a short step for the Court to hold that a rate fixed by the legislature itself, with no appeal to the courts, would violate due process of law. The way was now open for a decision which without seeming to reverse *Munn v. Illinois* would take most of the practical economic significance out of that decision by permitting the courts a general review of all rate-schedules fixed by legislative determination.

Justice Bradley in a cogent dissent pointed out that the majority decision practically overruled *Munn v. Illinois*. In that case the Court had presumably settled definitely that the rates charged by a business affected with a public interest were subject to public regu-lation. In the present case, the Court said in effect that public regu-lation must be reasonable and that what was reasonable was a judicial question. "On the contrary," said Bradley, the question of reasonableness "is pre-eminently a legislative one, involving considerations of policy as well as of remuneration." By undertaking to rule on the reasonableness of a legislative act, the judiciary was. in Bradley's view, determining a matter of policy ordinarily left to the legislature.

The present rate had been set by a commission, not by the legislature. Yet Bradley pointed out that it was "perfectly clear, and well settled by the decisions of this court, that the Legislature might have fixed the rates in question. . . . No one could have said that this was not due process of law." If the legislature could set the rate, Bradley asked, why not the commission?

Bradley might have put this inquiry the other way about: if the Court here insisted upon its right to review the reasonableness of a commission decision, why should it not in the future insist upon the right to review the reasonableness of direct legislative rate regulation by the legislature itself? In short, did it not imply its willingness to review the reasonableness of all state legislation regulating property?

To complete the evolution of substantive due process, it remained for the Court only to declare void a statute fixing rates directly through legislative enactment. The Court affirmed its power to do this in 1894 in *Reagan v. Farmers' Loan and Trust Co.*, although no statute was actually declared to be unconstitutional at this time. This step came in 1898 in *Smyth v. Ames*, wherein the Court held void a Nebraska statute setting intrastate freight rates. After protracted inquiry into the earning power of the railroads affected, the opinion concluded that the law imposed rates so low as to be unreasonable and thus to amount to a deprivation of property without due process of law.

DUE PROCESS AND FREEDOM OF CONTRACT

Substantive due process was at first concerned only with the protection of vested property rights against the police power of the states. It was property that could not be subjected to unreasonable restrictions. As yet the Court had said nothing of any substantive limitation upon the right of the states to regulate liberty. Yet it was a logical step for the Court to enlarge the substantive limitations of due process to include liberty as well as property. The legal instrument used to bring this about was the doctrine of freedom of contract.

Freedom of contract was a conception introduced into constitutional law directly from *laissez-faire* economics. There is virtually no other explanation for its appearance, for it certainly rested neither upon any specific constitutional principle, nor upon any well-established legal precedent. As we have seen, the old guarantee of liberty in due process had been entirely procedural—it merely threw certain safeguards about accused persons in criminal cases. The new doctrine asserted that when two parties came together to reach an agreement that was not contrary to public policy, the legislature had no right to interfere and to dictate the terms of that agreement or the conditions under which it should be carried out.

In *Allgeyer v. Louisiana* (1897) the Court entered into a comprehensive discussion of the liberty guaranteed by due process of law. Liberty, said the Court, included "not only the right of the citizen to be free from the mere physical restraint of his person, as by incarceration, but the term is deemed to embrace the right of the citizen to be free in the enjoyment of all his faculties; to be free to use them in all lawful ways; to live and work where he will; to earn his livelihood by any lawful calling; to pursue any livelihood or avocation, and for that purpose to enter into all contracts which may be proper, necessary, and essential to his carrying out to a successful conclusion the purposes above mentioned."

In reality, the concept of freedom of contract was to be used after 1900 mainly to invalidate state laws regulating conditions of labor. This became apparent as early as 1898, in *Holden v. Hardy*, when the Court considered whether or not a Utah statute limiting hours of labor in mines to eight hours a day was in violation of freedom of contract.

DUE PROCESS AND THE FIFTH AMENDMENT

Although the revolution in due process of law occurred through judicial interpretation of the Fourteenth Amendment, it will be recalled that there was also a due process of law clause in the Fifth Amendment, constituting a guarantee against the federal government. Early Supreme Court opinions, with the exception of the Dred Scott Case and *Hepburn v. Griswold*, interpreted the due process clause in the Fifth Amendment as extending purely procedural safeguards to the individual as against federal action. Presumably it expressed in a general way the same immunities expressed by the other clauses of the Fifth and Sixth Amendments in a specific way.

Once the substantive conception of due process of law had evolved, however, there was every prospect that the idea would be applied to the Fifth Amendment also. Although the federal govment had no general police powers except in the territories, it nevertheless possessed extensive regulatory powers over private property within limited spheres of jurisdiction. Congress, in exercising its authority over interstate commerce and taxation, in particular, frequently imposed extensive limitations upon private property rights and vested interests.

After several times suggesting that the due process clauses in the Fifth and Fourteenth Amendments meant substantially the same thing, the Court in *Adair v. United States* (1908) held void a federal statute prohibiting "yellow dog" labor contracts (by which employees agreed not to join labor unions) on the ground that the act impaired freedom of contract and so violated the due process clause of the Fifth Amendment. In a series of cases dealing with the federal commerce power, the Court ruled also that to be within due process, rail rates fixed by the Interstate Commerce Commission must be reasonable and not arbitrary or confiscatory. This was substantially the same conception, applied to federal legislation, as that advanced against state legislation under the Fourteenth Amendment.

It may be well to summarize the history of due process between 1870 and 1900 so that the extent of the constitutional revolution involved may be appreciated.

In the *Slaughterhouse Cases* the Court, disregarding the prior tentative association of due process and vested rights in the Dred Scott and Hepburn cases, had held that the due process clause of the Fourteenth Amendment had merely the traditional procedural content. It had denied the contention that due process constituted a substantive limitation upon the legislative capacity of the states. In *Munn v. Illinois* the Court had re-emphasized the capacity of state legislatures to regulate private property in the interest of the public welfare; and although it had by implication admitted the possibility of substantive due process, it had been concerned mainly with upholding state police power.

In a series of cases between 1877 and 1898, the Court gradually coupled vested rights to the due process clause, so that due process came to be a substantive limitation upon the power of a state to regulate private property in the interests of the public welfare. Liberty of contract also became a vested right, guaranteed by due process against unreasonable state legislation. Shortly after 1900 the substantive interpretation of due process was applied to the Fifth

Amendment, so that substantive due process also became a limitation upon congressional legislative power.

What constituted due process now became the most important consideration in constitutional law. Moreover, since judicial decision as to due process in reality involved passing judgment upon considerations of social and economic policy, substantive due process actually endowed the courts with a kind of quasi-legislative power. In 1890, accordingly, the judiciary stood on the threshold of a new era of power and prestige in the American constitutional system.

Chapter

20

The New Due Process and
Judicial Review—1890-1920

IN HUNDREDS of cases after 1890, the federal and state judiciaries developed a complex new law of substantive due process controlling state police power and federal legislative capacity. The content of due process underwent constant change and development, so that until 1937, at least, it was not possible at any one time to define absolutely the limits of substantive due process. From the time of the *Slaughterhouse Cases*, the Supreme Court consistently refused to lay down any inclusive definition or set of rules about due process; instead it preferred to develop the concept, as it remarked in 1877, by the method of "inclusion and exclusion." Yet the Court in the generation after 1890 succeeded fairly well in setting forth the fundamental nature of due process in a series of general propositions which remained moderately stable until 1937.

THE CONTENT OF DUE PROCESS

Due process was, broadly speaking, a general substantive limitation upon the police power of the state. Any state statute, ordinance, or administrative act which imposed any kind of limitation upon the right of private property or free contract immediately raised the question of due process of law. And since a majority of statutes of a general public character imposed some limitations upon private property or contractual right, the ramifications of due process were endless. Under the due process clause, the Supreme Court could and did consider the constitutionality of such varied statutes as a New York ten-hour law for bakers, a Massachusetts compulsory vaccination law, a Louisiana statute licensing foreign corporations, and an Illinois act compelling railroads to make at their own expense certain alterations for drainage purposes. Not in every instance was the statute found to be a violation of due process. In most cases the opposite was true; many more statutes were validated than were struck down. However, the Court insisted upon its right to examine the statute in question and to determine whether it constituted a legitimate exercise of the police power.

What constituted a legitimate exercise of the police power now became a judicial question, not merely a legislative question. Whereas formerly the Court had assumed that the decision of the legislature was conclusive as to the limits of the police power, the Court now reserved for itself the right to consider the whole question of whether the statute under review constituted a valid exercise of that power. Theoretically, the will of the legislature was still held in high respect. Actually the Court was often openly contemptuous of the reasons which had impelled legislatures to pass the legislation in question.

To be accepted as within the bounds of due process a statute must in the opinion of the court be "reasonable." This was the general and all-inclusive test that a law under review had to meet and pass. If the purpose for which the statute had been enacted was a reasonable one, if the act employed reasonable means to achieve its ends, if the means employed bore a reasonable and substantial relationship to the purposes of the act, and if the law imposed no unreasonable limitations upon freedom of contract or private vested right, then the Court would accept the law as a legitimate exercise of the police power.

Very closely associated with the concept of reasonableness was the requirement that a statute should not be "arbitrary." On most occasions where a law was found to be unreasonable it was also found to be arbitrary, an arbitrary statute being one "which restricts individual liberty or property right more severely than advantage to the community can possible justify."

The question of the reasonableness or arbitrariness of a law could not be settled by reference to any specific constitutional provision or any absolute principle of law. A reasonable law was one that seemed sensible, plausible, and intelligent to the judges who passed upon it. What constitutes sensible, plausible, and intelligent public policy, however, is largely a matter of the individual's economic and social philosophy—his standard of values. When the Court applied the test of reasonableness to legislation, therefore, it measured the law against its own economic and social attitudes. If in the light of these attitudes the law seemed intelligent, the justices upheld it; if not, they declared it unreasonable, arbitrary, and a violation of due process of law. There was often a capricious element in such judgment. The justices' opinion of what constituted "reasonable" legislation often depended upon the effectiveness of a lawyer's brief or upon the balance of the moment in the Court's membership.

DUE PROCESS AND THE REGULATION OF HOURS OF LABOR

The manner in which the Court used due process as a medium through which to pass upon the constitutionality of state social legislation in the light of the justices' social and economic theories may be illustrated by a consideration of the judicial history of state statutes regulating maximum hours for the employment of labor.

This issue first came before the Court in *Holden v. Hardy* (1898), a case involving the constitutionality of a Utah statute of 1896 prohibiting the employment of workingmen in mines, smelters, or ore refineries for more than eight hours in any one day, except in emergencies. By a vote of 7 to 2 the Court held the statute constitutional. Justice Henry B. Brown's opinion for the majority was a closely reasoned argument for preserving the flexibility of state police power as a necessary instrument to deal with the extraordinary amount of change then taking place in the social order. It was exceedingly important, he thought, "that the Constitution of the United States, which is necessarily and to a large extent inflexible and exceedingly difficult of amendment, should not be so construed as to deprive the states of the power to so amend their laws as to make them conform to the wishes of the citizens as they may deem best for the public welfare without bringing them into conflict with the supreme law of the land." He admitted the general right of free contract as set forth in *Allgeyer v. Louisiana* (1897), but at the same time emphasized the extent to which the right of contract was "subject to certain limitations which the state may lawfully impose in the exercise of its police powers." Examining briefly the Utah statute, he commented upon the hazardous and unhealthful character of mining as an occupation and the unequal bargaining power of employers and employees as sufficient justification for the law as a reasonable exercise of the state's police power.

Holden v. Hardy established no general precedent as to the constitutionality of statutes limiting hours of labor. In *Lochner v. New York* (1905) the Court, by a 5-to-4 majority, declared unconstitutional a New York statute limiting hours of labor in bakeshops to sixty hours in one week or ten hours in any one day. Justice R. W. Peckham, speaking for the majority, first cited the right of free contract as established in *Allgeyer v. Louisiana,* and emphasized further that the right to purchase or sell labor was an important part of the liberty guaranteed by the Fourteenth Amendment. He admitted that state police power might on occasion limit the right of free contract; indeed, he said, the Court had in the past been very liberal in accepting impairment of property or contract rights under state police power. But there were limits to the valid exercise of state police power; otherwise the Fourteenth Amendment would be without meaning.

Peckham then denounced the New York ten-hour law as unreasonable and void:

> There is no reasonable ground for interfering with the liberty of person or the right of free contract, by determining the hours of labor, in the occupation of a baker. There is no contention that bakers as a class are not equal in intelligence and capacity to men in other trades or manual occupations, or that they are not able to assert their rights and care for themselves without the protecting arm of the state, interfering with their independence of judgment and of action. They are in no sense wards of the state. Viewed in the light of a purely labor law, with no reference whatever to the question of health, we think that a law like the one before us involves neither the safety, the morals, nor the welfare, of the public, and that the interest of the public is not in the slightest degree affected by such an act. . . .

He went on to invoke the *argumentum ad horrendum*—the contention that if the present statute were valid there was no logical limit to the regulatory power of the state, and freedom of contract would be destroyed. "Not only the hours of employees, but the hours of employers, could be regulated, and doctors, lawyers, scientists, all professional men, as well as athletes and artisans, could be forbidden to fatigue their brains and bodies by prolonged hours of exercise, lest the fighting strength of the state be impaired."

Harlan wrote a dissent for himself, Edward D. White, and William R. Day, emphasizing the broad scope of the police power and the state's capacity to interfere with the right of free contract, and examining briefly some of the economic and social evidence as to the possible reasonable character of the New York law. But it was Justice Holmes who made the most effective attack upon the majority for injecting *laissez-faire* social theory into the content of constitutional law and substituting the Court's judgment upon public policy for that of the legislature. He wrote:

> This case is decided upon an economic theory which a large part of the country does not entertain. If it were a question whether I agreed with that theory, I should desire to study it further and long before making up my mind. But I do not conceive that to be my duty, because I strongly believe that my agreement or disagreement has nothing to do with the right of a majority to embody their opinions in law. It is settled by various opinions of this court that state constitutions and state laws may regulate life in many ways which we as legislators might think as injudicious, or if you like as tyrannical, as this, and which, equally with this, interfere with the liberty to contract. . . . The 14th Amendment does not enact Mr. Herbert Spencer's Social Statics . . . a Constitution is not intended to embody a particular economic theory, whether of paternalism and the organic relation of the citizen to the state or of *laissez-faire*. It is made for people of fundamentally differing views, and the accident of our finding certain opinions natural and familiar, or novel and even shocking, ought not to conclude our judgment upon the question whether statutes embodying them conflict with the Constitution of the United States.

It is possible that Holmes' brilliant rebuke in *Lochner v. New York* had some effect upon the other justices. Three years later, in *Muller v. Oregon* (1908), the Court unanimously upheld the constitutionality of an Oregon statute of 1903 prohibiting the employment of women in mechanical establishments, factories, and laundries for more than ten hours in any one day. The Oregon statute was substantially similar to a number of state acts then being enacted for the protection of the health and morals of women, and social workers and liberals generally were exceedingly anxious to secure a favorable judicial verdict on the law. At the request of Florence Kelley and Josephine Goldmark, both prominent social workers, the state of Oregon retained the noted Boston attorney Louis D. Brandeis to defend the constitutionality of the law before the Supreme Court.

Brandeis submitted to the Court a brief which disposed of the constitutional precedents in two pages, but which devoted over a hundred pages to statistics upon hours of labor, American and European factory legislation, and the health and morals of women. The logic behind the brief rested upon the premise that if the Court in fact passed upon legislation of this kind in the light of its reasonable character and plausible relation to the social welfare, then the best possible approach was to overwhelm the justices with direct and specific documentary evidence as to the wisdom and intelligence of the law under review.

The "Brandeis brief," as it was thereafter called, was a spectacular success, and set the precedent for many subsequent appeals to the Court of the same kind. Justice David Brewer in his opinion virtually admitted that Brandeis had succeeded in convincing the Court that the Oregon statute was a reasonable exercise of the state police power. He made the admission with some embarrassment, since it was virtually an open confession that social and economic philosophy and not mere constitutional precedent had been decisive in the Court's decision. "The legislation and opinions referred to in the margin," [1] said Justice Brewer,

> may not be, technically speaking, authorities, and in them there is little or no discussion of the constitutional question presented to us for determination, yet they are significant of a widespread belief that woman's physical structure, and the functions she performs in consequence thereof, justify special legislation restricting or qualifying the conditions under which she should be permitted to toil. Constitutional questions, it is true, are not settled by even a consensus of present public opinion, for it is the peculiar value of a written constitution that it places in unchanging form limitations upon legislative action, and thus gives a permanence and stability to popular government which otherwise would be lacking. At the same time, when a question of fact is debated and debatable, and the extent to which a special constitutional limitation goes is affected by the truth in respect to that fact, a widespread and continued belief concerning it is worthy of consideration. We take judicial cognizance of all matters of general knowledge.

This attempt to preserve the theory of a static written constitution and a body of constitutional law derived from that constitution by pure logic and precedent had a somewhat threadbare aspect. It was plain that the Court had in fact been overwhelmed by Brandeis' evidence as to the wisdom and intelligence and social ad-

---

[1] The substance of Brandeis' brief was reprinted in the margin of the Court's published opinion.

visability of legislation limiting female hours of labor. The fiction of judicial consistency could be maintained without too much difficulty, however, and Justice Brewer distinguished the present statute from that in *Lochner v. New York* by laying heavy emphasis upon the peculiarities of "woman's structure," and women's weak and indefensible position in society, so that the state was justified in interfering with female freedom of contract, although such interference would not be constitutional for men.

Nine years later, in *Bunting v. Oregon* (1917), the Court went even further, and accepted the constitutionality of an Oregon ten-hour statute applying both to men and women. The decision was the more remarkable because the law had a provision permitting employees to work not more than three hours overtime per day, provided they received additional pay at the rate of one and a half times the regular wage. The law thus appeared to regulate wages as well as hours of labor. It was this feature of the statute that most concerned the Court. But Justice Joseph McKenna's opinion disposed of the contention that the law regulated wages (and thereby possibly violated due process) with the assertion that the wage provisions were in the nature of a restrictive penalty for overtime rather than a permissive wage regulation. The law was therefore essentially a maximum-hours statute, not one regulating wages, and the Court proceeded to treat it as such. McKenna then made a brief inquiry into existing statutes regulating hours of labor and found that the Oregon law was not more restrictive than were those in force in other states. He concluded that the statute under review was a reasonable exercise of the state's police power and so constitutional. He did not even mention the embarrassing bakeshop precedent; but it was reasonable to suppose that the Court's decision in *Lochner v. New York* now stood silently overruled. The Court nevertheless in 1923 was to revive *Lochner v. New York* sufficiently to use it as precedent for overturning the constitutionality of a federal minimum wage law for the District of Columbia.[2]

DUE PROCESS AND OTHER ASPECTS OF SOCIAL LEGISLATION

The Court also brought its social philosophy to bear in passing upon the reasonableness, under due process, of a great variety of state police statutes imposing limitations upon private property or freedom of contract.

---

[2] See the discussion of *Adkins v. Children's Hospital* (1923), on pp. 656–658.

Jacobson v. Massachusetts (1905) is of interest in demonstrating how the Court could accept as constitutional a law imposing substantial limitations upon personal liberty where the justices approved of the social purpose of the legislation in question. This case involved the constitutionality of a Massachusetts statute providing for compulsory vaccination and imposing a fine of five dollars upon any person refusing to submit to free vaccination. Justice Harlan, in approving the reasonable character of the law, observed that "for nearly a century most members of the medical profession have regarded vaccination, repeated after intervals, as a preventive of small pox." As was usual in situations where the Court approved of the statute under review, Harlan emphasized the broad scope of state police power and the limitations upon the liberty secured by the Fourteenth Amendment. Liberty, he said, "does not import an absolute right in each person to be, at all times and in all circumstances, wholly free from restraint. . . . Real liberty for all could not exist under the operation of a principle which recognizes the right of each individual person to use his own, whether in respect of his person or his property, regardless of the injury that may be done to others."

On the other hand, a majority of the justices were unable to approve of the reasonable character or social purposes behind federal and state statutes prohibiting "yellow dog" contracts. This issue first came before the Court in *Adair v. United States* (1908), a case involving the constitutionality of Section 10 of the so-called Erdman Act, a congressional statute of June 1, 1898, which made it a misdemeanor for any employer engaged as an interstate carrier to require any person as a condition of employment to agree not to become or remain a member of a labor union. The statute, Harlan said, had no reasonable public character; it therefore violated freedom of contract and was unconstitutional as "an invasion of the personal liberty, as well as the right of property" guaranteed by the Fifth Amendment. Harlan's disapproval of the law's purpose and intent was patent throughout his opinion. It was "not within the functions of government" he said, "to compel any person, in the course of his business and against his will, to accept or retain the personal services of another, or to compel any person, against his will, to perform personal services for another." Harlan also held that the law exceeded the federal commercial power.[3] Both McKenna and Holmes dissented, holding that the law might fairly be interpreted as having

---

[3] See p. 563.

a reasonable public purpose and a reasonable relationship to the federal commerce power.

In *Coppage v. Kansas* (1915) the Court applied the precedent in *Adair v. United States* to hold unconstitutional a state statute forbidding yellow-dog contracts. Pointing out that the law did not differ in principle from that considered in the Adair case, Pitney emphasized that the right of an employer to buy labor on his own terms and the right of a laborer to sell on his terms were part of the freedom of contract protected by the Fourteenth Amendment. After a fairly elaborate discussion of freedom of contract as an essential ingredient in the whole process of human freedom, Pitney attacked the statute as one which had no reasonable or plausible relationship to the health, morals, and welfare of the community. The law was therefore void as a violation of the due process clause of the Fourteenth Amendment. Justices Holmes, Day, and Charles Evans Hughes dissented, Holmes restating briefly his contention in *Lochner v. New York*—that the Court ought not to substitute its judgment for that of the legislature in matters of public policy.

In *New York Central R.R. Co. v. White* (1917) the Court upheld the constitutionality of the New York Workmen's Compensation Act of 1914. The law set up an automatic schedule of compensation for payments in case of the accidental injury or death of an employee, without regard to any question of fault except in cases involving the employee's willful self-injury or injury as a result of drunkenness. The statute thus abrogated the "fellow-servant" and "contributory negligence" rules of the common law, whereby an employer had been held not liable for any injury sustained through the carelessness or fault of another employee nor for an injury sustained through the employee's contributory negligence. The law also set aside the common-law rule of "recognition of risk" whereby an employer was held not liable for injuries sustained by an employee who might reasonably have recognized the possibility of the accident as inherent in his work. The New York statute was in fact similar to many state compensation acts adopted about this time, some thirty states having enacted such legislation by 1915. Justice Pitney, speaking for a unanimous Court, made it plain that he approved of the general social purpose behind the law: "The act," he said, "evidently is intended as a just settlement of a difficult problem, affecting one of the most important of social relations." The subject regulated, Pitney added, had a "direct relationship to the common welfare" and therefore constituted a reasonable impairment of the right of free contract and a constitutional exercise of the police power.

In *Mountain Timber Co. v. Washington* (1917), the opinion on which was handed down at the same time, the Court accepted the constitutionality of the Washington Workmen's Compensation Act by a 5-to-4 majority. This statute differed from the New York law principally in that it provided for a system of enforced contributions by the employer to a state compensation fund whether or not any injuries had befallen the employer's own workmen. The New York law, by contrast, had merely required the employer to carry compensation insurance or to show ability to pay probable claims. Speaking for the majority, Justice Pitney said the Washington statute had a reasonable relationship to a matter of great importance to the public welfare. The contributions imposed upon employers, he added, were not so excessive as to amount to deprivation of property without due process of law, nor were they oppressive, since they were justified by the public nature of the object in view. Chief Justice White and Justices McKenna, Willis Van Devanter, and James McReynolds dissented without opinion.

In June 1917, three months after the foregoing decisions, the Court, in *Adams v. Tanner*, declared unconstitutional a Washington statute making it unlawful to receive fees from any person as a payment for aid in securing employment. Justice McReynolds' opinion observed first that the statute put an outright end to the employment agency business; the law was therefore one of prohibition, and not mere regulation. McReynolds thought such prohibition of a lawful public business lacked any adequate social justification. He considered it self-evident "that there is nothing inherently immoral or dangerous to public welfare in acting as paid representative of another to find a position in which he can earn an honest living. On the contrary, such service is useful, commendable, and in great demand." And he continued, "Because abuses may, and probably do, grow up in connection with this business, is adequate reason for hedging it about by proper regulations. But this is not enough to justify destruction of one's right to follow a distinctly useful calling in an upright way." Citing *Allgeyer v. Louisiana* as precedent for his assertion that the Fourteenth Amendment guaranteed the right "to earn a livelihood by any lawful calling," McReynolds denounced the statute at hand as arbitrary and oppressive and a violation of due process of law. Justice McKenna dissented briefly, while Brandeis wrote a lengthy dissenting opinion in which Holmes and Clarke concurred. Brandeis' opinion, filled with masses of detailed sociological data, cited the "vast evils" associated with the employment agency business as justification for the state's right to prohibit it entirely. Once again it was evident that the Court's acceptance or rejection of a police statute under the Fourteenth Amendment was essentially a function of the justices' social philosophy.

DUE PROCESS AND PUBLIC UTILITY RATES

Substantive due process had emerged primarily from the Court's review of state statutes prescribing rate structures for a variety of public utilities, railroads, grain elevators, and the like. As substantive due process broadened out into a constitutional doctrine supporting the general review of all state police statutes, the Court continued on appeal to examine the rate structures imposed upon public utilities in the light of the general proposition that such rates must be fair and reasonable, so as to allow the business in question a reasonable return on its property. A rate which had any arbitrary or confiscatory character or which did not permit the concern a fair return on its investment would be held to violate the due process clause of the Fourteenth Amendment.

The problem of what constituted a fair and reasonable return on a public utility corporation's investment was an exceedingly difficult one and almost invariably plunged the Court into the complexities of accountancy theory. No rate structure could be adjudged without reference to some estimated valuation of the property in question; this in turn meant that the Court was involved in the complexities of original cost versus replacement or earning capacity theories of evaluation, methods of apportioning the cost of doing business among the various services of a highly ramified public utility network, division of costs between interstate and intrastate rates, and many like problems. Very often these questions could be settled only by reference to highly technical accountancy theory. The Court tried to steer clear of this difficulty as far as possible by granting the rate schedules fixed by the state a prima facie validity, but the very fact of review usually imposed upon the Court an examination of rate theory. Thus in the *Minnesota Rate Cases* (1913), the Court announced that it would not interfere with the presumptive evidence of a fair rate as prescribed by the state, unless the evidence was clear as to the rate's confiscatory character, but in that very case, the Court found it necessary to examine such matters as the depreciation factor in the railroad's right of way, the methods of prorating the costs of state and interstate business, and the validity of various applications of cost-of-reproduction methods of computing the value of railroad properties.[4] Again, in *Northern Pacific Railway v. North Dakota* (1915), where the Court was concerned with the validity of a North Dakota statute fixing maximum intrastate rates for hauling coal, the Court made an elaborate examination of the prorata distribution of costs between interstate and intrastate freight rates to arrive at the conclusion that the statute was void as allowing the roads an inadequate return. And in *Norfolk and Western Railway Co. v. West Virginia* (1915), where the issue was the constitutionality of a state statute fixing intrastate passenger rates of two cents a mile, the Court used much the same methods in concluding that the rate was confiscatory and invalid.

Regardless of what theories of evaluation and rate analysis the Court adopted, there remained the question of what constituted a "fair" and "reasonable" return on a given investment. The Court never adopted a categorical theory of what constituted a reasonable return, but instead settled each case upon its merits. Perhaps it came the closest to enunciating a general philosophy of fair profits in *Willcox v. Consolidated Gas Co.* (1909), where the Court in effect stated that a return of 6 per cent was reasonable upon the property of a New York city gas company, a concern in which the element of business risk was reduced to a minimum. Thus the Court gave some recognition to the prevailing conception of a "normal" or "just" profit.

DUE PROCESS AND TAXATION

It will be recalled that some of the earlier cases involving the doctrine of vested interest had concerned the validity of various state revenue statutes. In *Loan Association v. Topeka* (1875), for example, the Court had held invalid a state tax law on the ground that the act authorized the expenditure of public taxes for private purposes and so transferred the property of A to B in violation of the basic nature of lawful constitutional government. With the emergence of substantive due process the Court began to pass upon the validity of state tax measures in the light of the more specific requirements of the due process and equal protection clauses of the Fourteenth Amendment.

A majority of due process tax cases involved questions of a state's jurisdiction to tax property held outside the state. The issue in such

---

4 The *Minnesota Rate Cases* are discussed at some length on pp. 572-578.

cases was essentially one of interstate jurisdictional relations in a federal system of government, and seemingly had little to do with due process of law as such. In *State Tax on Foreign Held Bonds* (1873), a case occurring before the rise of substantive due process, the Court had ruled that a state tax on railroad bonds held outside the state violated the obligation of contracts clause. Justice Field had observed that "property lying beyond the jurisdiction of the state is not a subject upon which her taxing power can be legitimately exercised."

With the rise of substantive due process, the Court reaffirmed the foregoing principle under the due process clause of the Fourteenth Amendment. Thus in *Delaware, Lackawanna and Western Railroad Co. v. Pennsylvania* (1905), the Court held invalid a Pennsylvania tax on the capital stock of a railroad where the state included $1,700,000 in coal, situated outside the state but owned by the road, as part of the capital stock in question. Justice Peckham first observed that a tax imposed directly on the coal would have been unconstitutional, and the tax here, he added, amounted to the same thing, since the Court had frequently ruled that a tax on the value of the capital stock of a corporation was a tax on the property in which that capital was invested. The tax therefore violated due process and was void.

The Court applied the same general principle in *Union Refrigerator Transit Co. v. Kentucky* (1905), a case involving the validity of a Kentucky tax on two thousand refrigerator cars owned by a corporation doing business within Kentucky, although very few of the cars in question were within the state's boundaries at any given time. Justice Peckham cited *State Tax on Foreign Held Bonds* as authority for the proposition that the state could not lawfully tax property located outside its jurisdiction. Such a levy, he said, was in the nature of an extortion rather than a lawful levy and violated due process of law. In *Buck v. Beach* (1907) the Court extended this principle to intangible property. Here the state of Indiana had attempted to collect a personal property tax upon certain notes deposited for security in a vault in Indiana, although the owner of the notes resided in New York and the borrowers were residents of Ohio. Justice Peckham observed first that "generally speaking intangible property in the nature of a debt may be regarded, for the purpose of taxation, as situated at the domicile of the creditor" and therefore within the tax jurisdiction of that state. In this instance, the paper deposited in Indiana was not the actual debt as property but merely the evidence thereof. The debt had no actual relationship to the jurisdiction of the state of Indiana, and "the enforcement of such a tax would be the taking of property without due process of law."

The general rule established in these cases—that a state could not lawfully tax property located outside its jurisdiction—led subsequently to the growth of a large body of case law on taxation and due process, too ramified to be analyzed at length here. Some idea of the importance of this type of due process tax law may be gained from Benjamin F. Wright's statement that between 1899 and 1937 the Court declared unconstitutional twenty-nine state tax laws which in some way discriminated against out-of-state enterprises or attempted to tax property not located within the jurisdiction of the state.[5]

In another group of cases, the Court was concerned with the question of certain fair and equitable procedures in levying taxes and assessments. The Court repeatedly held that due notice and an opportunity for a hearing for property owners was a prerequisite to due process of law in the assessment of taxes. Thus in *Londoner v. Denver* (1908) the Court held unconstitutional a street assessment by the city of Denver on the ground that the city council had enacted the tax without giving an opportunity for a full hearing to the landowners assessed. Although the property owners had been permitted to file complaints, Justice William H. Moody asserted that "a hearing, in its very essence, demands that he who is entitled to it shall have the right to support his allegations by argument, however brief; and if need be, by proof, however informal." The Court followed the same rule in *Turner v. Wade* (1920), where it held unconstitutional certain portions of the Georgia Tax Equalization Act. The act provided that the county board of assessors was empowered to examine property returns and correct them when necessary. Although the act provided for arbitration in case the taxpayer objected to his levy, Justice Day pointed out that the board of assessors "was not required to give any notice to the taxpayer, nor was opportunity given to him to be heard as of right before the assessment was finally made against him." Therefore the statute took property without due process of law.

In still another category of state tax cases, the Court held that there must be a reasonable relationship between the person or thing taxed, and any benefit which might accrue as a result of the tax. Thus

---

[5] Benjamin F. Wright, *The Growth of American Constitutional Law* (Boston, 1942), p. 160.

in *Myles Salt Co. v. Board of Commissioners* (1916), the Court held unconstitutional an assessment levied by a Louisiana drainage district, where the owner of the lands taxed showed that his property could not benefit from the tax and that the tax had been laid upon him merely as a means of raising revenue without regard to benefit derived. And in *Gast Realty and Investment Co. v. Schneider Granite Co.* (1916) the Court held unconstitutional a St. Louis city ordinance authorizing the erection of assessment districts for public improvements, where the districts were so bounded that certain properties within them would derive no benefit from prospective improvements. Justice Holmes said that since "the probability is that the parties will be taxed disproportionately to each other and to the benefit conferred, the law cannot stand against the complaint of the one so taxed in fact."

It might reasonably be supposed that the Court after 1895 would have extended the limitations of due process to prohibit taxation for a private purpose, but this did not occur. It may be recalled that in *Loan Association v. Topeka* (1875) the Court had denounced such a tax as contrary to the fundamental nature of constitutional government. But when, after 1895, various taxes were attacked before the Court as not levied for a public purpose, the Court showed itself unwilling to narrow the scope of "public use" unduly. Thus in *Fallbrook Irrigation District v. Bradley* (1896) the Court accepted the constitutionality of a California statute permitting groups of landowners by vote to organize themselves into irrigation districts which, in turn, had the authority to levy assessments upon all landowners within the district. Justice Peckham admitted that a law that levied taxes for other than a public purpose would violate due process; but he then added that what constituted public use of revenues was mainly a matter of local circumstances and that the Court must defer to the familiarity of the people in California with the circumstances surrounding the passage of such an act. Peckham concluded that irrigation constituted a public purpose within the decision of the people of California; hence the tax was devoted to a public use and the law was constitutional.

The Court adhered to this line of reasoning in *Jones v. Portland* (1917), where the issue was the constitutionality of a 1903 Maine statute authorizing any city or town to establish a fuel yard to sell wood and coal to the inhabitants. Thus such an enterprise might conceivably have been labeled a private business and taxation for it denounced as a violation of due process, but the Court refused to take this stand. Instead Justice Day asserted that "local conditions are of such a varying character that what is or is not a public use in a particular state is manifestly a matter respecting which local authority, has peculiar facilities for securing accurate information." In other words, the Court would ordinarily defer to whatever conception of public use was adopted by state and local authorities.

The Court's rule of noninterference with the judgment of state legislatures on matters of public use in relation to tax revenues was carried to its logical conclusion in *Green v. Frazier* (1920). Here the Court passed favorably upon the constitutionality of a series of North Dakota statutes creating a state industrial commission and authorizing the commission to engage in a variety of business enterprises, among them the operation of a state bank, a mill, and an elevator association to buy and sell all farm products, and a Home Building Association authorized to construct homes for citizens of the state. The state was empowered to issue bonds to capitalize these enterprises, and to pay for the bonds by taxation. These statutes seemingly put the state of North Dakota into private business on a large scale, but the Court again deferred to local circumstances and opinion as to what constituted public use. Justice Day pointed out that North Dakota had declared the various acts in question to have a public purpose, and he then cited *Jones v. Portland* to support the constitutionality of governmental business enterprise. *Loan Association v. Topeka* he distinguished, apparently on the ground that in the earlier case taxation had been for the benefit of a privately owned and operated enterprise as distinct from the publicly owned concerns benefiting from the tax under review.

THE RULE OF REASON AND JUDICIAL REVIEW

It is clear that the meaning of substantive due process as it developed after 1900 can be expressed by one phrase: "the rule of reason." Reasonableness, however, was not a quality of law specifically defined in the Constitution. It could not be related to any specific legislative limitation which the Constitution imposed upon the states such as that banning *ex post facto* laws. The one source upon which judges could draw when they decided for the first time whether a statute was reasonable was their own social and economic philosophy. If the law appeared to aim at objectives which the justices regarded as socially unwise, then frequently they ruled that it constituted an unreasonable or arbitrary interference with private property rights. If, on the other hand, the law strove for social objectives which the justices thought intelligent, they accepted it as a reasonable exercise of the states' police power.

The result was nothing less than the creation of a new type of judicial review, in which the Court examined the constitutionality of both state and federal legislation in the light of the judges' social and economic ideas. There had been occasional instances of this sort of judicial review in the early days of the court; for example, in *Terrett v. Taylor* (1815) Justice Joseph Story had held unconstitutional a Virginia statute confiscating church lands without referring to any constitutional clause but merely on the grounds that the act was "utterly inconsistent with a great and fundamental principle of republican government, the right of the citizens to the free enjoyment of their property legally acquired." And as has already been observed, the Court in certain early contract cases incorporated broad social generalizations in its opinions. In most instances, however, the Court did not consider it to be within its province to inquire whether legislation that came before it was reasonable or wise. Presumably such inquiry was a legislative function. In this earlier conception of judicial review it was the duty of the Court merely to pass upon the question of whether the law violated any provision of the Constitution. Both the law and the Constitution were subject to judicial interpretation, it is true, and judicial review, even of this limited character, was influenced substantially by the justices' social and political ideas. John Marshall, to take one instance, was a conservative nationalist, and he found ways and means of arguing conclusively for the constitutionality of strong national legislation. Yet Marshall did not presume to pass upon the wisdom or desirability of congressional legislation; he was concerned only with the question of whether Congress had acted within its authority under the Constitution. In theory, at least, he matched a written statute with the written Constitution.

The new judicial review was something very different. As has already been observed, in passing upon the wisdom and desirability of legislation under due process of law, the justices were in reality settling matters of public policy. This was a legislative rather than a judicial function. In democratic states men who decide whether laws are socially wise and desirable ordinarily sit in elective legislative bodies. They are sent there by their constituents to vote for or against measures in accordance with the interests of their constituents and in the light of their convictions as to the wisdom and expediency of the proposals upon which they pass. Legislative issues are commonly political rather than judicial in character, and as such are ordinarily settled in the political arena. But under the new judicial review, the Court, as well as Congress and the various state legislatures, now settled many issues of this kind.

The new judicial review thus made the Supreme Court a kind of "negative third chamber" both to the state legislatures and to Congress. Paralleling this development, the supreme courts of the various states became negative third chambers of their own state legislatures. The judicial chamber, it is true, had only a negative vote. It could not initiate legislation. Though limited in this way, its legislative power was nevertheless real. The judicial veto after 1890 constituted a powerful check upon the policies of every legislative chamber in the nation, a check exercised not only in terms of the requirements of the written constitution but also in terms of the social and economic ideas of the justices concerned. It was this fact which Justice Holmes had in mind when he observed in *Lochner v. New York* that the case was decided in accordance with an economic philosophy with which a large portion of the American people did not agree.

Paradoxically, the early twentieth century witnessed the general acceptance by judges of a theory of jurisprudence which denied the law-making capacities of the judiciary. The prevailing theory of jurisprudence around 1900 was that of "received law." This conception held that judges did not make or formulate law, but simply discovered and applied it. The Constitution, the theory held, was fundamental, absolute, and immutable. It contained, by implication, the answer to every constitutional question which might ever be raised in relation to any state or federal statute. The document was a written expression of certain fundamental principles of eternal right and justice. All that was necessary was for the Court to apply the appropriate word or clause of the Constitution to the law in question. Any constitutional issue could be solved by application of the suitable provisions in the Constitution, and the correct conclusion was presumably self-evident to any competent judge. This concept of jurisprudence Roscoe Pound in 1913 called the "slot-machine theory" of law.

Judges who adhered to the theory of received law were likely to deny strenuously that they were ever influenced by their view of the wisdom of legislation. They would deny even that the "rule of reason" in due process involved judicial discretion in any degree. They would deny also that the realities of social or economic life were any concern of theirs. Constitutional questions were to be settled specifically in accordance with the requirements of the written document. This theory was maintained squarely in the face of the rule of reason, in which it would appear to have been clear to any realistic observer that decisions of the Court were being arrived at in accordance with the social and economic philosophy of the judges who made them. In spite of the general acceptance of this theory, however, attorneys appearing before the Court after the presentation in 1908 of the Brandeis brief in *Muller v. Oregon* frequently included in their briefs materials demonstrating or denying the economic or social necessities behind the law in question. This was the real significance of the Brandeis brief; the repeated resort to its technique constituted a fairly general recognition by the legal profession that the Court did in fact pass upon the wisdom and desirability of legislation in deciding questions of due process.

As developed by the Court in the generation or so after 1890, substantive due process was essentially a conservative social instrument, which property-minded justices used to bulwark the vested rights and interests of a burgeoning American capitalism. However, substantive due process was not in and of itself a conservative device; on the contrary it could be used to infuse any given social philosophy which might dominate the Court into the existing social and legal structure. This fact was to become apparent many years later, when the Warren Court after 1960 was to invoke substantive due process not for the defense of property rights but to rid the statute books of "obsolete" or "restrictive" legislation which could not pass muster in the light of a new judicial generation's libertarian values. The legal logic which the Warren Court would one day invoke to strike down anti-birth control and anti-abortion laws would resemble strikingly that in *Lochner v. New York*. Only the philosophical premises and social goals would be radically different.

On occasion dissenting justices in the post-1890 era attacked the Court's tendency to decide the matter of reasonableness in the light of the justices' social philosophy. Justice Holmes' classic denunciation in *Lochner v. New York* has already been quoted. For thirty years thereafter Justice Holmes on notable occasions repeated his charge that the Court was in fact basing its decision upon its social predilections. In Justice Frankfurter's words, "Against this subtle danger of the unconscious identification of personal views with constitutional sanction Mr. Justice Holmes battled during all his years on the Court." [6] Justice Louis D. Brandeis, appointed to the

_____

[6] Felix Frankfurter, *Mr. Justice Holmes and the Supreme Court* (Cambridge, 1939), p. 34.

Court in 1914, came to occupy somewhat the same position; unlike Holmes, however, Brandeis tended to attack majority opinions as bad social thinking, whereas Holmes attacked the identification of either liberal or conservative social theory with the process as indefensible.

One important result of the new conception of the judicial function was a great increase in the resort to the judicial veto as applied to both state and national legislation. In the entire seventy-one years between the founding of the national government and secession, the Supreme Court had declared but two acts of Congress unconstitutional—in *Marbury v. Madison* and in *Dred Scott v. Sandford.* While in this same period the Court invalidated state laws with much greater frequency, even this exercise of the judicial veto was attended with considerable restraint. According to Benjamin F. Wright, there were some sixty cases before 1861 in which the Court declared state legislation void. After the Civil War, on the other hand, resort to the judicial veto increased steadily. Professor Wright reports that during the years 1874–1898 there were twelve decisions invalidating acts of Congress and 125 decisions declaring state legislation contrary to the Constitution.[7] After 1898 the Court invalidated acts of Congress with still greater frequency: there were about fifty such decisions between 1898 and 1937, while in the same period the Court invalidated state laws in some four hundred cases.

The explanation of this more frequent use of the judicial veto is to be found in part in the implications of the "rule of reason." As long as judges passed upon legislation mainly in accordance with the requirements of a written constitution, it was necessary only occasionally to declare a statute to be unconstitutional. However, when legislation had to meet the test of the justices' social philosophy, the chance that the law in question might be found wanting was much greater. It must be observed, however, that the increased use of the judicial veto can be accounted for in part merely by the great increase in the Court's volume of business. The Court was hearing many more cases at each term than in the early national era; hence the chances of invalidating a greater amount of legislation were proportionately increased.

It was also true that during this later period the states, in their efforts to deal with the social and economic problems induced by

---

[7] The foregoing figures are from Benjamin F. Wright, *The Growth of American Constitutional Law* (Boston, 1942). See also the Library of Congress pamphlet, *Provisions of Federal Law Held Unconstitutional by the Supreme Court of the United States* (Washington. 1936).

the industrial revolution, more frequently enacted legislation of a novel and experimental character, which posed new constitutional problems for the Court. Departure from traditional legislative patterns greatly increased the likelihood that some of the new legislative efforts would fail to meet the approval of the Court. When all allowances of this kind have been made, however, it remains true that the Court, after the rise of substantive due process and the new judicial review, was more willing than formerly to strike down state legislation as contrary to the Constitution.

The rise of substantive due process and the new concept of judicial review were factors in the partial failure of the states to deal adequately with the many social and economic problems growing out of the industrial revolution. Of equal importance in this failure, however, was the fact that most of the problems precipitated by the industrial revolution were regional or even national in scope, so that the area of sovereignty of any one state was not sufficiently broad to make possible the imposition of really effective controls. Rail rate problems, for example, were essentially national in character, and regulation by the various states could result only in a disjointed and confused regional and national rate pattern, or indeed in no pattern at all. The failure of the states to function effectively as the arbiters of American economic life became increasingly clear after 1885. The result was a growing demand for national economic controls and a federal program of regulation on the theory that only the national government could deal effectively with a national economy.

Chapter

21

The First Era of National Economic Regulation

As WE have seen, the comparative failure of the states to control economic and social life within their own boundaries had other causes than the interposition of the judiciary as a guardian of vested interests. This failure was also due to the very fact that the American economy had become a national one.

The development of the railroads first made clear the extent to which the great new industrial and commercial life of the nation was being intertwined in one vast network. A single great railroad crossed many states. The Pennsylvania Railroad, for example, cut across the borders of five states and had branch lines extending into many others. The policies of such a road, particularly in its rate structures, affected the welfare of the entire area it served—indeed, of the entire nation.

No one state could control effectively the rail rate structure within its own boundaries, for that structure was too closely bound up with a network extending into other states, in which the state attempting control had no authority. Intrastate rail regulation would at best mean dozens of unrelated and uncorrelated rate structures, with no rational organization of rates on a nationwide basis.

The great trusts that sprang up in industry during the last two decades of the nineteenth century were also nationwide. The Standard Oil Company, for example, became after 1882 a combination of some thirty-nine oil companies doing business in all the states in the Union. It refined oil in half a dozen states; it owned wells in eight widely scattered states; and it marketed in four continents. The huge combinations in steel, sugar, tobacco, and other commodities were hardly less impressive in financial power, size, and extent. As in the case of the railroads, it was not possible to impose a unified national policy upon any such industry by state legislation. Forty separate state laws did not constitute a unified control of the oil industry.

State regulation was made the more difficult by the fact that a corporation chartered in one state could do business in all the others under the constitutional provision by which each state must recognize the public acts of every other state. It became common policy for large-scale industries to incorporate in those states whose incorporation laws were most lenient toward the type of business concerned. This often meant incorporation in Delaware or New Jersey, where state legislation regulating the granting of corporate charters and controlling corporate enterprise was particularly lax.

Although by 1885 it was clear that the railroads and trusts were national phenomena and that they could not be effectively regulated by state law, there was for a long time comparatively little demand for national controls. The whole tradition of the nation's economic and legal thinking was against national regulation of economic life. The Constitution had not contemplated the imposition of an extensive national economic policy by the federal government. The potential authority over national economic life implicit in the commerce clause had been exercised only sporadically in the first century after 1787. Nearly all federal regulation of commerce had been confined to foreign commerce or water-borne domestic commerce, and had for the most part been concerned with mere detail. Much commercial activity was still regulated by state law; the concurrent right of the states to impose certain limited regulations upon interstate commerce within their boundaries had been recognized by the Supreme Court in *Cooley v. Board of Wardens* (1851) and had been confirmed as recently as *Munn v. Illinois* (1877). In short, federal authority over interstate and foreign commerce had hitherto been employed primarily as a negative rather than as a positive power, as a guarantee against state regulation having a restrictive or harmful effect upon normal commercial life.

Furthermore, few theorists before the late nineteenth century would have admitted that the right to regulate interstate commerce implied a general right in the national government to regulate all national economic life. John Marshall had indeed held in *Gibbons v. Ogden* (1824) that the federal commerce power was supreme and that it lawfully extended to all objects directly concerned with commerce, even though such regulation might incidentally affect the internal affairs of the states. Even Marshall, however, had admitted that the commerce power could not be made the basis for a regulation "of matters of pure domestic concern" to the states. The question of whether the federal government could regulate production, for example, did not even arise before the Civil War; and it seems evident that until the enactment of the Sherman Act in 1890, the commerce power was thought to comprehend only control over a variety of forms of interstate communication—highways, railroads, and marine shipping.

Yet the distinction between interstate commerce and economic matters of purely domestic concern to the states was every year becoming more archaic and artificial. By the late nineteenth century commerce and industry were so intertwined on a national scale that any effective regulation of commerce would of necessity include certain controls over manufacturing. The very existence of the great trusts, combinations in manufacturing, finance, and commerce, raised the question of whether commerce could be controlled effectively unless some restrictions were imposed upon manufacturing. The implications of economic reality had not yet affected constitutional theory, however, and it took more than half a century after the development of the tangled national network of production and trade for economic reality to find effective reflection in constitutional law.

The new masters of capitalism were, quite naturally, not interested in a federal regulatory program. While they sought and obtained from the national government numerous favors which meant increased earnings for industry, such as high tariffs and cheap railroad, timber, and mining lands, they were averse to effective federal economic controls. And in this attitude a majority of Americans usually concurred. The average citizen, in particular the average entrepreneur, was an individualist with but little understanding of the rapidity with which the small free enterprise of an earlier day was disappearing. Before 1885, most of the demand for the regulation of commerce and industry came from agrarian radicals, labor leaders, and certain unorthodox economic theorists.

Yet the malcontents had succeeded in raising some degree of public interests in the railroad and trust problems. Here the evils of uncontrolled private enterprise were so evident, so flagrant, and so widely publicized as to bring strong popular pressure for a degree of regulation on a national scale.

THE RAILROADS AND THE INTERSTATE COMMERCE
COMMISSION

Even before 1880 it was evident to many thoughtful persons that the abuses of railroad operation were a scandal to the nation. Rebates—the practice of refunding in secret to a shipper a portion of the established rate for a given haul—offered a method by which roads favored one business at the expense of another and so paved the way for the rise of monopoly. Pools and rate-fixing agreements ended competition between competing roads and were used as a monopolistic means to raise freight and passenger rates to high levels. Basing point systems, whereby shippers were obliged to pay the rate to a designated shipping point plus any additional mileage charges, and other distorted rate schemes favored certain industrial regions and certain corporations at the expense of others. As practices of this sort developed, the public began to demand regulatory measures, and indeed many railroad operators themselves began to recommend legal safeguards against cutthroat competition.

The states attempted to deal with this problem, although for reasons already made clear their efforts were not very effective. In the seventies, most of the states enacted legislation banning certain of the most evident abuses of the roads and also setting up commissions to enforce their laws. Most such commissions were authorized to conduct hearings into abuses, investigate violations of law, and issue orders to offending carriers to "cease and desist" from the violation in question. Very often the commissions were given the power to fix freight and passenger rates. Such regulation was established under the theory that the states retained power to regulate commerce within their own boundaries as well as to assert a certain incidental authority over interstate commerce in the absence of federal regulation.

Only gradually did the extent of the failure of state rail regulation attract attention. In 1874 a Senate committee under Senator William Windom of Minnesota publicized for the first time the extent of the evils practiced and recommended national legislation to enforce fair competitive practices. In 1878 the House of Representatives passed the Reagan bill, which would have imposed some degree of regulation upon the roads, but a railroad and trust lobby blocked the bill in the Senate. Several bills of similar intent were introduced into Congress soon after 1880, but as Congress was reluctant to oppose organized minority pressure and public opinion was not yet insistent, nothing came of these measures.

By 1886, however, the demand for reform commanded a strong measure of popular support, particularly in centers of agrarian unrest in the West and the South. In addition, the railroads had now come to realize the ruinous consequences of certain practices, so that many rail executives were ready to accept the necessity of some federal regulation as the only remedy. Two developments in that same year which brought to a head the demand for appropriate legislation were immediately responsible for the passage of the Interstate Commerce Act during the following year.

The Supreme Court, in *Wabash, St. Louis, and Pacific Railway Company v. Illinois* (1886), handed down a decision seriously impairing the legal capacity of the states to cope with the railroad problem. The case dealt with the validity of an Illinois statute prohibiting long-short haul rate discriminations. The state of Illinois sued to enjoin the Wabash road from charging more for a haul between Gilman, Illinois, and New York City than was charged for a haul between Peoria, Illinois, and New York City, a distance eighty-six miles greater. As most of the haul lay outside the state of Illinois, the case involved the validity of a regulation of interstate commerce by a single state.

The Court held that the Illinois statute was void as an intrusion upon the federal commerce power. In his opinion, Justice Miller observed that a state admittedly might regulate commerce entirely within its boundaries, and that such regulation might incidentally and remotely affect interstate commerce and still be valid. However, he said, the Illinois law attempted to regulate interstate commerce directly and so violated the Constitution. He virtually admitted that the decision gravely impaired the dictum that the states had a limited concurrent jurisdiction over interstate commerce, as recently expressed in *Munn v. Illinois* and the other *Granger Cases*. Yet he insisted that it never had been "the deliberate opinion of a majority of this court that a statute of a State which attempts to regulate the fares and charges of a railroad company within its limits, for a transportation which constitutes a part of commerce among the States, is a valid law."

The effect of the Wabash decision was to remove the interstate rail rate structure almost completely from state control. It thus made some kind of federal regulation imperative.

In 1886, also, a special Senate committee on railroads working under the chairmanship of Senator Shelby Moore Cullom of Illinois made its report recommending the passage of a comprehensive federal regulatory statute. The convincing body of evidence that it presented exposed nothing new; yet the report obtained far more publicity than any prior investigation, and the demand for regulation became too overwhelming for Congress to ignore.

The Interstate Commerce Act became law on February 4, 1887. Constitutional issues were scarcely touched upon during the debate that preceded the passage of the bill, for few questioned that the federal government had authority thus to regulate under the interstate commerce clause. Only Senator Leland Stanford of California had the temerity to suggest that transportation was not commerce and that a law regulating common carriers would therefore be unconstitutional. Stanford's rail interests were well known, and no one took his argument seriously.

The Interstate Commerce Act provided that all charges for rail transportation in interstate commerce should be reasonable and just, but did not attempt to define a reasonable and just rate. The law prohibited rebates, discriminatory rate agreements, long-short haul discriminations, pools, and rate-fixing agreements, and required the publication of all rate schedules.

The act entrusted enforcement to a five-man Interstate Commerce Commission, modeled generally on the state commissions of the time, the members to be appointed by the President with the consent of the Senate. The Commission had the power to hear complaints, to inquire into the books and accounts of railroads, to hold hearings, and to compel the attendance of witnesses. It was not specifically authorized to fix rates and charges, but it was empowered to issue cease-and-desist orders against any carrier found to be violating the provisions of the law. This clearly implied the power to issue orders against unreasonable rates, but whether it implied the power to fix a new rate for the one destroyed was very doubtful.

The Interstate Commerce Commission was the first permanent federal administrative board to which Congress delegated broad powers of a quasi-legislative, quasi-executive, and quasi-judicial nature. Its establishment was a landmark in American constitutional history.

In theory, at least, the Commission was a branch of the executive; its members were appointed by the President, and it was their duty to administer the law. The Commission also had certain functions similar to those of a court—namely, the holding of hearings, the taking of evidence, and the handing down of decisions which had the effect of court orders. Furthermore, its administrative orders had the effect of law and were based upon considerations of public policy; they were therefore quasi-legislative in character. The Commission thus cut squarely across the bounds of the three branches of the federal government.

The Commission and subsequent similar administrative boards actually represented a fundamental departure from the principle of the separation of powers. Why did this departure occur? The best explanation is the growing complexity and technical nature of the problems which confronted lawmakers. The mass of technical detail was in turn a direct reflection of the incredible complexity of the new economy. No one but a specialist-expert could hope to master certain problems—in this instance rate structures—which the government was now called upon to supervise and administer. Congressmen were first of all politicians and statesmen and seldom technical experts. They could not be expected to learn the details involved in the whole complex tangle of rail rates. All Congress could do, therefore, was to set up broad principles of policy, while the mastery of detail and the specific solution of numberless administrative problems were left to Commission experts. In founding the Commission, Congress thus recognized the indispensable place which the technical expert was coming to play in the governmental process.

THE COMMISSION AND THE COURTS—1887–1900

Within a few years after the establishment of the Interstate Commerce Commission, the Court had stripped it of most of its powers. The Court did not hold void any single part of the Interstate Commerce Act, but in a series of interpretative opinions it first denied to the Commission the power to fix rates, and then in another series of cases it impaired seriously the Commission's authority as a fact-finding body.

After some uncertainty expressed in early decisions, the Court finally denied to the Commission all positive rate-fixing power. In *Cincinnati, New Orleans, and Texas Pacific Railway Co. v. Interstate Commerce Commission* (1896), Justice Shiras observed for the Court that he could not find anything in the act that "expressly or by necessary implication" conferred the power to fix rates. Replying to the Commission's argument that the power to pass upon the reasonableness of existing rates necessarily implied the right to set a new rate by commission order, Shiras said that was "not necessarily so." The reasonableness of a particular rate, he held, "depends on the facts, and the function of the Commission is to consider these facts and give them their proper weight. If the Commission, instead of withholding judgment in such a matter until an issue shall be made and the facts found, itself fixes a rate, that rate is prejudged by the Commission to be reasonable."

A year later, in *Interstate Commerce Commission v. Cincinnati, New Orleans, and Texas Pacific Railway Co.* (1897) the Court denied the Commission these powers in even more categorical terms. As in the earlier case, the Commission had after hearing adjudged the railroad's rate structure to be unreasonable and had then ordered a new schedule of rates to be put in effect. In this instance, a lower court had certified the question of the Commission's rate-fixing powers to the Supreme Court. Justice Brewer, who delivered the majority opinion, first pointed out that "there is nothing in the act fixing rates," and he added that "no just rule of construction would tolerate a grant of such power by mere implication." Brewer then quoted at length from various state statutes to show the clear and unequivocal language invariably used in granting state commissions rate-fixing power, whereas the federal law used no such language.

In reality, Brewer and his colleagues were unwilling to grant a quasi-legislative function to an administrative body, since to do so appeared to violate the separation of powers. Rate-fixing by the Commission would have been essentially legislative in character, since the Commission's orders would have had the force of law. Therefore, said Brewer, the power to fix rates ought not to be exercised by a branch of the executive. "The power given," he said, "is the power to execute and enforce, not to legislate. The power given is partly judicial, partly executive and administrative, but not legislative." The idea that Congress might delegate quasi-legislative authority to the executive was too new to win the justices' acceptance.

The Commission, thus deprived of any positive rate-setting powers, now possessed only the negative right to declare that schedules already in effect were unreasonable. It could then issue cease-and-desist orders against such rates, and resort to the courts if the carriers refused to obey its orders. Theoretically the Commission might strike down one rate after another as illegal until the railroad finally established an acceptable rate, but such a method of control was hopelessly ineffective.

A few months later, in *Interstate Commerce Commission v. Alabama Midland Ry. Co.* (1897), the Court dealt a second heavy blow to the Commission by impairing its function as a fact-finding body. The act of 1887 had declared that the findings of fact upon which the Commission based its orders were to be accepted as conclusive by the courts. Clearly this implied that the court to which appeal was taken must accept the facts of the case as the Commission presented them and not ignore the Commission's findings by conducting an extensive original investigation of its own.

The Supreme Court, however, refused to accept this implication. Instead it ruled that the language of the act authorized the circuit courts as courts of equity to hear appeals from the orders of the Commission. This, said the Court, necessarily implied a right to investigate anew all facts in any case. "It has been uniformly held by the several circuit courts and the circuit courts of appeal, in such cases," said Justice Shiras' opinion, "that they are not restricted to the evidence adduced before the Commission, nor to a consideration merely of the power of the Commission to make the particular order under question, but that additional evidence may be put by either party, and that the duty of the court is to decide, as a court of equity, upon the entire body of evidence."

This decision further curtailed drastically the powers and usefulness of the Commission. The decisions it made could be reversed *in toto*, as to both facts and law, by the circuit courts. It was to become a frequent practice for the railroads to hold back important evidence and facts in any Commission hearing; on appeal these could then be presented to the courts in such a manner as to make the Commission's order appear to be ill-advised or even ridiculous. It is difficult to disagree with Justice Harlan, who in his dissent in the Alabama Midland Case observed, "Taken in connection with other decisions defining the powers of the Interstate Commerce Commission, the present decision, it seems to me, goes far to make that Commission a useless body for all practical purposes, and to defeat many of the important objects designed to be accomplished by the various enactments of Congress relating to interstate commerce."

Between 1898 and 1906, the Interstate Commerce Commission was little more than an agency for public information. It sometimes issued cease-and-desist orders, but it had little chance of sustaining these in the courts. Of the sixteen principal cases carried on appeal to the Supreme Court between 1897 and 1906, the Commission lost all but one.

PASSAGE OF THE SHERMAN ANTI-TRUST ACT

Meanwhile public attention was focusing upon the evils associated with the great trusts springing up in American industry.

The methods of trust combination were varied, although their purpose was always the same: the imposition of some degree of monopolistic control upon chaotic and cutthroat competition. Sometimes the combination was simply a price- or rate-fixing agreement. Sometimes production was allocated and profits were pooled and prorated among several participating firms. More spectacular were the great combinations which practically ended competition within an industry. Thus the Standard Oil Company, founded in 1882, was a trust combination of thirty-nine principal refining concerns which together dominated completely the business of producing, refining, and marketing oil in the United States. Likewise forty-odd independent sugar refiners were replaced in 1892 by a single firm, the American Sugar Refining Company. The trust controlled between 90 and 98 per cent of the sugar-refining business in the United States. Similar combinations were created in tobacco, leather, meat packing, and electrical goods. The United States Steel Corporation, organized in 1901, had the largest financial resources of all the trusts formed up to that time. This concern, originally capitalized at $1,450,000,000, controlled some 50 per cent of the nation's iron and steel manufacturing capacity, and the absorption of additional firms in 1907 raised this figure for a time thereafter to more than 70 per cent.

From the point of view of big business, combination was a sensible method of solving a serious problem. Unrestrained competition was ruinous and often led to bankruptcy, and combination appeared to be the only rational way to impose some limits upon cutthroat economic warfare. Viewed historically, the process of integration seems to have been a certain inevitable stage common to the development of large-scale industries in all capitalistic economies. Processes of combination substantially similar to those in America occurred also in Britain, France, and Germany.

Public opinion in the eighties and nineties, however, viewed the trusts in a different light. The trusts menaced the traditional structure of free private enterprise. They often destroyed the little fellow and replaced the open market with a closed semi-monopolistic one. Moreover, the ruthless and unscrupulous methods adopted by many trusts to attain their ends added greatly to their unsavory reputations. Rural areas in the South and West in particular came to look upon trusts as symbols of an economic revolution in which rich, powerful, and corrupt financiers and industrialists had grasped power and riches at the expense of small and helpless farm folk.

By 1890, the West and the South, as well as many eastern liberals, reformers, and small entrepreneurs, were in full hue and cry after the trusts. Many states passed antitrust laws, but by now it was generally recognized that the great trusts were nationwide combinations and that only the national government could deal with them effectively. In 1888, both major political parties demanded trust regulation by Congress, and the demand for federal regulation thereafter grew more insistent.

Senator John Sherman of Ohio took the lead in Congress in demanding the passage of a federal antitrust law. In 1888 and 1889 he introduced antitrust bills into Congress, but until 1890 neither house acted upon his proposals.

The session of 1890 was dominated by a conservative Republican majority, which might ordinarily have been expected to pay little attention to agrarian and liberal demands for an antitrust law. The Republican Party, however, was in a somewhat embarrassing position. Many Democrats and reformers were charging that Republican high-tariff policies were directly responsible for the rise of the trusts, since the tariff eliminated foreign competition. Congress was even then engaged in the passage of the McKinley Tariff Act, which was to raise tariff duties to unprecedented levels. If the Republican majority was to escape condemnation as the friend of the trusts. it was imperative that it take some very positive stand against industrial combinations. Sherman's bill had therefore the support of the regular party organizations in Congress. and there was little doubt of its passage in some form.

As originally introduced, Sherman's proposal made illegal all manufacturing combinations producing goods for interstate commerce. The bill thus raised an important constitutional question. Congress certainly had the power to regulate interstate commerce, but did it thereby have the power to regulate industrial combinations, merely because those combinations produced goods intended for interstate commerce? Senator James Z. George of Mississippi immediately attacked the constitutionality of Sherman's bill on this point. The power of Congress to regulate manufacturing, he said, could not rest upon the subsequent transportation of goods so produced. Several senators supported this view. They freely predicted that Sherman's measure, even if enacted by Congress, would eventually be declared unconstitutional by the Supreme Court.

Sherman's bill was open to the equally serious objection that it did not prohibit trusts as such, but only those formed with the intent to manufacture for interstate commerce. Several senators pointed out that intent would often be impossible of proof.

Two other methods of trust control were proposed in the Senate debates on the Sherman bill. Senator George suggested discriminatory federal taxes against industrial combinations as a constitutional method of regulation. This he supported with the plausible assertion that the federal government's right to use the power of taxation as a regulatory device had already been upheld by the Supreme Court. Senator George Vest of Missouri suggested an amendment which would have made state legislation the basis of federal action. His measure would have provided that whenever a state prohibited trusts within its own boundaries, it should then become unlawful for any carrier or producer to move the products of any trust in or out of that state. This scheme was not unlike that later embodied in the Webb-Kenyon Act of 1913, ultimately sustained by the Supreme Court, for controlling the traffic in liquor between wet and dry states. Vest's suggestion received little support, however, the basic objection being that it would result in irregular administration.

After some debate, Sherman's bill was referred back to the Senate Judiciary Committee and redrafted to eliminate the constitutional objections that had been raised. The new bill, reported for the committee by Senator George F. Hoar of Massachusetts, made illegal every contract, combination, and trust in restraint of trade or interstate and foreign commerce. Thus the bill left open the question whether a combination in production could be held to restrain commerce and so be construed as a violation of the law; this question was thrown upon the courts for a decision. It is probable that this was the intent of the authors of the measure.

In the debate on the revised bill, the question arose as to whether it prohibited all combinations in restraint of trade. If so, virtually every business contract or agreement, however innocent, would become illegal, since it might be construed as a limitation upon trade or commerce in some degree. Senator Hoar replied that the intent of the bill was to write the English common-law provisions on monopoly into federal law; that is, "monopoly" and "restraint of trade" were to be defined as in the English common law. Presumably, this would not make every contract of sale illegal, but only those which resulted in substantial control of some phase of industry or commerce by some one group or firm.

The revised Sherman bill became law on July 2, 1890, having encountered little organized opposition in either house. The statute was entitled "An Act to Protect Trade and Commerce against Unlawful Restraint and Monopolies." The important provisions of the law were embodied in Sections 1 and 2. Section 1 provided that

Every contract, combination in the form of trust or otherwise, or conspiracy, in restraint of trade or commerce among the several States, or with foreign nations, is hereby declared to be illegal. . . .

Section 2 declared that

Every person who shall monopolize, or attempt to monopolize, or combine or conspire with any other person or persons, to monopolize any part of the trade or commerce among the several States, or with foreign nations, shall be deemed guilty of a misdemeanor. . . .

The act provided appropriate punishments for violation of its provisions and further stipulated that the law might be enforced against any illegal combination by a suit in equity to dissolve it.

The critical constitutional question of whether the Sherman law prohibited manufacturers' trusts on the ground that they restrained interstate commerce was now a matter for the courts to decide. Unless the law was interpreted so as to control trusts in production it would be of little value and could be used only against those combinations formed strictly in interstate commerce—in railroads, steamship lines, and the like. It did not seem probable that the Supreme Court would yield an affirmative answer to this question, since the justices who were being called upon to interpret the law were the very ones who were even then developing the concept of due process of law as a constitutional rationalization of *laissez-faire* and vested interests and who were in the process of stripping the Interstate Commerce Commission of its power to fix rail rates.

THE SUGAR TRUST CASE: "MANUFACTURING IS NOT COMMERCE"

The Supreme Court first had occasion to interpret the Sherman Act in *United States v. E. C. Knight Co.*, decided in 1895, five years after the passage of the law. The case involved a suit brought by the government for the dissolution of the American Sugar Refining Company.

The government charged that this concern had, by contracts with four other defendants, gained control of more than 90 per cent of the manufacture of all refined sugar in the United States. The government contended that this constituted a substantial restraint upon commerce among the states, since the trust tended to raise prices and so restrict trade. It asked the voiding of the contracts upon which the trust rested and an injunction restraining the defendants from further violations of the Sherman law.

In denying the government's claim, Chief Justice Fuller, speaking for the majority, based his opinion upon a sharp distinction between manufacturing and commerce. "Commerce succeeds to manufacture, and is not a part of it," he said, and he went on to argue that the Sherman law was directed only against combinations in interstate commerce and could not be construed as invalidating those in production. He admitted that the present combination constituted a trust to monopolize the manufacture of sugar, but he held that it was not on that account illegal, for the trust was not in interstate commerce but in manufacturing.

Nor was it possible, said Fuller, to allow federal regulation of manufacturing merely upon the ground that production had an ultimate or indirect effect upon commerce. "It will be perceived," he said, "how far reaching the proposition is that the power of dealing with a monopoly directly may be exercised by the general government whenever interstate or international commerce may be ultimately affected. The regulation of commerce applies to the subjects of commerce and not to matters of internal police."

The Chief Justice then drew a sharp distinction between "direct" and "indirect" effects upon commerce. If a trust or monopoly had a direct effect upon commerce, then presumably it was subject to federal regulation. Combinations in manufacturing, however, were not of this kind: "Contracts, combinations, or conspiracies to control domestic enterprise in manufacture, agriculture, mining, production in all its forms, or to raise or lower prices or wages, might unquestionably tend to restrain external as well as domestic trade; but the restraint would be an indirect result, however inevitable and whatever its extent." Regulation of contracts of this kind was not a permissible exercise of federal power. "Slight reflection will show," he said, "that if the national power extends to all contracts and combinations in manufacture, agriculture, mining, and other productive industries, whose ultimate result may affect external commerce, comparatively little of business operations and affairs would be left for state control."

The Court's categorical distinction between commerce and manufacturing had some precedent. True, it has on occasion been contended with some force that the Constitutional Convention used the term "commerce" in a very broad eighteenth-century sense to comprehend all economic activity, including production, although not all historians accept this view. It is also true that John Marshall had repeatedly given an extremely broad connotation to the commerce power, although he observed that it did not comprise all forms of economic activity. And Justice Story in his *Commentaries*, though flatly denying that Congress had any authority to regulate manufacturing as such, nonetheless pointed out that such regulation might occur incidentally to the legitimate exercise of the commerce power.

However, after the Marshall era there was an increasing tendency to define the commerce power in limited terms. Thus Justice Daniel in *Veazie v. Moor* (1852) denied that the commerce power extended to manufacturing or agriculture. And in *The Daniel Ball* (1871) Justice Field in an otherwise nationalistic opinion on the federal commerce power stated that "whenever a commodity has begun to move as an article of trade from one state to another, commerce in that commodity between the states has commenced," the implication being that interstate commerce began when transportation or movement began. And in *Kidd v. Pearson* (1888) Justice Lamar observed that "no distinction is more popular to the common mind, or more clearly expressed in economic and political literature, than that between manufactures and commerce." It was this later stream of precedent, which viewed the commerce power as little more than control over interstate transportation and trade, to which Fuller appealed. One may hazard the guess that had John Marshall written the Sugar Trust opinion he would have pushed Fuller's precedents aside.

The Court's distinction between direct and indirect effects upon commerce had an amorphous and metaphysical quality—a quality that made it useful to legislative-minded jurists who were not averse to bringing their personal philosophy to bear in passing upon constitutional issues. In a later generation a conservative-minded Court was to invoke Fuller's distinction repeatedly in order to strike down congressional statutes attempting to assert control over some phase of the national economy.

The Court's distinction between manufacturing and commerce was not based upon economic reality. Whatever the situation in 1787, manufacturing had during the last decades of the nineteenth century become intimately associated with commerce. Some federal control over the instruments of production had become a necessary part of any effective national program for the promotion and control of interstate commerce.

More serious, the Court's distinction struck a hard blow at the doctrine of national ascendancy. That doctrine, as set forth by Marshall in *McCulloch v. Maryland* and *Gibbons v. Ogden*, held that the powers of Congress were paramount and that in their exercise Congress could lawfully invade the sphere of authority ordinarily reserved to the states whenever the matters affected had legitimate national ends. Some of Taney's opinions, it is true, had held that state and national authority constituted two mutually exclusive spheres of sovereignty and that Congress never could lawfully impinge upon the sphere reserved to the states. But the weight of decisions had been in the other direction. The powers of Congress were supreme within the federal field; those of the states were supreme only so long as they did not intrude upon federal authority. Chief Justice Fuller's distinction between commerce and manufacturing was completely at odds with this doctrine. Although it was evident that effective exercise of the commerce power now required some degree of national control over production, the Court nonetheless categorically set manufacturing aside as reserved unconditionally to the sovereign sphere of the states.

It seems fair to assume that in taking this position the Court was reluctant to concede any federal control over productive processes. Like all conservatives of the day, the justices were thoroughly imbued with the doctrine of *laissez faire*, and they viewed governmental controls over property as potential instruments in the hands of reformers and agrarian radicals who wished to assault the temples of private property and vested interest. The recent growth of substantive due process had indoctrinated the justices in the practice of relating their social philosophy to constitutional theory. Given this state of mind, it is understandable that the Court found plausible constitutional means to deny federal authority over production under the Sherman act.

United States v. Knight marked the beginning of a "twilight zone" between state and national powers—a zone in which neither the federal government nor the states could act. Certain economic problems it was obviously beyond the competence of the states to regulate; yet they were now constitutionally beyond the authority of the national government. The separate states could not regulate monopoly. They might regulate manufacturing within their own boundaries, but they could not impose comprehensive regulation upon a concern extending over a number of states. Nor could the national government impose the necessary controls upon such a business, for the Court had denied federal authority to do so. In other words, certain phases of national economic life lay outside the control of both the states and the national government. No more complete perversion of the principles of effective federal government can be imagined.

The Sugar Trust opinion for the time being vitiated in very large degree federal control of trusts and monopolies. The only successful prosecutions conducted by the government in the next few years were those directed against railroad rate combinations. Since a railroad was in itself a business directly engaged in interstate commerce, the issue in such cases was not federal control of production but the regulation of commerce itself, and the dictum in *United States v. Knight* did not apply. Thus in *United States v. Trans-Missouri Freight Association* (1897) the Court held that an "association" formed by several western railroads to fix rail rates was monopolistic in character and violated the Sherman law. In *Addystone Pipe and Steel Co. v. United States* (1899) the Court took at least one short step toward recognition of the intimate relationship between commerce and production. Here the Court held that a combination entered into by several pipe manufacturers, which divided the pipe market along regional geographic lines and which fixed the prices of pipe through collusive bidding by members of the combine, had a direct effect upon interstate commerce and was therefore illegal under the Sherman law. But decisions of this kind were rare.

IN RE DEBS: THE PULLMAN STRIKE

The Court might attack national supremacy when the federal government attempted to deal with monopoly, but it nevertheless found it possible at the same session to expound national supremacy and federal sovereignty in the most sweeping terms in the Debs case. The Court's inconsistency is apparent only in the realm of constitutional theory; on the economic plane it acted with complete consistency. For in the Debs case the Court used national supremacy to defend corporate property and law and order against labor union violence and anarchy.

In re Debs (1895) rose out of the great Pullman strike. In May 1894, the Pullman Car Company, because of the prevailing business depression, imposed a 20 per cent wage cut upon its employees. At the same time it maintained the high level of executive salaries and company dividends. Several thousand Pullman workers, organized within the American Railway Union, thereupon went out on strike. Under the leadership of Eugene V. Debs, the union presently resorted to a secondary boycott by refusing to move trains hauling Pullman cars. The strikers and their sympathizers shortly engaged in rioting and mob violence to block rail traffic. The result was the physical obstruction of interstate commerce and blockage of the mails in the region of Chicago and elsewhere in the nation.

President Grover Cleveland thereupon interfered in the strike to protect the mails and assure the free movement of interstate commerce. Over the protest of the governor of Illinois, Peter Altgeld, he despatched federal troops to the strike scene to keep order. At the same time the President's Attorney General sought and obtained an injunction in the Federal Circuit Court for Northern Illinois against further interference with the mails or with railroads engaged in interstate commerce. When violence and disorder continued, Debs and his associates were arraigned in federal circuit court, convicted of contempt, and sentenced to imprisonment.

In sentencing Debs the district court invoked the Sherman Act as authority for the injunction and for the convictions, on the ground that the strikers had engaged in a conspiracy in restraint of trade within the meaning of the law. The Court disregarded the objection that in enacting the antitrust law Congress had presumably been aiming at corporate trusts and not at labor union activities.

When Debs and his associates sought a writ of habeas corpus from the United States Supreme Court, the Court denied the writ. Justice Brewer made his opinion in *In re Debs* the occasion for a forceful exposition of national supremacy and the commerce power. The federal government, he said, had "all the attributes of sovereignty," and federal authority within its proper sphere was necessarily supreme over that of the states when the two came in conflict. "The strong arm of the national government," he said, "may be put forth to brush away all obstructions to the freedom of interstate commerce or the transportation of the mails." Resort to injunction, he added, was a proper remedy for securing the protection of commerce and the mails. He did not mention the Sherman law, as the circuit court had done, but instead he rested his opinion on the broadest possible grounds of national sovereignty and supremacy.

No one accepting the doctrine of national sovereignty could quarrel with the Court's language or reasoning, or with the decision.

In Cleveland's words, the Court had established "in an absolutely authoritative manner and for all time, the power of the national government to protect itself in the exercise of its functions." It is difficult to see how the administration or the Court could have acted otherwise. But there was irony in the fact that federal supremacy, so helpless to deal with the obstructions to interstate commerce imposed by monopolies and trusts, should be expounded so effectively against the leaders of a too-militant labor union.

THE FIRST INCOME TAX CASE

At the same session in which the Supreme Court decided *United States v. Knight* and *In re Debs*, it also rendered an unfavorable decision on the constitutionality of the federal income tax provisions incorporated in Wilson-Gorman Tariff Act of 1894. The two income tax cases, *Pollock v. Farmers' Loan and Trust Company* (1895) and *Pollock v. Farmers' Loan and Trust Company* (1895), illustrated another way in which the Court acted as the guardian of private vested rights and used its new quasi-legislative status to defeat attempts of the national government to cope with modern economic problems.

As a federal revenue measure, the income tax was not new. An income tax had been levied by Congress during the Civil War and had remained in effect until 1872. In *Springer v. United States* (1881) the Court in a unanimous decision had held this tax to be constitutional as applied to lawyers' professional earnings. Thus the new income tax seemed to involve no novel issue of federal power.

The income tax was a logical and obvious revenue device which recognized important shifts in the nature of taxable wealth that were occurring in the country. The older forms of wealth had been principally realty and personal property. Since the Constitution required that direct taxes be apportioned among the states, it was impracticable for the national government to tax realty. Congress therefore had hitherto depended primarily upon import duties and excises in raising federal revenue. The assets of the new industry, however, were primarily in the earning power of its capital investments, the visible symbols of which were stocks and bonds, the intangible property of banks, corporations, and private individuals scattered over the nation.

Eastern liberals and agrarian radicals of the West and South were insistent in their demands for an income tax. At the same time they attacked the tariff, which they condemned as a tax upon farmers and consumers. Thus the National Alliance and Industrial Union, a southern Populist group, demanded that the tariff be replaced with a "just and equitable system of graduated taxes on incomes." The 1892 platform of the Populist Party also voiced this demand. The Democratic platform upon which Cleveland was re-elected to the presidency in November of that year called for drastic downward revision of the tariff, but said nothing of an income tax. However, a majority of southern and western Democratic congressmen now strongly supported such a tax, while Cleveland apparently also accepted the tax in principle, although he opposed its immediate enactment as inexpedient.

A severe financial crisis and business depression struck the nation in 1893, and as a consequence the federal treasury encountered a series of quarterly deficits in 1893 and 1894. It was apparent that the Democratic Congress would be forced to seek out additional sources of federal revenue. The southern and western agrarians saw in the income tax an obvious solution of the government's financial difficulties. When the House in December 1893 began consideration of the Wilson bill for tariff revision, the proponents of the income tax, led by William Jennings Bryan of Nebraska, seized their opportunity and forced the incorporation of several income-tax sections in the bill. These provisions subsequently withstood the attacks of eastern Democrats and Republicans in both houses.

The Wilson-Gorman Act, which became law on August 15, 1894, effected a number of minor reductions in import duties. The income tax sections of the law levied a 2 per cent tax upon all kinds of income—rents, interests, dividends, salaries, profits, and the like. The act provided an exemption of $4,000, but, unlike the levies of a later day, the tax was not graduated.

A few months after passage of the Wilson-Gorman Act, *Pollock v. the Farmers' Loan and Trust Company* (1895), a case challenging the constitutionality of the statute's income-tax provisions, reached the Supreme Court. Pollock had sued as a stockholder to enjoin the company from payment of the tax. This was an astute method of attacking the constitutionality of the law, for an act of Congress of 1867 had specifically banned suits "for the purpose of restraining the assessment or collection of a tax." As Justice White very aptly observed in his dissenting opinion, the stockholder's suit ingeniously avoided this prohibition. Moreover, the case clearly constituted a collusive suit, since both parties obviously had the same interest in having the law declared unconstitutional. Ordinarily the Court will not consent to hear or decide collusive suits attacking the constitutionality of a federal statute. In spite of these dubious elements, the Supreme Court consented to review the Pollock case.

A brilliant array of legal learning, headed by Joseph Choate of New York and former Senator George Edmunds of Vermont, who were generally recognized as among the foremost lawyers of the day, appeared before the justices to attack the constitutionality of the income tax law. They were assisted by a battery of legal talent only slightly less distinguished. These gentlemen submitted one of the most elaborate briefs the Court had ever seen, a brief loaded with references to the Constitutional Convention, early American and English history, and works on economic theory.

Fundamentally the plaintiff's argument, as Chief Justice Fuller observed in his opinion, came down to three points. First was the contention that the tax was unconstitutional in so far as it levied a tax upon income from land. This claim was based upon the provisions in the Constitution (Article I, Section 2, and Article I, Section 9) that direct taxes must be levied among the states according to population. Taxes on land had always been classified as direct taxes. A tax on income from realty was equivalent to a tax on land. Therefore, plaintiff argued, the present law, in so far as it levied upon income from realty, was unconstitutional. An incidental additional claim was here entered: that since the sections of the law levying a tax upon income from land were inseparable from the other income tax sections, all those sections of the law dealing with the income tax were unconstitutional.

Second was the assertion that since the income tax exempted all persons and corporations earning less than $4,000 yearly and certain other corporations and associations, it violated Article I, Section 8, of the Constitution, which required that all taxes must be uniform throughout the United States.

Third was the claim that the law was invalid in so far as it levied upon the income of state and municipal bonds.

These arguments, except for the last, which was limited in application to a small category of income, were of questionable validity. Choate and Edmunds supplemented them, however, with a plea which was presumably much closer to their hearts—an impassioned appeal to the Court to defend the sacred rights of private property and the foundation of honest government against the assaults of the mob. Edmunds spoke in the following vein:

And this we call free government, a government of equal protection of the laws; we call it constitutional government. Three-fourths, nine-tenths of the people of this government, paying nothing toward carrying it on, shall be at liberty, under a Constitution which has been supposed always to protect the rights of minorities, to impose all the taxes of government upon those who own property amounting to more than $80,000, and nothing on those who own less. . . .

This would be followed by further invasions of private and property rights, as one vice follows another, and very soon we should have, possibly, only one per cent of the people paying the taxes, and finally a provision that only the twenty people who have the greatest estates should bear the whole taxation, and after that communism, anarchy, and then, the ever following despotism.

The technique of this argument, another example of the *argumentum ad horrendum,* is worth noting carefully, for it was used with increasing frequency in after years. It consisted essentially in dwelling upon the horrible results which would follow were the principles embodied in the legislation before the Court carried to a supposedly logical extreme, an extreme which in reality lay beyond all rational probability.

This kind of plea is intelligible if we recall the panicky state of the conservative mind between 1893 and 1896, when agrarian revolt, culminating in the Populist movement, loomed as a threat to the interests of sound property and government everywhere. The air was full of demands for monetary inflation, for government operation and ownership of railroads and other utilities, for abolition of the protective tariff. A series of bitter strikes was of recent memory: the Homestead strike of 1892, which had culminated in a pitched battle between the steel workers and Pinkerton detectives; the Pullman Company strike in Chicago, which Cleveland had finally squashed by the use of federal troops; the savage warfare of striking miners at Cripple Creek, Colorado. It was a day when the bitter unemployed men of Coxey's army marched in protest upon Washington—only to be arrested for walking on the grass! To conservatives of the day, the liberal, the populist, the socialist, the anarchist, and the communist were all of one stripe. The very foundations of American society seemed to be breaking up under radical attack. To damn the income tax as an anarchist assault upon the foundations of the American social order was an exceedingly clever approach to a Court dominated by a group of conservative property-minded justices. The argument did not fall upon deaf ears.

Chief Justice Fuller, who wrote the majority opinion, devoted most of his attention to the question of whether or not a tax upon income from land was in reality a direct tax. It would have been exceedingly simple for Fuller to reach a conclusion on this point, for there were two outstanding decisions of the United States Supreme Court to serve as precedents.

The first was *Hylton v. United States*, decided in 1796. It will be remembered that here the Supreme Court had been confronted with the validity of a federal tax upon carriages. A unanimous Court had held that the tax on carriages was not a direct tax, but an excise. Justice Paterson, who had been in the Constitutional Convention, had also expressed the belief that direct taxes, within the meaning of the Constitution, included only land and capitation taxes, an opinion in which Justice Chase concurred. This opinion had been quoted with approval by the Supreme Court numerous times during the succeeding century.

The second precedent was even more pertinent. As has already been observed, Congress had, during the Civil War, levied a tax upon incomes, which had remained in force until 1872. In *Springer v. United States* (1881) the Supreme Court had upheld the constitutionality of the Civil War statute, asserting that an income tax was not a direct tax within the meaning of the Constitution. In rendering this opinion the Court had quoted *Hylton v. United States* as precedent.

Taken together, *Hylton v. United States* and *Springer v. United States* had established a clear precedent, not merely as to the constitutionality of taxes upon income from land, but indeed as to all income taxes, with the possible exception of those levied upon state securities. Fuller, however, chose to ignore the force of these two precedents and instead sought to prove that the term "direct taxes" as used in the Constitution included "all taxes on real estate or personal property or the rents or income thereof." This contention he supported with an elaborate historical inquiry into the work of the Constitutional Convention of 1787, the state ratifying conventions, and early debates in Congress.

His appeal to history did not bear out his contention. If his evidence proved anything, it was merely that the term "direct taxes" had as of 1787 no certain and fixed meaning at all. In the Constitutional Convention, for example, Rufus King had "asked what was the precise meaning of direct taxation. No one answered." Fuller quoted this, and he quoted Luther Martin's letter to the Maryland legislature in which Martin had clearly implied that direct taxes meant capitation taxes and assessments on property. Also he quoted Albert Gallatin, who in 1796 had said that "direct taxes meant those paid directly from and falling immediately on the revenue." Evidence of this kind proved merely that in 1787 there was no general agreement as to what direct taxes were. Some men in 1787 apparently thought direct taxes included only capitation and realty taxes; others held that they included income; while still others defined direct taxes according to their status in theoretical economics. General agreement was absent. Yet in the face of this evidence, Fuller stated with no reservation that direct taxes, as of 1787, included "taxes on real estate or personal property or the rents or income thereof." This assertion prepared the way for his conclusion: that those portions of the present statute which provided for a tax upon the income from land established a direct tax, and were therefore unconstitutional.

Before Fuller could arrive at this conclusion, however, he had to dispose of the two embarrassing precedents of the Supreme Court itself. What of *Hylton v. United States?* Here Fuller emphasized that Justice Chase had merely said he was "inclined to think" that direct taxes included only capitation and land taxes; that is, he held that this portion of the Hylton opinion was not official, and was mere *obiter dictum.* Technically the Court had not defined direct taxes as such; it had merely decided that the tax on carriages was an excise.

What of *Springer v. United States?* Here Fuller disparaged the decision as precedent on the grounds that the case involved a tax on personal income which was derived from attorney's fees, and "not in any degree from real estate." The precedent thus narrowly construed did not in his opinion govern the question of the validity of a tax on the income from land.

Fuller thereupon concluded that taxes on income from land were not different from taxes on land itself, and were therefore unconstitutional. This, said Fuller, was well understood in 1787 and afterward. *Hylton v. United States* and *Springer v. United States* he construed as not relevant to the present decision.

In addition, Fuller's opinion held that those portions of the statute which laid a tax upon the income of state and municipal bonds were unconstitutional. Here he merely followed those precedents which prohibited the federal government from taxing state bonds.

Five other justices concurred with Fuller in the first two conclusions of his opinion. Only Justices Harlan and White dissented and in separate minority opinions argued that the tax was constitutional in its entirety.

There remained the far more important questions of whether the unconstitutionality of two parts of the tax law made void the entire statute and whether the entire income tax was void because it violated the principle of uniformity. Upon these crucial questions the Court was silent. The Chief Justice instead merely stated that the eight men participating in the decision—Justice Howell E. Jackson was ill at the time and took no part—were equally divided, 4 to 4, upon these questions and that the Court therefore rendered no opinion upon them.

It was at once evident that the decision was inconclusive, for the Court had refused to rule upon the constitutionality of the law as a whole. Yet by striking down part of the measure the Court had shown itself amenable to the arguments of the brilliant lawyers who had assailed the tax. The 4-to-4 decision was an open invitation for Choate, Edmunds, and their associates to return to the attack.

THE SECOND INCOME TAX CASE

Chief Justice Fuller had delivered his opinion in the first Pollock case on April 8, 1895. One week later, Choate and his associates asked for a rehearing. Their reason was the very plausible one that the inconclusive 4-to-4 decision of the Court upon the constitutionality of the law in its entirety made a clear decision upon this question imperative. This petition the Court granted, since Justice Jackson was expected to return to the bench shortly, and a majority opinion by a full Court might therefore be expected. Accordingly the case was reargued early in May, and on May 20 the Court in *Pollock v. The Farmers' Loan and Trust Company* (second case) handed down a second decision.

This time the opponents of the law won a complete victory, the Court striking down, 5 to 4, all the income-tax sections of the Wilson-Gorman Act as unconstitutional. Chief Justice Fuller based his opinion in the second Pollock case in part upon the point already decided in the first income tax opinion: that income taxes on realty were direct taxes and therefore unconstitutional. That is, the Court had already put taxes on income from land in a special category, separate from other income taxes; they were direct taxes, even though other income taxes conceivably were not.

Justice Fuller then proceeded to indulge in a major solecism. In the first case he had held that income taxes on land were in a separate category from other income taxes and were unconstitutional as being in effect taxes on land. Yet he now declared that he was unable to see any distinctive difference between a tax on income from land and taxes on income from other property. Although the Court had already held a tax on income from land to be void as falling in a special category, the Court now concluded that all taxes on income from all property were void, on the ground that it was not possible to distinguish between taxes on income from land and taxes on the income from other property. In a word, although the precedent of the first decision was followed, the carefully constructed special category for income taxes on land therein set up, having served its purpose, was now thrust aside. As Professor Corwin has neatly put it, "The ladder having served its purpose—having put the Court in the second story—is kicked down." [1]

There followed an involved historical analysis, in which Justice Fuller was obliged again to evade the clear-cut implications of *Hylton v. United States* and *Springer v. United States*. This he did by placing an excessively narrow construction upon the Hylton case, emphasizing the bad reporting in the decision and animadverting upon certain trifling elements of doubt as to the nature of a direct tax expressed by Justices Chase, Paterson, and Iredell in their opinions. The purpose of his argument was now precisely the opposite from that in the first case; there he had been concerned with proving conclusively the precise meaning of direct taxes as of 1787; now he was concerned with proving that the judicial precedents were historically weak. The apparently unanswerable *Springer v. United States* he did not even refer to; instead his opinion laid much stress upon certain vague English decisions as to the meaning of direct taxes.

Chief Justice Fuller then held that the unconstitutionality of the tax on income from all forms of property invalidated all the income-tax provisions of the law. Here the Court followed a well-established rule of statutory construction—that if the various parts of a statute are inextricably connected with one another in such degree as to warrant the assumption that the legislature intended the law to function as a whole, then if some portions of the statute are unconstitutional, the law must be treated as unconstitutional in its entirety. It was obviously impossible to regard the sections of the statute relating to income taxes on salaries, income taxes on businesses, income taxes on property, and the like, as separate and independent in character. Fuller therefore declared all the sections of the Wilson-Gorman Act relating to the income tax to be unconstitutional.

It is difficult to escape the conclusion that the two Pollock cases

---

[1] E. S. Corwin, *Court Over Constitution* (Princeton, 1938), p. 190.

constituted exceedingly unsound and unwise decisions on the part of the Court. The opinions disregarded one hundred years of decisions by the Court itself in which the meaning of a direct tax had been narrowly and definitely established. One can hardly argue that the Supreme Court ought on all occasions to follow the rule of *stare decisis*, for there have been occasions on which the Court has deliberately and consciously abandoned a set of precedents and has been applauded by enlightened liberals for doing so. In the income-tax cases, however, no rational justification seems to have existed for abandoning the older interpretation. For a century the tax practices of the federal government had been built upon the premise that direct taxes included only capitation and realty taxes.

There was a pre-eminently sound reason for this narrow construction. Apportionment of direct taxes among the states according to population was an archaic device. As Justice Paterson had pointed out in *Hylton v. United States*, the Convention had inserted the provision at the insistence of the southern states to protect their preponderant holdings in land and slaves against excessive taxation. By 1895 the clause had become obsolete and pointless. Moreover, from the beginning it worked not for justice but for injustice. Again, as Justice Paterson had observed, were a tax upon carriages to be apportioned among the states according to population, carriage-owners in those states having but few carriages in proportion to the states' population would be placed under an immense burden as compared to owners in states of equal population having many carriages.

By broadening indefinitely the category of direct taxes the Pollock cases threw doubt upon the entire excise structure of the federal government. For a hundred years, the federal government had levied a variety of taxes on the assumption that direct taxes included only capitation and land taxes. After 1895 no man could say with any certainty what taxes might be recognized as direct within the meaning of the Constitution and hence declared unconstitutional. Even the adoption in February 1913 of the Sixteenth Amendment did not clarify this matter, since it merely legalized income taxes as such.

The speciousness of Chief Justice Fuller's historical argument hardly needs further comment. He could not, in fact, show that in 1787 there was any general understanding about direct taxes.

Then, as already observed, the Court was not logically consistent in its two opinions. In the first case, the Court was able to quote with approval the Hylton case as establishing that direct taxes included taxes on land. Taxes on income from land were therefore held to fall in a special category. In the second case, the Court held that it was unable to perceive any difference between taxes on income from land and any other form of income tax, a clear denial of its premise in the first case. In spite of this, however, it used the first case as precedent in holding all income taxes unconstitutional.

Most significant was the way some of the justices evidently yielded to the demands of Choate and Edmunds that the Court constitute itself the guardian of property rights and vested interests. Here the Court's new legislative role was clearly displayed. The Court was asked to void the act in question in part upon the grounds that it was socially unwise—a purely legislative conception of the Court's powers. It is true that Justice Fuller in the second case denied that the Court had any interest or concern with the economic or social implications of the law. But Justice Field, who stood with the majority in both cases, wrote a concurrent opinion for the first decision in which he clearly revealed that social and economic considerations were uppermost in his mind. "The present assault upon capital," he said, "is but the beginning. It will be but the stepping stone to others, larger and more sweeping, till our political contests will become a war of the poor against the rich; a war constantly growing in intensity and bitterness."

The Court, in other words, was to constitute itself a guardian of property against revolution. If we recall the fervor with which Justice Field was working at this time to convert "due process of law" into a bulwark of property rights, this conception of the Court's function was not a surprising development.

The decision invalidating the entire income-tax law in the second case was made possible because one justice, whose identity is unknown, changed his mind on the constitutionality of the statute during the five weeks between the first and second decisions. It will be recalled that in the first case the justices were divided by a vote of 4 to 4 on the larger question of whether the law was void in its entirety, this tie vote having been made possible by the illness of Justice Jackson. But the identity of the four justices opposed to the constitutionality of the law *in toto* and the four who believed the law constitutional is unknown, for Chief Justice Fuller did not name them in his opinion.

In the second case, Justice Jackson returned to the Court and took part in the case. When the majority opinion was announced, he dissented and voted in favor of the constitutionality of the income-tax law. Three other justices—White, Harlan, and Brown—voted with him to make a minority of four in favor of upholding the law. But in the first case, four justices, names unknown, had also been in favor of the constitutionality of the law in its larger aspects. Had all four men in favor of the law in the first case again voted in favor of the law five weeks later, it is clear that, except for the provisions for taxes on income from land and income from state bonds, the law would have been declared constitutional by a vote of 5 to 4. Thus it is obvious that one of the original four men who favored the law in the first case shifted his vote in the second case and voted against the law's constitutionality.

Who was the justice who shifted his vote? Some deductions by the process of elimination are possible. It was not White, Brown, or Harlan, for they voted for the law in the second decision. The five justices who voted against the law in the second case were Fuller, Field, Shiras, Gray, and Brewer. Of these Justice Field plainly expressed himself in his concurrent opinion in the first case as opposed to the constitutionality of the law in its entirety, and Chief Justice Fuller was from the beginning clearly opposed to the entire law. This leaves only Justices Shiras, Gray, and Brewer. For many years Justice Shiras was thought by most students to have been the one who shifted in the second case. More recently doubt has been thrown on this supposition. Some present students are of the opinion that Justice Gray was the one who changed his vote; others believe it was Justice Brewer.

Regardless of who was responsible, the shift upset one hundred years of Supreme Court history as to what constituted direct taxes, made necessary the passage of the Sixteenth Amendment to the Constitution, and delayed the adoption of the income tax by the federal government for some nineteen years—far-reaching results to be produced by the constitutional doubts and vacillations of one anonymous justice.

THE IMPERIAL PROBLEM: THE INSULAR CASES

The impulse to national economic regulation and reform weakened perceptively after 1896. In part this was because the Supreme Court, controlled by justices devoted to the idea of a *laissez-faire* economic order, had administered repeated rebuffs to the movement. In part, also, the election of 1896, symbolizing as it did the failure of Populism and reformism and the triumph of a conservative-minded Republican political majority, badly discouraged the advocates of national economic reform. Finally, the war with Spain, the annexation of Hawaii, and the acquisition by peace treaty of an "American Empire" in the Caribbean and Pacific for a time shifted the focus of American public interest sharply away from internal political and economic questions to the issues associated with the sudden emergence of the United States as a "World Power."

The acquisition of Puerto Rico, the Philippines, Guam, and Hawaii precipitated a "great debate" between 1898 and 1900 over the new issue of "imperialism." At stake was the old question, now presented in a new guise, of the fundamental nature of the American Union. Hitherto it had always been assumed that the annexation of territory by the national government was a preliminary to its ultimate organization into new states, to be admitted to the Union on a basis of "co-ordinate equality." The United States, in short, was a union of "co-ordinate states" and the possession of western territories implied no system of colonialism or the subordination of "foreign peoples" whatever.

However, it now appeared to be difficult or impossible to apply co-ordinate statehood to the new overseas territories. Unlike the older West, the new acquisitions were geographically remote, already populous, and possessed of a civilization radically different from that in the United States. Were they, therefore, to be held indefinitely in a subordinate colonial condition? Was the United States, the original rebel against European colonialism, to become at last just another colonial power? These questions now gave rise to a great debate between "imperialists" and "anti-imperialists" over the political and constitutional issues involved.

The "imperialists," led by Theodore Roosevelt, Senator Henry Cabot Lodge, and Albert Shaw, editor of the Review of Reviews, argued that America's new stature as a world power made acquisition of an overseas empire both inevitable and desirable. They saw in colonies not only the control of sea-lanes and ocean areas essential to naval supremacy and the nation's maritime security, but also access to potential markets and raw materials of vast significance to the newly nationalized American industrial economy. The constitutional problem they solved by emphasizing national sovereignty and the long-established right of the federal government to acquire new territory—by purchase, treaty, or war. Moreover, they argued, such "colonies might be governed as Congress saw fit without assuming either future statehood or full application of all constitutional rights to the natives." The Constitution, in short, need not follow the flag.

The anti-imperialists, who included a few prominent Republicans led by Senator George Hoar of Massachusetts and most members of the Democratic party in Congress, showed themselves horrified by the prospect of a permanently subordinated American "colonial empire." Imperialism, they asserted, was a fundamental violation of the principle of equality laid down in the Declaration of Independence, the historic "co-ordinate" basis of the American Union, and the cherished American anti-colonial heritage. Imperialism and republicanism, Hoar asserted on the floor of Congress, were mutually incompatible.

Moreover, the establishment of a permanent colonial empire would constitute a gross violation of established constitutional precedent. The Union, they said, was a union of co-ordinate states, and territories properly were to be held in trust solely in preparation for co-ordinate statehood. Once the Philippines, Puerto Rico, and Guam were annexed, all the rights, obligations and limitations granted and imposed by the Constitution must be immediately extended to the people living there. *The Constitution, in short, must follow the flag.* Since such a constitutional state of affairs appeared to be neither practicable or feasible, the anti-imperialists also attacked the policy of annexation itself.

In Congress, the prospect of the annexation of Puerto Rico, Guam, and the Philippines, provided for in the as yet unratified treaty with Spain, precipitated a serious debate over the constitutional and political aspects of the imperialist question. On December 6, 1898, Senator George H. Vest of Missouri introduced the following resolution into the upper house:

> Resolved . . .
> That under the Constitution of the United States no power is given to the Federal Government to acquire territory to be held and governed permanently as colonies.
> The colonial system of European nations cannot be established under our present Constitution, but all territory acquired by the Government, except such small amounts as may be necessary for coaling stations, correction of boundaries, and similar governmental purposes, must be acquired with the purpose of ultimately organizing such territory into states suitable for admission into the Union . . .

A few days later Vest took the floor of the Senate to defend at length the constitutional policies implicit in his resolution. The anti-imperial character of the American Union, he observed, had first been set forth in the Declaration of Independence. It was inconceivable, he thought, that the Constitution, drafted only a few years later by the same men who had adopted the Declaration, could rest upon any other principle. Vest relied heavily upon Taney's opinion in the Dred Scott case, in which the former Chief Justice had argued at length that Congressional control of the territory was limited to preparation for statehood. The Fourteenth Amendment, Vest added, had confirmed the doctrine that "the fundamental idea of our American institutions is citizenship to all within the jurisdiction of the Government, except to the Indian tribes." The same principle must now be extended to the peoples in overseas "colonies," were such now to be acquired. Not to extend the Bill of Rights and the prospect of statehood to these peoples would commit the country to the same "monstrous colonial system" which had "destroyed all hope of republicanism in olden time."

A few days later, Senator Orville H. Platt of Connecticut, a leading "imperialist," answered Vest in a lengthy speech that apparently satisfied Republicans, at least, as to the constitutional right of the federal government to acquire and govern overseas possessions as it pleased. "Mr. President," said Platt, "we are a nation." This fact, he said, had "been written in blood which deluged the battlefields of the Civil War for four long years," and engraved with the sword "upon the heart of every true American." As a national entity, the United States possessed all sovereign powers except those "reserved to the states or to the people." (Here was an ingenious nationalistic reversal of the limitations of the Tenth Amendment!) The right to acquire territory, Platt pointed out, had been repeatedly recognized by the Court, beginning with *American Insurance Co. v. Canter*, and by both Story and Kent in their "Commentaries." Sovereignty, Platt added, also implied the right to govern territory as the republic pleased. The power of Congress over the territories, the discredited Dred Scott opinion to the contrary, "was clear and plenary," and "not limited by anything in the Constitution."

The Vest resolution, several times debated, never came to a vote, and in April the Senate by a narrow margin ratified the peace treaty with Spain, thereby settling the "colonial" question, at least as a matter of national policy. The United States now possessed an overseas "Empire"—one presumably not held antecedent to coordinate statehood.

It remained for the Supreme Court to define the precise constitutional status of the new "colonies." In a series of so-called *Insular Cases*, the Court after some uncertainty developed an "incorporation" doctrine which rationalized nicely the status of the new overseas possessions. In effect, this doctrine held that the Constitution did not automatically "follow the flag" but did so only when the United States, by treaty or act of Congress, first "incorporated" the territory in question within its limits.

The first of the Insular Cases, *DeLima v. Bidwell* and *Downes v. Bidwell*, reached the Supreme Court in 1901. In the former case, the collector of the Port of New York, after Puerto Rico's annexation to the United States, had collected import duties on sugar coming in from that island, exactly as though it were still a foreign nation. Thereupon the sugar's owners had sued the collector to recover the duties paid. The Downes case turned on the subsequent passage by Congress in 1900 of the so-called "Foraker Act," establishing a set of special duties upon imports from Puerto Rico. In the Downes case, the New York collector had imposed the stipulated duty upon a cargo of oranges. The owners thereupon had sued to recover the duty on the ground that the Foraker Act was unconstitutional in that it violated the requirement in Article I, Section 8, that all "duties, imports, and excises shall be uniform throughout the United States." Both cases obviously hinged upon whether and to what extent Puerto Rico was a "part" of the United States.

As it turned out, the Court was very badly divided upon this question. In *DeLima v. Bidwell*, a majority of five justices, speaking through Justice Brown, held that as a consequence of the treaty of peace with Spain, Puerto Rico was not a "foreign country" within the meaning of existing tariff laws, and that the duties in question accordingly had been collected unlawfully. Justices McKenna, White, Shiras, and Gray all dissented vigorously, arguing that in a practical sense Puerto Rico was not fully a part of the United States and that the tariffs in question therefore properly applied.

However, the presumption implicit in the *DeLima* decision was sharply reversed in *Downes v. Bidwell*, in which Brown joined the four dissenters from the DeLima case to make up a new majority. Central to Brown's opinion was his "extension" theory, in which he argued that the Constitution dealt with the states alone, and that Congress had historically possessed the power to decide whether the guaranties of the Constitution were to "extend" to a newly acquired territory. In this instance, he held, the Foraker Act demonstrated that Congress had decided not to extend the Constitution to that island; the import duties, accordingly, were constitutionally levied.

However, Justice White's concurring opinion setting forth his so-called "incorporation" doctrine was ultimately to be of far more constitutional significance than Brown's "extension" theory. Examining the historic precedents, White satisfied himself that in all past instances where territories had been treated as an integral part of the United States, they had been formally "incorporated," either by treaty or by act of Congress. The major question at issue in the present case, therefore, was this: "Had Puerto Rico, at the time of the passage of the act in question, been incorporated into and become an integral part of the United States?" The answer yielded by the language of the peace treaty and various acts of Congress being "no," the Constitution did not extend to Puerto Rico, and it followed that Congress lawfully could tax imports therefrom.

Chief Justice Fuller and Justices Harlan, Brewer, and Peckham firmly dissented from the majority opinions. They were of the belief that the Constitution automatically and without any discretion followed the flag wherever the United States had established its sovereignty. The theory of the majority of the Court, Fuller said, "substitutes for the present system of republican government, a system of domination over distant provinces in the exercise of unrestricted power." Harlan thought the majority decision "wholly inconsistent with the spirit and genius as well as with the words of the Constitution."

The incorporation theory, first presented merely as concurring opinion by Justice White, nevertheless presently was to triumph decisively. In *Hawaii v. Mankichi* (1903), the Court was confronted with an appeal from a manslaughter conviction in the Hawaiian courts, in which the accused had been brought to trial without a grand jury, and found guilty merely by a vote of nine out of twelve jurors. This procedure was clearly at odds with the guarantees in the Fifth and Sixth Amendments. If the Bill of Rights extended to Hawaii, the trial had violated the Constitution.

Justice Brown's majority opinion used the "extension" theory to find that Congress had not acted to extend certain benefits of the Bill of Rights, including the Fifth and Sixth Amendments, to Hawaii. The trial accordingly did not violate the federal Constitution. This time, however, Justice McKenna joined with White in a concurring opinion based upon the "incorporation" theory: Neither the resolution of annexation nor the Organic Act of 1900, they concluded, "had seemed to incorporate the Hawaiian Islands in the United States and make them an integral part thereof"; hence the Bill of Rights was not applicable.

Finally, in 1904, in *Dorr v. United States*, the incorporation doctrine gained a majority of the Court. This case, similar to that of Mankichi a year earlier, involved the issue of whether a criminal trial in the Philippines without traditional Anglo-Saxon indictment and a twelve-man petit jury violated the Constitution. Justice Day's opinion held briefly that "Until Congress shall see fit to incorporate territory ceded by treaty into the United States, we regard it as settled . . . that the territory is to be governed under the power existing in Congress to make laws for such territories and subject to such constitutional restrictions upon the power of that body as are applicable to this situation." Justice Harlan, still contending that the Constitution automatically followed the flag, could only comment that "Rome, Sparta and Carthage, at the time their liberties were lost, were strangers to trial by jury."

Thereafter, the incorporation doctrine moved steadily toward complete triumph. In *Rasmussen v. United States* (1905), a case involving the validity of six-man juries in Alaska, the Court found that Alaska had been substantially incorporated within the United States, so that the Fifth, Sixth and Seventh Amendments applied. Trial by six-man jury in this instance therefore was void. And in *Dowdell v. United States* (1911), eight justices concurred in Justice Day's opinion that the United States had not incorporated the Philippines and that criminal trial in the islands therefore did not require a twelve-man jury. Justice Harlan now stood all alone, defending to the last the position once advanced so eloquently by Senator Vest—that the Constitution in all its majesty followed the flag and that neither Congress, the executive, nor the courts properly could exercise any discretion in the matter.

By that time the "imperialist" question had ceased to be of any great moment to most Americans. A second and far more powerful wave of liberal nationalism and social change now was sweeping the country, exemplified by the reform measures of Theodore Roosevelt and the Progressive Movement. Once again the American people were demanding that problems beyond the competence of the states be dealt with by the national government.

Chapter

22

The Rise of Liberal Nationalism

In September 1901, as a result of the assassination of William Mc-Kinley, Theodore Roosevelt became President of the United States. While this event belonged in the category of political accidents, the powerful wave of nationalistic reform which began its sweep across the country almost coincidently with the accession of the new President had its roots deep in the American political scene. Within the next ten years the new reform movement was to bring about the development of a new federal "police power" as an instrument of national social reform, a substantial revival of the Sherman law and of federal trust prosecutions, and the passage of a new and more effective Interstate Commerce Commission Act. The constitutional issues raised in this new era of "liberal nationalism" set the stage for most of the subsequent constitutional controversies of the next thirty years.

THE DOCTRINE OF LIBERAL NATIONALISM

The popular impulse toward national reform, first manifested in the 1880's, had never died. It had merely been suppressed and diverted. William McKinley's victory over William Jennings Bryan in the presidential election of 1896 had thoroughly demoralized the agrarian radicals in the Populist and Democratic parties. Moreover, many middle-class people had been driven in alarm away from the idea of social reform because of the successive outbreaks of

548

class violence after 1890. For some time they were too frightened by the specter of revolution to care much about reform. The war with Spain also diverted the nation's attention from internal problems to foreign affairs and to the political controversies associated with America's sudden acquisition of a far-flung world empire. Not until after 1900 did the focus of national interest gradually turn back to internal affairs.

When it did turn back, it found that the old nationwide problems raised by America's industrial revolution were as far from solution as ever. Federal trust legislation was almost completely ineffective. The Sherman law, rendered harmless by the Supreme Court's intellectual calisthenics in the Knight case, was openly ignored. Meanwhile the trend toward the centralization and integration of American business and industry had continued. America saw the formation of the United States Steel Corporation, its first billion-dollar trust, during the year Theodore Roosevelt entered the White House. Railroad legislation, too, had become comparatively meaningless; since the courts had stripped the Interstate Commerce Commission of its authority, all the old evils—rebates, pools, regional discrimination and the like—flourished as in the days before 1887, although somewhat more covertly than before.

A host of new social problems also essentially national in character emerged after 1900. Public opinion demanded that the great corporations in production and commerce submit to some degree of control over their commercial and financial practices and their labor policies. As the reform movement grew, journalists and muckrakers brought other evils into the public forum for discussion and analysis—bad conditions in the meat-packing industry, child labor, employer liability, adulterated and spoiled foods, the traffic in women. Most liberals saw all the foregoing as nationwide problems demanding federal regulation.

There were two ways by which federal authority might be expanded to cover these problems. First, the Constitution might be amended. Most liberals, or Progressives as they presently called themselves, did not consider this a feasible approach to the problems at hand. Except for the amendments incident to the Civil War and Reconstruction, the Constitution had not been altered for a century, and most competent observers had concluded that because a small minority in a fraction of the states could block effectively any move for constitutional reform it was virtually impossible to amend the Constitution.

There remained the method of constitutional change by constitutional reinterpretation instead of formal amendment. This could conceivably be accomplished by the bold assertion of national authority by Congress and the President on the assumption that the necessary legislation would receive the sanction of the Supreme Court. It was this technique which met with the approval of President Roosevelt and other nationalistic liberals. It proposed to make the Constitution a living, growing instrument of national authority rather than a static charter of government. This would mean that the powers of the national government were not to be regarded as absolutely fixed but as subject to constant reinterpretation and reconstruction to keep abreast of the growth of American economic life.

THEODORE ROOSEVELT'S STEWARDSHIP THEORY

President Roosevelt was in many respects well fitted to serve as the leader of a strong liberal national movement. He had a dynamic and powerful personality that captured the popular imagination and inspired large numbers of people to follow him in whatever ideals he proclaimed. Roosevelt was psychologically incapable of accepting a secondary role in the government. Through his speeches and messages, his explosive symbol-making, and his ability to dramatize any cause he adopted, he made the presidency rather than Congress the center of national sovereignty and national leadership. In contrast most Presidents since Lincoln had been mediocre individuals who were well content to let the controls of government slip into the hands of Congress. Roosevelt literally insisted upon becoming the head of the state, and he had sufficient force of personality to make good his claim.

Roosevelt conceived of the presidency as a "stewardship," in whose care the common welfare and destiny of the American people were entrusted. Any matter concerning national welfare Roosevelt assumed to be his affair. He felt himself to be personally responsible for the safety, prosperity, and happiness of the entire United States.

The stewardship theory of presidential duties took Roosevelt far afield of the constitutionally prescribed functions of the presidency. Thus in the great coal strike of 1902, Roosevelt interfered and used the prestige of his office to force a settlement. So also, in the panic of 1907, Roosevelt stepped in to prevent the spread of a financial panic in Wall Street. In this instance, he took upon himself the responsibility for suspending the operation of the Sherman law in order to make possible a financial combination deemed desirable to check the panic.

Roosevelt revived the old Hamiltonian doctrine of inherent executive prerogative power which held that the President was not limited in authority by the enumeration of executive functions in the Constitution. To put it differently, the President could do anything which the Constitution or some act of Congress did not forbid him to do. Acting according to this concept, Roosevelt felt himself justified in settling a coal strike, quieting a financial panic, or arranging the finances of the Dominican Republic.

There were nevertheless grave difficulties in the way of Roosevelt's espousal of a nationalistic economic program. Both Congress and the Supreme Court were dominated by conservatives who had little interest in liberal nationalism. In the Senate a conservative Republican oligarchy, headed by Senators Nelson W. Aldrich of Rhode Island, Henry Cabot Lodge of Massachusetts, Mark Hanna of Ohio, Joseph B. Foraker of Ohio, John Spooner of Wisconsin, and Thomas Platt of New York, held a firm, almost dictatorial grip over the affairs of the upper chamber. Representative of big business and of state political machines, they were naturally opposed to legislation designed to control commerce or industry or to effect social reform. In the House the conservatives were almost equally entrenched. Joseph Cannon of Illinois, who became speaker in 1903, exercised a vigorous control over the lower chamber, usually in the interests of Republican conservatism.

Although by tradition the Republican party had been nationalistic in its constitutional theories, the conservative majority after 1900 turned increasingly toward strict constructionist and even states' rights arguments. In nearly every debate on progressive national legislation between 1901 and 1918, the Republican leadership was to raise the constitutional issue. In this, they were joined by many Democrats, particularly those from the South with its tradition of states' rights. Most conservatives thought of the Constitution as a document whose meaning remained absolutely fixed and unchanged except by the process of formal amendment, and to them the liberal attempt at constitutional reinterpretation appeared as a sophistical attempt to prove that the Constitution did not mean what it said.

The constitutional conservatives had their allies in the judiciary, although after 1900 the Court was in general tenor somewhat more liberal than it had been in the nineties. Still present from the property-minded bench of the last decade were three judges who had voted against the constitutionality of the income-tax law—Chief Justice Melville Fuller and Justices David Brewer and George Shiras. Justices Edward D. White and Henry B. Brown, who had voted for the income-tax law, were also still present; but White was on most occasions a conservative states' rights advocate and at best an indifferent champion of strong national government, and Brown was also a moderate conservative. Justice Rufus Peckham, a New York Democrat appointed by Cleveland in 1895, was definitely conservative in his attitude toward social legislation. Justice William R. Day, who replaced Justice Shiras in 1903, was a Republican lawyer and former Secretary of State under McKinley. Justice Day was to prove himself generally willing to accept moderate liberal nationalism, although he wrote the opinion in *Hammer v. Dagenhart* (1918) invalidating the first Child Labor Law. Justice William H. Moody, who replaced Justice Brown in 1906, had served as Roosevelt's Secretary of the Navy and Attorney General. During his four years on the Court he also proved to be a moderate liberal.

The two justices most in sympathy with liberal nationalism were John Marshall Harlan and Oliver Wendell Holmes. Justice Harlan, a Hayes appointee of 1877, was usually to be found on the nationalist side, although he wrote the opinion in *Adair v. United States* (1908) invalidating the federal statute outlawing railroad yellow-dog contracts. Justice Holmes, who was appointed by Roosevelt from the Massachusetts bench in 1902, was to become perhaps the most distinguished Supreme Court jurist of the early twentieth century. He was to vote against the government in the Northern Securities Case, but thereafter nearly always supported liberal nationalism. He based his judicial philosophy in considerable part upon a reluctance to impose judicial restraints upon legislative policy making. Essentially a skeptical conservative who was little interested in social reform as such, he nevertheless refused to countenance the resort to judicial review as a means whereby the Court might substitute its social theories for those of Congress. His famous dissent in *Lochner v. New York*, wherein he attacked the majority justices for their attempt to write *laissez-faire* economics into constitutional law, has already been cited.[1]

THE RISE OF A FEDERAL POLICE POWER:
THE LOTTERY AND OLEO CASES

The first important victory for the proponents of liberal nationalism was the recognition of a federal police power. Theoretically the

---

[1] See p. 495.

national government has no general police power, the right to legislate for the health, morals, and welfare of the community being reserved to the states. Nonetheless Congress after 1900 proceeded to attack a variety of social and economic problems, using its powers to regulate commerce and to tax as instruments of social reform. Although the intent of such legislation was patently the protection of the health, morals, and public welfare of the community, the Supreme Court between 1903 and 1915 accepted as constitutional a whole series of statutes of this kind and thus in effect recognized a growing sphere of federal police power.

The Court first recognized the use of the commerce power for police purposes in *Champion v. Ames* (1903). The case rose out of a relatively insignificant act of Congress passed in 1895 in an attempt to deal with the lottery problem. The law forbade the shipment of lottery tickets in interstate commerce. The real purpose of the law was not the regulation of commerce but the control of gambling, a matter that had previously lain entirely within the sphere of state police power.

By a vote of five to four, the Court held the lottery law to be constitutional. Justice Harlan, who spoke for the majority, dwelt at length upon the supreme and plenary power of Congress in the field of interstate commerce. "The power to regulate commerce among the several states," he said, "is vested in Congress as absolutely as it would be in a single government." This regulatory power could rightfully touch any problem that could be correctly construed as interstate commerce. There was nothing very revolutionary about this, and Harlan made his point by citing *Gibbons v. Ogden* and like precedents on the broad extent of the commerce power.

Harlan then held that Congress might lawfully impose absolute prohibitions upon portions of interstate commerce if it wished to do so. Harlan drove this point home with a forceful rhetorical question: "If lottery traffic, *carried on through interstate commerce*, is a matter of which Congress may take cognizance and over which its power may be exerted, can it be possible that it must tolerate the traffic, and simply regulate the manner in which it may be carried on?" [2]

There were ample precedents for Harlan's position here. Congress had several times laid absolute prohibitions upon certain types of commerce in pursuance of its power of regulation. The Embargo Act of 1807 was the most notable instance of this kind; here Con-

---

[2] The italics are in the original.

gress had prohibited all foreign commerce entirely. True, in this instance the prohibition had been exercised over foreign commerce and not over commerce between the states as in the lottery law; but unless one were prepared to argue that foreign commerce and commerce between the states lay in two separate and distinct categories, the embargo precedent was perfectly sound.

Harlan admitted that the logic of his opinion led "necessarily to the conclusion that Congress may arbitrarily exclude from commerce among the states any article . . . which it may choose, no matter with what motive, to declare shall not be carried from one state to another." This admission carried the further possible implication that Congress might conceivably use the commerce power to invade the sphere of sovereignty reserved to the states and thus to break down the federal character of the constitutional system. However, said Harlan, "it will be time enough to consider the constitutionality of such legislation when we must do so."

Chief Justice Fuller's dissent, in which Brewer, Shiras and Peckham concurred, centered on the intent or purpose behind the law. The real purpose of the statute, according to Fuller, was not the regulation of commerce but the suppression of lotteries. The measure therefore constituted a clear invasion of the police powers of the states under the pretense of regulating interstate commerce. Fuller warned that this conception of the commerce power would "defeat the operation of the 10th Amendment," and would break down all distinction between state and national authority. To his way of thinking, the present decision was a "long step in the direction of wiping out all traces of state lines, and the creation of a centralized government."

Fuller also challenged Harlan's two main assumptions: that the right to regulate commerce included the right to prohibit it entirely, and that federal power over interstate commerce was as extensive as that over foreign commerce. He cited no precedent against the power of Congress to prohibit interstate commerce entirely. However, had he searched the records of the slavery controversy, he would have found that the proponents of interstate trade in slaves had once argued against the constitutionality of any prohibition of the interstate traffic in slaves. And in at least one case, *Groves v. Slaughter* (1844), certain of the justices of the Supreme Court had accepted this argument.[3]

There were also precedents, although of somewhat dubious value. for Fuller's assertion that while the federal power over foreign

---

[3] See the discussion of *Groves v. Slaughter* on p. 337.

commerce was unlimited and supreme, that over interstate commerce was not. Madison in his later years had once mentioned the idea with approval. And in a few cases before and after 1900, the Supreme Court had suggested the distinction. The argument appears to draw but little plausibility from the wording of the Constitution, however, for the two types of commerce are mentioned without distinction in the same phrase.

Fuller's dissent closed on a dire note:

I regard this decision as inconsistent with the views of the framers of the Constitution, and of Marshall, its greatest expounder. Our form of government may remain notwithstanding legislation or decision, but, as long ago observed, it is with governments, as with religions: the form may survive the substance of the faith.

A year later, in *McCray v. United States* (1904), the Court sustained a federal police statute involving the use of an excise tax as an instrument of social control. In 1902 Congress, in response to powerful pressure from a national dairymen's lobby, had enacted a statute raising the excise on artificially colored oleomargarine to ten cents per pound but at the same time providing for a tax of but one-fourth cent per pound on oleomargarine free from artificial coloring. The obvious intent of the statute was not to raise revenue but to suppress the manufacture and sale of artificially colored oleomargarine, then being sold widely as butter. The statute was attacked in the courts on the ground that its true purpose was not taxation but the regulation of manufacturing, and that as such the law invaded the reserved powers of the states in violation of the Tenth Amendment. The tax was denounced also as being so heavy as to be confiscatory and hence in violation of the due process clause of the Fifth Amendment.

Justice White's opinion in *McCray v. United States* turned upon the Court's refusal to inquire into the motive or intent behind the tax or the result it produced. Laying down what amounted to a rule of judicial noninterference with federal tax statutes, he held that if Congress on the surface had power to levy the tax in question, then the Court could not inquire into the motive behind the law. "The decisions of this court from the beginning," he said, "lend no support whatever to the assumption that the judiciary may restrain the exercise of a lawful power on the assumption that a wrongful purpose or motive has caused the power to be exerted." Nor could the statute's result be considered. Since the tax was valid, regardless of motive, any invasion of the reserved powers of the states was incidental, and the law did not violate the Tenth Amendment. As for the Fifth Amendment, the result of the tax might well be the destruction of the oleomargarine business, but the statute could not thereby be said to be confiscatory and a violation of due process.

McCray v. United States opened potentially a vast area of federal social controls through the medium of taxation. On the basis of this decision there seemed to be no limits to the discretion of Congress as to either the motive behind a federal tax statute or the ultimate effect of the law. It remained only to be seen to what extent Congress would make use of the new power. Chief Justice Fuller and Justice Peckham dissented as they had in the lottery case, and Justice Brown joined them on this occasion.

EXPANSION OF THE FEDERAL POLICE POWER

In the decade after *Champion v. Ames* and *McCray v. United States* there occurred a general growth of federal police power. By 1916 nearly a score of statutes had been enacted, ostensibly either as regulation of interstate commerce or as tax measures, but actually as regulatory statutes aimed at specific social evils which liberal nationalists insisted required federal regulation. The most important statutes of this character using the commerce power were the Pure Food and Drug Law of 1906, the Meat Inspection Acts of 1906 and 1907, the White Slave Traffic Act of 1910, and the Child Labor Act of 1916. The most important statutes employing coercive or destructive taxation were the Phosphorus Match Act of 1912 and the Harrison Anti-Narcotics Act of 1914.

Every one of these statutes had much the same history behind its passage. Some widespread social evil or problem was brought to light, more often than not through the efforts of crusading writers— "muckrakers," as Theodore Roosevelt called them—in popular magazines and newspapers. The result was an aroused public opinion and a campaign for remedial federal legislation that eventually won sufficient popular support to push through an act of Congress.

The Pure Food and Drug Act, for example, was enacted in June 1906, after a protracted campaign in periodicals and the press against the menace of adulterated and spoiled foods. Much publicity was given the research of Dr. Harvey Wiley, a chemist in the Department of Agriculture, which demonstrated that the use of preservatives, coloring matter, and fradulent substitutes in the preparation of foods had become so common as to be "almost universal." Since many foods were now sold in nationwide markets, there was comparatively little chance of effective state regulation. In December 1905, President Roosevelt asked for federal legislation to control the evil, and a bill barring adulterated and misbranded foods from interstate commerce was thereupon introduced into Congress. Although several congressmen attacked the statute as an invasion of state police power, it nonetheless became law on June 30, 1906.

While the Pure Food Act was still a live issue, the nation became tremendously aroused over the situation in the meat-packing industry. A novel by Upton Sinclair, *The Jungle*, published in 1906, portrayed in terms of vivid realism the hard working conditions, the filth, and the general indifference to public welfare that prevailed in the great packing houses in Chicago. The whole country was swept by a wave of indignation. President Roosevelt responded by instigating an investigation which confirmed most of the charges that Sinclair had leveled. Although the packers had hitherto succeeded in resisting federal regulation as an invasion of state sovereignty and as socialistic, the pressure of public opinion aroused by the congressional revelations defeated their efforts to block legislation.

On June 30, 1906, the Meat Inspection Act became law, as part of a statute making appropriations for the Department of Agriculture. Branch offices under the Department of Agriculture were established at all packing houses which prepared meat for interstate commerce. Inspectors were to examine live animals for disease and carcasses for disease and putrefaction. Uninspected and rejected meat was banned from interstate commerce. In March 1907 Congress re-enacted the Meat Inspection Act, using virtually the same language as that in the 1906 law.

It is interesting to note that the commerce power was here used to effect the establishment of a local inspection service. Legally there was no direct way in which packers could be forced to submit to inspection; but if they did not, their products were banned from interstate commerce, so that practically they had no choice but submission.

Somewhat similar circumstances attended the passage of the White Slave Traffic Act of 1910, popularly known as the Mann Act. The Bureau of Immigration had long sought to cope with the international traffic in prostitutes by watching ports of entry. In 1907 Congress, in an attempt to make such control more effective, had enacted a statute making it a punishable offense to harbor an alien woman for immoral purposes within three years after her arrival in the United States. However, in *Keller v. United States*

(1909), the Supreme Court by a vote of six to three declared this act unconstitutional, Justice Brewer's majority opinion holding that the act attempted the local regulation of prostitution and hence invaded the police power of the states in violation of the Tenth Amendment. This decision made immigration controls over the traffic in prostitutes partially ineffective. Late in 1909 the Bureau of Immigration informed President William Howard Taft that much of the traffic in women was now carried on in commerce between the states and as such was beyond immigration controls.

Meanwhile a concerted agitation against the "white slave trade" had broken out in the press. An article by George Kibbe Turner in *McClure's* for November 1909 named New York City as one of the three world centers of the traffic. Taft was not the constitutional nationalist that Roosevelt had been, but in his annual message of December 1909 he hesitantly expressed the belief that an act prohibiting interstate and foreign traffic in women for immoral purposes might be constitutional. Representative James Robert Mann of Illinois shortly introduced such a measure in the House. The bill prohibited, under suitable penalties, the transportation of women for immoral purposes in interstate or foreign commerce. Although congressional conservatives attacked the bill as "an attempt to exercise police authority by the federal government under guise of regulating commerce among the states," public support for Mann's bill was so overwhelming that it passed Congress without protracted opposition, and became law on June 25, 1910.

The Child Labor Act of 1916 was another typical product of the Progressive era. Liberals, social reformers, and muckrakers alike had been attacking the evils attendant upon child labor in industry since the turn of the century. In 1906 Senator Albert J. Beveridge of Indiana had introduced a bill to prohibit carriers from moving the products of child labor in interstate commerce. The conservative majority had denounced the bill with tolerant amusement as "hopelessly unconstitutional," and it got nowhere. For the next ten years thereafter, bills of a similar character were nevertheless introduced into each Congress, and the drive for a federal child labor law gained strength with the Progressive tide. After 1913, President Woodrow Wilson lent his support to the demand for a child labor statute.

The Keating-Owen Child Labor Act became law on September 1, 1916, after an extensive debate as to the constitutionality of the measure. The House Labor Committee's report had defended the bill as a legitimate exercise of the plenary power of Congress over interstate commerce; but conservatives in both houses denounced the measure as a thinly disguised invasion of state police power. Most members of Congress voted for the law as a highly desirable statute, regardless of any doubts they entertained as to its validity under the Constitution.

The Child Labor Act of 1916 made it a misdemeanor for any manufacturer to ship in interstate commerce the product of any mine, quarry, factory, cannery, or like workshop, in which children under fourteen had been employed within thirty days of shipment. The statute imposed like restrictions upon manufacturers employing children between the ages of fourteen and sixteen for more than eight hours a day six days a week, or at night. The law was one of the outstanding achievements of the liberal national era. But it marked a frank invasion by the federal government of a field of labor relations in manufacturing, and as events were to demonstrate, it went beyond the limits of the Court's willingness to accept as constitutional the use of the commerce power for police purposes.

The Harrison Act, enacted on December 17, 1914, was the most notable and important federal statute to employ taxation as a federal police-power device. The United States had become a party to the Hague Convention of 1912 to suppress the traffic in narcotic drugs, and Congress passed the statute at the instance of Treasury Department authorities seeking to implement the treaty. The Harrison Act required all persons manufacturing or selling narcotic drugs to register with the Collector of Internal Revenue, to pay a tax of one dollar a year, to use certain prescribed blanks in recording all drug transactions, and to keep detailed records available for federal inspection. The statute also made it unlawful to manufacture, sell, or transport narcotic drugs except for legitimate commercial or professional purposes. It is evident that the tax levied was in fact simply a legal device invoked as a constitutional means for setting up an elaborate system of federal anti-narcotic controls. However, the law was passed by Congress virtually without opposition, the general sentiment being that the statute was socially highly desirable.

FEDERAL POLICE POWER IN THE COURTS

The new federal police legislation was at first accorded a very favorable reception in the Court. As Mr. Dooley, the creation of Finley Peter Dunne, had once remarked, "The Supreme Court follows the election returns," and perhaps the Court was merely reflecting the prevailing liberal national temper of the years between Theodore Roosevelt's inauguration and the first World War.

In *Hipolite Egg Co. v. U.S.* (1911), for example, the Court sustained the Pure Food and Drug Act, without reference to the angry differences of philosophy which had aroused the justices in the lottery case. The question before the Court was the validity of a federal order seizing several cases of preserved eggs. Justice Joseph McKenna's opinion reminded the appellants that there were very few limits to the federal commerce power. No trade could be "carried on between the states to which it does not extend" and the power was "complete in itself" and "subject to no limitations except those found in the Constitution." The opinion said nothing of the intent or purpose of Congress in enacting the law, nor of any distinction between foreign and interstate commerce. If any of the conservative justices disagreed with such an expression of extreme nationalism, they kept their opinions to themselves. There was no dissent.

Two years later, the Court in *Hoke v. United States* (1913) ruled favorably upon the constitutionality of the Mann Act. Answering the contention that the statute invaded the police powers of the states in violation of the Tenth Amendment, Justice McKenna declared explicitly that the commerce power could be used to promote the general welfare:

> Our dual form of government has its perplexities, state and nation having different spheres of jurisdiction, as we have said; but it must be kept in mind that we are one people; and the powers reserved to the states and those conferred on the nation are adapted to be exercised, whether independently or concurrently, to promote the general welfare, material and moral.

These were powerful words. They effectively disposed of the question of purpose, for the purpose of regulation need only have been the welfare of the American people. They seemed to lend conscious sanction to the Rooseveltian conception of national power: that the federal government could interpret its authority so as to adjust itself to the realities of new social conditions.

In spite of the foregoing precedents, the Supreme Court in *Hammer v. Dagenhart* (1918) invalidated the Child Labor Law by a 5-to-4 majority. This statute, said Justice Day, was not a regulation of commerce but an outright prohibition and as such was void. Here the Court revived the distinction between the regulation of commerce and outright prohibition, an idea that had apparently been discredited and discarded as a result of the Court's acceptance of the lottery, pure food, and white slave laws, all of which had imposed similar outright prohibitions. But Justice Day now asserted that in the earlier statutes the thing prohibited had been in itself harmful, and prohibition had been necessary to save commerce itself from contamination. The products of child labor, however, were in themselves harmless, and their movement in commerce was also harmless.

Justice Day then brought up once more the old issue of purpose. The real purpose of the present law, he said, was not to protect commerce, but to regulate child labor. The statute thus used subterfuge to invade the reserved powers of the states in violation of the Tenth Amendment. Justice Day thereupon formally revived the conception of dual federalism. "The grant of authority over a purely Federal matter," he said, "was not intended to deny the local power always existing and carefully reserved to the states in the 10th Amendment to the Constitution."

In his enthusiasm for placing restrictions upon federal authority, Justice Day even misquoted the Tenth Amendment. "In interpreting the Constitution," he said, "it must never be forgotten that the nation is made up of states, to which are entrusted the powers of local government. And to them and to the people the powers not expressly delegated to the national government are reserved." The word "expressly" is not in the Tenth Amendment, and was in fact specifically rejected by its framers.

Justice Day concluded with the *argumentum ad horrendum*: ". . . if Congress can thus regulate matters intrusted to local authority by prohibition of the movement of commodities in interstate commerce, all freedom of commerce will be at an end, and the power of the states over local matters may be eliminated, and thus our system of government be practically destroyed. . . ."

Justice Holmes' dissent, concurred in by Louis D. Brandeis, Joseph McKenna, and John H. Clarke, implied broadly that the majority had been influenced not so much by constitutional precedent as by the justices' social philosophy, which Holmes incidentally thought very bad. "If there is any matter upon which civilized countries have agreed," he said, "it is the evil of premature and excessive child labor. I should have thought that if we were to introduce our own moral conceptions where, in my opinion, they do not belong, this was preeminently a case for upholding the exercise of all its powers by the United States." As for Day's distinction between the present law and earlier police statutes, Holmes thought it specious: "The notion that prohibition is any less prohibition when applied to things now thought evil I do not understand."

The Court's decision in *Hammer v. Dagenhart* rendered uncertain and confused the constitutional status of federal police legislation. Obviously the decision was incompatible with *Champion* v. *Ames, Hipolite Egg Co. v. United States,* and *Hoke v. United States* The distinction made between things harmful in themselves and things merely producing harmful results lacked even metaphysical reality. Moreover, since 1903 the Court had repeatedly rejected the old Madisonian doctrine that Congress could regulate commerce but could not prohibit any phase of commerce outright. Finally, revival of the old issue of congressional purpose, emphatically rejected in *Champion v. Ames,* promised endless judicial complications and confusion, since it implied that the Court would inquire into the constitutionality of congressional purpose every time Congress enacted any regulation of commerce, however correct in form.

In short, the Court in *Hammer v. Dagenhart* broke sharply with the seemingly well-established liberal national tradition and returned to the spirit of strict construction and dual federalism. However, the Court's desertion of liberal nationalism was not unconditional. A few weeks later, in November 1918, the Court, in *Pittsburgh Melting Co. v. Totten,* ruled briefly that the Meat Inspection Act of 1906 was constitutional. The enactment of the law, said Justice Day in a unanimous opinion, was "within the power of Congress in order to prevent interstate and foreign shipment of impure or adulterated meat-food products."

The Court also accepted the Narcotics Act the following year, though by only a 5-to-4 majority. Justice Day's brief opinion in *United States v. Doremus* (1919) stated that Congress had complete discretion in levying taxes, subject only to the constitutional provision for geographical uniformity. Although Congress in levying a one-dollar tax subject to elaborate restrictive regulation had obviously intended to suppress the illicit drug traffic, Day waved aside the question of purpose: "The act may not be declared unconstitutional because its effect may be to accomplish another purpose as well as the raising of revenue." Why purpose was irrelevant here and not in the child labor case Day did not explain. Chief Justice White, speaking for the minority, showed more consistency when he attacked the law as "a mere attempt by Congress to exert a power not delegated; that is, the reserved police power of the states."

In spite of the government's victory in *United States v. Doremus,* it was evident thereafter that federal police statutes using taxation as an instrument of control now also rested on a somewhat uncertain constitutional foundation. A slight shift in personnel or opinion on the Court might well send taxation as a police device into the constitutional discard.

THE POLICE POWER AND RAILWAY LABOR

The regulation of railway labor was a sphere in which the Court early proved reluctant to recognize the constitutionality of the federal police power. During the liberal national era Congress enacted several statutes which attempted to regulate the relations of interstate carriers and their employees. The Court held unconstitutional two major statutes of this kind, and it confirmed a third only by the narrowest of majorities.

The Court's hostility to railway labor legislation first became apparent in *Adair v. United States* (1908), the so-called "yellow-dog" contract case. The Erdman Act, passed by Congress on June 1, 1898, had attempted to regulate certain broad phases of railway labor policy. Section 10 of the statute prohibited contracts by which any employee promised as a condition of employment not to join a labor union. Such agreements were familiarly known by labor as "yellow-dog" contracts. The same section of the act forbade also discrimination against any employee because of membership in any labor union or organization.

A majority of the Court thought Section 10 of the Erdman Act unconstitutional. Harlan's opinion called the statute an unreasonable violation of freedom of contract [4] and an interference with the right of employer and employee to negotiate on terms of employment which might be mutually agreeable. Hence the act was in violation of due process of law. Furthermore, Harlan saw no pertinent relationship between the subject of the act and interstate commerce. "We hold," said Harlan, "that there is no such connection between interstate commerce and membership in a labor organization as to authorize Congress to make it a crime against the United States for an agent of an interstate carrier to discharge an employee because of such membership on his part."

Justice Holmes thought differently. He believed that the law had a very obvious relationship to interstate commerce. "It hardly would be denied that some of the relations of railroads with unions of railroad employees are closely enough connected with commerce to justify legislation by Congress." As for the reasonableness of interfering with the right of free contract in employment, or even the deliberate promotion of labor unions by Congress, the question

---

[4] See p. 500 for a discussion of the due process aspects of the opinion.

was "one on which intelligent people may differ." Holmes thus intimated that the Court was substituting its conception of public policy for that of Congress.

The Court's attitude of hostility toward railroad labor appeared also in the *First Employers' Liability Cases* (1908). The federal Employers' Liability Act of June 11, 1906, had made every common carrier engaged in interstate commerce liable for the injury or death of any employee sustained in the carrier's employ. The statute had specifically abrogated the old "fellow-servant rule" of the common law, which had held an employer not liable for injuries to an employee suffered through the negligence of a fellow-workman. The statute had also modified the common-law rule of "contributory negligence," which had held the employer not liable for injuries to an employee suffered through the negligence or carelessness of the injured person. The act was similar to many laws then being enacted by the various states, experience with modern industrial conditions having revealed that the old common-law limitations upon employer liability were thoroughly outmoded and archaic.

By a majority of 5 to 4 the Court declared the Employers' Liability Act of 1906 unconstitutional, on the ground that the law invaded the sphere of intrastate commerce. The majority opinion, written by Justice White, admitted that Congress could lawfully regulate the employer liability of rail carriers engaged in interstate commerce. But the Court thought the wording of the statute was too sweeping in its all-inclusiveness. It put the relations of the carrier and *all* his employees under the terms of the act, whether or not a particular employe was directly engaged in interstate commerce. In reality, the Court could have construed the act more narrowly, to apply only to workers engaged in interstate commerce; in refusing to do this, the majority justices betrayed their underlying hostility to the measure.

The Court was widely divided in its decision. Only Day agreed completely with White's reasoning. The conservative bloc, Fuller, Peckham, and Brewer, concurred in White's decision holding the law invalid, but they refused to accept the opinion in its discussion of the extent of the commerce power. To their way of thinking, Congress had no right to regulate employer liability at all, since their view of interstate commerce was too narrow to include employer relationships of carriers. Four justices dissented outright on the grounds that the statute was constitutional. Moody, Harlan, and McKenna thought that Congress had a right to regulate all carrier liability, while Holmes thought the statute could have been read so as to make it constitutional.

Congress presently corrected the constitutional deficiency in the original liability statute by the enactment of a new law. The Federal Employers' Liability Act of April 22, 1908, was so drafted as to apply only to carrier liability for the injuries of employees actually engaged in interstate commerce. True to its implied promise in the *First Employers' Liability Cases*, the Court found no difficulty in holding the revised statute constitutional. Justice Willis Van Devanter's opinion in the *Second Employers' Liability Cases* (1912) was a persuasive brief for the right of Congress to regulate virtually every phase of carrier-employee relationships. Commerce, said Van Devanter, is an act. "It is performed by men, and with the help of things." These men and things are "the instruments and agents" of commerce. Therefore they can be regulated by commerce. The decision, a unanimous one, reflected the spirit of liberal nationalism on the Court at the height of the Progressive era.

In spite of the disturbing opinion in the Child Labor Case, the conception of federal police power was thoroughly established by the close of the Progressive era. While it suffered some reverses in the courts in the reactionary era after 1920, the idea did not die, and additional police statutes of substantial importance were to be enacted after 1920.

REVIVAL OF FEDERAL TRUST PROSECUTIONS: THE NORTHERN SECURITIES CASE

The Court in the Sugar Trust Case and a benevolent Republican administration had put the Sherman Law to rest as a menace to the trusts for a time after 1895. Public opinion, however, was not at rest. Newspapers and periodicals were full of articles denouncing the trusts as "monsters" or defending them as benevolent instruments of economic progress. More important was the voice of the voting public, which insistently demanded action against the evil of monopoly.

In his first annual message to Congress in December 1901, Roosevelt demanded a federal incorporation law and federal regulation of all concerns doing interstate business. Great corporations, he said, were all interstate organizations and ought to be subject to federal regulation, since it was utterly impossible to impose adequate state regulation upon them. He thought that a federal incorporation law would be constitutional under the interstate commerce power; but if this idea was not acceptable to Congress, he was prepared to ask for a constitutional amendment to give the federal government this right.

In response to the President's plea, Representative Charles E. Littlefield of Maine introduced a bill embodying part of Roosevelt's program. The proposed law did not provide for federal incorporation, but instead would have denied the facilities of interstate commerce to any firm which engaged in monopolistic practices through price discrimination, special privilege, rebates, or any other technique. Carriers would be prohibited from transporting goods produced in violation of the statute.

The Littlefield bill passed the House with strong administration support, but the conservative senatorial oligarchy led by Tom Platt of New York denounced the bill as utterly unconstitutional. Roosevelt, who had his more cautious moments, thereupon withdrew the support of the administration from the measure, and the bill died. This was but the first of several occasions on which Roosevelt failed to support his followers when they attempted to write his proposals into law. The difficulty with the bill was of course not alone its doubtful constitutionality. The conservative senatorial majority was shocked at the idea of such federal regulation of business.

In February 1903 Congress did enact a statute establishing a Department of Commerce and Labor and setting up a Bureau of Corporations within the department. The bureau had no regulatory powers, however, but was a mere statistics-gathering and publicity body. Roosevelt several times returned to his request for a federal incorporation law, but Congress thereafter treated his recommendations as so much verbiage.

Roosevelt's attack upon the trusts in the federal courts was more impressive. Since the Sugar Trust Case in 1895, the federal government had not prosecuted a single industrial combination. Beginning in 1902, however, Attorney General Philander C. Knox launched a series of suits against several important combinations and won a number of impressive victories. These brought the Sherman law back to life and considerably altered the constitutional status of trust legislation.

Knox's first big success was gained in *Northern Securities Co. v. United States* (1904). The case grew out of a battle between the Harriman and Hill railroad interests. In 1900, James J. Hill and his associate J. P. Morgan, owners of the Northern Pacific and Great Northern railroads, bought control of the Burlington railroad in order to secure a terminal line into Chicago. E. H. Harriman, who controlled the Union Pacific, was also interested in the Burlington line. He accordingly asked the Hill-Morgan group for permission to join with them in the purchase of the Burlington. Morgan and Hill refused, whereupon Harriman attempted to accomplish the same result by the grander scheme of buying control of the Northern Pacific in the open market. The resultant stock market scramble between Hill and Harriman brought about the so-called Northern Pacific Panic of 1901, in which for a few mad hours Northern Pacific stock sold for more than a thousand dollars a share.

Eventually Hill and Harriman compromised. They set up a holding company, the Northern Securities Company, capitalized at $400,000,000. Its stock was used to purchase control of the Northern Pacific and Great Northern roads. A board of directors representing both the Hill and the Harriman interests presided over the new concern. It was this trust which the Department of Justice now attacked in a suit in equity to dissolve the corporation. In December 1903 the case reached the Supreme Court.

Much to the surprise of the financial community at large, a 5-to-4 majority of the Court held that the Northern Securities Company was an unlawful combination within the meaning of the Sherman Act. Justice Harlan's majority opinion first attacked the defense argument that the holding company in question was the result of a mere stock transaction, not in itself commerce, and that the combination was therefore beyond the reach of the Sherman Law. Defense counsel here had relied heavily upon *United States v. Knight*, which had seemingly established the precedent that combinations not strictly in commerce were outside the meaning of the act.

This contention Harlan denied in sweeping terms. The act of 1890, he said, was aimed at all contracts, combinations, or conspiracies in restraint of trade, which "directly or necessarily" operate in restraint of commerce. The combination in question did not need to be in commerce. It could be simply a stock transaction or presumably even a manufacturing combine. It was necessary to show merely that the combination operated in restraint of commerce for it to become illegal under the Sherman Act.

Harlan turned next to the defense contention that if the Sherman law actually applied to the present combination, it was unconstitutional as an invasion of the sovereignty of the states and a violation of the Tenth Amendment. The corporation in question, the defense counsel had argued, was lawfully organized under the statutes of New Jersey. It was a state corporation. It had not violated any act of the state of New Jersey. Hence, interference with it by the federal government was an invasion of the sphere of state sovereignty.

Harlan attacked their line of argument as invalid; it amounted, he said, to an assertion that a state statute could confer immunity from federal law. As he put it: "It means nothing less than that Congress, in regulating interstate commerce, must act in subordination to the will of the states when exerting their power to create corporations." The defense argument, Harlan pointed out, constituted a denial of the paramount authority of the federal government within its own sphere of power. To claim that the act of a state could paralyze federal authority within the legitimate sphere of the national government was a direct attack upon national supremacy. Harlan concluded that "no such view can be entertained for a moment."

Chief Justice Fuller, and Justices Peckham, White, and Holmes all dissented. Fuller's opinion for the minority followed the established lines of *United States v. Knight* in its narrow definition of interstate commerce. The commerce power, Fuller said, did not extend to the regulation of corporations or stock transactions merely because the parties involved happened incidentally to be engaged in interstate commerce. In a separate opinion, Holmes implied that the present case paralleled *United States v. Knight* so closely that he could see no grounds for departing from that decision.

The principal significance of the Northern Securities Case was the extent to which it modified *United States v. Knight* by broadening the definition of commerce, insisting once more upon the paramount character of the commerce power, and virtually ignoring the more recent distinction between "direct" and "indirect" effects upon commerce. Any combination was unlawful, Harlan had said, merely if it had a restraining effect upon commerce. It is conceivable that some of the justices felt the force of the fact that the Northern Securities combination had been effected between railroads, which obviously were involved in interstate commerce in the most direct fashion possible. Yet Harlan's language was broad enough to apply to a trust in production, should occasion arise. The opinion, in short, revitalized the Sherman law. In the remainder of Roosevelt's term of office, the government commenced more than forty prosecutions under the Sherman Law, and many of them ended successfully.

The administration's most notable victory after the Northern Securities Case came in *Swift and Co. v. United States* (1905), in which the Court first formulated the "stream of commerce" doctrine. Here the government sought to enjoin a number of great packing houses from conspiring to manipulate and control livestock and meat prices in stockyards and slaughtering centers. The combinations in question had occurred in local yards, the animals in question were for the moment at rest there, and the sales involved were admittedly local transactions. But Holmes, speaking for the Court, emphasized the extent to which the animals and processed meat products moved in and out of the yards in interstate commerce, so that the supposedly local combination actually effected a combination in interstate commerce. "When cattle are sent for sale from a place in one state, with the expectation that they will end their transit, after purchase, in another, and when in effect they do so, with only the interruption necessary to find a purchaser at the stock yards, and when this is a typical constantly recurring course, the current thus existing is a current of commerce among the states, and the purchase of the cattle is a part and incident of such commerce." The Court's conservatives apparently considered this dictum to be harmless enough; the combination was in sales and not production, and there was no dissent. In reality, the "stream of commerce" doctrine was to become a basic legal concept in the expansion of the commerce power. The idea provided a logical premise under which production itself could later be held to be a part of commerce. Should this occur, the distinction between commerce and manufacturing would break down. This, in fact, is what happened after 1937.

THE RULE OF REASON

Eventually, much of the significance of the foregoing trust prosecutions was destroyed by the application of the so-called "rule of reason" to the Sherman law. In several early trust prosecutions the defense had attempted to introduce the English common-law conception of monopoly. Briefly, this held that not all combinations in restraint of trade were illegal but only those which were unreasonable, or against public interest. This contention first appeared in counsel's argument in the *Transmissouri Freight Association Case*,[5] where it had been emphatically rejected by the Court, Justice Peckham observing that "the plain and ordinary meaning" of the Sherman law prohibited all combinations in restraint of interstate commerce, not merely unreasonable ones.

However, the rule of reason was potentially too useful to be discarded. After 1901, a growing segment of public opinion, led

---

5 See p. 529.

by President Roosevelt, adopted the argument that there were "good" and "bad" trusts, that is, those whose business practices were in the public interest and those whose practices were not. The latter, Roosevelt's argument ran, ought to be prosecuted, the former left alone. For the Court to reject such a distinction might well imply acceptance of the argument espoused by Louis Brandeis: that all monopolistic big business was evil *per se*. And this a majority of justices, who were by and large sympathetic to large corporate interests, was not prepared to do.

The rule of reason made its appearance again in *Northern Securities Co. v. United States* (1904), where the conception evidently made some impression, for Holmes referred to it with respect. The persistence of counsel in pressing home this interpretation of the Sherman law in the face of repeated rebuffs recalls in striking fashion the manner in which the substantive conception of due process of law ultimately triumphed in the Court.

The Court formally recognized the rule of reason in *Standard Oil Co. v. United States* (1911). This case had grown out of a Roosevelt-inspired government prosecution against the oil trust. A United States district court decision had held the Standard Oil combination to be in violation of the Sherman Law and had ordered the company's dissolution into its component parts. This decision the trust then appealed to the Supreme Court.

The Court denied the appeal; yet the very words of Justice White's opinion recognized the rule of reason. White reviewed at length the law of monopoly and concluded that the historically correct interpretation of the Sherman Act was that it forbade only unreasonable combinations or contracts in restraint of trade. "Reasonable" monopolies, he held, were legal.

The implications of White's opinion were revealed two weeks later, in *United States v. American Tobacco Company* (1911), in which the Court passed on the government's suit against the tobacco trust. Although it ordered the American Tobacco Company to reorganize, the Court refused to impose absolute dissolution upon the concern, presumably on the grounds that the combination was not altogether an unreasonable one. Justice White's opinion put the full seal of approval upon the rule of reason with the amazing pronouncement that "the doctrine thus stated was in accord with all previous decisions of this court. . . ." This extraordinary attempt at legal consistency was too much for Justice Harlan to swallow, and in his dissent he remarked ironically that "this statement surprises me quite as much as would a statement that black was white or white was black."

The Court's acceptance of the rule of reason was altogether consistent with the judicial philosophy which had inspired the expansion of substantive due process. As has already been explained, due process had become whatever the Court held to be a "reasonable" exercise of legislative authority. What was reasonable or unreasonable was for the Court to decide. The same subtle distinction was now applied to monopoly cases. Unreasonable monopolies were illegal; but what constituted unreasonable monopoly was for the Court to decide. A "reasonable" trust was a "good" trust—that is, one which the Court found to be socially and economically acceptable.

After 1911, it proved virtually impossible to prosecute any great trust successfully, for almost any monopoly could put up a plausible argument for its social respectability and thus claim to be a "reasonable" combination. Thus in the arguments advanced in the shoe machinery trust case, *United States v. Winslow* (1913), counsel for the monopoly dwelt at length upon the corporation's high commercial character and the advances in technology which it had effected. The plea was successful. The government was able to show that the trust had been formed with intent to monopolize, that it almost completely controlled the industry, that it had frequently conspired to drive competition out of business. It was not enough. The Court held that the combination was a reasonable one, and hence not in violation of the Sherman law. Prosecution of the United States Steel Corporation a few years later in *United States v. United States Steel Corporation* (1920) produced the same argument of "economic legitimacy" and the same acceptance of the reasonableness of the trust by the Court.

These decisions paved the way for the unprecedented era of combination and monopoly in the America of the 1920's. As one authority has put it, "The merger movement of the 1920's was in effect simply a capitalization of the opportunities made available by the judicial legislation of 1911 as amplified and clarified by the outstanding decisions of the ensuing decade." [6]

THE REVIVAL OF THE INTERSTATE COMMERCE COMMISSION

More effective than Roosevelt's trust prosecutions was the revival of the Interstate Commerce Commission brought about by the pas-

---

[6] Myron W. Watkins, "Trusts," *Encyclopaedia of the Social Sciences*, XV, p. 117.

sage of the Hepburn Act in 1906 and by a subsequent series of Court decisions favorable to the new law. Since the Court's decisions in the Cincinnati and New Orleans case and in the Alabama Midland case, in 1897, the Interstate Commerce Commission had been moribund. It had no rate-setting powers; it could only issue "cease and desist" orders directed at specific rates. It was virtually impossible to enforce these orders in the courts. Since the Commission found it difficult to obtain evidence, and since the courts insisted upon a complete review of all the facts in a case, the Commission's orders were usually overturned on appeal.

This situation resulted in the renewal of all the evils the Commission had originally been set up to control. Rebates, pools, discriminatory practices against shippers, long- and short-haul discrimination had all been revived in force. The Elkins Act of 1903 checked rebates to some extent by making any deviation from published rates unlawful and subjecting both carrier and shipper to prosecution for the offense. The law was successful within a limited sphere, but left the broader aspects of the rail rate structure untouched.

By 1905, a majority of the general public as well as many big shippers and railroads were demanding more effective rail legislation. In response to Roosevelt's plea, the House in 1905 passed the Cullom bill, designed to enlarge the powers of the Interstate Commerce Commission. The Old Guard in the Senate blocked the measure, however, and instead set up a committee to investigate the entire railroad problem. The committee hearings merely confirmed what everybody knew—that grave abuses existed and a stronger law was needed.

In December 1905, Roosevelt again asked Congress to enact effective rate regulation. In response, Representative William P. Hepburn of Iowa introduced a bill which finally passed the House in February 1906. This measure gave the Commission ultimate rate-fixing powers, although it could not fix rates originally. The railroads could still publish their own rate schedules, but the Commission could take any rate under review on complaint, decide upon a fair and reasonable maximum rate, and order the railroad not to charge in excess of it.

As passed by the House, the Hepburn bill provided for very narrow review of the Commission's orders by the courts. It will be recalled that since the Alabama Midland case in 1897, the courts had exercised very broad review of the Commission's decisions, insisting upon a right to re-examine all the evidence *de novo* as well as the law in the case. This in effect had rendered the Commission little more than a fifth wheel, its entire work being duplicated by the courts. The Hepburn bill now provided that in reviewing a Commission order the court of appeal could decide only whether the order in question had been "regularly made"—that is, whether the Commission had observed the procedure prescribed by law. It was admitted in the House debates that the courts would also retain the right to decide that a given order was confiscatory or unreasonable and thereby in violation of due process. The courts could not, however, review facts, decide questions of policy, or try the case *de novo*.

When the Hepburn bill reached the Senate, the Republican Old Guard and conservative Democrats alike vigorously attacked both the Commission's proposed new rate-fixing powers and the provisions for narrow judicial review. In a long speech in late February, Senator Joseph B. Foraker of Ohio went so far as to assert that the power to fix rates was a purely judicial function; hence Congress itself did not possess the power and therefore could not delegate it to a commission. The proposed bill, he argued, was thus a gross violation of the separation of powers. As for narrow review, it would thrust policy-making discretion "without supervision or control" into the hands of a commission which "has erroneously decided almost every important case upon which it has passed judgment during the whole period of the nineteen years of its existence." In the weeks that followed, Senators John Spooner of Wisconsin, Nelson W. Aldrich of Rhode Island, Philander C. Knox of Pennsylvania, Henry Cabot Lodge of Massachusetts, and other conservatives took their cues from Foraker's speech, and for the most part centered their attacks upon the wisdom and constitutionality of "narrow review."

Eventually the conflict between the advocates of broad and of narrow review centered in the dispute between the respective merits of two amendments to the bill—the Long and Allison amendments. The former, offered by Senator Chester I. Long of Kansas on April 2, was understood to have been submitted at the instance of the President. By its terms, jurisdiction on appeals was lodged in the circuit courts, which had the power merely "to hear and determine in any such suit whether the order complained of was beyond the authority of the commission or in violation of the rights of the carrier secured by the Constitution."

In a brilliant speech, Long defended both the constitutionality and the wisdom of his amendment. Rate-setting was a legislative function, and provided Congress fixed certain broad limits of policy, the power could be delegated to a commission, he said. The courts were not policy-making bodies, and they should have no authority to review the "wisdom and policy" of the Commission's orders but should merely decide upon their legality and constitutionality.

Although the Long amendment was presumed to be an administration-sponsored measure, Roosevelt withdrew his support from it some days later. Why he did this is a matter of some controversy. It seems probable, however, that he was informed by Republican leaders in the Senate that they would not support the amendment and would rebel should he insist upon it. To avoid an open breach with the senatorial oligarchy, the President let it become known that he was no longer interested in the Long amendment.

Early in May, Senator William B. Allison of Iowa introduced an amendment as a substitute for the Long proposal. In place of the specific provisions for narrow review in the Long amendment, the Allison amendment was extremely vague in phraseology. It provided merely that the orders of the Commission should take effect within a reasonable time and should run for two years. Venue on appeals was to lie in the district court where the carrier had its principal office. No injunction or restraining order could be issued on less than five days' notice. The amendment made no effort to define the limits of judicial review and hence threw the whole matter into the hands of the courts for future definition.

Although the proponents of narrow review made every effort to defeat the Allison amendment, it was shortly adopted by a 2-to-1 majority. Subsequently the Hepburn bill passed the Senate by a vote of 71 to 3. After some resistance, the House concurred in the Allison amendment, and the Hepburn Act became law on June 29, 1906.

It remained to be seen whether the new law would prove more effective in operation than the old statute of 1887. Most important, the Hepburn Act plainly gave the Commission positive rate-setting powers, once a complaint had been filled and a hearing held on a particular rate. Also the burden of appeals was now placed upon the railroads and not upon the Commission. The critical question was how the courts would interpret their own powers of review. If they insisted upon the right to review policy and facts as well as law, the new act would have little meaning.

THE COMMISSION IN THE COURTS

Within the next few years, the Court virtually sustained the constitutional arguments of the congressmen who had insisted upon narrow review and upon the validity of the commission principle. Only a year after the passage of the Hepburn Act, the Supreme Court served notice in *Illinois Central Railroad Company v. Interstate Commerce Commission* (1907) that it would not investigate *de novo* all the facts of a case on appeal. It pointed out that the commission was a responsible tribunal, that its findings of fact were by law prima facie true, and that a "probative force" must be attributed to them. While in theory there was nothing revolutionary about this, the principle had hitherto been largely ignored.

Three years later, in *Interstate Commerce Commission v. Illinois Central Railroad Company* (1910), the Court had occasion to interpret directly the meaning of the Allison amendment. Its decision was a triumph for the principle of narrow review and the commission system. "Beyond controversy," said Justice White, "in determining whether an order of the Commission shall be suspended or set aside, we must consider (a) all relevant questions of constitutional power or right; (b) all pertinent questions as to whether the administrative order is within the scope of delegated authority under which it purports to have been made; and (c) . . . whether, even although the order be in form within the delegated power, nevertheless it must be treated as not embraced therein, because the exertion of authority which is questioned has been manifested in such an unreasonable manner as to cause it, in truth, to be within the elementary rule that the substance, and not the shadow, determine the validity of the exercise of the power." These words were in effect an endorsement of the principle embodied in the defeated Long amendment.

The Court then warned that it would not usurp the Commission's policy-making functions under the pretense of reviewing its decisions. The powers of review of the judiciary, the opinion held, "lend no support whatever to the proposition that we may, under the guise of exerting judicial power, usurp merely administrative functions by setting aside a lawful administrative order upon our conception as to whether the administrative power has been wisely exercised. Power to make the order, and not the mere expediency or wisdom of having made it, is the question."

This decision, shortly reinforced in several other cases, amounted to a signal triumph for the commission principle of administration. For if the Commission's orders were recognized as having an intrinsic validity, subject only to a review of power and constitutionality, then they would ordinarily have the effect of law; and the Commission's decisions on policy would almost invariably stand.

This was precisely what was necessary to make commission administration successful.

The Court also granted generous recognition to the new rate-fixing powers of the Commission. The test case came in 1910, when, after investigation, the Commission issued an order reducing class rates on certain western lines, and substituted a comprehensive rate schedule of its own. The Court, in *Interstate Commerce Commission v. Chicago, Rock Island, and Pacific Railway Company* (1910), accepted the validity of this order, which was in effect an assertion by the Commission of a general right of control over the rail rate structure. The Court hardly touched upon the question of whether such power could lawfully be delegated to an administrative commission.

In the Mann-Elkins Act of June 18, 1910, Congress delegated original rate-setting powers to the Commission. The law also created a Commerce Court whose function was to hear appeals from the Commission. As originally conceived, the Commerce Court appears to have represented an ingenious attempt to strip the Commission of its hard-won authority and to reinstate "broad review," for the bill would have permitted the new court to inquire into both findings of fact and the wisdom and expediency of Commission orders. Against these provisions in the bill, Robert M. LaFollette of Wisconsin, Albert J. Beveridge of Indiana, and other Senate liberals revolted successfully. As finally passed, the act conferred no extraordinary powers upon the new tribunal. The Commerce Court had only a brief and ineffective career and was abolished by Congress in 1913.

It now only remained for the Supreme Court to confirm the original rate-fixing powers of the Commission. The formal step came in *United States v. Atchison, Topeka, and Santa Fe* (1914). Here counsel for the road had argued that the grant by Congress of original rate-fixing powers to the Commission was an unconstitutional delegation of legislative authority. The Court replied by citing summarily a whole series of cases in which the delegation of quasi-legislative authority to the executive had been recognized as valid.

The Commission now had the grant of authority that it needed for a successful career. It had a broad degree of administrative discretion, which the Court recognized as legal. It was now recognized as a policy-making body, and the Court had served notice that the judiciary would not, under guise of judicial review, interfere with the Commission's policy-making function.

The Commission's triumph opened the way for a new era in government administration, in which the number and importance of executive boards was vastly increased. The movement really got under way in President Wilson's administration, with the establishment of three important administrative boards, the Federal Trade Commission, the Federal Tariff Commission, and the Federal Reserve Board.

THE INTERSTATE COMMERCE COMMISSION AND
NATIONAL ASCENDANCY

Not the least of the Interstate Commerce Commission's legal victories was that in which the Supreme Court recognized the Commission's control over intrastate commerce where that commerce affected interstate commerce directly. The decisions concerned were based upon the same principles of national ascendancy as that in the Northern Securities and Lottery cases, although the immediate constitutional issues were somewhat different.

The first opinion of this kind was delivered in the *Minnesota Rate Cases* (1913). The immediate question involved was the validity of a Minnesota Warehouse Commission order fixing rail rates within that state. While the order was concerned only with intrastate rates, it was admitted by both sides that it would have some effect upon the interstate rate structure. Justice Charles Evans Hughes' opinion upheld the validity of the state's regulation. Most of his opinion dealt with and powerfully emphasized the paramount authority of Congress over interstate commerce; but, taking his cue from the venerable *Cooley v. Board of Wardens*, he held that there was a sphere of state regulation of interstate commerce within which the states might act, provided the federal government had not yet assumed control. Hence the Minnesota commission's order was valid.

Then came the explosive part of the opinion. Interstate commerce and intrastate commerce, said Hughes, were nowadays so inextricably blended that the federal government probably had at least some power to regulate the latter. If by reason of this fact some federal regulation of intrastate commerce was necessary, it was for Congress to determine and apply the necessary regulation. Thus by implication the decision confirmed a certain degree of federal authority over the internal commerce of the states.

The full significance of the foregoing opinion emerged a year later in the *Shreveport Rate Cases* (1914), in which the Supreme Court sustained the Commission's authority to regulate intrastate rail rates. The case involved the rate structure of the Louisiana–east Texas region. It appeared that rates on the rail lines from Houston and Dallas eastward to east Texas cities were much lower than those for like distances from Shreveport, Louisiana, to the same east Texas cities. The result was serious discrimination against Shreveport in favor of Dallas and Houston.

The Interstate Commerce Commission attempted to correct this situation, and it accordingly issued an order forbidding the railroads in question to charge a higher rate from Shreveport to east Texas than from Houston and Dallas to east Texas. This order could have been complied with either by raising the intrastate rate from Houston and Dallas to east Texas, or by lowering the interstate rate from Shreveport to east Texas. However, the reduction of the interstate rate was impracticable, for it was part of a much larger regional rate structure. Hence the lower court had held that the Commission's order absolved the railroads in question from the obligation to obey the intrastate rate set by the Texas Railroad Commission.

On appeal, the Supreme Court upheld the validity of the Commission's order, even when interpreted as invalidating a purely intrastate rate. In his opinion, Justice Hughes dwelt at length upon the paramount powers of Congress over interstate commerce. This might sometimes make necessary some regulation of intrastate commerce, he said, for "Wherever the interstate and intrastate transactions of carriers are so related that the government of the one involves the control of the other, it is Congress, and not the state, that is entitled to prescribe the final and dominant rule."

Hughes inquired next into the question whether the present order was within the authority granted to the Commission by Congress. Again he reached an affirmative conclusion. The point rested upon Section 3 of the Interstate Commerce Act of 1887, which forbade any common carrier from giving undue advantage to one locality as against another. Here he recalled the *Minnesota Rate Cases*, which he distinguished sharply from the present situation. In the Minnesota cases an intrastate rate fixed by the state had had an incidental effect on interstate commerce, but there had been no attempt by either Congress or the Commission to regulate the Minnesota rate schedule; nor had the rate in question adversely affected interstate commerce. Hence the intrastate rate had been held valid. In the present case, however, the Federal government had acted through the Interstate Commerce Commission to invalidate an intrastate rate and in effect fix a new rate. This action was legal, for the Interstate Commerce Commission was empowered to maintain a reasonable interstate rate structure, and the local Texas rate had been found by the Commission to have an adverse effect upon interstate commerce. The Texas rate could therefore legally be set aside and a new rate fixed, for the paramount authority of the national commerce power made it both imperative and constitutional to do so.

In so far as the Court in the future should be willing to follow its own reasoning, this decision meant that federal authority could go to great lengths in the regulation of intrastate commerce, provided such regulation was incidental to some constitutional exercise of the national commerce power. Would not this principle, if given complete recognition, logically compel the Court to recognize that the federal government might regulate any matter ordinarily within the sphere of state authority if such regulation seemed necessary and incidental to some constitutional power of Congress? The larger implications of the *Minnesota Rate Cases* was clearly the same as that in the Lottery Case: the Court recognized the interpenetration of state and national economic life; yet it insisted upon the maintenance of national authority even though this might now mean a considerable invasion of the province originally reserved to the states. How far this expansion of federal sovereignty could be carried the Court was not prepared to say.

The Progressive Revolt

IN 1908, a triumphant Republican party had elected William Howard Taft to the presidency, brushing aside William Jennings Bryan's third and final bid for the office. Taft was virtually Roosevelt's personal choice as his successor, and the new President entered upon his duties with apparent assurance that he would be able to continue Roosevelt's policies and at the same time command the support of a Republican majority in Congress.

This prospect was not to be realized. Instead, a serious insurgent movement broke out in Republican ranks in both houses, so that by 1912 the Republican party had split into conservative and liberal wings, and the liberal insurgents were moving to organize the Progressive Party. The upheaval in Republican Party ranks was in considerable part the result of Taft's political ineptitude and Roosevelt's impatience with his successor's submission to the conservative senatorial oligarchy under Senator Aldrich.

In a more fundamental sense, however, Republican insurgency was a phase of the Progressive movement, which dominated American political life roughly between the turn of the century and American entry into World War I. The Progressive movement was, in its turn, rooted in the deep-seated agrarian unrest and urban discontent so apparent in the Populist revolt and in the reform movement which William Jennings Bryan had led within the Democratic Party. It is significant that many of the reforms which the Populists and Bryan Democrats advocated, among them control of the trusts, monetary and banking reforms, social welfare programs, the income tax, and the initiative, referendum and recall, reappeared in the Progressive era and eventually were incorporated in the Progressive Party's platform.

In the great urban centers of the North and East there had long been widespread conviction that the industrial revolution had given rise to serious social and economic evils and injustices that must be brought under national control. Henry George's classic exposition of single tax theory, *Progress and Poverty* (1879), was still enjoying wide circulation in the decade after 1900, as was Edward Bellamy's Utopian socialist novel, *Looking Backward* (1888), while Henry Demarest Lloyd's *Wealth Against Commonwealth* (1894) was regarded by Progressive reformers as a great classic.

This sentiment led to a series of reform movements in city government and in social and industrial welfare, some of which had their inception well before 1900. In Massachusetts, Democrats and liberal Republicans led by such men as Governor William E. Russell, Moorfield Storey, and Louis D. Brandeis joined forces to clean up urban government and to impose public controls upon privately owned gas, water, and traction utilities.

In Chicago, Jane Addams in 1889 founded Hull House, a pioneering institution in a generation-long crusade for better housing and social welfare for the city's poor. In 1893, Addams joined forces with Florence Kelley to obtain passage by the state legislature of a Factory Act imposing sanitary and safety provisions upon the state's industries as well as incorporating an eight-hourday provision presently held unconstitutional by the state Supreme Court. In 1899, Kelley moved to New York City, where as Secretary of the National Consumers League she at once assumed a prominent role in the campaign for tenement house reform and for state legislation protecting women against long hours, night work, and bad working conditions in industry.

In Detroit, Hazen Pingree, elected as a Republican reform mayor in 1889, fought successfully for gas and telephone rate controls, wrested concessions from the local traction company, established a municipal power plant, and initiated a comprehensive municipal garden plan to feed depression poor. And in Toledo, Samuel M. "Golden Rule" Jones, a wealthy reform-minded manufacturer who was elected mayor in 1897, broke with the regular Republican organization and went on to clean up the police department, establish free kindergartens and public playgrounds and advocate municipal ownership of public utilities.

After 1900, both municipal and state reform movements accelerated. In Cleveland, Thomas L. Johnson, a wealthy manufacturer and traction magnate who had read *Progress and Poverty* and had been converted to liberal reform, was elected mayor in 1901 and at once began a long fight for comprehensive city planning, a three-cent fare, tax reform, public parks and playgrounds, a modern sewage system, and adequate institutions for the handicapped and delinquent. In NewYork, Charles Evans Hughes as a special prosecutor exposed the corrupt and inefficient practices of the nation's leading insurance companies, an achievement that led to his election as governor in 1906. In this office, he antagonized party regulars with his successful advocacy of a state public utilities commission and his attack on race-track gambling.

Of great significance for the future of the Progressive Party was the career of Robert M. LaFollette, who became governor of Wisconsin in 1900. As governor, La Follette engaged in a long and spectacular battle with the railroads, trusts, and utility interests, to achieve effective rate regulation, antitrust laws, and a strong public utilities commission. His sponsorship of graduated income and inheritance taxes, workmen's compensation, maximum hours for women and children, and a state primary law, marked him as one of the nation's outstanding liberal Republicans. Elected to the Senate in 1906, La Follette speedily became the leader of the small but highly vocal group of Republican insurgents in the upper house.

In California, Hiram Johnson achieved fame as a special prosecutor in a spectacular bribery case involving railroads, public utilities, and a corrupt San Francisco city council. Partial success led to his election as a reform governor of California in 1910, and in 1912 he became Roosevelt's running mate on the Progressive Party's presidential ticket. In Chicago, George C. Cole, an enlightened political boss, organized the Municipal Voters' League, and began a long but ultimately unsuccessful fight to clean up Chicago politics. In Missouri, Joseph Folk, a St. Louis prosecutor, was more successful in his battle against utility and railroad lobbyists and bribery and eventually emerged as an outstanding reform governor of the state.

About 1906, a liberal Republican faction began to make its appearance in Congress, although for a time there was no sharp breakdown in party lines. La Follette first distinguished himself as a party rebel during the Senate debates on the Hepburn bill,[1] when he sponsored strong rail rate regulation, much to the disgust of the Republican regulars, who made a point of walking out of the chamber every time he spoke. Senator Albert J. Beveridge of Indiana, at the outset of his career a conservative Republican protectionist and imperialist, gradually drifted away from party regularity, and after 1906 underlined his new liberalism by championing the Meat Inspection Act, federal regulation of corporations, conservation, tariff reform, and in particular a federal child labor law. Senator Jonathan Dolliver of Iowa broke with Aldrich and the regular party organization in 1906 and soon emerged as an enemy of Republican protectionism and a supporter of federal rail rate regulation. Albert B. Cummins, a former reform governor of Iowa who entered the Senate in 1909, immediately joined the Progressive faction. William E. Borah of Idaho also lent support to the Senate liberals, as did Moses E. Clapp of Minnesota, who represented the more radical agrarian Republican elements in that state.

In the House, Charles A. Lindbergh of Minnesota, who entered the lower chamber in 1907 as a Republican, soon identified himself as a potential insurgent by his attacks on big business and his support for tariff reform and income and corporation taxes. Victor Murdock of Kansas, a former newspaperman with a typical Kansan Populist background, took his seat in 1909 and at once joined the liberal Republican faction. George W. Norris of Nebraska began his long and illustrious liberal career with his entrance into the House in 1908, where he soon assumed the leadership of the House insurgents.

By 1909, liberal Republicans and their Democratic sympathizers in and out of Congress were rapidly drawing together on a program of political and social reform. The Progressives believed that many of the problems created by the industrial revolution were national in scope and could be solved only by a broad program of federal controls. They were unanimous in desiring strong national legislation which would subject big business to a full measure of social control in the interests of public welfare.

Like the Jeffersonians of a century before, the Progressives had an abiding faith in the intelligence and good will of the American people. Fundamentally, their remedy for the failures of democracy was more democracy. Let the will of the people really reach into Congress, the courts, the state legislatures, and America could then

---

[1] See pp. 572ff.

solve its problems. This explains Progressive enthusiasm for the direct primary, and for the initiative, referendum, and recall. There was an unrealistic element of democratic idealism in the Progressive mind here; it remained to be seen whether more direct popular control of government would lead to a more efficient and equitable political order. In their enthusiasm, the liberals of the day too often forgot that democratic government requires strong party organization and discipline if it is to be effective and that an unorganized "will of the people" needs strong leadership and statesmanship if it is to find expression.

THE INCOME TAX AMENDMENT

It was the fight for a federal income tax law in the special session of 1909 which produced the first serious evidence that party lines in Congress were close to the breaking point. Here the threat of a Progressive-Democratic coalition forced the conservative Republican party leaders in both houses to make substantial concessions in order to hold party lines intact.

Liberal nationalists had never concealed their disgust with the constitutional status of income tax legislation after the two Pollock opinions of 1895. They believed that a federal income tax law was an indispensable means of reaching the intangible forms of property and wealth created by the industrial revolution and redressing what Progressives regarded as gross inequities in the distribution of national income. Yet all proposals to enact the necessary statute had been met with the seemingly unanswerable objection that the income tax was unconstitutional. The Supreme Court appeared to be an almost hopeless obstacle to the passage of a federal income tax law.

As the liberal faction in both parties in Congress grew stronger, however, it became more and more impatient with judicial restraint. In 1907 Roosevelt had recommended passage of an income tax law in his annual message to Congress. The Democratic platform of 1908 also had favored the tax, and William Howard Taft, the Republican candidate, had approved the income tax "in principle." Every session of Congress after 1905 had seen the introduction of one or more bills to levy an income tax, to enforce the old act of 1894, still technically on the statute books, or to legalize the tax by constitutional amendment.

The income tax amendment adopted by Congress in 1909 was a by-product of a congressional tariff fight. President Taft called Congress into special session in March in fulfillment of a campaign promise to reform the tariff. Early in April, while the Senate was engrossed in debating tariff schedules, Senator Joseph W. Bailey of Texas rose to present an amendment to the tariff bill virtually re-enacting the provisions of the old 1894 income tax law. The only difference of consequence was that Bailey's measure, in deference to the first income tax decision, would have exempted from taxation state, county, and municipal securities. He did not believe that the Court's opinion in the two Pollock cases was "a correct interpretation of the Constitution," and he did not think it "improper for the American Congress to resubmit the question to the reconsideration of that great tribunal." Bailey was a Southern conservative and had little sympathy with the income tax, but as a good party Democrat he was more than willing to embarrass the opposition majority with his bill. His measure called merely for a flat 3 per cent tax on all incomes above $5,000 and therefore did not suit the more ardent Progressives. Accordingly, Senator A. B. Cummins of Iowa, with La Follette's support, shortly introduced an amendment to the tariff bill calling for a graduated tax running up to 6 per cent on incomes above $100,000. The Cummins amendment proved to be too extreme to win general support, but Bailey's proposal attracted strong support from both liberal Republicans and Democrats.

When it became clear that the Bailey amendment stood an excellent chance for adoption, Senator Nelson W. Aldrich of Rhode Island, the Republican floor leader and administration spokesman, adopted extraordinary tactics to defeat the measure. Aldrich and Senator Henry Cabot Lodge of Massachusetts first introduced a substitute amendment proposing to levy a 2 per cent excise tax upon corporations. This tax Aldrich defended as constitutional, since the Supreme Court had ruled in 1898 that an excise tax on corporations, calculated as a percentage of corporate income, was not a direct tax within the meaning of the Constitution. He admitted that the real purpose of his proposal was to defeat the enactment of a general income tax law.

Since it still seemed likely that the Bailey amendment would be adopted, the Senate conservatives took the extraordinary step of presenting a constitutional amendment to legalize the income tax. This proposal was conceived solely as a device designed to defeat Bailey's proposal. Early in June, Senator Aldrich and other members of the Senate Finance Committee held a conference on strategy with President Taft. As a result of this meeting, Taft on June 16 sent a message to Congress recommending the passage of a constitutional amendment to legalize federal income tax legislation. The President pointed out that any law enacted without benefit of constitutional amendment would certainly face "protracted litigation" before it could be enforced. He also expressed concern lest Congress damage the prestige of the judiciary. Re-enactment of a law once held unconstitutional would "not strengthen public confidence in the stability of judicial construction of the constitution." Immediately after the President's message had been delivered to the Senate, the Finance Committee reported out the draft of a proposed amendment to the Constitution to legalize the income tax.

The appearance of the amendment threw the liberals into a quandary. They were convinced that once the amendment was submitted to the states the income tax would be dead, for there seemed but little chance that the amendment would secure approval by the necessary three-fourths of the states. They recognized the majority stratagem as an attempt to kill enactment of the tax, and apparently most of them believed that the diversion would be successful. Nevertheless, the Progressives could not bring themselves to vote against the amendment. They favored it in principle; hence they would vote for it even while condemning the tactics of the majority. Senator Cummins expressed this view when he declared he would vote for the amendment with the full understanding that its purpose was to defeat the Bailey clause and with the belief that the amendment would never become a part of the Constitution.

The majority strategy succeeded in its immediate objective. At the end of June, the Senate voted down Bailey's amendment to the tariff law, 45 to 31, and immediately thereafter it accepted the Aldrich amendment for a corporation franchise tax as a substitute. Early in July the Senate voted to submit the constitutional amendment by the impressive margin of 77 to 0.

Before the final vote, Senator Bailey and the Progressives made an unsuccessful attempt to get the Senate to provide for ratification by conventions in the several states rather than by state legislatures. They believed that if conventions were called for the specific purpose of voting on the amendment, it might possibly win ratification. The majority had no intention of increasing the chances of ratification and rejected the proposal.

A week later the House concurred in submitting the amendment. Before the representatives voted, they were treated to the amusing circumstance of hearing the majority floor leader, S. E. Payne of New York, the formal sponsor of the amendment before the House, denounce the income tax "as one that makes a nation of liars," and a "tax on the income of honest men which exempts the income of rascals." Cordell Hull of Tennessee responded to this somewhat too frank revelation of majority motives with a bitter speech in which he repeated the charge that the only purpose of the constitutional amendment was to kill the tax. But no liberal representative could vote against the amendment, and a few moments later the House passed it by a vote of 318 to 14.

Aldrich and Payne had won a Pyrrhic victory. Contrary to all expectations, the income tax amendment was ratified by one state legislature after another and was proclaimed in effect on February 25, 1913. It thus became the first constitutional amendment to secure adoption since Reconstruction days. Like its precursors of fifty years before, the Sixteenth Amendment heralded political and social changes little short of revolutionary. It inaugurated a new era in federal finance. Within a very few years the income tax was to become by far the most important source of federal revenue. The tax had an important effect upon the country's economic and social structure, for it partially shifted the growing burden of federal finance to the wealthy and in a measure served the very purposes of the agrarian radicals who had first suggested it as a device to effect the redistribution of income and wealth. It remains today one of the most important amendments to the Constitution.

THE REVOLT AGAINST THE SPEAKER

The Speaker of the House had since 1789 been a powerful figure in the federal government. His right to recognize members on the floor and to appoint all standing committees dated from the First Congress. From the beginning the privileges of the office had been exercised in the interest of personal power and party politics, and during the course of the nineteenth century a succession of great speakers, above all the masterful Henry Clay, had contributed to the growing prestige of the speakership.

In the post–Civil War era, the office had reached a new pinnacle of authority and prestige. This was in part because of the increased power of Congress, which had engaged and defeated President Johnson in the conflict over Reconstruction. Also, a long series of undistinguished Presidents, extending from Grant through McKinley, had strengthened congressional ascendancy over the executive. Further, the speaker derived much of his authority from the growing size of the House, which increased the necessity for effective discipline. In 1790 the House had had but 65 members; by 1860 the membership was 243; by 1906 it was 385; and by 1911 it had reached 433. No legislative body of this size could function effectively without strong discipline and organization, which it was the Speaker's function to impose.

Thomas B. Reed of Maine, who took the gavel in 1889 in the administration of Benjamin Harrison, was the most powerful Speaker up to that time. His influence stemmed in considerable part from his appointment and control of committees, especially the five-man Rules Committee, of which he was a member. This committee could and did recommend "special order" for any bill, this giving the measure priority on the House calendar and assuring its early passage. Reed also exercised to the full the Speaker's time-honored discretionary right to recognize members on the floor. This privilege had often been exercised for partisan purposes, but Reed went further in this respect than had any man before him. He invariably greeted representatives who sought recognition with the question: "For what purpose does the gentleman rise?" The implication was clear: any one who sought to revolt against the order of business prescribed by the Rules Committee could not even gain the floor.

Reed also destroyed the old minority tactic of refusing to answer a roll-call and then raising the plea of "no quorum" as a device for blocking House business. When a roll-call showed no quorum to be present, he merely instructed the clerk to enter the names of the silent members as "present." The first time he did this, he plunged the House into pandemonium. An infuriated Kentuckian rose to deny the speaker's right "to count me as present." Reed merely replied, "The Chair is making a statement of fact that the gentleman from Kentucky is here. Does he deny it?" The House laughed, and Reed won his point. The ruling weakened further the ability of the minority to resist Reed's absolutism.

Reed also used the party caucus for disciplinary purposes. The Republican majority in caucus was informed in advance of the coming legislative program and was also bound to co-operation, secrecy, and discipline. Majority members who were indiscreet enough to disobey this order were punished by expulsion from committees and by future oblivion.

The precedents established by Reed in the speakership prevailed from 1889 until 1910. Joseph Cannon of Illinois, familiarly known as "Uncle Joe," who became Speaker in 1903, had been trained in the Reed tradition, and until 1910 he wielded the gavel with all the arbitrary power of his preceptor.

The rise of the Progressive bloc in Congress opened up the possibility of an effective Progressive-Democratic attack on the Speaker's powers. The Progressives looked upon the office as it was then employed as an affront to their ideal of democratic self-government and as a reactionary bulwark against the passage of liberal social legislation. They were eager to co-operate with the Democrats in an effort to reduce Cannon's authority. Representative George W. Norris of Nebraska was the astute director of the campaign toward this end, undertaken with the able assistance of Charles A. Lindbergh of Minnesota, Irvine Lenroot and Henry Cooper of Wisconsin, and Victor Murdoch of Kansas.

The first victory of the rebels was the inauguration in March 1909 of "Calendar Wednesday." For years the reports of the more important committees had so monopolized the time of the House that there was little opportunity to consider the bills of individual members. Although a measure might be of the greatest significance, it had little chance of obtaining consideration by the House unless the all-important Rules Committee decided to give it priority. Needless to say, bills of which the speaker's machine disapproved never emerged from oblivion. The Progressives and Democrats now sought to remedy this situation by a proposed amendment to the House rules setting apart one day a week on which the speaker would be obliged to "call the calendar"—that is, to take up the business of the House in order, without regard to priorities fixed by the Rules Committee. A lengthy debate on the proposal ended in victory for the rebels, when a Progressive-Democratic vote forced adoption of the reform.

A year later, in March 1910, the Progressive-Democratic coalition after a protracted and bitter debate forced through a Norris-sponsored resolution abolishing the five-man Rules Committee. The resolution substituted a ten-man Committee on Rules elected by the House, the Speaker not being eligible for membership. The Speaker thus lost the right to control legislation on the floor, the most important source of his power.

The Speaker retained the right to make appointments to all other standing committees, but even that privilege was shortly taken from him. In the election of 1910, the Democrats secured control of the House, and when the new majority met in caucus in December 1911, they took from the new Speaker, Champ Clark of Missouri, the right to appoint committees and lodged it instead in the Chairman of the Ways and Means Committee, who in turn was to be elected by the House. Thus the chairman of the Ways and Means Committee, charged with organization of the House, emerged as an extremely powerful legislative leader. The Speaker still retained important elements of power. As presiding officer he could influence the course of debate, and if a popular and influential man, he might have an appreciable effect on legislation. He was, however, no longer the "dictator" of the Reed and Cannon days.

While the new arrangements better suited individual members of the House, it is doubtful whether they constituted altogether desirable reforms from the standpoint of legislative efficiency. The House was a large and unwieldy body, and to perform its duties effectively it required strong discipline. The Speaker had now lost the power to impose such discipline. Also, in certain respects, committee rule was a poor substitute for the Speaker's guiding hand in legislation. It might be argued that a more effective reform would not have reduced the Speaker's power so completely but rather would have made its exercise more open and more responsible to the will of the entire chamber.

The House now looked to the executive rather than to the Speaker for necessary discipline and legislative leadership. The reduction of the Speaker's authority therefore was one factor which tended to increase the power of the President. After 1913, on most occasions the real leader of Congress was the occupant of the White House.

THE SEVENTEENTH AMENDMENT

Election of United States senators by direct popular vote had long been advocated by many who felt that election by the legislatures of the several states was not consonant with the principles of democratic government. A constitutional amendment for this purpose had been offered in the House of Representatives as early as 1828. Forty years later, President Johnson in a special message to Congress had again recommended the reform.

The older conception of the Senate as a body representing the states as such rather than the people had for a long time precluded the change. The Senate also had certain nonlegislative functions in its power to ratify treaties and presidential appointments, which supposedly made it advisable to remove it from direct popular influence.

However, the Civil War had destroyed the idea of the states as sovereign political entities and had virtually ended the idea that they were represented as such in the Senate. The rise of economic unrest in the late nineteenth century also brought the Senate under fire. Agrarian radicals and reformers of the day frequently portrayed the Senate as filled with venal-minded corporation lawyers, retired millionaires, and corrupt state bosses, who represented the will of the "interests" and not that of the people. A cartoon of 1897 pictured the Senate in session as a group of overstuffed moneybags, each marked with the label of the "oil trust," "sugar trust," "money trust," and other corporate interests supposedly represented there.

Though exaggerated, such charges possessed a considerable element of truth. Senator H. B. Payne of Ohio was for years the faithful servant of the Standard Oil Company, and Senator Joseph Foraker of Ohio was later revealed as a pensionary of the same concern. Many senators had risen to high office as railroad and corporation lawyers. Still others—Tom Platt of New York, Matthew Quay of Pennsylvania, Boies Penrose of Pennsylvania, and Roscoe Conkling of New York—were the products of corrupt state political machines and boss politics.

A majority of the senatorial Old Guard were honorable and upright men of high personal integrity, but from the standpoint of agrarian radicals and Progressives they were too generally associated with large business enterprise, too conservative, and too far removed from popular democratic influences. Typical of this group were Marcus A. Hanna of Ohio (generally known as Mark Hanna), a retired steel manufacturer and President McKinley's friend and sponsor; Nelson W. Aldrich, a conservative Rhode Island statesman; John C. Spooner of Wisconsin; and the aristocratic Henry Cabot Lodge of Massachusetts. On the whole, these men were notably resistant to the kind of social legislation so frequently sponsored after 1900 by Progressives. Also, they were for the most part supporters of a high protective tariff and thereby incurred the opposition of agrarian interests in the South and West and of the Progressives, most of whom believed that excessive tariff duties served the interests of the trusts.

First the Populists, then the Bryan Democrats, and finally the liberal Republicans and Progressives advocated direct election of senators in the belief that the upper chamber would thereby become more democratic and more responsive to liberal forces. It was easy to get the necessary constitutional amendment through the House, but more difficult to secure adoption in the Senate, where most members regarded the proposal as a threat to their political security. The House passed the amendment in 1893, 1894, 1898, 1900, and 1902, but each time the measure reached the Senate, it was either ignored or voted down.

Meanwhile, however, the way for the amendment was being

prepared by the passage by various states of preferential primary laws. These statutes allowed the voters of a state to express their preference for United States senator. The state legislature then automatically ratified the vote of the people, in much the same manner that the electoral college acts in the choice of a President. Nebraska established the senatorial primary in 1875, but it was not until the turn of the century that the idea began to spread rapidly. By 1912, twenty-nine states had senatorial primaries, and were therefore in fact if not in theory choosing their senators by direct election. Since senators chosen in this fashion generally became supporters of a formal constitutional amendment for direct election, the Senate's resistance to the change weakened year by year.

The final impetus to reform came from the scandal attendant upon the Illinois legislature's election of William Lorimer to the Senate in 1911. The *Chicago Tribune* shortly published a story revealing that Lorimer's election had been brought about through wholesale bribery in the State assembly. The Senate refused to seat Lorimer, but the incident broke down the remaining resistance in the Senate to direct election. The amendment passed Congress by the necessary two-thirds majority in June 1911 and upon securing the necessary ratification by three-fourths of the states became the Seventeenth Amendment to the Constitution on May 31, 1913.

The composition of the Senate altered substantially after the amendment's adoption, and thereafter political bosses, retired millionaires, and corrupt corporate pensionaries were much less in evidence. To what extent the Seventeenth Amendment was responsible for this change is uncertain. The Progressive revolt destroyed many urban and state political machines, so that the states sent fewer political bosses to the Senate than formerly. Moreover, the growth of a somewhat irrational prejudice against men of great wealth in politics and the enactment of strict state and federal election laws made increasingly difficult the use of private fortune as a key to public office.

A new type of political leader was in the making—one who secured election to public office through the techniques of democratic leadership and mass psychology rather than the craftsmanship of the conservative elder statesman. Behind this development was the growth of vastly superior methods of communication—the press, the telephone, the automobile, and finally the radio. In the face of these instruments the conservative and colorless politician who operated through private contacts and personal manipulation had a much smaller chance of survival. The Seventeenth Amendment undoubtedly facilitated the appearance of the new type of statesman in the Senate, but the technological revolution was of even more importance.

THE PROGRESSIVE ATTACK ON THE JUDICIARY

The judiciary felt the full force of the Progressive attack upon undemocratic, oligarchical government. Well before the end of Theodore Roosevelt's second term, an undercurrent of bitter criticism against the courts was perceptible in America. During Taft's administration criticism broke into the open, and for the next few years liberals in both parties vied with one another in their condemnation of the judiciary. The main focus of attack upon the courts was the fashion in which they had handled social legislation. Decisions such as that in *Lochner v. New York*, invalidating the New York ten-hour bakeshop law, and *Adair v. United States*, declaring void the federal yellow-dog contract statute, had aroused the enmity of Progressives. Vitriolic propagandists denounced the courts as "tools of the trusts," stooges of "entrenched corporate interests," "enemies of the working man" and of the common social welfare. Calmer critics contended that judges were too often disciplined in a purely static conception of constitutional law, that they were in general extremely conservative in economic and social matters, and that as a result the courts acted as a drag upon reform and social progress.

True to the American tradition of formulating an economic or social argument in legalistic terms, the Progressives made a powerful attack upon the constitutionality of judicial review. Much of their argument was historical. The Constitutional Convention, they asserted, had never intended to give the courts the power to declare laws void; *Marbury v. Madison* was sheer judicial usurpation. An amazing amount of ink and oratory was poured forth in support of this claim. For example, a New York lawyer, Louis B. Boudin, contended in a series of highly partisan articles that there were no valid state cases of judicial review prior to 1787; that the members of the Constitutional Convention had never intended to sanction the practice; and that Marshall's argument for judicial review as presented in *Marbury v. Madison* was historically and logically unsound. This argument was answered by a number of thoughtful scholars, among them Andrew C. McLaughlin, Edward S. Corwin, and Charles A. Beard. After examination of the evidence these men all concluded that most members of the Convention apparently had taken judicial review for granted and that the action of the federal judiciary in assuming this function could hardly be construed as usurpation.

Other critics resorted to a theoretical attack upon judicial review. Certain arguments employed were very old, and could have been found in the writings of Jefferson, Jackson, or Lincoln. They may be summarized briefly as follows: (1) Under the doctrine of the separation of powers, there is no more reason for the judiciary to have the final right of constitutional interpretation than for the President or Congress to exercise the power. This was Jackson's old argument. (2) Most decisions holding laws unconstitutional are not in reality interpretations of the Constitution. Almost never does an act of Congress or of a state legislature violate specifically some provision of the written Constitution. Instead the law is found to violate some precept of social or economic philosophy held by the judges. This practice the Progressives denounced as in effect judicial legislation. (3) Five-to-four decisions on crucial constitutional questions are particularly obnoxious. Laws are not supposed to be declared invalid unless they are unconstitutional beyond a reasonable doubt. Yet 5-to-4 decisions reveal that there is actually room for very great doubt. (4) Judicial review is an utterly undemocratic method of settling constitutional questions. Its result is that a few men, removed from popular control, formulate the supreme law. (5) Judges are not fitted to interpret the Constitution in the light of modern social needs. Their training is legal, not economic or social. They tend to settle constitutional questions by legal precedents, most of which were formulated in the light of seventeenth- and eighteenth-century social conditions. Most judges do not understand modern society, and are incapable of formulating constitutional and legal precepts to meet modern conditions. This last argument was a favorite of Louis D. Brandeis and Theodore Roosevelt.

Every conceivable remedy was offered for the alleged evils of judicial review. Some writers, among them Louis B. Boudin, urged the outright abolition of the power of any court to declare any federal or state law void. Others, recognizing that the operation of the federal system required that some agency review state legislation, would have permitted the federal courts to void state legislation but would have abolished their right to declare acts of Congress unconstitutional. Another group, seeking to take advantage of the clause in the Constitution which permits Congress to define the jurisdiction of the federal courts, would have limited the federal judiciary's right to consider certain types of cases involving social and economic legislation. Other critics, among them George W. Norris and Hiram Johnson, would have prohibited the Supreme Court from declaring any act of Congress unconstitutional unless the decision was rendered by at least a 6-to-3 majority. Still other writers, among them Louis D. Brandeis, saw the remedy not in the abolition of judicial review, but rather in the social education of the bar and of the judiciary and in the growth of judicial self-restraint.

THE JUDICIAL RECALL

From a political viewpoint the most significant remedies advanced were those for the recall of judicial decisions on constitutional questions, and for the recall of judges. The two ideas came into prominence in Progressive circles about 1910, and Roosevelt, now out of office and associate editor of the *Outlook*, championed both reforms. Many other Progressives, among them LaFollette, Beveridge, and Norris, gave them support.

The recall of judges was the first of these proposals to enter the field of acute political controversy. In 1911 Congress took under consideration a joint resolution which would have admitted Arizona and New Mexico as states to the Union. The state constitution which Arizona had submitted to Congress provided for the recall of state judges by a majority of the popular vote. The provision precipitated considerable discussion on the floor of Congress, where it was hotly defended by Progressives in both houses. On August 11, 1911, Congress passed the resolution, but with the provision that the legislature of Arizona at the first state election should submit to the voters a constitutional amendment which, if adopted, would except all judicial officers from the recall.

There was grave question of the constitutional validity of this provision. In effect, it erected a condition subsequent to Arizona's admission, an issue which had been discussed at the time of the Missouri Compromise. Except where a property right of the federal government is concerned, there is no constitutional way in which Congress can force a state, once in the Union, to carry out the provisions of a condition subsequent. The effect of such agreements, if fulfilled, would be to create a Union of unequal states, as had been pointed out in the debates on the admission of Missouri.[2]

---

[2] In *Stearns v. Minnesota* (1900), the Court held constitutional a condition subsequent in the act admitting Minnesota to the Union, whereby Congress reserved the right to determine subsequently the disposition of federal public lands in the state. See also the discussion of the Missouri Compromise debates on pp. 251-256.

President Taft sent the resolution back to Congress with a veto. His veto did not mention the constitutional objections to imposing a condition subsequent upon Arizona but was based solely upon his objections to the recall of judges, which he termed "so pernicious in its effect, so destructive of the independence of the judiciary, so likely to subject the rights of the individual to the possible tyranny of a popular majority" that he felt obliged to "disapprove a constitution containing it." Recall, he held, would subject the judiciary to "momentary gusts of popular passion" and so destroy democratic processes. Taft went on to condemn radical solutions of the judicial problem on the ground that they were unnecessary. There were but few hidebound conservative judicial decisions, he said, and they did "not call for radical action."

Taft's veto forced Arizona to remove the constitutional provision in question. After admission, however, Arizona promptly amended her constitution to incorporate an even more drastic provision for the recall of judges. This provision was now entirely beyond the reach of Congress.

In 1912, attention shifted to the recall of judicial decisions, a proposed reform thought by many advocates to rest upon sounder grounds than that of the recall of judges. Colorado had a constitutional provision by which the people of the state could vote by referendum upon the constitutional issues involved in any decision of a Colorado court holding a state law unconstitutional. In January 1912, Roosevelt endorsed the Colorado plan in the *Outlook*. He also urged that the next New York state constitutional convention provide that the people be empowered to decide by popular ballot "what the law of the land shall be" in cases where "the courts of the state have refused to allow the people to establish justice and equity." Roosevelt conceded that when the federal Supreme Court finally passed upon a question of constitutionality, its interpretation ought to be allowed to stand. Prior to such a decision, however, the opinion of the people as to "what is or is not constitutional" should be final. A few days later Roosevelt endorsed this idea before the Ohio constitutional convention.

Roosevelt's sponsorship of this measure shocked many conservatives in both parties. It was in part responsible for his break with Philander Knox, Lodge, Root, and Taft, and for the fight inside the Republican national convention in June 1912, in which Roosevelt lost the nomination and bolted with his Progressive supporters to form the "Bull Moose" Party.

Judicial recall was subjected to thoughtful criticism by competent students of government and constitutional law, many of whom raised serious objections. Walter F. Dodd, a specialist in state government and constitutional law, pointed out that any attempt to force a popular interpretation of the federal Constitution overlooked the implications of Article VI of the Constitution. That provision bound state judges to uphold the federal Constitution regardless of anything in their own state constitutions and laws. Hence, it would be unconstitutional to force a state judge to accept a popular decision as to the constitutionality of a state statute, if that decision conflicted with the judge's conviction as to the requirements of the federal Constitution. It was this difficulty which caused the Progressive Party in 1912 to recommend only that decisions of state courts declaring state acts void under the provisions of state constitutions be subject to recall.

THE JUDICIARY ACT OF 1914

While "recall of decisions" gradually lost ground, a more moderate reform was finding support on the floor of Congress. Under the Judiciary Act of 1789, appeals could be taken from state courts to federal courts on Constitutional questions only when the state court had denied a "right, title, or claim" arising under the federal Constitution, treaties, or laws. As the reader is already aware, the intent of this section had been to insure the supremacy of federal law over state law. Were any claim under federal law denied by a state court, an appeal could be taken to the federal judiciary.[3] But no provision was made for appeals when a state court admitted a claim under federal law, since such action was not thought to be necessary.

This situation altered after 1900, when in numerous instances state courts began to find the law of their own states unconstitutional as violations of the due process clause of the Fourteenth Amendment. Since this was technically an admission of a claim raised under the federal Constitution, no appeal could be taken to the federal courts under existing law. This protected a reactionary state judge in an adverse decision on state legislation, for if the highest court in a state handed down such a decision, there was no way in which it could be overruled even by a state constitutional convention. This situation threatened to bring about a new regionalism in constitutional law. A certain type of state statute might be held constitutional un-

---

[3] See the discussion of the Judiciary Act of 1789 on pp. 162–164.

der the federal Constitution as interpreted in New York, void as interpreted in New Jersey, constitutional as interpreted in Illinois, and so on. In *Cohens v. Virginia*, Marshall had dwelt upon the danger of this evil, and the necessity of avoiding it through a system of appeals to the federal judiciary on constitutional questions. The same problem had now appeared in a new form, and there appeared to be no remedy available, unless Congress should by law broaden the basis of appeals to the federal courts.

The problem was given pointed expression in 1911, when the New York Court of Appeals in *Ives v. South Buffalo Railway Company* found the New York state employers' liability act unconstitutional under the Fourteenth Amendment. The opinion rejected with fine sarcasm the idea that social or economic objectives could have anything to do with the constitutionality of a law. Roosevelt, speaking through the *Outlook*, quoted "an eminent jurist" as saying that the case was "one more illustration of the principle that in many American courts property is more sacred than life." The decision was also attacked by eminent lawyers and students of constitutional law. Professor Ernst Freund of the University of Chicago Law School observed that "there is good reason to believe that the Supreme Court would sustain such a law." Shortly afterward, the supreme courts of both New Jersey and Washington held similar statutes to be constitutional. This absurd situation led the House Judiciary Committee to observe that "the Fourteenth Amendment means one thing on the east bank of the Hudson and the opposite thing on the west bank."

The remedy was a federal statute to permit appeals from state to federal courts on all questions arising under the federal Constitution and laws, regardless of whether or not the state court upheld a claim advanced under the federal Constitution. In 1911, the American Bar Association drafted a bill giving the Supreme Court the authority to accept writs of error from state courts in cases where the highest state court had sustained a federal right, as well as in those cases in which that right had been denied. The House promptly passed the bill by an overwhelming majority. The Senate Judiciary Committee, however, while approving of the general principle of the bill, amended the measure to provide for appeal upon writs of certiorari instead of writs of error.[4] This change was

---

[4] In modern federal practice, a writ of certiorari is a device for requesting review by a higher court, in cases where the higher court has a discretionary right to accept or reject the appeal. A writ of error, on the other hand, is a means of securing review by a higher court where federal law grants the appeal as of right.

made to provide the necessary review on constitutional questions, but at the same time to protect the already overloaded Court against a variety of other types of appeal. With this change, the Senate passed the bill, but the House failed to act on the Senate version. During 1913 the measure was crowded aside by the rush of administration legislation, but conservatives and liberals alike were agreed upon the desirability of the reform. Under the sponsorship of Senator Elihu Root of New York the bill quietly became law on December 23, 1914.

CONSTITUTIONAL REFORM IN THE STATES

Writing in 1914, a student of state government concluded "that it can no longer be doubted that a veritable constitutional revolution is sweeping through state government." Between 1900 and 1920 more than 1500 constitutional amendments were adopted in the various states of the Union, and in the period between 1900 and 1913 seven states adopted entirely new constitutions.

The driving force behind this movement was primarily the first article of the Progressives' faith: "let the people rule." Nearly all the constitutional changes adopted were designed to give the people a more direct share in popular government. Even staunch conservatives were affected by this attitude, as Elihu Root's speech before the New York state constitutional convention in 1915 bore witness. New York, Root said, had two governments, one the visible constitutional government of the people, the other the invisible government of party bosses. It was the invisible government that actually ruled the state. "The ruler of the state during the greater part of the forty years of my acquaintance with the state government has not been any man authorized by the Constitution or by the law." Instead, he said, the state had been ruled by Senators Roscoe Conkling and Thomas C. Platt, the latter for many years head of the New York state Republican machine. Root concluded that there was "a deep and sullen and long continued resentment at being governed thus by men not of the people's choosing," and he asked the convention to strip the "irresponsible autocracy of its indefensible and unjust and undemocratic control of government," and restore it to the people.

Root's words expressed a prevalent profound distrust of the established organs of state government and a belief that state legislatures could no longer be trusted with the control of public policy to the same extent as formerly. It will be recalled that early state constitutions were mere skeletal outlines of government, which had generally left the various assemblies free to do almost as they pleased. During the course of the nineteenth century there had been a growing tendency to impose constitutional controls upon the people's chosen representatives. In the last two decades of the century, in particular, a deep suspicion of legislative honesty and capacity, induced by repeated revelations of corruption and scandal in legislative halls, had grown up in the public mind. Too often the people of a state had seen it demonstrated that their government was in reality controlled by a venal party machine subservient to the interests of a great railroad, an industrial corporation, or an urban boss. They had learned to their sorrow that many a seat at Albany, Richmond, Harrisburg, or Springfield had a price—a price which more than one special interest was willing to pay.

In an effort to check legislative dishonesty and "restore government to the people," the states after 1900 adopted a growing number of amendments which imposed large restrictions upon the scope of legislative authority, competence, and discretion, and which specified legislative procedure and function in great detail. Large areas of special legislation were withdrawn from the control of the assembly entirely. Thus quite generally the power to fix rates for public utilities was handed to special commissions. Other amendments fixed tax schedules and specified permissible kinds of taxation, while still others forbade the enactment of special legislation for private interest groups. There were new provisions which established county seats, drew the boundaries of assembly districts, or fixed the salaries of public officials. Other provisions set up state factory inspection systems, limited the length of the working day for women, or set up workmen's compensation systems. Thus the typical state constitution came to resemble a statute book, mainly because the people no longer trusted the legislature to protect their interests or to exercise the degree of discretion which had once been accorded it.

The mass of restrictive and statutory material written into state constitutions made these constitutions sometimes run to extraordinary lengths. The Virginia constitution of 1776 was but seven pages long. By contrast, the Oklahoma constitution of 1907 covered fifty-eight pages of fine print totaling nearly forty thousand words. Ohio's constitution of 1912 was more than twenty thousand words in length, and Michigan's constitution of 1908 was about the same size. Frequent amendment often greatly increased the length of the original document. For example, California's constitution of 1879 was amended eighty-three times between 1894 and 1914, so that by the latter date it had reached a length of more than forty thousand words, nearly double its original size.

Through the initiative and referendum, constitutional reformers sought to encourage the people to write their own legislation directly over the heads of the assembly, or to veto the laws passed by their representatives. These twin instruments of direct popular participation in the legislative process were first advocated by the Populists and Bryan in 1896. In 1898, South Dakota wrote the initiative into its constitution by an amendment which permitted the people to present legislation to the assembly by petition. The legislature was permitted either to enact the law or to present an alternative proposal to the people. Oregon followed with a more famous reform in 1902, by which both constitutional amendments and ordinary legislation might be proposed by petition. These, in turn, were required to be submitted to the voters of the state for acceptance or rejection in a general election. This provision became a model for most states subsequently adopting the initiative and referendum. By 1914, eighteen states had adopted the initiative and referendum for ordinary legislation, and twelve of these permitted the device to be used for constitutional amendment as well.

Another device, the recall, was intended to place popular controls upon executive officers. A small percentage of the voters, usually about 8 per cent in statewide elections, could petition for a special election, in which the electorate could decide whether or not a specified official was to be removed from office. Oregon pioneered in this reform also, with a constitutional amendment adopted in 1908. By 1915, some eleven states had followed Oregon's lead, and seven of these permitted the recall of judges.

A highly effective instrument in the war against boss-dominated government was the direct primary, developed after 1903 as a substitute for county and state nominating conventions. In the rural society of mid-nineteenth-century America the convention had been a fairly effective instrument of popular will, but in the great urban centers of a later day it became subject to manipulation and abuse. By the late nineteenth century, state and local conventions were frequently controlled by the meanest type of local boss. The delegates, who usually included corrupt political hangers-on, saloonkeepers, brothel operators, and the like, were mere dummies assembled in convention to ratify the will of their masters. Meanwhile, beginning in 1867, a number of counties scattered across the country, most of them in the Middle West or South, adopted the direct primary by voluntary party rule.

A Wisconsin statute of 1903 abolished the state party convention as a nominating device and substituted the primary election, in which all the voters of a political party could nominate their chosen candidates by ballot. The movement thereafter spread rapidly. By 1912, thirteen states had adopted the state-wide direct primary, while by 1938 only two states retained the convention for all state nominations. In most cases the primary election was established by an act of the legislature, no constitutional amendment being deemed necessary; yet the change altered drastically the "living constitution" of state government.

These "radical" experiments in direct democracy were destined to realize neither the hopes of Progressives nor the fears of conservatives. Many a Progressive leader looked upon the initiative and referendum, the recall, and the primary as the greatest constitutional reforms since the days of 1787; through them the rascals would be swept from office and the intelligent will of an enlightened people would find expression. Some frightened conservatives, on the other hand, thought that direct democracy heralded the end of lawful representative government. President Taft said of the initiative that the "ultimate issue" was "socialism," and he denounced the recall of judges as giving "enormous power for evil" into the hands of corrupt bosses and "stirrers-up of social hate."

Actually no decisive change for good or evil followed upon these democratic reforms. Ordinary legislative processes went on much as before, while the laws passed by the people through the initiative and referendum were on the whole neither better nor worse than those of an earlier day. As for the recall, it was seldom used to rid government of the scoundrel in office. The most successful venture in direct democracy was the primary election, which, although it did not guarantee the nomination of superior candidates for office, could at least disrupt the smooth-running machine of a party boss who outraged public opinion too flagrantly. There has been a general decline in the influence and importance of corrupt party "bosses" since 1900, and municipal politics are certainly less corrupt today than they were in 1890. The party primary and improved governmental machinery have been to some extent responsible.

It was perhaps a weakness of the Progressive movement that it concentrated too much upon the reform of the mechanics of government, and too little upon the deep-seated social and economic institutions which gave rise to governmental corruption. The party boss was too often mere scum upon the surface of urban poverty, and the corrupt or stupid legislator merely the too-accurate image of special interest groups, organized minorities, or even deficient public intelligence or morality. These were not evils to be cured by stripping the Speaker of his powers or abolishing the party convention. Within its limits the Progressive movement accomplished certain desirable political and social reforms, but it did not bring about a wholesale regeneration of the entire social order, as certain ardent Progressives had hoped.

There was, in fact, little real radicalism in the Progressive era, in spite of the charges which frightened conservatives threw at liberal reformers. The Progressive movement expressed a widespread desire for certain controls upon great wealth and special interest, for certain mild social reforms, and for more direct democracy, but there was almost no wish to overturn the foundations of private property and constitutional government. There were no comprehensive theories damning the social order as totally beyond redemption. Rather the Progressive movement belonged to the stream of social reform which had begun in Jeffersonian Democracy and had found subsequent expression in the triumph of Jackson, the early Republican Party, and the Populist movement, and which would lead eventually to Wilson's New Freedom and ultimately to the New Deal. This tradition of reform accepted all the values of the "American dream" and sought to bring that dream closer to reality for the mass of Americans. Therein lay the source both of its weakness and of its recurrent vitality.

Chapter

24

Woodrow Wilson and the New Freedom

THE RISE of the Progressive faction in the Republican Party was climaxed by an open break in Republican ranks on the eve of the 1912 presidential election. Theodore Roosevelt, in a dramatic return to the national political arena, bolted the Republican convention in Chicago, and presently accepted the presidential nomination of the newly formed Progressive or "Bull Moose" Party. The Republicans renominated Taft, but Roosevelt's candidacy divided the Republican vote at the polls and thereby assured the election to the presidency of the Democratic candidate, Woodrow Wilson.

Two developments of especial significance for constitutional history occurred in Wilson's first administration. First, Wilson developed a new technique of executive leadership in initiating and effecting the passage of legislation. Second, Wilson brought about the enactment of an extensive reform program which was at once the culmination and a partial refutation of the ideals of liberal nationalism.

WILSON'S CONCEPTION OF THE PRESIDENT AS A PRIME MINISTER

Wilson was a college president turned politician. His practical experience in statecraft was confined to a two-year term as governor of New Jersey, but he was a brilliant historian and political theorist, and he had strong convictions concerning the President's relations with Congress. In 1883, while still a young university professor, he had published his *Congressional Government*, a study of the federal legislature. He had concluded that Congress had failed in its task of public leadership and had shown itself incapable of coping with the complex problems of modern society. Wilson had also expressed the belief that an effective program of legislation would require presidential formulation and leadership. He had condemned the doctrine of the separation of powers as inhibiting strong presidential leadership in legislation and had expressed admiration for the British parliamentary system with its automatic co-operation between executive and legislature. Parliament, he had observed, did not really originate legislation; it merely ratified or rejected the Cabinet's recommendations, seldom refusing its assent. This resulted, Wilson had concluded, in strong concerted leadership in government and in an absence of the paralysis so frequently present in relations between the American President and Congress.

Once in the White House, Wilson undertook to model his relations with Congress upon the British principle of executive ascendancy in legislation. He believed that this involved no unconstitutional usurpation of power. On the contrary, he found his authority to control legislation in Article II, Section 3, of the Constitution, which instructs the President to recommend to Congress such measures as the President judges necessary. Obviously Wilson's capacity to imitate the British parliamentary system was limited by the fact that he could not prorogue Congress or "go to the country" if it failed to do his bidding. He believed, however, that his own prestige and the Democratic Party's eagerness to achieve a successful reform program would compensate for the constitutional limits upon his coercive power.

In accordance with the foregoing ideas, Wilson presented Congress with a series of positive legislative measures, each framed to deal with one of the various problems that he proposed to solve. In co-operation with his intimate associates, various experts, and Democratic leaders in Congress, he worked out in careful detail a number of specific bills to cover each point in his program. The Federal Reserve Act, for example, was substantially the product of co-operation between Wilson, Representative Carter Glass of Virginia, and the economist H. Parker Willis, in consultation with various bankers, monetary specialists, and congressmen. The Underwood Tariff Act was evolved in numerous conferences between

Wilson, Glass, Senator LaFollette, and Representative Oscar Underwood of Alabama. The Clayton Anti-Trust Act and the Federal Trade Commission Acts were worked out by Wilson with the assistance of his intimate personal adviser, Colonel Edward M. House, the labor leader Samuel Gompers, Glass, and various congressmen.

When an important bill was ready for action, Wilson customarily appeared in person before Congress, delivered a short incisive message dealing solely with the measure in question, and urged its immediate passage. In thus appearing in person before Congress, Wilson revived a practice in disuse for over a hundred years. Washington and Adams had appeared personally before Congress, but Jefferson and his successors had ceased to follow this practice. Wilson's return to the custom had the effect of demonstrating his sharp concern and his immediate interest in the legislation he recommended.

Immediately following such a message, administration supporters introduced the bill into both houses of Congress. Although the President technically could not introduce legislation into Congress, all concerned knew that the measure in question was largely Wilson's own. The term "administration bill," occasionally heard in Roosevelt's time, now became common to describe measures formulated by the President. An administration bill was given the right of way by steering committees in both houses, and hence stood every chance of emerging as law. Unless the Democratic members of Congress wished to break openly with their own President, they were obliged to support the proposal.

While an administration bill was in process of passage, Wilson maintained a steady pressure upon Congress through frequent conferences with Senate and House leaders. In the early days of his administration, when his great reform program was being enacted, he appeared several times in the President's Room, off the Senate Chamber, to confer with Democratic leaders. It was plainly understood that he would not tolerate unreasonable delay or any substantial alteration in the text of a proposed law. When occasionally rebellion threatened an administration bill, Wilson did not hesitate to take the strongest measures to whip Congress into line. When, for example, he became convinced that various lobbyists were delaying the passage of the Underwood tariff bill, he went over the head of Congress to the people. In a dramatic message to the press, he attacked the "sinister interests" interfering with enactment of the law. Opposition to the measure thereupon collapsed, and the bill became law without further delay.

Wilson's theory of the President as a kind of prime minister worked out surprisingly well in practice, as even his opponents conceded. For a time he established something very like the British parliamentary system in Washington. Primarily, however, Wilson's success as a legislative leader rested upon his extraordinary capacity to rally national popular support to the ideals and the symbols he evoked, rather than upon his inadequate constitutional position. While Wilson made use of patronage and party discipline, he lacked the British prime minister's power to coerce the legislature with the threat of parliamentary dissolution followed by a general election. There is some evidence that Wilson considered the threat of his resignation as a coercive device when Congress in 1914 at first refused to pass his bill to equalize Panama shipping tolls, and again in 1917, when Congress rejected the armed merchant ship act. Resignation would at best have been an inadequate constitutional device with which to force his program upon Congress, but fortunately for Wilson's early success, his control of Congress before 1918 was so complete that his leadership was seldom challenged.

To many Americans the unprecedented position that Wilson exercised in the initiation and passage of legislation seemed at variance with the soundest traditions of the American constitutional system. Presidential control of legislation, they held, violated the principle of the separation of powers and usurped the functions of Congress. The ancient fear of executive prerogative and dictatorship was still very much alive in many minds, and a President who openly made his office more powerful than Congress seemed headed straight for dictatorship and despotism. From Wilson's time to the era of Richard Nixon many a politician declaimed against the new tyranny of the presidential office. Even those who recognized the necessity for strong presidential leadership at times experienced an uneasy feeling that a republic ought not to permit the concentration of so much power in the hands of one man.

In reality, Wilson's power was an expression of the strong forces of democratic nationalism at work in the nation. The common man had great aspirations and great fears—for his own welfare and for that of his country. He demanded that these be translated into some kind of positive political program, and he looked to Washington for statesmen who could do this. But as Wilson himself had observed, Congress was by its very nature incapable of responding to this demand. It was divided by partisan politics; and its various members, dependent upon local support for re-election, were for the most part concerned with local and sectional issues. They tended to view national issues not in the light of the total national welfare but in the light of sectional interest or the interests of constituents who might have influence upon their political fortunes. A strong President labored under no such disabilities. He was elected by the whole people in a great contest staged every four years with such dramatic emphasis that the nation's very future seemed to turn upon its outcome. The President, along with the flag and the Constitution, had become a symbol of the sovereignty and greatness of the United States. It was not difficult for a strong President to turn this situation to his own advantage.

Theodore Roosevelt was the first President after Lincoln to recognize the full strength of his position. His stewardship theory, which held the President to be the supreme guardian and protector of the nation's welfare, was a realistic analysis of popular sentiment about the presidential office. Roosevelt had the dramatic qualities and forceful personality of a great leader. Had he possessed a clear, consistent, and positive program of national reform, he probably would have had little difficulty in forcing Congress to accept his demands.

Wilson never formally enunciated Roosevelt's stewardship theory, but it is clear that he accepted the idea completely. He had the same understanding of the manner in which the common man now looked to the President for leadership, and he, too, had remarkable abilities as a popular leader. Further, he did what Roosevelt had failed to do—he presented Congress with a well-defined reform program, with the full understanding that his own prestige as a national leader was so great that the men on Capitol Hill could not refuse his demands. There was no intimation of despotism in Wilson's position, but many people, then and later, were slow to understand the profound difference between tyranny and strong executive leadership under responsible constitutional controls.

THE GROWTH OF EXECUTIVE ORDINANCE POWER

While Wilson successfully asserted in dramatic fashion the new technique of presidential leadership in legislation, other forces were at work to break down the doctrine of the separation of powers and to make the President a lawmaker in his own right. In theory, the execution of laws was a function entirely distinct from their enactment, and the legislature could not delegate any part of its lawmaking powers to the President. Actually, however, the line between lawmaking and administration had never been drawn so clearly as the niceties of constitutional theory appeared to require. It was impossible for Congress to draft a law in such detail as to cover every possible contingency arising under it. Congress had early recognized this fact by delegating a certain amount of minor "administrative discretion" to the President, Also, certain statutes, among them the Non-Intercourse Act of 1809, had made their enforcement contingent upon the appearance of certain conditions which the President was empowered to recognize. With a few important exceptions, however, congressional delegation of power to the executive had remained narrow in scope throughout most of the nineteenth century.

After 1890, however, there developed a trend toward the enactment of measures granting a much broader delegation of discretionary power to the executive. In addition, many of the new statutes carried with them a certain amount of authority to formulate policy. The reason for these developments has already been suggested: the modern problems of state were frequently so complex and so technical that they could be understood only by the expert. Furthermore, the administrative expert had to be granted a certain degree of discretion if he were to function efficiently. To meet these conditions Congress often found it advisable merely to sketch in the major objectives and policies aimed at in a statute, leaving the choice of means as well as minor decisions of policy to the executive.

In a series of important decisions between 1892 and 1911 the Court recognized this situation and substantially enlarged the doctrine of administrative discretion. *Field v. Clark* (1892), the first case of this kind, arose out of a provision in the Tariff Act of 1890, providing for reciprocal trade agreements with various nations, under which the United States would permit the free importation of sugar, molasses, coffee, tea, and hides. The statute also authorized the President to suspend free import and to levy a prescribed schedule of duties against the goods of any nation whenever in his opinion he was satisfied that the country in question was imposing "reciprocally unequal or unreasonable" duties on imports from the United States. A number of importers presently attacked this last provision as unconstitutional, contending that the law delegated legislative power to the President, and was therefore invalid because it was in conflict with Article I, Section 1, of the Constitution, which states that "all legislative powers herein granted shall be vested in a Congress of the United States, which shall consist of a Senate and a House of Representatives."

Justice Harlan's opinion rejected this plea. He admitted that the outright delegation of legislative power was unconstitutional: "That Congress cannot delegate legislative power to the President is a principle universally recognized as vital to the integrity and maintenance of the system of government ordained by the Constitution." But, said Harlan, the act in question did not violate this rule, for it left nothing "involving the expediency or the just operation" of the law to the President. The suspension of existing duties was absolutely required when the executive "ascertained the existence of a particular fact." Harlan concluded that "it cannot be said that in ascertaining that fact and in issuing his proclamation, in obedience to the legislative will, he exercised the function of making laws."

Thus the Court gave formal recognition to a distinction long existing in practice—that between the mere ascertainment of fact and actual policy making. This distinction became a fundamental one in the Court's subsequent attempts to distinguish between lawful and unlawful delegations of authority to the executive.

In *Buttfield v. Stranahan* (1904) the Court recognized that Congress might lawfully delegate to the executive certain policy-making decisions of a minor variety. The Tea Inspection Act of 1897 had given the Secretary of the Treasury the power to appoint a Board of Tea Inspectors, who were authorized to recommend certain standards in tea grading and to inspect and grade all imported tea. Tea which the board rejected as being below the standards thus established was to be denied entry by the customs authorities. This act went far beyond the delegation considered in *Field v. Clark*, for the executive was here empowered to fix standards which could then be enforced as law.

Did not this involve policy making, and hence an unlawful delegation of legislative power? The Court thought not. Congress, said Justice White, had fixed the "primary standard" and policy for the tea board to follow, and this was sufficient to insure the law's constitutionality. "Congress legislated on the subject as far as was reasonably practicable, and from the necessities of the case was compelled to leave to executive officials the duty of bringing about the result pointed out by the statute. To deny the power of Congress to delegate such a duty would, in effect, amount but to declaring that the plenary power vested in Congress to regulate foreign commerce could not be efficaciously exerted." In other words, the Court recognized that some policy making of a minor variety by the executive was legal "from the necessities of the case." It was sufficient for Congress to indicate its will and to fix the broad outlines of policy; the rest could lawfully be left to the executive.

In 1911, in the famous case of *United States v. Grimaud*, the Court extended the doctrine of administrative discretion to recognize that administrative rulings had the force of law and that violations of them might be punished as infractions of a criminal statute, if Congress should so provide. An act of 1891 had authorized the President to set aside public lands in any state or territory as forest reservations. In 1905, another statute transferred the administration of such lands to the Secretary of Agriculture and empowered him to make rules and regulations for their occupancy and use. The act further made violations of the secretary's rules subject to a fine of not more than $500 and imprisonment for not more than a year, or both. Under the authority of the 1905 act, the Department of Agriculture had issued certain regulations to limit grazing on such reserves. It was the constitutionality of these regulations which now came before the Court.

Justice Joseph R. Lamar in a brief opinion cited *Field v. Clark* and *Buttfield v. Stranahan*, and then concluded that "the authority to make administrative rules is not a delegation of legislative power, nor are such rules raised from an administrative level to a legislative character because the violation thereof is punishable as a public offense."

In short, by 1911 the Court had accepted as constitutional the delegation of a large element of administrative discretion to the executive. In theory, to be sure, the doctrine of the separation of powers remained unimpaired, and in each case that thereafter came before the Court, it carefully distinguished between "administrative discretion" and outright delegation of legislative power, the latter still being pronounced unconstitutional. In fact, however, this carefully drawn distinction was weakened by the Court's willingness to accept as constitutional delegations of authority far broader than those in the early constitutional period. It is significant that the Court spoke repeatedly of the "practical necessities of the case," thereby implying that the complexity and technical character of modern administrative processes required that Congress merely state broad objectives and major elements of policy and leave both detail and minor policy determination to administrative discretion. The theory that outright legislative power could not be delegated was certainly not dead, as the Court's denunciation of the National

Industrial Recovery Act in 1935 was to demonstrate. But from Wilson's time onward, presidents were to exercise something suspiciously like legislative power.

THE NEW BOARDS AND COMMISSIONS

The tendency of Congress to delegate quasi-legislative authority to the executive greatly increased during Wilson's presidency. Several of the statutes in Wilson's reform program made large grants of discretion to certain agencies of the executive. In many instances Congress created new executive boards and commissions for the express purpose of exercising control over certain areas of policy of a quasi-legislative character. Resort to the commission was apparently inspired in part by the judicial blessing which the Supreme Court bestowed upon the Interstate Commerce Commission between 1907 and 1914 and by the success of the Commission in administering the rail rate structure during that period.

Wilson's administration saw the establishment of no less than seven important commissions, not including the various wartime emergency boards erected in 1917 and 1918. The Federal Reserve Board, the first important new body to be established, was given extensive discretionary powers to control banking and credit, including the right to raise and lower the rediscount rate and to buy and sell federal bonds at its own discretion in order to control long-term credit operations.

The Federal Trade Commission, set up to administer antitrust legislation, was patterned closely upon the Interstate Commerce Commission. It had the same power to hold hearings, investigate complaints, and issue "cease and desist" orders to persons found to be carrying on unfair or monopolistic trade practices. Presumably, also, the act setting up the Board provided for narrow review, for the Board's findings of fact were to be considered prima facie true in any appeals to the courts.

The Federal Farm Loan Board, set up in 1916, was given extensive control over rural credits. The United States Shipping Board, erected in 1916, was given authority to construct and operate a merchant marine. The Railway Labor Board, established under the Transportation Act of 1920, had authority to mediate labor disputes. The Tariff Commission of 1916, on the other hand, was little more than an advisory body, for it could do nothing more than recommend certain policies to Congress. The Comptroller General of the United States, established by the Budget Act of 1921, was a kind of one-man commission supervising budgetary matters.

The anomalous and contradictory position of executive commissions, which exercised the functions of all three departments and yet belonged completely to none, shortly gave rise to a number of perplexing constitutional questions. Were the personnel of the various boards to be considered as a part of the executive department and as such subject to the President's orders and to his removal power? The members of the Interstate Commerce Commission, the Federal Reserve Board, the Federal Trade Commission, and the Farm Loan Board were appointed by the President with the consent of the Senate, and the boards in question were charged with the administration of the law. This implied that the boards were a part of the executive department and thereby subject to presidential control. However, the first Interstate Commerce Act had fixed the terms of commission members at seven years and had provided that they might be removed for "inefficiency, neglect of duty, or malfeasance in office." While this provision recognized the President's removal power, it placed limits upon it by enumerating the permissible causes for removal. Moreover, the fact that the statute fixed the term of office of members also constituted an implied limitation upon the President, since other subordinate executive officers were appointed for indefinite terms and for presidential pleasure. The acts creating the Federal Trade Commission and the Tariff Commission also fixed the commissioners' term of office and carried the same removal provisions as did the Interstate Commerce Act. The Federal Reserve Act, on the other hand, although it fixed the term of board members at ten years, said nothing about the President's removal power, while the act creating the Farm Loan Board fixed members' terms at seven years, but specified removal "for cause."

More significantly, the Transportation Act of 1920 made Railway Labor Board members removable for "neglect of duty or malfeasance in office, but for no other cause." This apparently implied congressional intent to confer upon the Board a large degree of independence from the President. The Budget Act of 1920 went even further and made the Comptroller General removable only by joint resolution of Congress; that official was thus placed entirely beyond presidential control.

The issue of presidential control over executive commissions ultimately involved a much broader constitutional question. If federal boards were mere subordinate executive agencies, not different in position from other government bureaus and officers, what was the point of creating them in the first place? Why not delegate power to a subordinate official in an already existing department? But if commissions were something more than mere subordinate agencies, was not the logical result an unconstitutional decentralization of executive power? Conceivably Congress could ultimately create a number of federal boards, charge them with the administration of the whole mass of federal law, and make the boards responsible to Congress rather than the President, thereby bringing about a revolutionary destruction of the President's powers and the establishment of a parliamentary government.

There is little evidence that the full import of these questions has ever been considered seriously, either by Congress or by the executive. There has been no inclination to drive the theoretical issues inherent in commission government to their logical extremities. It has never appeared necessary to answer categorically the question of whether or not an independent commission constitutes a theoretical violation of the doctrine of the separation of powers.

WILSON'S REFORM PROGRAM: THE NEW FREEDOM

Wilson sounded the keynote of his economic philosophy when he asserted during the 1912 campaign that "a comparatively small number of men control the raw materials, the water power, the railroads, the larger credits of the country, and, by agreements handed around among themselves, they control prices." Wilson, in other words, had never reconciled himself to the new industrial order. He opposed all trusts and monopolies as thoroughly bad, and in particular he viewed the integrated control of industry and finance by the great banks of New York as an unmitigated evil. Obviously there was something of agrarian radicalism in Wilson's intellectual heritage: he was the spiritual descendant of Thomas Jefferson, John Taylor of Caroline, William Jennings Bryan, and the Populists.

Wilson believed firmly in the continuance of a *laissez-faire* economy and a free market in America. The continuance of such an economy, he argued, could be assured only by ruthlessly smashing the great trusts, monopolies, and financial concentrations, which had already made great inroads upon the old free market of small entrepreneurs. The great trusts must be broken up, and the control of the great New York financial houses over money and banking must be ended. Only in this fashion could free enterprise and economic democracy be restored and preserved.

Wilson's uncompromising hostility toward all trusts and financial concentration was sharply different from the Progressive position.

Most Progressives did not condemn combination and monopoly as such, but rather the perversions of power practiced by certain "malefactors of great wealth." Roosevelt had drawn a distinction between "good" and "bad" trusts, a distinction accepted by the Supreme Court in the Standard Oil and American Tobacco cases. Most Progressives had been ready to recognize that certain giant combinations were inevitable, even desirable, provided only that they were subjected to appropriate governmental controls. But Wilson, like Brandeis, thought bigness as such to be an evil, and he viewed great combinations of financial and industrial power as incompatible with a free economy and a free society.

Wilson was by training a constitutional conservative. Like Jefferson and John Taylor before him he feared centralized government as well as centralized economic power. This meant that he rejected the liberal nationalist argument for the steady expansion of the sphere of national sovereignty as a means to solving new social and economic problems. In his *Constitutional Government*, a series of lectures published in 1908, he deplored the tendency to create new spheres of federal sovereignty under the guise of old established constitutional powers. He also regarded the rise of a federal police power as a subtle and pernicious perversion of the limited and derived character of federal sovereignty. He agreed with Chief Justice Fuller that a steady expansion of national authority by indirection would end in the destruction of the federal nature of the Union.

In theory, constitutional scruples of this kind should have confronted Wilson with some difficulties, once he sought to translate his economic philosophy into a legislative program. This difficulty was partially resolved in practice, however, by Wilson's heavy emphasis upon tariff reform and monetary legislation as his principal weapons in the attack upon financial combination and monopoly. Wilson believed that general downward revision of the tariff would strike a severe blow at monopoly by reintroducing international competition. Monetary and banking reform he looked upon as necessary to break the control of the New York banks over the country's monetary and banking system. Neither tariff reform nor revision of the banking and monetary system offered serious constitutional difficulties even to a constitutional conservative. Passage of the Underwood Tariff law, revising tariff duties downward about 30 per cent, and of the Federal Reserve Act therefore became cardinal points in his program. It seems clear, also, that Wilson's constitutional difficulties were reduced by the fact that he became somewhat less conservative in his constitutional philosophy once he was confronted as President with a variety of imperative national problems which could be solved only by the liberal interpretation of federal sovereignty.

The Federal Reserve Act, sponsored by Wilson and introduced into Congress in June 1913, became law on December 23, 1913, establishing extensive controls over the national banking system. The law created a seven-man Federal Reserve Board, which in turn exercised control over twelve district Federal Reserve Banks, each of which had extensive powers over money and national banking activities within its district. All national banks were required to become members of the federal reserve system, under penalty of the forfeiture of their charters should they refuse. Member banks were authorized to rediscount commercial paper at the federal reserve bank of their district under a carefully controlled system of reserves and rediscount rates. Manipulation of the rediscount rate by the various district federal reserve banks was expected to provide a method whereby the federal government could control the amount of commercial credit available and thereby exercise some control over the business cycle. Member banks were also authorized to put federal reserve notes into circulation—government obligations issued to the bank against commercial paper and a gold reserve on deposit with the district federal reserve bank. These notes were expected to give the monetary system a desired elasticity.

The federal government's right to establish and control a national banking system rested upon constitutional precedents established in the days of Hamilton and Marshall and seemingly raised little constitutional difficulty in the twentieth century. Although a few die-hard strict-constructionist Democrats in both houses raised the old Jeffersonian plea against the constitutionality of any national bank, this archaic argument attracted little support.

The House accorded more attention to the contention of Representative S. F. Prouty of Iowa, who attacked the constitutionality of the provision requiring member banks to subscribe a sum equal to one-fifth of their stock or 5 per cent of their deposits as a working capital fund for the district reserve banks, or to surrender their charters as an alternative. This section, Prouty said, violated the due process clause of the Fifth Amendment, since it impaired the obligation of contracts. However, Representative Andrew T. Montague of Virginia pointed out that the National Bank Act of 1864 had expressly reserved the right to amend the provisions of the law. National banks chartered under this act could scarcely claim that their charters were immune to congressional controls. Moreover, Montague observed, the Supreme Court had explicitly held in the *Sinking Fund Cases* (1879) that Congress had the right to place any reservations it wished upon the authority of any federal corporation created by act of Congress.

In the Federal Trade Commission Act and in the Clayton Anti-Trust Act, Wilson invoked the commerce power in his war against the trusts. The Federal Trade Commission Act, which became law on September 26, 1914, erected a five-man Federal Trade Commission, which was empowered to prevent "unfair methods of competition in commerce." Patterned after the Interstate Commerce Commission, the new board could receive complaints, hold hearings, gather evidence, compel the attendance of witnesses, and issue cease and desist orders where, after hearing, the Commission found unfair trade practices to exist.

The Clayton Anti-Trust Act of October 15, 1914, forbade certain trade practices whenever these lessened competition or created monopoly, notably price discrimination between different purchasers, exclusive selling agreements, holding companies, and interlocking corporate directorates. Important, also, were Sections 6 and 20, intended to serve as a "Magna Charta" for organized labor. Section 6 asserted that "the labor of a human being is not a commodity or article of commerce," and declared further that nothing in the government's antitrust laws was to be construed as forbidding the existence of labor unions or agricultural organizations or the lawful activities thereof. Section 20 forbade federal courts to issue injunctions in labor disputes, except where necessary to prevent irreparable injury to property for which there was no adequate remedy at law; while it further specifically forbade the issuance of federal injunctions prohibiting such activities as strikes, assembling to persuade others to strike, carrying on primary boycotts, persuading others to boycott, peaceably assembling, or doing any other thing otherwise lawful under the statutes of the United States.

Both of the foregoing statutes were conservatively drawn, and they aroused comparatively little debate in Congress upon their constitutional aspects. Several men in both houses attacked the section in the Clayton bill prohibiting discriminatory price agreements on the ground that contracts of sale were in no sense interstate commerce, and hence were beyond the legislative capacity of Congress. Regulation of contracts was attacked also as a violation of freedom of contract, and therefore illegal under the Fifth Amendment. Also, there was extended discussion of those sections of the

Clayton bill empowering persons held for trial in federal contempt cases to ask for trial by jury. This provision was intended as a remedy against the arbitrary conduct of many federal judges who indiscriminately issued federal injunctions in labor disputes and then convicted strikers in summary contempt proceedings. Several representatives nevertheless condemned the section, on the ground that a provision for jury trial in contempt proceedings was unconstitutional. Injunction and contempt proceedings were in equity, and the equity jurisdiction of the federal courts was specifically provided for in the Constitution. Since equity proceedings had historically never included the right of trial by jury, Congress, the argument ran, could not establish jury trial by law, for it could not interfere with a grant made by the Constitution directly to the federal courts.

Representative E. Y. Webb of North Carolina pointed out the weakness of this argument. The lower federal courts were the "absolute creatures" of Congress under the Constitution. Congress could therefore do what it liked with lower federal court procedure. Precedent, it may be observed, was on Webb's side. Congress had repeatedly regulated and prescribed federal court procedure in equity jurisdiction, beginning with the Judiciary Act of 1789.

The Federal Farm Loan Act, passed on July 17, 1916, sought in a constitutionally conservative fashion to extend some relief to agriculture through federal control over money and banking. The law set up federal land banks in each of the federal reserve districts and provided for a system of long- and short-range credits for farmers who wished to purchase land or to refinance old mortgages. A Federal Farm Loan Board was to supervise the system, the act providing significantly that its decisions on policy were not to be subject to review in the federal courts. Constitutionally the statute was conservative; in practice, it was an important implementation of Wilson's agrarian sympathies.

THE ADAMSON EIGHT-HOUR LAW

Wilson's most notable concession to the doctrine of liberal nationalism was his sponsorship, in September 1916, of the Adamson Act, which established an eight-hour law for railroad labor.

Wilson took this step to avert a general railroad strike then impending. Some months earlier the railway brotherhoods had presented to their employers a demand for a reduction of the standard working day from ten to eight hours, with payment of overtime at one and a half times the regular wage rate. The roads had refused this demand, whereupon their employees threatened to stage a general rail strike. Wilson then intervened with a proposal for arbitration. The roads accepted this offer, but their employees rejected it. The President thereupon suggested the general adoption of an eight-hour standard of work and wages, but the roads in turn refused to comply. At this point, the brotherhoods called a general strike on seventy-two hours' notice. Wilson believed that the impending strike threatened economic catastrophe, and to avert it he went before Congress and requested passage of a statute establishing an eight-hour day of work and wages as standard in railroad employment.

Congress responded with the passage of the Adamson Eight-Hour Act, which became law on September 3, 1916, in time to avert the strike. The statute provided that after January 1, 1917, eight hours should "be deemed a day's work" for purposes of reckoning wages on rail lines operating in interstate commerce. It further provided for presidential appointment of a three-man commission to "observe the operation and effects" of the eight-hour day, and to report its findings to the President. Pending report of the commission, the railroads were forbidden to reduce wages below the standards then in effect for the longer day. Shortly after passage of the act, the United States District Court for Western Missouri held that the law was unconstitutional, whereupon the government hastened an appeal to the Supreme Court.

In *Wilson v. New* (1917) the Supreme Court by a 5-to-4 majority reversed the lower court and held that the Adamson Act was constitutional. Chief Justice White's opinion emphasized the public character of rail transportation and the resultant extensive right of public regulation. The emergency character of the act, he said, did not make it less constitutional. While an emergency could not be made the source of new constitutional power, it nonetheless could furnish a proper occasion "for the exercise of a living power already enjoyed." Neither did the law violate due process. Although the act in effect fixed wages, evidently a matter of grave constitutional concern to all the justices, White emphasized that the wage-fixing provisions were temporary and were adopted only after the parties concerned had failed to exercise their private bargaining right. The Chief Justice therefore found these provisions to be constitutional, although he was careful not to imply a general right in Congress to fix all rail wages.

The four minority justices, led by Justice Day, all thought that the wage-fixing provisions of the Adamson Act were unconstitutional, on the ground that they were contrary to the time-honored formula forbidding "the taking of the property of A and giving it to B by legislative fiat," and so violated due process of law under the Fifth Amendment. Justices Pitney, Van Devanter, and Mc-Reynolds also were of the opinion that the law was not properly a regulation of interstate commerce, and therefore outside the federal commerce power. The obviously narrow interpretation of the scope of interstate commerce held by these justices boded ill for further attempts at broad federal regulation of the economic system, should the present minority on the Court subsequently become a majority.

TERMINATION OF WILSON'S REFORM PROGRAM

Diplomatic crisis and war brought Wilson's great reform program to an abrupt end in 1917. Thereafter the administration's energies centered upon winning the war and upon the issues of the peace. So ended the most comprehensive attempt at reorienting the American economic order which had been set in motion up to that time. Events were to demonstrate that Wilson had failed to alter substantially the drift of American economic life toward great industry, massive financial concentrations, and protectionism. Most of Wilson's reform measures remained on the books: the Federal Reserve Act, in particular, represented a permanent innovation in federal control of the nation's monetary and banking system. But the Clayton law and the Federal Trade Commission suffered severely from neglect and from unfriendly judicial interpretation, and the low-tariff Underwood Act was later replaced by the unprecedentedly high tariffs of 1922 and 1930. Wilson had acted fundamentally within the Jeffersonian agrarian tradition in his attack upon the centralization of private monetary power, protectionism, and the control of government by banking and manufacturing interests; but it was Hamilton's spirit, and not Jefferson's, which controlled national policy after 1920. Nevertheless, the ghost of Wilson's reform program was to rise again after 1933 to inspire several parts of the great program of controversial social legislation enacted under the second Roosevelt. The New Freedom was an important forerunner of the New Deal.

Chapter

25

The Constitution and World War I

THE ENTRY of the United States into war in 1917 brought about an abrupt change in the political objectives of the Wilson administration. Internal economic reform ceased to be the country's main concern, as the country embarked upon an enthusiastic crusade to crush the German foe and save the world for democracy.

War at once brought into sharp relief three important constitutional problems, none of them altogether new. These were the conflict between a decentralized constitutional system and the requirements of wartime centralization, the conflict between executive war powers and congressional legislative power, and the conflict between war powers and the Bill of Rights.

FEDERAL POWER IN WARTIME

In 1917 the United States experienced for the first time the full impact of war upon the modern social order. War, the nation soon learned, was no longer an isolated state activity, divorced from civil affairs and of little interest to the common citizen. Instead it involved every part of the nation's social and economic life. Both the Allies and the Central Powers had had this lesson driven home to them well before 1917, and the United States soon grasped the same reality. The imperative necessities of modern war posed a difficult constitutional issue: how could a total effort be reconciled with the limited extent of federal sovereignty? Did the war power suspend the federal system in wartime and so make constitutional the economic and social controls necessary to victory?

The extent of federal power in wartime became a major issue in Congress in June 1917, when the administration introduced the Lever Food Control Bill giving the federal government authority to deal with the impending food shortage and rising food prices. The preamble of this measure announced that for reasons of national defense it was necessary to secure an adequate supply and distribution of food and fuel. The food and fuel industries were therefore declared to be affected with a public interest and subject to federal regulation. It was made unlawful to waste, monopolize, fix prices, or limit production in foodstuffs. Whenever necessary, the executive was authorized to license the manufacture and distribution of foodstuffs, to take over and operate factories and mines, and to subject markets and exchanges to executive regulation. In "extreme emergencies" the President could impose schedules of prices upon any industry. The Lever bill was designed primarily to control food and fuel production, but its terms were so broad as to subject virtually the entire economic life of the nation to whatever regulation the President thought necessary for victory.

The bill at once precipitated a bitter debate in Congress, where much of the discussion hinged upon the federal war power. The bill's supporters contended that the war power could not be narrowly construed. Senator Frank B. Kellogg of Minnesota, for example, argued that in wartime the national government could "in fact do anything necessary to the support of the people during the war and to lend strength to the cause," an opinion concurred in by Senator Paul O. Husting of Wisconsin. More moderate was the position taken in the House by Representative Sidney Anderson of Minnesota, who contended simply that the federal government in wartime could do anything having a reasonable relationship to the war effort. This theory of the war power, it presently appeared, was accepted by a large majority in both houses of Congress.

The bill nevertheless drew fire from a vociferous minority in both houses. Senator James Reed of Missouri, an intransigent Democratic opponent of Wilson, attacked federal price and production controls as a violation of the Tenth Amendment, which he contended threw the burden of proof upon the proponents of any particular federal right in question. No federal right, he said, could be established by broad interpretation. This was good Jeffersonianism, but the argument was a bit archaic, what with a hundred or more years witnessing the growing triumph of national ascendancy and broad construction.

Senator Thomas W. Hardwick of Georgia, also a Democratic enemy of Wilson, advanced a more moderate claim. He admitted that Congress could do anything immediately and directly connected with the prosecution of the war, but he insisted that the outbreak of war did not immediately break down all the reserved powers of the states. The difficulty with this position was that a large majority in and out of Congress recognized how necessary federal food control was to the successful prosecution of the war. The House reflected this attitude when it passed the Lever bill late in June after only a week of debate. The measure was delayed in the Senate through an attempt to establish a congressional committee to direct the war effort,[1] but the bill eventually passed the upper house and became law on August 10, 1917.

While the Lever Act was the most dramatic instance in the first World War in which the federal government used the war power to invade a sphere of sovereignty ordinarily reserved to the states, there were numerous other measures of a similar character. Thus by various statutes, Congress authorized the President to force preferential compliance with government war contracts, to take over and operate factories needed for war industries, and to regulate the foreign language press of the country. In the War Prohibition Act, passed on November 21, 1918, Congress forbade the manufacture and sale of alcoholic liquors for the duration of the war. Other statutes, such as those for the wartime operation of the railroads, the censorship of the mails, the control of cable and radio communications, and the regulation of exports, were in part justified by the war emergency; but they could also be adjudged constitutional by other specific powers of Congress, notably that over interstate commerce. The Selective Service Act of May 18, 1917, establishing a wartime military draft, rested in part upon the constitutional provision empowering Congress to raise and support armies as well as upon the war power.

The important decisions bearing upon the extent of the federal war power were made by Congress and the President without guidance of the Supreme Court. Most of the critical war measures never came before the Court; and with one exception, the few that did reached the Court well after the Armistice, when the constitutional

[1] See p. 626.

issues involved were no longer of immediate significance. As in Civil War days, it would have been difficult or impossible for the Court to challenge successfully the constitutionality of a federal war activity while the war was in progress. One may assume that had the Court passed unfavorably upon vital war legislation while the war was still going on, ways and means would have been discovered to ignore or to circumvent the decision.

In the *Selective Draft Law Cases*, decided in January 1918, the Court unanimously upheld the constitutionality of the Selective Service Act of 1917. Chief Justice White found the constitutional authorization to impose compulsory military service in the clause empowering Congress to declare war and "to raise and support armies." He held that the power was derived, also, from the very character of "just government," whose "duty to the citizen includes the reciprocal obligation of the citizen to render military service in case of need and the right to compel it." He then pointed to the long historical record of compulsory military service in English and colonial law and in the American Civil War, to bolster his assertion that the power to draft men into military service was a necessary incidence both of the federal war power and of federal sovereignty. The Court's decision was obvious and inevitable, since it was evident that an adverse ruling upon the constitutionality of the draft would have interposed the Court's will directly athwart the national war effort.

Later decisions also sustained a broad interpretation of federal war powers. In the *War Prohibition Cases*, decided in December 1919, the Court upheld the validity of the War Prohibition Act, although the law had been passed after the signing of the Armistice. Justice Brandeis in his opinion simply assumed the validity of the act under the federal war power and held further that the signing of the Armistice did not make the statute inoperative or void, since the war power was not limited merely to insuring victories in the field but extended to the power to guard against renewal of the conflict. A few months later, in *Rupert v. Caffey* (1920), the Court again upheld the law. Brandeis' opinion rejected the plea that the act was an invasion of the states' police powers with the observation that "when the United States exerts any of the powers conferred upon it by the Constitution, no valid objection can be based upon the fact that such exercise may be attended by the same incidents which attend the exercise by a state of its police power."

In *Northern Pacific Ry. Co. v. North Dakota* (1919) the Court passed favorably upon the provision in the Army Appropriation Act of August 29, 1916, authorizing presidential seizure and operation of the railroads in wartime. Speaking for a unanimous Court, Chief Justice White observed that "the complete and undivided character of the war power of the United States is not disputable." He added that wartime federal operation could lawfully brush aside intrastate rate controls normally binding upon the roads in time of peace, since to interpret the exercise of the federal war power "by a presumption of the continuance of a state power limiting and controlling the national authority was but to deny its existence." In other words, the federal war power here broke in upon state authority and set aside the normal division between state and national power.

In *United States v. L. Cohen Grocery Co.* (1921) the Court invalidated Section 4 of the Lever Act (as re-enacted October 22, 1919), which had made it illegal to impose any unreasonable charge for food. But the Court's reason for taking this step was not that it thought the federal government could not fix prices in wartime. Instead, Chief Justice White's opinion held the law unconstitutional on the ground that the statute had failed to fix any standards for what constituted unjust prices, had fixed no specific standards for guilt, and had forbidden no specific act, and so violated the Fifth and Sixth Amendments, which prohibited the delegation of legislative power to the courts, the punishment of vague and inadequately defined offenses, and deprivation of the citizen's right to be informed of the nature of the accusation against him. In short, the law was unconstitutional not because it fixed prices, but because it failed to do so with any clarity. White's opinion said nothing of the larger constitutional issues implicit in the Lever Act, the Court presumably accepting as constitutional the main principle of the statute.

Thus the Court in several opinions recognized that the requirements of modern war left little of federalism in wartime. This was indeed little more than a judicial recognition of a condition already existing and of a truth so imperative that it would have been futile for the Court to deny its existence.

WILSON'S WAR DICTATORSHIP

Wilson has often been compared to Lincoln on the ground that both men were elevated to dictatorships by the exigencies of war. Yet the comparison must be made with some caution. Lincoln was faced with an internal war, for which there was no constitutional precedent, as well as a confusing constitutional problem growing out of the whole issue of secession. He solved the difficulties of his position by assuming certain arbitrary powers by virtue of his constitutional authority as commander in chief of the armed forces, and for several months he carried on a war against the secessionists by presidential fiat and without benefit of congressional authorization. Even after Congress had formally recognized the war, Lincoln took certain important steps—notably the Emancipation Proclamation and certain preliminary reconstruction decisions—without congressional authorization.

Wilson's position was somewhat different. The war was formally declared by Congress, and Wilson acted from the beginning by virtue of certain large grants of authority delegated to him by Congress. While he made frequent use of his authority as commander in chief, he was never obliged to take any fundamental step without the authorization of Congress.

If Wilson was in any sense a dictator, it was because Congress in certain spheres came close to a virtual delegation of its entire legislative power to the President for the duration of the war. Many federal war statutes merely described the objectives of the act in broad terms and then delegated to the President authority to enforce the law. Delegation of this kind went far beyond that considered in *Field v. Clark*, or *United States v. Grimaud*, for the war statutes in question erected no standards for executive guidance other than the general objectives of the law. Legislative delegation on this scale was unprecedented and little short of revolutionary.

This issue arose several times during the war, but was extensively discussed for the first time in the debates on the Lever Act. As already noted, the bill gave the President extraordinarily broad discretionary powers. He could license the manufacture and distribution of food and related commodities, take over and operate mines and factories, regulate exchanges, and fix commodity prices. No limits whatever were fixed upon his action in pursuance of any of these provisions so long as he deemed a particular step essential to secure the purposes of the act.

Administration supporters in both houses tried to defend delegation on this scale on the ground that adequate standards were erected by the announced purposes of the act. But as Senator Thomas W. Hardwick of Georgia pointed out in a discussion of the bill's price-fixing provisions, no standards whatever were provided except the general welfare and the successful conduct of the war. Most of the Republicans and a generous sprinkling of Democrats thought such delegation utterly unconstitutional. Representative George M.

Young of North Dakota voiced this position when he denounced the bill as an attempt to create a presidential dictatorship by law, an opinion echoed in the Senate by James Reed of Missouri.

This attitude led to a Senate attempt to establish a Joint Congressional Committee on the Conduct of the War, with the intent to effect a general congressional directorship over all war operations. While the Lever bill was in the upper house, Senator John Wingate Weeks of Massachusetts introduced an amendment providing for a congressional war committee, to be composed of ten men, three Democrats and two Republicans from each house. It was to study all problems arising out of the war, and to confer and co-operate with the President and other executive heads. It was also to possess extensive powers of investigation into all phases of war activity.

The proposed committee was modeled after a similar body established by Congress in 1861. It will be recalled that the Civil War committee had been inspired by Republican radicals dissatisfied with Lincoln's war efforts and the President's extraordinary assumption of power. Under Ben Wade's leadership the committee had arrogated to itself large powers of executive supervision and control and had been a constant source of annoyance to Lincoln.[2] Obviously, then, Weeks intended to place heavy shackles upon Wilson's war leadership. Ex-President Roosevelt, who bitterly distrusted Wilson and was now loud in his denunciation of the President, was in fact the principal inspiration for the Weeks amendment, but many congressmen of both parties, more than a little fearful of executive ascendancy, also supported the measure.

In the discussions on the Senate floor, both friends and enemies of the administration appealed to the authority of history to prove or disprove the wisdom of establishing another such committee. In an attempt to demonstrate that the Civil War committee had worked well, Republican Senators Joseph I. France of Maryland, Boies Penrose of Pennsylvania, and Laurence Y. Sherman of Illinois and Democratic Senators Reed and Hardwick quoted contemporary writers, the historians James Ford Rhodes and William H. Dunning, and even Wilson's historical works. In turn, Senator Lee Overman of North Carolina and Wilson's other supporters quoted John Hay, Gideon Welles, and Lincoln in an effort to show that the committee had worked badly and had embarrassed Lincoln's war effort. In the end, the Senate adopted a slight variant of the Weeks amendment by a vote of 51 to 31.

---

[2] See the discussion of the Civil War committee on pp. 387–388.

When the House took up the Senate amendments to the Lever bill, Wilson immediately made it clear that he regarded the proposed committee as an attempt to deprive him of executive leadership in the war. The committee would involve, he said, "nothing less than an assumption on the part of the legislative body of the executive work of the administration." He concluded with the warning that he would interpret the final adoption of the committee measure by Congress as a vote of lack of confidence in himself. Wilson's message killed the proposal, for the House eliminated it from the bill.

After the passage of the Lever Act on August 10, 1917, there was for the moment little further effective resistance to the delegation of broad legislative authority to the President. The Selective Service Act of May 18, 1917, had given the executive almost complete discretion to conscript an army as he saw fit. The Trading with the Enemy Act, which became law on October 6, 1917, gave the President discretionary authority to license trade with Germany, and to censor mail, cable, and radio communications with foreign states. A provision in the Army Appropriation Act of August 29, 1916, had already conferred upon the President the right to take over and operate common carriers in time of war. A joint resolution of Congress enacted July 16, 1918, authorized him to seize and operate telephone and telegraph lines.

Not until the Overman bill came before Congress in the spring of 1918 did Congress make any further show of resistance to presidential ascendancy. This bill, an administration measure introduced on February 6 by Senator Lee Overman of North Carolina, was inspired by a desire to introduce some order and flexibility into the chaotic welter of wartime bureaus, commissions, and other special agencies. The bill authorized the President to "make such redistribution of functions among executive agencies as he may deem necessary, including any functions, duties, and powers hitherto by law conferred upon any executive department. . . ." The act was to remain in force until a year after the close of the war, when all executive offices were to revert to their pre-war status. Thus the reorganization projected was not permanent, but merely a wartime emergency measure.

Obviously the Overman bill proposed to delegate an extraordinary measure of legislative discretion to the President. So broad and sweeping was its phraseology that the President could, for example, have transferred all the functions of the State Department to the War Department, or the functions of the Federal Reserve Board to the Treasury Department. Since these and similar executive units had been created and their functions defined by acts of Congress, the bill thus empowered the President to suspend during the war all past congressional statutes organizing the executive. No limits on executive discretion were specified, and no standards were erected, other than the President's decision that any given step was necessary to the efficient prosecution of the war.

The Overman bill reached the Senate floor in March 1918, and there the principal discussion centered on the constitutionality of the measure. Overman and other administration supporters contended that the bill made no actual substantive grant of legislative authority to the President, since he could create no new functions but could merely transfer those already in existence. The bill was justified also, argued Senator James Hamilton Lewis of Illinois, by the extraordinary powers which the President could lawfully exercise as wartime commander in chief. Oddly enough, Republican Senator Henry Cabot Lodge of Massachusetts admitted that in his opinion the President already possessed the powers delegated by the bill, since presidential war power existed by virtue of the Constitution, and not by act of Congress.

Some Democrats as well as Republicans joined in the attack on the constitutionality of the bill. Reed and Hardwick insisted that the bill could not be justified by the war power, since many departments and functions not related to the war could be affected by its terms. Republican Senator Frank B. Brandegee of Connecticut denounced the bill as an attempt to force Congress to "abdicate completely its legislative power and confer it upon the executive branch of the government," a sentiment concurred in by Senator Albert Cummins of Iowa. As in the debate on the Lever Act, the opposition emphasized the absence of adequate standards for executive guidance.

The Overman Act nevertheless passed the Senate on April 29, by a vote of 63 to 13, the size of the vote indicating that the great majority of senators were impressed with the need for the law and refused to allow constitutional doubts to interfere with the passage of the bill. But Senator Brandegee expressed the minority attitude in the Senate just before the voting began, when he offered an ironical amendment providing that "if any power, constitutional or not, has been inadvertently omitted from this bill, it is hereby granted in full." A few days later the House concurred in the passage of the bill, and it became law on May 20, 1918.

The Overman Act, like the Lever Act, demonstrated that all

ordinary restraints upon the delegation of legislative power to the President were largely put aside for the duration of the war. The rule that standards and guideposts must be provided was simply not observed. The Supreme Court never had an opportunity to pass upon the Overman Act. Had it done so, it might have found the delegation of legislative power constitutional under the extraordinary range of authority vested in the President as a wartime commander in chief. In no other fashion, however, would it have been possible to reconcile the law with the well-established limits on the delegation of legislative authority.

Wilson did not personally exercise all the tremendous authority delegated by Congress to the President. Instead he used his ordinance-making powers to establish a whole series of commissions, boards, bureaus, and government-owned corporations to carry on the multifarious wartime executive functions. Six major boards, each responsible to the President, exercised most of the vitally important functions incident to the conduct of the war. The Office of Food Administration, which in turn controlled the United States Food Administration and the Sugar Equalization Board, carried out the provisions of the Lever Act in managing the production and consumption of foodstuffs by price controls, licensing, and carrying out food conservation campaigns. The Office of Fuel Administration, which also derived its authority from the Lever Act, administered public and private consumption of coal during the war. The War Industries Board had complete authority over all war purchases and eventually came to exercise something like a complete dictatorship over all industry. The War Industries Board rested upon no statute whatsoever; it was created solely by virtue of the President's authority as commander in chief.

Carrier operation was eventually put under a Director General of the Railroads. The United States Shipping Board, created by Congress in 1916, acting through the Emergency Fleet Corporation, constructed and operated the necessary wartime merchant marine. The Export Trade Board, which derived its authority from the Trading with the Enemy Act, imposed general controls upon export and import trade. The Committee on Public Information, also created by the President solely by virtue of his war powers, exercised an informal censorship accepted voluntarily by the press, and it acted also as an information and propaganda bureau. In addition to these bodies there were a host of lesser committees, offices, and agencies, some authorized by law, some created by presidential fiat, some voluntary and informal, but all performing some wartime executive function.

Perhaps the principal significance of this extraordinary executive structure lay in the example it offered for later national emergencies. The first World War did much to accustom the American people to an enlarged conception of federal authority; and thus when the great economic crisis of the 1930's beset the nation, the country more readily accepted legislation which delegated various measures of legislative authority to the President and which invaded the traditional sphere of state authority. Still later, the President's power to erect emergency offices, commissions, and bureaus based upon his constitutional authority as commander in chief was again prominently exercised in World War II.

THE WAR AND THE BILL OF RIGHTS

The war brought into the open once more the old conflict between the Bill of Rights and military necessity. For all the conflict over the Alien and Sedition Acts and over Lincoln's policies, the wartime status of the first nine amendments was, in 1917, still vague and confused. Two things, however, could be said with certainty. First, the state of war did not suspend operation of the Bill of Rights; in fact, the Third and Fifth Amendments specifically mentioned wartime conditions. Further, the efficacy of the Bill of Rights in wartime had been confirmed in *Ex parte Milligan* (1866).[3] With this precedent in mind, the Wilson administration in 1917 immediately renounced any intention of suspending the Bill of Rights for the duration of the war. Second, it was equally clear from Civil War practice that the guarantees in the Bill of Rights were not necessarily the same under wartime conditions as in peacetime. Between these two extreme positions there was a vague and confused area of conflict between civil rights and the federal war power.

To an even greater extent than in Civil War days, it was the First Amendment, with its guarantees of free speech, free press, free assembly, and petition that caused most difficulty. Certain restrictions on freedom of speech and of the press were recognized by military and governmental officials as imperatively essential, both because of military necessity and because of the requirements of public morale. Furthermore, controls were demanded by an over-

---

[3] See pp. 417–419.

whelming proportion of the people, who were in no mood to listen to those opposing war with Germany.

While Congress adopted no general censorship law during the war, it did enact two statutes which, among other matters, imposed certain limitations upon press and speech. The Espionage Act adopted on June 15, 1917, included certain provisions for military and postal censorship. The amendment to the Espionage Act, which became law on May 16, 1918, and was often referred to as the Sedition Act of 1918, was more comprehensive and general in character.

The Espionage Act carried two principal censorship provisions. One section made it a felony to attempt to cause insubordination in the armed forces of the United States, to attempt to obstruct the enlistment and recruiting services of the United States, or to convey false statements with intent to interfere with military operations. The other established a postal censorship, under which treasonable or seditious material could be banned from the mails at the discretion of the postmaster general. A great many publications, including the *Saturday Evening Post* and the *New York Times*, as well as many radical and dissident periodicals and newspapers, were banned temporarily from the mails under this provision.

Under a broad interpretation of the federal war power, these provisions in the Espionage Act were undoubtedly constitutional, provided their application was not abused. Technically, a denial of the use of the mails does not constitute censorship, since the federal courts have several times held that the mails constitute an optional federal service, so that refusal to extend the facility does not deprive anyone of a constitutional right. As for the military censorship provisions, it may be observed first that it had never been supposed, either in 1791 or after, that the First Amendment created an absolute right of free speech under all circumstances. Freedom of speech, for example, does not protect a person who speaks in such a manner as to incite directly an illicit act. Freedom of speech and freedom of the press do not protect persons who commit libel or slander or who incite to riot. Presumably, then, freedom of speech and of the press could not protect a person who deliberately sought to obstruct the national war effort.

The difficulty in applying the law, however, arose from the fact that the statute sought to punish intent, and the definition of what constituted intent was exceedingly difficult to establish. In the past, common-law courts had attempted to establish intent in speech cases by inquiring into the degree of proximity between the spoken or written word and the illegal act supposed to have resulted. Most significantly, common law both in England and in America had since the eighteenth century rested upon the "rule of proximate causation." To prove intent under this rule, it was necessary to show a direct and immediate relationship between the spoken word and the illicit act. Printed or spoken statements of a general character remote from a particular illicit act were not illegal and did not make the speaker or writer an accessory. Mere "bad tendency" or "constructive intent" had not been sufficient to constitute a breach of the immunities of free speech.

The Supreme Court first passed upon the military censorship provisions of the Espionage Act in *Schenck v. United States* (1919), in which the Court borrowed the "rule of proximate causation" to create the "clear and present danger doctrine." The case involved an appeal from a conviction in the lower federal courts on a charge of circulating antidraft leaflets among members of the United States armed forces. Appellant's counsel contended that the Espionage Act violated the First Amendment and was unconstitutional.

In reply Justice Holmes wrote an opinion, unanimously concurred in by the Court, upholding the constitutionality of the Espionage Act. The right of free speech, he said, had never been an absolute one at any time, in peace or in war. "Free speech would not protect a man in falsely shouting fire in a theatre, and causing a panic." When a nation was at war, he added, "many things that might be said in time of peace are such a hindrance to its [war] effort that their utterance will not be endured so long as men fight," and "no court could regard them as protected by any constitutional right."

But Holmes made it quite clear that the Espionage Act did not supersede the First Amendment. He carefully distinguished between permissible and illicit speech in wartime, and in so doing brought to bear the doctrine of proximate causation of illegal deeds. "The question in every case," he said, "is whether the words used are used in such circumstances and are of such a nature as to create a clear and present danger that they will bring about the substantive evils that Congress has a right to prevent. It is a question of proximity and degree."

Thus the Court for the first time gave expression to the clear and present danger doctrine. Nearly forgotten during the remainder of the World War I period, the doctrine was to experience a powerful revival after 1937, and to become the principal judicial guide rule in First Amendment cases.

About two thousand cases involving the Espionage Act arose in the lower federal courts during the war. Unfortunately, in nearly all of them the rule of proximate causation and the clear and present danger doctrine were ignored. Vague statements criticizing the war, the administration, or the American form of government were usually accepted as having a "bad tendency" or constituting "intent" to bring about insubordination in the armed forces. Under the act, for example, pacifists were convicted for expressing a general opposition to all war; and a movie producer was convicted for showing a film on the American Revolution to a civilian audience. The Socialist leader, Eugene V. Debs, was convicted for merely exhorting an audience to "resist militarism, wherever found." If Holmes' later opinion in the Schenck case was correct, convictions of this character were based upon an incorrect interpretation of the law and were an unconstitutional infringement of the First Amendment.

In *Pierce v. United States* (1920), the Court adopted the "bad tendency" doctrine, ignoring "clear and present danger." The case, the last of a series rising out of the Espionage Act, involved a Socialist pamphlet attacking conscription and the war. It could not be shown that there was intent to interfere with the draft, nor was it shown that circulation of the pamphlet had any proximate effect on the war. Yet the Court, speaking through Justice Mahlon Pitney, held that the pamphlet might well "have a tendency to cause insubordination, disloyalty, and refusal of duty in the military and naval forces of the United States." Brandeis, with Holmes concurring, dissented vigorously. Quoting the Schenck opinion, Brandeis argued that it was necessary to prove "clear and present danger," and that mere "bad tendency" was not enough.

The Sedition Law of 1918 was enacted at the insistence of military men and a general public alarmed at the activities of pacifist groups, certain labor leaders, and a few over-publicized "Bolsheviks" and radicals. The law made it a felony to "incite mutiny or insubordination in the ranks of the armed forces," to "disrupt or discourage recruiting or enlistment service, or utter, print, or publish disloyal, profane, scurrilous, or abusive language about the form of government, the Constitution, soldiers and sailors, flag, or uniform of the armed forces, or by word or act support or favor the cause of the German Empire or its allies in the present war, or by word or act oppose the cause of the United States."

This phraseology came dangerously close to that of the odious Sedition Act of 1798. However, there was a difference. The 1918 law penalized criticism of the government and of the symbols of sovereignty when the criticism was made with intent to bring disrepute upon these symbols or to injure the nation's war effort. The act of 1798, on the other hand, forbade criticism of certain specific officers of the government—the President, members of Congress, and others named in the act. In short, the 1798 act prohibited criticism of individuals; the 1918 act, criticism of the government.

The Court had its first opportunity to pass on the Sedition Act of 1918 in *Abrams v. United States* (1919). Here the Court reviewed a conviction of appellants charged with violating the act by the publication of pamphlets attacking the government's expeditionary force to Russia. The pamphlets denounced the "capitalistic" government of the United States, called on the allied armies to "cease murdering Russians," and asked a general strike to achieve this purpose.

The majority opinion, written by Justice John H. Clarke, upheld the conviction and the statute. The purpose of the pamphlet, Clarke said, was to "excite, at the supreme crisis of the war, disaffection, sedition, riots, and . . . revolution." No such right could be protected by the First Amendment.

Justice Holmes, joined by Brandeis, dissented vigorously in the most eloquent and moving defense of free speech since Milton's *Areopagitica*. He thought that it had not been shown that the pamphlet had any immediate effect upon the government's war effort, or that it had been the appellant's purpose to have such effect. "Now nobody can suppose," he said, "that the surreptitious publishing of a silly leaflet by an unknown man, without more, would present any immediate danger that its opinions would hinder the success of the government arms or have any appreciable tendency to do so." If the sedition law were to be construed, he added, so as to prohibit all vigorous criticism of the government and its officials, there was clearly nothing to distinguish this law from the Sedition Act of 1798, long considered unconstitutional. He concluded with a powerful defense of the philosophy of free speech in a republican society:

> Persecution for the expression of opinions seems to me perfectly logical. If you have no doubt of your premises or your power and want a certain result with all your heart you naturally express your wishes in law and sweep away all opposition. To allow opposition by speech seems to indicate that you think the speech impotent, as when a man says that he has squared the circle, or that you do not care wholeheartedly for the result, or that you doubt either your

power or your premises. But when men have realized that time has upset many fighting faiths, they may come to believe even more than they believe the very foundations of their own conduct that the ultimate good desired is better reached by free trade in ideas,— that the best test of truth is the power of the thought to get itself accepted in the competition of the market; and that truth is the only ground upon which their wishes safely can be carried out. That, at any rate, is the theory of our Constitution. It is an experiment, as all life is an experiment. Every year, if not every day, we have to wager our salvation upon some prophecy based upon imperfect knowledge. While that experiment is part of our system I think that we should be eternally vigilant against attempts to check the expression of opinions that we loathe and believe to be fraught with death, unless they so imminently threaten immediate interference with the lawful and pressing purposes of the law that an immediate check is required to save the country.

The significance of the Pierce and Abrams decisions is evident. Thereafter, a general sedition act might be regarded as not unconstitutional under the First Amendment. In wartime the national government can probably punish as seditious any act which it regards as interfering in any manner with the war effort. The First Amendment, in short, does not altogether protect "open discussion of the merits and methods of a war." Whether this is a socially and politically desirable situation is hardly a legal or constitutional question. It involves rather the issue of the extent to which control of public opinion is necessary to the safety of the state in modern total war. (In the "limited" wars of the latter part of the twentieth century, notably in Korea and Vietnam, the government was to make no serious attempt to control public opinion.)

Contrary to the situation in the Civil War period, there was little disposition in 1917–18 to interfere with the procedural guarantees of correct indictment and trial extended by the Fifth Amendment. The first World War was fought outside the boundaries of the United States, and the nation itself was not in the field of military operations. Senator George E. Chamberlain of Oregon did indeed introduce a bill declaring the entire United States "a part of the zone of operations conducted by the enemy," and providing for summary trial by military tribunal of any person publishing anything endangering the successful conduct of military operations. Though this bill was clearly unconstitutional under the dictum in Ex parte Milligan, a few military leaders urged its passage. However, President Wilson formally condemned the measure as unconstitutional, and it did not come to a vote.

THE EIGHTEENTH AMENDMENT

The wartime atmosphere engendered a spirit of crusading reformism directly responsible for the passage of two constitutional amendments neither of which was directly concerned with the actual prosecution of the war. Both the Prohibition and the Woman Suffrage amendments, though the end products of long-prosecuted reform movements, finally triumphed because of the impetus given them by wartime psychology.

The prohibition movement antedated the Civil War, but it had made little lasting progress until caught up in the crusading enthusiasm for moral and social reform in the prewar liberal atmosphere. Only five states had adopted statewide prohibition acts before 1900, although by that time many other states had local option laws. Thereafter the movement spread rapidly, carried forward by the enthusiasm for reform characteristic of the Progressive era, by the entrance of women into public life, and by the political dexterity of the Anti-Saloon League, which lobbied effectively for its cause in state after state and in the halls of Congress. By 1916, nineteen states were entirely dry, and large portions of the remainder were dry under local-option laws.

Congress first recognized the prohibition movement with the passage of the Webb-Kenyon Act of March 1, 1913. This law, which forbade the shipment of liquor in interstate commerce into dry states, posed some serious constitutional questions. Whether or not the law took effect was dependent upon state acts, and the Webb-Kenyon act thus appeared to delegate congressional legislative power to the various states. The statute also posed the old question of a federal statute not applicable equally to all parts of the Union.

In *Clark Distilling Company v. Western Maryland Railway Company* (1917) the Supreme Court accepted the law as constitutional. Speaking through Chief Justice White, the Court ruled that the statute did not really delegate legislative power to the states, since Congress had fixed the conditions under which it went into effect. In this sense, also, it applied equally to all parts of the Union.

In 1913, the prohibitionists forced a constitutional amendment to a vote in the House of Representatives, where it was defeated. In 1917, Congress adopted prohibition by statute in the Lever Act as a wartime food-control measure, and on December 18 of the same year it voted to submit the Eighteenth Amendment to the states. Under the impetus of wartime enthusiasm and crusading fervor, the amendment was speedily ratified by the states, becoming a part of the Constitution on January 29, 1919. By the terms of the amendment, the manufacture, transportation, and sale of alcoholic liquor in the United States was prohibited, effective one year from the date of ratification. Congress and the states were given concurrent authority to enforce the amendment by appropriate legislation. The Volstead Act to provide for federal enforcement of the amendment became law on October 28, 1919.

The constitutionality of the Eighteenth Amendment was soon attacked in the courts. The situation was unique, for it was the first time that a constitutional amendment, presumably a part of the Constitution itself, had been attacked as unconstitutional. The case, *Rhode Island v. Palmer*, reached the Supreme Court in March 1920, where a large number of distinguished attorneys, among them Elihu Root, submitted briefs against the amendment.

The arguments offered against the amendment were extremely ramified; fundamentally, however, there were but two points at issue: First, counsel contended that the amendment had been illegally adopted. This point rested mainly upon the claim that the amendment had not been ratified by a valid two-thirds majority of both houses of Congress as required by the Constitution. The amendment had in fact passed each house by a two-thirds majority of those present, but counsel contended that the Constitution actually required passage by two-thirds of the total membership of each house. An additional count against the validity of ratification was the fact that Ohio had made ratification contingent upon a state-wide referendum, whereas the Constitution specified that amendments must be ratified either by state legislatures or by conventions, as Congress might direct. This contention was extremely weak, as the amendment had been adopted by all but two states in the Union, and to reject Ohio's vote would have had no effect upon the required three-fourths majority of the states.

Also, counsel advanced the far more extravagant claim that the very substance of the amendment was illegal and incapable of becoming a part of the Constitution. The Tenth Amendment, counsel argued, by specifically reserving the residual body of sovereign power to the states, had stated the very nature of the federal union, and was therefore unamendable, since the Constitution and the government it established would be destroyed were its substance altered. But the Eighteenth Amendment, they contended, constituted a radical invasion of the original police powers of the states in destruction of the Tenth Amendment, and thereby brought about a fundamental alteration in the distribution of powers between the states and the national government and a destruction of the original character of the Union, something that could not be done legally even by constitutional amendment. It was unconstitutional, counsel insisted, to use the process of amendment to destroy the very nature of the federal union.

This argument, though plausible was basically weak. Other amendments, notably the Thirteenth, Fourteenth, and Fifteenth, had altered the relations of the states and the national government. Moreover, neither the original Constitution nor the Tenth Amendment stated or implied any limits upon the amending power other than the provisions in Article V, which had prohibited any amendment altering the equal representation of a state in the Senate without its consent and which had also prohibited amendments abolishing the foreign slave trade before 1808.

Justice Van Devanter's opinion, handed down in June 1920, did not attempt analysis of any of these arguments; it merely dodged them. Without presenting any reasoning whatever to support his conclusions, Van Devanter said merely that passage of a constitutional amendment by two-thirds of a quorum in both houses was constitutional. He added that a state could not ratify by referendum, but that the amendment must nevertheless be considered as having been legally adopted and as being a valid part of the Constitution.

The Court, in short, displayed an apparent reluctance to be led into any discussion of the constitutionality of the amendment. This was undoubtedly a wise position, as an attempt by the Court to decide whether or not the substance of an amendment to the Constitution was valid would have gone far beyond any previously asserted right of judicial review. Such action would have implied that the Court could impose certain absolute limits upon the power of the people to alter their form of government through constitutional processes and would have opened the way to judicial review of all subsequent constitutional amendments.

The adoption of the Eighteenth Amendment was nevertheless unfortunate from a standpoint of constitutional theory, for the amendment was founded upon a bad constitutional principle. Instead of delegating to Congress the power to regulate the manufacture, transportation, and sale of alcoholic liquor, the amendment made absolute prohibition mandatory, and thus stripped Congress of all discretion in the matter. The Constitution thereby became in this respect a statute book rather than a frame of government. Admittedly the Thirteenth, Fourteenth, and Fifteenth Amendments had also imposed outright prohibitions of a statutory character. However, there had been practically no chance that the nation would change its mind about slavery, civil rights, or the principles of manhood suffrage, whereas the liquor issue was highly controversial. The Eighteenth Amendment deprived Congress of the right to resort to something less than outright prohibition if it later became obvious that controls of a different variety were desirable. Unless, therefore, Congress willfully decided to disobey the Constitution or chose to ignore the subject altogether, it had no choice but to pass an absolute prohibition law. The only discretion left to Congress was the means of enforcement. Much grief could have been spared the nation if the amendment had given Congress the right to control the manufacture, transportation, and sale of alcoholic liquors, lodging the power of legislative discretion where it belonged—in the Congress.

THE NINETEENTH AMENDMENT

Like its predecessor, the Nineteenth Amendment was the end product of a century-long crusade, begun in the 1830's, in the days of Lucretia Mott and Margaret Fuller. Although the suffragettes were at first ridiculed, the drive to give women the vote gained strength after the Civil War. The suffrage movement was a reflection of the profound change that was taking place in the status of women in the social order. In the last half of the nineteenth century, women had won an improved legal status in marriage, in the business and professional world, and in higher education. It was natural that a demand for the franchise should accompany this change.

Wyoming Territory gave women the vote in 1869. Six years later the Supreme Court, in *Minor v. Happersett* (1875), ruled that the Fourteenth Amendment had not conferred the vote upon women. By the turn of the century, four states had given women full franchise privileges. Thereafter the movement scored rapid political successes. Many Progressives endorsed women's suffrage, and in 1912 Theodore Roosevelt as the candidate of the Progressive Party advocated a constitutional amendment granting women the vote. As a Republican presidential candidate Charles Evans Hughes adopted the same position in the 1916 campaign. By the latter date eleven states had given women the right to vote.

Women now had an appreciable vote in state and national elections, and politicians could no longer afford to be indifferent to the suffrage movement, which was rapidly attaining landslide proportions. President Wilson, who had a somewhat mid-Victorian con-

THE CONSTITUTION AND WORLD WAR I

ception of women's role in society, was personally hostile to the crusade. But with the United States at war, and with a great increase in the number of women engaged in business and industry, it became clear in 1918 that the state of public morale dictated the wisdom of a constitutional amendment. Wilson therefore went before Congress in September 1918 and asked for passage of a suffrage amendment. Several months of dramatic conflict ensued, during which suffragettes picketed the White House, staged hunger strikes, and rallied their congressional supporters with parades and mass meetings.

Congress passed the amendment on June 4, 1919. Tennessee was the thirty-sixth state to ratify the measure, and the amendment went into effect on August 26, 1920.

Many reformers were confident that women's entry into politics would have a strong cleansing effect upon statecraft. It had little or no effect of this kind. It was found that women had for the most part the same political virtues and failings as their menfolk and that they were divided along much the same party, class, and sectional lines. The amendment doubled the number of people entitled to vote, but the effect upon political processes was otherwise slight.

THE TWILIGHT OF LIBERAL NATIONALISM

There was a final expression of liberal national sentiment in the early postwar era. The war itself had emphasized national sovereignty, and for the moment, also, the people had accepted strong federal controls over the economic system as a wartime necessity. The crusading spirit engendered by the war did not perish all at once, and there were certain evidences in the early postwar years of the old Progressive demand for national economic controls and federal reform legislation.

Congress, however, was without the strong executive leadership imposed by President Wilson earlier in his administration. Wilson, stricken dangerously ill in September 1919, was thereafter a broken man, incapable of asserting his former ascendancy over the legislature. For some months he was so completely incapacitated as to raise for the first time the serious question of the right of a Vice-President to assume office during a President's disability. The Constitution was silent on the question of how complete or how permanent the disability must be before the Vice-President was to assume power. It also said nothing of who was to decide the issues of fact involved. During Wilson's illness, Vice President Thomas Marshall made it clear that he did not care to accept the responsibility of assuming the office, and neither Congress nor the cabinet moved to confer its duties upon him. As a result, the nation was for some months virtually without a President. Secretary of State Robert Lansing settled certain current issues of policy by calling the cabinet together at intervals, an assumption of authority for which Wilson in indignation later forced his resignation.

Congress nonetheless enacted some important liberal national legislation between 1918 and 1921. The Transportation Act of 1920, enacted on February 28, 1920, was written altogether in the liberal national tradition. The law returned the railroads to private ownership and operation at the close of the war but at the same time confirmed in positive terms all the rate-setting powers of the Interstate Commerce Commission, which was now authorized to "initiate, modify, establish, or adjust rates," so that the carriers might earn a fair return under efficient management. The famous recapture clause authorized the Commission to recover one-half of all profits in excess of 6 per cent earned by any road. Recaptured earnings were to go into a revolving fund, out of which roads earning less than 4½ per cent were to receive additional compensation. The recapture provision went well beyond previous federal rail regulation, for it seriously modified the conception of the roads as private property. There was but little objection in Congress to the passage of the statute, although a few members objected to recapture as a violation of due process. The notion of federal rail rate regulation was becoming firmly embedded in the political mind.

The liberal national tradition was also evident in the Packers and Stockyards Act of August 15, 1921. The law was passed as a result of congressional inquiry into monopolistic conditions in meat packing, and it placed the meat packers' interstate business under strict federal control. Packers were forbidden to engage in "unfair, discriminatory, or deceptive practices in such commerce," or to attempt to establish a monopoly in business. The act also required all rates for handling livestock in the yards to be fair and nondiscriminatory. The Secretary of Agriculture was given authority to enforce the law through cease and desist orders, subject to appeal to the courts.

Although in 1918 the Supreme Court, in *Hammer v. Dagenhart*, had shown symptoms of a conservative reaction in invalidating the first child labor law, it nevertheless laid down a powerful statement of the doctrine of national supremacy in *Missouri v. Holland*

(1920). This case involved the validity of the Migratory Bird Act of 1918 and ultimately the validity of a treaty of 1916 between Great Britain and the United States for the protection of migratory birds. In the treaty, the two powers had agreed to establish closed seasons on several species of birds migrating annually between Canada and the United States, and the statute had been enacted in pursuance of this agreement. The state of Missouri shortly attacked the constitutionality of the statute and eventually carried the case to the Supreme Court.

Counsel for Missouri contended that the subject matter of both treaty and statute went beyond the enumerated powers of the federal government, invaded the powers of the states, and violated the Tenth Amendment. They pointed to the Migratory Bird Act of 1913, a statute similar to the 1918 law except that it had not been enacted in pursuance of a treaty. A lower federal court had declared the earlier law void as beyond the powers of Congress.

Justice Holmes, speaking for a majority of seven, rejected this argument. The treaty power, he said, was broader than the enumerated powers of Congress. "Acts of Congress are the supreme law of the land only when made in pursuance of the Constitution, while treaties are declared to be so when made under the authority of the United States." He thought it "open to question whether the authority of the United States means more than the formal acts prescribed to make the convention." He then implied that there might be limits to the treaty-making power but that they could not be ascertained in the same manner as those controlling congressional legislative authority. Rather, he said, the treaty-making power must be construed in the light of America's development as a great nation, and it was not lightly to be assumed that the power was inadequate to meet a given contingency. "With regard to that, we may add," he continued, "that when we are dealing with words that also are a constituent act, like the Constitution of the United States, we must realize that they have called into life a being the development of which could not have been foreseen completely by the most gifted of its begetters. It was enough for them to realize or to hope that they had created an organism; it has taken a century and has cost their successors much sweat and blood to prove that they created a nation. The case before us must be considered in the light of our whole experience, and not merely in that of what was said a hundred years ago."

Justice Holmes concluded with a straightforward defense of national authority on the grounds of national welfare and national necessity. "Here a national interest of very nearly the first magnitude is involved. It can be protected only by national action in concert with another power. . . . We see nothing in the Constitution that compels the government to sit by while a food supply is cut off and the protectors of our forests and of our crops are destroyed. It is not sufficient to rely upon the states. The reliance is vain, and were it otherwise, the question is whether the United States is forbidden to act."

The theoretical implications of this decision were astounding. If a treaty could accomplish anything of a national character so long as its subject matter were plausibly related to the general welfare, what limits were there to federal authority, if exercised in pursuance of the treaty-making power? The decision, in fact, seemed to open a serious breach in the limited character of federal sovereignty.

The surprising concurrence of six other justices, including the conservative McReynolds, in the Holmes argument, is perhaps best explained by observing that the statute and treaty did not impair or damage the interests of any powerful vested right. The treaty in question did not touch upon the fundamentals of the social order, seriously involve the sanctity of private property, nor even work any very important practical change in the extent of federal power. The theoretical implications of the opinion were in fact not subsequently translated into reality. The national government has not since brought about any significant change in its authority through the treaty-making power.[4]

THE END OF AN ERA

The liberal national spirit did not long survive in the postwar world. Symptoms of reaction were apparent even before the war ended. The Supreme Court, for example, had struck down the first child labor law in 1918, a good two years before Holmes wrote his opinion in *Missouri v. Holland.* America was rapidly entering upon a new era of postwar disillusionment, a period of material prosperity, fear of radicalism, and impatience with reform. A great revulsion against liberal nationalism was in the offing and was to find full expression after 1921.

---

[4] See the discussion of the Bricker Amendment, p. 816.

Chapter

26

Reaction and *Laissez Faire*

"AMERICA's present need is not heroics but healing; not nostrums but normalcy; not revolution but restoration." These words, uttered by Warren G. Harding in 1920, sounded the keynote of the new era.

America was entering upon an era of reaction and conservatism. The nation had been crusading for a generation, and it was now morally and spiritually weary. Since Theodore Roosevelt's day, politicians and the public had been fighting for or against one reform after another. There had been successive battles over rail rates, trusts, meat packing, the white slave trade, child labor, the monetary system, and a variety of state and local reform movements. The United States had then intervened in the great European war, and Americans had marched off to battle with all the emotional fervor of the Crusaders. Now the high flame of patriotism and moral enthusiasm had burned down into the ash of disillusionment.

In 1919 the Senate rejected the Versailles Treaty, and there died forthwith the hope that the United States would participate actively in the peace and in a new world order. Thereafter the spirit of isolationism mounted steadily, fostered by a growing cynicism about European democracy, a nostalgic longing for the nineteenth century, and a strong conviction that two great oceans had endowed America with an impregnable military security. Even before the war ended, a series of ugly conflicts had broken out between capital and labor, highlighted by a general strike in Seattle, the great steel strike of 1919, and the bloody Illinois coal wars of 1920–22. In 1919 a great Red scare began, inspired by Communist successes in Russia and central Europe. This fear was aggravated by the activities of a few bomb-throwing anarchists and of the Industrial Workers of the World, a small but lawless organization. The hysteria increased when, in the following year, 900,000 votes were polled by Eugene V. Debs, Socialist candidate for the presidency who was then in a federal penitentiary. In January 1919, Attorney-General A. Mitchell Palmer launched a gigantic two-year Red hunt, highlighted by mass arrests without benefit of habeas corpus, by hasty prosecutions, and by mass deportation of Communists and other radicals. Prohibition was a failure almost from the start, and in 1920 Americans began to hear of bootleggers, hooch, and home brew, and of the development of a sinister underworld of gangland conflict, erected on a foundation of misguided moral and constitutional reform.

Postwar prosperity also helped quench the last embers of reformist Progressivism. America was busy making money. After a brief economic recession in 1921, the United States entered an era of economic and industrial expansion unprecedented in all its booming history. National income, which in 1915 had been approximately thirty-five billion dollars, had risen by 1929 to more than eighty billions. Great new industries sprang up, pouring out a flood of goods and services on a scale formerly unknown. The production of durable consumption goods—a reliable index of the prosperity of the average man—increased 72 per cent between 1922 and 1929.

American political and constitutional philosophy in the twenties was formulated in direct response to the forces of reaction and prosperity. Most Americans now viewed reformers with suspicion and were inclined rather to listen with respect to the economic and political arguments of industrialists, financiers, and businessmen who had created the new deluge of wealth and material welfare. Business and industrial management asked above all that government refrain from disturbing the free play of creative individual initiative responsible for prosperity. Businessmen held that governmental controls were bad because they interfered with natural economic laws. In theory, this constituted a demand for an economic policy of complete *laissez faire*. In fact, however, the business community sough: not *laissez faire* but a minimum of restrictive legislation for management and a maximum of beneficent legislation for business enterprise. Thus the Republican high-tariff policy, which hardly comported with pure *laissez-faire* economic theory, was accepted as an integral part of American prosperity.

To some extent, all three departments of government shared in the task of translating the prevailing political and economic philosophy into state practice. In Congress there was a declining interest in reform legislation, reflected in the relative absence after 1921 of important new federal statutes regulating national economic life. President Calvin Coolidge, who often spoke the popular mind in the twenties, repeatedly attacked the doctrines of liberal nationalism. It was the Supreme Court, however, now generally regarded as the supreme arbiter of the constitutional system, that shouldered the task of translating dominant American political and economic beliefs into constitutional law. This fact gave the Court extraordinary prestige in the twenties, a prestige perhaps greater than it had ever enjoyed before. In 1924 President Coolidge expressed the prevailing attitude toward the Court when he called it the chief obstacle to the "deliberate and determined effort" then being made "to break down the guarantees of our fundamental law." The question, he added, "is whether America will allow itself to be degraded into a communistic and socialistic state, or whether it will remain American." The Court, he concluded, was the chief weapon in the patriot's battle to defend the American way of life.

It was in part historical accident, in part design, that caused the Supreme Court of the twenties to reflect so perfectly the prevailing political and economic milieu. Several of the judges appointed in the liberal national era emerged in the postwar period as the very embodiment of reactionary conservatism. Thus Justice James McReynolds, once Wilson's Attorney General, had originally fashioned a name for himself among liberals by the forthright character of his antitrust prosecutions; but after his appointment to the Court in 1914 he had gradually become more conservative and finally had emerged as a die-hard reactionary. Willis Van Devanter, a Taft appointee of 1910, had always been a somewhat unimaginative conservative except in matters that concerned Indian rights and conservation. Justice Joseph McKenna, a McKinley appointee of 1898, had once been a moderate liberal nationalist; now, however, he shifted with the times, and until his resignation in 1925 he supported generally if somewhat erratically the conservative majority.

These men were joined by several new appointees of conservative bent, named to the Court because the President understood and approved of their point of view. During his two and a half years in office, President Harding, who was completely in sympathy with his conservative Republican advisers, appointed four justices to the Court, all of whom were conservative property-minded lawyers. Ex-President William Howard Taft, undoubtedly the most able of the men appointed by Harding, was a staunch conservative who had always viewed the constitutional doctrines of liberal nationalism with some suspicion. In 1920, on the eve of his appointment as Chief Justice, he observed privately that it was of supreme importance to maintain the Court "as a bulwark to enforce the guarantee that no man shall be deprived of his property without due process of law." However, Taft was not an extreme reactionary. On occasion he seemed to recognize social reality, and he sometimes gave expression to a very genuine humanitarianism. George Sutherland, appointed in 1922, had been a conservative railroad lawyer and United States senator from Utah. Pierce Butler, a railroad attorney nominated the following year, was an extreme reactionary, blind to all the realities of social change. E. T. Sanford, appointed in 1923, had been a somewhat undistinguished federal district judge of southern Republican antecedents. Once on the Court, he assumed a consistently conservative position.

Two great jurists, Oliver Wendell Holmes and Louis D. Brandeis, were still present. The foundations of their legal and constitutional philosophy were decidedly different; yet the positions they adopted in actual cases before the Court were usually much the same. Brandeis, a progressive reformer and labor lawyer appointed by Wilson in 1916 over vigorous conservative protests, was not unwilling to write his liberal philosophy into his decisions. Father of the "Brandeis Brief," [1] he recognized and accepted the quasi-legislative capacity of the Court, and sought to make judicial decisions as liberal as possible. His opinions frequently were lengthy analyses of the economic and social situation behind the case at hand. Holmes, on the contrary, was "essentially a skeptical conservative with a radical theory of judicial review." [2] Comparatively little interested in social reform as such, he nevertheless refused to believe it a function of the Court to write its brand of economics into the Constitution or to interfere with social experimentation. As a result he often aligned himself with Brandeis in voting to uphold state and national legislation condemned by the conservative majority.

Justice Harlan Fiske Stone, appointed by Coolidge in 1925 to re-

---

[1] See pp. 496–497.

[2] This characterization is that of Professor Benjamin F. Wright, formerly of Harvard University and more recently of the University of Texas, in a note to the present authors.

place McKenna, immediately became an important addition to the ranks of the minority. Stone was a New York corporation lawyer, a former dean of Columbia University Law School, and Coolidge's Attorney General, whose antecedents, except in the area of civil liberties, hardly suggested his subsequent libertarianism. Soon after his appointment, however, he associated himself with Holmes and Brandeis in a series of dissents, and the notation "Holmes, Brandeis, and Stone dissenting" became a familiar one.

THE JUDICIAL TOOLS OF ECONOMIC CONSERVATISM: DUAL FEDERALISM AND NATIONAL SUPREMACY

The Court's conservative majority soon demonstrated an aptitude for the task of translating economic and political theory into constitutional law. It was not necessary to create new constitutional theory out of whole cloth, since a variety of useful constitutional ideas were already available. Thus when it came to questions of federal authority versus the rights of the states, the Court could draw upon either the doctrine of national supremacy or the newly reinvigorated notion of dual federalism, as suited its purposes. And when an issue arose concerning the legitimacy of state or federal regulation of private property, the opposing concepts of the police power and vested rights could be balanced nicely to achieve whatever economic or social result the majority justices thought desirable.

The doctrine of dual federalism was a particularly useful instrument for the Court's appraisal of congressional power. This concept, a relic of the Taney era, had for the most part been in eclipse since the Civil War, although Chief Justice Fuller had resorted to it in his opinion in *United States v. E. C. Knight* and again in his strenuous dissent in the Lottery Case.[3]

Proponents of dual federalism argued that the Tenth Amendment had decisively altered the nature of the American constitutional system. It had, they contended, abolished the unconditional supremacy of national powers over those of the states and created in its stead a dual system of sovereignty in which both the powers of the states and those of the federal government were alike inviolable. The consequence was that the powers reserved to the states could never be invaded or impaired even by an assertion of federal power specifically delegated to Congress by Article I, Sec-

---

3 See pp. 270-552 ff.

tion 8 of the Constitution. Nor could federal powers be recon-
strued merely because new national problems had arisen not
originally foreseen by the founding fathers.

A notable recent enunciation of dual federalism had occurred
in *Hammer v. Dagenhart* (1918), in which the Court had invalidated the Child Labor Act of 1916 as an invasion of the powers
of the states in violation of the Tenth Amendment. Congress in
February 1919 had thereupon enacted the Second Child Labor
Act, in an evident attempt to obviate the constitutional weaknesses
which the Court had discovered in the 1916 law. Instead of the
commerce power the new statute employed taxation as a regulatory device, imposing a tax of 10 percent upon the net profits of
any firm employing child labor. "Child Labor" was defined in the
same terms as in the 1916 law.

There were powerful precedents for this attempt to use the
federal taxing power as a regulatory device. At various times in
the past the Court had sustained as constitutional a 10 percent tax
upon state bank notes and a discriminatory tax upon oleomargarine.
Even more impressive was the Court's opinion in *United States v.
Doremus* (1919) upholding the Harrison Act of 1914, although
the nominal tax upon narcotics which this measure imposed had
been intended quite obviously to serve as the legal basis for the
federal regulation of the drug traffic.

But in spite of these precedents, the Court in *Bailey v. Drexel
Furniture Co.* (1922) declared the Second Child Labor Act unconstitutional as an invasion of the reserved powers of the states in
violation of the Tenth Amendment. Chief Justice Taft's majority
opinion turned in considerable part upon the sharp distinction he
drew between a tax and a penalty. In the first, he said, the primary intent was the collection of revenue; in the second, it
was regulation to accomplish some ulterior social purpose. The
analogy between the present act and the First Child Labor Law,
he concluded, was clear: both measures represented attempts to
"coerce the people of a state" without regard to the constitutional
limitations upon federal power.

Taft's distinction between a tax and a penalty was a valid one,
long recognized in constitutional law. But his argument ignored
the fact the Court had repeatedly accepted regulatory federal
taxes as constitutional, and his attempt to "distinguish" the taxes
on state bank notes, oleo, and narcotics was weak and unconvincing. His examination into congressional purpose once more invoked

a standard of constitutionality which the Court had repeatedly rejected in the liberal national era.

MAINTENANCE OF THE TRADITION OF NATIONAL SUPREMACY

In spite of the Court's resort to dual federalism in the child labor cases, the majority justices in most instances continued to accept the postulates of national supremacy and broad construction, particularly when the statute under review accorded with their economic and social theories.

Thus in a series of cases, the Court sustained the Transportation Act of 1920, which returned the railroads to private ownership after World War I. This law not only went unprecedentedly far in subjecting intrastate rail traffic to federal regulation, but interfered seriously with the concept of the railroads as private property in its "recapture" provisions.

In *Railroad Commission of Wisconsin v. C. B. and Q.* (1922), the Court unanimously upheld the Transportation Act's intrastate regulatory provisions. Taft's affirmation of the constitutionality of an Interstate Commerce Commission Order revising upward the Wisconsin intrastate rate structure went well beyond the dictum in the *Shreveport Rate Cases*. It was the Commission's duty under the 1920 law, Taft pointed out, to secure to the roads a fair income; were intrastate rates too low, a road would be obliged to charge higher interstate rates to guarantee a fair total return. Hence when necessary the Commission could revise intrastate rates even when these were not in direct competition with interstate rates. The practical effect was virtually to obliterate the distinction between interstate and intrastate rates as far as Commission control was concerned.

Two years later, in *Dayton-Goose Creek Railway Company v. United States* (1924), the Court upheld the Transportation Act's recapture provisions. Taft, again speaking for a unanimous Court, declared that a carrier was "not entitled, as a constitutional right, to more than a fair operating income upon the value of its properties" devoted to transportation. Nor was recapture confiscation, since by law recaptured earnings had never been the road's property at all.

The spirit behind these two cases was very different from that in the child labor opinions. A possible explanation is that railroads were, after all, "interstate commerce" in the narrowest possible construction of the term, and even conservative judges were willing to admit federal ascendancy in that sphere. Moreover, federal authority over the railroads was now so long established and so well recognized that the provisions embodied in the Transportation Act did little violence to the principles of conservative-minded men. The Court's function, in judicial eyes, might well be the protection of private property, but as Taft observed, a railroad was a public utility.

In *Stafford v. Wallace* (1922) the Court upheld the Packers and Stockyards Act of 1921. This statute provided for the regulation of meatpackers and stockyards handling products in interstate commerce. Basing his opinion upon *Swift and Co. v. United States*, Chief Justice Taft gave new emphasis to the stream of commerce doctrine. "The stockyards," he said, "are not a place of rest or final destination." They were "but a throat through which the current [of commerce] flows, and the transactions which occur therein are only incident to this current from the West to the East, and from one state to another." For the moment, the Court made little further use of the stream of commerce idea, but after 1937 the doctrine became the medium by which the Court escaped from the narrow transportation conception of interstate commerce and rationalized the federal control of production.

In *Brooks v. United States* (1925) the Court accepted the constitutionality of the National Motor Vehicle Theft Act of 1919. This statute forbade the movement of stolen automobiles in interstate commerce. It was clearly intended as a police measure, and like the first Child Labor Law, it laid an absolute prohibition upon the movement of things not in themselves harmful. Yet Chief Justice Taft's opinion, delivered for a unanimous Court, ignored the force of the child labor cases, and instead sustained the law with a brief reference to the pure food and drug and white slave cases as precedents.

Amusingly enough, the opinion actually stretched somewhat the meaning of interstate commerce, for it was open to some question whether or not the movement of stolen property by a thief was commerce in any real sense of the term. Actually, the law was an attempt to punish theft occurring before any movement took place. However, Taft made it clear that he approved strongly of the moral purpose behind the law, and he emphasized the importance of the law in controlling automobile thievery. In short, the Court held the law to be constitutionally acceptable, in part at least because it regarded its objective as socially desirable.

THE SHERMAN AND CLAYTON ACTS IN LABOR DISPUTES

The nationalistic conception of federal powers continued to show substantial vitality in a series of labor cases, where the Court used the Sherman and Clayton acts to protect employers from labor violence, secondary boycotts,[4] and similar practices which the Court interpreted as imposing unlawful restraints upon interstate commerce. The application of nationalistic constitutional doctrine in labor disputes had evident conservative implications for the protection of corporate property and vested right, and it is not surprising that the conservative majority on the Court sanctioned the continued resort to nationalism in this sphere.

As far back as 1908 the Court in *Loewe v. Lawlor* had ruled that secondary boycotts directed against an employer might constitute an unlawful interference with interstate commerce, and that persons resorting to such practices were liable under the Sherman Act. Resort to the Sherman Act to defeat labor union tactics had in turn inspired Congress to incorporate a number of provisions in the Clayton Anti-Trust Act of 1914 which were intended to protect labor unions from the limitations and penalties imposed in the federal antitrust laws. Thus Section 6 of the Clayton Act had provided that labor was "not a commodity or article of commerce," and that the antitrust laws should not be construed to forbid labor organizations as such nor their lawful pursuit of legitimate objectives. Section 20 had provided that "no restraining order or injunction shall be granted by any court of the United States . . . in any case between an employer and employees . . . unless necessary to prevent irreparable injury to property, or to a property right." This section also prohibited injunctions against peaceful persuasion of others to strike and injunctions against primary boycotts. All of these provisions were phrased somewhat vaguely and were somewhat general in character, and accordingly there remained some doubt as to the exact status of labor-union activities under the antitrust laws.

The Court did not pass upon the application of these provisions in the Clayton Act until 1921. Then, in *Duplex Printing Press Co. v. Deering* (1921), it held that certain labor-union practices might still constitute an illegal interference with interstate commerce and

---

[4] A primary boycott is one in which a labor union attempts to induce its members and friends to sever business relations with an employer with whom the union has a dispute. A secondary boycott is one in which the union attempts to induce its members and friends to coerce third parties, not concerned with the labor dispute in question, to sever business relations with the offending employer.

as such might be enjoined under the antitrust laws. The case involved a secondary boycott against an employer's product enforced in the New York area in order to win a strike against a factory in Michigan. Such a practice, said Justice Mahlon Pitney, had long been held to constitute an unlawful interference with interstate commerce. Section 6 of the Clayton Act, he pointed out, merely protected labor unions in "lawfully carrying out their legitimate objects"; since the secondary boycott was unlawful, it did not fall under the Clayton Act's protection.

Moreover, he held, the boycott was enjoinable under the antitrust laws, notwithstanding the provisions against labor injunctions in Section 20 of the Clayton Act. The restriction upon the right of injunction, said Pitney, must be construed very narrowly to apply only to the immediate parties concerned in the dispute—in this instance, to the men actually on strike. But the union calling the strike was not "substantially concerned" as an immediate party to the dispute, and its illegal boycotting activities in support of the strike were therefore enjoinable.

The practical effect of this opinion was to minimize the protections which the Clayton Act had thrown around labor unions in industrial disputes. "Unlawful" labor-union activity could still be enjoined and prosecuted under the antitrust laws. The anti-injunction provisions of the law had been gravely weakened, since the Court had ruled that a union conducting a strike was not an immediate party to the labor dispute in question and therefore was not entitled to the immunities of Section 20. Injunction proceedings and prosecutions against labor unions under the federal antitrust laws were thereafter fairly common throughout the 1920's.

In *Bedford Cut Stone Company v. Journeymen Stone Cutters' Association* (1927) the Court appeared to have forgotten completely the distinction between commerce and production laid down in *United States v. E. C. Knight Co.* In the Bedford case, the Court reversed a lower court decree denying an injunction against a stonecutters' union which had instructed its locals not to work on stone which had been cut by non-union labor. Although the resultant refusal to work was directed against building enterprises, although the stone itself had ceased to move in interstate commerce, and although the "boycotts" complained of were conducted on a purely local scale, the Court nonetheless denounced the refusal to work as an interference with the stream of interstate commerce. Since interstate commerce was held to be directly affected, it followed that there was a violation of the antitrust laws. In other words, the Court was willing enough to recognize the effect of production upon inter-state commerce when such recognition was necessary to protect a manufacturer against unreasonable interference by a labor union.

Thus, in the twenties there were two streams of constitutional thought upon the issue of national power. Sometimes the Court found itself in one, sometimes in the other. Its selection did not appear to be dictated so much by any logical constitutional principle as by the social and economic implications of the case at hand. When a nationalistic decision would serve the interests of conservative property rights the Court cheerfully cited precedents supporting the doctrines of national ascendancy. When a dual federalist decision appeared most appropriate, the Court cited *United States v. E. C. Knight Co.* and ignored the federal police power.

THE APOGEE OF DUE PROCESS OF LAW:
FEDERAL AND STATE SOCIAL LEGISLATION

As with dual federalism, substantive due process reflected adequately the prevailing economic and social philosophy of the 1920's. Substantive due process, as the reader will recall, was a modern application of the doctrine of limited government, asserting the supremacy of natural law and natural right. In theory the conception of limited government had not altered since its formulation in the eighteenth century. Actually, however, it had altered subtly, with the introduction of an additional body of natural law, now regarded as supreme and fundamental. The new natural law was the law of *laissez-faire* economics.

The tendency to associate *laissez-faire* economics with natural right, and in turn with due process of law, had been evident since the evolution of substantive due process. In the twenties, however, the association between the two ripened into a firm alliance, as the Court gave the doctrine broader scope and freer application than ever before. According to Professor Benjamin Wright, the Court under Chief Justice Taft (1921–30) invalidated state legislation in 141 cases, almost two-thirds of which involved the Fourteenth Amendment and due process. By contrast, between 1899 and 1921, the Court had vetoed state legislation in 194 cases, only about 90 of which involved the Fourteenth Amendment.[5] It thus appears that the Court invoked due process of law to invalidate state legis-

---

[5] Benjamin F. Wright, *The Growth of American Constitutional Law* (New York, 1942), p. 113.

lation more than half again as frequently after 1921 as it had in the previous twenty-two years. Although the volume of cases was greater in the twenties, the Court was undoubtedly now much more willing to invoke due process against objectionable state legislation than it had been in the prior two decades. Some of the legislation struck down in the twenties would before 1920 undoubtedly have been accepted as constitutional.

Significant, also, was the frank manner in which the Court on occasion now scrutinized the social and economic postulates underlying both state and federal legislation. This does not mean that the justices accepted legislation only when they approved of its social objectives. On the contrary, most legislation continued to be accepted as constitutional regardless of its social implications. But a statute seriously violating conservative *laissez-faire* social postulates was unquestionably examined more sharply than one which did not, and there was a greater likelihood that a "socially unsound" law would be declared void.

In a substantial proportion of the due process cases that came before the Court in this period, the statute in question fell foul of "liberty of contract." Such legislation frequently dealt with hours, wages, and working conditions of labor. Hence by its very nature it contained restrictions on free contract and could be found constitutional or unconstitutional as the judges believed it to be reasonable or not. Since interference with free contract usually also imposed certain limitations upon the use of property, the rights involved in freedom of contract merged to all intents and purposes with other property rights guaranteed by due process of law.

Adkins v. Children's Hospital (1923) illustrates the manner in which freedom of contract was now applied to strike down social legislation. Here the Court was concerned with the constitutionality of a District of Columbia minimum wage law, enacted by Congress in 1918. The statute had established a District Wage Board, with discretionary power to fix minimum wages for women and children in the District of Columbia.

In a 5-to-3 opinion, the Court declared this statute void as a violation of due process and the Fifth Amendment. Justice Sutherland, speaking for the majority, gave unprecedented scope to the doctrine of free contract. While he admitted that "there is, of course, no such thing as absolute freedom of contract," such freedom was "nevertheless, the general rule and restraint the exception. . . ." There were, he said, but four general categories of permissible restraint on free contract: (1) statutes fixing rates in businesses affected with a public interest; (2) statutes relating to contracts for public works; (3) statutes prescribing the character, methods, and time of wage payments; and (4) statutes fixing hours of labor. Since minimum wage legislation did not fall within any of the prescribed categories, it was unconstitutional.

Justice Sutherland then cited *Lochner v. New York*, the ten-hour bakeshop case, as direct precedent for holding the present law void. He was obliged to distinguish it from more recent cases in which the Court had accepted the constitutionality of statutes fixing hours of labor. In *Muller v. Oregon* (1908) the Court had validated a ten-hour law for women, and in *Bunting v. Oregon* (1917) the Court had presumably overruled *Lochner v. New York* entirely by accepting a statute imposing maximum hours of labor for both men and women. Sutherland rejected the two Oregon decisions as precedents on the ground that they dealt with hours of labor and not minimum wages. Why he could nonetheless cite *Lochner v. New York*, also an hours-of-labor case, as direct precedent, was not clear. He implied, however, that the Nineteenth Amendment granting the suffrage to women had destroyed the constitutional basis for special class legislation for women, since laws of this kind had rested upon the now discarded myth of "the ancient inequality of the sexes."

Sutherland then made a lengthy attack upon all minimum wage legislation as economically and socially unsound. It could not be demonstrated, he said, that such legislation actually raised wages, or that higher-paid women "safeguard their morals any more carefully than those who are poorly paid." Minimum wage laws also ignored the rights of the employer, leaving him "the privilege of abandoning his business as an alternative for going on at a loss." The good of society, he concluded, "cannot be better served than by the preservation against arbitrary restraints of the liberties of its constituent members."

Taft and Holmes in separate dissenting opinions both attacked the manifest legislative character of the majority opinion. Taft protested that "it is not the function of this Court to hold congressional acts invalid simply because they are passed to carry out economi, views which the court believes to be unwise or unsound." Holmes added that "the criterion of constitutionality is not whether we believe the law to be for the public good." Both also attacked Sutherland's resort to *Lochner v. New York* as a precedent for the present decision, Taft asserting that it was impossible for him to reconcile the Bunting and Lochner cases. Both dissenting justices thought that there was no adequate constitutional distinction between regulating hours and regulating wages. Both justices also attacked Sutherland's implication that the Nineteenth Amendment had altered the constitutional status of class legislation for women. "It will take more than the 19th Amendment," said Holmes, "to convince me that there are no differences between men and women and that legislation cannot take those differences into account."

Adkins v. Children's Hospital became the classic expression of the identification of *laissez-faire* economics with constitutional right. During the next few years the case was repeatedly cited as ample precedent for a broad interpretation of the scope of free contract. Under the precedent, several state minimum wage laws became inoperative on the plausible assumption that the Fourteenth Amendment imposed restraints upon the police power of the several states similar to those imposed by the Fifth Amendment upon the federal government. The decision served, too, as a general deterrent to state legislatures considering restrictive social legislation; for it was evident that laws of this variety could not now pass the Court's scrutiny, unless they clearly fell within one of the four criteria within which, according to Sutherland, limitation of the right of contract was constitutional.

The concept of "public interest," which Sutherland's opinion cited as one criterion under which extensive social controls might be valid, actually was destined to emerge in the 1920's carrying precisely the opposite implication. In the hands of the Court's *laissez-faire* minded majority it became a means of placing a large portion of all state regulatory legislation under the ban of the Fourteenth Amendment's due process clause.

The doctrine that a business affected with a public interest was subject to public regulation had first been formulated by Chief Justice Waite in *Munn v. Illinois* in 1877. Waite had refused to state categorically what "a public interest" was, but he had implied strongly that it was an attribute associated with an inherently monopolistic enterprise.

For a time thereafter the Court had vacillated uncertainly with respect to the relationship between monopoly and "public interest." In *Budd v. New York* (1892), it had hinted that a "practical" as well as a legal monopoly could be endowed with public interest and thus subject to regulation. Then in *Brass v. Stoeser* (1894), it had accepted as constitutional regulation of a business where no practical or legal monopoly existed. Finally, in *German Alliance Insurance Company v. Kansas* (1914), it had rejected altogether the monopoly conception. Justice McKenna's opinion had stated merely that there must be "a broad and definite public interest," and he had refused to restrict the concept further.

In the postwar era the Court swung back sharply toward a monopoly or "public utility" concept of public interest. The first evidence of such a development appeared in *Block v. Hirsch* (1919), in which the Court passed favorably upon a congressional statute imposing emergency rent controls upon wartime Washington. Justice Holmes' opinion declared that property rented in wartime was vested with a public interest and thus subject to public regulation. In a bitter dissent McKenna, Van Devanter, and McReynolds denied that rents were any matter of public concern and condemned the majority opinion as paving the way for socialism and the complete destruction of private property rights.

At length in *Wolff Packing Company v. Kansas Court of Industrial Relations* (1923), the Court returned to a monopoly or public utility concept of public interest. Under review was a Kansas statute declaring the food, clothing, fuel, transportation, and public utility businesses to be affected with a public interest, and vesting a three-man commission with the power to settle wage disputes in these industries by fixing wages and other terms of employment. Speaking for a unanimous Court, Chief Justice Taft said the state could not endow a business with public interest merely by a declaration that public interest existed. There were, he said, but three types of businesses affected with a public interest. First, there were those "carried on under authority of some public grant," which "expressly or impliedly imposes the affirmative duty of rendering a public service"—in short, public utilities. Second, there were certain occupations traditionally recognized as vested with a public interest, such as "keepers of inns, cabs, and grist-mills." And third, there were those businesses which "though not public at their inception, may fairly be said to have risen to be such, and have become subject in consequence to some government regulation."

Taft then went on to revive the public-utility-monopoly conception as the distinguishing characteristic of public interest. He admitted that in one sense all businesses were affected with a public interest, but added that in the legal sense the criterion was "the indispensable nature of the service and the exorbitant charges and arbitrary control to which the public might be subjected without regulation." Regulation of businesses not possessing this attribute was a violation of freedom of contract and of due process of law.

The Kansas statute therefore was void.

This conception of public interest constituted a return to the theory of *laissez-faire* economics in public regulation. The full social implications of Taft's opinion in the Wolff case became evident during the next decade, when the Court was to declare unconstitutional a series of state measures enacted to impose social controls upon a variety of private businesses.

Holmes and Brandeis remained silent in the Wolff case, but in *Tyson and Bros. v. Banton* (1927) they entered a powerful dissent against the majority justices' conception of public interest. Here the Court reviewed a New York statute declaring theater prices to be a matter affected with a public interest and regulating resale ticket prices. Sutherland, speaking for the Court, cited the three restrictive categories set forth in the Wolff case, pointed out that the theater business did not fall within any of them, and so held the law unconstitutional as a violation of free contract.

In a sharp dissent, Holmes attacked the doctrine of public interest as a conception now being invoked to destroy rather than to justify social controls. "I think," he said, "the proper course is to recognize that a state legislature can do whatever it sees fit to do unless it is restrained by some express prohibition in the Constitution of the United States, or of the State." The concept of public interest he considered to be a purely artificial one, "little more than a fiction intended to beautify what is disagreeable to the sufferers." Brandeis concurred in this opinion, while Stone wrote a separate dissent demonstrating how far the Court had now progressed in destroying the various criteria of social controls formerly accepted as valid. In substance, the minority justices were all virtually demanding that the entire conception of public interest be abandoned and replaced by a recognition of the general right of any state legislature to regulate private business whenever it thought the public welfare demanded it.

In *Ribnik v. McBride* (1928), the Court held unconstitutional a New Jersey statute licensing employment agencies and empowering a state commissioner of labor to refuse a license if the proposed schedule of fees were excessive. "An employment agency," Justice Sutherland said, "is essentially a private business." The Court, he observed, had already established that "the fixing of prices for food or clothing, or house rental or of wages to be paid, whether maximum or minimum" was beyond the legislative power, and he perceived "no reason for applying a different rule" to the regulation of employment agency fees.

In the same vein, the Court in *Williams v. Standard Oil Co.* (1929) invalidated a Tennessee statute authorizing a state commissioner of finance to fix gasoline prices within the state. Again Sutherland said simply that there was no power to fix prices unless the business was vested with a public interest, and in the present instance public interest was not present.

In *New State Ice Co. v. Liebmann* (1932) the Court went beyond the two foregoing cases to strike down an Oklahoma statute declaring the manufacture and sale of ice to be affected with a public interest and making a state license a prerequisite for engaging in the business. No issue of price fixing was involved here; however, the state was empowered by the law to withhold a license if the applicant could not show public necessity for his services. The Court held the law unconstitutional, on the ground that no public interest was present. In its absence restrictive licensing violated due process. Not until *Nebbia v. New York* (1934), with the nation in the grip of the great depression, was concept of public interest as defined in the theater ticket, employment agency, ice, and gasoline cases to be abandoned.[6]

Laissez-faire conservatism was also evident in a variety of other due process cases, in which the Court invalidated state police statutes on the ground that they imposed "arbitrary" or "unreasonable" restrictions upon private property or business enterprise. In *Pennsylvania Coal Co. v. Mahon* (1922) the Court held void a Pennsylvania statute forbidding the mining of coal in such a way as to damage surface habitations. Justice Holmes' opinion declared that the statute impaired the value of property in mines and so violated due process of law.

In *Jay Burns Baking Co. v. Bryan* (1924) the Court struck down a Nebraska statute fixing standard weights for bread. The evident purpose of the law was to minimize fraud. But Justice Butler, speaking for the majority, said that practical conditions would make it difficult to comply with the statute, and that because the law imposed an "intolerable burden" upon bakers, it was arbitrary, unreasonable, and in violation of due process. And in *Weaver v. Palmer Bros. Co.* (1926), the Court refused to accept a Pennsylvania statute prohibiting the use of shoddy in the manufacture of mattresses. Since shoddy could be effectively disinfected, Butler argued, the law bore no reasonable relationship

---

[6] See below, p. 692.

to the protection of public health and was thus "purely arbitrary" and at odds with the Fourteenth Amendment's due process clause.

The Court also employed the due process clause to protect business in its labor difficulties. Thus in *Truax v. Corrigan* (1921) the Court declared unconstitutional an Arizona statute forbidding state courts to grant injunctions against picketing. Chief Justice Taft said the statute violated due process by protecting palpable wrongful injuries to property rights. Moreover, since it singled out certain types of property (that involved in labor disputes) for exposure to wrongful injury, the law violated the equal protection clause of the Fourteenth Amendment. It is of some interest to observe that within a generation after this the Court was to hold that the right to engage in peaceful picketing was guaranteed by the Fourteenth Amendment.

In due process cases involving state police power there was a strong disposition on the part of Justices Holmes and Brandeis and, after 1926, Justice Stone, to attack the Court for using due process to implement its *laissez-faire* conservatism. In *Truax v. Corrigan*, for example, Holmes protested that "there is nothing that I more deprecate than the use of the 14th Amendment beyond the absolute compulsion of its words to prevent the making of social experiments that an important part of the community desires, in the insulated chambers afforded by the several states, even though the experiments may seem futile or even noxious to me and to those whose judgment I most respect." In *Jay Burns Baking Co. v. Bryan* Brandeis declared flatly that the decision was "in my opinion, an exercise of the powers of a superlegislature,—not the performance of the constitutional function of judicial review." However, Brandeis and Holmes themselves on occasion subscribed to the practice they criticized so severely—particularly where the statute in question was offensive to their own social predilections.

By the close of the twenties the Court, employing an expansive *laissez-faire* concept of vested property rights and a narrow and restrictive theory of public interest, had imposed unprecedented limits upon the state police power. Had this trend continued, there would before long have been little left of the former well recognized right of the states to impose regulations upon private property in the interest of the public welfare. The identity between *laissez-faire* social philosophy and the prevailing interpretation of due process was now very nearly complete. However, the economic cataclysm of the 1930's was to sweep away this identity completely and replace it with a broad acceptance of state social legislation unimpaired by any doctrine of vested rights.

DUE PROCESS AND CIVIL LIBERTIES IN THE TWENTIES

The Court's record in the 1920's in the field of civil liberties presents something of a paradox. On the one hand, the conservative majority justices manifested little of the solicitous regard for the rights of persons that they demonstrated generally for the rights of property.

On the other hand, the Court in the 1920's undertook for the first time to make the guarantees of the First Amendment applicable to the states through the due process clause of the Fourteenth Amendment. In taking this step, the majority justices were not much concerned with a libertarian approach to freedom of speech, press, and religion. But their action in bringing a portion of the federal Bill of Rights to bear against the states nonetheless was to open the way in the next fifty years for a vast expansion in the law of civil liberties—most of it libertarian-oriented.

Occasionally—particularly in cases devoid of any implications for the protection of left-wing minorities—the Court permitted itself to apply philosophic individualism to the protection of private rights. Thus in *Meyer v. Nebraska* (1923), the Court held void a Nebraska statute prohibiting the teaching of modern foreign languages to children in elementary schools. The liberty guaranteed by the Fourteenth Amendment, said Justice McReynolds, included the right to bring up one's children according to the dictates of individual conscience. The statute, he declared, invaded that right, and therefore violated the Fourteenth Amendment's due process clause. In the same vein, the Court in *Pierce v. Society of Sisters* (1925) struck down an Oregon law requiring children between the ages of eight and sixteen to attend public school. The statute, said Justice McReynolds, destroyed property rights in private schools and violated the right of parents to educate their children as they saw fit.

An early assertion that the guarantees of the First Amendment conceivably applied to the states came in a dissent by Brandeis in *Gilbert v. Minnesota* (1920). Here the Court upheld the constitutionality of a state statute punishing speech aimed at discouraging enlistment in the armed forces of the United States. Brandeis protested that the law in fact interfered with the right of a citizen of the United States to discuss a federal function—in this instance, the war power. The act, he hinted, therefore violated the Fourteenth Amendment.

In *Gitlow v. New York* (1925), the Court took the crucial step of incorporating the content of the First Amendment within the Fourteenth Amendment's due process clause. The case involved the validity of a New York statute punishing criminal anarchy— "the doctrine that organized government should be overthrown by force and violence." Justice Sanford found no difficulty in upholding the constitutionality of the law, since it merely punished advocacy of behavior "inherently unlawful" in a constitutional government. The Court also confirmed Gitlow's conviction under the act, in effect by applying the *Abrams* "bad tendency" doctrine to his Communist-oriented utterances.

But in the course of his opinion Justice Sanford declared that "we may and do assume that freedom of speech and of the press— which are protected by the 1st Amendment from abridgment by Congress—are among the fundamental personal rights and 'liberties' protected by the due process clause of the 14th Amendment from impairment by the states." Thus in an otherwise very conservative opinion, Sanford nonetheless opened the door upon what was to become a new era in the constitutional law of civil liberty.

Other cases soon followed confirming the new association between due process and the guarantees of the First Amendment. In *Whitney v. California* (1927), the Court upheld the constitutionality of a California criminal conviction under a statute defining and punishing criminal syndicalism—the advocacy of crime, sabotage, or terrorism as a means of accomplishing a political change or a change in industrial ownership. The statute, Sanford's opinion declared, was constitutional, since the utterance it made punishable—that "tending to incite to crime"—partook of the nature of a criminal conspiracy and was therefore outside the protection accorded free speech.

Thus Sanford again invoked the "bad tendency" doctrine. But Justice Brandeis, in a powerful concurring opinion in which Holmes joined, defended at length the theory of free speech in an open society, which he thought properly limited by the "clear and present danger" doctrine, although he conceded that the evidence of criminal conspiracy made the present conviction constitutionally valid.

In *Stromberg v. California* (1931), the Court declared invalid a California statute prohibiting the display of the red flag as an emblem of anarchism or of opposition to organized government. "It has been determined," said Chief Justice Charles Evans Hughes, "that the conception of liberty under the due process clause of the Fourteenth Amendment embraces the right of free speech." The statute in question, he held, was worded so broadly as conceivably to impose penalties upon peaceful and orderly opposition to government. It therefore violated due process of law.

And finally, at the same session the Court in *Near v. Minnesota* (1931) held unconstitutional a Minnesota statute providing for the suppression of any malicious, scandalous, or defamatory newspaper. Pointing out that the statute went well beyond existing standards of responsibility under libel laws, Chief Justice Hughes said the measure violated freedom of the press and hence the due process clause of the Fourteenth Amendment.

The Court further extended the new identity between the Fourteenth Amendment's due process clause and the Bill of Rights in *Powell v. Alabama* (1932), to include the Sixth Amendment's guarantee of a right to counsel for accused persons in criminal trials. The case, which arose out of the celebrated Scottsboro incident, involved an appeal from the Alabama courts from a conviction of several young black men for rape, in which petitioners charged that they had been denied right of access to counsel both before and during the trial. Justice Sutherland, speaking for a majority of seven, pointed out that the Sixth Amendment provided that in all criminal prosecutions, the accused shall enjoy the right of counsel, and he then went on to hold that failure of the Alabama trial court to give the defendants "reasonable time and opportunity to secure counsel was a clear denial of due process" as guaranteed by the Fourteenth Amendment.

This finding was in apparent contradiction to that in *Hurtado v. California* (1884), where the Court had specifically refused to identify due process as guaranteed by the Fourteenth Amendment with the full content of the Fifth Amendment, which included the requirement of indictment by a grand jury in all capital cases. Following the rule of construction that no part of the Constitution may be treated as superfluous, the Court in the Hurtado case had held that the guarantee of a grand jury must therefore not be included in the content of due process; otherwise the Fifth Amendment would not have extended the two guarantees separately. Obviously, by the same rule, none of the other guarantees of the first eight amendments would fall within the scope of the due process clause of the Fourteenth Amendment. While Sutherland did not specifically overrule *Hurtado v. California*, the authority of this precedent was for the time seriously impaired.

By 1932, therefore, the Court was embarked on an extension of the federal bill of rights as a limitation on state police power by incorporating certain of the first eight amendments in due process of law. How far this process might go in the future was as yet uncertain.[7]

OTHER CIVIL LIBERTIES ISSUES: ALIENS AND WIRETAPPING

Not surprisingly, the Court's treatment of other civil liberties issues in the twenties reflected the same conservative point of view which it brought to bear upon due process of law. Thus its disposal of cases involving the rights of aliens, in particular, mirrored the prevailing spirit of hostility toward foreigners generally. The average middle class "old American" of the twenties believed firmly that both the Communist and anarchist menaces and the contemporary alarming increase in urban crime were due to the presence of undesirable aliens in the country. Much contemporary xenophobic sentiment also was laden with religious and racial prejudice. Conservative Protestants feared and resented the recent heavy influx of Catholic immigrants from Italy and Poland, while the swarthy newcomers from southern and eastern Europe as well as those from Japan and Asia were looked upon as "unassimilable" and a threat to American racial purity.

Congress responded to this sentiment with a series of statutes to assist in the deportation of alien criminals and subversives and to place sharp new limits upon immigration from southern and eastern Europe and the Far East. An act of May, 1920, authorized deportation proceedings directed aganst aliens convicted of violating the 1917 Selective Service Act, the Espionage Act, or the 1918 Sedition Act. Successive immigration acts of 1921 and 1924 virtually banned Oriental immigration entirely and put the rest of the world on a "national origins" quota system which heavily favored "Nordic" northwest Europe at the expense of the southern and eastern portions of the continent.

The Court on its part adopted policies toward aliens very much in the spirit of the new alien and immigration laws. Thus in *Ozawa v. United States* (1922), the Court ruled that resident Japanese aliens were not eligible for citizenship. The Naturalization Act of

---

[7] For a discussion of more recent civil liberties cases see Chapter 29.

1906, at issue in the case, had not mentioned race; however, Sutherland's opinion held that the law must be interpreted in the light of other long-standing provisions of earlier acts which had banned citizenship by naturalization to all but whites and persons of African ancestry.

A year later, in *United States v. Bhagat Singh Thind* (1923), the Court extended the naturalization ban to Hindus. Sutherland admitted that persons from the Indian subcontinent might technically be "Caucasians," but ruled nonetheless that they were not "whites" in the popular or legal sense of the term. And in *Toyota v. United States* (1925), the Court ruled that even those Japanese aliens who had served honorably in the United States armed forces during the recent war were ineligible for citizenship, although a 1919 congressional statute for the naturalization of such aliens had not mentioned race.

The Court also found no difficulty in upholding the constitutionality of the various alien land laws which had been enacted in the last two decades by a number of Western states. These measures, aimed principally at Japanese farmers, prohibited aliens not eligible for citizenship from owning or leasing agricultural land. Such legislation, said Justice Butler in *Terrace v. Thompson* (1923), was a legitimate exercise of the state's police power. Moreover, the distinction it drew between citizens and aliens ineligible for citizenship constituted reasonable classification in the interest of the public welfare and hence did not violate the equal protection clause.

The Court also treated with indulgence federal legislation and procedures for the deportation of "undesirable" aliens. In *United States ex rel Bilokomsky v. Tod* (1923) the Court held constitutional deportation proceedings directed against an alien arrested on a charge of violating Pennsylvania's sedition act. The deportation hearing, Brandeis pointed out, was a civil and not a criminal proceeding. Accordingly, admissible evidence of the respondent's alien status properly included both his prior statement to an immigration officer and his refusal to answer questions on his citizenship put to him during the subsequent deportation hearing. Brandeis did not even touch upon the fact that the petitioner respondent had neither been convicted of any crime nor charged with unlawful entry into the United States.

A year later, in *Mahler v. Eby* (1924), the Court upheld the constitutionality of the 1920 statute ordering the deportation of aliens convicted of violating either the Espionage Act, the Sedition Act, or the 1917 Selective Service Act. The right to expel undesirable aliens, Taft first observed, was "a sovereign power necessary to the safety of the country." And although the statute under review had been enacted long after the commission of the offenses for which the appellants had been convicted, it was nonetheless not an *ex post facto* law, since the proceedings at issue were civil and not criminal in character. Nor did the law, Taft declared, involve an unconstitutional delegation of legislative power to the Executive.

Intimately related in spirit to the Court's stern stand against alien "undesirables" was the relatively free license the justices gave to electronic eavesdropping, which the advancing technology of the twenties had made available to the police for the first time. In *Olmstead v. United States* (1928), a badly divided Court, speaking through Chief Justice Taft, ruled 5 to 4 that wiretapping did not constitute "official search and seizure," either of a person or his material effects, or "an actual physical invasion of his home," in violation of the Fourth Amendment.

Curiously, it was the generally reactionary Justice Butler who in a carefully reasoned analysis condemned Taft's argument for ignoring the common sense historical meaning of the Fourth Amendment. Brandeis in another dissent declared bluntly that in his opinion it was "less evil that some criminals should escape than that the government should play an ignoble part." And Holmes, also dissenting, coined what was to become in later years a celebrated liberal aphorism: that wiretapping was "a dirty business." Notwithstanding the minority justices' doubts, the Olmstead dictum was to stand as good law into the 1960's, although a 1934 congressional statute was to make wiretap evidence inadmissible in federal courts.

THE BUREAUCRATIC MONSTER

A contention frequently advanced by conservatives in the twenties was that the federal government was in some danger of becoming a gigantic bureaucratic monster which would swallow up the activities of states and private enterprise alike. This argument was generally reinforced by reference to the rapid growth of federal expenditures, a growth presumably indicative of a dangerous increase in federal regulatory activities. In 1925, for example, the proponents of this contention could point out that the federal budget now amounted to over $3,000,000,000, an increase of some 300 per cent over the budget of $760,000,000 for 1916. By 1930, federal expenditures had mounted to almost $3,500,000,000.

This contrast exaggerated to a considerable extent the actual increase in federal functional activities. During the twenties the decline in the purchasing value of the dollar had inflated the budgetary figure. Calculated on the basis of the purchasing power of 1915 dollars, the federal budget in 1925 was but $1,791,000,000, and in 1930 just over $2,000,000,000. Moreover, nearly half the increase in federal expenditures of 1925 over 1915 went for non-functional purposes; that is, it was devoted to paying the interest and principal on the tremendous national debt incurred during World War I. Further, expenditures for national defense were now much greater than before the war, while expenditures for veterans' services had increased by more than 150 per cent.

The actual increase in federal functional expenditures, excluding monies expended for national defense, was a comparatively moderate one. In 1915, expenditures of this category had amounted to some 255 millions, while for 1925, if figured in 1915 dollars, they totalled 367 millions, and for 1930 some 513 millions, an increase of slightly more than 100 per cent in fifteen years.

This increase undoubtedly reflected a certain change in the functional character of the federal government. The government at Washington was becoming a huge service institution, performing countless informational, educational, and research activities for the general public and for special-interest groups. This type of activity had been increasing since 1900, and it continued to increase in the twenties, as private groups looked more and more to the federal government for various benevolent services which the separate states could not or would not undertake.

Thus, after 1920, there were significant increases in federal expenditures for services to business provided by the Department of Commerce, for federal conservation of natural resources, for direct aids to agriculture, and for grants-in-aid to the states for roads, maternity welfare, educational and vocational services, rural sanitation, and agricultural extension services. Services of this kind, once established, tended to expand rather than to contract. Not only were they convenient and useful to large numbers of citizens, but also they became vested interests of the bureaus which administered them and which worked for their continuance.

The constitutional basis for such services rested upon the federal power to spend money for the general welfare. The non-coercive character of most such services made it extremely difficult to bring their constitutionality before the courts, since they offered no opportunity to resist the assertion of federal authority. The old

Madisonian argument that Congress could not legally appropriate money for any purpose not within the enumerated powers of Congress was now seldom heard. Conservatives merely denounced the increase in federal services as contrary to the spirit of the American constitutional system without resting their position upon more precise legal grounds.

In spite of the prevailing spirit of *laissez-faire* conservatism, the twenties saw the creation of a few coercive and regulatory national agencies. Thus the Water Power Act of 1920 created a Federal Power Commission with authority to license and regulate power plants on the navigable streams of public lands. During the next decade, however, the board functioned so weakly that it was of little practical value or significance.

Radio broadcasting was another field into which the federal government extended its controls. Since 1912, radio transmission had been subject to extensive regulation and restriction, but the great growth of broadcasting after 1920 brought chaos to the ether and made additional controls imperative. The Radio Act of 1927 accordingly created a Federal Radio Commission, composed of five men appointed by the President for six-year terms. The commission was given extensive powers over radio transmission, including the right to classify radio stations, prescribe services, assign frequency bands, and regulate chain broadcasting. The act also gave the Secretary of Commerce a general right of inspection and regulation over radio operators and apparatus.

More controversial were the several attempts during the twenties to extend federal authority over agricultural production. American agriculture was in a chronic state of depression throughout the decade. Much additional land had been brought under cultivation during World War I, and following the contraction of demand after the War, agricultural prices had suffered a collapse from which they had not recovered. Chronic overproduction of the great agricultural staples kept prices low, while America's high-tariff policy diminished the possibility of expanding the foreign market to absorb the surplus. In 1927 Congress yielded to heavy pressure from agricultural interests and from western and southern congressmen and on February 25 enacted the McNary-Haugen Farm Bill. The measure provided for a series of equalization fees, to be paid by the growers of certain staple crops to a Federal Farm Board. The Board was empowered to use this money to dump crop surpluses abroad, to buy and sell agricultural products, and to make crop loans to farm co-operatives. The bill was clearly opposed to the prevailing temper of constitutional conservatism, for it extended national regulatory authority over agricultural production and thus not only invaded a sphere of authority traditionally reserved to the states but also interfered extensively with private property rights.

President Coolidge sent the bill back to Congress with a stinging veto, denouncing it as economically and constitutionally unsound. Attorney General John Sargent's opinion stated that the bill went far beyond the federal power over interstate commerce in attempting to fix commodity prices, and that it unconstitutionally put the federal government into the buying and selling of agricultural commodities. He was also of the opinion that equalization fees were unconstitutional. If the fees were taxes, they were invalid by virtue of the decision in the second Child Labor Case, for their purpose was not to raise revenue but to give the federal government illegal control over production. If they were not taxes, the fees took property without due process of law. Further, he said, in permitting farmers to determine when controls should be put into effect, the bill delegated congressional legislative power to private individuals and was unconstitutional upon this ground also. The veto was a typical expression of the Coolidge attitude toward the scope of federal authority, and the country at large appeared to agree with him. In 1928 Coolidge vetoed a second McNary-Haugen bill framed in the same general terms, and Congress sustained the veto.

In 1929, Congress enacted the less ambitious Agricultural Marketing Act. This law set up an eight-man Federal Farm Board and gave it authority to administer a $500,000,000 revolving fund to assist in the more effective marketing of agricultural commodities. The board was authorized to recognize private stabilization corporations and to make loans to the latter for the purchase and storage of surplus agricultural commodities. This statute did not attempt to regulate agricultural production, and it lacked any coercive character. As a price stabilization measure it was a failure.

The proposed Child Labor Amendment, adopted by Congress on June 3, 1924, represented the only serious attempt of the era to expand congressional authority by formal constitutional processes. This measure would have empowered Congress to regulate or prohibit child labor by appropriate legislation. However, the proposed amendment encountered general public indifference, while manufacturers' associations and certain religious groups also opposed it. By 1930, the amendment had secured ratification in but five states, while more than three-fourths of the states in the Union had rejected it. After 1933 a number of other states ratified the measure, but the proposed amendment never secured the ratification of three-fourths of the states necessary for its adoption.[8]

FEDERAL GRANTS-IN-AID

The grant-in-aid was the instrument through which the federal government extended many important social services in its new capacity as a service state. The grant-in-aid was an appropriation by the federal government to the states for some special purpose, certain stipulations being attached to the grant. These were, first, the formal acceptance of the grant by the legislature of any state accepting the grant; second, federal supervision and approval of state activities under the appropriation; third, state appropriation of a sum of money at least equal to that advanced by the federal government; and fourth, federal right to withhold the grant from any state violating the stipulated agreement.

Federal appropriations to the states were not altogether new. Notable early examples were the distribution of the federal surplus in 1837, various land grants, and the Morrill Act of 1862 granting federal lands to the states for agricultural colleges. Grants to the states increased in frequency after 1880, but before 1911 they lacked the provisions for systematic federal control characteristic of the modern grant-in-aid.

The Weeks Act, passed in 1911, established perhaps the first modern grant-in-aid. The statute appropriated money to the states for forest-fire prevention programs. A participating state was required to accept the grant by legislative act, to establish a satisfactory fire protection system of its own, and to appropriate to it a sum of money at least equal to the federal grant in prospect. State officials were to supervise the fire protection system, which was nonetheless subject to federal inspection and approval. The total congressional appropriation in the Weeks Act was but $200,000, but the law was the prototype of all subsequent grants-in-aid.

Several similar statutes were enacted during the next few years. These included the Smith-Lever Act of 1914, providing for state-federal agricultural extension work; the Federal Road Act of 1916, appropriating money for state highway programs; and the Smith-Hughes Act of 1917, granting money to the states for vocational education. In 1920 Congress enacted the Fess-Kenyon Act appro-

---

[8] The amendment has now become unnecessary by virtue of the extension of federal controls over production and acceptance of such controls by the Supreme Court. Congress prohibited child labor in the Fair Labor Standards Act of 1938, since held constitutional by the Supreme Court. See pp. 722ff.

priating money for disabled veteran rehabilitation by the states, and in 1921 it passed the Sheppard-Towner Act subsidizing state infant and maternity welfare activities. After 1921, no important grant acts were passed for several years, although the annual appropriations under existing statutes of this type were greatly increased. In 1925 grants-in-aid to the states totaled some ninety-three million dollars, compared with approximately eleven million dollars in 1915. Nearly all of the increase went to highway construction and educational projects.

The postwar conservative atmosphere gave rise to considerable hostility to the grant-in-aid, conservatives attacking it strongly as a threat to the essential nature of the federal system. Governor Frank O. Lowden of Illinois, for example, warned in 1921 that the grant-in-aid implied "the gradual breaking down of local self-government in America," and President Coolidge in his annual message of 1925 in speaking of grants to the states said that "local self-government is one of our most precious possessions. . . . It ought not to be infringed by assault or undermined by purchase." The real basis of objection to grants-in-aid was in all probability the fact that most federal revenues were collected in the wealthy, populous Northeast, while the distribution of grants was based upon both population and state area, so that the poorer South and West received a disproportionate return on federal funds. Moreover, grants-in-aid often went for so-called "social frills"—maternity welfare, vocational education, and the like—of which conservatives did not approve.

Opponents of the grant-in-aid based their constitutional objections upon two arguments. One, not very often raised after 1920, was the old Madisonian contention that federal funds could lawfully be spent only in connection with the enumerated powers of Congress. More frequently advanced was the assertion that the grant-in-aid was a subtle method of extending federal power and undermining state sovereignty. The device, constitutional conservatives said, enabled the national government to usurp functions properly belonging to the states. To the rebuttal that state acceptance of a grant was voluntary, they replied that state co-operation was not really voluntary, since the financial penalty for non-co-operation was so great as to force the states to accept the federal offer. If a state refused to co-operate, they said, its citizens nevertheless had to pay taxes to support the grant, and the funds were then paid out to the participating states.

In 1923 the Supreme Court had occasion to review this argument in *Massachusetts v. Mellon,* in which the state of Massachusetts challenged the constitutionality of the Sheppard-Towner Maternity Aid Act. Justice George Sutherland's opinion dismissed the suit for want of jurisdiction, on the grounds that the suit did not in reality arise between a state and citizens of another state. Instead, said Sutherland, it was an attempt on the part of the state to act as a representative of its citizens against the national government. "It cannot be conceded that a state, as parens patriae, may institute judicial proceedings to protect citizens of the United States from the operation of the statutes thereof." The Court also denied its jurisdiction on the ground that the constitutional issue raised by the state was a "political question," since the state was in effect asserting that Congress had invaded the realm of state power.

Though the Court thus denied its jurisdiction, Sutherland's opinion contained much obiter dicta implying that grants-in-aid were not coercive and were constitutional. "Probably it would be sufficient to point out," he said, "that the powers of the state are not invaded, since the statute imposes no obligation, but simply extends an option which the state is free to accept or reject." The statute did not "require the states to do or yield anything. If Congress enacted it with the ulterior purpose of tempting them to yield, that purpose may be effectively frustrated by the simple expedient of not yielding."

While the Court thus impliedly sanctioned the constitutionality of the grant-in-aid, public opinion of the day was such that for some years after 1921 grants were not extended into any important new field. Yet undeniably the grant-in-aid held potentialities for a large expansion of federal activities in fields ordinarily reserved to the states. After 1933, the number of grants-in-aid greatly increased and came to play an important part in the rise of a "new federalism."

THE EXECUTIVE IN THE TWENTIES

Liberal nationalism had called for strong executive leadership; reaction now called for a passive Presidency. Presidential leadership of the kind begun by Roosevelt and practiced by Wilson almost disappeared in the twenties. Harding, an ex-Senator with little or no sense of initiative, was nearly always willing to accept congressional leadership in legislation. Coolidge was less tractable; yet he had no positive program and offered Congress little leadership during his six years in office. He quarreled with Congress over taxation, a bonus for World War I veterans, and agricultural relief, but in the end Congress usually had its way. In the years of swift economic decay after 1929, Hoover, too, was able to assert but little control over Congress. Thus between 1921 and 1933 the Wilsonian concept of presidential leadership was largely discarded.

It was during the Coolidge era, nonetheless, that the Supreme Court decided that the President possessed the power to remove subordinate executive officials without regard to any process of senatorial assent. *Myers v. United States* (1926) involved an appeal from a decision of the Court of Claims rejecting a suit for back salary by a former postmaster whom Wilson had summarily removed from office. In a lengthy and detailed opinion Chief Justice Taft denied the appeal and confirmed the removal.

Taft's argument drew heavily upon the debate in the First Congress in 1789, in which Madison had argued that the Constitution charged the President with the faithful execution of the laws, and that he must be able to control his subordinates through removal when necessary if he was to be held responsible for his administration. The Chief Justice also cited with approval the contention advanced by Hamilton in his *Pacificus* essay of 1793: that the enumeration of executive powers in Article II, unlike that of congressional powers in Article I, was intended for emphasis only, and did not exclude the exercise of other powers by the President. A separate removal power, in other words, was an inherent part of a more general presidential prerogative power.

Taft then boldly defined the scope of the removal power to include minor executive officals as well as high policy making officers. Article II, Section 2 of the Constitution, Taft observed, provided that "Congress may by law vest the Appointment of such inferior officers, as they think proper, in the President alone, in the Courts of law, or in the Heads of Departments." The Supreme Court, the Chief Justice conceded, had ruled in *United States v. Perkins* (1896) that this provision gave Congress implicit control over the removal of inferior officers whose appointments it had lodged with department heads. Nonetheless, Taft declared, in those instances where Congress had left the appointment vested in the President, it could not then arbitrarily arrogate to itself or to others the executive's power over removals.

Taft's argument, while impressive, was open to serious objections. Madison's 1789 argument had been concerned with the appointment of a Secretary of Foreign Affairs, and his reasoning with respect to the President's responsibiliity for the control of his administration logically could apply only to high policy making officers. As Justices McReynolds and Brandeis pointed out in separate dissenting opinions, Congress had many times exercised its right to vest inferior appointments in the President or in cabinet officers, and had at the same time fixed the conditions for removal, frequently including a requirement for senatorial consent. To override such precedent with a vague assertion of a general executive prerogative in removals seemed doubtful reasoning. Taft also exaggerated when he asserted that Justice Joseph Story, Daniel Webster, and Chancellor James Kent as well as other statesmen of the past had accepted the 1789 congressional decision as decisive for all removals. Story apparently had disagreed with the decision, and had argued that Congress could revoke it at any time simply by legislating for removals.

The implications of the Myers decision were theoretically serious but in fact were hardly realized in practice. It could now be argued that civil service legislation which guaranteed the tenure of inferior executive officers was unconstitutional and that minor federal employees could now be removed by the President at will without the consent of the Senate. In fact, however, no one attacked the civil service tenure system as illegal. A further possible implication of the Myers decision was that members of independent federal regulatory commissions were now subject to removal at will by the President, even though in most instances the conditions for their removal had been stipulated by Congress. However the Court, in *Humphrey's Executor v. United States* (1935), was to refute this idea.

While the Court in the Myers case strengthened the hand of the President with respect to Congress, it balanced this in *McGrain v. Daugherty* by reinforcing the power of Congress to investigate the executive establishment, provided such investigations were staged pursuant to a legitimate exercise of congressional legislative power. The McGrain case grew out of a 1924 Senate investigation into the official conduct of Attorney General Harry M. Daugherty, who had come under severe attack because of his dubious associations with the principals in the disgraceful Teapot Dome scandal. The Senate investigating committee had issued a subpoena addressed to Mally S. Daugherty, the Attorney General's brother, ordering him to appear as a witness. When Mally Daugherty defied the subpoena, the Senate had issued a warrant for his arrest, in accordance with which the Senate Sergeant at Arms had taken him into custody. Daugherty then had appealed successfully to a federal court for a writ of habeas corpus, on the ground that the Senate had exceeded its constitutional powers.

Upon appeal, the Court in a unanimous decision reversed the order of the district court discharging the witness and confirmed in strong language the broad investigative powers of the Senate when exercised pursuant to its legislative function. The power of legislatures to stage investigations, Justice Van Devanter observed, was an ancient one and an "essential and appropriate auxiliary to the legislative function" itself. In the present instance, Van Devanter pointed out, the object of the Senate's inquiry was the administration of the Department of Justice—a matter properly "subject to regulation by congressional legislation." Pursuant to such an investigation, it followed, the Senate could constitutionally exercise its equally venerable right to issue warrants addressed to recalcitrant witnesses, and to arrest them where necessary in order to obtain their testimony.

Notwithstanding the broad investigative powers which the Court thus sanctioned in the two houses of Congress, legislative investigations after 1930 were to come under a cloud, in the main because Congress all too frequently allowed them to degenerate into inquisitorial trials only nominally related to the legislative process. In 1957, in *Watkins v. United States*, the Court, without overruling its McGrain dictum, was to speak sharply against congressional "trials" of this kind.[9] On the other hand, the crisis in the Presidency which developed after 1970 in the Nixon administration was to demonstrate anew what had been evident in the twenties: that, properly exercised, the congressional power of investigation was an important safeguard against the corruption and subversion of constitutional government.

FEDERAL ADMINISTRATIVE COMMISSIONS IN THE TWENTIES

The postwar reaction seriously damaged the prestige of federal administrative commissions. The Interstate Commerce Commission and the Federal Trade Commission, in particular, had been established in order to effect direct discretionary controls over certain phases of business activity. Public opinion in the postwar era, however, was sharply out of sympathy with the functions and methods of such boards.

After 1920 the Federal Trade Commission suffered a serious loss

---

[9] See below, p. 929.

of authority through a series of unfavorable court decisions. It was the Supreme Court's unwillingness to grant the Commission broad administrative discretion and the Court's insistence upon "broad review" that did the most damage. The Federal Trade Commission Act of 1914 had attempted to vest broad discretionary authority in the Commission, which was empowered to define unfair trade practices in accordance with what it believed to be the public interest. The Commission's findings of fact were to be accepted prima facie by the court of review if supported by evidence; presumably a finding that a particular practice was unfair was such a finding of fact. This definition of the Commission's powers in relation to the courts followed closely the pattern for the Interstate Commerce Commission established in the Hepburn Act. It will be recalled that the Supreme Court in interpreting the Hepburn Act had followed a self-imposed policy of narrow review in appeals from the Commission's decisions, and there was therefore some reason to believe that it would now treat the Federal Trade Commission's decisions in the same manner. Instead, the Court, in a series of decisions after 1920, not only reserved to itself the right to define what constituted an unfair trade practice, but it also gravely impaired the Commission's capacity as a fact-finding body. The result virtually destroyed the Commission's usefulness as an administrative agency.

The significant opinion outlining the Court's attitude came in *Federal Trade Commission v. Gratz* (1920). The Commission had found the practice, engaged in by certain manufacturers of cotton ties, of refusing to sell their product unless the purchaser also agreed to buy specified amounts of cotton bagging, to be an unfair trade practice and had issued to the respondent firms an order to cease and desist. The United States Circuit Court of Appeals had reversed the ruling, whereupon the Commission had appealed to the Supreme Court.

Justice McReynolds' majority opinion began by stating that "the words 'unfair method of competition' are not defined by the statute, and their exact meaning is in dispute." He added that "it is for the courts, not the Commission ultimately to determine, as a matter of law, what they include." Thus, although the law specifically gave the Commission the right to define unfair trade practices and gave the findings of facts supporting such a ruling a prima facie validity, McReynolds stated that since the Court had final power to interpret the law it also had final power to decide what constituted an unfair trade practice. McReynolds then proceeded to overrule the Commission's finding of an unfair trade practice in the present case, on the ground that the practice involved was not actually a harmful one. The decision had the effect of destroying the Commission's capacity to demarcate new areas of unfair trade practice, and thus it forecast the virtual destruction of the Commission's administrative discretion.

Had the Court been willing to accept as final Commission findings of fact supported by evidence, the Commission would still have been able to function with some efficiency. In fact, however, the Court in subsequent cases assumed a right of general review of all the facts *de novo*, on the ground that it could not otherwise determine whether the Commission's findings of facts were actually supported by the evidence. Thus, in *Federal Trade Commission v. Curtis Publishing Company* (1923) the Court, in overturning a "cease and desist" order against the publishing firm's exclusive sales contract, ignored the Commission's evidence in support of its findings that the exclusive sales contract in question was an unfair trade practice. Justice McReynolds in his opinion explained that "manifestly, the Court must enquire whether the Commission's findings of fact are supported by evidence. If so supported, they are conclusive. But, as the statute grants jurisdiction to make and enter, upon the pleadings, testimony, and proceedings, a decree affirming, modifying, or setting aside an order, the Court must also have power to examine the whole record and ascertain for itself the issues presented, and whether there are material facts not reported by the Commission." In short, the Commission's findings of fact had but little prima facie value, and the courts on appeal could consider the entire case anew.

In the decade after 1923, the Court in nearly all Federal Trade Commission cases followed its reasoning in the Gratz and Curtis opinions and so gave little weight to the Commission's findings of unfair trade practices and its findings of fact; instead it overturned the Commission's orders with monotonous consistency. The Commission thus occupied much the same relation to the courts as had the Interstate Commerce Commission before 1906. The Commission had little power, and the intent of Congress in erecting the body had been effectively frustrated.

To an extent this judicial tendency in the twenties to interfere with broad administrative discretion affected the Interstate Commerce Commission as well. In *St. Louis and O'Fallon Railway Company v. United States* (1929), for example, the Court reversed the Commission's ruling that a valuation of railroad assets in pursuance of the recapture clause in the Transportation Act of 1920 should be based upon original cost. Instead, the Court indicated that valuation must take into account reproduction cost. This decision the Court based on the argument that the Transportation Act required the Commission to estimate value in accordance with "the law of the land," and that the Court in *Smyth v. Ames* (1898) and in later cases had already decided that the law of the land required that replacement costs be considered.

In his dissent, Brandeis pointed out that the Commission was a fact-finding body whose duty was to weigh evidence and that the findings of fact by which it had arrived at a fair valuation were to be received, in the Court's own words, "with the deference due to those of a tribunal 'informed by experience' and 'appointed by law.' " In his belief, the Court, in overruling the Commission's analysis of evidence behind its decision that rates should be based on original cost, had invaded the commission's fact-finding sphere, just as it had already done with the Federal Trade Commission. Further, Brandeis pointed out, the practical effect of the ruling was to defeat the evident intent of Congress in the Transportation Act—to provide the public with adequate rail service at "the lowest cost consistent with full justice to the private owners."

THE CONSTITUTION AND THE NEW PROSPERITY

So it was that the vast prosperous, sprawling giant of American economy went its way comparatively unhindered by serious federal or state interference with the processes of business and industrial life. America's business and political leaders were practically unanimous in the belief that no new controls upon the economy were necessary. The constitutional system, in their opinion, wisely and correctly restricted the scope of federal activity and protected private property and free enterprise against unreasonable governmental interference. Most Americans shared these ideas. They were convinced that the nation's constitutional system, by thus protecting property, prepared the way for a new era of universal prosperity.

Thus inspired, a new wave of Constitution-worship swept the country. Statesmen, industrialists, financiers, and common folk frequently paid homage to a Constitution which they held responsible for America's wealth, happiness, and spiritual well-being. America's great charter was revered as an expression of certain eternal verities of good government, the more to be respected in an age when other nations seemed to be falling into the hands of Communist and Fascist despoilers of property and human liberty. Love of the Constitution as an uncrowned king was never so widespread as in the years after the first World War.

Thus the United States in the twenties moved on through a period of gigantic industrial, commercial, and financial development with but few effective controls upon the national economy. The ineffective character of federal trust controls inaugurated a period of dizzy combination in industry and finance. Holding companies mushroomed, especially in the fields of public utilities, railroads, and banking operations. Some of these were basically sound, but others were visionary, unsound, or even fraudulent both in organization and operation. Many of them, like the Insull empire, were to come crashing in ruins in the debacle of 1929–33. Uncontrolled investment banking operations dumped upon the public hundreds of millions in foreign securities, most of which ultimately proved to be worthless. Heavy industry, freed of the threat of prosecution for combination and price fixing, partially abandoned the free competitive price system in favor of "price leadership" or outright price fixing. Industry was becoming more and more efficient in production, but quasi-monopoly held up prices so that in a majority of cases the savings effected by industrial efficiency were not passed on to the public. Wages rose, but they failed to keep pace with the rise in over-all industrial capacity to produce goods. At the same time, technological improvements threw men out of work faster than they could be re-employed. For these reasons, mass purchasing power did not expand rapidly enough to absorb the increase in industrial output. Surplus corporate profits and big incomes, seeking investment outlets, poured into the securities market, skyrocketing stock and bond prices and precipitating an unprecedented era of stock market gambling. Agriculture, on the other hand, was already in a state of partial collapse. Most farmers had overexpanded as a result of the extraordinary demands for agricultural commodities during World War I. Operating in a free competitive market closely approximating the theoretical conditions of pure free enterprise, the farmer consistently overproduced the staple farm commodities in the face of collapsing agricultural prices. Well before 1929, most farmers were experiencing a deep depression.

The storm signals were flying long before 1929, but most Americans ignored them. President Herbert Hoover, taking office in March 1929, confidently predicted the greatest era of material prosperity in the world's history. Even then, however, the clock was ticking out the final moments of *laissez-faire* prosperity.

Chapter

27

The New Deal

In October 1929 the stock market wavered, broke, then crashed downward, inaugurating the most catastrophic economic collapse in American history. The dream of a new povertyless age was shattered; and in its place appeared a succession of ghastly economic nightmares. At first the Hoover administration and the nation's business leaders treated the great depression as no more than a passing flurry. But as unemployment passed the twelve-million mark, as industrial production fell below 50 per cent of the 1929 level, and as the entire banking structure threatened to collapse, it became evident that something was vitally wrong with the nation's economic life. According to orthodox economic theory, recovery should have set in automatically and in due course, but the expected development did not occur. The economic crisis inspired a great wave of social discontent which in turn produced a major political upheaval leading directly to what was to become a limited revolution in the American constitutional system.

As the depression continued its downward course, President Hoover recognized that the national government was properly concerned with the nation's welfare, and from time to time he initiated such relief measures as he believed advisable and within the sphere of federal sovereignty. Thus, in 1931, he secured the adoption of a moratorium on international debt payments; in 1932 he brought about the enactment of legislation creating the Reconstruction Finance Corporation, intended to rescue commercial, industrial, and financial institutions that were in difficulty by direct governmental loans; and in the same year he somewhat reluctantly accepted the necessity of direct federal appropriations to state and municipal governments for relief purposes.

Yet Hoover's deep-seated faith in a highly individualistic *laissez-faire* economy made him fundamentally unwilling to countenance a broad governmental program for either relief or social reform. He was committed to the belief that bureaucratic controls of private business were pernicious, that governmental interference with natural economic law was unwise and unnecessary, and that economic recovery would come about in due course through the inevitable corrective processes inherent in a system of untrammeled free enterprise.

Hoover's constitutional position in the great crisis flowed quite naturally out of his individualistic social philosophy. The federal government must be exceedingly careful not to overstep the constitutionally prescribed limits of its power. Constitutional change "must be brought about only by the straightforward methods provided by the Constitution itself." That is, he could not recognize the economic emergency as an adequate reason for the assertion of new federal powers and controls, no matter how badly needed they might be. In particular, Hoover was opposed to a broad construction of the federal commerce power. "If we are to stretch the Interstate Commerce provision to regulate all those things that pass state lines," he once observed, "what becomes of that fundamental freedom and independence that can rise only from local self-government?" In short, Hoover's faith in *laissez-faire* economics and constitutional conservatism made it impossible for him to launch a large-scale national attack on the depression.

In the presidential election of November 1932 the Democratic candidate, Franklin D. Roosevelt, scored an impressive popular and electoral college victory over President Hoover in the latter's attempt to win re-election. The election, which swept the Republican party from power only four years after its one-sided victory of 1928, was a clear indication of how completely the people at large had come to hold the President and the federal government responsible for the nation's economic welfare.

Hoover's defeat occurred largely because the electorate believed he had failed to deal adequately with the depression. Most voters ignored the Republican argument that the federal government had only a limited capacity to cope with the economic crisis, and in voting for Roosevelt they in effect demanded that the President and Congress assert sufficient national authority to deal with the emergency. Roosevelt's victory thus obviously implied a return to the constitutional postulates of liberal nationalism.

THE FIRST DAYS OF THE NEW DEAL

Franklin D. Roosevelt entered office in March 1933 with large Democratic majorities behind him in both houses of Congress and with a wave of public confidence in his capacity to deal with the emergency manifest in the country at large. He had once been a states' rights Democrat, and upon occasion had denounced the growth of federal power as "against the scheme and intent of our Constitution." In his inaugural address, however, he made it clear that he now believed in a flexible interpretation of the Constitution and in the legality of a federal program adequate to deal with the existing emergency. Accordingly, he at once initiated in Congress an extensive program of emergency reform legislation, establishing unprecedented controls over banking, finance, labor, agriculture, and manufacturing. A major portion of this program became law in an epoch-making "hundred days" after March 4, 1933.

At the moment Roosevelt entered office, a wave of bank failures of such proportion as to threaten the entire banking structure with complete collapse was sweeping the nation, while abnormal gold exports and panicky currency hoarding were undermining the stability of the monetary system.

To meet this situation, the President immediately declared a temporary "bank holiday" closing all banks in the nation. He also suspended gold exports and foreign exchange operations. He took these steps with but dubious legal authority, under certain provisions of the Trading with the Enemy Act of 1917. However, the Emergency Banking Act, rushed into law on March 9, 1933, ratified the President's action and made provisions for reopening banks under executive direction. The statute also required the surrender of all gold and gold certificates to the Treasury Department, the holders to receive an equivalent amount of other currency. This step was intended to stop currency hoarding and to prepare for a mildly inflationary devaluation of the currency.

A rider attached to the Agricultural Adjustment Act, enacted on May 12, authorized the President to adjust the gold content of the dollar, though it specified that he could not reduce the content to less than 50 per cent of the current amount. This provision reflected a belief, widely entertained at the time, that a reduction in the dollar's gold content would lead to a much-desired rise in prices, since it would lower the dollar's theoretical value. In accordance with this provision Roosevelt issued successive proclamations progressively lowering the dollar's gold content below the original 25.8 grains. The Gold Reserve Act of January 30, 1934, provided that the President should not in any event fix the gold content of the dollar at more than 60 per cent of its original value; accordingly the President on January 31 fixed the gold content of the dollar at 15 5/21 grains.

The retirement of gold from circulation and the reduction in dollar gold content made imperative the Joint Resolution of June 5, 1933, by which Congress canceled the "gold clause" in private contracts and in government bonds. Contracts of this type called for payment of a fixed amount of gold by weight as a precautionary device against destruction of the debt's real value through inflation. Their enforcement was not only impossible now that gold had been withdrawn from circulation, but if creditors successfully attempted to enforce collection in devalued dollars and demanded enough new dollars to make up the original theoretical gold value of the contract, the result would be a vast and inequitable increase in public and private indebtedness.

A second major group of statutes was concerned with agricultural relief. The most important of these measures was the Agricultural Adjustment Act of May 12, 1933, whose preamble declared that the prevailing economic crisis was in part the consequence of a disparity between agricultural prices and the prices of other commodities, a disparity that had broken down farm purchasing power for industrial products. This provision advanced, by implication, three different constitutional arguments to justify federal regulation of agriculture: the theory of emergency powers, the general welfare, and the effect of agriculture upon interstate commerce.

The announced purpose of the law was the restoration of agricultural prices to a pre-war parity level. This was to be accomplished by agreements between farmers and the federal government for reduction of acreage of production in seven basic agricultural commodities—wheat, cotton, corn, rice, tobacco, hogs, and milk —in return for federal benefit payments. Funds for benefit payments were to be secured by an excise tax to be levied upon processors of the commodity in question. The tax was to be at such a rate as to equal the difference between the current average farm price of the commodity and its "fair exchange" value, the latter being defined as that price that would give the commodity the same purchasing power as it had in the 1909–14 base period. Thus the act made use of the federal taxing power and the right to appropriate for the general welfare as the constitutional basis of agricultural control.

Other agricultural measures enacted at this time were intended to relieve the rural credit situation. A separate section of the Agricultural Adjustment Act authorized the Federal Land Banks to acquire farm mortgages and empowered the Federal Loan Commission to make loans to joint-stock land banks. In addition, the Farm Credit Act of June 16, 1933, authorized the Farm Credit Administration to create twelve "production credit" corporations, who were to invest funds in farmers' co-operatives authorized under the act. And the so-called Frazier-Lemke Act, enacted later, on June 28, 1934, permitted bankrupt farm mortgagors either to purchase the farm property in question over a period of six years, or to stay all proceedings for five years while paying rent for any portion of the property occupied, with the privilege of purchasing it at the expiration of the five-year period.

Perhaps the most famous New Deal statute enacted in the hundred days' emergency session was the widely heralded National Industrial Recovery Act of June 16, 1933. The introductory section declared that "a national emergency productive of widespread unemployment and disorganization of industry, which burdens interstate commerce, affects the public welfare, and undermines the standards of living of the American people, is hereby declared to exist." Thus the law cited the economic emergency, the relation between the economic crisis and interstate commerce, and the federal welfare power in an attempt to provide a constitutional foundation for federal regulation of industry.

The act then provided for "codes of fair competition" covering prices, wages, trade practices, and the like, to be drafted by trade or industrial groups and submitted to the President for approval and promulgation. Approved codes thereupon became the "standard of fair competition" in their respective trades or industries, an infraction of which was to be deemed a violation of the Federal Trade Commission Act. In other words, a promulgated code had the force of law. Section 7(a) of the measure required that every such code guarantee labor the right to collective bargaining, while still other sections provided for the regulation of interstate commerce in oil.

The statute thus contemplated the limited cartelization of American business and industry under a system of industrial self-government protected by federal sanctions. Needless to say, the underlying economic theory of the law was incompatible with previous federal trust policy, which had aimed at the preservation of a maximum of "free competition" in business.

A variety of other laws intended to stimulate production or employment deserve but brief mention here, as they posed no serious constitutional issues. The acts creating the Civilian Conservation Corps, which established reforestation camps for unemployed youths, the Federal Emergency Relief Administration, which made direct relief appropriations to the states, and the Home Owners Loan Corporation, which provided for the refinancing of home mortgages through federal savings and loan associations, could all be justified under the federal power to appropriate money for the general welfare. Since they involved no coercive controls, it was difficult to attack them in the courts, and the judiciary thus had no opportunity to pass upon their constitutionality.

More controversial, however, was the act of May 18, 1933, creating the Tennessee Valley Authority. The T.V.A. was organized as a government corporation, whose three-man board of directors was to be appointed by the President. The corporation was authorized to construct dams, reservoirs, power lines, and the like; to manufacture fertilizer and explosives for the War Department; and to sell all surplus power not used in its operations. The law in reality projected a gigantic rehabilitation and development program in the Tennessee Valley region, embracing flood control, power development, reforestation, and agricultural and industrial development.

The early days of the Roosevelt administration also saw the end of the great prohibition experiment. The Democratic platform of 1932 had called for the repeal of the Eighteenth Amendment, and Roosevelt as a candidate had also supported repeal. The overwhelming Democratic victory in November accordingly seemed to constitute a mandate, and the lame-duck Congress preceding Roosevelt's inauguration submitted, on February 20, 1933, the followed proposed amendment to the states:

Section 1. The eighteenth article of Amendment to the Constitution of the United States is hereby repealed.

Section 2. The transportation or importation into any state, territory, or possession of the United States for delivery or use therein of intoxicating liquors, in violation of the laws thereof, is hereby prohibited.

Section 3. This article shall be inoperative unless it shall have been ratified as an amendment to the Constitution by convention in the several states, as provided in the Constitution, within seven years from the date of the submission thereof to the states by Congress.

The proposed amendment was the first which Congress had submitted for ratification by conventions in the several states, and the exact procedure to be adopted in ratification became a matter of some discussion and controversy. Although many constitutional lawyers argued that Congress must prescribe the conditions under which the several state conventions would meet and ratify the amendment, Congress failed to act upon any of the various bills introduced for this purpose, so that the exact procedure became a matter of individual state law. In certain states, delegates were elected at large; in others, the district system was used. In most states, the people voted for delegates pledged for or against ratification. The delegates therefore did very little or no debating in convention, but merely voted as they had pledged. Ratification proceeded rapidly, and the proposal was proclaimed a part of the Constitution as the Twenty-First Amendment on December 5, 1933.[1] Meanwhile Congress, at Roosevelt's suggestion, had hastened the demise of prohibition by the passage of the so-called Beer Act. This measure, which became law on March 22, 1933, permitted the manufacture of alcoholic beverages containing not more than 3.2 per cent alcohol.

Considered in its entirety, the emergency program enacted under Roosevelt's leadership constituted a more far-reaching assertion of federal authority over national economic life than had hitherto been dreamed of in responsible political circles. Judicial precedents for using the commerce and taxing powers to assert control over industry and to effect certain police regulations did indeed exist, and were the Court to examine the recovery program in the light of these precedents, nearly all of it could pass constitutional muster. However, if the Court reviewed the National Industrial Recovery Act, the Agricultural Adjustment Act, and the statute creating the Tennessee Valley Authority in the spirit of *United States v. E. C. Knight Co.* or the Child Labor cases, most of the New Deal's grand design was doomed. Roosevelt's reform program thus inevitably precipitated a tremendous struggle between two opposing conceptions of national authority, a struggle fought out immediately in the courts, but ultimately decided in the arena of politics and public opinion.

---

[1] For a discussion of the constitutional aspects of the operation of the amendment, see pp. 743–744.

EXECUTIVE LEADERSHIP UNDER ROOSEVELT

The early days of the New Deal witnessed the restoration of a type of executive leadership over Congress strongly reminiscent of that exercised in the first year of the Wilson administration. Roosevelt's personal prestige was at the moment tremendous; his confident assertion that the great depression could be conquered, that "the only thing we have to fear is fear itself," caught the popular imagination and rekindled the nation's faith in itself at a moment of almost universal panic and despair. The President also commanded a large Democratic majority in both houses of Congress, a majority which well understood how completely its position depended upon a successful presidential program. In addition, Republican opposition in and out of Congress was for the moment silenced and demoralized by an economic collapse so severe as to convince a large majority of the public of the desirability of a powerful reform program. The need for haste also entered into the situation; Congress could ill afford to debate at length while urgent recovery measures awaited enactment.

As a result, there was little debate on constitutional issues or on the economic implications of the great programs Roosevelt submitted to Congress. Proposed statutes were drawn up in conference between the President, the various experts—early dubbed the "Brain Trust"—whom Roosevelt called upon for advice, party leaders, and the special-interest groups involved. Thus the National Industrial Recovery Act was the product of lengthy discussions between Roosevelt and certain business leaders; the Agricultural Adjustment Act, of conferences between Roosevelt, Secretary of Agriculture Henry Wallace, economists George Peek and Mordecai Ezekiel, and farm bloc leaders. Once presidential measures were submitted to Congress, however, they became "must legislation." As in the British parliamentary system, a refusal to act would have been no less than a major rebellion against the executive.

Congress yielded to the exigencies of the moment, but it had not surrendered its prerogative. As in Jackson's and Lincoln's time, executive ascendancy soon inspired charges that the President was a dictator conspiring to destroy representative government. But the fallacy of the dictatorship cry was soon revealed in the independent spirit exhibited in Congress once the emergency had passed.

Thus while F.D.R.'s influence with Congress remained strong, he nonetheless suffered a series of major defeats during his second term in his dealings with that body. Most notable was the dramatic failure in 1937 to persuade the two houses to adopt his plan for the reorganization of the federal judiciary.[1] Less spectacular but a substantial defeat nonetheless was the refusal of the House of Representatives in April 1939 to pass the President's Reorganization Bill, which would have restructured the federal bureaucracy in the interests of greater efficiency. This measure, which would have created two new executive departments—Social Welfare and Public Works—and which also would have expanded the White House staff, extended the application of the merit system, and placed several independent agencies and commissions in subordinate "line" positions in the appropriate departments, died on the floor of the House amid cries of "dictatorship" and an accusation by Senator David I. Walsh of Massachusetts that the President was attempting to plunge "a dagger into the very heart of democracy."

Earlier, the Supreme Court had imposed other constitutional limits upon the President's role. In *Humphrey's Executor v. United States* (1935), the Court held that the Chief Executive lacked constitutional authority to remove members of the various independent federal boards and commissions without senatorial consent. Humphrey, a member of the Federal Trade Commission, had been removed from office by Roosevelt in October 1933. After his death in February 1934, his executor sued in the Court of Claims to recover Humphrey's salary as a commissioner from his removal to his death, claiming his removal had been invalid. The Court held that the intent of Congress had been to confer upon the Commission independence of the President, and that the Commission was the agent of Congress and the judiciary, not of the executive. In reaching this conclusion, the Court specifically refused to apply the dictum in *Myers v. United States*, ruling that that precedent was limited to subordinate executive officers in the President's own departments. In other words, Humphrey's removal had been unlawful.

In short, while Franklin Roosevelt's tenure as Chief Executive undoubtedly must be seen as the beginning of a forty-year-long period of expanding presidential power and prerogative, he was by no means the dictator his enemies charged him with becoming. Sharp limits were imposed upon his decision-making capacity and his ability to influence the course of public policy by the separation of powers and the concomitant independence of Congress

---

[1] See above, pp. 714–718.

and the federal judiciary on the one hand and the constrictive forces of politics and public opinion on the other.

THE NEW DEAL BEFORE THE COURT

It was evident from the first that the Supreme Court's attitude toward the recovery program was a matter of extreme importance. Judges sympathizing with the New Deal social objectives and appreciating the liberal national tradition would find it easy to select a stream of precedents validating most of the New Deal measures. On the other hand, judges who sympathized with the conservative crescendo of protest against the New Deal's interference with private property rights and who accepted the traditions of *laissez-faire* economics and limited federal power would have little difficulty in finding justification for striking down as unconstitutional most of the important New Deal statutes.

The personnel of the Court now about to pass upon the constitutionality of the New Deal had not changed greatly since the mid-twenties. Four of the most consistent conservatives of the pre-depression era—George Sutherland, Willis Van Devanter, Pierce Butler, and James McReynolds—were still present. So also were Louis D. Brandeis and Harlan F. Stone, both of whom inclined strongly to the liberal national position.

The newcomers were Chief Justice Charles Evans Hughes and Associate Justices Benjamin Cardozo and Owen J. Roberts. Hughes had already enjoyed a long and distinguished career in law and politics when President Hoover nominated him to replace Chief Justice Taft in 1930. Successively Governor of New York, Associate Justice of the Supreme Court from 1911 to 1916, Republican presidential candidate in 1916, and Secretary of State from 1921 to 1925, he had achieved the feat of moving in conservative political circles and yet retaining much of his early reputation for liberalism. Cardozo, appointed in 1932, had served for years as a justice of the New York Court of Appeals and had a pre-eminent reputation as a legal scholar and a liberal. Roberts' position was less certain. He was a Pennsylvania Republican with a successful practice as a conservative attorney; yet he was thought to entertain Progressive sentiments, and President Hoover had named him as a liberal.

In the division between liberals and conservatives, Hughes and Roberts held the balance of power. Cardozo, Brandeis, and Stone could be counted on generally to vote in support of most New Deal measures. Van Devanter, Sutherland, McReynolds, and Butler were certain to vote consistently against the New Deal. On those occasions when both Hughes and Roberts supported the liberal minority, the New Deal could reasonably expect to win a victory, although by only a 5-to-4 majority. On the other hand, whenever either Roberts or the Chief Justice voted with the conservatives, the New Deal would lose the day. On the whole, the conservative position was the stronger one, for as matters developed Roberts usually voted against the New Deal, and Hughes frequently did. It must be remembered, also, that there were certain constitutional issues upon which the judges were united in opposition to the recovery program. Thus the National Industrial Recovery Act was to be invalidated by a unanimous Court.

Two opinions of 1934, neither of which directly involved federal legislation, gave some evidence that a majority of the justices might view the New Deal with some sympathy. In *Home Bldg. and Loan Association v. Blaisdell,* decided in January 1934, a majority of five justices held the Minnesota moratorium law constitutional. The decision was significant, for the statute declared a limited moratorium on mortgage payments, and the Court might easily have decided that it violated the obligation of contracts clause. Instead, Hughes' opinion skirted close to the proposition that an emergency might empower government to do things which in ordinary times would be unconstitutional. An emergency, said the Chief Justice, could not create power, but it could furnish the occasion for the exercise of latent power. He then went on to deny the proposition that the Constitution could not be altered by a process of growth or that it must "be read with literal exactness like a mathematical formula." The Constitution, he thought, could have a different meaning today from that which it had for the men who framed it. Significantly, the four conservatives dissented and repudiated the emergency as an excuse for modifying the force of the contract clause.

Two months later, in *Nebbia v. New York,* the Court broke with tradition even more sharply than it had in the Minnesota moratorium decision. Here the Court sustained the validity of a New York statute setting up a state milk control board and empowering the board to fix maximum and minimum milk prices. This was precisely the kind of legislation which the Court had with some consistency struck down in the 1920's as a violation of due process, on the grounds that the business regulated did not fall within the narrow conception of public interest then entertained by the Court. However, in a startling opinion Justice Roberts now chose to ignore the ice company and theater ticket precedents to lay down an extremely broad conception of public interest. "It is clear," he said, "that there is no closed class or category of businesses affected with a public interest." The touchstone, he added, was not state franchise or monopoly. Instead, he said, a state was in general free to adopt toward any business "whatever economic policy may reasonably be deemed to promote public welfare." The Court thus adopted the conception of public interest which had been advocated by the minority in the theater ticket and ice company opinions, and so virtually wrote an end to "affection with a public interest" as a constitutional issue. It was little wonder that McReynolds, speaking for the four minority justices, complained sharply that this was not due process as he had understood it and that the majority in his opinion was perverting constitutional law under stress of an emergency.

For the moment, then, the liberals on the Court held a precarious balance of power. A majority of the justices, including Hughes and Roberts, had in the Minnesota moratorium case accepted tentatively the doctrine of emergency power and the idea of dynamic constitutional change. In the Nebbia case that same majority had underwritten a statute going conspicuously far in imposing social controls upon vested property interests and had broken sharply with well-defined recent precedents in due process in order to do so. If the New Deal could command this same majority, much of its legislative program might be sustained.

Not until January 1935 did the Court finally review a New Deal statute. While this delay was not extraordinary, it is probable that the more important recovery measures might have come before the Court somewhat sooner if Attorney General Homer S. Cummings and his staff had not been maneuvering for time and an auspicious series of cases to argue before the Court. In the sixteen months after January 1935, however, the Court decided ten major cases or groups of cases involving New Deal statutes. In eight instances the decision went against the New Deal. Stricken down in succession were Section 9(c) of the National Industrial Recovery Act, the N.R.A. itself, the Railroad Pension Act, the Farm Mortgage law, the Agricultural Adjustment Act, the A.A.A. amendments, the Bituminous Coal Act, and the Municipal Bankruptcy Act. Only two measures, the emergency monetary enactments of 1933 and the Tennessee Valley Authority Act, were given approval in carefully circumscribed and conditional terms. In short, the Court in sixteen months destroyed a very large portion of the Roosevelt program.

THE "HOT OIL" CASES

The Court's first invalidation of a New Deal law came in January 1935, in *Panama Refining Co. v. Ryan*, a case involving the so-called "hot oil" provisions of the National Industrial Recovery Act. Section 9(c), standing apart from the provisions of the Act dealing with codes of fair competition, authorized the President to prohibit the transportation in interstate commerce of oil produced or stored in excess of the limitations imposed by states in order to bolster faltering oil prices and to conserve oil resources. Precedents for federal co-operation with state law enforcement existed, notably in the Webb-Kenyon Act, which had prohibited interstate transportation of liquor into states banning liquor imports.

Chief Justice Hughes, speaking for eight of the nine justices, held Section 9(c) unconstitutional as an invalid delegation of legislative power, on the grounds that it did not set adequate standards for executive guidance. The section itself, said Hughes, "establishes no criterion to govern the President's course. It does not require any finding by the President as a condition of his action. The Congress in §9(c) thus declares no policy as to the transportation of the excess production." Nor was Hughes able to discover in Title I, containing the act's general declaration of policy, any more specific restrictions upon executive discretion. He concluded, therefore, that executive orders issued by authority of Section 9(c) were "without constitutional authority."

The Court had thus for the first time held unconstitutional a statute which delegated quasi-legislative authority to the executive. Undoubtedly the discretion admitted in Section 9(c) was very large; yet it is questionable whether any considerable distinction existed between the provision and earlier instances of delegation already held constitutional. The Interstate Commerce Commission's discretion in rate setting, controlled only by the injunction that rates must be reasonable, was certainly as great, as was also the President's discretionary right to raise or lower tariff schedules under the Fordney-McCumber Tariff Act of 1922. Moreover, a standard for executive guidance was actually present in Section 9(c): the President could not proceed beyond the limitations imposed by the statute.

Hughes' opinion did not discuss other provisions of the Recovery

Act; yet it seemed certain that if the Court was unwilling to accept the relatively modest delegation of legislative authority granted in Section 9(c), then the fate of the far-reaching and ramified delegations of power effected by the codes of fair competition was already sealed, and the entire statute was doomed.

THE GOLD CASES

Immediately after the Hot Oil decision, the government won a substantial victory in the Gold Cases. All of these cases were concerned with the right of Congress to nullify the gold clause in private and public contracts, as it had done in the Joint Resolution of June 5, 1933. *Norman v. Baltimore and Ohio Railroad Co.* and a companion case, *United States v. Bankers Trust Co.*, arose in the lower federal courts out of bondholders' suits to enforce the gold clause against defendant railroads on outstanding bonds. Plaintiffs asked payment in an amount of devaluated currency equal in theoretical gold content to the original amount of gold stipulated in the contract, in effect a demand for a write-up of 69 per cent in the actual dollar value of the indebtedness. *Nortz v. United States* arose in the Court of Claims, where the plaintiff had sued to recover the theoretical difference between the gold content of some $10,000 in gold certificates which he had been forced to surrender to the government and the gold content of the money that had been issued to him in lieu of the certificates. In *Perry v. United States,* a case also certified from the Court of Claims, the owner of a ten-thousand-dollar government bond sued to recover the difference between the original theoretical gold value of the contract and its present gold value in new dollars.

The fundamental constitutional issue in all four cases was whether or not the national government could impair the obligation of contracts, public and private, in pursuance of the monetary power. Chief Justice Hughes, who wrote all three majority opinions, granted the government a substantial victory. In *Norman v. the Baltimore and Ohio Railroad Co.* he first decided the essential point that contracts for payment in gold were not commodity contracts but were in reality contracts for payment in money and hence, by implication, fell within the federal monetary power. Relying extensively upon the *Second Legal Tender Case,* wherein the Court had sustained the constitutionality of Civil War greenback legal tender issues, the Chief Justice dwelt at length upon the broad and comprehensive nature of all federal power and asserted finally the government's right to abrogate private contracts when they stood in the way of the exercise of rightful federal functions.

This opinion provided the cue for *Nortz v. United States*. Gold certificates, the Chief Justice ruled, were in reality currency, and not federal gold warehouse receipts. The plain implication was that the government had a right to replace them with other currency. More important, Hughes pointed out that the plaintiff had suffered only nominal damages and hence had no right to sue in the Court of Claims. Holding this point to be decisive, the Court refused to consider whether or not gold certificates were an express contract with the United States, and whether the Emergency Banking Act in requiring their surrender took property in violation of due process.

In *Perry v. United States*, the government suffered a nominal defeat. Hughes held that government bonds, as distinct from private obligations, were contractual obligations of the United States government. Congress, he asserted, could not break its own plighted faith, even in the subsequent exercise of its lawful powers. Hence the Joint Resolution of June 5, 1933, insofar as it abrogated the gold clause in United States government obligations, was unconstitutional. Hughes hastened to add, however, that the plaintiff had suffered no more than nominal damages and was hence not entitled to sue in the Court of Claims. The aspersion cast upon the Joint Resolution was henceforth without practical meaning.

In one of the bitterest minority opinions ever recorded, Justice McReynolds expressed the dissent of the four conservatives for all four cases. "Just men," he said, "regard repudiation and spoliation of citizens by their sovereign with abhorrence; but we are asked to affirm that the Constitution has granted power to accomplish both." Congress, he continued, under the guise of pursuing a monetary policy "really has inaugurated a plan primarily designed to destroy private obligations, repudiate national debts, and drive into the treasury all the gold in the country in exchange for inconvertible promises to pay, of much less value." Some of the language in McReynolds' oral opinion was too vitriolic for the formal record. At one point in his delivery he leaned forward and in a voice shaking with emotion proclaimed that "This is Nero at his worst. The Constitution is gone!"

It appears probable that the majority in the Gold Cases was more impressed by practical considerations than by theoretical issues of constitutional law. The government's emergency monetary policy was, in theory at least, a gigantic breach of obligation of contract.

But the gold policy had failed of its intended result, and acceptance of its constitutionality would have no practical effects, whereas enforcement of gold contracts in devalued dollars would have had a catastrophic effect on national economy. This Chief Justice Hughes recognized, when he observed in the Norman case that "it requires no acute analysis or profound economic inquiry to disclose the dislocation of the domestic economy" which enforcement would produce. One cannot but wonder, on the other hand, what attitude Hughes and Roberts would have taken had the government's policy been successful and creditors suffered a heavy real loss. The precedents behind Hughes' opinion were few and not so convincing that they could not have been set aside. The *Second Legal Tender Case*, the most relevant precedent, had merely decided that greenbacks were legal tender in payment of debts, and the cases had not specifically sanctioned the abrogation of gold clauses. On the contrary, in *Bronson v. Rodes* (1869), the Court had specifically construed the Legal Tender Act as not invalidating contracts calling for gold payments. Hughes might very conceivably have ignored the Legal Tender Cases and have ruled that abrogation of the gold clause in private and public contracts violated the due process clause of the Fifth Amendment.

The government's victory may also be explained in part by the fact that the Gold Cases did not involve the most controversial issue of liberal nationalism, the exercise of federal control over various aspects of production. In a general way, the broad and comprehensive character of the federal monetary power was already well established, and the emergency measures under review in the Gold Cases contemplated the creation of no new sphere of federal activity. When such issues were not raised, the New Deal could command a majority.

SCHECHTER V. UNITED STATES: THE "SICK CHICKEN" CASE

In May 1935 the full weight of judicial disapproval of Roosevelt's program was released, as the Court struck down New Deal statutes in three cases and imposed serious limitations upon the President's removal power in a fourth.

On May 6 the Court, in *Retirement Board v. Alton Railroad Co.*, voted 5 to 4 to invalidate the Railroad Retirement Pension Act. Justice Roberts in the majority opinion held that certain mechanical details of the pension law were arbitrary and unreasonable and so violated due process and the Fifth Amendment. More significantly, however, Roberts was of the opinion that the whole subject of old age pensions had no real relationship to the safety or efficiency of rail transportation and so lay outside the federal commerce power. The extremely narrow definition of interstate commerce here implied, namely, that the power did not extend even to certain matters directly related to transportation itself, not only labeled any future federal pension law unconstitutional but also presaged clearly what the Court's attitude would be toward other federal statutes resting on a broad interpretation of the commerce power.

Three weeks later, on May 27, 1935, the Court in a unanimous decision held the National Industrial Recovery Act to be unconstitutional. The President's strategists had long viewed with anxiety the inevitable judicial inquiry into the N.R.A. Attorney General Homer S. Cummings and the Department of Justice accordingly had sought to postpone the day of reckoning, awaiting the moment when they might present the Court with as favorable a case as possible. They had pressed the "Hot Oil" case to a decision in the hope that the special circumstances surrounding the oil industry might make a favorable impression upon the Court and that a victory in this case would pave the way for validating the act in its entirety. Instead, the Court had held Section 9(c) unconstitutional; and the pointed questions on the codes of fair competition directed at counsel from the bench indicated only too well what several justices thought of the entire statute.

To add to the government's troubles, the N.R.A. was collapsing of its own weight. In the first few months after its passage, the Recovery Act undoubtedly had some beneficial effects; it had raised wages, eliminated many sweatshops, and bolstered business morale. On the other hand, the codes of fair competition, though supposedly not monopolistic, had generally favored large enterprise and had injured the little businessman; moreover, many of the codes had been hastily drawn and were unworkable in detail. Once the immediate crisis had passed, the attempt to cartelize American business completely at one stroke also encountered much opposition. In short, the N.R.A. was crumbling, which meant that the Court would encounter comparatively little public reaction should it declare the law void. In these circumstances, the administration was obliged to move for a judicial decision or accept the statute's collapse through general disobedience. After striking one case from the docket, it finally carried *Schechter v. United States* through to decision, although a more unfavorable case for the government's purposes would have been difficult to imagine.

Schechter v. United States, destined to go down in Court history as the "Sick Chicken" case, involved an appeal from a conviction for violation of the code of fair competition for the live poultry industry of New York City. The defendants were slaughterhouse operators, who purchased on commission and sold to kosher retailers, the birds being slaughtered on their premises by schochtim in accordance with ancient Jewish ritual. The defendants had been convicted, among other counts, of violating the code's wage and hour provisions, ignoring the "straight killing" requirement, which prohibited selected sale to retailers of individual chickens from coops, and of selling an "unfit chicken."

Chief Justice Hughes' opinion took up three questions in succession: whether the law was justified "in the light of the grave national crisis with which Congress was confronted," whether the law illegally delegated legislative power, and whether the act exceeded the limits of the interstate commerce power.

Hughes settled the first question by observing that "extraordinary conditions do not create or enlarge constitutional power." He added that "such assertions of extraconstitutional authority were anticipated and precluded by the explicit terms of the Tenth Amendment." On this point Hughes' position was almost diametrically opposed to that in his recent opinion on the Minnesota moratorium law. Admittedly, in the Minnesota case the Court had been dealing with state power not subject to the limitations of the Tenth Amendment. Undoubtedly, however, Hughes viewed the Recovery Act with extreme distaste and hence found no occasion to rationalize constitutional change.

Hughes then passed to the issue of legislative delegation. Had Congress in authorizing the codes of fair competition fixed adequate "standards of legal obligation, thus performing its essential legislative function . . . ?" The Chief Justice thought not. In reality, he said, the codes embraced whatever "the formulators would propose, and what the President would approve, or prescribe, as wise and beneficent measures for the government of trades and industries." In short, trade groups had been given a blanket power to enact into law whatever provisions for their business they happened to think wise. With some feeling, Hughes asserted that such a delegation "is unknown to our law and is utterly inconsistent with the constitutional prerogatives and duties of Congress." If the codes had any validity, he continued, it must have been because they were promulgated by the President. Yet the act also fixed no real limits upon the President's code-making power, so long as he sought the vague objectives set forth in the statute's preamble. It therefore illegally delegated legislative power to the executive, and was void.

Behind Hughes' argument one senses two additional powerful objections to the N.R.A.'s code-making features, though these objections were nowhere clearly stated. First, the Court was appalled by the unprecedented magnitude of the delegation of legislative authority projected in the law. Previously delegation had been on a comparatively small scale; in this case Congress had given the President authority to draft regulations governing the whole vast sweep of the nation's economic life. Cardozo expressed this difficulty more specifically in his concurring opinion, when he said that "this is delegation run riot."

Second, the Court viewed with evident distaste the fact that code making was in the first instance carried out not by the President but by private business groups, the President merely putting his stamp of approval upon the codes. The law thus came close to a delegation to private individuals. Technically, perhaps, there were no grounds for objection, since the President promulgated the codes, but the break with traditional methods of quasi-legislative delegation was plain enough.

Finally, Hughes found that the poultry code under review attempted to regulate intrastate commercial transactions and hence exceeded the federal commerce power. He rejected the stream of commerce doctrine as not applicable, on the grounds that there was no "flow" in the Schechters' business, their transactions being conducted on a purely local basis. Hughes held also that the Schechters' business had only an indirect effect upon interstate commerce and so was beyond federal control. It will be recalled that the distinction between direct and indirect effect had first been raised in *United States v. Knight*, though Hughes himself nowhere referred to that somewhat discredited precedent. The distinction between direct and indirect effects, Hughes asserted, was "clear in principle," though he failed to assert what the distinguishing principle was. While the more realistic Cardozo observed that the distinction was merely one of degree, he nonetheless agreed that the connection between the Schechters' business and interstate commerce was remote in the extreme, and that if the local poultry business lay within interstate commerce, then all limitations upon federal authority were completely dissolved.

The Schechter case was in fact well calculated to expose all of the inherent weaknesses in the Recovery Act. It revealed the N.R.A.'s extreme detail of regulation and the extent to which the federal government had imposed regulation upon aspects of economic life which even the Court's liberals thought properly beyond federal control. And a prosecution for selling a "sick chicken" gave a touch of the ridiculous to the law. The New Deal certainly could have made a better showing had it been able to rest its case for the N.R.A. upon the steel or coal codes, where the industries were of national concern and obviously affected in considerable degree both interstate commerce and the general welfare. It is significant that the Court was unanimous in its stand upon the statute. Even Brandeis and Cardozo could not stomach the extraordinary delegation and minute regulation involved.

In *Louisville Bank v. Radford*, another opinion handed down on May 27, the Court declared the so-called Frazier-Lemke Act void. Justice Brandeis, speaking for a unanimous Court, first pointed out that unlike earlier federal and state laws, the Frazier-Lemke act compelled the mortgagee to surrender the property in question free of any lien without full payment of the debt. While the federal government could lawfully impair the obligation of contracts, it could not take private property, even for a public purpose, without just compensation. Since the act destroyed pre-existing creditor property rights under state law, it violated the Fifth Amendment and was therefore void.

The Court's rejection of the early New Deal measures was actually a stroke of fortune in disguise for President Roosevelt. The Schechter decision in particular relieved him of the embarrassment of junking an outworn recovery measure and at the same time provided him with political ammunition for the coming election and the great battle with the judiciary over constitutional reform already looming. A grim-lipped Chief Executive shortly told a press conference that the Court's reasoning took the Constitution "back to the horse and buggy days," and implied darkly that if the Court threw down the gauntlet on the issue of constitutional reform, he would gladly accept the challenge.

The administration, while discouraged by the outcome of the Schechter case, did not abandon its attempts to regulate industry. The summer of 1935 saw the passage of two landmarks in New Deal legislative policy, the National Labor Relations Act of July 5, 1935, and the National Bituminous Coal Conservation Act of August 30, 1935. Both of these acts imposed regulations upon industry in apparent defiance of the Schechter opinion and thus flung the issue of federal economic controls back at the Court. Roosevelt's position became even clearer when he wrote a letter to Representative J.

Buell Snyder of Pennsylvania asking Congress to pass the coal bill regardless of any doubts, "however reasonable," that it might have about the bill's constitutionality. On the basis of this letter the President was widely represented as urging Congress to disregard the Constitution. However, the Pension and N.R.A. decisions were not necessarily binding upon the Coal Act, whose constitutionality was at least open to question. Undoubtedly, however, the President was in part challenging the finality of the Court's interpretation of the Constitution.

UNITED STATES V. BUTLER: THE FALL OF THE A.A.A.

In January 1936 the Court invalidated the Agricultural Adjustment Act by a 6-to-3 vote, in a decision that revealed how bitterly divided the justices were on certain crucial constitutional issues involved in the New Deal.

United States v. Butler arose out of a district court order to the receiver for a bankrupt cotton-milling corporation directing the receiver to pay the processing taxes required under the A.A.A. Justice Roberts, who wrote the badly organized majority opinion, first observed that the so-called processing tax was properly not a tax at all but, like the tax in the Child Labor Case, was in reality but part of a system for the regulation of agricultural production. This did not necessarily mean, he added, that it was unconstitutional, but that it could not be held valid under the taxing power.

Roberts then inquired into the question of whether or not crop benefits could be justified under the general welfare clause, which authorizes Congress to "provide for the common defense and general welfare of the United States." He examined the theories advanced by Madison and Hamilton on the scope and meaning of the clause in question. Madison, he recalled, had asserted that the clause was merely introductory to the enumerated powers of Congress which followed it in Article I, Section 8, and that in itself it conferred no additional power upon Congress, since to admit otherwise would be to undermine the limited character of federal power. Hamilton, on the other hand, had argued that the welfare clause conferred a separate and distinct category of power upon the federal government beyond those enumerated in Article I, Section 8, and that in consequence of it, Congress had a general power to tax and appropriate for the general welfare. Summing up these arguments, Roberts concluded that Hamilton had been right: the federal government did indeed possess the power to appropriate for the general welfare apart from the other enumerated powers of Congress.

In the light of the foregoing conclusion, what now followed was little short of amazing. Crop benefits, Roberts declared, could not be justified under the welfare clause, because in reality they constituted a system of agricultural regulations projected under the guise of appropriations for the general welfare, in violation of the Tenth Amendment. The design for regulation was no less real because it was disguised under a system of voluntary crop controls. The farmer had no real choice but to accept benefits and submit to regulation. "The power to confer or withhold unlimited benefits is the power to coerce or destroy. . . . This is coercion by economic pressure. The asserted power of choice is illusory." Then followed the *argumentum ad horrendum*: The welfare power, if used in this fashion, could be used to impose federal regulation upon any phase of economic life, merely by purchasing compliance. Processing taxes were therefore void as part of an unconstitutional system of agricultural regulation.[2]

The heart of Roberts' argument lay in the limitations he imposed upon the general welfare clause. He admitted the separate right to appropriate for the general welfare, yet he denied that the government could impose any conditions upon those who accepted the grant. In short, he held that the government could give away its funds but that it could not stipulate how they should be used! This conclusion ignored the patent historical fact that in land grants and grants-in-aid the federal government had been "purchasing compliance" ever since 1802. The Court itself had answered Roberts' argument in *Massachusetts v. Mellon* (1923), in which Justice Sutherland had observed, concerning grants-in-aid, that a state could avoid submission merely by the process of not submitting, that is, by refusing the grant. Indeed, if Congress could not even stipulate how its own appropriations for the general welfare were to be used, then, as Justice Stone's dissent implied, the appropriations power was reduced to little more than inanity.

As Stone pointed out, Roberts was also in error in likening the processing tax to the penalty device considered in the Child Labor Case. The processing tax actually was not regulatory, and was not intended to be so. It was a mere revenue-raising device; regulation

---

[2] A week later, in *Richert Rice Mills v. Fontenot*, the Court also voided the processing taxes provided for in the Agricultural Adjustment Act of August 1935, merely by following the Butler precedent.

was effected by appropriation, not taxation. Stone might well have added that taxation for regulatory purposes lying outside the enumerated powers of Congress had more than once been accepted by the Court, the Child Labor Case to the contrary, as *McCray v. United States* and *United States v. Doremus* bore witness. He could have added the protective tariff, which also obviously was taxation for an ulterior purpose, the regulation of production. Roberts had, in fact, sought to meet the tariff analogy with the brief contention that the tariff had its basis in the commerce clause, not in the taxing power.

There was much spiritual comfort for New Dealers in Stone's sharp dissenting opinion. Not only did he expose mercilessly the weaknesses in Roberts' logic, but he also attacked the Court's tendency to legislate through the judicial power and so placed the onus of abusing constitutional interpretation squarely upon conservative shoulders. "A tortured construction of the Constitution," he observed, "is not to be justified by extreme examples of reckless congressional spending . . . possible only by action of a legislature lost to all sense of public responsibility. Such suppositions are addressed to the mind accustomed to believe that it is the business of courts to sit in judgment upon the wisdom of legislative action. Courts are not the only agencies of government that must be assumed to have the capacity to govern." These words took much of the sting from the often-reiterated conservative charge that the New Deal was engaged in a conspiracy to subvert the Constitution.

The administration also took heart from the fact that Stone, Brandeis, and Cardozo, three judges generally considered to be the most learned and intelligent men on the Court, had set their stamp of approval upon a New Deal reform of even more long-run importance than the Recovery Act. Moreover, the minority opinion in the A.A.A. case might in the future easily become a majority. A rumor given wide credence in Washington asserted that Chief Justice Hughes had at first believed the statute constitutional, but that he had ultimately voted with the majority only because he thought another 5-to-4 decision would seriously damage the Court's prestige. One or two Roosevelt appointments, inevitable if Roosevelt should win re-election in 1936, could easily change the entire constitutional status of agricultural regulation.

Congress did not accept *United States v. Butler* as the final word in agricultural regulation. Seven weeks later it enacted a new agricultural relief measure, the Soil Conservation Act. The new law sought to avoid the charge of coercion by payments of benefits for soil conservation programs. Also, the act levied no taxes, and thus avoided the charge of regulatory taxation. But crop control was still the obvious purpose underlying the law, and the Court might well have taken warning, for here was evidence of a strong congressional determination to resist judicial fiat, an intention to force through the major New Deal objectives even at the risk of a head-on collision with the judiciary.

In February 1936 the New Deal won a limited judicial victory, when, in *Ashwander v. Tennessee Valley Authority*, the Court upheld the validity of a contract between the Tennessee Valley Authority and the Alabama Power Company for the sale of "surplus power" generated by Wilson Dam. Hughes' opinion pointed out that the dam in question had been built for national defense and for the improvement of navigation, both objects specifically lying within the scope of federal power. The federal government's right to dispose of property legally acquired, he added, could not be denied.

CARTER V. CARTER COAL COMPANY

Four months later, in May 1936, the Court struck at another New Deal attempt to regulate production, this time invalidating the Bituminous Coal Act of 1935. This law, more familiarly known as the Guffey Act, had attempted to restore some measure of prosperity to a prostrated industry of national importance. For twenty years the conflict between capital and labor in coal mining had been particularly savage. Wages played a high part in the cost of production, and there was consequently an unusually strong temptation for the operators to cut wages in depressions and to resist wage increases in good times. Moreover, after 1925 the industry steadily lost ground to new fuels and as a consequence suffered from "overproduction" and ruinously low prices. The great depression aggravated both labor and market difficulties, and by 1933 the industry was in a state of collapse. The N.R.A. code brought some temporary relief, and the Guffey Act was an attempt to replace the N.R.A. with a new code.

The Guffey Act began by declaring that the coal industry was "affected with a national public interest," and that the production and distribution of coal directly affected interstate commerce and so made federal regulation necessary. The law created a National Bituminous Coal Commission and gave it authority to formulate a Bituminous Coal Code, regulating coal prices through district boards in various coal-producing areas. It also levied a tax of 15 per cent on all coal sold at the mine head, nine-tenths of which was to be remitted to producers who accepted the code provisions. A separate section, Part III, guaranteed collective bargaining and provided that wage contracts negotiated between operators producing two-thirds of the tonnage and half or more of the workers should be binding upon the entire industry. The Act specifically provided that the constitutionality of the labor and price-fixing sections should be considered separately and that neither should necessarily be invalidated should the other be declared void.

The act was immediately attacked in a stockholders' suit against an operating company, a procedure now become familiar for attacking federal legislation. Upon appeal, the Supreme Court, in *Carter v. Carter Coal Company* (1936), declared the entire act unconstitutional. Sutherland's opinion asserted that the "so called excise tax" was not a tax at all, but a penalty, and if validated would have to rest upon the commerce power. After a lengthy excursion into the nature of the federal Union, Sutherland declared the labor provisions of the act void on the grounds that they regulated an aspect of production having only an indirect effect upon interstate commerce. The difference between direct and indirect effects, he added, was one of kind and was absolute, not a matter of degree. His precedents, significantly, were the venerable *Kidd v. Pearson* and *United States v. Knight*, as well as *Schechter v. United States*. The stream of commerce doctrine, which might have applied, he discarded as inapplicable, on the grounds that the production in question had not yet begun to move at all. Sutherland concluded his argument against the labor provisions by remarking briefly that they also delegated legislative power to the executive, and were void under the precedent set in the Schechter case.

Having destroyed the labor sections, Sutherland now used this vantage point to invalidate the entire law. The act specifically provided that the voiding of either the price or the labor section of the act should not affect the constitutionality of the other section. Yet Sutherland contended that Congress would not have enacted the other sections of the law without the labor provisions, that the bone and sinew of the law was therefore gone, and that the price-fixing provisions were hence also unconstitutional. The act was thus void in its entirety.

The Carter case split the Court into three fragments. Butler, McReynolds, Van Devanter, and Roberts joined Sutherland in the majority opinion. Hughes wrote a concurring opinion agreeing that the labor provisions of the act were invalid, but holding that the Court erred in voiding the price-fixing provisions in defiance of the will of Congress. Cardozo wrote a sharp dissent, concurred in by Brandeis and Stone, contending that the price-fixing sections of the law regulated interstate commerce itself, and that even local coal sales directly affected interstate commerce. The difference between direct and indirect effects, he said, was merely one of degree, not of kind. In striking down the price-fixing sections of the law in defiance of the will of Congress, he added, the majority had seriously violated the "presumption of divisibility" in the law. In regard to the labor sections of the law, he thought the Court should not have passed upon these at all, since the case here anticipated a controversy that had not yet become real.

The most extraordinary thing about Sutherland's opinion was the absurdity of his contention that while the labor provisions of the act were only indirectly related to interstate commerce, they were nonetheless so intimately related to those portions of the law dealing with interstate commerce as to be inseparable from them. The inconsistency presented here merely revealed how hopelessly unreal was the attempt to draw any categorical distinction between direct and indirect effects upon commerce. Cardozo's contention that the difference was merely one of the degree of intimacy between commerce and the thing regulated was a far more realistic one.

Sutherland's position also came close to denying the supremacy of national powers over state powers. His argument, reduced to simplest terms, was that price fixing, which he nowhere denied was directly related to interstate commerce, was unconstitutional because it was unfortunately too closely bound up with matters directly reserved to the states. This line of reasoning, which would have pleased John C. Calhoun, was the direct opposite of that adopted by the Court in the *Shreveport Rate Cases* and in *Railroad Commission of Wisconsin v. C.B. and Q.*, where federal intrusion upon grounds reserved to the states had been allowed because the matter regulated was inextricably tangled up with a matter lying with the powers of Congress. In short, Sutherland had repudiated the entire argument for the supremacy of national powers and had ignored completely the great development in federal authority sanctioned by the Court itself since the Lottery opinion. Driven to choose between the logical implications of liberal nationalism and a return to categorical dual federalism, Sutherland had chosen the latter.

A week after the Carter decision, the Court in *Ashton v. Cameron County Water District*, in a 5-to-4 decision, voided the Municipal Bankruptcy Act of 1934. This law permitted municipalities and other political subdivisions of states to file petitions in voluntary bankruptcy. Although the statute required the assent of the state to such petitions, the Court, speaking through Justice McReynolds, nonetheless found it to be an interference with state finances, and an unconstitutional invasion of state sovereignty. Justice Cardozo, joined by Hughes, Brandeis, and Stone, dissented, protesting strongly that voluntary petitions to which the state itself gave assent could hardly be construed to invade state sovereignty. Again, however, Roberts' vote was decisive, and again the conservatives carried the day.

An appraisal of the New Deal's reception in Court reveals that the justices had three principal objections to the legislation they reviewed: First, the Court firmly rejected all attempts to extend federal authority over production. It denied in succession that interstate commerce, appropriations for the general welfare, or taxation could be used to this end. Second, the Court denied the constitutionality of legislative delegation to the executive on the scale attempted in the N.R.A. or the Guffey Act. Third, and more broadly, the Court refused to accept the conception of constitutional growth, either by evolution or through economic emergency.

The most important of these attitudes was the Court's stand on federal control over production; this issue evidently divided the justices most sharply. Even the fiction of a static constitutional system might have been preserved, and most of the New Deal still validated, had the justices admitted that production "directly" affected interstate commerce, and that the welfare and taxing powers were positive instruments of federal authority.

There are two probable explanations of the Court's opposition to federal control over production. First, several of the justices vigorously disagreed with the New Deal's social philosophy. They viewed Roosevelt's program as an assault upon private property and contractual rights and upon the time-honored fundamentals of the American economic system. One may suppose that if more effective arguments had not been at hand, the Court might well have resorted more frequently to due process of law to outlaw the New Deal.

Second, it is evident that the New Deal did involve a tremendous extension of federal authority, much of it at the expense of functions hitherto exercised by the states. Whatever the available constitutional precedents advanced by the government—and they were many and impressive—the fact remained that the new laws constituted a substantial alteration in the scope of federal powers and in state-federal relations. Such an alteration, the majority felt, somehow violated the fundamental nature of the Union itself, and they willingly called up all available precedents of strict construction and of dual federalism to refute it. Only Brandeis, Cardozo, and Stone were willing to accept the logical implications of the liberal-national argument and recognize a wide extension of federal authority over production. In the Schechter case, it is true, the three liberals voted with the majority, holding that the extension of federal authority over production was so extreme as to be inacceptable. The A.A.A. and Carter decisions, however, demonstrated that they were willing enough to rationalize federal controls over production when matters of great importance and nationwide scope were involved and no other constitutional difficulties were present.

The majority's unwillingness to accept the idea of constitutional growth is readily understandable. The idea, if accepted officially, would go far to undermine the postulates of judicial review. The Court's capacity to rationalize its role as arbiter of the constitutional system rested in large part on the "slot machine" theory of the constitution and jurisprudence, which held that the Court's constitutional findings were the inevitable result of the application of logic to a fixed written document.

The Court could present its findings as automatic and inescapable only as long as it insisted that the Supreme Law was absolute and fixed. Once the Court admitted the possibility of an evolving constitutional system, the question would inevitably arise: why is it the Court's peculiar duty and function to determine the degree to which evolution should be permitted? Are not the issues involved matters of public policy and are they not essentially legislative in character? It is significant that the three men most willing to accept federal power in new spheres of authority were also those who opposed the legislative conception of the Court's functions, as Stone's dissent in *United States v. Butler* made clear. They were willing to leave at least some of the crucial decisions involved in constitutional growth up to Congress and to the executive.

THE RISING CONSERVATIVE PROTEST

The Court's quarrel with the New Deal was only part of a larger conflict for which the lines of battle were forming even as the conservative justices made their viewpoint known. Whatever its constitutional orthodoxy, the New Deal was certainly a major assault upon the economic philosophy which had been in ascendancy in America since World War days. Franklin D. Roosevelt and his followers had flatly repudiated the notion of a self-regulated economic system and had accepted the thesis that the national welfare required extensive controls over big business, finance, and agriculture, as well as the use of governmental power to improve the lot of the socially unfortunate. If the President's followers were on occasion more than a little confused and divided about the methods to be adopted in reaching their objectives, there was little doubt about what economic groups in the population they favored. The New Deal had extended aid and comfort to organized labor, the farmer, and the unemployed. While certain of its enactments admittedly benefited business, it had imposed unprecedented controls upon banking, finance, and business management.

In short, the New Deal had drawn the lines of political conflict between clearly demarcated class interests. It rested its power upon the support of labor, agriculture, and the "little fellow," and although the President invited the support of all "honest" businessmen, he specifically repudiated the support of the "economic royalists." To America's great industrialists, bankers, lawyers, and newspaper editors—the men who had directed America's economic destinies in the past—and indeed to the mass of the upper-middle-class Americans who in one way or another were associated with those who held economic power, Roosevelt's program was an anathema. Had the President not assaulted the very citadels of capitalism and free enterprise upon which America had grown great and powerful? Did he not seek to improve the lot of the poor at the expense of the wealthy? Long before the Court stated its constitutional objections to the New Deal, many conservatives had become convinced that the President was a dangerous radical and that his program involved heresies hardly less hateful than those propounded by the revolutionaries in Russia.

The conflict was thus one between classes and economic interests; but just as in the days of the Revolution and the slavery controversy, the American tendency to express economic conflicts in legal and constitutional terms asserted itself. Even before the Court revealed its differences with the New Deal, many conservatives had linked together the economic and constitutional arguments used to attack the recovery program. In 1934 the Liberty League, organized by groups of eastern financiers and industrialists, sounded the battle cry with a denunciation of Roosevelt for "tinkering with the Constitution." Early in 1934, ex-President Hoover, in his *Challenge to Liberty*, denounced the New Deal as an attack upon free private enterprise and limited constitutional government, the two fundamentals of the American social order. However, as the Supreme Court in successive decisions revealed its own disapproval of Roosevelt's program, more and more conservatives rallied to the Court and to the constitutional argument in their stand against the New Deal.

Whether the conservative constitutional position as formulated by the Court and championed by the administration's enemies would ultimately prevail over the constitutional ideas adopted by the New Dealers was in reality dependent upon the political fortunes of the Roosevelt administration. Should the President win re-election in 1936, his victory would constitute a popular ratification of his policies, would demoralize the conservatives, and would almost certainly give the President the opportunity to appoint several justices of his own belief to the Court. The New Deal attitudes would then be written into constitutional law and the conservative constitutional argument would be discredited if not altogether destroyed. On the other hand, were Roosevelt defeated in 1936, at least a partial repudiation of New Deal policies would follow, while conservative control of the Supreme Court would be confirmed.

Thus the approaching election of 1936 took on the character of a national referendum on the Roosevelt policies whereby the New Deal's constitutional philosophy would either stand or fall.

Chapter

28

The Constitutional Revolution
in Federalism—1937-1947

IN NOVEMBER 1936 the Democratic Party won an overwhelming victory at the polls. The election confirmed the Roosevelt administration in power and inspired the President to attempt a reorganization of the judiciary in order to win control of that last remaining outpost of conservative constitutionalism. Although the President's plan failed of its immediate purpose, the Court nevertheless capitulated. In a remarkable series of opinions beginning in 1937, it accepted all of the outstanding New Deal reform measures, including much legislation passed to replace that which the Court had invalidated before 1937. In so doing, the Court wrote a new body of nationalistic constitutional law, and seemingly ended definitively the clash between dual federalism and liberal nationalism.

THE ELECTION OF 1936

The Republican attempt to fight the election of 1936 on constitutional grounds was destined to failure. Denunciation of the New Deal as unconstitutional usurpation counted for little with the average voter when weighed in the balance against Roosevelt's enormous popularity, a degree of economic recovery, and the appeal of a positive national program.

Moreover, there was an inherent strategic weakness in the Republican constitutional argument. The party repeatedly attacked the New Deal program as unconstitutional; but the conservative constitutional philosophy behind this attack made it impossible for the party to advance at the same time any convincing national program of its own. Thus the Republican platform adopted at Cleveland accused the Roosevelt administration of usurping the powers of Congress, flouting the authority of the Supreme Court, insisting upon the passage of unconstitutional laws, and invading the sovereignty of the states. Yet to meet the challenge of the New Deal program the Republican policy makers could offer nothing more positive than concerted state action, interstate compacts, grants-in-aid, and federal appropriations—all patently inadequate devices to deal with an economic crisis of such magnitude as the one the country was still experiencing. The Republican nominee, Alfred M. Landon, labored under the same fatal contradictions of theory and policy as beset the party platform. He was obliged to denounce the New Deal in the large as an assault upon the American constitutional system; yet political strategy obliged him to admit the desirability of many specific New Deal reforms and to promise Republican measures of similar effectiveness.

The Democrats, on the other hand, had only to insist upon the constitutionality and the necessity of their own program. "We know," said the platform adopted by the Democratic convention at Philadelphia, "that drought, dust storms, floods, minimum wages, maximum hours, child labor and working conditions in industry, monopolistic and unfair business practices cannot be adequately handled exclusively by 48 separate State legislatures, 48 separate State administrations, and 48 separate State courts. Transactions and activities which inevitably overflow State boundaries call for both State and Federal treatment." The platform avoided a direct attack upon the Supreme Court, and stated merely that the party had sought and would continue to seek reform only "through legislation within the Constitution." However, the party promised clarifying constitutional amendments should these be necessary to national reform.

When Roosevelt in November won re-election by a vast majority—the Republican candidate carrying only Maine and Vermont—the American people had in fact made a great constitutional decision. They put their stamp of approval upon Roosevelt's policies and thereby assured the eventual triumph of the constitutional arguments upon which the New Deal rested. It was now evident that if the Court maintained its opposition to the New Deal constitutional theories, it would find itself without adequate popular support, either in Congress or in the electorate. Further, it now became a practical certainty that several of the elderly conservative justices would either die or resign before Roosevelt left office, and that new appointments to the Court would convert the liberal minority into a majority.

ROOSEVELT'S COURT PLAN

The Court's opposition to the New Deal had roused bitter anger in the administration and among its supporters. As in past conflicts between executive and judiciary, the Court's enemies proposed to place some sort of check upon the judicial power. A variety of suggestions for judicial reform, very few of them new, were advanced in administration and congressional circles. The most extreme was a proposal for a constitutional amendment abolishing the Court's power to declare acts of Congress unconstitutional. Less drastic was the proposed amendment submitted by Senator Joseph O'Mahoney of Wyoming on March 11, 1937, to require a two-thirds vote of the Court whenever it declared an act of Congress unconstitutional. An amendment introduced by Senator Burton K. Wheeler of Montana on February 17, 1937, would have permitted Congress to validate laws previously declared unconstitutional by repassing them with a two-thirds vote of both houses. Others suggested simply a congressional enactment, similar to that passed in Reconstruction days, restricting the Court's appellate power in cases involving certain constitutional issues, while still others suggested that Congress enact a statute formally depriving the Court of the power to invalidate federal legislation.

On February 5, 1937, the President suddenly broke a long silence on the Court question by presenting Congress with a bill to reorganize the federal judiciary. The bill provided that whenever any federal judge who had served ten years or more failed to retire within six months after reaching his seventieth birthday, the President might appoint an additional judge to the court upon which the septuagenarian was serving. No more than fifty additional judges in all might be appointed under the act, and the maximum size of the Supreme Court was fixed at fifteen.

The message accompanying the bill deviously avoided the real purpose behind the proposal. The judiciary, Roosevelt said, was "handicapped by insufficient personnel" and by the presence of too many superannuated judges. Most old judges, the President added, were physically unable to perform their duties, and were antiquated in outlook—"little by little, new facts become blurred through old glasses fitted, as it were, for the needs of another generation." Privately, F.D.R. explained to Professor Felix Frankfurter of the Harvard Law School that he had arrived at the decision to press his Court proposal upon Congress "by a process of elimination." Adoption of a constitutional amendment to legalize necessary New Deal legislation would "in all probability" not be possible before "1941 or 1942." It was "my honest belief," the President wrote, that the nation could not afford to wait that long "to obtain effective social and economic legislation to bring it abreast of the times."

The President's plan was in reality a more or less refined court-packing scheme. It possessed some merit, but many weaknesses, not the least of which was its sophistry. It dodged the main issue of judicial power upon which so many liberals would willingly have gone forth to battle, while its emphasis upon old age as the core of the Court problem was particularly unfortunate. The Constitution was indeed deficient in not making some provision for the retirement of superannuated judges, and there had been notable instances in the past where judges incapacitated through age had refused to resign. As of 1937, however, the President's argument that age bred conservatism was particularly inept, for the oldest man on the Court, Justice Brandeis, was also the Court's greatest liberal, while Justice Roberts was under seventy. The President's contention that the federal judiciary was overworked was also unconvincing. The Supreme Court's docket had once been swamped, but the Judiciary Act of 1925, which gave the Court greater authority to reject certain types of cases, had solved this problem.

The President's plan had the merit of avoiding a constitutional amendment, and also it was clearly constitutional, since Congress specifically had power to fix the size of all federal courts. Moreover, there were several precedents for altering the Supreme Court's size. Thus the Judiciary Act of 1789 had fixed the number of justices at six; this number had been successively altered to five in 1801, to six in 1802, to nine in 1837, to ten in 1863, to seven in 1866, and finally to nine in 1869. In a sense, also, the President's plan was conservative, for it did not attack the institution of judicial review as such. Its implication was that nothing was fundamentally wrong with the judiciary beyond the present personnel of the Court, and this difficulty the plan would have corrected.

But from a standpoint of political expediency the plan was fatally weak. The thinly disguised court-packing plan evoked a powerful emotional response both in Congress and in the public against such an invasion of the sacred judicial precincts. The belief had long since grown up that the Court was an inviolable guardian of constitutional light and truth, holding forth far above the noisome sea of politics and secure against congressional meddling. The belief lacked historical reality; yet the public was unwilling to tolerate its violation. The conservative rallying cry—"hands off the Supreme Court"—was strong enough to build up a powerful sentiment of opposition not only among conservatives but among many liberals, who, though they acknowledged the Court's transgressions, still thought the plan wrong in principle.

The plan hopelessly split the Democratic majority in the Senate, despite yeoman work done by Senators Joseph Robinson of Arkansas and George W. Norris of Nebraska in support of the proposal. Democratic Senators Burton K. Wheeler of Montana, Carter Glass of Virginia, and Edward Burk of Nebraska led the attack upon the measure, while the Republican minority, presumably even more bitterly opposed to the plan, remained discreetly in the background.

Although it first appeared that the court plan would be enacted, several events decided the issue against the administration. Most important, between March and June the Supreme Court dramatically surrendered to the New Deal on several outstanding constitutional issues. In succession, the Court validated a state minimum wage law, the Farm Mortgage Act of 1935, the amended Railway Labor Act of 1934, the National Labor Relations Act of 1935, and the Social Security Act of 1935. It thus appeared that there was now no necessity for coercing the judiciary in order to push through the New Deal program, and that the Court bill could therefore be dropped.

It has long been assumed that the Court's spectacular series of reversals in these cases was simply a shrewd political maneuver designed to defeat Roosevelt's court plan—"the switch in time that saved nine." Recently published evidence, however, casts doubt upon any interpretation so simple. Justice Roberts, the "swingman" in *West Coast Hotel Co. v. Parrish* (1937), in which the Court by a five to four vote held a Washington state minimum wage law to be constitutional, had in fact decided some months earlier that the Court's position on such legislation, maintained ever since the much controverted Adkins decision in 1923, was wrong and ought to be abandoned. Only a legal technicality had prevented him from voting to overturn the Adkins decision in a similar New York case nearly a year earlier. In December 1936, after the Parrish case had been argued, Roberts announced his change of position to his fellow justices. However, Justice Stone's serious illness left the justices divided four to four on the decision and so prevented publication at that time of an opinion holding minimum wage legislation constitutional well before Roosevelt's court plan had become known. In short, Roberts' dramatic shift on minimum wage legislation reflected principled conviction on his part and not mere political opportunism.

This is not to say that Roberts and Chief Justice Hughes, whose change of position made possible the Court's validation that spring of the National Labor Relations and Social Security Acts, were naively unaware of the political implications of their altered stance. Both justices understood the meaning of the New Deal's overwhelming victory at the polls the previous November, and they realized full well that if the Court were to continue much longer to block social change it would in all probability be the Court and not the New Deal that would be broken.

Behind the scenes, in fact, the Chief Justice was working desperately to defeat Roosevelt's plan. In May Senator Wheeler, with a dramatic flourish, made public a letter from Hughes sharply attacking Roosevelt's argument that the Court needed more justices to keep abreast of its docket. "More justices," Hughes wrote, "meant more justices to hear, more justices to discuss, more justices to convince and to decide," and thus would delay rather than speed up the Court's work. Justice Brandeis, profoundly convinced that the President's proposal was a serious threat to the separation of powers in the American constitutional system, added his signature to Hughes's letter. Somewhat disingenuously, the Chief Justice assured Wheeler that he had had "no time" to obtain the signatures of the other justices. But it is now known that Justice Stone, at least, would have refused to sign the letter had he been asked. At all events, Hughes's letter did great damage in the Senate to the President's cause.

Justice Van Devanter resigned in May 1937, an event supporting the contention that the President would soon gain control of the Court without congressional intervention. The death of Senator Robinson soon thereafter deprived the administration of its Senate floor leader and also contributed to the defeat of the plan.

On June 14 the Senate Judiciary Committee reported out the bill unfavorably, by a vote of ten to eight. The majority report excoriated the plan's motives and methods. "The bill," it said, "applies force to the judiciary," and would "undermine the independence of the Courts." Its theory was "in direct violation of the spirit of the American Constitution," "and would permit alteration of the Constitution without the people's consent or approval. . . ." This report signaled the plan's demise, the Senate on July 22 rejecting the bill by voting, 70 to 20, to return it to the Judiciary Committee.

As a sop to the President, Congress enacted the Judiciary Reform Act, a mild and uncontroversial measure which became law on August 24. This statute provided that whenever any case arose in the federal courts involving the constitutionality of an act of Congress, the United States government might at its discretion become a party to the action, and that whenever a lower federal court declared an act of Congress unconstitutional an appeal might be taken immediately to the Supreme Court, to be heard and decided at the earliest possible time. These were desirable reforms, but they had little to do with the main issues of judicial power.

THE COURT ACCEPTS LIBERAL NATIONALISM

The President had lost a battle and won a war. In a remarkable series of decisions, beginning while the Court fight was at its height, the Court executed the most abrupt change of face in its entire history and accepted all the major constitutional postulates underlying the New Deal.

The first substantial intimation of the Court's new position came on March 29, 1937, in *West Coast Hotel Co. v. Parrish*, when Hughes and Roberts joined the liberal bloc to sustain a Washington minimum wage law. Only the year before the Court in *Morehead v. New York ex rel. Tipaldo* (1936) had held unconstitutional a similar New York statute, on the authority of *Adkins v. Childrens Hospital*. But now Chief Justice Hughes, speaking for the majority, announced that the Adkins decision had been wrong and should be overruled. He thrust aside the embarrassing Tipaldo precedent of the previous year with the assertion that in the Tipaldo case the Court had not re-examined the constitutionality of minimum wage legislation because it had not been asked to do so. This statement evaded the real point: that Justice Roberts, who had lined up with the conservatives in the Tipaldo case to invalidate the New York law by a 5-to-4 vote, had now reversed his stand so that the minority of a year before had become a majority. In his dissent for the four conservatives, Justice Sutherland pointed out that the Washington statute was in all essential respects similar to that in the Adkins case, and he bitterly attacked the theory that the meaning of the Constitution could change "with the ebb and flow of economic events."

In April the New Deal scored a further great victory, as Hughes and Roberts again joined the liberals in five decisions sustaining the National Labor Relations Act. This law imposed extensive and detailed controls upon labor-management relations in industry. Although it thus plainly attempted to regulate a phase of production, Chief Justice Hughes in *N.L.R.B. v. Jones and Laughlin Steel Corporation* (1937) thrust aside the Schechter and Carter precedents as "inapplicable." Resting his opinion mainly upon the "stream of commerce" doctrine, Hughes pointed out that the respondent steel firm drew its raw materials from interstate commerce and shipped its products back into that commerce. He bluntly rejected the old categorical distinction between direct and indirect effects upon commerce, which Roberts had accepted in the Carter case, and instead adopted Cardozo's contention in that case, that "the question is necessarily one of degree." And he concluded in the full vein of the liberal national tradition: "When industries organize themselves on a national scale, making their relation to interstate commerce the dominant factor in their activities, how can it be maintained that their industrial relations constitute a forbidden field into which Congress may not enter when it is necessary to protect interstate commerce from the paralyzing consequences of industrial war?"

The Court's findings in an accompanying case, *N.L.R.B. v. Friedman–Harry Marks Clothing Company* (1937), was even more significant. Here the respondent clothing firm was a small manufacturer whose production could not have had more than a negligible effect upon interstate commerce. Yet Hughes' opinion emphasized the interstate character of the clothing industry at large, and ignored the question of the actual effect production in the case at hand had upon commerce. McReynolds' dissenting observation that a "more remote or indirect interference with interstate commerce or a more definite invasion of the powers reserved to the states is difficult, if not impossible, to imagine," was an understandable one in the light of what the Court had said about the coal business the year before.

At the same time the Court held in *Associated Press v. N.L.R.B.* (1937) that the labor relations of newspapers and press associations were also subject to regulation under the Labor Relations Act. Petitioners had attacked the law as a violation of the First Amendment, on the ground that the statute permitted the federal government to dictate to the press the persons to be employed in preparing news and editorials and thus to control editorial policy, thereby curtailing freedom of the press. Justice Roberts' opinion rejected this contention as unsound and without relevance to the case at hand. The law, he said, did not regulate the press but only its labor relationships. "The publisher of a newspaper has no special immunity from the application of general laws," and the statute had "no relation whatever to the impartial distribution of news."

In May the Court reaffirmed its new-found nationalism in two opinions validating the Social Security Act. In *Stewart Machine Company v. Davis* (1937), the five liberal justices accepted the unemployment excise tax upon employers and the provisions for unemployment grants to states enacting satisfactory unemployment compensation laws. Cardozo's majority opinion contained an exceedingly nationalistic defense of the federal taxing power, which he held to be as comprehensive, except for specific constitutional limitations, as that of the states. And credits to the states, said Cardozo, were not an attempt to coerce the states, but were rather an instance of federal-state co-operation for a national purpose. Nor did the requirement that the state law conform to certain conditions before the federal government granted the credits alter the law's non-coercive character, since Congress was entitled to some assurance that state legislation was what it purported to be. In any event, Cardozo said, Congress had not obliged the states to enact any law, and states accepting benefits of the security system could hardly be said to be coerced when they could enter or withdraw from the arrangement at pleasure. By inference, this reasoning constituted a repudiation of Roberts' argument in *United States v. Butler* on the coercive nature of conditional federal appropriations, a repudiation which Roberts himself now apparently accepted.

In the second Social Security Act case, *Helvering v. Davis* (1937), Cardozo upheld the statute's old age tax and benefit provisions. The old age tax, he said, was a valid exercise of the taxing power, while of the benefit provisions he observed merely that "Congress may spend money in aid of the general welfare." His precedent for the latter statement was, ironically, *United States v. Butler*. Cardozo's two opinions went far to repudiate the entire theory of dual federalism, which had reached its apogee in the Butler case.

The administration's somewhat precarious majority on the Court was presently confirmed and strengthened by a series of resignations and new appointments, beginning with Justice Van Devanter's retirement in May 1937. A momentary furor occurred in September, when Senator Hugo Black of Alabama, whom President Roosevelt named to fill the Van Devanter vacancy, was "exposed" as having once been a member of the Ku Klux Klan. The connection was certainly an incongruous one for a liberal, but Black's record in the Senate had in fact been consistently progressive. Although his one-time Klan connection had been exposed in his last Alabama senatorial campaign, the National Association for the Advancement of Colored People had continued, in recognition of his liberalism, to lend him enthusiastic support. Justice Black's subsequent consistent liberalism on the Court soon silenced those who feared he might be a reactionary in disguise.

Other resignations and appointments soon followed. Justice Sutherland resigned in January 1938, his place being taken by Stanley Reed, who, as Solicitor General under Roosevelt, had repeatedly argued in defense of New Deal legislation before the Court. Justice Cardozo died in December 1938, and to the vacancy Roosevelt appointed Felix Frankfurter, a distinguished member of the Harvard Law School faculty and an informal adviser to the President. The Court lost another great jurist when age forced Justice Brandeis' resignation in March 1939. In his place, Roosevelt named William O. Douglas, formerly a Yale Law School professor and also a member of the Securities and Exchange Commission. The archconservative Butler died the following November, and to succeed him the President named Frank Murphy, former Philippine High Commissioner and Governor of Michigan. A year later, in February 1941, Justice McReynolds, the last remaining conservative opponent of the New Deal, submitted his resignation. The President filled the vacancy with Attorney General Robert H. Jackson, a staunch New Dealer who had attracted attention with his attacks upon "economic royalists."

Chief Justice Hughes resigned in June 1941, and the President thereupon paid tribute to Stone's long-standing liberal nationalism by appointing him to the Chief Justiceship. Stone's elevation broke through party lines, for the new Chief Justice had been a Republican and Attorney General under Coolidge. The vacancy occasioned by Stone's promotion went to Senator James Byrnes of South Carolina, long administration leader in the upper house. Justice Byrnes resigned in October 1942, and the President appointed Wiley Rutledge of Iowa to the vacancy in February 1943.

Thus, by 1943, the Supreme Court within six years had experienced a virtually complete change of personnel, so that control had passed completely into the hands of the Roosevelt appointees. The Court now obviously had a strongly New Deal flavor, evidenced especially in the repudiation of dual federalism and in civil liberties cases involving labor unions, racial minorities, and the like. The judicial future of the New Deal evidently was virtually assured.

THE NEW CONSTITUTIONAL LAW:
FEDERAL REGULATION OF LABOR

Even while these alterations in personnel were occurring, the Court was engaged in laying down the broad outlines of a new constitutional law, confirming the revolution begun in the spring of 1937.

In one large group of cases, the Court fully confirmed the implications of the initial labor board opinions with respect to federal controls over labor and production. In *Santa Cruz Fruit Packing Co. v. N.L.R.B.* (1938) the Court upheld the validity of a Labor Board order directed to a fruit-packing concern, only thirty-seven per cent of whose products moved in interstate commerce. Chief Justice Hughes, observing that the stream of commerce doctrine was not exactly applicable to the case, held that federal control was nonetheless valid, since labor disturbances at the plant had a substantial disruptive effect upon interstate commerce. Abandoning the old categorical distinction between direct and indirect effects, he said once more that the difference was "necessarily one of degree" and was not reducible to "mathematical or rigid formulas." Hughes' precedents were drawn from the earlier labor conspiracy cases, notably *Loewe v. Lawlor* (1908), and *United Mine Workers v. Coronado Coal Co.* (1922), wherein labor unions had been convicted of conspiracy to destroy interstate commerce, even though their activities had been immediately confined to stopping production.

In *Consolidated Edison Co. v. N.L.R.B.* (1938) the Court sustained federal control over the labor relations of a power company selling its output entirely within one state. Chief Justice Hughes pointed out that the company sold power to radio stations, airports, and railroads, which were in turn directly engaged in interstate commerce, and that the concern's relationship to interstate commerce was therefore sufficient to warrant federal control. Of like import was *N.L.R.B. v. Fainblatt* (1939), in which the Court sustained application of the National Labor Relations Act to a small-scale garment processor who delivered his entire output within the state. These cases meant that it was no longer necessary to show either an immediate stream of commerce or a large volume of business in order to establish federal authority. As long as a potential labor disturbance in the business in question would have a disruptive effect, however slight, upon interstate commerce, the labor relations of the business in question were subject to regulation.

The Court shortly employed the constitutional conceptions developed in the Labor Board cases to validate the Fair Labor Standards Act of June 25, 1938. This law prescribed an original minimum wage of twenty-five cents an hour and maximum hours of forty-four a week, subject to time and a half for overtime, for all employees engaged in interstate commerce or in the production of goods for interstate commerce.[1] In addition to those sections of the statute regulating wages directly, other provisions made it unlawful to ship in interstate commerce goods manufactured in violation of the minimum wage requirements of the statute. The act also prohibited the shipment in interstate commerce of the products of any establishment where child labor had been used in the previous thirty days. This provision constituted virtual re-enactment of the Child Labor Act of 1916. The statute thus plainly defied the dictum in the first Child Labor Case, as well as that in the Schechter and Carter opinions.

In *United States v. Darby* (1941) the Court found the Fair Labor Standards Act to be constitutional. The case involved a federal prosecution to enforce minimum wage standards upon an operator in the Southern lumber industry, in which wages in 1937 varied from ten to twenty-seven cents per hour, the average annual wage being $388.91. Justice Stone's opinion, for a unanimous Court, first analyzed and upheld the provisions prohibiting the movement of proscribed goods in interstate commerce. Formally overruling *Hammer v. Dagenhart* (1918), the first Child Labor Case, which he held to be a departure from sound principles, Stone said that the commerce power was complete, that Congress could lawfully employ absolute prohibition, and that the Court could not inquire into the motives behind an act of Congress. The sections by which Congress imposed direct federal regulation of wages were also valid, since Congress could "regulate intrastate activities where they have a substantial effect on interstate commerce." Stone's precedents here included the *Shreveport Rate Cases* (1914) and the recent Labor Board decisions. The Carter case he dismissed with the blunt observation that its dictum was limited by the other decisions cited. *Schechter v. United States* he did not even mention.

---

[1] The law prescribed subsequent successive elevations of the minimum wage level to forty cents an hour, and in two years the maximum work week was to be reduced to forty hours.

A year later, in *A. B. Kirschbaum v. Walling* (1942), another Fair Labor Standards Act case, the Court gave unprecedented scope to the conception of "production of goods for commerce." The employees in this case were not themselves engaged in production for commerce, but were employed merely in the maintenance and operation of a loft building where tenants did produce and sell ladies' garments into interstate commerce. There was no touchstone, said Justice Frankfurter, to separate employees engaged in interstate commerce from those who were not. The judicial task was rather one of accommodation between the assertion of new federal authority on the one hand and the historic functions of the individual states on the other. He added the somewhat startling assertion that the scope of the statute in question was not coextensive with the limits of congressional power over interstate commerce, thereby implying that the limits of federal authority over interstate commerce might well extend even beyond those established in the statute in question. At any rate, he said, the law specifically applied to employees "necessary to production," and that meant building employees here.

The Kirschbaum opinion left but few employees outside the scope of the commerce power. Subsequent opinions have for the most part followed that dictum. Thus in *Warren-Bradshaw Co. v. Hall* (1942), the Court accepted application of the law to operators of oil-well drilling rigs, although the drillers did not themselves produce for commerce. In *Walton v. Southern Package Corporation* (1944), the Court ruled that the act extended to a night watchman in a veneer plant, while in *Borden Co. v. Borella* (1945) it interpreted the statute to cover porters, elevator operators, and watchmen in a New York office building. However, employees of certain purely local activities are still beyond the protection of the law. Thus in *Walling v. Jacksonville Paper Co.* (1943) the Court held the law inapplicable to employees of wholesalers who purchased goods outside the state but distributed locally without advance orders. And in *10 East 40th St. Building v. Callus* (1945), the Court refused to extend the law to cover workers in an office building 26 per cent of whose tenants had manufacturing plants located elsewhere.

In still another line of cases, the Court upheld the constitutionality of the Norris–La Guardia Anti-Injunction Act of 1932. This statute had prohibited the issuance by any federal court of injunctions in labor disputes, except where unlawful acts had been threatened or committed, and where substantial and irreparable injury would result were relief not granted. It will be recalled that Section 20 of the Clayton Act had prohibited the issuance of federal injunctions in labor disputes unless necessary to prevent irreparable injury to property. However, in *Duplex Printing Press Co. v. Deering* (1921), the Court had virtually thrust aside Section 20 of the Clayton Act, with the opinion that the limitation upon injunctions must be interpreted very narrowly to forbid injunctions only against the actual employees involved in the dispute, so that the activities of the employees' union might in fact be enjoined. Further, the Court had pointed out in the Duplex case that the Clayton Act did not prohibit injunctions against "unlawful" labor activities. The Norris–La Guardia Act represented an attempt by Congress to undo the effect of the Duplex opinion and so restore the original intent of Congress in enacting Section 20 of the Clayton Act.

In *Lauf v. Shinner and Co.* (1938) the Court held briefly that the Norris–La Guardia Act was constitutional. There could be no question, said Justice Roberts, of the power of Congress to define the jurisdiction of the lower federal courts. The Court reached the same conclusion in *New Negro Alliance Co. v. Sanitary Grocery Co.* (1938), where Justice Roberts also noted that the evident purpose of Congress in passing the law had been to "obviate the results of the judicial construction" of the Clayton Act.

In *United States v. Hutcheson* (1941), the Court held that the Norris–La Guardia Act had in effect altered the status of criminal prosecutions against labor unions under the Sherman Anti-Trust Law. The case involved a criminal action under the Sherman Act against a carpenters' union which by a jurisdictional strike, picketing and boycotting a construction company, had allegedly interfered with interstate commerce. Justice Frankfurter's opinion infused the spirit of the Norris–La Guardia Act into Section 20 of the Clayton Act. He noted that under the Norris–La Guardia Act the union's activities would not be enjoinable in equity proceedings. It was absurd, he thought, to conclude that such action could still "become the road to prison" through criminal proceedings under the Sherman Act when it could not even be enjoined in equity proceedings. The Norris–La Guardia Act, he said, must be read broadly to alter the whole status of labor union activities under federal antitrust legislation.

However, in *Allen Bradley Co. v. Local Union No. 3* (1945), it became evident that certain types of labor union activity were still within the reach of the Sherman Act. Here an electricians' union had signed closed-shop agreements with a number of manufacturers and contractors. Both the union and the contractors had then conspired to boycott non-union manufacturers of electrical goods. Speaking through Justice Black, the Court held that by combining with employers and manufacturers, the union had stepped outside the protection of the Clayton and La Guardia Acts, and that its action could be enjoined under the Sherman Law.

This dictum was shortly somewhat beclouded, however, by the Court's opinion in *Hunt v. Crumboch* (1945). Here a union had made a closed-shop agreement with a large grocery concern, whereby the concern agreed to require all trucking concerns that worked for it to make closed shop agreements with the union. Subsequently the union refused to negotiate with one of the trucking concerns, with the result that that firm was obliged to maintain an open shop and so lost its hauling contract with the grocery firm.

Justice Black, speaking for five justices, held simply that the union had not violated the Sherman Act, since laborers singly or in concert could sell or refuse to sell their labor as they chose. Justice Roberts, dissenting, argued that the sole purpose of the union had been to drive the trucking concern out of business, and that such action was "clearly within the denunciation of the Sherman Act."

A logical concomitant of the enactment of various New Deal labor statutes and their ultimate acceptance by the Court was the passage by Congress of the Full Employment Act of 1946. This measure declared officially that it was now the responsibility of the national government to insure effective operation of the country's economic system, specifically with the objective of maintaining maximum employment, production, and purchasing power.

To this end, the 1946 law established a three-man Council of Economic Advisors charged with providing on-going analysis of the economy. On the basis of its studies, the Council was to advise the President and Congress as to appropriate fiscal, monetary, and spending policies. The economic assumptions behind the law quite evidently rested very heavily upon the theories of John Maynard Keynes, whose writings now constituted a kind of bible for the effective operation of a liberal capitalist economic order.

The Full Employment Act, when viewed in the light of pre-1937 constitutional law, was little less than revolutionary. Yet so obvious was its constitutional validity in terms of the post-1937 order of things that it was to encounter no effective challenge in the courts.

FEDERAL REGULATION OF AGRICULTURE

In another series of important decisions, the new Court accepted several new statutes imposing far-reaching federal controls upon agricultural production. For all practical purposes the Court thereby swept *United States v. Butler* into the scrap-heap.

In 1938 Congress made bold to enact a new Agricultural Adjustment Act. This statute, which became law on February 16, followed the 1933 act in citing the effect of agricultural production upon interstate commerce as the constitutional foundation for the law. Also, as was the case in the earlier law, its object was the attainment of parity prices for several of the principal agricultural commodities. Unlike the 1933 act, however, the new statute levied no processing taxes, nor did it directly impose any production quotas upon farmers. Instead, it provided for a system of marketing quotas for cotton, wheat, corn, tobacco, and rice. Whenever the Secretary of Agriculture found that the supply of any one of the foregoing commodities was too great, he was empowered to impose a marketing quota, subject to approval by referendum of two-thirds of the producers concerned. The act authorized the Secretary to assign individual quotas to each farm and fixed heavy penalties for marketing quantities in excess of such quotas.

In *Mulford v. Smith* (1939), the Court sustained the constitutionality of the new Agricultural Adjustment Act against an attack by several tobacco growers who sought to have their quotas set aside on the ground that the new law in effect regulated production and so invaded the reserved powers of the states in violation of the Tenth Amendment. But Justice Roberts, who had written the opinion in *United States v. Butler* invalidating the earlier Agricultural Adjustment Act, declared for the majority of the Court that the 1938 statute did not regulate production, but instead merely imposed market regulations at the "throat" of interstate commerce. Congress, he added, could lawfully limit the amount of any commodity to be transported in interstate commerce, even through the imposition of an absolute prohibition if it so desired. In this connection, he rejected the distinction so carefully drawn in *Hammer v. Dagenhart*, the first Child Labor Case, between things harmful in themselves and "ordinary" or "harmless" commodities. Answering the charge that the real purpose of Congress in enacting the statute was the regulation of production, he stated that "the motive of Congress in asserting the power to regulate commerce is irrelevant to the validity of the legislation." This repudiated the argument advanced in both the first and second Child Labor cases, that the Court could properly inquire into possible ulterior motives behind legislation that was otherwise constitutional and strike down the law if it discovered an intention to subvert the Tenth Amendment. Justice Roberts did not even mention *Hammer v. Dagenhart*, nor did he allude to *United States v. Butler*, wherein could be found his own lengthy exposition of the virtues of dual federalism.

It was evident that the precedent of the Butler case had now been discarded, even though it was not formally overruled. The practical effect of the imposition of marketing quotas was the regulation of agricultural production, the very thing attempted by Congress in the first Agricultural Adjustment Act and pronounced unconstitutional in the Butler opinion. Yet since the Court now refused to consider the motives of Congress in authorizing marketing quotas, the present statute was constitutional. In other words, Congress could constitutionally regulate agricultural production through control over commerce and so could accomplish by indirection that which the Court in the Butler case had said could not be done without violating the Tenth Amendment. Needless to say, Justices McReynolds and Butler, the shattered remnant of the Court's conservative bloc, dissented.

Three months before the Court's opinion in *Mulford v. Smith*, the Court in *Currin v. Wallace* (1939) had used the stream of commerce doctrine to validate the Tobacco Inspection Act of 1937. This law had established federal inspection and grading at tobacco auctions designated by the Secretary of Agriculture. The Court in the Currin case said simply that tobacco sales in which most of the commodity was about to move in interstate commerce were as much a part of that commerce as were grain and beef sales, over which federal inspection had already been sustained. The Court ignored the fact that the product in question had not yet begun to move, a distinction that had been strongly emphasized in the Carter opinion.

Finally, in June 1939, the Court, in *United States v. Rock Royal Cooperative* and in *Hood v. United States*, sustained the Agricultural Marketing Agreement Act of 1937. This law empowered the Secretary of Agriculture to maintain parity prices for a variety of agricultural commodities through the imposition of marketing quotas and price schedules. The Rock Royal and Hood cases involved the validity of certain orders of the Secretary fixing the price of milk paid to farmers in the New York and Boston interstate milksheds. Again the Court, speaking now through Justice Reed, held that since most of the milk sold eventually crossed state lines the local sales transactions in question were the beginning of interstate commerce and hence subject to federal control. Citing the *Shreveport Rate Cases*, the Court held that intrastate as well as interstate commerce in milk could be regulated, since the two admittedly commingled in moving to market. McReynolds and Butler, dissenting, thought the decision a violation of the "ancient doctrine" that Congress does not have "authority to manage private business affairs under the transparent guise of regulating commerce."

Later decisions served to confirm the ideas expounded in the foregoing cases. Thus in *United States v. Wrightwood Dairy* (1942) the Court again sustained the Agricultural Marketing Agreement Act, and held even that the federal government might lawfully regulate the price of milk sold wholly inside state lines and not commingled with interstate milk but merely sold in competition with it.

In *Wickard v. Filburn* (1942), the Court sustained the validity of the wheat-marketing quota provisions of the Agricultural Adjustment Act of 1938, even though Congress in 1941 had amended the statute to authorize the Secretary of Agriculture to fix marketing quotas for wheat which would include wheat consumed on the premises as poultry and livestock feed, as seed, and as household food, as well as for wheat sold into interstate commerce. Only wheat insulated by storage was exempt from the calculation of the total amount marketed and thus from the penalties imposed for marketing in excess of quotas. In a forceful opinion, Justice Jackson not only repudiated the old distinction between direct and indirect effects but also proceeded virtually to discard entirely the distinction between commerce and production as a constitutional touchstone. Questions of the power of Congress, he said, "are not to be decided by reference to any formula which would give controlling force to nomenclature such as 'production' and 'indirect' and foreclose consideration of the actual effects of the activity in question upon interstate commerce." And he continued, "Whether the subject of the regulation in question was 'production,' 'consumption,' or 'marketing' is, therefore, not material for purposes of deciding the question of federal power before us." The test of the power to regulate any local activity must hereafter, he said, be a practical economic one of the extent of economic effect the activity in question had upon interstate commerce. Applying this test, he found that wheat locally consumed did have an appreciable practical effect upon the price of wheat moving in interstate commerce; therefore wheat locally consumed was subject to federal regulation although it did not itself ever move in commerce at all. Jackson's words thus sounded the death knell of almost fifty years of categorical distinction between commerce and production and made it clear that in the future the Court would accept as constitutional the regulation of any activity, however local, if it could be demonstrated to have a practical economic effect upon commerce.

THE COMMERCE POWER AND COAL

In *Sunshine Anthracite Coal Co. v. Adkins* (1940), the Court accepted the Bituminous Coal Act of 1937, a statute that Congress had passed to replace the one invalidated in the Carter decision. The new act contained substantially the same provisions for price fixing and the regulation of competition as those in the old law, although in deference to the Carter opinion Congress had omitted the labor provisions of the earlier statute. Justice Douglas' opinion now held that fixing coal prices and establishing market rules was clearly written in the commerce power. As precedent he cited Justice Cardozo's dissenting opinion in the Carter case. As for the 19½ per cent penalty tax levied upon producers who failed to comply with the provisions of the law, Justice Douglas declared that it was clearly intended as a sanction to enforce the regulatory provisions of the statute, but it was not thereby unconstitutional, since Congress could lawfully "impose penalties in aid of the exercise of any of its enumerated powers." Asserting also that the act did not violate due process, Douglas observed: "If the strategic character of this industry in our economy and the chaotic conditions which have prevailed in it do not justify legislation, it is difficult to imagine what would." Douglas then repudiated definitively the existence of the "twilight zone," the area of sovereignty beyond the control of either state or national governments, with the observation that while there were evident limits on the power to regulate industry, "that does not mean that there is a no man's land between state and federal domains."

THE COMMERCE POWER AND FEDERAL REGULATION
OF PUBLIC UTILITIES

Between 1938 and 1946 the government won important victories before the Court in support of the constitutionality of the Public Utility Holding Company Act. This statute, which had become law on August 26, 1935, had been enacted in an attempt to eliminate certain abuses in the utility industry, among them pyramided holding companies, fictitious and watered capitalization, and the imposition of excessive rates upon the public. The act required gas and electric companies using the facilities of interstate commerce to register with the Securities and Exchange Commission under penalty of losing their right to use the mails or to engage in interstate commerce. Section 11, the so-called "death sentence" provision, required that after 1938 the Securities and Exchange Commission limit each holding company to the operation and control of a single integrated public utility system. Holding companies that were of a more complex structure were to be broken up into their integral parts through commission order.

After a protracted period of legal sparring in the lower courts, the Supreme Court in *Electric Bond and Share Company v. S. E. C.* (1938) upheld the registration provisions of the law. Chief Justice Hughes said that there was no serious question that the defendant companies were engaged in interstate commerce, since they operated in some thirty-two states, transmitted energy across state lines, sold energy in interstate commerce, and made continuous use of the mails and facilities of interstate commerce to carry on business. Registration, he added, was a legitimate instrument of congressional control over such businesses. The Court at the same time refused to be drawn into a larger discussion of the more controversial provisions of the statute. The constitutional point decided was in reality a narrow one, and the more vital "death sentence," Section 11, did not come before the Court until 1946.

Finally, in *North American Co. v. S. E. C.*, decided in April 1946, the Court upheld the constitutionality of Section 11 (b) (1) of the law. This provision, a portion of the "death sentence" section, authorized the Securities and Exchange Commission to act to bring about the geographic and economic integration of holding company systems engaged in interstate commerce in gas and electricity. To this end the provision empowered the commission to require holding companies engaged in interstate commerce to confine their activities to a stipulated area, and to dispose of their security holdings in other areas.

In the present case the Court was confronted with a commission order breaking up a public utility holding company controlling directly and indirectly some eighty corporations with an aggregate capital value of $2,300,000,000, doing business in some seventeen states and selling power across state lines. The appellant concern relied heavily upon the contention that it was merely an investment company and was not in itself engaged in interstate commerce. But as Justice Murphy's opinion for a unanimous Court pointed out, this was substantially the same attempted distinction as that which the Court had rejected as invalid forty years earlier in the Northern Securities case. The holding company, he said, could not "hide behind the façade of a mere investor"; the company not only had a "highly important relationship to interstate commerce and the national economy," but was "actually engaged in interstate commerce." Justice Murphy then presented an interpretation of the extent of the commerce power so broad as to make the federal government's authority under interstate commerce virtually coincident with the requirements of adequate national regulation of any phase of the economic system. "This broad commerce clause," he said, "does not operate so as to render the nation powerless to defend itself against economic forces that Congress decrees inimical or destructive of the national economy. Rather it is an affirmative power commensurate with the national needs. . . . And in using this great power, Congress is not bound by technical legal conceptions. Commerce itself is an intensely practical matter. . . . To deal with it effectively, Congress must be able to act in terms of economic and financial realities. . . ." He added briefly that the requirement for disposal of subsidiary holdings did not violate due process, since the provision was not confiscatory and required equitable means of disposal.

The following November, in *American Power and Light Co. v. S. E. C.* (1946), the Court upheld the constitutionality of Section 11 (b) (2) of the Public Utilities Holding Company Act. Section 11 (b) (2), another portion of the "death sentence" provisions, authorized the Securities and Exchange Commission to take all necessary steps to insure that "the corporate structure or continued existence of any company in the holding company system does not unduly or unnecessarily complicate the structure. . . ." Justice Murphy's opinion held that this phraseology clearly gave the commission the power to order the dissolution of unnecessarily complicated holding company structures. Such power, he said, was clearly within the power of Congress to regulate interstate commerce. The evils associated with unduly complicated holding company systems were "so inextricably entwined around the interstate business of the holding company systems as to present no serious question as to the power of Congress under the commerce clause to eradicate them." Citing the North American case, he reaffirmed "once more the constitutional authority resident in Congress by virtue of the commerce clause to undertake to solve national problems directly and realistically, giving due recognition to the scope of the state power." He added that Section 11 (b) (2) did not unlawfully delegate legislative power to the commission, since adequate standards for guidance were embodied in the act. Neither did it violate due process of law, since it was not confiscatory and provided for due notice and hearing.

THE INSURANCE BUSINESS AND INTERSTATE COMMERCE

On June 5, 1944, the Court handed down two highly significant opinions bringing the insurance business within the scope of the federal commerce power. In *Polish National Alliance v. N.L.R.B.*, the Court held unanimously that the activities of insurance companies affected interstate commerce and so were subject to regulation under the National Labor Relations Act. Justice Frankfurter's opinion carefully avoided any statement that the business of writing insurance contracts was in itself interstate commerce, a position that certain of his colleagues were unwilling to adopt. But in *United States v. Southeastern Underwriters Association* a majority of four justices went beyond the Polish Alliance opinion to hold that the insurance business was in itself interstate commerce, and so was subject to regulation under the Sherman Act. In reaching this conclusion the Court overturned a long series of Supreme Court decisions to the contrary beginning with *Paul v. Virginia* (1869). Justice Black, speaking for the majority, pointed out that all earlier decisions had been concerned with upholding state laws in the absence of federal regulation and that these decisions were therefore not conclusive as to the scope of federal power. He chose instead to cite historical evidence that the term "commerce" as of 1787 included insurance, and he cited, also, the sweeping language of Marshall's definition in *Gibbons v. Ogden*— "commerce is intercourse." Justice Black then argued at length that the business of insurance was so inextricably bound up with the processes of commerce that it must be considered as a part of that commerce in itself.

Justice Black held further that insurance contracts fell within the scope of the Sherman Act. He cited historical evidence that insurance companies were looked upon as trusts in the eighties and nineties, and he cited the absence of any positive evidence that Congress had intended to exclude insurance companies from the scope of the law. He concluded, therefore, that insurance companies were subject to the Sherman Act and could properly be convicted for its violation.

In a strong dissent, Chief Justice Stone objected that a long series of opinions had settled decisively that the business of writing insurance contracts was not in itself commerce, and he argued that the immediate effect of the present decision would be to withdraw from the states the regulation of the insurance business and to place it in the hands of the national government, which had no system of regulation at all other than the limited controls of the Sherman Act. In a separate dissent, Justice Jackson expressed the conviction that the insurance business "as a matter of fact" was in itself commerce, but he thought the "legal fiction" to the contrary had become so well established as the basis of federal and state legislative action that it ought to be preserved. Frankfurter, also dissenting, thought Congress could regulate insurance but had not intended to do so in the Sherman Act. Outside the Court, there was widespread editorial and legal criticism of the majority justices for having overturned a long-standing rule of constitutional law by a 4-to-3 decision.[2]

Criticism of the majority opinion in the Southeastern Underwriters case tended to obscure the significant fact that the justices had been unanimous in the conviction that the business of insurance, if not in itself commerce, nonetheless substantially affected commerce and so was subject to federal regulation in so far as it had such effect.

One result of the Court's decision that insurance contracts were themselves interstate commerce was to throw doubt upon the validity of existing state laws for the regulation of the insurance business. It was with this situation in mind that Congress enacted a statute, which became law on March 9, 1945, providing that "the business of insurance, and every person engaged therein, shall be subject to the laws of the several States which relate to the regulation or taxation of such business," and further, that "no Act of Congress shall be construed to invalidate, impair, or supersede any law enacted by any State for the purpose of regulating the business of insurance, or which imposes a fee or tax upon such business, unless such Act specifically relates" to such business. Another section of the act suspended application of the federal antitrust laws to insurance companies until January 1, 1948, after which the Sherman and Clayton Acts and the Federal Trade Commission Act were to be applicable to the extent that such business was not regulated

---

[2] For undisclosed reasons, Justices Roberts and Reed did not participate in the Southeastern Underwriters decision.

by state law. The statute also specified that the National Labor Relations Act and the Fair Labor Standards Act were to continue to apply to insurance companies. Thus Congress in effect stated that the various states could regulate the insurance business until the national government saw fit to supersede them. For the time being, Congress made the various states federal agents in the enforcement of a federal power, a device now familiar to the student of modern constitutional processes.

THE COMMERCE POWER AND NAVIGABLE STREAMS

In another group of opinions, the Court sanctioned federal control over navigable streams well beyond ideas hitherto held as to the limits of that authority. Previous decisions upholding federal authority over waterways had been based upon the proposition that the waterways in question were navigable in interstate commerce. Federal control had been sustained even when navigation was sporadic and difficult, and when the waterway in question lay entirely within one state. By implication, however, federal authority did not extend to the control over entirely non-navigable waters. However, in *United States v. Appalachian Electric Power Co.* (1940) the Court accepted federal control over the non-navigable upper reaches of an interstate stream, the New River in Virginia. Justice Reed's opinion said that since the stream might conceivably be made navigable by improvements, the Federal Power Commission could rightfully exercise control over dam-building, even though commercial navigation of this part of the stream was not at present feasible. Moreover, feasibility of navigation was not the only test of federal power over the stream. "Flood protection, watershed development, recovery of the cost of improvements through utilization of power are likewise parts of commerce control," while "water power development from dams in navigable streams is from the public's standpoint a byproduct of the general use of the rivers for commerce." In other words, flood control and power development had a legitimate relationship to the commerce power. Federal authority over waterways was thus extended far beyond the incidence of navigation.

The Court extended this concept in *Oklahoma ex rel. Phillips v. Atkinson* (1941). This case was concerned with the validity of a federal statute authorizing construction of a dam for flood-control purposes in the non-navigable upper reaches of the Red River. The state of Oklahoma had alleged that the primary purpose of the dam was the generation of power rather than flood control and that the statute authorizing construction therefore violated the Tenth Amendment. The Court, speaking through Justice Douglas, upheld the statute upon two grounds. First, he pointed out that one purpose behind construction of the dam was the promotion of navigation downstream. Second, he held, flood control had a vital relationship to the broader aspects of the commerce power. There was "no constitutional reason," he said, "why Congress or the courts should be blind to the engineering prospects of protecting the nation's arteries of commerce through control of the watersheds. There is no constitutional reason why Congress cannot, under the commerce power, treat the watersheds as a key to flood control on navigable streams and their tributaries." Moreover, the fact that power production was one objective in authorizing construction of the dam did not invalidate the project, since "the fact that ends other than flood control will also be served, or that flood control may be relatively of lesser importance, does not invalidate the exercise of the authority conferred on Congress."

The Atkinson and Appalachian cases thus placed federal authority over waterways upon a far broader constitutional basis than formerly. Flood control and waterway development were now recognized as of equal validity with maintenance of navigation as constitutional objectives of Congress. Also, the fact that Congress may have had objectives other than navigation or flood control— such as power development—did not invalidate an improvement project so long as it was concerned at any point with navigation or flood control. Finally, since an entire watershed area could be treated as a unity, federal authority was now extended to a program for the entire watershed, not merely the navigable portions of streams in that watershed.

THE SPENDING POWER AND PUBLIC WORKS

The new Court also went far beyond its earlier cautious approval of the Tennessee Valley Authority to place federal spending and public works projects practically beyond constitutional attack. It will be recalled that in *Ashwander v. T.V.A.* (1936) the Court, citing both the commerce and war power, had sustained the constitutionality of the Wilson dam and the sale of surplus power from that project, but that it had carefully refrained from passing upon other constitutional aspects of the Tennessee Valley Authority program. However, in *Alabama Power Co. v. Ickes* (1938), the Court, speaking through Justice Sutherland, denied the plea of several state-chartered power companies that it enjoin federal loans to municipalities for power projects. The plaintiff corporations, Sutherland said, had no right to be free of competition, nor could they attack federal appropriations merely as taxpayers. Since the Court would recognize neither of these grounds for action, the power companies were unable to show any impairment of legal right, and they therefore had no standing in court to attack the municipal plants in question.

This opinion was reinforced a year later in *Tennessee Electric Power Company v. T. V. A.* (1939). In this case, eighteen state-chartered power companies sought to enjoin the T. V. A. from the distribution and sale of electric power. They attacked the constitutionality of the Tennessee Valley Act on the ground that Congress had attempted, under the guise of its war and commerce powers, to assert authority over the generation of electric power, a subject matter not granted to it by the Constitution. Again the Court, now speaking through Justice Roberts, held that the appellants had no right to be free from competition and could not therefore show material interest or damage to a legal right to serve as a cause of action.

These two cases meant that for all practical purposes the federal spending power and federal public works projects were beyond federal judicial control. Since opponents of such programs could gain no judicial standing in court as having a material interest in attacking the constitutionality of such legislation, it was impossible to get the Court to pass upon the theoretical constitutional merits of a great regional improvement program such as that of the Tennessee Valley Authority,

STATE TAX LEGISLATION AND THE FEDERAL
COMMERCE POWER

In the course of broadening the scope of the federal commerce power, the Court after 1937 had occasion to pass upon a great variety of state statutes affecting interstate commerce, a majority of them involving the imposition of state taxes burdening interstate commerce or out-of-state business. In many instances, these statutes represented genuine attempts of hard-pressed local and state governments to find new sources of revenue. In most states returns from real and personal property taxes fell off drastically after 1929, while at the same time the expenses of municipal and state governments increased sharply, in large part because of the great rise in unemployment and poor-relief expenditures. The Court generally viewed sympathetically valid attempts to explore new sources of revenue, even where the tax in question went rather far in burdening interstate commerce. The Roosevelt-appointed justices who joined the Court after 1937 generally voted in favor of such legislation, in part apparently on the general principle of imposing as few limits upon governmental sovereignty as possible. The conservative justices remaining on the Court voted much more frequently to invalidate state legislation burdening commerce, but after 1937 they often found themselves in a minority.

However, many state tax laws enacted during the depression were in fact attempts to discriminate against interstate commerce or out-of-state business in favor of local business activity. Legislation of this kind occasioned considerable alarm among certain economic theorists, who foresaw the ultimate division of the United States into a number of more or less self-contained economic units—an eventuality rather dramatically described as "the Balkanization of the United States." This rather fearsome prospect remains decidedly remote; yet the tendency to discriminate by means of taxation against interstate commerce was undeniably a bad one, and was economically unsound. The Court invariably declared state legislation unconstitutional when the statute under review obviously represented a deliberate attempt to discriminate against out-of-state business or to erect an interstate trade barrier.[3]

---

[3] In passing upon state legislation burdening interstate commerce, the Court had available certain well-defined constitutional principles of long standing. Since *Willson v. Black Bird Creek Marsh Co.* (1829) and *Cooley v. Board of Wardens* (1851), it had generally been recognized that a state might, in the absence of federal legislation, impose certain local controls upon interstate commerce. It had also been well established, long before 1937, that a state might impose police controls or tax or inspection measures which incidentally restricted commerce to some degree, so long as the act in question was a bona fide police or revenue measure, did not unduly burden interstate commerce, and did not conflict with congressional regulation of the area of commerce in question.

However, state legislation which discriminated against interstate commerce under the guise of police regulations or revenue measures had long been held unconstitutional. For example, in *Ashbell v. Kansas* (1908), the Court had sustained the constitutionality of a Kansas Live-Stock Inspection Act which required a certificate of freedom from disease as a prerequisite for the transportation of cattle into the state, and in *Mintz v. Baldwin* (1903) the Court held constitutional a New York executive order that all cattle imported into the state for dairy and breeding purposes be certified free of Bang's disease. Further, in *Savage v. Jones* (1912), the Court upheld an Indiana statute requiring animal foods imported into the state to be inspected by a state chemist and labeled with a chemical description of content, and to pay an inspection license fee. All the foregoing were sustained as bona fide police statutes. On the other hand, the Court in *Minnesota v. Barber* (1890) held unconstitutional a Minnesota statute which made it illegal to offer for sale any meat other than that taken from animals passed by Minnesota inspectors within 24 hours of slaughter. Here the Court thought the law under review patently discriminated against meat products from other states and placed an undue burden upon interstate commerce. Likewise, in *International Text-Book Co. v. Pigg* (1910), a Kansas statute requiring a foreign corporation to file a business statement with state authorities as a condition precedent to carrying on business with the concern's customers within the state through the channels of interstate commerce was held unconstitutional as an attempted invasion of the federal commerce power.

For example, in *Ingels v. Morf* (1937), the Court held unconstitutional a California tax on automobile "caravans," which imposed a fee of $15 on each vehicle transported into the state for sale. Justice Stone's opinion observed that a tax burdening interstate commerce could be justified only as payment for some police, inspection, or administrative service rendered by the state. The tax under review purportedly was in payment for policing vehicle caravans, but Justice Stone pointed out that the state collected far more revenue under the act than it expended in police and administrative services. The law therefore burdened interstate commerce unjustifiably, and was invalid. On the other hand, when California passed a revised statute lowering the license fee to $7.50 for a six-month permit for "caravaning" a vehicle on the California state highways, the Court in *Clark v. Paul Gray, Inc.* (1939) found the new law constitutional.

In *Hale v. Bimco Trading Co.* (1939), the Court invalidated an obvious attempt to discriminate against out-of-state business. Here the state of Florida had levied a tax of fifteen cents a hundredweight on cement imported from outside the state. Nominally the tax was an inspection fee, but the state subjected domestic cement to no corresponding fee, while the statute in fact openly affirmed as its purpose the protection of the Florida cement industry against "unfair competition." Justice Frankfurter in holding the law void said that "no reasonable conjecture can here overcome the calculated discrimination against foreign commerce." Likewise, in *Best v. Maxwell* (1940) the Court held unconstitutional a North Carolina statute levying a $250 "privilege tax" upon any person, not a regular retail merchant of the state, who displayed samples in a hotel room or house rented temporarily for sales purposes. Justice Reed, speaking for a unanimous Court, said the tax "in practical operation" would work serious discrimination against interstate commerce, and was therefore invalid. On the other hand, in *Caskey Baking Co. v. Virginia* (1941), the Court accepted the constitutionality of a $100 annual fee imposed upon each vehicle used in peddling within the state, at other than the place of business of the vendor. The Court found the fee part of a comprehensive system of state taxation which did not discriminate against interstate commerce as such; hence the tax was valid.

Beginning with the depression, the retail sales tax became an important source of revenue for most state governments. This tax resulted in a number of important court decisions. Obviously it could not be levied upon goods that were indisputably moving in interstate commerce, but it was often difficult to distinguish precisely where the state's jurisdiction ended, the result being that a number of fine-drawn judicial decisions were necessary.

In *McGoldrick v. Berwind-White Co.* (1940), the Court held that a New York city sales tax on coal shipped into the city in interstate commerce, and there sold, was not unconstitutional. Justice Stone's opinion said that the only relation between the tax and interstate commerce was the fact that shipment had occurred immediately preceding the sale. The tax did not discriminate against interstate commerce and was legal. On the other hand, in *McLeod v. Dilworth* (1944), the Court held unconstitutional an Arkansas collection of a sales tax on a sale in Memphis, Tennessee, where the sale was consummated and title passed in Tennessee and the goods were subsequently shipped into Arkansas. Justice Frankfurter observed that Arkansas was attempting to exercise the prerogative of taxation beyond the jurisdiction of the state.

The tendency of many persons and firms to do business in interstate commerce in order to escape as far as possible from the burden of the sales tax led many states to enact so-called "use taxes" as a complementary levy. Here the state commonly levied a 2 or 3 per cent tax for the privilege of "use," on goods imported into the state and exempt from the sales tax. Although it appeared that the "use tax" was patently a device for evading the limitations upon taxing interstate commerce, the Court in *Nelson v. Sears Roebuck & Co.* (1941), held an Iowa use tax of 2 per cent valid when applied to out-of-state mail-order sales to persons within Iowa. Speaking through Justice Douglas, the Court emphasized that the state could properly tax use as distinct from the out-of-state sale. And in *General Trading Co. v. Tax Commission* (1944), the Court, speaking through Justice Frankfurter, held that the Iowa use tax could properly be applied to property shipped into the state of Iowa, even when both title and transaction had been consummated in Minnesota. Evidently in accepting the use tax, the Court was in part influenced by a sympathy for the revenue problems of the states and a determination not to infringe upon state prerogative any more than was absolutely necessary.

In *McCarroll v. Dixie Greyhound Lines* (1940), the Court invalidated an Arkansas statute which prohibited entry of any vehicle into the state having more than twenty gallons of gasoline in its tanks, without first paying the state gas tax on the balance in excess of twenty gallons. Justice McReynolds, speaking for the Court, said that while the state could levy a reasonable tax for the privilege of using state highways, the present tax could not be so construed, but instead must be interpreted as a simple tax on interstate commerce.

The case is notable because of the dissent of Justices Black, Frankfurter, and Douglas, who argued that judicial control of the taxation of interstate commerce had become unsatisfactory and that Congress ought to establish by statute a body of general rules for the states and courts to follow. "Spasmodic and unrelated instances of litigation," they said, "cannot afford an adequate basis for the creation of integrated national rules which alone can afford that full protection for interstate commerce intended by the Constitution." Justice Black was to repeat on other occasions his argument that state interference with interstate commerce was properly a subject for congressional solution rather than erratic judicial interpretation, but to date Congress has not acted upon the suggestion.

STATE POLICE POWER AND THE FEDERAL

COMMERCE POWER

In most instances the Court viewed with sympathy the attempts of the states to solve the variety of social problems confronting them by imposing local police regulations upon interstate commerce. Only in those instances in which state legislation deliberately interposed a discriminatory barrier to commerce, or in which state legislation intruded upon a sphere of commerce essentially national in character or pre-empted by Congress, did the Court refuse to accept state social legislation affecting interstate commerce.

In *Edwards v. California* (1941), the Court unanimously held unconstitutional the California "Okie Law," which made it a misdemeanor to transport an indigent person or pauper into the state. The obvious objective of the statute was to hold down the cost of the state's relief rolls. But Justice Byrnes, speaking for the Court, pointed out that the transportation of persons across a state line was interstate commerce, and went on to declare that the California act plainly erected "an unconstitutional barrier" to such commerce. No boundary to the permissible area of state police power, he said, "is more certain than the prohibition on the part of any single State to isolate itself from difficulties common to all of them by restraining the transportation of persons and property across its borders." It might well be, he added, that a state could by such expedients escape temporarily a problem common to all of them, but as Justice Cardozo had remarked in *Baldwin v. Seelig* (1935), "The Constitution was framed under the dominion of a political philosophy less parochial in range."

The Court's opinion seemed to be in part at odds with the old precedent of *New York v. Miln* (1837), where the Court had sustained New York's regulation of foreign immigration in order to protect itself against "a moral pestilence of paupers, vagabonds, and possibly convicts." However, Justice Byrnes doubted whether the transportation into California of individual indigent paupers constituted "a moral pestilence," and he intimated that the Miln precedent was in any event archaic.

In *Cloverleaf Co. v. Patterson* (1942), the Court struck down part of an Alabama pure food act as an interference with the federal commerce power. The law in question authorized the seizure of impure packing-stock butter while in the process of manufacture. However, a section of the federal internal revenue code, enacted on August 10, 1912, had established a system of inspection for the manufacture and reprocessing of packing-stock butter and also had authorized confiscation of renovated butter in interstate commerce if it contained unwholesome or deleterious materials.[4] Justice Reed, speaking for the majority, admitted that the federal law did not authorize seizure of packing-stock butter during manufacture, but held nonetheless that the entire process of manufacturing and distributing renovated butter had been subjected to such extensive federal regulation as to preclude state regulation even of the manufacturing process.

In an extremely vigorous dissent, Chief Justice Stone charged the majority with a radical departure from the "salutary rule" that congressional legislation was not to be deemed to have struck down any state law designed to protect health and safety unless the state law in question palpably conflicted with the act of Congress either in practical administration or policy. The present decision, he said, left both federal and state governments "powerless to condemn an article which is a notorious menace to health." Frankfurter, dissenting separately, pointed out that the majority opinion had created a new "twilight zone" between federal and state pure food laws.

The new Court in most instances willingly accepted as constitutional state police statutes whose evident purpose was to protect the health and welfare of the community. Thus in *Milk Board v. Eisenburg* (1939), the Court declared constitutional a Pennsylvania law empowering a state milk board to license milk dealers and fix prices, including that of milk transported into the state in interstate commerce. Justice Roberts, speaking for the majority, admitted that the

---

[4] Packing-stock butter is bulk tub butter. When rancid or off-flavor, it may be reprocessed with fresh milk, and is then known as renovated butter.

statute had an incidental effect on interstate commerce, but he held that the law was not necessarily unconstitutional on that account, since it did not discriminate against out-of-state milk nor place an undue burden upon commerce. In *California v. Thompson* (1941), the Court upheld a California statute requiring the licensing of agents who sold or negotiated for public transportation over the public highways of the state. Justice Stone called the law constitutional, under the rule enunciated in *Willson v. Black Bird Creek Marsh Co.* and *Cooley v. Board of Wardens*, whereby it had long been recognized that in the absence of federal intervention the states might constitutionally regulate certain matters of local concern which unavoidably involve some regulation of interstate commerce. And in *Parker v. Brown* (1943), Chief Justice Stone, speaking for the Court, passed favorably upon the validity of a California statute establishing an elaborate marketing control program for raisins. The law, he said, did not impose unduly restrictive burdens upon interstate commerce, nor did it violate the Agricultural Marketing Act or the Sherman Law.

One category of state statutes discriminating against interstate commerce—those regulating the importation of liquor into a state —were held to be constitutional as a result of the adoption of the Twenty-First Amendment. This became clear in *State Board of Equalization v. Young's Market Co.* (1936), when the Supreme Court ruled favorably upon a California statute which imposed a license fee of $500 for the privilege of importing beer into the state. Justice Brandeis, speaking for the Court, observed first that before the adoption of the Twenty-First Amendment, such a law undoubtedly would have been unconstitutional as imposing a direct burden upon interstate commerce. He then went on to say that the adoption of the amendment had made legal state tariffs upon the importation of liquor. To the argument that the amendment had been intended only to confer police powers upon the state to control the liquor traffic and not to burden interstate commerce, Brandeis replied that the Court could not rewrite the plain language of the amendment to give it that meaning. The Court reached the same conclusion in *Indianapolis Brewing Co. v. Liquor Control Commission* (1939), a case involving the constitutionality of a Michigan statute which forbade the sale within the state of beer manufactured in any state which discriminated against Michigan beer. Although the law admittedly discriminated against interstate commerce, the Court merely stated that since the Young case, a state's right to limit the importation of liquor was not controlled by the commerce clause.

The result of this interpretation of the Twenty-First Amendment has been to sanction a limited commercial warfare between the liquor businesses of the various states. Statutes discriminating against out-of-state liquor manufacturers through license or import duties or by outright prohibition have become common. There is no evidence that Congress intended to bring about this situation when it adopted the phraseology of the amendment; rather it seems probable that Congress intended merely to make it constitutionally possible for dry or partially dry states to protect their borders against a deluge of illicit liquor. However, the present condition does not seem to be remediable unless the Court in the future alters its interpretation of the amendment.

THE DECLINE OF SUBSTANTIVE DUE PROCESS OF LAW

After May 1937 the Court began a general retreat from the use of substantive due process as an instrument for the protection of vested interest and corporate property rights against state and federal social legislation. In the decade following the defeat of Roosevelt's court plan, the Court invalidated but one state statute imposing restrictions upon property or contractual rights as being contrary to the due process or equal protection clauses of the Fourteenth Amendment.

That instance occurred in *Connecticut General Life Insurance Co. v. Johnson* (1938) and was notable principally for Justice Black's dissenting opinion, in which he made an extraordinary attack upon the right of corporations to claim protection under the Fourteenth Amendment. The case involved the validity of a California statute taxing insurance premiums paid in Connecticut by foreign insurance companies doing business in California. All but Justice Black concurred in Justice Stone's opinion that the law violated due process in that it taxed property and business activity lying outside the state's jurisdiction.

"I do not believe the word 'persons' in the Fourteenth Amendment includes corporations," said Justice Black in his dissent. "Neither the history nor the language of the Fourteenth Amendment justifies the belief that corporations are included within its protection." Justice Black then cited Justice Miller's Negro-protection theory of the Fourteenth Amendment as advanced in the *Slaughterhouse Cases,* as supporting evidence for his contention that the Court had erred in *Santa Clara County v. Southern Pacific Railroad* (1886), when it had held that the word "persons" as used in the amendment included corporations.

Justice Black's lone dissent was not dignified by attention from the eight other justices, and his outburst was widely condemned in the legal press. Historically there was considerable basis for Black's contention, but it was doubtful that the Court would now reverse its long-standing dictum that a corporation was a person within the meaning of the Fourteenth Amendment. Such a reversal would have upset a body of legal precedent accumulated over a period of sixty years. Many liberals would have preferred to see an attack upon substantive due process as a far sounder ground upon which to oppose judicial interference with social legislation. Presumably Black did not take this step because he regarded substantive due process as a useful judicial weapon for the protection of civil rights against state legislation, and in fact the Court was to use substantive due process repeatedly for this purpose in the next few years. At any rate Black did not again advance the idea that corporations did not come within the protection of the Fourteenth Amendment. Apparently he dropped the idea as impracticable.

In any event, Black's colleagues shared his belief that the Fourteenth Amendment ought not commonly to be invoked to protect property rights against state social legislation. A notable instance of this new attitude occurred in *Madden v. Kentucky* (1940), a case involving the recently revived privileges and immunities clause of the amendment. The issue was the constitutionality of a Kentucky statute imposing an ad valorem tax on citizens' bank deposits outside the state five times as high as that imposed on deposits within the state. A Vermont income tax law involving a similar principle [5] had been held unconstitutional in *Colgate v. Harvey* (1936), in which Justice Sutherland had held that interstate business activity was one of the privileges and immunities of citizens of the United States and hence protected against state abridgment by the Fourteenth Amendment. [6] Now, however, Justice Reed specifically overruled *Colgate v. Harvey* to hold the Kentucky law valid. In pass-

---

[5] The Vermont law had exempted from taxation income from money loaned within the state, but had levied a tax upon income from money loaned outside the state.

[6] Until *Colgate v. Harvey*, the privileges and immunities clause of the Fourteenth Amendment had lain dormant, because of Justice Miller's holding in the *Slaughterhouse Cases* that the clause referred only to the privileges and immunities of national citizenship as distinct from that of the states (see pp. 473–477), and because of the Court's subsequent long-standing refusal to invoke the clause against state social legislation. In his dissent in *Colgate v. Harvey*, Justice Stone pointed out that "since the adoption of the Fourteenth Amendment at least forty-four cases have been brought to this Court in which state statutes have been assailed as infringements of the privileges and immunities clause. Until today, none has held that state legislation infringed that clause."

ing, he observed that "in the states there reposes the sovereignty to manage their own affairs except only as the requirements of the Constitution otherwise provide." These words implied a far more generous view of state police power than that entertained by the Court before 1937.

The new determination not to use the justices' own social philosophy as a constitutional guidepost was perhaps best expressed by Justice Frankfurter, in *Osborn v. Ozlin* (1940), in the course of an opinion upholding a Virginia statute regulating insurance brokerage contracts. It was immaterial, said Justice Frankfurter, "that such state actions may run counter to the economic wisdom of Adam Smith or J. Maynard Keynes, or may be ultimately mischievous even from the point of view of avowed state policy. Our inquiry must be much narrower. It is whether Virginia has taken hold of a matter within her power, or has reached beyond her borders to regulate a subject which was none of her concern because the Constitution has placed control elsewhere." These words recalled Holmes' dissent in *Lochner v. New York*, and placed the new majority's stamp of approval upon the great justice's conception of the judicial power in relation to the Fourteenth Amendment.

Thus the Court's new sense of judicial self-restraint meant the end of substantive due process as a check upon state economic legislation, although the Court did not formally repudiate the concept for many years. Finally in *Ferguson v. Skrupa* (1963), Justice Black, speaking for a unanimous Court in an opinion upholding a Kansas statute limiting the business of debt adjustment to lawyers, pronounced due process as an instrument for the protection of vested rights to be officially dead. The doctrine, he said, had been "long since discarded," so that courts no longer "substitute their social and economic beliefs for the judgment of legislative bodies." In reality the concept thus formally disposed of had been abandoned decades earlier. Only in the area of civil liberties did substantive due process remain alive—here it retained a great and growing vitality.

The quiet demise of substantive due process as a device for protecting vested rights greatly widened the field of economic regulation open to the several state legislatures, even as the Court, through its new interpretation of the commerce clause, was broadening the scope of federal legislative power. The result was the elimination of most of the old "twilight zone" between state and federal legislation, so that a long-standing grievance of liberals against the Court largely disappeared.

LONG-RANGE IMPLICATIONS OF THE
NEW ERA IN FEDERALISM

The "great retreat" by the Supreme Court in the spring of 1937 marked the beginning of a new era in federalism. Sufficient time has elapsed since then to enable us to assess with some confidence what the long-range effects of the limited constitutional revolution under Franklin Roosevelt have been for the federal system.

First, it now seems indisputable that there has occurred a permanent enlargement in the extent of federal power. Entire new areas of sovereignty hitherto entrusted to the states or to no government at all are now the subject of extensive federal regulation and control. Agricultural production and marketing, the sale of securities, labor-management relations, and flood control are perhaps the most important new areas of federal sovereignty. While none of them has been entirely withdrawn from state control, it is nonetheless true that federal policy for each of them is of far more importance than the regulatory measures of any of the states. This enlargement in federal authority has apparently been accepted as permanent by both major political parties and all shades of opinion. It is significant, for example, that when a Republican Congress in the spring of 1947 sought to redress what it regarded as certain of the inequities of the National Labor Relations Act, it did not even consider lessening federal controls; instead the new Taft-Hartley Law imposed certain additional regulations upon labor unions.

It is probable that the New Deal worked a permanent alteration in the American people's conception of the federal government's responsibility for the operation of the national economic system Earlier administrations had on occasion asserted the necessity for federal control over certain individual phases of the national economy—thus Theodore Roosevelt had preached trust-busting, conservation of natural resources, and rail rate regulation, and Woodrow Wilson had sponsored a broad program which included extensive regulation of the banking and financial system, tariff adjustment and tightening of the antitrust laws. But Franklin D. Roosevelt's administration was the first one to assume that it was the federal government's duty to assume responsibility for virtually all the important phases of the entire national economy—production, labor, unemployment, social security, money and banking, housing, public works, flood control, and the conservation of natural resources. It is true that this program was promulgated at a time of unprecedented economic crisis. But crisis appears to have become a characteristic part of the twentieth-century world, and federal responsibility for the solution of recurrent crises both in internal economy and in foreign affairs is something that most Americans now more or less take for granted. The public at large has at length accepted the validity of the old liberal national argument of Progressive days—that certain areas of economic activity are essentially national in character, that they are therefore beyond effective state control, and that only the federal government has the requisite prestige and nationwide authority to formulate policy and impose controls where they are needed.

"Dual federalism" is apparently dead beyond revival. This doctrine, it will be recalled, held that the federal government and the separate states constituted two mutually exclusive systems of sovereignty, that both were supreme within their respective spheres, and that neither could exercise its authority in such a way as to intrude, even incidentally, upon the sphere of sovereignty reserved to the other. The Court in *United States v. Darby* specifically repudiated this doctrine in favor of the doctrine of national supremacy—which points out that the Constitution makes federal law superior to state law and which holds accordingly that Congress may not be estopped in the exercise of any of its delegated powers merely because the performance of those powers may break in upon an area of sovereignty hitherto reserved to the states. It is highly improbable that in the future any attorney in pleading a case in federal court will argue that the Tenth Amendment worked an alteration in the federal system and gave permanent immunity to the states against federal invasion of their "reserved sphere."

The enlargement in the scope of federal sovereignty and the death of dual federalism have not brought about the destruction of the federal system or of the several states as essential members of that system. Federal functions have admittedly increased greatly since 1933, but the sphere of state activities has not undergone a decline; on the contrary, state functions have increased substantially since the inception of the New Deal. The decline of substantive due process of law has opened up a whole new area for experimentation in state social legislation which had hitherto been closed. Moreover, much New Deal legislation has depended upon the states as agencies for its implementation, so that instead of thrusting the states aside it has created a new state-federal partnership for the attainment of a common legislative objective. The Social Security Act of 1935, which makes the states the custodians of a large section of the social security program, is perhaps the most important statute of this kind. The United States Housing Act of 1937 makes use of this same device, as do the numerous grant-in-aid programs continued and expanded under the New Deal. In short, the states have a vital role to play in the "new federalism" as agents of national policy.

Interstate treaties, permissible under the Constitution where the contracting parties obtain the consent of Congress, have opened up another sphere of state activity. Since 1920, they have been used to solve a number of regional problems of some importance, particularly in the field of water-power projects and flood control. Thus an interstate compact of 1925 apportioned the Columbia River's waters between Montana, Idaho, Washington, and Oregon. And in 1937, Connecticut, Vermont, Massachusetts, and New Hampshire signed a Connecticut River flood control compact.

Certain political theorists have in recent years advocated the abandonment of existing state lines and the substitution of a number of regional units more in conformity with existing economic areas and with modern administrative requirements. This idea has secured a limited recognition in certain federal statutes, wherein the nation has been divided into regional districts for administrative purposes. The Federal Reserve Act of 1913 and the various federal communications acts, for example, have resorted to this device. However, the tradition of local and state government is obviously still far too strong to permit the outright destruction of existing states even were it desirable, and proposals for sweeping reorganization of state lines have received but little attention in practical politics.

Many observers in the late 1930's believed that the Constitutional "revolution" of 1937 would result eventually in a long-range decline of the power and prestige of the Supreme Court. Two forces, they predicted, would operate to this end. In the first place, the Court's "sovereign prerogative of choice" was gone. That is, it no longer had the power, when passing upon important congressional legislation dealing with commerce or taxing power, to choose between two streams of precedent, the one derived from the liberal national tradition and the other from dual federalism. Thus the Court, critics predicted, would lose its critical role as the arbiter of federal-state relations. Second, careful observers, recalling Stone's stern injunction that "Courts are not the only agencies of government that must be preserved to have the power to govern," noted that certain of the newer justices were decidedly devoted to a philosophy of "judicial self-restraint," and they predicted that the

Court would come more and more under the influence of this point of view. The combined result of these influences, critics predicted, would be a Court much less able and much less inclined to act as the final supreme arbiter of the constitutional system.

However, this expected long-range decline in the Court's prestige failed to occur. Instead, in the period following World War II, the Court recovered completely from whatever temporary loss of influence it had suffered after the constitutional "revolution" of 1937, and went on to demonstrate repeatedly that its decision-making process still was at the very heart of the "living" constitutional system.

Briefly this resurgence of the Court's power and prestige was to take place because the institution was to find for itself another area of decision in which it could exercise a new "sovereign prerogative of choice"—that of the resolution of constitutional problems arising from the clash between government power and private right. Thus the Court's decisions after World War II upon such issues as racial desegregation, separation of church and state, the control of Communist activity, and the apportionment of state legislatures all were to demonstrate anew the Court's role as the final arbiter of constitutional development. Ironically, by 1960 the Supreme Court was once again to be under severe attack for having arrogated to itself excess power "in defiance of the intent of the Fathers," although the criticisms of that era were to come generally from conservatives rather than from the "New Deal" type of liberals.

This conclusion—that in spite of the limited constitutional revolution of the 1930's, the Supreme Court, after all, was to maintain in the long run its old basic role in the constitutional system—now appears to be applicable also to the constitutional changes of the New Deal era generally. By solving the crisis in national sovereignty and federal-state relations, the reforms of the New Deal in the long run underwrote the stability and vitality of the old constitutional order generally. Like the great constitutional changes after the Civil War, those of the New Deal left the structure of the "old order" fundamentally intact. The "revolution" of 1937 did not break the continuity of American constitutional development in any decisive respect. In that sense it was not a revolution at all.

Chapter

29

The New Deal Era
in Civil Liberties

IT IS one of the interesting constitutional anomalies of the New Deal Era that the Supreme Court, even while it was engaged in sanctioning a tremendous expansion of federal and state power over economic and social matters, occupied itself at the same time with the formulation of an elaborate new constitutional law of civil liberties. This fact was the more remarkable if one remembers that the world at large witnessed in these years a progressive destruction by tyrannical governments of the ideals of liberty and human dignity which had been developed so painfully in western culture over the past three centuries. Even the entry of the United States into World War II did not disrupt the Court's preoccupation with its task of redefining, strengthening, and enlarging the scope of individual liberty and private right under the American constitutional system.

The Court had demonstrated some considerable concern with civil liberties and private rights from the early 1930's, Justices Brandeis, Cardozo and Stone consistently championing a liberal position in cases of this kind. However, with the advent of Justices Black and Douglas after the upheaval of 1937, the liberal position on civil liberties became dominant on the Court. These two justices were to constitute a kind of solid "liberal phalanx" on the Court for the next generation. Justices Murphy and Rutledge, who joined the Court in the next few years, were no less outspoken and emphatic upon civil liberties. Justice Frankfurter, whose respect for legislative prerogative and his espousal of the philosophy of judicial self-restraint were later to lead him to a conservative position on civil liberties questions, in this period also voted generally with the new civil liberties majority. As a consequence the Court now began to speak with a powerful and consistently liberal voice upon matters of personal freedom and individual right, as much in harmony with the general political tenor of the era as had been the Court's conservatism on such matters a decade or so earlier.

THE "MODERNIZATION" OF THE BILL OF RIGHTS

Broadly speaking, the New Deal Justices whom Roosevelt appointed after 1937 wished to interpolate a philosophy of economic democracy, political liberalism, and individual liberty into constitutional law. To this end they sought deliberately to "modernize" the Bill of Rights, formulating new constitutional guarantees to protect labor unions in strikes and picketing and championing the rights of racial and religious minorities.

The task the Court faced in attempting to develop a modernized body of civil liberties was no easy one. For one thing, the justices' libertarian outlook itself involved deep tensions, both between collective social interest and private right and between traditional rights long recognized by the courts and the rights which the justices were attempting to formulate. Conflicts of this kind appeared both in the Court's attempts to treat picketing in labor disputes as a form of free speech, and in the pamphlet peddling cases precipitated by the activities of Jehovah's Witnesses and other religious sects, where the religious liberty guaranteed by the First Amendment clashed with the long-established right of urban communities to regulate door-to-door peddling. In neither instance were there any self-evident answers at hand.

Modernization of the Bill of Rights also involved the Court in the difficult problem of defining further the newly established association between its provisions, in particular those of the First Amendment, and the guarantees of the Fourteenth Amendment. This association, it will be recalled, had first been enunciated in *Gitlow v. New York* (1925), and had been further strengthened in *Stromberg v. California* (1931) and *Near v. Minnesota* (1931).[1]

---

1 See above, pp. 664-665.

The result had been to bring a vast range of private rights, hitherto only under state protection, under the scrutiny and protection of the federal judiciary.

These cases left uncertain the question of whether the Fourteenth Amendment now included all the guarantees enumerated in the federal Bill of Rights. There was no logical solution of the problem immediately apparent. The due process clauses of the Fifth and Fourteenth Amendments presumably had the same meaning and content, except that they limited the federal and state governments, respectively. The Fifth Amendment would have been redundant within the Bill of Rights had it been construed to include freedom of speech—provided for in the First Amendment. Yet the Fourteenth Amendment was now construed to include freedom of speech. How much more of the Bill of Rights was to be construed as redundant and included within the phrase "due process of law?"

In *Palko v. Connecticut* (1937), the Court gave a partial answer to this question. This case was concerned with the constitutionality of a Connecticut statute permitting the state to take appeals from the decisions of the lower courts in criminal cases, and it thus presented the question of whether the Fourteenth Amendment embraced the guarantee against double jeopardy in the First Amendment. Justice Cardozo, speaking for the Court, answered in the negative. The Fourteenth Amendment, he said, did not automatically protect all the rights extended by the first eight amendments, but instead guaranteed only those "implicit in the concept of ordered liberty" and those principles of justice "so rooted in the traditions and conscience of our people as to be ranked as fundamental." Freedom of speech, for example, was such a right; trial by jury and immunity from double jeopardy were not. The Connecticut statute was therefore constitutional.

This interpretation restricted somewhat the scope of the Fourteenth Amendment in state civil liberties cases. But at the same time it opened the way for judicial development of a whole series of constitutional rights to be guaranteed by the Court as against the states which the Court might find to be "implicit in the concept of ordered liberty" in a modern democracy. Thus the technical constitutional means for the "modernization" of the Bill of Rights was now available; the Court needed merely to formulate new guarantees of liberty related to modern economic and social conditions. Paradoxically, this involved the creation of a vast new body of substantive due process law in the area of civil liberties at the very time when the Court had but lately terminated decisively the concept of due process as a bulwark for vested interest and property rights.

It is important to observe, also, that the Court tended constantly to enlarge the domain of "implicit in the concept of ordered liberty" with respect to rights reserved to the states. At least one member of the Court, Justice Black, in *Adamson v. California* (1948) adopted the position that the Court ought at once to declare the entire content of the federal Bill of Rights formally incorporated in the Fourteenth Amendment. He took this position on the ground that such incorporation had been the original intent of the amendment's framers. "My study of the historical events that culminated in the Fourteenth Amendment . . . persuades me," he asserted, "that one of the chief objects that the provisions of the Amendment's first section, separately, and as a whole, were intended to accomplish was to make the Bill of Rights applicable to the states." The Court had erred, he thought, in substituting "its own concepts of decency and justice for the language of the Bill of Rights." The Court now should return to "what I believe was the original purpose of the Fourteenth Amendment—to extend to all the people of the nation the complete protection of the Bill of Rights."

Justice Black's assertion, for which there was some historical evidence, was nonetheless attacked by Justice Frankfurter as ridiculous, and various scholars presently devoted themselves to arguing that Black's position was unsound. The Court, at all events, failed to adopt Black's theory whole cloth or in any formal way. Instead, over more than a decade, it was to move gradually toward the incorporation of more and more of the substance of the Bill of Rights within the Fourteenth Amendment, without coming fully to formal acceptance of Justice Black's thesis. Whether it would ever take this final step was to be still uncertain almost a decade and a half after Justice Black had enunciated the idea.

At all events, the Court found no difficulty in incorporating fully the guarantees of the First Amendment within the due process clause of the Fourteenth Amendment. The Court now used the First Amendment's guarantees to create new safeguards against restrictive state legislation with respect to speech, press and assembly, and religion. It threw new constitutional protection around picketing by labor unions, meetings in public parks, parades, pamphlet-peddling, the regulation of sound trucks, and the censorship of sacrilegious movies. Thus the guarantees of the First Amendment were "modernized" to apply to the constitutional exigencies of twentieth-century life.

Throughout most of the thirties and forties the Court majority adhered to a very broad interpretation of the scope of First Amendment rights, on occasion adopting a so-called "preferred position" doctrine and in other instances returning to the "clear and present danger" doctrine. The "preferred position" doctrine, as first set forth by Justice Stone in a now-celebrated footnote to his opinion, in *United States v. Carolene Products Co.* (1938), held that "there may be narrower scope for the operation of the presumption of constitutionality where legislation appears on its face to be within a specific prohibition of the Constitution, such as those of the first ten amendments, which are deemed equally specific when held to be embraced within the Fourteenth." That is, while under ordinary circumstances, the burden of legal proof was against those attacking the constitutionality of a statute, in First Amendment cases the burden of proof was to be reversed, and it became the obligation of the state to demonstrate that notwithstanding the prohibition on regulation in the First Amendment, the regulation in question was constitutional. Justices Murphy and Rutledge were vigorous exponents of the "preferred position" doctrine, as also were Black and Douglas, although the latter two justices on occasion came close to espousal of the doctrine that the First Amendment categorically prohibited all legislation restricting in any fashion the rights it guaranteed.

The so-called "clear and present danger" doctrine, it will be recalled, had first been enunciated by Justice Holmes in *Schenck v. United States* (1919). While not as extreme in its consequences as the "preferred position" doctrine, the "clear and present danger" doctrine also gave a very broad sweep to First Amendment rights and so brought a great range of state regulatory legislation under the Court's ban.

FREEDOM OF SPEECH: THE RIGHT TO PICKET

A notable example of the legal and philosophic difficulties the justices encountered in their attempts to "modernize" the Bill of Rights appeared in the development of the doctrine that picketing during the course of a labor dispute was a form of free speech protected by the First Amendment. For one thing, this approach involved a precipitous shift from the values of the "old" constitutional law with its primary concern for property rights. In *Truax v. Corrigan* (1921) the Court had struck down a state statute forbidding injunctions against picketing, on the ground that the law in question wrongfully exposed private property rights to possible injury. By contrast, the "free speech" approach to picketing, when carried to an extreme, minimized or even disregarded potential damage to private property rights and focused instead almost entirely on a right of free communication.

Complicating the matter still further was the fact that picketing, upon close examination, obviously involved other elements than mere freedom of expression. Picketing, many analysts pointed out, might indeed carry a "message" properly protected as free speech, but as a rule it was also intimately associated with a labor dispute or strike, which even when conducted peacefully was in fact a form of industrial warfare, however legitimate.

Moreover, picketing all too often did not confine itself to peaceful communication. Even when overtly abstaining from violence, it generally involved threats and intimidation aimed at both employers and nonstriking workers. Mass picketing went further; it often blocked plant entrances to employers and employees alike, while at worst it spilled over into rioting, violence, and even sabotage. Activities of the latter kind were the very antithesis of the "market place of ideas" upon which the original theory of the First Amendment rested. Not surprisingly, therefore, the legal and philosophical problems involved in the new "First Amendment" approach to picketing deeply troubled the justices and soon divided even the Roosevelt appointees on the Court into sharply opposing camps.

The Court took its first step toward the doctrine that picketing was a form of free speech protected by the First Amendment in *Senn v. Tile Layers Union* (1937). Here the majority justices upheld the constitutionality of a Wisconsin statute legalizing peaceful picketing. "Clearly," said Brandeis for the majority of five justices, "the means which the state authorizes—picketing and publicity—are not prohibited by the Fourteenth Amendment. Members of a union might, without special statutory authorization by a State, make known the facts of a labor dispute, for freedom of speech is guaranteed by the Federal Constitution." This language not only affirmed the constitutionality of the Wisconsin law; it also carried the implication that peaceful picketing was a form of free speech with which a state could not legally interfere.

How great was the difference between this point of view and that formerly entertained by the Court was emphasized by Justice Butler's vigorous dissent for himself and Justices Sutherland, Van Devanter, and McReynolds. Butler admitted that picketing by the parties of a labor dispute in order to better working conditions might sometimes be constitutional. In the present case, however, the union had attempted to force an employer to cease working as a tile-layer in his own establishment. Butler thought that the right to "carry on any of the common occupations of life" was guaranteed by the Fourteenth Amendment, and that the union's objection was therefore unlawful and a violation of due process. This argument relied heavily upon the Truax decision, which the majority had thrust aside as outworn.

Justice Brandeis' intimation that picketing was a form of free speech was confirmed in *Thornhill v. Alabama* (1940), in which the Court held "invalid on its face" an Alabama statute prohibiting peaceful picketing. "In the circumstances of our times," Justice Murphy said, "the dissemination of information concerning the facts of a labor dispute must be regarded as within that area of free discussion that is guaranteed by the Constitution." Free discussion of labor disputes, he added, was "indispensable to the effective and intelligent use of the processes of popular government to shape the destiny of modern industrial society." [2] In short, here was a new "fundamental constitutional right"—the right to picket—certainly one beyond the ken of the Joint Committee on Reconstruction which had drafted the Fourteenth Amendment in 1866.

The following year, in *American Federation of Labor v. Swing* (1941), the Court strengthened its new identification of picketing with free speech by holding that a state might not lawfully enjoin picketing merely because those carrying on the picketing were not parties to an immediate labor dispute. The case, which arose in Illinois, involved an unsuccessful attempt to unionize a beauty parlor, and the picketing in question had been accompanied by some violence as well as by the use of false and libelous placards. Justice Frankfurter made it clear that state courts might properly enjoin violent picketing under some circumstances; nonetheless, he found that in the present instance the Illinois court had issued the injunction in part on the ground that under Illinois law picketing was illegal when conducted by strangers to the employer. "Such a ban of free communication," Frankfurter declared, was "inconsistent with the guarantees of free speech" and therefore a violation of the Fourteenth Amendment. A year later, the Court reaffirmed this position in *Bakery and Pastry Drivers v. Wohl* (1942), when it held that a state could not lawfully enjoin a union from peaceful picket-

---

[2] In a companion case, Carlson v. California (1940), Justice Murphy delivered an opinion for the Court declaring unconstitutional a similar California statute.

ing, even when no labor dispute at all in the ordinary sense was involved.

However, it soon became evident that a majority of the justices believed that the right to picket was subject to certain limitations. Thus in *Milk Wagon Drivers Union v. Meadowmoor Dairies* (1941), a companion piece to the Swing case, the Court held that a state court might lawfully enjoin picketing marked by violence and the destruction of property. "It must never be forgotten," said Justice Frankfurter, "that the Bill of Rights was the child of the Enlightenment. Back of the guarantee of free speech lay faith in the powers of an appeal to reason by all the peaceful means for gaining access to the mind. But utterance in a context of violence can lose its significance as an appeal to reason and become part of an instrument of force. Such utterance was not meant to be sheltered by the Constitution." Significantly, Black, Reed, and Douglas dissented, holding that the injunction in question improperly went beyond the mere prohibition of violence and cut off the right of peaceable expression upon matters of public concern.

A year later, in *Carpenters and Joiners Union v. Ritter's Cafe* (1942), the Court found that a state could lawfully prohibit the picketing of an employer not involved in a labor dispute in order to bring pressure upon another employer who was so involved. Freedom of speech, said Justice Frankfurter for the majority, did not become completely inviolable merely by the circumstances of its occurring in the course of a labor dispute. He went on to balance the general police power of the state against the constitutional right of free speech precisely as the Court before 1937 had balanced vested rights against state police power in substantive due process cases. The state, Frankfurter thought, might reasonably prohibit the "conscription of neutrals." To hold otherwise, he said, would be to "transmute vital constitutional liberties into doctrinaire dogma." This time Black, Douglas, Murphy, and Reed dissented, contending that peaceful picketing, even against a neutral, was simple communication and ought not lawfully to be enjoined.

Quite plainly there was a serious difference of constitutional philosophy separating the majority and minority positions. The majority justices evidently believed that picketing, on occasion at least, involved elements other than mere communication—coercion, violence, intimidation, or conspiracy to accomplish unlawful ends. They believed also that the Court ought to recognize a discretionary right of the states to subject these elements to regulation and control. The minority, on the other hand, wished to treat picketing as mere free expression and as such entitled to a "preferred position" under the First Amendment, thereby making it very nearly immune from state attempts at regulation. Not until some years later was the conflict of theory and policy to be resolved.

FREEDOM OF SPEECH: PUBLIC MEETINGS AND PARADES

In another series of cases the Court used the guarantees of the First Amendment to erect new safeguards around individuals speaking at public meetings, staging parades, and the like. For some years the Court adhered closely to the doctrine that communication of this kind, even more than picketing, had a preferred constitutional position giving it at least partial immunity from state controls. The justices were especially quick to strike down statutes which imposed restrictive license requirements or "prior restraint" upon First Amendment activities as well as state or local ordinances which vested arbitrary discretion in local police officers in granting permits for meetings, parades, and the like.

The problem of state attempts to control public meetings first came before the Court in *Hague v. C.I.O.* (1939), a case involving the constitutionality of a Jersey City municipal ordinance requiring permits from a "director of public safety" for the conduct of public meetings. In the background of the case was a history of police violence in which labor-union meetings had been broken up, the dissemination of printed material forcibly stopped, and union organizers "run out of town."

By a vote of five to two, the Court found the ordinance in question unconstitutional. However, the majority justices reached this conclusion by various routes. Justices Black and Roberts thought that the "right peaceably to assemble" was one of the privileges and immunities of citizens of the United States guaranteed by the Fourteenth Amendment, and they cited *United States v. Cruikshank* in support of this position in holding the ordinance invalid. Justice Stone, with whom Justice Reed concurred, thought that the Court ought merely to hold that the ordinance violated the due process clause of the Fourteenth Amendment, and he protested against invoking the privileges and immunities clause. Chief Justice Hughes, who also concurred, thought that the right to discuss the National Labor Relations Act was properly a privilege of United States citizenship, but he believed that the record in the case better supported Stone's position otherwise. Justices McReynolds and Butler dissented, McReynolds expressing the opinion that "wise management of such intimate local affairs, generally at least, is beyond the competency of federal courts."

However, the Court soon made it clear that the rights of free speech and assembly were not absolutely immune to reasonable regulation under the state police power. In *Cox v. New Hampshire* (1941), Chief Justice Hughes delivered a unanimous opinion upholding a New Hampshire statute requiring a permit and license for organized parades. Regulation of the use of the streets, Hughes pointed out, was a "traditional exercise of control by local governments." He noted further that the New Hampshire law, as construed, gave the licensing board no arbitrary or discretionary power to exclude applicants, and that its regulatory powers existed only to prevent confusion resulting from overlapping parades and processions, to secure convenient use by other travelers, and to minimize the risk of disorder, all reasonable police requirements.

Another type of permissible local control emerged a year later in *Chaplinsky v. New Hampshire* (1942), when the Court upheld a conviction under a New Hampshire statute making it unlawful for any person to "address any offensive, derisive or annoying word to any other person who is lawfully in any street or public place." The defendant had addressed an impromptu street meeting with a denunciation of all organized religion as a "racket." Later he had cursed a complaining officer as a "God-damned racketeer" and the "whole government of Rochester" as "Fascists or agents of Fascists." Justice Murphy, speaking for a unanimous Court, observed that "there are certain well-defined and narrowly limited classes of speech, the prevention of which has never been thought to raise any constitutional problem. These include the lewd and obscene, the profane, the libelous, and the insulting or 'fighting' words— those which by their very utterance inflict injury or tend to incite an immediate breach of the peace." Utterances of this kind, Murphy thought, were "of such slight social value as a step to truth" that they were not entitled to any constitutional protection. The statute in question, construed to punish only this kind of speech, was therefore constitutional.

However, the justices continued to deal sternly with attempts on the part of the state to use the licensing of public meetings as a restrictive device. Thus in *Thomas v. Collins* (1945), the Court threw out a contempt conviction imposed by the Texas courts in pursuance of a statute requiring labor organizers to register with state officials and procure an organizer's card before soliciting membership in labor unions. The appellant had addressed an open mass meeting of oil workers, and in his speech he had deliberately solicited members for the C.I.O. oil union, in direct defiance of an anticipatory restraining order issued by the local courts.

Justice Rutledge, who delivered the majority opinion, held that the Texas statute, as applied in the present case, was unconstitutional. The great "indispensable democratic freedoms secured by the First Amendment," he asserted, had a constitutional priority which "gives these liberties a sanctity and a sanction not permitting dubious intrusions." Any attempt to restrict them "must be justified by clear public interest, threatened not doubtfully or remotely, but by clear and present danger."

Here was a classic statement of the "preferred position" theory of First Amendment rights; here, also, was the clear and present danger doctrine of World War I days, which the Court was now in the process of reviving. Rutledge also rejected the state's contention that solicitation of union membership was essentially a business activity and hence outside the protection of the First Amendment. "The idea is not sound," he said, "that the First Amendment's safeguards are wholly inapplicable to business activity." Justice Roberts, who wrote a dissenting opinion with which Stone, Frankfurter, and Reed concurred, argued that the states properly had a discretionary right to license public meetings in the interest of peace and order, an idea which was to triumph in the postwar era.

THE FIRST AMENDMENT AND PAMPHLET-PEDDLING

Meanwhile, the Court was engaged in an attempt to define exactly the area of constitutional liberty involved in pamphlet-peddling, a problem which gave the justices great difficulty. The confusion arose out of the fact that cases of this kind often involved commercial activity as well as elements of free speech, press, and even religion, and it was difficult or impossible to separate them in actual practice. The right of local communities to regulate peddling was well established at law. Nonetheless, several of the justices believed it important to protect the elements of free communication in such activity. As in the case of public meetings, it was the presence of "prior restraint" or of capricious or arbitrary licensing authority on the part of local officials which aroused the Court's hostility.

The Court took its departure on this problem in Lovell v. Griffin (1938), when it unanimously invalidated a city ordinance of Griffin, Georgia, prohibiting the distribution of pamphlets and literature without written permission from the city manager. The case was among the first of many involving the religious sect of Jehovah's Witnesses, who acknowledge allegiance to divine law alone—not to any political or temporal government or its statutes. Their difficulties with local and state police ordinances were to furnish much of the raw material for the Court's development of civil liberties doctrine in the next few years. The ordinance, said Chief Justice Hughes, "is such that it strikes at the very foundation of freedom of the press by subjecting it to license and censorship." He pointed out that it was precisely against the right to license publication that the original doctrine of freedom of the press had been evolved by John Milton and his contemporaries. Although the law in question limited distribution and not publication, it was nonetheless invalid, since liberty to publish without liberty to circulate "would be of little value."

The Lovell decision served as the basis for the court's finding a year later in *Schneider v. Irvington* (1939), in which it struck down four city ordinances which attempted to control the distribution of circulars, flyers, and the like. Justice Roberts, who spoke for the Court, first observed that freedom of speech reflected the "belief of the framers of the Constitution that exercise of [First Admendment] rights lies at the foundation of free government by free men." It followed that ordinances of Los Angeles, Milwaukee, and Worcester, Massachusetts, which banned outright the distribution of street literature as a means of preventing littering were void; the objective of clean streets, said Roberts, was insufficient to sustain the constitutionality of a law which prohibited a person "lawfully in the public street from handing literature to one willing to receive it." Roberts marked for special condemnation an osdinance of Irvington, New Jersey, which required a prior police permit for such distribution. To "require a censorship through license," he declared, "strikes at the very heart" of the First Amendment's guarantees.

The Court adopted a similar position in *Cantwell v. Connecticut* (1940). This case involved the constitutionality of a Connecticut statute prohibiting solicitation of money for any religious or charitable purpose without prior approval by the secretary of the public welfare council. Under the law, this official had the power to determine whether the cause in question was a bona fide religious one before approving solicitation. Justice Roberts' unanimous opinion declared the law void as a denial of religious liberty in violation of the due process clause of the Fourteenth Amendment. Justice Roberts admitted that the state had a general right to regulate solicitation, even for religious purposes, but he held that the secretary's power to withhold approval if he found the cause not a religious one an inadmissible "censorship of religion as a means of determining its right to survive." In short, it was the arbitrary quality of administrative control which destroyed the law's validity.

Subsequently the Court found some difficulty in adhering to the position taken in the Lovell and Cantwell cases. In *Jones v. Opelika* (1942), a majority of five justices upheld the constitutionality of a city ordinance of Opelika, Alabama, which required book-peddlers to procure a ten-dollar city license before doing business. Justice Reed's majority opinion emphasized that the constitutional rights guaranteed by the Fourteenth Amendment were "not absolutes" but that instead it was necessary to balance them against the general right of the states "to insure orderly living, without which constitutional guarantees of civil liberties would be a mockery." Obviously, he thought, the fact that the petitioners, members of Jehovah's Witnesses, had offered books for sale, gave the transactions a different character than the mere exercise of freedom of speech or religious ritual. "A book agent," he said, "cannot escape a license requirement by a plea that it is a tax on knowledge." Reed also distinguished the present case from *Lovell v. Griffin* on the ground that the earlier case had involved unjustifiable administrative discretion in the licensing power, an element not present here.

Chief Justice Stone wrote a vigorous dissent, in which Black, Murphy, and Douglas concurred. Stone thought the present case involved "more callous disregard of constitutional right" than that in *Lovell v. Griffin*. There, at least, he said, the defendant "would not have been compelled to pay a money exaction for a license to exercise the privilege of free speech."

A year later the dissenting minority again became a majority as the Court ruled in *Murdock v. Pennsylvania* (1943) that an ordinance licensing door-to-door sale and dissemination of religious tracts was unconstitutional. As in the Opelika case, petitioners were Jehovah's Witnesses engaged in door-to-door book sales. Justice Douglas, speaking for the new majority of five,[3] asserted that it "cannot be plainly said that petitioners were engaged in a commercial rather than a religious venture." While he admitted that religious groups were not "free from all financial burdens of govern-

---

[3] The Opelika minority became a majority in the Murdock case because Justice Byrnes, who had voted with the majority in the former case, resigned and was replaced by Justice Rutledge, who voted with Stone, Murphy, Black, and Douglas.

ment," the present tax in his opinion too closely resembled one exacted from a preacher "for the privilege of delivering a sermon." Douglas added that *Jones v. Opelika* now stood overruled.

In *Martin v. Struthers* (1943), decided the same day as the Murdock case, the same majority held unconstitutional an ordinance prohibiting doorbell-ringing, knocking on doors, and the like, for the purpose of distributing religious tracts and advertisements. Justice Black's opinion admitted that some police regulation of the right to distribute literature might on occasion be legal, but he insisted that the right in question was so "clearly vital to the preservation of a free society that, putting aside reasonable police and health regulations of time and manner of distribution, it must be fully preserved."

There were lengthy dissents by Reed, Roberts, Jackson, and Frankfurter, in both the Murdock and Struthers cases. Dissenting in the Murdock case, Justice Reed offered an extended historical interpretation of freedom of the press and religion, arguing that the authors of the Bill of Rights had merely intended to protect the right to be heard and the right to untrammeled ritual, and had never intended to grant a general immunity to either press or church from all incidence of taxation. In the light of the majority opinion he asked why a tax upon printing and publishing a newspaper could now be construed as constitutional, when a tax upon the distribution of literature was not.

In his dissent in the Struthers case, Frankfurter observed that the legislature ought to be given the greatest possible area of discretion in protecting the community against abuse. The Court could not, he thought, "however unwittingly, slip into the judgment seat of legislatures." Here was the old injunction against the substitution of judicial for legislative discretion in substantive due process.

The new majority nevertheless for the present maintained its position. In *Follett v. McCormick* (1944), the Court held invalid a city ordinance of McCormick, South Carolina, licensing all bookvending as applied to the peddling of religious books. The vending of religious books, said Justice Douglas, was essentially a religious occupation and could not be taxed. Justices Jackson, Frankfurter, and Roberts in dissent asked rhetorically, why not, then, exempt the press and all church property from taxation entirely, even though the property in question were commercially operated? Unmoved by this argument the Court, in *Marsh v. Alabama* (1946), upheld the right of a member of Jehovah's Witnesses to distribute religious tracts in a company-owned town, even though it was posted as private property and solicitation prohibited. And in *Tucker v. Texas* (1946), the Court upheld the right of religious solicitation on the grounds of a United States government-owned and -operated housing project.

DISSIDENT MINORITIES: REVIVAL OF THE CLEAR AND PRESENT DANGER DOCTRINE

The Roosevelt era witnessed a steady demand from a variety of sources for the control of Communists and other radical minorities who challenged in some fashion the fundamentals of the American social order. Paradoxically, it was a period in which many liberals and left-wing idealists, convinced that American capitalism was at least partially discredited, manifested interest or even sympathy with the Soviet Union and with Marxist theory generally. The New Deal itself also tended to promote an atmosphere of social experimentation and rapid social change.

In other segments of American society, however, the fear of radical and "un-American" ideas remained extremely high, and often expressed itself in concerted attempts at suppression. Thus numerous states enacted new statutes, many of them very vaguely worded, punishing seditious activity directed against the state or against the United States, and there was a wave of laws providing for loyalty oaths by teachers and other government employees. State legislative inquiries into Communist infiltration of colleges and labor unions became a familiar part of the American scene. The House Committee on Un-American Activities came into existence in 1938; thereafter its spectacular exposés of radical activity were never far from the headlines.[4]

In spite of concerted public pressure of this kind, however, the Roosevelt Court exhibited a fairly consistent determination to protect dissident political minorities against the suppression of their civil liberties, and to this end it invoked with fair consistency the "clear and present danger" doctrine. The practical effect was to underwrite a maximum of civil liberty for Communists and for other dissident minorities and to minimize the right of the state to suppress radical political activity in the interests of security.

DeJonge v. Oregon (1937), in which the Court invalidated conviction of a Communist under the Oregon criminal syndicalist law, was a notable example of the Court's attitude. Chief Justice Hughes' unanimous opinion pointed out that the sole charge against the

---

[4] See below, Chapter 32.

defendant was that he had participated in a Communist political meeting. There was no record that he had advocated violence, sabotage, revolution, or criminal behavior at the meeting or elsewhere, nor was he charged with having done so. "Peaceable assembly for lawful discussion," said Hughes, "cannot be made a crime." The conviction therefore was in violation of the defendant's constitutional right to freedom of speech and assembly.

Hughes had drawn upon a general philosophy of constitutional liberty rather than any specific legal doctrine. However, in *Herndon v. Lowry* (1937), the Court invoked the "clear and present danger" doctrine to invalidate the Georgia conviction of a Communist Party organizer charged with violating a state statute against inciting to insurrection. Justice Roberts' majority opinion cited with approval the proposition that the defendant's conduct, to be punishable, must show some immediate incitement to violence or insurrection. The evidence, he pointed out, wholly failed to show any such tendency; indeed, the state had not even demonstrated that the defendant had read the Communist literature in his possession advocating working-class unity and a Negro state in the South. As construed, he said, the statute punished mere bad tendency; it merely amounted to a "dragnet which may enmesh anyone who agitates for a change of government . . . an unwarrantable invasion of the right of free speech." Justices Van Devanter, McReynolds, Sutherland, and Butler dissented, arguing that the defendant's conduct properly was punishable under Georgia law.

The Court temporarily abandoned the "clear and present danger" doctrine in *Minersville School District v. Gobitis* (1940), in which it upheld the action of a Pennsylvania district school board in expelling two children from the public schools for refusal to salute the flag as part of a daily school exercise. The ritual in question was highly offensive to the members of Jehovah's Witnesses, who had attacked the requirement in the courts as an infringement of religious liberty.

Justice Frankfurter's majority opinion admitted that the case posed a nice dilemma between majority power and minority rights. But in this instance he thought the interests of the state more fundamental. The flag salute was intended to build up a sentiment of national unity, and "national unity is the basis of national security," since "the ultimate foundation of a free society is the binding tie of cohesive sentiment." The legislative judgment that the flag salute was a necessary means to this end therefore ought to be respected by the courts. Justice Stone alone dissented.

The Gobitis opinion was clearly at variance with the prevailing tendency of the Court to protect dissident minorities against punishment or coercion by the state. It is probable that the justices were deeply affected by the wave of patriotism then sweeping the nation as the United States prepared to battle for its life against Germany and Japan.

Three years later, in *West Virginia State Board of Education v. Barnette* (1943), the Court invoked the clear and present danger doctrine once more, to overrule the Gobitis precedent and declare unconstitutional a West Virginia flag-salute statute similar in all essentials to the earlier Pennsylvania board rule.[5] Justice Jackson, speaking for the new majority, pointed out that the refusal to salute did not at all interfere with the rights of other individuals. Emphasizing that censorship of expression was permissible "only when the expression presents a clear and present danger of action of a kind the State is empowered to prevent and punish," he argued that the present law went even beyond ordinary censorship to require the affirmance of positive belief. "To sustain the compulsory flag salute," he said, "we are required to say that a Bill of Rights which guards the individual's right to speak his own mind, left it open to the public authorities to compel him to utter what is not in his mind." Here was an argument for a "right of silence" equivalent in constitutional force to the other guarantees of the First Amendment.

In *Taylor v. Mississippi* (1943), decided the same day as the Barnette case, the Court held unconstitutional three convictions under a Mississippi sedition statute which made it a felony to encourage disloyalty to the United States or to encourage refusal to salute the flag. One defendant had been convicted only of encouraging refusal to salute the flag; two others, who had preached that all modern nations, including the United States, were in the grip of demons, had also been convicted of encouraging disloyalty to state and national governments. The flag-salute conviction Justice Roberts ruled out on the basis of the Barnette precedent; the other two defendants he freed on the ground that the statute as construed made it "a criminal offense to communicate to others views and opinions respecting governmental policies and prophecies concern-

---

[5] The reversal came about mainly because of a change of opinion on the part of Black, Murphy, and Douglas, while Justice Jackson, appointed in June, 1941, and Justice Rutledge, appointed in January, 1943, also voted against the West Virginia law. Stone had not changed his position, while Frankfurter, Roberts, and Reed continued to regard compulsory flag salutes as constitutional.

ing the future of our own and other nations." Again, there was no clear and present danger to American institutions or government.

The later flag-salute cases revealed a far greater determination to sustain the right of individual conscience and freedom of dissident communication than the Court had exhibited during World War I. However, *In re Summers* (1945) demonstrated that there was a limit to the Court's willingness to protect the right of free conscience against control by the state. The case involved the validity of an Illinois decision banning conscientious objectors to military service from admission to the state bar. Justice Reed pointed out for the majority that the federal government refused to grant citizenship to aliens who had refused military service, and he held that the Fourteenth Amendment did not prohibit the state from requiring military service as a condition for admission to the bar. Justices Black, Murphy, Douglas, and Rutledge dissented, contending that the state's action constituted an unreasonable intrusion upon freedom of opinion and religious liberty.[6]

FREE SPEECH AND EDITORIAL COMMENT

Meanwhile, the Court also had extended the clear and present danger doctrine to cover dissident editorial comment in the public press. In *Bridges v. California* (1941), the Court majority reversed a conviction for contempt of court imposed upon several newspaper editors and labor leaders because of their published comment upon litigation pending before the California courts. Again citing Holmes' "clear and present danger" doctrine, Justice Black added the requirement that the evils in prospect must be both substantial and serious. The supposed substantive evils inherent in criticism of the courts, he observed, were two: disrespect for the judiciary, and disorderly and unfair administration of justice. As for the first, Black thought that the "assumption that respect for the judiciary can be won by shielding judges from published criticism wrongly appraises the character of American public opinion." As for disorderly administration of justice, Black thought that to imply that mere adverse editorial criticism would "have a substantial influence upon the course of justice would be to impute to judges a lack of firmness, wisdom, or honor—which we cannot accept as a majority premise." In a lengthy dissent, Justice Frankfurter protested that the majority opinion had altered the Fourteenth Amendment so as

---

[6] See below, pp. 921–923, for a further exposition of the problem of political opinion and admission to the state bar.

to impair the historic right of state courts to preserve the impartial administration of justice.

The Court reached a like decision in *Pennekamp v. Florida* (1946). This case involved the conviction for contempt of court of a newspaper editor who had printed several editorials attacking the Florida courts for obstructing the process of criminal justice. As in the Bridges case, certain of the cases criticized were still awaiting final disposition or review. Justice Reed's opinion, holding the conviction in violation of the Fourteenth Amendment, first observed that the Bridges case had fixed reasonably well-marked limits to the power of courts to punish newspapers and others for comments upon or criticism of pending litigation. Reed admitted that it was not possible to define categorically what constituted a clear and present danger to the impartial administration of justice, but he held that editorial attempts to destroy faith in the integrity of judges and the efficiency of the courts did not constitute such a danger, since "we have no doubt that Floridians in general would react to these editorials in substantially the same way as citizens of other parts of our common country"; that is, they would weigh them and disregard them if found unfair. In a lengthy concurring opinion, Justice Frankfurter accepted the Court's decision but protested against the tendency to turn the "clear and present danger" doctrine into an "absolute formula," as well as the implication that the principle of free speech ought to protect newspapers against all interference with their attempts to influence the administration of justice.

BILLS OF ATTAINDER AND THE CONGRESSIONAL APPROPRIATIONS POWER

The New Deal Court's strong concern for the protection of civil liberties against attack by the state also appeared in *United States v. Lovett* (1946), in which the justices invoked the seldom-used constitutional prohibition against bills of attainder in order to defend three federal employees who had been made the victims of an attack by the Committee on Un-American Activities. The Committee had denounced Goodwin B. Watson, William E. Dodd, Jr., and Robert Morss Lovett as guilty of subversive activities against the United States.

After some debate, Congress had adopted a rider to a 1943 appropriations act providing that no funds available under any act of Congress should be paid out as salary or other compensation for government service to the three men in question, unless the President should appoint them to office before November 15, 1943, with the advice and consent of the Senate. In effect, this forced the removal of the men from the federal payroll, and they presently sued in the Court of Claims to recover unpaid portions of their salaries. The Court of Claims ruled in their favor, and the case was then certified to the Supreme Court.

Speaking through Justice Black, a majority of the Court held that the congressional provision was in effect a bill of attainder and therefore unconstitutional. "What is involved here," said Black, "is a congressional proscription of Lovett, Watson, and Dodd, prohibiting their ever holding a government job." Recalling the definition of a bill of attainder in *Cummings v. Missouri* as "a legislative act which inflicts punishment without a judicial trial," Black held that Congress plainly had intended to inflict punishment upon the three men in the form of a ban of their holding federal office, although they had not been subjected to any judicial proceedings. The section in question therefore violated Article I, Section 9, of the Constitution, and was void. In a concurring opinion, Justices Frankfurter and Rutledge agreed that Lovett, Watson, and Dodd were entitled to collect back pay through the Court of Claims, but they argued that the law in question lacked an essential quality of a bill of attainder in that it did not specifically adjudge the three men guilty of any offense and did not specifically ban them from office as a punishment for that offense.

LONG-RANGE SIGNIFICANCE OF THE NEW DEAL ERA IN CIVIL LIBERTIES

It is apparent upon analysis that the decisions of the Roosevelt Court in the field of civil liberties worked a revolution in the relation of the Court to the states and of government in general to the individual hardly less important than the revolution in federalism consummated about the same time. To put it differently, if the Court lost one "sovereign prerogative of choice" in the field of congressional versus state legislative power, it gained another such area of discretion and power in its capacity to weigh and determine the respective constitutional and social values of federal and state regulation of private rights as against its concern for the preservation of the integrity of individual liberty itself. This latter-day range of sovereign choice gave the Court an immense new power; in the post-war era it was to endow the Justices with a significance in the American constitutional order which for a time after 1938 they appeared to have lost.

Chapter

30

The Constitution and World War II

IN SEPTEMBER 1939, Hitler's legions plunged Europe into the chaos of World War II. This event virtually terminated the already diminished concern of the Roosevelt Administration and the American people with the internal political and constitutional issues incident to the New Deal; thereafter, national interest focused on the European war and the equally ominous program of Japanese imperialist expansion in eastern Asia. The United States managed to preserve an uneasy and increasingly dubious neutrality for more than two years, but after the fall of France in June 1940, President Roosevelt's program of aid to the Allies and frantic preparations for national defense absorbed public attention almost completely. The era of "neutrality" precipitated a severe crisis in foreign policy, which in turn raised constitutional issues of the utmost importance for American democracy.

PRESIDENTIAL PREROGATIVE AND THE CRISIS IN FOREIGN POLICY, 1939–1941

The crisis in foreign policy arose from the fact that the prospect of an unlimited German victory in Europe and the march of Japanese imperialism in East Asia both constituted major threats to the national interest of the United States. President Roosevelt very soon made it clear that he was aware of the menace and that he deemed it of vital importance for the United States to take steps to assist the enemies of Hitler and to balk Japanese expansion.

Conceivably, the President could have asked Congress for a declaration of war, as other chief executives confronted with major assaults upon American national interest from abroad had done in the past. However, at the moment, such a solution was not politically possible nor did the Roosevelt Administration deem it wise policy. The United States was not under immediate threat of attack and Congress would not have consented to embark on a "preventive" war. Moreover, the mood of the American people as they contemplated the conflict in Europe was a curiously bifurcated one. On the one hand, an overwhelming number of people sympathized with the Allied cause and agreed with President Roosevelt's estimate of the seriousness of the German threat; on the other hand, an equally large portion of the people believed that the United States ought to stay out of the war at almost any cost. This situation ruled out any open declaration of war on Germany, but it also made a program of aid to the Allies "short of war" politically feasible.

Accordingly, Roosevelt instituted a vigorous program of aid to the Allies and resistance to the Axis powers, in support of which he resorted to a variety of constitutional and legal devices. First and most important, he invoked to an extraordinary degree the executive prerogative in foreign policy. Second, he asserted the concept of an expanded presidential prerogative in a national emergency. Third, he sought and obtained legislation from Congress in support of his policy. Fourth, he issued a long series of executive decrees resting either on specific statutory authority or on his general constitutional powers. Fifth, he made extensive use of his authority as commander in chief of the Army and Navy to dispose of American armed forces in a fashion favorable to the Allies and ultimately to institute a "shooting war" against German submarines in the Atlantic.

Roosevelt carried the President's prerogative power in foreign policy to greater lengths than had any previous chief executive. However, this was not mere constitutional usurpation. The conception of a very broad executive prerogative in foreign policy had received extended support in both theory and practice ever since Alexander Hamilton had first set forth the idea in his *Pacificus* essays.[1] Moreover, the Supreme Court, in *United States v. Curtiss-*

---

[1] See p. 176, above.

Wright Export Corporation (1936), had only lately expounded with approval the same doctrine. Justice Sutherland's opinion had observed that "the very plenary and exclusive power of the President as the sole organ of the federal government in foreign relations" was "a power which does not require as a basis for its exercise an act of Congress, but which, of course, like every other governmental power, must be exercised in subordination to the applicable provisions of the Constitution." [2]

Roosevelt used his foreign-policy prerogative to conduct extended negotiations both in person and through the State Department with various belligerent governments, with the object of strengthening the Allied cause and diverting the course of German, Italian, and Japanese high policy. It also provided the constitutional support for a number of extraordinary executive agreements with foreign governments which Roosevelt effected in support of his program. The most significant of these, perhaps, were the Declaration of Panama, signed in October 1939, whereby the United States and nineteen Latin-American republics established the so-called "neutrality belt" around the western hemisphere and provided for a "neutrality patrol" of hemisphere waters; the "Destroyer-Base Deal," concluded with Great Britain in September 1940; and the so-called "Atlantic Charter," which Roosevelt and Prime Minister Churchill promulgated in August 1941.

The constitutionality of the executive agreement as an instrument of the President's prerogative in foreign policy had long been recognized in constitutional law.[3] However, the foregoing agreements went far beyond the usual scope of such arrangements. Under ordinary circumstances, they would either have been submitted to the Senate for ratification as treaties or made the basis for enabling legislation in Congress. In part, the President was able to avoid either recourse because he had the means at his disposal to execute them on his own authority. Thus, Roosevelt established the neutrality patrol simply by issuing the requisite order as commander in chief of the Navy. And the "Atlantic Charter," while it appeared on its surface to set up something like a military alliance and define the war aims of the "United Nations," was ultimately only a propa-

---

[2] The Curtiss-Wright case dealt with the validity of an embargo on arms shipments to the belligerents in the "Chaco War" between Bolivia and Paraguay, which President Roosevelt had imposed pursuant to discretionary authority granted him by a joint resolution of Congress passed in May 1934.

[3] See, for example, *United States v. Pink* (1942), where the Court went so far as to hold that executive agreements could in some instances be enforced in the courts as internal law.

ganda document requiring no specific implementation of a legislative kind.

However, the Destroyer-Base Deal presented far more serious constitutional difficulties. By this agreement, the President transferred fifty "overage" destroyers from the United States Navy to the British fleet. In return, the United States received ninety-nine-year leases to seven naval bases on British soil at strategic points in the Caribbean, West Indies, and North Atlantic. Roosevelt entered into this extraordinary arrangement on the basis of an official opinion from Attorney General Robert H. Jackson, who advised him that the transaction would be altogether constitutional and had adequate statutory authority.

However, Jackson's opinion rested on a dubious provision in an old statute of 1883 for the disposal of worn-out naval vessels and a section in a recently enacted statute of June 1940 which authorized the President to dispose of naval materials only when the Chief of Naval Operations "shall first certify that such material is not essential to the defense of the United States." The first of these laws had obviously been drafted for a purpose altogether different from the one at hand; the second had been written by the Senate in a specific attempt to guarantee against the transfer or disposal of war materials still useful to the United States. Jackson was obliged to argue that the 1940 law properly should be interpreted so that "not essential to the defense of the United States" would mean merely that it would serve the national interest to make the transfer, an interpretation which evidently nullified congressional intent in passing the law.

Moreover, the destroyer transfer was in apparently direct violation of an act of Congress of June 1917 which made it unlawful in any foreign war in which the United States was a neutral "to send out of the jurisdiction of the United States any vessel built, armed, or equipped as a vessel of war . . . with any intent or any agreement or contract, written or oral, that such vessel shall be delivered to a belligerent nation." This language stated a generally accepted principle of international law which Great Britain and the United States had originated in the Treaty of Washington in 1871 and which had been written into the Hague Convention of 1907. But Jackson interpreted the act as not applying in the present instance, since the vessels, he said, had not originally been built with any intent to deliver them to a foreign belligerent. Unhappily for this interpretation, a reading of the law makes it clear that the intent expressed in the statute relates to the delivery of the vessels to a foreign belligerent, not to their construction. A better argument was that of Professor Quincy Wright of the University of Chicago, who pointed out that the 1917 law was a criminal statute intended to control the acts of private persons; conceivably, it was not applicable to acts of the United States government.

It is difficult to escape the conclusion that President Roosevelt in executing the Destroyer-Base Deal acted on the basis of extremely dubious statutory authority. It is obvious, also, that the whole stuff of the agreement was such as would ordinarily have been made the subject of a treaty or an act of Congress. In effect, the President gave away a considerable portion of the United States Navy without adequate authority of law. Professor E. S. Corwin in a letter to *The New York Times* characterized the agreement as "an endorsement of unrestrained autocracy in the field of our foreign relations," and scouted Jackson's legalisms with the assertion that "no such dangerous opinion was ever before penned by an Attorney-General of the United States." Indeed, President Roosevelt himself had earlier expressed the opinion that the legal and constitutional difficulties in the way of the transfer were insurmountable.

Nonetheless, the President escaped any very severe condemnation in Congress or at the bar of public opinion. The country at large apparently was prepared to accede to "the law of necessity" rather than to cogent constitutional analysis, for it was overly evident the President's action heavily benefited American national interest.

To some extent, Roosevelt rested his foreign policy on the theory of an expanded presidential prerogative in a national emergency. On September 8, 1939, the President formally declared a limited state of national emergency to exist. This was done, he said, "solely to make wholly constitutional and legal certain necessary measures." And in May 1941 he proclaimed an "unlimited national emergency," for the purpose of repelling potential acts of aggression against the Western hemisphere.

There was substantial uncertainty concerning the constitutional status of these proclamations and the constitutional and legal situation that resulted from them. Neither cited any specific constitutional or statutory authority upon which they might be based. Congress itself was evidently in considerable doubt about the constitutional meaning of the "state of emergency," for on September 28, 1939, the Senate addressed a resolution to Attorney General Frank Murphy requesting him to report on "what executive powers are made available to the President under his proclamation of national emergency." Murphy refused to give the Senate any formal legal opinion on the matter, but he nonetheless told the Senate that "it is universally recognized that the constitutional duties of the Executive carry with them the constitutional powers necessary for their proper performance."

One consequence of the emergency proclamations was clear enough, however: they activated an impressive list of presidential powers which Congress by statute had stipulated could be exercised only in time of national emergency or state of war. Murphy accompanied his reply to the Senate with a long list of such statutes, clear evidence that Congress itself had repeatedly recognized that it might grant the President certain powers which were to be exercised only in time of national emergency. Modern delegation of this kind began with the National Defense Act of 1916, which had authorized the President, among other things, to make seizures of plants and communication facilities in time of national emergency or state of war. Other statutes gave the President emergency control of radio stations, the right to seize powerhouses and dams, to increase the size of the Army and Navy beyond authorized strength, to regulate and prohibit all Federal Reserve transactions, to seize any plant refusing to give preference to government contracts, and to take control of all communication facilities in the United States.

A more difficult constitutional question remained: did the proclamation of a national emergency expand the presidential prerogative in some general fashion without regard to any specific statutory authority? There was no doubt that various presidents, from Lincoln on, had acted upon the assumption that executive prerogative somehow increased greatly under the pressure of war or grave national emergency. The reader is already aware of Lincoln's extraordinary assumption of emergency power in the spring of 1861. Theodore Roosevelt's "Stewardship Theory," it will be recalled, had assumed that the President possessed a "mighty reservoir of crisis authority." [4] And Wilson's assumption of a broad executive prerogative in World War I, when he had acted to set up a variety of executive boards without any specific statutory authority, constituted another impressive precedent which influenced Franklin Roosevelt very heavily. The truth of the matter was that the President's emergency

---

[4] Clinton Rossiter, *Constitutional Dictatorship: Crisis Government in the Modern Democracies* (Ithaca, 1948), p. 219.

prerogative, within extremely broad limits, was subject principally to the political control of public opinion.[5]

The most notable legislative measures which Roosevelt sought in support of his foreign policy during the prewar crisis were the Neutrality Act of November 1939, repealing the embargo on private arms shipments to belligerents; the Lend-Lease Act of March 1941; and the Joint Resolution of November 1941, repealing the prohibition against American merchant vessels entering war-zone waters.

The most interesting constitutional element in these enactments was the very large delegation of quasi-legislative authority to the executive which they involved. Most extraordinary in this respect was the Lend-Lease Act, which in sweeping terms authorized the President to manufacture or procure any defense article for the government of any country "whose defense the President deems vital to the defense of the United States," and to sell, exchange, lease, lend, and otherwise dispose of such articles to the government in question as he saw fit. This was the kind of unlimited legislative delegation which the Supreme Court had only lately struck down in the Schechter and Carter cases. It must be remembered, however, that the Curtiss-Wright opinion had held that congressional delegation of legislative authority properly might be much broader in the area of foreign affairs than in domestic matters. Conceivably, this distinction rescued the constitutionality of the Lend-Lease Law.

Roosevelt's executive orders were a critically important aspect of his larger foreign policy. They poured forth in a steady stream, all being calculated to influence in some fashion the course of the world crisis. Characteristic were those terminating on six months' notice the United States–Japanese commercial treaty of 1911 (July 1939), placing an embargo on the export of aviation gasoline to Japan (July 1940), banning the sale of scrap iron and steel to Japan (October 1940), freezing Japanese financial assets in the United States (July 1941), establishing war zones under the Neutrality Law (November 1939), and declaring the Red Sea no longer a war zone (April 1941). Some of these had direct statutory authority; most of

---

[5] In the Steel Seizure Case, in 1952, the Supreme Court was to frown officially upon the idea of an expanded executive prerogative in time of emergency. However, President Truman's seizure of the steel industry was to be carried out in apparent direct defiance of a congressional statutory mandate, a situation somewhat different from that which Roosevelt faced during World War II. See pp. 811ff.

them did not and rested instead merely on the prerogative power in foreign policy.

There were numerous constitutional precedents for Roosevelt's use of his powers as commander in chief of the Army and Navy to influence foreign policy. President Adams had waged naval war with France in 1798 without formal authorization from Congress, and Wilson had used both the Army and Navy in punitive military expeditions against Mexico. There had been numerous small military expeditions against the Caribbean republics, all staged on presidential order, and there had been similar expeditions in China, notably the American participation in the suppression of the Boxer Rebellion in 1899. In particular, Presidents have felt quite free to order the Navy about in support of foreign policy and it was this tradition to which Roosevelt now resorted. His order to the Navy of October 1939 establishing the Neutrality Patrol in the western Atlantic was of this kind.

More controversial constitutionally was the process whereby Roosevelt instituted convoys for British merchant vessels carrying lend-lease supplies and subsequently commenced a shooting war against German submarines. The Lend-Lease Act itself had contained an ambiguous disclaimer that "nothing in this act shall be construed to authorize or to permit the authorization of convoying vessels by naval vessels of the United States." But in July 1941 the President ordered American armed forces to occupy Iceland, a step he took by virtue of an executive agreement with the newly independent Republic of Iceland and under his authority as commander in chief. The occupation of Iceland made convoying for the protection of American military supply ships an imperative necessity.

Accordingly, in August the President ordered the Navy to begin convoying American and British ships as far east as Iceland, although it was obvious that "convoys mean shooting and shooting means war." In defense of the President's action, it may be pointed out that this action was in a general way taken in support of a policy ratified by Congress, that of furnishing military supplies to the Allied powers, and that from a standpoint of international law the United States was hardly any longer a neutral in the European war.

In September 1941 the President on his own authority began an actual "shooting war" against German submarines in the Atlantic. The occasion was a supposed submarine attack against the destroyer *Greer*, then on convoy duty in the Greenland Straits. In retaliation, Roosevelt ordered the Navy to hunt down and destroy on sight the "rattlesnakes of the Atlantic." Here was a *de facto* war against a great power waged on presidential fiat and without the consent of Congress. John Adams had done much the same thing against France in 1798; however, it is probable that Adams had a far clearer congressional mandate than Roosevelt could have inferred from the Lend-Lease Law.

When Roosevelt's conduct in the international crisis between 1939 and 1941 is examined in the large, it appears to be closely analogous constitutionally to that of Lincoln in the Civil War crisis of April–July 1861. Each President confronted what he firmly believed to be a paramount threat to national security. In order to deal with the crisis, each assumed that the emergency endowed the executive with prerogative powers of a large and indefinite kind adequate to meet the emergency. Each took critically important steps without adequate statutory authority or in actual disregard of pertinent acts of Congress. Each believed that his conduct was justified by the necessity of saving the nation from disaster. And in each case, ultimately it was public and congressional recognition of the extraordinary character of the crisis which gave a kind of political sanction to the President's conduct.

Nonetheless, it is conceivable that had the state of affairs existing in the fall of 1941 lasted any great length of time, Roosevelt's continued use of the executive prerogative in foreign policy and his powers as commander in chief might have precipitated a major constitutional crisis. However, the attack on Pearl Harbor on December 7, 1941, and the declarations of war on Japan, Germany, and Italy which followed, averted a potential confrontation between the President and Congress over executive power.

THE FEDERAL GOVERNMENT IN WORLD WAR II

The task of organizing the federal government for the prosecution of World War II gave rise to much less constitutional controversy than had been the case in 1917. This was true mainly because the constitutional practices of World War I had pretty thoroughly broken down prior inhibitions about the scope of federal war power. As a consequence, the limitations inherent in the American constitutional system which in theory made it a poor instrument for waging total war had almost entirely been overcome.

The Supreme Court itself had recognized the force of this argument in the World War I era; later it had paid homage to an expansive theory of the federal war power. Thus in the Minnesota Moratorium case, Chief Justice Hughes had asserted that "the war *power* of the Federal Government . . . is a *power* to wage war successfully, and thus . . . permits the harnessing of the entire energies of the people in a supreme co-operative effort to save the nation." In the Curtiss-Wright case, the Court had taken an even more extreme position. Justice Sutherland had asserted that the power to wage war was inherent in national sovereignty, antedated the Constitution itself, and was not dependent upon the enumeration of federal powers in Article I, Section 8. This notion of the right to wage war as an "inherent power" was far more expansive than any enumerated power; as Professor Corwin has pointed out, it "logically guarantees the constitutional adequacy of the war power by equating it with the full actual power of the nation in waging war." [6]

This is not to say that the United States entered upon World War II with the doctrine established that there were absolutely no restraints either on the scope of federal sovereignty in war or on the means of exercising federal power in wartime. It was generally recognized that the specific prohibitions of the written Constitution remained in force, that national power, while vastly enlarged, was not without constitutional limits, and that private rights were still valid, although they were admittedly subject to certain limitations not ordinarily applicable in peacetime. These various limitations on federal power proved in practice to be by no means clear, however, and it remained for the progress of the war to mark them out by actual practice and occasional judicial decisions.

Both before and after Pearl Harbor, Congress enacted a series of critical statutes, all of which asserted vast federal powers for the prosecution of the war. These statutes were alike also in that they made tremendous grants of authority to the executive for the exercise of the powers over which Congress asserted its sovereignty.

Most important, perhaps, were the Selective Service Act of September 1940, and Lend-Lease Act of March 1941, the First War Powers Act of December 1941, the Second War Powers Act of March 1942, the Emergency Price Control Act of January 1942, and the War Labor Disputes Act of June 1943.

The Selective Service Act authorized the executive to inaugurate a comprehensive system of military conscription, although the United States was still technically at peace. The Lend-Lease Act, renewed repeatedly after Pearl Harbor, provided the President with

---

[6] E. S. Corwin, *Total War and the Constitution* (New York, 1947), p. 37.

carte blanche executive authority whereby some fifty billion dollars of war supplies were delivered to America's allies. The First War Powers Act, essentially a re-enactment of the Overman Act of World War I days, gave the President authority to reorganize all executive departments and independent commissions at his discretion for the effective prosecution of the war. The Second War Powers Act was a hodge-podge dealing with all manner of emergency grants of power to the executive; among other things, it gave the President comprehensive plant-requisitioning power, and control of overseas communications, alien property, the allocation of war-related materials and all defense contracts. The Emergency Price Control Act created an Office of Price Administration and a Price Administrator appointed by the President, and granted the Administrator a general power to regulate both rents and commodity prices. And the War Labor Disputes Act authorized executive seizure of plants closed by strikes or other labor disputes.

This body of legislation, creating as it did a vast and ramified federal dictatorship over the national economy, went far beyond the reaches of the Lever Act of World War I days. Yet the entire legislative program went through Congress with hardly a constitutional ripple. In part, this was because there was now a general acceptance of the all-inclusive scope of the federal war power. Also, Congress was far less disposed to quarrel with executive authority than it had been in 1861 or 1917; Congress and the President as a rule now constituted something like a working partnership for the prosecution of the war.

ROOSEVELT'S WARTIME "DICTATORSHIP"

The foregoing legislation in reality assumed the creation of a wartime executive mechanism modeled on Wilson's presidential "dictatorship" of 1917–1918. It was to this World War I precedent that Roosevelt now turned.

Roosevelt's notion of his war powers and emergency powers was at least as expansive as that of Lincoln and Wilson before him. Like Wilson, he created a vast executive mechanism for the conduct of the war, most of which rested originally upon no other direct authority than an executive order, "letter," or "directive." A bewildering succession of such decrees brought into being by the end of 1942 more than one hundred wartime offices, boards, commissions, autonomous corporations, and other agencies. So rapidly did the President create, reorganize, and reshuffle offices and functions that the result was a jumbled bureaucratic nightmare of multiple agencies and overlapping jurisdictions verging on utter chaos.

A great many of the wartime agencies were technically subordinate branches of the Office of Emergency Management. Established in May 1940 by an "Administrative Order" of the President, the Office of Emergency Management drew its authority specifically from the Reorganization Act of 1939. It thus served as a kind of legal cover for executive agencies which the President could not conveniently assign elsewhere. The O.E.M. speedily became a kind of White House management agency co-ordinating in some degree at least the wartime executive structure.

Principal O.E.M. agencies were the Office of Production Management (January 1941), the War Production Board (January 1942), the Office of Defense Transportation (December 1941), the War Shipping Administration (February 1942), the War Manpower Commission (April 1942), the War Labor Board (January 1942), the Office of War Information (June 1942), and the Office of Civilian Defense (June 1942).

The Office of Production Management was Roosevelt's first attempt at an agency to co-ordinate production for war. When it failed to function effectively, the President created the War Production Board, which soon established a virtual dictatorship over the mobilization of American industry. The Office of Defense Transportation co-ordinated land and coastal transportation, while the War Shipping Administration co-ordinated overseas shipping facilities. The War Manpower Commission had charge of the mobilization of the nation's manpower for war purposes, including the recruitment, training, and placement of workers in industry and agriculture. In December 1942, the President also put the Selective Service System under the War Manpower Commission's jurisdiction. However, the War Labor Board had general jurisdiction over collective bargaining. The Office of War Information was essentially a public-information and propaganda bureau, performing the same functions as the Creel Committee had exercised in 1918. And the Office of Civilian Defense was concerned primarily with protecting civilian communities against the threat of enemy bombing attack. This hardly exhausts the list of O.E.M. agencies, some twenty-nine of which were alive and functioning at the end of the war.

Outside the O.E.M., there existed a complex, sprawling bureaucracy of boards, commissions, offices, authorities, and autonomous corporations, only a few of which can be mentioned here. Very important was the office which Harry Hopkins occupied as Special

Assistant to the President. His functions, necessarily confidential in nature, were essentially those of an interdepartmental expediter and trouble shooter. The most important independent administrative agency was the Office of Price Administration, first set up in April 1941 without benefit of any statutory authority, to study plans for rationing and price fixing. However, the Emergency Price Control Act of 1942, as already observed, established the O.P.A. as an independent executive agency headed by an administrator appointed by the President with the advice and consent of the Senate.

The Board of Economic Warfare, another separate agency with some statutory powers, exercised control over exports and imports of strategic significance for war. The Office of War Censorship exercised a censorship over foreign communications, as authorized by the First War Powers Act. Beyond these, there were more than a hundred other independent war corporations, many of them virtually autonomous. The Rubber Reserve Corporation, the Defense Plant Corporation, and the Defense Supplies Corporation were but a few.

The precise constitutional status of most of these agencies was a matter of some uncertainty. The great majority of them had come into existence merely through a presidential order or directive and without the specific authority of any statute. Yet the fact was that in one fashion or another the President possessed almost unlimited authority to delegate his wartime authority virtually as he saw fit. In the first place, several of the emergency wartime statutes gave the President unlimited discretion to delegate the powers granted him by the law in question. The First War Powers Act was written in language so sweeping as to give the President the authority not only to shuffle functions among old agencies but also to create new agencies for war purposes.[7] The Second War Powers Act stipulated that "the President may exercise any power, authority, or discretion conferred on him by this section, through such department, agency, or officer of the Government as he may direct, and in conformity with any rules and regulations which he may procure." In addition, Congress repeatedly gave a belated statutory sanction to presidential agencies by appropriating money for their continued operations. Finally, the lower federal courts several times during the war rejected the argument that the President had improperly delegated his powers to an authorized agency; signifi-

---

[7] Although there was some ambiguity on this point in the law itself, the Supreme Court so decided in *Fleming v. Mohawk Wrecking and Lumber Co.* (1947).

cantly, the Supreme Court itself consistently refused to review such decisions.[8]

Many of the independent agencies technically had only advisory powers; yet in the tense atmosphere of wartime Washington, "advisory" directives were often in fact coercive in character. However, it proved impossible to develop a successful constitutional challenge in the courts against "advisory" instructions of this kind. Thus an attempt to secure judicial review of certain War Labor Board orders failed when the District of Columbia Court of Appeals held that the Board's "directives" technically were only advisory, imposed no sanctions, constituted only a moral obligation upon employers and workers, and hence were not subject to judicial review.[9]

However, the powers of the Office of Price Administration, which rested upon direct statutory authority, received some attention in the Courts. In *Yakus v. United States* (1944), the Supreme Court upheld the validity of those portions of the Emergency Price Control Act of 1942 which delegated to the O.P.A. the power to fix prices. Counsel had attacked the statute as attempting an unconstitutional delegation of congressional legislative power, on the grounds that the act was vague in purpose and fixed no adequate standards for executive guidance. However, Chief Justice Stone's opinion for the majority sustained the law as consistent with previously enunciated principles for the delegation of legislative power. He pointed out that the statute very clearly stated its objective as the stabilization of prices to prevent wartime inflation, that the act specified that prices must be fair and equitable, and that the Administrator was obliged to give due consideration, among other factors, to prevailing prices. These standards, Stone said, "were sufficiently definite and precise" that the Court was "unable to find in them an unauthorized delegation of legislative power." Technically, Stone did not pass upon the constitutional competence of Congress to fix prices under the federal war power, but it was obvious from the

---

[8] Thus in *Shreveport Engraving Co. v. United States* (1944), a United States Court of Appeals rejected the argument that the authority of the War Production Board rested upon improperly delegated power with the statement that "we think it may not be doubted that the Congress intended to and did make a general delegation to the office of the President of the authority to allocate critical war materials, and that the President, in his executive orders vesting the powers and charging the duties thus entrusted to him in others . . . was carrying out the congressional mandate and complying with it."

[9] *Employers Group of Motor Freight Carriers v. National War Labor Board* (1944).

tenor of his language that he thought this issue not open to serious consideration.[10]

In *Steuart and Bros. v. Bowles* (1944), the system of "indirect sanctions," whereby the O.P.A. imposed its controls upon the economy without formal resort to the judicial process, came under judicial scrutiny. The case involved the right of the O.P.A. to suspend fuel-oil deliveries to a retail oil dealer who had sold oil in violation of the coupon-ration system. The suspension obviously had some of the earmarks of an arbitrary administrative penalty imposed without benefit of any judicial process. But the Court refused to see the matter in this light. Speaking through Justice Douglas, it held that the suspension order was not "designed to punish petitioner" but only to promote the efficient distribution of fuel oil in accordance with the purposes of the law.

This was another way of saying that the Court refused to interfere with the principal coercive device whereby the various executive agencies gave practical force to their directives. Some indication of how important indirect sanctions were to the operation of the wartime executive machine may be gained from the fact that the War Production Board alone issued more than five thousand "penalty" orders of this sort during the war. When a Congressional committee in 1944 took under consideration a measure to forbid executive agencies to impose penalty sanctions except where they were specifically authorized by an act of Congress, a spokesman for the War Production Board protested in some dismay that the proposed law "would destroy our control completely." Significantly, Congress did not enact the proposal.

Actual seizure of industrial establishments was perhaps the most drastic sanction resorted to by the President in support of his "dictatorship." This was not a new device; Lincoln had made two or three seizures of railroads and telegraph lines during the Civil War, while Wilson had seized industrial establishments on eight different occasions for such varied reasons as labor difficulties and the failure to fill war orders satisfactorily. In a number of instances, he had acted without any specific statutory authority, depending merely upon his war powers.

In June 1941 Roosevelt seized the North American Aviation plant at Inglewood, California, mainly as a means of breaking up a

---

[10] The Court reached a similar conclusion in *Bowles v. Willingham* (1944), in which it passed favorably upon a rent-fixing directive of the O.P.A.

strike which threatened to paralyze vitally needed plane production. The executive proclamation announced merely that the President was acting pursuant to the powers vested in him by "the Constitution and laws of the United States, as President of the United States, and as Commander in Chief of the Army and Navy of the United States." How these conferred the right of seizure no one explained in any detail. Roosevelt made some six other seizures of this kind before the passage of the War Labor Disputes Act in 1943, all of them without citing any specific statutory authority. The War Labor Disputes Act, as already observed, belatedly gave the President general powers of plant seizure in support of the war effort. Thereafter, most of the forty-odd wartime seizures took place under the statutory authority of this law. One such seizure, that of Montgomery Ward and Company's nine plants in December 1944, led to protracted litigation in the lower courts, but the government returned the company's property in time to avert a ruling by the Supreme Court.

Perhaps the most extraordinary assertion of wartime executive power by President Roosevelt came when he threatened to nullify an act of Congress unless it were forthwith repealed. In a message to Congress on September 7, 1942, the President warned that he would set aside a section of the Emergency Price Control Act dealing with ceiling prices on farm products unless Congress forthwith repealed the provision. "In the event that the Congress should fail to act, and act adequately," he warned, "I shall accept the responsibility and I will act."

Here was a presidential claim of a right of executive nullification of a portion of a constitutional statute, solely on the ground that the law in question did not conform with the President's notion of what constituted intelligent national policy. No more extraordinary claim to executive prerogative has ever been advanced in the history of the American constitutional system. Only a theory of virtually unlimited wartime executive power could sustain the constitutional validity of the President's position. No test of the President's claim occurred, however, for Congress promptly complied with Roosevelt's request.

THE WAR DICTATORSHIP AND THE JAPANESE MINORITY

The unhappiest aspect of the presidential "dictatorship" during World War II was the Government's segregation and confinement of the Japanese-American minority. Some 112,000 persons of Japanese descent, more than 70,000 of whom were American citizens, were removed from their homes, separated from their jobs and property, and transferred to detention camps, where they were forcibly detained for periods up to four years. The official excuse for this program was that it was made necessary by the exigencies of war. Seemingly, it violated in a flagrant fashion the fundamentals of due process of law, although the Supreme Court was to accept it in part as constitutional.

Segregation and confinement of the Japanese-American minority had its origin on February 19, 1942, when President Roosevelt promulgated Executive Order No. 9066. This order authorized the Secretary of War and appropriate military commanders to prescribe military areas from which any or all persons might be excluded; and the right of other persons to enter, leave, or remain might be subjected to whatever restrictions the Secretary of War or appropriate military commanders might think necessary. The President issued this order solely upon his authority as commander in chief of the Army and Navy. However, Congress on March 21 enacted a statute embodying substantially the provisions of the original order, so that the segregation program also received legislative approval.

Meanwhile, on March 2, 1942, General J. L. DeWitt, commanding general of the Western Defense Command, designated by proclamation the entire Pacific coastal area as particularly subject to military attack and established Military Areas No. 1 and No. 2, comprising the entire region. The proclamation warned that subsequent notices would exclude certain classes of persons from the designated areas, or would permit them to remain only under suitable restrictions. On March 24, 1942, General DeWitt declared a curfew between the hours of 8:00 P.M. and 6:00 A.M. for German and Italian nationals and all persons of Japanese ancestry resident within Military Area No. 1, the coastal region.

A series of military orders directed against Japanese-Americans now followed. A proclamation of March 27 prohibited Japanese nationals and Americans of Japanese ancestry from leaving the coastal area except under future orders. Another order of May 9 formally decreed the exclusion of all persons of Japanese origin from the area. Thus Japanese-Americans were now under two contradictory orders—one prohibiting their departure except under future orders, and another excluding them from the same area. Compliance was possible only by reporting to one of a number of designated Civil Control Stations, where Japanese-Americans were gathered together and shipped out of the area to a number of so-called "Relocation Centers."

The "Relocation Centers" were in fact detention camps. They were operated by the War Relocation Authority, an executive agency created for this purpose by presidential order on March 18, 1942. In them, Japanese-Americans were detained for periods up to four years and then resettled outside the Pacific coastal area. In effect, therefore, the relocation program tore thousands of American citizens from their homes and subjected them to forcible confinement, although they had been convicted of no offense whatsoever.

The relocation program—astounding in its constitutional implications—first came before the Supreme Court in June, 1943, in *Hirabayashi v. United States*. The case concerned the conviction of an American citizen of Japanese descent who had been charged with violating the military curfew and with failure to report to a designated Civil Control Station. For technical reasons, however, the Court confined itself to a consideration of the constitutionality of the curfew order; thus it escaped the much larger issue of the constitutional validity of the segregation program in general.

Chief Justice Stone's opinion for a unanimous Court held that the Act of Congress of March 21, 1942, had clearly authorized the curfew order, and that the order lay within the combined congressional and presidential war powers and was constitutional. He emphasized the grave character of the national emergency which had confronted the nation in 1942, and the possible disloyalty of portions of the Japanese-American minority. The Court, he thought, ought not to challenge the conclusion of the military authorities that the federal war power be interpreted as broadly as possible. The curfew, Stone added, did not violate the Fifth Amendment, which, he pointed out, contained no equal protection clause. Discrimination based solely upon race was, he admitted, "odious to a free people whose institutions are founded upon the doctrine of equality"; for this reason, discrimination based upon race alone had in the past sometimes been held to violate due process. But in earlier cases, Stone pointed out, discrimination based upon race had been irrelevant to the national welfare; in the present case, race was not irrelevant, and Congress therefore had a right to take it into account.

Justices Murphy, Douglas, and Rutledge all wrote separate concurring opinions. Justice Murphy, in particular, made it clear that he found restrictions upon minority rights on the basis of race odious even in wartime. "Distinctions based on color and ancestry," he warned, " are utterly inconsistent with our traditions and our ideals."

The curfew order, he thought, bore "a melancholy resemblance to the treatment accorded to members of the Jewish race in Germany and other parts of Europe"; only the "critical military situation" on the West Coast had saved its constitutionality. It was obvious, in short, that Murphy considered the relocation program to be grossly unconstitutional. It was equally evident, however, that a majority of the justices were extremely reluctant to interfere with the program, principally because they were unwilling to dispute the considered judgment of military commanders as to what was necessary in order to win the war.

The validity of the West Coast exclusion orders finally came before the Court in December 1944, in *Korematsu v. United States*, a case involving the conviction of a Japanese-American who had remained in the region contrary to the military orders in question. Justice Black's majority opinion ruled briefly that the exclusion program, consideration of which he carefully separated from the detention program, had been within the combined federal war powers of Congress and the Executive. The crux of his argument was bare military necessity. It was imperative, he implied, to allow the Army to make decisions of this kind in wartime. Admittedly, the exclusion order worked hardship on the Japanese-American population. "But hardships are a part of war and war is an aggregation of hardships." Moreover, the exclusion program did not constitute racial discrimination as such; Korematsu had not been excluded because of his race but because of the requirements of military security. However, the opinion specifically refrained from passing upon the constitutionality of the relocation and confinement portions of the program, which Black said posed separate constitutional questions.

Justices Roberts, Murphy, and Jackson all entered vigorous dissents. Roberts thought it a plain "case of convicting a citizen as punishment for not submitting to imprisonment in a concentration camp, solely because of his ancestry," without evidence concerning his loyalty to the United States. He refused to accept Black's separation of the exclusion orders from the relocation and detention program. The appellant, he pointed out, had been under contradictory orders, which in reality "were nothing but a cleverly devised trap to accomplish the real purpose of the military authority, which was to lock him up in a concentration camp."

Justice Murphy wrote an equally vigorous dissent attacking exclusion itself as a program which "goes over the 'very brink of constitutional power' and falls into the ugly abyss of racism." He admitted that the argument of military necessity carried weight, but he insisted at the same time that the claim of military necessity must "subject itself to the judicial process" to determine "whether the deprivation is reasonably related to a public danger that is so 'immediate, imminent, and impending' as not to admit of delay and not to permit the intervention of ordinary constitutional processes to alleviate the danger." Japanese exclusion, he thought, could not possibly meet that test; instead, it was based upon an "erroneous assumption of racial guilt" and justified upon "questionable racial and sociological grounds not ordinarily within the realm of expert military judgment. . . ." The program at large, he concluded, flagrantly violated due process of law.

In a curious dissent, Justice Jackson virtually argued that war was an extra-constitutional activity above and beyond constitutional controls. He did not challenge the necessity of the Japanese relocation program, but he insisted that the military ought not then to come before the Court and attempt to incorporate the program within the framework of constitutional right.

In *Ex parte Endo*, decided the same day as the Korematsu case, the Court upheld the right of a Japanese-American girl, whose loyalty to the United States had been clearly established, to a writ of habeas corpus freeing her from the custody of the Tule Lake War Relocation Camp. Justice Douglas' opinion avoided any ruling upon the constitutionality of the confinement program in its entirety, but instead held merely that the War Relocation Authority had no right to subject persons of undoubted loyalty to confinement or conditional parole. "The authority to detain a citizen or to grant him a conditional release as protection against espionage or sabotage is exhausted," he said, "at least when his loyalty is conceded."

Douglas dodged the embarrassing question of whether the President's order and the Act of Congress behind it were not thereby at least in part unconstitutional by pointing out that neither statute nor executive order anywhere specifically authorized detention. Illegal detention, in other words, had technically resulted from the abuse of presidential orders by the War Relocation Authority. The larger constitutional issue—whether a citizen charged with no crime could be forcibly detained under orders of military authority in other than an immediate combat area—Douglas did not discuss at all. He distinguished the embarrassing precedent of *Ex parte Milligan*, where this had been in part an issue, by pointing out that in the present case confinement had been at the hands of civilian authorities. The distinction, it may be remarked, was at least debatable, since the present confinement had in fact taken place under direct orders from the military and without any proceedings in the civil courts.

Justices Murphy and Roberts wrote terse concurring opinions in the Endo case, making it plain that they did not altogether accept the Court's reasoning. Murphy said flatly that the detention program was "not only unauthorized by Congress or the Executive" but that the present case was but "another example of the unconstitutional resort to racism inherent in the entire evacuation program." In Murphy's opinion, Mitsuye Endo was not only entitled to an unconditional release but also was entitled to move freely into California. Justice Roberts centered his attack upon the Court's evasion of the constitutional issues inherent in the case. It was absurd, he said, to argue that Congress and the President had not sanctioned the relocation program; the Court's position ignored the obvious fact that Congress after full hearings had repeatedly passed full appropriations for the Relocation Authority, and the President had not exercised his power to alter its operations. The court, in short, had been "squarely faced" with an issue of constitutional right which it should have met head on. "An admittedly loyal citizen has been deprived of her liberty for a period of years. Under the Constitution she should be free to come and go as she pleases. Instead, her liberty of motion and other innocent activities have been prohibited and conditioned. She should be discharged."

There are strong grounds for concluding that the Supreme Court blundered seriously in the Hirabayashi, Korematsu, and Endo cases. As a result of the Court's opinions, it is now written into constitutional law that a citizen of the United States, set apart from his fellows only by race, may be expelled from his home, separated from his native community, forcibly transported to a concentration camp and there detained against his will, at least until his loyalty has been established. It is true that the Court accepted this program in the midst of a great war, and the Court rightly was unwilling to take any step which would interfere with the conduct of the war. But, as Justice Murphy pointed out, it does not follow that the Court must accept blindly the unlicensed judgment of military commanders that any given impairment of the Bill of Rights is absolutely essential to national safety.

It is precisely upon this point that the Court appears to have failed in its duty most seriously—it refused to examine the relocation program in the light of military necessity. There is little or no evidence that any substantial portion of the Japanese-American population was disloyal. There appears to be no reason whatever why the few potentially disloyal and seditious individuals in the larger group, practically all of whom were known to the Federal Bureau of Investigation and military intelligence, could not have been weeded out and subjected to whatever special controls were necessary. This is in fact what was done with the German-American and Italo-American minorities, the great majority of whose members were permitted their unconditional liberty.

The Court's refusal to examine these considerations put a stamp of approval upon a new relativism of "military necessity" in war-time civil liberties cases. In future wars, no person belonging to a racial, religious, cultural, or political minority can be assured that community prejudice and bigotry will not express itself in a program of suppression justified as "military necessity," with resulting destruction of his basic rights as a member of a free society. Bills of Rights are written in large part to protect society against precisely such a possibility, and insofar as they fail to do so they lose their meaning.

MILITARY GOVERNMENT IN HAWAII:
DUNCAN V. KAHANAMOKU

A second major instance of the wartime suppression of civil liberties by military authority occurred in Hawaii, where the Army erected a military government and for a time suspended all civilian governmental functions, including the writ of habeas corpus and the operation of the regular civil courts. Ultimately, the Supreme Court held that military government in Hawaii had been illegal although, significantly, it did not so rule until after the war ended.

On December 7, 1941, immediately following the attack on Pearl Harbor, the governor of Hawaii by proclamation suspended the writ of habeas corpus, placed the territory of Hawaii under martial law, and delegated to the commanding general, Hawaiian Department, his own authority as governor as well as all judicial authority in the territory. He took these steps under the Hawaiian Organic Act, adopted by Congress on April 30, 1900, which authorized such action "in case of rebellion or invasion, or imminent danger thereof, when the public safety requires it."

General Short at once proclaimed himself military governor of Hawaii and set up a military regime superseding the civil government. Order No. 4 of December 7 established military courts to try civilians in cases involving offenses against the laws of the United States or the Territory of Hawaii, or the rules and orders of the military authorities. Sentences imposed by these tribunals were not subject to review by the regular federal courts, and all regular civil and criminal courts were closed. Civil courts were shortly permitted to reopen as "agents of the commanding general," but they were prohibited from exercising jurisdiction in criminal cases and from empaneling juries. In February 1943 the President partially restored the independent functions of the civil governor and the regular courts. However, the writ of habeas corpus remained suspended, and military courts were still empowered to try civilians for violations of existing military orders. Military government was not terminated entirely until October 1944, at which time all threat of invasion had long since passed.

After much delay, the Supreme Court in February 1946 held in *Duncan v. Kahanamoku*, 6 to 2, that the establishment of military tribunals in Hawaii to try civilians had been illegal. The opinion avoided passing on the constitutionality of the suspension of the writ of habeas corpus, on the ground that the present appeal had been taken after the restoration of the writ in October 1944.

Black's opinion for the majority argued that the Hawaiian Organic Act of 1900 had not authorized military authorities to declare martial law except under conditions of actual invasion or rebellion. On the contrary, he pointed out, the Act had specifically extended the Constitution to the territory, so that civilians in Hawaii were entitled to the same guarantees of a fair trial as persons in other parts of the United States. Moreover, military trial of civilians was altogether contrary to American constitutional tradition. Congress had authorized it but once, in the Reconstruction Acts; and President Johnson had challenged that system with a series of vetoes "as vigorous as any in the country's history."

Chief Justice Stone in a concurring opinion disagreed with Black's contention that under martial law military authority was always properly subordinated to civil power. However, he thought the existence of a situation justifying the imposition of martial law was a question of fact properly subject to judicial determination. In the present case, no danger of invasion or public order had been shown to exist at the time of petitioner's trial; therefore military government at that time had been unconstitutional. Justice Murphy, also concurring, emphasized strongly the "open court" rule of *Ex parte Milligan*—that the military lacks any constitutional power either in peace or war to try civilians when the civil courts are open and functioning in normal fashion. Burton and Frankfurter, dissenting, thought the danger of invasion had been substantial enough throughout 1943 and 1944 to make continued military government in Hawaii constitutional.

The most surprising aspect of *Duncan v. Kahanamoku* was the Court's reluctance to rely more heavily upon *Ex parte Milligan* as a leading precedent. No doubt the explanation lies in the extent to which the Milligan decision had been criticized in recent years. Various commentators had pointed out that the exigencies of war on occasion may leave little room for so large a play of civilian authority in a possible field of military operations as the Milligan case insisted upon. Put differently, they argued that the "open court" rule may endanger national security. Also, the Milligan case had been said to lack realism in that it came after the close of the Civil War and was therefore in a sense an indulgence in a "peacetime luxury." Apparently, similar considerations motivated the Court in the Kahanamoku case. Only Justice Murphy was willing to stand by the rigid rule of the Milligan case, that military trial of civilians was unconstitutional except in an actual field of military operations.

MILITARY TRIAL OF ENEMY WAR CRIMINALS

A similar determination not to interfere with the conduct of the war undoubtedly was a large factor in the Court's refusal to extend the protection of the Bill of Rights to enemy military personnel charged with violations of the laws of war.

The question of whether enemy military personnel could claim the protection of the Constitution and the Bill of Rights first arose in *Ex parte Quirin* (1942), a case growing out of the arrest of eight members of the German military forces who had entered the United States in disguise with intent to commit acts of sabotage against American war industry. Following their capture in June 1942, the President ordered the saboteurs tried before a specially constituted military tribunal, on charges of violating the laws of war.

While their trial was still in progress, seven of the prisoners sought writs of habeas corpus before federal district courts and the Supreme Court. Late in July the Court consented to hear arguments for the writ. It then immediately denied the appeal without publishing a full opinion explaining why it did so. In October the Court published a unanimous opinion written by Chief Justice Stone, setting forth at some length the reasons for its decision three months earlier.

Stone's opinion held that the saboteurs were not entitled to other than summary military trial. The Chief Justice first examined and rejected the contention that the offenses for which the petitioners were being tried—violations of the laws of war—were defined neither in the Constitution nor in any federal statute and were therefore unknown to the law of the United States. In reply, Stone held that the Fifteenth Article of War, which authorized trial by military commissions of offenses under the laws of war, was sufficient statutory authorization for the present charge. The Chief Justice also denied the contention of counsel that the President was without adequate authority to establish the military commission, since he had departed slightly from the specifications of the Articles of War. Stone said merely that the national war power was sufficient to establish the commission, and he refused to separate congressional war power from the President's powers as commander in chief.

Finally, Stone denied that summary military trial of the saboteurs violated the guarantees of jury trial set forth in Article III, Section 2, of the Constitution and the procedural guarantees of civil trial extended by the Fifth and Sixth Amendments. Petitioners' counsel had pointed out that the Fifth Amendment exempts from its guarantees only "cases arising in the land or naval forces" of the United States. By implication, they had argued, the guarantees of civil procedure were extended to all other persons, including enemy military personnel. In reply, Stone said simply that there was "a long continued and consistent interpretation" by Congress and the courts to the contrary. Military tribunals, he pointed out, had long been held not to be courts within the meaning of the Constitution. It would be absurd, he concluded, to hold that the Constitution, which specifically withheld trial by jury from members of the American armed forces, nonetheless extended that right to enemy military personnel. Petitioners' plea was therefore held to be without merit.

Stone's entire opinion rested upon the highly dubious assumption that even though the saboteurs were prisoners of war in the hands of the military they nonetheless had certain rights under the Constitution. The assumption was at odds both with history and legal precedent. It is highly probable that the Constitutional Convention, many of whose members were well acquainted with the contemporary international law of war, did not intend to extend constitutional rights to enemy military personnel. Moreover, since 1776, the United States had always dealt with enemy war criminals by summary military procedure, as have all other states in the history of organized warfare. Perhaps, however, the justices were interested in impressing upon the totalitarian world the extraordinary degree to which the American constitutional system threw safeguards around accused persons—particularly since their speedy disposal of the appeal did not interfere in the least with Draconian military justice.

A possible implication of the Court's willingness to hear an appeal in the saboteurs' case was that the Constitution somehow threw its guarantees around all persons who in any fashion came under the authority of the United States. In that event, conceivably, the Constitution followed the flag into conquered Axis countries overseas. Not only surrendered enemy military personnel but perhaps also the entire civilian population of Germany, Italy, and Japan could to some extent claim the protection of the Constitution and the Bill of Rights.

However, *In re Yamashita* (1946) cut off the possibility of this development. The case involved an appeal by a captured Japanese general from his summary military conviction for violating the laws of war. As in the Quirin case, Yamashita's counsel had in effect argued that petitioner had been deprived of a fair trial in violation of the guarantees of the Fifth Amendment. But Chief Justice Stone's opinion in substance denied that Yamashita had any constitutional rights at all. Yamashita's conviction, he said, was subject to review only by higher military authority; he had no standing whatever in the civil courts under the Constitution. The Court thus silently overruled the major assumptions implicit in *Ex parte Quirin*.

Justices Rutledge and Murphy both dissented vigorously. Rutledge pointed out the discrepancy between the Court's present position and that in the saboteurs' case, and then went on to argue that the guarantees extended by the Constitution applied whenever and wherever the authority of the United States was exercised, except under actual conditions of combat. Murphy argued that failure to extend the guarantees of the Fifth and Sixth Amendments to Yamashita was not only grossly unconstitutional but also would hinder the "reconciliation necessary to a peaceful world."

The Court's position in the Yamashita case made possible large numbers of subsequent trials of enemy military and political personnel by summary military procedure and without the interference of American civil courts. Whether the Nuremberg trials, for example, were a happy development in American jurisprudence and international law is a matter of some dispute. Justices Rutledge and Murphy certainly had the virtues of both consistency and humanitarianism on their side, but it is indisputable that past American practice accorded more closely with the Court's stand.

THE CRAMER AND HAUPT TREASON CASES: WHAT IS AN OVERT ACT?

An interesting sequel to the saboteurs' case was a pair of treason trials which gave the Supreme Court its first opportunity in history to expound the meaning of Article III, Section 3, of the Constitution, which defines the offense of treason against the United States. The critical question in both cases was the meaning of the phrase "overt act" as set forth in the Constitution.[11] In the first case, the Court defined the meaning of "overt act" so narrowly as to make convictions for treason extremely difficult if not impossible except where the defendant formally enlisted himself in the service of an enemy power. In the second case, however, the Court substantially modified its stand.

The first case, *Cramer v. United States* (1945), came to the Court on appeal from the conviction of a naturalized American citizen of German background who had befriended two of the Nazi saboteurs during the brief time they had remained at large in New York City. Cramer had voluntarily met with the saboteurs, had eaten with them and had conversed with them at some length. The prosecution had argued that these activities constituted overt acts within the meaning of the constitutional requirement, and that the testimony of the F.B.I. agents met the constitutional requirement that there be two witnesses to the acts in question. The trial judge had adhered to this interpretation in his charge to the jury, which had accordingly returned a verdict of "guilty."

By a vote of five to four the Supreme Court reversed the conviction and set Cramer free. The critical legal issue, Justice Jackson's majority opinion made clear, was whether the Constitution required that the overt act in question must manifest virtually on its face an obvious intent to commit treason, or whether the treasonous character of an act innocent in itself might be demonstrated by surrounding testimony and evidence. Jackson adopted the first point of view almost unconditionally. While he admitted that an overt act might in itself be innocent and gain its traitorous character from the intent involved, he held that the evidence of two or more witnesses to the act in question must establish its traitorous intent beyond a reasonable doubt. He bulwarked this argument with an elaborate

---

[11] Article III, Section 3, provides that "no person shall be convicted of Treason unless on the Testimony of two Witnesses to the same overt Act, or on Confession in open Court."

historical survey of the law of treason, in which he contended among other things that the Constitutional Convention of 1787 had undoubtedly intended to write the restrictive view of "overt act" into the Constitution. Jackson leaned heavily, also, upon the restrictive interpretation presented by Lord Reading in the famous English treason trial of Sir Roger Casement in 1915, and a 1917 opinion of Judge Learned Hand. In the present case, Jackson then pointed out, Cramer's overt act as established in Court had consisted merely of social intercourse with the enemy, and the testimony of the witnesses involved had not established any traitorous intent. The Court therefore concluded that Cramer's guilt had not been established.

The majority justices in the Cramer case were undoubtedly motivated by a high-minded conviction that in a constitutional democracy the offense of treason ought to be defined as narrowly as possible. While the weight of historical precedent was against the Court, there was some authority for Jackson's argument, as the Reading and Hand opinions made clear.

The difficulty with the Court's position, as Justice Douglas pointed out for the minority,[12] was that it made subsequent convictions for treason all but impossible, primarily because it was now necessary to establish the intent of the overt act itself through the testimony of two witnesses. This requirement, Douglas contended, was at odds with both history and the intent of the framers of the Constitution. At all events, the Cramer case threatened to stand on a par with Marshall's narrow definition of "levying war" in the Burr trial in very nearly writing the offense of treason out of federal criminal law.

However, in *Haupt v. United States* (1947), another case growing out of the saboteurs' activities, the Court modified substantially the force of its restrictive interpretation of what constituted an overt act. Hans Haupt, the father of one of the saboteurs, had given shelter to his son, attempted to secure him a job in a factory manufacturing the Norden bombsight, and helped him to purchase an automobile. On the strength of testimony by the required two witnesses to these acts, the trial court had convicted the elder Haupt of treason. As in Cramer's case, the overt acts in question were admittedly innocent in themselves. Indeed they conceivably could be interpreted as evidence of nothing more than the natural concern of a father for his son and not of intent to aid the enemy.

---

[12] Chief Justice Stone and Justices Black and Reed joined Douglas in dissent.

The Court nonetheless voted eight to one to sustain Haupt's conviction. Justice Jackson, who again wrote the majority opinion, argued that the present case differed fundamentally from Cramer's in that there could be no question that Haupt's acts were "helpful to an enemy agent" and had "the unmistakable quality which was found lacking in the Cramer case of forwarding the saboteur in his mission." Justice Murphy alone dissented, arguing with some force that the Court had departed from its stand in the Cramer case.

The Haupt conviction opened the way for a number of treason prosecutions of American nationals who had lent assistance to the Nazis or Japanese during the war. In several of these cases the defendant had committed his alleged act of treason while in the enemy country. For example, Douglas Chandler, an American "Lord Haw-Haw," was convicted of treason in 1948 on the strength of his Berlin radio broadcasts for Germany during the war. This raised the interesting question of whether an American could commit treason while in a foreign country, or whether on the contrary treason, like most other felonies, had territorial limits and must be committed within the jurisdiction of the United States.

In *Kawakita v. United States* (1952), the Court put this question to rest, ruling that treason was an offense without territorial limits and might be committed by an American national while in a foreign country. The case was the more interesting because the defendant possessed dual citizenship under Japanese and American nationality laws. Moreover, there was some evidence that in leaving the United States and going to Japan he had divested himself of United States citizenship prior to his assistance to the enemy. A majority of the Court nonetheless agreed with Justice Jackson that Kawakita had properly been convicted of treason in spite of his dubious national status.

OTHER WARTIME CIVIL LIBERTIES ISSUES:
DENATURALIZATION AND ESPIONAGE CASES

It is notable that during World War II, in spite of the disgraceful treatment of the Japanese minority, the political atmosphere in the country was far more open and free from repression than it had been during World War I. There was no counterpart in 1941–1945 to the semihysterical suppression of German culture which had occurred in 1917. The nation's great symphony orchestras continued to play the music of Bach, Beethoven, Brahms, and Mozart to enthusiastic audiences; college and school boards con-

tinued to encourage the teaching of German language and literature; and German-language newspapers and magazines quietly
continued to publish. There was little overt censorship of the press,
and nothing to correspond to the government's 1918 action in
banning the *New York Times* and *Saturday Evening Post* from
the mails. Even sauerkraut retained its traditional name, undergoing no such absurd transformation to "liberty cabbage" as had
occurred in 1917–1918.

The wartime political atmosphere on the Supreme Court both
reflected and contributed to the prevailing spirit of libertarianism.
Thus in *Schneiderman v. United States* (1943), the Court reversed,
six to three, a lower federal court decision revoking a certificate
of naturalization obtained by a petitioner who at the time of his
original naturalization proceedings had been a member of the Communist Party. The government had argued that Party membership
was decisive evidence that petitioner had not been "attached to the
principles of the Constitution and well disposed to the good order
and happiness of the United States," as the law required. His certificate of naturalization hence had been fraudulently obtained.

Murphy's opinion rejected this argument. He first declared
firmly that while naturalization admittedly was a privilege controlled by Congress and not a constitutional right, the Court would
refuse to construe "general phrases" in the naturalization statutes
in such a way as to "circumscribe liberty of political thought."
Communist Party membership, he pointed out, had not been illegal
as of 1927. Moreover, an examination of the principles of the Communist Party led him to the conclusion that membership in that
organization was "not absolutely incompatible" with loyalty to the
Constitution. Hence, he concluded, the government had not rested
its case upon the "clear, unequivocal, and convincing evidence"
which successful denaturalization proceedings properly required.
Chief Justice Stone, whom Frankfurter and Jackson joined in dissent, protested that membership in the Communist Party, contrary
to Murphy's conclusion, was in fact "utterly incompatible" with
loyalty to the Constitution.

A year later, in *Baumgartner v. United States* (1944), the Court
again reversed a denaturalization finding, aimed this time at a professed Nazi sympathizer. Frankfurter's opinion drew back slightly
from the "clear, unequivocal, and convincing" formula Murphy
had invoked in the Schneiderman case. The evidence in a denaturalization proceeding, he held, must be "clear and unequivocal" and of such a character as to "leave no troubling doubt in

deciding a question of such gravity." Murphy, concurring with Black, Douglas, and Rutledge, insisted that the proper formula for such proceedings was the "clear, unequivocal, and convincing" one of the Schneiderman decision.

In *Hartzel v. United States* (1944), the majority justices applied the Schneiderman formula to reverse a conviction under Section 3 of the Espionage Act of 1917, which made punishable wartime attempts to cause insubordination, disloyalty, mutiny or refusal of duty in the armed forces, or willfully to obstruct the recruiting or enlistment services of the United States. The petitioner had circulated articles vilifying Jews, the English, and the President of the United States and had in effect called for both an alliance with Germany and conversion of the war into a racial conflict. Recipients had included high military personnel. But Murphy's opinion held that the government had not succeeded in establishing by "clear, convincing, and unequivocal evidence" the petitioner's intent to violate the law. Since intent was an essential ingredient in the statute, the conviction must be overturned. Reed, dissenting along with Frankfurter, Douglas, and Jackson, protested that it had been altogether reasonable for the trial jury to conclude from the evidence that the petitioner's purpose had been "to undermine the will of our soldiers to fight the enemy."

THE SIGNIFICANCE OF WORLD WAR II FOR CONSTITUTIONAL GOVERNMENT

It is evident that American constitutional government met the challenge of total war between 1941 and 1945 as it had in 1861 and 1917. There was, in fact, a striking similarity between the nature of the constitutional problems which arose in all three eras. In each instance the war crisis exposed something of the inner inconsistency between the nature of constitutional government and the requirements of national security and military policy. In each instance the executive solved the problem of the effective conduct of the war by establishing a kind of quasi-constitutional dictatorship, erected in part on a statutory basis and in part merely on the presidential prerogative as commander in chief in wartime. In each instance, also, there was some interference with civil liberties in the name of the larger war effort. In World War II, however, this interference was limited largely to forced segregation of the Japanese minority and the imposition of military government on Hawaii.

Most important, the spirit of constitutional government once more survived the exigencies of war. Once more the remarkable flexibility of the American constitutional system had been demonstrated; it could adjust rapidly to the requirements of war and then return as rapidly to the institutions of peace.

As the United States entered upon a new postwar era, however, it became evident that perhaps the supreme test of constitutional government was yet to come. The Constitution had met the test of total war; could it also meet the test of survival in a world which lived in a perpetual state of international crisis and half-war lasting not for two or four years but for decades and perhaps generations? Not long after 1945 it became evident that this was perhaps the gravest constitutional question of the twentieth century.

Chapter

31

The Constitution and the Cold War

AT THE CLOSE of World War II the United States occupied a position of power and pre-eminence among the nations of the world rivaled in the past only by the Roman and British empires. Vast industrial capacity, immense financial resources, large population and a high level of technical culture made the United States a new colossus of the West. American military power stretched over half the earth, from West Berlin to Japan. American economic ascendancy was equally evident. Many billions of dollars poured into Europe and Asia through the successive media of UNRRA, the Marshall Plan, and Point Four in American efforts to work the economic rehabilitation of a war-ravaged world.

In 1945, the United States joined with the other victorious Allied powers at San Francisco in the organization of the United Nations, a new experiment in world peace through collective security. Here was an "entangling alliance" projected on a world scale, yet the Senate ratified the Charter with hardly a murmur of dissent, so radically had the national understanding of America's role altered since the days of the Versailles Treaty.

Unfortunately the new era of collective security did not bring peace to the world. Soon after the close of the fighting in World

War II, a "Cold War" developed between the "Iron Curtain" countries and the West that made any real peace impossible. The Western nations and the members of the Soviet Bloc alike soon came to live under the continuous threat of atomic war. Both felt obliged to maintain their military establishments and their national economies virtually on a war footing. Both built up elaborate systems of military alliances, dominated by the North Atlantic Treaty Alliance in the West and the Warsaw Pact in the East, in an effort to supplement the fragile guarantees of collective security extended by the United Nations. No more than the United Nations did these alliances bring any real stability to the world. Instead, successive diplomatic crises over Greece, Berlin, Hungary, Suez, and Cuba, interspersed with bloody "little wars" in Korea, Laos, and Vietnam, more and more dominated the international scene.

The pressures and tensions generated by the Cold War were also responsible in considerable part for the emergence of a whole series of internal constitutional problems, many of them fraught with grave implications for the future of constitutional liberty. For a decade or more the United States lived in an almost continuous state of proclaimed national emergency, with all that this implied in a constitutional sense. The constitutional crisis precipitated in 1952 by President Truman's seizure of the steel industry would demonstrate dramatically how difficult it was to reconcile normal constitutional government with the requirements of a chronic condition of national emergency.

The Cold War, with its crisis psychology and accompanying concern for security, was also responsible to some extent for the conservative political reaction that enveloped the United States in the decade after 1945. In 1946 the Republican Party scored its first congressional victory in almost twenty years; thereafter a coalition of northern Republicans and conservative southern Democrats took over control of both houses, and in the next several years pushed a series of counter-reform measures onto the books, including the Taft-Hartley Labor Relations Act of 1947, the McCarran, or Internal Security, Act of 1950, and the McCarran-Walter Immigration Act of 1952.

The conservative reaction also was accompanied by a powerful "Red Scare," far more persistent and pervasive in its political and constitutional consequences than that which had swept the country in the early 1920's.

To a surprising extent the postwar Supreme Court, although

made up mainly of Old New Dealers and Democrats, reflected the conservative spirit now abroad in the land. The intellectual leader of the Court was undoubtedly Felix Frankfurter, who, in his earlier career as a Harvard Law School professor and intimate personal advisor to F.D.R., had been incautiously described by enemies of the Roosevelt administration as "a red-hot radical," but who in decision after decision now demonstrated an increasing respect for legislative discretion, state police power, and society's concern for stability, security, and continuity. Justice Jackson, who had once upon a time talked and acted like a somewhat populistic enemy of great corporate wealth, now took on something of the same conservative shading, as did Justice Reed, who earlier had been a middle-of-the-road New Dealer.

Meanwhile President Truman, whether by design or not, strengthened the tendency of the Court toward moderate conservatism with the appointment of four successive justices of middle-of-the-road political sentiments. Frederick M. Vinson, whom the President named to the Chief Justiceship in 1946 upon Stone's death, was a somewhat conservative Democratic Kentucky Congressman who had never been associated with the more extreme phases of the New Deal. Harold H. Burton, appointed in 1945 upon the resignation of Justice Roberts, was a former Republican Senator from Ohio whom Truman nominated apparently in an effort to give the Court some bipartisan balance. Tom Clark, whom Truman named in 1949 to succeed Justice Murphy upon the latter's death, was a conservative Texan who had served since 1945 as Attorney General. And Sherman Minton, who succeeded Justice Rutledge a few weeks later, was a former Democratic Senator from Indiana and more recently a judge of the United States Court of Appeals who entertained political views rather similar to those of Clark. Together with Frankfurter, Jackson, and Reed, the four new appointments by 1950 gave the Court a more distinctively conservative flavor than it had possessed at any time since the Roosevelt appointments following the constitutional crisis of 1937.

President Eisenhower's appointments at first seemingly confirmed the somewhat conservative political balance the Court already had achieved under Truman. Chief Justice Earl Warren, whom the President named to the Court in 1953 upon Vinson's death, was eventually to emerge as a very strong libertarian activist, but at the time of his nomination he was known only as a mildly liberal Republican who had enjoyed great popularity as governor of California and who had served as Thomas E. Dewey's running mate in the 1948 presidential campaign. John Marshall Harlan, grandson of the late distinguished associate justice of the same name, was a New York lawyer whom Eisenhower named to the Court in 1955 following Jackson's death; his career on the Court was to be characterized by a consistent moderate conservatism. William J. Brennan, who joined the Court in 1956 upon Minton's resignation, was a former Associate Justice of the New Jersey Supreme Court and a Democrat with a reputation as a very moderate liberal. And Charles E. Whittaker, appointed in 1957 upon Reed's resignation, was a Kansas City lawyer of moderate Republican sentiments who only months earlier had been named to the United States Court of Appeals.

Thus for about twelve years the Court was controlled by moderate conservatives who adopted a cautious policy of judicial self-restraint and respect for legislative prerogative and discretion. To some observers the course they plotted seemed to justify the prediction advanced by E. S. Corwin some years earlier that the Court as a consequence of the constitutional crisis of 1937 now was destined to take a back seat in the power structure of the federal government. Only in Negro civil rights cases did the Court in the Truman and early Eisenhower years show a tendency to controversial judicial activism of the sort that in the later Warren period was to characterize its behavior more generally.

THE CONSTITUTION AND COLLECTIVE SECURITY:
THE "GREAT DEBATE"

American membership in the United Nations and the new alliances had some substantial effect upon the constitutional balance of power between the President and Congress. Thus American consent to participation in the application of military sanctions against an aggressor state was at the discretion of the United States delegate to the Security Council, who in turn was under the control of the President and the Secretary of State. Technically, a U.N. "police action" would not be war, but it was probable that in practice this would prove to be a distinction without a difference.

Congress itself presently recognized the practical force of this situation with the passage of the United Nations Participation Act of 1945. Section 6 of this law authorized the President to negotiate military agreements with the Security Council to earmark American military contingents for the Council, subject to congressional approval of the agreements negotiated. The act further provided that the President "shall not be deemed to require the authorization of Congress" to make such forces available to the Council in any specific collective security action. In short, Congress here recognized that the President could now commit the United States to a venture in military sanctions under the Charter without congressional consent. Technically, agreements of the kind provided for in the act were not subsequently negotiated. In fact, this mattered little, as the Korean War presently demonstrated.

A similar constitutional problem arose in 1949 when the Senate undertook consideration of the North Atlantic Treaty. Article 5 of this agreement stipulated that an armed attack against any one of the signatory states was to be deemed an attack against them all. In the event of such an attack, each of the other parties to the treaty was to lend assistance "by taking such action as it deems necessary, including the use of armed force, to restore and maintain the security of the Atlantic area." This provision had been drafted very carefully so as to avoid any specific obligation on the part of the United States to go to war, an obligation which would have violated the constitutional control by Congress of the power to declare war. The Senate Committee on Foreign Relations was thus able to report that the "treaty in no way affects the basic division of authority between the President and Congress as defined in the Constitution." Senator Arthur Vandenberg of Michigan, who championed the treaty on the Senate floor, also insisted that the technical obligation assumed under the treaty was merely to give assistance at the discretion of the United States. Formal participation in any war, he said, would still require the consent of Congress.

It was obvious, however, that the President might deploy American armed forces in such a fashion that were any of the signatory states attacked the United States would immediately become heavily engaged in fighting. War would then become virtually inevitable. Concern for this possibility led Senator Arthur Watkins of Utah to offer a reservation to the treaty declaring that the United States assumed no obligation to render military assistance to its allies in the event of attack "unless in any particular case Congress . . . shall by joint resolution so provide." However, the Watkins reservation was immediately voted down by a top-heavy majority, plain indication that the Senate realized that the President in fact would be able to commit the United States to war under the treaty, even though Congress still possessed the right to make a formal declaration.

The Korean War all too soon provided a dramatic illustration of the President's war-making powers under collective security. Following the attack by North Korea on the South Korean Republic, the Security Council on June 25, 1950, adopted a resolution calling upon the North Korean forces to withdraw and asking United Nations member-states to "render every assistance in the execution of this resolution." On June 27, President Truman announced that in accordance with the Council's request he had ordered American military forces into the fighting in Korea. The President took this action in spite of the fact that the United States had never signed any specific agreement with the United Nations assigning American forces to the Council for police purposes.

Thus presidential discretion alone took the United States into a large-scale *de facto* war. Technically the Korean "police action" was not war in a formal constitutional sense, for war was never declared by Congress. However, Congress was perforce constrained to underwrite the President's policy, which it did through the passage of comprehensive war legislation and military appropriations for the war's prosecution. The Korean "police action" ultimately proved to be the fourth largest war up to that time in American history; it cost some 30,000 lives and scores of billions of dollars and placed the nation on a partial war footing for some three years.

The events of the next two decades did little to weaken the executive prerogative in war-making which President Truman in 1950 had exercised so decisively. When Truman early in 1951 announced that he intended to send four divisions to Germany in support of American obligations under the North Atlantic Treaty, Senator Robert A. Taft of Ohio responded with an embittered speech in which he charged that the President had "usurped power and violated the Constitution and laws of the United States" by intervening in Korea and now proposed to repeat the offense. But in the "Great Debate" that followed, several Senators, among them Tom Connally of Texas and Paul Douglas of Illinois, came to the President's defense, while Truman, in a series of press releases, insisted that he possessed the power to move troops anywhere without the consent of Congress, although he conceded that he might on occasion consult with individual members of the two houses as a "practical matter."

The outcome of the "Great Debate" was a victory for the presidential war prerogative. In April, the Senate staged a calculated retreat with the passage, 69 to 21, of a weak resolution expressing "approval" of the President's intention to send troops to Germany but adding that it was "the sense of the Senate" that "in the interests of sound constitutional processes, and of national unity" the Chief Executive ought to obtain the approval of Congress to "the assignment of American troops abroad" in the future.

To all intents and purposes the issues surrounding the question of presidential war-making prerogative now were very nearly settled. President Eisenhower, notably careful in his recognition of congressional war-making prerogative, in 1955 obtained the support of a joint resolution of Congress authorizing him to use armed force to defend the offshore Nationalist Chinese Islands should he see fit to do so. But when in 1958, Eisenhower, confronted with a sudden crisis in the Middle East, abruptly moved troops into Lebanon, his action caused scarcely a ripple in Congress. In 1962, President Kennedy took the same step without serious congressional objection, both in Thailand and in Vietnam. And in October of that year, in response to the Soviet emplacement of missiles in Cuba, Kennedy upon his own authority proclaimed a naval "quarantine" of Cuba, a move that lacked the formal character of an act of war under international law only because he avoided use of the word "blockade." In short, presidential control of the war power now appeared to have become primary and that of Congress secondary, and there appeared to be very little that aroused Senators, the Court, or anyone else could do about it. The massive presidential military intervention which took place in Vietnam after 1964 heavily reinforced this conclusion.

THE CONTINUED EXERCISE OF FEDERAL WAR POWERS

Hostilities in World War II had ended in August 1945, but the speedy development of the "Cold War," the consequent delay in the negotiation of peace treaties with Germany and Japan, and the onset of the Korean War kept the United States technically at war for the next several years and resulted in maintaining indefinitely large portions of the wartime emergency government. On December 31, 1946, the President issued a proclamation officially terminating hostilities, and in July 1947, Congress enacted a joint resolution which repealed a great variety of wartime statutes and set termination dates upon others. However, some 103 wartime statutory provisions still remained active. And in signing the joint resolution the President noted that the emergencies declared in 1939 and 1941 continued to exist and that it was "not possible at this time to provide for terminating all war and emergency powers."

Thereafter, Congress, the President, and the courts continued to assume the existence of a state of wartime emergency. In June 1947, Congress enacted a new Housing and Rent Act which continued the rent-control system established in the Emergency Price Control Act of 1942. A new Rent Control Act passed in 1949 continued rent controls in defense areas but provided for decontrol at the option of state and local governments. In 1948, Congress enacted a new Selective Service Law; thereby it put the draft on a regular "peacetime" basis, although there was no imminent prospect of hostilities as had been the case in 1940. And with the outbreak of the Korean War, Congress in 1950 passed the Defense Production Act, which established once more general presidential control over the economy for war purposes. A new executive proclamation of war emergency followed in December. Thereafter, the President by executive order created the Office of Defense Mobilization and the Office of Price Stabilization for executive regulation of the war economy.

The dangers for constitutional government in all this were evident enough. If the state of emergency became a permanent affair the constitutional barriers upon the scope of peacetime federal power and upon the executive power of the President in time might crumble away.

The Court itself expressed uneasy awareness of this possibility in *Woods v. Miller* (1948), a case involving the constitutionality of the Housing and Rent Act of 1947. Justice Douglas, who spoke for the Court, found no difficulty in sustaining the constitutionality of the statute, pointing merely to the World War I cases wherein the Court had held that the federal war power did not terminate with the close of hostilities but instead included the power "to remedy the evils which have arisen from its rise and progress." Nonetheless Douglas observed with some apprehension that "We recognize the force of the argument that the effects of war under modern conditions may last for years and years, and that if the war power can be used in the days of peace to treat all the wounds which war inflicts on our society, it may not only swallow up all other powers of Congress but largely obliterate the Ninth and Tenth Amendments as well." In a concurring opinion Jackson expressed "explicit misgivings" about the continuance of federal war power which he found to be "the most dangerous to free government in the whole catalogue of powers."

A few months later, in *Ludecke v. Watkins* (1948), a minority of four justices expressed even greater concern over the continued exercise of federal war powers. The case involved a review of a deportation order issued under the authority of the now ancient Alien Enemies Act of 1798. A majority of the Court, speaking through Justice Frankfurter, found that the war powers of the President under the act were not limited to the state of actual hostilities and that the deportation order was therefore constitutional. But Justice Black, in a vigorous dissent in which Douglas, Murphy, and Rutledge joined, objected that "the idea that we are still at war with Germany in the sense contemplated by the statute here is a pure fiction." It was high time, he thought, to return to peacetime methods of handling alien cases.

THE STEEL SEIZURE CASE: A CHECK TO PRESIDENTIAL EMERGENCY POWER

However, it was President Truman's seizure of the steel industry that presently called forth the full measure of the Court's condemnation of emergency government.

The Steel Seizure case grew out of President Truman's efforts to avert a long-threatened strike which promised to have a catastrophic effect on the prosecution of the Korean War. Efforts at compromise through the Wage Stabilization Board ended in failure, and early in April 1952 the United Steel Workers of America called a nationwide strike to begin on April 9.

On the eve of the walkout, the President issued an executive order to Secretary of Commerce Charles Sawyer instructing him to take possession of the steel mills and operate them in the name of the United States Government. The order cited the national emergency proclaimed on December 16, 1950, and the necessity of maintaining uninterrupted steel production for the Korean War and the atomic energy program. The President issued the order by virtue of his authority "under the Constitution and laws of the United States" and as commander in chief, but did not cite any specific statutory authority. Secretary Sawyer immediately issued a seizure order to the companies. The President reported the seizure to Congress in a special message in which he invited legislative action should that body think it necessary. However, Congress took no action, although a great many members subjected the President's seizure to severe criticism.

From a constitutional point of view, the most extraordinary fact about the seizure order was its total lack of statutory authority. The Selective Service Act of 1948 and the Defense Production Act of 1950 both authorized the seizure of industrial plants which failed to give priority to defense orders, but neither mentioned seizure to resolve labor disputes. Moreover, Congress in enacting the Taft-Hartley Act in 1947 had considered and rejected just such a proposal, and had instead incorporated in the law a provision permitting the President to obtain an injunction postponing for eighty days any strike threatening the national welfare. However, President Truman had chosen to ignore this procedure, in part because the strike already had been delayed more than eighty days by the Wage Stabilization Board, and had instead fallen back upon his general executive prerogative. In short, here was an assertion of executive prerogative power rivaling those of Lincoln, Wilson, and Franklin Roosevelt.

The steel companies immediately attacked the constitutionality of the seizure in the federal courts. Judge Pine of the United States District Court for the District of Columbia presently issued a preliminary injunction restraining the Secretary of Commerce from continuing in possession of the mills. The District of Columbia Court of Appeals thereafter stayed the injunction; further legal maneuvering brought the case to the Supreme Court.

By a six to three vote the Court in *Youngstown Sheet and Tube Co. v. Sawyer* (1952) held that the President's steel seizure was an unconstitutional usurpation of legislative power. Justice Black's brief and rather summary majority opinion avoided the more complex constitutional aspects of the case and rested instead squarely upon the separation of powers and a summary rejection of the theory of executive prerogative. After observing that there was "no statute that expressly authorizes the President to take possession of property as he did here," Black rejected in succession the propositions that the President's powers as commander in chief authorized the seizure or that some inherent executive prerogative flowing from the Constitution itself supplied the necessary authority. Although the President's order "resembled a statute in form" it was nonetheless invalid, for the Constitution limited the President's role in law-making "to the recommending of laws he thinks wise and the vetoing of laws he thinks bad." The seizure, it followed, was unconstitutional and void. Significantly, Black had avoided any discussion whatever of expanded executive prerogative in times of emergency.

There were lengthy concurring opinions by the other five majority justices. Frankfurter placed special weight upon the fact that the President had ignored "the clear will of Congress" on plant seizures as expressed in the Taft-Hartley Act. He did not totally reject the notion of executive prerogative, but he thought the history of plant seizures during World War I and World War II showed no such sweeping pretensions to emergency prerogative power as did the present action. Douglas, like Black, was shocked by "the legislative nature of the action taken by the President." Jackson, on the other hand, attempted to distinguish three circumstances of executive prerogative: first, when the President acted in pursuance of a specific statute or constitutional provision; second, when he acted in the absence "either of a congressional grant or denial of authority," and third, when he took "measures incompatible with the expressed or implied will of Congress." In the last instance, he thought, presidential prerogative power was at its lowest ebb. Burton, like Frankfurter, found decisive the President's violation of the strike settlement procedures set forth in the Taft-Hartley Act. Clark alone of all the majority specifically subscribed to the theory of an expanded executive prerogative "in times of grave and imperative national emergency." Such a grant, he thought, "may well be necessary to the very existence of the Constitution itself." Nonetheless the President's violation of the procedures for strike settlement laid down by law obligated him to agree that the present seizure was unconstitutional.

Chief Justice Vinson wrote a lengthy and spirited dissent, in which Reed and Minton joined. The main weight of his argument was that in a grave national crisis the President must necessarily exercise a very large degree of discretionary prerogative power. "Those who suggest that this is a case involving extraordinary powers should be mindful that these are extraordinary times." He made much of the fact that the President's seizure in a general way had been in support of declared congressional policy as set forth in the Mutual Security Program and appropriations for the Korean War. He offered a very broad construction of the provision in Article II of the Constitution that the President "shall take care that the laws be faithfully executed." He cited Lincoln's extraordinary actions at the outbreak of the Civil War, Cleveland's use of the army to protect the mails and interstate commerce, Wilson's creation of wartime agencies without statutory authority, and Franklin Roosevelt's seizure of the North American plant before Pearl Harbor, again without statutory authority. He concluded that President Truman's seizure of the steel industry was altogether within this tradition; there was, he thought, "no basis for claims of arbitrary action, unlimited powers, or dictatorial usurpation of Congressional power."

On the surface, the Supreme Court had sharply repudiated the twin theories of inherent executive prerogative in internal affairs and an expanded executive prerogative in national emergencies. But one may well express some doubt whether a future Court in an even graver national emergency would succeed in adhering to the Steel Seizure precedent. Significantly, the United States in 1952 was not involved in a major declared war; plainly the majority justices felt that the nation probably could afford the luxury of a temporary interruption of steel production even in the face of the Korean War. One might well argue that it was in the nature of the twentieth-century crisis of civilization that national emergencies would occur repeatedly and that future Presidents would inevitably use prerogative power in some fashion in an attempt to solve them. Chief Justice Vinson's argument on the growth of the executive prerogative as a fact of constitutional life had very great pragmatic force.

THE UNITED NATIONS AND FEDERAL-STATE RELATIONS

A constitutional issue that commanded considerable public attention in the postwar era was that arising out of the potential impact of the United Nations Charter and the U.N. Covenant on Human Rights upon federal-state relations. The fear that the Charter, a duly ratified treaty and as such the supreme law of the land, would impose new civil rights obligations upon the states enforceable in the federal courts caused a major furore in Congress and in conservative legal circles, and led to near-passage by the Senate of the Bricker Amendment to limit application of treaties as internal law.

The problem first attracted attention with the Supreme Court's handling of *Oyama v. California* (1948), in which the justices had at hand the California Alien Land Law forbidding ownership of lands by aliens ineligible for citizenship. The Court carefully refrained from invalidating the law generally, but ruled cautiously that application of the statute in the particular case at hand violated the equal protection clause of the Fourteenth Amendment. However, Justices Black and Murphy, in concurring opinions joined in by Douglas and Rutledge, expressed the belief that the law in question also was void because it conflicted with Article 55 of the United Nations Charter, whereby the United States had pledged itself to "promote . . . universal respect for, and observance of, human rights and fundamental freedoms for all without distinction as to race, sex, language, or religion." "How can this nation be faithful to this international pledge," Black asked, "if state laws which bar land ownership and occupancy by aliens on account of race are permitted to be enforced?" As if in response to Black's stricture, a California district court presently ruled, in *Fujii v. State* (1950), that the Alien Land Law was indeed invalid in that it violated the civil rights guarantees incorporated in Article 55 of the Charter, now the supreme law of the land.

The Oyama and Fujii decisions inspired a flurry of commentary among constitutional experts and leading political figures. If the United Nations Charter were a self-executing treaty, then as supreme law it might well set aside numerous state and federal statutes in areas both of civil rights and vested interests. Moreover, under the half-forgotten dictum of *Missouri v. Holland,* which now suddenly flared into importance, the treaty power might serve as the foundation for expanded congressional legislative authority beyond that set forth in Article I, Section 8 of the Constitution. The result conceivably could be a serious disturbance in federal-state relations.

Much of the immediate discussion turned on the question of whether the Charter was indeed a self-executing treaty. Judge Manley O. Hudson, a noted authority on international law, wrote that the Fujii decision had been based upon the "mistaken idea" that treaties were necessarily self-executing without supporting federal legislation. The Charter, he thought, constituted merely a vague declaration of national intent; it could become effective as internal law only to the extent that Congress enacted supporting statutes. Professor Zechariah Chafee of the Harvard Law School adopted much the same position. As if to support this interpretation, the California Supreme Court upon appeal ruled in *Fujii v. State* (1952) that the district court had erred in holding that Article 55 had of itself voided the Alien Land Law; instead, said the court, the law was invalid solely because it violated the Fourteenth Amendment's equal protection clause. On the other hand, Professor Quincy Wright of the University of Chicago, a noted authority on international law and federal treaties, argued that the original California district court decision had been correct, and he backed up his stand with citations showing that the federal Supreme Court itself had considered treaties to be non-self-executing only when they obviously needed legislative support, in instances such as criminal jurisdiction, tariffs, military law, and the like.

This discussion did little to quiet the qualms of constitutional conservatives, whose fears were further aroused by possible forthcoming United States ratification of the International Covenant on Human Rights, then in the process of preparation by the U.N. Human Rights Commission. This document would have bound signatory states to an elaborate series of legal guarantees of the kind found in the first eight amendments to the Constitution and in the various state bills of rights. Was it not possible that mere ratification of the forthcoming Covenant, even without supporting legislation from Congress, might work some fundamental revolution in the scope of state legislative power as against private rights? And even if the new Covenant were not self-executing, might it not constitute the basis for enlarged federal legislation in the area of private rights? State Department officials argued in reply that the Human Rights Covenant was not intended to be a self-executing treaty, and that in any event the document provided that each signatory state was to give it force only "in accordance with its constitutional processes."

In spite of such assurances, there was soon widespread agitation for a constitutional amendment to limit the scope of the federal treaty power. During 1951 and 1952, the legislatures of Colorado, California, and Georgia petitioned for such an amendment. And in February, 1952, the House of Delegates of the American Bar Association recommended to Congress an amendment to provide that "a provision of a treaty that conflicts with any provision of this Constitution shall not be of any force and effect."

In response to demands of this kind, Senator John Bricker of Ohio in February, 1952, introduced a comprehensive constitutional amendment, the first portion of which followed the Bar Association's proposal. The "Bricker Amendment," after some changes in wording, read as follows:

Section 1. A provision of a treaty which conflicts with this Constitution shall not be of any force and effect.

Section 2. A treaty shall become effective as internal law only through legislation which would be valid in the absence of a treaty. *Section 3.* Congress shall have the power to regulate all Executive and other agreements with any foreign power or international organization. All such agreements shall be subject to the limitations imposed on treaties by this article.

Thus Senator Bricker and his supporters sought to negate the possibility, implicit in the Court's opinion in *Missouri v. Holland*, that a treaty could enlarge federal power at the expense of the states, and equally that a treaty might be internally self-enforcing without the consent of Congress. Unless *Missouri v. Holland* were overruled, said Dean Clarence Manion of Notre Dame University Law School, the "Constitutional integrity of the states of the Union . . . and the sovereign independence of the United States" itself would "continue to be menaced by the threatened supremacy of treaty law."

The provision in the Bricker Amendment seeking to bring executive agreements under congressional control was an afterthought, growing out of the partisan controversy then being pursued over the late President Franklin Roosevelt's extensive resort to this device in his conduct of foreign relations. "The Bricker Amendment," said Senator Andrew Schoepel of Kansas in debate, "would restrain some future Roosevelt who might be tempted to indulge in another spree at Yalta."

Opponents of the Bricker Amendment in reply asserted that it constituted a very serious assault upon both the doctrine of national ascendancy and upon executive control of foreign relations. They centered their fire on the so-called "which clause" in Section 2, stipulating that treaties were to become effective as internal law only through legislation which would be valid in the absence of a treaty. This language, they pointed out, constituted a serious impairment of the treaty provision in Article VI, Section 2 of the Constitution, which had been written specifically to enable the national government to make treaties upon matters which ordinarily lay within the province of the States. As for the provision calling for congressional regulation of executive agreements, critics added, it would not even have reached such arrangements as those entered into at Cairo, Yalta, and Potsdam, which had been negotiated under the President's powers as commander-in-chief rather than by virtue of his prerogative in foreign affairs. But the greatest concern expressed by the Bricker Amendment's opponents was that if adopted it would break in upon the President's conduct of foreign affairs so decisively as to make an effective foreign policy impossible.

By January, 1953, Senator Bricker was able to announce nonetheless that no less than sixty-four members of the Senate had promised to sponsor his proposal. Thereafter, however, opposition swiftly mounted. President Eisenhower announced his "unalterable opposition" to the amendment, and Secretary of State John Foster Dulles, who earlier had indicated some sympathy for the proposal, now took up the cudgels for the administration. Senator Alexander Wiley, a leading Republican opponent, announced in January, 1954, that twenty-six out of twenty-seven deans of principal law schools throughout the United States had declared their opposition to the amendment.

In February, 1954, the Senate voted 60 to 31, one vote short of the required two-thirds constitutional majority, for a modified version of the Bricker Amendment, omitting the "which clause" and toning down somewhat the language on executive agreements. With this defeat the amendment rapidly lost its political force, and by the late 1950's it had become a dead issue. Meanwhile the Supreme Court resolved the problem in some part by acceding to the proposition that treaties were, after all, subject to certain constitutional limitations.

MILITARY POWER OVERSEAS: A NEW "INSULAR" PROBLEM

The Court's strictures on the treaty power were to occur in connection with a series of new "Insular Cases," arising this time out of the constitutional problems which inhered in America's far-flung military bases overseas.

America's postwar military bases on foreign soil generally came into existence by virtue of a treaty of alliance between the United States and the foreign nation in question, the 1949 twelve-nation North Atlantic Treaty being the prototype of such arrangements. The ordinary rule of international law would have given the foreign ally complete sovereignty over all persons within its boundaries. However, the exigencies of military discipline required that the United States retain jurisdiction over its military personnel stationed on such bases, at least in connection with military duties. Convenience also dictated that American civilian personnel attached to these bases—families, civilian employees, and the like— also be subject for some purposes to American sovereignty.

The United States and its allies solved this problem by the

negotiation of so-called Status of Forces Agreements whereby the United States and its ally defined the respective jurisdiction of the two sovereignties over American military and civilian personnel stationed on the ally's soil. Technically these were executive agreements made in pursuance of the basic treaty of alliance. Again, the NATO Status of Forces Agreement of 1951 was the prototype for arrangements of this kind; others followed with Spain, Morocco, Saudi Arabia, Japan, Iran, and so on.

The peacetime exercise of American military authority on foreign soil inevitably gave rise to a number of vexing constitutional problems. In *United States ex rel. Toth v. Quarles* (1955), the Court for the first time faced the question of whether or not military jurisdiction extended to former servicemen who had committed criminal offenses while in uniform overseas. Robert Toth, a former enlisted man in the United States Air Force, had served overseas in Korea and subsequently been honorably discharged. Five months later he was arrested at his home in Pittsburgh by Air Force police on a charge of murdering a citizen of Korea during his service in that country, and without further legal amenities was flown overseas to Korea to stand trial before a court-martial. The Air Force had acted under Article 3 (a) of the Uniform Code of Military Justice Act of 1950 which authorized the arrest and military trial of former members of the Armed Forces accused of offenses committed while in uniform. Subsequently, Toth had been freed on a writ of habeas corpus. The appeals process presently brought the case to the Supreme Court.

Justice Black's majority opinion held Article 3 (a) unconstitutional, declaring that "such an assertion of military authority over civilians" could not "be sustained on the power of Congress 'to raise and support armies,' 'to declare war,' or to 'punish offenses against the law of nations,' " or upon "the President's power as Commander-in-Chief, or on any theory of martial law." Moreover, he added, such an expansion of court-martial jurisdiction "necessarily encroaches on the jurisdiction of federal courts set up under Article III of the Constitution," and it would also bring "enormous numbers" of civilians under the jurisdiction of courts-martial with a consequent impairment of the right of jury trial. To the objection that the Court's decision might well result in allowing ex-service men guilty of serious felonies while in uniform to go unpunished, Black pointed out that Congress might well follow the suggestion of the Judge Advocate-General of the Army, who had recommended that Congress confer jurisdiction upon the federal courts to try this type of offense. Justices Reed, Burton, and Minton, dissenting, protested that the Court's decision had resulted in freeing a man accused of murder without possibility of trial.

The Court majority very obviously had been motivated by the traditional over-all constitutional doctrine of the subordination of military authority to civil government. Black's concluding statement practically amounted to a declaration that constitutional liberty made it imperative that those portions of Article I, Section 8, empowering Congress to authorize military jurisdiction were to be subjected to a kind of Jeffersonian strict construction as a means of maintaining an open constitutional system and a free democratic society.

The constitutional questions involved in the military trial of civilians accompanying the Armed Forces overseas also involved more difficulty and perplexity. Here the basic constitutional question was not merely one of the extent of military authority over civilians—in this instance, serving overseas with the Armed Forces—but also the extent to which the "Constitution followed the flag" outside the United States for American citizens overseas, so that they could claim the protections of the Bill of Rights. These issues arose in the companion cases of *Reid v. Covert* (1956) and *Kinsella v. Krueger* (1956), in which the Court was to reverse itself dramatically within the space of a single year.

The Reid and Kinsella cases had substantially identical origins and presented substantially similar legal problems. In both instances the wife of a member of the Armed Forces stationed overseas had murdered her husband. Thereafter, each had been brought to trial before an overseas court-martial under Article 2 (11) of the Uniform Code of Military Justice Act, which had conferred court-martial jurisdiction on the Armed Forces over all persons accompanying the Armed Forces outside the continental limits of the United States. In each instance, also, the United States military courts exercised jurisdiction over the defendant by virtue of a Status of Forces Agreement between the United States and Great Britain and Japan respectively, whereby the two allies had ceded "exclusive jurisdiction" over all offenses committed by members of the Armed Forces and the civilian component of these forces and their dependents, when the offenses in question did not involve local nationals.

Each woman, after trial, had been sentenced to life imprisonment and thereafter committed to a civilian federal prison for women in the United States. Each had thereupon secured release on a writ of habeas corpus issued by a federal district court, which in each instance held Article 2 (11) unconstitutional. In each case, the government had then sought and obtained *certiorari* to the Supreme Court. The ultimate constitutional questions in each case were the same: first, the extent to which the Constitution and the Bill of Rights were applicable beyond the boundaries of the United States—the old Insular Cases problem; second, the "Bricker" question—whether the treaty-power may validate by its own force a provision which conflicts with other portions of the Constitution; and third, the venerable issue of the allowable extent of military jurisdiction over civilians.

Justice Clark's majority opinion, substantially delivered for both cases in *Kinsella v. Krueger*, virtually thrust aside treaty and military jurisdiction issues and treated the case as presenting little more than an "Insular" problem. The only major constitutional question, Clark said, was whether an American citizen residing abroad but under the authority of the United States was entitled to trial before an "Article III" Court as a matter of constitutional right. This question the Court answered in the negative. For precedents Clark cited first *American Insurance Company v. Canter*, which had long ago validated the power of Congress to establish legislative-type courts in the territories. He also relied heavily upon *In re Ross* (1891), in which the Court had upheld the constitutional power of Congress to create consular courts overseas having extraterritorial jurisdiction over Americans residing on foreign soil, in which the Court had gone so far as to assert that Americans living abroad had no constitutional rights as such at all. Finally, he briefly cited the Insular Cases, in which the Court had repeatedly denied the applicability of the Bill of Rights to areas which Congress had not "incorporated" within the United States. The Reid case was disposed of in a second brief opinion, on the authority of the Kinsella decision.

In a "reservation" to the majority opinion, Justice Frankfurter observed sharply that the Court had utterly ignored the distinction between the civil and military classes of jurisdiction drawn so incisively in the Toth case. Chief Justice Warren and Justices Black and Douglas dissented outright, stating briefly that by the decision "the military is given powers not hitherto thought consistent with our scheme of government."

A year later, however, the Court in a rehearing on both cases voted six to two to overturn the earlier Reid and Kinsella decisions completely. In *Reid v. Covert* (1957) and *Kinsella v. Krueger* (1957), it now found both defendants to have been tried unconstitutionally and declared that Article 2 (11) of the Uniform Code of Military Justice might not lawfully be applied to civilian trials in capital cases. The Court was so badly divided, however, that there was no majority opinion.

Justice Black, who wrote the "plurality" opinion for himself, Warren, Brennan, and Douglas, developed three points in his argument. First, he categorically extended the protection of the Bill of Rights to citizens subject to United States sovereignty abroad. "We reject the idea," Black declared, "that when the United States acts against citizens abroad it can do so free of the Bill of Rights." The Bill of Rights, in short, followed the flag, so far as citizens were concerned.

Second, Black ruled, treaties were subject to the limits of constitutional supremacy, just as were Acts of Congress. The NATO Status of Forces Agreement between the United States and Great Britain could not act to impair or suspend the constitutional rights of citizens overseas. "No agreement with a foreign nation," he asserted, "can confer power on the Congress, or on any other branch of the government, which is free from the restraints of the Constitution." There was, Black asserted somewhat astonishingly, "nothing new or unique about what we say here." Even *Missouri v. Holland*, he thought, said nothing to the contrary.

Third, Black reinforced his argument with an extensive history of the principle of the subordination of military to civilian authority in Anglo-American law. Quoting *Ex parte Milligan* and *Toth v. Quarles* as his precedents, he pointed out that in the latter case the defendant at least had been in uniform at the time of the alleged offense; here the two defendants "had never served in the Army in any capacity."

Accordingly the Court ordered the two women in question forthwith released from custody. Clark and Burton, now reduced to a dissenting minority of two, argued that an "Article III" trial had not been feasible and that the trial of civilians attached to the Armed Forces overseas was "reasonably related" to the constitutional power of Congress, as set forth in Article I, Section 8, to provide for the trial of persons "in the land and naval forces of the United States."

That the guarantees of the Constitution did not necessarily "follow the flag" for American military personnel stationed overseas, however, became clear a few weeks later when the Court rendered its decision in *Wilson v. Girard* (1957). Private William Girard, while on duty guarding a rifle range in Japan, had killed a Japanese woman scavenging on the range. A dispute thereafter had developed between Japanese officials and United States Army authorities as to jurisdiction over the offense in question. The language of the 1952 Status of Forces Agreement with Japan gave the United States a "primary right" to try American military personnel for offenses committed "in line of duty" but gave Japan jurisdiction over such personnel for "all other offenses." Immediately at issue was the subtle distinction between an offense committed "in line of duty" and an offense "while on duty." After prolonged dispute, the Army and the State Department had waived jurisdiction, whereupon Girard had sought a writ of habeas corpus from a federal district court, whence the matter had come to the Supreme Court for review. Meanwhile American public opinion had become seriously aroused at the prospect that a Japanese court might be allowed to try an American soldier for an "offense" which conceivably amounted to nothing more than a conscientious execution of his orders.

The Court, in a terse, unanimous *per curiam* decision, denied Girard's plea. Under international law, the justices pointed out, a sovereign has exclusive jurisdiction to punish all offenses against its laws committed on its soil. Hence jurisdiction in the ordinary course of events belonged to Japan. Accordingly the Court found "no constitutional or statutory basis" upon which to found an objection to the United States waiver of jurisdiction. Girard, thereafter tried by a Japanese court and convicted of manslaughter, received only a light prison sentence—far lighter, in all probability, than would have been the case had he been tried by an American court-martial.

In any event the Girard case did not touch upon the issue in overseas trials with which the justices obviously were most deeply concerned—court-martial jurisdiction over civilians as against the right of such persons to an Article III trial. But in a series of cases after 1957, a majority of the justices showed themselves determined to give the greatest possible sweep to the force of the second Reid-Covert opinion, so that civilians serving with American armed forces abroad consistently found themselves relieved of the onus of trial by court-martial. A majority of the justices, it was evident, were determined to construe the sweep of military jurisdiction for the armed forces under the grant in Article I, Section 8 as narrowly as possible. And it was now clear, also, that a treaty, no matter how construed, could not weaken the applicable force of the Bill of Rights.

LONG-RANGE SIGNIFICANCE OF THE COLD WAR

For a time in the late 1950's and early 1960's it appeared that the American people were beginning to adjust to the new role of the United States in world affairs and indeed to the Cold War itself as continuing facts of national existence. The internal political, social, and constitutional readjustments required by the new order of things had for the most part been completed, while the sense of psychic shock Americans had for a time experienced in contemplating the new world in which they lived appeared for a time to be passing away.

The fact remained, however, that the new order of things brought about by the revolutionary changes in America's world position showed every evidence of being permanent. The complex alliance system, with its military and economic concommitants, the balance of terror between the two superpowers, and the bloody little second level crises and confrontations, promised to continue for decades to come, in spite of some evidences that the United States and the Soviet Union might eventually achieve a kind of limited *modus vivendi*. And what the subtler long-range meaning of all this was for a constitutional system evolved originally out of an eighteenth-century conception of the nature of sovereignty and limited government no man could tell.

Chapter

32

Civil Liberties in the Cold War Decade: Liberty versus Security

THE DECADE that followed the close of World War II proved to be one of some considerable retrenchment and even retreat on the part of the Supreme Court in the general area of civil liberties. The conservative mood of the moment brought a subtle shift in political values—from a primary concern for individual freedom and the open society to a desire for stability, order, and security. This change found its way into the decisions of the Court, as the majority justices repeatedly gave at least some recognition to the spirit that now dominated the American people. Even the powerful anti-Communist movement, by all odds the most irrational expression of the new demand for security, won some acceptance from the justices, who almost of necessity bent before the storm of public excitement.

The Court, in adjusting its decisions on First Amendment issues to the nation's prevailing conservative mood, resorted repeatedly to two general constitutional concepts: judicial self-restraint and a "balance" between individual and community rights. The doctrine of judicial self-restraint, whose leading proponent now was Justice Frankfurter, had been very well summarized in Justice Stone's famous dissenting aphorism in *United States v. Butler* back in 1936—that "Courts are not the only agency of government that must be assumed to have the capacity to govern." Thus the doctrine required the justices to yield a very large measure of deference to the legislature in critical constitutional questions, to shun the technique formerly so fashionable of writing judicial legislation into the Court's opinions, and to avoid, whenever possible, holding either state or federal legislation unconstitutional. It was by means of judicial self-restraint, for example, that Frankfurter found it possible to reconcile himself to certain dubious provisions of the Taft-Hartley Act and of the Smith Act which otherwise he might have voted to declare unconstitutional.

The other principal instrument of First Amendment conservatism was the new "balancing" philosophy on civil liberties, which, after the war, came very largely to replace the "preferred position" doctrine so popular with Stone, Murphy, Rutledge, and other libertarians in the era after 1937. The Court's conservatives, led by Frankfurter and Jackson, now refused to treat First Amendment liberties as having any absolute or near-absolute character, and instead deliberately "balanced" them against the police power of the states, insisting that on occasion individual liberty must yield to society's desire for order, security, and stability. Justices Black and Douglas still adhered firmly to the older "preferred position" libertarianism, but for the moment, at least, their voices were reduced to those of a dissenting minority. Only in constitutional questions having to do with the rights and liberties of the Negro did the majority justices join them in an insistent judicial activism of the kind that was again to become characteristic of the Court in the Warren era.

CIVIL LIBERTIES AND THE COLD WAR CRUSADE
AGAINST COMMUNISM

Perhaps the most difficult body of First Amendment questions with which the postwar Court had to deal were those arising out of the Cold War crusade against the menace of internal Communism. The anti-Communist movement, it may be observed, was compounded of a modest element of intelligent concern for public security in an age of international conspiracy and espionage and a very large component of emotionalism, irrationalism, and downright hysteria.

The fundamental premise of anti-Communism was fairly simple: It held that the American Communist Party, in cooperation with the Soviet Union, was engaged in a gigantic conspiracy to envelop the United States in a network of espionage, to penetrate the government and pervert and paralyze American politics, and finally to destroy the American constitutional system in violent revolution. There was sufficient truth in all this, as the Hiss, Rosenberg, Coplin, and Abel cases demonstrated, so that it could not be dismissed simply as a tissue of sheer fantasy. Soviet espionage and American Communist Party puppetry did indeed create a genuine security problem—one best handled by F.B.I. counter-intelligence, by security checks administered under proper constitutional safeguards to persons holding "sensitive" government positions, and so on. But that the American Communist Party, an organization that by 1950 had shrunk to less than 20,000 faithful and had lost completely whatever shred of public influence and prestige it had once possessed, could serve as a serious instrument for the violent overthrow of the government of the United States was an idea which could be entertained seriously only by the profoundly naive, the politically unsophisticated, and those with deeply disturbed and confused minds.

Unfortunately, large numbers of the American people were indeed badly frustrated, confused, and disturbed by the fearful social pressures and tensions generated by the new age of crisis and chaos. The consequence was an unhappy interlude of hysteria and repression, in which Senator Joseph McCarthy of Wisconsin could build an impressive political following out of his fabricated charges that the State Department and the Army were riddled with Communist agents; Senator Edward Jenner of Indiana could with political immunity label General George C. Marshall an infamous traitor and a Communist agent; and the head of the rightwing John Birch Society could denounce President Dwight D. Eisenhower as a dedicated instrument of the Communist conspiracy.

The anti-Communist crusade burned itself out after a time, as all irrational social movements must in a reasonably enlightened constitutional democracy, but before it did so it had a severe if temporary repressive impact upon American civil liberties. Both the federal government and the states adopted a great variety of security measures, some of them exceedingly harsh or capricious, intended to guard against the dangers of Red-controlled infiltration, subversion, and revolution. These included the incorporation by Congress of an anti-Communist affidavit provision in the Taft-Hartley Labor Relations Act of 1947; enactment of the McCarran Internal Security Act of 1950 and the Communist Control Act of

1954; prosecution by the Department of Justice of leading Communist Party officials for violation of the sedition sections of the Smith Act of 1940; a series of far-ranging investigations into the Communist menace conducted by the House Committee on Un-American Activities and the Senate Internal Security Sub-Committee; and the adoption by the federal government and the states of a variety of employee security programs intended to ferret out Communists and Communist sympathizers in government service. All of these devices restricted or impaired personal liberty in one fashion or another, and thus posed anew for Court and country the ancient conflict between the authority of the state and private constitutional right.

PROSECUTION OF COMMUNISTS IN THE COURTS: THE DOUDS AND DENNIS CASES

The Court first had occasion to deal with the legal aspects of the postwar anti-Communist drive in *American Communications Association v. Douds* (1950), a case arising out of the registration provisions of the Taft-Hartley Act. This statute, in itself a product in part of the conservative reaction to the New Deal, carried a section requiring labor union officials to file affidavits disavowing membership in the Communist Party. The Communications Union, which had a record of rather serious Communist infiltration, had refused to comply with this provision of the law, and instead attacked it in the courts, claiming that it violated freedom of speech, assembly, and thought as guaranteed by the First Amendment, and also that it constituted a bill of attainder.

However, Chief Justice Vinson's majority opinion found the affidavit requirement to be a constitutional exercise of the federal commerce power. He admitted very frankly that "Congress has undeniably discouraged the lawful exercise of political freedom." However, he said, the Court thought it wise to bow to the considered legislative judgment that the law was necessary to protect commerce against a serious danger of disruptive strikes.

The Court thus saved the constitutionality of the oath requirement by exercising "judicial self-restraint" and by treating it as a commercial regulation rather than as limitation upon free speech. Yet there was a great force in Justice Jackson's concurring comment that "if the statute before us required labor union officers to forswear membership in the Republican Party, the Democratic Party, or the Socialist Party, I suppose all would agree that it was unconstitutional. But why, if it is valid as to the Communist

Party?" Frankfurter, also concurring, thought "Congress had cast its net too indiscriminately" in the law, while Black, dissenting, asserted that the statute despoiled the "fundamental principle" that "beliefs are inviolate."

Far more provocative of constitutional controversy was the Court's decision a year later in *Dennis v. United States* (1951), in which the much-disputed Smith Act passed constitutional muster, as the Court upheld the conviction of eleven principal Communist Party officers under the law.

The Smith Act, technically known as the Alien Registration Act, had been first introduced in 1935 and passed by Congress in 1940, virtually unnoticed in the excitement of the current war crisis. The most significant part of the law, the "advocacy" section, made it unlawful to "advocate, abet, advise, or teach . . . overthrowing any government of the United States by force or violence," forbade publication of printed matter "advising or teaching" such overthrow, prohibited the organization of groups so to teach or to advocate, and forbade conspiracy to commit any of the foregoing acts. Another provision, the so-called "membership clause," forbade "knowing" membership in any group advocating forcible overthrow of the government. The Act did not mention the Communist Party as such, but it was obvious that it had been inspired principally by alarm at Communist activities.

The Smith Act was little used for a number of years, although the government in 1941 procured the conviction under the law of several obscure Minneapolis Trotskyites, and in 1943 it resorted to the act in an indictment and unsuccessful prosecution in a mass trial of some twenty-eight small-time American Fascists.

In 1948, however, the Department of Justice moved against the leadership of the American Communist Party itself, procuring Smith Act indictments against twelve principal party officers. The indictments did not allege any actual conspiracy to overthrow the government by force or violence, but charged merely that the defendants had conspired to form groups advocating such overthrow and had conspired to teach such ideas. Obviously, any rigorous application of the "clear and present danger" doctrine would have made it extremely difficult to sustain the constitutionality of convictions on such a charge. However, the trial court, the court of appeals, and the Supreme Court all subsequently tended to treat the indictments as though they charged direct conspiracy to overthrow the government.

A celebrated trial in New York City before Judge Harold

Medina presently resulted in a verdict of "guilty" for all eleven defendants brought to trial, and the Court of Appeals in turn sustained the conviction. Judge Learned Hand's appellate opinion virtually set aside the "clear and present danger" doctrine, and substituted instead a kind of "sliding scale" rule for sedition cases. The greater the potential evil, he argued, the more remote might be the possibility of its being brought about, and a prosecution nonetheless sustained as constitutional. Such a theory came close to a return to the "bad tendency" doctrine of World War I days. However, the Supreme Court was presently to adopt Judge Hand's standard as its own.

Upon appeal, the Supreme Court, in *Dennis v. United States* (1951), sustained the eleven convictions in question, upheld the constitutionality of the "advocacy" section of the Smith Act, and incorporated Hand's "sliding scale" rule in constitutional law. Nominally Vinson's opinion accepted the "clear and present danger" doctrine; in reality, it destroyed the force of this old Holmes-Brandeis guide rule almost completely. "Obviously," Vinson said, the doctrine "cannot mean that before the government may act, it must wait until the putsch is about to be executed, the plans have been laid, and the signal is awaited." In each case at hand, he continued, "the Court must ask whether the gravity of the 'evil,' discounted by its improbability, justifies such invasion of free speech as is necessary to avoid the evil."

Frankfurter and Jackson concurred in lengthy separate opinions, while Black and Douglas registered brief and bitter dissent. Frankfurter, making it clear that he accepted the constitutionality of the Smith Act only under his rule of deference to legislative discretion, observed soberly that "in sustaining the conviction before us, we can hardly escape restriction on the interchange of ideas." Jackson, on the other hand, advocated junking the "clear and present danger doctrine" outright for conspiracies of the present size and extent, although he would have saved it "for hot-headed speeches on a street-corner . . . or parading by some zealots behind a red flag." Black and Douglas, by contrast, labeled the Smith Act "unconstitutional on its face" as a "virulent form of prior censorship of speech and press," and ridiculed the notion that the Communist Party constituted any real revolutionary threat. Douglas also pointed out carefully that the Court had assumed existence of an actual conspiracy to overthrow the government, although "the fact is that no such evidence was introduced at the trial."

To all intents and purposes, the Court now had revived the "bad tendency" doctrine of World War I under another name. Moreover, it had sanctioned the government's use of a legal weapon whereby it could conceivably destroy the Communist Party completely by prosecuting its principal officers under the law and lodging them safely behind bars.

In the next six years the Department of Justice procured Smith Act conspiracy indictments of some one hundred and twenty-eight "second-string" Communist Party officers. There were "little" Smith Act trials in Seattle, Detroit, Los Angeles, Pittsburgh, New York, Cleveland, Philadelphia, Baltimore, Honolulu, Denver, New Haven, and St. Louis. Nearly one hundred convictions resulted, the government obtaining "guilty" verdicts in practically every instance where the defendant had not already renounced party membership. The government also procured indictments of nine Communists under the membership clause of the Smith Act, and obtained convictions against five of them. Had this process continued for any great length of time, the government might well have destroyed the Party entirely, or at least driven it completely underground. Beginning in 1957, however, the Supreme Court was to administer a series of sharp checks to Smith Act prosecutions, which by the 1960's virtually brought such suits to an end.[1]

LEGISLATION AGAINST THE COMMUNIST PARTY: THE MC CARRAN ACT AND THE COMMUNIST CONTROL ACT

While the Department of Justice proceeded against Communist Party leaders in the courts, members of both parties in Congress hastened to adopt additional anti-Red statutes that would assist in breaking up the Communist conspiracy. In the spring of 1950, after several years of controversy, Congress enacted the so-called Internal Security Act, popularly known as the McCarran Act, a measure of almost incredible complexity, whose basic purpose was to force the Communist Party to register with the government as a "subversive organization."

The McCarran Act first declared that there existed a "world Communist conspiracy," the object of which was to establish a Communist dictatorship in the United States, and that American Communists therefore constituted a "clear and present danger" to the security of the United States. In accordance with this finding of fact, the law then provided for the registration of "Communist-action" and "Communist-front" organizations with a Subversive

---

[1] See p. 976, below.

Activities Control Board.[2] Should a suspected front organization fail to register, the Attorney General was empowered to petition the Board for a registration order, which could then hold hearings and issue such an order if it found that the group in question was indeed an "action" or "front" organization. Board orders, however, were subject to a right of appeals to the courts. Other provisions of the law made it illegal to conspire to establish a "totalitarian dictatorship" in the United States, imposed virtually prohibitive limitations upon the entry into the United States of aliens with Communist connections, and permitted the compulsory detention, after presidential proclamation of an "internal security emergency" and hearing and appeal, of any person who "probably will conspire with others to engage in acts of espionage and sabotage."

President Truman vetoed the McCarran bill, condemning the registration provisions as "the greatest danger to freedom of speech, press, and assembly since the Sedition Act of 1798." In spite of a considerable liberal outcry, however, Congress promptly enacted the bill over Truman's veto by large majorities in both houses. (Ironically, the liberal Democratic bloc in the Senate, anxious not to be tarred with the Communist brush, had pressed for adoption of the security detention provisions of the law.)

The McCarran Act was to prove peculiarly ineffective in actual operation. Although the Subversive Activities Control Board in April, 1953, duly found that the Communist Party was indeed a "Communist front" organization, the Party refused to register. The fifteen-year battle which thereafter ensued in the courts finally was to end in the registration provisions of the law being held unconstitutional. By the time this occurred, both the act and the Board had become virtually dead letters.[3]

Four years after passage of the McCarran Act, in 1954, with Senator McCarthy's "revelations" concerning Communists in the Eisenhower administration rocking the country, a group of Senate liberals led by Hubert Humphrey, apparently hoping to kill off campaign charges that their party was "soft on Communism," introduced a bill to make membership in the Communist Party a crime. The Eisenhower administration strongly opposed the measure, in large part because it feared that it would present individual Communists with a plausible pretext for not registering under the

---

[2] The Communist Control Act of 1954 added a new category of groups required to register—that of "Communist-infiltrated" organizations.

[3] See pp. 911ff., below.

McCarran Act, on the ground that registration now would amount to self-incrimination in violation of the Fifth Amendment. Accordingly, the bill was amended to outlaw the Communist Party but not to make Party membership itself a crime. In this form the bill was enacted into law by an overwhelming vote of both houses.

The Communist Control Act of 1954, as this measure became known, proved to be inoperative from the beginning. It presented numerous grave constitutional questions—conceivably it violated both the First and Fifth Amendments and amounted also to a bill of attainder—and the Department of Justice wisely ignored it, so that no general test of the provisions of the law ever arose.

THE FEDERAL LOYALTY PROGRAM

Far more significant in their immediate impact upon civil liberties were the successive loyalty programs for federal employees launched by the Truman and Eisenhower administrations in an effort to root out Communists and other disloyal and subversive persons from government service.

Federal loyalty programs antedated the postwar Communist scare, having had their beginnings in a series of executive orders beginning in 1940 growing out of wartime security requirements. In 1943, President Roosevelt set up an Interdepartmental Committee on Loyalty Investigations that handled federal loyalty checks for the next several years.

Pressure for a more rigorous executive loyalty program rose sharply in the postwar era. The *Amerasia* scandal, which broke in 1945, seemingly threw serious doubts upon the loyalty of several federal officials, while the defection in Canada about this time of Igor Gouzenko from his Soviet masters exposed the existence of a widespread Communist spy network in North America. The spectacular revelations in the next year or so of Whittaker Chambers and Elizabeth Bentley also served to focus attention on the employee security problem. In the congressional election of 1946, Republican candidates made "Communists in government" an important campaign issue.

Accordingly, in November, 1946, President Truman established a Temporary Commission on Employee Loyalty to investigate the problem and to recommend more effective federal security measures. In March, 1947, in accordance with the Commission's findings, the President issued Executive Order 9835, setting up a comprehensive new federal loyalty program. The order directed the F.B.I. to conduct loyalty checks of all federal employees and to forward any derogatory information to the loyalty boards herewith established in all principal federal bureaus. When any person was accused of disloyalty, the board in question was to conduct hearings to determine whether "reasonable grounds exist for belief that the person involved is disloyal to the United States." Membership in any organization designated by the Attorney General as "totalitarian, Fascist, Communist, or subversive" was to be the principal ground for establishing such belief. An accused person was entitled to a hearing before his board, in which he might be represented by counsel, and to present counter-evidence on his behalf. However, he could not examine the F.B.I. files in question, nor was he entitled to learn the name of his accusers. He did have a right of appeal to his agency head and ultimately to a Loyalty Review Board, whose findings, although technically only advisory, were, in fact, final.

The Truman Loyalty Program was immediately put into general operation. Between 1947 and 1953 the loyalty of some 4,750,000 federal employees was scrutinized, some 26,000 "cases" created thereby being referred to various loyalty boards for further investigation. Of these, some 16,000 were ultimately given loyalty clearance, some 7,000 resigned or withdrew applications while under investigation, and 560 persons were actually removed or denied employment on loyalty charges. Meanwhile several "sensitive" departments and agencies, among them the State, Defense, Army, Navy, Air Force, Commerce, and Justice Departments, the Economic Cooperation Administration, the National Security Resources Board, and the Atomic Energy Commission, each developed its own programs under various special statutory authorizations, while the Attorney General's office by 1953 had designated some 200 organizations as "subversive."

Despite the serious constitutional difficulties implicit in all this, Senator McCarthy's attacks in 1950 charging widespread Communist infiltration of the State Department, put the Truman administration on the defensive once more. Accordingly, in April, 1951, the President issued Executive Order 10241, which inaugurated a new and far more strenuous loyalty program. Fundamental to the new procedures was the provision that an employee now could be discharged after a hearing which found that there was a "reasonable doubt as to the loyalty of the person involved to the Government of the United States." In other words, the government now did not have to prove disloyalty; instead it merely had to find "reasonable doubt" of an employee's loyalty, a far easier task. In the next two years 179 additional federal employees were discharged under the "reasonable doubt" formula.

In spite of these measures, the Republicans made "Communism in government" a major issue in the 1952 election, and President Dwight D. Eisenhower came into office pledged to clean up the Communist "conspiracy" in Washington. On April 27, 1953, accordingly, Eisenhower promulgated Executive Order 10450, setting up still another executive loyalty program. The fundamental criterion for discharge after hearing now became simply a finding that the individual's employment "may not be clearly consistent with the interests of national security." Seven categories of "security criteria" were set up. These included sexual immorality and perversion; drug addiction; conspiracy or acts of sabotage, treason or unauthorized disclosure of classified information; and refusal to testify before authorized government bodies on grounds of possible self-incrimination. Obviously these offenses involved much more than mere disloyalty or possible Communist affiliation; instead, they covered virtually every possible ground on which an employee might be released as unsatisfactory. In October, 1954, the Eisenhower administration announced that there had been more than 8,000 security program releases under the President's order, but it soon became clear that only 315 persons had actually been discharged for loyalty reasons.

Both the Truman and Eisenhower loyalty programs provoked serious constitutional controversy. Critics charged that the programs violated procedural due process in that persons were too often discharged for "a state of mind" rather than for an overt act; that "evidence" of disloyalty often consisted of nothing more than "guilt by association"; that the accused was often the victim of "faceless informers" whom he could neither confront nor cross-examine; and that the programs in the large amounted to a form of virulent censorship seriously at odds with the First Amendment. They also argued that the Attorney General's List of Subversive Organizations constituted virtually an executive bill of attainder.

In reply, the defenders of the programs pointed out that the Supreme Court itself had repeatedly held that there was no constitutional right of federal employment and that the government had an undoubted right to assure itself of the loyalty of its public servants. Opponents of loyalty programs, they said, had confused the hearings with criminal proceedings, which they were not, for they made no finding of guilt and inflicted no punishment. Seth W. Richardson, Chairman of the Loyalty Review Board, argued further that the F.B.I. could not investigate disloyalty effectively if it were obliged to reveal its sources of information. And as for guilt by association, he said, its use amounted to no more than recognition of the old adages that "birds of a feather flock together" and "a man is known by the company he keeps."

The Supreme Court long demonstrated a distinct reluctance to come to grips with the central constitutional issues involved in loyalty programs, probably because of the justices' natural reluctance to move against a coordinate branch of the government. Strangely, in two early cases, *Bailey v. Richardson* (1951) and *Joint Anti-Fascist Committee v. McGrath* (1951), the Court came closer to attacking the vital constitutional questions at stake than it was to do again for some time.

In the Bailey case, the justices were confronted with a decision of the Court of Appeals of the District of Columbia holding that a loyalty board ruling barring an employee of the Federal Security Agency from federal employment for three years constituted a bill of attainder, and so was unconstitutional. The Appeals Court had sustained the removal under the well-recognized principle that there is no constitutional right to federal employment and that due process in removal was therefore not necessary. Nor was the First Amendment any bar to removal, since it had long been established that the Constitution did not bar removals from office for political reasons.

The Supreme Court confirmed the Bailey decision, four to four without opinion. However, in their opinions in the McGrath case, Black, Douglas, and Jackson all took occasion to condemn the procedures in the Bailey removal as illustrative of the fashion in which "the entire loyalty program grossly deprives government employees of the benefits of constitutional safeguards."

In the McGrath case, several justices cast a pall of doubt upon the Attorney General's List of Subversive Organizations. The plaintiff organization had sued to remove its name from the list, and the Court, by a vote of five to three, sustained this plea. Justice Burton's opinion, avoiding constitutional questions, held merely that the presidential order establishing the loyalty program had not authorized the Attorney General arbitrarily to designate an organization as subversive without other justification. But Justices Black, Frankfurter, Douglas, and Jackson in concurring opinions all attacked directly the constitutionality of the list as "an evil type of censorship," as "a violation of the First Amendment," as an "executive bill of attainder," and as involving procedures "so devoid of fundamental fairness as to offend the due process clause of the Fifth Amendment."

The Bailey and McGrath decisions seemingly implied that the Court stood on the verge of a comprehensive analysis and probable condemnation of the constitutionality of federal loyalty programs generally. Instead, however, the Court for the next several years disposed of successive loyalty cases upon marginal technical grounds. Thus in *Peters v. Hobby* (1956), a case involving a Yale professor of medicine discharged by a Loyalty Review Board as a security risk and barred from federal employment for three years, the Court held merely that his discharge was without authorization under Executive Order 9835 and that he was entitled to have the Board finding expunged from the government records. However, since his original term of employment had expired, he was not entitled to be rehired.

And in *Cole v. Young* (1956), the Court reversed the discharge of an inspector in the Food and Drug Administration who had been released on the ground that his employment was "not clearly consistent with the national interest." This procedure, the Court held, although authorized by the Summary Suspension Act of 1950, properly applied only to "sensitive" positions involving "possible internal subversion and foreign aggression." Since Cole's position had been a "non-sensitive" one, his discharge had been unlawful. Both the Peters and Cole opinions carefully skirted the crucial constitutional questions involved. Not until several more years had passed, when the furore over loyalty programs had largely died down, did the Court finally come to grips with the fundamental constitutional issues they posed.

STATE LOYALTY PROGRAMS

When it came to state loyalty programs, however, the Court early showed far less reluctance to confront the major constitutional questions at issue. Such programs, developed like those of the federal government in response to the pressures and tensions of the McCarthy era, generally had as their starting point a loyalty oath whereby the government employee, under pain of discharge, was obliged formally to swear to a denial of membership in the Communist Party and other subversive organizations, and to repudiate belief in any doctrine of the revolutionary overthrow of the government by force and violence. Quite generally, also, state loyalty programs provided for the discharge of employees who, as witnesses before legislative investigating committees, refused to answer questions about Communist Party affiliation. Needless to say, such programs required the discharge of persons exposed as having Communist Party or other affiliations.

In the early 1950's a conservative Court majority worked out a fairly consistent body of constitutional law with respect to state loyalty programs. Their position rested on the premise that there was no inherent right to state employment, and that the states had a constitutional right to obtain adequate assurance, by oath, affidavit, and the like, that an employee was not engaged in subversive activity and did not subscribe to the overthrow of the federal or state government by force or violence. The majority justices imposed only one sure constitutional limitation upon such affidavits—they must require the disavowal only of *knowing* membership in subversive organizations, as contrasted with membership innocent of any understanding of subversive purpose. On occasion, also, the Court viewed with suspicion oaths requiring retroactive disavowal of subversive affiliations, although this was not enough to condemn a loyalty statute out of hand. In any event, the Court as a rule held discharges for refusal to testify as to Party affiliation to be constitutional, if accompanied by adequate procedural safeguards. Justices Black and Douglas dissented with fair consistency from the majority position, holding that state loyalty programs violated First Amendment guarantees, that provisions requiring retroactive disavowal of subversive membership constituted bills of attainder, and that loyalty discharges also violated procedural due process of law.

The majority position in state loyalty programs first became clear in *Gerende v. Election Board* (1951), a case involving the constitutionality of a Maryland law requiring every candidate for public office to file an affidavit disavowing belief in overthrow of the government by force and violence and membership in any subversive organization. The Court in a *per curiam* decision held the law constitutional—on the specific assurance of the Maryland attorney general that the law required disavowal only of "knowing" membership in such organizations.

A few weeks later, in *Garner v. Board of Public Works* (1951), the Court upheld the validity of a Los Angeles city ordinance requiring employees to disavow by affidavit their belief in violent overthrow and also to execute an oath that they had not belonged to any subversive organization for the past five years. Justice Clark's majority opinion once more drew vital distinction between "knowing" and innocent membership, but brushed aside the contention that the retroactive feature of the law constituted it a bill of attainder. Justice Frankfurter, dissenting in part, thought the law did not distinguish adequately between knowing and innocent membership, while Burton, Black, and Douglas, dissenting, argued that the retroactive feature condemned the measure as a bill of attainder similar to those held void in *Cummings v. Missouri* and *Ex Parte Garland*.

The following year, in *Adler v. Board of Education* (1952), the conservative justices prevailed once more, as the Court passed favorably upon the highly controversial New York Feinberg Law. This statute, enacted in 1949, implemented an earlier provision of the state code that prohibited the appointment of any person who advocated or taught the overthrow of the government of the United States by force and violence. The law required the State Board of Regents to publish a list, after notice and hearing, of all subversive organizations advocating such overthrow. Membership in any such organization thereafter was to constitute prima facie evidence of such advocacy and to disbar the individual in question from either appointment or retention as a public-school teacher.

Justice Minton, speaking for the majority, restated the oft-repeated dictum that there was no constitutional right to public employment, and went on to find it to be "both the right and the duty" of public-school authorities "to screen . . . teachers . . . as to their fitness to maintain the integrity of the public schools as part of an ordered society." The Court undoubtedly had been influenced by the fact that the law contained no retroactive features, provided for the listing of subversive organizations only after notice and hearing, and permitted teachers to offer evidence of innocent membership. Black and Douglas, in dissent, nonetheless attacked the law as another of "those rapidly multiplying legislative enactments that make it dangerous—this time for schoolteachers—to think or say anything except what a transient majority thinks at the moment."

Only when a statute imposed retroactive disavowal which at the same time failed to distinguish between innocent and knowing subversive membership did the justices unite to strike the offensive enactment down. Thus in *Wieman v. Updegraff* (1952), the Court unanimously declared void a retroactive disavowal oath for teachers and state officers that failed to make such distinction. Clark's opinion, emphasizing the critical difference between the present law and those in the Garner and Adler cases, declared

sternly that "indiscriminate classification of innocent with knowing activity must fall as an assertion of arbitrary power."

But the Updegraff decision was an exception to the trend of the
times. It was the Adler opinion that symbolized the postwar Court
approach to the disavowal of subversion. Significantly, this decision was to stand for fifteen years, until the Warren Court,
animated by vastly different values in a profoundly changed era,
finally struck it down.[4]

POSTWAR CONSERVATISM IN CIVIL LIBERTIES: PICKETING

The same general conservatism that manifested itself in the postwar Court's treatment of the problems of Communism and subversion were evident also in its approach to a variety of other civil
liberties questions, among them picketing, freedom of assembly,
and group libel.

The shift in the majority justices' point of view was particularly
apparent in their treatment of the problem of picketing. It will be
recalled that beginning in *Senn v. Tile Layers Union* (1937) and
later in *Thornhill v. Alabama* (1940) and *American Federation of
Labor v. Swing* (1941), the New Deal Court had taken the position that peaceful picketing was a form of free communication
protected by the First Amendment and that the states under no
circumstances could prohibit or enjoin it. Only in *Carpenter and
Joiners' Union v. Ritter's Cafe* (1942), had the Court majority,
led by Justice Frankfurter, implied that picketing might involve
something more than mere free expression, and that as a consequence the states under some circumstances might subject it to
regulation under their police power.

It was the Frankfurter view of the matter that came to prevail
more and more in the postwar decade, as the Court moved toward
a new position—that picketing was so bound up with elements of
economic coercion, restraint of trade, labor relations, and other
social and economic problems that a very large measure of discretion in regulating it must be restored to the states. Only a minority
of justices, which included on occasion Black, Minton, and Reed,
maintained the old "picketing is pure free speech" position, and
even they admitted that picketing in a context of violence, disorder, or conspiracy for grossly unlawful ends might be prohibited.

The Court's first clear recognition in the postwar era that picketing involved something more than mere communication came in
Giboney v. Empire Storage and Ice Co. (1949). Here the Court,

---

[4] See the discussion of *Keyishian v. Board of Regents* (1967), pp. 927f., below.

speaking through Justice Black, unanimously sustained a Missouri injunction prohibiting picketing that had been intended to force an employer into an agreement in violation of the state's anti-trust laws. "It is clear," said Black, "that appellants were doing more than exercising a right of free speech or press. . . . They were exercising their economic power to compel Empire [Storage] to abide by union rather than state regulation of trade."

A possible implication of the Giboney decision was that a state might regulate or prohibit picketing whenever it was directed toward ends the state considered socially undesirable. The following year, in *Hughes v. Superior Court* (1950) and *International Brotherhood of Teamsters v. Hanke* (1950), the Court gave overt expression to this doctrine. In the Hughes case, the Court, speaking through Justice Frankfurter, sustained an injunction against peaceful picketing carried on with the objective of forcing a supermarket to hire Negroes on a racial quota basis. No statute prohibited quota hiring, and the case differed sharply from the Giboney precedent in that the injunction at issue rested merely upon the judge's decision that the picketing involved violated sound public policy and not upon any formal legislative prohibition.

Justice Frankfurter's opinion first enunciated the new "conservative" theory of picketing. "While picketing is a mode of communication," he said, "it is inseparably something more and different." "It sought," he said, "to exert influences, and it produces consequences, different from other modes of communication." A racial quota system, he added, was a matter for proper regulation by the state's police power, and if California wanted to establish a policy "against involuntary employment along racial lines," it could prohibit picketing for that objective.

In the Hanke case, the majority justices virtually adopted the position that a state might prohibit picketing even when directed to an end in itself perfectly lawful. The case involved an injunction prohibiting picketing intended to compel the self-employed proprietor of a small auto shop to adopt the union shop. Labeling picketing a "hybrid" of free speech and "other elements," Frankfurter emphasized the Court's "growing awareness that these cases involved not so much questions of free speech as review of the balance struck by a state between picketing that involved more than 'publicity' and competing interests of public policy." Not surprisingly, Black, Minton, and Reed dissented, pointing out quite accurately that the Court now had virtually abandoned the position that peaceful picketing for lawful purposes was a form of free speech protected by the First Amendment.

Any remaining doubt concerning the Court's new position vanished in *International Brotherhood of Teamsters, Local 695 v. Vogt* (1957), in which the justices sustained a Wisconsin injunction issued in pursuance of a state statute prohibiting peaceful picketing directed against an employer in the absence of a labor dispute. While Frankfurter admitted that a state could not "enact blanket regulations against picketing," it was nonetheless entitled to exercise virtually unlimited discretion in controlling the social objectives for which picketing was conducted. Since there was a "rational basis for the inferences" the Wisconsin court had drawn concerning "the purpose of the picketing," the injunction was lawful. Black and Douglas, dissenting, protested that "the Court had now come full circle," and "today . . . signs the formal surrender." Thus with the Vogt decision, picketing virtually ceased to be a First Amendment right, the Court recognizing instead an all but unlimited power in the several states to regulate the practice for whatever rational purpose they wished. An important phase of the latter New Deal constitutional era thereby passed into history.

OTHER FIRST AMENDMENT ISSUES: FREEDOM OF ASSEMBLY, PAMPHLET-PEDDLING, GROUP LIBEL, AND CAPTIVE AUDIENCES

The same tendency to restore a large measure of discretionary police power to the states so apparent in the Court's review of picketing practices was evident also in its treatment of a variety of First Amendment cases involving assembly, pamphlet-peddling, and group libel laws. Here, after some initial uncertainty, the Court emphasized very heavily the "balancing" argument—that First Amendment rights were not to be considered as absolute or even preferred, but rather must be weighed against the right of the state to protect the public welfare.

In *Terminiello v. Chicago* (1949), the Court was confronted with a peculiarly difficult aspect of the conflict between First Amendment rights and the interest of the community in protecting law and order. Terminiello, an unfrocked priest of extreme right-wing sentiments, had been convicted of disorderly conduct following a public address in Chicago, in which he had attacked his Jewish opponents as "filthy scum," and had accused them of an organized conspiracy to inoculate the entire German population with syphilis. The speech had produced a near riot, which in turn had led to Terminiello's arrest and trial. The circumstances of Terminiello's conviction were peculiar, however, in that the actual disturbance had been precipitated not by Terminiello or his followers but by persons in his audience outraged by what he had to say. The case thus produced a nice constitutional question: Could a speaker, himself guilty of no disorder, be punished for a breach of the peace on the part of those who objected to ideas he expressed?

By a vote of five to four, the Court, applying the "clear and present danger" doctrine, overturned Terminiello's conviction. Justice Douglas' majority opinion was extraordinary in that it turned upon a point not even raised in the lower courts—the constitutionality of the Illinois statute under which Terminiello had been tried. The trial judge, interpreting the law for the jury, had asserted that it made punishable "speech which stirs the public to anger, invites dispute, brings about a condition of unrest or creates a disturbance."

So construed, Douglas said, the Illinois law was unconstitutional. The right of free speech, he admitted, was "not absolute," but it could be suppressed only in the face of a "clear and present danger of a serious and substantive evil that rises far above public inconvenience, annoyance, or unrest." The opinion made it quite clear that Douglas thought it intolerable to punish a person merely because his ideas led to violence on the part of those who resented what he said. Vinson, Frankfurter, Jackson, and Burton dissented, their opinions attacking the majority decision for declaring unconstitutional a statute whose validity technically was not before the Court at all, and for the majority justices' "doctrinaire" disregard of the rights of the states in free speech matters. Jackson, in particular, castigated the Court's decision, warning that the majority had best beware, lest its destruction of state police power "turn the Bill of Rights into a suicide pact."

Two years later, in *Feiner v. New York* (1951), the conservative Terminiello minority became a majority, as the Court wrote Jackson's argument into law. The Feiner case involved conviction of a street orator under a New York statute forbidding speaking on the streets "with intent to provoke a breach of the peace." The facts closely resembled those in Terminiello, in that the disturbance had been created not by the speaker but by persons who resented the defendant's remarks. Chief Justice Vinson's majority opinion affirming the conviction pointed out that the lower courts had found evidence of a "genuine attempt to arouse Negro people against the whites," while there was no evidence that the police had interfered merely because of the opinions Feiner had expressed. Black, Douglas, and Minton dissented, Black protesting that the "petitioner has been sentenced to the penitentiary for the unpopular views he expressed," so that "this conviction makes a mockery of the free speech guarantees of the First and Fourteenth Amendments."

Meanwhile, in a series of pamphlet-peddling cases, the Court moved back very close to the position it had occupied in *Jones v. Opelika* (1942), only to abandon it in *Murdock v. Pennsylvania* and *Martin v. Struthers* the following year—that the commercial element in door-to-door solicitation was sufficiently prominent to justify a city license requirement even when elements of freedom of religion or freedom of speech were involved. Thus in *Breard v. Alexandria* (1951), the Court sustained a municipal ordinance forbidding canvassers from calling upon private residences except when invited to do so. Justice Reed's opinion for the majority asserted that "opportunists, for private gain, cannot be permitted to arm themselves with an acceptable principle, such as . . . freedom of the press, and proceed to use it as an iron standard to crush the living rights of others to privacy and repose." Here again was the same regard for state police power and community order which the Court now so frequently manifested. Black and Douglas, the remnant of the Murdock and Struthers majority, dissented on the ground that the Court had departed from those precedents.

The following year, in *Beauharnais v. Illinois* (1952), the Court moved still farther toward a recognition of state police power discretion in pamphlet-peddling, when it accepted the constitutionality of an Illinois criminal libel law. The law in question forbade the distribution of printed material that "exposes the citizens of any race, color, creed, or religion to contempt, derision, or obloquy, or which is productive of breach of the peace or riots." The defendant, head of a so-called "White Circle League," had been convicted under the law after distributing inflammatory pamphlets calling for "one million self-respecting white people to unite to prevent the white race from being mongrelized by the Negro."

By a five to four vote, the Court upheld the conviction. Justice Frankfurter's opinion for the majority developed the somewhat novel idea of "group libel" in defense of the statute. He first quoted with approval the Cantwell and Chaplinsky opinions upholding the right of the state to punish expressions of "the lewd and obscene, the profane, the libelous and the insulting or 'fight-ing' words." If the state properly could punish language of this kind when aimed at an individual, Frankfurter observed, then the Court could not "deny the state power to punish the same utter-ances directed at a defined group."

Obviously the concept of "group libel" greatly broadened state police power at the expense of First Amendment rights, and Black, Douglas, Reed, and Jackson all entered strenuous dissents. Black and Douglas protested that the Court's new dictum "degrades the First Amendment to a 'rational basis' level," by which they meant that instead of applying the "preferred position" doctrine the ma-jority now balanced First Amendment rights against the state police power. Jackson's criticism was different and more con-servative: he thought the Court should apply the "clear and present danger" test in cases of this kind.

In *Burstyn v. Wilson* (1952), however, the Court refused to apply the group libel principle to validate censorship of a movie whose theme was particularly offensive to certain religious sects. The case involved a much controverted film, *The Miracle*, an Italian production portraying the seduction of a half-witted peasant girl by a man whom she believes to be St. Joseph, and the subse-quent "miraculous" birth of her child. The New York Board of Regents, charged by law with film censorship in that state, had first licensed the film's exhibition and then rescinded the license after a strenuous campaign by Catholic officialdom denouncing the picture as "a sacrilegious and blasphemous mockery of Chris-tian religious truth." The Regents had acted under a New York law that made it unlawful to "treat any religion with contempt, mockery or ridicule." Conceivably the Court could have accepted the statute as a prohibition against group criminal libel like that in *Beauharnais v. Illinois*.

Instead, the Court, speaking through Justice Clark, unanimously declared New York's censorship of *The Miracle* to be a violation of the First Amendment. Clark's opinion, surprisingly, resorted to the now all-but-abandoned "preferred position" doctrine to assert that a state could not ban a film merely as "sacrilegious." Such a standard, Clark said, would set both censors and courts "adrift upon a boundless sea of conflicting religious views" and might well result in favoring one religion against another in violation of the First Amendment prohibition on religious "establishment."

The Miracle decision was one of the very few occasions in which the postwar Court abandoned its generally conservative position on the relationship between the First Amendment and state police power. Unquestionably the justices in reaching their conclusion had been influenced very heavily by the fact that the connection between censorship and the campaign for suppression staged by organized religion had been uncomfortably close. For the moment, the decision gave films a very broad right of F st Amendment immunity, an immunity that stood until the Wa en Court modified it substantially nearly a decade later.[5]

"Captive audience" cases involved the Court in still anouner phase of the attempt to balance state police power and First Amendment rights. At issue was the constitutionality of state laws or city ordinances attempting to regulate or forbid sound trucks, street amplifying devices, and advertising broadcasts on public vehicles. Cases of this kind were especially perplexing in that they involved conflict between two sets of First Amendment rights— that of freedom of expression, as against a contrary right of individuals not to be compelled to listen against their will to the utterances of others. The Court after some uncertainty solved this problem by recognizing a broad right of regulation in the states, without, however, insisting outright that "captive audience" techniques categorically violated a First Amendment-guaranteed right of privacy.

The captive audience question first reached the Court in *Saia v. New York* (1948), in which the justices voted five to four to strike down a city ordinance giving the chief of police discretionary power to license sound trucks and amplifying equipment in the public parks. Justice Douglas' opinion treated the law as a simple instance of "prior license" and studiously ignored any question of a contrary right of the listener to privacy. Frankfurter, with whom Reed and Burton joined in dissent, protested that "surely there is not a constitutional right to force other people to listen." Jackson, dissenting even more forcibly, warned that the majority position actually threatened to make the very right of free speech "ridiculous and obnoxious."

A year later, in *Kovacs v. Cooper* (1949), the Court overturned the Sa a precedent almost completely, holding constitutional a Trenton ordinance that prohibited outright the operation of sound truck emitting "loud and raucous noises." Justice Reed's opinion made it evident that he thought it a perversion of the right of free speech to guarantee sound trucks a captive audience. "The unwill-

---

[5] See pp. 968, 969f., below.

ing listener," he said, "is practically helpless to escape this interference with his privacy except through the protection of municipal regulation." It was not quite clear from this whether sound trucks that did not emit "loud and raucous noises" also could be constitutionally banned, but Frankfurter and Jackson, concurring, treated the Saia precedent as rightfully reversed.

However, the new majority was not quite willing to defend a categorical right of privacy in the absence of regulatory legislation. This became clear in *Public Utilities Commission v. Pollak* (1952), in which the Court reversed a District of Columbia Court of Appeals decision which had held that the practice of Washington bus companies in playing radio programs on their vehicles violated a Fifth Amendment-guaranteed right of privacy. Burton's opinion for the six majority justices rejected this argument, and denied also that such broadcasts violated the First Amendment unless the companies were to broadcast government propaganda. Oddly, Justice Douglas, who had consistently defended sound trucks against government regulation, now dissented, expressing the conviction that "the sanctity of thought and belief" implicit in the First Amendment made it imperative to recognize "a constitutional right to be left alone."

SEPARATION OF CHURCH AND STATE:
RELIGION IN THE SCHOOLS

A particularly explosive issue involving First Amendment rights was that which arose out of a series of cases involving state support of one sort or another for organized religion in either parochial or public schools. The amendment's prohibition on an "establishment of religion" and its guarantee of religious freedom had been at issue at least peripherally in several cases of the later New Deal era, notably in the Flag Salute Cases and in those dealing with the peddling of religious books. Now, however, the Court confronted the far more controversial question of just how far cooperation between church and state might go without violating one or both of the amendment's injunctions on the subject.

The root of the controversy lay in the difficulty of defining precisely the line of separation between church and state in American life. Almost no one disagreed in the abstract with the principle of separation, which had led to the First Amendment's prohibition upon "establishment." Yet the fact was that church and state historically had rubbed shoulders in a variety of ways. There were chaplains in Congress, in the armed forces, and in state legislatures;

the states often granted tax exemption to church property and gave some support, direct or indirect, to parochial schools, and so on. Each of these points of contact was potentially one of public debate and dispute.

The postwar controversy over "religion in the schools" arose out of a sharp and growing division of public opinion in America between certain conservative and liberal groups over the appropriate role of religion in public life. The prevailing "Cold War" atmosphere promoted the conviction of a great many religious minded people, already alarmed at the growth of secularism in American life, that the country was in danger of losing its religious heritage because of hostility on the part of the state, that the public schools were "Godless" or irreligious, and that the state ought to counter secularism and irreligion either by providing religious instruction in the public schools or at least through active cooperation with the churches in their programs of religious instruction.

In response to pressures generated by religious conservatives, state assistance to religion in the public schools—through school prayers, classes in religion, or released time—grew very rapidly in the decade after the war. A survey conducted by the National Education Association in 1956 found that about half of the states had statutes which either recognized or permitted the reading of the Bible in the public schools. A 1961 survey was to show that about one-third of the nation's school districts required classroom prayers, this practice being most common in the South and Northeast. Released-time programs existed in some 2,600 communities scattered through forty-three states. Programs of this kind badly frightened many liberal Protestants and most persons of Jewish faith, who saw in them a serious threat to that separation of church and state which protected an important aspect of their personal liberties.

A closely related issue was that of federal and state aid to parochial schools. A protracted and recurrent controversy went on in Congress over this question, as supporters of parochial school aid, conceding that direct federal appropriations to church-supported schools posed monumental constitutional and political difficulties, concentrated their efforts on bills providing for subsidies for bus transportation, school lunches, free textbooks, and so on. Such measures, their supporters argued, appropriated money for children without regard to where they went to school and were therefore constitutional. This approach achieved some modest successes. Thus the School Lunch Act of 1946, which included parochial schools in its grant-in-aid program to the states, won large support in Congress and something like general public approval.

On the other hand, a series of bills introduced by Representative Ralph Barden of North Carolina, providing for large-scale grants-in-aid to state public-school programs, generally met defeat year after year, in considerable part because of Catholic opposition to provisions specifically barring assistance to parochial schools as unconstitutional. When Eleanor Roosevelt in her newspaper column expressed approval of this feature of the 1949 Barden bill as compatible with the principle of separation of church and state, Cardinal Spellman of New York wrote her a bitter public letter charging her with giving vent to anti-Catholic prejudice. Their subsequent public reconciliation did nothing to heal the underlying deadlock in national policy, which was to continue scarcely unmitigated for the next two decades. Meanwhile the issue of aid to parochial schools was fought out also in one fashion or another in a majority of the nation's state legislatures.

The approach of the postwar Court to the "religion in the schools" question was essentially cautious and somewhat conservative. Except in one or two instances where the issue of an "establishment of religion" was clear cut the justices showed themselves inclined to compromise. Thus by divided votes the Court gave somewh t questioning approval both to tax-supported parochial school busing and to a released-time program.

It was the busing question that first brought the "religion in the schools" controversy before the Court. At issue in *Everson v. Board of Education* (1947) was the procedure set up by a local New Jersey school board, in accordance with the provisions of a 1941 state law, authorizing the reimbursement of parents who paid school bus expenses either to public schools or to Catholic parochial schools. By a five to four vote the Court held both board rule and state law to be constitutional. Justice Black's opinion for the majority justices first paid homage at some length to Jefferson's celebrated proposition that "the clause against the establishment of religion by law was intended to erect 'a wall of separation' between church and state." But then, somewhat surprisingly in view of the earlier tenor of his argument, Black found that while the law and board rule might well "approach the limits" of the state's discretionary power, they were nonetheless constitutional.

Jackson, Frankfurter, Rutledge, and Burton all dissented. Jackson, with whom Frankfurter concurred, observed sharply that the language of the majority opinion reminded him of Byron's heroine

Julia, who "whispering 'I will ne'er consent'—consented." And Rutledge, in a lengthy historical review, concluded that the New Jersey law did indeed violate the establishment clause as Jefferson had construed it and that it was unconstitutional.

In spite of the Court's somewhat hesitant concession in the Everson case, it soon became evident that nearly all the justices were still strongly committed to a fairly broad interpretation of the establishment prohibition in the First Amendment. In *McCollum v. Board of Education* (1948), the Court held unconstitutional an elaborately organized system of religious instruction in the public schools of Champaign, Illinois. The program in question was carried on by a private organization, the Champaign Council on Religious Education. But Justice Black's opinion pointed out that the classes in question were held in tax-supported buildings with instructors subject to approval by the superintendent of schools, so that "the State's compulsory education system thus assists and is integrated with the program of religious instruction carried on by separate religious sects." Such an arrangement, Black concluded, "falls squarely under the ban of the First Amendment." Justice Reed alone dissented, arguing that the Court had broken with the traditional interpretation of the establishment clause.

On the other hand, in *Zorach v. Clauson* (1952), the Court accepted a New York City released-time program as constitutional. Justice Douglas' majority opinion, carefully distinguishing the present circumstances from those in the McCollum case, pointed out that the New York program operated outside school property and without school personnel and did not involve the use either of public buildings or public teachers. "The wall of separation" between church and state, he said, was not absolute. Americans, Douglas added, were "a religious people whose institutions presuppose a Supreme Being," and he thought it "obtuse reasoning" to use the First Amendment to support a "philosophy of hostility to religion." Black, Frankfurter, and Jackson all dissented, Jackson observing rather bitterly that "the wall of separation between church and state has become even more warped and twisted than I anticipated."

The Everson, McCollum, and Clauson cases hardly settled the constitutional aspects of "religion in the schools" or the impact of the establishment and freedom of religion clauses upon American society generally. Controversy over church-state relations and religion in the schools was to continue into the 1960's, when the

Warren Court was to re-enter the controversy and precipitate a powerful new public debate on the whole question.

By the late 1950's the political atmosphere in the United States was changing perceptibly once more. The "Red Scare," somehow badly discredited and in disrepute after Senator McCarthy's disastrous encounter with the brilliant attorney Joseph Welch in the 1954 Senate hearings on Communism in the Army, was rapidly receding into the background. The Cold War hardly had faded, but its internal political consequences underwent alteration, as the American people learned to live with the fact of what appeared to be permanent international involvement and even the hideous threat of hydrogen warfare.

Meanwhile a host of internal social problems pressed in upon the nation, while the Court, entering upon a new and almost unprecedented era of judicial activism under the leadership of Chief Justice Earl Warren, found itself involved in its attempted solution in a fashion that had never occurred before. The first major symptom of the Court's new activism was its extraordinary leadership in attacking the plight of the American Negro. Indeed, the Court's attempt to solve the problem of racial segregation by judicial decision played a major part in precipitating a new constitutional, political, and social revolution in the status of the black American.

Chapter

33

The Constitution, the Warren Court, and the "Black Revolution"

THE PROFOUND REVOLUTION in the status of the Negro, which assumed such prominence in American national life in the generation after World War II, had its roots deep in the republic's history. Even in the decades after 1890, when the black American's old Reconstruction dream of first-class citizenship sank to a cruel nadir, there were silent forces at work beneath the surface to improve the Negro's economic and social position in American life.

Thus in the opening years of the twentieth century, a Negro professional and white-collar class made its appearance in the larger northern cities, its ranks steadily augmented by the black American's access to universal free public education, his passionate thirst for knowledge and self-improvement, and his capacity, once properly trained, to gain access to first-class universities and professional schools. In spite of fearful discrimination, the new Negro elite steadily built up its resources in property, education, and professional status, and entered more and more into a middle-class way of life generally.

By the 1920's, the Negro population in certain northern cities, its ranks augmented by the heavy migration out of the South incident to World War I, was substantial enough to wield some political power. In Chicago, Negroes traded votes with Mayor William Hale Thompson's corrupt urban political machine for jobs in the police department and the city bureaucracy, a lax policy toward rent evictions, equal access to certain bathing beaches and parks, and a primitive but fairly effective system of poor relief. Similar informal alliances prevailed in New York between Negroes and Tammany Hall and in Philadelphia between that city's long-established black population in the Vare organization.

The New Deal gave the Negro his first taste of national political power. Black Americans suffered frightfully in the Great Depression, and when the Democrats swept into office in 1933, Negroes abandoned for the most part their allegiance to the Republican Party and entered into the loose coalition of labor union members, unemployed workers, intellectuals, farmers, and traditional southern Democrats upon which Franklin Roosevelt rested his potent New Deal organization. Support for F.D.R. yielded Negroes numerous positions in the lower ranks of the federal bureaucracy, easy access to W.P.A. jobs and welfare rolls, admission to public housing projects, and improved economic security generally, in another demonstration of the intimate relationship between political influence and social betterment.

World War II vastly accelerated the forces at work to improve the Negro's position in the country. The severe labor shortage increased the demand for black workers and served thereby to break down at least some of the barriers to the entry of Negroes into various craft unions, the professions, and higher-paid jobs generally. In addition, certain labor leaders, those of the CIO in particular, deliberately destroyed the "color line" in their unions, often not without substantial resistance from their rank-and-file membership.

Meanwhile the Roosevelt administration, uncomfortably aware of the stark contrast between the easy professions of equalitarianism in its wartime propaganda and the shocking reality of widespread racial injustice in the country, moved cautiously toward a limited policy of integration. At the President's instance, the government expanded the employment of Negroes in the federal bureaucracy, established by executive order in 1941 a Fair Employment Practices Commission, wrote "no discrimination" clauses into war contracts, and in a few instances allowed Negroes to qualify for officers' commissions in racially unsegregated units in the armed forces. More important than any of this, perhaps, was the silent change taking place in the minds and hearts of millions of white

Americans who were rapidly coming to realize that segregation and economic discrimination based upon race were anachronisms in a twentieth-century democracy.

By 1945, the revolution in the position of the Negro had become too powerful to be halted, and in the ensuing decades it swept forward in a vast new tide of constitutional, economic, and social change. Taking advantage of their new-found political and economic power, Negro leaders staged a massive assault in the courts upon the citadels of legalized segregation and discrimination, in education, transportation, voting, and housing. The black American's principal instrument in this campaign was the Legal Defense and Educational Fund of the National Association for the Advancement of Colored People, generally known simply as the NAACP. Under the leadership of Thurgood Marshall, the Defense Fund's brilliant general counsel, the NAACP "marched on the Supreme Court," where it won victory after victory in its drive to realize the first Justice Harlan's famous dissenting dictum—that "the Constitution is color-blind."

Both in the Vinson and Warren eras, the Supreme Court manifested an extraordinary consistency in its condemnation of legalized segregation. In marked contrast to the numerous rifts and divisions that characterized their approach to such varied problems as Communist political activity, legislative apportionment, birth control, obscene literature, and separation of church and state, the justices until about 1964 stood shoulder to shoulder in their decisions touching state-supported racial discrimination. Only after the black revolution in the mid-1960's had entered a new and more radical phase and the Court on occasion confronted the difficult and complex problems associated with sit-ins, mass demonstrations, white backlash in housing, and so on, did its members sometimes split into the liberal and conservative blocs that for some time had characterized their decisions in other major areas of constitutional development.

To some extent the Court's consistent stand against segregation reflected the swelling tide of public opinion nearly everywhere outside the South that legal segregation ought to be done away with. The justices who made up the Court's membership in the decade after 1945—Vinson, Black, Douglas, Frankfurter, Rutledge, Murphy, Clark, Jackson, and Burton—had, except for the last named, been schooled in the practical politics of the New Deal, where they had imbibed not only a large measure of racial equalitarianism but also had been taught to appreciate fully the political significance of the black American's recent entry into national life.

Nor did President Eisenhower's appointments to the Court weaken its determined stand against racial injustice. Chief Justice Warren, who took his position just in time to participate in the celebrated decision in *Brown v. Board of Education* outlawing racial segregation in the public schools, soon demonstrated that he was at one with his colleagues in matters touching racial segregation. Eisenhower's subsequent appointments to the Court—Harlan, Brennan, Whittaker, and Stewart—were, with the possible exce)-tion of Justice Brennan, cut from somewhat more conservative political cloth than their predecessors, but on questions of race they fell in readily enough with the new Chief Justice and with their remaining New Deal brethren.

The four appointments Presidents Kennedy and Johnson made to the court in the 1960's actually strengthened, if that was possible, the justices' libertarian stance on matters of race. Byron R. White, whom President Kennedy nominated in 1962 upon the retirement of Justice Whittaker, was a former all-American football player, prosperous Denver lawyer, and Deputy Attorney General under Robert Kennedy, whose middle-of-the-road tendencies and precise and incisive legal mind soon marked him above all as "a lawyer's judge." But White's dissents in matters of race were confined to a few marginal and difficult sit-in and housing cases; for the rest, he adhered to the libertarian tradition. Arthur J. Goldberg, whom President Kennedy named to the Court later in 1962 when ill health forced Justice Frankfurter into retirement, was a prominent labor lawyer and former Secretary of Labor in Kennedy's cabinet, who soon demonstrated that he was more than willing to implement his powerful liberal convictions with a consistent judicial activism, both in civil rights and civil liberties generally. Justice Abe Fortas, an influential Washington lawyer and friend of President Johnson whom the latter appointed upon Goldberg's resignation in 1965, proved to be another judicial activist, who, on racial questions, was thoroughly at home with his liberal colleagues. Finally, Thurgood Marshall, long-time general counsel of the NAACP, who, upon his appointment to the Court by President Johnson in 1967, became the first Negro in American history to sit upon the nation's highest tribunal, quite obviously was destined to take a stand on racial matters consistent with the cause he had long argued so ably.

Although the Court was in a sense "following the election returns" in its decisions on matters of race, it also moved out in front of public opinion in such cases, assuming a novel role as a leader in the process of social change quite at odds with its traditional position as a defender of legalistic tradition and social continuity. So pronounced was the Court's activist leadership in what presently assumed the proportions of a sweeping racial reform movement that the Court for some years stood almost alone among the three branches of the national government in its quest for racial equality for the black American. The Truman administration between 1947 and 1952 did sponsor civil rights legislation in Congress, but its efforts met with consistent failure. The Eisenhower administration on its part adopted an attitude of studied neutrality toward the Court's desegregation decisions, although in 1957 and again in 1960 it was to intervene forcibly if reluctantly to uphold the desegregation orders of federal courts against deliberate attempts at nullification by state officialdom.

At length in 1957, Congress also joined the battle for racial desegregation, and in the next eleven years it enacted five major pieces of legislation enlisting federal sovereignty in support of desegregation, racial justice, and Negro political rights. But it was the Supreme Court's long and lonely stand for justice for black Americans which, more than any other single instrument of government, brought the Negro far along the path in his century-old quest for first-class citizenship in the American constitutional system.

THE BREAKDOWN OF LEGALIZED SEGREGATION IN HOUSING AND TRANSPORTATION

The most important constitutional battle over legalized segregation eventually was to be that fought over "separate but equal" school systems in the South. Well before the Court's now celebrated 1954 decision in *Brown v. Board of Education,* however, the Court had made it unmistakably clear that all was not well with the Plessy dictum, which so long had reconciled racial segregation with the Fourteenth Amendment. This was most evident in the successful attack conducted by the NAACP upon restrictive racial covenants in housing and upon segregated interstate transportation.

Restrictive racial covenants, a time-sanctioned institution of American urban life, were perhaps even more common in the North than in the South. Agreements of this kind customarily bound the property owners in a particular neighborhood to sell only to other "members of the Caucasian race." In *Corrigan v. Buckley* (1926), the Court had ruled that such covenants constituted mere private agreements and were not state action within the meaning of the Fourteenth Amendment. The Court also had refused to apply the Fifth Amendment to the outlawing of restrictive covenants in the District of Columbia.

In *Shelley v. Kraemer* (1948), however, the Court, in a unanimous five-justice opinion, ruled that judicial enforcement of restrictive covenants constituted state action and so violated the Fourteenth Amendment. Adhering very carefully to the distinction drawn in the Civil Rights Cases, Chief Justice Vinson agreed that restrictive covenants in themselves did not constitute state action. But judicial enforcement, he asserted, involved the powers of the state and so ran afoul of the equal-protection clause. In a companion case, *Hurd v. Hodge* (1948), the Court held that judicial enforcement of restrictive covenants in the District of Columbia not only violated the Civil Rights Act of 1866 but was also inconsistent with the public policy of the United States when such action in state courts had been ruled illegal.

Destruction of segregation in interstate transportation facilities began on the eve of World War II, when the Court, in *Mitchell v. United States* (1941), held that denial of a Pullman berth to a Negro when such facilities were available to whites was a violation of the Interstate Commerce Act. Chief Justice Hughes' opinion took its stand upon Congressional implementation of the commerce power and not upon the Fourteenth Amendment. However, Hughes implied broadly that discrimination in Pullman facilities, if practiced by a state, would violate the equal-protection clause.

Five years later, in *Morgan v. Virginia* (1946), the Court again used the interstate-commerce approach to invalidate a Virginia statute requiring racial segregation on public buses moving across state lines. The great diversity of state statutes dealing with segregation in transportation, Justice Reed's opinion implied, interfered with the uniformity of interstate commerce and thus made such laws invalid. Ironically, Reed's precedent for such a position was *Hall v. DeCuir* (1878), in which the Court had invalidated as an invasion of the commerce power a Louisiana statute prohibiting racial discrimination in public carriers. Justice Burton pointed out in dissent that if the Court were to maintain this position with any consistency, then by analogy all state laws prohibiting racial segregation in interstate commerce also were unconstitutional.

However, the Court obviously was not aiming at absolute legal consistency but rather at the destruction of segregation in transportation. This became evident in *Bob-Lo Excursion Co. v. Michigan* (1948), a case involving the constitutionality of a provision in the Michigan Civil Rights Act guaranteeing full and equal accommodations on public carriers.. A local steamship line, following a whites-only policy, had refused a ticket to a Negro girl for transportation to a nearby Canadian resort island; criminal prosecution of the company had followed. Here the state obviously was involved in the regulation of foreign commerce, and the logic of the Morgan case implied that the law in question was invalid.

However, Justice Rutledge's majority opinion emphasized the purely local character of the foreign transportation in question and so found the Michigan law constitutional under the Court's dictum in *Cooley v. Pennsylvania Port Wardens*. Significantly, Black and Douglas, concurring, thought the law ought to be sustained as an implementation of the equal-protection clause, regardless of any interference with commerce. Vinson and Jackson, holding to legal consistency, contended that the act was invalid under the DeCuir and Morgan precedents.

The Court struck another judicial blow at segregation in transportation in *Henderson v. United States* (1950), invalidating racial discrimination in railroad dining-car facilities. At stake was the practice, then common in several Southern states, of setting up a curtained-off section of the dining car for Negroes. Justice Burton found this to be a violation of the Interstate Commerce Act of 1887, which forbade railroads "to subject any particular person to any undue or unreasonable prejudice or disadvantage." Thus another long-standing segregation technique succumbed to the Court's new position.

The Morgan and Henderson opinions undoubtedly lay behind an order of the Interstate Commerce Commission, announced in November, 1955, terminating all racial segregation in trains and buses crossing state lines. The order also banned discrimination in auxiliary rail and bus facilities, waiting rooms, rest rooms, restaurants, and the like. The Commission, finding its inspiration in the Henderson dictum, now held that racial discrimination in transportation violated the Interstate Commerce Act of 1887. Though this step reversed long-standing policy, the Commission defended its order in the "lights of reason and experience" and as enabling it to "preserve the self-respect and dignity of citizenship in a common country."

THE CONSTITUTIONAL BATTLE OVER SCHOOL SEGREGATION

At the center of the constitutional battle over the Negro's status was the NAACP's attack upon school segregation in the South. So true was this that the Supreme Court's decision in *Brown v. Board of Education of Topeka* (1954), presently came to symbolize for the American people generally the Court's determination to destroy segregation on grounds of incompatibility with the equal-protection clause of the Fourteenth Amendment and the requirements of twentieth-century constitutional democracy generally.

At the close of World War II, legalized school segregation prevailed virtually everywhere in the South and border states, extending to some communities in Indiana, Illinois, and Kansas. Eighteen states had statutes making mandatory the segregation of white and Negro children, while six others permitted segregation at the discretion of local school boards. The constitutionality of such laws rested upon the assumption that the "separate but equal" doctrine of the Plessy case properly could be applied to education, although the Supreme Court technically had never so decided.

The first judicial intimation that all was not well constitutionally with state school segregation antedated World War II. *Missouri ex rel. Gaines v. Canada* (1938) arose out of the refusal of the University of Missouri, a state institution, to admit a Negro applicant to its law school. Although Missouri had no law school for Negroes, the state in accordance with established policy had offered to pay the student's expenses at any of the law schools in neighboring states which admitted Negroes.

However, Chief Justice Hughes' majority opinion held that Missouri's refusal to admit the applicant to the state law school violated the equal-protection clause of the Fourteenth Amendment. "By the operation of the laws of Missouri," said Hughes, "a privilege has been created for white law students which is denied to Negroes by reason of their race." The state's offer of fees in another state, he ruled, "does not remove the discrimination."

The Gaines decision did not imply technically that there was anything legally wrong with the "separate but equal" doctrine. The Court merely had found that Negro students had a right of access to a "white" educational institution where no "separate but equal" facility for Negroes existed. Careful observers soon concluded, however, that the South's entire system of segregated educational institutions was in serious trouble. Separate facilities for Negroes throughout the South—in buildings, libraries, trained teacher personnel, and academic standards—were notoriously *un*-equal to those for whites. This fact might ultimately lead to a judicial conclusion that equality and segregation were intrinsically incompatible with one another. Throughout the South, now made sharply aware of the precarious legal position of the "separate but equal" dictum, there was a concerted movement to improve Negro school facilities.

The NAACP's postwar assault on segregation deliberately selected higher education in the South as the most promising sector for its attack upon school segregation. In part this was because the number of Negroes seeking collegiate and professional education was relatively small, so that the "threat" to the Southern social order was not as extensive. In part, also, Southern mores somehow regarded the presence of a few Negroes in institutions of higher learning as less a threat to the caste system than was "indiscriminate mixing" in elementary and high-school education. It was also obviously more difficult—often even impossible—to make segregated facilities in university and professional education even approximately equal in a pragmatic sense to those for whites, so that the precedent in the Gaines case could be capitalized upon more fully here than in elementary education.

The first victory in the NAACP's postwar campaign came in *Sipuel v. Board of Regents* (1948), another case involving a state's refusal to admit a qualified student to the state law school. The *per curiam* opinion for a unanimous Court said simply that as long as Oklahoma furnished white persons with legal education, "petitioner is entitled to secure legal education afforded by a state institution." Denial of the applicant's admission violated the equal-protection of the Fourteenth Amendment.

It soon became clear that the Court's attitude toward equal educational facilities for Negroes in higher education would speedily make segregation on this level a practical impossibility. In *Sweatt v. Painter* (1950), the Court refused to admit that a Texas state law school, established specifically to meet the requirement of equality for Negroes in legal education, could satisfy the demands of the equal-protection clause. The petitioner, in accordance with the requirements of state law, had been denied admission to the University of Texas law school. A state court had thereupon ordered the Texas school authorities to furnish Sweatt with "substantially equal facilities" for legal education. To meet this demand, the state had established a Negro law school as an adjunct of the University of Texas. Sweatt had refused to attend this institution, but when the Texas courts again refused to admit him to the "white" law school of the University, he took an appeal to the federal courts.

Chief Justice Vinson's unanimous opinion held that the Negro law school established by the state did not in fact furnish Negroes with true equality in legal education. The Chief Justice pointed out the obvious advantages of the regular university law school in library, buildings, faculty, prestige, and the like, and concluded that "it is difficult to believe that one who had a free choice between these law schools would consider the question close." Sweatt's exclusion from the University therefore violated the equal-protection clause of the Fourteenth Amendment. The opinion carefully refrained from any review of the "separate but equal" rule, but it was obvious that the line of argument adopted by the Court could be used to force the admission of Negroes into virtually any graduate professional school in the South.

Like implications for segregation in higher education were apparent in *McLaurin v. Oklahoma State Regents* (1950), decided the same day as the Sweatt case. Here a Negro by legal action had compelled the state of Oklahoma to admit him to the graduate school of the state university. However, the school authorities thereafter had required him to sit in a special class section marked "reserved for colored," to use a special desk in the library, and to eat at a special table at mealtime. Chief Justice Vinson's opinion held that in-school segregation of this kind also was unconstitutional. The restrictions in question, Vinson said, impaired McLaurin's "ability to study, to engage in discussion and exchange views with other students, and, in general, to learn his profession," so that "appellant is handicapped in his pursuit of effective graduate instruction." He concluded that "state-imposed restrictions which produce such inequalities cannot be sustained."

So far, the "separate but equal" rule technically stood intact. It was obvious, however, that the trend of judicial reasoning implied that the next step might be a finding that racial segregation in the schools was by definition intrinsically incompatible with the requirements of the Constitution. The legal leap involved in reaching this conclusion was a substantial one, however, and the courts might well have hesitated to take it lightly.

After some further sparring, a group of five school segregation cases came before the Supreme Court in the fall of 1952. Four of these, from Delaware, Virginia, South Carolina, and Kansas, involved state segregation laws, a fifth touched school segregation in the District of Columbia. The cases speedily became a *cause célèbre*, as a battery of highly trained attorneys led by John W. Davis for the Southern states and Thurgood Marshall for the NAACP took over the preparation of briefs. Following initial argument by counsel, the Court after some delay ordered the cases re-argued with special attention to the question of whether Congress and the states in adopting the Fourteenth Amendment had in fact intended to ban segregated schools. Evidently, the justices were much troubled, also, about both the means and the consequences of a sudden abolition of school segregation throughout the South, for they asked counsel to discuss how the decision ought to be put into effect should the Court find that segregated schools were unconstitutional. Both sides now filed further lengthy briefs, and Attorney General Herbert Brownell also submitted a brief for the Department of Justice arguing that segregation violated the Fifth and Fourteenth Amendments and ought properly to be declared unconstitutional.

After a long silence, the Court in *Brown v. Board of Education* (1954) and *Bolling v. Sharpe* (1954) decided unanimously that school segregation, both in the states and in the District of Columbia, violated the Constitution. Chief Justice Earl Warren's opinion was remarkable for its avoidance of both legal and historical complexities. It was not possible, he thought, to decide whether the authors of the Fourteenth Amendment had intended to ban school segregation. But he thought it obvious that in the light of twentieth-century conditions, school segregation imposed an inferior status upon Negro children. Segregation, said the Chief Justice, generated a "feeling of inferiority" in Negro children as to their status in the community; the damage to their minds and hearts might well be so grave that it could never be undone. School segregation laws therefore violate the equal-protection clause of the Fourteenth Amendment. He added that the "separate but equal" doctrine of *Plessy v. Ferguson,* insofar as it applied to schools, now stood formally overruled.

In the District of Columbia case, Warren found briefly that segregation here was not "reasonably related to any proper governmental objective" and that it amounted to an improper restriction of "liberty under law," in violation of the due process clause of the Fifth Amendment. Moreover, he said, it was absurd to suppose that the Constitution permitted the national government to maintain segregated schools when it forbade that practice to the states.

Hence segregation in the District of Columbia also was unconstitutional.

In a very real sense, Warren's opinion amounted to a piece of judicial legislation. The Court had dismissed the historical question of congressional intent with a wave of the hand; it had disregarded or reversed long-standing precedents which implied constitutional validity for school segregation; and it had conspicuously refused to support its conclusion with any subtle constitutional analysis. Instead it had presented a simple sociological argument on the impact of segregation on the status of the Negro. Not without reason, opponents of segregation hailed Warren's opinion as a "piece of judicial statesmanship." Southern conservatives, on the other hand, condemned the decision as a usurpation of legislative function and a violation of traditional state-federal relations.

The Court, in deciding the case, significantly had issued no enforcement order; instead it asked counsel to re-argue once more the means of implementing the decision. Thus very astutely it separated its enunciation of the constitutional ban on segregation from the far more perplexing question of how Southern society was to adjust itself to the new standard. Quite conceivably, this careful separation of principle from enforcement had enabled the justices to unite in a unanimous decision; certainly it saved them from the issuance of a judicial order which would have proved impossible of enforcement.

In May, 1955, the Court, after re-argument, handed down its order in *Brown v. Board* (second case), implementing the earlier decision. It found its answer to the difficult enforcement problem by invoking the principles of equity law, which, as Warren's opinion pointed out, "has been characterized by a practical flexibility in shaping its remedies." Accordingly, the Court remanded the cases to the several lower courts concerned and ordered them to work out equitable solutions to eliminate "the variety of obstacles" admittedly involved, to admit the parties of the cases "to the public schools on a racially non-discriminatory basis with all deliberate speed."

In a certain sense, the Court's resort to equity principles to enforce the Brown decision was both self-contradictory and precedent-breaking. On the one hand, the Court had found that the plaintiff schoolchildren had a categorical right under the Fourteenth Amendment to attendance at racially non-segregated schools. At the same time, the Court had done what it had never done before—by implication denied these same children a full and instant implementation of this constitutional right. In a legal sense this was unprecedented and almost absurd; in a pragmatic sense it was vitally necessary to provide the flexibility and necessary delays that the imposition of something like a social revolution on the South now entailed. This was the meaning of the curiously contradictory phrase, "with all deliberate speed," which soon came to characterize, both legally and popularly, the second Brown decision.

"INTERPOSITION" AND "MASSIVE RESISTANCE": LITTLE ROCK, NEW ORLEANS, AND OXFORD

The second Brown decision signaled the opening of a protracted legal and political battle over school desegregation, which soon spread throughout the length and breadth of the South. A few places in the upper South, among them Washington, D.C., and Louisville, Kentucky, moved immediately to comply with the Brown and Bolling decisions, so that by 1957, integration, much of it only nominal, had been effected in approximately seven hundred school districts out of some three thousand below the Mason and Dixon line. But after an initial period of uncertainty, virtually all of the region formerly enlisted in the Confederacy resorted to what Senator Harry F. Byrd of Virginia presently called "massive resistance," in an effort to block implementation of the Brown decision. Segregationist tactics, while generally dubious in the extreme from a constitutional point of view, were nonetheless comparatively successful. Ten years after the Court's order, in the school year 1964–1965, only a little more than two per cent of the black students in the eleven former Confederate states were in attendance at integrated schools.

The most dramatic southern legal move calculated to defeat school integration was the attempt to invoke the long-dead doctrine of "interposition" by the states against federal sovereignty. "Interposition," it will be recalled, was the constitutional theory that Madison and Jefferson had incorporated in the Virginia and Kentucky Resolutions of 1798, in which the legislatures of those states had "interposed" against the Alien and Sedition Laws, declaring them to be null and void. Although nothing had been heard of this idea for more than a century, several southern states, among them Virginia, South Carolina, Georgia, Alabama, Mississippi, Louisiana, and Arkansas, presently adopted "interposition" resolutions aimed at the Brown decisions.

Thus the Georgia legislature, speaking almost in the language of the South Carolina Nullification Ordinance of 1832, in February, 1956, adopted a resolution declaring the Brown dictum "null, void, and of no effect" within the limits of the state. Alabama, in November, 1956, adopted a constitutional amendment commanding the state legislature to oppose "in every constitutional manner the unconstitutional desegregation decisions" of the Court. The Louisiana legislature simply declared the Brown decisions "unconstitutional," while Virginia, avoiding any resort to "null and void" language, spoke merely of "illegal encroachment" by the Court upon the sovereignty and autonomy of the states.

All this ignored in almost pathetic fashion the outcome of the Civil War and the long evolutionary process which had lodged firmly in the Supreme Court the final power to interpret the Constitution. The Supreme Court itself was presently to quote with approval the dictum of a lower federal court that "interposition" was "not a constitutional doctrine," that is, it could not be treated seriously as a legal idea. Yet interposition, if constitutionally absurd, nonetheless became the philosophic basis for much of the southern resistance movement in the next few years, notably in Arkansas and Louisiana.

More formidable in an immediate sense were the various school laws adopted by the southern states as a part of their "massive resistance" programs. These included pupil-placement laws intended to enable local school boards to shuffle children among school districts so as to maintain segregation, repeal of compulsory school attendance acts to permit parents to withdraw children from integrated public schools, acts providing for indirect support of segregated private schools through tuition payments to parents, statutes threatening to withdraw tax support from any school system that submitted to integration, "freedom of choice" plans that allowed a pupil to select his own school, and laws providing for the outright closure of the public schools as a last resort if all other evasive devices failed.

The NAACP on its part countered "massive resistance" with an equally massive program of litigation in the southern states. By the end of 1956, it had filed more than fifty desegregation suits in the South, and it instituted scores of others in the next few years. Very often these suits spilled over into spectacular political maneuvering and even into rioting and violence necessitating the imposition of martial law.

The first dramatic instance of this sort occurred in Little Rock,

Arkansas, where the state's defiance of federal court orders for the gradual desegregation of the city's all-white high school finally obliged President Eisenhower to call out units of the United States Army to compel submission to federal sovereignty. The crisis had its beginnings when the Little Rock Board of Education secured federal court approval for the admission, beginning in September, 1957, of a small number of Negro students to the school. The Arkansas Chancery Court thereupon attempted to intervene, issuing an injunction barring the Board from proceeding with its desegregation plans. However, Judge Ronald Davies, then presiding as a visiting judge on the Arkansas federal bench, countered this move with a new writ voiding the state court's injunction and ordering the Board to proceed as planned.

Governor Orval Faubus, now heavily committed to the die-hard segregationist cause, thereupon called out the Arkansas National Guard. On September 2, guard forces, acting under the Governor's proclamation alleging the necessity for maintaining law and order, effectively barred prospective Negro students from entering the white high-school building. A new series of court orders from Judge Davies commanding immediate compliance with the integration plan went disregarded. At this juncture the state of Arkansas had succeeded by the use of force in effectively nullifying a series of federal court orders.

After some hesitation, President Eisenhower at length intervened. A conference between Faubus and the President failed to produce any result, whereupon Attorney General Herbert Brownell, Jr., acting on the President's instructions, sought and obtained an injunction against the Governor, ordering him and the National Guard to cease forthwith from blocking enforcement of the federal court orders in question. The Governor thereupon withdrew the National Guard. However, when Negro students again attempted to enter the high school, they were prevented from doing so by a large and ugly tempered mob.

Accordingly, the President, on September 25, dispatched several companies of the United States Army to Little Rock, in effect putting the city under martial law. He took this action under Section 333, Title 10, of the United States Code, which, as Brownell pointed out, authorized the President to suppress insurrection and unlawful combinations that hindered execution of either state or federal law. Mob resistance immediately disappeared, and several Negro students thereupon entered the school without further interference. Regular Army units remained on guard at the school until late November, when they were replaced by a contingent of the state National Guard, called into federal service for this purpose.

The Little Rock conflict presently afforded the Supreme Court an opportunity to read Arkansas officialdom an elementary lesson in constitutional law. In the summer of 1958, the Little Rock School Board succeeded in obtaining a thirty-month stay against integration on the ground that "conditions of chaos, bedlam, and turmoil" made this necessary. The United States Court of Appeals, however, reversed the stay, and the Supreme Court thereupon assembled in special session in August to hear arguments on the case. On September 12, in a unanimous decision in *Cooper v. Aaron* (1958), confirmed the Appeals Court order, without then publishing any opinion.

The Court's opinion in *Cooper v. Aaron*, published in late September and signed personally by every one of the justices, constituted a solemn admonition to the state of Arkansas on the folly and futility of attempting to frustrate the sovereign will of the Supreme Court and the national government. Admitting that the Little Rock School Board had acted in good faith, the Court pointed out that the recent disturbances were "directly traceable" to action by Arkansas officials "which reflect their own determination to resist this Court's decision in the Brown case." The constitutional rights of Negro children, the Court warned, "can neither be nullified openly and directly by state legislators or state executive officials nor nullified indirectly by them by evasive schemes for segregation." No state official, the Court continued sternly, "can war on the Constitution without violating his oath to support it . . . else . . . the Constitution becomes a solemn mockery." And as if to impress both Arkansas and the South at large with the fact that any hope of overturning the Brown decision was utterly without foundation, the Court concluded: "Since the first Brown opinion, three new justices have come to the Court. They are as one with the justices still on the Court who participated in that basic decision as to its correctness and that decision is now unanimously reaffirmed. The principles announced in that decision and the obedience of the states to them, according to the command of the Constitution, are indispensable for the protection of the freedoms guaranteed by our fundamental charter for all of us. Our constitutional ideal of equal justice under law is thus made a living truth." Further to emphasize the solemnity of these pronouncements, all nine justices signed the opinion.

The clash of wills between Arkansas and the Court was not yet quite played out. Confronted with the decision in *Cooper v. Aaron*, Faubus immediately signed into law two bills adopted by the Arkansas legislature a few days earlier authorizing him to close the high schools of Little Rock and to withhold funds from these schools. A proclamation issued at the same time closed the schools for the ensuing school year.

In June, 1959, however, a three-judge federal district court declared both Arkansas closure statutes unconstitutional under the due process and equal protection clauses of the Fourteenth Amendment, and in August the Supreme Court in *Faubus v. Aaron* (1959) affirmed without opinion. In September, the Little Rock high schools quietly reopened, this time on an integrated basis.

Further state-federal confrontations over school desegregation presently ensued in Louisiana and Mississippi, the result in each instance being a victory for federal authority. A federal district court order of May 1960, calling for the gradual desegregation of the New Orleans public school system, led to a complex legal battle between the court and Louisiana officialdom. The battle climaxed in November, when the state legislature, meeting in special session, adopted a statute that purported to "interpose" the sovereignty of the state against federal-ordered school desegregation. Other statutes made desegregation a criminal act, placed control of the New Orleans schools in the hands of a special eight-man legislative committee, and denied accreditation, free textbooks, and financial aid to desegregated schools.

This kind of direct defiance of federal sovereignty inevitably encountered the same fate as it had in Arkansas. Judge Skelly Wright immediately blocked the legislature's seizure of the schools with a new injunction keeping control in the Board's hands. The Eisenhower administration, watching the situation closely, dispatched large numbers of United States marshals to New Orleans to make certain that Wright's order was obeyed. On November 14, as resistance collapsed, two New Orleans schools underwent token integration.

A few days later, the three-judge federal district court declared void the new Louisiana interposition statute and eighteen other new segregation statutes adopted by the Louisiana legislature at its recent special session. Judge Wright's opinion reviewed briefly and contemptuously the history and theory of the doctrine of interposition that he held to be "a preposterous perversion" of the

Constitution, which, if taken seriously, was "illegal defiance of constitutional authority", and, if otherwise, no more than "an escape valve through which legislators blow off steam to reduce their tensions." Twelve days later, in *United States v. Louisiana* (1960), the Supreme Court affirmed the lower court's decision *per curiam*, with a terse one-sentence opinion approving the latter's denunciation of the interposition doctrine. Thus a second and even more clearly defined attempt at state defiance of federal authority through "interposition" ended in failure.

However, the explosive Meredith riot at the University of Mississippi in late September, 1962, presently demonstrated only too dramatically that the South's attempted resort to "massive resistance" was far from over. Following a protracted legal battle, the Supreme Court earlier that month had confirmed a federal Appellate Court order requiring officials of the University forthwith to admit as a student one James Meredith, a Negro citizen of the state. At this juncture, Governor Ross Barnett, invoking all the symbols of state sovereignty and interposition, virtually took charge of the University. Using state and local police, the governor blocked a series of attempts by Meredith, now escorted by United States marshals, to register. The United States Court of Appeals thereupon found Barnett guilty of contempt, and imposed a conditional fine upon him of $10,000 a day unless he should purge himself. On September 29, President Kennedy, after vainly attempting to get Barnett to recede, issued a proclamation addressed to the officials and people of the state of Mississippi, warning them to cease their resistance to federal authority. On the next day, a Sunday, University officials reluctantly capitulated, and agreed to allow Meredith, now accompanied by several hundred United States marshals, to register the next morning.

That night a massive riot approaching the proportions of an outright insurrection broke out in and around the college campus at Oxford. Thereupon President Kennedy, who obviously had hoped to avoid resort to direct federal military intervention such as had occurred at Little Rock, sent several thousand regular United States Army troops to the town, as well as several units of the Mississippi National Guard which already had been called into federal service. Overt resistance thereupon collapsed, and Meredith registered and began attending classes. Within a year several Negroes were registered quietly at the University. So terminated yet another experiment with the now thoroughly discredited interposition doctrine.

"MASSIVE RESISTANCE" AND "FREEDOM OF CHOICE"
IN VIRGINIA

Meanwhile Virginia's attempt to block school desegregation, first through "massive resistance" and later by means of a system of tax subsidies for private schools combined with outright closure of the schools, headed for final collapse and repudiation by the Supreme Court. In December, 1955, the state adopted a constitutional amendment incorporating the so-called "Gray Plan," to allow the legislature and local governing bodies to support private schools through a system of tuition grants. In September, 1956, the General Assembly, meeting in special session, adopted a series of "massive resistance" laws. One measure, a pupil placement law, provided that all children must remain in their present schools unless their transfer was approved by a special three-man board. Another provision of this law cut off state funds to any board resorting to mixed schools. Still another act provided for the outright closing of any school or schools where the federal courts had ordered integration and all other evasive devices had failed.

Several of these measures ran into difficulties in the Virginia courts. In January, 1959, the Virginia Supreme Court declared unconstitutional both the law closing desegregated schools and that cutting off state funds from such schools.[1] The legislature thereupon abandoned its "massive resistance" program and adopted an indirect procedure for defying federal integration orders. To this end, the Assembly, in April, 1959, repealed the remainder of the 1956 legislation, but at the same time it also struck the state's compulsory school attendance laws from the books and made school attendance a matter of local option. The Assembly also adopted a new tuition grant program for students attending private schools.

Several school boards, taking advantage of the new legislation, thereupon closed their schools. But in the next two years, a series of federal court orders forced the opening of integrated public schools in Front Royal, Norfolk, Arlington, and Charlottesville, Governor Almond meanwhile confessing himself helpless to do anything about the matter.

By 1962, only the schools of Prince Edward County, where one of the original desegregation suits that reached the Court with *Brown v. Board* had commenced back in 1951, were still closed.

---

[1] *Harrison v. Day*, 200 Va. 439.

Here, in 1956, the County Supervisors had resolved that they would not finance public schools "wherein white and colored children are taught together." And when the United States Court of Appeals in June, 1959, ordered the County School Board forthwith to admit students to the white high school without regard to race and to also plan immediately for the desegregation of the elementary schools, the supervisors responded by refusing to levy any school taxes.

Cut off from support, Prince Edward County schools failed to open in the fall of 1959 and remained closed for the next several years. In 1960, the legislature adopted a tuition grant program for parents sending their children to private schools, while the Prince Edward Supervisors not only made a supplementary tuition grant but also granted property tax credits up to twenty-five per cent for contributions to private schools in the county. Thus subsidized, the so-called Prince Edward School Foundation established a private white school system in the county, but Negro children, whose parents rejected an invitation to form a like private school system for blacks, remained without any schools whatever. At length, after long and complex legal maneuvering, a federal suit commenced by the NAACP Legal Defense Fund on behalf of the county's Negro children reached the Supreme Court.

In *Griffin v. County Board of Prince Edward County* (1964), that tribunal held that county authorities in closing the public schools and at the same time subsidizing private white schools had "denied petitioners the equal protection of the laws." Justice Black, in an opinion delivered for a virtually unanimous Court, not only upheld the injunction granted originally by the federal district court banning the county's system of tuition grants and tax credits, but also informed the district court that it had the power, at its discretion, to order the County Board of Supervisors to levy school taxes and to command the Board of Education to reopen the public schools. "The time for mere 'deliberate speed,' " Black warned sternly, "has run out." In an accompanying opinion, Justices Clark and Harlan expressed disagreement with the majority ruling that the federal courts could order Prince Edward County's public schools reopened, but otherwise joined in the Court's opinion. That fall Prince Edward County's public schools quietly reopened, as its long defiance of the two Brown decisions at last finally collapsed.

Thus the Supreme Court served notice that the period of equity grace originally granted southern school boards through the "all deliberate speed" formula in "Brown II" had at length ended. From now on the Court was to insist upon integration "forthwith." All this, however, hardly implied that school integration thereafter picked up any great momentum in the South. On the contrary, both in Virginia and elsewhere, a great majority of the local school boards in the states of the former Confederacy continued to operate dual segregated school systems, secure in the knowledge that local white public opinion overwhelmingly supported their stand and that any attempt to force any given school district to desegregate would require a long and expensive court fight. Not until after 1967, when the impact of Title VI of the Civil Rights Act of 1964, with its provision prohibiting federal financial assistance to schools practicing racial segregation, began to make itself felt, did the pace of integration increase somewhat.

FREEDOM OF CHOICE PLANS: THE GREEN
AND HOLMES DECISIONS

Southern school boards, frustrated in their attempts at direct defiance of the federal courts, also were engaged in careful exploration of other and more subtle techniques for subverting the Brown decisions. Beginning about 1963, so-called "freedom of choice" plans spread rapidly throughout the South. These plans nominally allowed any child, white or black, to attend any appropriate school which he wished within his school district. At the same time they relied upon the force of local custom and economic and social sanctions to confine black children within what were in fact segregated schools.

In a number of cases after 1963, "freedom of choice" plans won the approval of southern-oriented federal district judges directing the process of desegregation, thereby further adding to the plausibility and prestige of such schemes. The so-called "guidelines" for desegregation prepared in 1967 by the Department of Health, Education, and Welfare in accordance with Title VI of the Civil Rights Act of 1964 also granted a conditional executive approval to such plans, treating them as acceptable if they were a part of a court-approved desegregation plan or could be considered a step in the process of effective desegregation. In *Goss v. Board of Education of Knoxville* (1963), the Supreme Court in effect indicated its displeasure with such schemes when it held unconstitutional a city "free transfer" plan that allowed any child, white or black, to transfer out of any school in which he found himself in a racial minority. But the Goss decision, somewhat restrictive in character, hardly made an end to "freedom of choice" plans generally.

At length, in *Green v. County Board of New Kent County* (1968), the Court, without condemning freedom of choice plans outright, placed them under a grave constitutional cloud. The plan at issue, which had been instituted in a lightly populated county in eastern Virginia, allowed children in the first eight grades annually to opt which of two pre-existing schools, one traditionally white and one black, they wished to attend. The respondent school board had attempted to argue before the Court that the Fourteenth Amendment, after all, could not be read as requiring compulsory school integration, and that its plan, which allowed Negro children to attend any school they wished, therefore was constitutional.

The Court refused to accept this argument. It ignored, said Justice Brennan, the thrust of "Brown II," which had deliberately called for "the dismantling of well-entrenched dual systems," and had charged school boards "with the affirmative duty to take whatever steps might be necessary to convert to a unitary system in which racial discrimination would be eliminated root and branch." Hence "freedom of choice" plans could be regarded as constitutionally acceptable only when they offered a "real promise of aiding a desegregation program" and where there were no alternative means to that objective "readily available."

It was by no means clear, however, that the Court's uncompromising stand in favor of integrating the South's dual school systems would be successful in the near future. Ominously, the Court in the fall of 1969 appeared to lose the support of the Attorney General's office, when the Nixon administration, apparently engaged in a cautious policy of wooing the South on the school question, came out in favor of delay in effecting integration in the dual school systems in the South. In August, the United States Court of Appeals at New Orleans had granted some thirty-three school districts in Mississippi an indefinite stay in a lower court integration order, providing they took "significant steps" in the course of the coming school year toward disestablishment of their dual school systems. Upon appeal to the Supreme Court by the NAACP, the Attorney General's office intervened in favor of delay, arguing that it was "simply unreal to talk of instant desegregation" of the South's dual school systems, and that it would be necessary to perfect "workable plans" before school integration of the kind contemplated in the present case could be effected.

Predictably, the Supreme Court rejected this plea. In a unanimous *per curiam* decision handed down in late October, the Court, in *Alexander v. Holmes* (1969), declared once more that the "all deliberate speed" formula was "no longer constitutionally permissible," and instructed the Appellate Court forthwith to order the Mississippi school districts involved in the case "to begin immediately to operate as unitary school systems within which no person is to be effectively excluded from any school because of race or color." Significantly, Chief Justice Warren Burger, whom President Nixon had appointed to replace Chief Justice Warren upon the latter's resignation from the Court the previous June, joined in the Court's decision.

By 1970, some thirty per cent of the black children in the South attended schools at least nominally integrated. Title VI of the Civil Rights Act of 1964 was now beginning to have a substantial impact upon school integration below the Mason and Dixon line. This provision, which prohibited discrimination based upon race in any state program receiving federal financial assistance, was interpreted by the Department of Health, Education and Welfare as banning federal education grants to school boards in the South which failed to develop "affirmative action" programs of the kind the Court had referred to in the Green case. The consequence was that one school board after another hastened to comply with H.E.W. affirmative action regulations, lest it be cut off from federal funds.

By 1973 *de jure* school segregation in the South had virtually disappeared. The center of interest in the continuing conflict over school segregation had already visibly shifted to the great urban centers of the North, where massive postwar in-migration of blacks had created an unprecedented problem of *de facto* school segregation, based not upon law but upon racial population distribution. [2]

THE DESTRUCTION OF OTHER STATE SEGREGATION LAWS:
THEATERS, PARKS, BUSES, AND INTERMARRIAGE STATUTES

Curiously enough, the Court's decision in "Brown I" had a substantially greater immediate impact upon the fabric of state segregation laws in the South with respect to other types of state-

[2] See below, pp. 1002–1008.

operated or state-regulated facilities than it did upon the region's dual school system. The decision, in fact, was the signal for a general attack by the Legal Defense Fund and its associates upon state laws providing for mandatory racial segregation in public parks, swimming pools, theaters, athletic contests, and the like. Almost invariably the federal district court where the suit had been commenced held that the Brown decision had outlawed the old Plessy "separate but equal" rule, not only for schools but for all public facilities of whatever kind, so that the statute under review violated the equal protection clause. The Supreme Court in turn without exception confirmed decisions of this kind without opinion. In those few cases where the lower court had managed to rationalize the statute in question as constitutional, the Court invariably remanded the case *per curiam* to the lower court for further proceedings "not inconsistent with *Brown v. Board.*"

Significantly, the Court in these cases from the beginning refused to allow application of the "all deliberate speed" rule from "Brown II," demanding instead integration forthwith. And since the integration of parks, theaters, and the like apparently offered less challenge to southern mores than did school integration, and since such facilities also were peculiarly vulnerable to the boycotts and crusades that Martin Luther King and other Negro leaders were to wage within the next few years, the Court's orders ultimately commanded a substantially larger element of compliance in the South than was the case with segregated southern school systems.

From a technical point of view, the decisions invalidating segregation in public facilities were of two kinds. Sometimes a state law directly commanding segregation either in a state or private facility was at issue; here the Court had no difficulty in finding that the statute violated the equal protection clause. Typical of such decisions were those abolishing racial segregation in municipal bathing beach facilities, on city-owned golf courses in public parks, at public athletic events, on city bus lines, and in state and county courthouses and courtrooms.[3] Significantly, the Court consistently refused to allow the application of the "all deliberate speed" rule to the desegregation of state and municipal facilities or to state laws imposing racial segregation on private facilities, or to accept legal evasions or delays of other kinds.

In a second group of cases, the Court struck down racial segre-

---

[3] *Baltimore v. City of Dawson* (1955); *Holmes v. City of Atlanta* (1955); *Watson v. Memphis* (1963); *State Athletic Commission v. Dorsey* (1959); *Gayle v. Browder* (1956); *Evers v. Dwyer* (1958); *Johnson v. Virginia* (1963).

gation or discrimination which in the immediate instance was practiced by private parties, but where the authority of the state loomed
in the background. Thus the Court invalidated the exclusion of
Negroes from a private theater located in a public park, and from
a private restaurant operating in a county courthouse.[4]

Cases of this kind early raised the question of whether or not
the Court was in effect engaged in subtly destroying the distinction between state and private action, as originally set forth in the
Civil Rights Cases of 1883. However, in *Burton v. Wilmington
Parking Authority* (1961), the Court went on record officially to
the contrary. The case involved the constitutionality of segregation in a private restaurant located on the premises of a municipal
parking authority. Clark's opinion took pains specifically to reaffirm the principle of the Civil Rights Cases as "embedded in our
constitutional law." But the Court nonetheless held that the connection between the restaurant and the municipality was intimate
enough to categorize the former's policies as "state action" within
the meaning of the Fourteenth Amendment. A year later, in
Turner v. Memphis (1962), the Court applied the same general
rule in a *per curiam* decision to invalidate racial segregation in a
private restaurant leased from the city at a municipal airport; the
Court observed briefly that since the Burton decision there was
"no serious constitutional issue to decide."

Perhaps the ultimate in the Court's determination to break
down state-imposed racial segregation came with its invalidation
of southern statutes forbidding sexual relations or intermarriage
between the white and black races. The Court long manifested
great reluctance to interfere with laws of this kind, in all probability because it recognized the extreme sensitivity of southern
whites in matters of "miscegenation." But at length, in *McLaughlin v. Florida* (1964), the Court struck down as unconstitutional
under the equal protection clause a Florida law that prohibited
cohabitation between unmarried whites and blacks. Justice White's
opinion, which reversed an earlier decision in *Pace v. Alabama*
(1882) upholding a state act that subjected interracial fornication
and adultery to special penalties, held simply that the law now
under review trenched upon "constitutionally protected freedom
from invidious discrimination based upon race," and was therefore

---

[4] *Muir v. Louisiana Park Theatrical Association* (1955); *Derrington v. Plummer*
(1957). The Court held that racial segregation in a private restaurant operating in
an interstate bus terminal was in violation of the Interstate Commerce Act. *Boyn-
ton v. Virginia* (1960).

void. Three years later, in *Loving et ux. v. Virginia* (1967), the Court voided Virginia's miscegenation statute. "Under our constitution," said Justice White, "the freedom to marry or not to marry a person of another race resides with the individual and cannot be infringed by the state." Again, the law under review violated the equal protection clause.

THE SIT-IN CASES: DIFFICULTIES WITH THE LIMITS OF STATE ACTION

The difficulties of defining the precise limits of "state action" were particularly apparent in a series of so-called "sit-in" cases, several of which came before the Court in the five years or so beginning in 1961.

"Sit-ins" represented a new and more radical technique developed by black leaders and their supporters, as the civil rights movement passed from its earlier legalistically oriented phase to involvement in "civil disobedience" and other forms of direct action. The sit-in pattern was a fairly standard one. A group of young Negroes "invaded" a restaurant serving only whites and demanded service, refusing to leave when ordered to do so by management or the police. Arrest and prosecution for trespass, disturbing the peace, or the like then followed. Occasionally, also, sit-ins took place in hotels, libraries, courthouses, and even in jails.

The Court found itself exceedingly perplexed in deciding various sit-in cases to find some rule under which it might reasonably classify the racial discrimination imposed as state rather than private action. The difficulty was that by traditional standards the refusal to serve a customer in a private restaurant—one not located in a state facility and where no state law commanded the discrimination in question—was mere private discrimination and so fell outside the aegis of the Fourteenth Amendment. The Court might have solved this dilemma by wiping out entirely the old distinction between state and private action, as Justice Douglas on occasion apparently was prepared to do, but in a pluralistic society where the right of private discrimination was a widely recognized fact of daily life, this solution promised to open a veritable Pandora's box of constitutional difficulties. (What of the right of a church, for example, to exclude members not of its faith, or of a private club to limit its membership to whites or blacks, Catholics, Protestants, or Jews?)

The Court also flirted with a second possible rule, derived from

Shelley v. Kraemer, where the Court had held that privately negotiated restrictive covenants were in themselves not illegal but that
any attempt to enforce them in the courts automatically became
state action invalid under the equal protection clause. By this
theory, a private restaurant operator had a right to engage in
discrimination, but the state had no right to arrest or prosecute
sit-in "offenders." Close to this idea was the further legal theory
that when a restaurant owner discriminated in accordance with
current local custom enforceable by police and the courts, he was
in fact taking action required by state policy whether or not any
specific segregation law was involved. Finally, Justice Douglas on
occasion argued that restaurants, hotels, and the like were engaged
in a form of public activity closely akin to the services extended
by the state in operating swimming pools, parks, libraries, and
other state-owned facilities and that discrimination in such places
hence might be said to involve state action.

But no one of these theories captured a consistent majority of
the justices, so that the Court very often settled sit-in cases upon
somewhat narrow technical grounds. Almost invariably it ruled in
favor of the Negro petitioners, but it did so without creating any
broad new rule of what constituted state action. Thus in *Garner
v. Louisiana* (1961), the first sit-in case to reach the Court, the
justices reversed the conviction of a group of Baton Rouge sit-in
demonstrators who had been arrested and convicted for disturbing
the peace. The convictions, Warren's opinion held, were "totally
devoid of evidentiary support" for such a charge. Douglas, concurring, thought that the Court should have held that Louisiana
was itself enforcing a policy of racial segregation, while Harlan
would have ruled the convictions unconstitutional for vagueness
under the Louisiana statute as applied.

Again, in *Taylor v. Louisiana* (1962), where petitioners had
been convicted for a breach of peace after "invading" a bus waiting room reserved for whites, the Court once again held the convictions invalid for lack of evidentiary support, since the record
showed that the petitioners had been "quiet, orderly, and polite,"
and there had been no threat of violence in their intrusion upon a
transportation facility where segregation in any event was illegal
under federal law. And in *Edwards v. South Carolina* (1963),
where a group of Negroes had invaded the Statehouse grounds and
been arrested for a breach of the peace after failure to move on,
Justice Stewart's opinion found not only that petitioners had been

lawfully exercising their right to freedom of speech and assembly but also that the convictions were unsupported by evidence and were unconstitutional for vagueness.

On the other hand, in *Peterson v. Greenville* (1963) and *Lombard v. Louisiana* (1963), the Court moved close to the theory that arrests for sit-ins meant in effect that the state was supporting a segregation policy and that the convictions were therefore illegal under the equal protection clause. In the Peterson case, where the defendants had been arrested for a lunch-counter sit-in after the management had excluded them under a local segregation ordinance, Chief Justice Warren's opinion found that the restaurant management in excluding Negroes had done "precisely what the law requires," so that the state "to a significant extent" had become involved in the segregation practice in question, thereby removing it from the sphere of private action. The subsequent convictions for trespass therefore violated the equal protection clause. In the Lombard case, where arrests for trespass had followed a New Orleans lunch-counter sit-in, there had been no local segregation law, but Warren's opinion emphasized that the restaurant had acted in accordance with a policy announced by the mayor, and that its management, in asking petitioners to leave, had asserted that "we *have* to sell to you at the rear of the store," and had "called the police as a matter of routine procedure." Therefore, said Warren, it was "the voice of the state directing segregated service," and the convictions could not stand.

Thus far the Court in handling sit-in appeals had exhibited a substantial unanimity, but the following year, in *Bell v. Maryland* (1964), its united front broke down very badly. Here the Court confronted an appeal from the conviction of twelve Baltimore sit-in demonstrators who had been tried for violation of a Maryland criminal trespass law. Subsequent to the convictions, Maryland had enacted a new public accommodations statute forbidding the owners and operators of restaurants and like places to deny any person service because of race. In other words, petitioners' "offense," had it occurred subsequent to the enactment of the new act, would no longer have constituted a crime under Maryland law.

Justice Brennan's opinion for the Court refused to consider the larger constitutional questions involved, and instead merely vacated the judgment of the Maryland Court of Appeals confirming the conviction, and remanded the case to that court for further consideration in the light of Maryland's new public accommodations law. But six of the other justices refused to accept any such easy disposition of the case. Douglas wrote a long opinion arguing that the Court should face up squarely to the constitutional issue involved, which he defined as the right of equal access to public accommodations for all persons regardless of race or class. This right he found to be inherent in the historic purposes of the Thirteenth, Fourteenth, and Fifteenth Amendments, and also to be an incidence both of national citizenship and of the right to travel. He concluded that the old common law of public carriers—i.e., the obligation to serve all comers on an equal footing—should now become the "common law" of the Thirteenth and Fourteenth Amendments and, as such, applied to restaurants, which, he said, were in the modern world "as essential to travel as are inns and carriers."

Goldberg, who, like Douglas, technically concurred in the Court's decision, also examined the history of the Fourteenth Amendment, to conclude that the amendment had been intended to bind the states to enforce the common-law guarantees of equal access to public facilities. State enforcement of private segregation therefore violated the equal protection clause.

Justice Black, who in the next several years was to take exception on numerous occasions to the more precedent-breaking libertarian decisions of the Court majority in civil rights cases, dissented at length in an opinion joined also by Harlan and White. The Maryland trespass law under which petitioners had been convicted, Black protested, was perfectly constitutional. "The Fourteenth Amendment of itself," he insisted, "does not compel either a black man or a white man running his own private business to trade with anyone else against his will." Furthermore, persons practicing such discrimination, no matter how bigoted, had a right to call upon the state for the defense of their property, as had been the case here. "It would betray our whole plan for a tranquil and orderly society," he said, "to say that a citizen, because of his personal prejudices, . . . cannot call for the aid of officers sworn to uphold the law and preserve the peace." Black carefully distinguished *Shelley v. Kraemer*, observing that restrictive covenants enforceable in the courts had had the effect of state or municipal zoning laws, prohibiting a sale to which both parties were willing participants. But when a party refused to enter into a private contract, the state must protect him in that decision.

A series of accompanying cases, decided at the same time as *Bell v. Maryland*, served further to emphasize the Court's now hopeless division on the sit-in issue.[5] Thus the Court's hitherto virtually unanimous stand on all consequential issues involving racial segregation was at length shattered. Fortunately, the enactment by Congress at this juncture of the Civil Rights Act of 1964 decisively altered the constitutional issues involved in sit-down and other public accommodation cases and thereby restored a large measure of judicial unity on such matters once more.

THE DRIVE FOR COMPREHENSIVE FEDERAL CIVIL RIGHTS LEGISLATION: THE FRANCHISE

The Civil Rights Act of 1964 was the high point in a long and ultimately successful drive by northern liberals for comprehensive new federal civil rights legislation that eventually resulted in the enactment of five major civil rights statutes over a period of eleven years: The Civil Rights Acts of 1957, 1960, and 1964; the Voting Rights Act of 1965; and the Fair Housing Act of 1968. Thus for the first time since the Reconstruction era, federal legislative power was brought to bear to support the black American's hundred-year-old demand for civil and political equality.

The early campaign for federal civil rights legislation concentrated upon three issues: protection of voting rights, enactment of an anti-lynch law, and adoption of a federal fair employment practices statute. Of these measures, proposals for federal legislation to protect Negro voting rights seemingly offered the most promise of success and the least constitutional difficulties.

The Negro's new political awakening had in fact already resulted in a great increase in participation by black Americans in the electoral process, particularly in the South. The NAACP, for

---

[5] In *Griffin v. Maryland* (1964), the majority justices reversed the conviction of five Negroes who had refused to leave a private amusement park, on the ground that the arresting officer was both a park employee and a deputy sheriff, thereby establishing decisively the element of "state action" necessary to invoke the equal protection clause. In *Bouie v. City of Columbia* (1964), the same majority reversed the conviction of two Negro sit-down demonstrators, holding that lack of fair notice to petitioners that refusal to leave constituted a crime had resulted in a denial of due process of law. And in *Barr v. City of Columbia* (1964), the majority threw out a conviction of sit-in petitioners who had been tried both for trespass and breach of the peace, citing the Bouie decision as precedent on the trespass conviction and lack of evidence to support the breach of peace charge. In all three of these cases, Black, Harlan, and White dissented and voted to uphold the convictions, citing Black's Bell opinion as the basis for their position. Douglas, on the other hand, concurred in all three cases on the basis of his Bell opinion, while Goldberg, joined by Warren, did the same in the Bouie and Barr cases. Only in *Robinson v. Florida* (1964) did the Court preserve its united stand, as it unanimously reversed a sit-in conviction under the *Peterson v. Greenville* precedent, since the evidence made it clear that state policy itslf required separate facilities.

example, estimated that some 3,000,000 Negroes voted in the 1948 presidential election, compared with only 1,000,000 in 1940. Much of this increase came from the lower South, where, even in Georgia and Mississippi, particularly in urban areas, Negroes now were going to the polls in increasing numbers.

The Court, always fairly vigilant in the protection of the Negro's right to vote, also was demonstrating a new interest in checking state legislation which sought by one device or another to nullify the Fifteenth Amendment. A favorite device that emerged in the southern states in the 1920's and 1930's was the so-called "white primary" law, which barred Negroes from participation in the Democratic Party primary, where in most southern states the out- come of the regular election was at that time in fact decided.

In *Nixon v. Herndon* (1927), the Court held the Texas "white primary" law unconstitutional. Curiously, Justice Holmes's opinion did not rest on the Fifteenth Amendment, but instead labeled the law "a direct and obvious" infringement of the equal protection clause, in that the statute classified and discriminated among per- sons by color alone.

Thereafter several southern states, with direct "white primary" legislation now outlawed, sought to accomplish the same end by allowing political parties to organize as "private clubs" and hence to fix their own qualifications for membership. Thereafter, various state Democratic Party organizations, acting under such laws, barred blacks from participation in their "private" primary elec- tion. This technique proved temporarily successful, when the Court in *Grovey v. Townsend* (1935) held that under such legis- lation state conventions could lawfully restrict party membership to whites, since by law the party now was a private organization and therefore not subject to the limitations imposed on state action under the Fourteenth and Fifteenth Amendments.

The Townsend decision was obviously at odds with the consti- tutional revolution already under way in the Negro's civil and political status, and it shortly was repudiated. In *United States v. Classic* (1941), a case dealing with ballot-box tampering by state officials in a primary election, the Court held that the federal gov- ernment could lawfully regulate a state primary, where such an election was an integral part of the machinery for choosing candi- dates for federal office. A possible implication of this decision was that the guarantees of the Fifteenth Amendment extended to state primary elections. Finally, in *Smith v. Allwright* (1944), the Court specifically reversed the Townsend decision. Justice Reed's opinion pointed out that since the state of Texas had delegated to the Democratic Party the right to fix the qualifications for party membership, the party convention in barring Negroes constituted "state action" within the meaning of the Fifteenth Amendment. The exclusion of Negroes by the Party was therefore unconstitutional.

From time to time thereafter the Court disposed of other state devices designed to evade the force of the Fifteenth Amendment. Thus in *Schnell v. Davis* (1949), the Court refused to review the decision of a lower federal court declaring void Alabama's so-called Boswell Amendment, which provided that voters in order to register must be able to "understand and explain" any article in the state constitution. Significantly, local election officials were to administer the law. The federal district court had labeled the law a "patently unconstitutional" scheme to evade the Fifteenth Amendment. (It was "devices" of the kind, outlawed in the Boswell case, which the Civil Rights Act of 1964 would seek to eliminate.) In *Terry v. Adams* (1953), the Court extended the principles of the Allwright decision to cover private primaries held by the altogether unofficial but highly influential "Jaybird Party," whose nominees in a Texas county thereafter invariably received local Democratic nominations. The Court held simply that the "Jaybird Party" had in fact become a part of the state's election machinery, so that its elections were covered by the Fifteenth Amendment. And in *Gomillion v. Lightfoot* (1960), the Court unanimously declared invalid an Alabama law that had carefully redrawn the boundaries of the city of Tuskegee in such a way as to exclude from the city all but a small fraction of that municipality's former Negro residents and thus had excluded them from participating in the city's elections. The law, said the Court in a unanimous opinion, constituted an obvious attempt to subvert the Fifteenth Amendment.

One device that for a time remained outside the reach of the Court was the so-called poll tax, whereby a state required the payment of a small head tax as a prerequisite to voting. Such laws were commonplace in the nineteenth century, but beginning about 1890 they died out almost everywhere except in the South, where they were retained as a fairly effective instrument to prevent Negro voting. As of 1948, seven southern states retained the tax, which by law was usually retroactive and cumulative, so that a citizen who at length decided to exercise the franchise found himself obliged to pay a sum which might well amount to thirty or forty dollars. Confronted with such an obstacle, the more indigent voter, white or black, speedily found himself overcome anew with a vast indifference with respect to the election at hand. The Southern Conference on Human Welfare in 1938 condemned the poll tax as "patently a device for disfranchising Negroes." But the Supreme Court, in *Breedlove v. Suttles* (1937), ruled that the tax, properly administered, did not violate either the equal protection clause or the Fifteenth Amendment and was constitutional.

Abolition of the poll tax, at least in federal elections, was an early and long-time objective of liberal proponents of federal civil rights legislation. Supporters of such a law pointed to the provision in Article I, Section 4 of the Constitution, which permitted Congress to regulate the "time, place, and manner" of holding federal elections. Abolition of the poll tax, they asserted, would be a proper regulation of the "manner" of holding such elections. Southern congressmen in rebuttal cited the obvious fact that the Constitution made both federal and state elections primarily a matter of state responsibility, and pointed out also that the Court itself had accepted the poll tax as constitutional. They argued therefrom that congressional abolition of the tax would be unconstitutional.

Poll tax repealer bills were introduced at every session of Congress for the next generation after 1937, although for a long time there was little hope of their passage. Typical of such measures was the bill introduced in 1941 by Senator Claude Pepper of Florida, which provided that the poll tax was not to be deemed a qualification for voting within the meaning of Article I, Section 2 of the Constitution. The Soldiers' Vote Act of 1942 abolished the poll tax as a franchise requirement for members of the armed forces for the duration of the war. But postwar attempts at general abolition met with consistent failure, until adoption of a constitutional amendment, together with passage of the Civil Rights Act of 1964 and Voting Rights Act of 1965, and a Supreme Court decision declaring such taxes unconstitutional, finally eliminated them as a feature of the American political scene.[6]

THE CIVIL RIGHTS CAMPAIGN: ANTI-LYNCHING AND F.E.P.C. BILLS

The campaign for enactment of a federal anti-lynching statute and a federal fair employment practices law encountered a far more formidable constitutional obstacle than did that for Negro voting rights—the familiar fact that Congress, under the dictum set

---

[6] See below, p. 899.

forth in the Civil Rights cases, had no comprehensive police power with respect to the private rights of one individual as against another. This fact, along with southern political opposition, was sufficient to block all legislation in both areas for a generation.

As of 1940 there were but two federal statutes, both of them products of the Reconstruction era, which could conceivably be construed as of some value in protecting Negroes against lynching, violence, or intimidation. Section 51, Title 18, of the United States Code, derived from the Enforcement Act of 1870, forbade conspiracies to deny any person the rights "secured to him by the Constitution and laws of the United States." Section 52, Title 18, a remnant of the Civil Rights Act of 1866, made it a misdemeanor willfully to deprive any person under color of state law of rights "secured or protected by the Constitution or laws of the United States or to subject any person to different pains or penalties on account of race."[7]

These measures in reality were of very limited efficacy. The Civil Rights Section in the Department of Justice, which Attorney General Frank Murphy established in 1939, at first expressed the hope that these two provisions might be made the basis of an adequate federal anti-violence program. However, this expectation was speedily doomed to disappointment. Section 51 had repeatedly been interpreted by the Supreme Court—for example, in *Logan v. United States* (1892) and in *United States v. Powell* (1909)—to mean little more than the right of a person to be free from violence by officials while in federal or state custody.

Until 1941, Section 52 had never been subjected to scrutiny by the Supreme Court, but the provision quite evidently applied only to the misuse of power against individuals by state officials. In *United States v. Classic* (1941), the Court confirmed this restrictive interpretation of Section 52. And in *Screws v. United States* (1945), the Court, speaking through Justice Douglas, held that Section 52 could be construed as constitutional only if applied to state officials who acted "under color of law" to deprive a person of a specific right secured to him by the Constitution or laws of the United States. Significantly, Roberts, Jackson, and Frankfurter thought Section 52 unconstitutional on its face. Thus Sections 51 and 52, far from proving themselves in practice to be effective federal anti-lynch laws, ultimately served only to emphasize the constitutional difficulties involved in such legislation.

Nonetheless, the leaders of the liberal bloc in Congress, begin-

---

[7] Section 51 has since become 18 U.S.C. 241; Section 52 is now 18 U.S.C. 242.

ning in 1946, regularly introduced anti-lynch proposals. A 1947 bill sponsored by Senators Robert Wagner of New York and Wayne Morse of Oregon, for example, defined the right not to be lynched as an attribute of national citizenship, guaranteed also by United States adherence to the United Nations Covenant. And a bill introduced by Representative Clifford Case of New Jersey also declared it to be a "federal right" not to be lynched, and provided for prosecution of any person infringing that right. But such proposals, and numerous others like them, got nowhere.

Enactment of a federal fair employment practices statute posed fewer constitutional difficulties than did a federal anti-lynching law, the Court's sweeping affirmation in *United States v. Darby* (1941) of federal authority over labor relations affecting interstate commerce making it highly probable that such a measure would be held constitutional. In 1941, as already observed, President Roosevelt established a Federal Fair Employment Practices Commission by executive order, essentially as a wartime emergency measure, and Congress appropriated money for this body annually until 1945. A National Council for a Permanent Fair Employment Practices Commission, organized in June, 1944, was able to enlist both Senators Robert F. Wagner of New York and Arthur Capper of Kansas as honorary co-chairmen. By the war's end, nearly all northern leaders of both major political parties were at least nominally in favor of a federal F.E.P.C. statute, and in 1945 no less than thirteen measures to that end were introduced in the House alone. Thereafter, F.E.P.C. bills were a regular feature of every Congress, but for a long time they received no great attention.

FROM THE TRUMAN CIVIL RIGHTS PROGRAM TO THE CIVIL RIGHTS ACTS OF 1957 AND 1960

The postwar campaign for a comprehensive new federal civil rights act may fairly be said to have begun in 1946, when President Truman appointed a fifteen-man Commission on Civil Rights to investigate the situation in the nation at large. The commission, under the chairmanship of Charles E. Wilson of the General Motors Corporation, spent a year in the analysis of the problem. It reported that the nation of late had made great progress in the area of civil rights, but that further legislation was needed to close the gap between the American equalitarian ideal and actual practice.

In February, 1948, accordingly, President Truman sent a special message to Congress, based upon the Commission report, calling for the enactment of a comprehensive new federal civil rights statute. Recommended measures included creation of a Joint Congressional Committee on Civil Rights, establishment of a Federal Civil Rights Commission, and statutory creation of a Civil Rights Division in the Department of Justice. The President also asked for provisions outlawing the poll tax in federal elections, extending federal protection against lynching, and establishing a Fair Employment Practices Commission.

The Truman civil rights recommendations remained bottled up in Congress for the next several years. In part the difficulty lay in the general atmosphere of postwar conservative reaction, in which the public showed itself more concerned with catching Communists than with protecting Negro rights.

However, the great obstacle in Congress to the successful enactment of a new civil rights law was the virtual absence of cloture in the Senate. Rule XXII of that body provided that cloture in debate could be imposed only upon the vote of a "constitutional two-thirds majority," that is, by sixty-four Senators. The rule further stipulated that there could be no cloture whatsoever in any debate to amend Rule XXII. Thus the rule not only made cloture all but impossible if an obdurate minority wished to filibuster; it also made it vastly difficult to change the rule itself.

Moreover, a majority of the Senate, even including many northern liberals, evidently had considerable affection for Rule XXII, for attempts to amend it for a long time went down to defeat by substantial majorities. A 1953 attempt by a northern liberal bloc met defeat, 70 to 21. And a 1957 major assault, conducted under the leadership of Senator Clinton Anderson of New Mexico, failed 55 to 38. In 1959 the Senate finally consented to amend the rule to provide cloture by a simple two-thirds majority of the Senators present, but the rule still presented an almost insuperable obstacle to cloture if a recalcitrant minority wished to hold the floor.

By 1956, the political atmosphere with respect to civil rights legislation nonetheless was undergoing substantial change. Northern Democrats had become acutely aware that the southern Democratic stand on civil rights had badly damaged the party's strength, not only in presidential campaigns but also in northern congressional elections. Republican politicians, by contrast, seized upon the civil rights issue as a means whereby the all-important northern Negro vote might be wooed away from its old New Deal political allegiance. Republican platforms in 1952 and 1956 were strong and unequivocal in their demand for comprehensive civil rights legislation, and Eisenhower's Vice President, Richard Nixon, was an avowed member of the NAACP. The civil rights question, in short, posed an issue upon which Republicans now eagerly seized and which Democrats were obliged to meet.

In January, 1956, the Eisenhower administration laid before Congress a somewhat limited civil rights "package," its main features borrowed from the earlier Truman civil rights program. The resultant bill passed the House in June, but thereafter died of calculated strangulation in the Senate Judiciary Committee. In January, 1957, however, a liberal coalition in the two houses of Congress took control and drove through to passage by lopsided majorities the Civil Rights Act of 1957, which President Eisenhower signed into law in September.

The Civil Rights Act of 1957, the first such law to be enacted by Congress since the close of Reconstruction, was an extremely modest measure, devoted largely to strengthening the judicial enforcement of voting rights in the South. The act established a temporary six-man Commission on Civil Rights, charged with investigating alleged franchise discriminations based upon race, and instructed it to make its final report within two years. (Subsequent special acts extended the Commission's life indefinitely.) Other provisions empowered the Attorney General to seek injunctions to prevent interference with the right to vote, made it a federal offense to intimidate or coerce anyone in order to interfere with the exercise of the franchise, and empowered federal courts to try criminal contempt cases without juries, where the punishment to be imposed was a fine of not more than $300 and imprisonment for not more than forty-five days. The law also fixed for the first time the qualifications of federal jurors, making eligible all citizens over twenty-one who could read and write, who had been a resident for one year of the judicial district in question, and who had not been convicted of a crime.

The new Civil Rights Commission, under the chairmanship of John Hannah, President of Michigan State University, reported to the President in September, 1959. The recent Civil Rights Act, the report made clear, had been of doubtful efficacy—"no one had yet been registered through the civil remedies" it provided. Accordingly, the Commission recommended a system of federal registration for disfranchised Negro voters. In the face of some dissent offered by southern members of the Commission, it also called for a federal statutory requirement that state voting records be preserved for five years, a provision making it a criminal offense to deprive anyone of the right to vote in a federal election, establishment of the Commission as a permanent investigatory body, denial of federal grants to institutions of higher learning practicing segregation, and a constitutional amendment abolishing literacy tests as a franchise requirement. The Commission also recommended that it be empowered to act as an advisory and conciliatory board in school desegregation cases.

These recommendations resulted presently in the enactment of another very modest law: the Civil Rights Act of 1960. President Eisenhower's annual message to Congress in January, 1960, called for a new civil rights law providing for a system of voter-referees appointed by the federal courts to protect the right to vote. Once more a liberal biparty coalition took control of affairs, forced the administration bill to the House floor by the threat of a discharge petition, and secured passage by an overwhelming majority after a five-week debate. In the Senate, a moderate bloc under the leadership of Lyndon Johnson of Texas first broke a protracted southern filibuster and then guided the House bill to passage, virtually unchanged, 71 to 18. President Eisenhower signed the measure early in May.

The Civil Rights Act of 1960, like its predecessor of three years earlier an extremely limited statute, made mandatory the preservation of state records of federal elections for at least twenty-two months, and provided for the appointment by federal courts of voter-referees empowered to receive applications from any person allegedly denied the right to vote, which might result ultimately in a court order declaring the person qualified to vote. Other provisions made arson and bombing federal crimes, where the offenders crossed state lines, authorized the establishment of schools for members of the armed forces when local state facilities were not made available for such persons, and provided for a $1,000 fine and a year's imprisonment for anyone convicted of obstructing the orders of a federal court. (In its original form, this last provision had been aimed only at defiance of school integration orders, but at the insistence of southern Senators it had been broadened to include all court orders.)

THE POLL TAX AMENDMENT AND THE
CIVIL RIGHTS ACT OF 1964

Neither the Civil Rights Act of 1957 nor that of 1960 made any very considerable impact upon the growing racial crisis in the country. School integration was making very little progress; further, the 1963 report of the Commission on Civil Rights made it clear that in at least one hundred hard-core counties in the lower South, Negro registration, in spite of the 1957 and 1960 laws, had risen to only 8.3 per cent of the eligible black voters.

Meanwhile the rapid spread of sit-ins and freedom marches, the rise to prominence of new civil rights leaders such as James Farmer and Martin Luther King, and the burgeoning of the Black Muslims whose most charismatic leader, Malcolm X, was openly advocating black revolution and the establishment of a Negro republic, all testified to the growing sense of outrage in the Negro community generally and to the fact that the civil rights "revolution" was moving into a new stage, characterized by civil disobedience, direct action, and even the resort to violence. In the lower South, also, there was an ominous rise in white violence, as reactionaries countered sit-downs and freedom marches with mass arrests, intimidation, and, on occasion, even with bombings and the murder of civil rights workers.

Both the administration of John F. Kennedy and the liberal bloc in Congress soon became convinced that further federal legislation was imperative. Their first move was against the poll tax. In August, 1962, the liberal coalition passed and sent to the states a constitutional amendment abolishing the poll tax in federal elections. Ratification took place with surprising rapidity, the Twenty-Fourth Amendment becoming a part of the Constitution in February, 1964. A year later, in *Harman v. Forssenius* (1965), the Supreme Court brought the new amendment to bear when it ruled that a Virginia law, passed in anticipation of the amendment's ratification, which imposed a special federal registration requirement on persons not paying the poll tax in state elections, violated the new constitutional prohibition. All this meant but little, for the Supreme Court presently was to outlaw entirely all poll taxes, both state and national.[8]

In June, 1963, President Kennedy, now thoroughly aroused to the explosive character of the nation's racial crisis, submitted to Congress proposals for a new civil rights act, the most comprehensive since Reconstruction. The President asked for a prohibition upon the denial of equal facilities to any person in restaurants, hotels, and the like; authorization for school desegregation suits to be instituted by the Attorney General; a ban on job discrimination because of race; statutory creation of an Equal Employment Opportunity Commission; a prohibition on racial discrimination in all

---

[8] See below, p. 899.

federally funded programs; the establishment of a Community Relations Service to advise on the adjustment of racial conflicts; and a new and more comprehensive system of federal voter registration. The President's message carried a note of extreme urgency. The price of inaction, he warned, might well be that "leadership on both sides" in the civil rights crisis would "pass from the hands of reasonable and responsible men to the purveyors of hate and violence."

In spite of the President's demand for haste, both houses proceeded with something like "all deliberate speed." A House Judiciary subcommittee under its chairman, Representative Emanuel Celler of New York, after leisurely hearings, drafted a very strong bill that prohibited all discrimination in all facilities affecting interstate commerce and in all state-licensed enterprises—this last a reflection of the Douglas view of the sweep of permissible federal regulation under the equal protection clause. So strong was the measure that the Kennedy administration became alarmed. At its insistence, Title II was amended to exempt certain small enterprises—"Mrs. Murphy's boarding house"—and the compromise bill at length was approved at the end of October. However, the hostile attitude of Representative Howard Smith of Virginia, chairman of the House Rules Committee, and the disruptive impact of the assassination of President Kennedy in November frustrated further action in 1963.

In January, 1964, the liberal coalition in the House, now supported by a formidable civil rights lobby, representing among other organizations the AFL-CIO, the National Council of Churches, several veterans' organizations, numerous Catholic and Jewish clergy, and the NAACP, used the threat of a discharge petition to force the bill out onto the floor. Passage followed, 290 to 130, on February 10. In the Senate, Everett Dirksen of Illinois, the minority leader, took charge behind the scenes, maneuvering carefully between liberals and conservatives and working some seventy amendments into the bill to assuage the constitutional doubts of marginal opponents. On June 10, the Senate voted 71 to 29 for cloture, and passage of the bill itself followed on June 19, 73 to 27, almost as an anticlimax. "This is a sad day for America," declaimed Senator Strom Thurmond of South Carolina, while Jacob Javits of New York countered with the observation that this was "one of the Senate's finest hours." More astute, perhaps, was Dirksen's widely quoted remark: "Stronger than all the armies is an idea whose time has come."

The heart of the Civil Rights Act of 1964 was to be found in Title II, which, in language reminiscent of the repudiated Civil Rights Act of 1875 nearly a century earlier, declared all persons to be entitled to "the full and equal enjoyment" of the facilities of inns, hotels, motels, restaurants, motion picture houses, theaters, concert halls, sports arenas, and the like, "without discrimination or segregation" because of "race, color, religion or national origin." These guarantees were applicable to any establishment if it "affects commerce or if discrimination is supported by state action." This last was said to be present if discrimination was carried on under color of law, was required by local custom or usage enforced by state officials, or was required by the state itself.

Other provisions of the new law ranged over a wide variety of civil rights problems. Title III authorized the Attorney General to file suits for the desegregation of public facilities other than public schools. Title IV required the Commissioner of Education to conduct a survey of the lack of availability of equal educational facilities because of race, color, religion, or national origin, and also authorized him to "render school boards technical assistance" in preparing desegregation plans. It also authorized the Attorney General on complaint to institute suits for the desegregation of public schools.

Title V empowered the Civil Rights Commission to investigate all situations where citizens were deprived of the equal protection of the laws because of race, color, religion, or national origin. Title VI prohibited discrimination on account of race, color, religion, or national origin in any program receiving federal financial assistance. Title VII created a five-man Equal Employment Opportunity Commission, banned discrimination in employment on account of race, color, religion, or national origin by employers, labor unions, and employment agencies, and gave the new commission the power through investigations, hearings, and civil actions to enforce the law. Title X established the new Community Relations Service, and instructed it to assist communities in resolving "disputes, disagreements, or difficulties" relating to discriminatory practices based upon race, color, religion, or national origin.

Title I, virtually a separate statute, incorporated a variety of measures intended to promote effective federal enforcement of the right to vote. It prohibited any person acting under color of law from applying any discriminatory standard to a prospective voter different from those applicable to other voters in the same district, and it also forbade any denial of the right to vote because of any error in the registration proceedings. The law also put state literacy tests for the franchise under very restrictive controls. It forbade outright the employment of any such test in federal elections unless it was administered in writing and required of all prospective registrants, and it stipulated also that there was to be a "rebuttable presumption" that any person who had completed the sixth grade in a public school possessed sufficient "literacy, comprehension and intelligence to vote in a federal election."

TITLE II IN THE COURTS: THE HEART OF ATLANTA
AND MC CLUNG CASES

Title II of the new act, embodying its "public accommodations" provisions, was not long in meeting and passing a crucial test of constitutionality. In December, 1964, less than six months after the act's passage, the Court unanimously sustained Title II as a legitimate exercise of the commerce power.

In *Heart of Atlanta Motel v. United States* (1964), Justice Clark, who delivered the opinion of the Court, declared that Congress possessed "ample power" under its authority to regulate interstate commerce to forbid racial discrimination in motels and hotels serving interstate travelers and thus "affecting commerce." The crucial constitutional test, Clark said, was whether the activity to be regulated concerned "commerce which affects more than one state" and bore a "real and substantial relationship" to the national interest. Clark also brought an old "liberal-national" doctrine to bear: It was not material, he said, that Congress in regulating interstate commerce might also in fact be "legislating against moral wrongs." As precedent he cited the long series of federal "police power" cases dealing with the "white slave" trade, pure food and drug laws, federal regulation of hours and wages, interstate prohibitions upon gambling, and so on. Significantly, Clark carefully refrained from invoking the equal protection clause. This enabled him to dismiss as not "apposite" the embarrassing precedent of the Civil Rights Cases, where an earlier Court had invalidated the public accommodations provisions of the Civil Rights Act of 1875.

Clark followed essentially the same line of reasoning in a companion case, *Katzenbach v. McClung* (1964), to hold that the prohibition in Title II upon racial discrimination in restaurants was a constitutional exercise of the commerce power. The case presented the Court with a particularly sharp test of the applicability of the law, since "Ollie's Barbeque," the Birmingham eating place whose discriminatory practices were at issue, did not serve out-of-state customers, and the only possible basis for bringing it under the aegis of the law was that it drew from out of the state "a substantial portion of the food served."

In spite of the fact that service to interstate travelers technically was not at issue, however, Clark's opinion emphasized nonetheless that the congressional inquiry prior to passage of the law had been "replete with testimony of the burden placed on interstate commerce by discrimination in restaurants." In any event, Clark held, Ollie's place came within the purview of the law because a substantial portion of the food it served came from outside the state. Nor did it matter, said Clark with a citation to the 1942 precedent of *Wickard v. Filburn,* that the quantity of food involved amounted only to a very small portion of all the foodstuffs moving in interstate commerce. And after disposing of a number of technicalities, Clark concluded that in passing Title II Congress had "acted well within its power," and "we herewith declare it valid."

Justices Black, Douglas, and Goldberg all wrote separate concurring opinions applicable to both the Heart of Atlanta and McClung cases. Black emphasized particularly that his dissenting opinion in *Bell v. Maryland* did "not in the slightest affect my conclusion that Title II of the 1964 act was valid under the commerce and necessary and proper clauses." Douglas on his part made it clear that he would have preferred to have seen the Court rest its decisions upon the equal protection clause, a course that would have made it unnecessary thereafter to determine whether or not a particular public facility "affected commerce" within the provisions of the statute. Goldberg also would have preferred to have the Court involve the equal protection clause to sustain Title II, since, he said, the law's concern, after all, was with "the vindication of human dignities and not mere economics."

In still another companion case, *Hamm v. City of Rock Hill* (1964), the Court held that passage by Congress of Title II had in effect abated both pending and future state criminal trespass prosecutions in sit-in cases. Justice Clark's reasoning for the majority was decidedly tortuous and involved. In sum, he argued that the new federal act had substituted a federally protected right for what formerly had constituted a crime. And since under federal law any such substitution would have required an abatement of a pending federal criminal prosecution, the doctrine of national supremacy here made it imperative to abate any parallel state prosecution also. To this line of reasoning, Justice Black vigorously dissented, pointing out that the Court had disregarded an 1871 congressional statute saving pending criminal prosecutions against abatement through new legislation unless Congress specifically so required. Harlan, Stewart, and White also joined in dissent, Harlan observing succinctly that abatement "strikes a jarring note" when it "is applied to affect the legislation of a different sovereignty."

All this was of little moment as against the fact that the Court now had sanctioned federal legislative controls reaching far into spheres of private discrimination hitherto regarded as beyond the reach of federal law. The time-honored distinction between state and private action, which even now the Court had carefully preserved, promised in the future to become increasingly sterile.

THE VOTING RIGHTS ACT OF 1965: BACKGROUND AND PASSAGE

For some time, Negro leaders, among them Roy Wilkins of the NAACP, James Farmer of CORE, and Martin Luther King, had been demanding passage of a more effective federal statute to protect the right to vote. Neither the Civil Rights Act of 1957 nor its 1960 counterpart had proved particularly effective in decisively breaking long-established southern discriminatory franchise practices, although Negro voting, especially in urban areas in the South had increased substantially. The federal Commission on Civil Rights dramatized the problem in its 1963 reports, pointing out that one hundred so-called "hard-core counties" in the lower South had lately succeeded almost completely in blocking Negro attempts to vote.

The Civil Rights Division of the Department of Justice in fact was already actively engaged in a series of battles to extend Negro voting south of the Mason and Dixon line. On paper, at least, the results of this effort promised to be impressive. Thus in *Anderson v. Martin*, decided in January, 1964, the Court unanimously held unconstitutional a Louisiana statute requiring the state secretary of state to designate on the ballot the race of all candidates for public office. The law, said Justice Clark, deliberately invited invidious discriminatory classification on the basis of race and so violated the equal protection clause.

Again, in *Louisiana v. United States* (1965), the Court invalidated a so-called "discrimination test" embodied in Louisiana's constitution and laws, whereby registration officials in local parishes exercised virtually unlimited discretion in administering a test requiring prospective voters to "give a reasonable interpretation" of any provision in the state or federal constitutions. The law, said Justice Black's opinion for a unanimous Court, was "not a test but a trap," and violated both the Fourteenth and Fifteenth Amendments. And in a companion case, *United States v. Mississippi* (1965), the Court, reversing a three-man lower court decision, ruled that the Attorney General properly could sue both the state of Mississippi and its Board of Registration Commissioners to block enforcement of the discriminatory literacy "devices" incorporated in the state's constitution and laws. Both the Louisiana and Mississippi actions, significantly, had been brought by the Attorney General under the Fifteenth Amendment Enforcement Act, adopted in 1870, long before enactment of Title I of the 1964 Civil Rights Law.

Meanwhile, events in and around Selma, Alabama, were impelling President Johnson and the liberal bloc in Congress toward new legislative endeavors to protect Negroes in the exercise of the franchise. Selma was a city in the so-called "black belt," where, as federal statistics revealed, Negro registration and voting had made almost no progress. Early in 1965, Martin Luther King launched a series of "marches," directed first against Selma and then against Montgomery, the Alabama state capital, calculated to force an increase in Negro voting. White officials fought back with state troopers, clubs, guns, dogs, and tear gas. At the height of the disorders, hoodlums murdered the Rev. James Reeb of Boston and then Mrs. Viola Liuzzo of Detroit, who, with hundreds of other white civil rights enthusiasts, had come South to participate in King's campaign. An enraged northern liberal community thereupon poured some 25,000 persons, many of them leading citizens in their home communities, into Selma to participate in a massive new "march" on Montgomery, which President Johnson protected by mobilizing the Alabama National Guard.

In Washington, both the President and the liberal bloc in both houses now took advantage of the Selma crisis to promote passage of a drastic new federal statute designed to force even the most recalcitrant portions of the South to yield to the black American's demand for the franchise. On March 15, following the Reeb murder, the President appeared in person before Congress to demand action on a new Voting Rights Bill, which he requested in the name of the "long-suffering men and women" who had "peaceably protested the denial of their rights as Americans."

Enactment of the new measure, it soon became clear, was virtually a foregone conclusion. Senate Minority Leader Everett Dirksen once again directed strategy in the upper house, where southern opposition this time proved to be demoralized and feeble.

Final passage came in August, the President proclaiming as he signed it: "Today we strike away the last major shackles of those fierce and ancient bonds of slavery."

The Voting Rights Act of 1965 was designed specifically to eliminate franchise discrimination against Negroes in the South, in particular that achieved through resort to literacy devices, educational tests, and the like. The law automatically suspended the use of such "devices" in any state or subdivision thereof where the Attorney General found them to be in use and where the Director of the Census determined that less than fifty per cent of the persons of voting age were registered or had voted in the presidential election of 1964. Such suspension, once in effect, was not reviewable by any court and was to remain in force for five years.

The law also provided for the appointment of federal "examiners" to supervise elections in states practicing discrimination in violation of the Fifteenth Amendment. Whenever the Attorney General instituted legal proceedings against any state to enforce the guarantees of the Fifteenth Amendment the court was to authorize the appointment of such officers by the Civil Service Commission. Examiners were authorized to prepare lists of eligible voters regardless of any existing registration list, and were to enforce the right of such persons to vote by inspection of polling places on election day.

In addition, the act carried a provision which, in effect, set aside New York State's law requiring literacy in English as a prerequisite for the franchise, for the benefit of the Spanish-speaking Puerto Rican population of New York City. To this end, the act prohibited any state from making the right to vote of persons educated in "American-flag schools," where a language other than English was used, conditional upon the ability to read and write English. Still another provision of the law made a finding that the poll tax had been used in some states to "deny the constitutional right of citizens to vote," and it directed the Attorney General to institute suits against such taxes—in effect to test their constitutionality.

Immediately after passage of the Voting Rights Act, the Attorney General by proclamation extended coverage under the new law to South Carolina, Alabama, Alaska, Louisiana, Mississippi, Virginia, twenty-six counties in North Carolina, and one county in Arizona. In November, coverage was extended to two more counties in Arizona, one county in Hawaii, and one in Idaho. A veritable welter of suits and counter suits intended to block or effect operation of the law followed within the next few months. After some delay, the Supreme Court agreed to hear arguments in *South Carolina v. Katzenbach* (1966), in which South Carolina, invoking the original jurisdiction of the Supreme Court in cases to which a state is a party, had sued the Attorney General, asking that the Court declare unconstitutional those portions of the Voting Rights Act dealing with literacy "devices" and with the appointment and functions of federal examiners. South Carolina's standing to sue was open to some doubt, for the action evidently ran counter to the decision in *Massachusetts v. Mellon* (1923), in which the Court had ruled that a state could not interpose its sovereignty between its citizens and the operation of federal law. In spite of this evident difficulty, however, a majority of the justices had consented to hear arguments in the case. At the Court's invitation, a majority of the states of the Union also submitted briefs either supporting South Carolina or the Attorney General.

South Carolina's argument, although immensely complex, actually came down to three main points. First and most important was the claim that Congress in enacting the statute had exceeded its legislative powers under the enforcement clause of the Fifteenth Amendment, and thereby encroached on the reserved powers of the states. This argument carried the assumption that the courts alone could supervise in detail state voting procedures with respect to the amendment, and that congressional power to enforce the amendment's guarantees could be exercised only in the most general terms. Second, South Carolina contended that the coverage formula in the act, by subjecting only certain states to special treatment, violated the principle of the equality of states in the Union. Third, the state claimed that the law, by barring judicial review of administrative findings, constituted a bill of attainder and also impaired the principle of the separation of powers.

Chief Justice Warren's opinion for a near-unanimous Court, while long and intricate, rejected South Carolina's principal arguments almost out of hand. Congress, the Chief Justice emphasized, possessed broad legislative powers under the amendment and might "use any rational means to effectuate the constitutional prohibition of racial discrimination in voting." To emphasize the point, he quoted the celebrated broad construction formula laid down by John Marshall in *McCulloch v. Maryland*: "Let the ends be legitimate . . ." The doctrine of the equality of states, Warren continued, applied only to the terms of admission to the Union and "not to the remedies for local evils which have subsequently appeared." Finally, citing *Massachusetts v. Mellon*, Warren dismissed the bill of attainder argument with the assertion that a state had no standing to sue "as the parent of its citizens . . . against the federal government, the ultimate *parens patriae* of every American citizen." The portions of the Voting Rights Act under review, the Chief Justice concluded, were constitutional as "a valid means for carrying out the commands of the Fifteenth Amendment."

In an accompanying opinion, Justice Black attacked as unconstitutional those portions of the Voting Rights Act that prohibited a state under coverage of the law from amending its franchise legislation without the consent of the Attorney General. Otherwise, Black agreed, the law was a valid exercise of congressional power.

A few weeks later, in *Katzenbach v. Morgan* (1966), the Court passed favorably upon the portion of the law which in effect outlawed New York's English literacy requirement in order to guarantee the franchise to the state's Spanish-speaking population. A three-man federal district court had held the provision unconstitutional, on the ground that it invaded the reserved powers of the states in violation of the Tenth Amendment. On appeal, the Court now reversed. Justice Brennan's opinion emphasized once more the broad sweep of congressional legislative authority in the implementation of its delegated powers—in this instance in enforcement of the equal protection clause of the Fourteenth Amendment. Brennan also dismissed as "inapposite" several earlier decisions holding state literacy tests constitutional, notably that in *Lassiter v. Northampton Election Board* (1959), since these cases had been decided in the absence of federal legislation. This time, Justice Harlan, in a dissent joined by Justice Stewart, protested that Congress in enacting the provision under review had in effect made an arbitrary ruling that New York's literacy law violated the equal protection clause; thereby, he said, Congress unconstitutionally had invaded the functions of the judiciary.

Meanwhile in March, the Court had completed the destruction of the poll tax, by ruling in *Harper v. Virginia Board of Elections* (1966) that such taxes introduced "wealth or payment of a fee as a measure of a voter's qualifications" and so imposed "an invidious discrimination . . . that runs afoul of the equal protection clause." Accordingly, said Justice Douglas for the majority, the decision in *Breedlove v. Suttles*, in which the Court had held to the contrary, now stood overruled. Both Justices Harlan and Black entered strong dissents. Black accused the majority of using the "old 'natural law-due process' formula" simply to legislate out of existence a state statute it did not like, while Harlan, making much the same point, charged the Court with tailoring its opinion to the "current egalitarian notion" of the moment, in violation of Holmes's celebrated warning in his Lochner dissent against judicial legislation. At all events, the poll tax, already reduced by law and constitutional amendment to state elections in only four states of the Union, now was completely dead.

The Voting Rights Act shortly proved to have a remarkable impact upon Negro resort to the franchise in the South. In 1964, less than 1,500,000 blacks had been registered in the eleven states of the Old Confederacy; by 1969, under the impetus of the new law, that figure had risen to some 3,100,000, an increase of more than 100 per cent. Increased Negro voting in turn led to a remarkable rise in the number of blacks holding elective office. By 1969, nearly five hundred Negroes held elective office in the states of the lower South alone, including the vice-mayor of Atlanta and mayors of small cities in Mississippi and North Carolina.

CONGRESS, THE WARREN COURT, AND RACIAL DISCRIMINATION IN HOUSING

The elimination of racial discrimination in the sale and rental of housing was still another area in which Congress presently brought its legislative powers to bear in the national racial crisis. In the background of this development was a rapid increase in *de facto* community racial segregation in the great cities of the country, particularly in the North and West, where large numbers of whites, frightened by the unprecedented influx of blacks into the inner cities, had fled to the suburbs. Here, in spite of the fact that restrictive covenants now were technically illegal, a cautious network of "understandings" between home owners, real estate dealers and local governmental officials kept these communities "lily-white." Angry Negroes, frustrated in their attempts to escape from slum-ridden urban ghettos, in turn fought to obtain state and municipal "fair housing" laws which would compel property owners and their agents to sell or rent to anyone regardless of race. Frightened whites responded in many instances by demanding confirmation by statute of the old common-law rule that a property owner might lawfully restrict the sale of his property to buyers of his own choice—a polite euphemism for a right to refuse to sell to Negroes or other "undesirables."

For years various liberal groups had been campaigning both for state and federal open housing laws. A National Committee Against Discrimination in Housing, a loose alliance of churches, labor unions, and civil rights organizations established in 1950, played a major role in securing passage by 1965 of open housing statutes, ordinances, or administrative rules in some seventeen states and sixty cities throughout the country. Unhappily, the fair housing drive also produced a fairly severe "white backlash," as conservatives forced through various laws confirming the common-law "freedom of choice" in realty sales.

In California, the white backlash led ultimately to the Supreme Court. In 1964, the voters of that state by referendum approved Proposition 14, a constitutional amendment providing that the state could not interfere with the right of any person to sell or rent or "to decline to sell or rent" his property to "such persons as he in his absolute discretion chooses." Proposition 14 had the effect of repealing a variety of California statutes and constitutional guarantees against racial discrimination in housing, notably the Rumford Fair Housing Act of 1963, and as such precipitated a long legal battle in the courts.

At length, in *Reitman v. Mulkey* (1967), the Supreme Court upheld the decision of the California Supreme Court, which had ruled Proposition 14 to be a violation of the Fourteenth Amendment. The California Court, Justice White's majority opinion pointed out, had treated Proposition 14 as one in which the state had "expressly authorized and constitutionalized the right to discriminate." Agreeing with this analysis, White concluded that "the right to discriminate is now one of the basic policies of the state," and thus significantly involved the state in private racial discrimination. Proposition 14 hence violated the equal protection clause. Douglas in a concurring opinion argued that in any event the realty business not only was carried on by means of state licensing but also in effect involved zoning, "a state and municipal function," so that state action was unquestionably involved. But Justice Harlan, in a sharply worded dissent concurred in by Black, Clark, and Stewart, contended that Proposition 14 was in fact "neutral on its face," so that the Court was able to reach its conclusion only through the assumption that "this requirement of passive official neutrality is camouflage," an interpretation he did not think could be sustained.

Meanwhile Congress, spurred on by the Johnson administration, moved somewhat uncertainly toward the enactment of a national fair housing law. The House in August, 1966, passed a bill to prohibit racial or religious discrimination in the sale or rental of housing, including a proviso exempting owner-occupied properties of four units or less—"Mrs. Murphy's boarding house" again. But the hostility of Senator Dirksen, who denounced the house bill as "absolutely unconstitutional," effectively killed all action in the Senate for the next two years.

At length, in the spring of 1968, Senate leaders worked out a compromise whereby the liberal bloc accepted a "rider" to the bill making it unlawful to cross state lines to incite a riot. This agreement served to break a seven-week southern filibuster, and the Senate finally passed the amended measure on March 8, 60 to 19. The assassination of Martin Luther King early in April spurred the House into concurrence, 250 to 171, and on April 11, the President signed the bill into law.

The central feature of the Civil Rights Act of 1968, as the new measure technically was known, was to be found in Title VIII, in effect a federal fair housing law. This provided for a general ban on racial and religious discrimination in the sale and rental of housing, to be imposed in three time stages, culminating in December, 1969. Only dwellings of four units or less sold without the services of a broker were exempted from the law. A separate provision of the statute, Title I, incorporated the new anti-riot measure. Other provisions of the law confirmed certain Indian rights to reservation self-government.

Within weeks of the enactment of the new federal housing law, the Supreme Court took matters into its own hands by ruling in *Jones v. Mayer Co.* (1969) that an obscure but long-standing portion of the federal code—42 U.S.C.1982—actually prohibited all racial discrimination, private as well as public, in the sale or rental of property. Section 1982, which provided that "all citizens of the United States shall have the same right . . . as is enjoyed by white citizens thereof to inherit, purchase, lease, sell, hold, and convey real and personal property," had originally been enacted as a part of the Civil Rights Act of 1866, and hence rested not upon the equal protection clause but upon the enforcement provision of the Thirteenth Amendment.

Justice Stewart's opinion for the Court first recalled that in 1948

in *Hurd v. Hodge* the Court had invoked Section 1982 to hold
invalid the judicial enforcement of restrictive covenants in the
District of Columbia, in part on the theory that government action
was involved in enforcement parallel to that in state enforcement
of such agreements, already held to be in violation of the Fourteenth Amendment. Now, however, the Court extended the force
of Section 1982 to include purely private racial discrimination in
no wise supported by government action. To support such a finding, Justice Stewart inquired at length into the historical circumstances surrounding the passage of the Civil Rights Act of 1866,
and came to the conclusion that the law had been intended to wipe
out both government-supported and purely racial private discrimination as "badges and incidences of slavery." Significantly, Stewart took sympathetic note of the recent enactment of Title VIII,
although technically it was not involved in the present action.
Justice Harlan, in a strenuous and lengthy dissent joined in by
Justice White, contended that the majority's interpretation of
Section 1982 was historically incorrect, and that the law as
presently applied was unconstitutional.

In *Hunter v. Erickson* (1969), the Court a few months later
again found occasion to comment favorably upon the newly
enacted federal housing law, this time in striking down a provision
of the city charter of Akron, Ohio, which had wiped that municipality's fair housing ordinance off the books. In certain respects
the situation rather resembled that in *Reitman v. Mulkey*. Akron
had adopted its fair housing ordinance in 1964, but thereafter the
electorate had by referendum amended the city charter to provide
that any ordinance which regulated the sale or rental of real property must be approved by a majority of the voters in a general
election before it could take effect. The new charter provision
thus had rendered the fair housing ordinance inoperative.

The Court, speaking through Justice White, found no difficulty
in holding the charter provision invalid as a violation of the equal
protection clause. Unlike the ambiguous circumstances in the
Mulkey case, where no specific law commanding discrimination
had existed, the Court here was confronted with a law that resorted to "an explicitly racial classification treating racial housing
matters differently" from other legislative problems. The ordinance, said Justice White, thus "disadvantaged those who would
benefit from laws barring racial, religious or ancestral discriminations," and was clearly unconstitutional. Justice Black alone dissented, reiterating the argument that "the Equal Protection Clause

does not empower this Court to decide what ordinances or laws a State may repeal."

THE WARREN COURT AND THE BLACK REVOLUTION: A SUMMARY

By the close of the Warren era in June 1969, it was apparent that the Court had succeeded in staging something like a "constitutional revolution, limited," in the field of civil rights, comparable in scope to that which had occurred in the law of national economic regulation following the great constitutional crisis of 1937. In the South, *de jure* segregation was rapidly becoming a thing of the past. A solid body of new constitutional law had developed which made it extremely unlikely that the nation at large would ever again revert to the legal myths of the "separate but equal" era.

At the same time, there were several ominous developments already apparent, which were destined to shape the dimensions of the continuing civil rights controversy of the 1970's. One was the shifting focus of the controversy itself, which now was beginning to center upon the problem of *de facto* segregation in the great metropolitan areas of the North and West. The social issues involved here were vastly more complex than those which the Court formerly had confronted in the South. Moreover, the appearance of a severe nationwide white "backlash" threatened to cut the ground out from beneath the Court's position, should it adopt as firm and uncompromising a stand against Northern *de facto* segregation as it had with respect to *de jure* segregation a decade or so earlier.

The election of Richard Nixon to the presidency in November 1968 was in part a product of the white "backlash." The result was to be the emergence in the 1970's of a "moderate" majority on a Court whose approach to civil rights issues would be vastly more cautious than that which had characterized the Warren era. In short, as the new decade dawned, it was evident that the ultimate answers to the great fundamental issues posed by America's racial problem were no longer as obvious or as free from doubt as had once been the case in the optimistic era of *Brown v. Board*.

Chapter

34

The Warren Court and Political Dissent: A New Era of Libertarianism

THE PRECEDENT-BREAKING DECISIONS of the Supreme Court under Chief Justice Warren in the field of desegregation and civil rights were paralleled in the fifteen years between 1954 and 1969 by the development of a powerful body of libertarian-oriented constitutional law in the field of civil liberties. The Court now engaged in a distinct shift in position with respect to the treatment of Communists, subversives, political dissidents, and "far-out" groups generally. In the process, the Court "reinterpreted," reversed, modified, or simply ignored a considerable body of constitutional law that had been written in the so-called "McCarthy Era" between 1949 and 1954, and in so doing returned the Court to the libertarian attitude toward radical political activity that had prevailed in the days of the De Jonge and Herndon cases.

Public reaction, which in the late 1950's began to shift away from hysteria and excessive anxiety toward the activities of Communists and the menace of political radicalism that had prevailed earlier, undoubtedly had something to do with the success of the Warren Court in introducing a new era of libertarian values into the judicial process. By no means, however, did the shift in public opinion account entirely for the Court's changing position, for the majority justices were obliged to brave a very considerable body of dissident conservative views in order to maintain their position. The Court's new stance, in fact, was to be explained in considerable part also by a set of accidental circumstances that, after 1954, brought together on the Supreme Bench a bloc of justices who entertained powerful philosophic convictions in favor of the values of an open society and First Amendment rights. Chief Justice Warren and the veteran New Deal Justices Black and Douglas made up the original core of this libertarian bloc. After 1957, they were joined by Justice Brennan who soon demonstrated that he was as libertarian in his beliefs as his older judicial brethren. The liberal political philosophy of these men was to make itself felt not only in the field of political dissidence but also in the law of libel, in matters having to do with the separation of church and state, and in the maintenance of First Amendment rights generally.

Control of the Court by the libertarian bloc was at first not altogether complete. For a time between about 1958 and 1962 a conservative group of justices, made up of Frankfurter, Clark, Harlan, Whittaker, and Stewart, maintained a somewhat precarious ascendancy in most of the Court's decisions in the field of political dissidence. These men, greatly influenced by Frankfurter's philosophy of judicial self-restraint, were less inclined than the libertarian activists to challenge directly the judgment of Congress on Communist controls, while they also resorted frequently to the so-called "balancing philosophy" which held that First Amendment rights must be weighed against considerations of general public welfare. But with the resignations of Frankfurter and Whittaker in 1962 and the successive appointments of Justices Goldberg and Fortas, control of First Amendment cases passed decisively into the hands of the Court's libertarian activists who thereafter built up an elaborate new body of First Amendment-oriented constitutional law. So firmly was the new law established by the close of the Warren era in 1969 that few constitutional experts thought it likely that much of it would be discarded in the future, even by a possible new conservative-oriented judicial majority.

THE WARREN COURT AND THE SMITH ACT:
THE YATES AND SCALES DECISIONS

The first clear evidence of the Warren Court's attitude toward Communist controls in relation to First Amendment Rights came in *Yates v. United States* (1957), in which the majority justices overturned the conviction of several "second-string" Communists who had been indicted in the wave of prosecutions that followed the government's victory in the Dennis decision. Without formally repudiating the "sliding scale" standard set forth in the Dennis opinion, the Court nonetheless now erected a stern new standard for evaluating convictions under the Smith Act, so rigorous as to render successful prosecution under that measure difficult in the extreme.

Justice Harlan, who in this instance joined with the Court's libertarian majority, first addressed his opinion to the meaning of the section in the Smith Act prohibiting the organization of subversive groups, which, among other things, petitioners were accused of violating. He construed this clause very narrowly, to include within its sweep only the original act of setting up such a group and not any continuing process of proselytising and recruiting. But since the Communist Party in its modern form had been established in 1945 and since the federal three-year statute of limitations applied to prosecutions under the act, the Court's interpretation meant that Communist Party officials now were immune to prosecution under the organization section, unless they were to be so foolish sometime in the future as to "organize" their Party anew once more.

Harlan then drew a careful distinction between advocacy of subversive action and mere advocacy of doctrine. Only the former class of acts, he emphasized, could be prosecuted constitutionally under the limitations of the First Amendment. The "essential distinction," he emphasized, "is that those to whom advocacy is addressed must be urged to *do* something, now or in the future, rather than merely believe in something." All this meant that the government now would be obliged to prove a nexus of specific acts having to do with advocating, planning, or teaching the necessity of the violent overthrow of the government. Mere proof of the propagation of the writings of Marx or Lenin would not do, as the lower court, following the Dennis dictum, had "erroneously supposed."

Accordingly, the Court cleared five of the defendants completely, holding the evidence in their cases to be hopelessly insufficient for conviction, while it remanded the cases of nine other defendants for retrial. Black and Douglas, concurring, thought the Smith Act ought to have been declared unconstitutional outright. Justice Clark, who alone dissented, argued with some force that the Court's fine-drawn distinction between the present circumstances and those in the Dennis case were "too subtle and difficult to grasp."

The requirement of the Yates opinion that the government now show a nexus of specific acts of advocacy of revolution brought an abrupt end to the main body of Smith Act prosecutions then under way. After some delay, the Department of Justice quashed the indictments against the nine Communists whose cases the Court had remanded for retrial, on the ground that it could not meet the new "evidentiary requirements" for conviction. In only one "advocacy" trial subsequent to the Yates decision, that in Denver, did the government succeed in obtaining a conviction, only to suffer a reversal in the Court of Appeals on grounds not related to the Smith Act. Ultimately, some thirty additional indictments under the act including those from Denver, were quietly dropped in the next three years, while in several instances United States Courts of Appeals, guided by the Yates opinion, reversed convictions already obtained in the district courts.

There remained the possibility that the government might prosecute Communists successfully under the Smith Act provision forbidding "knowing" membership in a group advocating forcible overthrow of the government. Many legal experts believed that this section had been rendered meaningless, if not repealed outright, by the compulsory registration provisions of the McCarran Act, which, when taken in connection with the older law, seemed to compel compulsory self-incrimination in violation of the Fifth Amendment. In spite of this difficulty, the government in 1954 instituted several prosecutions under the membership clause, apparently in part with the deliberate intention of testing the controverted provision.

At length, in Scales v. United States (1961), the Court gave the membership clause its constitutional blessing. In so doing, however, it attached to the clause the "evidentiary requirements" for conviction set forth in the Yates opinion, thereby making it as difficult to obtain convictions under the membership provision as under the advocacy section. Harlan's opinion for the majority first distinguished carefully between "knowing" membership and mere passive membership in a subversive organization. The former, he said, could be established only by applying the Yates formula, which thus required the government to demonstrate that the defendant possessed an understanding of the group's revolutionary purposes and that he had deliberately participated in activities directed to such an end.

So construed, Harlan said, the Smith Act membership clause, judged by the now familiar "balancing" test, met the test of constitutionality. In the present case, he added, the government had indeed established a nexus of evidence showing both understanding and advocacy of action so that petitioners had been properly convicted. Warren, Black, Douglas, and Brennan, in separate dissenting opinions, protested that the majority had "practically rewritten the statute" to save the membership clause from McCarran Act repeal, while they also attacked the "balancing" test as impairing the very liberties the First Amendment was designed to protect.

In a companion case, *Noto v. United States* (1961), the Court actually reversed a membership clause conviction, on the ground that the trial court evidence was not sufficient to sustain it. Thereby the Court reinforced its Scales warning that it would in fact apply the sternest of evidentiary standards in membership clause appeals, requiring a convincing nexus of "particular evidence in a particular record" to sustain a conviction.

Not surprisingly, the government, following the Scales and Noto decisions, quietly dropped several membership clause indictments. The Smith Act nominally was still on the books, but prosecutions under it terminated.

PENNSYLVANIA V. NELSON: THE COURT BAN ON STATE
PROSECUTIONS FOR SEDITION AGAINST THE UNITED STATES

Meantime, in *Pennsylvania v. Nelson* (1956), the Court banned outright, state prosecutions for sedition against the United States, simply by ruling that Congress already had decisively pre-empted the field of sovereignty in question. The Nelson case involved an appeal from a conviction in the Pennsylvania courts of a leading Communist Party member who had been indicted for conspiracy to overthrow the government of the United States by force and violence. Chief Justice Warren's opinion for the Court stated three grounds for the conclusion that there was no longer any room for state action against this offense. First, he said, "the scheme of federal regulation" of sedition through the Smith Act, the Communist Control Act of 1954, and the McCarran Act was "so pervasive" as to make reasonable the inference that Congress had left no room for the states to supplement it. Second, federal interest in the field of sovereignty in question was "so dominant" as to "preclude enforcement of state laws on the same subject." Third, enforcement of state sedition acts presented "a serious danger of conflict with the administration of the federal program." Federal pre-emption of the field of sedition prosecutions against the United States, the Chief Justice added carefully, did not preclude the states from punishing this crime when and if Congress should decide to withdraw from the field, nor did it estop a state from punishing acts of violence, sabotage, or "sedition against the state itself."

The Chief Justice did not say so, but the Court may well have reached its conclusion in part because of the reactionary character of the Pennsylvania statute under review, which Warren termed "strangely reminiscent of the Sedition Act of 1798." Justice Reed, in a dissent in which Burton and Minton joined, pointed to the language of the federal criminal code guaranteeing the joint jurisdiction of the federal and state courts over offenses against the United States, and concluded therefrom that Congress had in fact intended no such "pre-emption" as the Court now held to be the case.

The Nelson decision was extremely unpopular with certain conservatives, who believed it might hamper effective prosecution of dangerous radicals generally. Some forty-two states at this time had laws on their books punishing sedition, criminal anarchism, or criminal syndicalism. Most prominent of these measures was the New York Criminal Anarchy Act, which had been enacted in 1902 and which later had served as a model for the Smith Act. Twenty other states had adopted legislation of this kind during and immediately after World War I, while still other state legislation was a product of the more recent anti-Communist movement. The validity of all was now in doubt.

Accordingly, in January, 1957, Representative Smith of Virginia, a leading conservative Democrat and the author of the federal statute that bore his name, introduced into the House of Representatives a measure, H.R. 3, intended to set the Nelson decision aside. H.R. 3 declared that "No act of Congress shall be construed s indicating an intent on the part of Congress to occupy the field in which such act operates, to the exclusion of any state laws on the same subject matter, unless such act contains an express provision to the effect or unless there is a direct and positive conflict between such act and the state law, so that the two cannot be reconciled or consistently stand together."

The Smith proposal undoubtedly would have produced vast confusion in the field of state-federal relations, and the Eisenhower administration, speaking through Attorney General William Rogers, immediately opposed it as such. The House nonetheless twice passed the Smith Resolution by substantial margins, in July, 1958, and again in June, 1959. Significantly, the Senate refused to act, and the Nelson dictum remained "the law of the land."

The Warren Court continued to recognize that state prosecutions for sedition against the state itself were constitutionally permissible. However, in *Dombrowski v. Pfister* (1965) the Court put such legislation under a further serious constitutional onus when it ruled the Louisiana Subversive Activities Criminal Control Act unconstitutional for vagueness. This measure had been drafted in language virtually identical with the Smith Act, but Chief Justice Warren's opinion held the law unconstitutional on its face for failure to specify clearly an identifiable criminal offense and also because the procedural safeguards set forth in the law were not adequate.

Again, in *Brandenberg v. Ohio* (1969), the Court in a *per curiam* opinion voided the Ohio Criminal Syndicalism Act of 1919, which had made it a crime to "advocate . . . the duty, necessity, or propriety of crime, sabotage, violence or unlawful methods of terrorism as a means of accomplishing industrial or political reform." "The constitutional guarantees of free speech," the Court said, "do not permit a state to proscribe advocacy of the use of force . . . except where such advocacy is directed to inciting or producing imminent lawless action . . ." In so declaring, the Court specifically overruled *Whitney v. California* (1927), in which an almost identical state statute had been ruled valid some forty years earlier. Oddly, the Court's language seemed to suggest a possible revival of the "clear and present danger" doctrine, an intimation that Black and Douglas in concurring opinions firmly repudiated. At all events, the Dombrowski and Brandenberg cases seemed to leave comparatively little room for prosecution under state "Little Smith Acts" generally. Even "knowing" Party membership by this time was immune from prosecution, while "advocacy" now would have to be tied to immediate acts of revolution or criminal violence.

THE WARREN COURT AND THE MC CARRAN ACT:
THE REGISTRATION BATTLE

In another somewhat tortuous series of cases the Warren Court at length rendered virtually unenforceable the registration provisions of the much disputed McCarran Act. The first blow fell in 1956, when in *Communist Party v. Subversive Activities Control*

Board the Court overturned a Board ruling of April 1953, which had ordered the Party to register as a Communist-action group. Justice Frankfurter's majority opinion held that the government's case against the Party had been hopelessly tainted by the resort to the "testimony of witnesses who are professional informers, have committed perjury, and are completely untrustworthy."

The protracted and painful attempt to force the Party to register now began all over again. Once more, after hearings, the S.A.C.B. ordered the Party to register, and once more the Party appealed to the courts. At length, in *Communist Party v. Subversive Activities Control Board* (1961), the Supreme Court in a five to four decision confirmed the new Board order. In one of the longest opinions in the Court's history, Justice Frankfurter held that the evidence at hand had demonstrated that the Party was indeed a Communist-action group within the meaning of the McCarran Act. Nor did the registration provisions of the statute constitute a bill of attainder, he said, since they merely set up certain criteria for identifying Communist-action groups generally and not for imposing punishment on the Party as such. Nor did the registration provisions constitute prior restraint in violation of the First Amendment. Numerous other federal statutes, he pointed out, required registration and disclosure, among them the Federal Corrupt Practices Act, the Federal Registration of Lobbying Act, and the Foreign Agents Registration Act. Registration, he admitted, involved some controls over individual liberty, but again it was a question of "balancing" private rights against the public interest in disclosure.

Frankfurter carefully avoided passing upon the crucial question of whether compulsory registration constituted forced self-incrimination in violation of the Fifth Amendment. The present order, he pointed out, did not oblige any individual Party member to register; it would be time enough to pass upon the self-incrimination issue when and if the Party's officers, upon being ordered to register, were to claim the constitutional privilege in question.

Chief Justice Warren and Justices Black, Douglas, and Brennan all dissented at length in separate opinions. Warren thought that the S.A.C.B. had once again relied upon tainted testimony while he argued also that under the statute a Communist-action group must be construed only as one engaged in direct advocacy of the overthrow of the government by force and violence. Black protested vehemently that the McCarran Act "embarks this country, for the first time, upon the dangerous venture of outlawing groups that preach doctrines that nearly all Americans detest." Douglas, more restrained, stated that he could accept compulsory registration of the Party as constitutional, but expressed the belief that the requirement that Party officers sign the registration statement constituted obvious self-incrimination in violation of the Fifth Amendment.

Superficially it appeared that the Party and its officers had at long last been brought to book, but, as might have been expected, the Party's officers simply defied the Court decision, as well as subsequent notice from the Department of Justice setting November 19, 1961, as the deadline date for Party registration. When this date passed without any Party action, the government sought and obtained a criminal indictment against the Party for its refusal to comply with the law, and it also presently obtained an S.A.C.B. order directing various officers of the Party to register personally. This last action was taken under Section 8 of the McCarran Act, which required such registration of the individual members of any Communist-action organization that had failed to comply with a Board registration order. Once again a Board order met defiance, as the Party's officers refused to register personally, and again appealed to the courts.

This time, in *Albertson v. Subversive Activities Control Board* (1965), the Party's officers, after fighting their case through the lower courts, won a clean-cut victory. In a unanimous opinion written by Justice Brennan, the Supreme Court held that compliance by Party officers with the S.A.C.B.'s individual registration order would require them to fill out registration blanks containing information that was obviously self-incriminatory and thus in violation of the Fifth Amendment.

Brennan's opinion rejected outright the government's argument that compulsory registration amounted to no more than was involved in filling out an income tax return. Tax returns, he observed, were "neutral on their face and directed at the public at large," whereas registration here was aimed at "a highly selected group inherently suspected of criminal activities." Nor did the immunity provision in the McCarran Act save the Board order, since the information the government obtained still could be used for "investigatory leads" that might well result in prosecution under a variety of federal sedition statutes. The lower court decision sustaining the Board order accordingly was reversed.

The Albertson opinion also wrecked the criminal prosecution of the Communist Party for failure to register which was then under way. In December, 1961, the government in a district court trial had obtained a criminal conviction of the Party for failure to register, only to have the United States Court of Appeals for the District of Columbia in 1963 throw out the conviction and order a new trial, on the ground that the government had failed to prove that the Party could have found an officer who could have registered for it without undergoing the onus of self-incrimination. A second district court trial and conviction then followed.

In March, 1967, the Appellate Court again threw out the Party's conviction, declaring as it did so that the registration provisions of the McCarran Act were "hopelessly at odds" with the constitutional guarantees against self-incrimination. Thus a lower federal court did what the Supreme Court up to that time technically had not undertaken to do—declare the McCarran Act's registration provisions to be outright unconstitutional. It was evident from the appellate opinion, however, that the judges had drawn heavily upon the Albertson opinion in reaching their conclusion.

The Justice Department now confessed defeat, announcing that it would not appeal the appellate court decision. The practical consequence, as *The New York Times* put it, was to reduce the McCarran Act to "an empty shell," its main provisions invalidated or rendered unenforceable. By March, 1967, the government over the years had attempted to secure the registration of some twenty-three allegedly subversive organizations, among them the Labor Youth League, The National Council of Soviet-American Friendship, the Civil Rights Congress, and the Dubois Clubs of America. In every instance it had failed.

The Subversive Activities Control Board now became moribund. In January, 1968, Congress, after protracted controversy between conservatives, led by Senators Eastland of Mississippi and Dirksen of Illinois, and liberals, led by William Proxmire of Wisconsin, enacted a compromise law which provided that unless the S.A.C.B. held at least one hearing and instituted at least one hearing in the next year it was to go out of existence in June, 1969. A request in July, 1968, by Attorney General Ramsey Clark that the Board institute registration proceedings against seven alleged Communists saved the S.A.C.B. from extinction, but it remained evident that the Board was finished as an effective instrument of government.

THE WARREN COURT AND COMMUNISTS IN DEFENSE
INDUSTRIES AND LABOR UNIONS

Meanwhile in another major series of decisions having to do with Communists in industry, the Warren Court not only struck down a 1959 law banning Communists from serving as officers in labor unions but also voided another section of the McCarran Act—this one prohibiting the employment of the members of any Communist-action group in any national defense facility.

United States v. Brown (1965) had to do with a provision in the Labor-Management Reporting and Disclosure Act of 1959 that made it a crime for any person to serve as an officer or employee of a labor union, except in a minor clerical capacity, who was now a member of the Communist Party or had been within the past five years. The law in question had been adopted to replace the affidavit provisions of the Taft-Hartley Act and was designed to accomplish the same objective—the protection of the national economy from the danger of sabotage and politically inspired strikes. Presumably the measure raised much the same constitutional questions as those involved in the Douds decision in which the Taft-Hartley affidavit provisions had passed constitutional muster.

However, in a five to four decision the Court now held the Disclosure Act provision unconstitutional as a bill of attainder. Chief Justice Warren's opinion for the majority rejected the government argument that the law was merely regulative and not punitive, asserting that "it would be archaic," in arriving at a modern definition of bills of attainder, "to limit the definition of 'punishment' to retribution" in the traditional sense, and that the present provision, considered in any contemporary context, did indeed impose punishment. Warren carefully distinguished the present law from that reviewed in the Douds decision, pointing out that in the latter instance a Communist could become eligible for union office merely by resigning from the Party, whereas here the five-year prohibition made any such maneuver impossible. Justice White, in a dissenting opinion in which Clark, Harlan, and Stewart joined, protested that the majority had "obviously overruled" the Douds decision, and had construed the attainder clause in Article I, section 9, to forbid "precisely what was validated in Douds."

Two years later, in *United States v. Robel* (1967), the Court struck another blow at the now-tattered McCarran Act by holding unconstitutional the provision in Section 5 of that law that made it unlawful for a member of a Communist-action group under orders to register to enter upon employment in any plant defined as a "national defense facility." Chief Justice Warren, who spoke for the majority in a five to two decision, castigated the provision in question as one that "sweeps indiscriminately across all types of association with Communist-action groups without regard to the quality or degree of membership" and so ran "afoul of the First Amendment." The provision, he pointed out, failed to make any distinction between knowing and innocent Party membership and failed likewise to distinguish between sensitive and non-sensitive positions in industry. Justice White, with whom Harlan joined in dissent, argued that the right of association upon which the Chief Justice seemingly depended, was not even mentioned in the Constitution and was in any event "not absolute," while the Communist threat, which the majority ignored, was "real and substantial," and Congress in this instance had taken appropriate measures to control it.

THE WARREN COURT, COMMUNISTS, AND THE PASSPORT QUESTION

The same broad conception of an open society and a determination to protect the rights of dissident political minorities that had been present in the Brown and Robel opinions were evident also in a series of cases in which the Warren libertarian majority swept away most of the administrative and statutory restrictions on the issuance of passports to Communists and other "subversive persons." In the process still another section of the McCarran Act fell by the wayside.

The Passport Act of 1926, upon which modern passport administration long had been based, had by implication granted the State Department the authority to deny passports only to applicants with criminal records or who lacked United States citizenship. In 1949, however, the Department formulated new rules under which it also denied passports to Communist Party members or persons closely affiliated with the Party. Thereafter the Department at one time or another denied various members of the Communist Party the right to travel abroad.

The McCarran Act carried a provision that made it a felony

for any member of a Communist organization which had registered or was under final orders to register to apply for a passport or to attempt to use one already issued. However, since the Party, at least until the 1961 decision in *Communist Party v. S.A.C.B.*, had successfully resisted any "final" registration order, this provision at first remained inactive. The Immigration and Nationalities Act of 1952 made possession of a passport a necessary prerequisite to an American citizen's entering or leaving the country, but attached no specific conditions to passport issuance. Hence, the Department continued merely to enforce its own rules denying passports to Communist Party members.

At length, in *Kent v. Dulles* (1958), the Court ruled that the Department's informal policy lacked any adequate statutory base and was illegal. "The right to travel," Justice Douglas declared for the majority, "is a part of the 'liberty' of which the citizen cannot be deprived without due process of law under the Fifth Amendment." The Court, he added, would be "faced with important constitutional questions" were it to hold that Congress "had given the Secretary of State the authority to withhold passports to citizens because of beliefs or associations." In the absence of such legislation, Douglas declared, "the Secretary may not employ that standard to restrict the citizen's right of free movement." Clark, Burton, Harlan, and Whittaker, dissenting, thought that the various statutes enacted earlier had in fact granted the State Department the authority Douglas said it lacked.

Although from one point of view, the Kent opinion was an exercise in judicial self-abnegation, the decision nonetheless raised something of a political storm. Several well-known Communists, among them the singer Paul Robeson, obtained passports within the next year or so. President Eisenhower in a special message urged Congress to remedy the situation, while the State Department also asked for authority to deny passports "for any reason related to foreign policy." In September, 1959, the House responded by passing, 371 to 18, a bill allowing the Department to deny passports to Communists who were knowingly engaged in furthering the international Communist movement. However, the Senate, apparently unfavorably impressed by the State Department's "uncooperative attitude," refused to act and the bill died.

The Court's decision in *Communist Party v. S.A.C.B.* in 1961 presumably put the Communist Party under final orders to register and thus made operative the passport provisions of the McCarran Act. Accordingly, the Department of State in January, 1962, issued new regulations denying passports to Communist Party members but granting such persons preliminary hearings with a right of confrontation and providing for the issuance of a passport where the F.B.I. insisted upon preserving the anonymity of an accusing witness. Within the next year or so the Department revoked the passports of a number of leading Communist figures, among them Elizabeth Gurley Flynn, J. A. Jackson, editor of the *Daily Worker*, and Herbert Aptheker, the Party's leading historian-intellectual. The result was further litigation and another rebuke to the government.

In *Aptheker v. Secretary of State* (1964), the Court held that Section 6 of the McCarran Act, which contained the passport provisions, was unconstitutional on its face as a restriction of the right of travel guaranteed by the Fifth Amendment. There were, said Justice Goldberg, three major things wrong with this portion of the law. In the first place, it swept within its terms "both knowing and unknowing" Party members, a now familiar deficiency that doomed the section in question as "an assertion of arbitrary power." Second—a closely related point—the law treated as immaterial the Party member's "degree of activity in the organization and his commitment to its purposes." Finally, the statute arbitrarily excluded any consideration of the purpose of the applicant's proposed travel abroad, so that an innocent "visit to a sick relative" and suspect Party activity alike fell under the law's ban and could not be curbed constitutionally except in a wartime emergency. Clark, Harlan, and White, dissenting, argued that the Court's much vaunted distinction between knowing and unknowing membership was not applicable to the litigants in the present case, all of whom were "knowing" members, and they protested further that in any event the law was "reasonably tailored" to accomplish a legitimate congressional purpose.

Although these decisions left comparatively little of the government's legal and administrative prohibitions on Communist travel abroad, there still remained certain restrictions imposed by the Department of State upon travel by anyone to Communist-bloc countries. In *Zemel v. Rusk* (1965) the Court held that such restrictions were properly authorized by the act of 1926. It soon became clear, however, that the rules in question sadly lacked teeth. In *Laub v. United States* (1965) the Court, speaking through Justice Fortas, refused to equate travel without a passport with travel to a forbidden area, even one designated as such on the passport in question. It thus appeared that the Department's rules intended to restrict travel to Communist-controlled areas abroad were unenforceable. Justice Douglas' aphorism—that "freedom of movement is the very essence of our free society"—came close to expressing the heart of the Court's position, considerations of national security to the contrary notwithstanding.

Closely associated with the Court's insistence upon freedom of travel abroad was its intervention to preserve freedom the mails from abroad. In *Lamont v. Postmaster General* (1965) the Court struck down a "rider" in the Employees Salary Act of 1962 which provided that mail originating in a foreign country, except for sealed letters, could be intercepted by the Post Office and examined to determine whether or not it was Communist propaganda. Whenever the Postmaster General so determined, the intercepted material was to be detained and the prospective recipient notified thereof. Intercepted material was to be delivered only at the addressee's specific request.

Speaking through Justice Douglas, a unanimous Court now held the 1962 "rider" unconstitutional, on the ground that "it requires an official act (viz., returning the reply card) as a limitation on the unfettered exercise of the addressee's First Amendment rights." The provision, Douglas declared sternly, was "at war with the 'uninhibited, robust, and wide-open' debate and discussion that are contemplated by the First Amendment." The decision produced ominous growls from conservatives in Congress, but no action followed.

THE WARREN COURT AND LOYALTY PROGRAMS:
THE FIRST PHASE, 1956–1962

Federal and state loyalty programs constituted still another phase of the postwar drive against Communism that the Warren Court now laid under sharp restrictions and controls.

The Court, it will be recalled, had long exhibited a distinct reluctance to bring federal loyalty programs under sharp judicial scrutiny, apparently in part because it hesitated to interfere in the operations of a coordinate branch of the government. Thus in *Peters v. Hobby* (1955), *Cole v. Young* (1956), and *Service v. Dulles* (1957), the justices had settled cases on technical, administrative, and statutory grounds, studiously avoiding the more profound constitutional issues lurking beneath the surface.

At length, however, in *Greene v. McElroy* (1959), the Court moved close to an outright adverse constitutional judgment on certain federal security procedures. The case involved an official of a private firm engaged in defense contract work, who, on the basis of anonymous information, had been denied clearance to classified information by the Army, Navy, and Air Force Personnel Security Board. As a consequence, he had lost an $18,000 job.

Once more the Court decided the case on technical grounds, ruling merely that the Defense Department had lacked adequate statutory authority for the procedures in question. But Chief Justice Warren's opinion expressed open shock at the government's resort to "faceless informers," and observed sternly that the Court would be unwilling in any event to accept a security program "which is in conflict with our long accepted notions of fair procedures" without "explicit authority from either the President or Congress." So strong was the Chief Justice's condemnation of the procedures in question that Frankfurter, Harlan, and Whittaker dissociated themselves therefrom in a brief concurring statement. But at the same time, Justice Clark's dissent, in which he depicted the majority opinion as holding that a citizen had "a constitutional right to have access to the Government's military secrets," drew a stern rebuke in a brief rebuttal from Harlan.

Congressional conservatives thereafter attempted unsuccessfully to overturn the Greene decision, which nonetheless resulted in a distinct improvement in the constitutional safeguards in the government's security programs. In February, 1960, the House passed virtually unnoticed a measure introduced by Representative Walter of Pennsylvania that would have specifically authorized the Secretary of Defense to establish an industrial security program "designed to protect from disclosure" all classified information affecting the national security.

A few days later, however, President Eisenhower issued a new executive order setting up a new industrial security program with vastly improved procedural safeguards, including hearings and the right of confrontation under all circumstances. For the past several years, in fact, the government had been steadily improving procedures in its various loyalty programs, with the result that constitutional controversy over them after 1960 largely died down. At all odds, such programs thereafter escaped judicial scrutiny.

State loyalty programs were a decidedly different matter. The Warren Court, it will be recalled, had inherited a fairly clear body of constitutional doctrine with respect to such, which in general granted state loyalty programs approval if they distinguished between knowing and unknowing membership in subversive organizations, defined subversive activity with some precision, maintained fair procedures, and did not attempt to impose retroactive disavowal or penalties. Even the much controverted New York Feinberg Law had passed muster by these standards.[1]

For several years, the Warren Court vacillated somewhat uncertainly with respect to state loyalty programs, the justices being divided closely between liberal and conservative blocs on the question, so that the outcome of a particular case often hinged on the position of one or two justices in either "camp." Thus in *Slochower v. Board of Higher Education of the City of New York* (1956), the liberal bloc momentarily prevailed as Justice Clark joined the majority to invalidate the arbitrary discharge of a Brooklyn College professor who, in testifying before the Senate Internal Security Subcommittee, had invoked the Fifth Amendment in response to questions as to former possible Communist Party affiliations. The New York Board, citing a provision in the city charter, had treated his refusal to testify as tantamount to a resignation, and had dismissed him without charges, notice, hearing, or any opportunity to explain.

Justice Clark's opinion holding the discharge "arbitrary" and invalid under the Fourteenth Amendment, made it clear that the justices had been moved both by the summary character of the discharge and by the assumption that guilt automatically attached to anyone who invoked the constitutional privilege against self-incrimination. "We must condemn the practice," the Court said, "of imputing a sinister meaning to the exercise of a person's constitutional rights under the Fifth Amendment." The opinion carefully distinguished the Adler case, where discharge had taken place only after notice and hearing and adequate opportunity to establish innocent membership. Justices Reed, Burton, Minton, and Harlan all dissented, generally on the ground the Slochower's discharge had taken place merely because of his failure to cooperate with public authorities, carried no imputation of guilt, and thus had been based upon reasonable grounds.

A year later, the liberal bloc, still in precarious control, drew upon the Slochower and Wiemann precedents to overrule two state decisions denying applicants admission to the state bar. *Schware v. New Mexico Board of Bar Examiners* (1957) involved exclusion of a candidate for the bar on a variety of grounds: his alleged former membership in the Communist Party, his one-time use of a protective alias, and an old record of arrests in labor disputes.

---

[1] See above, p. 839.

Justice Black's majority opinion, emphasizing that the facts showed Schware to be "a man of high ideals with a deep sense of social justice," held that there was no evidence that his former membership in the Communist Party had demonstrated "anything more than a political faith in a political party," and accordingly found that the failure to grant Schware a license had been arbitrary and in violation of due process.

A companion case, *Konigsberg v. California* (1957), dealt with a bar applicant whose petition had been denied because of his refusal to answer questions about former Communist Party affiliations. Konigsberg had not invoked any immunity against self-incrimination, but instead had stood upon "a right of privacy" under the First and Fourteenth Amendments. Justice Black's opinion declared that "the mere fact of Konigsberg's past membership in the Communist Party, if true, without anything more, is not an adequate basis for concluding that he is disloyal or a person of base character," and ruled accordingly that denial of his license to practice law violated the due process clause of the Fourteenth Amendment. Frankfurter, Harlan, and Clark, dissenting in both the Schware and Konigsberg cases, protested that the Court's decisions "violated the limits of federal jurisdiction" over what was properly a discretionary state matter.

The Schware and Konigsberg decisions, which exhibited very much the same attitude toward civil liberties as that in the Watkins and Yates cases of about the same time, provoked something of a minor uproar in legal circles and in Congress. The Annual Conference of Chief Justices of the States attacked the decisions as "the high-water mark . . . in denying to a state the power to keep order in its own house." And in Congress, Senator Jenner of Indiana introduced a bill in the 1957 session to deny the Court any appellate jurisdiction in cases of this kind, while Senator Butler of Maryland presented substantially the same measure the following year. However, both proposals failed of enactment.

A year later the Court itself, with its internal balance of power shifted slightly, started a retreat from the Slochower, Konigsberg, and Schware decisions. *Beilan v. Board of Education* (1958), in which the new judicial stance first manifested itself, concerned a Philadelphia schoolteacher who had been discharged after first refusing to answer questions from the superintendent as to possible Communist Party affiliations and who immediately thereafter had invoked the Fifth Amendment before the House Un-American Activities Committee. However, the school board had been careful to make "incompetence" the technical grounds for discharge and not any charge of disloyalty or criminality.

Justice Burton, who delivered the majority opinion holding the discharge constitutional, conceded that Beilan in becoming a schoolteacher certainly "did not give up any right to freedom of speech, belief, or association," but added emphatically that "he did, however, undertake obligations of frankness, candor and cooperation in answering inquiries made of him" by his school board. His discharge, accordingly, was not "arbitrary," and had not violated the Fourteenth Amendment. Burton carefully distinguished the Slochower and Konigsberg precedents, where action aimed at the individual had been based not upon any alleged lack of competence but upon a challenge to loyalty.

In a companion case, *Lerner v. Casey* (1958), Justice Harlan's majority opinion upheld the discharge of a New York subway employee who had been discharged after invoking a privilege against self-incrimination in response to an inquiry by transit authorities as to possible Communist Party affiliations. Harlan pointed out that Lerner, in contrast to both Wiemann and Slochower, technically had been fired not because of any inference of Party membership but because of a finding that he was "of doubtful trust and reliability." So construed, his discharge did not violate due process.

Chief Justice Warren and Justices Black, Douglas, and Brennan entered vigorous dissenting opinions in both the Beilan and Lerner cases. The alleged grounds for discharge, they protested, were "a transparent denial of reality." Both men, they thought, had been discharged simply because they had refused to answer questions about possible Communist Party affiliations, a procedure that Douglas declared "cannot be squared with our constitutional principles."

The slender conservative majority prevailed once more in *Nelson and Globe v. County of Los Angeles* (1960), a case that involved two social workers who, in response to the usual questions on Communist Party affiliations, had resorted to the Fifth Amendment before the House Un-American Activities Committee. Thereafter they had been released from employment under a California state statute that made it the duty of state employees to answer such questions on pain of discharge.

Justice Clark, speaking for the five majority justices who sustained Globe's discharge, had the somewhat embarrassing task of distinguishing the circumstances of the present case from those in the Slochower opinion, which he also had written. Slochower's discharge, Clark said, had rested upon "a built-in inference of guilt . . . derived solely from Fifth Amendment claims," whereas here, discharge rested not upon any such inference but solely upon a "failure of the employee to answer," grounds which did not violate due process. Black, Douglas, and Brennan, dissenting, expressed the belief that in distinguishing the Slochower case, Clark had construed a distinction without a difference.[2]

It remained only for the conservative majority to overturn the Schware and Konigsberg opinions. This step came in *Konigsberg v. State Bar of California* (1961), a sequel to the earlier case of the same title. Following the Court's 1957 decision, the state bar examiners had held a new hearing for Konigsberg, had again addressed to him questions as to possible Communist Party membership, and when he had again refused to answer, invoking his rights under the First Amendment, had again denied his application. This time, however, the committee had based its decision technically not on a finding of bad moral character but upon the grounds that continued refusal to answer constituted a systematic obstruction of the examiner's proceedings.

This time the justices voted five to four to sustain the discharge. Harlan's majority opinion first observed that the discharge now resed upon petitioner's "systematic obstruction" of the state bar hearing, and not upon any finding of possible Party affiliation as such. Harlan then employed the "balancing" test, to hold that in this instance First Amendment rights must be subordinated to the state's ascendant interest in protecting the integrity of the legal profession. As in the Beilan and Lerner cases, Warren, Douglas, Black, and Brennan dissented, objecting that the Court could sustain the California Board's action only by refusing to look at the "real reason behind the ruling."

That even the conservative bloc of justices would unite with their more libertarian brethren against a loyalty statute afflicted with fundamental constitutional defects became evident in *Cramp v. Board of Public Instruction of Orange County* (1961), decided a few months after the second Konigsberg case. Here the Court passed a unanimous adverse judgment on a Florida statute that required each state employee to subscribe to an oath that he had never lent "aid, support, advice, counsel, or influence to the Com-

---

[2] The Court divided four to four on the Nelson case, and therefore sustained Nelson's discharge without opinion. Chief Justice Warren, a Californian, did not participate in either decision.

munist Party." Although Justice Stewart in his opinion agreed that by the interpretation of the Florida court the law in question applied only to knowing support of the Party, he pointed out that the law undertook to forbid nothing specific, such as advocacy of Party membership or of violent overthrow of the government. Accordingly, he concluded, the law was "afflicted with the vice of unconstitutional vagueness," a defect "further aggravated" by the fact that it "touched upon individual freedoms affirmatively protected by the Constitution." It thus fell under the ban of the Fourteenth Amendment.

THE WARREN COURT AND LOYALTY PROGRAMS: THE LIBERTARIAN VICTORY, 1962–1969

Following the Cramp decision, the new libertarian majority on the Court took over control of adjudging state loyalty programs, just as it did also with respect to McCarran Act registration, passport issuance, Communist employment in industry, and so on. The consequence was the evolution of an almost wholly new body of constitutional law concerning loyalty oaths, state employment of Communists, and the like, which for the most part rendered obsolete the constitutional standards that had been developed in the early 1950's for evaluating such programs. Whereas earlier a majority of loyalty programs had won cautious judicial approval, now a whole series of such fell victim to adverse judgment by the newly dominant libertarian bloc on the Court, very often because the majority justices concluded that an act under review suffered from the "fatal flaw" of unconstitutional vagueness—the standard first delineated for this purpose in the Cramp case.

The new libertarian control of the Warren Court on state loyalty programs first became evident in *Baggett v. Bullitt* (1964), in which the Court struck down a complex of loyalty statutes from the state of Washington. Involved were two separate loyalty oaths. A 1931 law, which applied only to teachers, obliged them to swear to support the Constitution and laws of the United States and to "promote respect for the flag and institutions" of the United States. A 1955 act applicable to all state employees required them to disavow being "a subversive person," earlier defined in a 1951 law virtually in Smith Act terms as one who advocated, abetted, advised, or taught the overthrow of the government of the United States or of the state of Washington by force or violence. The 1955 law also automatically defined members of the Communist Party as "subversives."

Justice White, who spoke for a majority of seven justices, held after analysis that both laws at issue suffered from the same "vice of unconstitutional vagueness" as had been present in the Cramp case. It was impossible, he declared, to define with any precision from the wording of the statutes just what constituted subversive activity under the law. In addition, White said, the laws required a disavowal of "revolution," a vague concept that involved "any rapid or fundamental change," and might mean mere advocacy of "repeal of the twenty-second amendment" or of "participation by this country in a world government." Accordingly, Justice White concluded, the two principal statutes before the Court offended due process, a vice aggravated by the fact that they dealt with First Amendment liberties.

Two years later, in *Elfbrandt v. Russell* (1966), the majority justices again applied the "vice of vagueness" standard to invalidate, five to four, an Arizona statute that required state employees to take an oath to support the Constitution of the United States and the constitution and laws of the state and to defend them against all enemies. A gloss that had been spread upon the statute by the state legislature made it an offense punishable as perjury to subscribe to the oath and later to commit an act calculated to overthrow the government by force and violence or "knowingly and wilfully" to become or remain a member of the Communist Party.

Justice Douglas, in analyzing the law, pointed out that as in the Cramp and Baggett cases it was impossible to know with any certainty the sweep of the law's provisions—whether it applied to one who supported Communist Party candidates or to one who, for example, merely attended an international conference where Communists were present. Nor was it constitutionally permissible since the Aptheker passport decision, Douglas said, to proscribe "knowing membership" in the Communist Party, without any showing of "specific intent" to subscribe to the Party's unlawful objectives. In short, Douglas concluded, the law "threatened the cherished freedom of association protected by the First Amendment," and was unconstitutional.

Thus the Court in substance declared not only that a state could not impose an oath upon its employees requiring them to disavow "knowing" Communist Party membership, but also that it could not forbid such "knowing" membership to its employees or make such membership a crime. This stand evoked a strongly worded dissent from Justice White, author of the Baggett opinion, in which he pointed out that the Court in a long series of cases beginning

with the Gerende decision had ruled that states could indeed prohibit knowing membership in the Communist Party and could discharge those who refused "to affirm or deny" such membership
under oath.

Finally, in *Keyishian v. Board of Regents of the University of
the State of New York* (1967), the Court struck down New
York's much controverted Feinberg Law, which an earlier conservative majority had carefully validated in the Adler case fifteen
years earlier. The present case involved a complex series of state
loyalty statutes of which the Feinberg Law was but a single part.
These measures included, among others, a 1917 law that required
the removal of public-school teachers guilty of "treasonable or
seditious" utterances, and a 1939 statute that forbade the employment by the state of any person who advocated overthrow of the
government by force and violence or who held membership in a
group so advocating. The Feinberg Law proper, enacted in 1949,
required the Board of Regents of the State University to prepare
a list of subversive organizations, and also to draw up rules and
regulations for the exclusion from employment of teachers who
fell under the ban imposed in the foregoing provisions, while it
also made membership in the Communist Party prima facie evidence of disqualification for appointment or retention in the public-
school system.

Justice Brennan's opinion for the five majority justices first side-
stepped the Adler decision by ruling that the question of "unconstitutional vagueness" had not been before the Court at that time.
Brennan then declared that both the words "treasonable" and
"seditious" in the 1917 law were "dangerously uncertain" in meaning, were reminiscent of the "dangers fatal to First Amendment
freedoms" in the Sedition Act of 1798, and were entangled in the
vast area of uncertainty and confusion that surrounded New
York's criminal anarchy laws.

It was not mere vagueness, however, that tainted the Feinberg
complex. The whole plan, Brennan thought, made it a "highly
efficient *in terrorem* mechanism" whose "result must be to stifle
that free play of the spirit which all teachers ought especially to
cultivate and practice." Brennan admitted that the Feinberg provisions of the complex had been sustained in the Adler decision, but
added that the "constitutional doctrine which has emerged since
that time has rejected its major premise . . . that public employment may be conditioned upon a surrender of constitutional rights
which could not be abridged by government action," i.e., in this

instance, knowing membership in the Communist Party. The law, in short, was void both for vagueness and for its intrusion on First Amendment freedoms.

Justice Clark, in an embittered dissent in which Harlan, Stewart, and White joined, first attacked with derisive sarcasm the "blunderbuss fashion in which the majority couches its artillery of words." The language that the Court now struck down, he pointed out, had been borrowed from various federal statutes, and in particular from the Smith Act, which had already passed constitutional muster. As for Brennan's assertion that more recent cases had rejected the Adler opinion's major premise, Clark observed flatly that they "have done no such thing."

The spirit of the Keyishian opinion was present, also, in *Whitehill v. Elkins* (1967), in which the Court a few months later declared invalid a teachers' oath imposed by the Regents of the University of Maryland, which called for a disavowal by the recipient that he was engaged "in one way or another" in any "attempt to overthrow the government of the United States or the State of Maryland . . . by force and violence." The oath, Justice Douglas declared, must be read in connection with the state's Ober Act, which defined a subversive person as one who conspired to overthrow or alter the government. The word "alter," read into the Regents' oath, Douglas said, tainted it with vagueness and a lack of "precision and clarity," and carried with it "a possible offensive capricious application" that could "deter the flowering of academic freedom as much as successive suits for perjury." Observing that "we are in the First Amendment field," Douglas thereupon ruled that the oath technically fell under the ban of the Fourteenth Amendment's due process clause. Harlan, dissenting for himself, White, and Stewart, thought that the majority opinion, without actually undertaking to overrule the Gerende case, had undertaken to "by-pass that decision by reasoning that defies analysis."

The Baggett, Elfbrandt, Keyishian, and Whitehill opinions left very little of the structure of constitutional law that the Vinson Court had built around loyalty oaths and procedures in the early 1950's. No longer could a state require a disavowal even of "knowing" membership in the Communist Party or other subversive organization. Since "knowing" membership in the Party was in itself now declared legal, and since a state could not even by implication forbid to its employees the exercise of civil liberties possessed by all citizens, discharge for refusal to subscribe to such an oath was now branded as unconstitutional, in a kind of fusion between due process of law and First Amendment rights. Curiously, the Court technically had not overturned the Gerende decision and its companion cases, but whether a state could now salvage anything from a judicial position so hostile to loyalty oaths generally was a matter of some doubt.

THE WARREN COURT AND CONGRESSIONAL INVESTIGATIONS

Of great significance in the altered climate of civil liberties in the country was the series of sharp checks the Warren Court administered to the far-ranging inquiries into subversive activities that had been carried on by congressional investigating committees since the founding of the Committee on Un-American Activities in the late 1930's. As the reader is well aware, inquiries of this kind all too often had had only a nominal legislative purpose; they were, instead, inquisitorial "trials," freed from most of the restraints of procedural due process of law. Attempts to alter this situation through judicial intervention substantially failed in the Vinson era, the Court apparently being determined to avoid any direct confrontation on the subject with the legislative branch of the government.

At length, in 1957, the Warren Court in *Watkins v. United States* consented to bring judicial sanctions to bear against the House Un-American Activities Committee. This case involved an appeal from a contempt conviction of a witness who had invoked the First Amendment as a basis for his refusal to answer certain questions concerning his former Communist Party associates.

Chief Justice Warren, in a rambling and diffuse opinion for the majority, held the conviction invalid. In the final analysis, his decision turned on a finding that both the House resolution creating the Committee and the Committee's own definition of the subject under investigation were so extremely vague that the witness could not be assured of an adequate "standard of specificity" with respect to the pertinency of the questions asked him. Hence his indictment for contempt suffered from "the vice of vagueness" and so violated the due process clause of the Fifth Amendment.

Before reaching this conclusion, however, the Chief Justice read the House Committee a lengthy lecture on constitutional law. Broad as the congressional investigative power was, he warned, it was "not unlimited." There was "no general authority to expose the private affairs of individuals without justification in terms of the function of Congress," nor was "Congress a law enforcement or trial agency." And without quite saying so, he implied broadly that inquiry into private affairs based upon a hopelessly vague committee charge violated a First Amendment right of privacy. In a sharp dissent, Justice Clark deplored the majority decision as a "mischievous curbing" of an essential function of Congress.

In *Sweezy v. New Hampshire* (1957) decided the same day, the Court applied the Watkins line of reasoning to a state legislative investigation. Acting under a legislative authorizing resolution, the Attorney General of New Hampshire had subpoenaed a visiting professor at the state university and had attempted to question him concerning his lectures, his Socialist Party affiliations, and the like. The witness, standing on his First Amendment rights, had refused to answer.

After dwelling upon the importance of protecting First Amendment rights, "particularly in the academic community," Warren again condemned the legislative charge as so vague that the inquiry suffered from "an absence of authority." Petitioner's conviction therefore violated his rights under the Fourteenth Amendment.

Thus the Warren Court, at the moment in control of a libertarian majority, had adopted for itself a great part of the contemporary body of criticism of legislative inquiries. In the long run the Warren Court's strictures against private exposure unrelated to legislative needs, against vagueness of committee charge, upon the necessity of "pertinency" in a line of questioning, and in favor of First Amendment rights were to emerge as principal judicial guideposts in a strongly libertarian approach to legislative inquiries generally.

Before this development became clear, however, the temporary control exercised over the Court between 1958 and 1962 by the conservative majority of the moment for a time put the Watkins opinion virtually "on the shelf." Thus in *Barenblatt v. United States* (1959), the Court handed down a decision which on the surface seemed largely to destroy the force of the Watkins precedent. A witness, called before the House Un-American Activities Committee in the course of an investigation into Communism in higher education, had invoked his rights under the First Amendment, and thereafter had been convicted under 2 United States Code, Section 192 (the old 1857 contempt statute). In his appeal, he had relied heavily upon the Watkins case as precedent, arguing that the vagueness of the Committee's charge made it impossible to establish the pertinency of its question.

However, Justice Harlan, somewhat astonishingly, now denied that vagueness in the Committee's charge had been the basis for the

Court's finding of a lack of pertinency in the Watkins decision. In any event, he held, "a persuasive gloss of legislative history" made the Committee's charge from the House altogether clear, and this in turn made technically pertinent questions concerning Communist affiliations in higher education. Nor could First Amendment rights prevail here. The right of congressional inquiry, he said, touched upon the nation's "ultimate right of self-preservation itself," so that "the balance between the individual and the governmental interests here at stake must be struck in favor of the latter." In a vigorous dissent, Justice Black, joined by the Chief Justice and Justices Douglas and Brennan, condemned the Court's departure from the principles of the Watkins case, and deplored resort to the "balancing test" on First Amendment rights as amounting to the proposition that the Amendment's guarantees would not be enforced "unless the Court believes it reasonable to do so."

Again, there was a New Hampshire companion case, *Uphaus v. Wyman* (1959), growing out of a witness's refusal to answer questions or produce documents in an inquiry into higher education conducted by the state's attorney general under an authorizing resolution of the legislature. Clark's opinion for the majority abruptly rejected the argument of want of pertinency, and also dismissed the plea that First Amendment rights had been violated. Instead, he said, the "investigation had been undertaken in the interests of self-preservation," so that "public interests overbalance the private ones." Again, Brennan, Warren, Black, and Douglas dissented. Brennan's opinion insisted that there had been no "discernible legislative purpose" in the inquiry, condemned "exposure for the sake of exposure," and declared that the state had not demonstrated any ascendant public interest "sufficient to subordinate appellant's constitutionally protected rights."

In *Wilkinson v. United States* (1961) and *Braden v. United States* (1961), a pair of cases arising out of the operations of the House Un-American Activities Committee, the conservative bloc again asserted its momentary control. The circumstances involved had about them an odor suspiciously like that of deliberate persecution. The two petitioners were journalists who had followed a subcommittee to an Atlanta hearing on Communism in Southern industry, and thereupon had been subpoenaed by the subcommittee in what appeared to be a calculated act of harassment. Both had refused to allow the subcommittee to question them about possible Communist Party affiliations, invoking their rights under the Fifth Amendment, but also challenging in both cases "in the most fundamental sense," the very legality of the Committee itself. Indictment, trial, and conviction under Section 192 had followed.

Justice Stewart's terse majority opinions in the two cases held in succession that the subcommittee investigation had been properly authorized, that it had had a valid legislative purpose, and that the questions asked had been pertinent to the investigation at hand. Applying the balancing test, he ruled, also, that the witnesses' rights had not been violated. Accordingly, petitioners had been lawfully convicted under Section 192. Justice Black, in a strongly worded dissent which the Chief Justice and Douglas and Brennan joined, argued that the cases involved "nothing more or less than an attempt by the House Un-American Activities Committee to use the contempt power of the House of Representatives as a weapon against those who dare to criticize it."

The conservative bloc on the Court, even then in the process of losing its controlling position, prevailed once more in *Hutcheson v. United States* (1962), as the justices by a four to two vote sustained the contempt conviction of a witness who had refused to answer a series of questions put to him by the Senate's so-called McClellan Committee, which was then in the process of investigating "improper activities" in the labor-management field. The witness, who was under indictment on a grand jury "fixing" charge in Indiana, was aware that under Indiana law any resort on his part to the Fifth Amendment might be used as evidence against him in criminal proceedings in that state, and he had as a consequence carefully refused to claim any privilege against self-incrimination. Instead he had based his refusal to testify upon the grounds that the questions put to him were not pertinent to any subject the Committee was authorized to investigate and further that his Fifth Amendment rights were threatened in that his answers might aid the prosecution in his pending state trial. Indicted and brought to trial under Section 192, he had thereupon claimed that the Committee's line of questioning on a matter pending in a state criminal trial had threatened him with self-incrimination in violation of the Fifth Amendment (a different Fifth Amendment right than that claimed earlier), and further that the questioning had served no legislative purpose and had amounted only to exposure for exposure's sake.

Justice Harlan, with whom only Clark and Stewart joined, rejected both these claims. Observing first that under *United States v. Murdock* (1931), possible incrimination under state law was not a proper grounds for pleading the Fifth Amendment in a federal proceeding, he pointed out that in any event, petitioner in his appearance before the Committee had repeatedly disclaimed any intention of relying upon his right not to incriminate himself. To allow him to do so now, Harlan said, would "enable a witness to toy with a committee," which was entitled to know the grounds upon which a witness refused to answer. Further, the questioning at hand had been pertinent to the Committee's charge, had lain well within the authority of Congress, and did not involve "exposure for the sake of exposure." Justice Brennan concurred in a separate opinion to make up the Court majority, but Chief Justice Warren, with whom Douglas joined in dissent, argued forcefully that the Committee's line of questioning had violated the witness's Fifth Amendment rights in that it had placed him on the horns of a "three-pronged dilemma," in which he faced prosecution whether he answered truthfully, pleaded his Fifth Amendment privilege against self-incrimination, or committed perjury.

Even at this time, it was possible to muster a majority of the justices, through a shift of Brennan and Stewart, to condemn congressional investigations that the Court considered to be mere fishing expeditions conducted for the sake of exposure and without clear reference to a clear committee charge. *Russell v. United States* (1962), decided within days of the Hutcheson case, was in fact well calculated to expose the constitutional weaknesses in the more irresponsible type of congressional inquiry. The case involved appeals by six different persons who had been tried and convicted under Section 192 after refusal to testify, in two instances before the House Committee on Un-American Activities and in the other cases before the Senate Internal Security Sub-Committee. Both committees of late had been engaged in general fishing expeditions into Communist activities, the House Committee, in particular, apparently for the purpose of exposure and harassment rather than for legislative purposes.

Stewart's opinion for the four majority justices who voted to reverse the convictions found all six indictments defective for "failure to identify the subject under congressional subcommittee inquiry." As a consequence, he said, the indictments did not support the claim that the line of questioning pursued by the subcommittee had been pertinent to the Committee charge. In turn this meant that the indictments were wanting in one fundamental constitutional guarantee to which all accused persons were entitled: "To be apprised, with reasonable certainty, of the nature of the indictment against him." Stewart's analysis made it clear that it was the general probing character of the inquiries at issue, without benefit of a specific committee charge, that the Court found most offensive. Clark and Harlan, in dissent, insisted that a simple assertion of pertinency in the indictments was all that the precedents called for.

Thus the Court had used a technical point in the indictments related to pertinency to reverse convictions where the majority's principal concern in fact had been the protection of First Amendment rights. This conflict between committee prerogative and First Amendment rights became more overt in *Gibson v. Florida Legislative Investigating Committee* (1963), in which the Court in a five to four decision upset the conviction of a local NAACP official who had refused to produce membership lists subpoenaed by a state legislative committee. The committee had been seeking to ascertain whether fourteen persons previously identified as Communists were in fact members of the local NAACP chapter.

Justice Goldberg first observed that this involved an obvious "conflict between individual rights of free speech and association and governmental interest in conducting investigations." The crucial point, he made clear, was that there was no compelling evidence of "a nexus of relationship" between the NAACP and Communist Party activity, so that the Committee had failed to establish the "adequate foundation for inquiry," necessary before it could intrude upon First Amendment rights. To put it differently, the committee had engaged in a mere fishing expedition, against which First Amendment rights were sacrosanct. Clark, Harlan, White, and Stewart, dissenting, expressed the belief that the Court had imposed a serious and unprecedented limitation upon the legislative power to "investigate the Communist Party and its activities."

Yellin v. United States (1963), decided on a somewhat different point, exhibited the same concern of the majority justices for the protection of First Amendment rights, which the Court in this instance defined as a right to immunity from the casual exposure of Communist Party activities. Speaking through Chief Justice Warren, the five majority justices ruled that the House Committee on Un-American Activities had erred in denying a witness his request for a closed hearing, a refusal arrived at contrary to the Committee's own rules. The refusal to consider the consequences for the witness of possible unfavorable exposure, the Court said, had tainted the subsequent indictment and conviction under Section 192.

Justice White, who entered a dissent in which Clark, Harlan, and Stewart concurred, pointed out that the witness at the original hearing had challenged the right of the Committee to "investigate into areas protected by the First Amendment," and had also attacked the validity of the House authorizing resolution, but had said nothing of his earlier request for a closed hearing. The case, White thought, should have been settled on the issues raised by the petitioner in his hearing and not on the basis of a defective committee procedure not asserted by the witness at the time.

Insistence upon the protection of a witness against casual exposure of left-wing affiliations was again evident in *DeGregory v. Attorney General of New Hampshire* (1966), in which the Court reversed a state conviction for contempt resting upon refusal of a witness to answer questions having to do with his Communist Party activities in a rather distant past. Both the First and Fifth Amendments, Justice Brennan said, stood "as a barrier" against any such casual "state intrusion of privacy." "The information being sought," he pointed out, "was historical, not current," and the First Amendment protected witnesses against any such "use of the power to investigate enforced by the contempt to probe at will and without relation to existing needs." Harlan's dissenting opinion, in which Stewart and White concurred, would have affirmed the New Hampshire conviction under the Barenblatt precedent.

Gojack v. United States (1966), arose as a sequel to the Russell case of four years earlier. The petitioner, who had been one of the defendants freed by the earlier Russell decision, had been reindicted, tried, and convicted under a corrected bill of particulars. But Justice Fortas, who now spoke for a unanimous Court, found that "the failure of these proceedings is more fundamental" than a "mere omission from the indictment . . . of the subject of inquiry" being conducted by the subcommittee. Not only was there no record of any resolution by the main Committee authorizing the subcommittee inquiry in question; there also was no resolution or record defining the jurisdiction of the subcommittee. The subcommittee's activities, in short, had never been properly authorized; it had exercised a mere "roving commission" without any "clear chain of authority from the House." The "jurisdiction of the courts," Fortas admonished, "cannot be invoked to impose criminal sanctions for any such inquiry." Petitioner's conviction under Section 192 accordingly was again reversed.

The stern stand on First and Fifth Amendment rights that the Court adopted with respect to congressional investigations after 1962 was doubtless responsible in considerable part for the decline in prestige, activities, and "headline capacity" that the House Committee on Un-American Activities and the Senate Internal Security Subcommittee suffered in the late 1960's. The House Committee, in particular, became the subject of repeated attacks in the press and by liberal congressmen. The latter succeeded in slashing substantially the Committee's operating appropriations, although they failed several times by lopsided votes in their efforts to abolish the Committee outright.

Finally, in January, 1969, the Democratic majority in the House gave the Committee a substantial infusion of liberal blood, with the appointment of Claude Pepper of Florida and Louis Stokes of Ohio, the latter a brother of the Negro mayor of Cleveland. It was about this time that *The New York Times* labeled the Committee an utter failure, pointing out that of the 133 contempt citations the Committee had imposed between 1950 and 1966, only five had resulted in convictions, while in the thirty years of its existence the Committee had reported only five bills that had become law. In February, nonetheless, the House turned back, 262–133, a new attempt by the liberal Democratic bloc to abolish the Committee outright.

However, the House this time adopted the recommendation of its new chairman, Representative Richard Ichord of Missouri, that the Committee's name be altered and its charge somewhat limited. The Committee became the House Internal Security Committee, and was now charged merely with the investigation of totalitarian groups and groups seeking to overthrow the government by force and violence, thus eliminating the portion of the original charge calling for the investigation of "un-American propaganda." It seemed probable, however, that it was the Court's new stand and the change in the spirit of the times, rather than any minor alteration in Committee name and charge that might well bring an end in the future to the kind of far-ranging inquiries which had characterized its activities since the days of Martin Dies and Francis Walter.

Thus by the end of the Warren era, legislative inquiry for investigative purposes immediately unrelated to the enactment of legislation had suffered a substantial decline, both in prestige and effectiveness, in large part as a result of the Court's strictures. Here, as with the black revolution, it had been the Court which had fashioned the new era, with Congress, the Executive, and finally society at large trailing along in its wake. However, legislative inquiry for investigative purposes was by no means finished, as the spectacular 1973 probe by the Senate's Ervin Committee into the conduct of the Nixon administration was to demonstrate so dramatically.

Chapter

35

The Warren Court and the
New Egalitarianism

THE CONSISTENT CONCERN the Warren Court exhibited for racial justice and civil liberties was in reality only one manifestation of a general responsiveness of the justices to the powerful new egalitarian drive that dominated American life during these years. The Court, of course, did not initiate the new populistic trend any more than it was responsible ultimately for the revolution in the status of the black American. On the contrary, the unparalleled growth of egalitarianism in American life—which far overshadowed the somewhat limited social democracy of earlier generations—was in itself a response to numerous and variegated forces at work in the country. The vast and continued rise in the productivity of the economic system, which enabled a larger and larger percentage of people to achieve a middle-class standard of living; the emergence of organized labor as a part of the political and economic "establishment"; the full entry into the mainstream of American culture of various minority groups, (such as Italians, Jews, and Poles), who only lately had occupied the "airless back rooms" of the great urban slums but who now constituted social, political, and economic forces to be reckoned with; the corresponding comparative political and social decline from their old ascendancy of the

WASPs, or "White Anglo-Saxon Protestants"—all these were responsible in some degree for the new egalitarian spirit that pervaded American society in the generation after 1945. Integral to the new egalitarianism, also, was the extraordinary expansion in higher education, in itself a product both of unprecedented prosperity and the new aspiration to middle-class living of the sons and daughters from working-class and immigrant backgrounds who poured into business and the professions a flood of educated men and women, most of whom were libertarian in outlook and aggressively egalitarian in the point of view they adopted toward politics and society.

The Court's leadership in the egalitarian movement in American society added up to a new era of judicial activism quite at odds with the "twilight" interlude of judicial self-restraint that had prevailed between 1937 and 1953. Unquestionably the Court was "legislating" once more, in part in a manner reminiscent of the fashion in which it had written its economic and social predilections into constitutional law in the era of *Lochner v. New York*. The great difference was that whereas in the earlier period the Court had used substantive due process and the doctrine of vested rights to strike down state and federal social legislation on behalf of vested corporate interests, it now was using a new substantive interpretation of the Fourteenth Amendment to expand the guarantees of the Bill of Rights on behalf of the new egalitarianism, the new freedom from restraint, and the new privacy. To put it differently, formerly the Court for the most part had played a conservative role in the social order; now its role had become libertarian, reformist, and, in the eyes of some conservatives, even "radical."

The result was a new avalanche of criticism directed at the Court, much of it from conservative and even extreme right-wing political sources, but a substantial portion of it also from concerned moderates and responsible legal technicians. The gist of the most careful argument was that the Court had unwisely fashioned itself into a kind of permanent libertarian constitutional convention, which sat from day to day intent on solving all of the political and social ills of the country through a continuous process of judicial intervention. To this end, the Court's critics charged, the justices disregarded precedent and long-standing rules of law and on occasion even resorted to spurious "law office history" in order to endow their decisions with a superficial constitutional plausibility. All this, critics continued, seriously violated the democratic process in that it "imposed" reform without regard to majority will or the normal legislative organs for effecting social change. Further, they asserted, it "diminished the rule of law" in American society, while it was at last self-defeating in that many of the Court's reforms somehow failed in actual practice, creating new evils in place of those supposedly remedied. "Indeed," concluded Philip B. Kurland of the University of Chicago Law School, a principal acerbic critic of the Supreme Tribunal, "if, as has been said, the road to hell is paved with good intentions, the Warren Court had been among the great road builders of all time."

Other critics, more vociferous and less restrained in their attacks, accused the Court variously of "violating states rights," scheming to "mongrelize the races," protecting "vicious criminals," and "deliberately destroying the Constitution" which the justices "have sworn to uphold." Some agreed even with the demand of the John Birch Society that Congress "impeach Earl Warren."

Undoubtedly the best reply to these critics was that which pointed to the importance of the reforms the Court had achieved through the judicial process. The Court's destruction of the "rotten borough" system in the state legislatures and in Congress, its defenders argued, almost certainly could have been achieved in no other fashion, since neither Congress nor the various state legislatures had any inclination to tackle the job. Without it, the Court's advocates declared, constitutional democracy might have died of "self-strangulation." The same defense could be offered on behalf of the Court's reform of criminal procedure, its elimination of anti-birth control legislation now gravely at odds with society's actual morals and practices, its long, lonely crusade in favor of the black American, and so on. The Court, its friends proclaimed, had always been a political instrument deliberately manipulating the political balance of power; nothing had changed, they said, except that the judicial process at length was being brought to bear in favor of a progressive, democratic, libertarian society.

THE WARREN COURT AND THE APPORTIONMENT REVOLUTION

Apart from its leadership in the black revolution, the most significant piece of egalitarian reformist activism in which the Warren Court engaged was its imposition of the "one man, one vote" principle upon representation in state legislatures and in Congress. By this means the Court brought its new egalitarianism to bear upon a portion of the "living constitution" hitherto largely isolated from the judicial process. Thereby it worked a substantial redistribution of power in the country's political life.

The Court's interference in state legislative and congressional apportionment had its inception in one of the most conspicuous scandals of modern American constitutional history: the gross malapportionment both of the great majority of American state legislatures and of state delegations to the national House of Representatives. This situation had come about over the years simply because rural-dominated state legislatures had persisted in ignoring the vast shifts in population produced by the great growth of the country's cities in the twentieth century. In all too many instances, state legislatures, fearful of the political consequences that equitable redistricting would mean for the rural-urban balance of power, deliberately flouted provisions in their own constitutions requiring periodic redistricting, both of their own houses and of their state congressional delegations. The result was a species of constitutional deformity that gravely imperiled the democratic political process.

Some idea of the proportions the problem had assumed may be obtained by a survey of the apportionment situation on the eve of the Court's epoch-making 1962 decision to intervene. As of 1960, thirty-six of the American state constitutions embodied specific provisions requiring periodic redistricting of the legislature, usually on the basis of the decennial census. But in spite of such provisions, twelve state senates and another twelve state houses of representatives had not been reapportioned for thirty years or more. There had been no reapportionment in Delaware since 1897, and none in Alabama and Tennessee since 1901.

There had been fairly extensive state legislative reapportionment in the 1950's, twenty-eight senates and thirty-one lower houses being restructured during the decade. However, this generally had involved resort of some sort to the so-called "federal principle," whereby each electoral district received at least one vote regardless of population, so that the original requirement of the state constitution for districting according to population alone underwent substantial modification.

The result of all this very often was a gross distortion of anything like equitable representation. In California, for example, the population of the state senate's county districts varied from six million for Los Angeles down to a mere 14,000 for the least populous rural district in the state. In Florida, senate districts ranged in population from a maximum of 900,000 to a minimum of 9,500, a difference that apportionment experts expressed as a "variance ratio" of 98 to 1. In Vermont, the population differential for districts in the lower house extended from a maximum of 33,000 to a minimum of 238, a variance ratio of about 140. Population disparities in congressional apportionment were as a rule less striking, ranging from variance ratios of 6.9 in Michigan and 4.4 in Texas, down to 1.3 in Iowa and 1.1 in Maine. Taken in the large, American state legislative and congressional apportionment by 1960 had taken on a suspicious resemblance to the ancient ill-famed English "rotten borough" system of the eighteenth century.

For more than a generation, political reformers had attempted to get the Supreme Court to interfere in apportionment, but that tribunal had consistently refused to do so, on the ground that apportionment involved "a political question" and hence was not subject to adjudication by the courts. The most pertinent precedent was *Colegrove v. Green* (1946), in which the Court by a four to three vote had refused to invalidate the Illinois Apportionment Act of 1901. Plaintiffs had contended that the statute in question violated both the equal protection clause and the federal Congressional Apportionment Acts of 1911 and 1929. "Appellants," Frankfurter declared for the majority justices, "ask of this Court what is beyond its power to grant." Legislative apportionment, he explained, fell in the category of cases having "a peculiarly political nature and therefore not meet for judicial determination." Black, Douglas, and Murphy had dissented, the former protesting that the "complaint presented a justiciable case and controversy," in which "appellants had standing to sue."

Colegrove v. Green dealt with congressional apportionment and not with that of state legislatures, but the principle the Court enunciated obviously covered both types of cases. In the next few years the Court several times turned back apportionment cases without opinion, on the basis of the Colegrove precedent.

That the Court might at last be moving toward a change in its position, however, became apparent in *Gomillion v. Lightfoot* (1960), where, it will be recalled, the Court had struck down an Alabama law redrawing the boundaries of Tuskegee, Alabama, so as to exclude Negroes from the city franchise. In the Gomillion case the Court acted under the aegis of the Fifteenth Amendment, but it was apparent that it would be only a very short step to a finding that the boundaries of state and congressional legislative districts were also subject to judicial scrutiny.

Baker v. Carr (1962), in which the Court at length abandoned its long-standing self-imposed prohibition upon judicial interference in apportionment matters, began with a suit in a federal district court in Tennessee attacking the constitutionality of that

state's 1901 law apportioning the general assembly, on the ground
that it violated the equal protection clause. When that court, acting
on the basis of *Colegrove v. Green*, refused to interfere, the suit
went on appeal to the Supreme Court.

This time the Court threw both precedent and the "political
questions" doctrine overboard, to hold by a six to two vote that
state legislative apportionment properly was subject to judicial
scrutiny and possible remedy under the equal protection clause.
The Court's opinion, delivered by Justice Brennan, decided three
principal points—that the federal courts properly possessed jurisdiction of the subject matter of the case; that the case presented a
"justiciable cause of action"; and that appellants had "standing to
challenge" the Tennessee statute in question.

The crucial issue, Brennan made clear, was whether or not the
case presented a "justiciable cause of action," that is, whether or
not legislative apportionment was a "political question" and hence
not subject to judicial scrutiny. Brennan reviewed at length the
various categories of "political questions" which the Court had
recognized in the past—foreign relations, the duration of hostilities
in war, the ratification of constitutional amendments, the status of
Indian tribes, and the guarantee to the states of a republican form
of government—and concluded that each of these possessed one
or the other of two essential elements. In certain instances, the
Constitution committed the matter at hand to "a coordinate political department," so that it was ascendantly one for control by
Congress or the President. In other instances, the controversy before the Court was characterized by "a lack of judicially discover-
able and manageable standards for resolving it."

State legislative apportionment, Brennan now found, involved
neither of these elements. In reaching this conclusion, Brennan rejected respondent's claim that the present case properly arose under
the Constitution's guarantee to the states of a republican form of
government, and hence was controlled by the application of the
"political questions" doctrine thereto in *Luther v. Borden* (1842).
The present case, Brennan held, was not such, but was simply one
of "arbitrary and capricious" state action. Nor was *Colegrove v.
Green* a barrier to the present decision, Brennan held, since even
there, four justices actually had treated apportionment as a justiciable matter. Far more significant as a precedent, Brennan thought,
was the recent decision in *Gomillion v. Lightfoot*, where the Court
had deliberately rejected the claim that redefinition of district
boundaries by a state legislature lay beyond judicial control.

Accordingly, the Court decided that the present case indeed presented a justiciable cause of action. However, it did not immediately undertake to pass upon the merits of the Tennessee apportionment controversy as such. Instead, it merely remanded the case to the lower federal court once more, to arrive at a decision and hand down orders that would in turn be subject to review on appeal.

Frankfurter and Harlan both dissented at length, each joining also in the other's opinion. Frankfurter denounced the Court's decision as "a massive repudiation of the experience of our whole past in asserting destructively novel judicial power," insisting that the case at hand, despite the majority opinion, indeed involved a "republican form of government" question and so was controlled by *Luther v. Borden.* Harlan thought that there was "nothing in the Federal Constitution to prevent a state, acting not irrationally, from choosing any electoral structure it thinks best suited to the interests, temper, and customs of its people," while he also examined at some length the apportionment system in Tennessee, in order to refute to his own satisfaction the argument that it was "so unreasonable as to amount to a capricious classification of voting strength."

The Court's decision in *Baker v. Carr* unleashed something like a veritable avalanche of new apportionment litigation in the several states, along with a general legislative scramble to adjust to the Court's ruling. By the end of 1963, federal suits attacking apportionment of the legislature had been instituted in thirty-one states, while like suits had been commenced in the state courts of nineteen other states. In no less than twenty-four states, the courts already had declared at least one house of the state legislature to be unconstitutionally apportioned, or had postponed final decision on the issue in order to allow the legislature to correct the situation. Meanwhile, twenty-six states had adopted new state legislative apportionment plans, either by legislation or by constitutional amendment, and in twelve states suits already had been commenced attacking one or another of these plans supposedly drafted in conformity with the Court's new apportionment stance.

All this took place amidst vast legal confusion, for the Court, in refusing to pass on the merits of the Tennessee situation, had failed thereby to furnish any standards by which either state legislatures or the lower state and federal judiciary could proceed. Such questions as how large a variance ratio the Court would find acceptable; whether or not so-called "federal" plans employing some kind of area representation were constitutional; whether or not a state in apportioning itself might recognize sectional, party, class, geographic, historical, and class factors as well as population; and whether or not an apportionment plan, otherwise dubious, might receive some additional constitutional sanction if the people by formal referendum gave it their approval, were matters upon which both legislatures and the lower courts alike remained altogether in the dark.

THE NEW APPORTIONMENT RULE: ONE MAN, ONE VOTE

The first clear intimation of what the Court's new apportionment standard might be came in March, 1963, in *Gray v. Sanders*, in which the majority justices struck down Georgia's so-called "county unit" rule. This system of representation assigned each county in the state a number of so-called "votes," or "units," determined only in part by population, and required all successful candidates for nomination to state offices in primary elections to poll a majority of such unit votes. The plan discriminated heavily against the votes of citizens in the more populous counties, and a three-man federal district court had issued an injunction against it, forbidding the state thereafter to employ any unit scheme that resulted in greater disparities among voters than those that existed between voters of different states through the operation of the electoral college in national presidential elections.

On appeal, the Supreme Court held the entire county unit rule plan unconstitutional as a violation of the equal protection clause. Justice Douglas, who spoke for a majority of eight, further condemned as "inapposite" the attempt of the lower court to fix guidelines by analogy with the federal electoral college system. "The conception of political equality from the Declaration of Independence to Lincoln's Gettysburg Address, to the Fifteenth, Seventeenth, and Nineteenth Amendments," he said, "can mean only one thing—one person, one vote." Justice Harlan in a lone dissent protested that the "one man, one vote" rule "flies in the face of history," and "is constitutionally untenable."

Gray v. Sanders technically was a voting rights case and not one having to do with legislative apportionment, so that, as Justices Stewart and Clark pointed out in a concurring opinion, it could not properly be read as dealing with "the basic ground rules implementing *Baker v. Carr*." Nonetheless, the broad sweep of Douglas's language made it highly probable that application of the "one man, one vote" rule to apportionment would not be long in forthcoming.

This expectation was fulfilled a year later in *Wesberry v. Sanders* (1964), in which the Court employed the "one man, one vote" principle to declare void a 1931 Georgia congressional apportionment law. Justice Black, who wrote the majority opinion, delved deeply into early American history to determine to his own satisfaction that the provision in Article I, Section II of the Constitution, which directed the apportionment of representatives among the states according to population, had been intended by the Philadelphia Convention to assure that "as nearly as is practicable one man's vote in a congressional election is to be worth as much as another's." In an embittered dissent, Justice Harlan pointed out, correctly enough, that Black's historical analysis had confused the debate in the 1787 Convention over the apportionment of representatives *between* the states with the present matter of apportionment of representatives *within* the states.

Despite Harlan's dissent, the Court now was firmly embarked upon its campaign to apply simple majoritarianism to all legislative apportionment. Four months later, in *Reynolds v. Sims* (1964), the Court applied the "one man, one vote" principle to strike down both the existing apportionment of the Alabama state legislature and a complex proposal for reform that combined representation by population with a so-called "federal" plan. Restrictions on the right to vote, declared Chief Justice Warren sternly for the majority of eight, "strike at the heart of representative government." The Wesberry decision, he added, had "clearly established that the fundamental principle of representative government in this country is one of equal representation for equal numbers of people, without regard to race, sex, economic status, or place of residence within the state." The "federal analogy" he dismissed as "inapposite and irrelevant to state legislative redistricting schemes." Warren conceded that on occasion "some deviation from the equal population principle" might be permissible to achieve "some flexibility" and to avoid gerrymandering, but he warned that "neither history alone nor economic or other sorts of group interests are permissible factors in attempting to justify disparities from population-based representation." "One man, one vote," in other words, was virtually a pure and intractable rule.

In five other principal companion cases, decided the same day as *Reynolds v. Sims*, the Court struck down legislative apportionment schemes in New York, Maryland, Virginia, Delaware, and

Colorado, in each instance simply by applying the "one man, one vote" rule. The last of these, *Lucas v. Forty-Fourth General Assembly of Colorado* (1964), was of particular significance, for the plan in question not only came fairly close to establishing a straight population ratio (the variance ratio in the Colorado House of Representatives was only 1.7 to 1), but it also had been approved as a constitutional amendment in a popular election. However, the plan did take account of the division of the state into certain "natural" geographic districts, and the Chief Justice, who spoke for a majority of six, observed simply that the apportionment of the state senate, where a variance ratio of about 3.6 to 1 was involved, incorporated "departures from population-based representation too extremes to be acceptable." Further, he said, the plan's employment of multimember delegations for the more populous districts in the upper house deprived the people of such districts of the "intimate and direct" representation to which they were entitled. The plan therefore violated the equal protection clause and was unconstitutional.

In a lengthy and detailed minority opinion, Justice Harlan registered his vigorous dissent in all six apportionment cases. Warren's argument, he declared, rested both upon bad history and bad constitutional theory. The decisions, he remarked in some bitterness, "cut deeply into the fabric of our federalism," and would "result in a radical alteration in the relationship between the states and the federal government." The Court's whole performance, he added, rested upon the "mistaken view . . . that every major social ill in this country can find its cure in some kind of 'constitutional principle,' and that this Court should 'take the lead' in promoting reform when other branches of government fail to act." Justice Stewart, who filed a somewhat more limited dissent for himself and Justice Clark, confined his attack to a condemnation of the "one man, one vote" principle, since he thought it "unanswerably demonstrated" that this was not the system predominantly practiced in America, either in the past or today." And in language strongly reminiscent of Holmes's Lochner dissent, he protested that the Court had taken a "long step back into that unhappy era" when the justices proceeded on the assumption that "the demands of the Constitution were to be measured not by what it says, but by their own notions of wise political theory." Both Harlan and Stewart, in short, accused the Court once again of engaging in judicial legislation.

THE DRIVE FOR AN APPORTIONMENT AMENDMENT

As might be expected from decisions having so profound an impact upon the political balance of power within the country, *Reynolds v. Sims* and its companion cases produced a rumbling explosion of discontent both in and out of Congress that gave rise to a substantial movement for a remedial constitutional amendment.

As early as December, 1962, the 16th Biennial General Assembly of the States, sponsored by the Council of State Governments, approved, 26 states to 10, a proposed amendment stipulating that no part of the federal Constitution was to apply to apportionment within the states, and also stripping the federal courts of jurisdiction in all apportionment cases. This "prescription" proved to be too extreme for moderate political tastes, and it died after the conservative-minded House of Delegates of the American Bar Association condemned it as unwise and unworkable. Thereafter, agitation for congressional intervention in the apportionment controversy died down for a time.

However, the decision in *Reynolds v. Sims* and its companion cases reawakened the conservative demand for action. Between June and August of 1964 alone, more than 130 bills providing for a legislative check upon the Court's control of apportionment were introduced into the House of Representatives. When the House Judiciary Committee failed to act on any of these, Representative William V. Tuck of Virginia forced a so-called "court ripper bill" onto the floor. This measure, which would have stripped the federal judiciary of all jurisdiction over apportionment cases, met prompt condemnation in liberal and moderate circles; Walter Lippmann attacked it repeatedly in his daily column, and Professors Eugene V. Rostow and Thomas I. Emerson of the Yale Law School condemned it as a "blow at the Constitution itself." On August 18, nonetheless, the House passed the Tuck bill, 218–175. However, as tempers cooled, support for the Tuck bill faded. In late September, the Senate put the question aside by adopting, 44 to 38, a "sense of the Senate" resolution asking the courts to allow "adequate time" for consideration by the states of a possible apportionment amendment.

Early in January, 1965, accordingly, Senator Dirksen introduced a proposed amendment which, as modified, provided that "the people of a state may apportion one house of a bicameral legislature, using population, geography, and political subdivisions as factors as they deem appropriate. The amendment also would have allowed the same type of weighting in apportioning a unicameral legislature, provided, however, that in either case the people approved the proposed plan in a popular referendum. Further, the plan would have required submission to the people in the same election of an alternate plan of apportionment based upon "substantial equality of population," and it stipulated also that any "federal plan" as approved must be resubmitted to the state's electorate within two years following each decennial census.

A subcommittee under Senator Birch Bayh of Indiana presently began hearings on the Dirksen proposal, which meanwhile won approval in principle from the House of Delegates of the American Bar Association and from both Houses of the California Legislature. When the Bayh committee failed to act, Dirksen resorted to a parliamentary artifice to force his amendment onto the Senate floor.

The debate that followed divided the Senate along liberal and conservative lines without much regard to party, Senator Paul Douglas of Illinois taking leadership of those seeking to defeat Dirksen's proposal. Walter Mondale of Minnesota, Robert Kennedy of New York, William Proxmire of Wisconsin, and George McGovern of South Dakota charged variously that Dirksen's scheme constituted "legalized ballot-box stuffing" and would "impede the progress of civil rights" for the Negro and "perpetuate the rotten borough system" in American politics. On the other hand, George Murphy of California argued that the amendment would make possible "balanced legislatures" and would serve as a barrier "against the extremes of rural domination and city domination."

On August 4, at the close of debate, the Dirksen amendment went down to defeat, 57 yeas to 39 nays. A modified Dirksen draft, support for which was mobilized by a well-financed publicity campaign throughout the country, also met rejection in January, this time by a vote of 55 to 38.

Meanwhile other conservatives had launched a drive for a federal constitutional convention, to be called by Congress upon petition from the legislatures of two-thirds of the states in accordance with the provision in Article V of the Constitution, whose task it would be to draft and submit to the states an apportionment amendment. By the summer of 1967, the legislatures of no less than thirty-two of the states, only two short of the constitutional majority required to impel Congress to act, had petitioned for an "apportionment convention."

However, the amendment for a federal apportionment convention soon ran into unforeseen difficulties. Many state legislatures, whose members now held office as a result of apportionment plans adopted in accordance with the Baker and Sims decisions, were having second thoughts about the wisdom of such a convention. Further, the various state petitions to Congress were couched in a great variety of legal phraseologies and did not "jibe" with one another. Careful constitutional lawyers pointed out that it was doubtful whether the various petitions constituted a uniform request to Congress, while many also expressed agreement with Senator Douglas when he warned that he regarded Congress as empowered at its discretion not to act upon such a call, and predicted in fact that it would not were the demand to arise.

It became clear, upon close analysis of the problem, that it would also be extremely difficult to structure any such federal apportionment convention intelligently. Were it to be set up in accordance with the distribution of electoral votes, for example, the country would face the prospect of a federal convention called to amend the "one man, one vote" rule that was itself at least mildly malapportioned under the new Supreme Court rule. And in a straight "one man, one vote" convention, were each state to have at least one vote, the resultant body would have to consist of at least 800 delegates, an impossibly large number for intelligent debate. And so the movement for a federal convention, like that for congressional submission of a constitutional amendment, faltered and died.

THE ONE MAN, ONE VOTE PRINCIPLE RECONFIRMED

For a time after 1964, the Court, having at length laid down a clear and decisive rule for the guidance of the inferior judiciary in apportionment cases, showed remarkably little inclination to interfere in the details of state and lower federal court apportionment procedures. It was soon evident, however, that the majority justices had no intention of retreating from the "one man, one vote" rule; in fact, if necessary, they were prepared to apply it more rigidly than ever.

Thus in *Swann v. Adams* (1967), the Court held unconstitutional a Florida apportionment statute that involved a variance ratio for the state senate of only 1.3 to 1, and, for the house, of only 1.41 to 1. Justice White's opinion for the majority admitted that under the Sims precedent "absolute mathematical exactness or precision is not required," but declared the law void nonetheless because of the state's failure to explain adequately certain "peculiar deviations" from the norm embodied in the plan. Harlan and Stewart alone dissented.

The Court thereafter used the Swann precedent to invalidate a variety of apportionment laws that deviated only slightly from the "one man, one vote" rule. And in *Avery v. Midland County* (1968), the Court brought county and city government under the purview of the "one man, one vote" rule for their legislative bodies.

Advocates of the "one man, one vote" rule at first believed that the new principle would result in an increase in the relative political strength of the Democratic Party at the expense of the Republicans, since the former presumably stood to gain from its massive support in the great cities. But this calculation, it soon became clear, failed to take into account the extraordinary growth in the past generation of the suburbs around the principal metropolitan areas, most of which were predominantly Republican and which siphoned off most of the new representative strength lost by rural Republican districts.

Other critics pointed out that simple majoritarianism in representation was seriously at odds with the tradition of American representative government, which historically had attempted, as Madison had explained in *The Federalist*, to give balanced recognition to a congeries of minority and pluralistic interest groups. And other commentators argued that the "one man, one vote" rule quite possibly strengthened opportunities for gerrymandering and other forms of legislative skullduggery, so that in the long run American legislative bodies might prove to be no more "representative" of that elusive thing called majority will than they had been before the apportionment upheaval. The only certainty in all this was that time alone could assess adequately the validity of such criticism.

THE WARREN COURT AND THE REFORM OF
CRIMINAL PROCEDURE

In the late 1950's, the Warren Court entered upon a radical reform of the foundations of criminal procedure in the United States, in considerable part by bringing the guarantees of fair procedure in criminal justice, which were already in effect in the federal courts, to bear upon the operation of criminal trials in the states. This involved further extension of the guarantees of the federal Bill of Rights, particularly the Fourth, Fifth, and Sixth Amendments, as limitations upon the states, through the medium of the Fourteenth Amendment.

Conceivably the Court might have accomplished this by embracing completely Justice Black's argument, as set forth in his celebrated opinion in *Adamson v. California*, that the Fourteenth Amendment had been intended by its framers to incorporate all the guarantees of the first Nine Amendments to the Constitution. However, a majority of the justices, even now, refused to subscribe to this doctrine; instead, they continued to pay formal homage to the dictum set forth by Justice Cardozo, in *Palko v. Connecticut*, that the Fourteenth Amendment, properly construed, had incorporated only those guarantees of the Bill of Rights that were "fundamental to ordered liberty." To put the matter differently, the Court continued formally to adhere to the so-called "selective incorporation" doctrine even while it continuously widened the area of incorporation.

The great portion of the new developments in criminal procedure were egalitarian in spirit, in that they benefited the weak, impoverished, friendless, and helpless, who had somehow become entangled in the toils of the law. And here, as elsewhere, the Court in its new activism frequently broke with precedent, or called up novel history to justify its apparent disregard for its own past. And again the result filled both the press and the law journals with volumes of controversy.

One of the most interesting examples of the way in which the Court brought state criminal procedure under federal judicial supervision was its application to the states of the long-standing federal rule, derived from the Fourth Amendment, that forbade the admission into criminal trials of evidence obtained through illicit searches and seizures—those conducted without lawful warrants and without "probable cause." This so-called "exclusionary rule" had first been enunciated in *Weeks v. United States* (1912), where the Court had in effect accepted the argument that the exclusion of illicitly obtained evidence was the only effective way of discouraging illegal searches.

However, in *Wolf v. Colorado* (1949), Justice Frankfurter, who spoke for a majority of six justices, had refused to apply the Weeks exclusionary rule to the states, on the ground that it was not fundamental to the concept of ordered liberty. The broad guarantees of the Fourth Amendment, he had conceded, did indeed apply to the states. But the exclusionary rule, he had added, was not intrinsic to the amendment's guarantees; instead it was a mere application of procedure about which men devoted "to the protection of the right of privacy might give different answers." Curiously, Justice Black, who had delivered himself of his Adamson opinion only a year earlier, had concurred, although Douglas, Rutledge, and Murphy, early exponents of the coming humanitarian activism, had dissented.

Domination of the Warren Court by the new egalitarianism inevitably brought reversal of the Wolf decision. In *Mapp v. Ohio* (1961), the Court applied the Weeks exclusionary rule to state criminal procedure. Clark's opinion for the six majority justices pointed out that more than half of the states now adhered of their own accord to the exclusionary rule on illicitly seized evidence, and that it had become evident that other remedies to enforce the guarantees of the Fourth Amendment were "worthless and futile." Further, to bring the Fourth and Fourteenth Amendments into line with one another, Clark said, would eliminate illicit collusion between state and federal officials in law enforcement and hence was but the dictate of "common sense." Justice Harlan, in a dissent in which Frankfurter and Whittaker also joined, protested that the reasoning of the majority was "notably unconvincing" and that the present decision threatened to damage "the preservation of a proper balance between state and federal responsibility in the administration of criminal justice."

A similar concern for egalitarianism, humanitarianism, and protection of the interests of the poor and helpless was apparent in the Warren Court's decision bringing the guarantees of the right to counsel set forth in the Sixth Amendment within the content of the Fourteenth Amendment's due process clause. As early as 1932, in *Powell v. Alabama*, a case growing out of the notorious Scottsboro rape trials, the Supreme Court had ruled that the failure of a state court to make adequate provision for counsel for defendants who were young, illiterate, friendless, far from home, and faced by a violently hostile body of public opinion, violated the due process guarantees of the Fourteenth Amendment.

A few years later, however, in *Betts v. Brady* (1942), the Court applied the "selective incorporation principle" in refusing to hold that the Sixth Amendment guarantee of counsel in criminal cases required the states to provide counsel in all criminal trials where the accused was unable to furnish his own attorney. The Sixth Amendment, said Justice Roberts, "applies only to trials in federal courts." Access to counsel, Roberts added, was "not a fundamental right, essential to a fair trial." Black, Douglas, and Murphy had dissented from the Court's finding.

Domination of the Court by the Warren libertarian majority doomed the Betts decision to an early demise. Reversal came in *Gideon v. Wainwright* (1963), in which Justice Black, speaking for the new majority, declared that the earlier ruling represented "an abrupt break" with the Court's "own well-considered precedents," and must now formally be overruled. The Sixth Amendment guarantee of counsel thus now became applicable to the states as a provision of the Bill of Rights "fundamental to a fair trial." This time even Justice Harlan concurred, although he protested that the Betts precedent was "entitled to a more respectful burial than has been accorded" by the majority opinion. At the same time, in *Douglas v. California* (1963), the Court majority extended the state's obligation to guarantee counsel for indigents through the first appeals process, this time over the protest of Clark, Harlan, and Stewart.

Douglas v. California was in reality also one of a series of cases in which the Warren majority undertook to guarantee convicted indigents various rights incident to possible appeal. In *Griffin v. Illinois* (1956), the Court had held that if a state granted the right of appeal in criminal cases, then it must as a matter of right furnish free court transcripts to indigent prisoners if this was a necessary means to such review. And in *Draper v. Washington* (1963), the Court found that a state could not deny indigent prisoners access to free transcripts, even where the trial court had ruled that the assignment of errors for possible appeal was "patently frivolous." This time Justice White, joined by Clark, Harlan, and Stewart, had dissented, protesting that the majority decision placed state appellate courts in an "inflexible procedural straight jacket."

One of the most controversial procedural matters handled by the Warren Court was the time-honored issue of the pretrial rights of accused persons. Attention now centered particularly on the matter of coerced confessions, which, it presently became clear, was in part related to a possible right of access to counsel in the pretrial process. It was of course an ancient rule of the English common law that police could not torture a confession out of an accused person and then use his statement against him to obtain a conviction in open court. It was this guarantee to which the Court had given indignant expression in *Brown v. Mississippi* (1936), in holding that police torture to wring a confession out of a Negro arrested for an alleged rape-murder violated the Four-teenth Amendment's due process clause. The Warren Court now undertook some considerable refinement of this venerable common-law rule.

Thus in *Haynes v. Washington* (1963) the Court threw out the conviction of a petitioner who had been convicted of robbery, in part by means of a confession that the police had obtained by holding the accused incommunicado, questioning him repeatedly, and refusing him permission to call either his wife or an attorney. Nominally, at least, the confession had been voluntary—there had been no torture, deprival of food, overt threats, or even uninter-rupted questioning for long periods of time. But Justice Goldberg, who wrote the opinion for the majority, declared nonetheless that holding the prisoner incommunicado meant that his confession had been "obtained in an atmosphere of substantial coercion" and so violated the due process clause of the Fourteenth Amendment. Justice Clark, in a dissent concurred in by Harlan, Stewart, and White, protested that the majority ruling constituted an "abrupt departure" from earlier court decisions, in that the confession was substantially the product of the defendant's free will.

A year later, in *Escobedo v. Illinois* (1964), the Court ruled inadmissible in a murder trial a confession obtained through a police examination in which the accused had been repeatedly denied an opportunity to consult with an attorney and in which police failed to inform him of "his absolute constitutional right to remain silent." Justice Goldberg's opinion first recalled the deci-sion in *Gideon v. Wainwright*, categorically extending the right to counsel in all state and federal criminal trials, and then ruled that since in an accusatory inquiry the adversary system already had begun to operate against a defendant, denial to him of counsel at this stage and failure to warn him of his constitutional rights violated the guarantee of assistance of counsel in the Sixth Amend-ment. Again, Harlan, Stewart, Clark, and White dissented, Justice Stewart declaring that the majority decision in his opinion in fact perverted "precious constitutional guarantees" and frustrated "the vital interests of society in preserving . . . honest and purposeful police investigation." [1]

Two years later, in *Miranda v. Arizona* (1966), the Court found

---

[1] The logical companion piece to the Escobedo decision had come a few weeks earlier in *Massiah v. United States* (1964), in which the Court had held that ad-mission of statements made by a defendant after indictment but without benefit of counsel also violated the Sixth Amendment.

occasion to deal even more extensively with the constitutional issues involved in police interrogation. This time, in a new legal departure, it coupled the in-custody interrogation rights of potential defendants to the Fifth Amendment guarantee against self-incrimination. At hand were four different cases in which the police had questioned a suspect extensively without advising him of his right to have an attorney present or of his right to refuse to answer. In each instance a confession had resulted (in the Miranda case to kidnapping and forcible rape). Thereafter the confession had been admitted into evidence in the resulting criminal trial and had been the basis, in part at least, for the convictions that had resulted. Technically the question before the Court was the admissibility of the confessions into evidence in the trials.

The Court, speaking through Chief Justice Warren, threw out all four confessions as obtained in violation of the defendants' Fifth Amendment privilege against self-incrimination. "We hold," said the Chief Justice, "that when an individual is taken into custody, the privilege against self-incrimination is jeopardized, and positive safeguard must be employed to protect the privilege." Warren spelled out with "some specificity" what these procedural safeguards must be. They included an obligation to inform the suspect of his "right to remain silent," to warn him that any statement he made, "exculpatory or inculpatory," might be "used as evidence against him," and that he had a "right to the presence of an attorney, either retained or appointed," during the interrogation.

Justices Clark, Harlan, Stewart, and White, all members of a fairly recognizable "conservative bloc" with respect to the revolution in criminal procedure under way, dissented from the Court's decision. Harlan protested that the thrust of the majority's new rule was to "negate all pressures" on suspects and "ultimately to discourage any confession at all," to the great detriment of general community welfare. Harlan and White also objected to the new linkage between pretrial rights and the self-incrimination privilege in the Fifth Amendment, White declaring emphatically that the supposed connection "has no significant support in the history of the privilege or in the language of the Fifth Amendment."

Quite evidently, both the Warren Court majority's profound humanitarian sense and its equally strong instinct for egalitarianism were at work in the Miranda decision. Conceivably, also, Warren and his majority brethren were assisted in their decision by an abiding suspicion that modern techniques of police interrogation still smelled suspiciously of the ancient coercive devices of the "third degree," even though, as the Chief Justice conceded, modern interrogation was primarily "psychological rather than physically oriented." Finally, the Miranda decision was indicative of the vast concern of the Warren Court for individual privacy, a concern present in a large range of decisions, including those on birth control and obscene movies and literature.

One of the most significant decisions in the application of the Bill of Rights to state criminal procedure came in *Duncan v. Louisiana* (1968), in which the Court for the first time held that the right to jury trial, guaranteed in federal criminal procedure in the Sixth Amendment, now extended to the states through the due process clause of the Fourteenth Amendment. The case at hand involved appeal from a Louisiana conviction for battery—a misdemeanor under Louisiana law—in which the defendant had been denied his request for jury trial and thereafter sentenced to sixty days imprisonment and a $150 fine. Said Justice White for the majority: "Because we believe that trial by jury in criminal cases is fundamental to the American scheme of justice, we hold that the Fourteenth Amendment guarantees of a right of jury trial in all criminal cases which—were they to be tried in a federal court—would come within the Sixth Amendment's guarantee. . ."

The Court's decision, interestingly enough, led to a renewal of the "Adamson controversy," this time between Black and Harlan, as to whether or not the framers of the Fourteenth Amendment had intended Section I to embrace the content of the Bill of Rights. The jury process, Harlan protested in dissent, was not "fundamental to ordered liberty"; further, he insisted, "neither history, nor sense, supports using the Fourteenth Amendment to put the states in a constitutional strait-jacket with respect to their own development in the administration of criminal or civil law." To which the constitutional historian can only observe that Harlan's argument, however much historical evidence could be mobilized in its support, was by the close of the Warren era already largely lost by default, so far as contemporary constitutional practice was concerned.

THE NATIONALIZATION OF THE LAW OF LIBEL

A major interest of the Warren Court, closely akin to its concern for humanitarianism and egalitarianism, was that which it manifested for an increased range of private freedom of both action and expression, free from the threat of state interference and control. It was this interest that found expression, among other things, in the Court's nationalization of the law of libel, which it now brought within the aegis of the First Amendment.

Historically, the law of private, or tort, libel held that certain classes of defamatory statements, among them the imputation to another of a criminal offense, affliction with a heinous disease such as syphilis or leprosy, lack of competence in one's chosen trade or profession, an accusation of gross misconduct in public office, and, later, a lack of chastity in a female, rendered the publisher liable for damages. The classic defense in a libel suit for damages was the actual truth of the allegedly false utterance. The burden for such proof fell upon the defendant, but if offered successfully, it rendered the libel "justified" and the publisher immune to damages therefor.

All defamatory statements were customarily said to be actuated by malice. When, however, a defamatory utterance had been published through simple error or in good faith it was said to carry "simple malice." But a deliberately false or defamatory statement or a statement published with reckless disregard for its truth or falsity was said to carry "special malice" or "actual malice," a conception presently to become of great importance in the Supreme Court's nationalization of the law of libel.

Important, also, in the Supreme Court's present intervention was the concept of privilege, which held that certain classes of utterances were immune to damage suits, either because of their character or because of the status of the person who uttered them. Privilege, the law held, was of two kinds: absolute and qualified. The utterances of public officials in their official capacity—the official reports of legislative bodies, executive offices, and the like— carried absolute privilege. On the other hand, the utterances of certain classes of persons in a professional capacity—among them lawyers and physicians—carried qualified privilege, which protected their utterer under most circumstances.

The most controversial aspect of tort libel law was the threat to free and open criticism of public officials and other personages in the public eye. Newspapers, rival politicians, and other commentators who were guilty even of simple error in criticizing such persons very often laid themselves open to heavy suits for damages, a fact that quite conceivably had as great a deterrent effect upon free and open political criticism as had prosecutions for seditious libel in the eighteenth century.

Nor was the fact that truth was a defense an adequate safeguard for newspapers and others engaged in responsible public political discussion. In the first place, defamatory statements, even when uttered in good faith or as a result of obvious error, constituted "simple malice" and laid the publisher open to a potentially devastating damage suit. In the second place, what constituted "truth," particularly in the political realm, was often a matter of interpretation rather than absolute fact, and a jury, dealing with such a matter as an allegation of anti-Semitism or of violation of a public trust, might unexpectedly find the disputed statement to be "false." Finally, demonstration of the truth, particularly in financial matters, might in itself be so fearfully expensive that the mere threat of a libel action would dampen free public discussion by newspapers and others.

Libel law thus involved a dilemma for intelligent public policy. To wipe out entirely the right of the victims of defamatory statements to sue for damages would have allowed the vicious and irresponsible free rein to damage the innocent without remedy. On the other hand, the threat of private libel actions was unquestionably a serious limitation upon open and free discussion of a kind vital to the welfare of a great constitutional democracy.

By the opening of the twentieth century, the courts in many states were solving this conflict of values by recognizing the necessity for a very great degree of freedom to criticize public officials free from the threat of actions for damages of even simple and innocent error. It was in this spirit that the Supreme Court of Kansas in 1908, in *Coleman v. McLennan*, formulated the rule that the Supreme Court of the United States was to adopt nearly a half-century later. Political criticism of public officials, the Kansas court held, should carry qualified privilege and be free from damage suits, except where the publisher resorted to "deliberate falsehood and malice." The whole area of public criticism of political officials, in short, was to be treated as very nearly outside the law of libel, except where deliberate, malicious falsehood was concerned.

Historically, the law of defamation had been almost entirely a matter for the state courts, the Supreme Court having consistently refused to recognize that it involved any federal question or constitutional issue, except under a few special circumstances. In *Near v. Minnesota* (1931), it had voided the issuance of an injunction by the state court to suppress an allegedly libelous publication, holding that such suppression violated the two-hundred-year-old rule against "prior restraint." In *Beauharnais v. Illinois*

(1959), it will be recalled, it had upheld the constitutionality of a curiously reactionary Illinois group libel law. And in *Barr v. Matteo* (1959), it had declared the publications of federal officials to be invested with absolute privilege, even "within the outer perimeter of their duties." But for a long time it resisted all attempts to bring the law of libel under the aegis of the First Amendment.

At length, in *New York Times v. Sullivan* (1964), the Court stepped into the picture, in effect adopting the McLennan rule and investing it with a First Amendment sanction. *The New York Times* case had its origin in an advertisement published in the paper, signed by sixty-four clergymen and other persons of some prominence, charging the police and city commissioners of Montgomery, Alabama, with instituting an "unprecedented wave of terror" in their attempts to suppress various desegregation activities of Negro college students, Martin Luther King, and their white supporters. Significantly, several of the statements in the advertisement were erroneous, at least in detail, and a Montgomery city commissioner had promptly sued *The Times* for libel. The Alabama trial court had found the disputed statements to be libelous *per se*, and had refused to instruct the jury that for the defendant to be liable he must have published the statements with "actual malice," that is, as deliberate or reckless falsehood. The result had been a $5,000,000 judgment against *The Times*, which the Alabama Supreme Court had affirmed.

In a unanimous decision, the United States Supreme Court overturned the Alabama judgment for "failure to provide the safeguards for freedom of speech and of the press that are required by the First and Fourteenth Amendments." The First Amendment, said Justice Brennan's opinion, required that public criticism of governmental officials be invested with qualified privilege. Citing *Coleman v. McLennan* as his major precedent, Brennan ruled that henceforth a public official, in order to recover damages for a publication criticizing his official conduct, would be obliged to show "actual malice" on the part of the publisher. This Brennan now defined as publication of a false defamatory statement "with knowledge that it was false or with reckless disregard of whether it was false or not."

Significantly, in concurring opinions, Black, Douglas, and Goldberg expressed the belief that the Court's opinion did not go far enough. Justice Black, for example, would have invested the press with "an absolute immunity for the way in which public officials do their public duty," a position with which Douglas agreed. Justice Goldberg, a little more cautious, warned only that any such rule of absolute immunity ought not to extend to defamatory statements directed against "the private conduct of a public official or private citizen."

It soon became clear that a majority of the justices were not prepared to make *The New York Times* "actual malice" rule applicable to political discussion of all "public personages," in or out of office. Thus in *Rosenblatt v. Baer* (1966) the Court, in another opinion written by Justice Brennan, declared carefully that the new rule ought to apply to those "among the actual hierarchy of government employees who have, or appear to have, substantial responsibility for the control of public affairs." *The New York Times* formula, in other words, presumably was to be limited in its scope to policy-making governmental officers. Douglas and Black thought it "dangerous" to limit the rule in this fashion, but Stewart and Harlan, adopting a far more constricted view, argued that *The Times* rule should be applied only "where a state's law of defamation has been converted into a law of seditious libel."

Finally, in *Curtis Publishing Co. v. Butts* (1967) and *Associated Press v. Walker* (1967), a pair of cases disposed of with a single opinion, the Court formulated a new libertarian standard by which to judge libel suits for public personages other than governmental officials. The Curtis case arose out of an article in the *Saturday Evening Post* that accused "Wally" Butts, the athletic director at the University of Georgia, of conspiring to "fix" a football game with the University of Alabama. General Edwin Walker's suit against the Associated Press had its origins in his activities on the campus of the University of Mississippi at the time of the massive Meredith riots in late September, 1962. An A.P. dispatch had described the former army general as having led a charge against the federal marshals who had been sent to the campus to preserve order. Neither Butts nor Walker was a government officer of any kind; thus the two cases afforded the Court a clear opportunity to decide whether *The Times* actual malice rule ought to be extended to anyone other than public officials.

The Court majority refused to do so. Instead, Justice Harlan's opinion laid down a new formula, intended to "strike a balance between the interests of the community in free circulation of information and those individuals seeking damages for harm done by the circulation of defamatory falsehood." "A 'public figure' who is not a public official," Harlan held, may recover damages for defamation "on a showing of highly unreasonable conduct" on the part of the publisher, "constituting an extreme departure from the standards of investigating and reporting ordinarily adhered to by responsible publishers." Applying this formula, the Court confirmed the state court's award of damages in the Butts case and reversed the Texas court decision granting damages to Walker.

The Court was badly split in its Butts-Walker decision. Chief Justice Warren, who concurred in the result, thought nonetheless that it was a mistake to depart from the application of *The Times* rule in the present instance, while Brennan and White, also adhering to that formula, thought the cases should be remanded for new trials in accordance with it. But Black, with whom Douglas concurred, thought Harlan's new formula "wholly inadequate" to protect freedom of the press, and would have thrown both suits out of court.

Thus the Court now found itself split four or five different ways on the precise reach of the newly nationalized law of libel. A majority of the justices, excepting perhaps only Harlan and Stewart, were willing to apply *The Times* formula to all policy-making government officials and perhaps to lower governmental officials as well. But there agreement ended. Black and Douglas were close to holding that the whole concept of civil as well as criminal libel law ought to be outlawed entirely under the First Amendment for all public political discussion. Warren, Brennan, and White thought *The Times* rule should extend at least to all public personages, such as Butts and Walker. And Harlan and Stewart apparently wanted *The Times* rule limited to impersonal suits against private persons, that is, when such suits came close to prosecutions for seditious libel. The situation, in short, had become one of considerable confusion; indeed, Justice Black in his Butts opinion aptly described the Court as "sinking into the same helpless quagmire in the field of libel in which it is helplessly struggling in the field of obscenity." [2]

THE RIGHT OF PRIVACY: THE BIRTH CONTROL AND "HILL" DECISIONS

One of the major libertarian concerns of the 1960's was that for a constitutional right of privacy. The notion of privacy as a legal right was not altogether new. No such right had existed in older common law, but a variety of courts since the 1890's had recog-

---

[2] See below, pp. 966–973.

nized it in one fashion or another, on occasion relating it to the law of libel in the sense of an individual's right to be free from exposure through irresponsible utterance. Hitherto, however, the right of privacy had been without any formal constitutional foundation. But now from time to time the justices, as they expounded upon the right of immunity from illegal search and the right to remain silent in the face of police interrogation, asserted that the right in question was an aspect of a larger right—the right of the individual to protect certain sacred precincts of his private life from intrusion by others or by the state.

In *Griswold v. Connecticut* (1965), in which the Court outlawed state legislation prohibiting the use of contraceptives and the dispensing of birth control information to married couples, the justices gave even more specific recognition to a constitutional right of privacy. The Griswold decision represented the culmination of a long drive by the opponents of anti-birth control legislation to remove laws of this kind from the books of the various states, the Court itself having several times earlier refused to touch the question, conceivably because of implicit recognition of its extreme sensitivity. Now, however, the justices, responding in all probability to a widespread change in attitudes and values on the part of a large portion of American society, at length consented to pass on the merits of the old 1879 Connecticut birth control law.

Justice Douglas, who delivered the opinion of the Court, declared the Connecticut statute to be invalid as an invasion of a constitutional right of marital privacy. The "specific guarantees in the Bill of Rights," he declared, "have penumbras formed by emanations from those guarantees that give life and substance." Such "penumbras," guaranteeing "zones of privacy" for the individual, he found to lie around the guarantees of the First, Fourth, and Fifth Amendments as "protection against all governmental invasions of the sanctity of a man's home." Douglas also mentioned briefly the Ninth Amendment, with its stipulation protecting those rights of the people not specifically enumerated in the first eight amendments, as contributing to a constitutional right of privacy, a right presumably now projected as a limitation upon the states through the instrumentality of the Fourteenth Amendment. Applying the concept of a constitutional right of privacy to the Connecticut law, Douglas found that its provisions, particularly the one prohibiting the use of contraceptives by married persons, violated a "marital right of privacy," and was unconstitutional.

Although Douglas had delivered the "opinion of the Court,"

virtually all the justices had something to say concerning the matter at hand. Harlan, who concurred, nonetheless objected to the Court's opinion because he thought it implicitly rested on the "incorporation doctrine." The Connecticut law was invalid, he thought, simply because it violated "basic values 'implicit in the concept of ordered liberty' " guaranteed by the Fourteenth Amendment. Goldberg, with whom Warren and Brennan concurred, rejected the "incorporation doctrine," but nonetheless dwelt heavily also upon the implications of the Ninth Amendment as protecting rights not specifically enumerated in the first eight amendments and, by derivation, therefore a right of privacy in marriage. Justice White first pointed out that the Connecticut law imposed a very serious limitation upon personal liberty and then found that the rationale advanced by the state in defense of the measure—the discouragement of illicit sexual intercourse—had no reasonable relationship to the law's actual prohibitions.

From all this Justices Black and Stewart vigorously dissented. The majority justices, Black asserted, were in reality invoking "the same natural law—due process philosophy" used in *Lochner v. New York* and long since discredited, and he also ridiculed as bad history Goldberg's interpretation of the Ninth Amendment. "Every student of history knows," he said, "that it was intended to limit the federal government to the powers granted expressly or by necessary implication." And Justice Stewart, conceding that the Connecticut statute was "an uncommonly silly law," pointed out that Douglas' opinion did not even declare specifically what portion of the Bill of Rights, if any, the law infringed. "To say that the Ninth Amendment has anything to do with this case," he added, "is to turn somersaults with history."

It is difficult to escape the conclusion that the Court in the Griswold case was, as Justice Black asserted, engaged in a piece of activist judicial "legislation." Very clearly, almost all the justices thought the Connecticut statute "an uncommonly silly law"—one at odds with the mores of a substantial majority of the American people. Since the internal political and religious situation in the various states made repeal of state anti-birth control statutes extremely unlikely, the Court registered a new libertarian consensus by finding such legislation to be a violation of the "liberty" guaranteed by the Fourteenth Amendment.

A very different aspect of the "right of privacy" appeared in *Time v. Hill* (1967), where the Court applied *The New York Times* libel formula—"knowing falsity or reckless disregard of the truth"—to an alleged press invasion of a family's private life. The Hill case grew out of the publication by *Life* magazine of a series of pictures taken from a play that portrayed in highly fictionalized fashion an incident in which escaped convicts had invaded the Hill home and held the members of the family captive for several hours. The *Life* story identified the play as based originally on the Hill family's experience, but failed to make clear its fictionalized character. The *Life* story contained nothing libelous or disgraceful in any way concerning the Hill family, but Hill nonetheless promptly sued the publishers of the magazine for invasion of his privacy. He brought his action under a provision of the New York civil code that forbade invasions of privacy for commercial purposes. An award of damages, adjusted in a retrial, had ultimately been appealed to the United States Supreme Court.

That Court, speaking through Justice Brennan, set aside the judgment. The trial judge, Brennan said, should have instructed the jury that it could return a verdict of liability only if it found "that the statements in the article were made with knowledge of their falsity or in reckless disregard of the truth." In other words, the Court borrowed *The New York Times* "actual malice" libel formula and applied it to a privacy suit. In defense of this position, Brennan argued that "exposure of the self to others in varying degrees is a concomitant of life in a civilized community," and that the Court would "create a grave risk of serious impairment of the indispensable service of a free press in a free society" if it saddled publications with "the impossible burden of verifying to a certainty the facts associated in news articles with a person's name, picture, or portrait, particularly as related to non-defamatory matter."

Again there was extensive commentary by the other justices. Black, whom Douglas joined in a concurring opinion, protested that the Court once more had resorted to a "balancing" act to protect First Amendment rights, and warned that if the Court could today "create a right of privacy superior to the right of a free press" then the Court tomorrow could "create more rights that balance away other cherished Bill of Rights freedoms." Harlan, dissenting, thought the "knowing falsity" formula too narrow to protect privacy in an instance such as this where "the market-place of ideas could hardly function," and he would have allowed judicial sanctions where an erroneous story created "a severe risk of irremediable harm to those momentarily exposed to it and powerless to protect themselves against it."

It is evident that in *Time v. Hill* a libertarian-formulated "right of privacy" ran squarely up against another long-established right cherished by judicial libertarians—that of a free press. Inevitably, perhaps, "privacy" pretty well lost the encounter. What Justice Brennan and the majority did essentially was to define any "newsworthy" story as constitutionally protected except where the publisher had resorted to "deliberate falsity or a reckless disregard for the truth." And what constituted a "newsworthy" story, Brennan made clear, was to be determined, after all, by a news medium's decision that the matter at hand was worth publishing. Thus, in spite of Justice Black's concern, the sphere of constitutional protection the majority had accorded the press in its potential invasions of privacy appeared to be extremely broad.

THE WARREN COURT AND OBSCENITY: A CONSTITUTIONAL "DISASTER AREA"

As Justice Black had implied in his dissent in the Butts-Walker case, the Court's attempts to formulate a new law of First Amendment rights with respect to pornographic literature and obscenity ran into even more difficulties than was the case with libel and privacy. No less than five distinct constitutional positions eventually emerged among the justices with respect to obscene publications, a situation that inspired one commentator to label the new law of obscenity "a constitutional disaster area." In reality, this situation reflected certain deep-rooted philosophic differences among members of the Court, not only with respect to the meaning and sweep of the First Amendment but also in the very conception of obscenity itself.

Earlier Supreme Court decisions had foreshadowed something of the difficulties in which the Warren Court was to find itself in its attempts to establish constitutional guidelines with respect to obscene publications. As far back as *Chaplinsky v. New Hampshire* (1942), Justice Murphy had declared categorically for a unanimous Court that "the lewd and obscene" lay outside the protection of the First Amendment.[3] On the other hand, in *Winters v. New York* (1948), the Vinson Court, speaking through Justice Reed, had invalidated as too sweeping and vague a New York law that attempted to prohibit as obscene those publications devoted mainly to "bloodshed, lust, or crime." Here were two major boundaries of constitutional policy with respect to the control of obscene publi-

---

[3] See above, p. 760.

cations that the Warren Court was to accept without much question: Obscene publications, once properly classified as such, were not entitled to the protection of the First Amendment. But not all that was salacious or morally objectionable by traditional puritanical standards was necessarily legally obscene. The problem thus became one of definition: How was legal obscenity to be defined?

The Warren Court first confronted this problem in *Butler v. Michigan* (1957), in which it invalidated unanimously a Michigan statute prohibiting the sale of books and magazines "tending to incite minors to violent or depraved or immoral acts." To attempt to "quarantine the general reading public against books not too rugged for grown men and women in order to shield juvenile innocence," Frankfurter declared, "is to burn down the house to roast the pig." By implication, this language rejected a long-standing English legal definition of obscenity, first advanced in *Regina v. Hicklin* (1868), which had defined as legally obscene all "pornographic material" incorporating even isolated passages that might sexually arouse "particular susceptible persons"—in this instance minors. However, the problem of evolving a positive American definition still remained.

A few weeks later, in a pair of companion cases, *Roth v. United States* (1957), and *Alberts v. California* (1957), which the Court disposed of in a single opinion, the majority justices attempted to formulate both a comprehensive legal definition of obscenity and a statement of First Amendment principles as they bore upon obscene publications. The Roth case involved the validity of postal censorship of obscene materials under a long-standing federal statute, a practice that Justice Brennan's opinion upheld as a "proper exercise of the postal power."

At issue in the Alberts case was the validity of a California law prohibiting the circulation of obscene literature which the courts of that state had defined as that which "offends the conscience of the community." This law, also, Brennan found to be constitutional. "Implicit in the history of the First Amendment," he explained, was "the rejection of obscenity as utterly without redeeming social importance"; hence it did not lie "within the area of constitutionally protected free speech." At the same time Brennan in effect adopted the California court's definition of obscenity: "Whether to the average person, applying contemporary community standards, the dominant theme of the material as a whole appeals to prurient interests."

Already, it was apparent, the obscenity problem was fragmenting the Court. Justice Harlan, dissenting in the Roth case, expressed the belief that the limitations upon congressional power properly limited federal postal censorship to the suppression of hard-core pornography; by contrast, he would have allowed the states a broad range of discretion under their police powers in the definition and suppression of obscenity. Douglas and Black, dissenting in both cases, thought the Court's "community conscience" standard inflicted punishment "for thoughts provoked, not for overt acts or anti-social conduct," and could not be squared with the First Amendment.

The Roth definition of obscenity was destined to serve the Court as its standard of reference in such cases for several years. Apparently simple, it actually involved reasoning suspiciously circular in character. The "appeal to prurient interest" now became the critical test of obscenity; yet this elusive quality, which the Court carefully separated from a mere literary concern with the mysteries of sex, was nowhere defined. And the notion of "contemporary community standards" implied that the definition of obscenity might vary with the shifting sands of public opinion.

Two years later, in *Kingsley International Pictures Corporation v. Regents* (1959), the members of the Court demonstrated anew their diversity of opinions on the obscenity problem, even as they united to strike down unanimously a New York statute under which that state's Board of Regents had censored a film version of D. H. Lawrence's *Lady Chatterley's Lover*. What the Regents had done, Justice Stewart's opinion declared, "was to prevent the exhibition of a motion picture because that picture advocates an idea," i.e., that adultery might on occasion be "a desirable, acceptable, and proper form of behavior." Censorship of this kind, Stewart held, "struck at the very heart of constitutionally protected liberty" under the First Amendment, and both the statute that permitted it and the Regents' censorship were unconstitutional.

There were five other concurring opinions. Douglas and Black each condemned the New York law as involving "prior restraint," expressing the belief that all prior censorship of films "violated First and Fourteenth Amendment rights." Clark thought the New York law too vague and so in violation of due process. Frankfurter and Harlan, with whom Whittaker concurred, agreed with Stewart's ruling but thought Stewart had gone too far in condemning the New York law as outright unconstitutional, since it need not have been read as categorically requiring the censorship of ideas.

The Kingsley case concealed rather than exposed the profound difficulties in the Roth definition of censurable obscenity, but in *Manuel Enterprises v. Day* (1962) Justice Harlan, speaking for the majority, entered upon an extensive refinement of the Roth formula. At issue was postal suppression of three magazines devoted principally to a portrayal of nude males and evidently intended primarily for homosexuals. For published material to be defined as obscene, Harlan now declared, it must be characterized both by "patent offensiveness and indecency" and "prurient interest" appeal. Furthermore, Harlan said, the Roth formula as applied to federal censorship called for "a national standard of decency" rather than any local community standard, since federal law necessarily must reconcile a great diversity of community and cultural backgrounds. Judged by these standards, he declared, the magazines involved in the present case were not obscene and were entitled to the protection of the First Amendment. Justice Brennan, in a concurring opinion in which the Chief Justice and Douglas also joined, argued that federal postal law, properly construed, did not authorize postal censorship under any circumstances. But Justice Clark in dissent blasted his judicial brothers for a decision that would require the Post Office "to be the world's largest disseminator of smut."

How completely divergent were the varying views of the several justices on the obscenity problem became even more apparent in *Jacobellis v. Ohio* (1964). This case, which came on appeal from the Ohio Supreme Court, involved a state criminal conviction for exhibiting an allegedly obscene movie, *Les Amants,* which portrayed the story of an unhappy marriage and which, near its close, presented an explicit love scene conceivably involving sexual intercourse.

Justice Brennan, who announced the decision of the Court in an opinion in which only Justice Goldberg joined, first defended the Court at some length from the charge, in effect levied in Black's concurring opinion, that in deciding obscenity cases in accordance with constitutional principles the Court was arrogating to itself the function of a "supercensor." He then declared his adherence to the Roth "prurient interest" standard for adjudging obscenity. That formula, he admitted, was "not perfect," but "any substitute would raise equally difficult problems." He warned, however, that a mere portrayal of sex was not in itself "sufficient to deny material the constitutional protection of freedom of speech and press," and that to be proscribed, any such portrayal must be " 'utterly' without social importance." Here Brennan added a new ingredient of his own—a finding that the material in question "goes substantially beyond customary limits of candor in description or representation of such matters." In addition, he incorporated Harlan's *Manual* requirement that the "contemporary community standard" of judgment required by the Roth formula must be national and not local; otherwise "the constitutional limits of free expression in the nation would vary with state lines." So adjudged, he now declared, *Les Amants* was not obscene.

Five other justices concurred without joining the Brennan opinion. Black, joined by Douglas, attacked the Court's role as "Supreme Board of Censors" and reaffirmed his belief that any censorship of movies abridged the freedom of the press guaranteed by the First Amendment. Justice Stewart explained that he had concluded that "under the First and Fourteenth Amendments criminal laws in this area are limited to hard-core pornography." He admitted that he could not define what this was, but he declared firmly that "I know it when I see it, and the motion picture involved in this case is not that." Justice White concurred without opinion.

On the other hand, Chief Justice Warren, with whom Clark joined, dissented on the ground that enforcement of the Roth rule ought to be confided to state and lower federal courts and that the Supreme Court should accept their judgments as binding, "provided there is sufficient evidence in the record upon which a finding of obscenity could be made." And Justice Harlan, also dissenting, reiterated his now familiar belief that the "States are constitutionally permitted a greater latitude" in defining obscenity than was the federal government.

Between the Roth-Alberts decision and that in the Jacobellis case, the Court had failed to sustain in a single instance any obscenity conviction appealed from a lower tribunal, and certain astute observers concluded that the justices, in spite of their great diversity of opinion, had for all practical purposes adopted a "hard-core pornography" definition of what was suppressible consistent with the First Amendment. But in *Ginzburg v. United States* (1966) that supposition was rudely shattered, as the Court sustained a federal conviction involving a fine and prison sentence imposed upon a publisher charged with violating the federal postal censorship laws.

The specific constitutional issue in the Ginzburg case was whether or not the "context of production, sale, and publicity" attendant upon the marketing of disputed materials might be taken into account in adjudging them to be obscene, when in fact the materials standing alone might not be adjudged as such under the Roth standard. Justice Brennan, who spoke for the five majority justices, answered this question in the affirmative. At issue were three publications: *Liaison*, a biweekly newsletter filled with smutty jokes and sensationalist pseudomedical sex stories; *Eros*, a high-priced hardcover magazine devoted to an "intellectual" examination of erotica; and *The Housewife's Handbook on Selective Promiscuity*, a medically specific sexual biography of an anonymous female. Justice Brennan finally avoided the question of whether this material, standing alone, met the Roth test for obscenity; instead he pointed out that "leer of the sensualist" pervaded the advertising for the three publications and that in fact Ginzburg had been engaged in the "sordid business of pandering." The appellant's marketing methods thus had tainted the materials themselves, so that a criminal conviction for mailing them did not offend the First Amendment.

As might be expected, Brennan's opinion elicited vigorous dissent from the minority justices. Black, in addition to stating his now-familiar extreme libertarian view of the First Amendment, charged that the majority had rewritten the federal obscenity statute to convict Ginzburg of an offense "Congress never thought about." Douglas thought Ginzburg had in fact been convicted of pandering merely for resorting to a lurid "advertising technique as old as history." Stewart, adhering to his "hard-core pornography" theory, thought also that Ginzburg had been denied due process, since he had in fact been convicted merely of pandering, an offense unknown to federal law. And Harlan, holding also to his belief that the federal government could ban only hard-core pornography from the mails, accused the majority of "an astonishing piece of judicial improvisation," i.e., in effect writing into law a new federal pandering act.

In *Mishkin v. New York* (1966), a companion case to Ginzburg's, the Court brought to bear its new notion of pandering as an element in obscenity to sustain the conviction of a New York publisher for violating that state's obscenity laws. The case had a peculiar twist in that much of the material was of interest only to homosexuals, so the defense had argued that it did not meet the Roth standard of "prurient interest appeal" for the average person. Emphasizing that the appellant's books dealt with "raw sex," Brennan's majority opinion rejected this contention out of hand. Brennan also rejected summarily the defense argument that *scienter* was wanting in appellant's offense, i.e., that he had been unaware of the nature of his offense. His activity, said Brennan, was "not innocent but calculated purveyance of filth." Again Black and Douglas in dissent stated their libertarian view of the First Amendment and protested the Court's new censorship role; again, also, Stewart protested that the books at hand were "not hard-core pornography." Harlan at the same time concurred on the basis of his double standard for federal and state obscenity.

That there was, in fact, no promise of a new stability in the momentary majorities achieved in the Ginzburg and Mishkin cases was apparent in the Court's decision in *Memoirs v. Massachusetts* (1966), in which it reversed by a vote of six to three a Massachusetts Supreme Court judgment that *Fanny Hill*, the notorious eighteenth-century account of a prostitute's intimate sexual experiences, was obscene and thus subject to suppression. Justice Brennan, who now spoke for a very different majority, first undertook to redefine the Roth standard for adjudging obscenity: It must be established, he said "that (a) the dominant theme of the material taken as a whole appeals to a prurient interest in sex; (b) the material is patently offensive because it affronts contemporary community standards relating to the description or representation of sexual matters; and (c) the material is utterly without redeeming social value."

This last point provided the cue to the Court's decision. The Massachusetts Court had observed that the book "need not be unqualifiedly worthless before it can be deemed obscene"; this, said Brennan, was reversible error, since a book must be *"utterly* without redeeming social value" to be adjudged obscene. Justice Clark, protesting in dissent that he could not "stomach" the present decision, pointed out accurately enough that Brennan in requiring that a disputed work be *"utterly"* without social value had injected a new element into the Roth standard. Harlan, adhering in dissent to his double federal-state standard, also pointed to the "significant transformation" the majority opinion had worked in the Roth formula. And Justice White, also dissenting, thought that the Court's decision actually rejected the basic premise of the Roth opinion— that obscene material was not constitutionally protected precisely *because* it was inherently and utterly without social value.

It thus appears that the Court in the 1960's had more difficulty with the concept of the constitutional law of obscenity than with any other area of constitutional law it confronted. The reason for this, as various analysts have made clear, lay not so much in any failure of the Court as in the weakness of the very concept of obscenity itself. "Obscenity, at bottom, is not crime," one writer has observed; "obscenity is sin." As "sin," obscenity reflects the shifting social, ethical, and religious values of a complex pluralistic society, and its precise legal definition, as the Roth standard itself makes clear, is almost impossible. Given this fact, the Court's move into the legal field as a "supercensor" inevitably led it into a constitutional quagmire.

THE WARREN COURT AND THE "ESTABLISHMENT OF RELIGION"

Like the Vinson Court before it, the Warren Court found itself obliged to deal with the issue of church-state relations, and in particular the question of sectarian prayer in the public schools. From its predecessor the Warren Court had inherited the Jeffersonian concept that the First Amendment clause prohibiting an establishment of religion imposed a "wall of separation" between church and state. This concept enjoined both upon the federal government and upon the states a sharp policy of noninvolvement, nonsupport, and stern neutrality, not only between competing sects but also between faith and disbelief. It was this concept of separation of church and state that Justice Black had formulated in the Everson and McCollum cases, and which a majority of the justices of the Warren Court now embraced. The result precipitated another wave of severe criticism from conservative religious sources directed toward the Court's "atheism" and "animosity toward religion," which for a time appeared to be serious enough to give rise to a proposed constitutional amendment modifying the establishment clause.

The Warren Court first confronted the "establishment" question in 1961, in a series of cases dealing with the constitutionality of Sunday closing laws. *McGowan v. Maryland* involved the constitutional status of Maryland's so-called "Blue Laws," which banned a great variety of Sunday retail business activities, but at the same time allowed numerous exceptions for resort and entertainment enterprises. Potentially, at least, the legislation at issue posed a dilemma for the Court. A strict Jeffersonian application of the establishment clause would require the justices to hold Maryland's "Blue Laws" presumably unconstitutional. To do so, however, would strike down a state policy not only long established but also one that had gained renewed support in late years in many communities because of the desire of conservative businesses to protect themselves from more aggressive retail competitors who desired to operate on Sunday.

The Court dodged this dilemma very nicely by treating Maryland's Blue Laws as essentially secular in purpose. Chief Justice Warren's opinion for the majority dealt with two principal constitutional questions—whether or not the laws in question violated the equal protection clause and whether or not they constituted an "establishment of religion." Warren dismissed the "equal protection" question almost summarily, observing that the state had "a wide scope of discretion in enacting laws that affect some groups of citizens differently than others." He then examined the history of Maryland's Blue Laws at great length, and concluded that while such legislation had originally been religious in purpose, its objective now had become almost entirely secular—to provide "a Sunday atmosphere of recreation, cheerfulness, and enjoyment." The disputed laws, he concluded, hence were constitutional. In a companion case, *Two Guys from Harrison-Allentown v. McGinley* (1961), the Court resorted to like reasoning and to the McGowan precedent to hold constitutional a Pennsylvania Sunday retail closing law.

Still another companion case, *Braunfeld v. Brown* (1961), presented a more difficult constitutional issue. At issue was the application of the Pennsylvania Sunday closing law to an orthodox Jewish establishment which, under rabbinical law, would be obliged to close also on Saturday. Application of the state statute to the business in question would involve the proprietor in a serious dilemma—he must either violate the precepts of his religion or accept a severe competitive hardship. The law thus raised an additional constitutional issue: possible interference "with the free exercise of the appellant's religion."

Again Chief Justice Warren avoided the dilemma implicit in the case by holding that "the Sunday law simply regulates a secular activity," and by pointing out that much existing state legislation imposed secular obligations upon individuals in direct or indirect violation of their religious principles. Legislation advancing legitimate secular goals but which imposed an "indirect burden on religious observances," in other words, was constitutional. The Chief Justice disposed of a fourth companion case, *Gallagher v. Crown Kosher Supermarket* (1961), where the validity of a Massachusetts Sunday retail closing law as applied to an orthodox Jewish business was again at issue, in the same fashion.

Justice Douglas entered a vigorous dissent in a single opinion covering all four Sunday closing cases. "The parentage of these laws," he declared, "is the Fourth Commandment; and they serve and satisfy the religious predispositions of our Christian communities." Hence, he asserted, they constituted not only "an establishment of religion," but also "an interference with the 'free exercise' of religion . . . contrary to the constitutional mandate." Justices Brennan and Stewart also dissented in the Braunfeld and Crown Kosher cases, arguing that the state in neither case had shown any "compelling interest" to justify the "substantial though indirect" violation of appellants' religious liberty involved.

The scheme of "secular motivation" thus had enabled the Court to escape from a potentially difficult constitutional problem. But no such convenient avenue of logic was available to the Court, however, in the series of cases that arose in the next year or so involving the constitutionality of religious services in the public schools. Here the majority justices, adhering sharply to the Jeffersonian interpretation of the establishment clause, declared such devotionals invalid, and thereby precipitated a storm of controversy that was to persist for several years.

In the first such case, *Engel v. Vitale* (1962), the Court found itself called upon to pass upon the constitutionality of a twenty-two word "non-sectarian" prayer that various local New York school boards had adopted in pursuance of its recommendation by the State Board of Regents. By a six to one majority, the justices declared that recitation of the Regents' Prayer violated the "establishment clause" of the First Amendment. There was "no doubt," said Justice Black's opinion, that "a daily class invocation of God's blessing . . . is a religious activity." It was "no part of government," he observed further, "to compose official prayers for any group of the American people to recite as a part of a religious program carried on by the government." The "establishment clause," Black added, was not irreligious in spirit; instead it "relied on the belief that a union of government and religion tends to destroy government and degrade religion."

A year later, in *School District of Abington Township v. Schempp* (1963), the Court drew heavily upon the Engel precedent to declare unconstitutional a Pennsylvania statute which required that "at least ten verses from the Holy Bible" be read daily, without comment, in all public schools of the state. Justice Clark's majority opinion focused upon the concept of "the wholesome neutrality" toward religion that he found embodied in the establishment clause, and which, he warned, not only forbade "governmental preference of one religion over another," but also, since the Everson decision, prohibited all "laws which aid one religion" or "aid all religion . . ." This meant that any law, "to withstand the strictures of the establishment clause, "must carry a "secular legislative purpose." And since the Pennsylvania law before the Court required religious exercises, as such, it was in violation of the First Amendment.

Several concurring opinions and one dissenting opinion made it evident that the concept of a "wholesome neutrality" had given the justices considerable difficulty. Douglas filed a short concurring opinion in which he expressed the belief that the Pennsylvania law violated the establishment clause both because it called for "a religious exercise" and because it expended public funds for a religious purpose. On the other hand, both Brennan and Goldberg expressed great uneasiness that the Court's injunction of strict neutrality between religion and non-religion might have too wide a sweep in banning "every vestige of cooperation between religion and government, however slight." And Justice Stewart, entering the lone dissent once more, objected that the present decision would lead not to a true neutrality with respect to religion but rather to the "establishment of a religion of secularism."

The "prayer" and "Bible reading" decisions together precipitated a sharp renewal of the long-standing controversy over the role of religion in the public schools, which of late had tended to die down. Conservative criticism of the Court's stance, both by clerical and lay leaders, was for the most part exceedingly severe. Thus Cardinal Spellman declared himself to be "shocked and frightened" by a decision that "strikes at the heart of the Godly tradition in which America's children have so long been raised," while Herbert Hoover, now a patriarchal Republican Party figure, demanded that Congress forthwith submit to the states a constitutional amendment confirming the right to religious devotion in all government agencies. And Senator Robert C. Byrd of West Virginia warned that "somebody is tampering with America's soul."

However, the Court was not without its defenders, most of them drawn from liberal Protestant and Jewish circles. The Anti-Defamation League, for example, hailed the Engel decision as "a splendid reaffirmation of a basic American principle," while Dean Maurice Kelley, an official of the National Council of Churches, expressed the opinion that "many Christians would welcome" the Engel decision, which "protects the religious rights of minorities" and "guards against the development of 'public school' religion."

In Congress, the Engel and Schempp decisions led to a drive for a constitutional amendment to affirm a constitutional right to voluntary public-school prayers and religious services. Some ten such proposals were introduced into the House alone in the days following the Engel decision, while the decision in the Schempp case the following June brought about the introduction of another twenty-odd amendments. By August, 1966, more than 150 such proposals had been introduced in the Senate or the House.

Ultimately, however, the campaign for a "prayer amendment" foundered. Representative Emanuel Celler of New York, Chairman of the House Judiciary Committee, was openly hostile to the idea and he succeeded in keeping all such proposals in the lower chamber from reaching the floor. In September, 1963, Representative Frank J. Becker of New York, a principal sponsor of such an amendment, began a sustained drive to obtain the 218 signatures necessary to force his proposal onto the floor for a vote, but by the following June it was evident that he had failed. Even the inclusion in the Republican Party platform of 1964 of a somewhat equivocal plank supporting a prayer amendment failed to resuscitate Becker's campaign.

In March, 1966, Senator Dirksen brought the "prayer amendment" drive back to life momentarily, with the introduction of a constitutional amendment stipulating that "nothing in the constitution" was to prohibit school authorities from "providing for or permitting the voluntary participation by students or others in prayer." The "common man," Dirksen declaimed, "is going to have his way" on the school prayer question, and would not be dissuaded, he warned, by "highly sophisticated arguments" to the contrary. But it soon became apparent that effective organized support from clerical and lay religious leaders for Dirksen's proposal was now almost completely wanting. And when, in September, 1966, the Dirksen amendment finally came to a vote, it went down to defeat 49 yeas to 37 nays, nine votes short of the two-thirds majority required for passage. Thereafter support for a "prayer amendment" died away.

As the "prayer amendment" issue lost force, the public interest increasingly was drawn to another "establishment" question—the matter of federal and state appropriations for private sectarian schools. The growing crisis in school financing that beset local boards of education in the late 1950's and in the 1960's, particularly in the larger cities, served to give renewed force to the longstanding demand for comprehensive federal legislation in support of state and local public education. But as in the days of the lengthy impasse over the Barden grant-in-aid bills of the early 1950's, the deadlock over the inclusion of private sectarian schools in such a measure for a long time effectively blocked passage of all such proposals. In addition, the Kennedy administration, sensitive to the fact that the President was the first Catholic Chief Executive in the nation's history, announced in 1961 through Attorney General Robert F. Kennedy that it regarded federal grants-in-aid to parochial schools as in violation of the guarantees of the First Amendment.

In January, 1965, however, President Lyndon Johnson, who as a Protestant was far less vulnerable to charges of pro-Catholic bias and who also was doubly secure politically by virtue of his recent overwhelming victory at the polls, called upon the Congress to enact a $1.5 billion grant-in-aid bill for assistance to primary and secondary education. The bill, which contemplated assistance for a great variety of school educational programs, was specifically worded to provide for grants both to public and to private sectarian and secular schools. Under heavy administration pressure, the bill passed both houses of Congress by overwhelming majorities and became law in April. A last-minute attempt by Senator Sam Erwin of North Carolina to include a provision allowing taxpayers' suits to test the constitutionality of the law ended in failure.

The Elementary and Secondary Education Act of 1965, as the new measure was known, at once drew the legal fire of strong proponents of separation of church and state, who argued that the inclusion of parochial schools in the law's benefits rendered these provisions unconstitutional under the establishment clause. Suits to attack the law's constitutionality, however, seemingly faced an insurmountable obstacle: the precedent set in *Frothingham v. Mellon*, the 1923 Maternity Act grant-in-aid decision, apparently barred taxpayers' suits to attack the constitutionality of the new law, by denying such persons standing to sue.[4]

However, in *Flast v. Cohen* (1968), the Court, speaking through Chief Justice Warren, reversed the judgment of a lower court to rule that taxpayers properly had standing to sue to attack the constitutionality of the new law. The Frothingham decision, said Justice Warren, had rested upon obsolete policy considerations "not consistent with modern conditions," and he went on to imply that in any event taxpayers' suits to enforce the guarantees of the

---

[4] See above, pp. 673–674.

establishment clause ought to be given special standing by the Court. The Flast decision implied that massive federal appropriations for education which included support for church-related schools might be ruled unconstitutional in the future. However, no such development was to occur.[5]

Meanwhile the crisis over school finances had precipitated a series of legislative and judicial battles in the various states over the issue of what had commonly become known as "parochiad," i.e., state legislative appropriations for parochial schools. Proponents of such legislation argued that parochial schools, about ninety per cent of which were Roman Catholic in affiliation, relieved the state of a heavy burden of educational support, and thus ought properly to be included in state appropriations for local boards of education. Direct support for sectarian schools, supporters of parochiad admitted, was almost certainly unconstitutional, but they pointed to the Everson decision as precedent for their contention that appropriations for lunches, textbooks, laboratory facilities, and the like could be held constitutional as educational services to be extended to all children without regard to religion or where they attended school. Opponents of parochiad, on the other hand, replied firmly that appropriations of this kind would constitute an establishment of religion in violation of the First Amendment.

On this issue the Court proved to be decidedly more sympathetic to a sectarian-oriented argument than it had been on the prayer and Bible-reading questions. In *Board of Education v. Allen* (1968), a majority of the justices voted to uphold the constitutionality of a 1965 New York law that required local public-school boards to furnish free textbooks without charge to all children enrolled in grades seven through twelve, both in public and private schools, if such schools complied with the state compulsory education law. Chief Justice Warren's opinion, relying heavily upon the Everson precedent, found that the act was basically an attempt to extend "the benefits of state laws to all citizens without regard for their religious affiliations." Citing the formula in the Schempp case, he found that the primary purpose of the law was secular, and that it "neither advances nor inhibits religion." Accordingly it met the test of the establishment clause.

Black, Douglas, and Fortas all registered strong dissents from the majority ruling. Black, recalling his powerful affirmation of the separation of church and state principle in his Everson opinion,

---

[5] See below, pp. 994–998.

protested that the Court in its present decision had taken "a great stride" in the direction of a state religion. Douglas pointed out that the law actually allowed parochial schools to choose the particular textbooks they wanted, and then illustrated by specific example his contention that many so-called secular textbooks used in parochial schools were in fact religion- and sectarian-oriented. And Fortas, echoing Black's argument, condemned as a "transparent camouflage" the notion that textbooks under the law were furnished to children without regard to religion and not to parochial schools as such.

Thus as the Warren Court era drew to a close, the long-established legislative and constitutional inhibitions on federal and state appropriations for sectarian schools at length appeared to be breaking down. The Allen decision seemingly cleared the way for large-scale state appropriations for parochial-school activities not specifically religious in character, while federal grants-in-aid for the same purpose now were an accomplished fact. Time was to demonstrate, however, that the apparent thrust of the Allen decision was misleading. The Burger Court was presently to prove itself to be as devoted to the "wall of separation" theory of church-state relations as its Warren predecessor had been. It was to modify substantially much of the Warren's Court's libertarian-oriented constitutional law, but the Everson-McCollum tradition was to remain unimpaired.

Chapter

36

President Nixon and the Burger Court

In November 1968, Republican candidate Richard Nixon defeated Hubert Humphrey in one of the most closely contested elections for the Executive Office in the twentieth century. It was already evident that the President-elect intended to use his appointive power to remodel the Supreme Court in the image of his own conservative value system. On several occasions during the campaign he had severely criticized the Warren Court, which he charged with "seriously hamstringing the peace forces in our society and strengthening the criminal forces." Nixon's elevation to the presidential office thus presaged a new political battle between liberal and conservative political interests for control of the Court, both in Congress and in the nation at large.

THE FIGHT FOR CONTROL OF THE COURT

In fact, the battle for control of the Court had begun even before the election. In June 1968, Chief Justice Warren, now 77 years of age, submitted his resignation to President Johnson, to take effect upon Senate confirmation of his successor. This procedure presumably opened the way for Johnson to nominate and to secure confirmation of a suitably libertarian successor to Warren before the fall election. But in the event that this tactic did not succeed, Warren's resignation then might be postponed indefinitely.

This stratagem, if it was such, was doomed to failure. As Warren's successor, President Johnson nominated Associate Justice Abe Fortas, a close personal and political friend, a brilliant legal craftsman, and a libertarian activist. But an unprecedented Senate filibuster sent the Fortas nomination down to defeat, amid cries of "cronyism" and charges of an unethical attempt to "steal" the Chief Justiceship from the incoming President. With Nixon's election, Warren bowed to the inevitable. In December, he once more announced his resignation, to take effect the following June.

In May 1969, on the very eve of Warren's retirement, a minor scandal forced Fortas to resign from the Court. A story in *Life* magazine revealed that Fortas had accepted a $20,000 retainer fee for legal services from promoter-financier Louis Wolfson, who subsequently had been convicted and sent to prison for stock jobbing. Fortas had broken no law, his legal services had had nothing to do with Wolfson's criminal activities, and he had in fact returned Wolfson's fee some months earlier. But the impropriety was evident, and after some hesitation, Fortas resigned. Nixon now had two Court nominations in hand.

In June, President Nixon nominated Judge Warren Earl Burger of the Federal Court of Appeals for the Eighth Circuit, a former prominent Eisenhower Republican, to be Chief Justice. Burger had a reputation as a fairly hard-line "law and order" judge, but the Senate liberals had been demoralized by the Fortas resignation, and he won confirmation, 74 to 3, with scarcely a murmur of dissent.

However, Nixon's attempt to choose Fortas' successor ran into difficulties. The President first nominated Judge Clement Haynsworth of the Court of Appeals for the Fourth Circuit. But Haynsworth, a conservative Southerner, had a distinctly segregationist reputation in civil matters, and the Senate liberal bloc, now thoroughly aroused, rallied to defeat the nomination in December, 45 to 55.

The President then submitted to the Senate the name of G. Harrold Carswell, a Judge of the Court of Appeals for the Fifth Circuit and another conservative Southerner. But not only did Carswell enjoy a well-known record as a last-ditch champion of segregation and white supremacy; he also suffered from a painful lack of intellectual distinction and legal scholarship. Dean Louis Pollak of the Yale Law School pronounced Carswell to be "gravely deficient" both in legal skills and in "larger constitutional wisdom," while Senator Robert Griffin of Michigan, a Carswell supporter, inadvertently compared his literary style to that of a "plumber's manual." In April, a liberal coalition defeated the nomination, 45 to 51. The next day an angry President announced that "with the Senate as at present constituted," confirmation of a Southern strict constructionist was impossible; accordingly his next Court nominee would be from outside the South.

The President turned next to Judge Harry A. Blackmun of the United States Court of Appeals for the Eighth Circuit, a personal friend of Chief Justice Burger. Blackmun, a somewhat colorless federal tax specialist, provoked almost no opposition in the Senate, which presently confirmed him without debate, 94 to 0. Meanwhile, an ill-considered attempt by Representative Gerald R. Ford of Michigan to secure the impeachment of Justice Douglas ended in failure, when the House Judiciary Committee, after extended study, reported that no sound basis for impeachment existed.

In any event, time was on Nixon's side. In September 1971, Justice Black, now old and ill, reluctantly retired, to die only eight days later. And at the end of the month, Justice Harlan, long a pillar of moderate conservatism and judicial self-restraint, also announced his retirement.

Not surprisingly, the President's attempt to replace Black and Harlan with two additional conservative justices gave him further difficulty. An arrangement worked out by Attorney General John Mitchell whereby the American Bar Association would give an advance private screening to potential Court nominees proved disastrous from the administration's point of view, as the A.B.A. rejected virtually out of hand several Nixon suggestions as "not qualified."

At length, in mid-October, President Nixon went on television to announce his two nominees: Louis Powell, a distinguished Virginia lawyer who had been severely critical of the Warren Court's stance in civil liberties, and William H. Rehnquist, an Arizona Goldwater Republican whom Harvard Law Professor Paul Freund described as "very conservative" but with "a brilliant and powerful mind." In early December 1971, the Senate approved both names by lopsided majorities. Thus, by the end of 1971, Nixon had succeeded in placing four of his nominees on the Court.

THE BURGER COURT AND CIVIL LIBERTIES:
FAIR TRIAL PROCEDURE

Within the next several years, principally as a consequence of the conservative role adopted by the Nixon appointees, the Supreme Court shifted substantially to the right in its treatment of a variety of civil liberty and civil rights issues. The charge sometimes advanced in libertarian circles that the Burger Court "consistently out-Wallaced George Wallace" hardly was justified. Nonetheless the Court's movement away from the liberal-oriented reformism of the Warren era was very often impressive, while the cleavage in both law and social philosophy between the Warren Court veterans and the Nixon appointees was frequently profound.

This was particularly evident, after a transitional period, in the Court's disposition of cases involving the procedural guarantees of the Bill of Rights. Here the four Nixon justices, joined on occasion by Stewart or White, gravely altered Fourth Amendment search and seizure law, substantially weakened the *Miranda* precedent guaranteeing the pretrial rights of accused persons, and even broke in upon the time-honored common-law provisions of twelve-man juries and unanimous verdicts in criminal cases.

In civil rights matters, also, there was a distinctly conservative shift. The substantial unanimity which the Warren Court had exhibited in school desegregation cases disappeared, as the Nixon justices, while acceding to the general principle of "affirmative action," administered a heavy rebuff to interdistrict busing in the North.

On the other hand the libertarian reformist activism which had so characterized the Warren era by no means disappeared entirely. Often this was because the five Warren Court veterans banded together as a bloc, a situation particularly evident in the Court's treatment of the death penalty cases. On occasion, however, one or more of the Nixon justices assumed a libertarian activist stance. This occurred, for example, in the Court's disposition of the problem of anti-abortion laws. And in "establishment" and "free exercise" cases arising under the First Amendment, the Nixon appointees proved to be for the most part powerful adherents of the "separationist" tradition which had dominated the Court in church-state matters since the Everson decision in 1947.

It was in its treatment of the Fourth Amendment exclusionary rule—that evidence obtained in violation of the guarantees of that amendment was inadmissible in a subsequent criminal prosecution —that the Burger Court's "law and order" stance eventually became most evident. Between 1969 and 1971, the Warren holdover justices managed by and large to maintain the defendant-oriented libertarian tradition so much in evidence since the Mapp decision.

After this transitional era, however, the Nixon appointees took control.

Thus in *Vale v. Louisiana* (1970), the Court ruled that a warrantless search of a house in front of which the police had just made a narcotics arrest was illegal. The police, said Justice Stewart, should have obtained a search warrant. Significantly, Burger joined in Black's protest that the Court's decision made "unnecessarily difficult the conviction of those who prey upon society."

The force of the *Vale* ruling was offset only in part by the Court's decision in *Chambers v. Maroney* (1970), in which the majority justices accepted as constitutional a warrantless car search conducted after the police had first arrested the petitioner and then towed his car to the police station. The vital distinction, it appeared for the moment, was between warrantless search of a home and a like search of a car.

But a year later, in *Whiteley v. Warden* (1971), a six-man "Warren" majority rejected as unlawful a car search which had actually been conducted under a warrant. The warrant, Harlan pointed out, had been based merely upon an informer's tip unsupported by other evidence; hence it did not rest upon "probable cause," as the Fourth Amendment required. Both Burger and Blackmun joined in Black's indignant dissent. The decision, said Black, was "calculated to make good people believe our Court actually enjoys frustrating justice by turning criminals loose upon society."

Two months later, in *Coolidge v. New Hampshire* (1971), a five-justice "Warren" majority again invalidated a car search based upon a defective warrant. The difficulty this time, said Stewart, was that the New Hampshire attorney general who had issued the writ was not a "neutral and detached magistrate" as the Constitution implicitly required. Nor did police station search fall under the traditional highway "plain view" rule which might have validated it otherwise. Burger, in a protest in which Black, White, and Blackmun joined, objected that the Court's opinion "strained and distorted warrant law and threw it into confusion."

Only a week later, in *United States v. Harris* (1971), a new Burger majority gained control. At issue was the validity of a warrant resting on an anonymous informer's tip, presumably a question already settled decisively by the Whitely and Coolidge precedents. Instead, Burger's opinion attacked what he called "mere hypertechnicality" in warrant affidavits, and emphasized that "a policeman's knowledge of a suspect's reputation," a "practical consideration of everyday life," properly was sufficient to support a warrant application.

Harlan, Douglas, Brennan, and Marshall, by contrast, thought the warrant in question fatally defective. It failed, said Harlan, to meet a critical test: that "the informer's description of criminal behavior accurately reflects reality." In fact the shift to the Court's *Harris* stance from that of *Whiteley* and *Coolidge* had taken place simply because Stewart and White had changed sides.

In the next four years, the Nixon justices, aided by Stewart or White, moved steadily if somewhat erratically toward an outright "law and order" stance on Fourth Amendment issues. Thus in *Cady v. Dombrowski* (1973), the Court accepted as valid a warrantless search of a drunken Chicago policeman's car by Wisconsin police following a highway accident, although no probable cause for the search had existed. In *Schneckleth v. Bustamente* (1973), the majority accepted a warrantless search as "voluntary" and therefore legal, although police failure to warn the suspect that he had a right not to submit meant that its "voluntary" character was largely without meaning.

Again, in *United States v. Robinson* (1973), the majority in an extraordinary "law and order" decision accepted as valid a warrantless on-the-spot search of a car after a traffic arrest, in effect sanctioning a police right to conduct such a search without a shadow of probable cause, for whatever evidence of crime the police chose to look for. Finally, in *United States v. Calandra* (1974), the Court sharply limited the Fourth Amendment exclusionary rule itself, holding that illegally seized evidence might be presented to a grand jury (in distinction to a trial jury). To hold otherwise, Powell declared, would be to "delay and disrupt" grand jury proceedings in an unacceptable fashion.

Thus, as of 1975, the Fourth Amendment exclusionary rule, while still technically valid, had been gravely weakened. Whether it could survive the Court's new "law and order" posture much longer was not yet clear.

THE BURGER COURT AND THE FIFTH AMENDMENT: SELF-INCRIMINATION

Beginning in 1971, the Burger Court also adopted a stern "law and order" stance with respect to the Fifth Amendment's guarantee against compulsory self-incrimination. The Warren Court, it will be recalled, had evolved elaborate safeguards against the forced disclosure of evidence by a criminal suspect. The high point of this development had been the 1966 *Miranda* decision requiring the police to inform a suspect undergoing questioning that he had a right to remain silent, that anything he might say could be used against him, and that he was entitled to counsel during such pretrial interrogation. The new Burger majority did not overrule *Miranda* directly, but in several decisions it seriously damaged its authority.

This first became evident in *Harris v. New York* (1971), where the issue was the validity of a pretrial confession obtained without *Miranda* safeguards. Since the petitioner claimed also that his confession had been coerced rather than given voluntarily, the Court conceivably might have disposed of the case under the ancient common-law rule that coerced confessions were inadmissible in evidence.

Instead, Chief Justice Burger in his opinion for the five-man majority first observed somewhat astonishingly that petitioner "makes no claim of coercion." He then ruled that while the disputed confession could not be used "directly" as a part of the prosecutor's case, it nevertheless could be introduced to impeach the credibility of the defendant on the witness stand. Brennan, in a hotly worded dissent, protested that it was "monstrous" that "the courts should aid or abet the law-breaking police officer," as the majority now contemplated.

More than any other single case, *Harris v. New York* symbolized for many libertarians what they conceived to be the Burger Court's "scandalous" disregard of basic civil liberties. Nor did the Court retreat from its Harris "credibility" rule. Four years later, in *Oregon v. Hass* (1975), it again allowed incriminating evidence obtained from a defendant to be used to attack his credibility, once he had given contrary testimony.

Meanwhile the Court also adopted a "law and order" approach to the problem of immunity from prosecution for those compelled to give potentially incriminating testimony. A long series of decisions, beginning with *Counselman v. Hitchcock* (1892), had held that testimony could be compelled in the face of the Fifth Amendment guarantee only by granting a witness "transactional immunity"—that is, immunity from subsequent prosecution for any offense thus disclosed, even though the government might later be able to fashion a case independent of the witness's testimony. A series of congressional immunity statutes had taken account of the *Counselman* rule.

But in 1970, Congress, acting under heavy "law and order" pressure, enacted a new statute providing that a witness who claimed protection under the Fifth Amendment could be compelled to testify merely by granting him "use immunity"—that is, a guarantee merely that any evidence elicited from the witness could not be used against him. By the same token, the government would remain free to fashion a case out of evidence independently secured, even though the original knowledge of the crime in question came from the witness's testimony.

In *Kastigar v. United States* (1972), the Court, speaking through Justice Powell, found the 1970 use-immunity statute to be constitutional. Although Powell could find but one marginal precedent to support his argument, he insisted that the disputed act was entirely consistent with the *Counselman* decision and with other decisions since that time. Douglas and Marshall in dissent contended that the 1970 law in fact represented an unconstitutional attempt on the part of Congress "to dilute the self-incrimination clause."

THE BURGER COURT AND THE RIGHT TO COUNSEL

The Burger Court subjected the Sixth Amendment's guarantee of the right to counsel for accused persons to somewhat inconsistent treatment: it broadened the guarantee even while it weakened its force through a "law and order" interpretation.

Thus in *Argersinger v. Hamlin* (1972), the Court extended the guarantee of a right to counsel in state criminal trials, first assured for felony prosecutions in *Gideon v. Wainright*, to include trials for all criminal offenses, no matter how petty, provided possible imprisonment was involved. "Absent a knowing waiver," Justice Douglas now declared, "no person may be imprisoned for any offence, whether classified as petty, misdemeanor, or felony, unless he was represented by counsel at his trial." Powell, dissenting, thought it would have been best to have conferred upon trial judges in petty cases a discretionary right to decide whether the intricacies of the case at hand required assignment of counsel in order to assure due process.

Argersinger, in which several "Warren" justices joined, was a thoroughly libertarian decision. But in *Kirby v. Illinois* (1972), decided at the same time, the Court substantially limited the right to counsel in the pretrial process, and thereby damaged somewhat both the *Escobedo* and *Miranda* precedents. At issue was the Warren's Court's stern exclusionary rule, laid down in *Wade v. United States* (1967), providing that police line-up identifications in which the defendant had not been represented by counsel might not be introduced into a subsequent criminal trial.

Notwithstanding the *Wade* decision, Justice Stewart now found that a long line of cases had clearly established that the right to counsel began only upon "the initiation of formal adversary proceedings," and not before. The *Escobedo* and *Miranda* decisions he dismissed as not appropriate; they dealt, he said, only with the Fifth Amendment guarantee against compulsory self-incrimination and not with the right to counsel as such.

Technically the Kirby decision did not overrule the Wade precedent, since the suspect, unlike that in *Wade*, had not as yet been formally charged with any offense. But, as Justice Brennan's angry dissent for the four other "Warren" justices emphasized, the wound inflicted upon Wade, Escobedo, and Miranda was obvious. A year later in *United States v. Ash* (1973), the Court took still another step away from Wade and Miranda, when it ruled that a pretrial photographic lineup without presence of counsel also did not violate the Sixth Amendment.

THE BURGER COURT AND JURY TRIAL

The Sixth Amendment's guarantee of a right to jury trial in criminal cases was another aspect of criminal procedure upon which the Burger Court adopted a fairly consistent "law and order" stance. The Warren Court had enlarged the jury trial guarantee, extending it to the states in *Duncan v. Louisiana* (1968), although it had limited it to felony prosecutions.

During the Warren-Burger transitional era, the Court had actually enlarged further the state jury trial guarantee, acting in *Baldwin v. New York* (1970), to extend the right to include all petty misdemeanors punishable by six months imprisonment or more. Justice White's opinion justified the "six months line," as representing already established "common practice of the states." Burger in a dissent almost archaic in flavor protested that the Sixth Amendment had not been written as a command to the states and that in any event the jury trial guarantee historically had applied only to serious crimes.

Even as the Court broadened the jury trial guarantee, however, it weakened it by ruling in *Williams v. Florida* (1970), that six-man jury trials were constitutional. The twelve-man jury, Justice

White argued, had come about merely through historical accident. Moreover, he contended rather too boldly, a jury of twelve
members was not necessarily any more advantageous to a defendant than one of six members. Harlan, who in a separate opinion
attacked both White's history and his statistics, concurred only
because he believed the Palko "ordered liberty" standard ought to
be preserved. Marshall, accepting Harlan's analysis, concluded that
six-man juries were downright unconstitutional.

Further damage to the twelve-man jury guarantee came two
years later when the Court in companion cases, *Johnson v. Louisiana*
(1972) and *Apodaca v. Oregon* (1972), by five to four votes sustained the constitutionality of state laws permitting nine to three
and ten to two verdicts, respectively. Justice White, whom Burger,
Blackmun, and Rehnquist joined, declared somewhat ingenuously
that "this Court has never held jury unanimity to be a requisite
of due process of law." But Justice Powell, concurring only because he refused to accept the "incorporation doctrine," demonstrated decisively in a separate opinion that both twelve-man juries
and unanimous verdicts long had been "universally accepted both
in common law and constitutional law." And Douglas, dissenting
outright, attacked the majority's attempt to develop a "watered
down version of the Bill of Rights."

THE DEATH PENALTY DECISION:
A DELAYED WARREN COURT TRIUMPH

Thus in cases having to do with the procedural guarantees of
the Bill of Rights the four Nixon justices—almost always voting
as a bloc and with the supprt of one or two of the Warren Court
justices—were able to check sharply the Court's libertarian activism and modify substantially "fair trial" law. On the other hand,
when the five Warren veterans themselves voted as a bloc, they
were still able to decide major issues in a fashion consistent with
the Court's humanitarian activist tradition.

A dramatic demonstration of this situation came in June 1972,
in *Furman v. Georgia*, as the five Warren holdover justices joined
together to declare unconstitutional two state statutes imposing
the death penalty in murder and rape convictions, on the ground
that they violated the Eighth Amendment's prohibition against
cruel and unusual punishment. Technically the Court did not declare the death penalty unconstitutional *per se* in all instances.
Nevertheless the decision cast a pall of doubt upon capital punish-

ment laws in some forty states as well as upon several federal statutes providing for the death penalty—among them the so-called Lindbergh Kidnapping law, the Aircraft Piracy Act, and the Presidential Assassination Act.

The *Furman* decision found the nine justices deeply divided in their reasoning. Only Brennan and Marshall held that the death penalty, viewed in the light of the conditions of modern society, was unconstitutional under all circumstances. Brennan, in order to reach this conclusion, first reviewed the judicial history of the Eighth Amendment's "cruel and unusual punishment" clause, to conclude that it had "an expansive and vital character"—i.e., that it was open to continuous judicial reinterpretation. This in turn enabled him to set up a modern constitutional standard by which any punishment must be judged: "whether or not it comports with human dignity." He then found that society's rejection of the death penalty as not so comporting was now virtually total; so little enforced was the death penalty that it no longer had any adequate deterrent effect. Capital punishment provisions therefore now must be adjudged invalid in all instances as in violation of the Eighth Amendment.

Marshall's reasoning was very close to Brennan's. He also thought that the Eighth Amendment "must draw its meaning" from the "evolving standards" of social decency in a "maturing society." Unlike Brennan, however, Marshall did not contend that contemporary society totally rejected the death penalty; instead he argued that it *would* reject the penalty if it knew all the facts.

Douglas, Stewart, and White on their part cautiously refused to conclude that the death penalty was unconstitutional under all circumstances. Douglas thought the death penalty as commonly imposed—"sparsely, selectively, and spottily to unpopular groups" —that is, upon blacks, the poor, and the ignorant—violated the equal protection clause. Stewart and White also emphasized the rare and capricious circumstances under which capital punishment was inflicted. The death penalty, Stewart observed, was "cruel and unusual" in the "same way that being struck by lightning" was cruel and unusual. But he warned at the same time that he regarded racial discrimination in imposition of the death penalty as "not proved"; moreover, he refused to reject unconditionally society's right to retribution as an element in punishment.

The four Nixon appointees, in turn, charged the five majority justices with enacting reformist social legislation under the guise of interpreting the Constitution. "In a democratic society," Burger admonished, "legislatures are constituted to respond to the will and therefore the moral values of the people." The four minority justices also attacked the social theorizing of the majority as inadequate. There was, they insisted, no clear evidence upon which to base a conclusion that the death penalty was without deterrent effect, that it was racially biased in application, or that it was imposed so rarely as to imply its total rejection by organized society.

The decision in *Furman v. Georgia* by no means disposed decisively of the capital punishment issue. Three of the five majority justices had rested their arguments in part on the rare and capricious element in the penalty. Ironically, as both Burger and Powell pointed out, were the death penalty to be made mandatory by statute, this constitutional weakness would be removed.

Within the next three years, this observation by Burger and Powell took on a large measure of reality. Between 1972 and mid-1975, some thirty states, acting in response to the *Furman* decision, enacted mandatory capital punishment laws. These acts made automatic the imposition of the death penalty for a variety of offenses: typically for murder committed while the offender was engaged in resisting arrest, for the murder of a police officer, for murder by a felon already incarcerated for another crime, or for murder incident to the commisison of a rape or certain other major felonies.

Meanwhile, in March 1973, President Nixon asked Congress to make mandatory imposition of the death penalty upon conviction of a defendant for any of twelve federal crimes; among them treason, espionage, airplane hi-jacking, assassination of government officials, and kidnapping where the victim met death. However, Congress failed to respond to the President's plea.

By mid-1975 there were some 200 persons in the United States confined in death-rows, their executions delayed for the moment while the courts struggled with the constitutional issues involved in their respective sentences. Meanwhile the Supreme Court itself heard arguments in a new series of death-penalty appeals. Almost certainly the Court was destined to speak again, either to confirm the harsh new mandatory laws or to consign the death penalty to the constitutional rubbish heap for good and all.

THE ABORTION DECISIONS:
FURTHER LIBERTARIAN LAW-MAKING

A year after the *Furman* decision, the Court, in another dramatic piece of humanitarian-liberal activism, handed down two decisions declaring unconstitutional two principal state antiabortion statutes and sharply limiting the power of the states to impose prohibitory regulations upon abortion. Three of the Nixon justices—Burger, Backmun, and Powell, joined four of the Warren holdovers to make up the seven to two Court majority—ample evidence that the new conservatives were hardly opposed to activist judicial lawmaking when they believed the occasion called for it.

The abortion cases, *Roe v. Wade* (1973) and *Doe v. Bolton* (1973) rather resembled *Furman* in that they had arisen more or less directly as a result of a sustained drive in the previous decade by reformists and humanitarian-minded libertarians. The campaign in New York, in particular, had attracted national attention. In 1970, a liberal coalition in that state, acting with the support of Governor Nelson Rockefeller, drove through to enactment a law permitting abortion for any reason in the first twenty-four weeks of pregnancy. By contrast, a powerful antiabortion 1972 Michigan campaign, whose sponsors rallied their supporters with the slogan "abortion is murder," resulted in the adoption by referendum of a stringent new antiabortion law. However, the State Supreme Court presently struck this measure down as unconstitutional.

The Texas statute under review in *Roe v. Wade* was typical of many such laws enacted during the latter half of the nineteenth century. It made abortion a criminal offense, and excepted only operations performed to save the life of the woman in question.

By contrast, the Georgia statute challenged in *Doe v. Bolton* had been adopted in 1968 and reflected rather recent reformist tendencies in abortion law. Patterned after a section in the American Law Institute's Model Penal Code, the act made abortion a crime, but excepted operations performed pursuant to a physician's "best clinical judgment" that (1) continued pregnancy might endanger either the life or the health of the woman, (2) that the prospective child might be born "with a grave, permanent, and irremedial mental or physical defect"; or (3) that pregnancy "had resulted from forcible or statutory rape." The law also limited abortions to Georgia residents and required that such operations be performed only in certified hospitals.

Justice Blackmun's majority opinion in *Roe v. Wade* first reviewed at length the history of the theology, ethics, and law of abortion, to conclude that there had been no generally recognized long-standing moral or legal prohibition on abortion operations, and that the antiabortion laws now prevailing in the American states were of relatively recent origin. He also found that of the three original objectives of antiabortion legislation—the discouragement of illicit sexual behavior, the protection of women against a medically hazardous operation, and the protection of fetal life—only the last had any contemporary validity. Even here, he declared, the state's interest was a very limited one, since it had long been clear that a fetus was not a person within the meaning of the Fourteenth Amendment.

Accordingly, Blackmun balanced a conditional right of privacy for women contemplating abortions with an even more conditional right of the state to protect the fetus as a prospective person. In the first trimester of pregnancy—a period when a properly performed abortion is safer than childbirth itself—he ruled that a woman's right to decide upon an abortion was a private matter between her and her physician, with which the state could not constitutionally interfere. In the second trimester, when the medical problems attendant upon an abortion became serious, the state might lawfully regulate such operations for the "protection of maternal health," although the decision as to whether or not to terminate a pregnancy was still solely one for the woman alone.

Only in the third trimester, Blackmun declared, when the fetus achieved viability—the potential to survive if born—did the state have a constitutional right to prohibit abortion outright. Even here, the state could not constitutionally prohibit abortions to save the life or health of the mother. The Texas statute, it followed, violated the right of privacy guaranteed by the Fourteenth Amendment, and was unconstitutional.

Blackmun's opinion in *Doe v. Bolton* confirmed the finding of a three-man district court that the Georgia statute's three conditions stipulated for lawful abortions constituted, again, an unconstitutional invasion of the right of privacy. In effect, the court now struck them out of the law. Blackmun's opinion also invalidated the hospital and residence requirements attached to the law as violative of the right of privacy and of the equal protection clause, respectively. Justices White and Rehnquist entered vigorous dissents, labeling both decisions "an extravagant exercise" of "raw judicial power."

The court's abortion decisions were deeply offensive to many political and religious conservatives. Senator James L. Buckley of New York, a Catholic and a member of his state's Conservative Party, promptly introduced into the Senate a proposed constitutional amendment to restore to the states the power to regulate and to prohibit abortions. And a 1974 act of Congress creating a

Legal Services Corporation prohibited use of its funds to provide legal assistance to procure an abortion.

Numerous state legislatures and courts in communities where conservative religious influence was strong meanwhile continued virtually to ignore the *Roe* and *Doe* decisions. In June 1972, the Pennsylvania legislature overrode a gubernatorial veto to enact a stringent new antiabortion statute. And in February 1975, a Massachusetts trial court convicted a black Boston physician, Dr. Kenneth Edelin, of manslaughter following his performance of a presumably legal second trimester abortion.

However, many liberal Protestant and Jewish spokesmen were emphatic in their praise of the Court's stand. Early in 1975, the federal Civil Rights Commission also spoke out against the Buckley amendment, whose chance of passage, it appeared, was exceedingly dim. Meanwhile thirty-one states enacted some fifty-seven new abortion statutes, most of them tailored to take account of the Supreme Court's stand. And a survey early in 1975 by the Planned Parenthood Association of America appeared to demonstrate that while the number of legal abortions in the United States had jumped more than fifty percent between 1972 and 1973 alone, the number of recorded postabortion deaths fell from more than 300 annually in the 1960's to 47 in 1973. The Court's libertarian abortion "legislation," it thus appeared, had in all probability worked something very like a permanent alteration in both law and social practice in America.

CHURCH-STATE QUESTIONS: PAROCHIAD

The Burger Court continued the very strong separationist stand on the relationship of church and state which the Warren Court had adopted in the *Vitale* and *Schempp* decisions. Several of the Nixon appointees, it presently became clear, were moderately strong separationists; Justice Powell, in particular, emerged as virtually a successor to Justice Black in his advocacy of "wall of separation" doctrine. Chief Justice Burger on his part attempted to develop a kind of compromise between separationist and accommodationist positions, but in the final event he proved unable to win a majority of his judicial brethren to his position. On the other hand, the Court majority also refused to go along with Justice Douglas, who steadfastly opposed all forms of assistance to church-related institutions, however remote and indirect the resultant aid to religion might be.

Chief Justice Burger's compromise approach first manifested itself in *Walz v. Tax Commissioners* (1970) in which the Court by an eight to one vote accepted the constitutionality of a New York law exempting church-owned real property from taxation. Similar exemptions, the Chief Justice pointed out, obtained in all fifty states; moreover, the practice was at least two hundred years old and was "deeply embedded in our national life." Tax exemption, Burger continued, could not properly be equated with direct monetary grants to churches. On the contrary, he thought, it probably did more to preserve "a benevolent neutrality" toward organized religion than would church taxation, what with its potential element of entanglement. Douglas alone dissented.

The *Walz* decision led some analysts to conclude that the Court might now be willing to accept direct state financial assistance to parochial schools—"parochiad" as it was becoming known. Nationally the parochiad question was again provoking serious controversy. The Catholic Church had for some time found itself involved in an increasingly severe financial crisis in its system of parochial school support. Several leading Catholic organizations, among them the U.S. Catholic Conference, the National Catholic Educational Association, and the Knights of Columbus, now were conducting intensive lobbying campaigns in the states for the passage of parochiad bills. Conservative Protestant and Jewish religious leaders also were sympathetic to such legislation.

By 1971, thirty-three states had adopted parochiad programs of one sort or another for church-related schools. Assistance ranged from free textbooks, busing, and health services, to tuition grants, parental tax credits, and direct teacher salary subsidies. Because of the 1968 *Allen* decision there was some reason to believe that the Court might declare such legislation constitutional.

But in *Lemon v. Kurtzman* (1971), the Court balked, as it declared subsidy laws both in Rhode Island and in Pennsylvania unconstitutional. The Rhode Island law under review provided salary supplements up to fifteen percent for teachers of secular subjects in parochial schools. The Pennsylvania statute in question authorized the State Superintendent of Public Instruction to "purchase" certain "educational services" from private schools. In practice this involved reimbursing parochial schools for teachers' salaries, textbooks, and the like.

The fatal difficulty with both laws, Chief Justice Burger now declared, was that they involved "excessive entanglement" between church and state. There were three major requirements, Burger held, which a law affecting church-state relations must meet in order to pass muster constitutionally: it "must be secular in purpose"; its "primary effect must be neither to advance nor inhibit religion"; and it must not "foster an excessive entanglement with religion."

It was this last test which both the Rhode Island and Pennsylvania acts failed. Parochial schools, Burger pointed out, were steeped in a profoundly religious atmosphere which made virtually impossible any "prophylactic measures" to guarantee that state assistance did not violate the establishment clause. Douglas and Black, in a lengthy concurring opinion, thought the two laws of necessity would involve a "pervasive monitoring" of parochial schools, which in itself would "make a shambles of the establishment clause." White alone dissented, arguing that no actual "entanglement" had in fact been demonstrated.

However, the Court refused to extend its *Lemon* logic to church-related colleges and universities. In *Tilton v. Richardson* (1971), the Court passed favorably, five to four, upon the Higher Education Facilities Act of 1963, in which Congress had provided for federal construction grants "for institutions of higher education." The law specifically banned construction of buildings for religious purposes, but did not exclude church-related schools from its benefits.

In his opinion Chief Justice Burger argued that there were significant differences between collegiate education and that on the primary and secondary level, which allowed the federal act to clear the constitutional barrier. There was no evidence, he thought, that religion had "seeped into the use" of any of the buildings which had been constructed on the campuses of the church-related schools in question. He concluded that only that provision of the law which allowed an institution to convert a subsidized building to a religious purpose after twenty years must be held in violation of the Establishment Clause. In an indignant dissent, Douglas protested that there was no vital constitutional difference between the state legislation voided in *Lemon* and the federal act which the Court now accepted.

The *Lemon* decision hardly put the parochiad question to rest. In the next three years fifteen states, most of them in the northeast and with heavy Catholic populations, passed laws at-

tempting by means of a variety of techniques to provide parochial schools with a measure of financial assistance. The Court,
nonetheless, persisted in its strongly separationist stance.

Thus in *Committee for Public Education and Religious Liberty
v. Nyquist* (1973), the Court struck down three distinct parochiad
programs which the New York legislature in 1972 had incorporated in its education and tax laws. One law provided for direct
money-grants to nonpublic schools attended by children from
low-income families for the "maintenance and repair" of school
equipment and facilities. Another provided for tuition reimbursement for low-income parents of children attending nonpublic
schools, while a third allowed parents who failed to qualify for
tuition reimbursement to claim state income tax credits for private
school tuition payments.

Justice Powell's opinion for the majority found all three programs in violation of the Establishment Clause. "Maintenance and
Repair" and "tuition reimbursement," he declared, violated the
"effect test"—that is, their primary effect was to subsidize and
advance the religious mission of sectarian schools. As for the income tax credit program, it constituted "a charge made upon the
state for the purposes of religious education"; hence it also violated the Establishment Clause. In a separate opinion Burger and
Rehnquist agreed that the "maintenance and repair" program violated the Establishment Clause, but contended that tuition reimbursement and tax credits were "indistinguishable in principle"
from the aid programs approved years earlier in the *Everson* and
Allen cases, and hence should be allowed.

The *Lemon* and *Nyquist* decisions seemingly put to rest indefinitely the issue of state appropriations for primary and secondary
schools. A few marginal support programs, theoretically for the
child rather than the school, remained—the principal one being the
busing of parochial school children. In Congress and the state legislatures a few diehards now advocated a tuition voucher plan,
whereby children in both public and private schools would be
given tuition chits redeemable at the public treasury. A number
of proposed constitutional amendments providing for parochiad
also went into the congressional hopper. But it seemed probable
that in the future church-related schools would be obliged to look
to private sources to solve their admittedly desperate financial
problems.

THE BURGER COURT AND THE PORNOGRAPHY PROBLEM

A further instance of the Burger Court's comparative conservatism in its treatment of social issues was its deliberate attempt to increase the sphere of governmental regulatory power over hardcore pornography.

In *Miller v. California* (1973), the Court by a five to four vote in effect sustained a conviction under a California statute which prohibited the knowing sale of obscene matter. At the outset Chief Justice Burger deliberately rejected as a "burden impossible to discharge," the *Memoirs* version of the Roth formula—that the material under review be adjudged to be "utterly without redeeming social value." In its place, he postulated still another version of the Roth formula:

(a) whether the average person, applying contemporary community standards, would find that the work, taken as a whole, appeals to prurient interest;

(b) whether the work depicts or describes, in a patently offensive way, sexual conduct specifically defined by applicable state law; and

(c) whether the work, taken as a whole, lacks serious artistic, political or scientific value.

Burger then rejected sharply the idea of a national community standard for obscenity, such as that called for in the *Manuel* and *Jacobellis* cases, as "an exercise in futility" and "not constitutionally sound." Instead, he declared, trial courts ought to measure obscenity by local community standards; these admittedly might vary widely between, for example, a little Mississippi town and New York City or Las Vegas.

In an accompanying case, *Paris Adult Theater I v. Slaton* (1973), the Court applied the new Miller standard to hold constitutional a civil prosecution against an allegedly pornographic film which had portrayed at length scenes of simulated fellatio and cunnilingus. Burger's opinion denied emphatically that any right of privacy, such as that which the Warren Court had set forth to protect the exhibition of obscene films in a person's home, could be extended to protect the display of obscene materials in a public theater.

Burger then went on to deliver himself of a number of philosophic propositions about the obscenity problem in general. The state, he declared, had an undoubted legitimate interest in maintaining "the quality of life and the total community environment." The Minority Report of the President's Commission on Obscenity and Pornography, he pointed out, had contended that there was "at least an arguable correlation between obscene material and crime." Admittedly the connection was not absolutely demonstrable, but legislatures quite properly frequently acted upon the basis of unprovable assumptions. Regulation of so-called "adult movies," it followed, was altogether constitutional, provided the state complied with the First Amendment standards set forth in *Miller*.

As might well have been expected, the Court's new Miller-Slaton stance drew sharp fire from several of the Warren Court veterans. Douglas, still insisting that the First Amendment did not allow "any implied exceptions in the case of obscenity," protested that the Court's new formula had opened the way to send a man to prison under standards "which until today were not a part of the law." And Brennan, whom Stewart and Marshall joined in dissent, thought the Court had rejected both "fundamental First Amendment premises" and the Roth rationale.

Conceivably the substitution both of the *Miller* standard for the now rejected *Memoirs* formula and of variable local community standards in place of the former national requirement might well have led to a new era of suppression throughout America of sexually explicit movies, books, and magazines. In fact, nothing like this occurred. Instead, in spite of some flurries of police activity, so-called "x-rated" films and "adult" bookstores continued to be very much a part of the national urban scene. Most Americans, it appeared, now agreed with the position adopted by the majority in the Report of the President's Commission on Obscenity: that there was no convincing link between obscenity and other manifestations of antisocial behavior or criminal activity. A permissive public stance involving minimal legal controls over pornography, it followed, might after all be the most intelligent public policy.

Curiously, while the Burger Court enlarged substantially governmental power to suppress pornographic art and literature, it narrowed at the same time the authority of the states to punish casual obscene public utterance. Since the 1942 decision in *Chaplinsky v. New Hampshire*, lewd, profane and insulting utterances or "fighting words" presumably had been outside the protection of the First Amendment.

But in *California v. Cohen* (1971), a Court still under the domination of Warren veterans very nearly repudiated the *Chaplinsky* doctrine. The Cohen case involved the appeal of a young man tried and convicted under an "offensive conduct" statute for entering a California courthouse wearing a sweater emblazoned with the provocative slogan "Fuck the Draft."

Justice Harlan's opinion emphasized that the defendant had merely been engaged in the "communication" of the ideas his slogan represented. The slogan, while vulgar in the extreme, was not pornographic within the meaning of the Roth-Albert standard, since it contained no exotic element. Nor did it constitute an invasion of the privacy of an unwilling audience, since those who found it offensive had merely to avert their eyes to protect themselves. Harlan also rejected out of hand the propositions that the states could suppress such an utterance either as "guardians of the public morality," or on the ground that its display might cause a "violent reaction" disturbing the public peace.

In short, the appellant's scurrilous slogan was communication protected by the First Amendment, and the statute under which the state had attempted to suppress it was unconstitutional. Justice Blackmun in a dissent joined by Burger and Black, argued convincingly that the Court in fact had effectively disregarded the force of the *Chaplinsky* precedent.

Somewhat surprisingly, the Cohen dictum survived the successive changes in the Court's personnel in the next year. In *Gooding, Warden v. Wilson* (1972), the Court struck down the Georgia "offensive language" conviction of a black man who had threatened a police officer with "white son of a bitch, I'll kill you." Justice Brennan, speaking for the majority, thought there was "no likelihood that the person addressed would make an immediate violent response"; the utterance was therefore protected by the First Amendment. This conclusion, Chief Justice Burger protested, was bizarre.

Employing a standard much like that in *Cohen*, the Court in *Hess v. Indiana* (1973) reversed the conviction of a campus antiwar demonstrator who had told a crowd of followers that "we'll take the fucking street later." Significantly, Justice Powell now joined with the majority, although Burger, Blackmun, and Rehnquist dissented.

In short, the Burger Court, while nominally preserving the Chaplinsky doctrine, very nearly divested it of practical meaning.

SCHOOL DESEGREGATION: CROSS-DISTRICT BUSING

Like procedural due process and the death penalty, school desegregation was an issue which eventually was to divide the Burger Court decisively, in the main between the Warren veterans and the Nixon appointees. The unity which the Warren Court had preserved in school desegregation matters, from Brown I and II to *Green v. County Board*, now was to be sharply shattered.

Part of the Court's difficulty lay in the fact that the social, political, and legal issues involved in school desegregation began to alter rapidly after 1967. Between Brown I and the *Green* case, the Court had faced a relatively simple constitutional and legal situation: the fact of *de jure* segregation in the South, which the Court insisted violated the equal protection clause. For a long time, the South, aided in part by the "all deliberate speed" formula, had been able for the most part to avoid anything more than nominal compliance with the Brown decisions.

But about 1967, pressure from the Department of Health, Education and Welfare for "affirmative action" programs pursuant to the Civil Rights Act of 1964 began to produce dramatic results in the Southern states. One school system after another below the Mason and Dixon Line moved to reluctant compliance, lest it be cut off from a variey of federal aid programs. By 1973 *de jure* school segregation had been effectively terminated almost everywhere in the South.

Meanwhile the NAACP focused its attention increasingly upon the great cities of the North. Here the legal situation was radically different from that below the Mason-Dixon line. In Chicago, Detroit, Cleveland, New York, Philadelphia, Boston, and so on, statutory school segregation either had never existed or had been done away long since. Nonetheless the school systems in the great metropolitan areas were characterized to an extraordinary degree by segregation along racial lines. As a rule, the schools of the inner city core now were almost entirely black, while those of the outer city belt and the surrounding suburbs were almost entirely white. By 1975, some 71.5 per cent of the children in Detroit's schools were black. Similar situations existed in New York, Chicago, Philadelphia, Boston, and Cleveland, while in Washington, D.C., where the schools had been officially desegregated after Brown II, black children now made up virtually one hundred percent of the student body.

From a legal point of view, segregation of this kind had two fundamental characteristics. First, on the surface, at least, it was very largely *de facto* rather than *de jure* in character. For the most part it was a product of the ecology of urban growth, having been brought about by the massive black immigration into Northern cities after World War II. It had frequently been promoted by subtle school board policies—school districting, student transfers, curriculum distinctions, and the like. But as it now existed it could not be done away with simply by an order to end *de jure* segregation, even where a court found that some *de jure* segregation in fact existed. Second, any court order aimed at desegregation of the schools of a great metropolitan region, if it were to be effective, would have to be directed not only at the schools of the core city but also at the white schools of the outer suburban belt.

The principal social tool available to cope with metropolitan segregation of this kind was cross-district busing. Legally this meant ordering outer-belt school districts which, although "lily white," had never engaged in *de jure* segregation to embark upon cooperative desegregation with the inner city. Cross-district busing involved inconceivably complex concommitant problems of interdistrict taxation, finance, community pressure, and the like, which again could hardly be solved simply by issuing court orders.

Public opinion, always a factor to be reckoned with in any difficult legal situation, also had altered greatly since the days of Brown I and Brown II. Then a Northern public, willing enough to subscribe to a considerable measure of libertarian idealism on racial questions as long as the solution did not strike too close to home, had lent substantial support to a succession of Supreme Court decisions and congressional enactments aimed almost entirely at achieving desegregation in the South. Thus the Southern white population had found itself arrayed as a distinct minority against the population of the country at large.

But as the focus of school desegregation shifted rapidly to the great metropolitan regions of the North, Northern white public opinion also underwent a dramatic shift. Fear of court-ordered metropolitan integration and cross-district busing was undoubtedly a component in the white "backlash" that figured so prominently in President Nixon's overwhelming victory in the election of 1972. And, true to Mr. Dooley's venerable aphorism that the "Supreme Court follows the election returns," the sharp alteration in Northern public opinion on school segregation presently found expression in the decisions of the Supreme Court itself.

Swann v. Charlotte-Mecklenburg Board of Education (1971), the case in which the Court first expounded what were destined to become the guidelines for its approach to Northern metropolitan desegregation, arose not in the North but in Charlotte, North Carolina. Here a federal district court had ordered an affirmative action plan for the Charlotte-Mecklenburg School District which not only restructured attendance zones but also employed a school pairing technique that necessitated extensive intracity busing.

In a unanimous opinion, the Court upheld the district court's order. Chief Justice Burger's opinion, which deliberately undertook "to provide some guidelines" for affirmative action, emphasized very heavily the broad equity powers of the lower federal courts in such programs. School pairings and grouping and interschool busing, he declared, were all legitimate instruments of the Court's equity power.

But even as the Court upheld affirmative action in seemingly sweeping terms, Burger posted a series of "red lights," warning that there were sharp limits beyond which the lower courts might not go. The courts, he declared, could act only upon the basis of "a finding of constitutional violation"—that is, that *de jure* segregation existed. Moreover, he asserted, the imposition of rigid racial quotas in a school system was not constitutionally acceptable. Nor did the continued existence of some one-race schools within a school system necessarily mean that it was still legally segregated. Finally, Burger warned, while busing was a legitimate affirmative action tool, it must not be employed so as to risk children's health or disrupt the educational process.

In all this there was a decided measure of judicial ambiguity; conceivably this had made possible the justices' united stand. But it was also apparent that the limitations Burger's opinion had stipulated, if applied sharply to Northern metropolitan *de facto* school segregation, might well make effective affirmative action programs in that region extremely difficult to implement.

The *Swann* decision had been unanimous, but in the next three years the Court's unanimity disappeared. In *Wright v. Council of the City of Emporia* (1972), the five "Warren" justices united to declare unconstitutional an attempt by the school board of a small North Carolina city to withdraw from the Greenville County School District and set up a district of its own. Significantly, the Emporia Board had taken this action only two weeks after a federal district court had ordered into effect an NAACP-devised school pairing plan which would have integrated completely all black and white children in the county on a grade-by-grade basis.

The racial ratio in the united system would have been 66 per cent black and 34 per cent white; by contrast, the new splinter district would have been 52 per cent black and 48 per cent white.

Justice Stewart's opinion rejected sharply the argument that Emporia's "dominant purpose" had been merely to improve the quality of education. Formation of the splinter district, he found, would have "a substantially adverse effect" on desegregation of the county district. As such, it was unconstitutional. In a dissent for the four Nixon appointees, Chief Justice Burger accused the majority of adopting "a pointless racial balancing approach" and of allowing the district court to abuse its equity powers.

The depth of the rupture within the Court was hardly dispelled by the unanimity it displayed in a companion splinter-district case, *United States v. Scotland Neck Board of Education* (1972). Here the justices struck down as unconstitutional an attempt to form a separate school district in North Carolina's Halifax County, which would have been 57 per cent white and 43 per cent black, as compared with an original district, not yet integrated, in which the ratios were 28 per cent white and 72 per cent black. Evidently the Nixon appointees had regarded as decisive the variation between these percentages and those in the *Wright* case.

The split between the Warren Justices and Nixon appointees was again evident in *Bradley v. School Board of the City of Richmond* (1973). Here the Court deadlocked, four to four, without opinion, in its review of a Court of Appeals decision reversing a district court order calling for an elaborate multicounty integration plan for the schools of metropolitan Richmond, Virginia. The Circuit Court, quite evidently following the Swann dictum, had ruled that there was no evidence of *de jure* segregation. Hence cross-county integration which included the suburban districts in question was not constitutionally justified. The Supreme Court's tie vote, precipitated by Justice Powell's abstention and Justice White's vote with the other Nixon appointees, technically affirmed the appellate court decision. However, the ominous import of the Court's four to four division for the future of interdistrict integration in the great metropolitan regions of the North was evident enough.

The Court's decision in *Keyes v. School District No. 1, Denver, Colorado* (1973), brought into even sharper relief the practical difficulties and constitutional problems involved in Northern urban school integration. Here a federal court had ruled that the schools of the Park Hill district in Denver had been segregated *de jure,* as a result of a deliberate policy of racial segregation pursued by the Denver School Board. However, the court had refused to accept the NAACP argument that a finding of *de jure* segregation for Park Hill necessarily implied that the entire Denver system was segregated *de jure.* Instead, in an odd throwback to *Plessy v. Ferguson,* it had found that the city's core schools, whether segregated *de jure* or *de facto,* were educationally inferior, and had ordered the Denver Board to provide them with "substantially equal facilities."

Upon appeal, the Supreme Court in a seven to two decision rejected the district court's attempt to "fractionate" the Denver school system. The laws of evidence, Justice Brennan declared, dictated that a finding of *de jure* segregation in one part of a school system established a "primary case of intentional segregation" in all of Denver's core city schools, which could be rebutted only by decisive evidence to the contrary. In the absence of such proof, the school board had "an affirmative duty to desegregate the entire system, 'root and branch.' "

In separate concurring opinions, Justices Douglas and Powell both expressed the opinion that the distinction between *de facto* and *de jure* segregation, upon which the Court had relied so heavily in the *Swann* case, had outlived its usefulness. Douglas thought that the Court should rule simply that all racial segregation, whether it resulted from intentional state action or from impersonal social forces, violated the equal protection clause.

Powell on the other hand argued that the Court now should formulate constitutional principles for dealing with desegregation upon a national rather than upon a merely regional basis. This amounted to an assertion that the *de jure–de facto* distinction obliged the South to bear the entire weight of desegregation while allowing the North to escape the consequences of its own more subtle discriminatory policies. But Powell also took the occasion to express his "profound misgivings" at the prospect of "large-scale or long-distance" busing in metropolitan areas, which he feared would result in the surrender of "balance," "equity," and "flexibility" in educational policy.

At length, in July 1974, the Court in *Milliken v. Bradley* rejected, five to four, a comprehensive interdistrict integration plan for the school systems of metropolitan Detroit. The plan in question sought to integrate Detroit's schools, now nearly three-quarters black, with those of fifty-three outlying suburban school districts, all of them overwhelmingly white, principally by means of school matching and an interdistrict busing plan.

The plan was based upon a district court ruling that *de jure* segregation existed in Detroit's schools because of past "action and inaction" by city and state officials. Significantly, however, there had been no finding that *de jure* segregation existed in any of the suburban school districts. Instead, the district court had included them simply because integration of the schools of metropolitan Detroit had ceased to have any great meaning. Nonetheless the Court of Appeals, after long and complex litigation, had confirmed the interdistrict busing plan.

Upon appeal, the Supreme Court reversed. Chief Justice Burger's majority stated the fundamental constitutional issue at the outset: whether a federal court could impose a multidistrict affirmative action plan to remedy *de jure* segregation in a single district, in the absence of any claim that the other districts involved had operated segregated schools. Burger's answer, drawn directly from his *Swann* opinion, was a firm "no." "Without an interdistrict violation and an interdistrict effect," he declared, "there is no constitutional wrong calling for an interdistrict remedy."

Burger also emphasized the potential financial, administrative, logistical, and jurisdictional problems that would be attendant upon the creation of a "vast new super school district." The result, he intimated, might well be to turn the federal courts into a *de facto* legislative authority, and to "deprive the people of control of schools through their elected representatives." Accordingly, the Court vacated the interdistrict busing order and instructed the district court to fommulate an integration plan for the Detroit schools alone.

Justices Douglas, Brennan, White, and Marshall all entered strenuous dissents. The Court, Douglas declared, "had put the problems of our society back to the period that antedated the 'separate but equal' regime of *Plessy v. Ferguson*." And Marshall protested bitterly that the Court's "giant step backward" would allow the state "to profit from its own wrong," accelerate white flight to the suburbs, and "perpetuate for years to come the separation of the races" into two cities—one white and one black.

As Marshall himself recognized, the Court's decision was in considerable part "a reflection of a perceived public mood." In the North, white public opinion of late had turned very heavily against interdistrict busing, while substantial portions of the Negro community now also opposed what one Detroit black leader called "the invidious racial implications" and "dubious educational benefits" associated with transporting black school children to white schools.

In New York, the State Board of Regents was now engaged in a careful strategic retreat from its former heavy commitment to school integration, repudiating both quotas and racial ratios for any such purpose. And in Boston, mob violence virtually paralyzed implementaton of a federal court order which called merely for intradistrict integration, without suburban participation. Significantly, the Ford administration at first refused to interfere, although the result was something suspiciously like mob nullification.

Elsewhere, in Louisville and Indianapolis, lower federal courts went ahead with metropolitan integration plans. But it now appeared probable that only a major shift in public opinion and the eventual appointment to the Court of new justices heavily committed to integration could throw judicial desegregation machinery into high gear once more.

AFFIRMATIVE ACTION IN HIGHER EDUCATION: THE DE FUNIS CASE

Another facet of the "affirmative action" problem arose out of the program of the Department of Health, Education and Welfare to correct racial and sexual discrimination in the nation's colleges and universities. Beginning about 1967, HEW, acting under authority derived from Title VI of the Civil Rights Act of 1964, demanded that institutions of higher education develop comprehensive plans directed toward increasing the enrollment of blacks, Chicanos, American Indians, and other racial and cultural minorities. HEW also demanded affirmative action plans to increase the percentages of female and minority group faculty members and to raise both the rank and salaries of such individuals. It sought also to equalize funds and opportunities for male and female students in athletic programs, vocational education, dormitory facilties, and so on. The penalty for noncompliance by an institution was the loss of lucrative federal contracts for research, building funds, and the like, which for a prestigious university might amount to several score million dollars.

Affirmative action programs of this sort raised a serious constitutional problem: was inverse discrimination by race, sex, or national origin compatible with the equal protection clause of the Fourteenth Amendment? The argument for inverse discrimination, achieved in part by racial and sexual hiring and admissions quotas, was that it was constitutionally acceptable in order to correct past violations of the equal protection clause. Opponents of such programs replied that discrimination by race, sex, and the like was flatly incompatible with the Fourteenth Amendment no matter how laudable the objective.

Most university administrators claimed that in any event their institutions had never discriminated against blacks, women, and other minorities, in either faculties or student bodies. The small numbers of female faculty members, they contended, reflected the relative paucity of women entering the academic profession. A like reason, they declared, accounted for the small numbers of minority students in undergraduate programs and professional schools—only a very few qualified black, Indian, or Chicano applicants sought admission.

Affirmative action programs, many university officials insisted, also threatened to substitute an arbitrary standard of equality for the traditional academic standard of competitive excellence. Such a shift in values, they argued, menaced seriously the capacity of institutions of higher education to do scientific research, to generate social theory, and to train superior minds.

In *De Funis v. Odegaard* (1974), the Supreme Court found itself face to face for the first time with inverse racial discrimination, in this instance in a law school affirmative action admissions program. At issue in the case was the petition of a white student of Jewish background who had been denied admission to the University of Washington Law School. De Funis's aptitude scores and undergraduate grades had been reasonably good, but the Washington Law School had had an affirmative action program which gave admissions priorities to blacks, Chicanos, Indians, and other racial minorities. Law school officials as a consequence had rejected De Funis's application even while they had admitted thirty-six minority students with lower scores than his. Thirty of these had had scores so low that they could not possibly have secured admission except for their race.

De Funis had thereupon secured an injunction from the state courts effecting his admission, on the ground that he had been the victim of "invidious racial discrimination" in violation of the equal protection clause. Although on appeal he had lost his case in the Washington Supreme Court, he had, by successive legal maneuvers, succeeded in continuing his studies in the Washington law school until well into his final year. Attorneys for the school now assured the United States Supreme Court that De Funis would in any event be allowed to graduate, regardless of the outcome of his present petition.

Accordingly, the Court by a five to four vote dismissed De Funis's petition as moot, on the ground that no true adversarial position now existed between the two parties involved. This decision, legally plausible, also enabled the Court to avoid coming to grips with an almost unresolvable complex of issues in law and social policy. Justice Brennan, joined by Douglas, White, and Marshall, dissented, protesting that the issues involved in the case were real, and that the Court's action "clearly disserves the public interest."

Justice Douglas was not content to let the matter rest there. In a lengthy dissent replete with contradictions and ambiguities, he argued the case for and against affirmative action. "The consideration of race as a measure of an applicant's qualifications," he conceded, "normally introduces a capricious and irrelevant factor working an invidious discrimination." On the other hand, he contended, law school aptitude tests reflected "the dimensions and orientation of the organization man"; thereby they did "a disservice to minorities." Accordingly, he thought, there was "sufficient warrant for a school to put minorities into a separate class in order better to probe their capacities and potentials," even though there was "no constitutional right for any race to be preferred."

Douglas' agony of ambivalence of course settled nothing. Instead it seemed certain that the affirmative action question, reflecting as it did social and political issues of vital contemporary significance, would very soon confront the Court once more.

THE VOTING RIGHTS ACT OF 1970: OREGON V. MITCHELL

The Voting Rights Act of 1970 presented still another aspect of the civil rights movement on which the "Warren" justices and the Nixon appointees differed on the constitutional issues involved. This measure extended for another five years the supervisory sections of the Voting Rights Act of 1965, but it also incorporated three additional provisions: it fixed the minimum voting age in both national and state elections at eighteen; it banned literacy tests outright; and it fixed state residential requirements in presidential elections at thirty days. This last provision in effect nullified all existing state laws fixing franchise residence requirements in such elections, since these without exception imposed state residence requirements prior to voting of from six months to one year or more.

The provision enfranchising eighteen-year-olds was the end result of a campaign conducted by a variety of interest groups. Since the 1940's proponents of the reform, pointing out that eighteen-year-olds were liable to military service, had argued that "if you're old enough to fight, you're old enough to vote." Voting age reform advocates argued also that eighteen-year-olds now constituted an important portion of the nation's work force, and that they were far better educated than had been the case in the days when the venerable twenty-one years age limitation had first arisen in English law.

For some years voting age reform won few converts. Georgia adopted an eighteen-year-age franchise requirement in 1943, as did Kentucky in 1945, while Hawaii and Alaska in 1959 fixed voting age at nineteen and twenty, respectively. But the Michigan constitutional convention of 1961–1962 after extensive debate voted to retain the twenty-one-year limitation, as did the New York constitutional convention of 1965.

Thereafter, champions of voting age reform took their case to the halls of Congress. At length, in 1970, they won a decisive victory. The necessary provision in the Voting Rights Act went through Congress without serious opposition, as both liberal Democrats and Republican conservatives lent it their support.

A few months later, in *Oregon v. Mitchell* (1971), the 1970 Voting Rights Act came under the Court's scrutiny. So badly did the justices fragment on the constitutionality of the eighteen-year-old franchise rule and the thirty-day presidential residence requirement in presidential elections that no "opinion of the Court" was possible. Instead, Justice Black, who found himself in the majority upon all four principal constitutional issues involved announced the Court's decisions in an opinion in which no other justice joined.

By five to four votes, the Court held constitutional the franchise provision for eighteen-year-olds as applied to national elections but unconstitutional as applied to state elections. Four justices— Douglas, Brennan, White, and Marshall—thought the provision constitutional in its entirety, while four others—Burger, Stewart, Harlan, and Blackmun—thought it altogether unconstitutional.

Justice Black thus became the "swing man" for both portions of the Court's decision.

Black, with whom Douglas, Brennan, White, and Marshall concurred, thought Congress had the power to act in national elections by virtue of the authority granted it in Article I, Section 4 of the Constitution, to regulate "the time, places, and manner of holding elections for Senators and Representatives." But Black also thought it "a plain fact of history" that the framers had "never imagined that Congress would set the qualifications" for the franchise in state elections, a conclusion with which Burger, Stewart, Harlan, and Blackmun all agreed. Harlan, in a lengthy excursion into constitutional history, argued also that Congress in adopting the Fourteenth Amendment had not intended to convey to itself any authority over the franchise or over political rights generally.

Literacy tests and the abolition of residency requirements in presidential elections gave the Court less difficulty. By unanimous vote the justices confirmed the constitutionality of the nationwide provision on literacy tests, as authorized by congressional power to enforce the Fifteenth Amendment. (The literacy test provision was, after all, little more than an extension of the literacy test provisions of the 1965 law, which the Court had accepted in *South Carolina v. Katzenbach* and *Katzenbach v. Morgan.*)

Eight of the nine justices also joined in holding constitutional the thirty-day residence requirement in presidential elections. However, lines of reasoning varied widely from justice to justice. Black thought the requisite congressional power involved was derived from its authority to regulate federal elections, while Douglas argued that the right to vote for national officers was "a privilege and immunity of national citizenship," derived from the first section of the Fourteenth Amendment.

Brennan, developing a different "privileges and immunities" argument, contended that Congress properly could protect the right to interstate travel by removing the residential "penalty" the states had imposed thereon. And Justice Stewart, implicitly making very much of the same point, simply cited Justice Miller's century-old opinion in the Slaughter House cases. Harlan alone found himself unable to accept the constitutionality of the thirty-day rule. Thus the "privileges or immunities" clause of the Fourteenth Amendment, virtually dormant for a hundred years, suddenly took on a measure of vitality.

It is doubtful that extension of the franchise to eighteen-year-

olds worked any very considerable change in the American political system. As had been the case with women's suffrage following the adoption of the Nineteenth Amendment, the newly
enfranchised voters tended to reflect almost exactly the voting
pattens, ideology, and political allegiance of those already voting,
so that their addition to the electorate changed very little the
balance of power betwen parties, classes, and interest groups. No
"youth bloc" appeared in American politics, nor did the symbols,
tactics, or political myths of parties and politicians alter perceptibly. Eighteen-year-olds, in short, were for the most part simply
absorbed quietly into the mainstream of American political life.

Far more significant was the renewal of the Voting Rights Act
generally, with its system of federal examiners and federal registration in the states of the lower South. Between 1965 and 1975,
these provisions effected a dramatic increase in Negro voting,
which by the latter date in these states approximated seventy-five
per cent of the white vote. Meanwhile the number of black officeholders in the states of the former Confederacy rose from 500 in
1969 to about 2,000 in 1975. Nearly a score of American cities,
including Detroit, Atlanta, and Los Angeles now had black
mayors.

In July 1975, despite the pleas of Southern Senators and Representatives that the measure was no longer needed, Congress once
more extended the life of the Voting Rights Act, this time for a
period of seven years. It also made applicable the system of federal
examiners to states and districts with heavy Spanish-speaking or
Indian populations, so that Texas, Colorado, California, Alaska,
and portions of New York now fell under these provisions. Significantly, both houses passed the extension act by overwhelming
majorities, while in the Senate a bipartisan coalition easily invoked
cloture to frustrate a Southern filibuster. Thus by 1975, the Voting Rights Act's mechanisms and procedures bade fair to become
a more or less permanent part of the American political scene.

THE FUTURE OF THE BURGER COURT

By 1975, the four Nixon appointees to the Supreme Court had
assumed very nearly complete control of that tribunal's decision-
making process. Analysis of the Court's decisions during the
1974–1975 term revealed that the Nixon appointees voted as a
four-man block between eighty and ninety per cent of the time,
and that when they did so they controlled the decision at hand

an astonishing ninety-eight per cent of the time. This situation came about in considerable part because on most occasions either Stewart or White voted with the Nixon appointees, and in some part through the absence of Douglas, who because of illness was unable to participate in the latter portion of the session.

Yet Chief Justice Burger and his three conservative colleagues were by no means mere political instruments of the Nixon administration. In the crisis which beset the American presidency after 1970, the Court was to demonstrate on several occasions its devotion to the idea of constitutional supremacy and the independence of the judiciary. In so doing it preserved successfully the popular image of the Court as the ultimate oracle of the Constitution.

Chapter

37

President Nixon and the Crisis

in the Presidency

ON AUGUST 9, 1974, Richard Nixon, in a move unprecedented in American history, resigned from the office of President of the United States. He did so, manifestly, to avoid impeachment by the House of Representatives for "high crimes and misdemeanors" and subsequent trial by the Senate. Indeed at the moment of Nixon's resignation, his impeachment had already been voted by the House Judiciary Committee.

The precipitating factor both in Nixon's decision and in the House proceedings against him was his complicity after the fact in the so-called Watergate burglary of June 1972, in which agents of the White House, acting on direct orders, had burglarized the Washington headquarters of the Democratic Party. In reality, however, the Watergate scandal, while no trifling matter, was nothing more than a catalyst in a far more serious constitutional crisis: the assumption by the President of the United States of a series of extraordinary powers which when taken collectively marked the emergence of what historian Arthur M. Schlesinger, Jr., has called "The Imperial Presidency."

President Nixon's arrogation of power in no instance involved entirely new assertions of authority. On the contrary, the "Imperial Presidency" had roots extending back at least to Franklin

Roosevelt's time. But Nixon's assertion of executive prerogative, if not new, was unquestionably on an unprecedented scale. It was this fact, combined with the aura of corruption and lawlessness which surrounded his administration, that finally drove him from office.

THE PRESIDENT, FOREIGN POLICY, AND THE WAR POWER

It was in the field of foreign affairs and war-making that the assertion of presidential prerogative by Nixon appeared most blatant; yet it was precisely in this area that the precedents for the President's actions were most impressive. The resort to armed force unsanctioned by Congress as an instrument of foreign policy had been growing steadily since the days when Franklin Roosevelt in 1941 had waged an undeclared war against Nazi submarines in the Atlantic. Truman's plunge into large-scale war in Korea in 1950, Truman's movement of several "trip-wire" divisions to Germany in 1951, Kennedy's 1962 naval "quarantine" of Cuba, and Johnson's action in 1965 in landing the marines in Santo Domingo had further damaged the constitutional prerogative of Congress to declare war.

In the beginning, the American military intervention in Vietnam had a more adequate constitutional foundation. The so-called "Tonkin Gulf" joint resolution adopted by Congress in August 1964, authorized the President to "repel any armed attack against the forces of the United States and to prevent further aggression" in Southeast Asia. Whether the Tonkin Gulf Resolution in fact amounted to a formal declaration of war is uncertain; most members of Congress apparently thought not, although Senator Sam Ervin of North Carolina declared that it was. Whatever the Tonkin Gulf Resolution's legal status, President Johnson thereafter relied upon it and upon his inherent constitutional powers as Commander-in-Chief to stage a massive war in Southeast Asia.

Under President Nixon the constitutional status of the war in Southeast Asia altered substantially. In the spring of 1970, the President ordered an invasion of Cambodia, thereby commencing a new war in a foreign state at least nominally neutral. In so doing, Nixon consulted Congress not at all; instead he rested his action solely upon his constitutional powers as Commander-in-Chief, as he had done for some time in Vietnam. Thereafter a disillusioned Congress, aroused at length by outraged public opinion, sought to bring hostilities in Southeast Asia to a close, but for a long time its efforts proved almost completely unavailing.

In January 1971, the two houses repealed the Tonkin Gulf Resolution. Conceivably this action withdrew from the President further constitutional authority to conduct hostilities in Southeast Asia. In fact, however, repeal had no visible impact either upon the conduct of hostilities or upon the intermittent presidential diplomatic negotiations for peace, although the President was already "winding down" the involvement of American ground forces·in Vietnam.

In January 1973, the President finally terminated American military operations in Vietnam, by means of an armistice negotiated with North Vietnam and the Viet Cong. But the air war against the Cambodian "rebels" continued until Congress, in June 1973, finally voted to cut off all supplies for its support.

Meanwhile the Supreme Court had persistently rejected all attempts to involve it in the constitutional controversy over the President's prosecution of an undeclared war. In 1967 it twice refused to grant certiorari from lower court decisions upholding plenary Executive war powers. Again, in 1970, the Court let stand a unanimous Court of Appeals decision in *Massachusetts v. Laird*, holding that since the President in carrying on the Vietnam war had acted "with steady congressional support," the Constitution had "not been breached."

Finally, in August 1973, a district court ruled the war in Cambodia unconstitutional and issued an injunction against its continuance. But an Appellate Court order immediately stayed the injunction. And when Justice Douglas vacated the stay, a telephone poll of the other justices by Justice Marshall reinstituted the stay. Thereupon, in *Holtzman v. Schlesinger* (1973), the Appellate Court, now free to proceed, invoked the doctrine of "political questions" to hold that the federal courts could not intervene against a presidential war.

In October 1973, Congress passed, over President Nixon's veto, a War Powers Act, designed to impose some congressional control over Executive war-making. This measure, sponsored in 1972 and again in 1973 by Senator Jacob Javits of New York, provided that, in the absence of a formal declaration of war by Congress, a President could initiate hostilities only under four conditions: to repel an attack on the United States; to protect American armed forces overseas; to protect the lives of Americans abroad; or to fulfill the specific statutory military obligations of the United States. Such action, the new law provided, could not be continued more than sixty days without congressional consent.

It was doubtful, however, whether the War Powers Act constituted any very serious check upon presidential war-making prerogative. On the contrary, its permissive provisions were so broad, critics pointed out, that they might well be used in the future to sanction virtually any kind of military action a President wished to initiate. The War Powers Act, in short, came uncomfortably close to confirming arbitrary Executive war-making prerogative rather than checking it.

Yet the strong public reaction against the Vietnam war undoubtedly cost the President, for the moment at least, something of his discretionary war powers. In the spring of 1975, President Gerald Ford, faced with the imminent collapse of South Vietnam under heavy assault from Hanoi, felt obliged to ask congressional permission before undertaking to furnish the Saigon government with badly needed war supplies. Congress, after some sparring with the Executive, refused. It remained to be seen whether this rebuff represented a permanent check to long-established Executive war-making prerogative.

THE GROWTH OF INTERNAL EXECUTIVE PREROGATIVE POWER

Since 1917, the exigencies of war had promoted the growth of a general executive prerogative power not only in foreign policy but also in internal affairs. Both World War I and World War II had stimulated an extraordinary exercise of presidential prerogative power, based only in part upon statutory authority. This trend was checked temporarily when, in 1952, even while the Korean War was in progress, the Supreme Court denied categorically in the celebrated *Steel Seizure* case that a general internal executive law-making power existed.[1] For a time after the Korean War, the exercise of presidential prerogative power in internal affairs was in abeyance.

With the Vietnam war, the exercise of presidential prerogative power blossomed once more. During the Johnson administration the process was cautious, restrained, and based for the most part upon plausible statutory authority. But even before the Watergate scandal broke, as Professor Alexander Bickel of the Yale Law School later observed, Nixon was "well on his way to an extraordinary dominance" over the entire structure of government. Former

---

[1] See pp. 811–814.

Justice Abe Fortas thought Nixon's actions added up to an "attempted *coup d'etat;* a fundamental alteration—a subversion—of our basic constitutional structure." And historian Arthur Schlesinger, Jr., argued that Nixon sought to base his "imperial presidency" upon a Napoleon-like conception of plebiscitary power; that is, extraordinary executive authority sanctioned not by the Constitution but by popular ratification at the polls.

More specifically, President Nixon impounded monies appropriated by Congress on such a scale as to give him virtually an unlimited line-item veto over appropriation bills, in obvious defiance of the Constitution. He deliberately resorted to selective enforcement of federal law, in evident disregard of his constitutional mandate to "take care that the laws be faithfully executed." He resorted also to a dubious and unprecedented use of the pocket veto to suppress congressional measures of which he disapproved. He appealed to the courts in an unsuccessful attempt to impose "prior restraint" upon the publication of the so-called *Pentagon Papers,* which he regarded as an embarrassment to his administration. He engaged in an extraordinary but virtually unchallenged manipulation of the nation's economy, basing his authority principally upon a series of venerable but unrepealed proclamations of emergency, some of them extending back to 1933. He instituted a far-reaching program of internal wiretapping and Executive espionage in an attempt to strengthen governmental security against "subversives." And he climaxed all this by challenging the subpoena powers of the federal courts, in an effort to conceal his administration's complicity in the Watergate scandal.

In exercising this vast array of dubious Executive authority, President Nixon depended hardly at all upon the Cabinet, which had been in decline as a policy-making instrument since Franklin Roosevelt's time. This situation had come about originally as a consequence of F.D.R.'s propensity to depend upon a variety of intimate advisors—Rexford Tugwell, Raymond Moley, Ben Cohen, Harry Hopkins, and so on—without regard to the official status of such individuals.

Under Presidents Truman, Eisenhower, Kennedy, and Johnson, individual cabinet members had on occasion exercised very considerable influence and power, particularly in matters of foreign policy, as the roles of Dean Acheson, John Foster Dulles, Charles Wilson, Robert McNamara, and Dean Rusk had demonstrated. But President Nixon allowed his cabinet, with the exception of an occasional cabinet officer, most notably Attorney General John

Mitchell and Secretary of State Henry Kissinger, to fall back into a near-powerless obscurity.

Instead, access to President Nixon's inner circle was limited to a small staff of White House administrative assistants, whose role was somewhat reminiscent of Andrew Jackson's "Kitchen Cabinet," except that their positions were more formalized. Employment of administrative assistants by the President had been authorized by the Executive Reorganization Act of 1939. But from FDR to Johnson, the role played by White House assistants had been hardly more than that of highly competent executive secretaries, possessed of no real influence or power. Nixon's principal administrative assistants—H. R. Haldeman, John Ehrlichman, John Dean, Egil Krogh, and so on—were in fact powerful ministers of state, whose advice very largely shaped the internal policies of the Nixon administration.

Through the isolation from Congress, the press, public opinion, and the American people which this closed executive staff system involved, the President experienced a grievous loss of contact with day-to-day political reality. This insulation from reality was to contribute decisively to the administration's tragic decline and ultimate fall from power.

IMPOUNDMENT: AN UNOFFICIAL LINE-ITEM VETO

Perhaps Nixon's most specific violation of the constitutional limitations of the presidency was his impoundment of monies voted by Congress for purposes which he did not approve. The result was not only to give him what amounted to a line-item veto over the provisions of congressional appropriation acts, but also to arrogate to the Executive a virtually uncontrollable power to block any federal program whatever involving the expenditure of money.

Nixon's impoundment program was by no means without some precedent. Jefferson in 1803 had held up a $50,000 gunboat appropriation for a short time (though merely to ascertain what model was most advisable), while Grant in 1876 had interpreted a congressional appropriation for public works as not "obligatory" in view of the current economic depression. And Franklin Roosevelt in 1941, anticipating the will of Congress, had suspended expenditures on public works not related to the war effort. Even as he acted, however, FDR had assured Congress that impoundment could not constitutionally be used to "nullify the express will of Congress."

More to the point were the impoundments by Presidents Truman, Kennedy, and Johnson between 1949 and 1969 of funds for military appropriations of one sort or another. But in virtually every one of these instances, impoundment could be justified either by the permissive language of the appropriation act itself or by the President's action in obtaining the unofficial consent of Congress. Military impoundment, it also could be argued, was also a special case which conceivably fell within the President's powers as Commander-in-Chief.

President Nixon's impoundments, the first of which occurred in 1969, were without precedent in frequency, in the amount of money involved, and in purpose. By the end of 1973, the President had impounded monies from more than one hundred different federal programs, involving aggregate expenditures of more than $15 billion.

Many of Nixon's impoundment actions had to do with federal programs for pollution control, housing, assistance to public education, and the like. For the first time, impoundment represented the imposition upon federal policy of a philosophy of state contrary to that upon which Congress had acted. The President, in other words, was doing what FDR in 1941 had warned he could not properly do: substituting his legislative will for that of Congress. But Nixon, in a celebrated press conference in January 1973, defended his right to make national policy through impoundment, in particular with respect to prices and tax policy. His constitutional right to do so was, he declared, "absolutely clear."

In February 1975, some months after President Nixon had resigned his office, the Supreme Court in effect condemned the entire Nixon impoundment program as illegal. At issue in *Train v. City of New York*, was the power of the President under the provisions of the Federal Water Pollution Control Act of 1972 to refuse to allot to the states for expenditure a total of $6 billion appropriated by Congress for the fiscal years 1973 and 1974.

Justice White's opinion for a unanimous Court drew a careful distinction between the mandatory language of the law with respect to the allocation of the appropriation itself and the discretionary power of the act's administrator to refuse to "obligate" funds to a project where the state had not complied with the provisions of the law. The wording of the statute, White held, left the President no power to withhold "allocation" of the sums appropriated, and his action in doing so had been in violation of law. White's language carefully avoided any reference to the constitutional limits of presidential power, but the implications of his opinion were none-theless clear: the entire Executive impoundment program, except where authorized by permissive statutory language, had been illegal.

Meanwhile, in July 1974, Congress adopted a Congressional Budget and Impoundment Control Act, which attempted to deal with the impoundment problem by statute. This statute required the President to recommend to Congress in a special message any proposal to impound funds. Thereafter either house might effect a rejection of the proposal by a resolution of disapproval. This measure, together with the Court's decisive stand, promised to dispose of the impoundment issue as a major constitutional question unless—as seemed improbable—the new act failed to pass the Court's scrutiny.

SELECTIVE LAW ENFORCEMENT AND THE POCKET VETO

Impoundment was in effect a kind of selective law enforcement; by it, the President decided upon his own authority which appro-priation acts he would recognize and which he would nullify. Closely related to this form of executive nullification was Nixon's decision from time to time not to enforce one statute or another of whose policy implications he disapproved. His procedure here was reminiscent of Roosevelt's warning to Congress in 1942 that he would refuse to enforce certain provisions of the Emergency Price Control Act unless Congress repealed them forthwith. But there was one important difference: FDR had asked Congress for repeal; Nixon on two notable occasions imposed executive nullification without bothering to ask Congress for repeal.

In July 1969, the Nixon administration announced formally that the Department of Justice and the Department of Health, Educa-tion and Welfare would no longer enforce Title VI of the Civil Rights Act of 1964. This was the provision which prohibited dis-crimination based upon race, color, religion, or national origin in programs receiving federal financial assistance, and which required a fund cutoff in those instances in which HEW ascertained that such discrimination existed. A federal district court pronounced the administration's action to be illegal, but no change in administrative practice resulted. The implications were clear: the Nixon ad-ministration was pursuing a policy toward racial discrimination inconsistent with the intent of the law.

Another dramatic step was taken in January 1973 when the administration decided to dismantle the Office of Economic Opportunity, an agency created by statute as a part of Lyndon Johnson's ill-starred campaign to end poverty. The Nixon-appointed OEO director, acting under presidential order, thereupon set to work to liquidate the agency's personnel and to terminate its field activities.

The legal excuse offered for this action was simply that the President had decided not to include an appropriation for OEO in his forthcoming budget message to Congress. A federal district court ruling partially checked the formal process of dismantling, but the OEO nonetheless headed for innocuous obscurity.

The reverse of this process was President Nixon's attempt to endow an administrative agency created by Congress with functions it had not authorized. The Subversive Activities Control Board, whose activities had been checked sharply by the Supreme Court in 1965 in the Albertson case, had for some time been moribund. But in July 1971, the President, acting without congressional authority, issued an executive order endowing the SACB with certain new administrative functions. Congress, indignant, responded in 1972 with a statutory provision denying the agency any funds for its new functions. In practice this made little difference, since the SACB remained moribund.

Still another "legislative" device adopted by President Nixon was his unprecedented and highly unorthodox use of the "pocket veto." Article I, Section 7, of the Constitution allows the President to kill a bill enacted by Congress within ten days of an adjournment simply by failing to sign it into law. The language of the Constitution poses a constitutional question of some importance: what is an "adjournment?"

In 1929, in the *Pocket Veto Case*, the Court had ruled that the President could constitutionally impose a pocket veto at the end of a session of Congress, as well as at the adjournment incident to the ending of a Congressional term. The President's right to resort to a pocket veto during an even shorter adjournment—a holiday recess of a few days—remained uncertain. But in *Wright v. United States* (1938) the Court ruled that during a short recess (in this instance one of three days), the Secretary of the Senate had the constitutional power to receive a veto message. The plain implication of Chief Justice Hughes' opinion was that the pocket veto could not properly be applied to an adjournment of only a few days.

But in December 1970, President Nixon nonetheless imposed a pocket veto on a bill adopted by Congress during its Christmas recess. The bill, Family Practice of Medicine Act, involved appropriations of some $225 million for hospital and medical school support, and had been adopted by the two houses by overwhelming majorities eight days before the recess. Two days after the recess commenced, however, President Nixon announced that he was refusing to sign the law, and that because of the pocket veto provision he would also refuse to return it to Congress. The President's strategy was evident: instead of a two-thirds majority veto, which he would exercise were he to return the measure to Congress with a veto message, he had in effect endowed himself in this instance with an absolute veto. Senator Jacob Javits of New York declared in indignation that the President's pocket veto was "illegal." In 1972 and again in 1973 Congress appropriated monies intended to give the "vetoed" law force and effect; however, Nixon in turn ignored the appropriation acts.

THE PRESIDENTIAL SECURITY SYSTEM

Meanwhile President Nixon established an elaborate White House-controlled security and espionage system, intended both to protect the country against subversives and the Executive Office against disclosure of confidential materials either to Congress or to the nation generally. The entire system posed grave constitutional questions, under both the Bill of Rights and the separation of powers.

Early in his administration, President Nixon expressed dissatisfaction with the system of security against subversive activity established by the Federal Bureau of Investigation under J. Edgar Hoover. In its place, he sought to develop a system of his own. In July 1970, the President endorsed and promulgated secretly a so-called Decision Memorandum prepared by Tom Huston, a youthful White House staff member, which authorized a comprehensive program for surveillance of those Americans who "pose a major threat to our internal security."

The Huston Memorandum called for the warrantless search of domestic mails, infiltration by government agents into radical student organizations on university campuses, the monitoring of all overseas mail, cable, and phone communications by American citizens, and outright burglary of both offices and private homes where surveillance authorities thought it necessary. The President at the same time ordered warrantless wiretaps placed on thirteen members of the National Security Council as well as on several newspapermen. None of this rested on any statutory authority.

The Huston security program was blatantly unconstitutional on its face. Ironically, J. Edgar Hoover, who hitherto had hardly established a reputation as a defender of constitutional liberty, forthwith denounced the program as illegal and unacceptable. The President thereupon ordered the plan abandoned.

In reality, it is doubtful that the Huston program involved anything very new. Hearings by the Senate Internal Security Subcommittee in September 1975, established that the CIA had for some years been intercepting and reading mail addressed to American citizens from Iron Curtain countries. The FBI, testimony made clear, in the previous twenty years had engaged in large-scale warrantless wiretapping and interception of private mail, including on one occasion that of President Nixon himself. Moreover, it had carried out more than one hundred burglaries—all in the name of internal security.

In any event, Executive-authorized domestic espionage, mail searches, and the like continued. Early in 1971, the President set up an Intelligence Evaluation Committee to coordinate undercover White House espionage activities. In July, following the controversy over publication of the so-called *Pentagon Papers*, the President also established a special White House espionage unit—shortly dubbed the "Plumbers"—and placed Egil Krogh in charge. In effect, Nixon gave Krogh and the "Plumbers" carte blanche authority to engage in whatever forms of espionage they thought necessary in the interests of national security.

The "Plumbers" immediately embarked upon a program of nationwide espionage altogether unauthorized by any statutory or constitutional authority. It was a "Plumbers" task force which in late August burglarized the office of the psychiatrist who had treated Daniel Ellsberg, the dissident Defense Department employee who had purloined the *Pentagon Papers* for *The New York Times*. So outrageous were the "Plumbers'" antics that John Ehrlichman, astonished and indignant, dissolved the unit in December 1971. But the "Plumbers'" personnel, still available, were presently reassigned to "CREEP"—the White House-controlled Committee to Re-elect the President. It was a CREEP task force which, in June 1972, staged the bungled burglary of the Democratic National Committee in the Watergate apartment complex.

THE SUPREME COURT AND THE NIXON SECURITY SYSTEM

The Supreme Court early found occasion to condemn important portions of the Nixon security program as unconstitutional. Publication in June 1971, by *The New York Times* and the *Washington Post*, of the *Pentagon Papers*, the Defense Department's "inside" history of American involvement in war in Southeast Asia, precipitated the first contretemps between the Executive and the Judiciary. At issue in this instance was the administration's attempt to invoke "prior restraint" to suppress publication of materials it considered to be damaging to national security.

Both newspapers rejected out of hand an initial administration request to halt publication of the disputed *Papers*. Attorney General Mitchell thereupon sought and obtained from a federal district court in New York City a temporary injunction halting publication by *The New York Times*, on the ground that it would cause "grave and irreparable" injury to the United States, and also was in violation of Title 18, Section 793, of the Espionage Act of 1917 forbidding the "communication" of defense information harmful to the security of the United States. The Court of Appeals for the Second Circuit shortly in effect sustained the injunction. Meanwhile, a district court in Washington, D.C., and the Court of Appeals for the District of Columbia refused the government's plea for an injunction against publication by the *Washington Post*. Immediate appeal to the Supreme Court from both appellate court decisions followed.

In a brief *per curiam* opinion, the Court in *New York Times Co. v. United States* (1971), observed that "any system of prior restraints comes to this court bearing a heavy presumption against its constitutional validity." The government, the opinion continued, had not met the "heavy burden" involved; accordingly it reversed the outstanding injunction against *The New York Times* and confirmed the District of Columbia decision, thereby removing all further restraint upon publication. As was customary, the *per curiam* opinion was unsigned, but every one of the nine justices entered either a concurring or dissenting opinion.

For Justices Black and Douglas, both of whom subscribed to an absolutist view of the freedom of the press guaranteed by the First Amendment, the constitutional problem at hand was simple: under no circumstances could the courts ever impose prior restraint by injunction, no matter how great was the threat to national security. Justice Brennan's denunciation of prior restraint also was very nearly categorical, but he did concede guardedly that in wartime there might be "a single, extremely narrow class of cases in which the First Amendment's ban on prior judicial restraint may be overridden."

Justices White, Stewart, and Marshall, on the other hand, all centered their argument upon the absence of any adequate statutory authority enabling the federal courts to issue prior-restraint injunctions in national security cases. Both White and Marshall pointed out that Congress in debating passage of the Espionage Act in 1917 had specifically rejected a provision empowering the Executive to seek such injunctions, so that Section 793 properly could not be read as authorizing them. Instead, they pointed out, Congress in enacting the 1917 law had relied upon the traditional power of the government to punish offenses through criminal prosecution in the courts.

Chief Justice Burger and Justices Harlan and Blackmun, dissenting, all emphasized the "almost irresponsibly feverish" fashion in which the Court had disposed of the case. Vital facts, Harlan protested, were still unknown and vital questions of law remained unexplained. All three justices also repudiated what Blackmun called "First Amendment absolutism," implying that the courts should have been more flexible in adjusting the conflict between First Amendment rights and national security. Accordingly, the three dissenters would have affirmed the injunction against *The New York Times*, pending further argument conducted under what Harlan called "full ground rules."

Thus, for the first time, a demand for the imposition of prior restraint in the name of national security clashed head-on with the guarantees of the First Amendment. In this instance, prior restraint lost. But a close reading of the Stewart, Brennan, White, and Marshall opinions makes it clear that the libertarian triumph was by no means unconditional. Lying just below the surface of several of the opinions was a half-expressed agreement with the proposition that in a national security crisis of the first magnitude—involving, for example, wartime troop movements or battle plans—the administration would have obtained its injunction.

Even as the Court spoke, a bloody *de facto* war was indeed in progress. But the administration's lawyers had been unable to convince a majority of the justices that publication of the *Pentagon Papers* presented any very considerable threat to national security. Had they succeeded in doing so, it seems probable that the outstanding injunction against the *Times* would have been confirmed.

A year later, in *United States v. United States District Court* (1972), the President's system of wiretapping for domestic security surveillance purposes also ran afoul of the Court. At issue in the case was the constitutionality of warrantless security surveillance, conducted by the Attorney General's office on the authority of the President, of a defendant accused of bombing a CIA office in Ann Arbor, Michigan.

The government claimed that such surveillance, conducted without prior judicial approval, constituted "a reasonable exercise of the President's power . . . to protect the national security." Attorney General Mitchell argued, also, that the administration had acted pursuant to Section 2511 of the Omnibus Crime Control and Safe Streets Act of 1968, which provided among other things that nothing contained in the act "shall limit the constitutional power of the President to take such measures as he deems necessary to protect the United States against the overthrow of the government by force or other unlawful means or against any clear and present danger to the structure and existence of the Government."

Justice Powell, who spoke for a unanimous Court, first pointed out that the President could not properly derive any authority from Section 2511. The legislative history of that provision, he declared, demonstrated that it was no more than "an expression of Congressional neutrality" with respect to any constitutional powers which the President might have in the field of domestic security. The provision could not be read as an attempt by Congress to endow him with any extra-constitutional grant of power.

Powell then turned to a more fundamental issue: the President's claim to an "inherent power" to conduct electronic surveillance for domestic security purposes without judicial approval. Acts of sabotage against the government, he conceded, "were elementary truths"; yet the fact remained that domestic security cases involved "a convergence of First and Fourth Amendment values" which made it imperative to safeguard proper constitutional procedures. The price of lawful public dissent, he continued, must not be a dread of subjection to an unchecked surveillance power. Accordingly, Powell rejected outright the argument that internal security matters were "too subtle and complex" to permit Fourth Amendment guarantees to be observed.

The decision in *United States v. United States District Court* handed down only two days after the Watergate burglary, resulted in a flurry of Justice Department orders terminating security wiretaps. The check to warrantless electronic surveillance, however, was illusory. Large-scale wiretapping by government officers, with the express or implied consent of the administration, continued.

WATERGATE: NIXON'S FIGHT AGAINST IMPEACHMENT

In November 1972, President Nixon won reelection by the largest popular and electoral majority in American history. It was possible to read the outcome of the contest between him and Democratic candidate George McGovern as a validation of sorts for the theory of the plebiscitary presidency. Under the terms of this theory the Chief Executive could properly exercise a general prerogative power in the conduct of his office without any very nice regard for the limitations which the Constitution imposed upon him, provided only that he recognized that his assumed authority was subject to popular ratification through the electoral process. Had not Nixon proceeded to destroy his administration through his participation in a criminal conspiracy to conceal White House complicity in the Watergate burglary, the concept of the plebiscitary presidency undoubtedly would have been vastly strengthened by the close of his second term of office.

On the surface, the Watergate break-in on June 17, 1972 had little to do with high constitutional theory. But in the two years between President Nixon's instructions for a "coverup" and his final resignation, the "Watergate affair" came to represent far more in the public mind than a mere burglary. Instead, it now symbolized an administration with little regard for the ethics of public office or for the legal limitations imposed by the Constitution and federal law upon the President's conduct of the great affairs of state.

Thus, the Nixon administration had attempted to pressure the Internal Revenue Service into employing income tax investigations as a weapon with which to pillory its political enemies. At the same time there had been an inexplicable carelessness in the President's own income tax returns: a gift of the President's papers to the National Archives had been falsely back-dated in order to allow a tax credit actually ruled out by a recently enacted federal statute fixing a cut-off date for credits of this kind. And there had been other gross administration improprieties: in the handling of private and corporate gifts for campaign purposes, and in the reckless fashion in which the President had spent government monies to improve his private estates at San Clemente and Key Biscayne. In all this, administrative lawlessness and malfeasance merged with the constitutional crisis over the President's extraordinary exercise of Executive power to become a single issue in the public mind.

The lengthy political crisis over "Watergate" came to focus

upon two major constitutional issues: "executive privilege" and the scope of the impeachment power. Executive privilege had to do with the alleged constitutional right of the President to withhold documents from Congress and from the courts. The issue was not a new one in American history. President Washington in 1792 had insisted upon his right to withhold certain papers from the House of Representatives in connection with General St. Clair's defeat by the Ohio Indians. Again, in 1795, he had refused a request from the House of Representatives for Executive papers having to do with the negotiation of the Jay Treaty. And in 1807 Jefferson had successfully defied a *subpoena duces tecum* directed to him by John Marshall, presiding as a United States Circuit Judge in the Burr treason trial.

Thereafter other Presidents, when it suited their interest to do so, had refused congressional requests for executive documents. In a notable modern case, President Truman in 1948 had successfully defied a House resolution directing him to turn over whatever executive papers its committees found necessary "to properly perform their duties." The President, said Truman in a general order to all Executive Departments, would determine on the basis of "the public interest in each case" when papers were to be handed over to Congress or its committees. The Eisenhower, Kennedy, and Johnson administrations subsequently adopted much the same position. And in 1954 Attorney General Herbert Brownell claimed an "uncontrolled discretion" for the Executive in deciding whether or not to comply with congressional requests for documentary materials. Curiously, however, the President's right to withhold papers from Congress had never been tested before the Supreme Court.

"Executive privilege," with respect both to Congress and to the federal courts, now became a major constitutional issue, as the Nixon administration fought to conceal its involvement in the Watergate break-in and the subsequent coverup conspiracy. In February 1973, as the press succeeded in bringing to light many of the details of the Watergate break-in, the Senate voted 77 to 0 to establish a seven-man Select Committee to inquire into "illegal, improper, or unethical activities" in connection with the recent election.

The Select Committee's hearings, staged between May and late August under the dramatic chairmanship of Senator Sam Ervin of North Carolina, directly implicated former Attorney General

Mitchell in the break-in and the President himself in the subsequent coverup. Equally important, the hearings brought to light the existence of a more or less complete set of tape recordings of Nixon's private conversations with the White House staff.

The Ervin Committee thereupon sought to obtain by subpoena five critically important tapes it believed would assist its investigation, only to encounter a firm presidential refusal. "I cannot and will not," Nixon declared, "consent to giving any investigatory body private presidential papers."

The Ervin Committee thereupon voted unanimously to appeal to the courts. But in mid-October federal district Judge John Sirica rejected the Committee's plea for a *subpoena duces tecum* directed to the President. The long-standing tradition of executive privilege with respect to congressional demands for executive documents had been decisive.

Presidential defiance of a subpoena addressed to the Executive by the federal courts proved to be a different matter. Early in May 1973, a Senate resolution had established the Office of Special Prosecutor by agreement with Attorney General Elliott Richardson and had endowed the Prosecutor with sweeping powers to investigate the Watergate scandal. Richardson in turn had named Harvard Law School Professor Archibald Cox to the new position.

On July 23, Cox addressed a *subpoena duces tecum* to the President, ordering him to produce a series of Presidential tapes covering the period from June 20, 1972 to April 15, 1973 before a grand jury of the District of Columbia. Two days later, Nixon formally refused to comply, declaring that "it would be inconsistent with the public interest and with the Constitutional position of the presidency" for him to do so. When Judge Sirica directed Nixon to comply with the subpoena, the President's lawyers took an appeal to the Circuit Court for the District of Columbia, claiming that the district court order "threatened the continued existence of the presidency as a functioning institution."

In mid-October, the Circuit Court ruled, five to two, in *Nixon v. Sirica* (1973),[2] that the President's claim of executive privilege was in this instance invalid, and that the President must comply with the subpoena. The majority judges conceded that presidential conversations are "presumptively privileged." But it was for

---

[2] 487 F 2nd 700.

the courts to determine whether "a mere assertion of privilege" was sufficient to overcome the need of the party subpoenaing the document in question.

In the present instance, the opinion concluded, the President's invocation of executive privilege "must fail in the face of the uniquely powerful showing made by the special prosecutor." Significantly, the court relied rather heavily for precedent upon the *subpoena duces tecum* which Chief Justice John Marshall had addressed to Jefferson during the Burr trial.

The President now attempted to arrange a compromise with Cox, whereby the Prosecutor would agree to accept an authenticated summary of the nine contested tapes in place of the tapes themselves. As might have been expected, Cox refused. Nixon thereupon invoked his authority as Chief Executive: he ordered Cox "as an employee of the Executive Branch to make no further attempt by judicial process" to obtain the tapes in question. But, in a defiant press conference, Cox pointed out that Nixon in reality was refusing outright to obey a direct order of the appellate court.

The President thereupon directed Richardson to remove Cox from office. However, both Richardson and Assistant Attorney General William Ruckelshaus in turn refused to obey Nixon's order and forthwith resigned. Ultimately Assistant Attorney General Robert Bork, who was now precipitated suddenly into the Attorney General's office, executed the President's order.

In discharging Cox, Nixon was undoubtedly upon firm constitutional ground. Cox was technically an employee of the Executive Department, and the President's right to remove subordinate executive officers, which Presidents Jackson and Andrew Johnson had heatedly defended, had been undisputed since the Supreme Court's decision in the Myers case.[3]

Politically, however, "The Saturday Night Massacre," as the press dubbed Nixon's action, was disastrous. All across the nation, an outraged people, including party leaders, newspaper editors, students, university professors, and businessmen, attacked Cox's discharge as an outrageous violation of elementary public morality. The President, the *Baltimore Sun* declared, had "lost touch with truth and principle." *The New York Times*, the *Detroit News*, and the *Atlanta Journal* called for the President's immediate resignation.

---

[3] See above, pp. 675–677.

Thus pressured, Nixon capitulated. "The President does not defy the law," the President's attorney Charles Alan Wright declared a few days later, as he promised Judge Sirica to deliver the contested tapes forthwith. But the fact of the matter was that Nixon now was very nearly destroyed politically.

THE AGNEW RESIGNATION AND CONGRESSIONAL STEPS TOWARD NIXON'S IMPEACHMENT

The Cox "firestorm," as presidential aide Alexander Haig called it, led to the first serious consideration by congressional leaders of the possibility of Nixon's impeachment. The idea of the President's impeachment also had been rendered more palatable by the forced resignation of Vice President Spiro Agnew in early October and his subsequent replacement by Representative Gerald Ford of Michigan.

In late September it had become apparent that there was a strong likelihood that Agnew would be indicted by a federal court in Maryland on a charge of income tax evasion. In an effort to avoid such a development, Agnew had asked the leaders of both parties in the House of Representatives to move for his impeachment, arguing that as Vice President he was immune to the criminal processes of the courts and that impeachment was the only appropriate mode of procedure against him. But House leaders, after consultation, had refused to accept Agnew's contention and had declined to intervene. Thereafter Attorney General Richardson had worked out an arrangement in accordance with which Agnew had agreed to plead *nolo contendere* [4] to a single count of income tax evasion but had been allowed to resign as Vice President without the imposition of any further punishment by the court.

Agnew's resignation, the first such since that of Calhoun in 1832, brought the provisions of the Twenty-Fifth Amendment into play. Section 2 of that amendment stipulated that "whenever a vacancy occurs in the office of Vice President, the President shall nominate a Vice President who shall take office upon confirmation by a majority vote of both Houses of Congress." With Agnew's resignation, accordingly, President Nixon submitted Ford's name to the two houses for the vacated office. Ford was a staunchly conservative Republican and political ally of the administration, but he enjoyed a high reputation for personal integrity, and his confirma-

---

[4] Literally, "I do not wish to contest," i.e., in effect, an admission of guilt.

tion by Congress came a few weeks later without serious opposition.

Meanwhile, in late October, Speaker Carl Albert of the House of Representatives called in Representative Peter Rodino, Chairman of the House Judiciary Committee, and asked him to launch an impeachment inquiry very quietly. In response, Rodino assembled a staff under John Doar, a former Justice Department lawyer, and told it to begin gathering evidence.

The Doar staff immediately ran into a serious constitutional problem: the long-standing uncertainty over what constituted an impeachable offense. The difficulty lay in the Constitution's laconic provision in Article II, Section 4, that the President, Vice President, and other civil officers of the United States were impeachable for "Treason, Bribery, or other high Crimes and Misdemeanors." Treason was defined elsewhere in the Constitution itself, while bribery was a well-defined common law offense.

But what did "other high crimes and misdemeanors" mean? Did it mean that impeachable offenses were limited to serious common-law felonies, specific statutory crimes, and specific violations of the Constitution itself? Or were gross negligence in office, neglect of correct Constitutional procedure, or a general "aura" of corruption in a President's administration also impeachable? To put the matter differently, was impeachment essentially a quasi-judicial process for removing an official charged with a crime? Or might it also be deemed to be a quasi-political process for removing an official whose main offense lay in a gross breach of public trust? Since it was not yet at all certain that Nixon had committed any specific felony, the issue of the President's impeachability for some time appeared to turn on the answer to these questions.

Raoul Berger of the Harvard Law School argued that in England and the United States impeachment had traditionally been a quasi-political process for removing an official who had breached the public trust in some gross fashion. Both the Doar staff and Democratic majority in the House Judiciary Committee obviously were heavily influenced by Berger's argument.

To a constitutional historian, the precedents were not so clear. In Britain, before the rise of cabinet government, impeachment unquestionably had been a political device whereby Parliament removed a Minister of the King it found objectionable. But impeachment of this kind disappeared after Walpole's time—rendered obsolete by the cabinet system of government. In America the delegates to the Constitutional Convention of 1787 had specifically rejected a proposal by Mason and Gerry to make "maladministration" an impeachable offense, after Madison had objected that such a provision would make the President removable at "the pleasure of the Senate."

In the first Congress Madison himself had implied that a President might be impeachable for the misdeeds of his subordinates—something close to "maladministration" once more. But in the two major impeachment trials of the nineteenth century—those of Justice Chase and President Johnson—acquittal had followed failure by the House lawyers to establish clearly that the "defendant" had committed either a statutory offense or a serious crime.

Not unexpectedly these two conflicting interpretations of the impeachment process now spilled over into a public argument between the President's lawyers and the Doar staff. In a memorandum of February 20, 1974, the Committee staff contended that impeachment was a "remedial measure" and "constitutional safety valve" whereby a President might be removed for "substantial misconduct" not necessarily of a specifically criminal nature. But in a counter-memorandum of February 27, the President's lawyers argued that "high crimes and misdemeanors" must be read to require the commission of a specific criminal offense by an executive officer. American history, they declared, supported only this interpretation. In the forceful vernacular of the moment, this became the "smoking gun" theory of impeachment. For a time, lacking hard evidence of a specific Nixon criminal or statutory offense, the Judiciary Committee stalled.

But on March 1 a Washington grand jury, acting upon evidence submitted to it by Leon Jaworski, Cox's successor as Special Prosecutor, brought in indictments charging Mitchell, Ehrlichman, Haldeman, and four other White House aides with conspiracy to defraud the United States and conspiracy to obstruct justice. Significantly, the grand jury named the President as an unindicted co-conspirator. And in mid-April the Special Prosecutor issued a new *subpoena duces tecum* directed to Nixon requiring the surrender of certain additional tapes needed for the forthcoming criminal trial.

The desperate President responded once more by attempting to quash the subpoena. The dispute between him and the Special Prosecutor, Nixon's lawyers now argued, was essentially "intra-Executive" in character and was therefore "non-justiciable." The district court, they again contended, was without authority to review an assertion of executive privilege by the President. Meanwhile the President, in a frantic attempt to clear himself of the criminal charges now pressing in upon him, published a carefully edited version of the disputed tapes—a move that served only to damage him further politically.

On May 20, Judge Sirica denied the President's motion to quash the Jaworski subpoena. Judge Sirica based his decision upon the Appellate Court's opinion in *Nixon v. Sirica* the previous fall. Thereafter, the President's lawyers and the Special Prosecutor in a series of petitions and cross-petitions brought the dispute over the tapes to the Supreme Court.

On July 24, the Court in a unanimous eight-justice opinion ruled in *United States v. Nixon* (1974) that the President must obey the Special Prosecutor's subpoena. Chief Justice Burger's opinion first declared that the intra-Executive character of the present dispute was no bar to its justiciability. The Attorney General, Burger pointed out, had, by regulations with the force of law, vested in the Special Prosecutor authority to sue in the name of the United States as well as explicit authority to contest the invocation of executive privilege. In this instance they had given rise to a "traditionally justiciable controversy."

Burger then rejected sharply the President's claim that he possessed an "absolutely unqualified privilege" against any judicial process. The need for presidential privacy, Burger conceded, did indeed justify a "presumptive privilege" for executive communications. At the same time, however, both the rule of law and respect for the integrity of the judicial process made it imperative for the courts to weigh any such claim against the importance of assuring the production in court of relevant evidence and ultimately of protecting the system of criminal justice itself.

In such matters as military affairs and the conduct of foreign policy, Burger implied, a claim of executive privilege might well be virtually absolute. But in other fields the proper procedure was to treat the documents at issue as presumptively privileged and then to allow the prosecutor to rebut that presumption. A district court, Burger added, would then bear "a very heavy responsibility" to protect the privacy of the papers committed to its care.

The Court's decision broke down the President's last defenses against either impeachment or forced resignation. Even as the Court spoke, the House Judiciary Committee was moving swiftly to bring in a bill of impeachment. In mid-May the Committee had, on its own authority, attempted once more to subpoena

White House tapes and documents—this time those it considered to be relevant to possible impeachment proceedings. Once more the President had refused, citing the separation of powers, judicial precedent, and executive privilege. The Committee by return letter had rebuked the President and then had moved to review the evidence for impeachment assembled by its staff.

In late July, on the eve of the Court's decision, the Judiciary Committee staged a series of televised evening debates on the impeachment question. The argument for the most part followed party lines. Several hard-line Republicans, led by Albert Wiggins of California, advanced the "smoking gun" theory of impeachment: there was no hard evidence, they contended, that the President had been guilty of a specific criminal offense or specific violation of law; it followed, therefore that he could not properly be impeached.

In reply, Democratic Congressmen, led by Robert Drinan of Massachusetts, Don Edwards of California, and John Conyers of Michigan, promulgated the "maladministration" theory of impeachment. Emphasizing the enormity of Nixon's breach of public trust, they argued for the necessity of impeachment as a means of maintaining the integrity of the Executive office and the viability of the Presidential system of government, without regard to "hard" evidence. Significantly, several Republicans, led by Tom Railsback of California, Hamilton Fish of New York, and William Cohen of Maine, broke away from their Republican colleagues to accept the "maladministration" argument, evidence for which Doar's staff had assembled so carefully.

The Committee concluded by voting three articles of impeachment against the President. Article I, a carefully constructed bipartisan compromise, charged that Nixon had "prevented, obstructed, and impeded the administration of justice," in "violation of his constitutional duty to take care that the laws be faithfully executed." The bill of particulars made it clear that this had to do with the Watergate break-in.

Article II charged the President with conduct "violating the Constitutional rights of citizens, impairing the due and proper administration of justice . . ." and "contravening the laws governing agencies of the executive branch. . . ." Here the bill of particulars dealt, among other things, with Nixon's attempted manipulation of the Internal Revenue Service, with his "misuse" of the FBI, and with his maintenance of a secret White House investigative unit with its unlawful utilization of the CIA.

Article III charged the President with ignoring the subpoenas of the House Judiciary Committee itself, by which the Committee had attempted to obtain materials relevant to the impeachment process. Two additional articles, ultimately rejected, would have charged Nixon with illicitly bombing Cambodia and with corruptive manipulation of his personal and partisan finances.

At this point Nixon faced almost certain impeachment by the House of Representatives and possible conviction in the Senate. But before the full House could act, the President resigned. The Supreme Court's decision in *United States v. Nixon* had brought the beleaguered Chief Executive face to face with the realization that the contents of the fateful tapes must now at long last become public.

At the President's own suggestion, his lawyers now reviewed the tape of June 23, 1972, in which Nixon had ordered his staff to use the CIA to abort the Watergate investigation. Lawyers James St. Clair, Leonard Garment, and Fred Buzhardt listened; swiftly they decided that the President must resign. Republican members of the House and Senate, who now for the first time learned the full details of the President's complicity, agreed. The actual resignation, skillfully manipulated by the lawyers and by presidential aide Alexander Haig, followed a few days later.

LONG-RANGE IMPLICATION OF THE NIXON PRESIDENTIAL CRISIS

The constitutional crisis which led to Nixon's forced resignation from office hardly solved the cluster of problems associated with the rise of the "Imperial Presidency." But it did throw into bold relief certain strengths and limitations of twentieth-century constitutional government.

The crisis demonstrated dramatically that the idea of constitutional government and the rule of law still command tremendous reverence and prestige in America. This was the meaning of the sense of outrage which the American people at large manifested as the extent of the Nixon administration's betrayal of public trust became evident.

The Nixon crisis was not merely the product of the irresponsible behavior of a lawless Chief Executive; on the contrary, it was also in considerable part precipitated by what appeared to be a growing hiatus in the American system of constitutional government. Since Franklin Roosevelt's time, Presidents have been confronted with a deepening dilemma: the American constitutional system carries as a basic premise the proposition that Congress alone makes major national policy. The President, by contrast, cannot legislate but is charged by the Constitution to "take care that the laws be faithfully executed."

Since the great crisis of the spring of 1933, if not earlier, Presidents have found it necessary both to formulate and to execute major national policy. On occasion they have succeeded in making Congress a willing or unwilling partner in the process; all too frequently, both in foreign policy and in domestic affairs the President has cut constitutional corners in his execution of the "stewardship" which every Chief Executive since the first Roosevelt has taken for granted. Nixon thus was only the latest of a succession of Presidents to become restive under the constitutional restraints imposed by limited government and the separation of powers, although his departure from prescribed constitutional limitations was more clear-cut than that of any of his predecessors.

The outcome of the Nixon crisis may well mean that for the present, at least, the American people will no longer tolerate a broad sweep of executive prerogative in the presidential office. If that is indeed the case, one can then predict with some confidence the emergence of a new constitutional crisis at no very distant future date—one centering on the inability of the Congress to perform adequately its constitutionally appointed task of formulating policy. To put the matter differently, the future of constitutional government in the United States appears to depend in some considerable part upon the ability of the American people to solve the problem of the locus of responsible power in Washington.

In a larger sense the ultimate fate of constitutional government in the United States lies hidden deep within the future evolution of the nation's social fabric. Constitutional government depends ultimately for its viability upon the continued existence of a society in which a great majority of men and women are bound together by a common awareness of certain ideas of justice, liberty, and order, and who are aware of the meaning of those ideas for the destiny of the nation.

Perhaps the most disturbing aspect of the Nixon crisis is that an entire coterie of men who showed little or no understanding of the profound principles underlying constitutional government in the United States were able for some years to exercise effective control of the presidential office. They were at length repudiated.

But the kind of challenge they posed can be met successfully in the future only as long as American society is knit together powerfully by a sense of destiny arising out of a common devotion to the underlying values of constitutional liberty.

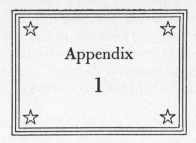

Articles of Confederation

To ALL to whom these Presents shall come, we the undersigned Delegates of the States affixed to our Names send greeting.

Whereas the Delegates of the United States of America in Congress assembled did on the fifteenth day of November in the Year of our Lord One Thousand Seven Hundred and Seventyseven, and in the Second Year of the Independence of America agree to certain articles of Confederation and perpetual Union between the States of Newhampshire, Massachusetts-bay, Rhodeisland and Providence Plantations, Connecticut, New York, New Jersey, Pennsylvania, Delaware, Maryland, Virginia, North-Carolina, South-Carolina and Georgia in the Words following, viz.

"Articles of Confederation and perpetual Union between the States of Newhampshire, Massachusetts-bay, Rhodeisland and Providence Plantations, Connecticut, New-York, New-Jersey, Pennsylvania, Delaware, Maryland, Virginia, North-Carolina, South-Carolina and Georgia.

ARTICLE I. The stile of this confederacy shall be "The United States of America."

ARTICLE II. Each State retains its sovereignty, freedom and independence, and every power, jurisdiction and right, which is not by this confederation expressly delegated to the United States, in Congress assembled.

ARTICLE III. The said States hereby severally enter into a firm league of friendship with each other, for their common defence, the security of their liberties, and their mutual and general welfare, binding themselves to assist each other, against all force offered to, or attacks made upon them, or any of them, on account of religion, sovereignty, trade, or any other pretence whatever.

ARTICLE IV. The better to secure and perpetuate mutual friendship and intercourse among the people of the different States in this Union, the free inhabitants of each of these States, paupers, vagabonds and fugitives from justice excepted, shall be entitled to all privileges and immunities of free citizens in the several States; and the people of each State shall have free ingress and regress to and from any other State, and shall enjoy therein all the privileges of trade and commerce, subject to the same duties, impositions and restrictions as the inhabitants thereof respectively, provided that such restrictions shall not extend so far as to prevent the removal of property imported into any State, to any other State of which the owner is an inhabitant; provided also that no imposition, duties or restriction shall be laid by any State, on the property of the United States, or either of them.

If any person guilty of, or charged with treason, felony, or other high misdemeanor in any State, shall flee from justice, and be found in any of the United States, he shall upon demand of the Governor or Executive power, of the State from which he fled, be delivered up and removed to the State having jurisdiction of his offence.

Full faith and credit shall be given in each of these States to the records, acts and judicial proceedings of the courts and magistrates of every other State.

ARTICLE V. For the more convenient management of the general interests of the United States, delegates shall be annually appointed in such manner as the legislature of each State shall direct, to meet in Congress on the first Monday in November, in every year, with a power reserved to each State, to recall its delegates, or any of them, at any time within the year, and to send others in their stead, for the remainder of the year.

No State shall be represented in Congress by less than two, nor by more than seven members; and no person shall be capable of being a delegate for more than three years in any term of six years; nor shall any person, being a delegate, be capable of holding any office under the United States, for which he, or another for his benefit receives any salary, fees or emolument of any kind.

Each State shall maintain its own delegates in a meeting of the States, and while they act as members of the committee of the States.

In determining questions in the United States, in Congress assembled, each State shall have one vote.

Freedom of speech and debate in Congress shall not be impeached or questioned in any court, or place out of Congress, and the members of Congress shall be protected in their persons from arrests and imprisonments, during the time of their going to and from, and attendance on Congress, except for treason, felony, or breach of the peace.

ARTICLE VI. No State without the consent of the United States in Congress assembled, shall send any embassy to, or receive any embassy from, or enter into any conference, agreement, alliance or treaty with any king, prince or state; nor shall any person holding any office of profit or trust under the United States, or any of them, accept of any present, emolument, office or title of any kind whatever from any king, prince or foreign state; nor shall the United States in Congress assembled, or any of them, grant any title of nobility.

No two or more States shall enter into any treaty, confederation or alliance whatever between them, without the consent of the United States in Congress assembled, specifying accurately the purposes for which the same is to be entered into, and how long it shall continue.

No State shall lay any imposts or duties, which may interfere with any stipulations in treaties, entered into by the United States in Congress assembled, with any king, prince or state, in pursuance of any treaties already proposed by Congress, to the courts of France and Spain.

No vessels of war shall be kept up in time of peace by any State, except such number only, as shall be deemed necessary by the United States in Congress assembled, for the defence of such State, or its trade; nor shall any body of forces be kept up by any State, in time of peace, except such number only, as in the judgment of the United States, in Congress assembled, shall be deemed requisite to garrison the forts necessary for the defence of such State; but every State shall always keep up a well regulated and disciplined militia, sufficiently armed and accoutred, and shall provide and constantly have ready for use, in public stores, a due number of field pieces and tents, and a proper quantity of arms, ammunition and camp equipage.

No State shall engage in any war without the consent of the United States in Congress assembled, unless such State be actually invaded by enemies, or shall have received certain advice of a resolution being formed by some nation of Indians to invade such State, and the danger is so imminent as not to admit of a delay, till the United States in Congress assembled can be consulted: nor shall any State grant commissions to any ships or vessels of war, nor letters of marque or reprisal, except it be after a declaration of war by the United States in Congress assembled, and then only against the kingdom or state and the subjects thereof, against which war has been so declared, and under such regulations as shall be established by the United States in Congress assembled, unless such State be infested by pirates, in which case vessels of war may be fitted out for that occasion, and kept so long as the danger shall continue, or until the United States in Congress assembled shall determine otherwise.

ARTICLE VII. When land-forces are raised by any State for the common defence, all officers of or under the rank of colonel, shall be appointed by the Legislature of each State respectively by whom such forces shall be raised, or in such manner as such State shall direct, and all vacancies shall be filled up by the State which first made the appointment.

ARTICLE VIII. All charges of war, and all other expenses that shall be incurred for the common defence or general welfare, and allowed by the United States in Congress assembled, shall be defrayed out of a common treasury, which shall be supplied by the several States, in proportion to the value of all land within each State, granted to or surveyed for any person, as such land and the buildings and improvements thereon shall be estimated according to such mode as the United States in Congress assembled, shall from time to time direct and appoint.

The taxes for paying that proportion shall be laid and levied by the authority and direction of the Legislatures of the several States within the time agreed upon by the United States in Congress assembled.

ARTICLE IX. The United States in Congress assembled, shall have the sole and exclusive right and power of determining on peace and war, except in the cases mentioned in the sixth article—of sending and receiving ambassadors—entering into treaties and alliances, provided that no treaty of commerce shall be made whereby the legislative power of the respective States shall be restrained from imposing such imposts and duties on foreigners, as their own people are subjected to, or from prohibiting the exportation or importation of any species of goods or commodities whatsoever—of establishing rules for deciding in all cases, what captures on land or water shall be legal, and in what manner prizes taken by land or naval forces in the service of the United States shall be divided or appropriated—of granting letters of marque and reprisal in times of peace—appointing courts for the trial of piracies and felonies committed on the high seas and establishing courts for receiving and determining finally appeals in all cases of captures, provided that no member of Congress shall be appointed a judge of any of the said courts.

The United States in Congress assembled shall also be the last resort on appeal in all disputes and differences now subsisting or that hereafter may arise between two or more States concerning boundary, jurisdiction or any other cause whatever; which authority shall always be exercised in the manner following. Whenever the legislative or executive authority or lawful agent of any State in controversy with another shall present a petition to Congress, stating the matter in question and praying for a hearing, notice thereof shall be given by order of Congress to the legislative or executive authority of the other State in controversy, and a day assigned for the appearance of the parties by their lawful agents, who shall then be directed to appoint by joint consent, commissioners or judges to constitute a court for hearing and determining the matter in question: but if they cannot agree, Congress shall name three persons out of each of the United States, and from the list of such persons each party shall alternately strike out one, the petitioners beginning, until the number shall be reduced to thirteen; and from that number not less than seven, nor more than nine names as Congress shall direct, shall in the presence of Congress be drawn out by lot, and the persons whose names shall be so drawn or any five of them, shall be commissioners or judges, to hear and finally determine the controversy, so always as a major part of the judges who shall hear the cause shall agree in the determination: and if either party shall neglect to attend at the day appointed, without showing reasons, which Congress shall judge sufficient, or being present shall refuse to strike, the Congress shall proceed to nominate three persons out of each State, and the Secretary of Congress shall strike in behalf of such party absent or refusing; and the judgment and sentence of the court to be appointed, in the manner before prescribed, shall be final and conclusive; and if any of the parties shall refuse to submit to the authority of such court, or to appear or defend their claim or cause, the court shall nevertheless proceed to pronounce sentence, or judgment, which shall in like manner be final and decisive, the judgment or sentence and other proceedings being in either case transmitted to Congress, and lodged among the acts of Congress for the security of the parties concerned: provided that every commissioner, before he sits in judgment, shall take an oath to be administered by one of the judges of the supreme or superior court of the State where the cause shall be tried, "well and truly to hear and determine the matter in question, according to the best of his judgment, without favour, affection or hope of reward:" provided also that no State shall be deprived of territory for the benefit of the United States.

All controversies concerning the private right of soil claimed under different grants of two or more States, whose jurisdiction as they may respect such lands, and the States which passed such grants are adjusted, the said grants or either of them being at the same time claimed to have originated antecedent to such settlement of jurisdiction, shall on the petition of either party to the Congress of the United States, be finally determined as near as may be in the same manner as is before prescribed for deciding disputes respecting territorial jurisdiction between different States.

The United States in Congress assembled shall also have the sole and exclusive right and power of regulating the alloy and value of coin struck by their own authority, or by that of the respective States—fixing the standard of weights and measures throughout the United States—regulating the trade and managing all affairs with the Indians, not members of any of the States, provided that the legislative right of any State within its own limits be not infringed or violated—establishing and regulating post-offices from one State to another, throughout all the United States, and exacting such postage on the papers passing thro' the same as may be requisite to defray the expenses of the said office—appointing all officers of the land forces, in the service of the United States, excepting regimental officers—appointing all the officers of the naval forces, and commissioning all officers whatever in the service of the United States—making rules for the government and regulation of the said land and naval forces, and directing their operations.

The United States in Congress assembled shall have authority to appoint a committee, to sit in the recess of Congress, to be denominated "a Committee of the States," and to consist of one delegate from each State; and to appoint such other committees and civil officers as may be necessary for managing the general affairs of the United States under their direction—to appoint one of their number to preside, provided that no person be allowed to serve in the office of president more than one year in any term of three years; to ascertain the necessary sums of money to be raised for the service of the United States, and to appropriate and apply the same for defraying the public expenses—to borrow money, or emit bills on the credit of the United States, transmitting every half year to the respective States an account of the sums of money so borrowed or emitted,—to build and equip a navy—to agree upon the number of land forces, and to make requisitions from each State for its quota, in proportion to the number of white inhabitants in such State; which requisition shall be binding, and thereupon the Legislature of each State shall appoint the regimental officers, raise the men and cloath, arm and equip them in a soldier like manner, at the expense of the United States; and the officers and men so cloathed, armed and equipped shall march to the place appointed, and within the time agreed on by the United States in Congress assembled: but if the United States in Congress assembled shall, on consideration of circumstances judge proper that any State should not raise men, or should raise a smaller number of men than the quota therof, such extra number shall be raised, officered, cloathed, armed and equipped in the same manner as the quota of such State, unless the legislature of such State shall judge that such extra number cannot be safely spared out of the same, in which case they shall raise officer, cloath, arm and equip as many of such extra number as they judge can be safely spared. And the officers and men so cloathed, armed and equipped, shall march to the place appointed, and within the time agreed on by the United States in Congress assembled.

The United States in Congress assembled shall never engage in a war, nor grant letters of marque and reprisal in time of peace, nor enter into any treaties or alliances, nor coin money, nor regulate the value thereof, nor ascertain the sums and expenses necessary for the defence and welfare of the United States, or any of them, nor emit bills, nor borrow money on the credit of the United States, nor appropriate money, nor agree upon the number of vessels of war, to be built or purchased, or the number of land or sea forces to be raised, nor appoint a commander in chief of the army or navy, unless nine States assent to the same: nor shall a question on any other point, except for adjourning from day to day be determined, unless by the votes of a majority of the United States in Congress assembled.

The Congress of the United States shall have power to adjourn to any time within the year, and to any place within the United States, so that no period of adjournment be for a longer duration than the space of six months, and shall publish the journal of their proceedings monthly, except such parts thereof relating to treaties, alliances or military operations, as in their judgment require secresy; and the yeas and nays of the delegates of each State on any question shall be entered on the Journal, when it is desired by any delegate; and the delegates of a State, or any of them, at his or their request shall be furnished with a transcript of the said journal, except such parts as are above excepted, to lay before the Legislatures of the several States.

ARTICLE X. The committee of the States, or any nine of them, shall be authorized to execute, in the recess of Congress, such of the powers of Congress as the United States in Congress assembled, by the consent of nine States, shall from time to time think expedient to vest them with; provided that no power be delegated to the said committee, for the exercise of which, by the articles of confederation, the voice of nine States in the Congress of the United States assembled is requisite.

ARTICLE XI. Canada acceding to this confederation, and joining in the measures of the United States, shall be admitted into, and entitled to all the advantages of this Union: but no other colony shall be admitted into the same, unless such admission be agreed to by nine States.

ARTICLE XII. All bills of credit emitted, monies borrowed and debts contracted by, or under the authority of Congress, before the assembling of the United States, in pursuance of the present confederation, shall be deemed and considered as a charge against the United States, for payment and satisfaction whereof the said United States, and the public faith are hereby solemnly pledged.

ARTICLE XIII. Every State shall abide by the determinations of the United States in Congress assembled, on all questions which by this confederation are submitted to them. And the articles of this confederation shall be inviolably observed by every State, and the Union shall be perpetual; nor shall any alteration at any time hereafter be made in any of them; unless such alteration be agreed to in a Congress of the United States, and be afterwards confirmed by the Legislatures of every State.

And whereas it has pleased the Great Governor of the world to incline the hearts of the Legislatures we respectively represent in Congress, to approve of, and to authorize us to ratify the said articles of confederation and perpetual union. Know ye that we the undersigned delegates, by virtue of the power and authority to us given for that purpose, do by these presents, in the name and in behalf of our respective constituents, fully and entirely ratify and confirm each and every of the said articles of confederation and perpetual union, and all and singular the matters and things therein contained: and we do further solemnly plight and engage the faith of our respective constituents, that they shall abide by the determinations of the United States in Congress assembled, on all questions, which by the said confederation are submitted to them. And that the articles thereof shall be inviolably observed by the States we respectively represent, and that the Union shall be perpetual.

In witness whereof we have hereunto set our hands in Congress. Done at Philadelphia in the State of Pennsylvania the ninth day of July in the year of our Lord one thousand seven hundred and seventy-eight, and in the third year of the independence of America.

The Constitution of the United States

WE THE PEOPLE OF THE UNITED STATES, in Order to form a more perfect Union, establish Justice, insure domestic Tranquility, provide for the common defence, promote the general Welfare, and secure the Blessings of Liberty to ourselves and our Posterity, do ordain and establish this Constitution for the United States of America.

ARTICLE. I.

Section. 1. All legislative Powers herein granted shall be vested in a Congress of the United States, which shall consist of a Senate and House of Representatives.

Section. 2. The House of Representatives shall be composed of Members chosen every second Year by the People of the several States, and the Electors in each State shall have the Qualifications requisite for Electors of the most numerous Branch of the State Legislature.

No Person shall be a Representative who shall not have attained to the Age of twenty five Years, and been seven Years a Citizen of the United States, and who shall not, when elected, be an Inhabitant of that State in which he shall be chosen.

Representatives and direct Taxes shall be apportioned among the several States which may be included within this Union, according to their respective Numbers, which shall be determined by adding to the whole Number of free Persons, including those bound to Service for a Term of Years, and excluding Indians not taxed, three fifths of all other Persons. The actual Enumeration shall be made within three Years after the first Meeting of the Congress of the United States, and within every subsequent Term of ten Years, in such Manner as they shall by Law direct. The Number of Representatives shall not exceed one for every thirty Thousand, but each State shall have at Least one Representative; and until such enumeration shall be made, the State of New Hampshire shall be entitled to chuse three, Massachusetts eight, Rhode-Island and Providence Plantations one, Connecticut five, New-York six, New Jersey four, Pennsylvania eight, Delaware one, Maryland six, Virginia ten, North Carolina five, South Carolina five, and Georgia three.

When vacancies happen in the Representation from any State, the Executive Authority thereof shall issue Writs of Election to fill such Vacancies.

The House of Representatives shall chuse their Speaker and other Officers; and shall have the sole Power of Impeachment.

Section. 3. The Senate of the United States shall be composed of two Senators from each State, chosen by the Legislature thereof, for six Years; and each Senator shall have one Vote.

Immediately after they shall be assembled in Consequence of the first Election, they shall be divided as equally as may be into three Classes. The Seats of the Senators of the first Class shall be vacated at the Expiration of the second Year, of the second Class at the Expiration of the fourth Year, and of the third Class at the Expiration of the sixth Year, so that one third may be chosen every second Year; and if Vacancies happen by Resignation, or otherwise, during the Recess of the Legislature of any State, the Executive thereof may make temporary Appointments until the next Meeting of the Legislature, which shall then fill such Vacancies.

No Person shall be a Senator who shall not have attained to the Age of thirty Years, and been nine Years a Citizen of the United States, and who shall not, when elected, be an Inhabitant of that State for which he shall be chosen.

The Vice President of the United States shall be President of the Senate, but shall have no Vote, unless they be equally divided.

The Senate shall chuse their other Officers, and also a President pro tempore, in the Absence of the Vice President, or when he shall exercise the Office of President of the United States.

The Senate shall have the sole Power to try all Impeachments. When sitting for that Purpose, they shall be on Oath or Affirmation. When the President of the United States is tried, the Chief Justice shall preside: And no Person shall be convicted without the Concurrence of two thirds of the Members present.

Judgment in Cases of Impeachment shall not extend further than to removal from Office, and disqualification to hold and enjoy any Office of honor, Trust or Profit under the United States: but the Party convicted shall nevertheless be liable and subject to Indictment, Trial, Judgment and Punishment, according to Law.

Section. 4. The Times, Places and Manner of holding Elections for Senators and Representatives, shall be prescribed in each State by the Legislature thereof, but the Congress may at any time by Law make or alter such Regulations, except as to the Places of chusing Senators.

The Congress shall assemble at least once in every Year, and such Meeting shall be on the first Monday in December, unless they shall by Law appoint a different Day.

Section. 5. Each House shall be the Judge of the Elections, Returns and Qualifications of its own Members, and a Majority of each shall constitute a Quorum to do Business; but a smaller Number may adjourn from day to day, and may be authorized to compel the Attendance of absent Members, in such Manner, and under such Penalties as each House may provide.

Each House may determine the Rules of its Proceedings, punish its Members for disorderly Behaviour, and, with the Concurrence of two thirds, expel a Member.

Each House shall keep a Journal of its Proceedings, and from time to time publish the same, excepting such Parts as may in their Judgment require Secrecy; and the Yeas and Nays of the Members of either House on any question shall, at the Desire of one fifth of those Present, be entered on the Journal.

Neither House, during the Session of Congress, shall, without the Consent of the other, adjourn for more than three days, nor to any other Place than that in which the two Houses shall be sitting.

Section. 6. The Senators and Representatives shall receive a Compensation for their Services, to be ascertained by Law, and paid out of the Treasury of the United States. They shall in all Cases, except Treason, Felony and Breach of the Peace, be privileged from Arrest during their Attendance at the Session of their respective Houses, and in going to and returning from the same; and for any Speech or Debate in either House, they shall not be questioned in any other Place.

No Senator or Representative shall, during the Time for which he was elected, be appointed to any civil Office under the Authority of the United States, which shall have been created, or the Emoluments whereof shall have been encreased during such time; and no Person holding any Office under the United States, shall be a Member of either House during his Continuance in Office.

Section. 7. All Bills for raising Revenue shall originate in the House of Representatives; but the Senate may propose or concur with Amendments as on other Bills.

Every Bill which shall have passed the House of Representatives and the Senate shall, before it become a Law, be presented to the President of the United States; If he approve he shall sign it, but if not he shall return it, with his Objections to that House in which it shall have originated, who shall enter the Objections at large on their Journal, and proceed to reconsider it. If after such Reconsideration two thirds of that House shall agree to pass the Bill, it shall be sent, together with the Objections, to the other House, by which it shall likewise be reconsidered, and if approved by two thirds of that House, it shall become a Law. But in all such Cases the Votes of both Houses shall be determined by yeas and Nays, and the Names of the Persons voting for and against the Bill shall be entered on the Journal of each House respectively. If any Bill shall not be returned by the President within ten Days (Sundays excepted) after it shall have been presented to him, the Same shall be a Law, in like Manner as if he had signed it, unless the Congress by their Adjournment prevent its Return, in which Case it shall not be a Law.

Every Order, Resolution, or Vote to which the Concurrence of the Senate and House of Representatives may be necessary (except on a question of Adjournment) shall be presented to the President of the United States; and before the Same shall take Effect, shall be approved by him, or being disapproved by him, shall be repassed by two thirds of the Senate and House of Representatives, according to the Rules and Limitations prescribed in the Case of a Bill.

Section. 8. The Congress shall have Power To lay and collect Taxes, Duties, Imposts and Excises, to pay the Debts and provide for the common Defence and general Welfare of the United States; but all Duties, Imposts and Excises shall be uniform throughout the

United States;

To borrow Money on the credit of the United States;

To regulate Commerce with foreign Nations, and among the several States, and with the Indian Tribes;

To establish an uniform Rule of Naturalization, and uniform Laws on the subject of Bankruptcies throughout the United States;

To coin Money, regulate the Value thereof, and of foreign Coin, and fix the Standard of Weights and Measures;

To provide for the Punishment of counterfeiting the Securities and current Coin of the United States;

To establish Post Offices and post Roads;

To promote the Progress of Science and useful Arts, by securing for limited Times to Authors and Inventors the exclusive Right to their respective Writings and Discoveries;

To constitute Tribunals inferior to the supreme Court;

To define and punish Piracies and Felonies committed on the high Seas, and Offences against the Law of Nations;

To declare War, grant Letters of Marque and Reprisal, and make Rules concerning Captures on Land and Water;

To raise and support Armies, but no Appropriation of Money to that Use shall be for a longer Term than two Years;

To provide and maintain a Navy;

To make Rules for the Government and Regulation of the land and naval Forces;

To provide for calling forth the Militia to execute the Laws of the Union, suppress Insurrections and repel Invasions;

To provide for organizing, arming, and disciplining, the Militia, and for governing such Part of them as may be employed in the Service of the United States, reserving to the States respectively, the Appointment of the Officers, and the Authority of training the Militia according to the discipline prescribed by Congress;

To exercise exclusive Legislation in all Cases whatsoever, over such District (not exceeding ten Miles square) as may, by Cession of particular States, and the Acceptance of Congress, become the Seat of the Government of the United States, and to exercise like Authority over all Places purchased by the Consent of the Legislature of the State in which the Same shall be, for the Erection of Forts, Magazines, Arsenals, dock-Yards, and other needful Buildings;—— And

To make all Laws which shall be necessary and proper for carrying into Execution the foregoing Powers, and all other Powers vested by this Constitution in the Government of the United States, or in any Department or Officer thereof.

Section. 9. The Migration or Importation of such Persons as any of the States now existing shall think proper to admit, shall not be prohibited by the Congress prior to the Year one thousand eight hundred and eight, but a Tax or duty may be imposed on such Importation, not exceeding ten dollars for each Person.

The Privilege of the Writ of Habeas Corpus shall not be suspended, unless when in Cases of Rebellion or Invasion the public Safety may require it.

No Bill of Attainder or ex post facto Law shall be passed.

No Capitation, or other direct, Tax shall be laid, unless in Proportion to the Census or Enumeration herein before directed to be taken.

No Tax or Duty shall be laid on Articles exported from any State.

No Preference shall be given by any Regulation of Commerce or Revenue to the Ports of one State over those of another: nor shall Vessels bound to, or from, one State, be obliged to enter, clear, or pay Duties in another.

No Money shall be drawn from the Treasury, but in Consequence of Appropriations made by Law, and a regular Statement and Account of the Receipts and Expenditures of all public Money shall be published from time to time.

No Title of Nobility shall be granted by the United States: And no Person holding any Office of Profit or Trust under them, shall, without the Consent of the Congress, accept of any present, Emolument, Office, or Title, of any kind whatever, from any King, Prince, or foreign State.

Section. 10. No State shall enter into any Treaty, Alliance, or Confederation; grant Letters of Marque and Reprisal; coin Money; emit Bills of Credit; make any Thing but gold and silver Coin a Tender in Payment of Debts; pass any Bill of Attainder, ex post facto Law, or Law impairing the Obligation of Contracts, or grant any Title of Nobility.

No State shall, without the Consent of the Congress, lay any Imposts or Duties on Imports or Exports, except what may be absolutely necessary for executing it's inspection Laws: and the net Produce of all Duties and Imposts, laid by any State on Imports or Exports, shall be for the Use of the Treasury of the United States; and all such Laws shall be subject to the Revision and Controul of the Congress.

No State shall, without the Consent of Congress, lay any Duty of Tonnage, keep Troops, or Ships of War in time of Peace, enter into any Agreement or Compact with another State, or with a foreign

Power, or engage in War, unless actually invaded, or in such imminent Danger as will not admit of delay.

ARTICLE. II.

Section. 1. The executive Power shall be vested in a President of the United States of America. He shall hold his Office during the Term of four Years, and, together with the Vice President, chosen for the same Term, be elected, as follows

Each State shall appoint, in such Manner as the Legislature thereof may direct, a Number of Electors, equal to the whole Number of Senators and Representatives to which the State may be entitled in the Congress: but no Senator or Representative, or Person holding an Office of Trust or Profit under the United States, shall be appointed an Elector.

The Electors shall meet in their respective States, and vote by Ballot for two Persons, of whom one at least shall not be an Inhabitant of the same State with themselves. And they shall make a List of all the Persons voted for, and of the Number of Votes for each; which List they shall sign and certify, and transmit sealed to the Seat of the Government of the United States, directed to the President of the Senate. The President of the Senate shall, in the Presence of the Senate and House of Representatives, open all the Certificates, and the Votes shall then be counted. The Person having the greatest Number of Votes shall be the President, if such Number be a Majority of the whole Number of Electors appointed; and if there be more than one who have such Majority, and have an equal Number of Votes, then the House of Representatives shall immediately chuse by Ballot one of them for President; and if no Person have a Majority, then from the five highest on the List the said House shall in like Manner chuse the President. But in chusing the President, the Votes shall be taken by States, the Representation from each State having one Vote; A quorum for this Purpose shall consist of a Member or Members from two thirds of the States, and a Majority of all the States shall be necessary to a Choice. In every Case, after the Choice of the President, the Person having the greatest Number of Votes of the Electors shall be the Vice President. But if there should remain two or more who have equal Votes, the Senate shall chuse from them by Ballot the Vice President.

The Congress may determine the Time of chusing the Electors, and the Day on which they shall give their Votes; which Day shall be the same throughout the United States.

No Person except a natural born Citizen, or a Citizen of the United States, at the time of the Adoption of this Constitution, shall be eligible to the Office of President, neither shall any Person be eligible to that Office who shall not have attained to the Age of thirty-five Years, and been fourteen Years a Resident within the United States.

In Case of the Removal of the President from Office, or of his Death, Resignation, or Inability to discharge the Powers and Duties of the said Office, the Same shall devolve on the Vice President, and the Congress may by Law provide for the Case of Removal, Death, Resignation or Inability, both of the President and Vice President, declaring what Officer shall then act as President, and such Officer shall act accordingly, until the Disability be removed, or a President shall be elected.

The President shall, at stated Times, receive for his Services, a Compensation, which shall neither be encreased nor diminished during the Period for which he shall have been elected, and he shall not receive within that Period any other Emolument from the United States, or any of them.

Before he enter on the Execution of his Office, he shall take the following Oath or Affirmation:—"I do solemnly swear (or affirm) that I will faithfully execute the Office of President of the United States, and will to the best of my Ability, preserve, protect and defend the Constitution of the United States."

Section. 2. The President shall be Commander in Chief of the Army and Navy of the United States, and of the Militia of the several States, when called into the actual Service of the United States; he may require the Opinion, in writing, of the principal Officer in each of the executive Departments, upon any Subject relating to the Duties of their respective Offices, and he shall have Power to grant Reprieves and Pardons for Offences against the United States, except in Cases of Impeachment.

He shall have Power, by and with the Advice and Consent of the Senate, to make Treaties, provided two thirds of the Senators present concur; and he shall nominate, and by and with the Advice and Consent of the Senate, shall appoint Ambassadors, other public Ministers and Consuls, Judges of the supreme Court, and all other Officers of the United States, whose Appointments are not herein otherwise provided for, and which shall be established by Law; but the Congress may by Law vest the Appointment of such inferior Officers, as they think proper, in the President alone, in the Courts of Law, or in the Heads of Departments.

The President shall have Power to fill up all Vacancies that may happen during the Recess of the Senate, by granting Commissions which shall expire at the End of their next Session.

Section. 3. He shall from time to time give to the Congress Information of the State of the Union, and recommend to their Consideration such Measures as he shall judge necessary and expedient; he may, on extraordinary Occasions, convene both Houses, or either of them, and in Case of Disagreement between them, with Respect to the Time of Adjournment, he may adjourn them to such Time as he shall think proper; he shall receive Ambassadors and other public Ministers; he shall take Care that the Laws be faithfully executed, and shall Commission all the Officers of the United States.

Section. 4. The President, Vice President and all civil Officers of the United States, shall be removed from Office on Impeachment for, and Conviction of, Treason, Bribery, or other high Crimes and Misdemeanors.

ARTICLE. III.

Section. 1. The judicial Power of the United States, shall be vested in one supreme Court, and in such inferior Courts as the Congress may from time to time ordain and establish. The Judges, both of the supreme and inferior Courts, shall hold their Offices during good Behaviour, and shall, at stated Times, receive for their Services, a Compensation, which shall not be diminished during their Continuance in Office.

Section. 2. The judicial Power shall extend to all Cases, in Law and Equity, arising under this Constitution, the Laws of the United States, and Treaties made, or which shall be made, under their Authority;—to all Cases affecting Ambassadors, other public Ministers and Consuls;—to all Cases of admiralty and maritime Jurisdiction;—to Controversies to which the United States shall be a Party;—to Controversies between two or more States;—between a State and Citizens of another State;—between Citizens of different States,—between Citizens of the same State claiming Lands under Grants of different States, and between a State, or the Citizens thereof, and foreign States, Citizens or Subjects.

In all Cases affecting Ambassadors, other public Ministers and Consuls, and those in which a State shall be Party, the supreme Court shall have original Jurisdiction. In all the other Cases before mentioned, the supreme Court shall have appellate Jurisdiction, both as to Law and Fact, with such Exceptions, and under such Regulations as the Congress shall make.

The Trial of all Crimes, except in Cases of Impeachment, shall be by Jury; and such Trial shall be held in the State where the said Crimes shall have been committed; but when not committed within any State, the Trial shall be at such Place or Places as the Congress may by Law have directed.

Section. 3. Treason against the United States, shall consist only in levying War against them, or in adhering to their Enemies, giving them Aid and Comfort. No Person shall be convicted of Treason unless on the Testimony of two Witnesses to the same overt Act, or on Confession in open Court.

The Congress shall have Power to declare the Punishment of Treason, but no Attainder of Treason shall work Corruption of Blood, or Forfeiture except during the Life of the Person attainted.

ARTICLE. IV.

Section. 1. Full Faith and Credit shall be given in each State to the public Acts, Records, and judicial Proceedings of every other State. And the Congress may by general Laws prescribe the Manner in which such Acts, Records and Proceedings shall be proved, and the Effect thereof.

Section. 2. The Citizens of each State shall be entitled to all Privileges and Immunities of Citizens in the several States.

A Person charged in any State with Treason, Felony, or other Crime, who shall flee from Justice, and be found in another State, shall on Demand of the executive Authority of the State from which he fled, be delivered up, to be removed to the State having Jurisdiction of the Crime.

No Person held to Service or Labour in one State, under the Laws thereof, escaping into another, shall, in Consequence of any Law or Regulation therein, be discharged from such Service or Labour, but shall be delivered up on Claim of the Party to whom such Service or Labour may be due.

Section. 3. New States may be admitted by the Congress into this Union; but no new State shall be formed or erected within the Jurisdiction of any other State; nor any State be formed by the Junction of two or more States, or Parts of States, without the Consent of the Legislatures of the States concerned as well as of the Congress.

The Congress shall have Power to dispose of and make all needful Rules and Regulations respecting the Territory or other Property belonging to the United States; and nothing in this Constitution shall be so construed as to Prejudice any Claims of the United States, or of any particular State.

Section. 4. The United States shall guarantee to every State in this Union a Republican Form of Government, and shall protect each of them against Invasion; and on Application of the Legislature, or of the Executive (when the Legislature cannot be convened) against domestic Violence.

ARTICLE. V.

The Congress, whenever two thirds of both Houses shall deem it necessary, shall propose Amendments to this Constitution, or, on the Application of the Legislatures of two thirds of the several States shall call a Convention for proposing Amendments, which, in either Case, shall be valid to all Intents and Purposes, as Part of this Constitution, when ratified by the Legislatures of three fourths of the several States, or by Conventions in three fourths thereof, as the one or the other Mode of Ratification may be proposed by the Congress; Provided that no Amendment which may be made prior to the Year One thousand eight hundred and eight shall in any Manner affect the first and fourth Clauses in the Ninth Section of the first Article; and that no State, without its Consent, shall be deprived of it's equal Suffrage in the Senate.

ARTICLE. VI.

All Debts contracted and Engagements entered into, before the Adoption of this Constitution, shall be as valid against the United States under this Constitution, as under the Confederation.

This Constitution, and the Laws of the United States which shall be made in Pursuance thereof; and all Treaties made, or which shall be made, under the Authority of the United States, shall be the supreme Law of the Land; and the Judges in every State shall be bound thereby, any Thing in the Constitution or Laws of any State to the Contrary notwithstanding.

The Senators and Representatives before mentioned, and the Members of the several State Legislatures, and all executive and judicial Officers, both of the United States and of the several States, shall be bound by Oath or Affirmation, to support this Constitution;

but no religious Test shall ever be required as a Qualification to any Office or public Trust under the United States.

ARTICLE. VII.

The Ratification of the Conventions of nine States, shall be sufficient for the Establishment of this Constitution between the States so ratifying the Same.

Done in Convention by the Unanimous Consent of the States present the Seventeenth Day of September in the Year of our Lord one thousand seven hundred and Eighty seven and of the Independance of the United States of America the Twelfth. In witness whereof We have hereunto subscribed our Names,

G? WASHINGTON—Presid^t
and deputy from Virginia

New Hampshire	{ John Langdon Nicholas Gilman
Massachusetts	{ Nathaniel Gorham Rufus King
Connecticut	{ Wm Saml Johnson Roger Sherman
New York	} Alexander Hamilton
New Jersey	{ Wil: Livingston David A. Brearley. Wm Paterson. Jona: Dayton
Pensylvania	{ B Franklin Thomas Mifflin Robt Morris Geo. Clymer Thos FitzSimons Jared Ingersoll James Wilson Gouv Morris

Delaware	{ Geo: Read Gunning Bedford jun John Dickinson Richard Bassett Jaco: Broom
Maryland	{ James McHenry Dan of St Thos Jenifer Danl Carroll
Virginia	{ John Blair— James Madison Jr.
North Carolina	{ Wm Blount Richd Dobbs Spaight. Hu Williamson
South Carolina	{ J. Rutledge Charles Cotesworth Pinckney Charles Pinckney Pierce Butler.
Georgia	{ William Few Abr Baldwin

Amendments to the Constitution

ARTICLES IN ADDITION TO, and Amendment of the Constitution of the United States of America, proposed by Congress, and ratified by the Legislatures of the several States, pursuant to the fifth Article of the original Constitution.

ARTICLE I.

Congress shall make no law respecting an establishment of religion, or prohibiting the free exercise thereof; or abridging the freedom of speech, or of the press; or the right of the people peaceably to assemble, and to petition the Government for a redress of grievances.

ARTICLE II.

A well regulated Militia, being necessary to the security of a free State, the right of the people to keep and bear Arms, shall not be infringed.

ARTICLE III.

No Soldier shall, in time of peace be quartered in any house, without the consent of the Owner, nor in time of war, but in a manner to be prescribed by law.

ARTICLE IV.

The right of the people to be secure in their persons, houses, papers, and effects, against unreasonable searches and seizures, shall not be violated, and no Warrants shall issue, but upon probable cause, supported by Oath or affirmation, and particularly describing the place to be searched, and the persons or things to be seized.

ARTICLE V.

No person shall be held to answer for a capital, or otherwise infamous crime, unless on a presentment or indictment of a Grand Jury, except in cases arising in the land or naval forces, or in the Militia, when in actual service in time of War or public danger; nor shall any person be subject for the same offence to be twice put in jeopardy of life or limb; nor shall be compelled in any criminal case to be a witness against himself, nor be deprived of life, liberty, or property, without due process of law; nor shall private property be taken for public use, without just compensation.

ARTICLE VI.

In all criminal prosecutions, the accused shall enjoy the right to a speedy and public trial, by an impartial jury of the State and district wherein the crime shall have been committed, which district shall have been previously ascertained by law, and to be informed of the nature and cause of the accusation; to be confronted with the witnesses against him; to have compulsory process for obtaining witnesses in his favor, and to have the Assistance of Counsel for his defence.

ARTICLE VII.

In Suits at common law, where the value in controversy shall exceed twenty dollars, the right of trial by jury shall be preserved, and no fact tried by a jury, shall be otherwise re-examined in any Court of the United States, than according to the rules of the common law.

ARTICLE VIII.

Excessive bail shall not be required, nor excessive fines imposed, nor cruel and unusual punishments inflicted.

ARTICLE IX.

The enumeration in the Constitution, of certain rights, shall not be construed to deny or disparage others retained by the people.

ARTICLE X.

The powers not delegated to the United States by the Constitution, nor prohibited by it to the States, are reserved to the States respectively, or to the people. [The first ten amendments went into effect December 15, 1791.]

ARTICLE XI.

The Judicial power of the United States shall not be construed to extend to any suit in law or equity, commenced or prosecuted against one of the United States by Citizens of another State, or by Citizens or Subjects of any Foreign State. [January 8, 1798.]

ARTICLE XII.

The Electors shall meet in their respective states, and vote by ballot for President and Vice-President, one of whom, at least, shall not be an inhabitant of the same state with themselves; they shall name in their ballots the person voted for as President, and in distinct ballots the person voted for as Vice-President, and they shall make distinct lists of all persons voted for as President, and of all persons voted for as Vice-President, and of the number of votes for each. which lists they shall sign and certify, and transmit sealed to the seat of the government of the United States, directed to the President of the Senate;—The President of the Senate shall, in the presence of the Senate and House of Representatives, open all the certifi cates and the votes shall then be counted;—The person having the greatest number of votes for President, shall be the President, if such number be a majority of the whole number of Electors appointed; and if no person have such majority, then from the persons having the highest numbers not exceeding three on the list of those voted for as President, the House of Representatives shall choose immediately, by ballot, the President. But in choosing the President, the votes shall be taken by states, the representation from each state having one vote; a quorum for this purpose shall consist of a member or members from two-thirds of the states, and a major ity of all the states shall be necessary to a choice. And if the House of Representatives shall not choose a President whenever the right of choice shall devolve upon them, before the fourth day of March next following, then the Vice-President shall act as President, as in the case of the death or other constitutional disability of the President.—The person having the greatest number of votes as Vice-President, shall be the Vice-President, if such number be a majority of the whole number of Electors appointed, and if no person have a majority, then from the two highest numbers on the list, the Senate shall choose the Vice-President; a quorum for the purpose shall consist of two-thirds of the whole number of Senators, and a majority of the whole number shall be necessary to a choice. But no person constitutionally ineligible to the office of President shall be eligible to that of Vice-President of the United States. [September 25, 1804.]

ARTICLE XIII.

Section 1. Neither slavery nor involuntary servitude, except as a punishment for crime whereof the party shall have been duly convicted, shall exist within the United States, or any place subject to their jurisdiction.

Section 2. Congress shall have power to enforce this article by appropriate legislation. [December 18, 1865.]

ARTICLE XIV.

Section 1. All persons born or naturalized in the United States, and subject to the jurisdiction thereof, are citizens of the United States and of the State wherein they reside. No State shall make or enforce any law which shall abridge the privileges or immunities of citizens of the United States; nor shall any State deprive any person of life, liberty, or property, without due process of law; nor deny to any person within its jurisdiction the equal protection of the laws.

Section 2. Representatives shall be apportioned among the several States according to their respective numbers, counting the whole number of persons in each State, excluding Indians not taxed. But when the right to vote at any election for the choice of electors for President and Vice President of the United States, Representatives in Congress, the Executive and Judicial officers of a State, or the members of the Legislature thereof, is denied to any of the male inhabitants of such State, being twenty-one years of age, and citizens of the United States, or in any way abridged, except for participation in rebellion, or other crime, the basis of representation therein shall be reduced in the proportion which the number of such male citizens shall bear to the whole number of male citizens twenty-one years of age in such State.

Section 3. No person shall be a Senator or Representative in Congress, or elector of President and Vice President, or hold any office, civil or military, under the United States, or under any State, who, having previously taken an oath, as a member of Congress, or as an officer of the United States, or as a member of any State legislature, or as an executive or judicial officer of any State, to support the Constitution of the United States, shall have engaged in insurrection or rebellion against the same, or given aid or comfort to the enemies thereof. But Congress may by a vote of two-thirds of each House, remove such disability.

Section 4. The validity of the public debt of the United States, authorized by law, including debts incurred for payment of pensions and bounties for services in suppressing insurrection or rebellion, shall not be questioned. But neither the United States nor any State shall assume or pay any debt or obligation incurred in aid of insurrection or rebellion against the United States, or any claim for the loss or emancipation of any slave; but all such debts, obligations and claims shall be held illegal and void.

Section 5. The Congress shall have power to enforce, by appropriate legislation, the provisions of this article. [July 28, 1868.]

ARTICLE XV.

Section 1. The right of citizens of the United States to vote shall not be denied or abridged by the United States or by any State on account of race, color, or previous condition of servitude——

Section 2. The Congress shall have power to enforce this article by appropriate legislation.——[March 30, 1870.]

ARTICLE XVI.

The Congress shall have power to lay and collect taxes on incomes, from whatever source derived, without apportionment among the several States, and without regard to any census or enumeration. [February 25, 1913.]

ARTICLE XVII.

The Senate of the United States shall be composed of two senators from each State, elected by the people thereof, for six years; and each Senator shall have one vote. The electors in each State shall have the qualifications requisite for electors of the most numerous branch of the State legislature.

When vacancies happen in the representation of any State in the Senate, the executive authority of such State shall issue writs of election to fill such vacancies: Provided, That the legislature of any State may empower the executive thereof to make temporary appointments until the people fill the vacancies by election as the legislature may direct.

This amendment shall not be so construed as to affect the election or term of any senator chosen before it becomes valid as part of the Constitution. [May 31, 1913.]

ARTICLE XVIII.

After one year from the ratification of this article, the manufacture, sale, or transportation of intoxicating liquors within, the importation thereof into, or the exportation thereof from the United States and all territory subject to the jurisdiction thereof for beverage purposes is hereby prohibited.

The Congress and the several States shall have concurrent power to enforce this article by appropriate legislation.

This article shall be inoperative unless it shall have been ratified as an amendment to the Constitution by the legislatures of the several States, as provided in the Constitution, within seven years from the date of the submission thereof to the States by Congress. [January 29, 1919.]

ARTICLE XIX.

The right of citizens of the United States to vote shall not be denied or abridged by the United States or by any State on account of sex.

The Congress shall have power by appropriate legislation to enforce the provisions of this article. [August 26, 1920.]

ARTICLE XX.

Section 1. The terms of the President and Vice-President shall end at noon on the twentieth day of January, and the terms of Senators and Representatives at noon on the third day of January, of the years in which such terms would have ended if this article had not been ratified; and the terms of their successors shall then begin.

Section 2. The Congress shall assemble at least once in every year, and such meeting shall begin at noon on the third day of January, unless they shall by law appoint a different day.

Section 3. If, at the time fixed for the beginning of the term of the President, the President-elect shall have died, the Vice-President-elect shall become President. If a President shall not have been chosen before the time fixed for the beginning of his term, or if the President-elect shall have failed to qualify, then the Vice-President-elect shall act as President until a President shall have qualified; and the Congress may by law provide for the case wherein neither a President-elect nor a Vice-President-elect shall have qualified, declaring who shall then act as President, or the manner in which one who is to act shall be selected, and such person shall act accordingly until a President or Vice-President shall have qualified.

Section 4. The Congress may by law provide for the case of the death of any of the persons from whom the House of Representatives may choose a President whenever the right of choice shall have devolved upon them, and for the case of the death of any of the persons from whom the Senate may choose a Vice-President whenever the right of choice shall have devolved upon them.

Section 5. Sections 1 and 2 shall take effect on the 15th day of October following the ratification of this article.

Section 6. This article shall be inoperative unless it shall have been ratified as an amendment to the Constitution by the legislatures of three-fourths of the several States within seven years from the date of its submission. [February 6, 1933.]

ARTICLE XXI.

Section 1. The eighteenth article of amendment to the Constitution of the United States is hereby repealed.

Section 2. The transportation or importation into any State, Territory or possession of the United States for delivery or use therein of intoxicating liquors, in violation of the laws thereof, is hereby prohibited.

Section 3. This article shall be inoperative unless it shall have been ratified as an amendment to the Constitution by convention in the several States, as provided in the Constitution, within seven years from the date of the submission thereof to the States by the Congress. [December 5, 1933.]

ARTICLE XXII.

Section 1. No person shall be elected to the office of the President more than twice, and no person who has held the office of President, or acted as President, for more than two years of a term to which some other person was elected President shall be elected to the office of the President more than once. But this Article shall not apply to any person holding the office of President when this Article was proposed by the Congress, and shall not prevent any person who may be holding the office of President, or acting as President, during the term within which this Article becomes operative from holding the office of President or acting as President during the remainder of such term.

Section 2. This article shall be inoperative unless it shall have been ratified as an amendment to the Constitution by the legislatures of three-fourths of the several States within seven years from the date of its submission to the States by the Congress. [February 27, 1951.]

ARTICLE XXIII.

Section 1. The District constituting the seat of government of the United States shall appoint in such manner as the Congress may direct:

A number of electors of President and Vice-President equal to the whole number of Senators and Representatives in Congress to which the District would be entitled if it were a State, but in no event more than the least populous State; they shall be in addition to those appointed by the States, but they shall be considered, for the purposes of the election of President and Vice-President, to be electors appointed by a State; and they shall meet in the District and perform such duties as provided by the twelfth article of amendment.

Section 2. The Congress shall have the power to enforce this article by appropriate legislation. [March 29, 1961.]

ARTICLE XXIV.

Section 1. The right of citizens of the United States to vote in any primary or other election for President or Vice President, for electors for President or Vice President, or for Senator or Representative in Congress, shall not be denied or abridged by the United States or any State by reason of failure to pay any poll tax or other tax.

Section 2. The Congress shall have power to enforce this article by appropriate legislation. [January 23, 1964.]

ARTICLE XXV.

Section 1. In case of the removal of the President from office or of his death or resignation, the Vice President shall become President.
Section 2. Whenever there is a vacancy in the office of Vice President, the President shall nominate a Vice President who shall take office upon confirmation by a majority vote of both Houses of

Congress.

Section 3. Whenever the President transmits to the President pro tempore of the Senate and the Speaker of the House of Representatives his written declaration that he is unable to discharge the powers and duties of his office, and until he transmits to them a written declaration to the contrary, such powers and duties shall be discharged by the Vice President as Acting President.

Section 4. Whenever the Vice President and a majority of either the principal officers of the executive departments or of such other body as Congress may by law provide, transmit to the President pro tempore of the Senate and the Speaker of the House of Representatives their written declaration that the President is unable to discharge the powers and duties of his office, the Vice President shall immediately assume the powers and duties of the office as Acting President.

Thereafter, when the President transmits to the President pro tempore of the Senate and the Speaker of the House of Representatives his written declaration that no inability exists, he shall resume the powers and duties of his office unless the Vice President and a majority of either the principal officers of the executive departments or of such other body as Congress may by law provide, transmit within four days to the President pro tempore of the Senate and the Speaker of the House of Representatives their written declaration that the President is unable to discharge the powers and duties of his office. Thereupon Congress shall decide the issue, assembling within forty-eight hours for that purpose if not in session. If the Congress, within twenty-one days after receipt of the latter written declaration, or, if Congress is not in session, within twenty-one days after Congress is required to assemble, determines by two-thirds vote of both Houses that the President is unable to discharge the powers and duties of his office, the Vice President shall continue to discharge the same as Acting President; otherwise, the President shall resume the powers and duties of his office. [February 10, 1967.]

ARTICLE XXVI.

Section 1. The right of citizens of the United States, who are eighteen years of age or older, to vote shall not be denied or abridged by the United States or by any State on account of age.

Section 2. The Congress shall have power to enforce this article by appropriate legislation [June 30, 1971.]

Appendix 3

Glossary of Legal Terms

Abatement, plea in: A plea addressd to a court which, without disputing the justice of the plaintiff's claim, objects to the place, mode, or time of asserting it.

Ad hoc: "For this special purpose"—for example, an ad hoc court.

Admiralty court: A court having jurisdiction over controversies arising out of acts, torts, crimes, and the like, occurring at sea.

Apellant: The party who takes an appeal from a decision in an inferior court to a superior tribunal.

Cloture: The procedure in a parliamentary body whereby debate is terminated.

Comity: The practice of cooperation and accommodation, as between courts, the various states of the Union, or foreign nations—for example, the recognition by one state of the court decisions or public acts of another.

Common law: The body of court-made law, inherited from England, which state courts generally use, subject to modifications by constitutions, statute law, and American precedent.

Court-martial: A court for the trial of military personnel. In U.S. law one established under the power delegated to Congress in Article I, Section 8 to make rules for the government of the military forces and hence not established under Article III of the Constitution.

De facto: ("In fact," or "in reality"): Applicable to any governmental authority that for the moment, at least, maintains its existence regardless of any lawful or constitutional basis—for example, the Confederate state governments.

Defendant: The party against whom relief or recovery is sought in an action or suit.

De jure: ("Of right," legitimate, lawful): Applicable to any governmental authority founded upon a correct legal basis.

Equity law: A system of law, originally administered in England by a separate set of tribunals, which is intended to provide certain forms of remedial justice not ordinarily available at common law—for example, by means of an injunction.

Ex post facto law: A law passed after the commission of an act, retroactively defining the act as a crime and prescribing punishment.

Freehold: An estate in real property (land or buildings), held free of any rents, burdens, or obligations to another.

Injunction: A prohibitive order issued by a court under its equity jurisdiction, forbidding a defendant to do some act which may damage the plaintiff.

Obiter dictum: Any part of the opinion of a court entirely unnecessary to the decision of the case at hand, and hence regarded as not binding precedent for future decisions.

Petitioner: Generally, one who addresses an application or plea to a court for the exercise of its power. In U.S. Supreme Court practice, a party who appeals his case to the Court on a writ of certiorari.

Per curiam: A phrase used to describe an opinion presented by the whole Court rather than by any one judge. Generally confined to very brief and summary disposition of the case at hand.

Plaintiff: One who brings a legal action in a lawsuit against another.

Rem, action in: A legal proceeding against a "thing" rather than an action against a person—for example, a suit to recover possession of a piece of property.

Respondent: In appellate jurisdiction, the person who defends against an appeal.

Statute: Any law formally enacted by a legislative body.

Subpoena: An order issued by a court or other governmental agency compelling the attendance of a witness.

Writ of certiorari: A writ granted at the discretion of a superior court, directed to an inferior tribunal, to enable the former to examine the lower court's opinion. Nowadays the principal method whereby the Supreme Court takes appeals from lower tribunals.

Writ of error: A writ issued by an appellate court directing an inferior court to submit to it the records of a case in which final judgment has been entered, for examination for possible errors in law, and for possible reversal, modification, or confirmation of the judgment. Formerly a common mode of appeal to the U.S. Supreme Court.

Writ of habeas corpus: ("You have the body"): A writ directing an official to produce a prisoner in court with an explanation of the reasons for the prisoner's detention.

Writ of mandamus: ("We command"): An order directed to an executive, administrative, or judicial officer commanding him to perform some duty associated with his office.

Selected Readings

WORKS OF GENERAL VALUE

Andrew C. McLaughlin, *A Constitutional History of the United States* (1935), contains excellent material on the period from the Revolution through Reconstruction but relatively little on constitutional developments after 1885. Homer C. Hockett, *The Constitutional History of the United States, 1776–1876* (1939), 2 vols., is a somewhat old-fashioned constitutional history emphasizing political developments. Carl B. Swisher, *American Constitutional Development* (1954), presents much valuable material on twentieth-century constitutional problems. Benjamin F. Wright, *The Growth of American Constitutional Law* (1942), is a valuable synthesis of judicial-constitutional development. Association of American Law Schools, ed., *Selected Essays on Constitutional Law* (1938), 4 vols., hereinafter referred to as *Selected Essays*, comprises a collection of notable essays in constitutional law and history gathered from the nation's legal periodicals. Leonard Levy, ed., *American Constitutional Law: Historical Essays* (1966), is another useful collection. Paul Freund, ed., *The History of the Supreme Court of the United States* (1971–   ), 11 vols., published by the Oliver Wendell Holmes, Jr., Devise, is not yet finished, but, when completed, it will provide scholars with an extremely detailed and comprehensive history of the Court and its work from the pre-Marshall era to 1941. The separately authored and titled volumes of this study already in print are discussed below. Charles Warren, *The Supreme Court in United States History* (1937), 2 vols, contains a wealth of material on the Court's role in politics and history. Henry J. Abraham, *Justices and Presidents: A Political History of Appointments to the Supreme Court* (1974), provides, despite some minor errors, a good short survey of the political considerations which have determined the Court's composition. Robert G. McCloskey, *The American Supreme Court* (1960), is an excellent brief history. Leon Friedman and Fred L. Israel, eds., *The Justices of the United States Supreme Court 1789–1969: Their Lives and Opinions* (1969), 4 vols., provides more detail, but the ninety-seven biographical sketches which it contains are by thirty-seven different authors, and the quality is quite uneven. Arthur E. Sutherland, *Constitutionalism in America: Origins and Evolution of Its Fundamental Ideas* (1965), emphasizes English legal background. Lawrence M. Friedman, *A History of American Law* (1973), is excellent on the colonial period and also provides an effective overview of the broad legal context within which nineteenth century constitutional development took place. William W. Crosskey, *Politics and the Constitution in the History of the United States* (1953), 2 vols., advances the insupportable thesis that the Constitutional Convention intended to establish a unitary state, but contains much valuable material otherwise. Alan Barth, *Prophets with Honor: Great Dissents and Great Dissenters in the Supreme Court* (1975), emphasizes civil rights and civil liberties. Charles Miller, *The Supreme Court and the Uses of History* (1969), is an intelligent and provocative analysis of the types of historical inquiries in which Justices have engaged and the purposes for which they have used history in their opinions.

Henry S. Commager, ed., *Documents of American History* (1968), is the modern documentary source book for the student of constitutional history. F. N. Thorpe, ed., *The Federal and State Constitutions, Colonial Charters and Other Organic Laws* (1909), 7 vols., is a convenient collection of colonial charters and state constitutions. James M. Smith and Paul Murphy, eds., *Liberty and Justice: A Historical Record of American Constitutional Development* (1958, 1968), presents the basic documents virtually as a constitutional history. Zechariah Chafee, Jr., ed., *Documents on Fundamental Human Rights* (1951), 3 vols., has many useful early documents, including charters and state constitutions.

Stanley I. Kutler, ed., *The Supreme Court and the Constitution: Readings in American Constitutional History* (1969, 1977), is a fine historical casebook. Paul Kauper, *Constitutional Law: Cases and Materials* (1966), is an excellent general casebook, and, because of its historical orientation, Gerald Gunther, *Constitutional Law: Cases and Materials* (1975), is also useful. Alpheus T. Mason and William Beaney, *The Supreme Court in a Free Society* (1959), employs a historico-analytical approach to constitutional law, as does C. Hermann Pritchett, *The American Constitution* (1968). E. S. Corwin, *The Constitution and What It Means Today* (1958, 1975), is a brief classic. Bernard Schwartz, *A Commentary on the Constitution of the United States* (1963, 1968), 5 vols., is excellent on constitutional law but outdated in its history. Edward Dumbauld, *The Constitution of the United States* (1964), analyzes the historical and legal meaning of the Constitution, clause by clause. E. S. Corwin, ed., *The Constitution of the United States, Analysis and Interpretation* (1953), annotates the Constitution with Supreme Court cases to 1952. Louis Henkin, *Foreign Affairs and the Constitution* (1972), brilliantly explicates the conduct of foreign affairs under the constitution.

United States Supreme Court reports are available in three principal editions. The official Government Printing Office publication of the reports, *United States Reports,* is cited more briefly as *U.S.* [Example: 274 *U.S.* 179.] The *Supreme Court Reporter* is cited as *S. Ct.* [Example: 65 *S. Ct.* 847.] The *Lawyers' Edition* is cited as *L. Ed.* [Example: 69 *L. Ed.* 234.] Until 1882, Supreme Court decisions were published by private reporters and commonly cited by their names. [Examples: 1 *Cranch* 38; 3 *Peters* 136; 7 *Wallace* 94.]

CHAPTER 1. ENGLISH AND COLONIAL ORIGINS

Stanley N. Katz, "The Origins of American Constitutional Thought," *Perspectives in American History*, III (1969), reviews recent writings on late seventeenth and eighteenth century British constitutional thought and development and relates these to the American experience. Charles M. Andrews, *The Colonial Period of American History* (1935–39), 4 vols., is predominantly political and constitutional in content. H. L. Osgood, *The American Colonies in the Seventeenth Century* (1904–1907), 3 vols., is an older work with a similar approach. A detailed study on the joint-stock companies can be found in W. R. Scott, *The Constitution and Finance of English, Scottish and Irish Joint Stock Companies to 1720* (1910–12), 3 vols. Charles P. Lucas, *Beginnings of English Overseas Enterprise* (1917), is a good brief study. W. F. Craven, *Dissolution of the Virginia Company* (1935), has pertinent constitutional material. A. C. McLaughlin, *Foundations of American Constitutionalism* (1932), contains essays on the joint-stock company and on the influence of early Separatism in colonial constitutional theory. Francis D. Wormuth, *The Origins of Modern Constitutionalism* (1949), contains interesting ideas. J. G. A. Pocock, *The Ancient Constitution and the Feudal Law: A Study of English Historical Thought in the Seventeenth Century* (1957), analyzes attitudes toward the British constitution at the time when settlement of the American colonies was beginning. G. P. Gooch, *The History of English Democratic Ideas in the Seventeenth Century* (1898), is a study of Puritan political theory. Margaret Judson, *The Crisis of the Constitution: An Essay in Constitutional and Political Thought in England, 1603–1645* (1949), argues for the similarity of Puritan and Royalist political ideas. Jean Moura and Paul Louvet, *Calvin: A Modern Biography* (1932), is useful for its treatment of the implications of Calvinism for political theory. H. D. Foster, "The Political Theories of Calvinists before the Puritan Exodus to America," *American Historical Review*, XXI (April 1916), is worth reading, as is H. L. Osgood, "The Political Ideas of the Puritans," *Political Science Quarterly*, VI (March, June 1891). George M. Trevelyan, *England under the Stuarts* (1930), is enlightening both on religious controversy and on Stuart colonial policy. Godfrey Davies, *The Early Stuarts, 1603–1660* (1937), is a study of considerable merit. Robert Emmet Wall, *Massachusetts Bay: The Crucial Decade 1640–1650* (1972), deals with a number of constitutional issues, as does Mary Jeane Anderson Jones, *Congregational Commonwealth: Connecticut 1636–1662* (1968). Warren Billings, "The Growth of Political Institutions in Virginia 1634 to 1676," *William and Mary Quarterly*, XXXI (April 1974) is also valuable. A detailed constitutional study of a proprietary colony is William R. Shepherd, *History of Proprietary Government in Pennsylvania* (1896). J. S. Bassett, *The Constitutional Beginnings of North Carolina, 1663–1729* (1894), is old but still valuable. Louise P. Kellogg, "The American Colonial Charter," *American Historical Association Reports, 1903*, Vol. I, discusses Stuart proprietary policy. Relevant charters are in Henry S. Commager, ed., *Documents of American History* (1968); William MacDonald, ed., *Select Documents Illustrative of the History of the United States, 1776–1861* (1897); *Documentary Source Book of American History, 1606–1913* (1916); and Zechariah Chafee, Jr., ed., *Documents on Fundamental Human Rights* (1951), 3 vols.

CHAPTER 2. A CENTURY OF COLONIAL GOVERNMENT

H. L. Osgood, *The American Colonies in the Eighteenth Century* (1924), 4 vols., is devoted to political and constitutional development. George Dargo, *Roots of the Republic: A New Perspective on Early American Constitutionalism* (1974), is a useful survey, but its tone is less than dispassionate, and some of its self-consciously revisionist conclusions are dubious. Michael Kammen, *Deputies and Liberties: The Origins of Representative Government in Colonial America* (1972), introduces a collection of documents with an outstanding essay. Bernard Bailyn, *The Origins of American Politics* (1968), also offers valuable insights. Mary P. Clarke, *Parliamentary Privilege in the American Colonies* (1943), is a good treatment of colonial legislative organization and procedure. A. E. McKinley, *The Suffrage Franchise in the Thirteen English Colonies in America* (1905), is still a rewarding study on colonial voting requirements. A recent study, Chilton Williamson, *American Suffrage from Property to Democracy, 1760–1860* (1960), contends that the colonial suffrage was much more broadly based than previously supposed. Robert Emmet Wall, Jr., "The Decline of the Massachusetts Franchise 1647–1666," *Journal of American History*, LIX (September 1972), demonstrates that the percentage of freemen in several towns in that colony went down in the middle seventeenth century, but Robert E. Brown, *Middle-Class Democracy and the Revolution in Massachusetts, 1691–1780* (1955), argues that colonial Massachusetts eventually became a middle-class democracy. Robert F. and Katharine Brown, *Virginia: 1705–1788: Democracy or Aristocracy?* (1964), extends the Brown thesis to Virginia. Roy N. Lokken, "The Concept of Democracy in Colonial Political Thought," *William and Mary Quarterly*, XVI (October 1959), argues that Brown's thesis misconstrues the nature of colonial "democracy" and David C. Skaggs, *Roots of Maryland Democracy 1753–1776* (1973) finds it untenable for that colony. Michael Zuckerman, "The Social Content of Democracy in Massachusetts," *William and Mary Quarterly*, XXV (October 1968), although conceding that the right to vote was widespread there, contends that important policy decisions were made outside the formal electoral process. Robert Zemsky, *Merchants, Farmers, and River Gods: An Essay on Eighteenth Century American Politics* (1971), demonstrates that most Massachusetts voters and legislators willingly deferred to the will of a ruling elite. In "Peaceable Kingdoms: The New England Town from the Perspective of Legal History," *American Journal of Legal History*, XV (October 1971), Kinvin L. Wroth challenges the contention of Michael Zuckerman, *Peaceable Kingdoms: New England Towns in the Eighteenth Century* (1970), that the towns were the basic means of social control in New England, arguing that the legal system there was an independent and effective instrument of social control. William E. Nelson, "The Legal Restraint of Power in Pre-Revolutionary America: Massachusetts as a Case Study 1760–1775," *American Journal of Legal History*, XVIII (January 1974), demonstrates that Americans in one colony were extremely successful in restraining governmental power. B. F. Wright, "The Origin of Separation of Powers in America," *Economica*, XIII (May 1933), is an admirable brief survey. Malcolm P. Sharpe, "The Classical American Doctrine of the Separation of Powers," *University of Chicago Law Review*, II (April 1935), contains valuable theoretical observations. Lucille Griffith, *The Virginia House of Burgesses, 1750–1774* (1963), is an excellent detailed study. George Edward Frakes, *Laboratory for Liberty: The South Carolina Legislative Committee System 1719–1776* (1970), argues that committees played an important role in the development of colonial notions of legislative supremacy. Jack P. Greene, *The Quest for Power: The Lower House of Assembly in the Southern Royal Colonies, 1689–1776* (1963), emphasizes the colonial drift toward autonomy. The same author's "Political Mimesis: A Consideration of the Historical and Cultural Roots of Legislative Behavior of the British Colonies in the Eighteenth Century," *American Historical Review*, LXXV (December 1969), emphasizes colonial recapitulation of the "Glorious Revolution." J. R. Pole, *Political Representation in England and the Origins of the American Revolution* (1966), emphasizes the Whig tradition of "mixed government" in the colonies. L. W. Labaree, *Royal Government in America* (1930), is mainly a study of the royal governors. L. W. Labaree, *Royal Instructions to British Colonial Governors, 1670–1776* (1935), provides an excellent collection. E. B. Greene, *The Provincial Governor* (1898), is a useful work. There is good material on the colonial courts and judiciary in Richard B. Morris, *Studies in the History of American Law, with Special Reference to the Seventeenth and Eighteenth Centuries* (1930), and in Charles Warren, *A History of the American Bar* (1911). The first volume of the Holmes Devise *History of the Supreme Court of the United States*, Julius Gobel, Jr., *Antecedents and Beginnings* (1971), is also useful on this subject. Marvin K. Singleton, "New Light on the Chancery Side of Virginia's Evolution to Statehood," *Journal of American Studies*, II (October 1968), and Herbert Alan Johnson, "The Prerogative Court of New York 1686–1776," *American Journal of Legal History*, XVIII (April 1973) are valuable specialized studies. Anton-Hermann Chroust, *The Rise of the Legal Profession in America* (1965), 2 vols., is rich but badly organized. George A. Billas, *Law and Authority in Colonial America* (1965), has several useful essays. David H. Flaherty, ed., *Essays in the History of Early American Law* (1969), is especially valuable. The same author's *Privacy in Colonial New England* (1972), and "Law and the Enforcement of Morals in Early America," *Perspectives in American History*, V (1971), are also useful. Zechariah Chafee, Jr., "Colonial Courts and the Common Law," *Massachusetts Historical Society Proceedings*, LXVIII (1944), is a superior short study. Mark DeWolfe Howe and Louis F. Eaton, Jr., "The Supreme Judicial Power in the Colony of Massachusetts Bay," *New England Quarterly*, XX (September 1947), is also useful, while Paul M. McCain, *The County Court in North Carolina Before 1750* (1954), is valuable too. On the role of the courts in colonial politics see Stanley N. Katz, "The Politics of Law in Colonial America: Controversies over Chancery Courts and Equity Law in the Eighteenth Century," *Perspectives in American History*, V (1971), and Jerome J. Nadellhaft, "Politics and the Judicial Tenure Fight in Colonial New Jersey," *William and Mary Quarterly*, XXVIII (January 1971). Katz, ed., *Brief Narrative of the Case and Trial of John Peter Zenger* (1963, 1973), is also useful. Paul M. Hamlin and Charles Baker, *The Supreme Court of Judicature of the Province of New York, 1691–1704* (1959), 3 vols., is a valuable technical work. Benjamin F. Wright, *American Interpretations of Natural Law* (1931), contains two excellent chapters on colonial political theory. Lawrence H. Leder, *Liberty and Authority: Early American Political Ideology* (1968), is an extremely important book. J. W. Gough, *John Locke's Political Philosophy* (1950), shows the relationship of Locke's ideas to American theory, but Ronald E. Pynn, "The Influence of John Locke's Political Philosophy on American Political Traditions," *North Dakota Quarterly*, XLII (1974), raises serious doubts about the extent of Locke's influence on the colonies. T. H. Breen, *The Character of the Good Ruler: A Study of Puritan Political Ideas in New England 1630–1730* (1970), documents a substantial change in Puritan political thought during the period which it covers. Alice M. Baldwin, *The New England Clergy and the American Revolution* (1928), shows the prevalence of natural-law theory and the doctrine of limited government in eighteenth-century New England. Clinton Rossiter, *Seed-time of the Republic: The Origins of The American Tradition of Political Liberties* (1953), analyzes the ideas of principal colonial political thinkers. There are sketches of Roger Williams, Thomas Hooker, and other colonial political theorists in Vernon L. Parrington, *Main Currents in American Thought* (1927), Vol. 1. Perry Miller, *The New England Mind: From Colony to Province* (1953), is useful for political theory. James Ernst, *Roger Williams* (1932), and S. H. Brockunier, *The Irrepressible Democrat: Roger Williams* (1940), are biographies presenting Williams as a prototype of a modern liberal-democrat. This point of view is criticized severely in Perry Miller, *Roger Williams: His Contribution to the American Tradition* (1953), and in Alan Simpson, "How Democratic Was Roger Williams?," *William and Mary Quarterly*, XIII (January 1956). Edmund S. Morgan, *Roger Williams: The Church and the State* (1967), in turn differs with the Miller thesis. William G. McLoughlin, *New England Dissent 1630–1833: The Baptists and the Separation of Church and State* (1971), 2 vols., is an important work. G. A. Cook, *John Wise: Early American Democrat* (1952), emphasizes Wise's democratic ideas. Its thesis is at odds with Raymond P. Stearns, "John Wise of Ipswich Was no Democrat in Politics," *Essex Institute Historical Collections*, XCVII (January 1961). E. S. Corwin, "The 'Higher Law' Background of American Constitutional Law," *Harvard Law Review*, XLII (December 1928, June 1929), reprinted in *Selected Essays*, I, and as a Cornell University Press Paperback (1955), is a classic essay on early natural rights theory. L. K. Wroth and H. B. Zobel, eds., *Legal Papers of John Adams* (1965), 3 vols., includes Adams' documents on the Writs of Assistance Case, together with a valuable explanatory essay. The Writs of Assistance Case is also discussed in O. M. Dickerson, "Writs of Assistance as a Cause of the American Revolution," *The Era of the American Revolution* (Studies Inscribed to E. B. Greene) (1939), and in Theodore F. T. Plucknett, "Bonham's Case and Judicial Review," *Harvard Law Review*, XL (November 1926), reprinted in *Selected Essays*, I.

The over-all development of the British imperial system is traced and analyzed in G. L. Beer, *Origins of the British Colonial System* (1908), and in G. L. Beer, *The Old Colonial System* (1912). On relations between the colonies and England in the late seventeenth and early eighteenth centuries see David S. Lovejoy, *The Glorious Revolution in America* (1972) and Philip S. Haffenden, *New England in the English Nation 1689–1713* (1974). O. M. Dickerson, *American Colonial Government, 1696–1765* (1912), is a good study of the Board of Trade. Mary P. Clarke, "The Board of Trade at Work," *American Historical Review*, XVII (October 1911), is also useful. C. M. Andrews, "The Royal Disallowance," American Antiquarian Society, *Proceedings* (October 1914), and Elmer B. Russell, *The Review of American Colonial Legislation by the King in Council* (1915), are helpful in their treatment of disallowance. George A. Washburne, *Imperial Control of the Administration of Justice in the Thirteen American Colonies, 1684–1776* (1923), is a study of the Privy Council's function in the review of appeals from colonial courts. H. J. Smith, *Appeals to the Privy Council from the American Plantations* (1950), is an exhaustive technical work. E. R. Turner, *The Privy Council of England in the Seventeenth and Eighteenth Centuries* (1928), is also detailed and specialized. A. M. Schlesinger, "Colonial Appeals to the Privy Council," *Political Science Quarterly*, XXVIII (June, September 1913), is a useful brief survey. Ella Lonn, *The Colonial Agents of the Southern Colonies* (1935); James J. Burns, *The Colonial Agents of New England* (1935); and M. G. Kammen, *A Rope of Sand: The Colonial Agents, British Politics and the American Revolution* (1968), are all useful. Lawrence Harper, *The English Navigation Laws: A Seventeenth Century Experiment in Social Engineering* (1939), emphasizes general colonial obedience to the acts of trade. But Dora May Clarke, *The Rise of the British Treasury: Colonial Administration in the Eighteenth Century* (1960), emphasizes growing colonial autonomy, while T. C. Barrow, *Trade and Empire: The British Customs Service in America, 1660–1775* (1967), argues that "salutary neglect was a deliberate British policy." James A. Henretta, *"Salutory Neglect": Colonial Administration Under the Duke of Newcastle* (1972), contends that the major interest of British leaders was in colonial patronage. A. C. McLaughlin, "The Background of American Federalism," *American Political Science Review*, XII (May 1918), presents the old British Empire as a great federal state. Efforts to achieve cooperation among the North American colonies themselves are discussed in Harry M. Ward, *"Unite or Die": Intercolony Relations 1690–1763* (1971), and John V. Jezierski, *"Imperii in Imperio: The 1754 Albany Plan of Union and the Origins of the American Revolution,"* *North Dakota Quarterly*, XLII (September 1974).

CHAPTER 3. THE AMERICAN REVOLUTION

Merrill Jensen, *The Founding of a Nation: A History of the American Revolution, 1763–1776* (1968), is an excellent general survey presenting the Revolution as due to a concurrence of various political and social forces. Stephen Kurtz and James H. Hutson, eds., *Essays on the American Revolution* (1973), is an important collection. John Parker and Carol Arness, eds., *The American Revolution: A Heritage of Change* (1975), and Library of Congress, *Library of Congress Symposia on the American Revolution: Papers Presented at the Second Symposium May 10 and 11, 1973* (1973), also contain significant contributions by noted scholars. Bernard Knollenberg, *Growth of the American Revolution 1766–1775* (1975), is useful and provocative, although disjointed, because the author died before completing it. Knollenberg, *Origins of the American Revolution, 1759–1766* (1960), emphasizes the significance of British constitutional decisions in the early part of the Revolutionary crisis. L. H. Gipson, *The British Empire Before the American Revolution*, Vol. X: *The Triumphant Empire: Storm-Clouds Gather in the West, 1763–1776* (1961); Vol. XI: *The Triumphant Empire: Rumblings of the Coming Storm* (1965); and Vol. XII: *The Triumphant Empire: Britain Sails into the Storm* (1965), are Britain-oriented but emphasize the obsolete character of the old British constitution. Bernard Donoughue, *British Politics and the American Revolution* (1964), emphasizes American refusal to submit any longer to colonialism. Edward Channing, *History of the United States* (1912), Vol. III, is still valuable, particularly for its emphasis on constitutional issues. C. H. Van Tyne, *The Causes of the War of Independence* (1922), and John C. Miller, *Origins of the American Revolution* (1943), also are still useful. O. M. Dickerson, *The Navigation Acts and the American Revolution* (1951), is excellent on British commercial policy in the Revolutionary era. F. P. Wickwire, *British Subministers and Colonial America, 1766–1783* (1966), emphasizes the role of the permanent ministry in British formulation of policy toward America after 1763. Carl Ubbelohde, *The Vice-Admiralty Court and the American Revolution* (1960), is a valuable special study. Edmund S. and Helen M. Morgan, *The Stamp Act Crisis: Prologue to Revolution* (1953), is excellent. Hiller B. Zobel, *The Boston Massacre* (1970), is good on the legal facets of that incident and on the trial which followed it. S. E. Morison, ed., *Sources and Documents Illustrating the American Revolution, 1764–1788* (1923, 1965), is a valuable brief source book. Bernard Bailyn, *Pamphlets of the American Revolution, 1750–1776*, Vol I: *1750–1765* (1965), is an invaluable primary source, whose excellent introductory essay is reprinted as Bailyn, *The Ideological Origins of the American Revolution* (1967). Also important is this author's *The Ordeal of Thomas Hutchinson* (1974). Alan Rogers, *Empire and Liberty: American Resistance to British Authority 1755–1763* (1974), takes Bailyn's thesis that it was eighteenth century America's assimilation of Whig political ideology which was responsible for the Revolution and attempts to explain why such ideas were so widely accepted in the colonies. Louis Hartz, "American Political Thought and the American Revolution," *The American Political*

Science Review, XLVI (June 1952), is also worthwhile. C. H. McIlwain, *The American Revolution: A Constitutional Interpretation* (1923, 1958), defends the view that the colonies were not properly subject to Parliament's authority. R. L. Schuyler, *Parliament and the British Empire* (1929), disputes this analysis. Randolph G. Adams, *Political Ideas of the American Revolution* (1922, 1958), provides a comprehensive discussion of the theories of dominion status. Thad W. Tate, "The Social Contract in America 1774–1787: Revolutionary Theory as a Conservative Instrument," *William and Mary Quarterly*, XXII (July 1965), shows how an idea used to justify the break with England was also employed to check unwanted change at home. Gordon Wood, *The Creation of the American Republic, 1776–1787* (1969), treats both Revolutionary ideas and constitutional development. Daniel Boorstin, *The Genius of American Politics* (1953), argues that the Revolution was a movement to defend constitutional democracy. James M. Kirby, *Men in Rebellion: Higher Governmental Leaders and the Coming of the American Revolution* (1973), emphasizes the frustrations of office holders denied upward mobility within the governmental structure by extensive plural office holding.

Pauline Maier, *From Resistance to Revolution: Colonial Radicals and the Development of American Opposition to Britain 1765–1776* (1972), is a provocative and important interpretation of America's break with England. For a general account of the crisis of 1774–76, Carl Becker's *The Eve of the Revolution* (1920) is a competent treatment. Less satisfactory is John M. Head, *A Time to Rend: An Essay on the Decision for American Independence* (1968). Julian Boyd, *Anglo-American Union: Joseph Galloway's Plans to Preserve the British Empire* (1941), presents a sympathetic interpretation of the Galloway plan. J. M. Leake, *The Virginia Committee System and the American Revolution* (1917), is a study of the committees of correspondence in that state. E. C. Burnett, *The Continental Congress* (1941), comprises the definitive work of scholarship on that body. H. A. Cushing, *History of the Transition from Provincial to Commonwealth Government in Massachusetts* (1896), and J. Paul Selsam, *The Pennsylvania State Constitution of 1776* (1936), are the best studies of the constitutional aspects of revolution within a state. C. H. Lincoln, *The Revolutionary Movement in Pennsylvania* (1901), and H. J. Eckenrode, *The Revolution in Virginia* (1916), are more general in character. James Hutson, *Pennsylvania Politics: The Movement for Royal Government and its Consequences* (1972), argues that in Pennsylvania the effort to replace proprietary with royal rule prepared the colonists temperamentally for revolution. Charles Barker, *The Background of the Revolution in Maryland* (1940); Donald Kemmerer, *Path to Freedom: The Struggle for Self-Government in Colonial New Jersey, 1703–1776* (1940); Oscar Zirchner, *Connecticut's Years of Controversy, 1750–1776* (1949); T. J. Wertenbaker, *Give Me Liberty: The Struggle For Self-Government in Virginia* (1958); and E. P. Douglass, *Rebels and Democrats: The Struggle for Equal Political Rights and Majority Rule During the American Revolution* (1955), are all useful on the rise of constitutional democracy during the Revolutionary controversy.

By far the most brilliant work on the philosophy and content of the

Declaration of Independence is Carl Becker, *The Declaration of Independence* (1922, 1942, 1958). Herbert Friedenwald, *The Declaration of Independence* (1904), is useful. John H. Hazelton, *The Declaration of Independence* (1906), is a detailed specialized study. Edward Dumbauld, *The Declaration of Independence and What It Means Today* (1950), presents a historical interpretation of each passage of the Declaration. Useful background is supplied by J. M. Bumstead, "Things in the Womb of Time: Ideas of American Independence 1633 to 1763," *William and Mary Quarterly*, XXXI (October 1974), and Paul W. Adams, "Republicanism in Political Rhetoric Before 1776," *Political Science Quarterly*, LXXXV (September 1970).

CHAPTER 4. THE FIRST STATE CONSTITUTIONS AND THE ARTICLES OF CONFEDERATION

Allan Nevins, *The American States During and After the Revolution, 1775–1789* (1924), contains material on the adoption of various state constitutions between 1776 and 1783. Jackson Turner Main, *The Sovereign States 1775–1783* (1973), also devotes considerable attention to this subject, characterizing these early state constitutions as moderate products of compromise between democratic and Whig ideologies. Fletcher M. Green, *Constitutional Development of the South Atlantic States, 1776–1860* (1930), analyzes the early Southern state constitutions. Benjamin F. Wright, "The Early History of Written Constitutions in America," *Essays in History and Political Theory in Honor of C. H. McIlwain* (1936), is a brief summary of theory and ideas behind early state constitutions. W. F. Dodd, "The First State Constitutional Conventions, 1776–1783," *American Political Science Review*, II (November 1908), summarizes the conventions and their work. Wood, *Creation of the Republic*, also contains valuable materials, as does Jackson Turner Main, *The Upper House in Revolutionary America, 1763–1788* (1967). H. A. Cushing, *History of the Transition from Provincial to Commonwealth Government in Massachusetts* (1896), and Samuel E. Morison, "The Struggle over the Adoption of the Constitution of Massachusetts, 1780," Massachusetts Historical Society, *Proceedings*, L (October 1916; June 1917), include essential material on Massachusetts constitutional development. However, Robert J. Taylor, ed., *Massachusetts, Colony to Commonwealth: Documents on the Formation of Its Constitution* (1961), presents documents at odds with Morison's thesis. Oscar Handlin, *The Popular Sources of Political Authority: Documents on the Massachusetts Constitution of 1780* (1966), is similar in emphasis to Taylor. Jere R. Daniell, *Experiment in Republicanism: New Hampshire Politics and the American Revolution 1741–1794* (1970), offers a solid analysis of constitution making in that state. For information on the Pennsylvania and Vermont constitutions see two articles by John N. Schaeffer, "A Comparison of the First Constitutions of Vermont and Pennsylvania," *Vermont History*, XLIII (Winter 1975), and "Public Consideration of the 1776 Pennsylvania Constitution," *Pennsylvania Magazine of History and Biography*, XCVIII (October 1974).

Corwin, "The 'Higher Law' Background" (see bibliography, Chapter 1, above), deals with the background of judicial review. E. S. Corwin, "The Progress of Constitutional Theory between the Declaration of Independence and the Meeting of the Philadelphia Convention," *American Historical Review*, XXX (April 1925), includes a discussion of the emergence of judicial review in the Revolutionary era. A. C. McLaughlin, *The Courts, the Constitution and Parties* (1912), has some material on early judicial review. Patrick T. Conley, "Rhode Island's Paper Money Issue and *Trevett v. Weeden* (1786)," *Rhode Island History*, XXX (August 1971), examines the background and results of a state court decision which looms large in most discussions of that subject. Charles G. Haines, *The American Doctrine of Judicial Supremacy* (2nd ed., 1932), is a scholarly study of the origins and development of judicial review. Jonathan Elliot, ed., *The Debates in the Several State Conventions on the Adoption of the Federal Constitution* (1836), 5 vols., includes the congressional debate on adoption of the Articles of Confederation. A. C. McLaughlin, *The Confederation and the Constitution* (1905), is a classic treatment of the Confederation era. A more recent study which views the Articles as an experiment in democracy is Merrill Jensen, *The Articles of Confederation: An Interpretation of the Social-Constitutional History of the American Revolution* (1940, 1959). Merrill Jensen, *The New Nation: A History of the United States during the Confederation, 1781–1789* (1950), maintains the same thesis. This interpretation should be contrasted with that in B. F. Wright, *Consensus and Continuity, 1776–1787* (1958). John Fiske, *The Critical Period of American History* (1888), although outmoded, also presents an interpretation which may be compared to advantage with that in Jensen. H. B. Adams, *Maryland's Influence upon Land Cessions to the United States* (1885), is still the authoritative study on this topic. Jennings B. Sanders, *Evolution of Executive Departments of the Continental Congress, 1774–1789* (1935), is a scholarly work. Charles C. Thach, *The Creation of the Presidency, 1775–1789* (1922), also contains materials on the Confederation executive. The judicial function of the Confederation Congress is discussed in J. C. B. Davis, "Federal Courts Prior to the Adoption of the Constitution," 131 *U.S.* Appendix, in J. F. Jameson, "The Predecessor of the Supreme Court," *Essays in the Constitutional History of the United States* (1889).

CHAPTER 5. THE CONSTITUTIONAL CONVENTION

Max Farrand, ed., *The Records of the Federal Convention of 1787* (1911, 1937), 4 vols., contains Madison's notes as well as other contemporary source material and is indispensable to any study of the Convention. W. U. Solberg, ed., *The Federal Convention and the Formation of the Union of American States* (1958), is a useful brief collection of documents, as is Adrienne Koch, ed., *Notes and Debates in the Federal Convention of 1787* (1966). A. C. McLaughlin, *The Confederation and the Constitution* (1905), emphasizes the essentially nationalistic character of the Convention's work. Max Farrand, *The Framing of the Constitution of the United States* (1913), treats personalities and political issues rather than the problem of sovereignty. Charles Warren, *The Making of the Constitution* (1929), is virtually a day-by-day study of the Convention. Max Farrand, *The Fathers of the Constitution* (1913), is a brief survey of the Convention. Carl Van Doren, *The Great Rehearsal: The Story of the Making and Ratifying of the*

Constitution of the United States (1948), is a popular work, as are also Catherine Drinker Bowen, *Miracle at Philadelphia: The Story of the Constitutional Convention, May to September, 1787* (1966), and Clinton Rossiter, *1787: The Grand Convention* (1966). William P. Murphy, *The Triumph of Nationalism: State Sovereignty, the Founding Fathers and the Making of the Constitution* (1967), overemphasizes the Convention's rejection of states rights. Christopher Collier, *Roger Sherman's Connecticut: Yankee Politics and the American Revolution* (1971), treats the Connecticut Compromise effectively. Howard A. Ohline, "Republicanism and Slavery: Origins of the Three Fifths Clause in the United States Constitution," *William and Mary Quarterly,* XXVIII (October 1971), is good, too. Irving Brant, *James Madison: Father of the Constitution* (1950), and Charles P. Smith, *James Wilson, Founding Father, 1742–1798* (1956) are both valuable. R. G. McCloskey, ed., *The Works of James Wilson* (1967), 2 vols., is a useful primary source. M. R. Zahniser, *Charles Cotesworth Pinckney: Founding Father* (1967), is another useful biography of a Convention figure. So are Paul S. Clarkson and R. Samuel Jett, *Luther Martin of Maryland* (1970), and John J. Reardon, *Edmund Randolph: A Biography* (1974). Helen Miller, *George Mason: Gentleman Revolutionary* (1975), and Max M. Mintz, *Gouverneur Morris and the American Revolution* (1970), are of lower quality. Arnold A. Rogow, "The Federal Convention: Madison and Yates," *American Historical Review,* LX (January 1955), contains useful insights. Broadus Mitchell, *Alexander Hamilton, Youth to Maturity 1755–1788* (1957), treats Hamilton's Convention role, as does Clinton Rossiter, *Alexander Hamilton and the Constitution* (1964), a somewhat uncritical work. Gerald Stourzh, *Alexander Hamilton and the Idea of Republican Government* (1970), analyzes Hamilton's political philosophy. Charles A. Beard, *The Supreme Court and the Constitution* (1913), probably exaggerates the number of delegates who regarded judicial review favorably. Charles Warren, *Congress, the Constitution and the Supreme Court* (1925), presents somewhat the same conclusions. E. S. Corwin, *Court over Constitution* (1938), subjects Beard's findings to criticism. Madison's attitude toward judicial review is discussed in E. M. Burns, *James Madison, Philosopher of the Constitution* (1938). Ralph Ketchum, *From Colony to Country: The Revolution in American Thought 1750–1820* (1974), contains useful information on both Madison's political thought and the Constitution itself. Charles A. Beard's highly controversial study, *An Economic Interpretation of the Constitution of the United States* (1913, 1935, 1962), has lately been subjected to severe criticism. Robert E. Brown, *Charles Beard and the Constitution* (1953,) and Forrest McDonald, *We the People: The Economic Origins of the Constitution* (1958), attack both Beard's methodology and his conclusions. McDonald, in his *E Pluribus Unum: The Formation of the American Republic 1776–1790* (1965), downplays the significance of economic and social interests in motivating those who supported the Constitution. H. S. Commager, "The Constitution: Was It An Economic Document?" *American Heritage* (December 1958), labels the Constitution a political, and not an economic document. Lee Benson, *Beard and Turner* (1960), criticizes the methodology of both Beard and his critics, while J. T. Main, *The Anti-Federalists: Critics of the Constitution, 1781–7788* (1962), in turn makes a "vigorous counter-statement" defending Beard's argument. Douglass Adair, "The Tenth Federalist Revisited," *William and Mary Quarterly*, VIII (January 1951), is also critical of the Beard thesis. Robert E. Thomas, "A Re-appraisal of Charles A. Beard's 'An Economic Interpretation of the Constitution of the United States,'" *American Historical Review*, LVII (January 1952), is an interpretative defense. E. James Ferguson, *The Power of the Purse: A History of American Public Finance 1776–1790* (1961), emphasizes the relationship between public finance and the movement for constitutional reform, while Frederick W. Marks, *Independence on Trial: Foreign Affairs and the Making of the Constitution* (1973), stresses the importance of foreign policy considerations. Another provocative interpretation is that offered by Stanley Elkins and Eric McKitrick, "The Founding Fathers: Young Men of the Revolution," *Political Science Quarterly*, LXXXVI (1961). Wood, *Creation of the Republic* is valuable on this subject also. Staunton Lynd, *Class Conflict, Slavery and the United States Constitution: Ten Essays* (1968), is "new left" in flavor.

CHAPTER 6. RATIFICATION OF THE CONSTITUTION

Jonathan Elliot, ed., *The Debates in the Several State Conventions on the Adoption of the Federal Constitution* (1836), 5 vols., gives the debates in the various state ratifying conventions. Merrill Jensen, ed., *The Documentary History of the Ratification of the Constitution* (1976–   ), 2 vols., is a definitive collection, prepared with the support of the National Historical Publications and Records Commission, which will eventually include 15 volumes. *The Federalist* is available in a number of editions. A convenient volume of *The Federalist* is the Modern Library Edition. Two valuable recent editions are B. F. Wright, ed., *The Federalist* (1961), and Jacob E. Cooke, ed., *The Federalist* (1961). Irving Brant, "Settling the Authorship of The Federalist," *American Historical Review*, LXVI (October 1961), throws new light on a long-disputed question. A. T. Mason, "The Federalist —A Split Personality," *American Historical Review*, LVIII (April 1952), emphasizes the contradictory ideas in *The Federalist*. Martin Diamond, "Democracy and The Federalist: A Reconsideration of the Framers' Intent," *American Political Science Review*, LIII (March 1959), also is worthwhile. Nearly all important contemporary literature on the ratification controversy is gathered together in Paul L. Ford, ed., *Essays on the Constitution . . . 1787–1788*, (1892), and in *Pamphlets on the Constitution* (1888). Herbert A. Johnson, Charles T. Cullen, and Nancy G. Harris, eds., *The Papers of John Marshall* (1974), Vol. I, contains the speeches made by the future Chief Justice during the Virginia ratifying convention. Bernard Donahoe and Marshall Smelser, "The Congressional Power to Raise Armies: The Constitutional and Ratifying Conventions 1787–1788," *Review of Politics*, XXXIII (1971), emphasizes the importance of the subject of central government military power in the ratification debates. O. G. Libby, *The Geographical Distribution of the Vote of the Thirteen States on the Federal Constitution 1787–1788* (1894), is indispensable for an understanding of sectional alignment for and against the Constitution. Alpheus T. Mason, *The States Rights Debate: Anti-Federalism and the Constitution* (1964); R. A.

Rutland, *The Ordeal of the Constitution: The Anti-Federalists and the Ratification Struggle* (1966); Cecelia Kenyon, ed., *The Anti-Federalists* (1966); and Main, *The Anti-Federalists*, all analyze anti-Federalist thought and activities. There are a number of studies of state ratification controversies; most valuable are Samuel B. Harding, *The Contest over the Ratification of the Federal Constitution in the State of Massachusetts* (1896); Joseph B. Walker, *A History of the New Hampshire Convention . . . 1788* (1888), reprinted in *Massachusetts Historical Society Collections*, 5th series, II, III, 6th series, IV; C. E. Miner, *Ratification of the Federal Constitution by the State of New York* (1921); J. B. McMaster and F. D. Stone, *Pennsylvania and the Federal Constitution, 1787–1788* (1888); L. I. Trenholme, *Ratification of the Federal Constitution in North Carolina* (1932); and Linda G. DePauw, *The Eleventh Pillar: New York State and the Federal Constitution* (1966), and Norman K. Risjord, "Virginians and the Constitution: A Multivariant Analysis," *William and Mary Quarterly*, XXXI (1974). The most recent work on holdout Rhode Island is Irwin H. Polishook, *1774–1795: Rhode Island and the Union* (1969). Philip A. Crowl, "Anti-Federalism in Maryland, 1787–1788," *William and Mary Quarterly*, IV (October 1947), argues that the Libby thesis needs considerable qualification in Maryland. Richard P. McCormick, *Experiment in Independence: New Jersey in the Critical Period, 1781–1789* (1950), supports a similar thesis. Main, *The Anti-Federalists*, is also valuable on the ratification controversy. Edward P. Smith, "The Movement toward a Second Constitutional Convention," in J. F. Jameson, ed., *Essays in the Constitutional History of the United States* (1889), provides a study of a little-remembered trend. On the general significance of the Constitution in American history and life see the collection of essays in Conyers Read, ed., *The Constitution Reconsidered* (1938).

CHAPTER 7. ESTABLISHING THE NEW GOVERNMENT

The inauguration of the new federal government in 1789 has often served as the point of beginning for historical studies, both general and specialized. Among the general surveys which include constitutional developments are John C. Miller, *The Federalist Era, 1789–1801* (1960), Nathan Schachner, *The Founding Fathers* (1954), and J. A. Krout and D. R. Fox, *The Completion of Independence* (1944). Joseph Dorfman, *The Economic Mind in American Civilization, 1860–1865* (1946) shows clearly the relationship between economic ideas and constitutional theory. Vernon L. Parrington, *Main Currents in American Thought*, Vol. I, presents brilliant analyses of the constitutional philosophies of such leaders as Adams, Hamilton, and Jefferson. Congressional discussion of constitutional issues as well as the formulation of legislation can be traced in detail in the official *Annals of the Congress of the United States* (1834–1856), 42 vols., for this period from 1789 to 1824. R. M. Bell, *Party and Faction in American Politics: The House of Representatives, 1789–1801* (1973) provides a useful quantitative analysis of voting behavior.

Washington's role in establishing the new government continues to be assessed variously. A recent comprehensive and well balanced treatment is James T. Flexner, *George Washington and the New Nation, 1783–1793*

(1969) and *George Washington: Anguish and Farewell (1793-1799)* (1972). Forrest McDonald, *The Presidency of George Washington* (1974) is a fresh treatment which emphasizes the great importance of Hamilton's economic program for the success of the new government. For a good, general treatment of the Adams administration one should see Page Smith, *John Adams* (1962), 2 vols. E. S. Corwin, *The President: Office and Powers* (1948), analyzes the development of presidential authority, beginning with Washington's administration. Comprehensive and convenient is William M. Goldsmith, *The Growth of Presidential Power: A Documented History*, 3 vols. (1974). Volume I: *The Formative Years* extends through Jackson's presidency. Lloyd M. Short, *The Development of National Administrative Organization in the United States* (1923) describes the organization of the early executive departments, while Leonard D. White, *The Federalists: A Study in Administration* (1948) is a detailed study of the infant federal bureaucracy. Raoul Berger, *Executive Privilege: A Constitutional Myth* (1974) is a careful analysis of this controversial issue with detailed attention to the Federalist Era.

Greatly increased interest in civil rights has led to new studies of the Bill of Rights. Bernard Schwartz, *The Bill of Rights: A Documentary History*, 2 vols., contains practically all of the relevant documents from English and Colonial antecedents through the ratification of the first ten amendments. Other valuable treatments are Edward Dumbauld, *The Bill of Rights and What It Means Today* (1957), Robert A. Rutland, *The Birth of the Bill of Rights, 1776-1791* (1955), Irving Brant, *The Bill of Rights: Its Origin and Meaning* (1966), and Leonard Levy, *Legacy of Suppression: Freedom of Speech and Press in Early America* (1960). Other special studies include Leonard Levy, *Origins of the Fifth Amendment: The Right Against Self-Incrimination* (1968), Clyde E. Jacobs, *The Eleventh Amendment and Sovereign Immunity* (1972), and Richard Hofstadter, *The Idea of a Party System: The Rise of Legitimate Opposition in the United States, 1780-1840* (1969).

Some of the important constitutional implications of foreign policy are treated in S. F. Bemis, *Jay's Treaty, A Study in Commerce and Diplomacy* (1923), C. M. Thomas, *American Neutrality in 1793, A Study in Cabinet Government* (1931), and C. R. Ritcheson, *Aftermath of Revolution: British Policy Toward the United States, 1783-1795* (1969).

Of the many books on the federal judicial system and the Supreme Court in particular, the following recent studies should be of special value to serious students: The Oliver Wendell Holmes Devise *History of the Supreme Court of the United States*, 9 massive volumes projected. Volume I, Julius Goebel, Jr., *Antecedents and Beginnings to 1801* (1971) devotes more attention to British and American antecedents, the framing and adoption of the Constitution, the formulation of the Bill of Rights and the adoption of the Judiciary Act of 1789, than it does to the early Supreme Court, but all of it is good. Leon Friedman and Fred L. Israel, *The Justices of the United States Supreme Court: Their Lives and Major Opinions* (1969), 4 vols., is comprehensive, judicious, and convenient. Raoul Berger, *Congress v. the Supreme Court* (1969) is a critical analysis of the origin and continuing nature of judicial review. Charles Warren, *The Supreme Court in United*

States History (1937) is comprehensive and Federalist-oriented. Charles G. Haines, *The Role of the Supreme Court in American Government and Politics, 1789–1835* (1944) contains a detailed discussion sympathetic to the Jeffersonians. Richard B. Morris, *John Jay: The Nation and the Court* (1967) is brief and relevant.

The constitutional-political issues of the Adams administration receive critical analysis in S. J. Kurtz, *The Presidency of John Adams: The Collapse of Federalism* (1957), J. J. Dover, *The Adams Federalists* (1953), and Ralph A. Brown, *The Presidency of John Adams* (1975). Valuable but variable studies of the controversial Alien and Sedition Acts are James M. Smith, *Freedom's Fetters: The Alien and Sedition Laws and American Civil Liberties* (1956) and John C. Miller, *Crisis in Freedom: The Alien and Sedition Acts* (1951). Kathryn Turner, "Federalist Policy and the Judiciary Act of 1801," *William and Mary Quarterly*, XXII (Oct. 1965) and Erwin C. Surrency, "The Judiciary Act of 1801," *American Journal of Legal History* (April 1958) are good interpretations.

CHAPTER 8. THE RISE OF JEFFERSONIANISM

Thomas Jefferson and his ideas continue to challenge historians two centuries after the famous Declaration of Independence. Although the old classic, Henry Adams, *History of the United States During the Administration of Jefferson and Madison* (1890–91), 9 vols., is still valuable it has been superseded by two excellent and comprehensive treatments: Dumas Malone, *Jefferson and His Time* (1948–1974) 4 vols., of which the last two volumes on Jefferson as President are particularly relevant for this chapter; and Merrill D. Peterson, *Thomas Jefferson and the New Nation: A Biography* (1970). Both authors, however, seem to be unduly critical of Alexander Hamilton and John Marshall. Another classic is Charles A. Beard's *Economic Origins of Jeffersonian Democracy* (1915) which emphasizes the economic differences between Jeffersonians and Federalists. Eugene T. Mudge, *The Social Philosophy of John Taylor of Caroline* (1939) analyzes the thought of one of Jefferson's chief advocates. Other good, brief interpretations are Avery O. Craven, *Democracy in American Life* (1941); Charles M. Wiltse, *The Jeffersonian Tradition in American Democracy* (1960); and Richard B. Davis, *Intellectual Life in Jefferson's Virginia, 1790–1830* (1964). Irving Brant, *James Madison: Father of the Constitution* (1950) is excellent in scholarship and readability but less satisfactory in analytical qualities. Leonard D. White, *The Jeffersonians: A Study in Administrative History, 1801–1829* (1951) emphasizes administrative policies and practices. E. S. Corwin, *The President: Office and Powers, 1787–1957* (rev. ed. 1957) is generally insightful and is especially valuable for various conceptions of the presidential office.

The organizational aspects of the Republican opposition to the Federalists is discussed in Eugene P. Link, *Democratic Republican Societies* (1942); in Noble E. Cunningham, Jr., *The Jeffersonian Republicans: The Formation of Party Organization, 1789–1801* (1957); and in Cunningham, *The Jeffersonian Republicans in Power: Party Operations, 1801–1809* (1963). The Virginia and Kentucky Resolutions are analyzed in F. M. Anderson,

"Contemporary Opinion of the Virginia and Kentucky Resolutions," *American Historical Review*, V (October 1899; July 1900). Alpheus T. Mason, "The Nature of Our Federal Union Reconsidered," *Political Science Quarterly*, LXV (December 1950), restates the argument that Madison was the "grandfather of the Civil War." The standard work on the Twelfth Amendment to the Constitution is Lolabel House, *A Study of the Twelfth Amendment of the Constitution of the United States* (1901). Everett S. Brown, *The Constitutional History of the Louisiana Purchase* (1920), discusses the various constitutional issues involved in the acquisition of the Louisiana Territory.

CHAPTER 9. THE TRIUMPH OF JEFFERSONIAN REPUBLICANISM

For this period also the monumental studies of Henry Adams, Dumas Malone, and Merrill D. Peterson, mentioned above, provide the basic facts and interpretations for understanding the controversial administration of Jefferson. Useful special treatises include Noble E. Cunningham, *The Jeffersonian Republicans in Power*; Marshall Smelser, *The Democratic Republic, 1801–1816* (1968), and Norman Risjord, *The Old Republicans: Southern Conservatism in the Age of Jefferson* (1965).

The major conflicts between Jefferson and his Congressional supporters and the Supreme Court under John Marshall continue to bring forth new analyses and interpretations. Albert J. Beveridge, *The Life of John Marshall* (1916–1919) 4 vols., the monumental biographer of the great Chief Justice, deals in detail with the various constitutional and political issues and still stands as a kind of grand defense of the federal judiciary. Additional materials and interpretations are in Charles Warren, *The Supreme Court in United States History* (1937). Leonard Baker, *John Marshall: A Life in Law* (1974) presents a fresh, more personal biography, with some new insights, especially regarding the Burr trial and personal relationships among the justices.

The growth of judicial review and the arguments resulting therefrom have been repeatedly analyzed. Richard E. Ellis, *The Jeffersonian Crisis: Courts and Politics in the Young Republic* (1971) is an excellent constitutional analysis with emphasis upon the major divisions within the Jeffersonian party and upon political reform in the States. Judicial review is emphasized also in E. S. Corwin, *The Doctrine of Judicial Review* (1914) and Charles G. Haines, *The American Doctrine of Judicial Supremacy* (1932). Louis B. Boudin, *Government by Judiciary* (1932) 2 vols., is an elaborate but extremely partisan and hostile treatment of the origin and growth of judicial review. Raoul Berger, *Impeachment: The Constitutional Problem* (1973) has a fresh analysis of the intent of the framers of the Constitution and of the nature of impeachment during the Jeffersonian period. A useful objective account is Richard B. Lillich, "The Chase Impeachment," *American Journal of Legal History* (January 1960).

The conspiracy of Aaron Burr continues to defy historical resolution, while the Burr trial persists as a challenging and enticing subject. In addition to the Beveridge and Baker biographies listed above, the following treatments are valuable: Thomas P. Abernethy, *The Burr Conspiracy* (1954),

W. F. McCaleb, *The Aaron Burr Conspiracy* (1903), and Bradley Chapin, *The American Law of Treason: Revolutionary and Early National Origins* (1964). Robert Faulker, "John Marshall and the Burr Trial," *Journal of American History*, LIII (September 1966), defends Marshall against the traditional charges of biased motives in this matter.

Malone and Peterson give much attention to the Embargo and the Constitutional issues involved. Louis M. Sears, *Jefferson and the Embargo* (1927), is primarily a political study but it contains some constitutional material. Madison's efforts to deal with the controversial foreign situation of Jefferson's and his own administration and the resultant War of 1812 are sympathetically treated by Irving Brant, *James Madison*, Volumes IV, V, and VI, and by Ralph Ketcham, *James Madison* (1971). Old but valuable collections of documents are Henry Adams, ed., *Documents Relating to New England Federalism, 1800–1815* (1877) and H. V. Ames, ed., *State Documents on Federal Relations* (1906). The notorious Hartford Convention is discussed in detail in S. E. Morison, *The Life and Letters of Harrison Gray Otis* (1913), 2 vols., and in James M. Banner, *To the Hartford Convention: The Federalists and the Origins of Party Politics in Massachusetts, 1789–1815* (1969).

CHAPTER 10. NATIONALISM VERSUS SECTIONALISM

The slow and irregular development of American nationalism in the generation after 1815 is carefully analyzed in Merle Curti, *The Roots of American Loyalty* (1946). George Dangerfield, *The Era of Good Feeling* (1951) has much valuable material on politico-constitutional questions, while Shaw Livermore, *The Twilight of the Federalist Party, 1815–1830* (1962) is a well-balanced account of the influence of sectional forces upon national development. Frederick Jackson Turner's *The Significance of Sections in American History* (1932) is a collection of his interpretative essays on sectionalism. Although emphasizing social and economic factors, R. C. Buley, *The Old Northwest: Pioneer Period, 1815–1840* (1950) 2 vols., is a good survey of the key section for this period. The important personal contributions to the constitutional controversies of this period are clearly revealed in the biographies of the leading statesmen: Irving Brant, *James Madison*, Vol. VI; Henry Ammon, *James Monroe: The Quest for National Identity* (1971); Chase C. Mooney, *William H. Crawford, 1772–1834* (1974); Charles M. Wiltse, *John C. Calhoun, Nationalist, 1782–1828* (1944); G. G. Van Deusen, *The Life of Henry Clay* (1937); B. C. Clark, *John Quincy Adams: "Old Man Eloquent"* (1932); Samuel F. Bemis, *John Quincy Adams* (1949–1956) 2 vols.; Richard N. Current, *Daniel Webster and the Rise of National Conservatism* (1955) and C. M. Fuess, *Daniel Webster* (1930) 2 vols. At the present time major publication programs are producing what will doubtless be the really definitive editions of the papers and documents of the outstanding leaders of the period between 1800 and 1860.

Some of the major politico-constitutional issues have received specialized treatment. Good analyses of the sectional clashes over federal land policies can be found in Roy M. Robbins, *Our Landed Heritage: The Public Domain, 1776–1836* (1942) and in Malcolm Rohrbough, *The Land Office*

Business (1968). The controversial second national bank is comprehensively treated in R. C. H. Catterall, *The Second Bank of the United States* (1903) and in T. P. Givan, *Nicholas Biddle, Nationalist and Public Banker, 1786–1844* (1959). Bray Hammond, *Banks and Politics in America, from the Revolution to the Civil War* (1957) is highly critical of Jackson's bank policy. J. S. Young, *A Political and Constitutional Study of the Cumberland Road* (1904) emphasizes constitutional aspects of the internal improvement program, while Ronald E. Shaw, *Erie Water West: A History of the Erie Canal, 1792–1854* (1966) has an excellent treatment of that famous project.

The slavery controversy has one of the most extensive, interesting, and varied bibliographies in the whole of American history and new books continue to appear almost every year. While key general books on slavery and abolitionism are listed under Chapter 14, notice should be taken here of treatments of the Missouri controversy and compromise: Jesse Carpenter, *The South as a Conscious Minority* (1930); F. C. Shoemaker, *Missouri's Struggle for Statehood, 1804–1821* (1916); and Homer C. Hockett, *The Constitutional History of the United States* (1939), 2 vols. C. R. King, ed., *The Life and Correspondence of Rufus King* (1894–1900), 6 vols., throws additional light on the Northern constitutional position regarding Missouri. To appreciate fully the comprehensive scope of constitutional arguments as well as the intensity of sectional feelings over Missouri, one should follow the extensive debates in the *Annals of Congress*.

CHAPTER 11. JOHN MARSHALL AND JUDICIAL NATIONALISM

John Marshall dominates the literature in this field as he dominated its history. A good introduction and clear analysis of constitutional development and interpretation during the Marshall period are contained in E. S. Corwin, *John Marshall and the Constitution* (1919) and R. K. Newmyer, *The Supreme Court under Marshall and Taney* (1968). Beveridge, *The Life of John Marshall*, Vols. III and IV, provides an interesting account of Marshall's public life and a thorough discussion, sympathetic to the Chief Justice, of the important constitutional decisions of the period. Leonard Baker, *John Marshall: A Life in Law* (1974) presents some new insights into Marshall's judicial career and his life in general. Charles Warren, *The Supreme Court in United States History* (1937), 2 vols., has good background material and generally presents the Supreme Court in a favorable light, as does S. J. Konefsky, *John Marshall and Alexander Hamilton: Architects of the American Constitution* (1964). Charles G. Haines, *The Role of the Supreme Court in American Government and Politics, 1789–1835* (1944) takes exception to Beveridge's and Warren's conservative and nationalistic interpretation of Marshall and the Court and argues that a Jeffersonian interpretation of the Constitution during the period might well have had a salutary effect upon later American development. Louis Boudin, *Government by Judiciary* (1932) 2 vols., is extremely critical of much of the constitutional interpretation of this era. Robert R. Faulkner, *The Jurisprudence of John Marshall* (1968) presents Marshall as a classic eighteenth century Whig liberal.

Other jurists also left their impact upon constitutional development.

Joseph Story, *Commentaries on the Constitution of the United States* (1891) 2 vols., is a classic on the American constitutional system, and reveals Story's scholarship, conservatism, and nationalism. Gerald T. Dunne, *Justice Joseph Story and the Rise of the Supreme Court* (1970) is a valuable recent interpretation. Elizabeth K. Bauer, *Commentaries on the Constitution, 1790–1860* (1952) analyzes both Story's work and that of the states' rights theorists. Newmyer, "A Note on the Whig Politics of Justice Joseph Story," *Mississippi Valley Historical Review*, XXXV (December 1961) is a valuable interpretation. John T. Horton, *James Kent: A Study in Conservatism* (1939) is an admirable study of another great jurist. Donald G. Morgan, *Justice William Johnson, the First Dissenter: The Career and Constitutional History of a Jeffersonian Judge* (1954) presents an excellent analysis of the justice who most consistently adhered to the Jeffersonian interpretation of the Constitution. Maurice G. Baxter, *Daniel Webster and the Supreme Court* (1966) portrays well the impact of Webster's thought and eloquence upon the justices of the Court.

Benjamin F. Wright, *The Contract Clause of the Constitution* (1938), contains a valuable discussion of the issues raised in the contract cases. Fresh interpretations are also in C. P. McGrath, *Yazoo: Law and Politics in the New Republic: The Case of Fletcher v. Peck* (1966), and in Wallace Mendelson, "New Light on Fletcher v. Peck and Gibbons v. Ogden," *Yale Law Journal*, LVIII (March 1949). Early interpretation of the commerce power is ably analyzed in Felix Frankfurter, *The Commerce Clause under Marshall, Taney and Waite* (1937) and more recently in Maurice G. Baxter, *The Steamboat Monopoly: Gibbons v. Ogden, 1824* (1972). Information on Virginia's conflict with the Supreme Court is contained in Eugene T. Mudge, *The Social Philosophy of John Taylor of Caroline* (1939). Curtis Nettels, "The Mississippi Valley and the Federal Judiciary, 1807–1837," *Mississippi Valley Historical Review*, XII (September 1925), describes the attitude of the West toward Marshall's nationalism and conservatism.

CHAPTER 12. THE NULLIFICATION CONTROVERSY

The background of developing Southern discontent is presented in A. O. Craven, *The Coming of the Civil War* (1942, 1957); R. S. Cotterill, *The Old South* (1936); Charles S. Sydnor, *The Development of Southern Sectionalism, 1819–1848* (1948); Clement Eaton, *A History of the Old South: The Emergence of a Reluctant Nation* (1975); and J. G. VanDeusen, *Economic Bases of Disunion in South Carolina* (1928). Craven's book especially emphasizes the extent of agricultural depression in the older section of the South between 1800 and 1832. Also thought-provoking is Eugene D. Genovese, *The Political Economy of Slavery* (1965).

The Indian removal controversies continue to arouse interest and concern among historians. A thoughtful background work is Wilcomb E. Washburn, *The Indian in America* (1975). Bernard W. Sheehan, *Seeds of Extinction: Jeffersonian Philanthropy and the American Indian* (1973) argues that the good intentions of the Jeffersonians toward the Indians actually worked against them. Francis P. Prucha, *American Indian Policy*

in the Formative Years: the Indian Trade and Intercourse Acts, 1780–1834
(1962) emphasizes the link between removal and the civilization program.
Ronald N. Satz, *American Indian Policy in the Jacksonian Era* (1975)
presents the critical nature of Indian-white relationships and a judicious
analysis of the Indian policy of both Congress and President. Old but still
valuable are U. B. Phillips, *Georgia and States' Rights* (1902) and Wilson
Lumpkin, *Removal of the Cherokee Indians from Georgia* (1907) 2 vols.
Marion L. Starkey, *The Cherokee Nation* (1946) stresses the lack of real
constitutional protection for the Indians. Beveridge, *The Life of John
Marshall*, analyzes the Supreme Court's position on the Indian issues, while
Leonard Baker, *John Marshall*, emphasizes the efforts of the Cherokees
to obtain protection from the Government.

William W. Freeling, *Prelude to Civil War: The Nullification Controversy in South Carolina, 1816–1836* (1966), argues that slavery and not the
tariff was the actual issue in the 1832 crisis. Constitutional theory in the
crisis is analyzed ably in Major L. Wilson, " 'Liberty and Union,' an
Analysis of Three Concepts Involved in the Nullification Controversy,"
Journal of Southern History, XXXIII (August 1967). C. S. Boucher, *The
Nullification Controversy in South Carolina* (1916), is still useful. Calhoun's
transformation from nationalist to states-rightist is carefully analyzed in
Charles M. Wiltse, *John C. Calhoun, Nationalist, 1782–1828: Nullifier,
1829–1839; Sectionalist, 1840–1850* (1944–1951), 3 vols. Margaret L. Coit,
John C. Calhoun: American Portrait (1950), is a briefer but excellent treatment. G. M. Capers, *John C. Calhoun, Opportunist: A Reappraisal* (1960)
and Richard N. Current, *John C. Calhoun* (1966), both downgrade
Calhoun's stature. The old source for Calhoun's important writings and
speeches, Richard Cralle, *The Words of John C. Calhoun* (1864) 6 vols.,
is gradually being superseded by the multi-volume *The Papers of John C.
Calhoun*, edited by W. E. Hemphill, now in process of publication.
Calhoun's role in the nullification controversy receives detailed treatment
in Wiltse's Volume II, in Arthur Styron, *The Cast-Iron Man: John C.
Calhoun and American Democracy* (1935), and in Jesse Carpenter, *The
South as a Conscious Minority*. August O. Spain, *The Political Theory of
John C. Calhoun* (1951), is a clear exposition of the South Carolinian's
basic ideas. An able analysis of Calhoun's constitutional position from a
nationalistic viewpoint is in A. C. McLaughlin, *Foundations of American
Constitutionalism* (1932). Vernon Parrington, *Main Currents in American
Thought*, II, has a stimulating discussion of Calhoun's constitutional philosophy as a defense of the minority position of the South. The difference
between Calhoun's concept of the Union and that of Madison in 1798 is
discussed in E. S. Corwin, "National Power and State Interposition,
1787–1861," *Michigan Law Review*, X (May 1912), reprinted in *Selected
Essays*, III.

CHAPTER 13. DEMOCRACY AND JACKSONIANISM

The second quarter of the nineteenth century was one of the most
turbulent and controversial periods in American history, and both contemporary and later interpretations reflected these qualities. The pace was

set by the romantic French visitor Alexis de Tocqueville, whose penetrating insights and fertile imagination led him to characterize American society of the early 1830's as egalitarian, fluid, and dynamic, in his *Democracy in America*, 2 vols. (various editions). Many later historians have made similar interpretations, while others have focused upon the more seamy side of American democracy, and still others have pointed to the wide discrepancies in American society. From 1890 to the 1930's Frederick Jackson Turner repeatedly emphasized the great influence of the frontier and "the West" as the dominant influences in society and government. See his *The United States, 1830–1850* (1935), a good, comprehensive survey, and his *The Frontier in American History* (1920), containing his now famous essays on the significance of the frontier in the growth of democracy. This point of view is challenged by Benjamin F. Wright in "American Democracy and the Frontier," *Yale Review*, XX (Winter 1931). A fresh and stimulating interpretation is in Richard A. Bartlett, *The New Country: A Social History of the American Frontier, 1776–1890* (1974).

National political developments are discussed in G. G. VanDeusen, *The Jacksonian Era, 1828–1848* (1959), while William McDonald, *Jacksonian Democracy, 1829–1837* (1906) and J. S. Basset, *Life of Andrew Jackson* (1911) 2 vols., are thorough but generally critical of Jackson. Arthur M. Schlesinger, Jr., *The Age of Jackson* (1945) presents a stimulating defense of Jackson and his policies. Schlesinger draws his material very largely from eastern sources and argues that the economic as well as the ideological basis of Jacksonian democracy was in the Northeast and not the West. His interpretation should be compared with that of Lee Benson, *The Concept of Jacksonian Democracy: New York as a Test Case* (1961), who presents quantitative evidence to show that ethnic and religious factors were often more important in politics than social and economic issues. Recently Edward Pessen has challenged the simplified versions of American society and government in his *Jacksonian America: Society, Personality and Politics* (1969) and especially in his *Riches, Class, and Power Before the Civil War* (1973). James R. Sharp, *The Jacksonians versus the Banks: Politics in the States after the Panic of 1837* (1970) has a good analysis of the continuing controversy over banks in the states. Merle Curti, *Growth of American Thought* (1943), is a careful appraisal of the egalitarian forces operating during the Jacksonian period. R. H. Gabriel, *The Course of American Democratic Thought* (1940), has a stimulating analysis of the basic elements of the American democratic faith. A more recent and penetrating analysis of American popular attitudes and constitutional ideas is in Rush Walter, *The Mind of America, 1820–1860* (1975). Sydney E. Ahlstrom, *A Religious History of the American People* (1972) is a monumental history of American religions, including their impact upon the growth of democracy.

One of the most valuable studies of the growth of democracy as reflected in state constitutions is Fletcher M. Green, *Constitutional Development in the South Atlantic States, 1776–1860* (1930). Benjamin F. Wright, "Political Institutions and the Frontier," D. R. Fox, ed., *Sources of Culture in the Middle West* (1934), argue that the East preceded the frontier West in the development of constitutional democracy. A. O. Craven, *Democracy in American Life* (1941), stresses the contributions of the West to democracy. K. H. Porter, *A History of Suffrage in the United States* (1918), contains an account of the movement for suffrage extension. Merrill Peterson, ed., *Democracy, Liberty and Property: The State Constitutional Conventions of the 1820's* (1966), contains much useful material. Bayrd Still, "An Interpretation of the Statehood Process, 1800 to 1850," *Mississippi Valley Historical Review*, XXIII (September 1936), contrasts the state constitutions around mid-century with earlier ones, emphasizing the tendency to limit legislative authority. Other valuable sectional and state studies of the growth of democracy are T. P. Abernethy, *From Frontier to Plantation in Tennessee* (1932); A. B. Darling, *Political Changes in Massachusetts, 1824–1848* (1925); T. C. Pease, *The Frontier State, 1818–1848* (Centennial History of Illinois, II, 1918); and F. P. Weisenburger, *The Passing of the Frontier, 1825–1850* (The History of the State of Ohio, III, 1941); Alice E. Smith, *The History of Wisconsin. Vol. I: From Exploration to Statehood* (1973). The repeated attempts to democratize the federal Constitution by amendment are discussed in H. V. Ames, *The Proposed Amendments to the Constitution of the United States during the First Century of its History* (1896).

James S. Chase, *Emergence of the Presidential Nominating Convention, 1789–1832* (1973) covers this important political development. Marquis James, *Andrew Jackson: Portrait of a President* (1937) is a thoughtful interpretation of Jackson's role in enhancing the importance of the presidential office. James C. Curtis, *The Fox at Bay: Martin Van Buren and the Presidency, 1837–1841* (1970) is a competent study of the President who had to follow Jackson. George Poage, *Henry Clay and the Whig Party* (1936) is useful for an understanding of the position of the Whigs on constitutional and political issues. Vernon Parrington, *Main Currents in American Thought*, II, analyzes the constitutionalism of Webster and Story. Leonard D. White, *The Jacksonians: A Study in Administrative History* (1954) has much useful constitutional material. The chief documents relating to Jackson's authority as President are presented, with elaborate interpretation, in William M. Goldsmith, *The Growth of Presidential Power: A Documented History* (1974), Volume I. *The Oliver Wendall Holmes Devise History of the Supreme Court of the United States*. Vol. V: *The Taney Period, 1836–1864* (1974) by Carl B. Swisher has a comprehensive and detailed account of the Court and its decisions during this critical period. Swisher's earlier *Roger B. Taney* (1935) is a careful study of the Chief Justice which does much to counteract former unfavorable interpretations. Other studies of Jacksonian judges are Charles W. Smith, Jr., *Roger B. Taney, Jacksonian Jurist* (1936); F. P. Weisenburger, *The Life of John McLean: A Politician on the United States Supreme Court* (1937); A. A. Lawrence, *James Monroe Wayne: Southern Unionist* (1943); and John P. Frank, *Justice Daniel Dissenting: A Biography of Peter V. Daniel* (1964).

The Taney Court is analyzed at length also in Charles G. Haines and F. H. Sherwood, *The Role of the Supreme Court in American Government and Politics* (1957). Wright, *The Growth of American Constitutional Law,* shows that the Jacksonian judges did not overthrow as much of Marshall's constitutional law as earlier historians had indicated. Wright, *The Contract Clause of the Constitution*, also minimizes the difference between Taney's and Marshall's interpretation of this clause. Stanley I. Kutler, however, in *Privilege and Creative Destruction: The Charles River Bridge Case* (1971) argues persuasively that the rights of the proprietors of the old bridge were sacrificed unjustly and unnecessarily through the doctrine of so-called creative destruction. E. S. Corwin, *The Commerce Power versus States Rights* (1936), argues effectively that the comprehensive federal commerce power incorporated into the Constitution in 1787 was progressively undermined by states' rightist statesmen and jurists after 1830. Also valuable for judicial interpretation are Felix Frankfurter, *The Commerce Clause under Marshall, Taney and Waite* (1937), and G. C. Henderson, *The Position of Foreign Corporations in American Constitutional Law* (1918). R. P. Longaker, "Andrew Jackson and the Judiciary," *Political Science Quarterly*, LXXI (September 1956) is a valuable interpretative article.

Chapter 14. the slavery controversy and sectional conflict

The best recent studies of the abolitionist movement are Dwight Dumond, *Anti-Slavery: The Crusade for Freedom in America* (1961), marred slightly by a somewhat polemical tone; Louis Filler, *The Crusade Against Slavery, 1830–1860* (1960), a more general work; and Aileen Kraditor, *Means and Ends in American Abolitionism: Garrison and His Critics on Strategy and Tactics 1834–1850* (1969), an examination of the variety and conflict within the abolitionist movement. Gerald Sorin, *Abolitionism: A New Perspective* (1972) synthesizes recent scholarship on the subject. Martin Duberman, ed., *The Anti-Slavery Vanguard: New Essays on the Abolitionists* (1964), is useful also. Winthrop D. Jordan, *White Over Black: American Attitudes Toward the Negro, 1550–1812* (1968), is valuable for background. Old but still useful are A. B. Hart, *Slavery and Abolition* (1906); G. H. Barnes, *The Anti-Slavery Impulse, 1830–1844* (1933); and Dwight Dumond, *The Anti-Slavery Origins of the Civil War* (1939). Two excellent studies of the Negro's contributions to the anti-slavery crusade are Benjamin Quarles, *Black Abolitionists* (1969), and Jane H. and William Pease, *They Who Would Be Free: Blacks' Search for Freedom 1830–1860* (1974).

H. T. Catterall, *Judicial Cases Concerning American Slaves and the Negro* (1926–1937), 5 vols., contains source material on personal liberty and sojourner laws. J. C. Hurd, *The Law of Freedom and Bondage* (1862), 2 vols., includes much material on these topics, but it is badly organized. Robert M. Cover, *Justice Accused: Antislavery and the Judicial Process* (1975), somewhat exaggerates the racism of the American legal order, but Kermit C. Hall, "Federal Judicial Reform and Proslavery Constitutional Theory: A Retrospective on the Butler Bill," *American Journal of Legal History*, XVII (April 1973), demonstrates the control which Southern slaveholding interests maintained over the structure of the federal judicial system. Clement Eaton, "Censorship of the Southern Mails," *American Historical Review*, XLVIII (January 1943), is a scholarly appraisal. Russell B. Nye, *Fettered Freedoms: Civil Liberties and the Slavery Crisis 1830–1860*

(1963), discusses the gag rule and other attacks on freedom of expression inspired by the Southern defense of slavery. W. H. Siebert, *The Underground Railroad* (1898), discusses the early fugitive slave act and the personal liberty laws, while Allen Johnson, "The Constitutionality of the Fugitive Slave Acts," *Yale Law Journal*, XXXI (December 1920), is a careful analysis. Leonard Levy, *The Law of the Commonwealth and Chief Justice Shaw* (1957), is extremely valuable on the Fugitive Slave Laws and other slavery questions in the Massachusetts Courts. The most comprehensive treatment of the sectional conflict from 1846 to 1857 is Allan Nevins, *Ordeal of the Union* (1947), 2 vols. M. M. Quaife, *The Doctrine of Non-Intervention with Slavery in the Territories* (1910), is exhaustive and scholarly. Eric Foner, "The Wilmot Proviso Revisited," *Journal of American History*, LVI (September 1969), and Chaplin W. Morrison, *Democratic Politics and Sectionalism: The Wilmot Proviso Controversy* (1967), are both useful. Arthur Bestor, "State Sovereignty and Slavery, A Reinterpretation of Pro Slavery Constitutional Doctrine," *Journal of the Illinois State Historical Society* (Summer 1961), argues for the inconsistency of pro-slavery constitutional theory. A. C. McLaughlin, *Lewis Cass* (1899). contains material on popular sovereignty, including Cass's Nicholsen letter. Frederick J. Blue, *The Free Soilers: Third Party Politics 1848–1854* (1973), is a good, if not always entirely persuasive, analysis of political anti-slavery. A. O. Craven, *The Coming of the Civil War* (1942, 1957), written from what most historians would regard as a Southern point of view, has an account of the crisis of 1850, as does the same author's *The Growth of Southern Nationalism, 1848–1861* (1953). A. C. Cole, *The Whig Party in the South* (1913), also contains material on the background of the Compromise of 1850. Holman Hamilton, *Prelude to Conflict: The Crisis and Compromise of 1850* (1964), is especially valuable. "The Correspondence of Robert Toombs, Alexander H. Stephens, and Howell Cobb," American Historical Association, *Report*, II (1911), is one of the best single sources for Southern constitutional theories on slavery and the Union.

CHAPTER 15. CRISIS AND SECESSION—1851–1861

David M. Potter, *The Impending Crisis, 1848–1861* (1976) provides broad coverage of this period. T. C. Smith, *Parties and Slavery, 1850–1859* (1906), presents a well-balanced account of political and constitutional conflict in the fifties. James Ford Rhodes, *History of the United States from the Compromise of 1850* (1900–1928), 9 vols., Vol. I, 1850–1854; Vol. II, 1854–1860, is good literary history and has valuable constitutional material, somewhat biased in favor of the North. Allan Nevins, *The Ordeal of Union* (1947), 2 vols., is a detailed, readable work, also Northern in emphasis. Craven, *The Coming of the Civil War*, summarizes from a Southern point of view. William Barney, *The Road to Secession: A New Perspective on the Old South* (1972), is a recent short work. James C. Malin, *The Nebraska Question, 1852–1854* (1953), is a valuable general work. F. H. Hodder, "The Railroad Background of the Kansas-Nebraska Act," *Mississippi Valley Historical Review*, XII (June 1925), is useful for an understanding of the motives behind Douglas' bill. Robert R. Russel,

"The Issues in the Congressional Struggle over the Kansas-Nebraska Bill," *Journal of Southern History*, XXIX (May 1963), is excellent on constitutional questions, as is the same author's "Constitutional Doctrine with Regard to Slavery in the Territories," *Journal of Southern History*, XXXII (November 1966). G. F. Milton, *The Eve of Conflict* (1934), defends Douglas' doctrines, and Robert W. Johannsen, *Stephen A. Douglas* (1972), contends that his commitment to popular sovereignty was a matter of principle rather than political expediency. Vincent C. Hopkins, *Dred Scott's Case* (1951), is a competent general work although not definitive. H. T. Catterall, "Some Antecedents of the Dred Scott Case," *American Historical Review*, XXX (October 1924), is a study of the case before it reached the Supreme Court. C. B. Swisher, "Dred Scott One Hundred Years After," *Journal of Politics* (May 1957), is a useful summary of contemporary doctrine. There are good discussions of Taney's opinion in Carl B. Swisher, *Roger B. Taney* (1935) and *The Taney Era* (1974), and in Charles W. Smith, Jr., *Roger B. Taney, Jacksonian Jurist* (1936). E. S. Corwin, "The Dred Scott Decision in the Light of Contemporary Legal Doctrines," *American Historical Review*, XVII (October 1911), emphasizes the distinction between Taney's opinion and Calhoun's constitutional doctrines. F. H. Hodder, "Some Phases of the Dred Scott Case," *Mississippi Historical Review*, XVI (June 1929), discusses the role of McLean and Curtis in influencing the Court to pass on the question of slavery in the territories. F. P. Weisenburger, *The Life of John McLean: A Politician on the United States Supreme Court* (1937), and G. T. Curtis, *The Life and Writings of Benjamin Robbins Curtis*, I (1879), also have passages throwing light on McLean's and Curtis' part in the case, as does Richard H. Leach, "Justice Curtis and the Dred Scott Case," *Essex Institute Historical Collection* (January 1958). Stanley I. Kutler, ed., *The Dred Scott Decision: Law or Politics* (1967), includes the opinions and examples of contemporary reaction to the decision, as well as several of the articles noted above. Roy F. Nichols, *The Disruption of American Democracy* (1948), is a superior work on the period 1856–1861. James H. Rawley, *Race and Politics: Bleeding Kansas and the Coming of the Civil War* (1969), is also excellent.

Paul M. Angle, ed., *Created Equal? The Complete Lincoln-Douglas Debates of 1858* (1958) is a valuable collection. D. E. Fehrenbacher, "Lincoln, Douglas, and the Freeport Question," *American Historical Review*, LXVI (April 1961), challenges the view that Douglas' doctrine was decisive in splitting the Democratic party. Stanley Campbell, *The Slave Catchers: Enforcement of the Fugitive Slave Law 1850–1860* (1970), and Norman L. Rosenberg, "Personal Liberty Laws and Sectional Crisis 1850–1861," *Civil War History*, XVII (March 1971), are both valuable on Northern resistance to the tough 1850 fugitive slave law. Lincoln's role in the secession crisis, as well as his constitutional philosophy, receives judicious appraisal in J. G. Randall, *Lincoln the President* (1945–1952), 4 vols., and in D. M. Potter, *Lincoln and his Party in the Secession Crisis* (1942). Arthur Bestor, "The American Civil War as a Constitutional Crisis," *American Historical Review*, LXIX (January 1964), emphasizes inconsistencies in southern constitutional theory. Ollinger Crenshaw, *The Slave States in the Presidential Election of 1860* (1945); Reinhard H. Luthin,

The First Lincoln Campaign (1944); and D. F. Dumond, *The Secession Movement, 1860–1861* (1931), are all useful on the secession crisis, as are R. A. Wooster, *The Secessionist Conventions of the South* (1962), and Charles Robert Lee, *The Confederate Constitutions* (1963). A. C. Cole, "Lincoln's Election an Immediate Menace to Slavery in the States," *American Historical Review*, XXXVI (July 1931), and J. G. de R. Hamilton, "Lincoln's Election an Immediate Menace to Slavery in the States," *American Historical Review*, XXXVII (July 1932), argue the constitutional interests. R. G. Gunderson, *Old Gentlemen's Convention: The Washington Peace Conference of 1861* (1961), and J. L. Keene, *The Peace Convention of 1861* (1961) are both useful. Catherine M. Tarrant, "To 'insure domestic Tranquility': Congress and the Law of Seditious Conspiracy 1859–1861," *American Journal of Legal History*, XV (April 1971), offers an interesting new perspective on the failure of efforts to prevent the Civil War.

CHAPTER 16. THE CIVIL WAR

Allan Nevins, *The War for the Union* (1959–1971), 4 vols., has described and analyzed the Civil War as an heroic and tragic conflict over the nature of American nationality, participated in by some thirty million people. Doubtless he came closer to capturing the full drama and the significance of the great struggle than anyone before him, and his achievement is not likely to be equaled in the future. The most comprehensive and well-balanced single-volume treatment of the War is J. G. Randall and David Donald, *The Civil War and Reconstruction* (rev. ed. 1969); especially valuable for students is the very extensive and well-organized bibliography. Recent and most important for constitutional issues is Harold M. Hyman, *A More Perfect Union: The Impact of the Civil War and Reconstruction on the Constitution* (1973). Hyman argues very persuasively that northern victory not merely preserved the pre-1861 Union but made the Constitution a much stronger and more effective national instrument. Another new comprehensive work, by a British historian, Peter J. Parish, *The American Civil War* (1975) presents many interesting judgments and viewpoints. A fresh and reflective account of developments leading to civil war is in David M. Potter, *The Impending Crisis, 1848–1861* (1976). Of the many versions of the War from the Southern side two of the most perceptive and well-written are Clement Eaton, *A History of the Southern Confederacy* (1954) and the more recent Frank E. Vandiver, *Their Tattered Flags: The Epic of the Confederacy* (1970). Benjamin Quarles, *The Negro in the Civil War* (1953) is both scholarly and comprehensive. R. H. Gabriel, *The Course of American Democratic Thought* (1940), and A. O. Craven, *Democracy in American Life* (1941), show the impact of the Civil War upon the development of democracy. More specialized books help to fill out the almost staggering account of the War. A. C. Cole, *The Irrepressible Conflict* (1934), is a good analysis of social and economic conditions in both North and South, before and during the War. E. Merton Coulter, *The Confederate States of America, 1861–1865* (1951) is a thorough and balanced study of the struggle for Southern independence. F. L. Owsley, *State Rights in the Confederacy* (1925), shows that the Confederacy contained to a large degree the seeds of its own destruction. R. W. Patrick, ed., *The Opinions of the Confederate Attorneys-General* (1950), a valuable technical work, lends weight to the same conclusion. Two virtually contemporaneous accounts, written by participants in the Civil War, one defending the Confederacy and the other the Union, are still of value and interest. A. H. Stephens, *A Constitutional View of the Late War Between the States* (1868–1870), 2 vols., is a partisan defense of Southern constitutional theory and practice. Likewise John Nicolay and John Hay, *Abraham Lincoln: A History* (1890), 10 vols., is a detailed, strongly Union account, containing much source material. The most penetrating studies of Lincoln as a great war leader struggling to maintain the Union and the American constitutional system are J. G. Randall, *Lincoln the President* (1945–1955), 4 vols.; Carl Sandburg, *Abraham Lincoln: The War Years* (1939), 4 vols.; and Benjamin Thomas, *Abraham Lincoln: A Biography* (1952). Many of Lincoln's most relevant state papers are conveniently presented and soundly interpreted in William M. Goldsmith, *The Growth of Presidential Power: A Documented History*, Vol. II (1974). Benjamin Quarles, *Lincoln and the Negro* (1962) is an excellent account of the President's changing views on crucial racial issues.

The critical role of Great Britain in the outcome of the War is carefully described in E. D. Adams, *Great Britain and the American Civil War* (1924) 2 vols. Brian Jenkins' more recent analysis, *Britain & the War for the Union*, Vol. 1 (1974) stresses crucial British neutrality based upon that government's firm beliefs that the Union could not win the War and that British intervention would jeopardize the security of Canada. D. P. Crook, *The North, the South, and the Powers, 1861–1865* (1974) focuses more sharply than anyone previously has done upon the total European ramifications of the Civil War and their effect upon the outcome. Valuable also for the international aspects of the War are Martin Duberman, *Charles Francis Adams 1807–1886* (1960); G. G. Van Deusen, *William Henry Seward* (1967); and David Donald, *Charles Sumner and The Rights of Man* (1970).

For strictly constitutional issues and developments, J. G. Randall, *Constitutional Problems under Lincoln* (rev. ed. 1951), contains a careful and thorough analysis. Harold Hyman's *A More Perfect Union* presents challenging new viewpoints and repudiates the lingering states' rights ideology in American historiography. Clinton L. Rossiter, *The Supreme Court and the Commander in Chief* (1951) argues vigorously that strong presidential leadership in times of great national crisis is necessary and wise. Fred Shannon, *The Organization and Administration of the Union Army, 1861–1865* (1928), 2 vols., reveals how states' rights sentiments and practices in the Northern states interfered seriously with the creation of a national army. State-federal relations also are dealt with in William B. Hesseltine, *Lincoln and the War Governors* (1948). E. S. Corwin, *The President* (1948) emphasizes Lincoln's expansive conception of the presidential office. Benjamin Thomas and Harold Hyman, *Stanton: The Life and Times of Lincoln's Secretary of War* (1962), emphasizes Stanton's immense organizational abilities. Wilfred E. Binkley, *President and Congress* (1947), discusses Lincoln's unusual relations with the Radicals. Radical congressional attempts to obtain a more important part in the direction of the war are ably discussed in T. Harry Williams, *Lincoln and the Radicals* (1941), while Hans L. Trefousse, *The Radical Republicans: Lincoln's Vanguard for Racial Justice* (1969), emphasizes a similarity between Lincoln's ultimate values and those of the Radicals. See also M. R. Cain, *Lincoln's Attorney General, Edward Bates of Missouri* (1965). The nature, extent, and significance of Northern political opposition to Lincoln, the Union government, and the War itself continues to be interpreted variously. Wood Gray, *The Hidden Civil War: The Story of the Copperheads* (1942), considers the extreme political opposition to be serious, even dangerous to the war effort, while Frank L. Klement, *The Copperheads in the Middle West* (1960) thinks the Republicans grossly exaggerated the danger of Copperhead opposition and activities. Klement's more recent *The Limits of Dissent: Clement S. Vallandigham & the Civil War* (1970) is an excellent account of that vital constitutional issue. See also Kenneth Stampp, *Indiana Politics During the Civil War* (1949), and William E. Parrish, *A History of Missouri*, Vol. 3 (1973). William L. King, *Lincoln's Manager: David Davis* (1960) has a good analysis of the famous Milligan case and Supreme Court opinions. Constitutional and political problems involved in the use of loyalty oaths during the War are discussed in Harold M. Hyman, *To Try Men's Souls: Loyalty Tests in American History* (1959). The part played by the Supreme Court in deciding constitutional issues is described by Carl B. Swisher in *History of the Supreme Court of the United States*, Vol. V: *The Taney Era, 1836–1864* (1974); David M. Silver, *Lincoln's Supreme Court* (1956); and Charles Warren, *The Supreme Court in United States History* (1937), 2 vols; Swisher, *Roger B. Taney* (1935) and *Stephen J. Field, Craftsman of the Law* (1930); and Charles Fairman, *Mr. Justice Miller and the Supreme Court, 1862–1890* (1939). Fairman, *The Law of Martial Rule* (1930) is a good discussion of military arrests and martial law.

CHAPTER 17. RECONSTRUCTION: THE PRESIDENTIAL PHASE

There has been a revolution in Reconstruction historiography in the last decade or so, and much of what was written before that time is now outmoded. Randall and Donald, *The Civil War and Reconstruction* (1961), which now carries Professor Donald's recent scholarship, is a valuable introduction. Eric McKitrick, *Andrew Johnson and Reconstruction* (1961); La Wanda and John H. Cox, *Politics, Principle and Prejudice, 1865–1866: Dilemma of Reconstruction America* (1963); W. R. Brock, *The American Crisis: Congress and Reconstruction, 1865–1877* (1963); Kenneth M. Stampp, *The Era of Reconstruction, 1865–1877* (1965); David Donald, *The Politics of Reconstruction* (1965); and James H. McPherson, *The Struggle for Equality: Abolitionists and the Negro in the Civil War and Reconstruction* (1964), all reflect the new scholarship. Rembert W. Patrick, *The Reconstruction of the Nation* (1967), and A. O. Craven, *Reconstruction: The Ending of the Civil War* (1969), synthesize the old and new outlooks. Harold Hyman, ed., *New Frontiers of the American Reconstruction*

(1966), has several valuable essays reflecting recent scholarship, as does Kenneth Stampp and Leon Litwack, eds., *Reconstruction: An Anthology of Revisionist Writings* (1969).

Harold Hyman, *A More Perfect Union,* is much the best work available on the constitutional aspects of Reconstruction. Charles Fairman, *History of the Supreme Court of the United States,* Vol. V: *Reconstruction and Reunion 1864–1888,* Pt. I (1971), contains a wealth of information on constitutional developments, including many which did not directly or immediately affect the Court, but it is verbose, badly organized, and lacking in focus. Herman Belz, *Reconstructing the Union: Theory and Policy During the Civil War* (1969), is an excellent account of the first steps toward reconstruction. W. A. Dunning, *Reconstruction, Political and Economic, 1865–1877* (1907, 1962), remains a valuable classic, as does the same author's *Essays on the Civil War and Reconstruction* (1904). H. K. Beale, *The Critical Year* (1930), is also still useful. E. Merton Coulter, *The South During Reconstruction, 1865–1877* (1947), deals with conditions within the Southern states. William C. Harris, *Presidential Reconstruction in Mississippi* (1967), is a valuable recent study. Fawn Brodie, *Thaddeus Stevens: Scourge of the South* (1959), is largely devoted to Reconstruction problems. George Bentley, *A History of the Freedmen's Bureau* (1955), is an adequate work. A more recent and imaginative treatment is William S. McFeely, *Yankee Stepfather: General O. O. Howard and the Freedmen* (1968). W. A. Fleming, *Documentary History of Reconstruction* (1905, 1907), 2 vols., contains documents still not easily available elsewhere. Theodore B. Wilson, *The Black Codes of the South* (1965), is virtually an apologetic for the codes.

The best general work on the adoption of the Fourteenth Amendment is still H. E. Flack, *Adoption of the Fourteenth Amendment* (1908), a study surprisingly modern in tone. Also useful is Joseph B. James, *The Framing of the Fourteenth Amendment* (1956). Benjamin B. Kendrick, *The Journal of the Joint Committee of Fifteen on Reconstruction* (1914), is still very valuable. Jacobus Ten Broek, *The Anti-Slavery Origins of the Fourteenth Amendment* (1951), finds the amendment's wellsprings in prewar antislavery idealism. The now-discredited conspiracy theory of the amendment is analyzed in A. C. McLaughlin, "The Court, the Corporation, and Conkling," *American Historical Review,* XLVI (October 1940); in L. B. Boudin, "Truth and Fiction about the Fourteenth Amendment," *New York University Law Quarterly Review,* XVI (November 1938); in James Russell, "The Railroads and the Conspiracy Theory of the Fourteenth Amendment," *Mississippi Valley Historical Review,* XLI (March 1955); in Howard J. Graham, "The Conspiracy Theory of the Fourteenth Amendment," *Yale Law Journal,* XLVII, XLVIII (January, December 1938), reprinted in *Selected Essays,* I; and in H. J. Graham, *Everyman's Constitution: Historical Essays on the Fourteenth Amendment, The Conspiracy Theory and American Constitutionalism* (1968), an indispensable collection. Alexander M. Bickel, "The Original Understanding and the Segregation Decision," *Harvard Law Review,* LXIX (November 1955), argues that the amendment was not intended to prohibit segregation in public schools. This interpretation should be compared with that in A. H. Kelly,

"The Fourteenth Amendment Reconsidered: The Segregation Question," *Michigan Law Review*, LIV (June 1956); and in H. J. Graham, "Our Declaratory Fourteenth Amendment," *Stanford Law Review*, VII (December 1954). The South's response to the amendment is analyzed in J. B. James, "Southern Reaction to the Proposal of the Fourteenth Amendment," *Journal of Southern History*, XXII (November 1956). The same author's "Is the Fourteenth Amendment Constitutional," *Social Science*, L (Winter 1975), examines the numerous irregularities in the adoption and ratification of the Amendment. H. M. Hyman, *The Era of the Oath: Northern Loyalty Tests During the Civil War and Reconstruction* (1954), treats the constitutional aspects of loyalty oaths of the day.

CHAPTER 18. RADICAL CONGRESSIONAL RECONSTRUCTION

Randall and Donald, *The Civil War and Reconstruction;* McKitrick, *Andrew Johnson and Reconstruction;* Franklin, *Reconstruction after the Civil War;* Cox and Cox, *Politics, Principle and Prejudice;* Brock, *The American Crisis;* Stampp, *Reconstruction;* Donald, *The Politics of Reconstruction;* Craven, *Reconstruction;* Hyman, *A More Perfect Union;* Fairman, *Reconstruction and Reunion;* Stampp and Litwack, eds., *Reconstruction;* and Hyman, ed., *New Frontiers,* all have valuable materials on congressional Reconstruction. Dunning, *Reconstruction, Political and Economic,* and Dunning, *Essays on Reconstruction,* are also valuable. Michael Les Benedict, *A Compromise of Principle: Congressional Republicans and Reconstruction, 1863–1869* (1974), emphasizes the role played by moderates and conservatives in shaping Republican reconstruction policy. The military reconstruction acts may be found in Fleming, *Documentary History of Reconstruction,* II. Michael Les Benedict, *The Impeachment and Trial of Andrew Johnson* (1973) is the best study of that subject. Also useful is Hans L. Trefousse, *Impeachment of a President: Andrew Johnson, the Blacks, and Reconstruction* (1975). The same author's *Benjamin Franklin Wade: Radical Republican From Ohio* (1963), is excellent, as is David Donald, *Charles Sumner and the Rights of Man* (1970). William Gillette, *Politics and the Passage of the Fifteenth Amendment* (1965), also is very valuable, although its interpretation should be compared with La Wanda and John H. Cox, "Negro Suffrage and Republican Politics: The Problem of Motivation in Reconstruction Historiography," *Journal of Southern History*, XXXIII (1967). J. M. Mathew, *Legislative and Judicial History of the Fifteenth Amendment* (1909), is still useful, particularly on the amendment in the courts. Everett Swinney, "Enforcing the Fifteenth Amendment, 1870–1877," *Journal of Southern History*, XXVIII (May 1962), discusses Negro voting in latter Reconstruction years. Paul Lewinson, *Race, Class, and Party: A History of Negro Suffrage and White Politics in the South* (1932, 1959), deals with post-Reconstruction emasculation of the amendment. J. Morgan Koasser, *The Shaping of Southern Politics: Suffrage Restriction and the Establishment of the One-Party South 1880–1910* (1974), employs sophisticated quantitative techniques to determine the impact of changes in electoral laws and procedures. Stanley Kutler, *Judicial Power and Reconstruction Politics* (1968), a significant

revisionist work, reassesses the relationship of the Court to the Radicals.
Bernard Schwartz, *From Confederation to Nation: The American Con-
stitution 1835–1877* (1973), is much more traditional in its conclusions.
Stanley Kutler, "Ex Parte McCardle: Judicial Impotency? The Supreme
Court and Reconstruction Reconsidered," *American Historical Review*,
LXXII (April 1967), argues that the Court in the McCardle case acted
from principle, not expediency. William Van Alstyne, "A Critical Guide
to Ex Parte McCardle," *Arizona Law Review*, XV (1973), combines
history with an excellent analysis of the Court's opinion. William M.
Wiecek, "The Reconstruction of Federal Power, 1863–1875," *The American
Journal of Legal History*, XIII (1969), emphasizes the growth of federal
judicial power during Reconstruction. This theme receives further elabora-
tion in the same author's "The Great Writ and Reconstruction: The
Habeus Corpus Act of 1867," *Journal of Southern History*, XXXVI
(November 1970) and in David J. Hoeveler, Jr., "Reconstruction and the
Federal Courts: The Civil Rights Act of 1875," *Historian*, XXXI (August
1969). Charles Fairman, "Mr. Justice Bradley's Appointment to the Supreme
Court and the Legal Tender Cases," *Harvard Law Review*, LIV (April,
May 1941), is a careful study of the "Court packing" charge. Allen Nevins,
Hamilton Fish: The Inner History of the Grant Administration (1936),
presents evidence that Grant knew that Stone and Bradley would vote
to sustain the Legal Tender Acts, although he exacted no pledge from them.

School segregation during Reconstruction is discussed in Louis R. Harlan, "Desegregation in New Orleans Public Schools During Reconstruction," *American Historical Review*, LXVII (April 1962), while A. H.
Kelly, "The Congressional Controversy over School Segregation, 1867–
1875," *American Historical Review* (April 1959), analyzes the background
of the Civil Rights Act of 1875. The 1875 act is also treated in James Mc-
Pherson, "Abolitionists and the Civil Rights Act of 1875," *Journal of Amer-
ican History*, LII (December 1965), and John S. Ezell, "The Civil Rights
Act of 1875," *Mid-America*, L (October 1968). Leonard Levy and H. B.
Phillips, "The Roberts Case; Source of the Separate But Equal Doctrine,"
American Historical Review, LVI (April 1951), demonstrates the link
between the Roberts and Plessy cases. J. T. Dorris, *Pardon and Amnesty
Under Lincoln and Johnson: The Restoration of the Confederates to Their
Rights and Privileges, 1861–1898* (1953), is useful.

Paul H. Buck, *The Road to Reunion* (1937), and C. Vann Woodward,
*Reunion and Reaction: The Compromise of 1877 and the End of Recon-
struction* (1951), are both very valuable on the late Reconstruction era.
So is Keith Polakoff, *The Politics of Inertia: The Election of 1876 and the
End of Reconstruction* (1973), which sheds needed light on the mystifying
election of Justice David Davis to the Senate, which destroyed the political
balance of the Electoral Commission. Philip S. Paludan, *A Covenant with
Death: The Constitution, Law, and Equality in the Civil War Era* (1975),
argues, on the basis of an examination of the ideas of five Northern constitutional authorities, that Reconstruction failed because traditional federalism restrained the national government from doing what was necessary
to protect the rights of Southern blacks. Michael J. Horan emphasizes the
tenacity of *laissez-faire* ideas in his not altogether convincing "Political

Economy and Sociological Theory as Influences upon Judicial Policy-Making: The Civil Rights Cases of 1883," *American Journal of Legal History*, XVI (January 1972). P. L. Haworth, *The Hayes-Tilden Disputed Election of 1876* (1906), is still useful. Alan Westin, "The Case of the Prejudiced Doorkeeper," in John Garraty, ed., *Quarrels that Have Shaped the Constitution* (1962, 1964), is more valuable on the Civil Rights Cases, while C. Vann Woodward, "The Case of the Louisiana Traveler," in Garraty, ed., *Quarrels*, is useful on the background of *Plessy v. Ferguson.* Paul Oberst, "The Strange Career of *Plessy v. Ferguson,*" *Arizona Law Review*, XV (1973), is also excellent. Edward G. White, "John Marshall Harlan I: The Precursor," *American Journal of Legal History*, XIX (January 1975), is a solid analysis of the judicial philosophy adhered to by the Justice who entered lonely but forward-looking dissents in both Plessy and the Civil Rights Cases.

CHAPTER 19. THE REVOLUTION IN DUE PROCESS OF LAW

Loren Beth, *The Development of the American Constitution 1877–1917* (1971), is a broad survey, topically organized, which discusses all aspects of national and state constitutional development between the end of Reconstruction and American entry into World War I. The early history of the doctrine of vested rights is discussed in E. S. Corwin, "The Basic Doctrine of American Constitutional Law," *Michigan Law Review*, XII (February 1914). On the relationship between the doctrine of vested rights and the obligations of contract clause, see Benjamin F. Wright, *The Contract Clause of the Constitution* (1938). The early history and meaning of due process of law are treated in C. H. McIlwain, "Due Process of Law in Magna Charta," *Columbia Law Review*, XIV (January 1914), and in E. S. Corwin, "The Doctrine of Due Process of Law Before the Civil War," *Harvard Law Review*, XXIV (March, April 1911), both reprinted in *Selected Essays*, I. R. L. Mott, *Due Process of Law* (1926), has useful chapters on early due process. Walton H. Hamilton, "The Path of Due Process of Law," in Conyers Read, ed., *The Constitution Reconsidered* (1938), makes significant comments upon the development of due process between the Slaughterhouse Cases and *Smyth v. Ames.* C. G. Haines, "Judicial Review of Legislation in the United States and the Doctrine of Vested Rights," *Texas Law Review*, II, III (June, December 1924), reprinted in part as "The History of Due Process after the Civil War," in *Selected Essays*, I, is a good survey. S. J. Buck, *The Granger Movement* (1913), is the standard book on the economic background of *Munn v. Illinois* and the other Granger Cases, while George H. Miller, *Railroads and Granger Laws* (1973), is a revisionist work which challenges Buck's interpretation. George H. Miller, "Origins of the Iowa Granger Law," *Mississippi Valley Historical Review*, XL (March 1954), is also useful. B. P. McAllister, "Lord Hale and Business Affected with a Public Interest," *Harvard Law Review*, XLIII (March 1930), reprinted in *Selected Essays*, II, discusses the relationship of *Munn v. Illinois* to the public-interest doctrine. Harry N. Scheiber examines the antecedents of that doctrine in a superb article, "The Road to Munn: Eminent Domain and the Concept of Public Purpose in the State Courts," *Perspectives in American History*, V (1971). Ernst Freund, *The Police Power* (1904), includes a discussion of *Munn v. Illinois*. Charles Fairman, "The So-called Granger Cases, Lord Hale, and Justice Bradley," *Stanford Law Review*, V (July 1953), is also valuable. Carl B. Swisher, *Stephen J. Field, Craftsman of the Law* (1930), treats Justice Field's role in the emergence of substantive due process. Charles Fairman, *Mr. Justice Miller and the Supreme Court, 1862–1890* (1939), is also important. C. Peter Magrath, *Morrison R. Waite: The Triumph of Character* (1963), is a mature study. On liberty of contract, see C. E. Shattuck, "The True Meaning of the Term 'Liberty' in Those Clauses in the Federal and State Constitutions Which Protect Life, Liberty, and Property," *Harvard Law Review*, IV (March 1891); Roscoe Pound, "Liberty of Contract," *Yale Law Journal*, XVIII (May 1909); and Charles Warren, "The New Liberty under the Fourteenth Amendment," *Harvard Law Review*, XXXIX (February 1926), all reprinted in *Selected Essays*, II. Alan Jones, "Thomas M. Cooley and Laissez Faire Constitutionalism: A Reconsideration," *Journal of American History*, LIII (March 1967), assesses Cooley's role in the new constitutional law. Herman Belz, "The Constitution in the Gilded Age; The Beginnings of Constitutional Realism in American Scholarship," *American Journal of Legal History*, XIII (January 1969), challenges traditional notions about the nature of constitutional thought in the decades after Reconstruction.

CHAPTER 20. THE NEW DUE PROCESS AND JUDICIAL REVIEW—1890–1920

R. L. Mott, *Due Process of Law* (1926), is an adequate general survey of substantive due process before 1926. One of the most concise summaries of the new due process is to be found in Benjamin F. Wright, *The Growth of American Constitutional Law* (1942). Felix Frankfurter, *Mr. Justice Holmes and the Supreme Court* (1938, 1961), has an appendix tabulating and describing briefly all cases before 1939 in which the Supreme Court held state action invalid under the Fourteenth Amendment. Ray A. Brown, "Police Power—Legislation for Health and Personal Safety," *Harvard Law Review*, XLII (May 1929), is a valuable study of the balance between the police power and state social legislation. Felix Frankfurter, "Hours of Labor and Realism in Constitutional Law," *Harvard Law Review*, XXIX (February 1916), is a detailed survey of maximum-hours cases before 1916. Sir Frederick Pollock, "The New York Labor Law and the Fourteenth Amendment," *Law Quarterly Review*, XXI, is a contemporary critique of the Lochner opinion. Frank R. Strong, "The Economic Philosophy of Lochner: Emergence, Embrasure and Emasculation," *Arizona Law Review*, XV (1973), is a more recent article, but a myopic one, which delivers far less than its title promises. Thomas Reed Powell, "The Judiciality of Minimum Wage Legislation," *Harvard Law Review*, XXXVII (March 1924), reprinted in *Selected Essays*, I and II, is very useful, as is Breck P. McAllister, "Public Purpose in Taxation," *California Law Review*, XVIII (January, March 1930), reprinted in *Selected Essays*, I. Maurice H. Merrill, "Jurisdiction to Tax—Another World," *Yale Law Journal*, XLIV (February 1935), reprinted in *Selected Essays,* I, is a study of the application of due process to the taxation of out-state property. Charles G. Haines, *The American Doctrine of Judicial Supremacy* (2nd ed., 1932), is a good general study of judicial review as a constitutional, political, and social institution. R. E. Cushman, "The Social and Economic Interpretation of the Fourteenth Amendment," *Michigan Law Review,* XX (May 1922), discusses the role of due process in the new judicial review. A. M. Kales, "New Methods in Due Process Cases," *American Political Science Review,* XII, reprinted in *Selected Essays,* I (May 1918), calls the Supreme Court an American House of Lords. The social and economic implications of judicial review are also treated in Max Lerner, "Constitution and Court as Symbols," *Yale Law Journal,* XLVI (June 1937), reprinted in *Selected Essays,* I; in Roscoe Pound, "The New Feudal System," *Kentucky Law Journal,* XIX (November 1930), reprinted in *Selected Essays,* II; and R. L. Hale, "Judicial Review versus Doctrinaire Democracy," *American Bar Association Journal* (1924), reprinted in *Selected Essays,* I. Frankfurter, *Mr. Justice Holmes and the Supreme Court,* is an excellent short study of Holmes' legal and constitutional philosophy. Many of Holmes' constitutional ideas emerge in the Holmes-Pollock Letters (1941), the correspondence between Holmes and Sir Frederick Pollock, 1874–1932. Max Lerner, ed., *The Mind and Faith of Justice Holmes* (1943, 1954), contains extracts from Holmes' opinions, speeches, and letters, as well as excellent brief commentaries. Felix Frankfurter, ed., *Mr. Justice Brandeis* (1932), is a valuable collection of essays on Brandeis' thought and work. A. T. Mason, *Brandeis, A Free Man's Life* (1946), is a scholarly biography. The same author's *Brandeis: Lawyer and Judge in the Modern State* (1933), is a useful brief study.

CHAPTER 21. THE FIRST ERA OF NATIONAL ECONOMIC REGULATION

I. L. Sharfman, *The Interstate Commerce Commission* (1931–1937), 5 vols., a detailed and technical work, has much material on the early history of the commission. Ari and Olive Hoogenboom, *A History of the ICC: From Panacea to Palliative* (1976), is a shorter and more general survey. John Moody, *The Railroad Builders* (1930), is a good elementary study of railroad practices and abuses between 1870 and 1910. Harold U. Faulkner, *Politics, Reform and Expansion, 1890–1900* (1959), is excellent for general background material on the early era of national economic regulation. Gabriel Kolko, *Railroads and Regulation, 1877–1916* (1965), contains valuable materials, but its main theme, that the railroads courted regulation, is questionable. It should be compared with Albro Martin, "The Troubled Subject of Railroad Regulation in the Gilded Age," *Journal of American History,* LXI (September 1974), and also with E. A. Purcell, "Ideas and Interests: Businessmen and the Interstate Commerce Act," *Journal of American History,* LIV (December 1967). John Moody, *The Truth About the Trusts* (1904), and H. D. Lloyd, *Wealth against Commonwealth* (1894), are useful in throwing light upon contemporary liberal and agrarian resentment toward the trust movement. W. H. Hamilton and Douglass Adair, *The Power to Govern* (1937), contend that in 1787 the term "commerce" generally comprehended all business activity including manufacturing. Felix

Frankfurter, *The Commerce Clause under Marshall, Taney and Waite* (1937), traces the evolution of the interstate commerce power in the nineteenth century. E. S. Corwin, *The Commerce Power versus States Rights* (1936), analyzes certain theoretical limitations on the commerce power, including "direct" and "indirect" effects upon commerce. Hans B. Thorelli, *The Federal Anti-Trust Policy: Origination of an American Tradition* (1955), is valuable on Sherman Law background. Joe A. Fisher, "The Knight Case Revisited," *Historian*, XXXV (May 1973), is an interesting article, which blames the Sugar Trust decision on the incompetence of the government attorneys who handled the case, rather than on the biases of the Court. Allan Nevins, *Grover Cleveland* (1932), includes a discussion of the Pullman strike. The Debs case is discussed in Felix Frankfurter and N. V. Greene, *The Labor Injunction* (1930), and in Charles O. Gregory, *Labor and the Law* (1946), both very useful works. John D. Hicks, *The Populist Revolt* (1930), is the best general treatment of the agrarian political upheaval that led to passage of the income tax law of 1894. Sidney Ratner, *American Taxation* (1942), contains a good account of the legislative history of the 1894 law and of its subsequent history in the courts. E. S. Corwin, *Court over Constitution* (1938), includes a chapter analyzing the Pollock decisions. Louis B. Boudin, *Government by Judiciary* (1932), 2 vols., a decidedly partisan study of judicial review, has a highly critical analysis of the same cases. Nevins, *Cleveland* contains an appendix discussing the question of which justice shifted his vote in the cases. The same matter is touched upon in Charles E. Hughes, *The Supreme Court of the United States* (1928). Arnold M. Paul, *Conservative Crisis and the Rule of Law: Attitudes of Bar and Bench, 1887–1895* (1960), has valuable chapters on both the Debs and Income Tax cases, while Gerald G. Eggert, *Richard Olney: Evolution of a Statesman* (1974), also discusses both of these cases, and Knight as well. Willard L. King, *Melville Weston Fuller: Chief Justice of the United States, 1888–1910* (1950), is a competent biographical study. W. F. Swindler, *Court and Constitution in the Twentieth Century: The Old Legality, 1889–1932* (1969), relates politics and the work of the Court in an effective journalistic style.

CHAPTER 22. THE RISE OF LIBERAL NATIONALISM

The most persuasive interpretation of late nineteenth and early twentieth century American history is that offered by Robert Weibe in *The Search for Order 1877–1920* (1967). Accepted liberal theories about the nature of Progressive reform and the forces pushing for federal regulation of economic activity during the period are challenged by Gabriel Kolko, *The Triumph of Conservatism: A Reinterpretation of American History 1900–1916* (1963), and by James Weinstein, *The Corporate Ideal in the Liberal State 1900–1918* (1968). Lewis L. Gould, ed., *The Progressive Era* (1974), is a collection of well-done essays by scholars who eschew the New Left rigidity of Kolko and Weinstein. Two useful examinations of early twentieth century legal and constitutional thought are David Wigdor, *Roscoe Pound: Philosopher of Law* (1974), and Herman Belz, "The Realist Critique of Constitutionalism in the Era of Reform," *American Journal of Legal History*, XV (October 1971). Henry Pringle, *Theodore Roosevelt* (1931), presents a good general account of the first Roosevelt's administration. George E. Mowry, *The Era of Theodore Roosevelt, 1900–1912* (1958), is also very useful. E. S. Corwin, *The President: Office and Powers* (1948), discusses Roosevelt's stewardship theory. E. E. Morison and John Blum, eds., *The Letters of Theodore Roosevelt*, 8 vols., (1951–1954), is indispensable to a thorough understanding of Roosevelt's political and constitutional ideas. On Justice Holmes' attitude toward federalism, see again Frankfurter, *Mr. Justice Holmes and the Supreme Court*. F. B. Clark, *Constitutional Doctrines of Justice Harlan* (1915), emphasizes Harlan's nationalism. Corwin, *The Commerce Power versus States Rights*, analyzes the Lottery case at some length. Robert E. Cushman, "Social and Economic Controls through Federal Taxation," *Minnesota Law Review*, XVIII (June 1934), reprinted in *Selected Essays*, III, is a survey of taxation as an instrument of federal police power. R. Alton Lee, *A History of Regulatory Taxation* (1973) is a book-length treatment of the same subject. H. U. Faulkner, *The Quest for Social Justice, 1898–1914* (1931), discusses the passage of the Pure Food and Livestock Acts. "Purefood" politics and law are also analyzed in detail in Oscar E. Anderson, "The Pure Food Issue: A Republican Dilemma, 1906–1912," *American Historical Review*, LXI (April 1956). C. C. Regier, *The Era of the Muckrakers* (1932), contains material on the background of federal police statutes. B. H. Meyer, *History of the Northern Securities Case* (1906), is detailed and scholarly. A. H. Walker, *History of the Sherman Law* (1910), is a study of early antitrust cases. I. L. Sharfman, *The Interstate Commerce Commission* (1931–1937), discusses the Hepburn Act and the Commission's subsequent revival, as does the Hoogenbooms' *History of the ICC*. Stephen B. Wood, *Constitutional Politics in the Progressive Era: Child Labor and the Law* (1968), is an excellent study. Joseph McLean, *William Rufus Day: Supreme Court Justice from Ohio* (1946), is a competent biography.

CHAPTER 23. THE PROGRESSIVE REVOLT

Mowry, *The Era of Theodore Roosevelt*, is again useful, as is Claude Bowers, *Beveridge and the Progressive Era* (1932), a colorful study of Progressive issues and personalities. Swindler, *Court and Constitution*, is useful on the Court in the Progressive period. Donald Carl Leavitt, "Attitude Change on the Supreme Court 1910–1920," *Michigan Academician*, IV (Summer 1971), is a sophisticated analysis of judicial voting patterns which goes a long way toward explaining the Court's response to Progressive legislation. Donald F. Anderson, *William Howard Taft: A Conservative's Conception of the Presidency* (1973), attempts to explain Taft's failure as a Chief Executive. H. F. Pringle, *The Life and Times of William H. Taft* (1939), 2 vols., includes material on the fight between Progressives and conservative Republicans in Congress. Ratner, *American Taxation*, has a section on the passage of the income tax amendment. John D. Buenker, "Urban Liberalism and the Federal Income Tax Amendment," *Pennsylvania History*, XXXVI (April 1969), is also helpful on this subject. The same author's "The Urban Political Machine and the Seventeenth

Amendment," *Journal of American History*, LVI (September 1969), emphasizes contributions made to Progressive era constitutional change by a group not usually associated with reform. G. B. Haynes, *The Senate of the United States: Its History and Practice* (1938), also tells the story of the Seventeenth Amendment. P. D. Hasbrouk, *Party Government in the House of Representatives* (1927), analyzes the Reed rules and the rebellion against Cannon. John D. Baker, "The Character of the Congressional Revolution of 1910," *Journal of American History*, LX (December 1973), contends that the fight against Cannon was not really part of the Progressive reform movement. W. F. Willoughby, *Principles of Legislative Organization and Administration* (1934), has a chapter on the speakership. E. S. Corwin, *Court over Constitution* (1938), is a more recent critique. The origins of the judiciary act of 1914 are discussed in Felix Frankfurter and J. M. Landis, *The Business of the Supreme Court* (1928). A. T. Mason, *The Supreme Court From Taft to Warren* (1958) contains observations on the Supreme Court during the Progressive era. E. P. Oberholtzer, *The Referendum in America* (1911), and W. B. Monroe, *Initiative, Referendum and Recall* (1912), have valuable contemporary material on these reforms.

CHAPTER 24. WOODROW WILSON AND THE NEW FREEDOM

Ray Stannard Baker, *Woodrow Wilson: Life and Letters* (1927–1939), 8 vols., is a detailed and exhaustive study. Baker, *The Public Papers of Woodrow Wilson* (1925), 3 vols., is a convenient source of Wilson's messages and state papers. W. E. Dodd, *Woodrow Wilson and His Work* (1925), is a good short biography. Arthur Link, *Woodrow Wilson and the Progressive Era* (1954), is also a competent general study. Arthur Link, *Woodrow Wilson: The New Freedom* (1956), the second volume of a definitive biography, has a vast amount of political and constitutional material. Woodrow Wilson, *Congressional Government* (1885), and Woodrow Wilson, *Constitutional Government in the United States* (1908), are indispensable to an understanding of the development of Wilson's constitutional ideas. Robert E. Cushman, *The Independent Regulatory Commissions* (1941), is an illuminating study of the constitutional and administrative aspects of federal commissions. Joseph P. Chamberlain, *The Judicial Function in Federal Administrative Agencies* (1942), is a useful work. E. S. Corwin, *The President* (1940), also discusses constitutional issues involved in commission government. Carl McFarland, *Judicial Control of the Federal Trade Commission and the Interstate Commerce Commission Trust and Corporation Problems* (1929), includes material on the Federal Trade Commission Act and the Clayton Act. D. D. Martin, *Mergers and the Clayton Act* (1959), is valuable. W. O. Weymouth, *The Federal Reserve Board* (1933), contains sections on the passage and constitutional aspects of the Federal Reserve Act. Passage of the Adamson Act and its constitutional aspects are considered in Edward Berman, *Labor Disputes and the President* (1924). The fight over the appointment of Brandeis to the Court is treated in A. L. Todd, *Justice on Trial: The Case of Louis D. Brandeis* (1964).

CHAPTER 25. THE CONSTITUTION AND WORLD WAR I

F. L. Paxson, *America at War, 1917–1918* (1939), contains much detail on wartime constitutional problems. Ray Stannard Baker, *Woodrow Wilson: Life and Letters* (1927–1939), 8 vols., is also valuable. Wilson's war powers are discussed in Corwin, *The President* (1948). William F. Willoughby, *Government Organization in War Time and After* (1919), is a study of wartime agencies. A brilliant examination of the most important of these agencies is Robert D. Cuff, *The War Industries Board: Business-Government Relations During World War I* (1973). Harold A. Van Dorn, *Government-Owned Corporations* (1926), includes a discussion of federal wartime corporations. C. B. Swisher, "The Control of War Preparations in the United States," *American Political Science Review*, XXXIV (December 1940), treats various constitutional aspects of federal wartime activity. C. R. Van Hise, *Conservation and Regulation in the United States During the World War* (1917), is a valuable contemporary analysis of food-control. James R. Mock, *Censorship, 1917* (1941), is a somewhat general nontechnical discussion. Zechariah Chafee, *Free Speech in the United States* (1948), has a penetrating discussion of wartime civil-liberties cases. Also valuable are Fred D. Ragan, "Justice Oliver Wendell Holmes, Jr., Zechariah Chafee, Jr., and the Clear and Present Danger Test for Free Speech," *Journal of American History*, LVIII (June 1971), and Gerald Gunther, "Learned Hand and the Origins of Modern First Amendment Doctrine: Some Fragments of History," *Stanford Law Review*, XXVII (February 1975). H. C. Peterson and Gilbert C. Fite, *Opponents of War 1917–1918* (1957) is an encyclopedic treatment of wartime repression. C. B. Swisher, "Civil Liberties in War Time," *Political Science Quarterly*, LV (September 1940), is also informative. Garry N. Scheiber, *The Wilson Administration and Civil Liberties, 1917–1921* (1960) is a valuable analytical study. William Preston, Jr., *Federal Suppression of Radicals, 1900–1933* (1963), is excellent on the IWW, but less satisfactory in its treatment of governmental attacks on Communism. Zosa Szajowski, "Double Jeopardy— The Abrams Case of 1919," *American Jewish Archives*, XXIII (April 1971), is a well-researched article which discusses many facets of a case usually remembered only for Holmes' dissent. The woman's suffrage movement and adoption of the Nineteenth Amendment are treated exhaustively in Elizabeth Cady Stanton *et al.*, *The History of Woman Suffrage*, 6 vols. (1887–1922). Eleanor Flexner, *A Century of Struggle: The Woman's Rights Movement in the United States* (1959) is a scholarly, objective study. Aileen Kraditor, *The Ideas of the Woman Suffrage Movement 1890–1920* (1965), is also excellent. David Morgan, *Suffragists and Democrats: The Politics of Woman Suffrage in America* (1972), focuses on the period from 1916 until the ratification of the Nineteenth Amendment four years later. Stanley Lemons, *The Woman Citizen in the 1920's* (1973), discusses the legal problems of women during the succeeding decade and the efforts of the National Woman's Party to obtain a constitutional amendment guaranteeing equality of the sexes. *Missouri v. Holland* is analyzed in

Julian P. Boyd, "The Expanding Treaty Power," *Selected Essays*, III, and in Wm. B. Cowles, *Treaties and Constitutional Law* (1941).

CHAPTER 26. REACTION AND LAISSEZ FAIRE

Frederick L. Paxson, *The Post-War Years: Normalcy, 1918–1923* (1948), is a sound and readable general account, as are John D. Hicks, *Republican Ascendancy, 1921–1933* (1960), and W. E. Leuchtenberg, *The Perils of Prosperity, 1914–1932* (1958). Paul Murphy, *The Constitution in Crisis Times* (1972), contains the best survey of constitutional development in the 1920's. The anti-radical hysteria of the early twenties is analyzed in detail in Stanley Coben, *A. Mitchell Palmer: Politician* (1963), and Robert Murray, *Red Scare: A Study in National Hysteria 1919–1920* (1955). Chafee, *Free Speech in the United States*, is the classic work on the great First Amendment cases of the decade. Also valuable are Paul Murphy, *The Meaning of Freedom of Speech: First Amendment Freedoms from Wilson to FDR* (1972) and the same author's "Communities in Conflict 1919–1930" in Alan Reitman, ed., *The Pulse of Freedom: American Liberties 1920–1970s* (1975). David B. Tyack, "The Perils of Pluralism: The Background of the Pierce Case," *American Historical Review*, LXXIV (October 1968), provides useful information on the origins of one of the major civil liberties cases of the 1920's. Swindler, *Court and Constitution*, is rich on judicial detail from the twenties. Wood, *Constitutional Politics*, is now the best analysis of the Child Labor Cases, but R. G. Fuller, *Child Labor and the Constitution* (1929), is still useful. Constitutional analysis of other labor decisions in the twenties may be found in Gregory, *Labor and the Law;* in Edwin E. Witte, *The Government in Labor Disputes* (1932); and in Edward Berman, *Labor and the Sherman Act* (1930). Alpheus T. Mason, *William Howard Taft: Chief Justice* (1965), emphasizes the constructive technical role Taft played as the Court's head, but Stanley Kutler, "Chief Justice Taft, National Regulation and the Commerce Clause," *Journal of American History*, LI (March 1965), analyzes certain of Taft's legal inconsistencies. David Danielski, *A Chief Justice Is Appointed* (1964), tells the political story behind Harding's nomination of Taft, while Paul M. Holsinger, "The Appointment of Supreme Court Justice Van Devanter: A Study of Political Preferment," *American Journal of Legal History*, XII (October 1968), discusses how one of his conservative colleagues obtained a seat on the Court. Alpheus T. Mason, *Brandeis: A Free Man's Life* (1946), emphasizes that great jurist's essential conservatism. Melvin I. Urofsky, *A Mind of One Piece: Brandeis and American Reform* (1971), also offers useful insights. S. J. Konefsky, *The Legacy of Holmes and Brandeis: A Study in the Influence of Ideas* (1956), contains excellent material on the two great "dissenters" of the twenties. Max Lerner, ed., *The Mind and Faith of Justice Holmes;* and Francis Biddle, *Justice Holmes, Natural Law and the Supreme Court* (1961), are also valuable. J. F. Paschal, *Mr. Justice Sutherland: A Man Against the State* (1951), is sympathetic but critical. H. Woody, *The Growth of the Federal Government, 1915–1932* (1934), analyzes the expansion of federal functions in the twenties. The statistics on federal growth and expenditures in President's Research

Committee, *Recent Social Trends in the United States* (1933), are pertinent to this subject. Federal Agricultural programs of the twenties are treated in John D. Black, *Agricultural Reform in the United States* (1929). V. O. Key, Jr., *Administration of Federal Grants to States* (1937); H. J. Bitterman, *State and Federal Grants in Aid* (1938); and A. F. MacDonald, *Federal Aid: A Study of the American Subsidy System* (1928), are all competent studies of the grant-in-aid. The history of the spending power is analyzed in E. S. Corwin, "The Spending Power of Congress Apropos the Maternity Act," *Harvard Law Review*, XXXVI (March 1923). T. R. Powell, "The Supreme Court and State Police Power, 1922-1930," *Virginia Law Review*, XVII, XVIII (April, May, June, November, December 1931; January 1932), is a general survey of due process in the twenties. T. R. Powell, "The Judiciality of Minimum Wage Legislation," *Harvard Law Review*, XXXVII (March 1924), reprinted in *Selected Essays*, II, discusses the Adkins case. The new identity between due process and the First Amendment is discussed in Charles Warren, "The New 'Liberty' under the Fourteenth Amendment," *Harvard Law Review*, XXXIX (February 1926), and Klause H. Heberle, "From Gitlow to Near: Judicial Amendment by Absent-Minded Incrementalism," *Journal of Politics*, XXXIV (May 1970). George Foster, Jr., "The 1931 Personal Liberties Cases," *New York University Law Quarterly Review* (September 1931), and Harvey Shulman, "The Supreme Court's Attitude on Liberty of Contract and Freedom of Speech," *Yale Law Review*, XLI (December 1931), both reprinted in *Selected Essays*, II, are also very useful. The concept of public interest in the twenties is ably treated in Maurice Finklestein, "From Munn v. Illinois to Tyson v. Banton: A Study in the Judicial Process," *Columbia Law Review*, XXVI (November 1927). Walton H. Hamilton, "Affectation with a Public Interest," *Yale Law Journal*, XXXIX (June 1930), and Breck P. McAllister, "Lord Hale and Business Affected with a Public Interest," *Harvard Law Review*, XLIII (March 1930), both reprinted in *Selected Essays*, II, are profitable reading. E. S. Corwin, "Tenure of Office and the Removal Power under the Constitution," *Columbia Law Review*, XXVII (April 1927), reprinted as "The President's Removal Power under the Constitution" in *Selected Essays*, IV, is a thoughtful treatment of the Myers case. James Hart, *Tenure of Office under the Constitution* (1930), discusses the Myers case at length, and there is also pertinent material in Corwin, *The President* (1948), in Paul McFarland, *Judicial Control of the Federal Trade Commission and the Interstate Commerce Commission* (1932), and in Myron W. Watkins, "An Appraisal of the Work of the Federal Trade Commission," *Columbia Law Review*, XXXII (February 1932).

CHAPTER 27. THE NEW DEAL

William E. Leuchtenberg, *Franklin D. Roosevelt and the New Deal: 1932-1940* (1963), is a highly competent general survey of the New Deal and its politics, while Charles and Mary Beard, *America in Mid-Passage* (1939), still has some value. Mario Einaudi, *The Roosevelt Revolution* (1959), and Dexter Perkins, *The New Age of Franklin Roosevelt, 1932-*

1945 (1957), are also useful, while Paul Conklin, *FDR and the Origins of the Welfare State* (1967), possesses valuable insights. Denis W. Brogan, *The Era of Franklin D. Roosevelt* (1950), is a beautifully written short study. James M. Burns, *Roosevelt: The Lion and the Fox* (1960), is careful, thoughtful, and objective. Arthur M. Schlesinger, Jr., *The Age of Roosevelt*, 3 vols. (1957–1960), is detailed, well-written, and pro-New Deal in bias. Edgar E. Robinson, *The Roosevelt Ledaership, 1933–1945* (1955), a rambling and diffuse work, is anti-New Deal in bias. Dixon Wecter, *The Age of the Great Depression* (1948), is also valuable. Rexford Guy Tugwell, *F.D.R.: Architect of an Era* (1967), is biased but useful. *The Public Papers and Addresses of Franklin D. Roosevelt* (1938), 5 vols., comprises a valuable source collection. Murphy, *The Constitution in Crisis Times* has a chapter on the impact of the Depression. Corwin, *The Commerce Power versus States Rights* (1936), is an analysis of the conflicting interpretations of the commerce power that lay in the background of the New Deal constitutional crisis. Robert H. Jackson, *The Struggle for Judicial Supremacy* (1941), tells the story of the conflict between the New Deal and the Court from the standpoint of one of the participants. Robert L. Stern, "The Commerce Clause and the National Economy, 1933–1946," *Harvard Law Review*, LIX (May, July 1946), written by a government lawyer, is an excellent general treatment of the New Deal's program in the courts. A. H. Cope, *Franklin D. Roosevelt and the Supreme Court* (1952), is also a valuable study. E. S. Corwin, *Constitutional Revolution, Ltd.* (1941), presents an account of changing constitutional doctrines under the New Deal and of their ultimate acceptance by the Supreme Court. C. H. Pritchett, *The Roosevelt Court* (1948), is an excellent general study of the Court under the New Deal. The constitutional ideas behind the Minnesota moratorium case are analyzed in Jane Perry Clark, "Emergencies and the Law," *Political Science Quarterly*, XLIX (June 1934). V. D. Paris, *Monetary Policies of the United States, 1932–1938* (1938), contains much material on the constitutional aspects of New Deal monetary policy. John P. Dawson, "The Gold-Clause Decisions," *Michigan Law Review*, XXXIII (March 1935), is profitable reading. The Schechter case is analyzed at length in E. S. Corwin, "The Schechter Case—Landmark or What?," *New York University Law Quarterly Review*, XIII (January 1936), and in Thomas Reed Powell, "Commerce, Pensions, and Codes," *Harvard Law Review*, XLIX (November, December 1935). Another interesting article on this case is Frank Freidel, "The Sick Chicken Case," *Quarrels That Have Shaped the Constitution* (1962, 1964). The background to the Schechter case is ably covered in Bernard Bellush, *The Failure of the NRA* (1975). J. A. C. Grant, "Commerce, Production, and the Fiscal Power of Congress," *Yale Law Journal*, LXV (March, April 1936), is also pertinent. Paul Murphy, "The New Deal Agricultural Program and the Constitution," *Agricultural History* (October 1955), analyzes the A.A.A. Russell L. Post, "Constitutionality of Government Spending for General Welfare," *Virginia Law Review*, XXII (November 1935), is a good general examination of the constitutional issues in the A.A.A. case. Chas. S. Collier, "Judicial Bootstraps and the General Welfare Clause: The AAA Opinion," *George Washington Law Review*, IV (January 1936), and John W. Holmes, "Federal Spending Power and States Rights,"

Michigan Law Review, XXXIV (March 1936), are also valuable. Helen Martell, "Legal Aspects of the Tennessee Valley Authority," *George Washington University Law Review,* VII (June 1939), is a good constitutional study of the federal power program. Certain general observations on the Court's constitutional position under the New Deal may be found in E. S. Corwin, *The Twilight of the Supreme Court* (1934), and in Dean Alfange, *The Supreme Court and the National Will* (1937). Samuel Hendel, *Charles Evans Hughes and the Supreme Court* (1951), is a careful and competent study, Merlo J. Pusey, *Charles Evans Hughes* (1951), 2 vols., is detailed but rather uncritical, while Dexter Perkins, *Charles Evans Hughes and American Democratic Statesmanship* (1956), is a somewhat laudatory short study. J. F. Paschal, *Mr. Justice Sutherland: A Man Against the State* (1951), perhaps overestimates Sutherland's stature. William F. Swindler, *Court and Constitution in the 20th Century: The New Legality 1932–1968* (1970), provides a good sketch of the Hughes Court and also discusses its response to the Roosevelt legislative program. William Harbaugh, *Lawyer's Lawyer: The Life of John W. Davis* (1973), is a brilliant biography of a conservative constitutional lawyer who fought the New Deal in court.

CHAPTER 28. THE CONSTITUTIONAL REVOLUTION IN FEDERALISM—1937–1947

Leonard Baker, *Back To Back: The Duel Between F.D.R. and the Supreme Court* (1967), is a popular work, valuable for its political insights. W. E. Leuchtenberg, "The Origins of Franklin D. Roosevelt's 'Court-Packing' Plan," *Supreme Court Review* (1966), is excellent. Max Freedman, annotator, *Roosevelt and Frankfurter: Their Correspondence, 1928–1945* (1967), also throws new light on certain aspects of the fight. Joseph Alsop and Turner Catledge, *The 168 Days* (1938), is an accurate contemporary account. Fred Rodell, *Nine Men: A Political History of the Supreme Court of the United States from 1790–1955* (1955), has a valuable chapter on F.D.R.'s plan, as does Murphy, *Constitution in Crisis Times,* while Beard and Beard, *America in Mid-Passage,* also gives a good account of the conflict. William Droze, George Wolfskill, and William E. Leuchtenberg, *Essays on the New Deal* (1969), contains a perceptive paper by Leuchtenberg on the Court fight. Roberts' role in the Court's turnabout is discussed in John W. Chambers, "The Big Switch: Justice Roberts and the Minimum Wage Cases," *Labor History,* X (Winter 1969), and in Charles A. Leonard, *A Search for a Judicial Philosophy: Mr. Justice Roberts and the Constitutional Revolution of 1937* (1971). Richard C. Cortner, *The Jones & Laughlin Case* (1970), is valuable on both the background and the results of the revolution of 1937. Corwin, *Constitutional Revolution, Ltd.,* provides an excellent general interpretation of the Court's acceptance of the New Deal after 1937. C. Hermann Pritchett, *The Roosevelt Court: A Study in Judicial Politics and Values, 1937–1947* (1948), is also excellent on the post-1937 Court, as is E. S. Corwin, "The Passing of Dual Federalism," *Virginia Law Review,* XXXVI (February 1950). Carl B. Swisher, *The Growth of Constitutional Power in the United States* (1946), also deals with constitutional developments after 1937, while there are also able chapters on the post-1937 Court in Benjamin F. Wright, *The Growth of American Constitutional Law* (1942), and William F. Swindler, *Court and the Constitution*, is useful too. Robert L. Stern, "The Commerce Clause and the National Economy," *Harvard Law Review*, LIX (May, July 1946), traces the history in the courts of New Deal commerce legislation, as does John I. Ganoe, "The Roosevelt Court and the Commerce Clause," *Oregon Law Review*, XXIV (February 1945). The history of the Fair Labor Standards Act in the courts is treated in detail in E. Merrick Dodd, "The Supreme Court and Organized Labor, 1941–1945," *Harvard Law Review*, LVIII (September 1945), and in E. Merrick Dodd, "The Supreme Court and Fair Labor Standards, 1941–1945," *Harvard Law Review*, LIX (February 1946). A. L. Humes, "Trend of Decisions Respecting Power of Congress to Regulate Interstate Commerce," *American Bar Association Journal*, XXVI (November 1940), is valuable on post-1937 developments in the regulation of interstate commerce, while Paul R. Benson, *The Supreme Court and the Commerce Clause 1937–1970* (1970), is also a competent study.

The Polish Alliance and Southeastern Underwriters cases are discussed in T. R. Powell, "Insurance as Commerce," *Harvard Law Review*, LVII (September 1944). The problem of state interference with interstate commerce is treated in great detail in a series of articles under the title, "Governmental Market Barriers: a Symposium," in *Law and Contemporary Problems*, VIII (April 1941). E. W. Adams, "State Control of Interstate Migration of Indigents," *Michigan Law Review*, XL (March 1942), is also useful. E. S. Corwin, "Dissolving Structure of Our Constitutional Law," *New Jersey Law Journal*, LXIX (March 1946), makes important generalizations about the trends of American federalism and constitutionalism. James T. Patterson, *The New Deal and the States: Federalism in Transition* (1969), is a good survey, although the author's generalizations often outrun his evidence. John D. Sprague, *Voting Patterns of the United States Supreme Court: Cases in Federalism 1889–1959* (1968), is an unsatisfactory quantified study. Samuel J. Konefsky, *Chief Justice Stone and the Supreme Court* (1945), is a careful analysis of Stone's work and thought. There is a chapter on the Stone Court in Robert G. McCloskey, *The Modern Supreme Court* (1972), and Alpheus T. Mason, *Harlan Fiske Stone: Pillar of the Law* (1956), is also valuable. John P. Frank, *Mr. Justice Black: The Man and His Opinions* (1949), and Charlotte Williams, *Hugo L. Black: A Study in the Judicial Process* (1950), are both still useful. Valuable for background are Virginia Van der Veer Hamilton, *Hugo Black: The Alabama Years* (1972), and William E. Leuchtenberg, "A Klansman Joins the Court: The Appointment of Hugo L. Black," *University of Chicago Law Review*, XLI (Fall 1973). J. Woodford Howard, Jr., *Mr. Justice Murphy: A Political Biography* (1968), is a superior work containing valuable legal materials. Samuel Konefsky, Jr., ed., *The Constitutional World of Mr. Justice Frankfurter* (1949), and Helen Thomas, *Felix Frankfurter: Scholar on the Bench* (1960), are both very useful. Joseph P. and Jonathan Lash, *From the Diaries of Felix Frankfurter* (1975), reveal the tensions within the Stone Court. Fowler V. Harper, *Justice Rutledge and the Bright Constitution* (1965), is uncritical in scholarship and hasty in organization and style. Eugene C. Gerhart, *America's Advocate: Robert H. Jackson* (1958), is useful. Herman Belz, "Changing Conceptions of Constitutionalism in the Era of World War II and the Cold War," *Journal of American History*, LIX (December 1972), is an insightful analysis of American constitutional thought from the 1930's to the 1970's.

CHAPTER 29. THE NEW DEAL ERA IN CIVIL LIBERTIES

Paul Murphy, *Constitution in Crisis Times* and Jerald S. Auerbach, "The Depression Decade," in Reitman, ed., *The Pulse of Freedom* are both good introductions to the subject of civil liberties in the New Deal era. E. S. Corwin, *Liberty Against Government: The Rise, Flowering and Decline of a Famous Judicial Concept* (1948), is an illuminating historical and theoretical analysis of the idea of civil liberty. Alfred H. Kelly, ed., *Foundations of Freedom in the American Constitution* (1958), contains several useful essays. Very useful also is H. S. Commager, *Majority Rule and Minority Rights* (1950). Paul Freund, "The Supreme Court and Civil Liberties," *Vanderbilt Law Review*, IV (April 1951), is an excellent general interpretative essay on the law of civil liberties. "Civil Liberties—a Symposium," *University of Chicago Law Review*, XX (Spring 1953), contains a number of useful articles on a variety of problems. Zechariah Chafee, Jr., *Freedom of Speech in the United States* (1948), is the latest edition of a now classic work. Virginia Wood, *Due Process of Law, 1932–1949* (1951), is useful on various civil liberties problems. Charles Fairman, "Does the Fourteenth Amendment Incorporate the Bill of Rights? The Original Understanding," *Stanford Law Review*, II (December 1949), attacks the validity of Justice Black's thesis. William Crosskey, "Charles Fairman, 'Legislative History,' and the Constitutional Limitations on State Authority," *University of Chicago Law Review*, XXII (Autumn 1954), rebuts Fairman's thesis and is answered in turn by Charles Fairman, "A Reply to Professor Crosskey," *University of Chicago Law Review*, XXII (Autumn 1954). Also useful on the Bill of Rights "debate" is Charles L. Black, Jr., "Mr. Justice Black, the Supreme Court, and the Bill of Rights," *Harper's Magazine* (February 1961). The early debate over picketing as a form of free speech is set forth in L. Teller, "Picketing and Free Speech," *Harvard Law Review*, LVI (October 1942), and E. M. Dodd, "Picketing and Free Speech: A Dissent," *Harvard Law Review*, LVI (January 1943). R. L. Hough, "The Jehovah's Witnesses Cases in Retrospect," *Western Political Quarterly* (March 1953), and "Freedom of Speech and Assembly in Streets and Other Public Places," *George Washington Law Review*, XIX (June 1951), are both useful. David Manwaring, *Render Unto Caesar: The Flag Salute Controversy* (1962), is a careful, competent study.

CHAPTER 30. THE CONSTITUTION AND WORLD WAR II

Richard Polenberg, *War and Society: the United States 1941–1945* (1972), is the best domestic history of the war years, but Murphy, *Constitution in Crisis Times* is more reliable on civil liberties and constitutional developments generally. William Preston, "Shadows of War and Fear," in Reitman, ed., *The Pulse of Freedom* is also good on wartime civil liberties. E. S. Corwin, *Total War and the Constitution* (1947), emphasizes the extent to which President Roosevelt broke through "normal" constitutional processes in the war crisis. Clinton Rossiter, *Constitutional Dictatorship: Crisis Government in the Modern Democracies* (1948), is a careful scholarly analysis of constitutional government in modern war. Bernard Schwartz, "The War Power in Britain and America," *New York University Law Quarterly Review*, XX (July, October 1945), is another valuable comparative study. Clinton Rossiter, *The Supreme Court and the Commander-in-Chief* (1951), interprets carefully the Court's handling of war problems. Robert E. Sherwood, *Roosevelt and Hopkins: An Intimate History* (1948), throws considerable light on the origins of the destroyer-base deal. Robert H. Jackson, "A Presidential Legal Opinion," *Harvard Law Review*, LXVI (June 1953), is the former Attorney General's defense of his destroyer-base opinion. Arthur T. Vanderbilt, "War Powers and Their Administration," *Annual Survey of American Law, 1942* (1945), presents an exhaustive analysis of the wartime administrative machinery. War Production Board Historian and Staff, *Industrial Mobilization for War* (1947), is an excellent comparable study. Eliot Janeway, *The Struggle for Survival: A Chronicle of Economic Mobilization in World War II* (1951), emphasizes the chaos in the wartime bureaucracy. Nathan Grundstein, "Presidential Subdelegation of Administrative Authority in War-time," *George Washington Law Review*, XVI (April 1948), demonstrates the extent to which the courts accepted the constitutionality of the wartime executive mechanism. J. L. O'Brian and M. Fleischmann, "The War Production Board Administrative Policies and Procedures," *George Washington Law Review*, XIII (December 1944), treats "indirect" wartime administrative sanctions. Louis Smith, *American Democracy and Military Power: A Study of Civil Control of the Military Power in the United States* (1951), treats World War II military rule in useful detail. Jerome Kerwin, *Civil-Military Relationship in American Life* (1948), is a valuable general survey. Charles Fairman, "The Supreme Court on Military Jurisdiction: Martial Rule in Hawaii and the Yamashita Case," *Harvard Law Review*, LIX (July 1946), and J. Garner Anthony, "Hawaiian Marital Law in the Supreme Court," *Yale Law Journal*, LVII (November 1947), are both excellent special studies. Cyrus Bernstein, "The Saboteur Trial: A Case History," *George Washington Law Review*, XI (February 1943), is a careful, detailed treatment. Morton Grodzins, *Americans Betrayed: Politics and the Japanese Evacuation* (1949); Leonard Bloom and Ruth Keiner, *Removal and Return* (1949); and Jacobus ten Broek, E. N. Barnhart, F. W. Matson, *Prejudice, War and the Constitution: Japanese-American Evacuation and Resettlement* (1954), and Roger Daniels, *Concentration Camps U.S.A.: Japanese Americans and World War II* (1971), all emphasize the dubious legal and constitutional aspects of the wartime Japanese-American detention program. E. V. Rostow, "The Japanese American Cases—A Disaster," *Yale Law Journal*, LIV (June 1945), is a vigorous indictment of both government policy and the critical court decisions involved. A. F. Reel, *The Case of General Yamashita* (1949), argues that there were serious constitutional inequities in Yamashita's trial. Charles Fairman, "Some New Problems of the Constitution Following the Flag," *Stanford Law Review*, I (June 1949), is a careful analysis of the constitutional aspects of postwar military trials of German and Japanese war criminals. Willard Hurst, *The Law of Treason in the United States* (1971), surveys the development of treason law and analyzes the World War II cases. Both Mason, *Harlan Fiske Stone* and Howard, *Mr. Justice Murphy* are excellent on the World War II years.

CHAPTER 31. THE CONSTITUTION AND THE COLD WAR

Edwin Borchard, "The Charter and the Constitution," *American Journal of International Law*, XXXIX (October 1945), discusses the impact of the UN charter on the constitutional locus of the war power. Jacob D. Hyman, "Constitutional Aspects of the Covenant," *Law and Contemporary Problems*, XIV (Summer 1949), deals with the same subject. Constitutional aspects of the North Atlantic Treaty receive treatment in Heindel Kalijarvi and F. O. Wilcox, "The North Atlantic Treaty in the United States Senate," *American Journal of International Law*, XLIII (October 1949). The impact of the human rights provisions of the charter on constitutional rights and federal law is cogently analyzed at length in Zechariah Chafee, Jr., "Federal and State Powers under the UN Covenant on Human Rights," *Wisconsin Law Review* (May, July 1951). M. G. Pauken, "Charter and Constitution: The Human Rights Provisions in American Law," *Vanderbilt Law Review*, IV (April 1951), is also useful, while Lawrence Preuss, "Some Aspects of the Human Rights Provisions of the Charter and Their Execution in the United States," *American Journal of International Law*, XLVI (April 1952), is a valuable note on the same subject. Manley O. Hudson, "Charter Provisions on Human Rights in American Law," *American Journal of International Law*, XLIV (July 1950), and Charles Fairman, "Finis to Fujii," *American Journal of International Law*, XLVI (October 1952), are both useful on the Fujii case. Bricker amendment "politics" are discussed in Glendar Schubert, "Politics and the Constitution: The Bricker Amendment During 1953," *Journal of Politics*, XVI (May 1954). The argument for a constitutional amendment restricting the treaty power is set forth in F. E. Holman, "Treaty Law Making: A Blank Check for Writing a New Constitution," *American Bar Association Journal*, XXXVI (September 1950), and in E. P. Deutsch, "Peril in the Treaty-making Clause," *American Bar Association Journal*, XXXVII (September 1951). Cogent arguments against the Bricker Amendment appear in Zechariah Chafee, Jr., "Amending the Constitution to Cripple Treaties," *Louisiana Law Review*, XII (May 1952), and in A. E. Sutherland, "Restricting the Treaty Power," *Harvard Law Review*, LXV (June 1952), reprinted in Robert G. McCloskey, ed., *Essays in Constitutional Law* (1957). Worth reading, also, is Craig Matthews, "The Constitutional Power of the President to Conclude International Agreements," *Yale Law Journal*, LXIV (January 1955). The new "Insular" problem and related issues of military jurisdiction over civilians are discussed in Sedgwick N. Green, "Applicability of American Laws to Overseas Areas Controlled by the United States," *Harvard Law Review*, LXVIII (March 1955); Arthur Sutherland, Jr., "The

Flag, the Constitution, and International Agreements," *Harvard Law Review*, LXVIII (June 1955); Gordon D. Henderson, "Courts-Martial and the Constitution; the Original Understanding," *Harvard Law Review*, LXXI (December 1957); Frederick B. Wiener, "Courts-Martial and the Bill of Rights: The Original Practice," *Harvard Law Review*, LXXII (November, December 1958); and William G. McLaren, "Military Trials of Civilians," *American Bar Association Journal*, XLV (March 1959). Joseph W. Bishop, "Court-Martial Jurisdiction over Military-Civilian Hybrids: Retired Regulars, Reservists, and Discharged Prisoners," *University of Pennsylvania Law Review*, CXII (January 1964), and Chief Justice Earl Warren, "The Bill of Rights and the Military," *New York University Law Review*, XXXVII (April 1962), are both valuable. Samuel P. Huntington, "Civilian Control and the Constitution," *American Political Science Review*, L (September 1956), argues that the Constitution itself obstructs civilian control. William B. Aycock and Seymour W. Wurfel, *Military Law under the Uniform Code of Military Justice* (1955), is a useful general survey. Alan Westin, *The Anatomy of a Constitutional Law Case* (1958), assembles primary sources on the Steel Seizure Case. E. S. Corwin, "The Steel Seizure Case—A Judicial Brick Without Straw," *Columbia Law Review*, LIII (January 1953); also reported in McCloskey, *Essays;* and Paul Kauper, "The Steel Seizure Case: Congress, the President and the Supreme Court," *Michigan Law Review*, L (December 1952), are valuable. Both Swindler, *Court and Constitution* and McCloskey, *Modern Supreme Court* have chapters on the Vinson period. Murphy, *Constitution in Crisis Times* is also helpful.

CHAPTER 32. CIVIL LIBERTIES IN THE COLD WAR DECADE: LIBERTY VERSUS SECURITY

A number of studies deal extensively with civil liberties in the decade after World War II. Among them are Walter Gellhorn, *American Rights: The Constitution in Action* (1960); O. K. Frankel, *The Supreme Court and Civil Liberties* (1960); and Milton S. Konvitz, *Fundamental Liberties of a Free People* (1957). John W. Caughy, "McCarthyism Rampant," in Alan Reitman, ed., *The Pulse of Freedom*, is a useful overview. Alfred H. Kelly, ed., *Foundations of Freedom* (1958), has a number of valuable essays on First Amendment rights in the Cold War. The best book on Senator McCarthy is Robert Griffith, *The Politics of Fear: Joseph R. McCarthy and the Senate* (1970). Robert K. Carr, *The House Committee on Un-American Activities* (1952), is a classic of its kind. Alan Barth, *Government by Investigation* (1955), is severely critical in vein, as is Walter Goodman, *The Committee: The Extraordinary Career of the House Committee on Un-American Activities* (1968). C. H. Pritchett, *Civil Liberties and the Vinson Court* (1958), is a fine special study. Recent revisionist scholarship attributes the development of McCarthyism to the foreign policy and political rhetoric of the Truman Administration. The most important works in this school are Athan Theoharis, *Seeds of Repression: Harry S. Truman and the Origins of McCarthyism* (1971), and Richard Freeland, *The Truman Doctrine and the Origins of McCarthyism: Foreign Policy, Domestic Politics, and Internal Security 1946–1948* (1972). The Communist problem in the McCarthy era is dealt with in Harold W. Chase, *Security and Liberty: The Problem of Native Communists, 1947–1955* (1955); in C. H. Pritchett, *The Political Offender and the Warren Court* (1958); and in Kelly, *Foundations of Freedom.* Earl Latham, *The Communist Controversy in Washington: From the New Deal to McCarthy* (1966), gives some credibility to charges of Communists in government. Smith Act prosecutions have not yet received detailed analysis, but Robert Mollan, "Smith Act Prosecutions: The Effect of the Dennis and Yates Decisions," *University of Pittsburgh Law Review,* XXVI (June 1965), provides a good summary of most of the relevant litigation. Wallace Mendelson, "Clear and Present Danger: From Schenck to Dennis," *Columbia Law Review,* LII (March 1952) and "Clandestine Speech and the First Amendment—A Reappraisal of the Dennis Case," *Michigan Law Review,* LI (February 1953); E. S. Corwin, "Bowing out 'Clear and Present Danger,' " *Notre Dame Lawyer,* XXVII (Spring 1952); J. A. Gorfunkel and J. W. Mack, II, "Dennis v. United States and the Clear and Present Danger Rule," *California Law Review,* XXXIX (December 1951); Eugene V. Rostow, "The Democratic Character of Judicial Review," *Harvard Law Review,* LVI (December 1952); and Louis Boudin, "Seditious Doctrines and the 'Clear and Present Danger' Rule," *Virginia Law Review,* XXXVIII (February, April 1952), provide a variety of viewpoints on the Dennis decision. Michal R. Belknap, "The Fight for the Right to Counsel," *Ohio History,* LXXXV (Winter 1976), emphasizes the role of local bar associations in halting the Smith Act prosecutions. John P. Sullivan and David N. Webster, "Some Constitutional and Practical Problems of the Subversive Activities Control Act," *Georgetown Law Journal* (Winter 1957–1958), is a valuable study of the McCarran Law. The Communist Control Act of 1954 receives treatment in "Constitutional Law—Federal Anti-Subversive Legislation—The Communist Control Act of 1954," *Michigan Law Review,* LIII (June 1955), and in Carl A. Auerbach, "The Communist Control Act of 1954: a Proposed Legal-Political Theory of Free Speech," *University of Chicago Law Review,* XXX (Winter 1956).

On the Truman Loyalty Program, Eleanor Bontecou, *The Federal Loyalty-Security Program* (1953), is careful and moderate in tone, as is John H. Schaar, *Loyalty in America* (1957). Athan Theoharis, "Escalation of the Loyalty Program," in Barton Bernstein, ed., *Politics and Policies of the Truman Administration* (1970), is a stinging New Left critique. Alan D. Harper, *The Politics of Loyalty: The White House and the Communist Issue* (1969), on the other hand, adopts a basically pro-Truman position. Seth W. Richardson, "The Federal Employee Loyalty Program," *Columbia Law Review,* LI (May 1951), is a reasoned defense of the Truman program by the former chairman of the Loyalty Review Board. The Eisenhower Loyalty Program is analyzed at length in Report of the Special Committee of the Association of the Bar of the City of New York, *The Federal Loyalty-Security Program* (1956). Other useful material may be found in Morton Grodzins, *The Loyal and the Disloyal* (1956); in Ralph S. Brown, *Loyalty and Security: Employment Tests in the United States* (1958); and in "Symposium—Federal Loyalty-Security Programs," *Ohio State Law Journal,* XVIII (Summer 1957). Walter Gellhorn, ed., *The States and*

Subversion (1952), deals with several state loyalty programs of the day, while Lawrence Chamberlain, *Loyalty and Legislative Action: A Survey of Activity by the New York Legislature, 1919–1949* (1951), is a detailed study of New York's sedition legislation. Milton Greenberg, "Loyalty Oaths: An Appraisal of the Legal Issues," *Journal of Politics,* XX (August 1958), also is valuable.

The postwar conservative approach to picketing is treated in J. Tanenhaus, "Picketing as Free Speech: The Growth of the New Law of Picketing From 1940 to 1952," *Cornell Law Quarterly,* XXXVIII (Fall 1952); and in Edgar A. Jones, Jr., "The Right to Picket: Twilight Zone of the Constitution," *University of Pennsylvania Law Review,* CII (June 1954). Hostile and captive audience problems are analyzed in "Free Speech and the Hostile Audience," *New York University Law Review,* XXVI (July 1951); and in C. J. Black, "He Cannot Choose But Hear: The Plight of the Captive Auditor," *Columbia Law Review,* LIII (November 1953). On group libel, see Loren P. Beth, "Group Libel and Free Speech," *Minnesota Law Review,* XXXIX (January 1955); and Jay Murphy, "Free Speech and Interest in Local Law and Order," *Journal of Public Law,* I (Spring 1952). Melville Nimmer, "The Constitutionality of Official Censorship of Motion Pictures," *University of Chicago Law Review,* XXV (Summer 1958) is a good analysis.

There is a vast body of literature on Church-State relations since World War II. Leo Pfeffer, *Church, State and Freedom* (1953), is an exhaustive analysis. Fund for the Republic, ed., *Religion and the Free Society* (1958), is a useful symposium, while Roy F. Nichols, *Religion and American Democracy* (1959), is also valuable. Loren P. Beth, *The American Theory of Church and State* (1958), is moderate and well balanced. Paul Kauper, *Religion and the Constitution* (1964), combines legal and social theory. Philip B. Kurland, *Religion and the Law: Of Church and State and the Supreme Court* (1962), is also valuable. Richard E. Morgan, *The Supreme Court and Religion* (1972), is a perceptive but occasionally confusing analysis. Mark DeWolfe Howe, *The Garden and the Wilderness: Religion and Government in American Constitutional History* (1965) is a superior essay relating contemporary constitutional law to early American religious theory. The New Jersey bus and Champaign School prayer cases receive treatment in E. S. Corwin, "The Supreme Court as National School Board," *Law and Contemporary Problems,* XIV (Winter 1949). Frank J. Sorauf, "Zorach v. Clawson, The Impact of a Supreme Court Decision," *American Political Science Review,* LIII (September 1959); Paul Kauper, "Church, State and Freedom: A Review," *Michigan Law Review,* LII (November 1954); and Paul Kauper, "Released Time and Religious Liberty: A Further Reply," *Michigan Law Review,* LIII (November 1954), all deal with the released-time controversy.

CHAPTER 33. THE CONSTITUTION, THE WARREN COURT,
AND THE "BLACK REVOLUTION"

Very good for general background are Benjamin Muse, *Ten Years of Prelude: The Story of Integration Since the Supreme Court's 1954 De-*

cision (1964), and *The American Negro Revolution: From Non-Violence to Black Power* (1968), by the same author. Samuel P. Wiggins, *The Desegregation Era in Higher Education* (1966), is also generally valuable. Mary Francis Berry, *Black Resistance/White Law: A History of Constitutional Racism in America* (1971), argues that for years the federal government employed the Constitution as an instrument for sustaining a racist society. Loren Miller, *The Petitioners: The Story of the Supreme Court of the United States and the Negro* (1966), contends that throughout American history the relationship between the Court and blacks has been a guardian-ward one. Archibald Cox, *The Warren Court: Constitutional Decision as an Instrument of Social Reform* (1968), is extremely useful on all recent civil rights problems. Valuable historico-legal surveys are to be found in Milton R. Konvitz, *A Century of Civil Rights* (1961), and in Robert H. Harris, *The Quest for Equality: The Constitution, Congress, and the Supreme Court* (1960). "Equality Before the Law: A Symposium on Civil Rights," *Northwestern University Law Review*, XIV (July-August, 1959), and "Race Relations and Integration," *Annals*, CCCIV (March 1956), are still useful. *Buchanan v. Worley* and early residential segregation are discussed in Roger L. Rice, "Residential Segregation by Law, 1910–1917," *Journal of Southern History*, XXIV (May 1968). Clement E. Vose, *Caucasians Only: The Supreme Court, The NAACP and the Restrictive Covenant Cases* (1959), is an excellent technical study. Louis Henkin, "Shelley v. Kramer: Notes for a Revised Opinion," *University of Pennsylvania Law Review*, CX (February 1962), is very good. Robert C. Dixon, Jr., Civil Rights in Transportation and the I.C.C.," *George Washington Law Review*, XXXI (October 1962), is a valuable historical survey. Daniel T. Kelleher, "The Case of Lloyd Lionel Gaines: The Demise of the 'Separate-but-Equal' Doctrine," *Journal of Negro History*, LVI (October 1971), discusses the first major victory won by the NAACP in its fight against segregation in education. Richard Kluger, *Simple Justice: The History of Brown v. Board of Education and Black America's Struggle for Equality* (1976), is an exhaustively researched and comprehensive work. Alfred H. Kelly, "The School Desegration Case," *Quarrels That Have Shaped the Constitution* (1962, 1964), traces the background and discusses the plaintiffs' strategy. William Harbaugh, *Lawyer's Lawyer: The Life of John W. Davis* (1973), has a chapter which examines the case from the perspective of an attorney on the losing side. The man who headed the NAACP team which defeated Davis is the subject of Randall W. Bland's premature and rather disappointing biography, *Private Pressure on Public Law: The Legal Career of Justice Thurgood Marshall* (1973). S. Sidney Ulmer, "Earl Warren and the Brown Decision," *Journal of Politics*, XXXIII (August 1971), credits Warren with achieving unanimity in the case. Leon Friedman, ed., *Argument: The Oral Argument Before the Supreme Court in Brown v. Board of Education of Topeka* (1969), is a very valuable primary source.

Albert P. Blaustein and C. C. Ferguson, Jr., *Desegregation and the Law: The Meaning and Effect of the School Segregation Cases* (1957), is a very useful historical and constitutional analysis. Southern efforts to thwart desegregation are chronicled in Numan V. Bartley, *The Rise of Massive*

Resistance: Race and Politics in the South During the 1950's (1969); Neil
R. McMillen, *The Citizens Council: Organized Resistance to the Second
Reconstruction 1954–1964* (1971); and Francis Wilhoit, *The Politics of
Massive Resistance* (1973). The general situation in southern desegregation
as of 1963 is set forth in statistical detail in *Civil Rights '63: 1963 Report
of the United States Commission on Civil Rights*, an indispensable study.
Alexander M. Bickel, "The Decade of School Desegregation: Progress and
Prospects," *Columbia Law Review*, LXIV (February 1964), is a very useful
analysis. Robert L. Carter, "The Warren Court and Desegregation," *The
Warren Court: A Critical Analysis* (1968), is a valuable brief legal survey,
as is Marian Edelman Wright, "Southern School Desegregation 1954–1973:
A Judicial-Political Overview," *Annals*, CCCVII (May 1973). Harrell R.
Rodgers, Jr., "The Supreme Court and School Desegregation: Twenty
Years Later," *Political Science Quarterly*, CXXXIX (Winter 1974–1975),
not only discusses court cases, but also provides statistics showing the
actual amount of desegregation achieved since 1954. Morris D. Forposch,
"The Desegregation Opinion Revisited: Legal or Sociological," *Vanderbilt
Law Review*, XXI (December 1967); Lawrence W. Knowles, "School
Desegregation," *North Carolina Law Review*, XIII (October 1963); "Racial
Imbalance," *Virginia Law Review*, L (April 1964); and Jack Greenberg,
"The Supreme Court, Civil Rights and Civil Dissonance," *Yale Law Journal*,
LXXVII (July 1968), all examine various aspects of school desegregation
since Brown I and II. HEW guidelines in re school desegregation are
analyzed in Editorial Staff, "The Courts, HEW, and Southern School
Desegregation," *Yale Law Journal*, LXXVII (December 1967); in Editorial
Staff, "School Desegregation and the Office of Education Guidelines,"
Georgetown Law Journal (November 1966); and in James R. Dunn, "Title
VI, The Guidelines and School Desegregation in the South," *Virginia Law
Review*, LIII (January 1967). Russell H. Barnett, *Integration at Ole Miss.*
(1965), is the story of the Meredith crisis at that institution. Bob Smith,
They Closed Their Schools: Prince Edward County, Virginia, 1961–1964
(1965), is useful. "Symposium—De Facto Segregation," *Western Reserve
Law Review*, XVI (May 1965), has several useful articles. Thomas P.
Lewis, "The Sit-In Cases: Great Expectations," *Supreme Court Review*
(1963), is an excellent general survey. M. G. Paulsen, "The Sit-In Cases of
1964: 'But Answer There Came None,'" *Supreme Court Review* (1964),
is also valuable. J. W. Anderson, *Eisenhower, Brownell, and the Congress:
The Tangled Origins of the Civil Rights Bill of 1956–1957* (1964), is useful
on the 1957 law, while Claudia Mitchell, "The Warren Court and Congress:
A Civil Rights Partnership, *Nebraska Law Review*, XLVIII (November
1968), discusses passage of both the 1957 and 1960 laws. C. C. Ferguson,
Jr., "Civil Rights Legislation 1964: A Study of Constitutional Resources,"
Federal Bar Journal, XXIV (Winter 1964), analyzes content and constitu-
tionality of the 1964 law. Ira Michael Heyman, "Civil Rights 1964 Term:
Responses to Direct Action," *Supreme Court Review* (1965), examines in
detail the Heart of Atlanta, McClung, and Hamm cases, as does H. T.
Quick, "Public Accommodations: A Justification of Title II of the Civil
Rights Act of 1964," *Western Reserve Law Review*, XVI (May 1965).
Sanford Jay Rosen, "The Law and Racial Discrimination in Employment,"
California Law Review, LIII (August 1965), gives a history of employment

discrimination and fair employment legislation. Richard K. Beng, "Equal Employment under the Civil Rights Act of 1964," *Brooklyn Law Review*, XXXI (December 1964), and G. L. Bryenton, "Employment Discrimination: State F.E.P. Laws and the Impact of Title VII of the Civil Rights Act of 1964," *Western Reserve Law Review*, XVI (May 1965), examine the F.E.P. content of the 1964 law. Donald S. Strong, *Negroes, Ballots, and Judges: National Voting Rights Legislation in the Federal Courts* (1968), surveys the 1957, 1960, 1964, and 1965 laws and voting rights. Charles V. Hamilton, *The Bench and the Ballot: Southern Federal Judges and Black Voters* (1973), is also valuable on this subject. Warren Christopher, "The Constitutionality of the Voting Rights Act of 1965," *Stanford Law Review*, XVIII (October 1965); Alexander Bickel, "The Voting Rights Cases," *Supreme Court Review* (1966); and Elbert P. Tuttle, "Equality and the Vote," *New York University Law Review*, XLI (April 1966), all examine the impact of the Voting Rights Act of 1965. Gerhard Casper, "Jones v. Mayer: Clio, Bemused and Confused Muse," *Supreme Court Review* (1968), examines the Civil Rights Act of 1866 in relation to *Jones v. Mayer*. James M. Galbraith, "The Unconstitutionality of Proposition 14: An Extension of Prohibited State Action," *Stanford Law Review*, XIX (November 1966); Charles L. Black, Jr., "Forward: State Action, Equal Protection, and California's Proposition 14," *Harvard Law Review*, LXXXI (November 1967); and Kenneth L. Korst and Harold W. Horowitz, "Reitman v. Mulkey: A Telophase of Substantive Equal Protection," *Supreme Court Review* (1967), are also useful.

CHAPTER 34. THE WARREN COURT AND POLITICAL DISSENT:
A NEW ERA OF LIBERTARIANISM

Murphy, *Constitution in Crisis Times* is good on all aspects of the work of the Warren Court. Swindler, *Court and Constitution* also devotes several chapters to it. Alexander Bickel, *Politics and the Warren Court* (1965); Samuel Krislov, *The Supreme Court and Political Freedom* (1968); and Walter Berns, *Freedom, Virtue and the First Amendment* (1957), are all useful on the Court's handling of political dissent. Thomas I. Emerson, "Toward a General Theory of the First Amendment," *Yale Law Journal*, LXXII (April 1963), is also valuable, as is Earl Latham, *The Communist Controversy in Washington* (1966). C. H. Pritchett, *The Political Offender and the Warren Court* (1958), is still useful, as is A. H. Kelly, ed., *Foundations of Freedom*. C. H. Pritchett, *Congress versus the Supreme Court, 1957–1960* (1961), analyzes conflicts between Court and Congress over several security questions. Valuable general articles also include Robert G. McCloskey, "Reflections on the Warren Court," *Virginia Law Review*, LI (November 1965); Harry Kalven, Jr., " 'Uninhibited, Robust, and Wide-Open'—a Note on Free Speech and the Warren Court," *Michigan Law Review*, LXVII (December 1968); and William J. Brennan, Jr., "The Supreme Court and the Meiklejohn Interpretation of the First Amendment," *Harvard Law Review*, LXXIX (November 1965). Robert B. McKay, "The Preference for Freedom," *New York University Law Review*, XXXIV (November 1959), deals with balancing theory in civil liberties, as do also Laurent B. Frantz, "The First Amendment in Balance," *Yale Law Journal*, LXXI (July 1962); and Raymond L. Wise, "Is Dennis

Really a Menace?," *University of Florida Law Review*, XV (Fall-Winter 1962). The Yates and Scales cases receive treatment in Editorial Staff, "Judicial Technique and the Communist Party: The Internal Security and Smith Acts Construed," *University of Cincinnati Law Review*, XXXI (Spring 1962); in Robert Mollan, "Smith Act Prosecutions: The Effect of the Dennis and Yates Decisions," *University of Pittsburgh Law Review*, XXVI (June 1965); and in Kathleen L. Barber, "The Legal Status of the American Communist Party, 1965," *Journal of Public Law*, XV (1966). On the Brandenberg Case, see Frank E. Strong, "Fifty Years of Clear and Present Danger: From Schenck to Brandenberg—and Beyond," *Supreme Court Review* (1969). John H. Masefield. "The Albertson Case: The Conflict Between the Privilege Against Self-Incrimination and the Government's Need for Information," *Supreme Court Review* (1966), is excellent on the demise of the McCarran Act. David Kairys, "The Bill of Attainder Clauses and Legislative and Administrative Suppression of Subversives," *Columbia Law Review*, LXVII (December 1967), is very good on the Brown case, while Gerald Gunther, "Reflections on Robel: It's Not What the Court Did but the Way It Did It," *Stanford Law Review*, XX (June 1968), is useful on the Robel case. The Warren Court's handling of the passport question is treated in Joseph L. Rauh, Jr., "Restrictions on the Right to Travel," *Western Reserve Law Review*, XIII (December 1961); in Lawrence L. Velvel, "Geographic Restrictions on Travel: The Real World and the First Amendment," *Kansas Law Review*, XV (October 1966); and in Carl L. Salans and Richard A. Frank, "Passports and Area Restrictions," *Stanford Law Review*, XX (May 1968). Later aspects of the federal loyalty-security program are treated in Felix Rackow, "The Federal Loyalty Program: Politics and Civil Liberty," *Western Reserve Law Review*, XII (September 1961); in Michael C. Slotnick, "The Anathema of the Security Risks," *University of Miami Law Review*, XVII (Fall 1962); and in Frank C. Newman, "Federal Agency Investigations: Procedural Rights of the Subpoenaed Witness," *Michigan Law Review*, LX (December 1961). The Court's treatment of state loyalty programs is analyzed in Harry Kalvan and Roscoe T. Steffen, "The Bar Admission Cases: An Unfinished Debate Between Justice Harlan and Justice Black," *Law in Transition*, XXI (Fall 1961); in James E. Leahy, "Loyalty and the First Amendment—A Concept Emerges," *North Dakota Law Review*, XLIII (Fall 1966); in Jerold H. Israel, "Elfbrandt v. Russell, The Demise of the Oath," *Supreme Court Review* (1966); in Arval A. Morris, "Washington's Loyalty Oath and 'Guiltless Knowing Behavior,'" *Washington Law Review*, XXXIX (October 1964); and in Editorial Staff, "Loyalty Oaths," *Yale Law Journal*, LXXVII (March 1968). Walter Goodman, *The Committee* (1968), is excellent on the later phases of The House Committee on Un-American Activities.

CHAPTER 35. THE WARREN COURT AND THE NEW EGALITARIANISM

Archibald Cox, *The Warren Court: Constitutional Decision as an Instrument of Reform* (1968), is excellent on the Warren Court's handling of a variety of reform issues. Philip B. Kurland, *Politics, the Constitution, and the Warren Court* (1970), is highly critical of what the author regards as the Court's excessive activism. Alexander M. Bickel, *The Supreme Court and the Idea of Progress* (1970), predicts eventual abandonment of some of the most important principles developed by Warren and his colleagues. There are also a number of useful brief surveys in Richard H. Sayler, Barry B. Boyer, and Robert E. Gooding, Jr., eds., *The Warren Court: A Critical Analysis* (1968). Richard Cortner. *The Apportionment Cases* (1970), is probably the best book on that subject. Robert Dixon, *Democratic Representation: Reapportionment in Law and Politics* (1968); and Robert B. McKay, *Reapportionment: The Law and Politics of Equal Representation* (1964), are both excellent detailed studies. Ward E. Y. Elliot, *The Rise of Guardian Democracy: The Supreme Court's Role in Voting Rights Disputes 1845–1969* (1974), offers a good analysis of the Warren Court's reapportionment decisions, but is weak on the kind of historical background supplied by William Wieck, *The Guarantee Clause of the U.S. Constitution* (1972). Generally useful articles include A. E. Banfield, "Baker v. Carr: New Light on the Constitutional Guarantees of Republican Government," *California Law Review*, L (May 1962); Robert Dixon, "Legislative Apportionment and the Federal Constitution," *Law and Contemporary Problems*, XXVII (Spring-Summer 1962); S. H. Friedelbaum, "Baker v. Carr: The New Doctrine of Judicial Intervention and Its Implications for American Federalism," *University of Chicago Law Review*, XXIX (Summer 1962); Robert B. McKay, Political Thickets and Crazy Quilts: Reapportionment and Equal Protection," *Michigan Law Review*, LXI (February 1963); and Robert McCloskey, "The Reapportionment Case," *Harvard Law Review*, LXXVI (November 1962); and Robert B. McKay, "Reapportionment: Success Story of the Warren Court," *Michigan Law Review*, LXVII (November 1968).

Search and seizure is discussed in Arlen Specter, "Mapp v. Ohio: Pandora's Problems for the Prosecutor," *University of Pennsylvania Law Review*, CXI (November 1962); in Dale W. Broeder, "The Decline and Fall of Wolf v. Colorado," *Nebraska Law Review*, XLI (December 1961); in Edmund W. Kitch, "Katz v. United States: The Limits of the Fourth Amendment," *Supreme Court Review* (1968); and in A. Kenneth Pye, "The Warren Court and Criminal Procedure," *Michigan Law Review*, LXVII (December 1968), and in Robert B. McKay, "Mapp v. Ohio, the Exclusionary Rule, and the Right of Privacy," *Arizona Law Review*, XV (1973). Right to counsel and restrictions on police interrogation are treated in Jerold H. Israel, "Gideon v. Wainwright: The Art of Overruling," *Supreme Court Review* (1963); in William W. VanAlstyne, "In Gideon's Wake: Harsher Penalties and the Successful Criminal Appellant," *Yale Law Journal*, LXXIV (March 1965); in Donald C. Dowling, Jr., "Escobedo and Beyond: The Need for a Fourteenth Amendment Code of Criminal Procedure," *Journal of Criminal Law, Criminology, and Political Science*, LVI (June 1965); in David Robinson, Jr., "Massiah, Escobedo and Rationales for the Exclusion of Confessions," *Journal of Criminal Law, Criminology, and Political Science*, LVI (December 1965); in Lawrence Herman, "The Supreme Court and Restrictions on Police Interrogation," *Ohio State Law Journal*, XXV (Fall 1964); and in Yale Kamisar, "A Dissent from the

Miranda Dissents: Some Comments on the 'New' Fifth Amendment and the Old 'Voluntariness' Test, *Michigan Law Review*, LXV (November 1966).

A great variety of articles discuss nationalization of the law of libel. These include Barry Mason, "Defamation of Public Officials—Free Speech and the New Constitutional Standard," *UCLA Law Review*, XII (August 1965); Donald Meiklejohn, "Public Speech and the First Amendment," *Georgetown Law Journal*, LV (November 1966); Arthur L. Barney, "Libel and the First Amendment—A New Constitutional Privilege," *University of Virginia Law Review*, LI (January 1965); Editorial Staff, "The Scope of First Amendment Protection for Good Faith Defamatory Error," *Yale Law Review*, LXXV (March 1966); Editorial Staff, "The Vindication of the Reputation of a Public Official," *Harvard Law Review*, LXXX (June 1967); and Harry Kalven, Jr., "The Reasonable Man and the First Amendment: Hill, Butts, and Walker," *Supreme Court Review* (1967). Alfred H. Kelly, "Constitutional Liberty and the Law of Libel: A Historian's View," *American Historical Review*, LXXIV (December 1968), treats historical backgrounds.

The Court's birth control decision and its relationship to the new "right of privacy" are analyzed in Thomas I. Emerson, "Nine Justices in Search of a Doctrine," *University of Michigan Law Review*, LXIV (December 1965); in Robert G. Dixon, Jr., "The Griswold Penumbra: Constitutional Charter for an Expanded Law of Privacy?," *University of Michigan Law Review*, LXIV (December 1965); in Paul Kauper, "Penumbras, Peripheries, Emanations, Things Fundamental and Things Forgotten: The Griswold Case," *University of Michigan Law Review*, LXIV (December 1965); in Robert B. McKay, "The Right of Privacy: Emanation and Intimation," *University of Michigan Law Review*, LXIV (December 1965); in Mitchell Franklin, "The Ninth Amendment as Civil Law Method and its Implications for the Republican Form of Government: Griswold v. Connecticut," *Tulane Law Review*, XL (April 1966); William M. Beaney, "The Griswold Case and the Expanded Right to Privacy," *Wisconsin Law Review* (1966); and in Ernst Katin, "Griswold v. Connecticut: The Justices and Connecticut's 'Uncommonly Silly Law,'" *Notre Dame Lawyer*, XLII (June 1967). The "right to privacy" receives more general treatment in Robert B. McKay, "Self Incrimination and the New Privacy," *Supreme Court Review* (1967); in J. Skelly Wright, "Defamation, Privacy, and the Public Right to Know: A National Problem and a New Approach," *Texas Law Review*, XLVI (April 1968); in M. B. Nimmer, "The Right to Speak from *Times* to *Time:* First Amendment Theory Applied to Libel and Misapplied to Privacy," *California Law Review*, LVI (August 1968); and in W. O. Bertelsman, "The First Amendment and Protection of Reputation and Privacy—New York Times v. Sullivan and How It Grew," *Kentucky Law Review*, LVI (Summer 1968).

Harry Kalven, Jr., "The Metaphysics of the Law of Obscenity," *Supreme Court Review* (1960), is useful on the theoretical problems involved in controlling pornography. C. Peter McGrath, "The Obscenity Cases: The Grapes of Roth," *Supreme Court Review* (1966), is excellent on the Ginzberg, Mishkin, and Fanny Hill cases. Louis Henkin, "Morals and the

Constitution: The Sin of Obscenity," *Columbia Law Review*, LXIII (March 1963), attempts to distinguish between the immoral and the obscene. Other valuable articles on the constitutional aspects of obscenity include Editorial Staff, "More Ado About Dirty Words," *Yale Law Review*, LXXV (July 1966); John P. Frank, "Obscenity: Some Problems of Values and the Use of Experts," *Washington Law Review*, XLI (August 1966); Henry P. Monaghan, "Obscenity, 1966: The Marriage of Obscenity Per Se and Obscenity Per Quod," *Yale Law Review*, LXXVI (November 1966); John E. Semonche, "Definitional and Contextual Obscenity: The Supreme Court's New and Disturbing Accommodation," *U.C.L.A. Law Review*, XIII (August 1966); Samuel Krislov, "From Ginzburg to Ginsberg: The Unhurried Children's Hour in Obscenity Legislation," *Supreme Court Review* (1968); and O. John Rogge, "The High Court of Obscenity," *University of Colorado Law Review*, XLI (February 1969).

On the Warren Court and the "establishment" and "free exercise" guarantees, see Nichols, *Religion and American Democracy* (1959); Beth, *The American Theory of Church and State* (1958); Kauper, *Religion and the Constitution* (1964); and Howe, *The Garden and the Wilderness* (1965). Other valuable discussions may be found in Leo Pfeffer, "Court, Constitution, and Prayer," *Rutgers Law Review*, XVI (1962); in Edmund Cahn, "On Government and Prayer," *New York Law Review*, XXXVII (December 1962); in "Religion and the Constitution—A Symposium on the Supreme Court Decisions on Prayer and Bible Reading in Public Schools," *Journal of Public Law*, XIII (1964); in Jonathan Weiss, "Privilege, Posture and Protection: Religion in the Law," *Yale Law Journal*, LXXIII (March 1964); in Donald A. Gianella, "Religious Liberty, Nonestablishment, and Doctrinal Development; Part I: The Religious Liberty Guarantee," *Harvard Law Review*, LXXX (May 1967); in Marc Galenter, "Religious Freedom in the United States: A Turning Point?," *Wisconsin Law Review* (1966); in Myron S. Rudd, "Toward an Understanding of the Landmark Federal Decisions Affecting Relations Between Church and State," *University of Cincinnati Law Review*, XXXVI (Summer 1967); in Alan Schwartz, "No Imposition of Religion: The Establishment Clause Value," *Yale Law Review*, LXXVII (December 1968); and in Joseph M. Dodge, II, "Free Exercise of Religion: A Sociological Approach, *Michigan Law Review*, LXVII (February 1969).

CHAPTER 36. PRESIDENT NIXON AND THE BURGER COURT

Aware that the retirement of Earl Warren signaled the end of one of the most revolutionary eras in American constitutional history, scholars, anxious to determine whether the years to come will be ones of advance, consolidation, or reaction, have devoted considerable attention to the Burger Court, and the literature on it, although largely confined to the law reviews, is already quite extensive. Louis M. Kohlmeir, Jr., *God Save This Honorable Court!* (1974), is a severe attack on the Burger Court and Nixon's Supreme Court policy. John P. Frank, "Conflict of Interest and U.S. Supreme Court Justices," *American Journal of Comparative Law*, XVIII (1970), discusses Fortas at great length, and also deals briefly with

Haynsworth and Carswell. Edward N. Beiser, "The Haynesworth Affair Reconsidered: The Significance of Conflicting Perceptions of the Judicial Role," *Vanderbilt Law Review*, XXIII (March 1970), is a sound article by a political scientist. Joel B. Grossman and Stephen L. Wasby, "The Senate and Supreme Court Nominations: Some Reflections," *Duke Law Journal*, MCMLXXII (August 1972), devotes substantial attention to the Haynesworth and Carswell affairs, and the same authors' "Haynsworth and Parker: History Does Live Again," *South Carolina Law Review*, XXIII (1971), notes some interesting parallels between Haynsworth and the last Supreme Court nominee before him to suffer Senate rejection. The formation of the Burger Court and the major decisions rendered by that body during its first four terms are concisely analyzed in William F. Swindler, "The Court, the Constitution, and Chief Justice Burger," *Vanderbilt Law Review*, XXVII (April 1974). Philip B. Kurland, "The 1971 Term: The Year of the Stewart-White Court," *Supreme Court Review*, MCMLXXII (1972) is excellent on the transition from liberal Court to conservative one. "The Burger Court and the Constitution," *Columbia Journal of Law and Social Problems*, XI (Fall 1974), contains evaluations by NAACP lawyer Jack Greenberg, practicing attorney Harriet Pilpol, and law professor Monard G. Paulson. Less sweeping in coverage is "Symposium—The Burger Court: New Directions in Judicial Policy Making," *Emory Law Journal*, XXIII (Summer 1974). Haig Bosmajian, "Chief Justice Warren Burger and Freedom of Speech," *Midwest Quarterly*, XV (Winter 1974), examines the views expressed by the new leader of the Court, both before and after he became Chief Justice, and predicts that he is likely to adopt a negative position on freedom of speech questions. Both Gerald Gunther, "In Search of Quality on a Changing Court: The Case of Justice Powell," *Stanford Law Review*, XXIV (June 1972), and A. E. Dick Howard, "Mr. Justice Powell and the Emerging Nixon Majority," *Michigan Law Review*, LXX (January 1972), express more optimistic views about the future performance of another new member of the Court. Despite talk in some circles about a judicial reaction, Alpheus Mason, "The Burger Court in Historical Perspective," *Political Science Quarterly*, LXXXIX (March 1974), contends that the major pillars of the Warren Court's constitutional edifice, although somewhat eroded, remain substantially intact, and sees its expansion of the Bill of Rights as a permanent achievement. P. Allan Dionisopaulos, "The Uniqueness of the Warren and Burger Courts in American Constitutional History," *Buffalo Law Review*, XXII (Spring 1973), argues that there are actually substantial similarities between the two Courts. The one area in which this is not true, he concedes, is procedural due process.

Leonard Levy, *Against the Law: The Nixon Court and Criminal Justice* (1974), a book which is somewhat intemperate in tone but utterly devastating in effect, characterizes Burger and the Justices who generally vote with him in such cases as pro-prosecution, result-oriented, conservative activists and charges them with weakening the Fourth, Fifth, and Sixth Amendments, and with writing opinions lacking in judicial craftsmanship. An equally stinging rebuke is Alan M. Dershowitz and John Hart Ely, "*Harris v. New York:* Some Anxious Observations on the Candor and Logic of the Emerging Nixon Majority," *Yale Law Journal*, LXXX (May 1972). Herman B. Gerringer, "Burger Court and the Bill of Rights, Part II," *Trial Lawyers Quarterly*, VIII (Spring/Fall 1972); Arthur J. Goldberg, "Forward–The Burger Court 1971 Term: One Step Forward, Two Steps Backward," *Journal of Criminal Law, Criminology and Police Science*, LXIII (December 1972); and Marshall J. Hartman, "Forward–The Burger Court–1973 Term: Leaving the Sixties Behind Us," *Journal of Criminal Law and Criminology*, LXVI (December 1974), all demonstrate the essentially reactionary nature of recent decisions in the criminal justice field. The last triumph of Warren Court liberalism fares no better at the hands of Daniel B. Polsby, "The Death of Capital Punishment? *Furman v. Georgia*," *Supreme Court Review*, MCMLXXII (1972), which contends that in this case the majority failed to make a convincing argument for its proposition that the death penalty constituted cruel and unusual punishment. Charles L. Black, Jr., *Capital Punishment: The Inevitability of Caprice and Mistake* (1974) argues that the system by which we choose those who are to die, as penalty for crime, is so unreliable that it cannot decently be used and strives to ward off a conservative reexamination of the issue. The abortion decision receives sharp criticism in John Hart Ely, "The Wages of Crying Wolf: A Comment on *Roe v. Wade*," *Yale Law Journal*, LXXXII (April 1973), and Richard A. Epstein, "Substantive Due Process by any Other Name: The Abortion Cases," *Supreme Court Review*, MCMLXXIII (1973). Philip B. Heymann and Douglas E. Barzelay, "The Forest and the Trees: *Roe v. Wade* and Its Critics," *Boston University Law Review*, LIII (July 1973), is more favorable, but criticizes the Court for failing to make effective use of available precedents. Laurence H. Tribe, "Forward: Toward a Model of Roles in the Due Process of Life and Law," *Harvard Law Review*, LXXXVII (November 1973), is also useful on the abortion decision. Three excellent discussions of the parochiad problem are Donald A. Ginnella, "Lemon and Tilton: The Bitter and the Sweet of Church-State Entanglement," *Supreme Court Review*, MCMLXXI (1971); Richard E. Morgan, "The Establishment Clause and Sectarian Schools: A Final Installment?" *Supreme Court Review*, MCMLXXIII (1973); and Paul G. Kauper, "The Supreme Court and the Establishment Clause: Back to *Everson*," *Case Western Reserve Law Review*, XXV (Fall 1974). Philip B. Kurland, "The Supreme Court, Compulsory Education, and the First Admendment's Religion Clauses," *West Virginia Law Review*, LXXV (April 1973), criticizes the Yoder decision. Although only a student note, the anonymous "In Quest of a 'Decent Society': Obscenity and the Burger Court," *Washington Law Review*, XLIX (November 1973), is a very good discussion of its subject. Lucius J. Barker, "Black Americans and the Burger Court: Implications for the Political System," *Washington University Law Quarterly*, MCMLXXIII (Fall 1973), and Inez Reid Smith, "Cast Aside by the Burger Court: Blacks in Quest of Justice and Education," *Notre Dame Lawyer*, IL (October 1973), both examine a variety of decisions affecting blacks and conclude that the Burger Court has adopted a rather negative stance where they are concerned. Owen M. Fiss, "The Fate of an Idea Whose Time Has Come: Anti-discrimination Law in the Second Decade

after *Brown v. Board of Education,*" *University of Chicago Law Review,*
XLI (Summer 1974), is an excellent analysis, and one which is a bit
more sanguine in tone. Robert Herbst, "The Legal Struggle to Integrate
Schools in the North," *Annals,* CDVII (May 1973), and Norman C.
Amaker, "Milliken v. Bradley: The Meaning of the Constitution in School
Desegregation Cases," *Hastings Constitutional Law Quarterly,* II (Spring
1975), are both useful on busing and Northern school desegregation. The
affirmative action and reverse discrimination problems receive extensive
discussion in "DeFunis: The Road Not Taken," *Virginia Law Review,*
LX (October 1974); "DeFunis Symposium," *Columbia Law Review,*
LXXV (April 1975); Richard A. Posner, "The DeFunis Case and the
Constitutionality of Preferential Treatment of Racial Minorities," *Supreme
Court Review,* MCMLXXIV (1974); and John Hart Ely, "The Constitutionality of Reverse Racial Discrimination," *University of Chicago
Law Review,* XLI (Summer 1974). William Cohen, "Congressional Power
to Interpret Due Process and Equal Protection," *Stanford Law Review,*
XXVII (February 1975), discusses *U.S. v. Mitchell.* Gerald Gunther,
"Forward: In Search of Evolving Doctrine on a Changing Court: A Model
for a Newer Equal Protection," *Harvard Law Review,* LXXXVI (November 1972), is an important article, which suggests how the Court may
handle a number of problems in the future.

CHAPTER 37. PRESIDENT NIXON AND THE CRISIS IN THE PRESIDENCY

The abuses of the Nixon years have inspired a reassessment of the
Presidency and its role in the American system of government, which
is perhaps best exemplified by Arthur M. Schlesinger, Jr., *The Imperial
Presidency* (1973). Also useful for tracing the expansion of the office and
its powers is William M. Goldsmith, ed., *The Growth of Presidential
Power: A Documentary History* (1974), 3 vols., which combines docu-
ments with informative headnotes. America's protracted involvement in
the undeclared Vietnam War inspired a flood of books and articles on
Presidential warmaking. Alexander M. Bickel, "Congress, the Court and
the Power to Wage War," *Chicago-Kent Law Review,* XLVIII (Fall/
Winter 1971), argues that this country has allowed too much warmaking
power to flow into the hands of its Chief Executive. Charles A. Lofgren,
"War-Making Under the Constitution: The Original Understanding,"
Yale Law Journal, LXXVI (March 1972), contends that those who framed
and ratified the Constitution intended that Congress should initiate all
wars, undeclared as well as declared. Raoul Berger, "War Making by the
President," *University of Pennsylvania Law Review,* CXXI (November
1972) and Thomas F. Eagleton, *War and Presidential Power* (1974) also
argue for Congressional supremacy in this field. Richard F. Haynes, *The
Awesome Power: Harry S. Truman as Commander in Chief* (1973),
examines the growth of Presidential military power after 1945 and the
resultant emasculation of Congressional authority. John Norton Moore,
Law and the Indo-China War (1972), argues that there was adequate legal
and constitutional basis for the military actions taken by Johnson and
Nixon in Vietnam. Leon Friedman and Burt Neuborne, *Unquestioning*

Obedience to the President: The ACLU Case Against the Illegal War in Vietnam (1972) and Stanley Faulkner, "War in Vietnam: Is it Constitutional?" *Georgetown Law Journal*, XLVI (1968), view the matter much differently. William Van Alstyne, "Congress, the President, and the Power to Declare War: A Requiem for Vietnam," *University of Pennsylvania Law Review*, CXXI (November 1972), expresses the opinion that while the Gulf of Tonkin Resolution may have constituted sufficient Congressional authorization for the conduct of the war, Nixon acted illegally when he continued hostilities after it was repealed. William Rogers, "The Constitutionality of the Cambodian Incursion," *American Journal of International Law*, LXV (January 1971), is a criticism of Nixon's actions by his former Secretary of State. John Norton Moore, "Legal Dimensions of the Decision to Intercede in Cambodia," *American Journal of International Law*, LXV (January 1971), defends the President. Also useful on the subject of executive warmaking are "Symposium—The Constitution and the Use of Military Force Abroad," *Virginia Journal of International Law*, X (December 1969), and J. Terry Emerson, "War Powers Legislation," *West Virginia Law Review*, XIV (August/November 1971). William B. Spong, Jr., "The War Powers Resolution Revisited: Historic Accomplishment or Surrender," *William and Mary Law Review*, XVI (Summer 1975), is a valuable legislative history and analysis by a former Senator who was the floor manager for the bill. Peter Rodino, Jr., "Congressional Review of Executive Action," *Seton Hall Law Review*, V (Spring 1975), another article by a prominent legislator, attributes Nixon era conflicts over war powers and impoundment to a lack of cooperation between the President and Congress. Abner J. Mikva and Michael Hertz, "Impoundment of Funds—The Courts, the Congress and the President: A Constitutional Triangle," *Northwestern University Law Review*, LXIX (July-August 1974); Harold J. Levinson and Jon C. Mills, "Impoundment: A Search for Legal Principles," *Florida Law Review*, XXVI (Winter 1974); and Louis Fisher, "Impoundment of Funds: Uses and Abuses," *Buffalo Law Review*, XXIII (Fall 1974), are all excellent articles. Nile Stanton, "The Presidency and the Purse: Impoundment 1803–1973," *Colorado Law Review*, XLV (Fall 1973), is a concise history. For a brief discussion of the pocket veto problem and a proposed solution to it, see Arthur Selwyn Miller, "Congressional Power to Define the Presidential Pocket Veto Power," *Vanderbilt Law Review*, XXV (March 1972). Charles Nesson, "Aspects of the Executive's Power over National Security Matters: Secrecy Classifications and Foreign Intelligence Wiretaps," *Indiana Law Journal*, XLIX (Winter 1974), is by a Harvard Law School professor who defended Daniel Ellsberg. Valuable for judicial reaction to several facets of the Nixon Administration internal security system is Jerrold L. Becker, "The Supreme Court's Recent National Security Decisions: Which Interests Are Being Protected," *Tennessee Law Review*, XL (Fall 1972).

Theodore H. White, *Breach of Faith: The Fall of Richard Nixon* (1975), is an excellent account of the Watergate crisis. Carl Bernstein and Bob Woodward, *All the President's Men* (1974), and *The Final Days* (1976), are by the reporters whose persistent probing uncovered much of the Watergate cover-up conspiracy, and, while the lasting importance of these books is questionable, they make fascinating reading. *The Watergate Hearings: Break-in and Cover-up* (1973), which reports the testimony before Senator Sam Ervin's Select Committee on Presidential Campaign Activities, is an invaluable primary source; so is *The White House Transcripts* (1974), despite the significant inaccuracies and omissions which mar Nixon's version of the Watergate-related conversations recorded by his taping system. Probably the best article on *United States v. Nixon* is Paul Freund, "Forward: On Presidential Privilege," *Harvard Law Review*, LXXXVIII (November 1974), but there are good ones by Raoul Berger, Gerald Gunther, Louis Henkin, Kenneth L. Karst, Philip Kurland, Paul J. Mishkin, Leonard Ratner, and William Van Alstyne, all in "Symposium: *United States v. Nixon*," *U.C.L.A. Law Review*, XXII (October 1974). Raoul Berger, *Executive Privilege: A Constitutional Myth* (1974), is a heavily documented historical account which appeared just in time to blast the foundations from under Nixon's claim that the President had an inherent right to withhold tapes and documents and to forbid testimony by his aides. Although influential, Berger's book has not escaped criticism, and, while that in Ralph K. Winter, "The Seedlings for the Forest," *Yale Law Journal*, LXXXIII (July 1974), seems to be inspired mainly by that reviewer's liking for executive privilege, Abraham Sofaer, "Book Review," *Harvard Law Review*, LXXXVIII (November 1974), does raise some apparently valid questions about Berger's historical scholarship. Archibald Cox, "Executive Privilege," *University of Pennsylvania Law Review*, CXXII (June 1974), is particularly interesting, because its author was fired from his position as Watergate Special Prosecutor for vigorously pressing Nixon to turn over his tapes. Norman Dorson and John H. F. Shattuck, "Executive Privilege, Congress, and the Court," *Ohio State Law Journal*, XXXV (1974), is also a useful article. Raoul Berger, *Impeachment: The Constitutional Problems* (1973) is a brilliantly researched and extremely influential historical treatise. Ira Goldberg, "An Essay on Raoul Berger's Thesis for Judicial Intervention in the Process of the Removal of the President of the United States," *Wisconsin Law Review*, MCMLXXIV (1975), takes issue with one aspect of Berger's analysis. *Impeachment of Richard Nixon, President of the United States: The Final Report of the Committee on the Judiciary of the House of Representatives* (1975) is an invaluable primary source on the proceedings which carried Nixon to the verge of House impeachment and set the stage for his resignation. Among the numerous books and articles on the future of the American system of government inspired by the Watergate crisis, some of the best are "American Political Institutions after Watergate—A Discussion," *Political Science Quarterly*, LXXXIX (Winter 1974–1975); Donald W. Howard, ed., *Crisis in Confidence: The Impact of Watergate* (1974); and William F. Swindler, "The Constitution After Watergate," *Oklahoma Law Review*, XXVIII (Summer 1975).

Table of Cases

The reference in italics indicates the page on which the principal treatment of a case begins. Where two page references appear in italics, they indicate detailed treatments of a case from two different points of view.

Index

Abatement, 894
Abolitionist movement, 334ff., 341, 354, 369
Abortion, 984, 992ff.
Acheson, Dean, 1019
Act of 1807, banning foreign slave trade, 247, 248
Adams, John, 186, 188, 190, 191, 778f.; Alien Acts, 187; appearance before Congress, 606; cabinet, 175; commercial treaty with Britain, 102; constitutional and political concepts, 204; Continental Congress (first), 78; Declaration of Independence, 83, 84; electoral votes, 158; judicial appointments, 190; minister to Great Britain, 113fn.; Townshend Acts, opposition to, 72; veto power of president, 173f.
Adams, John Quincy: "gag rule," quoted on, 336; Indian treaty rights, 285; internal improvements program, 246; slavery-extension controversy, 345; Wilmot Proviso, 345
Adams, Samuel: Circular Letter, drafting of, 72; Constitutional Convention, not named a delegate, 113fn.; Continental Congress (first), 78; England, controversy with, 73; parliamentary authority, quoted on, 74f., 79f., 86f.; ratification, 148; religious liberty, 76; Townshend Acts, opposition to, 72
Adamson Eight-Hour Act (1916), 618f.
Addams, Jane, 581
Administration bill, 606
Administration of Justice Act (1774), 76
Administrative Commissions, federal, 677ff.
Administrative discretion, doctrine of, 609ff.

Admiralty, High Court of, 53f.
Admission of states: Compromise of *1850*, 336, 343, 348ff., 354, 358f.; Constitutional provisions, 249f.; Missouri Compromise, 247ff., 357ff., 595; preparation of territories, 364, 542ff.; restrictions on new states, 251f.
"Adult" bookstores, 1000
Agnew, Spiro, 1033
Agrarianism, 195f.
Agricultural Adjustment Act (1933): 689, 728; gold rider, 684f.; invalidated, 702ff.; provisions, 685f.
Agricultural Adjustment Act (1938); provisions, 727; sustained, 727ff.
Agricultural Marketing Act (1929), 671, 743
Agricultural Marketing Agreement Act (1937), 729
Agriculture: after Revolutionary War, 103f.; after World War I, 681; federal control, 670f., 727ff.; marketing quotas, 630; processing tax, 702ff., 727; relief statutes, 685, 704f.; tobacco inspection, 728
Agriculture, Secretary of: marketing quotas, imposition of, 727ff.; Packers and Livestock Act, 642, 652; public lands, administration of, 611
Agriculture, United States Department of: packing-house inspection, 557; public lands, 611
Aircraft Piracy Act, 991
Alabama: Boswell Amendment, 883; foreign corporations, legislation, 327; interposition resolutions, 864; legislative apportionment, 941, 946; libel laws, 960; Negro suffrage, 440, 883, 896, 942; nullification, opposition to, 297; picketing statute, 757; pure food

(1864), 616
National Bituminous Coal Commission, 705f.
National Bituminous Coal Conservation Act (1935): invalidated, 705ff.; passed, 701f.
National Catholic Educational Association, 996
National Committee Against Discrimination in Housing, 901
National Consumers League, 581
National Council of Soviet-American Friendship, 914
National Council for a Permanent Fair Employment Practices Commission, 886f.
National debt: Confederation, 102, 105, 167; Hamilton program, 167f., 206; War of 1812, 312, 313; World War I, 669
National Defense Act (1916), 776
National emergency, 775ff.
National Education Association, 848
National Industrial Recovery Act (1933), 335fn., 612, 686f., 689, 693; "hot-oil" provisions, 335fn., 694; unconstitutionality, 698f.
National Labor Relations Act (1935), 716, 717, 747; "communist-infiltrated" unions, 915ff.; insurance companies, 733; passed, 701; upheld, 719f.
National Recovery Administration, 693, 698f.; codes of fair competition, 686, 698, 699; weaknesses, 701
National Republicans, 312
National Security Council, 1024
National supremacy, 529, 530, 531, 707, 748, 894; and implied powers, 272ff.; maintenance of tradition, 651ff.
Nationalism: American, 116, 136f., 257ff., 420; failure of first movement for, 541; in first Congress, 159; judicial, 257–283
Nationalism, liberal: 548–579; doctrine of, 548ff., 604, 615f.; Interstate Commerce Commission, revival of, 571ff.; Interstate Commerce Commission in the Courts, 574ff.; police power, federal, 522ff.; police power in the courts, 559ff.; railway labor and police power, 563ff.; return of, 684; rule of reason, 569ff.; stewardship theory of Theodore Roosevelt, 550ff.; Supreme Court acceptance of, 717ff.; trust prosecutions, revival of, 565ff.; twilight of, 641ff.
Natural law, theory of, 35ff., 63f., 84f., 346, 470f.
Naturalization Act (1740), 53
Naturalization Act (1906), 666f.

Navigable streams, and commerce power, 735ff.
Navigation Acts (1600–1696), 46, 47, 52, 53, 59, 70
Navy, Articles for the Government of the, 389
Navy Department, Destroyer-Base deal, 773ff.; establishment of, 161; Presidential use of, 778
Nebraska: bread, standard weight, 661; foreign language teaching in schools, 663; intrastate freight rates statute, 488; senatorial primary established (1875), 592; territory, organization, 357f.
Nebraska Bill, 358, 359
Negro suffrage: disfranchisement after Reconstruction, 464ff.; Fifteenth Amendment, 442f., 455f., 462ff.; grandfather laws, 465; poll tax, 465, 883, 884, 889, 890; primaries, 465, 882f.; Tuskegee boundaries redrawn, 883, 942; voters, 440, 441, 853, 881, 882, 887, 889, 890; Voting Rights Act (1965), 895ff.
Negroes: alteration in social climate, 852ff.; "Black Codes," 428, 429; citizenship, 253ff., 363f., 431ff., 438, 856; Civil Rights Act (1866), 431ff.; Constitutional revolution in position, 851, 852ff., 890f.; discrimination in employment, 841, 853f., 881, 886f.; Freedmen's Bureau, 429ff., 443; Jacksonian constitutions, 305f.; lynching, 884ff.; Truman program, 886f.; white backlash, 904f.; See also Civil Rights Acts; Fourteenth Amendment; Negro suffrage; Scott, Dred; Segregation, racial; Slavery; Thirteenth Amendment
Nelson, Samuel: basic war power, quoted on, 388; commerce power, 329ff.; Scott, Dred, 365ff., slavery, 361, 362
Neutrality Act (November, 1939), 777
Neutrality belt, 773
Neutrality Patrol (1939), 773, 778
New Deal, 682–711; Agricultural Adjustment Act, fall of, 702ff.; Carter v. Carter Coal Company, 705ff.; civil liberties. 751ff:; conservative protest against 709ff.; due process, 708; end of, in civil liberties, 801ff.; first days of, 684ff.; free enterprise, attack on, 710; gold cases, 695ff.; hot-oil cases, 694f.; Negro rights, 852ff.; New Freedom, forerunner of, 620; not a revolution, 750; political minorities under, 765ff.; Schechter v. United States: the "sick chicken"